Technical Draughtsmanship

Second Edition

Éanna O Broin

Gill and Macmillan

Published in Ireland by
Gill and Macmillan Ltd
Goldenbridge
Dublin 8
with associated companies throughout the world
© Éanna O Broin 1986 and 1991
0 7171 1652 2
Origination in Ireland by Keywrite

All rights reserved.
No part of this publication may be copied,
reproduced or transmitted in any form or by
any means, without permission of the publishers.
Photocopying any part of this book is illegal.

Acknowledgment
The publishers wish to thank the University
of London and the Imperial College of
Science and Technology for permission
to reproduce the drawings on
pages 240 and 241.

Photocopying
prohibited
by law

For Christina

CONTENTS

Preface — iv

Part 1: Plane and Solid Geometry
1. Introduction — 1
2. Revision — 8
3. Area Conversions and Graphic Calculation — 23
4. Scales — 35
5. Orthographic Projection — 43
6. Auxiliary Projection — 61
7. Pictorial Projection — 73
8. Points, Lines and Planes in Space — 91
9. The Oblique Plane — 107
10. Spheres and Tangent Planes — 121
11. Sections and Intersections — 131
12. Development — 145
13. Envelopments — 169
14. Loci — 173
15. Conics — 187

Part 2: Professional Practice
16. The Profession — 201

Part 2A: Engineering Applications
17. An Engineering Project — 211
18. Engineering Structures — 219
19. Fabrication — 227
20. Pipework and Assembly — 235
21. Mechanisms — 245
22. Engines — 265
23. Limits and Fits — 279

Part 2B: Building Applications
24. A Building Project — 285
25. Surveying and Mining — 293
26. Building Structures — 309
27. Building Geometry — 323
28. Presentation Drawings — 331

Appendices

Examination Hints — 347

Tables — 348

Glossary — 350

Index — 351

PREFACE

This book is a response to the new Technical Drawing syllabus for the Leaving Certificate Ordinary and Higher Level courses. It covers both the Engineering and the Building Application options, as well as the common Plane and Solid Geometry sections of the course. As a complete course of study, this book forms a good and sound introduction for any potential draughtsman.

Two colours have been used throughout to help in the explanation of drawing procedures. Red lines will correspond to construction lines.

Each page has a title block for easy reference, a letter H being added to indicate Higher Level topics.

In most cases 'short-cut' methods have been avoided, as have constructions involving an exceptional set of circumstances.

Each chapter is followed by a set of exercises designed to consolidate and extend the student's comprehension. The questions relate directly to the text and do not try to emulate an examination, ample examples of examination questions being already available.

This book has been written to satisfy the needs of a student interested in this truly fascinating subject and it is hoped that, above all, it will prove true in that respect.

Éanna O Broin
Good Counsel College
New Ross
1986

ADDENDUM (SECOND EDITION)

In the last five years the syllabus has taken shape and classroom use has suggested some improvements to this work. The second edition revises and enlarges the text, making it more rounded and complete.

Éanna O Broin, 1991.

PART 1
PLANE AND SOLID GEOMETRY

CHAPTER 1
INTRODUCTION

This chapter contains some notes on equipment and on drawing hidden lines, something which is essential to good draughtsmanship.
Many headaches can be avoided by adopting a clear logical procedure for drawing and especially for inking. One such approach is outlined on page 6.

CONTENTS
A Note on Equipment	*Page* 2
Using the Set Squares	3
Lines and Hidden Lines	4
Title Blocks and Lists	5
Order of Drawing and Inking	6
Preliminary Exercises	7

Photocopying prohibited by law

①

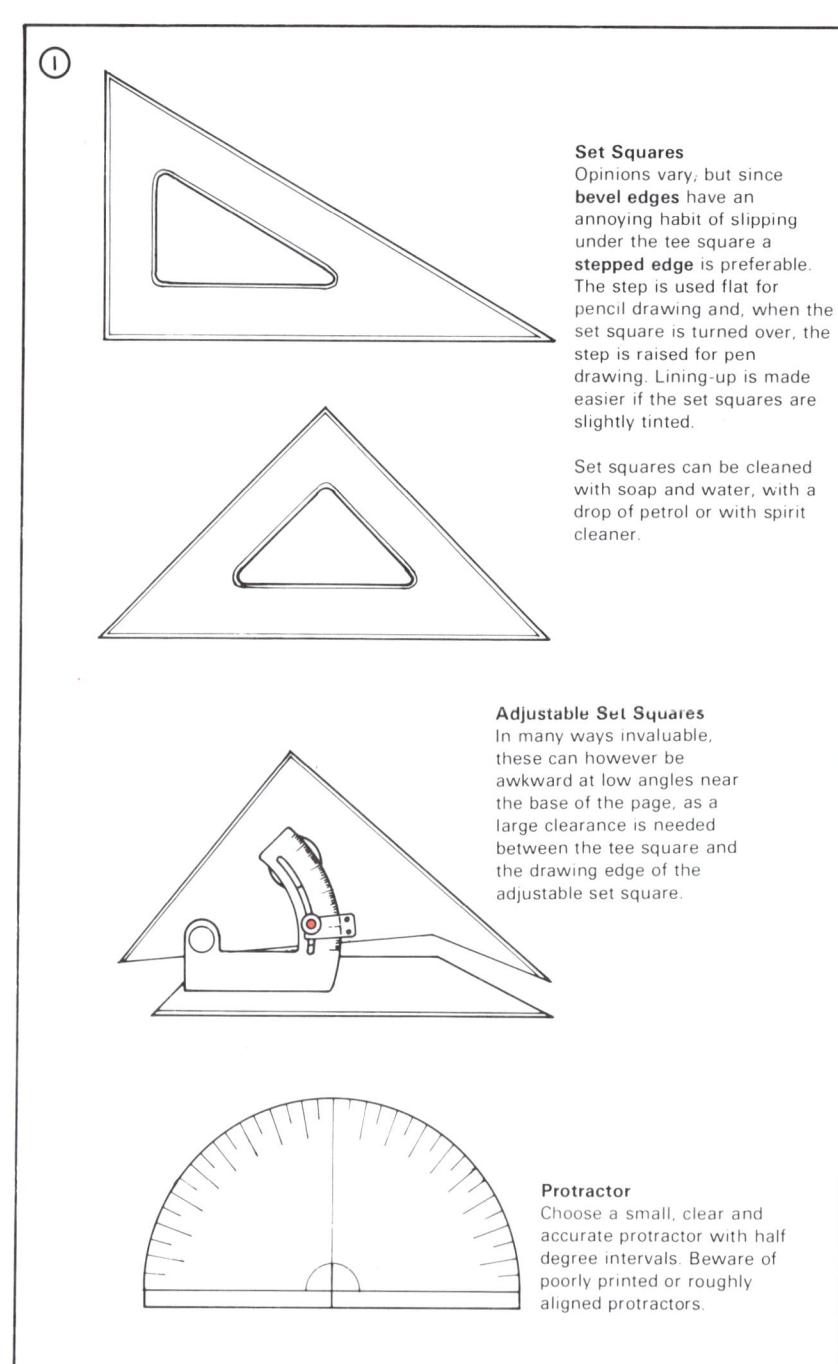

Set Squares
Opinions vary; but since **bevel edges** have an annoying habit of slipping under the tee square a **stepped edge** is preferable. The step is used flat for pencil drawing and, when the set square is turned over, the step is raised for pen drawing. Lining-up is made easier if the set squares are slightly tinted.

Set squares can be cleaned with soap and water, with a drop of petrol or with spirit cleaner.

Adjustable Set Squares
In many ways invaluable, these can however be awkward at low angles near the base of the page, as a large clearance is needed between the tee square and the drawing edge of the adjustable set square.

Protractor
Choose a small, clear and accurate protractor with half degree intervals. Beware of poorly printed or roughly aligned protractors.

②

Half section · Half section · Half section · Half section

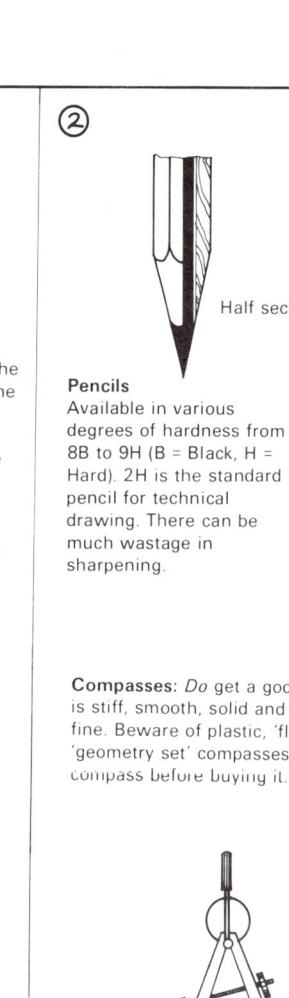

Pencils
Available in various degrees of hardness from 8B to 9H (B = Black, H = Hard). 2H is the standard pencil for technical drawing. There can be much wastage in sharpening.

Clutch Pencils
Generally a good buy, these use 2mm leads with hardly any wastage. A special parer is needed. Some pencils boast a parer within the cap but these are a mixed blessing since the parings can make their way onto the drawing.

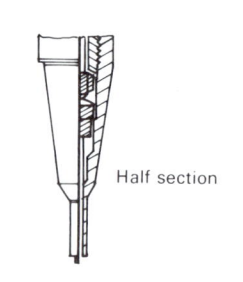

Fine Lead Pencils
These are a disappointment. Leads vary from 0.3 to 0.9mm in thickness. Good with soft leads but hard leads need a very light touch indeed.

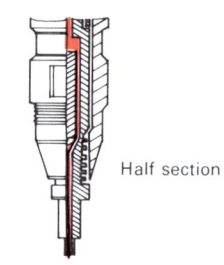

Draughting Pens
For inking you may use a very fine felt tip but for a lot of ink work a few draughting pens will be needed. These pens are expensive. Normally a 0.18 and 0.5mm will suffice. Do not let them lie around for long uncapped, as the ink dries and clogs the nibs.

Compasses: *Do* get a good compass that is stiff, smooth, solid and whose point is fine. Beware of plastic, 'flashy' or thin 'geometry set' compasses. Always test a compass before buying it.

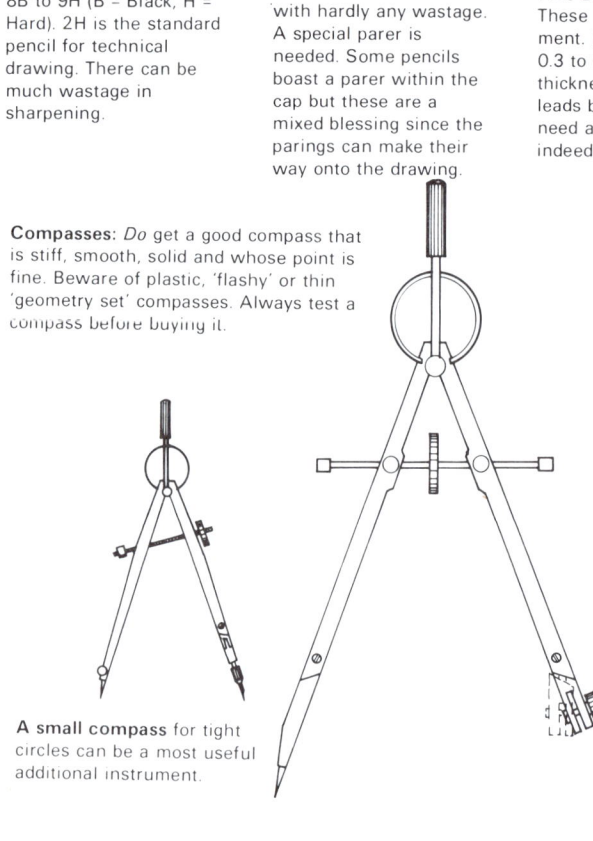

Some Common Nib Sizes
0.13
0.18
0.25
0.35
0.5
0.7
0.9
1.0
1.2

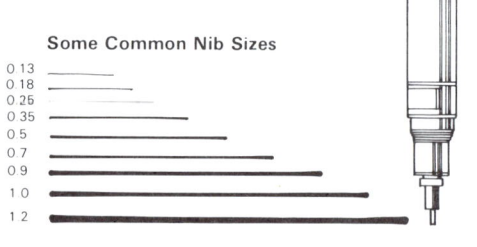

The finer the nib, the more expensive it will be. Clean pens regularly with lukewarm, soapy water. Do not dismantle the inside plunger as it will not go back easily and once it bends it is useless. Also be careful when tightening the cap since the plastic will split if overtightened.

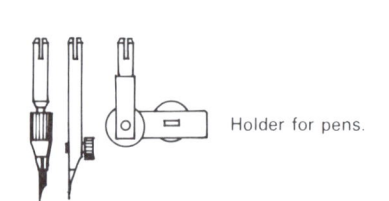

A small compass for tight circles can be a most useful additional instrument.

Holder for pens.

Note: *Good, well cared-for instruments will work long and well for you, but bad instruments are a constant vexation.*

Technical Draughtsmanship
A Note on Equipment
Introduction 1

① THE SET SQUARES

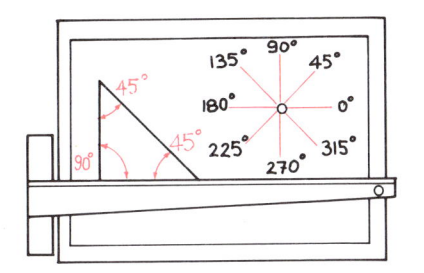

Eight different angles can be constructed with a **45°** set square. Thus a circle may be divided into eight equal parts. This set square is also vital when transposing measurements in an orthographic projection.

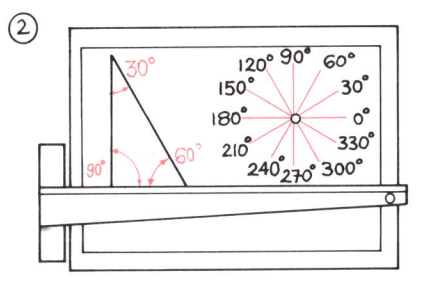

②

Twelve different angles can be drawn using a **30°-60°** set square. A circle may thus be divided into twelve: a most useful construction.

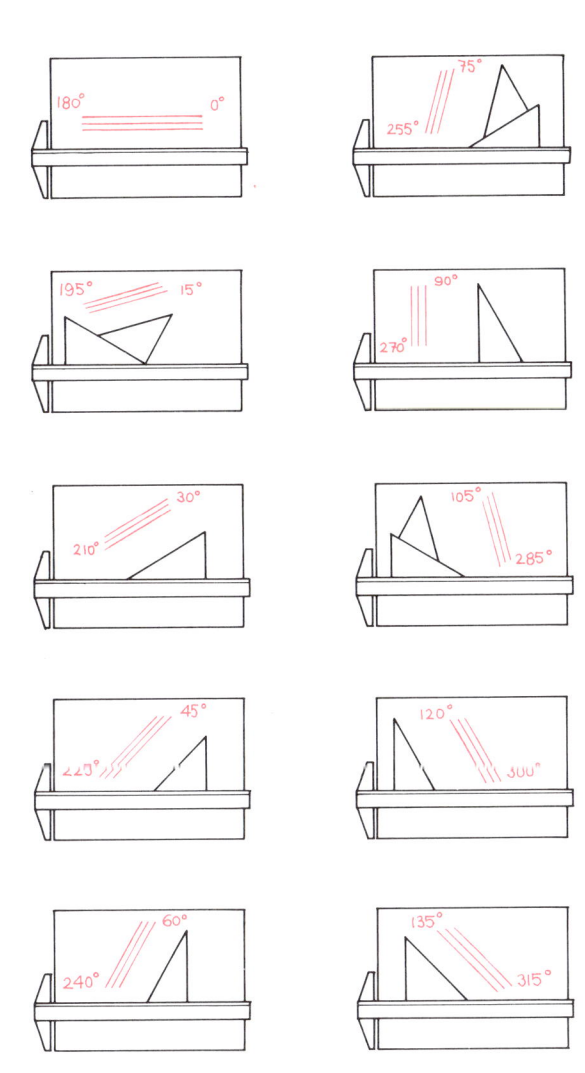

③ USING BOTH SET SQUARES

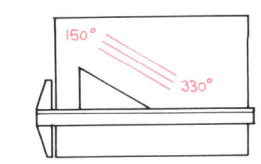

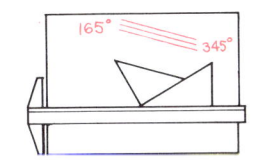

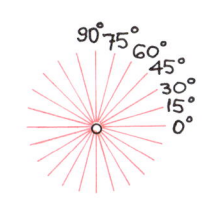

By using both set squares twenty-four angles can be drawn. In this way a circle can be divided into twenty-four equal sections, or the usual twelve divisions can be subdivided. This is especially useful in linkage, development and cycloidal drawings.

④ Parallel Lines

Sit a set square on the tee square and move them until the tee square is steady and the set square is against the given line. Now slide the set square along the tee square to draw parallel lines.

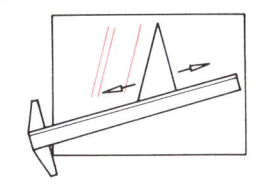

⑤ Lines Perpendicular

Arrange the set square and tee square as below. Then, by turning over the set square, perpendicular lines can be drawn.

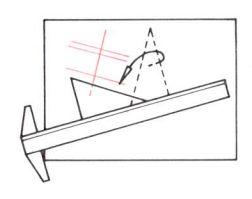

Technical Draughtsmanship
Using the Set Squares
Introduction 2

Type of Line	Example of Line	Application of Line
Continuous (thick)	————————————	Visible Outlines and Edges.
Continuous (thin)	————————————	Dimension and Leader Lines, Projection and Extension Lines and for Hatching.
Short Dashes (thin)	– – – – – – – –	Hidden Outlines and Edges.
Chain (thin)	— - — - — - —	Centre Lines, Pitch Circles and for the Extreme Positions of moving parts.
Chain (thick)	— - — - — - —	A feature subject to special requirements.
Short Chain (thin)	— - — - — - —	A feature located in front of Cutting Plane.
Chain (thick at ends and at changes of direction, otherwise thin)	— - — - — - —	Cutting Planes
Continuous irregular (thin)	～～～～～	Limits of Partial Views, Sections or Short Break Lines.
Continuous with short zig-zags (thin)	—/\/\/\—	Long Break lines.

HIDDEN LINE TECHNIQUE

Begin with a dash and not with a gap.

Dashes meet without a gap.

Dashes meet at corners without a gap.

Dashes meet at corners without a gap.

One exception is when a line continues as a hidden line. Then begin the hidden line with a gap.

Hidden arcs begin with a dash and not a gap.

Again, where an arc continues as a hidden arc an exception is made and the hidden arc is started with a gap.

Two hidden arcs meet at a dash and not at a gap.

Technical Draughtsmanship
Lines and Hidden Lines
Introduction 3

① **A Standard Title Block Arrangement**

Labels (top to bottom):
- Notes
- 8mm margin (on A3 sheet)
- List of items, members, corrections etc.
- Tolerances and units of measurement
- Projection symbol
- Issue data: checked, approved, rechecked etc.
- Finish specifications
- Firm's title
- Drawing's title
- Scale ratio
- Drawing number

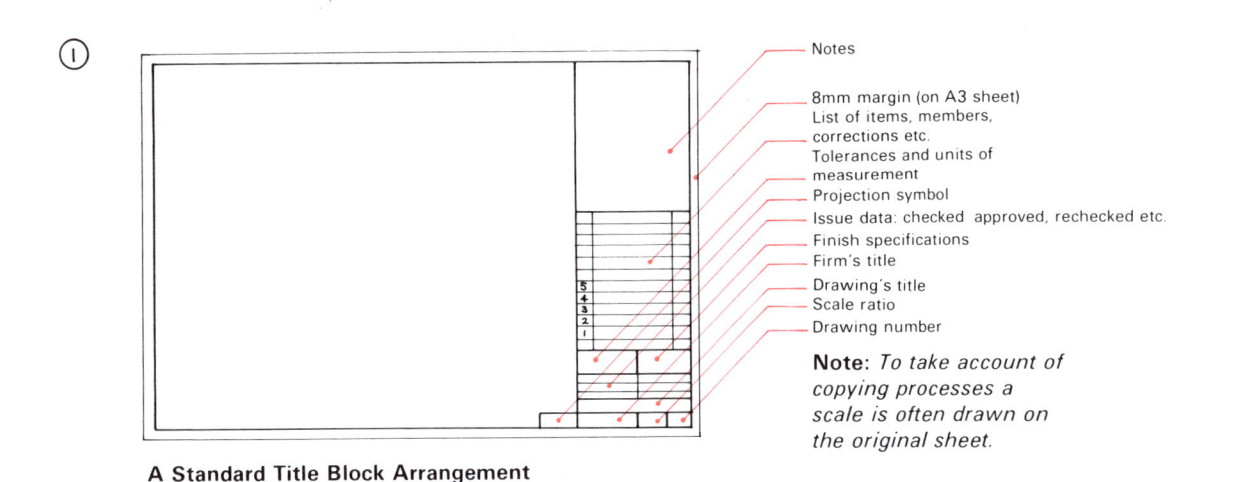

Note: *To take account of copying processes a scale is often drawn on the original sheet.*

② **An Alternative Block Arrangement (with grid)**

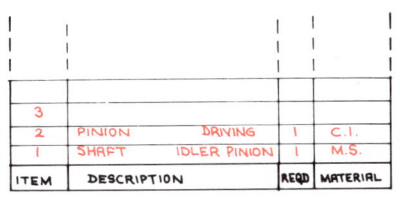

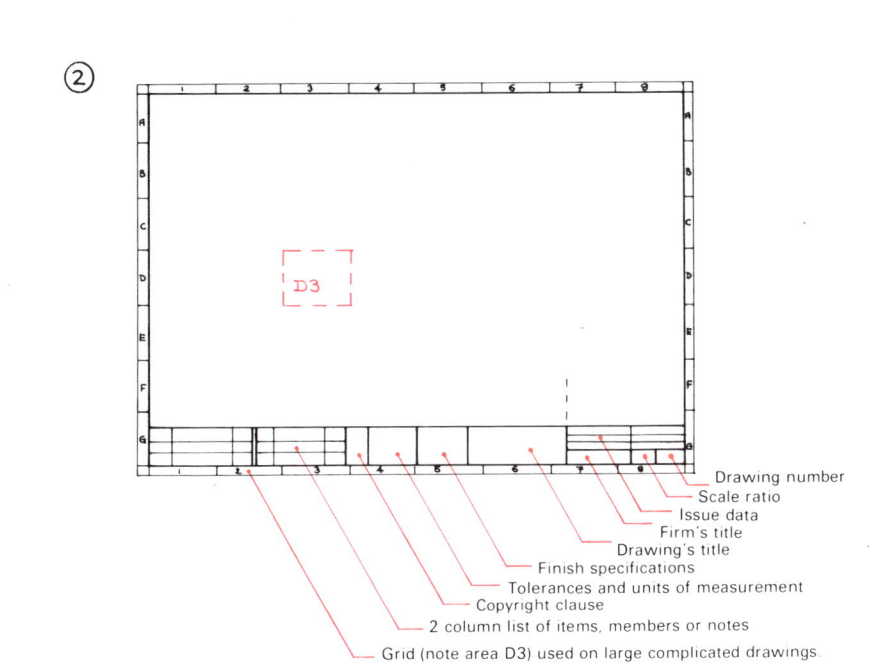

Labels:
- Drawing number
- Scale ratio
- Issue data
- Firm's title
- Drawing's title
- Finish specifications
- Tolerances and units of measurement
- Copyright clause
- 2 column list of items, members or notes
- Grid (note area D3) used on large complicated drawings.

③ **A Material List for an Assembly Drawing.** Note how it grows upwards. *C.I.* is cast iron and *M.S.* is mild steel.

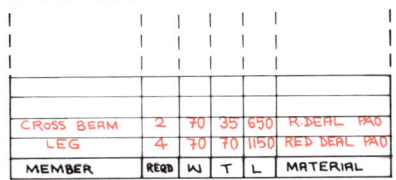

ITEM	DESCRIPTION		REQD	MATERIAL
3				
2	PINION	DRIVING	1	C.I.
1	SHAFT	IDLER PINION	1	M.S.

④ **A Cutting List for a Cabinet Drawing,** where *W* is width, *T* is thickness and *L* is length. *PAO* means "planed all over".

MEMBER	REQD	W	T	L	MATERIAL
CROSS BEAM	2	70	35	650	R. DEAL PAO
LEG	4	70	70	1150	RED DEAL PAO

⑤ **A suggested Title Block for students.** Dimensions are for an A3 sheet. These may be halved for A4 and doubled for A2.

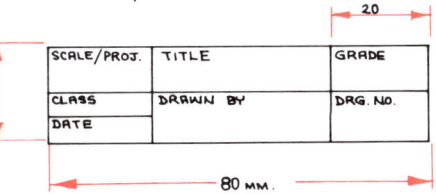

SCALE/PROJ.	TITLE	GRADE
CLASS	DRAWN BY	DRG. NO.
DATE		

(80 mm × 20)

⑥ **The Title Block used throughout this book.** **N.T.S.** means 'not to scale'. If **H** is used it refers to the Higher Level course.

BOOK TITLE		
PAGE TITLE		
SCALE / PROJ.	CHAPTER / PAGE	PART OF COURSE / AREA / LEVEL

Title Blocks are usually located in the bottom right hand corner of the page. Each specialist industry would modify the basic block to suit its particular needs.

Technical Draughtsmanship
Title Blocks and Lists
N.T.S	Introduction 4

① Drawing Procedure

STAGE 1
Lay out the overall spaces required and the margins. See Stage 6 for the finished drawing.

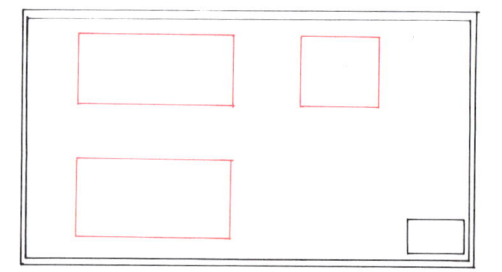

STAGE 2
Locate main Centre Lines and mark further measurements on these.

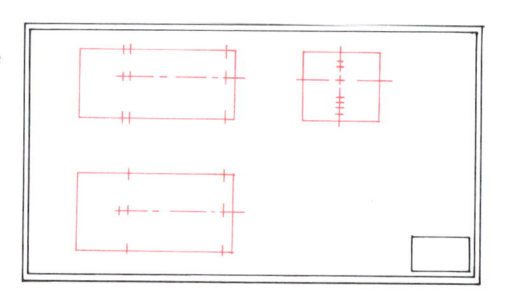

STAGE 3
Draw in the Circles and Arcs.

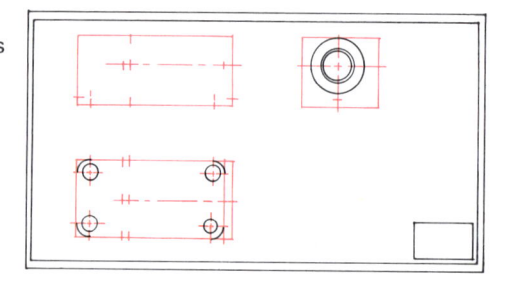

STAGE 4
The projections of the circles and Tangents to arcs are drawn.

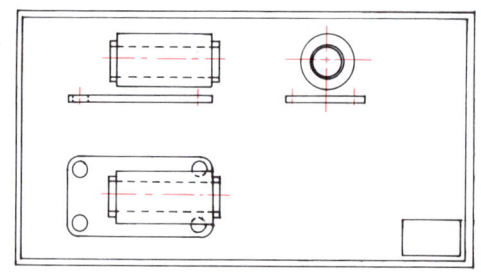

STAGE 5
Complete the three views.

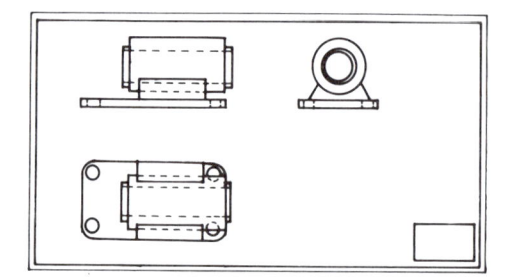

STAGE 6
Add Titles, Dimensions, Lists, etc.

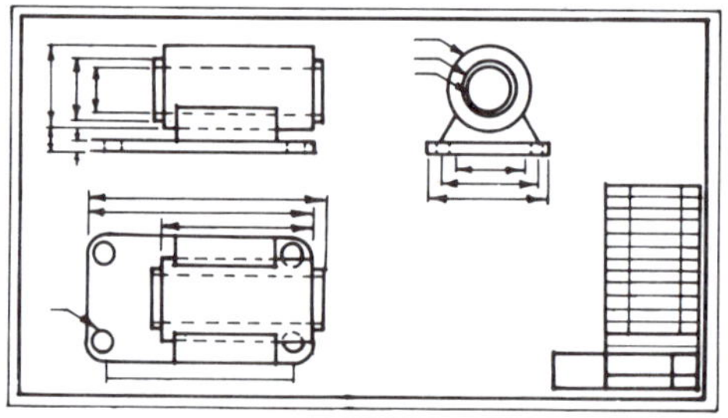

Note: *If tracing a drawing draw any changes to be made first.*

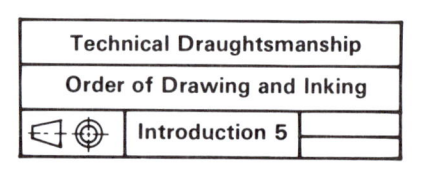

A methodical approach to inking will avoid innumerable headaches. The list below is based on common sense and experience.

② Inking Procedure

1. Main centre lines.
2. Small circles and arcs.
3. Large circles and arcs.
4. Hidden circles and arcs.
5. Irregular curves.
6. Horizontal lines.
7. Vertical lines.
8. Inclined Lines.
9. Hidden lines.
10. Extension and Dimension lines
11. Arrowheads and figures.
12. Notes and titles.
13. Border lines
14. Check for lines missed or mistaken.

Note: *Draw away from a gathering point of ink lines to avoid blots. It also helps to have a piece of scrap paper under your hand when inking, to avoid causing grease spots.*

| Technical Draughtsmanship |
| Order of Drawing and Inking |
| Introduction 5 |

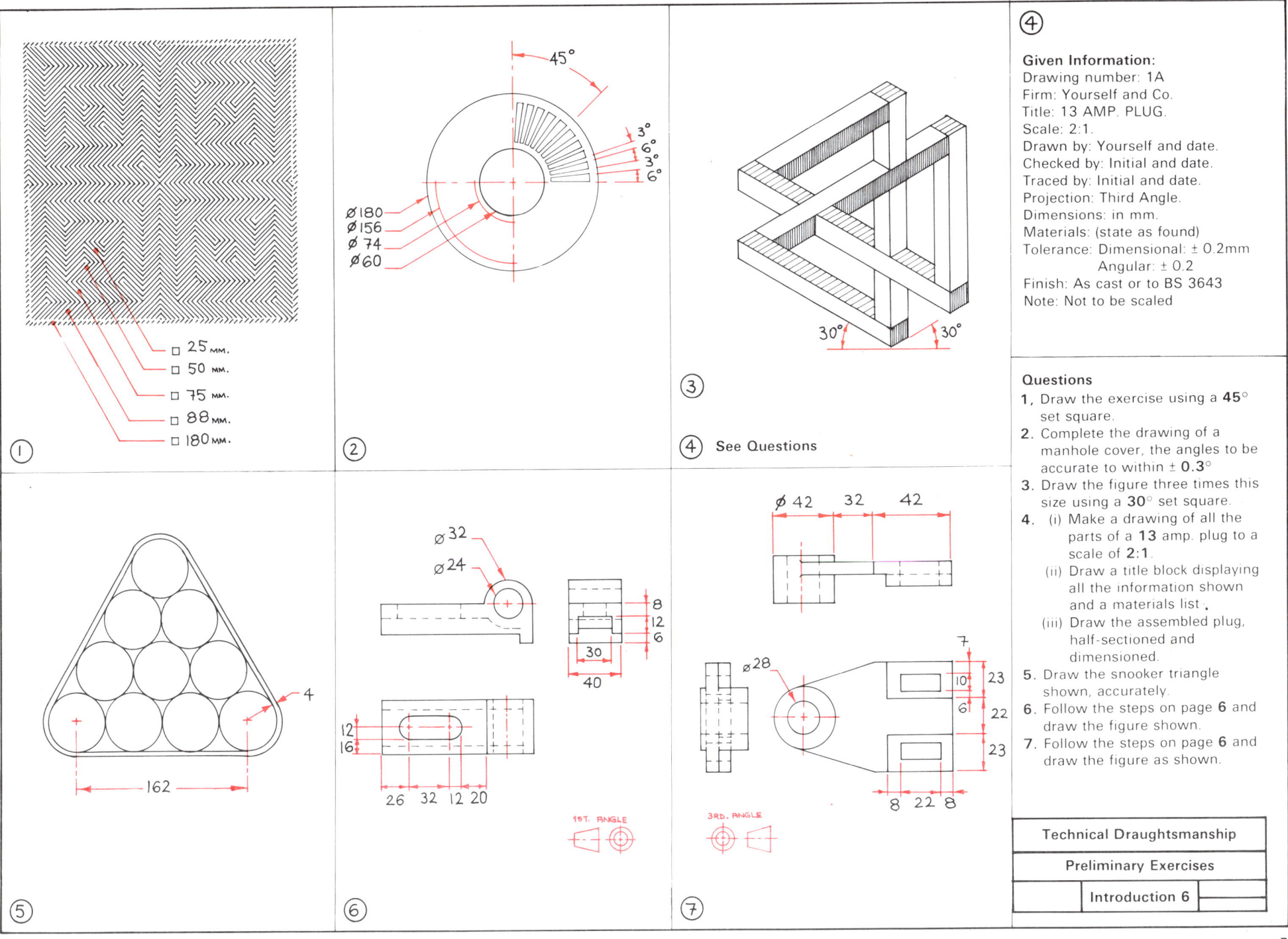

④

Given Information:
Drawing number: 1A
Firm: Yourself and Co.
Title: 13 AMP. PLUG.
Scale: 2:1.
Drawn by: Yourself and date.
Checked by: Initial and date.
Traced by: Initial and date.
Projection: Third Angle.
Dimensions: in mm.
Materials: (state as found)
Tolerance: Dimensional: ± 0.2mm
　　　　　　Angular: ± 0.2
Finish: As cast or to BS 3643
Note: Not to be scaled

Questions

1. Draw the exercise using a **45°** set square.
2. Complete the drawing of a manhole cover, the angles to be accurate to within ± **0.3°**.
3. Draw the figure three times this size using a **30°** set square.
4. (i) Make a drawing of all the parts of a **13** amp. plug to a scale of **2:1**.
   (ii) Draw a title block displaying all the information shown and a materials list.
   (iii) Draw the assembled plug, half-sectioned and dimensioned.
5. Draw the snooker triangle shown, accurately.
6. Follow the steps on page **6** and draw the figure shown.
7. Follow the steps on page **6** and draw the figure as shown.

Technical Draughtsmanship
Preliminary Exercises
Introduction 6

PART 1

**CHAPTER 2
REVISION**

Here is a short outline of the basic geometric ideas and constructions.
You should make absolutely sure you know these pages before proceeding further.
Should your memory slip you can refer back here.

CONTENTS

Lines, Angles and Triangles	*Page* **9**
Quadrilaterals and Polygons	**10**
Regular Solids	**11**
Basic Constructions	**12**
Polygons and Pentagons	**13**
Triangle Constructions	**14**
The Circle and its Properties	**15**
Tangents and Tangent Arcs	**16**
Circle Constructions 1	**17**
Circle Constructions 2	**18**
Inscribing	**19**
Exercises	**20**

1 LINES

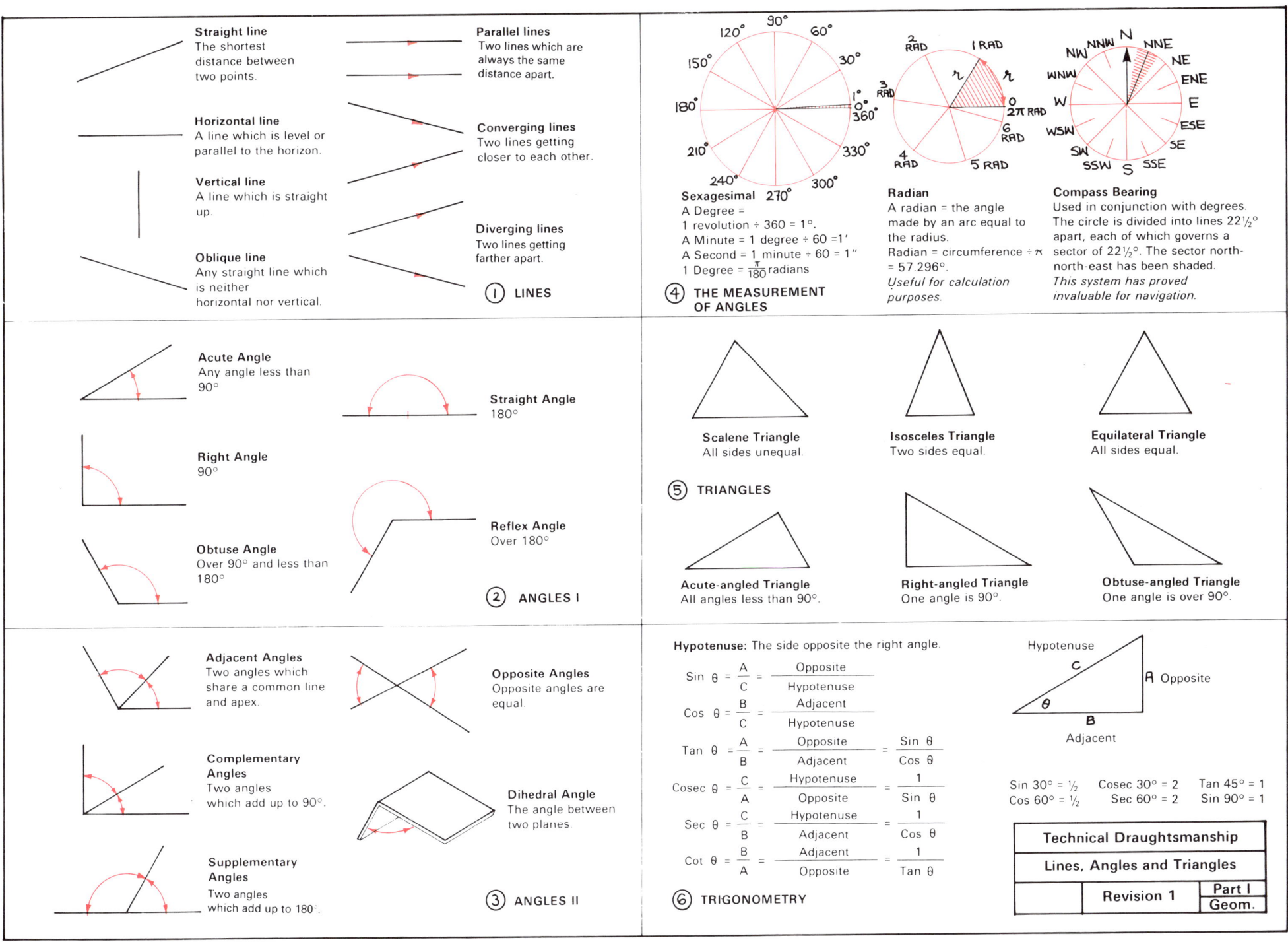

Straight line — The shortest distance between two points.

Horizontal line — A line which is level or parallel to the horizon.

Vertical line — A line which is straight up.

Oblique line — Any straight line which is neither horizontal nor vertical.

Parallel lines — Two lines which are always the same distance apart.

Converging lines — Two lines getting closer to each other.

Diverging lines — Two lines getting farther apart.

2 ANGLES I

Acute Angle — Any angle less than 90°

Right Angle — 90°

Obtuse Angle — Over 90° and less than 180°

Straight Angle — 180°

Reflex Angle — Over 180°

3 ANGLES II

Adjacent Angles — Two angles which share a common line and apex.

Complementary Angles — Two angles which add up to 90°.

Supplementary Angles — Two angles which add up to 180°.

Opposite Angles — Opposite angles are equal.

Dihedral Angle — The angle between two planes.

4 THE MEASUREMENT OF ANGLES

Sexagesimal
A Degree =
1 revolution ÷ 360 = 1°.
A Minute = 1 degree ÷ 60 = 1'
A Second = 1 minute ÷ 60 = 1"
1 Degree = $\frac{\pi}{180}$ radians

Radian
A radian = the angle made by an arc equal to the radius.
Radian = circumference ÷ π
= 57.296°.
Useful for calculation purposes.

Compass Bearing
Used in conjunction with degrees. The circle is divided into lines 22½° apart, each of which governs a sector of 22½°. The sector north-north-east has been shaded.
This system has proved invaluable for navigation.

5 TRIANGLES

Scalene Triangle — All sides unequal.

Isosceles Triangle — Two sides equal.

Equilateral Triangle — All sides equal.

Acute-angled Triangle — All angles less than 90°.

Right-angled Triangle — One angle is 90°.

Obtuse-angled Triangle — One angle is over 90°.

6 TRIGONOMETRY

Hypotenuse: The side opposite the right angle.

$\sin \theta = \dfrac{A}{C} = \dfrac{\text{Opposite}}{\text{Hypotenuse}}$

$\cos \theta = \dfrac{B}{C} = \dfrac{\text{Adjacent}}{\text{Hypotenuse}}$

$\tan \theta = \dfrac{A}{B} = \dfrac{\text{Opposite}}{\text{Adjacent}} = \dfrac{\sin \theta}{\cos \theta}$

$\text{cosec } \theta = \dfrac{C}{A} = \dfrac{\text{Hypotenuse}}{\text{Opposite}} = \dfrac{1}{\sin \theta}$

$\sec \theta = \dfrac{C}{B} = \dfrac{\text{Hypotenuse}}{\text{Adjacent}} = \dfrac{1}{\cos \theta}$

$\cot \theta = \dfrac{B}{A} = \dfrac{\text{Adjacent}}{\text{Opposite}} = \dfrac{1}{\tan \theta}$

Sin 30° = ½   Cosec 30° = 2   Tan 45° = 1
Cos 60° = ½   Sec 60° = 2   Sin 90° = 1

Technical Draughtsmanship
Lines, Angles and Triangles
Revision 1 — Part I — Geom.

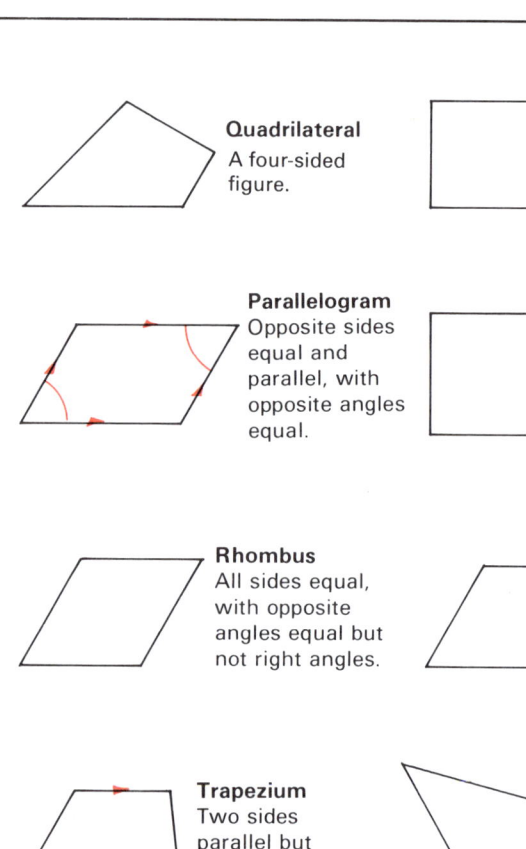

Quadrilateral
A four-sided figure.

Rectangle
Opposite sides equal and all angles 90°.

Parallelogram
Opposite sides equal and parallel, with opposite angles equal.

Square
All sides equal and all angles 90°.

Rhombus
All sides equal, with opposite angles equal but not right angles.

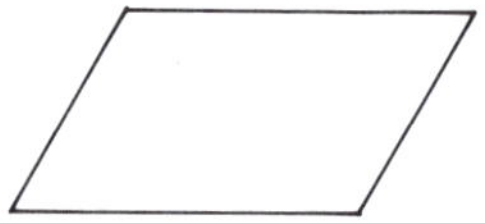

Rhomboid
Opposite sides equal and parallel, with opposite angles equal but not right angles.

Trapezium
Two sides parallel but unequal in length.

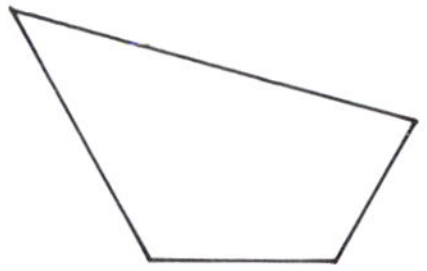

Trapezoid
No two sides parallel.

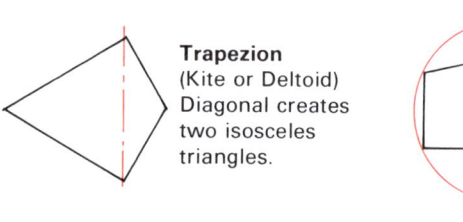

Trapezion
(Kite or Deltoid) Diagonal creates two isosceles triangles.

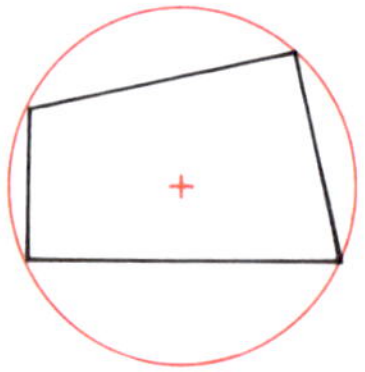

Cyclic Quadrilateral
Any quadrilateral all of whose corners can be touched by a single circle.

QUADRILATERALS:
① *All* the above are quadrilaterals. The rhombus, rhomboid, rectangle and square are also parallelograms.

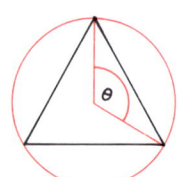

Equilateral Triangle
$\theta = 120°$
Three equal sides.

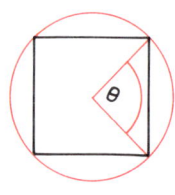

Square
$\theta = 90°$
Four equal sides

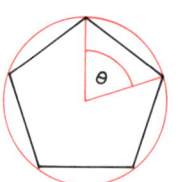

Pentagon
$\theta = 72°$
Five equal sides.

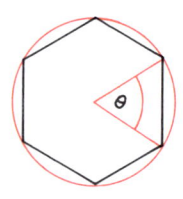

Hexagon
$\theta = 60°$.
Six equal sides.

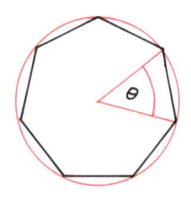

Heptagon
$\theta = 51.5°$
Seven equal sides

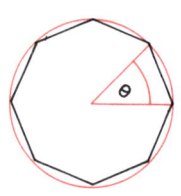

Octagon
$\theta = 45°$.
Eight equal sides.

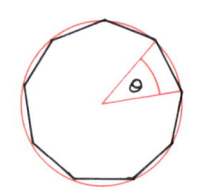

Nonagon
$\theta = 40°$
Nine equal sides.

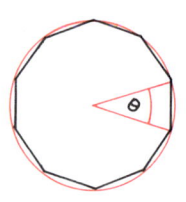

Decagon
$\theta = 36°$.
Ten equal sides.

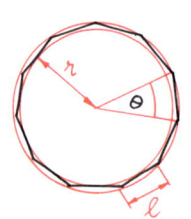

Regular Polygon
$\theta = 360 \div n$
Area = $\dfrac{n l r}{2}$

where **n** is the number of sides, **l** the length of side and **r** the radius of the inscribed circle.

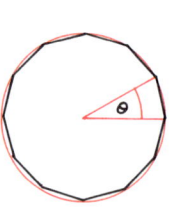

Dodecagon
$\theta = 30°$.
Twelve equal sides.

REGULAR POLYGONS: ② Any many-sided plane figure whose sides are equal and whose interior angles (θ) are equal.

Technical Draughtsmanship
Quadrilaterals and Polygons
Revision 2 — Part I — Geom.

Triangular
Ends are triangles.

Rectangular
Ends are rectangles.

Cube
Ends and sides are square.

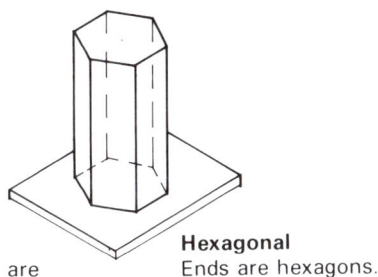

Hexagonal
Ends are hexagons.

Cylinder
Ends are circular.

① **PRISMS:** A prism has two ends that are similar, equal and parallel. *The word is Greek and means "a piece sawn off". Look around a woodwork room and you will find plenty of prisms.*

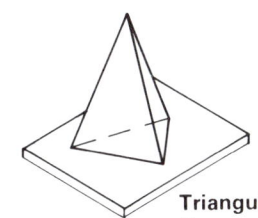

④ **CYLINDER**

Triangular
Base is a triangle

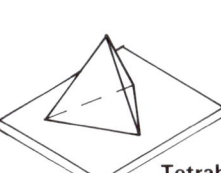

Tetrahedron
Base and sides are equilateral triangles.

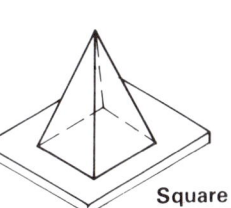

Square
Base is square.

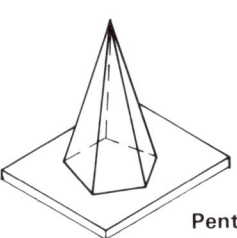

Pentagonal
Base is a pentagon.

Cone
Base is circular.

② **PYRAMIDS:** A pyramid has a polygon as a base and sloping sides that meet at a point called the apex. *The word is Greek but nobody is sure of its origin.*

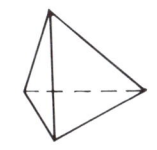

⑤ **CONE**

Tetrahedron
Four equilateral triangular sides.

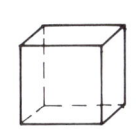

Cube
Six square sides.

Octahedron
Eight equilateral triangular sides.

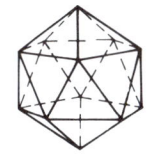

Icosahedron
Twenty equilateral triangular sides.

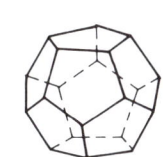

Dodecahedron
Twelve pentagonal sides.

A *solid* may be described as:
Right: upright, as shown here.
Oblique: leaning.
Cut: simply cut.
Truncated: when a piece is cut off.
A Frustrum: when it is cut off parallel to the base.

③ **REGULAR POLYHEDRA:** There are only five solids whose faces are all identical. Plato mentioned them and they are often called **The Platonic Solids**. *At one time philosophers thought that these solids formed the basis of all creation. Polyhedra is Greek for 'many faces'.*

Technical Draughtsmanship
Regular Solids
Revision 3 — Part 1 Geom.

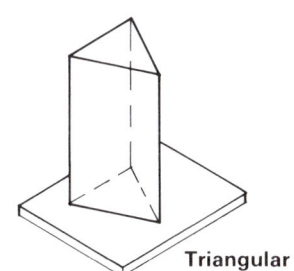

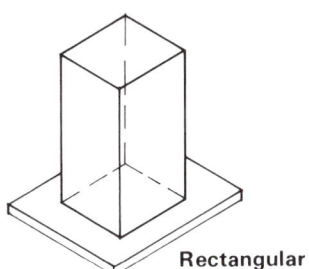

①

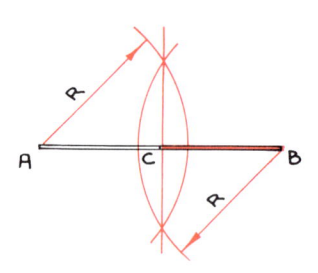

To bisect a line
- Radius **R** may be any length obviously over half of **AB**.

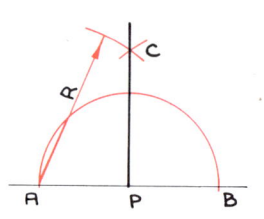

To erect a perpendicular at P
- **AB** is a semicircle about **P**.
- **R** is any radius greater than **AP**.

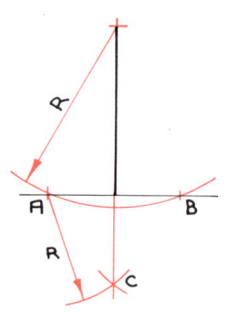

To drop a perpendicular from P to line AB
- Radius **R** is any length that will reach the line **AB**.

②

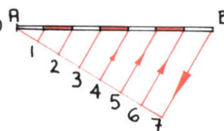

To divide a line into parts (e.g. seven)
- At any acute angle from **A** set out a true scale of seven parts.
- Then **B** is joined to **7** and the other divisions are drawn parallel.

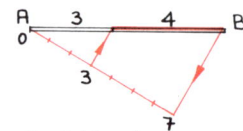

To divide a line into a given ratio (e.g. 3:4)
- The construction is clear from the diagram.

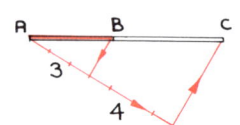

To extend a line in a given ratio (e.g. 3:4)
- The construction is clear from the diagram.

③

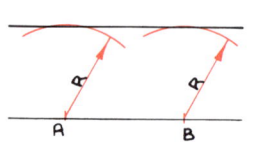

To draw a line parallel to a given line
- The construction is clear from the diagram.

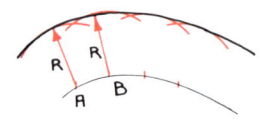

To draw a curve parallel to a given curve.
- The construction is clear from the diagram.

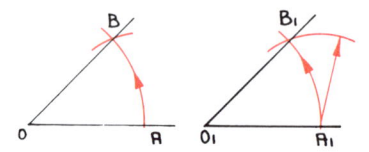

To copy a given angle
- With centre **O** swing an arc **AB**.
- With centre **O₁** swing an equal arc **A₁B₁**.
- With centre **O₁** measure the distance to **B**.
- Transfer this to centre **A₁** and fixing **B₁** draw the angle.
- Angle **AOB** = angle **A₁O₁B₁**.

④

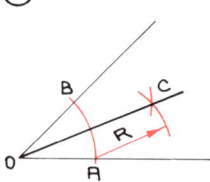

To bisect an angle
- With centre **O** strike an arc (**AB**).
- Radius **R** can be of any chosen length.
- **OC** is the bisector.

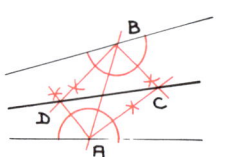

To bisect an angle (not given the apex) I.
- **AB** is drawn wherever you wish.
- Bisect each of the supplementary angles at **A** and **B** to find **C** and **D**.
- **CD** is the bisector.

To bisect an angle (not given the apex) II 
- Draw a line parallel to and at a chosen distance from **AB**.
- Draw a second line parallel to and at the same distance from **CD**.
- Their intersection gives **E**.
- **F** is found in a similar way.
- **EF** is the bisector.

⑤

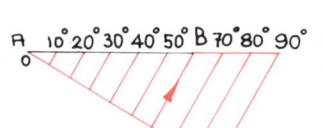

Scale of chords:
- Given **AB** divide it into *six* parts (always).
- Index these as 0° to 60°.
- Once the divisions are set they may be extended to 90°.

Using the scale of chords to construct an angle, (e.g. 40°) 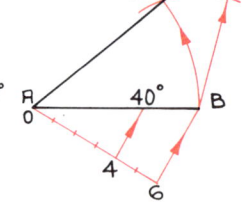
- Find 40° as previously.
- With centre **A** swing an arc towards **C**.
- With centre **B** and radius **A**40° locate point **C**.
- Angle **BAC = 40°**.

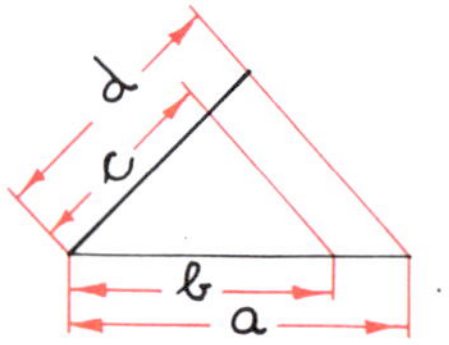

Given a, b and c to find d so that a:b::c:d. (find the fourth proportion)
- Lay out **a** and **b** as shown.
- At any acute angle draw **c**.
- Join **c** to **b**.
- From the end of **a** draw a line *parallel* to find **d**.

⑥

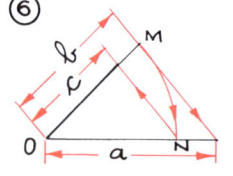

Given the extremes a and b to find the mean c so that a:c::c:b
- Set **b** at any acute angle to **a**.
- With centre **o** swing **M** to meet **a** at **N**.

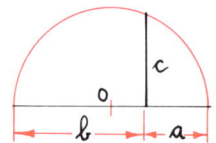

An alternative way of finding the mean a:c::c:b
- Draw a semicircle on **ab**.
- **c** is perpendicular where **a** meets **b** and is the Mean Proportion.

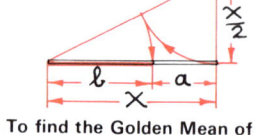

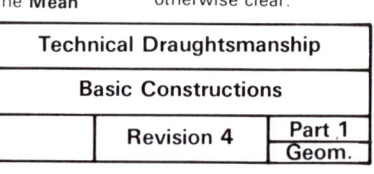

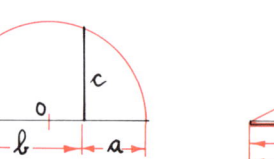

To find the Golden Mean of line x so that a:b::b:(a + b)
- **x = a + b**.
- The construction is otherwise clear.

Note: *There is only one Golden Mean proportion. This is ($\sqrt{5}+1$) ÷ 2 or* **1.618**. *This was considered the one true and perfect division and was even seen as symbolic of the Son of God.*

Technical Draughtsmanship	
Basic Constructions	
Revision 4	Part 1
	Geom.

①

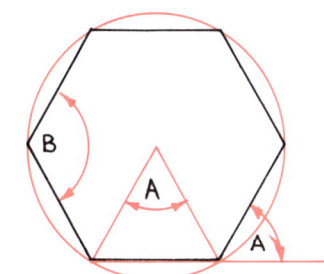

Angles in Regular Polygon
- The angle $A = \dfrac{360°}{n}$
- n is the number of sides.
- The angle $B = 180° - A°$

Note: *Although the best way to construct a Polygon is with a protractor it is nonetheless useful to know other constructions. The Pentagon is somewhat special and has often been considered magical due to its many elegant constructions.*

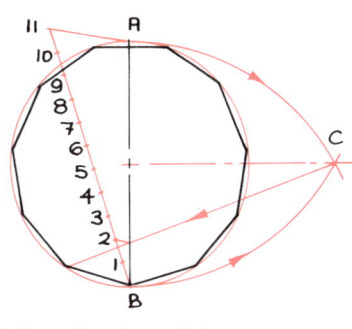

②

Polygon in a given circle
- Divide the diameter into the same number of parts as there are sides on the required polygon.
- With **A** as centre swing **B** towards **C**.
- With **B** as centre swing **A** to fix **C**.
- Join **C** through the *second* division to find **D**.
- Step off the sides.

Note: *The second division is always the one used.*

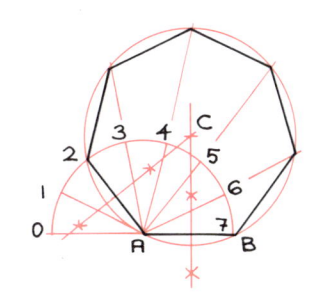

Polygon given a side AB (alternative method)
- With **A** as centre and **AB** as radius draw a semicircle.
- Divide the semicircle into the same number of parts as the required polygon has sides.
- **A2** will be a side of the polygon.
- The bisectors of **AB** and of **A2** will meet at **C**, the centre of the circumcircle.

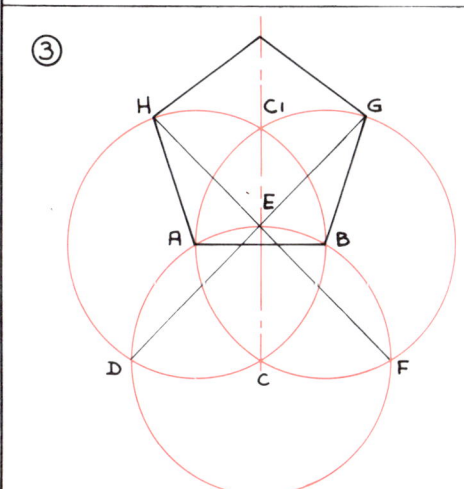

③

To construct a pentagon given side AB (Method I)
- With **A** as centre and **AB** as radius draw a circle.
- With **B** as centre draw a similar circle to intersect the first circle at **C** and **C1**.
- Join **C** to **C1** and extend.
- With centre **C** draw a third similar circle.
- Join **D** through **E** to find **G**.
- Join **F** through **E** to find **H**.
- Complete the pentagon.

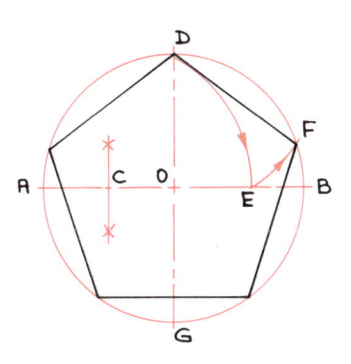

To construct a pentagon in a given circle
- Draw the diameters **AB** and **DG**.
- Bisect **OA** to find **C**.
- With **C** as centre swing **D** down to **E**.
- With **D** as centre swing **E** to **F**.
- **DF** is one side. Step off the others.

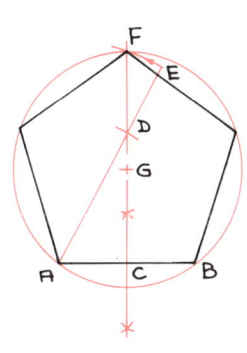

To construct a pentagon given side AB (method II)
- Bisect **AB** and extend.
- Measure **AD** = **AB**.
- Join **A** to **D** and extend.
- With centre **D** and radius **AC** swing an arc **E** to **F**.
- Bisect the diagonal from **F** to find the circumcentre **G**.

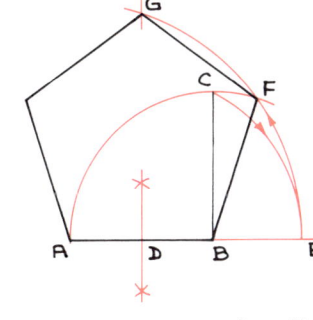

To construct a pentagon given side AB (Method III)
- With centre **B** and radius **AB** draw an arc towards **E**.
- Erect a perpendicular at **B** to **C**.
- Bisect **AB**.
- With centre **D** swing **C** to **E**.
- With centre **A** and Radius **AE** fix **F** and **G**.

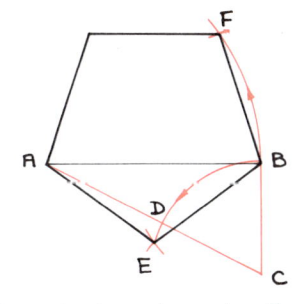

To construct a pentagon given the diagonal (AB)
- Make **BC** = ½ **AB**.
- With centre **C** swing **B** to **D**.
- With centre **A** swing **D** towards **E**.
- With centre **B** and Radius **AD** locate **E**.
- With centre **A** swing **B** towards **F**.
- With centre **B** and Radius **AD** fix **F**.
- Complete the pentagon.

Technical Draughtsmanship		
Polygons and Pentagons		
Revision 5	Part I	Geom.

①

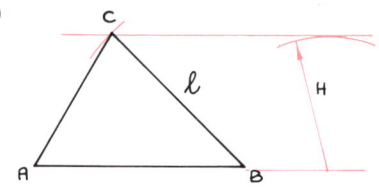

A triangle given base AB, one side l and altitude H.
- Draw base **AB**.
- Parallel, and at a distance **H**, draw a line.
- With centre **B** and Radius **l** fix point **C** on the line.
- Complete the triangle.

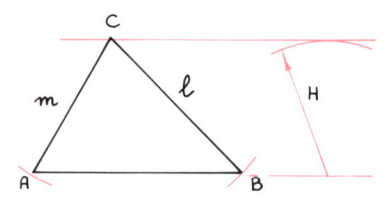

A triangle given two sides l and m, and altitude H.
- Draw two parallel lines a distance of **H** apart.
- On the line choose a point **C**.
- With **C** as centre and **l** as radius fix **B**.
- With **C** as centre and **m** as radius fix **A**.

②

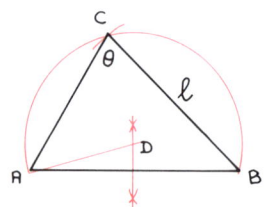

A triangle given the base AB, one side l and the apex angle
- Bisect the base **AB**.
- From **A** draw an angle of 90°−θ, angle **BAD**, to fix centre **D**.
- With **D** as centre and **AD** as radius draw a circle.
- With centre **B** and radius **l** fix point **C**.

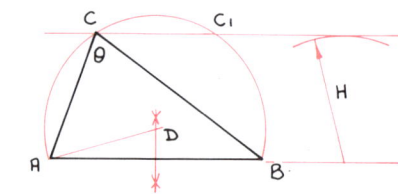

A triangle given the base AB, the altitude H and the apex angle θ.
- Proceed as before, letting angle BAD = 90°− θ
- Use **H** to find **C** as shown.
- **C1** is a valid alternative position.

Note: *D may be outside the triangle. Also these constructions can be used to find a triangle known to be inscribed.*

③

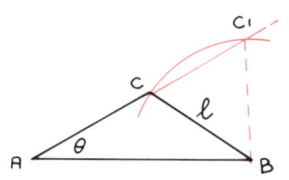

A triangle given the base AB, a base angle θ and side l that is opposite the given angle.
- Draw **AB** and set out angle **θ**.
- With **B** as centre and **l** as radius fix point **C**.
- Notice the two possible positions of **C**. Both are valid.

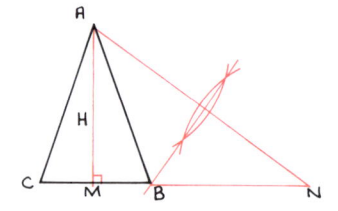

An isosceles triangle given the perimeter and the altitude H.
- Draw **MN** = ½ the perimeter.
- At **M** erect a perpendicular of altitude **H** to find **A**.
- Join **N** to **A** and bisect. The bisector cutting **MN** at **B**.
- Make **CM** = **MB** and draw the triangle.

④

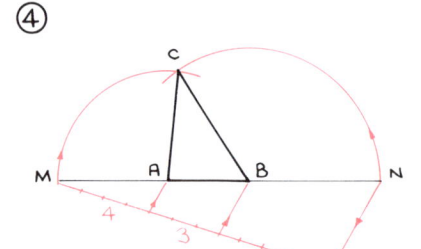

A triangle given the perimeter MN and the ratio of the sides (e.g. 4:3:5).
- Draw the perimeter **MN**.
- Divide **MN** into the ratios 4:3:5 as shown to get the base **AB**.
- With **A** as centre swing **M** towards **C**.
- With **B** as centre swing **N** to fix **C**.

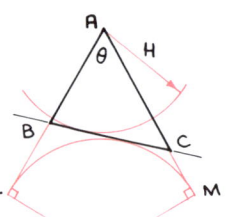

A triangle given the perimeter, the apex angle θ and the altitude H.
- Take a point **A** and set out **θ** letting AL = AM = ½ the Perimeter.
- Erect perpendiculars at **L** and at **M** to meet at **N**.
- With **N** as centre swing **L** to **M**.
- With **A** as centre and **H** as radius swing an arc.
- **BC** is on a tangent to both arcs, there being two possible solutions.

⑤

A triangle given the perimeter, the base AB and the altitude H. 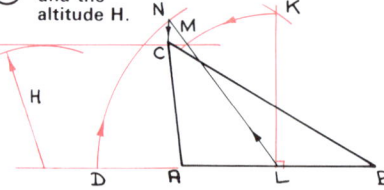
- Bisect **AB** at **L** and let LD = (½ the perimeter − AB).
- Erect a perpendicular at **L** and with centre **A** and radius LD find **K**.
- At distance **H** from the base draw a line.
- With centre **L** swing **D** towards **N** and from **K** onto the line at **M**.
- Join **L** to **M** and extend to **N**.
- Drop a perpendicular from **N** to find **C**.

A triangle given the base AB, the altitude H, and the ratio of the other two sides (e.g. 3:7). 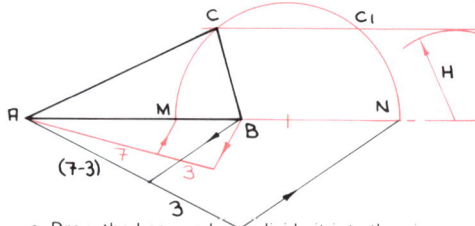
- Draw the base and divide it into the given ratio to find **M**. Note the largest ratio is *first*.
- From **A** set a line with the ratios as shown in black. Use this to find **N**.
- At distance **H** draw a line.
- On **MN** draw a circle cutting the line at **C** and **C1**.
- Draw the triangle **ABC** or **ABC1**.

⑥

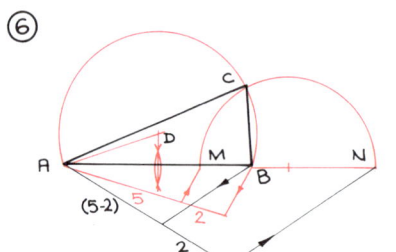

A triangle given the base AB, the ratio of the two other sides (e.g. 5:2) and the apex angle θ.
- This is a mix of constructions 2 and 5ii above.
- Divide **AB** into the given ratio (largest first) to find **M**.
- From **A** set a line with ratios as shown in black. Use this to find **N** and draw semicircle **MN**.
- Bisect **AB** towards **D** and from **A** set an angle of 90°−θ to fix **D**.
- With **D** as centre and radius AD find point **C**.

Note: *Give yourself plenty of room for this construction.*

Note: *Many of these problems can also be solved using the simple trigonometry on page 9.*

Technical Draughtsmanship
Triangle Constructions
Revision 6 — Part I Geom.

①

Concentric Circles are circles drawn about the same centre.

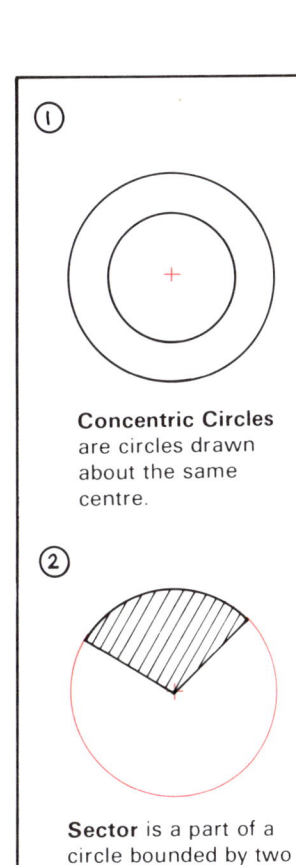

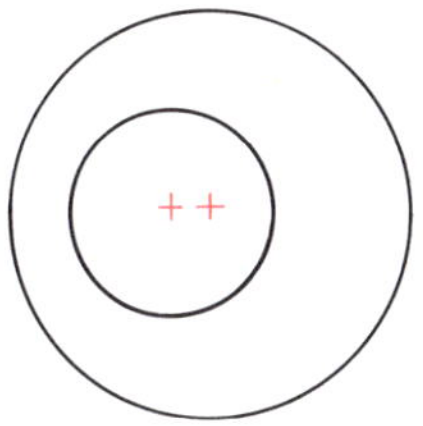

Eccentric Circles are circles drawn about different centres.

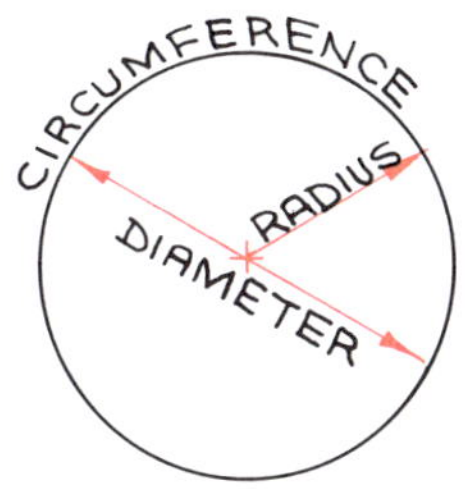

Diameter = 2 x radius
Circumference = $2\pi r$

②

Sector is a part of a circle bounded by two radii.

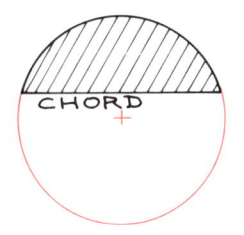

Segment is a part cut from a circle by a chord.

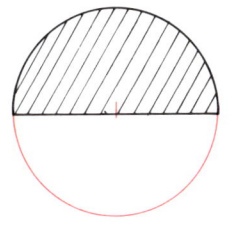

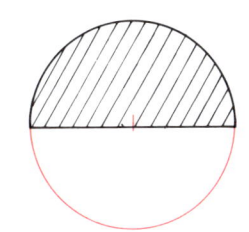

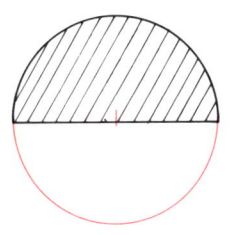

Semicircle is half a circle.

③

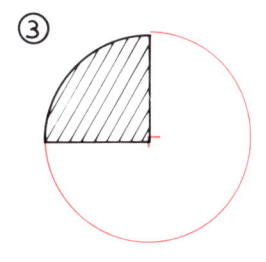

A Quadrant is a quarter of a circle.

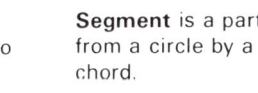

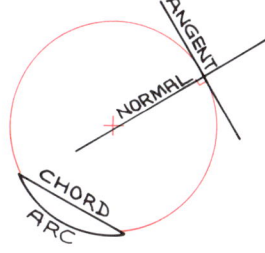

A Chord is any line drawn across a circle.
An Arc is any part of the circumference of a circle.
A Tangent is a line that touches a circle at one point only.
A Normal is at right angles to a tangent and passes through both the point of tangency and the centre of the circle.

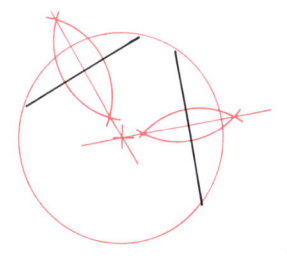

The Bisectors of Chords are normals and pass through the centre of the circle.

④

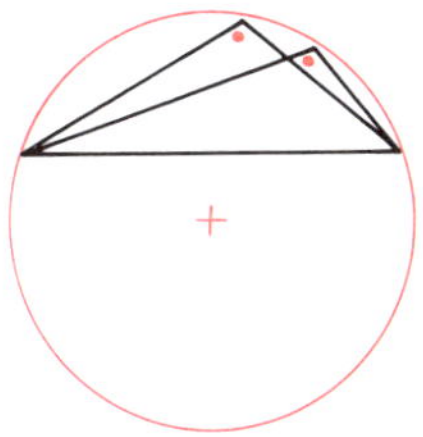

Angles in a segment less than half a circle are equal and obtuse.

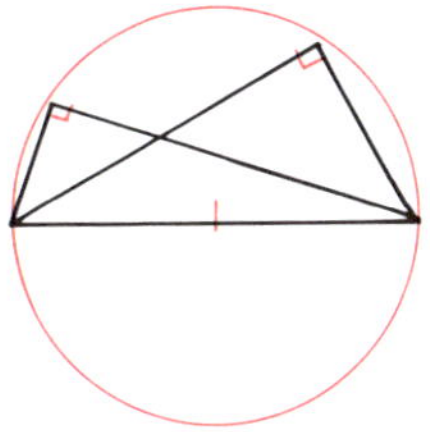

All **angles in a semi-circle** are right angles.

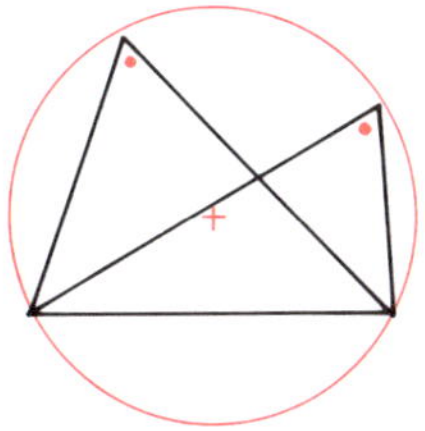

Angles on a segment over half a circle are equal and acute.

⑤

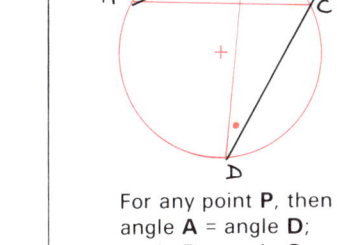

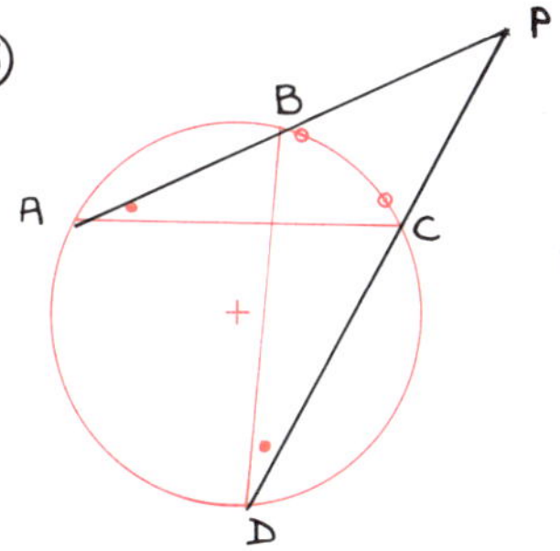

For any point **P**, then angle **A** = angle **D**; angle **B** = angle **C**
AP x PB = CP x PD

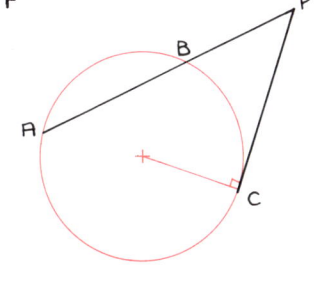

For any point **P** and if **PC** is a tangent, then **PA x PB = PC²**.

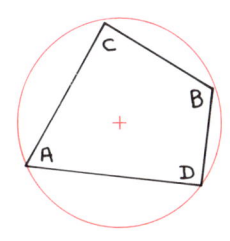

For any **Circumscribed Quadrilateral**
A + B = 180° = C + D.

⑥

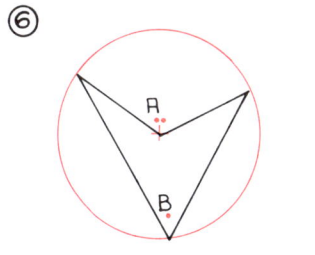

The angle at the centre of a circle is twice that at the perimeter.
A = 2B

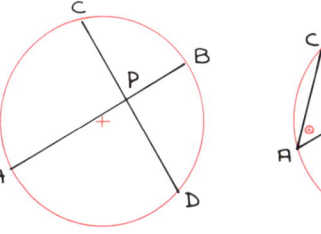

If two chords cross at P, then
AB x PB = CP x DP

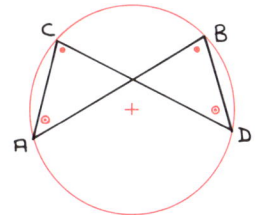

Join the ends of two chords, then **angle at A = angle at D** and **angle at B = angle at C**.

Technical Draughtsmanship		
The Circle and its Properties		
	Revision 7	Part I Geom.

① To draw a tangent at P.
- Join **C** to **P** and extend.
- Erect a perpendicular at **P**.
- This will be the tangent.

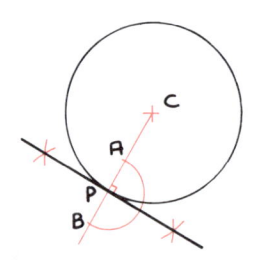

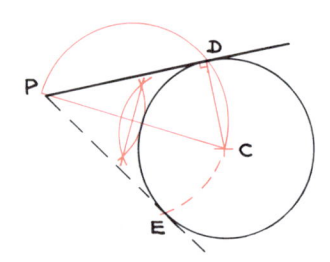

To draw a tangent from P.
- Join **P** to **C** and bisect.
- Draw a semicircle on **PC** cutting the circle **C** at **D**.
- **PD** is the tangent.

② Tangent to an arc at P.
- With **P** as centre draw a circle.
- Bisect **AB** to get **CD**.
- Set the tangent at **P** perpendicular to **CD**.

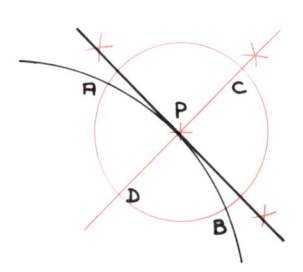

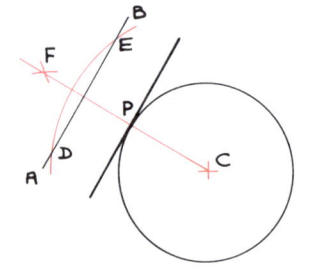

Tangent parallel to a given line AB.
- With centre **C** draw an arc across the line at **D** and **E**.
- Erect a perpendicular on **DE** to get **FC**.
- **P** is the point of tangency.
- Draw the tangent parallel to **AB**.

③ An external tangent to two equal circles.
- Join **A** to **B**.
- Erect perpendiculars to **C** and **D**.
- Draw the tangent **CD**.

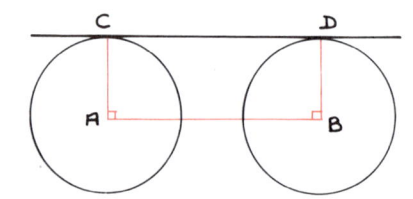

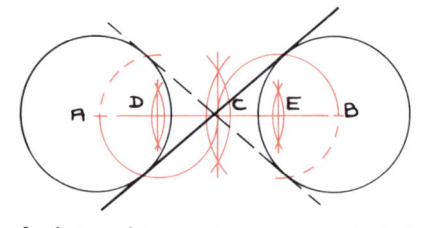

An internal tangent to two equal circles.
- Join **A** to **B** and bisect (**C**).
- Bisect **AC** and with radius **DC** draw an arc to find **F**.
- Find **G** in a similar way.
- **FG** is the tangent.

④ External tangent to two given circles.
- With centre **A** draw an auxiliary circle of radius **R-r**.
- Join **A** to **B** and bisect.
- Draw a semicircle **AB** cutting the auxiliary circle at **D**.
- Draw **ADE** and **BF** parallel.
- **EF** is the tangent.

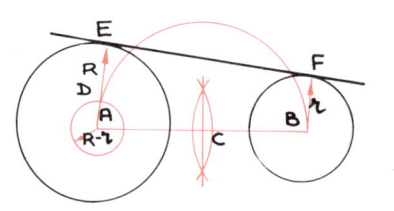

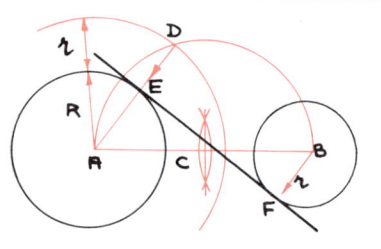

Internal tangent to two given circles.
- With centre **A** draw an auxiliary circle of radius **R+r**.
- Join **A** to **B** and draw a semicircle on **AB** cutting the auxiliary circle at **D**.
- Draw **DEA** and **BF** parallel.
- **EF** is the tangent.

⑤ Tangent arc to two given circles.
- **X** is a given distance.
- Arcs are struck from **A** and **B** to locate **C** as shown.

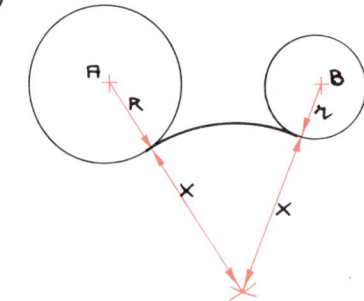

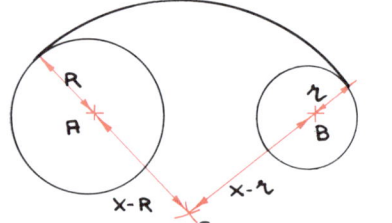

Tangent arc to enclose two given circles.
- **X** is a given distance.
- Arcs are struck from **A** and **B** to locate **C** as shown.

⑥ Internal tangent arc to two given circles.
- **X** is a given distance.
- An arc is struck from **A** and **B** to locate **C** as is shown above.

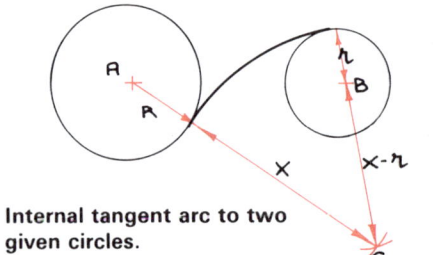

Note: *Tangents are difficult. So, if there are tangents in a drawing tackle them first.*

Technical Draughtsmanship
Tangents and Tangent Arcs
Revision 8 — Part I Geom.

①

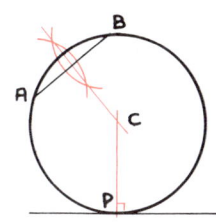

The centre of a circle
- The centre lies on a line at right angles to any point of tangency **P**. This line **CP** is called a **Normal**.
- The centre lies on the bisector of any chord **AB**.

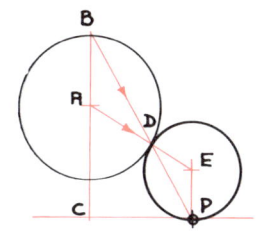

A circle to touch circle A and point P.
- Draw a vertical diameter from **B** and extend towards **C**.
- Draw a horizontal line from **P** to **C** and a perpendicular at **P** towards **E**.
- Join **B** to **P** cutting circle **A** at **D**.
- From **A** through **D** find **E**.

②

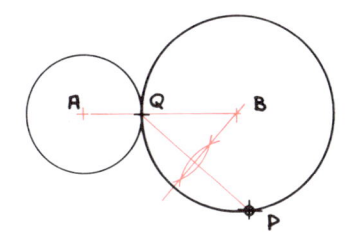

A circle to touch circle A at point Q and to pass through point P.
- From **A** draw a line through **Q** towards **B**.
- Join **Q** to **P** and bisect.
- The bisector will fix centre **B**.

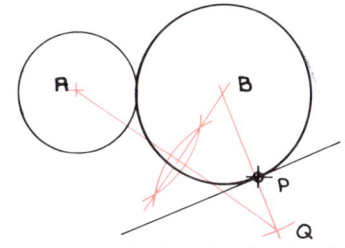

A circle to touch circle A and a given line at point P.
- The line must be a tangent.
- Erect a perpendicular at **P** towards **B** and extend it so that **PQ** is equal to the radius of circle **A**.
- Join **A** to **Q** and bisect.
- The bisector will fix centre **B**.

③

A circle through two points A and B and to touch a given line. (Method I) 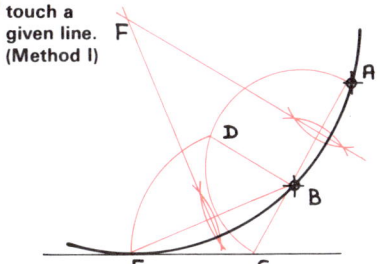
- Join **A** to **B**. Bisect and extend to meet the line at **C**.
- Draw a semicircle on **AC** and erect a perpendicular at **B** to **D**.
- With **C** as centre swing **D** on to the line at **E**.
- Join **E** to **B** and bisect to fix centre **F**.

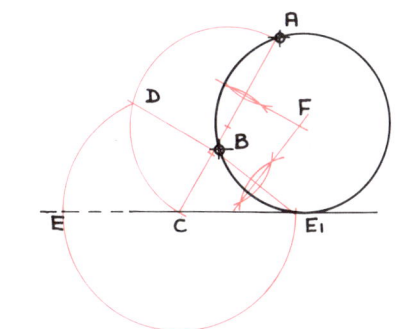

A circle through two points A and B and a given line. (Method II).
- The method is as before but **D** is swung *past* **E** until it meets the line a second time at **E₁**.

④

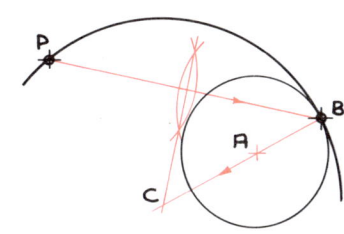

Circle to enclose a given circle A to touch it at B and to pass through a point P.
- Join **P** to **B** and bisect.
- From **B** through centre **A** fix centre **C**.

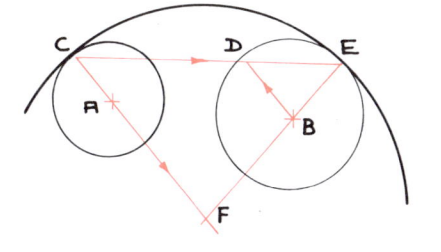

Circle to touch and enclose two given circles A and B.
- Take any point **C** on circle **A** and draw a line through its centre towards **F**.
- At centre **B** draw a line **BD** parallel to **CA**.
- Join **C** to **D** and extend to **E**.
- From **E** through **B** fix centre **F**.

⑤

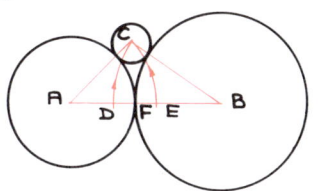

A circle C to touch two given circles A and B.
- Join **A** to **B**.
- Mark **D** and **E** so that **DF** = **FE** = radius of circle **C**.
- With centre **A** swing **E** towards **C**.
- With centre **B** swing **D** to fix centre **C**.

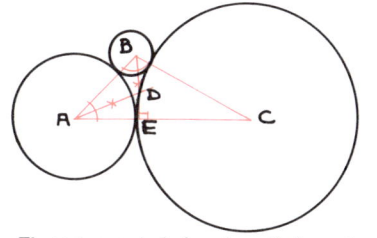

Three tangent circles given their centres A, B and C.
- Join **A** to **B** to **C**.
- Bisect angles **ABC** and **BAC** to find the circumcentre **D**.
- Drop a perpendicular from **D** to **E**.
- Draw circles **A** and **C** through **E**.
- Draw circle **B**.

⑥

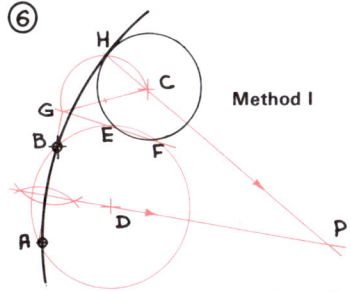

Method I

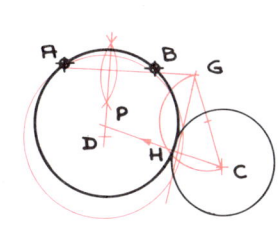

Method II
As previously, except that the semicircle is erected on the other side of the line **CG**.

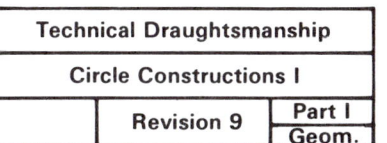

A circle through two points A and B and to touch a circle C.
- Join **A** to **B** and bisect.
- Choose a centre **D** on the bisector and draw a circle through **A** and **B** to cut circle **C** at **G**.
- Join **G** to **C** and erect a semicircle cutting circle **C** at **H**.
- From **H** through **C** fix centre **P**.

Technical Draughtsmanship
Circle Constructions I
Revision 9 — Part I — Geom.

17

①

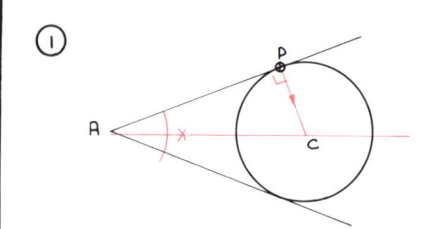

A circle to touch two lines and point P on
- Bisect the angle between the lines and extend the bisector.
- From P drop a perpendicular to find centre C on the bisector.

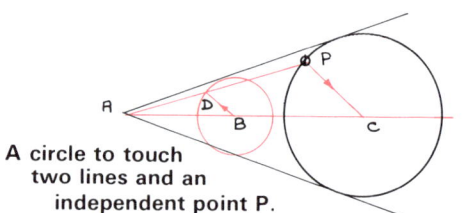

A circle to touch two lines and an independent point P.
- Bisect the angle between the lines.
- With any centre B draw a circle touching both lines.
- Join P to A cutting the circle at D.
- Join B to D and draw PC parallel.

Note: Point D may have an alternative position that is also valid. The circles often overlap.

②

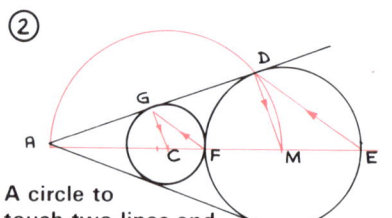

A circle to touch two lines and a given tangent circle (M).
- Bisect A and extend the bisector.
- On AM draw a semicircle, cutting the circle at D.
- Join E to D and D to M.
- Parallel to ED draw FG.
- Parallel to DM draw GC.
- C is the centre and CF the radius.

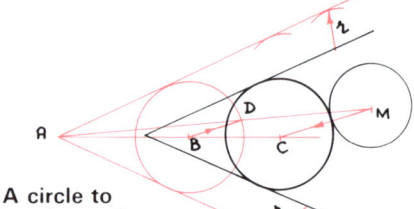

A circle to touch two lines and a given circle (M).
- Parallel to the two lines draw two new lines at a distance equal to the radius of M.
- Bisect A and extend the bisector.
- At any centre B draw a circle touching both outside lines.
- Join M to A cutting the circle at D.
- Join B to D and draw MC parallel.

③

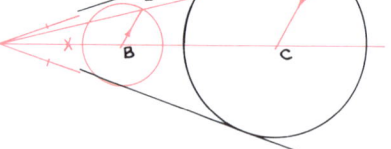

One of the above problems when the lines are not joined.
- Extend the lines to locate A.
- Proceed as usual.

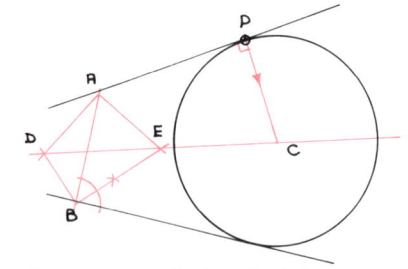

When it is not practical to find the meeting point of the lines.
- Locate the bisector as shown on page 12.
- Proceed as usual.

Note: This construction is of limited use.

④

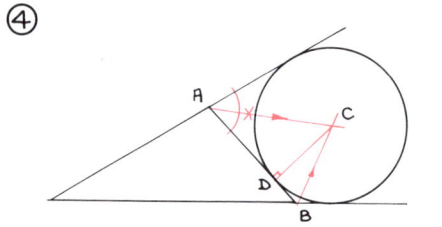

To escribe a circle to a triangle.
- Extend any two sides of the triangle.
- Bisect the exterior angles formed (A and B) to find C.
- From C drop a perpendicular to D.
- C is the centre and CD the radius.

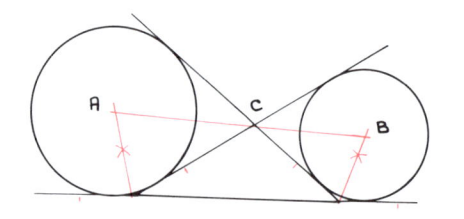

To escribe two circles to a triangle.
- Same procedure as previously.

Note: The centres A and B are in line with an apex C. Where would the third centre lie?

⑤

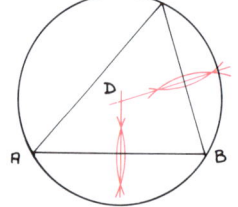

To escribe a circle around a given triangle (ABC).
- Bisect any two sides and extend the bisectors to meet at D.
- D is the centre and DA the radius.

Note: The centre (D) may lie outside the triangle.

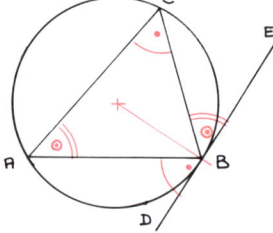

Some properties of an escribed triangle.
- DE is drawn as a tangent at B.
- Angle ACB = angle ABD.
- Angle CAB = angle CBE.

⑥

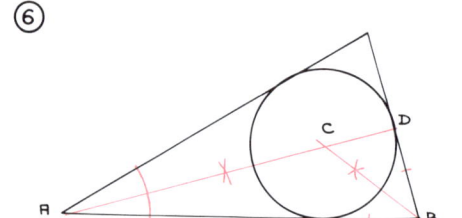

Inscribe a circle in a triangle.
- Bisect any two angles (A and B) to find C.
- Extend a bisector to D.
- C is the centre and CD the radius.

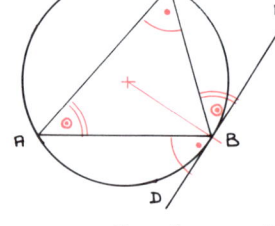

Note:
Describe means 'write down' or draw.
Escribe (originally exscribe) means 'draw outside'.
Inscribe means 'draw inside'.

Technical Draughtsmanship		
Circle Constructions 2		
Revision 10	Part I	Geom.

① **To inscribe a circle in a sector.**
- Bisect the angle at **A** and extend to **D**.
- At **D** draw a tangent **BC**.
- Complete the triangle **ABC**.
- Bisect the angle at **C** (or **B**) to fix centre **F**. Radius is **FD**.

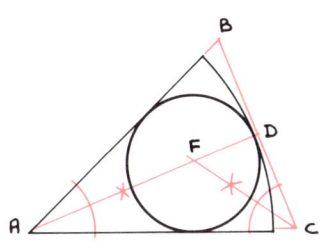

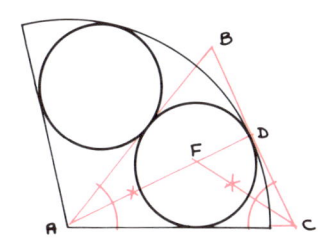

To inscribe two circles in a sector.
- Bisect the angle at **A**.
- Take each subsector and proceed as before.

④ **To inscribe a square in a semicircle.**
- Erect a perpendicular at **B**.
- With centre **B** swing **A** up to meet the perpendicular at **D**.
- Join **D** to the centre **C** of the semicircle cutting it at **E**.
- With **E** as one corner draw the square.

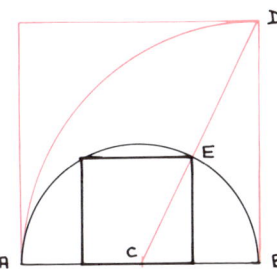

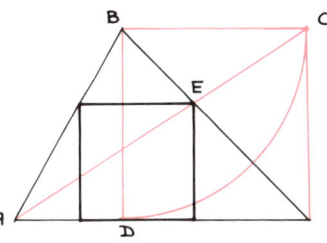

To inscribe a square in a triangle.
- From **B** drop a perpendicular to **D** and set **BC** at right angles to **BD**.
- With centre **B** swing **D** to **C**.
- Join **C** to **A** cutting the triangle at **E**.
- With **E** as a corner draw the square.

② **To inscribe circles within a circle (e.g. five)**
- Divide the circle into five sectors.
- Proceed as before for each.

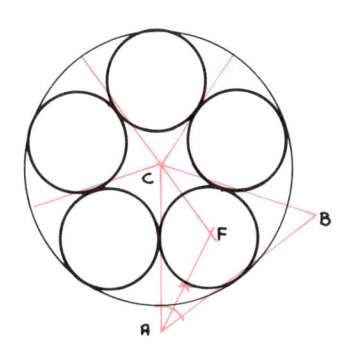

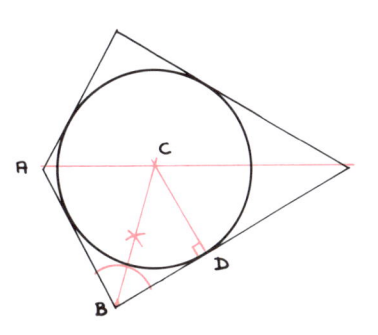

To inscribe a circle in a trapezoid.
- Bisect the angle at **A**.
- Bisect the angle at **B** to fix centre **C**.
- Drop a perpendicular to get radius **CD**.

⑤ **To inscribe a square in a trapezoid**
- Join **B** to **C** and set **BD** at right angles to **BC**.
- With centre **B** swing **C** to **D**.
- Join **D** to **A** cutting the trapezoid at **E**.
- With **E** as a corner draw the square.

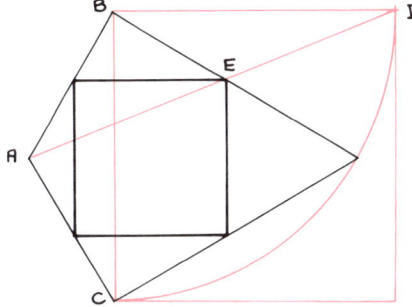

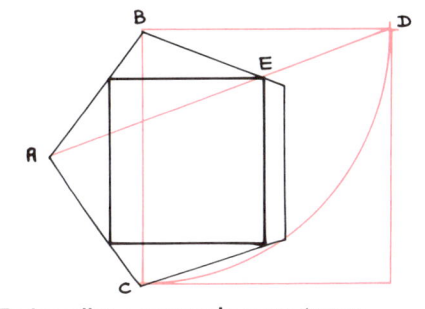

To inscribe a square in a pentagon
- Join **B** to **C** and set **BD** at right angles to **BC**.
- With centre **B** swing **C** to **D**.
- Join **D** to **A** cutting the pentagon at **E**.
- With **E** as a corner draw the square.

③ **To inscribe circles in a polygon. (e.g. four in an octagon)**
- Divide the polygon into either trapezoids, as here, or triangles.
- Using the appropriate method proceed as before for each.

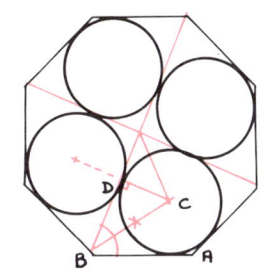

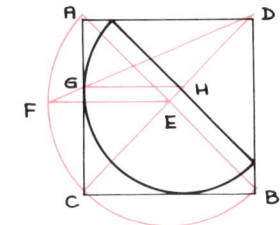

To inscribe a semicircle in a square.
- Draw the diagonals **AB** and **CD** crossing at **E**.
- With **E** as centre draw the semicircle **AB**.
- Draw a horizontal line **E** to **F**.
- Join **D** to **F** cutting **AC** at **G**.
- Parallel to **EF** draw **G** to centre **H**.

⑥ **To inscribe a square in a sector.**
- Join **B** to **C** and set **BD** at right angles to **BC**.
- With centre **B** swing **C** to **D**.
- Join **D** to **A** cutting the sector at **E**.
- With **E** as a corner draw the square.

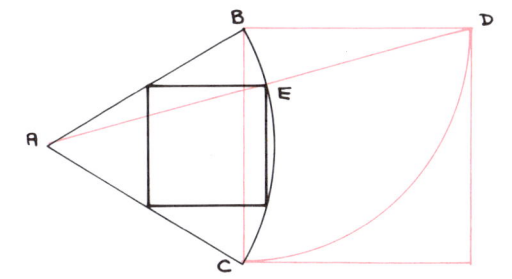

Note: See also the drawing of Tracery in **Part 2B**, *page* **324**, *and page* **30**.

Technical Draughtsmanship
Inscribing
Revision 11 — Part I — Geom.

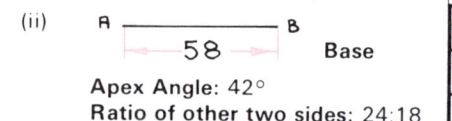

QUESTIONS

1. (i) Divide the three lines into **5**, **7** and **9** equal pieces respectively.
   (ii) Divide the three lines into the **ratio 3:5**, **6:11** and **9:7** respectively.
   (iii) Extend each line in the **ratio 3:4**, **7:2** and **5:11** respectively.

2. Bisect the angles between the diverging and converging lines.

3. On the three lines by scale of chords construct angles of **40°**, **55°** and **70°** respectively.

4. Given three lines find a fourth so that **a:b::c:d**, i.e. find a fourth proportional.

5. Given two lines find a third so that **a:c::c:b**, i.e. given the extremes find the mean proportional.

6. Find the Golden Mean of each line so that **a:b::b:(a + b)**.

7. (i) With side **AB** construct a Hexagon, a Nonagon and a Dodecagon.
   (ii) Using an alternative method construct on side **CD** a Heptagon and a Decagon.

8. Within each circle draw a Pentagon, an Octagon and a Dodecagon.

9. Use three different methods draw three pentagons of side **AB**.

10 to 15. Construct the triangles from the information given.

All measurements are in millimetres.

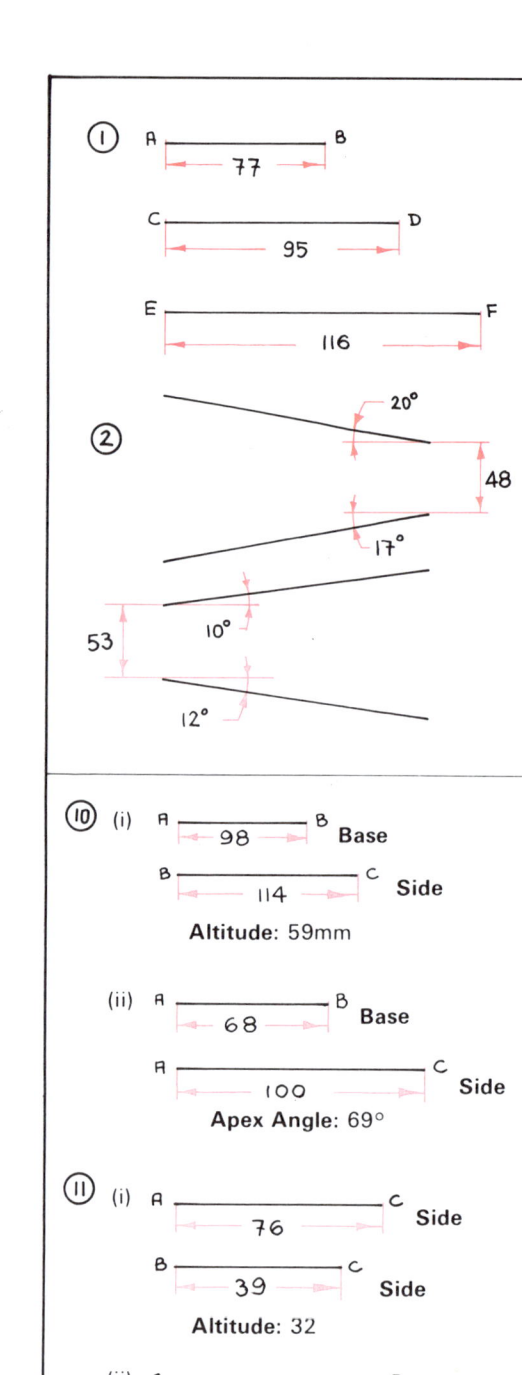

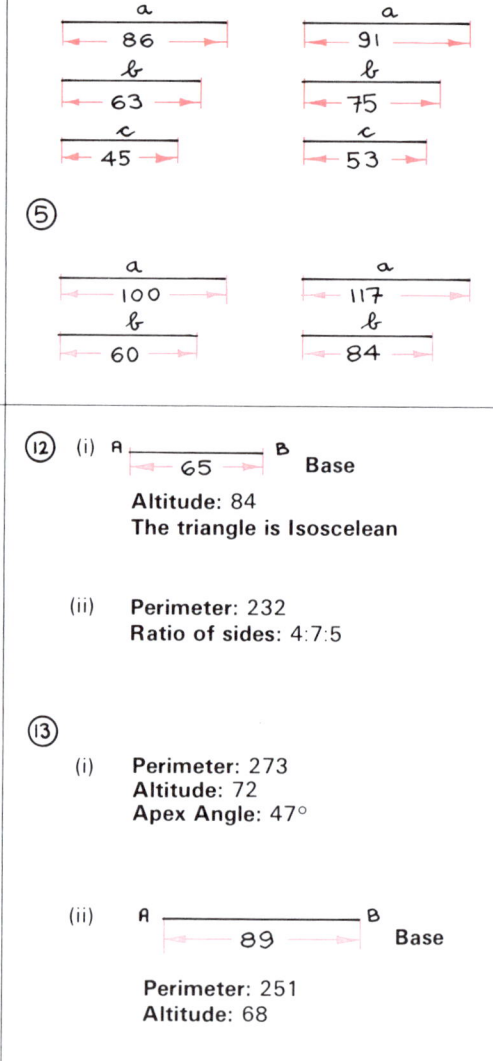

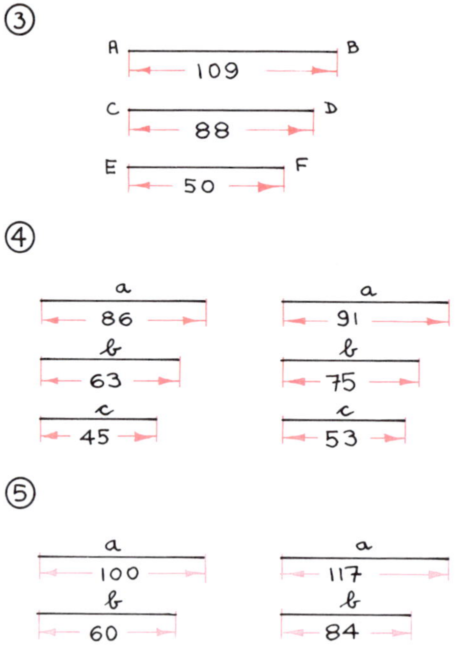

Technical Draughtsmanship		
Exercises 1		
N.T.S.	Revision 12	Part I Geom.

Exercise data

1. AB = 77, CD = 95, EF = 116

2. 20°, 17°, 10°, 12°; dimensions 48, 53

3. AB = 109, CD = 88, EF = 50

4. a = 86, b = 63, c = 45 ; a = 91, b = 75, c = 53

5. a = 100, b = 60 ; a = 117, b = 84

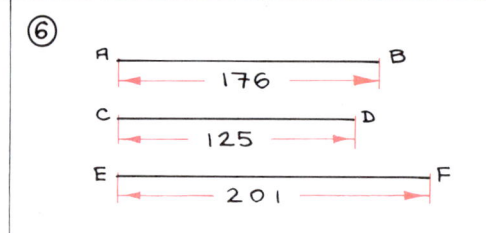

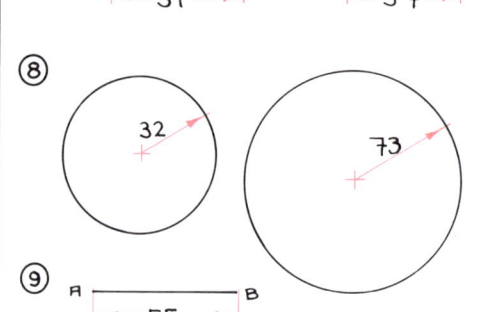

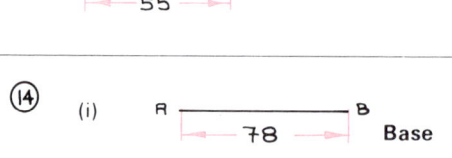

6. AB = 176, CD = 125, EF = 201

7. AB = 31, CD = 57

8. Circles of radius 32 and 73

9. AB = 55

10. (i) Base AB = 98, Side BC = 114, Altitude: 59mm
   (ii) Base AB = 68, Side AC = 100, Apex Angle: 69°

11. (i) Side AC = 76, Side BC = 39, Altitude: 32
   (ii) Base AB = 81, Altitude: 42, Apex Angle: 56°

12. (i) Base AB = 65, Altitude: 84, The triangle is Isoscelean
   (ii) Perimeter: 232, Ratio of sides: 4:7:5

13. (i) Perimeter: 273, Altitude: 72, Apex Angle: 47°
   (ii) Base AB = 89, Perimeter: 251, Altitude: 68

14. (i) Base AB = 78, Altitude: 31, Ratio of other two sides: 3:5
   (ii) Base AB = 59, Altitude: 29, Ratio of other two sides: 2:7

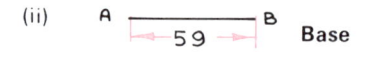

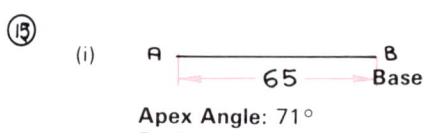

15. (i) Base AB = 65, Apex Angle: 71°, Ratio of other two sides: 48:32
   (ii) Base AB = 58, Apex Angle: 42°, Ratio of other two sides: 24:18

QUESTIONS

All measurements are in millimetres

1. In each case draw a tangent to the circle at **P** and from **Q**.
2. Draw a tangent to the arc at **P**. Point **C** is centre of the arc.
3. Construct a tangent to the circle parallel to **AB**.
4. Draw the pulley system.
5. Draw the chain link.
6. Draw the plan of a clearing lever.
7. Carefully draw the casting in both **first** and **third** angle projection.
8. Measure and draw the hand set of a telephone to a dimensional tolerance of ± **0.3mm**.
9. Draw a circle to touch the given circle and to pass through point **P**. Repeat for point **Q**.
10. Find a circle to touch the given circle at **P** and to pass through point **Q**.
11. Draw a circle to touch the given circle, and the line **AB** at point **P**. Repeat for **Q**.
12. (i) Draw a circle to pass through **P** and **Q**, and to touch the line **AB**.
    (ii) Using a different method, draw a circle through **P** and **Q** to touch line **AB**.
13. Enclose the given circle in a circle that will touch it at **Q** and pass through point **P**.
14. Draw a circle to touch and enclose the two given circles.
15. Show a circle of radius **21 mm** that touches the given circles.
16. Draw a tangent circle of radius **33mm** to the given circles.
17. With centres **A**, **B** and **C** draw three tangent circles.
18. Using two different methods draw a circle through **P** and **Q** to touch the given circle.

Technical Draughtsmanship		
Exercises 2		
N.T.S.	Revision 13	Part I
		Geom.

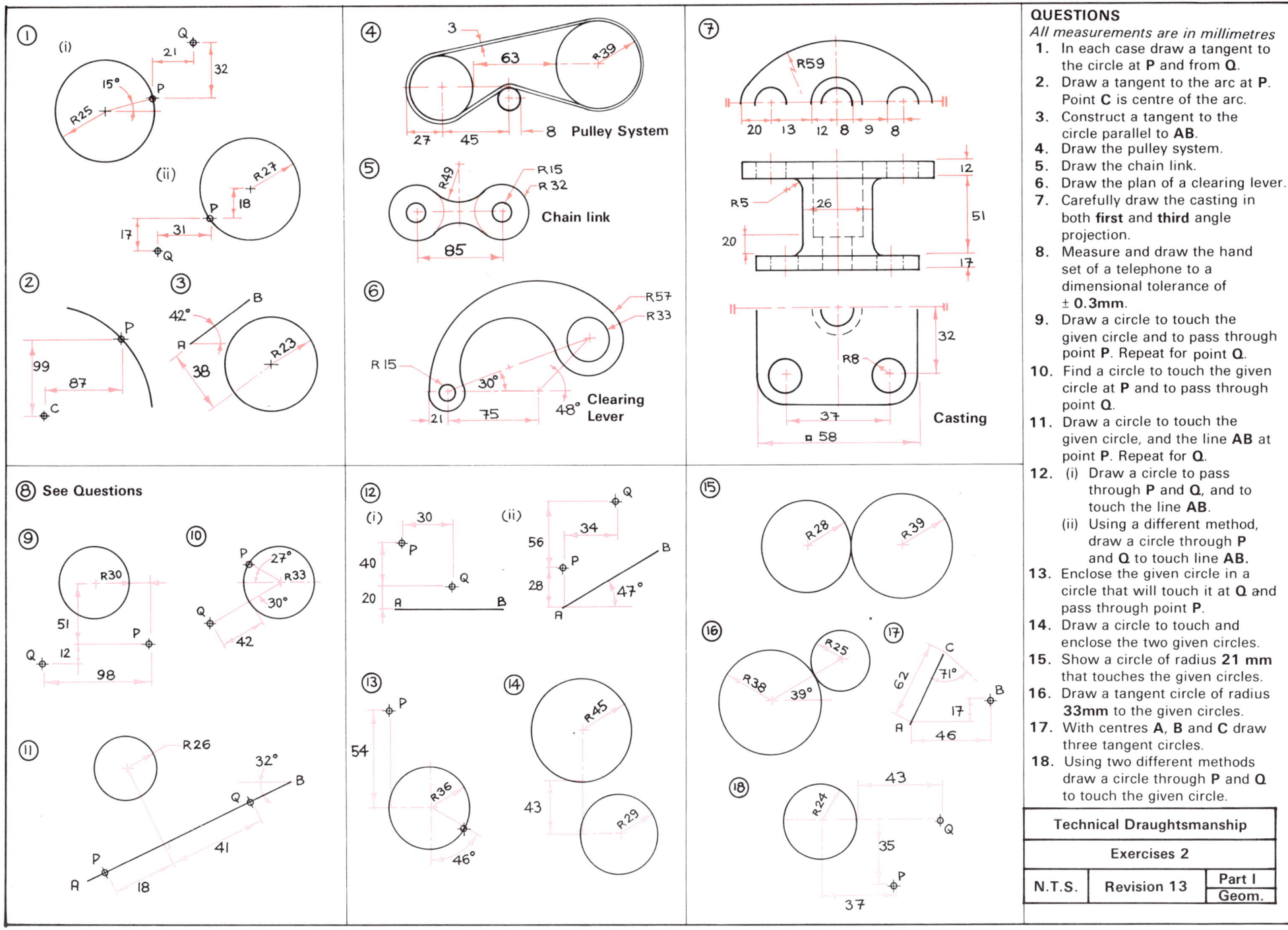

QUESTIONS

1. In each case draw a circle through **P** tangent to both lines.
2. In each case draw a circle to touch both lines and the given circle.
3. Using a different method in each case draw a circle through point **P** to touch both lines.
4. Escribe three circles to the given triangle.
5. Draw the two triangles from the information given and escribe a circle around each.
6. Draw the given figure.
7. Draw a tangent circle of radius **22mm** in each complementary angle.
8. Draw two circles of radius **20 mm** to touch each other and one given line each.
9. Construct the given figure.
10. Complete the inscribed triangles of base **AB** and apex angle **40°**.
11. Draw two circles to touch the given cirlce and two sides of the triangle **ABC**.
12. Draw a circle to touch the given arc and the line at **P**. Draw another to touch at point **Q**.
13. Inscribe 7 tangent circles.
14. Inscribe 3 tangent circles in a hexagon of side **AB**, and **5** in a decagon of side **CD**.
15. Draw the first figure, and inscribe a square in the second.
16. Inscribe a square in the first triangle and a semicircle in the second.
17. Inscribe a square in each figure.
18. Inscribe 5 equal and touching squares in the first circle and **7** in the second.
19. Inscribe 4 touching squares in the first and **7** in the second figure.
20. Inscribe a semicircle within a square within each figure.
21. Draw the four Rose Windows. Each has a radius of **50mm**.

Technical Draughtsmanship		
Exercises 3		
N.T.S.	Revision 14	Part I
		Geom. H

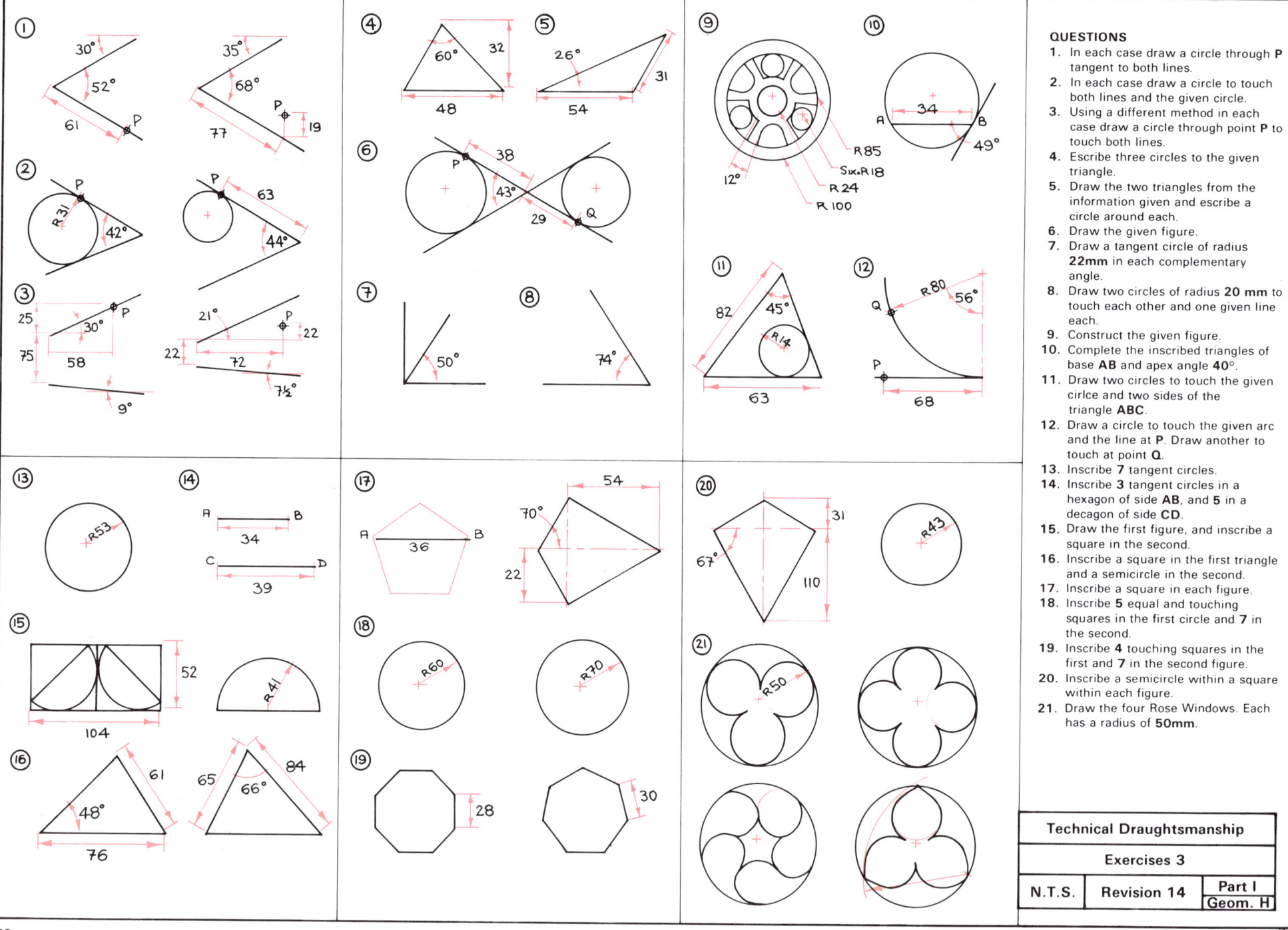

PART 1

CHAPTER 3
AREA CONVERSIONS AND GRAPHIC CALCULATION

Sheet metalwork and pattern-making of any kind deal with surface area, both for design and for costing. To relate different surface areas is also very useful for surveying and land distribution.
Geometry surpasses arithmetic in the examples on page 28, where simple operations can fix such numerically awkward quantities as π, $\emptyset$, or the square root of **2**.

CONTENTS
Area Formulae	*Page* **24**
Area Conversion 1	**25**
Area Conversion 2	**26**
Area Conversion 3	**27**
Graphic Calculation	**28**
Subdivision of Figures	**29**
Reduction and Enlargement 1	**30**
Reduction and Enlargement 2	**31**
Sample Problems	**32**
Exercises	**33**

Photocopying prohibited by law

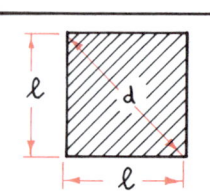

Square

Area = $l^2 = \dfrac{d^2}{2}$

$l \simeq 0.7d \quad d \simeq 1.4l$

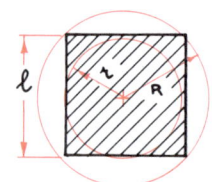

Inscribed Square

Area = $2R^2 = 4r^2$

$l = 2r \simeq 1.4R \quad R \simeq 0.7l$

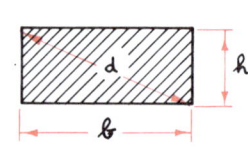

Rectangle

Area = bh

$d = \sqrt{b^2 + h^2}$

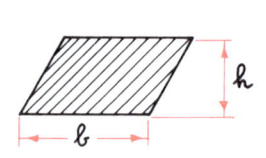

Rhomboid

Area = bh

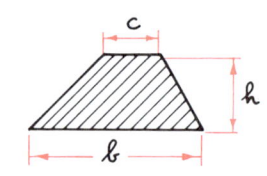

Trapezium

Area = $\left(\dfrac{b+c}{2}\right) h$

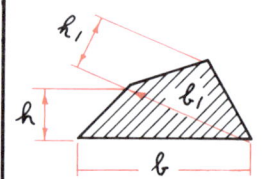

Trapezoid I

Area = $\dfrac{bh}{2} + \dfrac{b^1 h^1}{2}$

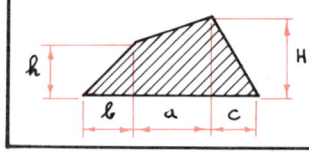

Trapezoid II

Area = $\dfrac{1}{2}[(H+h)a + bh + cH]$

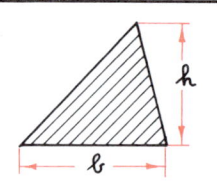

Triangle

Area = $\dfrac{bh}{2}$

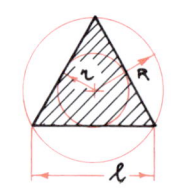

Inscribed Equilateral Triangle

Area $\simeq 5.2r^2 \simeq 1.3R^2 \simeq 0.43l^2$

$r = 0.3l \quad R = 2r = 0.6l$

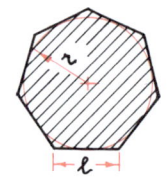

Regular Polygon

Area = $\dfrac{nlr}{2}$

l: length of one side
n: number of sides
r: radius of inscribed circle.

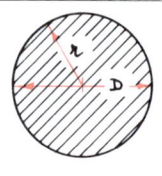

Circle

Area = πr^2

Perimeter = $\pi D = 2\pi r$

$\pi \simeq \dfrac{22}{7} \simeq 3.1416$

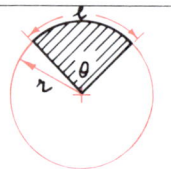

Sector of a Circle

Area = $\dfrac{\pi r^2 \theta}{360} = \tfrac{1}{2} r l$

$l = \dfrac{\pi r \theta}{180}$

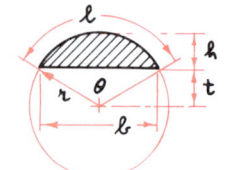

Segment of a Circle

Area = $\dfrac{rl - bt}{2}$

$t = r - h \quad l = \dfrac{\pi r \theta}{180}$

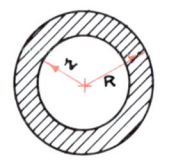

Ring

Area = $\pi (R^2 - r^2)$

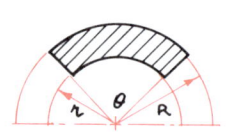

Sector of a Ring

Area = $\dfrac{\pi \theta (R^2 - r^2)}{360}$

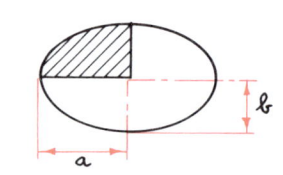

Ellipse

Shaded area $\simeq \pi ab$

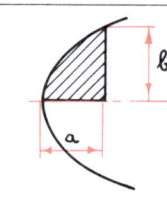

Parabola

Shaded area = $\tfrac{2}{3} ab$

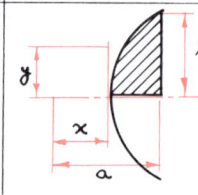

Hyperbola

Shaded area = $\dfrac{ab}{2} - \dfrac{xy}{2}$

where **MN** is an asymptote

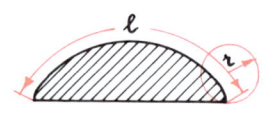

Cycloid

Area = $3\pi r^2$
(three times area of the generating circle)

$l = 8r$

Note: *You should know these formulae by heart.*

Technical Draughtsmanship
Area Formulae
Areas 1 — Part I Geom.

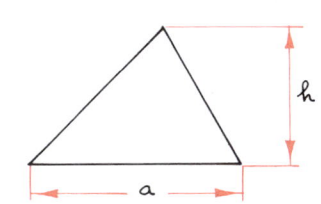

①
To construct a triangle equal in area and on the same base as a given triangle.

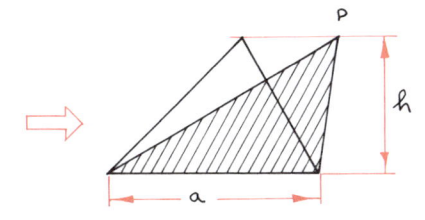

- The given triangle is of base **a** and altitude **h**.
- area = $\frac{a}{2}h$
- $\frac{a}{2}$ is not changed.
- Therefore, if **h** is not changed, the area is unchanged.
- So, parallel to the base at a distance **h** draw a line.
- Then *any* point **P** on this line will be the apex of a triangle equal in area to the given triangle.

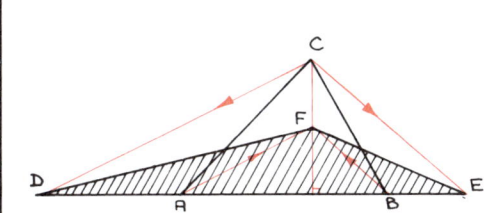

②
A triangle equal in area to ABC but of different base DE.

- Join **C** to **D** and parallel draw **A** towards **F**.
- Join **C** to **E** and parallel draw **B** to fix apex **F**.
- DEF is equal in area to ABC.

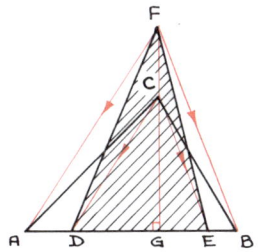

A triangle equal in area to ABC but of different altitude GF.

- Set **GF** to the new altitude.
- Join **F** to **A** and parallel draw **C** to **D**.
- Join **F** to **B** and parallel draw **C** to **E**.
- DEF is equal in area to ABC.

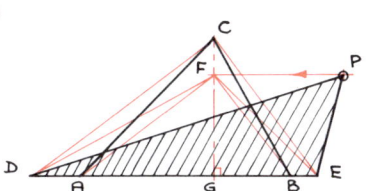

③
A triangle equal in area to ABC and with apex at point P.

- From **P** draw a line parallel to the base.
- Convert ABC to DEF (new altitude) as before.
- Now convert DEF to DEP as shown above (same base, same height).
- DEP is equal in area to ABC.

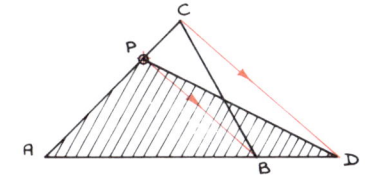

A triangle equal in area to ABC with apex at point P on side AC.

- Join **P** to **B** and parallel draw **C** to **D**.
- Triangle ADP is equal in area to ABC.

④
To construct a rectangle equal in area to triangle ABC.

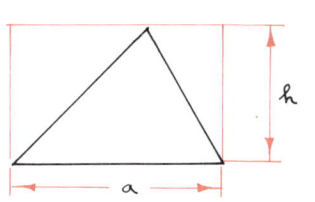

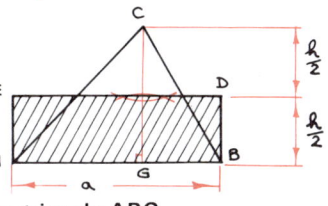

- Area of a triangle is $\frac{a}{2}h$
- Area of a rectangle is **ah**
- *Therefore with the same base and altitude the rectangle is twice the area of the triangle. If the height of the rectangle were halved, then it would equal the area of the triangle.*
- From **C** drop a perpendicular to find the altitude **CG**.
- Bisect **CG**.
- On base **AB** and of height (**CG** ÷ 2) draw rectangle ABDE equal in area to ABC.

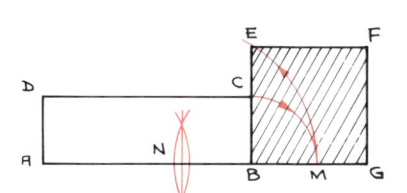

⑤
To construct a square equal in area to a given rectangle

- Extend **AB** and with centre **B** swing **C** down to **M**.
- Bisect **AM** to find **N**.
- Extend **BC** towards **E**.
- With centre **N** swing **M** to **E**.
- **BE** is one side of the square BEFG that equals the area of ABCD.

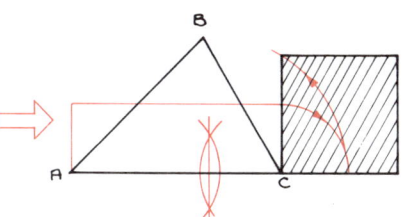

To construct a square equal in area to triangle ABC.

- First convert the triangle to a rectangle as above.
- Then convert the rectangle to a square.

⑥
A parallelogram equal in area to triangle ABC

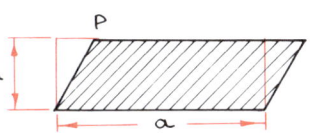

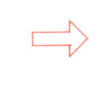

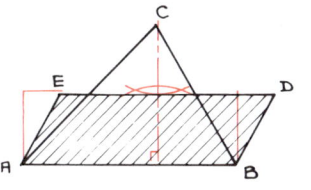

- *Area of a rectangle is* **ah**
- *Area of a parallelogram is also* **ah**.
- *So given the same base and altitude the areas are equal for any point* **P**.
- Convert the triangle to a rectangle as previously.
- Then convert the rectangle to a parallelogram as shown here.

Technical Draughtsmanship		
Area Conversion 1		
	Areas 2	Part I
		Geom.

①

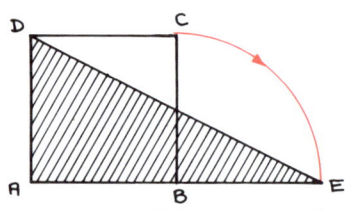

To convert a square ABCD to a triangle of equal area AED.
- Extend **AB** towards **E**.
- With centre **B** swing **C** to fix **E**.

To convert a square ABCD to two squares the sum of whose areas equals ABCD. 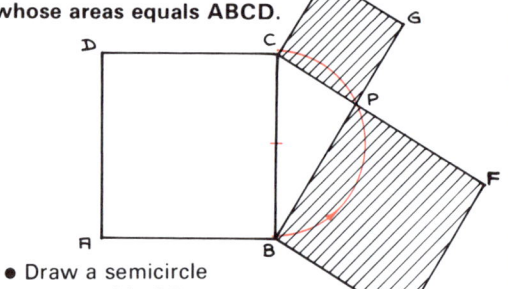
- Draw a semicircle on one side **CB**.
- Take *any* point **P** on the semicircle.
- **CP** is the side of one square and **BP** the side of the other required square.
- This is based on **The Theorem of Pythagoras**.

②

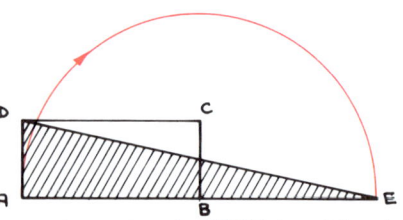

To convert a rectangle ABCD to a triangle of equal area AED.
- Extend **AB** towards **E**.
- With centre **B** swing **A** around to fix **E**.

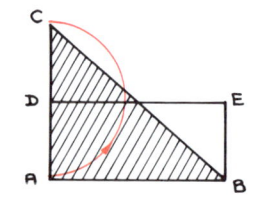

An alternative method
- Extend **AD** towards **C**.
- With centre **D** swing **A** up to fix **C**.

③

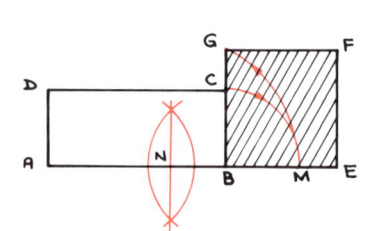

To convert a rectangle to a square of equal area.
- A reminder of the construction explained on page **25**.

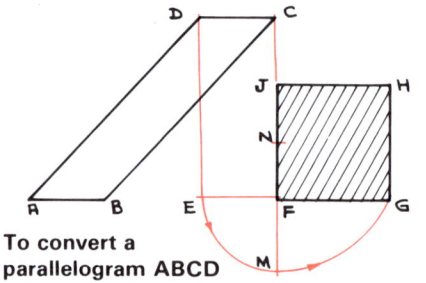

To convert a parallelogram ABCD to a square of equal area FGHJ
- Convert **ABCD** to the rectangle **EFCD**.
- Extend **CF** towards **M**.
- With centre **F** swing **E** around to fix **M**.
- Bisect **CM** and extend **EF** towards **G**.
- With centre **N** swing **M** to fix side **FG**.
- Complete the square **FGHJ**.

④

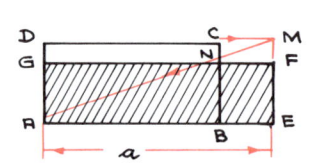

To change the base but not the area of a rectangle ABCD.
- Draw the new base **A** and erect a perpendicular at **E**.
- Extend **DC** to **M**.
- Join **M** to **A** and find **N**.
- Draw **G** through **N** to complete **AEFG**.

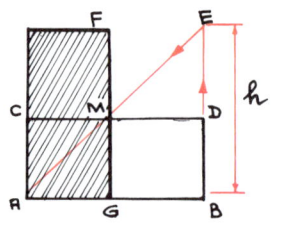

To change the altitude but not the area of a rectangle ABCD.
- Extend **BD** to new altitude **BE**.
- Join **A** to **E** and find **M**.
- Parallel to **BDE** draw **GMF**.
- Complete the shaded rectangle.

⑤

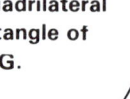

To convert a quadrilateral ABCD to a rectangle of equal area ABFG. 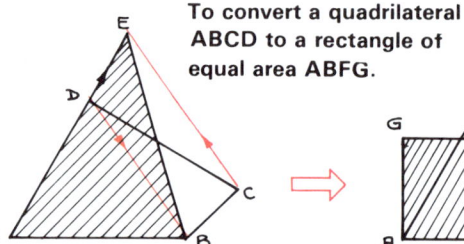
- Extend **AD** towards **E**.
- Join **D** to **B**, and parallel draw **C** to fix apex **E**.
- Triangle **ABE** is equal in area to **ABCD**. 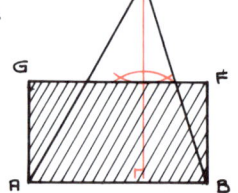
- Convert the triangle **ABE** to the required rectangle **ABFG** as shown on page **25**.

⑥

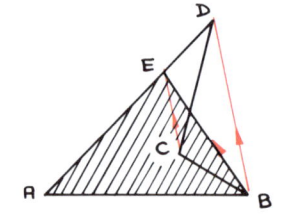

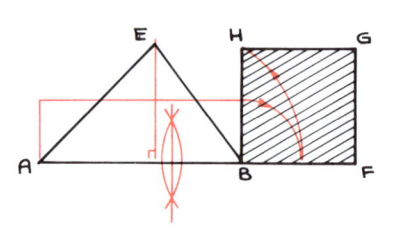

To convert a quadrilateral ABCD to a square of equal area.
- Join **D** to **B** and parallel draw **C** to **E**.
- Join **B** to **E**. The triangle **ABE** is equal to the quadrilateral **ABCD**.
- Now convert this, first to a rectangle and then to a square, as on page **25**.

Technical Draughtsmanship	
Area Conversion 2	
Areas 3	Part I Geom.

① **To convert a regular polygon (e.g. a pentagon) to a triangle of equal area DEC.**

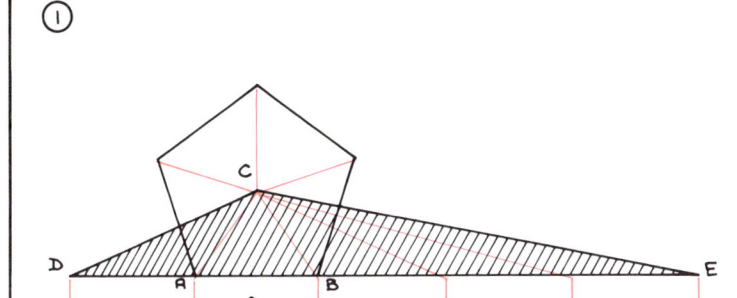

- Extend the base **AB** to be the length of the perimeter. Here **DE** is five times **AB**.
- Join **C** to **D** and to **E**.
- **DEC** is equal in area to the polygon.

Note: This is so because the bases and altitudes of the five triangles shown are equal.

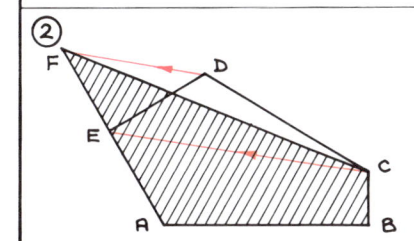

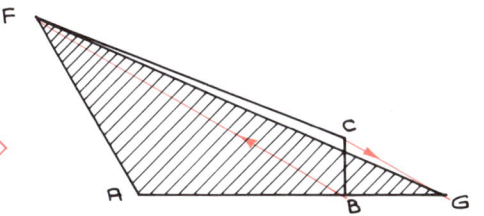

② **To convert an irregular polygon ABCDE to a triangle of equal area (Method I)**

- Extend **AE** towards **F**.
- Join **C** to **E** and parallel draw **D** to fix **F**.
- The quadrilateral **ABCF** is equal in area to the polygon **ABCD**.
- Now convert the quadrilateral to a triangle as shown on page **26**.
- The triangle **AGF** is equal in area to the original polygon.

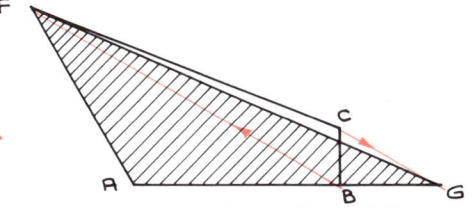

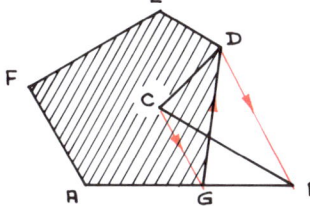

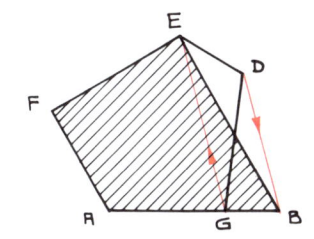

③ **To convert an irregular polygon ABCDEF to a triangle of equal area (Method II)**

- Join **D** to **B** and parallel draw **C** to **G**.
- Join **G** to **D**. The five sided polygon **AGDEF** is equal in area to the six sided **ABCDEF**.
- Continue by conversion to reduce the number of sides by one until a triangle is reached.

Note: No matter how many sides are in question, the approach is the same. Reduce the number of sides by one at a time until you have a triangle. This can then be converted to other shapes.

④ **A graphic demonstration of the area of a circle.**

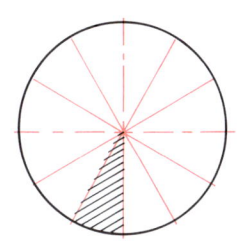

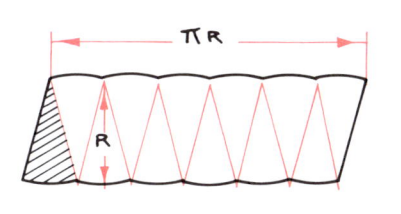

- By laying the sectors side by side as shown, a parallelogram of base πR and altitude **R** is made.

$Area = \pi R^2$
$\pi R = \frac{1}{2}$ *circumference*

⑤ **To convert a circle A to a square of equal area CFGE.**

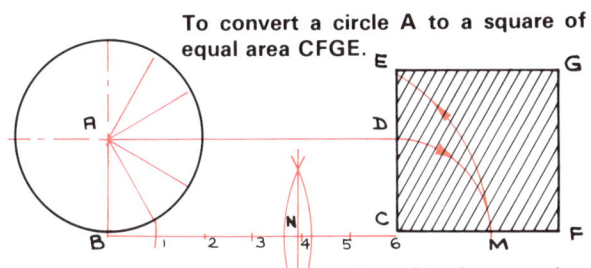

- Divide the circle into sectors.
- Either by calculation ($r \times \pi$) or by stepping off approximate arc lengths lay out **BC**.
- With altitude **r** complete the rectangle **BCDA** which is equal in area to the circle.
- Convert the rectangle to the required square in the usual way.

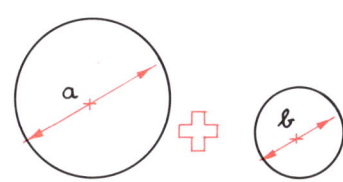

⑥ **To construct a circle equal in area to the sum of two circles.**

- Set the two diameters at right angles to each other and complete the triangle **ABC**.
- On **AC** with radius ½ **AC** draw the required circle.

Note: How could the process be used in reverse?

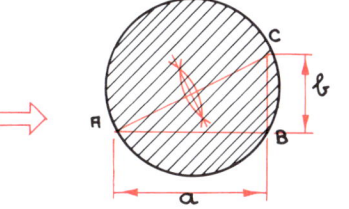

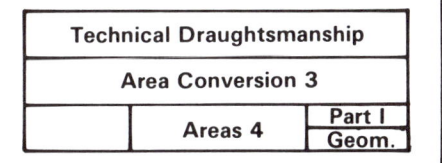

Technical Draughtsmanship		
Area Conversion 3		
Areas 4		Part I Geom.

①

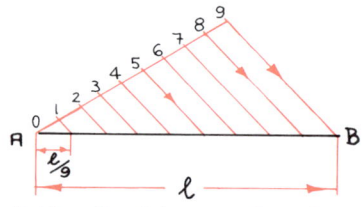

To divide a line into a number of equal parts (e.g. nine)
- Set off a real scale at any acute angle to **A**.
- Join **9** to **B** and draw the other divisions parallel.

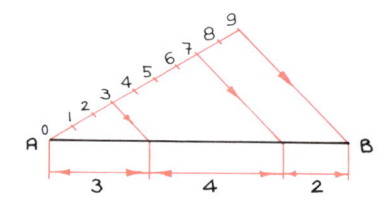

To divide a line into a given ratio (e.g. 3:4:2)
- Set off a real scale at any acute angle to **A**.
- Add the ratios 3 + 4 + 2 = 9.
- Join **9** to **B** and draw the other points parallel at **3** and **7** (i.e. 3 + 4).

②

To calculate square roots (Method I)
- Starting from a unit square and with **C** always as centre, this series can continue indefinitely.

③

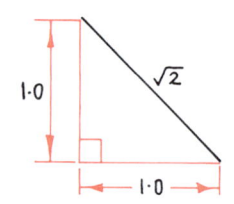

To calculate square roots (Method II)
- Start with a right-angled triangle with two sides of unity.
- This series can continue for some time but is more prone to inaccuracies due to the angles involved.

④

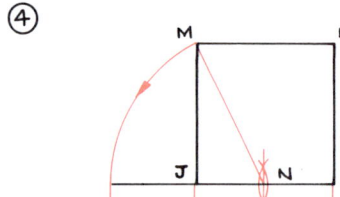

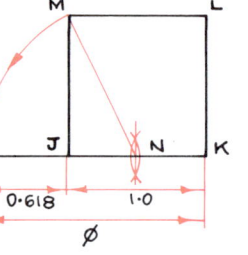

To find the Golden Mean (ø). Method I (given one proportion **A** = line **JK**)
- Draw a square on **JK** and extend one side.
- Bisect the side **JK** and with **N** as centre swing **M** onto the line as shown.

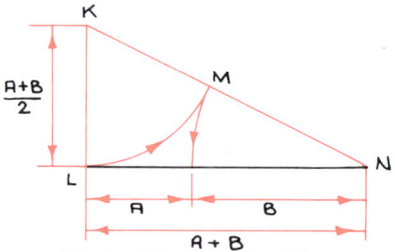

Method II (given **A + B**)
- Set (A + B) ÷ 2 at right angles to **A + B**.
- With **K** as centre swing **L** to **M**.
- With **N** as centre swing **M** down to separate **A** and **B**.
- **A** is the **extreme** and **B** is the **mean** proportional.

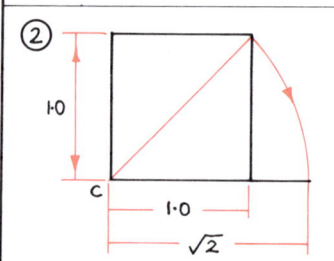

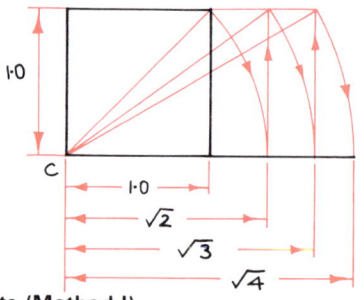

⑤

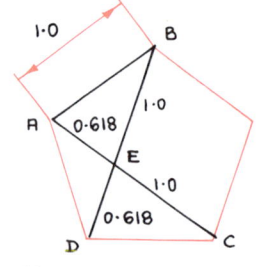

Method III
- Within a regular pentagon each diagonal will divide another at the Golden Mean point (**E**).

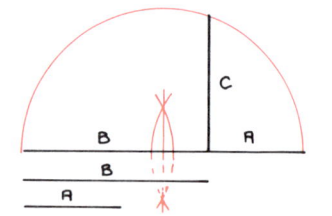

To find a mean proportional C so that A:C::C:B.
- Bisect **A + B** and erect a semicircle.
- At the point where **A** meets **B** erect a perpendicular, which will be the required proportional **C**.
- **A** and **B** are **extreme** and **C** the **mean** proportional.

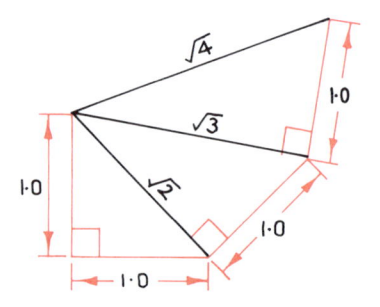

A **ratio** is a comparison of two different sizes, quantities or areas:
  Ratio **A:B** (e.g. 2:4).
A **proportion** is a comparison of two ratios.
  Proportion **A:B::C:D** (e.g. 2:4::3:6)
If **C** is made the same as **B** we get a continuous proportional series and only need three elements to set up the proportions:
  A:B::B:C (e.g. 2:4::4:8)
Here **B** is called the **mean** proportional with **A** and **C** the two **extreme** proportionals.
Can even this be simplified? Yes, if the third term is made up using the first two:
  A:B::B:(A + B).
There is one and only one proportion for **A + B** that works. And it appears frequently in music, art, science and geometry. The Greeks called it Phi (ø) or **The Golden Proportion**.
ø = A + B = ($\sqrt{5}$+1)/2 = **1.61803398875...!**

Technical Draughtsmanship		
Graphic Calculation		
Areas 5	Part I	Geom.

①

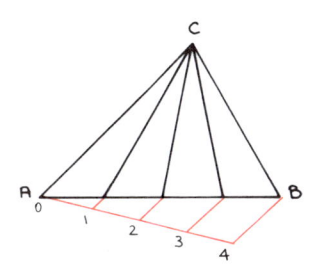

To divide a triangle into a number of equal pieces from the apex (e.g. four).
- From **A** set out a real scale to four units.
- Join 4 to **B** and draw the other divisions parallel to divide **AB** into four equal parts.
- Join each to apex **C** to complete the division of the triangle.

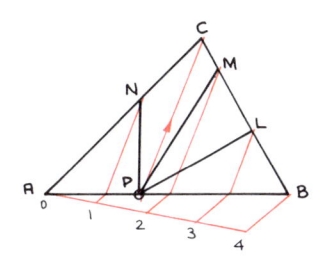

To divide a triangle into a number of equal pieces from point P (e.g. four)
- Divide the base as before.
- Join **P** to **C** and parallel draw lines from each division to find **L**, **M** and **N**.
- Join **P** to **L**, **M** and **N** to divide the triangle into equal areas.

②

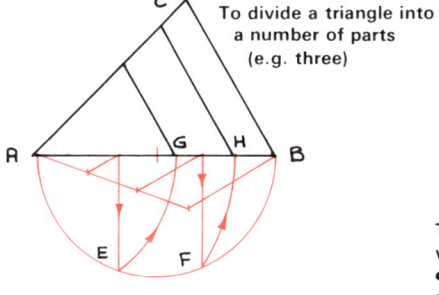

To divide a triangle into a number of parts (e.g. three)
- Draw a semicircle on **AB**.
- Divide **AB** into three parts and at each division drop a perpendicular to find **E** and **F**.
- With centre **A** swing **E** to **G** and **F** to **H**.
- Parallel to **CB** draw lines from **G** and **H** to divide the triangle.

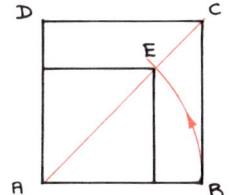

To divide a square into two equal areas, one of which is itself a square.
- Draw the diagonal **AC**.
- With centre **A** swing **B** to **E**.
- Complete the square with **AE** as diagonal.

③

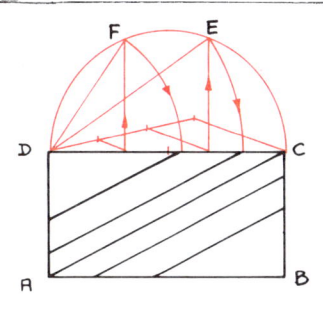

To divide a rectangle into an even number of parts diagonally (e.g. six)
- Draw the diagonal **AC** dividing the rectangle into two equal triangles.
- Divide each triangle into three parts, as explained above.

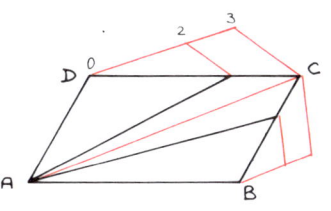

To divide a parallelogram into an uneven number of equal parts (e.g. three) from corner A
- Draw the diagonal **AC** lightly.
- Divide each triangle into one and a half parts, as shown.

④

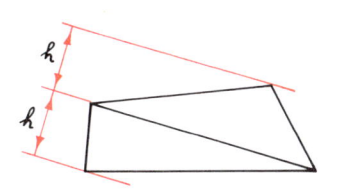

Principle: *Both of the triangles have the same base and the same altitude. Therefore they have the same area.*

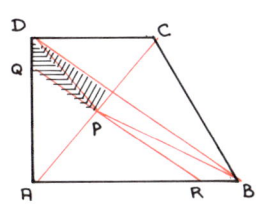

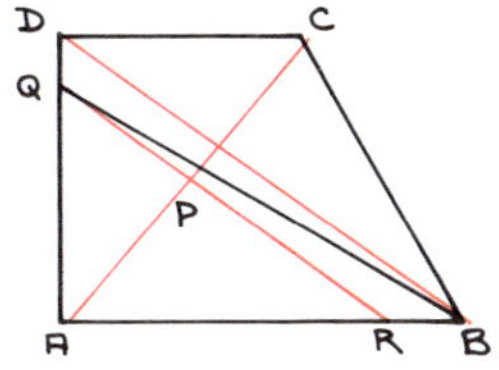

To divide a quadrilateral into two equal parts from a corner B.
- Join **A** to **C** and bisect to find point **P**.
- Join **B** to **D** and parallel draw a line through **P** to find **Q**.
- Join **B** to **Q** to divide the quadrilateral into two equal pieces **QAB** and **BCDQ**.

Note: △**APD** = ½ △**ACD**; △**ABP** = ½ △**ACB**; *The principle is then to reduce* **ABPD** *to a triangle.*

⑤

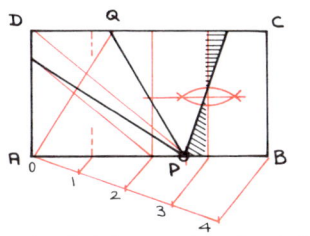

To divide a rectangle into a number of parts from P (e.g. four)
- Divide the rectangle into four equal vertical strips.
- Bisect the first two division lines at **M** and **N**.
- Draw the first two divisors from **P** through **M** and **N**.
- This leaves quadrilateral **PQDA** to be halved from **P**, as above.

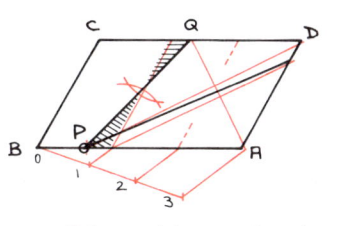

To divide a parallelogram into a number of equal parts (e.g. three)
- The procedure is similar to the previous one, the difference being that the initial divisions are oblique and not vertical.

⑥

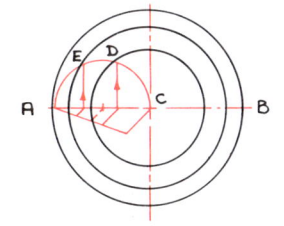

To divide a circle into a number of equal parts (e.g. three).
- Draw a semicircle on **AC**.
- Divide **AC** into three equal parts and erect a perpendicular at each division to find **D** and **E** on the semicircle.
- With centre **C** draw a circle through **D** and through **E**.
- Each ring is equal in area.

An alternative method (e.g. five) 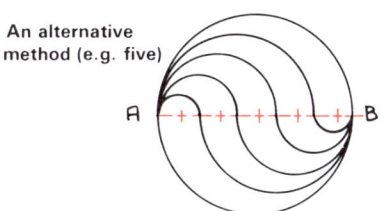
- Divide **AB** into *ten* equal pieces.
- Place a centre at each division and draw semicircles as shown.
- *The Yin-Yang symbol is of this construction.*

Technical Draughtsmanship		
Subdivision of Figures		
Areas 6	Part 1	Geom.

29

① To increase (or decrease) a given figure (e.g. increase ABCD)

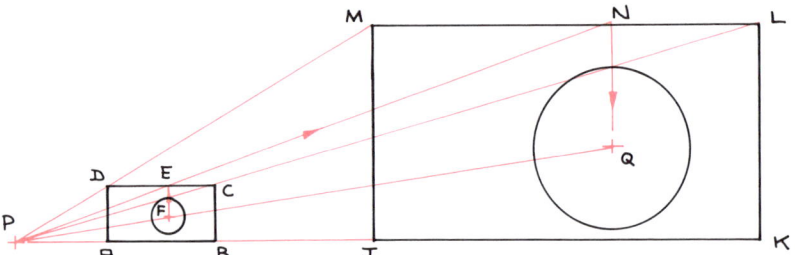

- Choose any point **P** to one side of the given figure (but not too close by). If **P** is in line with **AB** it will make things a little neater.
- From **P** draw a line through each corner of the figure.
- Choose the size of **JK** and draw the similar figure **JKLM**, each side being parallel to its original.
- To locate a point **F** bring it onto the side at **E**. Project to **N** and down to **O**.

Note: This process is known as either **Polar** *or* **Radial Projection**.

② To increase a figure in a given ratio (e.g.

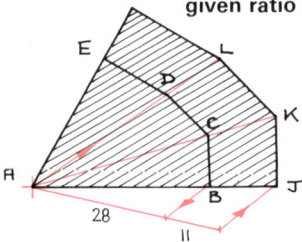

- Place the projection point at a corner **A** of the given figure.
- Set off the ratio and project the similar figure **AJKLM** as shown.

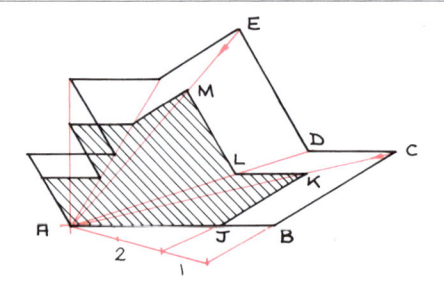

To decrease a figure in a given ratio (e.g.

- This is the same process, with the exception that the scale at **A** is set to reduce as shown.

③

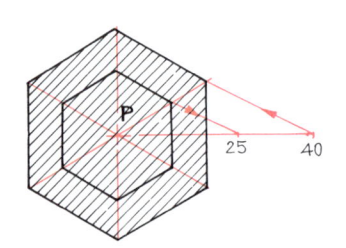

To increase a figure in a given ratio (25:40).
- **P** can be taken inside the figure as shown here.
- Set a scale from **P** and proceed as before.

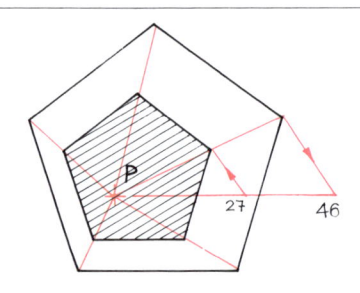

To decrease a figure in a given ratio (46:27).
- Here **P** is taken as off-centre but this makes no difference to the procedure.

④ Changing Areas

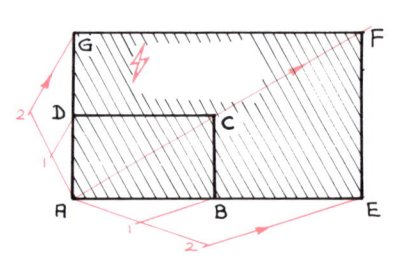

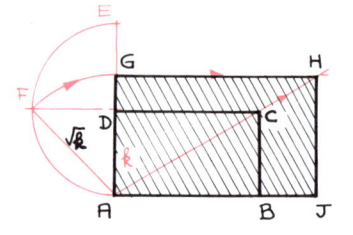

The Pitfall
- By extending all the sides to twice their length, gives not twice, but *four* times the area.

- Given **ABCD**: With centre **D**, set the semicircle **AFE**.
- The line **AF** is the square root. Swing this onto the line at **G** and complete the rectangle on the diagonal.
- The area **AJHG** is twice the area **ABCD**.

⑤ To enlarge a rectangle in area by 1:2

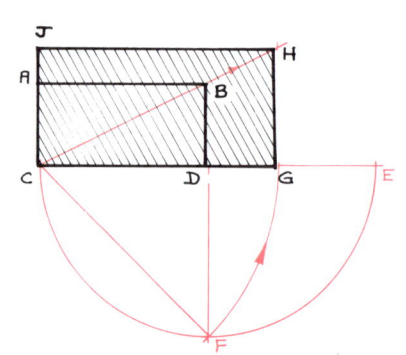

- Here the above principle is used on the long side. The result is the same: **CGHJ** is twice the area of **ABCD**.

⑥ To reduce a rectangle in area by 2:1 (half)

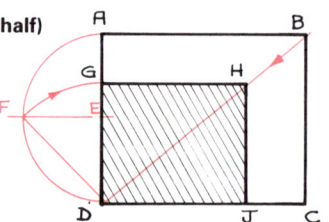

- Set a semicircle on one side, then swing **DF** onto the side at **G**.
- From **G**, construct the rectangle **GHJD**, using the diagonal to find **H**.
- The rectangle **GHJD** is half the area of **ABCD**.

Note: The square root can also be found as on page 28.

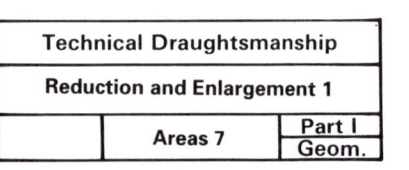

Technical Draughtsmanship	
Reduction and Enlargement 1	
Areas 7	Part I / Geom.

① Area enlargement by a given ratio (e.g. 2:5)

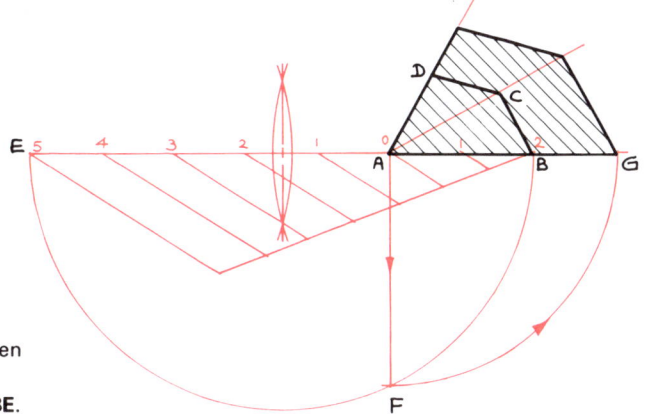

- Extend the baseline **AB** to the given proportion.
- Bisect and draw a semicircle on **BE**.
- Drop a perpendicular from **A** to the semicircle at **F**.
- With **A** as the centre, swing **F** to find the new base at **G**.
- The rest is a straightforward polar projection.

③ Area reduction by a given ratio (e.g. 3:1)

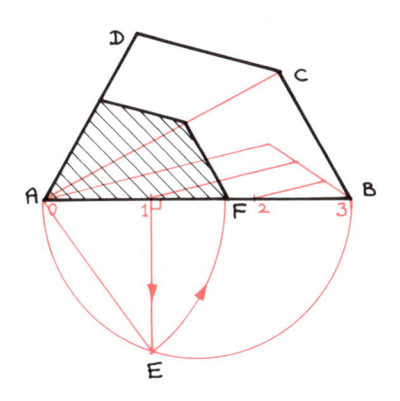

- Divide the baseline **AB** into three.
- Draw a semicircle on **AB**. From point **1**, drop a perpendicular to find **E**.
- With **A** as centre, swing **E** to find the new base **AF**.
- Complete the reduced figure by polar projection.

② To enlarge the given figure by 6:11

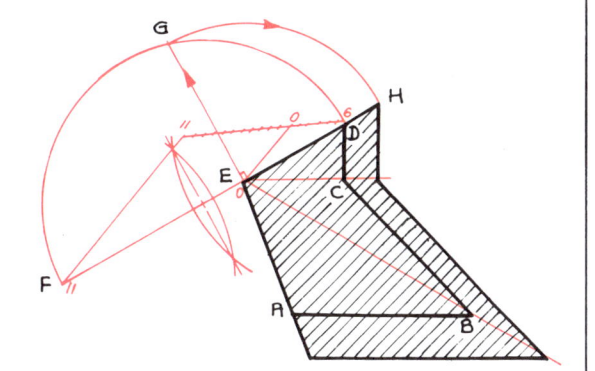

- Here a shorter side **ED** has been taken as a baseline. The rest is as above.
- Extend **ED** to **F** in the proportion **6:11**.
- Draw a semicircle on **FD** and drop a perpendicular from **E** to **H**.
- With **E** as centre, swing **H** to find the new line at **G**.
- Complete the figure by polar projection.

④ To reduce the given figure by 7:3

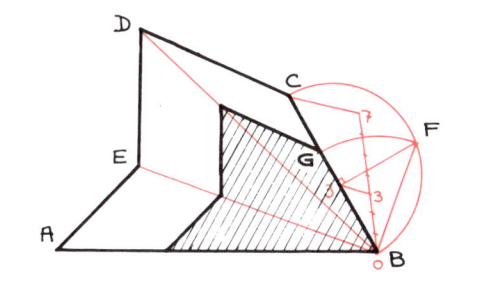

- Here side **BC** has been taken as a baseline. The rest is as above.
- Divide **BC** into seven.
- Draw a semicircle on **BC**. Drop a perpendicular from point **3** to find **F**.
- With centre **B**, swing **F** to find **G** and complete the reduced figure.

Technical Draughtsmanship		
Reduction and Enlargement 2		
	Areas 8	Part 1 Geom.

31

①

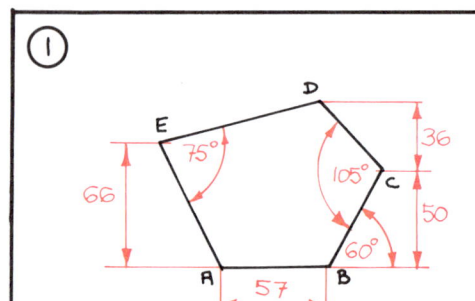

The Problem

- Construct a square that is twice the area of **ABCDE**.

Stage 1
- Mark out **A, B, C, D**.
- Point **E** is the problem.
- If **E** is **75°**, then the other two angles of triangle **EAD** must add up to **105°**.
- So, set up one possible set of angles (**45°** and **60°**) to find one possible **75°** at position **F**.
- Using the principle from page 15, Fig. 4, find the centre **S** and draw the circle to locate **E**.

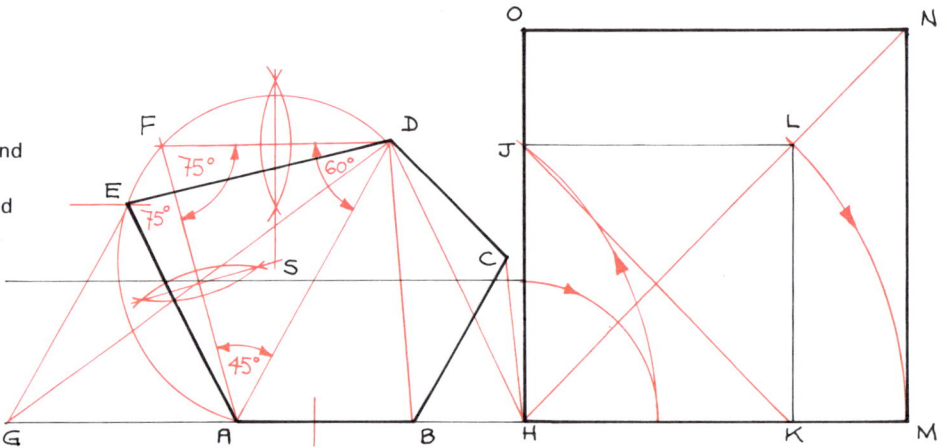

Stage 2
- Convert the figure to the square **HJLK**.
- As the diagonal is the square root, swing it to **M** and complete **HMNO**.

②

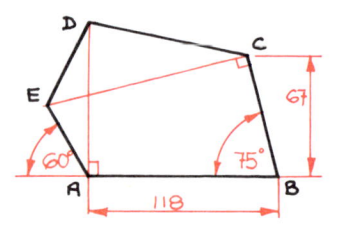

The Problem
- Given that the perimeter of **ABCDE** is 373mm, draw a rectangle that will have **1.5** times the area and be of altitude 60mm.

Stage 1
- Mark out **A, B, C, E**. Point **D** is the problem.
- The perimeter is given and there is **145mm** left for **CD** and **ED**.
- Take any break up of this (e.g. **80 + 65**), and find the point **F**.
- Try other combinations (**100 + 45** etc.), to plot the path **FGH**.
- Use this to pinpoint **D**.
- **FGDH** is part of an ellipse. Why?

Stage 2
- Convert the figure to rectangle **JKLM**.
- Extend **LK** to **N** where **KN** is 1.5 times **LK**.
- Find **Q** and draw the rectangle **JKQR**.
- The area of **KQRS** is 1.5 times that of **ABCDE**.

Stage 3
- Now extend the end wall to the height **60mm** at **S**.
- Join **S** to **J** and find **T**.
- Draw **UV** through **T** and complete the rectangle **JUVW**.

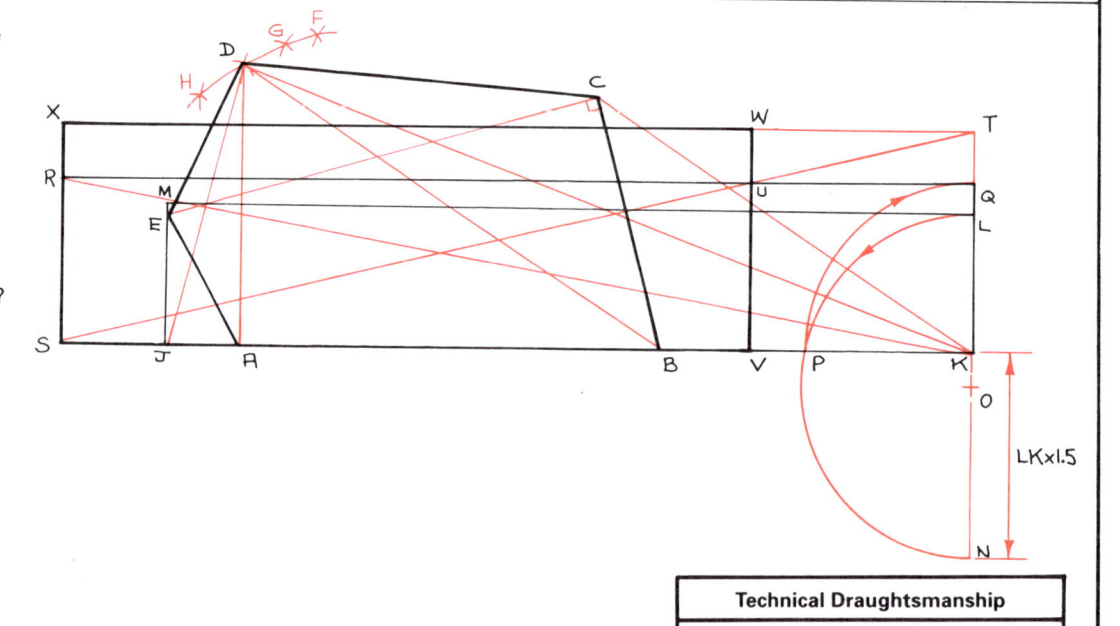

Technical Draughtsmanship

Sample Problems

Areas 9 — Part 1 — Geom. H

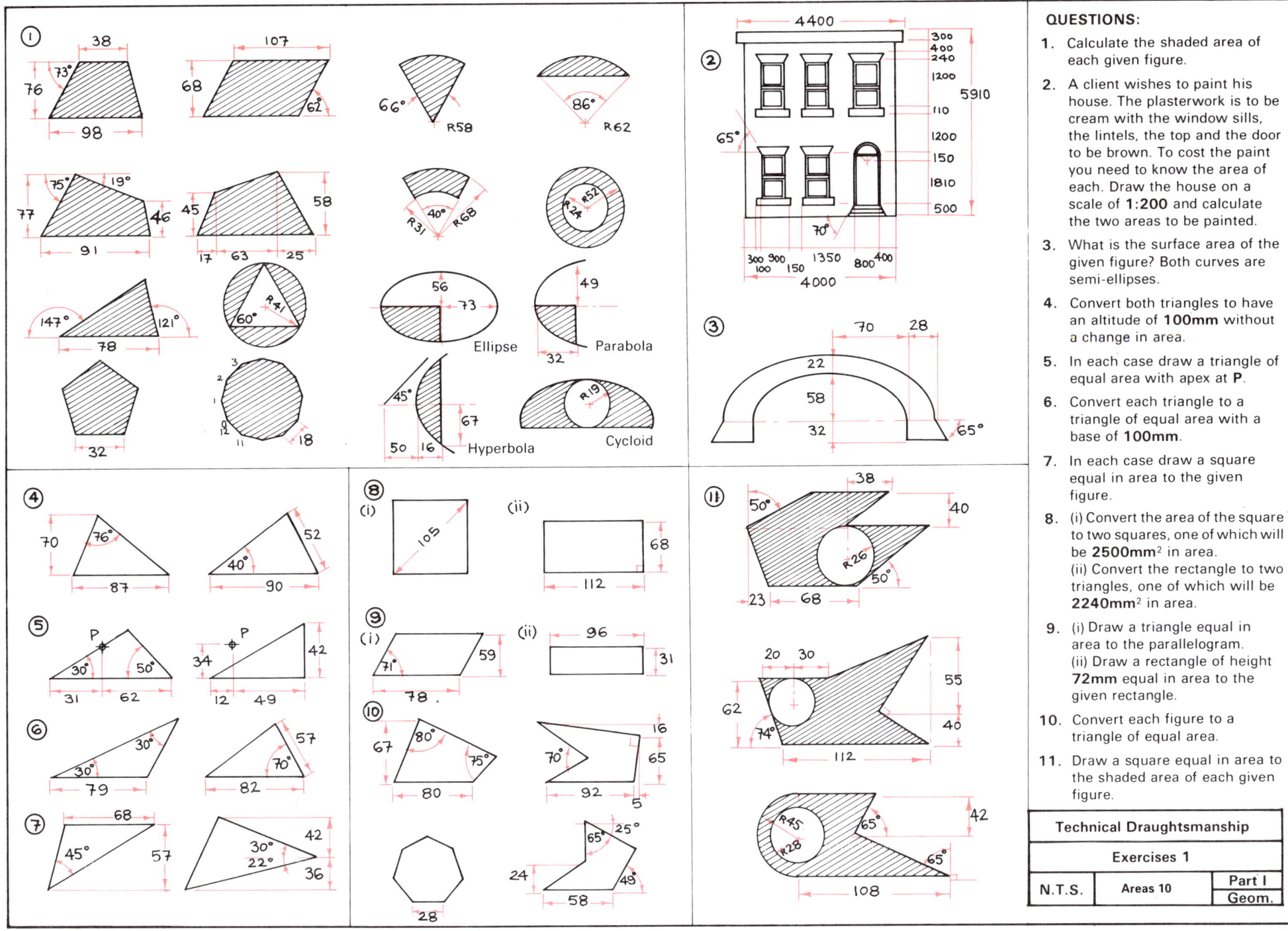

QUESTIONS:

1. Calculate the shaded area of each given figure.

2. A client wishes to paint his house. The plasterwork is to be cream with the window sills, the lintels, the top and the door to be brown. To cost the paint you need to know the area of each. Draw the house on a scale of **1:200** and calculate the two areas to be painted.

3. What is the surface area of the given figure? Both curves are semi-ellipses.

4. Convert both triangles to have an altitude of **100mm** without a change in area.

5. In each case draw a triangle of equal area with apex at **P**.

6. Convert each triangle to a triangle of equal area with a base of **100mm**.

7. In each case draw a square equal in area to the given figure.

8. (i) Convert the area of the square to two squares, one of which will be **2500mm²** in area.
   (ii) Convert the rectangle to two triangles, one of which will be **2240mm²** in area.

9. (i) Draw a triangle equal in area to the parallelogram.
   (ii) Draw a rectangle of height **72mm** equal in area to the given rectangle.

10. Convert each figure to a triangle of equal area.

11. Draw a square equal in area to the shaded area of each given figure.

Technical Draughtsmanship		
Exercises 1		
N.T.S.	Areas 10	Part I Geom.

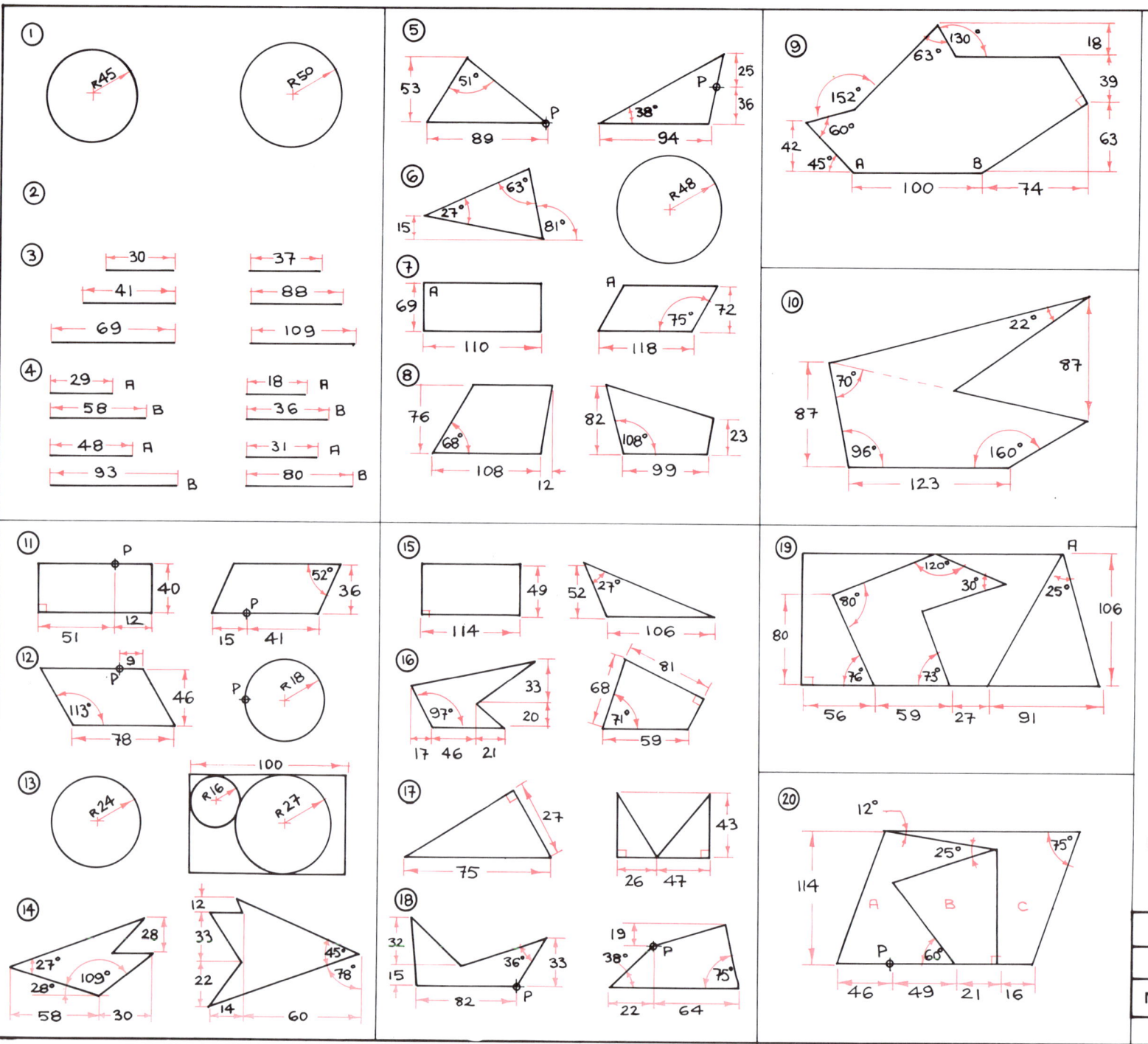

QUESTIONS

1. (i) Convert the first circle to a square of equal area.
   (ii) Draw two squares, one of side **74mm**, whose combined area is equal to that of the given circle.
2. Find the $\sqrt{5}$ graphically using two different methods.
   (i) Taking each of the three lines as **A**, for each find a line **B** so that **A:B::B: (A + B)**.
   (ii) Each of these lines represents **A + B** so that **A:B::B: (A + B)**. Separate **A** from **B** in each case
4. In each of the four cases find a mean proportional **C**, so that **A:C::C:B**.
5. Divide each triangle into five equal parts from point **P**.
6. Divide the triangle into four equal parts and then convert the circle to two equal squares.
7. Divide each figure first into five equal parts from **A** and then into six parts parallel to a diagonal from **A**.
8. Divide both figures into two equal parts.
9. Reduce the figure to a triangle of equal area on base **AB**.
10. Draw a square equal in area to the given figure.
11. Divide each figure into five equal areas from point **P**.
12. Divide each figure into four equal areas from point **P**.
13. Draw and divide each circle into three equal areas.
14. Draw figures similar to the given figures but **1.7** times their size.
15. Decrease the area of each figure to **0.68** the given size.
16. For each figure draw a triangle equal to **0.85** times the given area.
17. In each case draw a square equal to **1.2** times the given area.
18. With **P** as polar centre project a figure similar to the given figure but reduced in a ratio of **28:41**.
19. Two farmers have bought the four fields. From corner **A** divide the area in half with one line. What area has each farmer?
20. Redivide the figure into three equal parts from point **P**. What proportion of the overall area had **A**, **B** and **C** represented?

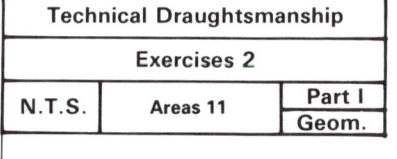

Technical Draughtsmanship		
Exercises 2		
N.T.S.	Areas 11	Part I
		Geom.

PART I

CHAPTER 4
SCALES

Technical drawings are almost always for use in manufacture, construction or design. It is vital that dimensions and sizes be understood by those looking at your drawings. Imagine a computer chip circuit and a traffic flow diagram presented without a clear indication of the scale. One may be a thousand times larger than its real size, while the other may represent half of Europe! Scales are vital. At times, great accuracy is required and diagonal or vernier scales may be used to achieve this, e.g. in the design of clock parts.

CONTENTS
Plain Scales	*Page* **36**
A Scale Drawing	**37**
Diagonal Scales	**38**
Vernier Scales	**39**
Exercises	**40**

A table of the most commonly used scales: *Scale rules can be bought that have already been calibrated to a variety of useful scales, or you can make one up yourself.*

Scale Ratio	Application	An Equivalent Ratio
1 : 50 000	Location maps	1 cm = half a kilometre
1 : 10 000		1 cm = 100 metres
1 : 2500	Site maps	1 cm = 25 metres
1 : 1250		
1 : 500	Site plans	1 cm = 5 metres
1 : 200	General arrangement	1 cm = 2 metres
1 : 100		1 cm = 1 metre
1 : 50		1 cm = half a metre
1 : 25	Plans, components, sections	1 cm = a quarter metre
1 : 10		1 cm = 10 cm
1 : 5	Details	A fifth of the real size
1 : 2		Half real size
1 : 1	Patterns	Real size
2 : 1	Fine details	Twice the size
5 : 1		Five times real size
10 : 1		1 cm = 1 mm
20 : 1		1 cm = 0.5 mm

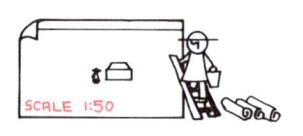

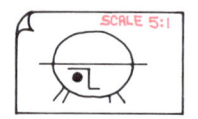

A series of scales illustrated.
Scale 1 : 1 is 'life size'
The size on your drawing is *always* quoted first and its relation to the real size of the object, second.

1 : 50

In your . In real
drawing ˙ life size

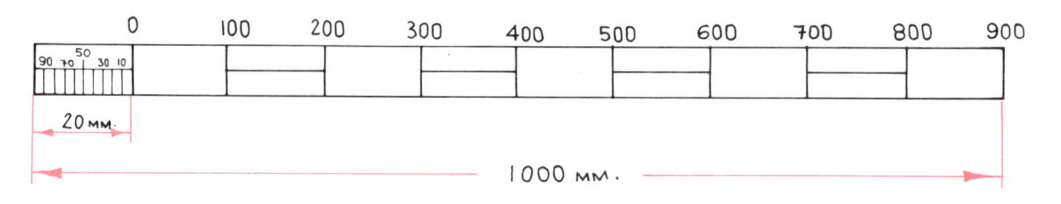

A scale drawn to represent up to one metre. Notice how the first section is measured backwards from **O**. In practice this makes quick accurate measurement easier as it means the rest of the scale need not be cluttered with detailed measurement.

Technical Draughtsmanship
Plain Scales
Scales 1	Part I Geom.

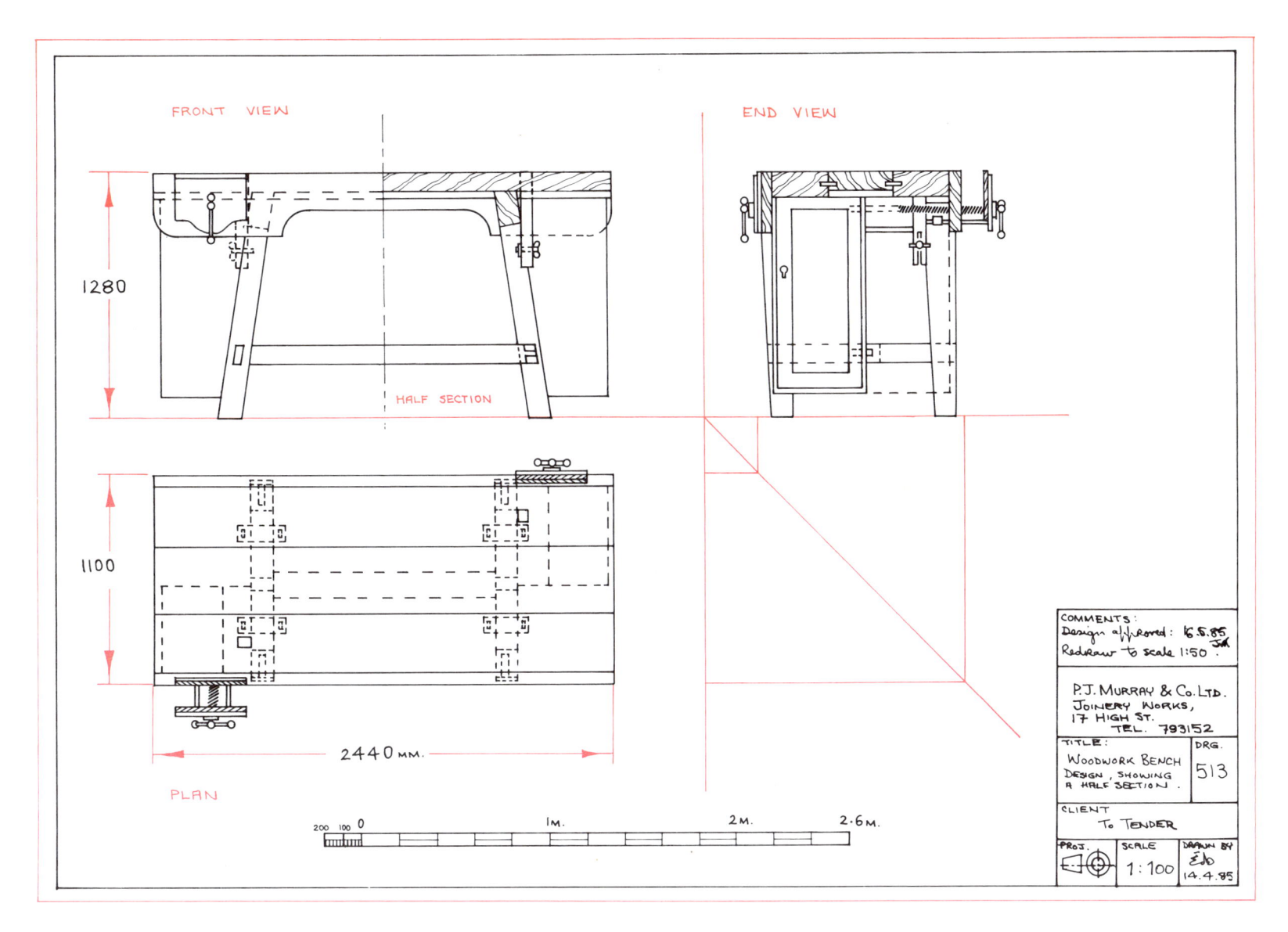

Note:
- The measurements quoted are *always* the real size and not the drawing size.
- As printing or copying processes can distort a drawing, it is useful to draw a plain scale on the sheet. Such a scale can settle many arguments. Draw the scale long enough to be of practical use.

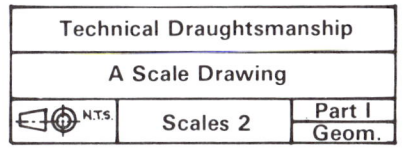

Technical Draughtsmanship
A Scale Drawing
Scales 2 — Part 1 Geom.

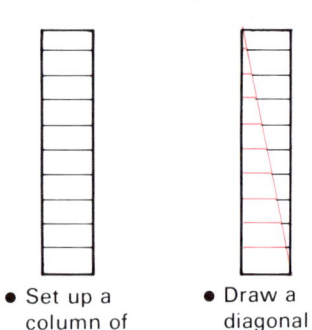

- Set up a column of ten steps
- Draw a diagonal

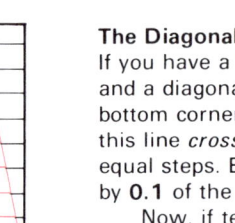

The Diagonal Scale

If you have a ladder of ten steps and a diagonal line from one bottom corner **A** to the top **B**, then this line *crosses* the ladder in ten equal steps. Each step increases by **0.1** of the width of the column.

Now, if ten columns were put together you would get the arrangement shown on the right, which can clearly measure to one hundredth of a unit. This is a diagonal scale rule and is used when high tolerance drawing is required.

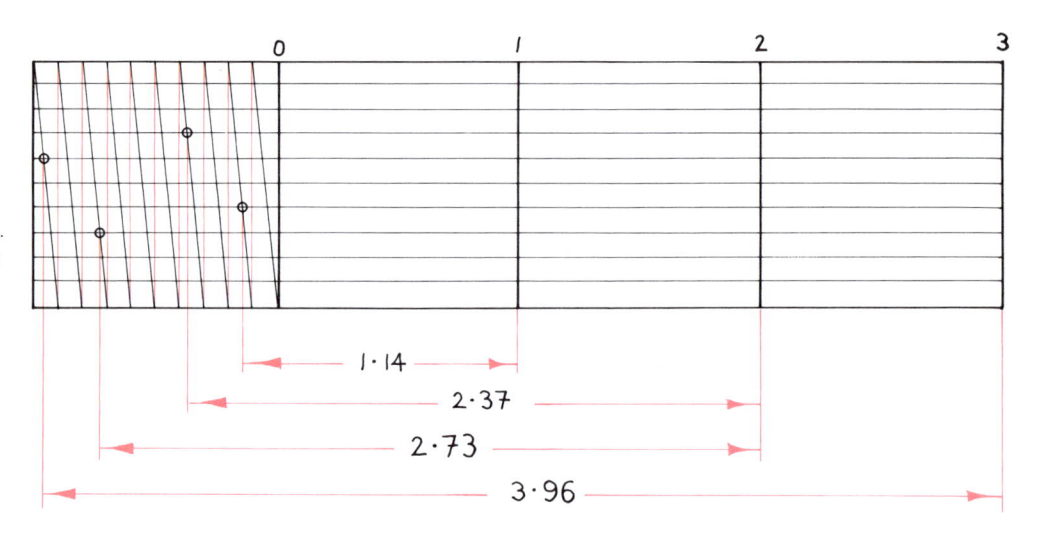

1·14
2·37
2·73
3·96

A diagonal scale can be used to subdivide any size of unit into hundredths. These scales are often set up to help draft a particularly accurate drawing that will later be reduced to working size, e.g. the pattern for a clock piece.

What exact measurements are indicated by the circled points?

Notes:
- Normally clarity is improved by marking the top and bottom divisions and drawing only the diagonals and not the columns.
- It does not matter much how high the columns are but steps of less than 2 mm are hard to see clearly.
- The diagonal scale was much more important before the metric system became so familiar, as inches were troublesome to subdivide.

Here the scale is of smaller units. Can you name the four circled points? Where would these measurements be: **0.27**; **3.79**; **4.04**; **1.69** and **2.93**?

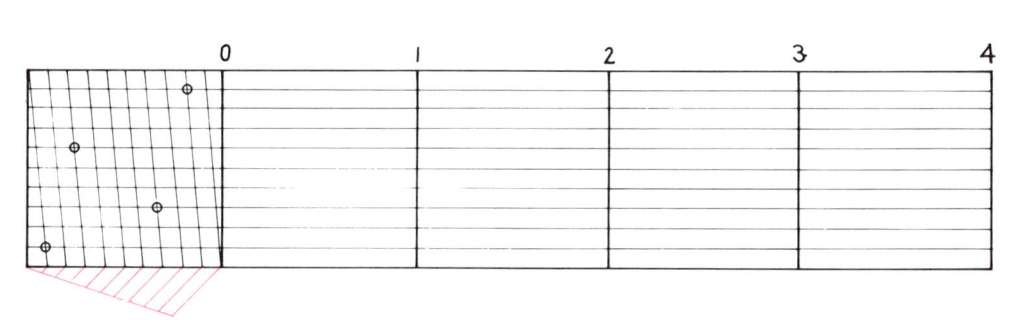

Technical Draughtsmanship		
Diagonal Scales		
Scales 3	Part I Geom.	

38

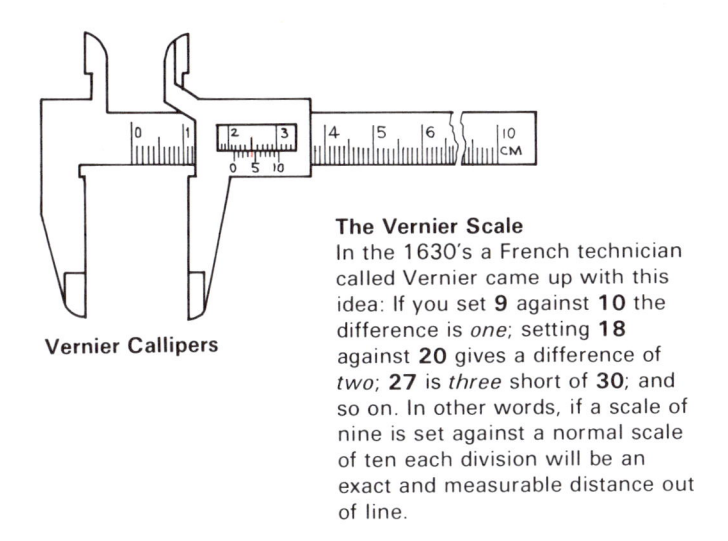

Vernier Callipers

The Vernier Scale
In the 1630's a French technician called Vernier came up with this idea: If you set **9** against **10** the difference is *one*; setting **18** against **20** gives a difference of *two*; **27** is *three* short of **30**; and so on. In other words, if a scale of nine is set against a normal scale of ten each division will be an exact and measurable distance out of line.

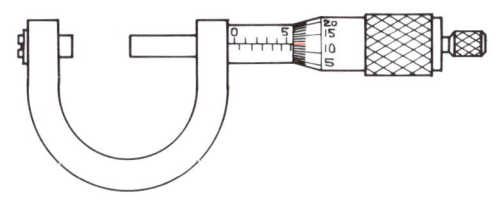

Vernier Micrometer Screw

By arranging the sliding scale on a ring and moving it along a spiral path (see p. **176**), it was found to be easier to read and to use the Vernier Scale.
However the straight Vernier Scale is still the more versatile.

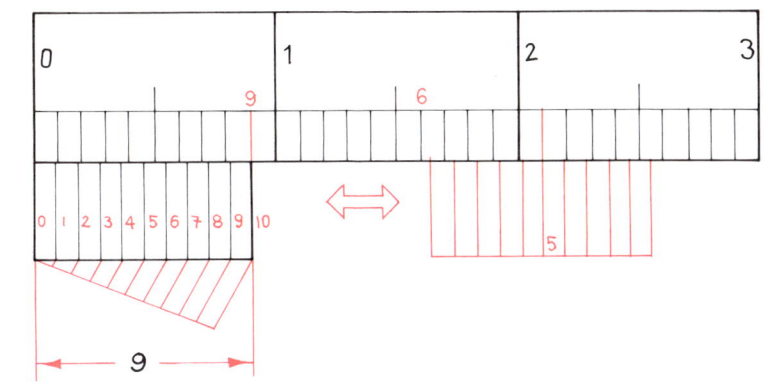

Plain Scale

Sliding Vernier Scale

To construct a Vernier Scale to read up to two decimal places
- Divide **90** standard units into ten subdivisions.
- Set this against a standard scale of **100** that is also divided into ten divisions.
- Here each line of the sliding scale is **0.01** nearer the lines on the fixed scale. So if it takes five divisions before the two scales are in line, then the offset was **0.05**. The measurement shown in the above diagram is **1.65**.

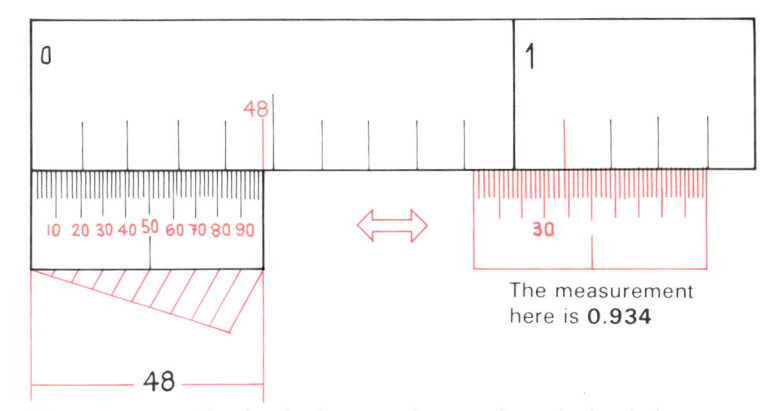

Plain Scale

Sliding Vernier Scale

The measurement here is **0.934**

To construct a Vernier Scale to read up to three decimal places
- Divide **48** standard units into one hundred subdivisions.
- Set this against a standard scale of **100** units that has been divided into ten divisions.
- This means that each line of the sliding scale is **0.001** nearer the lines on the fixed scale.

Technical Draughtsmanship
Vernier Scales
Scales 4 — Part I / Geom.

QUESTIONS

1. In each case:
   (i) Chose and draw a suitable diagonal scale and
   (ii) Draw both the given figure and a triangle equal in area to the given figure.

2. Using an appropriate diagonal scale draw the race track accurately. Then incorporate the markings of the other given sports within the boundary of the track.

3. In each case:
   (i) Draw the figure using an appropriate scale and
   (ii) Draw a square equal in area to the given figure.

4. Draw the three bicycle frames specified in the given table to a tolerance of ± **0.02 mm**.
   Make a vernier scale from thin card to read to **0.01 mm**.

A	580	600	520
B	555	570	518
C	585	600	580
D	410	410	425
E	270	270	275
F	74°	73°	93°
G	106°	107°	87°

All lugs : **1.8 mm** thick

All measurements are in millimetres

Technical Draughtsmanship		
Exercises 1		
N.T.S.	Scales 5	Part I / Geom.

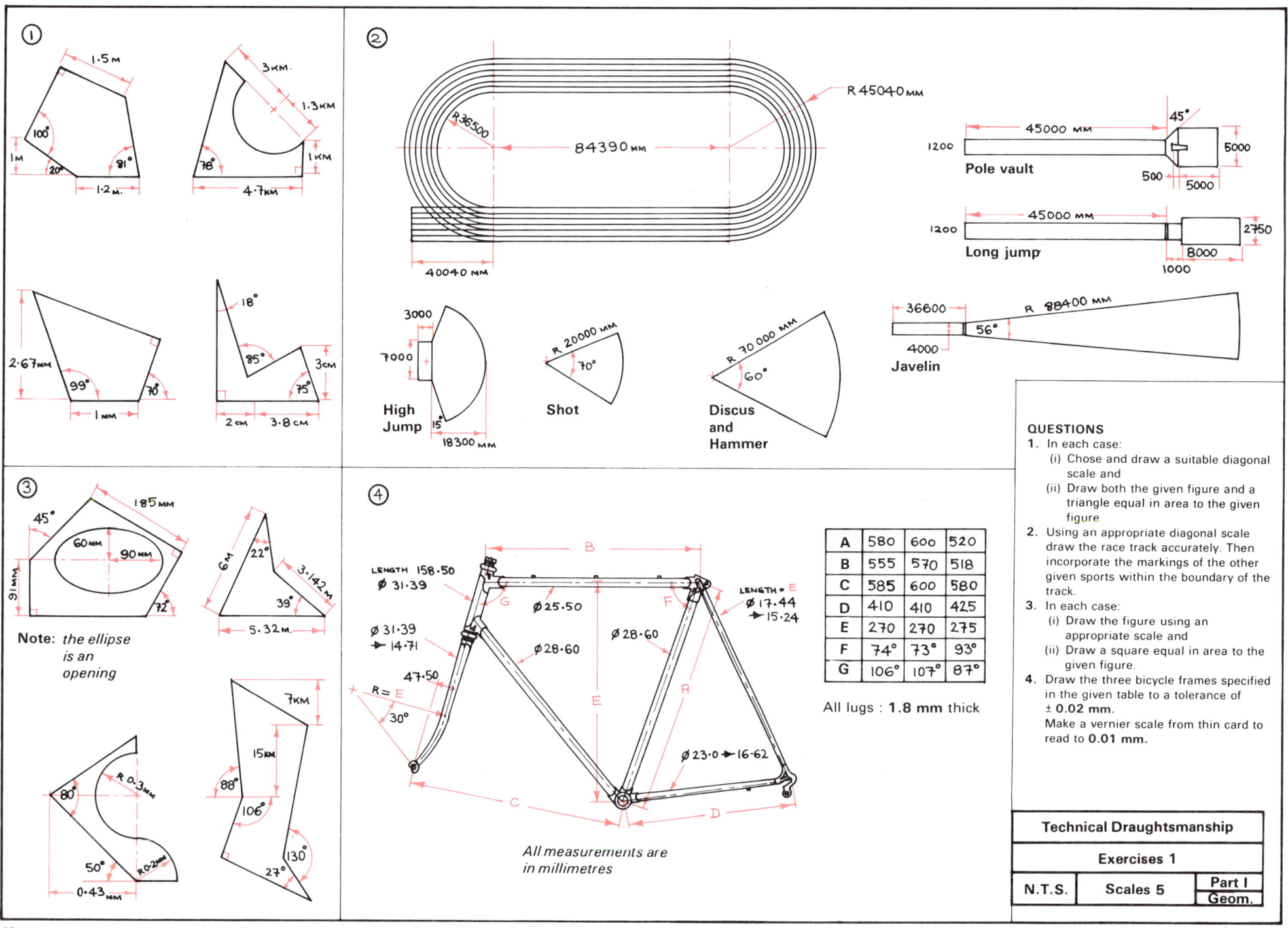

Questions

1. Scale each drawing to fit an **A4** size sheet. Then draw each figure. Mark the scale clearly on your drawings.
2. Using a diagonal scale draw each figure to fit on an **A4** sheet. Do not draw the figure too small or construction will be difficult.
3. This is a sketch brought back from a survey. To an appropriate scale, draw up the location map from the given information.
4. Using a diagonal scale draw the clock mechanism.
5. Choose an appropriate scale and draw both views, legend and dimensions.

Technical Draughtsmanship

Exercises 2

Scales 6 — Part I / Geom.

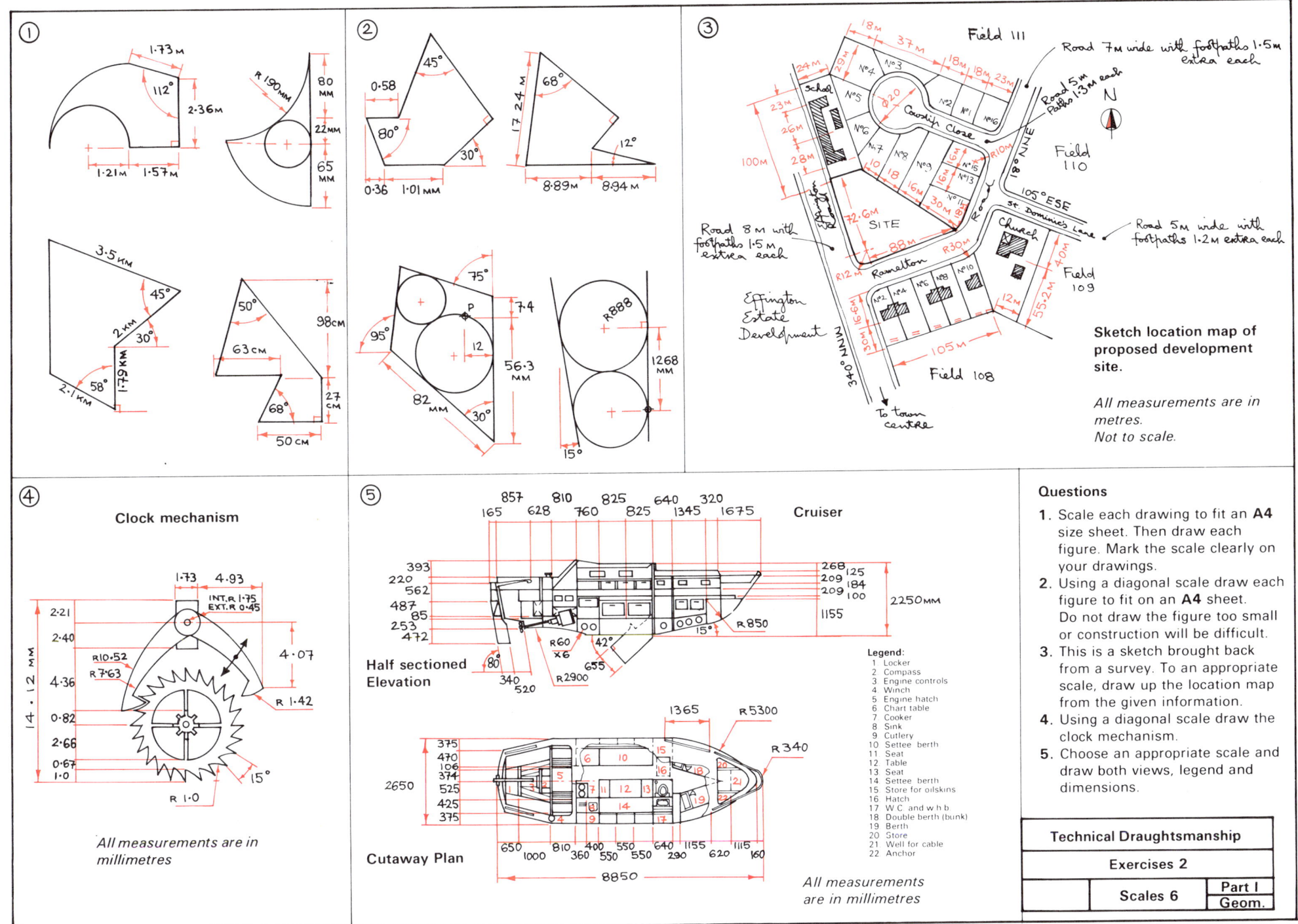

Figure 3 — Sketch location map of proposed development site.

All measurements are in metres.
Not to scale.

Figure 4 — Clock mechanism

All measurements are in millimetres

Figure 5 — Cruiser

Half sectioned Elevation

Cutaway Plan

Legend:
1. Locker
2. Compass
3. Engine controls
4. Winch
5. Engine hatch
6. Chart table
7. Cooker
8. Sink
9. Cutlery
10. Settee berth
11. Seat
12. Table
13. Seat
14. Settee berth
15. Store for oilskins
16. Hatch
17. W C and w h b
18. Double berth (bunk)
19. Berth
20. Store
21. Well for cable
22. Anchor

All measurements are in millimetres

①

Elevation

Plan

Nursery School:
Reconstruct the plain scale shown to suit an enlargement of the drawings of a nursery school. Then redraw the given views and project an end view of the school.

1M 0 1 2 3 4 5 6 7 8 9M

②

Front View   **End View**

Half section

Pulley:
Construct a vernier scale and draw the pulley to a tolerance of ± **0.04 mm**. Choose your own scale carefully. Also project a plan of the pulley.

Technical Draughtsmanship
Exercises 3
Scales 7   Part I   Geom. H

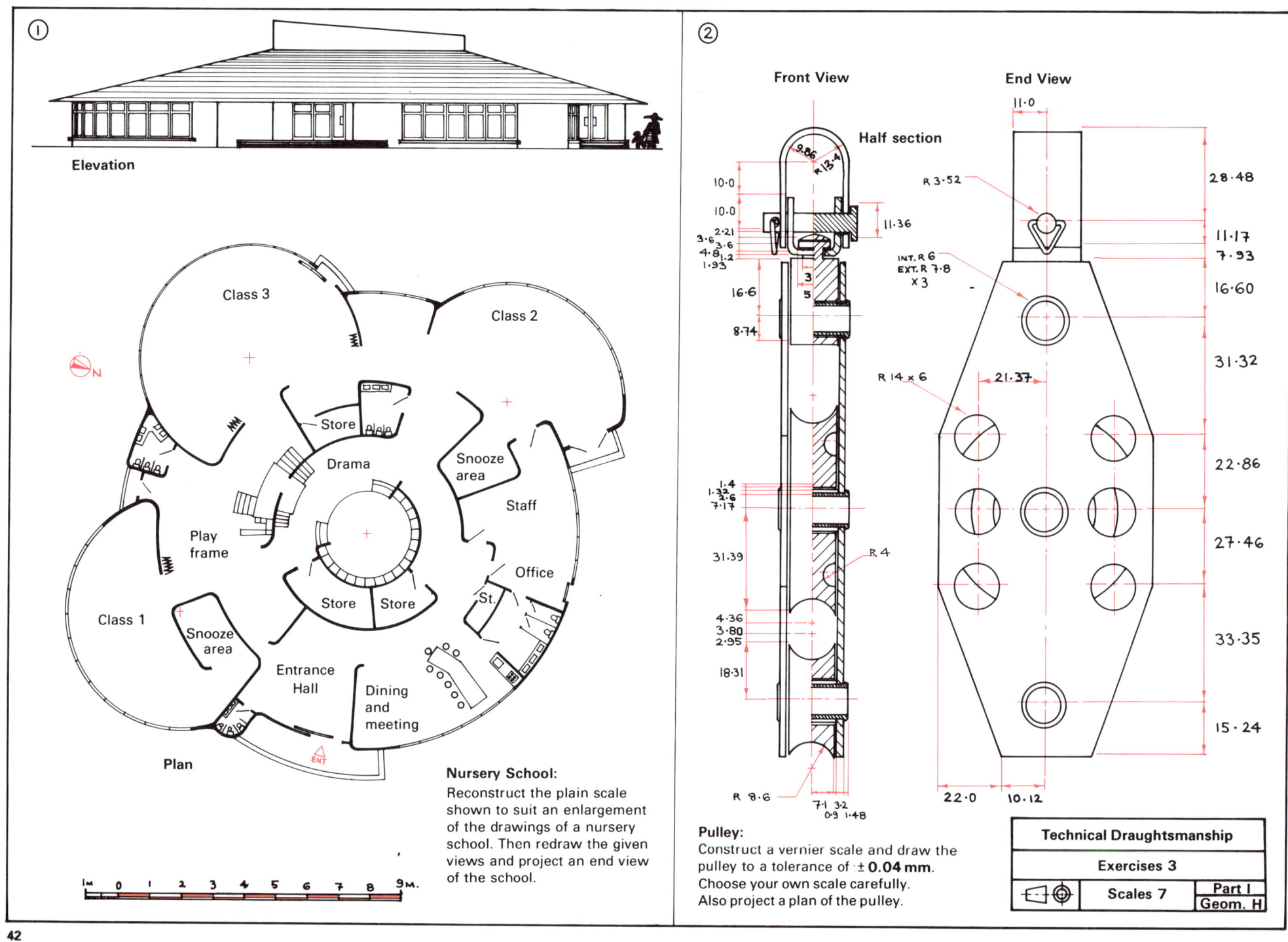

PART I

CHAPTER 5
ORTHOGRAPHIC PROJECTION

If lines run parallel from points on an object to corresponding points on a flat surface you have a view in orthographic projection. This idea was present in Stone Age cave drawings at Lascaux, Altamira, in Egypt and in Ancient Greece. But one view cannot fully define an object. By the early Renaissance, artists like Dürer and Uccello used a system of three related orthographic views. Finally, in the eighteenth century a French engineer worked out a standardized system — now known as first angle projection. This became, and still is, the basis of all technical drawing.

CONTENTS
Projection Systems 1	*Page* **44**
Projection Systems 2	**45**
Projections compared	**46**
First Angle (European)	**47**
First and Third Angles	**48**
A First Angle Projection	**49**
A Third Angle Projection	**50**
True Length of a Line	**51**
True Shape	**52**
Three Regular Polyhedra	**53**
The Icosahedron	**54**
The Dodecahedron	**55**
Inscribing Polyhedra	**56**
Two Sample Problems	**57**
Exercises	**58**

Photocopying prohibited by law

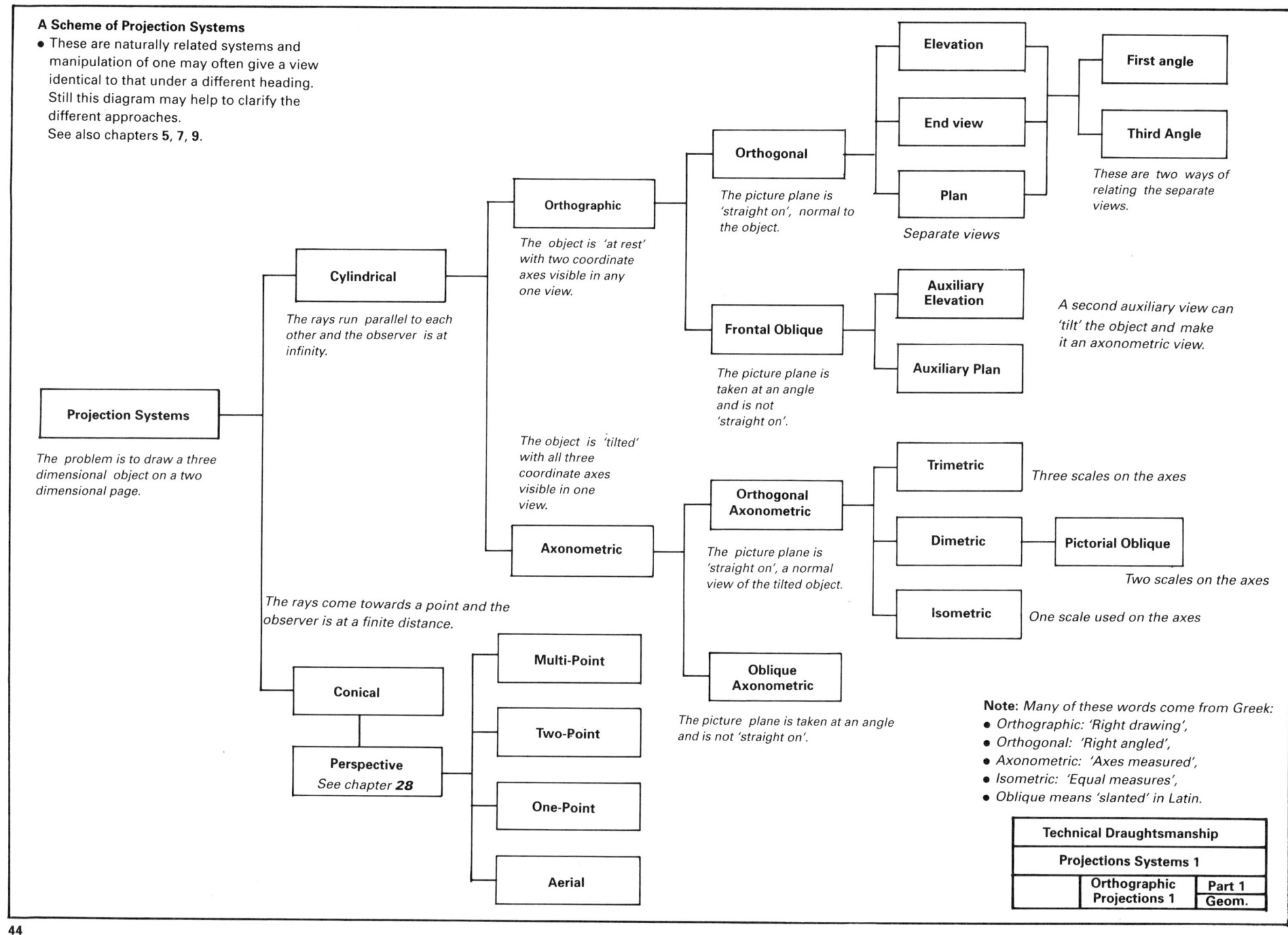

A Scheme of Projection Systems
- These are naturally related systems and manipulation of one may often give a view identical to that under a different heading. Still this diagram may help to clarify the different approaches.
See also chapters **5, 7, 9**.

```
Projection Systems ──┬── Cylindrical ──┬── Orthographic ──┬── Orthogonal ──┬── Elevation ──┬── First angle
                     │                 │                  │                ├── End view    └── Third Angle
                     │                 │                  │                └── Plan
                     │                 │                  └── Frontal Oblique ──┬── Auxiliary Elevation
                     │                 │                                        └── Auxiliary Plan
                     │                 └── Axonometric ──┬── Orthogonal Axonometric ──┬── Trimetric
                     │                                   │                            ├── Dimetric ── Pictorial Oblique
                     │                                   │                            └── Isometric
                     │                                   └── Oblique Axonometric
                     └── Conical ── Perspective ──┬── Multi-Point
                                                  ├── Two-Point
                                                  ├── One-Point
                                                  └── Aerial
```

The problem is to draw a three dimensional object on a two dimensional page.

The rays run parallel to each other and the observer is at infinity.

The rays come towards a point and the observer is at a finite distance.

The object is 'at rest' with two coordinate axes visible in any one view.

The object is 'tilted' with all three coordinate axes visible in one view.

The picture plane is 'straight on', normal to the object.

Separate views

The picture plane is taken at an angle and is not 'straight on'.

The picture plane is 'straight on', a normal view of the tilted object.

The picture plane is taken at an angle and is not 'straight on'.

These are two ways of relating the separate views.

A second auxiliary view can 'tilt' the object and make it an axonometric view.

Three scales on the axes

Two scales on the axes

One scale used on the axes

Perspective
*See chapter **28***

Note: Many of these words come from Greek:
- Orthographic: 'Right drawing',
- Orthogonal: 'Right angled',
- Axonometric: 'Axes measured',
- Isometric: 'Equal measures',
- Oblique means 'slanted' in Latin.

Technical Draughtsmanship		
Projections Systems 1		
	Orthographic Projections 1	Part 1
		Geom.

① ORTHOGRAPHIC
Orthogonal

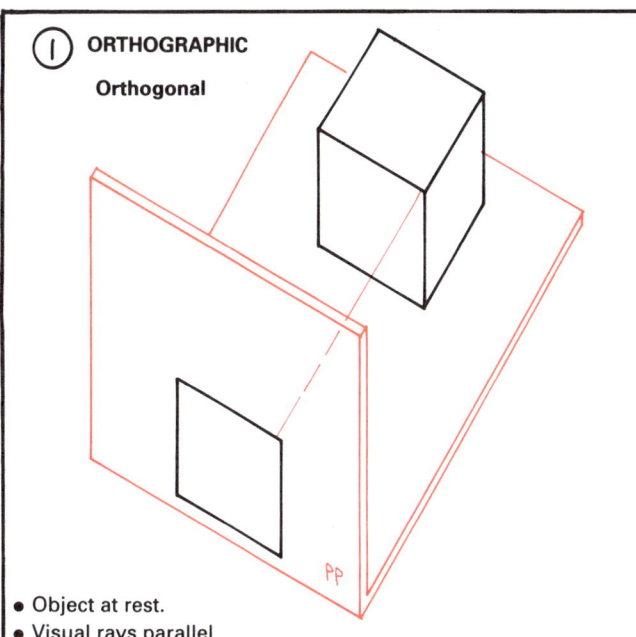

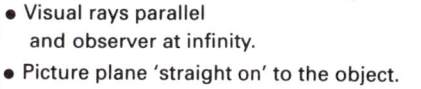

- Object at rest.
- Visual rays parallel and observer at infinity.
- Picture plane 'straight on' to the object.

② ORTHOGRAPHIC
Oblique

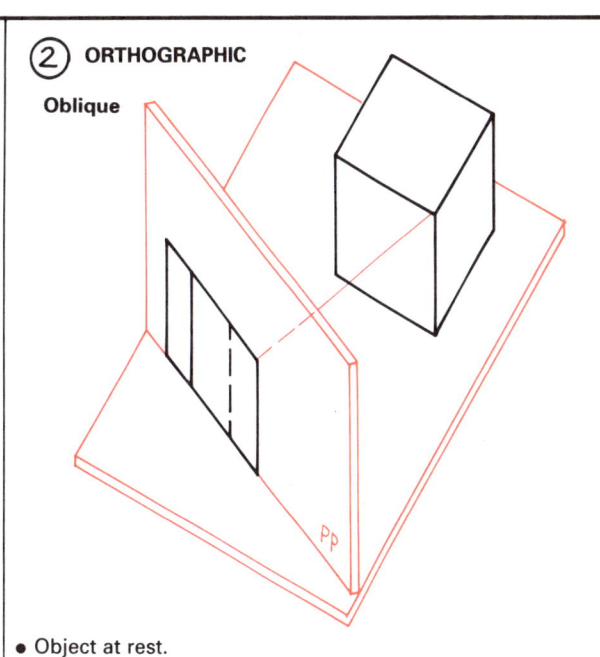

- Object at rest.
- Visual rays parallel with observer at infinity.
- Picture plane at an angle to the object.

③ AXONOMETRIC
Orthogonal

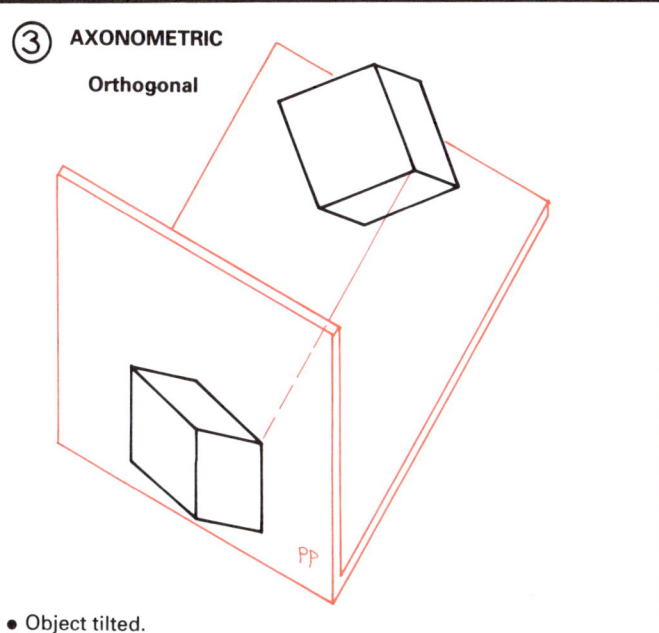

- Object tilted.
- Visual rays parallel with observer at infinity.
- Picture plane 'straight on' to the object.

④ AXONOMETRIC
Oblique

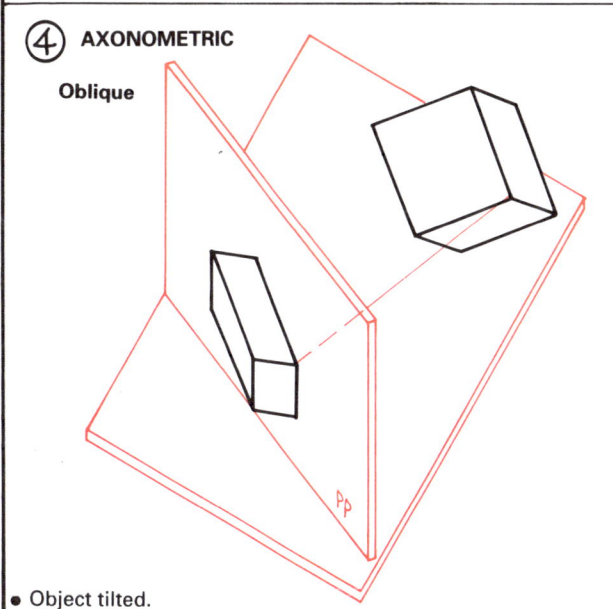

- Object tilted.
- Visual rays parallel and observer at infinity.
- Picture plane at an angle to the object.

⑤ CONICAL PROJECTION
Perspective

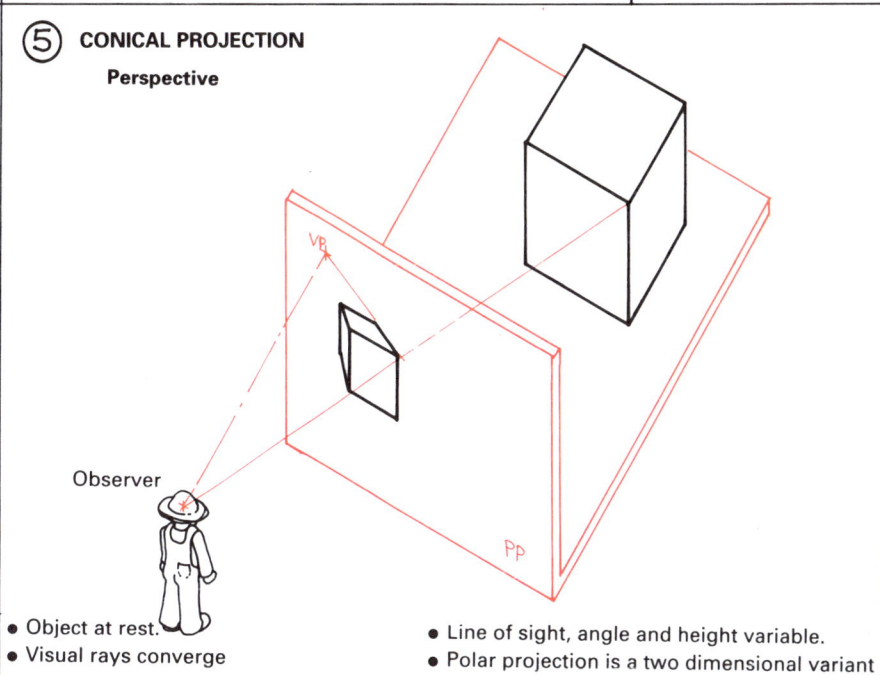

- Object at rest.
- Visual rays converge with observer at a finite distance.
- Line of sight, angle and height variable.
- Polar projection is a two dimensional variant of this approach.

Note:
- This may seem like a lot of jargon, but, if you get the different approaches clear, then you will be able to increase your own control.

Technical Draughtsmanship	
Projection Systems 2	
Orthographic Projection 2	Part 1
	Geom.

45

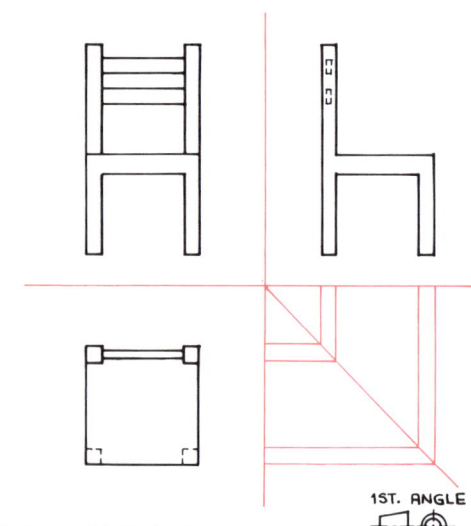

Oblique Projection

Orthographic Projection
Three views, front, left side and plan are drawn to scale and give detailed information about the object. This arrangement is sometimes called **European projection**. When the system was perfected by Gaspard Monge, Napoleon ordered it to be kept a military secret for over fifteen years.

1ST. ANGLE

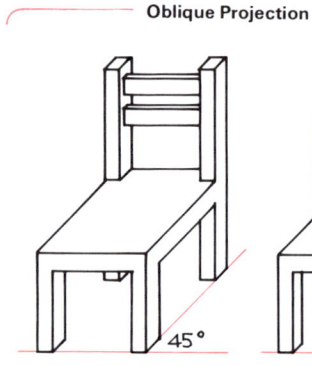

Cavalier Projection
Originally used by cavalry officers to draw houses or towns. All the measurements are to scale. Lines that are vertical or horizontal in a front view are unchanged, while the side view is set along the oblique axis of **45°**. There is often visual distortion (notice how long the seat seems) when using this system.

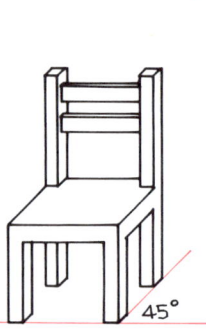

Cabinet Projection
Used by cabinet makers, this system avoids the visual distortion of cavalier projection by simply dividing all the oblique lines by *two*. the drawing works a lot better but cannot now be easily used for measurement.

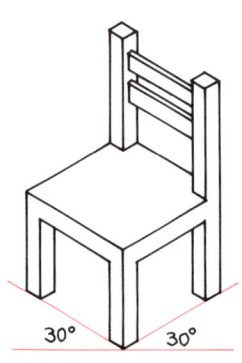

Isometric Drawing
By introducing a *second* oblique axis the sense of seeing a third dimension is enhanced. These axes are both at **30°**, and the measurements are all to scale. Isometric is Greek for 'equally measured'.

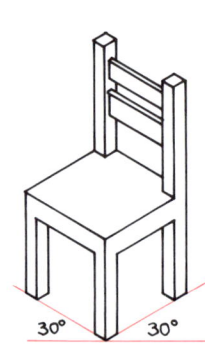

Isometric Projection
This avoids the very chunky look of an isometric drawing. One oblique axis is measured to scale while a special isometric scale is used on the other axis.

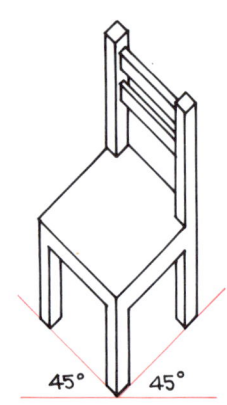

Planometric Projection
Here the sum of the oblique angles is **90°**. Any combination may be used (**60°/30°**, **45°/45°**, **50°/40°** etc.). All measurements are to scale and right angles are unaffected. This means that tracing can be done directly from a plan. Hence 'plan-o-metric'.

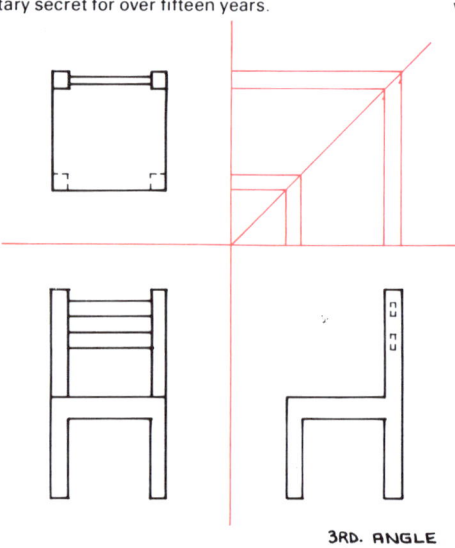

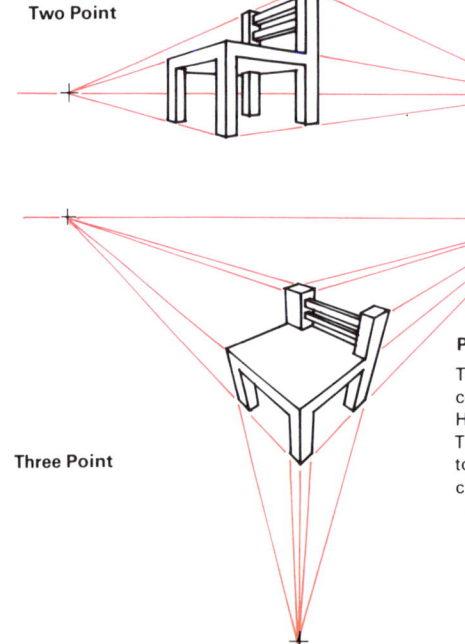

Two Point

One Point

Three Point

Orthographic Projection
Here the three views are front, right side and plan. This arrangement is also known as **American Projection**.

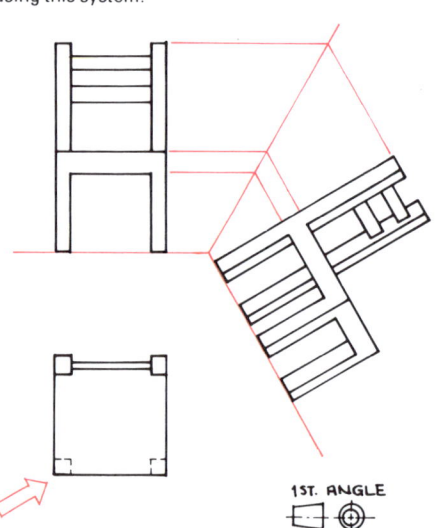

3RD. ANGLE

Auxiliary Projection
Sometimes a standard view of an object may be a little confusing. Auxiliary views can be constructed to show the object from *any* stand-point. See Chapter **6**.

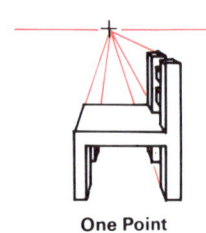

1ST. ANGLE

Perspective Projection
The sense of seeing a third dimension is most convincing when a perspective projection is used. Here lines converge at a chosen point, or points. These drawings are slow to construct and difficult to scale but are very impressive to non-technical clients — see Chapter **28**.

Technical Draughtsmanship		
Projections Compared		
Orthographic Projection 3	Part I	Geom.

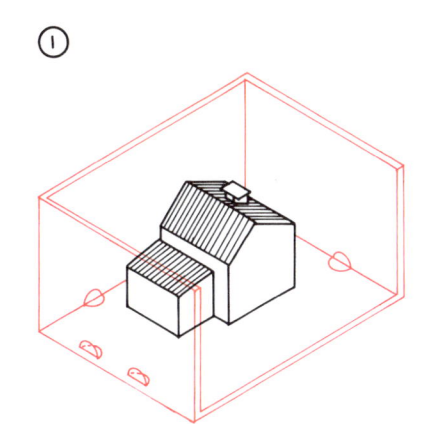

①
- Imagine an object placed in an open box with hinged sides.

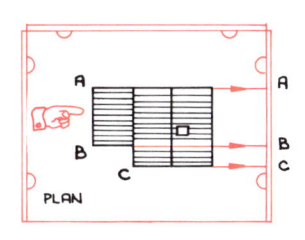

②
- Looking straight down you see a **plan**.
- To draw the **left side** look towards it and project points back onto the box-wall behind it.

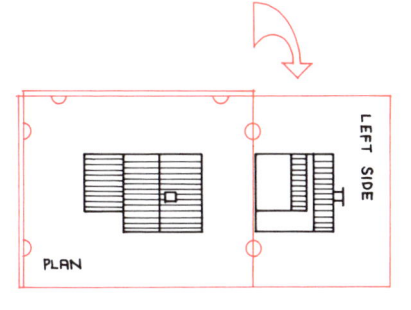

③
- Flatten that wall and you have a view of the **left side**.
- Flattening a plane is technically called **rabatment**

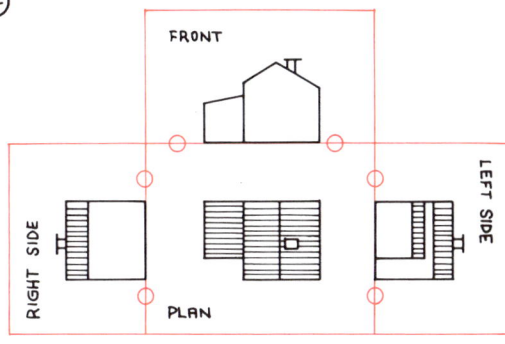

④
- Do the same for the **right side** and the **front**.
- This is an **orthographic projection** but you would get a crick in your neck reading it. So...

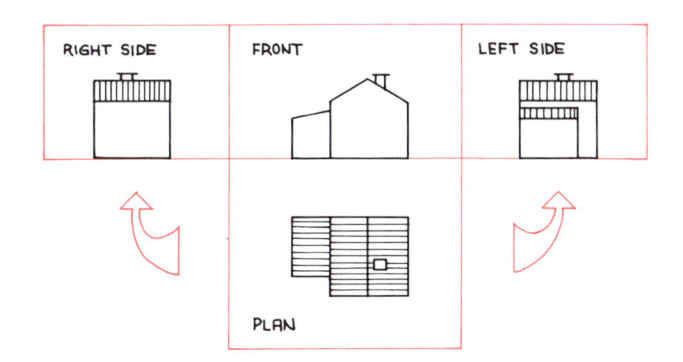

⑤
- Swing both sides up level with the front.

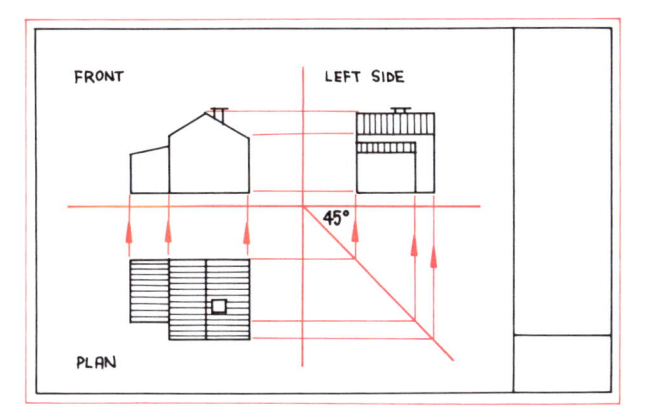

⑥
- Normally three views give enough information about the object.
- A **45°** line allows us to transfer measurements from one view to another.

Pitfall:
- If you put a view on the wrong side, the plan gets turned inside out.

Note:
- Rabat comes from French and means to 'beat down'.
- Orthographic comes from Greek orthos meaning 'right' or 'correct' and graphos to 'describe' or 'draw'.

Technical Draughtsmanship		
First Angle (European)		
	Orthographic Projection 4	Part I Geom.

47

①

FIRST ANGLE

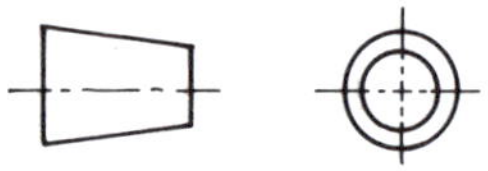

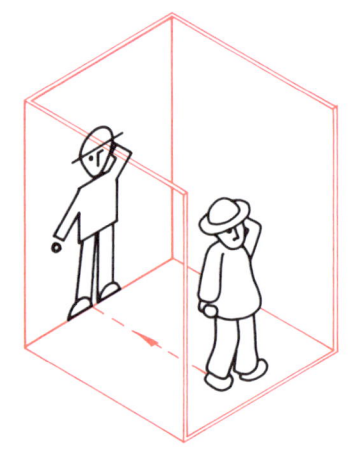

First angle (European) projection
The image is projected from the figure *back* onto the glass box around it.
If you stand to the left the view will be projected onto the right wall, at the *far* side of the figure, much as you would project a silhouette onto a wall.

- The standard arrangement of views for first angle projection.

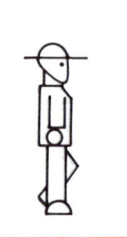

Right side — Left side — Plan

②

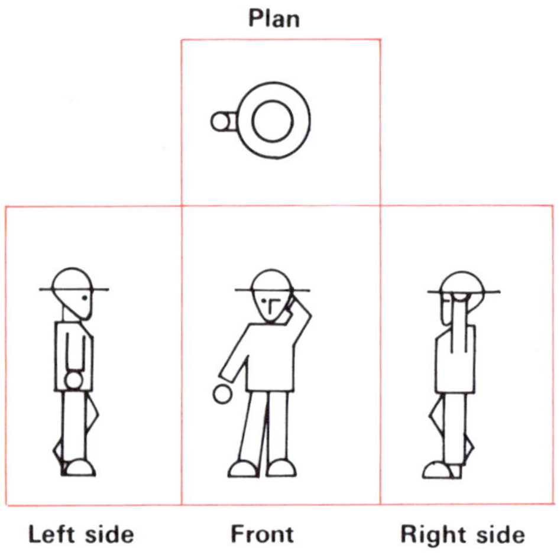

THIRD ANGLE

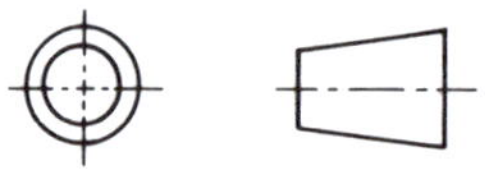

Third angle (American) projection
The image is seen on the glass sheets *in front* of the figure. Notice the difference in the side view positions. If you stand to the left the view will be seen on the *near* side wall, like a tracing on the glass.

Plan
Left side — Front — Right side

- The standard arrangement of views for third angle projection.

③

Angles
The idea of **1st** and **3rd** angles is not as baffling as it sounds. Cut two rectangles of cardboard and fit them together to form a cross.

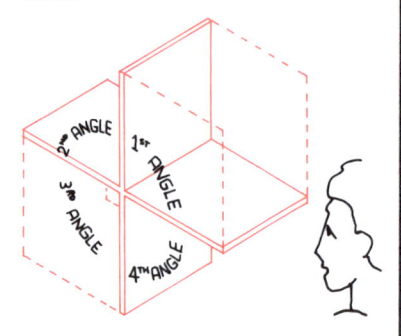

Now flatten the cross. It will be clear that you can have either **1st** and **3rd** angles opened out *or* **2nd** and **4th** angles, but not both at the same time. Since first and third angles are familiar and most useful, we always choose them.

- The two systems were in use long before they were named by angles.
- The Angle of Projection **must** be stated either in words or by symbol on a drawing.
- Third angle projection is gaining ground in Europe at the moment, but, except for Holland, is not yet dominant.

Technical Draughtsmanship
First and Third Angles

| Orthographic Projection 5 | Part I Geom. |

FRONT VIEW

Ø 65
Ø 63
Ø 59
Ø 57
Ø 42
Ø 40
Ø 37
Ø 36
Ø 12

8 14 29 19 3
5 3
4 2 2
5 6
17
15
16
5
72
6
14
8 12 6 2 12 30 25 5
140

END VIEW

32
14
2 4
3 16
1 5
53
8
16 2 12 3 10 7 8 14 3 9

PLAN

14 15 4 8 4 7 10 28
Ø 12
Ø 24
Ø 19
4
16
3
6
8 15
2
8
5
2
7
5
12
3
10
84

INT Ø 20
EXT Ø 24
INT Ø 6
EXT Ø 10
INT Ø 10
EXT Ø 18

All measurements are in millimetres.

Here is an example of **First Angle** projection.
Draw the camera on an **A3** sheet. The drawing will take up most of the sheet so position the views carefully. Your scale will be **1 : 1**.

Technical Draughtsmanship
A First Angle Projection
Orthographic Projection 6	Part 1 Geom.

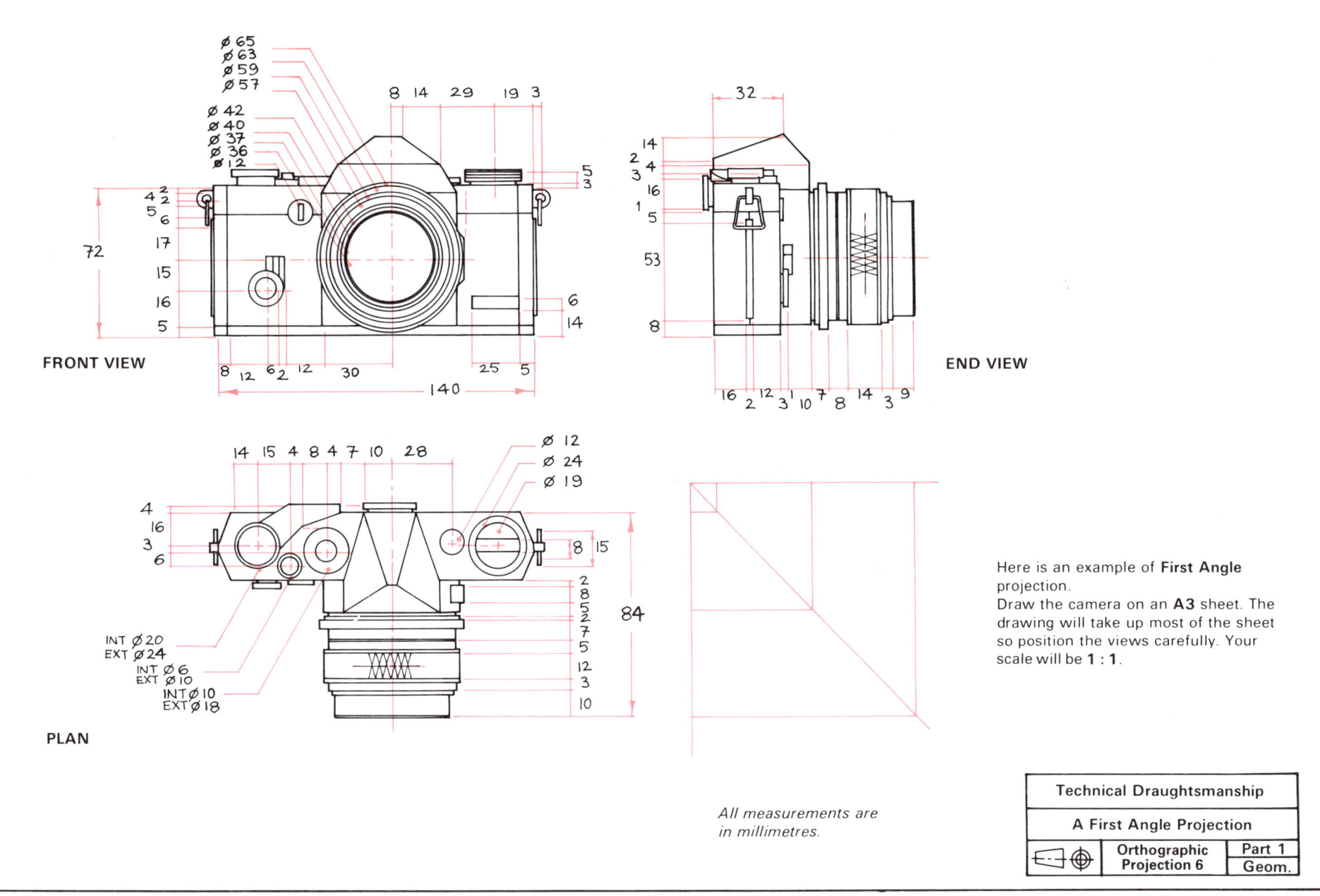

49

PLAN

This is an example of **Third Angle** Projection. Draw the screw down valve on an **A3** sheet. Take care to get the hatching right and to position the views. Your scale will be **1 : 2**.

All measurements are in millimetres.

Detail at A

FRONT VIEW
With Half Section

END VIEW

Technical Draughtsmanship	
A Third Angle Projection	
Orthographic Projection 7	Part I / Geom.

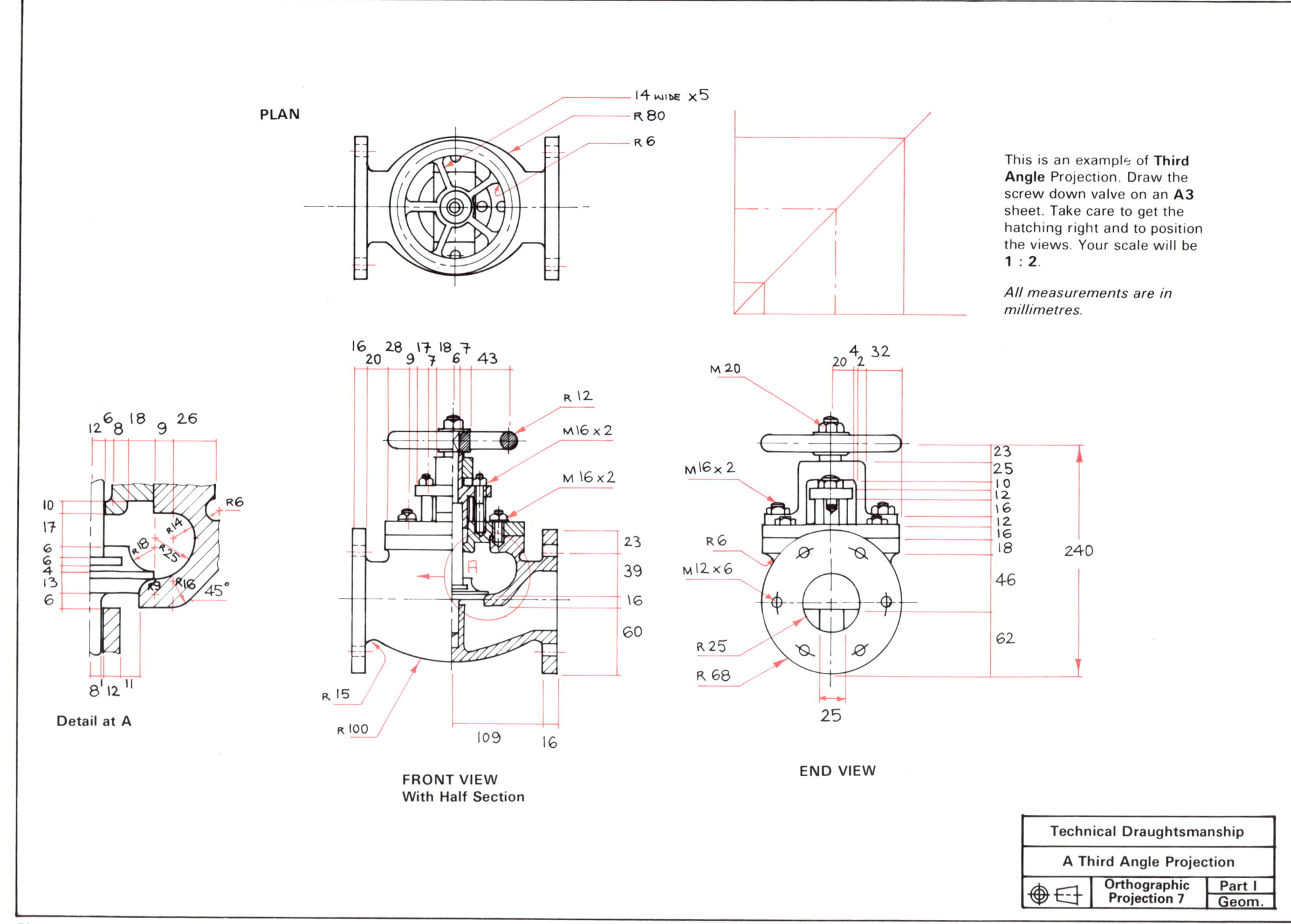

50

① The Problem of True Length

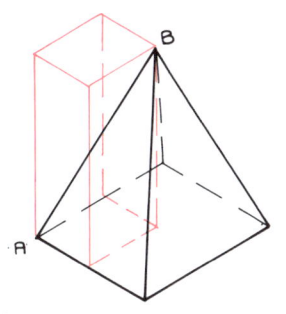

Sketch

- Line **AB** is leaning with regard to one of the principal planes.
- Because **AB** is leaning, you cannot measure it from either the elevation or the plan.
- You have to find its **true length**.

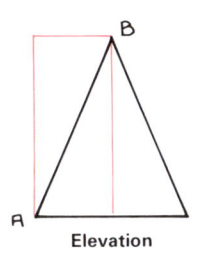

Elevation

Plan

The solution: Step 1:

Sketch

- Here line **AB** has been isolated.
- Notice in the sketch that a triangle can be drawn by setting l at right-angles to h, where l is the apparent length on the plan and h is the apparent height in elevation.
- Such a triangle will have **AB** in true length as its hypotenuse.

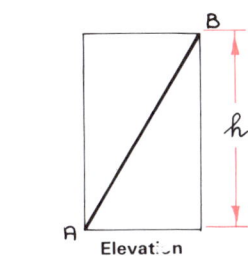

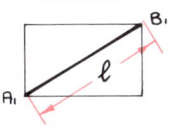

Elevation

Plan

- With centre **B** swing **A** to **C**.
- Project **C** to **D**.
- Join **B** to **D**.
- **BD** will be the true length of **AB**.
- This process is called **Rabatment**.

Step 2

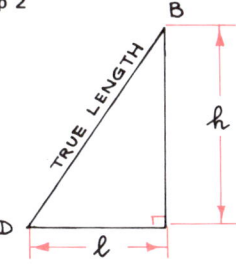

A true length diagram

- Sometimes it is better to simply set up the triangle in a separate diagram.
- Transfer l and h with pointers.

---

② An example of a true length problem

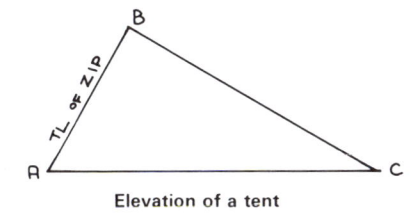

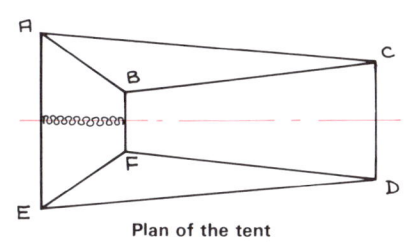

Elevation of a tent

Plan of the tent

- In order to design a pattern for the tent all the true lengths are needed.
- First check for lines that are already true lengths. The base is flat on the ground, therefore, **AC, CD, DE** and **EA** are true lengths on the plan.
- As **BF** is parallel to the ground then it too is true length on plan.
- The zip appears in its true length on the elevation. Why?
- That leaves **AB, BC, EF** and **FD** to be found.

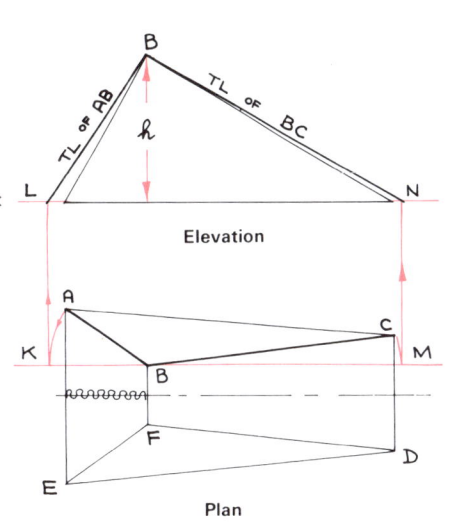

Elevation

Plan

- **AB** is similar to **EF** and **BC** is similar to **FD**. So there are only two true length problems.
- For **AB**: draw a horizontal line through **B**.
- With **B** as centre swing **A** onto this line at **K**.
- Project **K** up to **L** on the elevation.
- Join **B** to **L**. This is the true length of **AB**, and of **EF**.
- For **BC**: with **B** as centre swing **C** onto the horizontal line at **M**.
- Project **M** up to **N** on the elevation.
- Join **B** to **N**. This is the true length of **BC**, and of **FD**.

Notes:

- *True length calculations are very important.*
- *See Chapter 8, page 95 for a second method of finding true lengths.*
- *See also Chapter 12, page 145.*
- *See also Chapter 27, page 326.*

Technical Draughtsmanship
True length of a line

| N.T.S. | Orthographic Projection 8 | Part I Geom. |

① The Problem of True Shape:

Elevation / **End view** / **Plan**

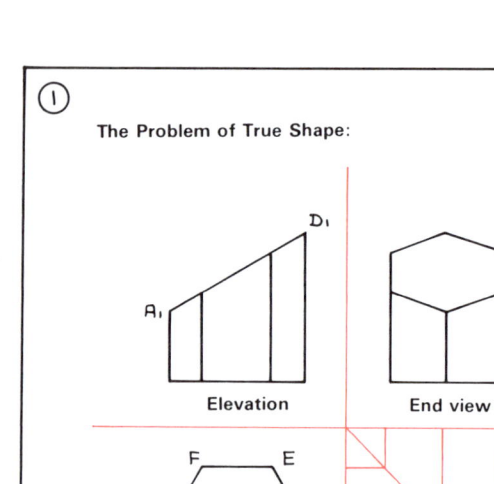

- Because surface A_1D_1 is sloping in all three standard views some of its sides are *not* true lengths and nowhere is its true shape visible.

A solution

True Shape

- On elevation draw a horizontal line from A_1.
- With A_1 as centre swing B_1, C_1 and D_1 onto this line at **K**, **L** and **M**.
- By projecting down from **MA**, and over from the plan, fix the points and draw the true shape.

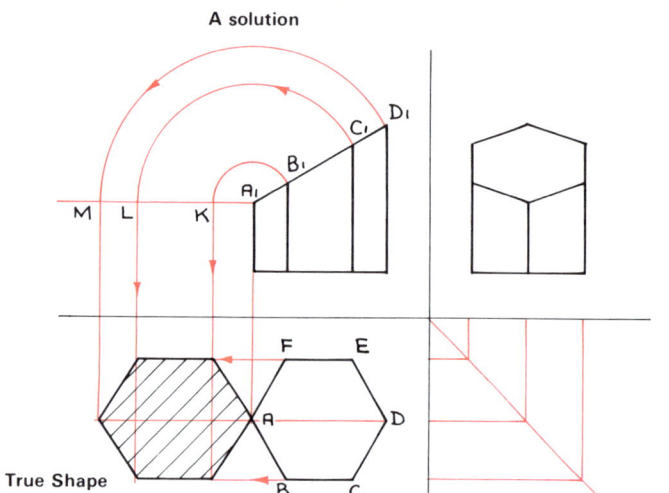

This process is known as Rabatment.

② Rabatting a curved surface

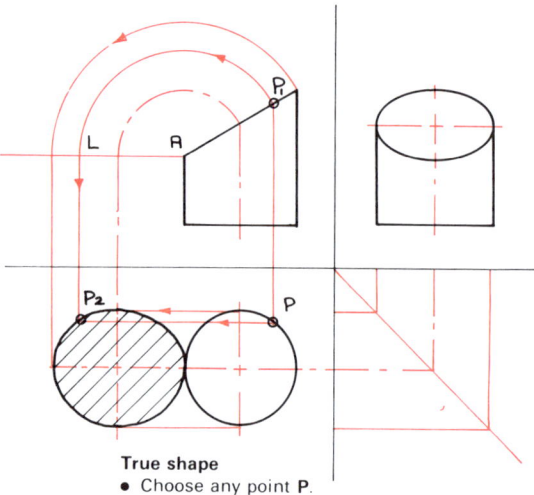

True shape

- Choose any point **P**.
- Project **P** to P_1 and towards P_2.
- With centre **A** rabat P_1 to **L**.
- From **L** project down to fix point P_2 of the true shape.

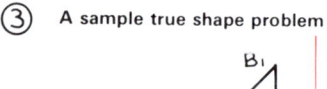

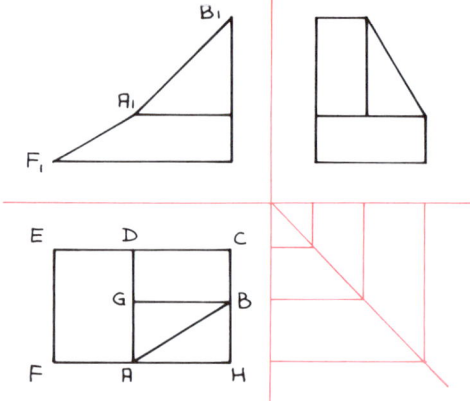

③ A sample true shape problem

- Check which areas could be rabatted.
- T **GBCD1** and **FADE**.
- Notice that **AHB** and **ABG** cannot be simply swung down flat.

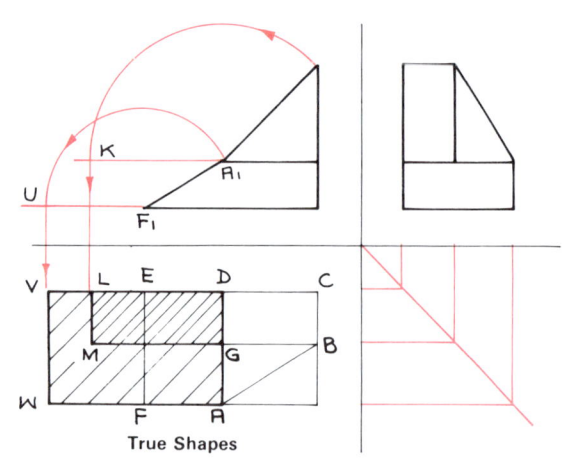

True Shapes

Step 1:
- On elevation draw a horizontal line from A_1.
- With centre A_1 swing B_1 onto this line at **K**.
- Project **K** to define **LMGD**, the true shape of **GBCD**.
- Similarly rabat F_1A_1 to find **VWAD**, the true shape of **FADE**.

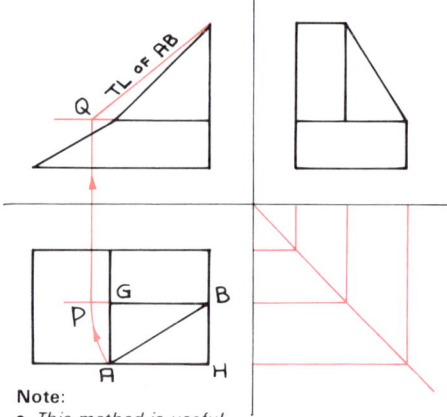

Step 2:
- We still have to determine the true shapes of **AHB** and **ABG**.
- The only line that can not be measured on the given views is **AB**.
- Proceeding as on page **51** find the true length of **AB**.
- All the measurements now being known the true shape of **AHB** and **ABG** can be drawn.

Note:
- *This method is useful but of limited practical application.*
- *See also page **145**, Chapter **12**.*
- *See also page **326**, Chapter **27**.*
- *Rabatment is French for 'to beat down' or 'to flatten'.*

Technical Draughtsmanship		
True Shape		
	Orthographic Projection 9	Part I / Geom.

52

①

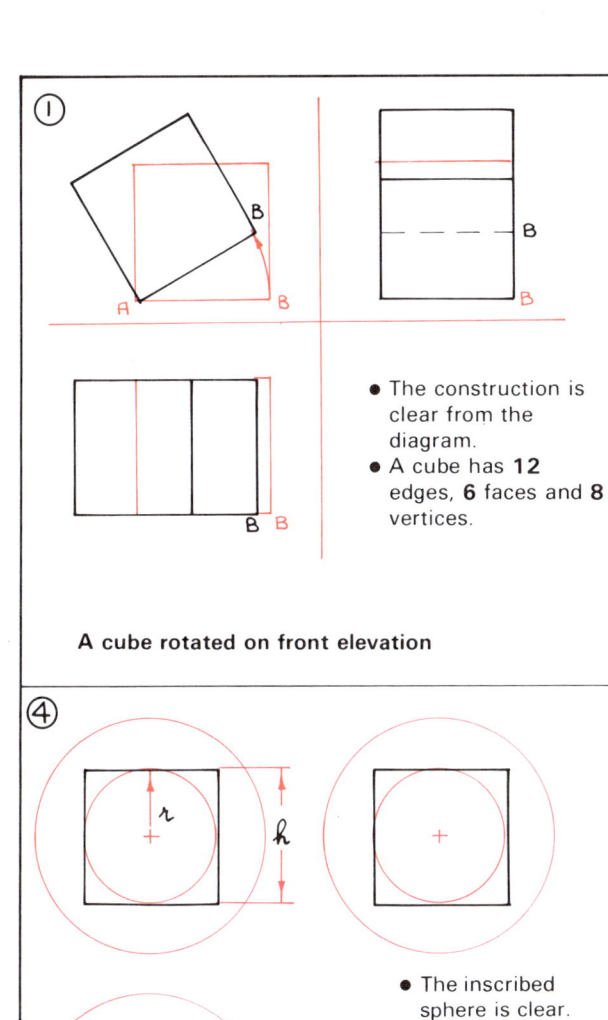

A cube rotated on front elevation

- The construction is clear from the diagram.
- A cube has **12** edges, **6** faces and **8** vertices.

②

A tetrahedron rotated on end view

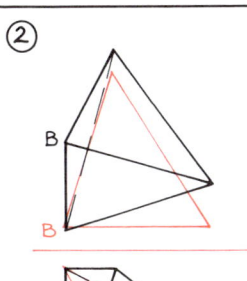

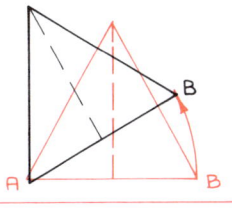

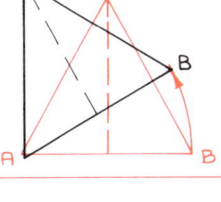

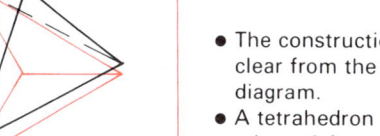

- The construction is clear from the diagram.
- A tetrahedron has **6** edges, **4** faces and **4** vertices.

③

An octahedron rotated on plan

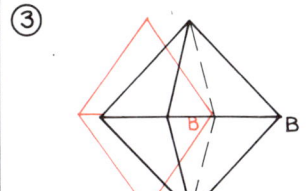

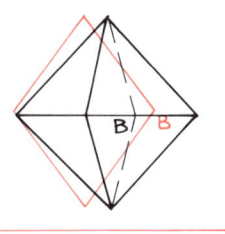

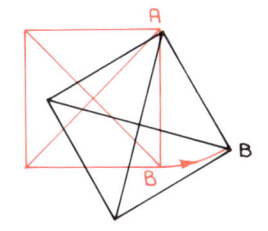

- The construction is clear from the diagram.
- An octahedron has **12** edges, **8** faces and **6** vertices.

④

To inscribe and circumscribe a cube

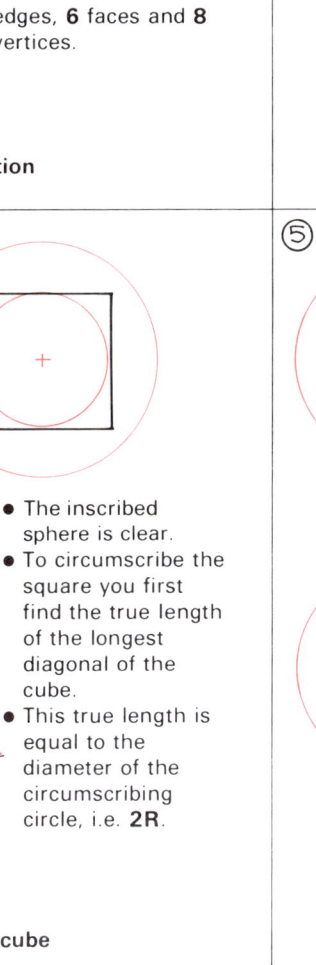

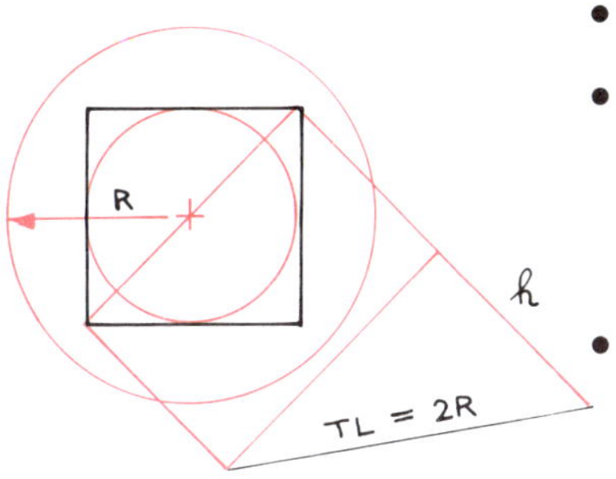

- The inscribed sphere is clear.
- To circumscribe the square you first find the true length of the longest diagonal of the cube.
- This true length is equal to the diameter of the circumscribing circle, i.e. **2R**.

⑤

To inscribe and circumscribe a tetrahedron

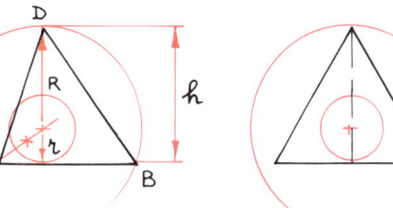

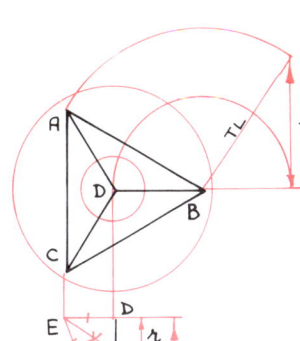

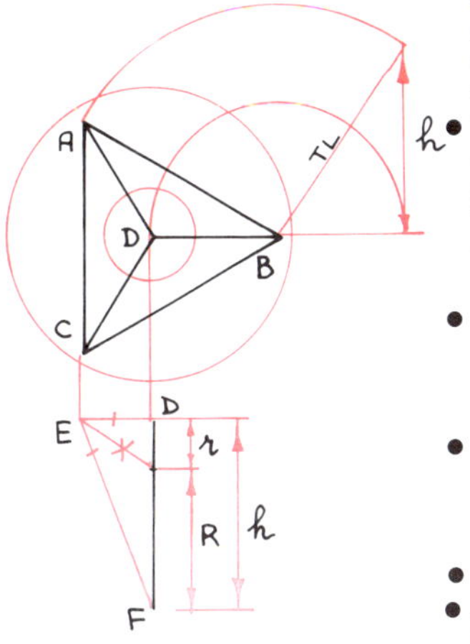

- The centre of both spheres will be equidistant from each of the four corners of the tetrahedron.
- To find that centre on elevation drop a perpendicular from **D**. Then bisect angle **DCB** to fix the centre. Both radii will be clear, as **R + r = h**.
- Alternatively start with the plan and project out the distance from **D** to **AC**, as shown.
- Set the height at right angles to this and complete the triangle **EDF**.
- Bisect angle **DEF** to find **r** and **R**.
- A method of finding the height from a plan is also shown.

⑥

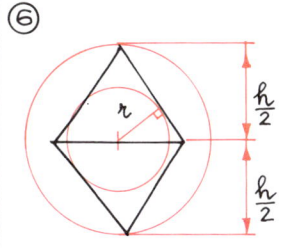

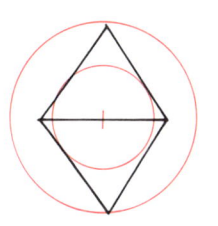

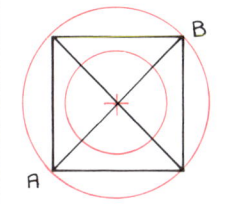

To inscribe and circumscribe an octahedron

- **AB** = h = **2R**
- The radius of the inscribing circle is obtained from an elevation as shown.

Note: *If any of these solids appear in awkward positions rotate, or project, easier views before proceeding.*

Technical Draughtsmanship
Three Regular Polyhedra

| Orthographic Projection 10 | Part I Geom. H |

53

Procedure, step by step

① 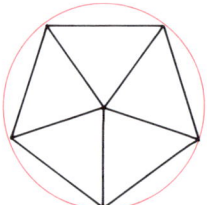
- Draw a pentagon in a circle and join the corners to the centre. See page **13**.

② 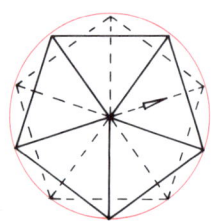
- By projecting lines from the centre, lightly draw a 'ghost' pentagon.

③ 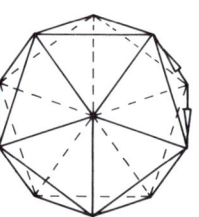
- Join the corners of the two pentagons.
- This is a *plan* of an icosahedron.

④ 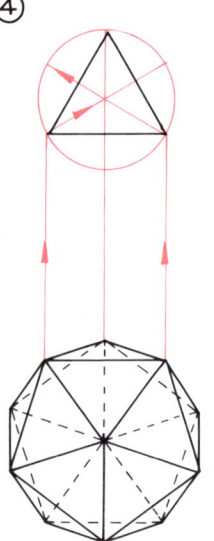
- Take one side of a pentagon in the plan and project it up to form the base of a triangle.
- Bisect the angles of the triangle and inscribe it.

⑤ 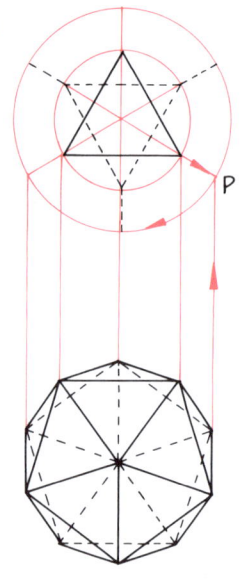
- Draw a 'ghost' triangle.
- From the plan bring up an outside dimension line towards **P**.
- Extend a bisector to fix point **P**.
- Using the same centre as before, draw a circle through point **P**.

⑥ 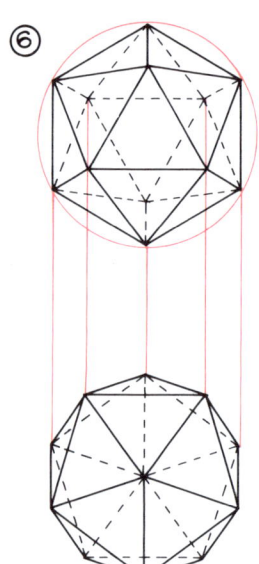
- Extend each bisector to meet the outside circle.
- Draw the hexagon joining these and, with the help of the plan, draw in the remaining lines, as shown.

The finished views

Front View

Left Side View

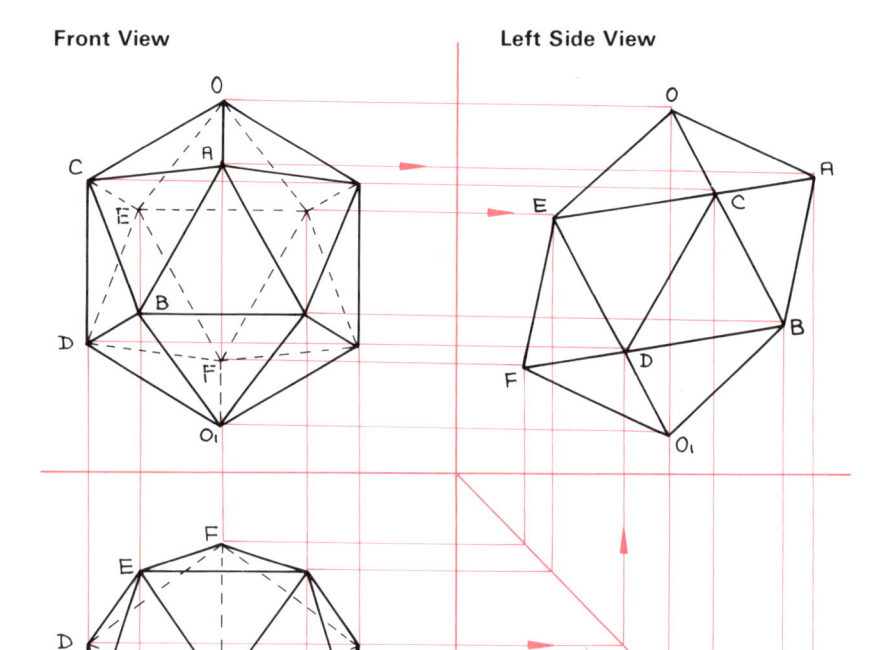

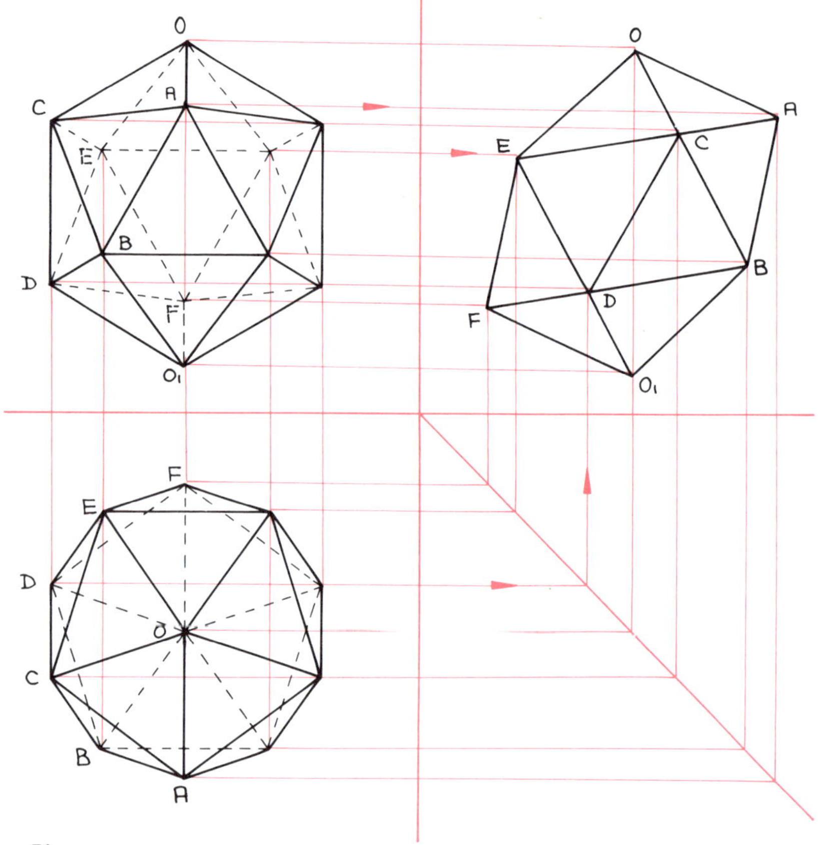

Plan

- Index the points of the plan and front elevation. Bring these together by projection to locate the left side view.

Notes:
- The Icosahedron has **30** *edges*, **20** *faces* and **12** *vertices*.
- The flu virus is an Icosahedron.

Technical Draughtsmanship
The Icosahedron
Orthographic Projection 11 — Part I — Geom. H

54

Front View   **Left Side View**

① Inscribe two pentagons in a circle of your choice.

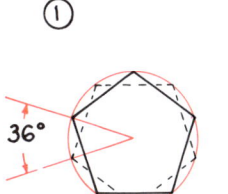

② Join two adjacent apices and extend the line.
Draw a line from the centre through a third adjacent apex to meet the first line at **P**.
Draw a circle through **P**.

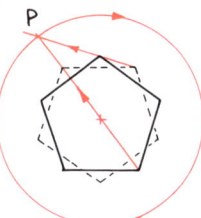

③ Extend lines from the centre through the apices to the outside circle.
Join these outside points.
This is a plan of a dodecahedron.

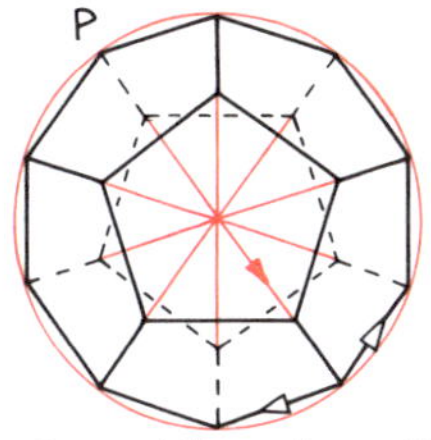

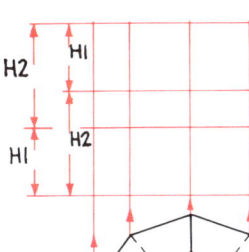

④ Finding the heights for the elevations presents two true-length problems.
Take the lengths from the base pentagon and by matching these to their apparent lengths on the sloping sides, the heights can be calculated. This is shown in the above diagram.

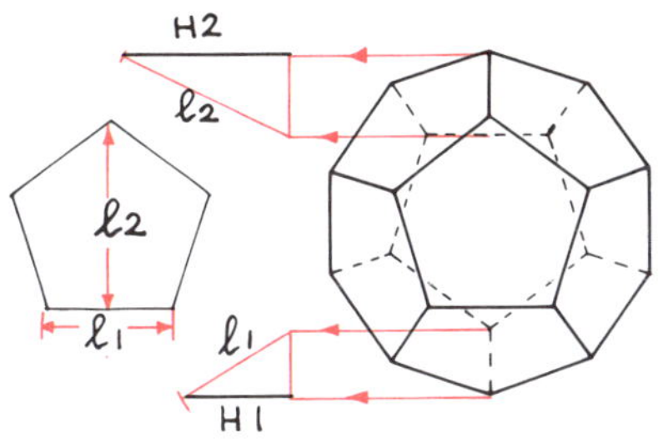

⑤ Set the heights up as shown and bring up the width lines from the plan.
Notice how the heights alternate.

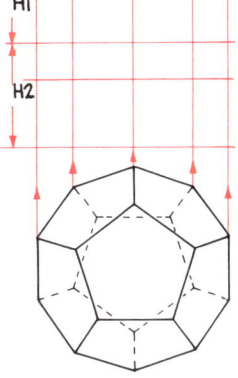

⑥ With help from the plan, locate each point and draw in the lines joining them.

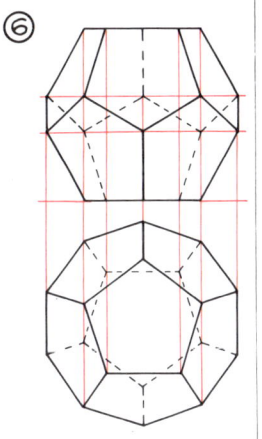

Procedure, step by step

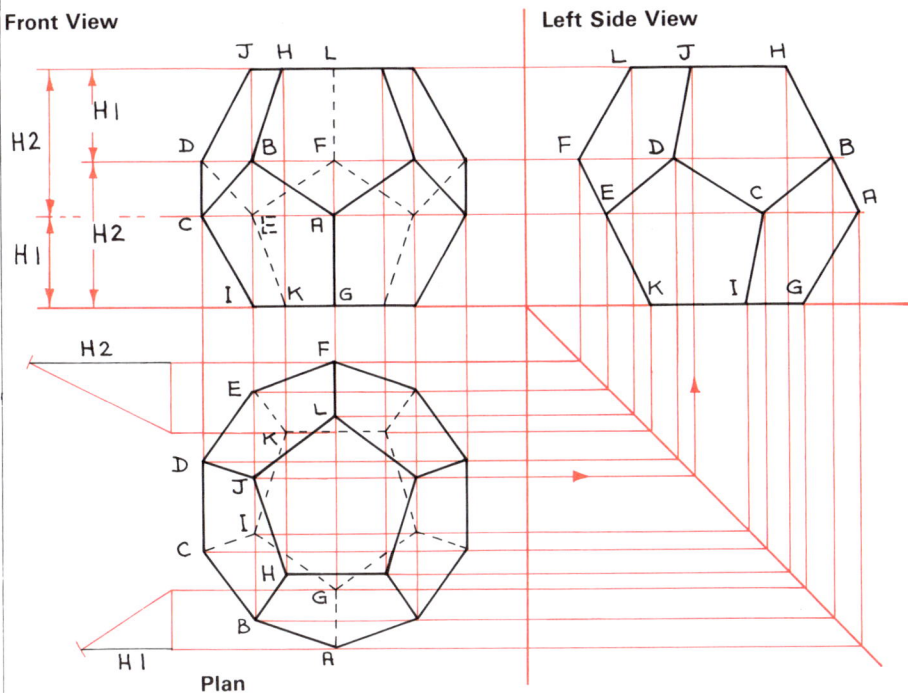

- Index the points on the plan and front elevation. Bring these together by projection to locate the left side view.

The finished views

Note:
- *The Dodecahedron has* **30** *edges,* **12** *faces and* **20** *vertices.*

Technical Draughtsmanship
The Dodecahedron
Orthographic Projection 12 — Part I — Geom. H

55

① To inscribe and circumscribe an icosahedron.

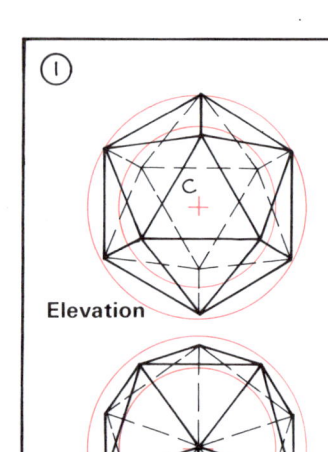

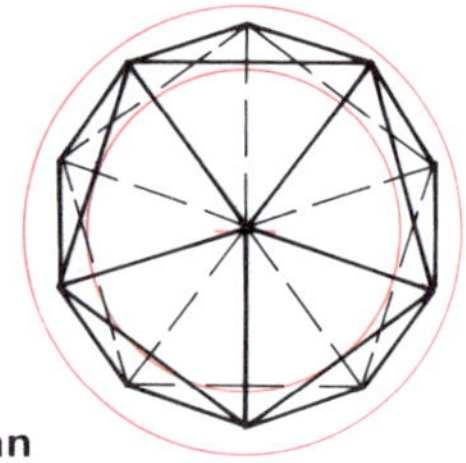

Elevation
End view 
Plan

- Both radii are best found on the end view.
- **AB** is the longest diagonal and is equal to the diameter of the circumscribing circle.
- The centre **C** is most easily found on elevation, as shown.
- Again on end view, draw the inscribed circle tangent to **AC** and to **BD**.

② To inscribe and circumscribe a dodecahedron.

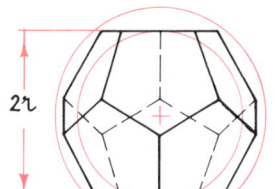

Elevation
End view 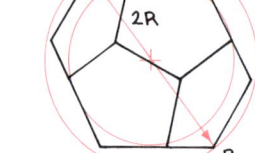
Plan 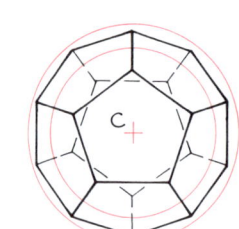

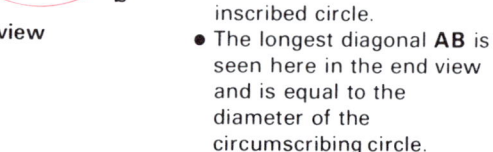

- The height of the dodecahedron is equal to the diameter of the inscribed circle.
- The longest diagonal **AB** is seen here in the end view and is equal to the diameter of the circumscribing circle.
- The centre **C** for both circles is most easily found on the plan, as shown.

③ To inscribe a series of polyhedra within each other

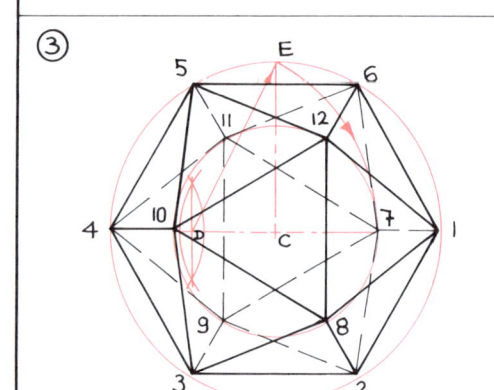

- Draw an icosahedron.
- A dodecahedron within the icosahedron. 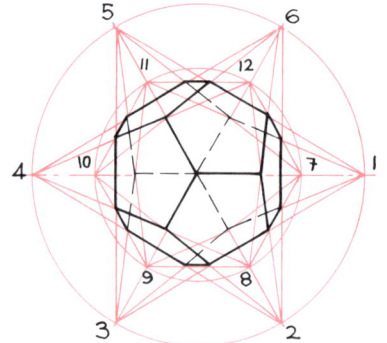
- A cube within the dodecahedron. 
- A tetrahedron within the cube. 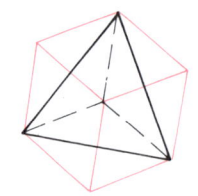
- An octagon within the tetrahedron. 
- Within the octagon, an icosahedron once again. 

Notes:
- *Each of the platonic solids relates to each other very clearly and this relationship is often phi (ø ≙ 0.618).*
- *The refraction graphs that are the nearest we can now get to seeing the atomic nature of a substance show what appear to be geometric patterns of light-energy.*

| Technical Draughtsmanship |
| Inscribing Polyhedra |
| Orthographic Projection 13 | Part I Geom. H |

56

The Problem

- This is the elevation of a cube of side **40mm**. Draw its plan and elevation, showing with it an inscribed and a circumscribed sphere.

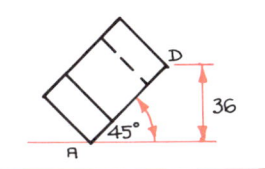

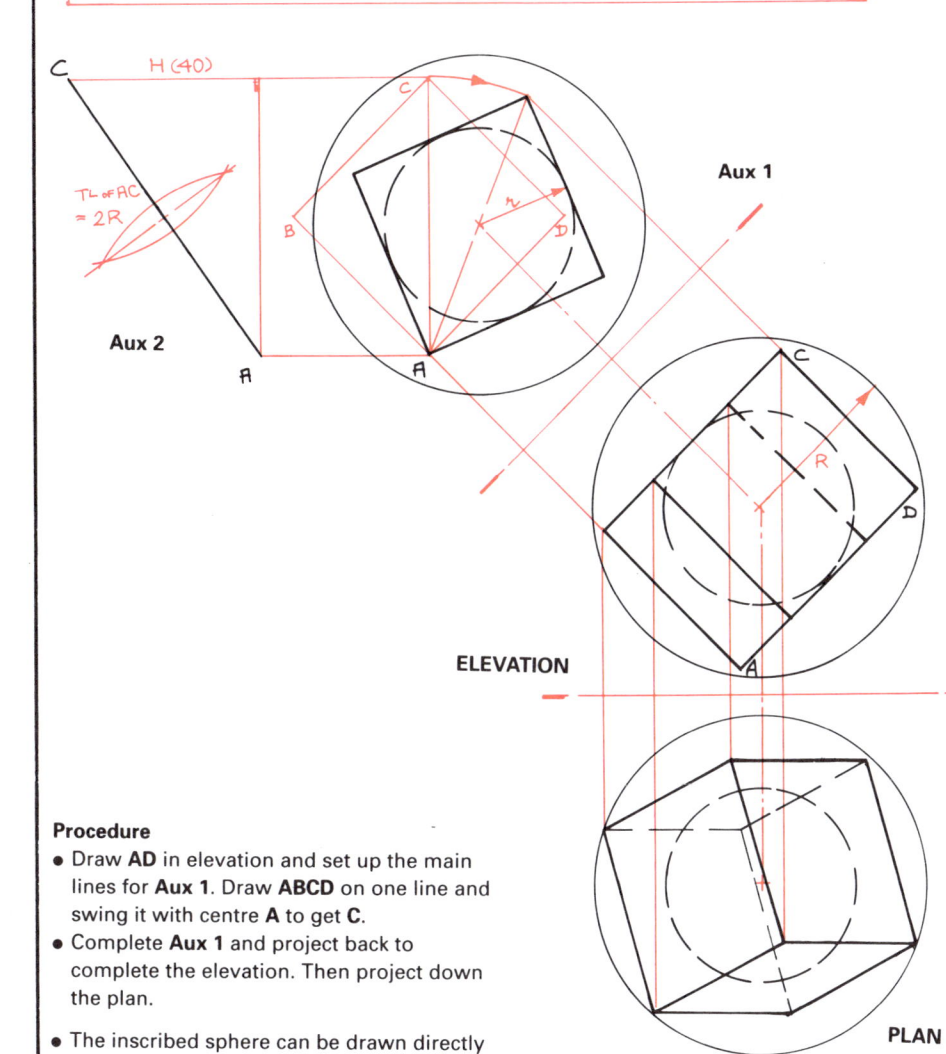

Procedure

- Draw **AD** in elevation and set up the main lines for **Aux 1**. Draw **ABCD** on one line and swing it with centre **A** to get **C**.
- Complete **Aux 1** and project back to complete the elevation. Then project down the plan.
- The inscribed sphere can be drawn directly onto **Aux 1** and projected back.
- For the circumscribed sphere, the radius will be half of the true length of a diagonal. To get this, set up **Aux 2** in order to get the true length of **AC**.

The Problem

- This is the plan of a tetrahedron of side **60mm**. Draw this in plan and in elevation. **BC** is parallel to the **VP**.

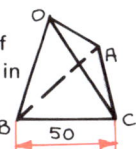

Heights:
A: 0mm
B: 12mm

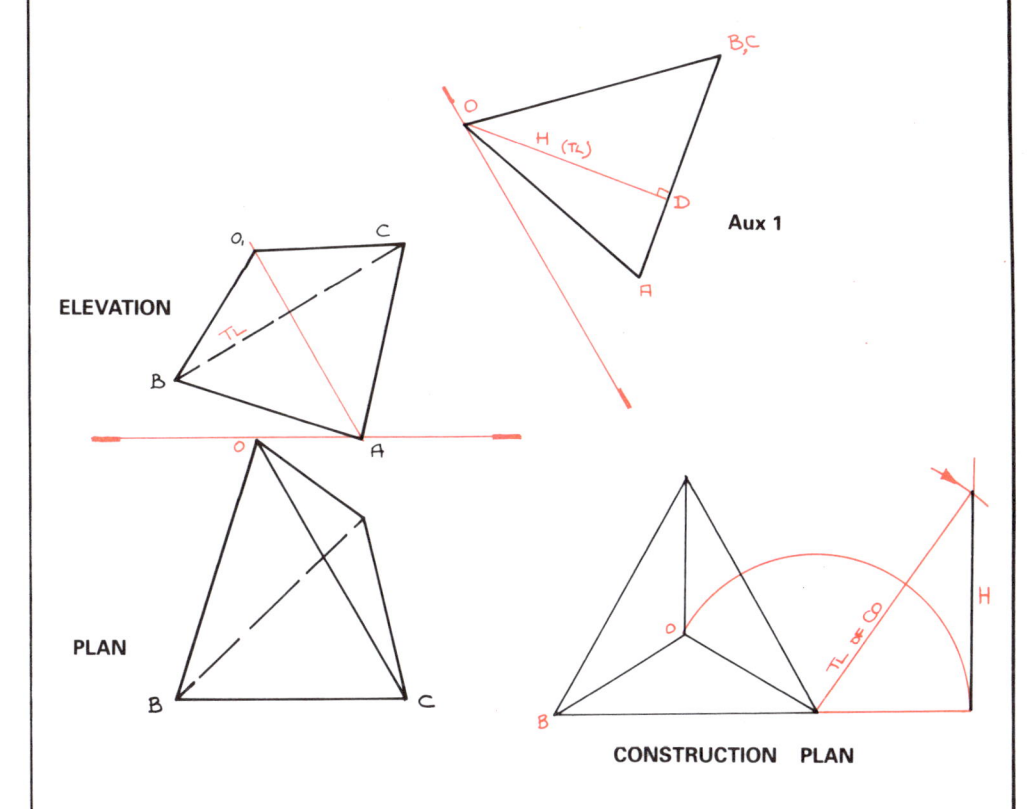

Procedure

- As **BC** is parallel to the **VP**, it will be a true length on elevation. Draw this and bisect to find **A**.
- Project a point view of **BC** onto **Aux 1**. This will be an edge view of the base. Why?
- Set the perpendicular height **H**, to locate **O** and then work it all back to the plan.

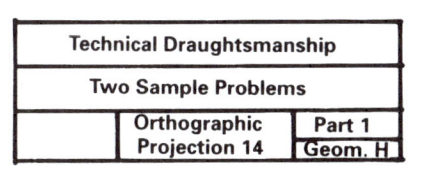

Technical Draughtsmanship		
Two Sample Problems		
Orthographic Projection 14	Part 1	Geom. H

57

Questions

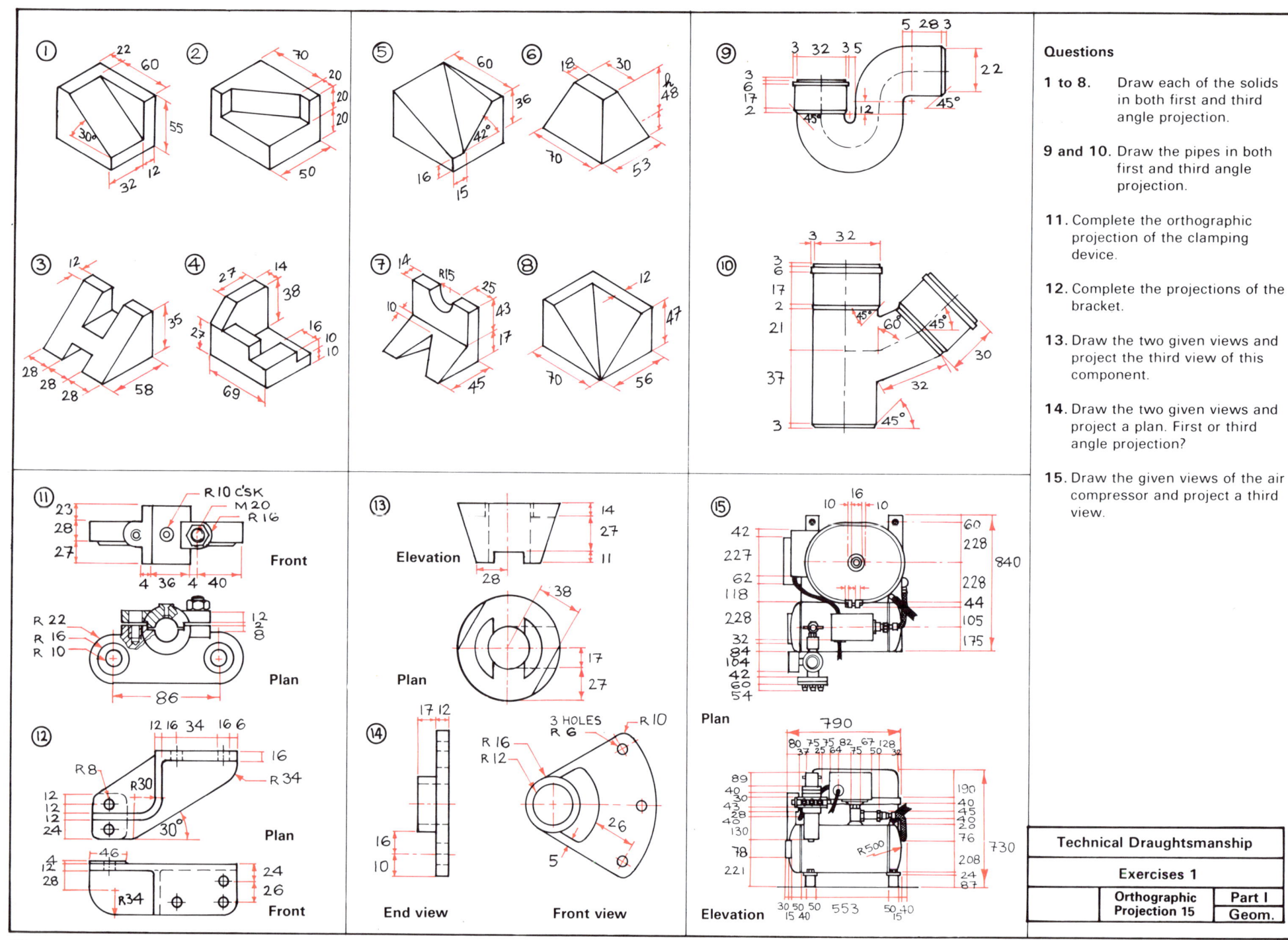

1 to 8. Draw each of the solids in both first and third angle projection.

9 and 10. Draw the pipes in both first and third angle projection.

11. Complete the orthographic projection of the clamping device.

12. Complete the projections of the bracket.

13. Draw the two given views and project the third view of this component.

14. Draw the two given views and project a plan. First or third angle projection?

15. Draw the given views of the air compressor and project a third view.

Technical Draughtsmanship	
Exercises 1	
Orthographic Projection 15	Part I
	Geom.

Questions

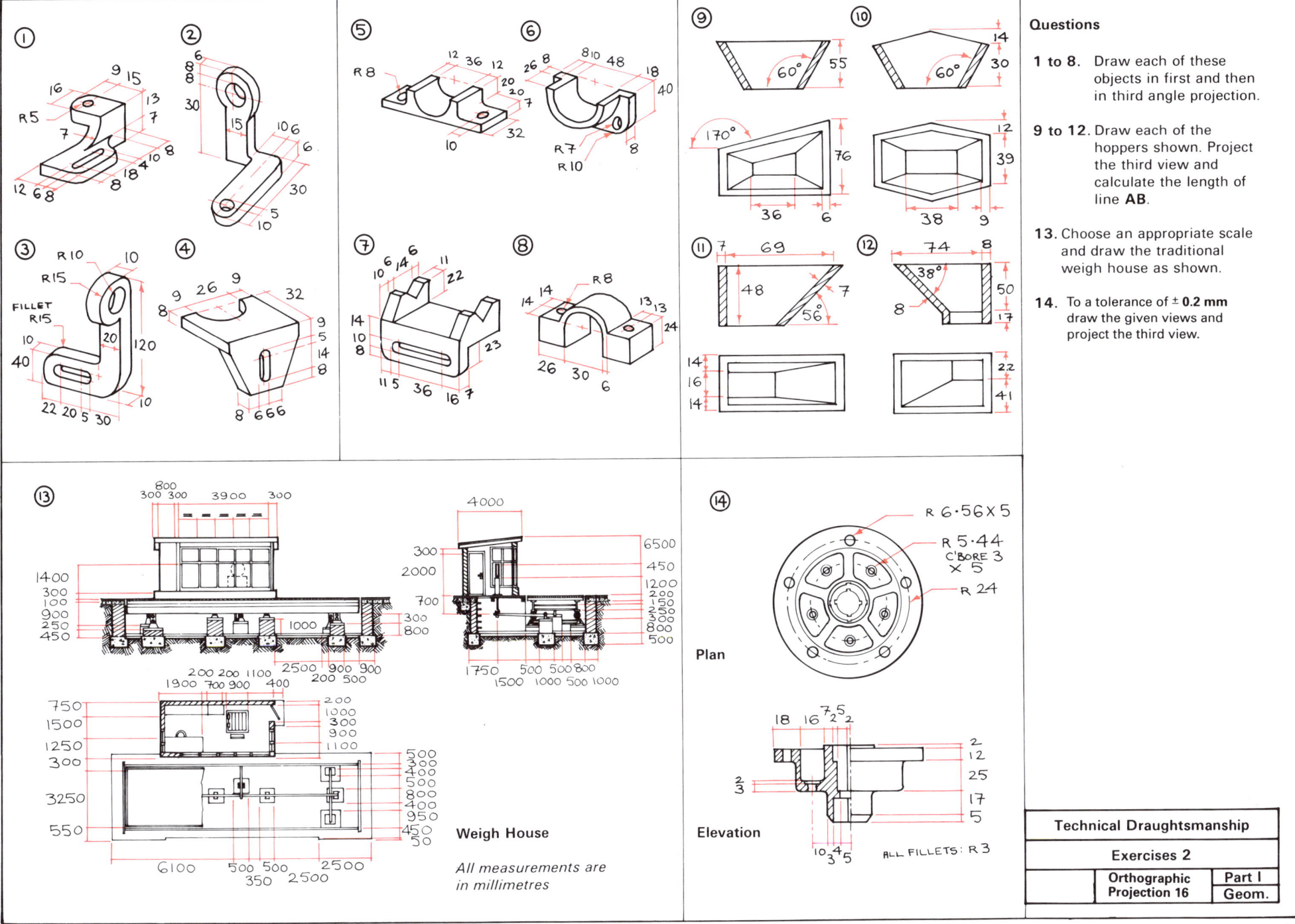

1 to 8. Draw each of these objects in first and then in third angle projection.

9 to 12. Draw each of the hoppers shown. Project the third view and calculate the length of line **AB**.

13. Choose an appropriate scale and draw the traditional weigh house as shown.

14. To a tolerance of ± **0.2 mm** draw the given views and project the third view.

Weigh House

All measurements are in millimetres

Plan

Elevation

Technical Draughtsmanship		
Exercises 2	
Orthographic Projection 16	Part I Geom.	

59

Questions

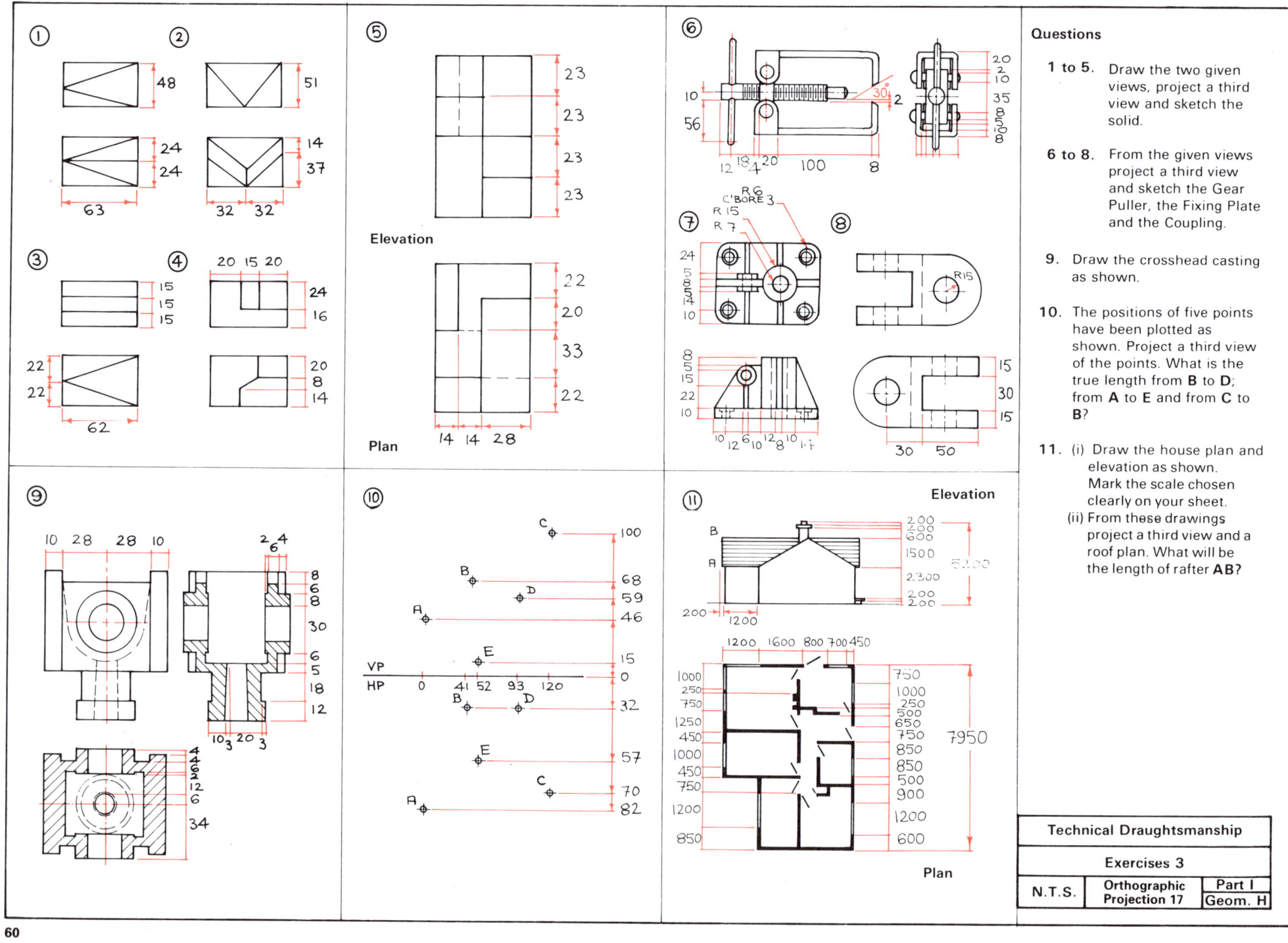

1 to 5. Draw the two given views, project a third view and sketch the solid.

6 to 8. From the given views project a third view and sketch the Gear Puller, the Fixing Plate and the Coupling.

9. Draw the crosshead casting as shown.

10. The positions of five points have been plotted as shown. Project a third view of the points. What is the true length from **B** to **D**; from **A** to **E** and from **C** to **B**?

11. (i) Draw the house plan and elevation as shown. Mark the scale chosen clearly on your sheet.
(ii) From these drawings project a third view and a roof plan. What will be the length of rafter **AB**?

Technical Draughtsmanship

Exercises 3

N.T.S. | Orthographic Projection 17 | Part I Geom. H

PART 1

CHAPTER 6
AUXILIARY PROJECTION

There are times when the three standard views of an object have surfaces that are still unclear or difficult to dimension. An extra view will often solve these problems.
An auxiliary view is an extra orthographic view. This can be projected from a standard view and allows us to see the object from *any* angle. Once an auxiliary view is constructed it may then be used as a basis for a second auxiliary view.

CONTENTS

	Page
Procedure, step by step	62
The Angle Projection Method	63
Projecting Curves	64
A Third Angle Projection	65
A Second Auxiliary View	66
A Second View: third angle	67
Multiple Auxiliary Views	68
Multiple Views: third angle	69
Exercises	70

Photocopying prohibited by law

① To project an auxiliary elevation

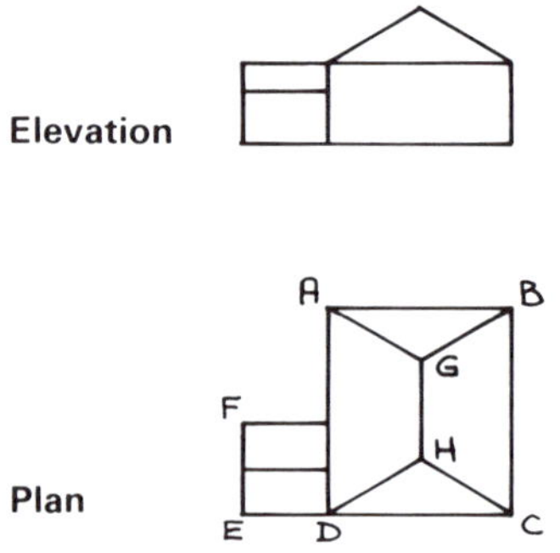

Step 1:
- Draw the plan and elevation of the object.
- Index the main points.

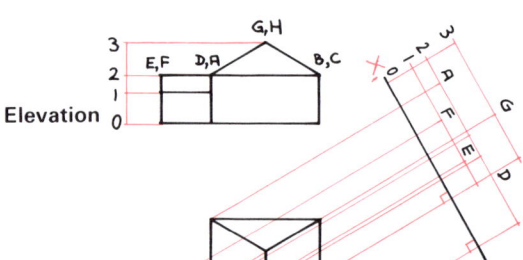

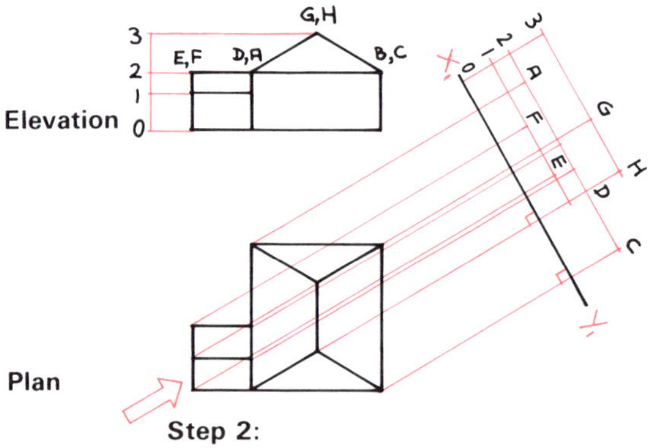

Step 2:
- To the side of the elevation set up a scale of heights.
- Draw the auxiliary plane X_1Y_1.
- From the plan project the points across the auxiliary plane at right angles.

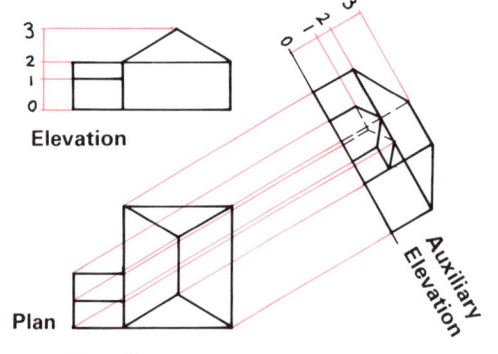

Step 3:
- Measure the heights of each point using the elevation heights.
- Join the points, finishing a clearly visible surface first.
- Complete the **auxiliary elevation**.

② To project an auxiliary plan

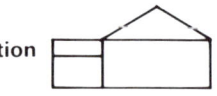

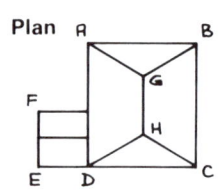

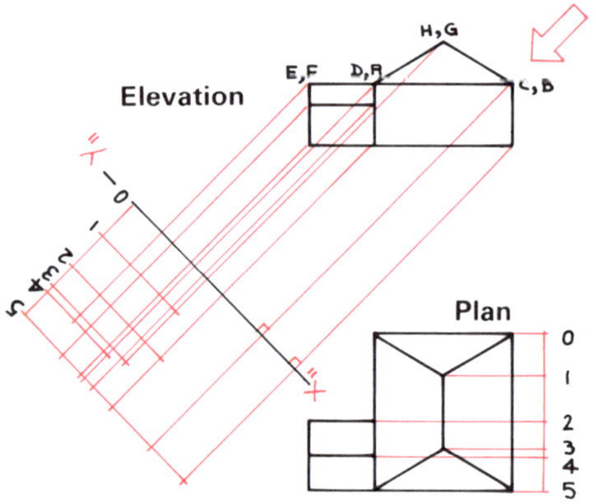

Step 1:
- Draw the given plan and elevation.
- Index the main points.

Step 2:
- On the plan, measure the points, moving *away* from the elevation.
- Draw the auxiliary plane $X_1 Y_1$.
- From the elevation project the points across the auxiliary plane at right angles.

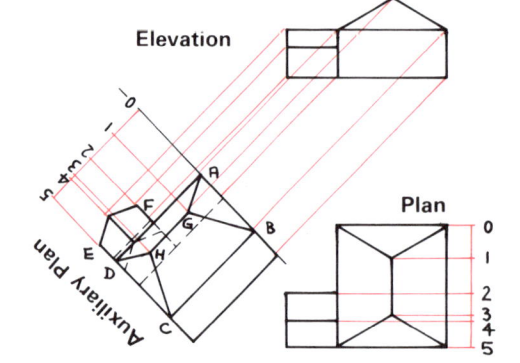

Step 3:
- Using the measurements from the plan locate the position of each point.
- Join up the points and draw a visible surface first.
- Complete the **auxiliary plan**.

③ The principle

At times the three views have surfaces that are still unclear or hard to dimension. An extra view is needed.

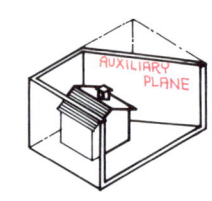

Imagine an object in a box as before. Now put in a new side panel, an **auxiliary plane**.

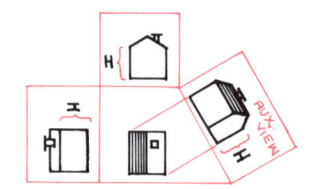

Open out the box. An **auxiliary view** can be seen on the auxiliary plane.

Note:
- *An auxiliary view can be projected from any view.*
- *An elevation can only be projected from a plan and a plan can only be projected from an elevation.*
- *The dimensions for a plan come from a plan.*
- *The dimensions or heights for an elevation come from an elevation.*

Technical Draughtsmanship
Procedure, step by step
Auxiliary Projection 1 — Part I Geom.

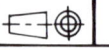

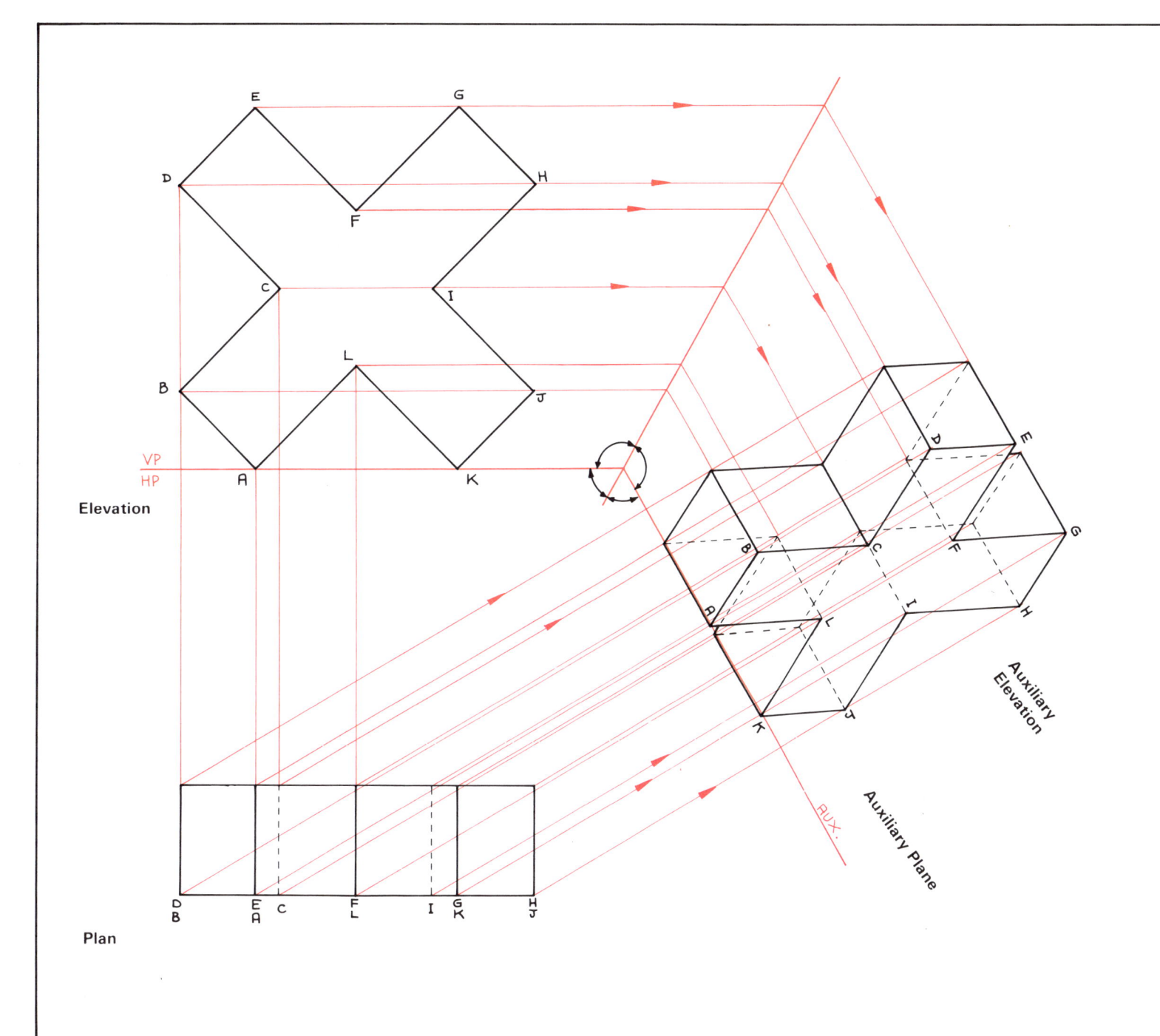

Projecting measurements onto an auxiliary view

One very useful way of transferring measurements to auxiliary views is shown here.

- Calculate the angle between the new auxiliary plane and the original plane lines:

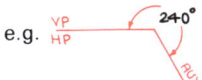

  e.g. 240°

- Bisect this angle:

  e.g. 120° / 120°

- This bisector can then be used to transfer measurements as shown.

- Both auxiliary elevations and auxiliary plans can be drawn using this system, which is called the **angle projection method**.

Note: *this method is very useful for single auxiliary projections but is **not** a good idea when a second projection is required.*

Technical Draughtsmanship
The angle projection method

| | Auxiliary Projection 2 | Part I Geom. |

63

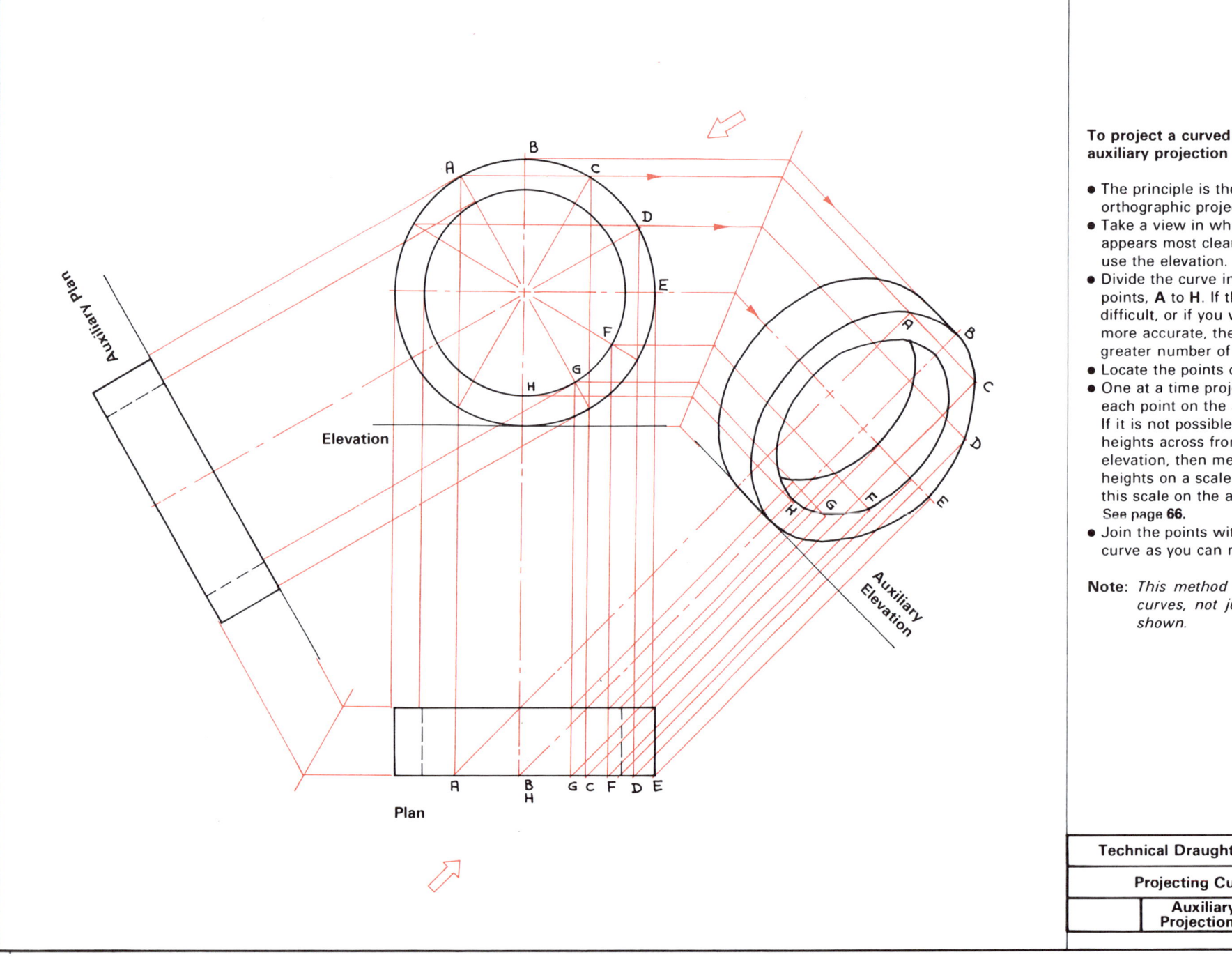

To project a curved surface with auxiliary projection

- The principle is the same as for orthographic projection.
- Take a view in which the curve appears most clearly, in this case use the elevation.
- Divide the curve into a number of points, **A** to **H**. If the curve is difficult, or if you want to be more accurate, then take a greater number of points.
- Locate the points on the plan.
- One at a time project and locate each point on the auxiliary view. If it is not possible to project the heights across from the elevation, then measure these heights on a scale and redraw this scale on the auxiliary view. See page 66.
- Join the points with as smooth a curve as you can manage.

Note: *This method applies to all curves, not just the circle shown.*

Technical Draughtsmanship	
Projecting Curves	
Auxiliary Projection 3	Part I Geom.

Plan

Auxiliary Plan

Elevation

End View

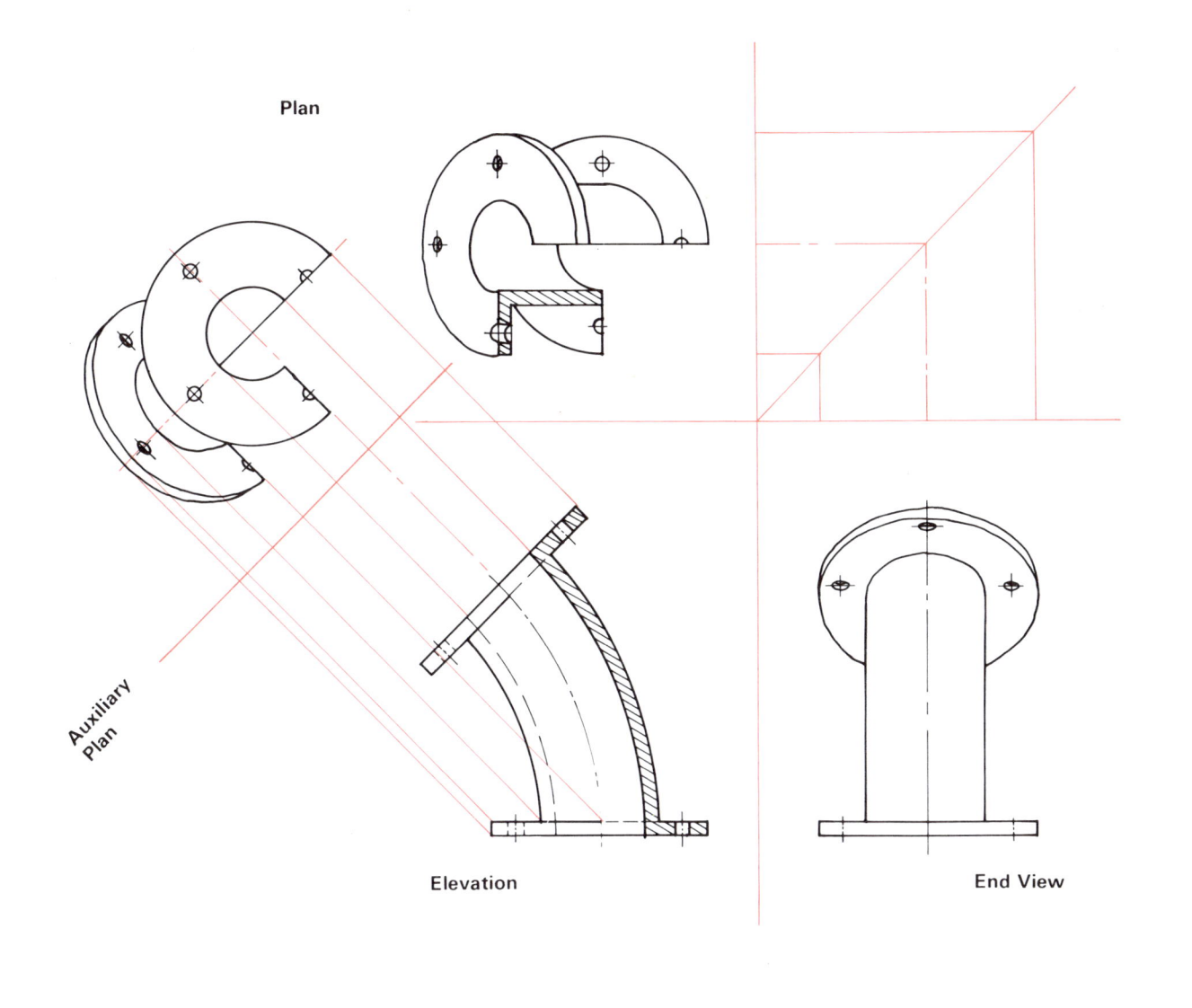

An auxiliary projection in third angle, with half section

- Third angle auxiliary projection is similar to first angle.

- The main difficulties have to do with your own bias. If you have been trained in European projection methods the third angle can be confusing.

- It is good to practise the projections you are least familiar with in order to eliminate weak points in your training.

- The construction itself is clear from the drawing.

Technical Draughtsmanship		
A Third Angle projection		
Auxiliary Projection 4	Part I	Geom.

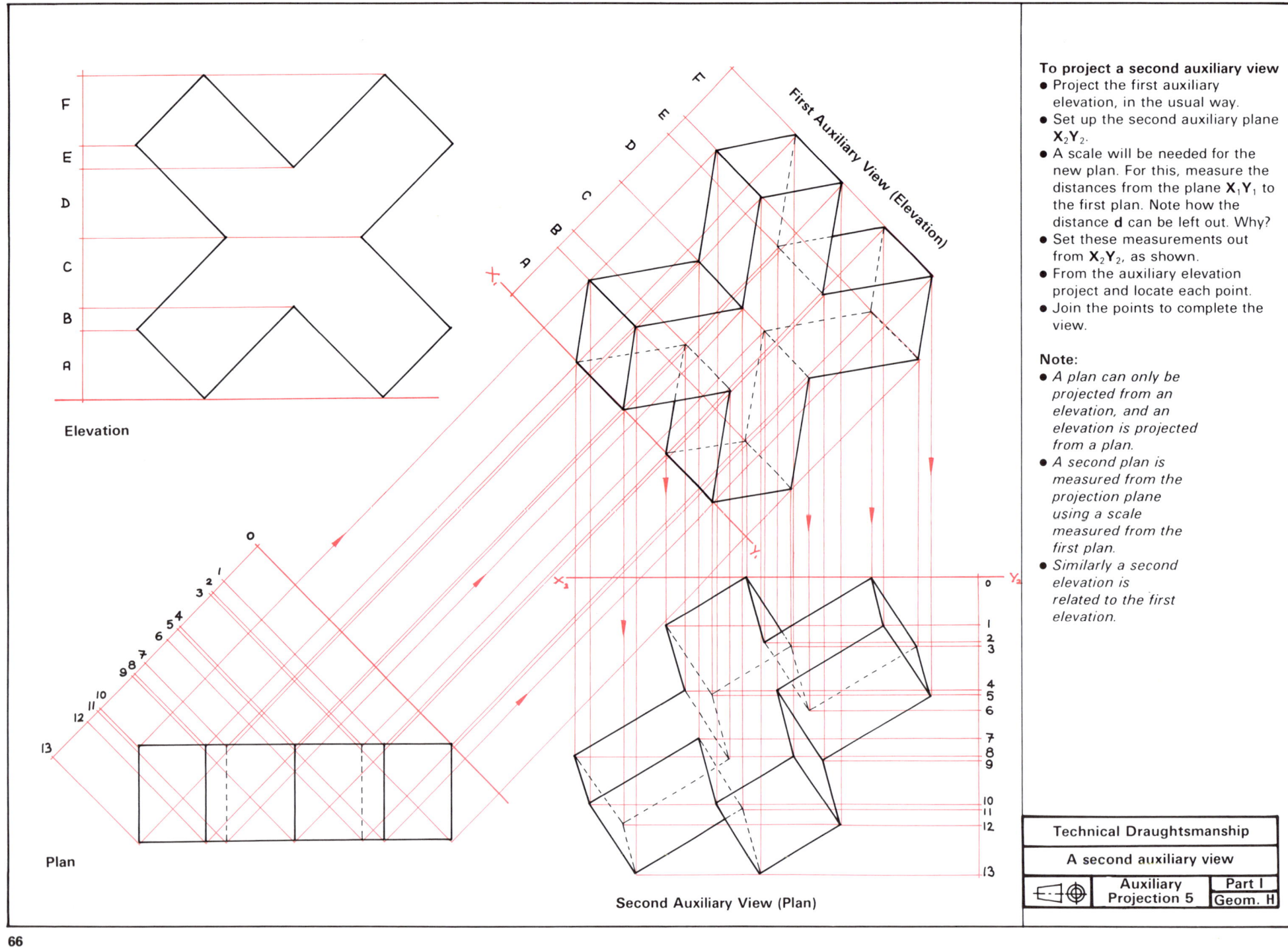

To project a second auxiliary view
- Project the first auxiliary elevation, in the usual way.
- Set up the second auxiliary plane X_2Y_2.
- A scale will be needed for the new plan. For this, measure the distances from the plane X_1Y_1 to the first plan. Note how the distance **d** can be left out. Why?
- Set these measurements out from X_2Y_2, as shown.
- From the auxiliary elevation project and locate each point.
- Join the points to complete the view.

Note:
- *A plan can only be projected from an elevation, and an elevation is projected from a plan.*
- *A second plan is measured from the projection plane using a scale measured from the first plan.*
- *Similarly a second elevation is related to the first elevation.*

Elevation

First Auxiliary View (Elevation)

Plan

Second Auxiliary View (Plan)

Technical Draughtsmanship
A second auxiliary view
Auxiliary Projection 5 | Part I Geom. H

First Auxiliary View (Elevation)

Plan

Second Auxiliary View (Plan)

Elevation

End View

- This is in **Third Angle** projection.
- The principles are as before, and the construction will be clear from the drawings.

Technical Draughtsmanship

A second view: third angle

Auxiliary Projection 6 | Part I
Geom. H

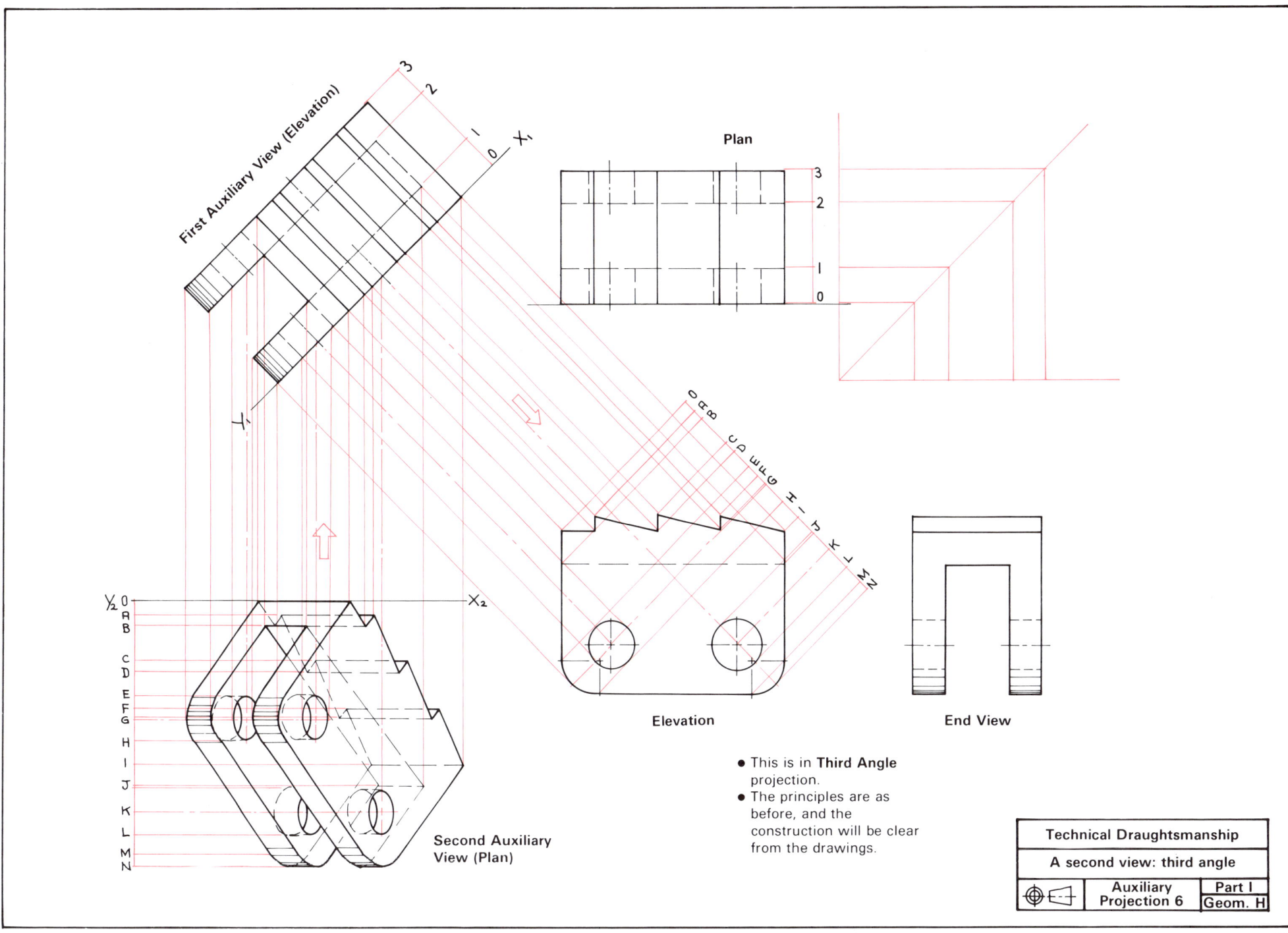

67

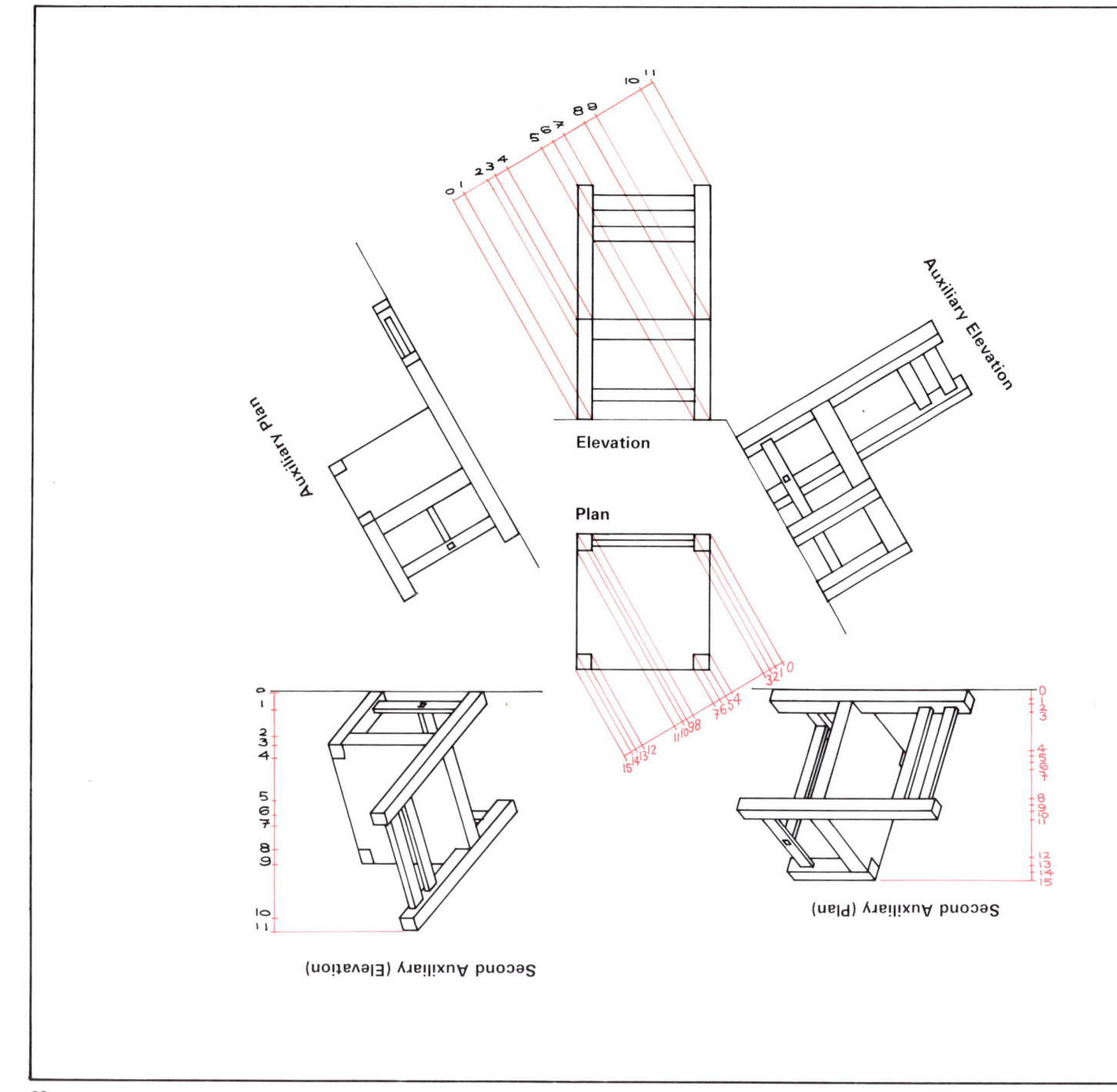

Multiple auxiliary views

- There is no end to the number of auxiliary views that you can project.

- These can be taken from any viewing angle and from either plan or elevation.

- Once an auxiliary view is constructed it can be used as a basis for second auxiliary projections, which can in turn form the basis of third auxiliary projections and so on, ad infinitum.

- The construction will be clear from the drawing.

Technical Draughtsmanship

Multiple auxiliary views

| Auxiliary Projection 7 | Part I Geom. H |

- The constructions will be clear from the drawings.

Second Auxiliary View (Elevation)

Plan

Auxiliary Plan

Auxiliary Elevation

Auxiliary Elevation

Elevation

Technical Draughtsmanship
Multiple views: third angle
Auxiliary Projection 8 — Part I Geom. H

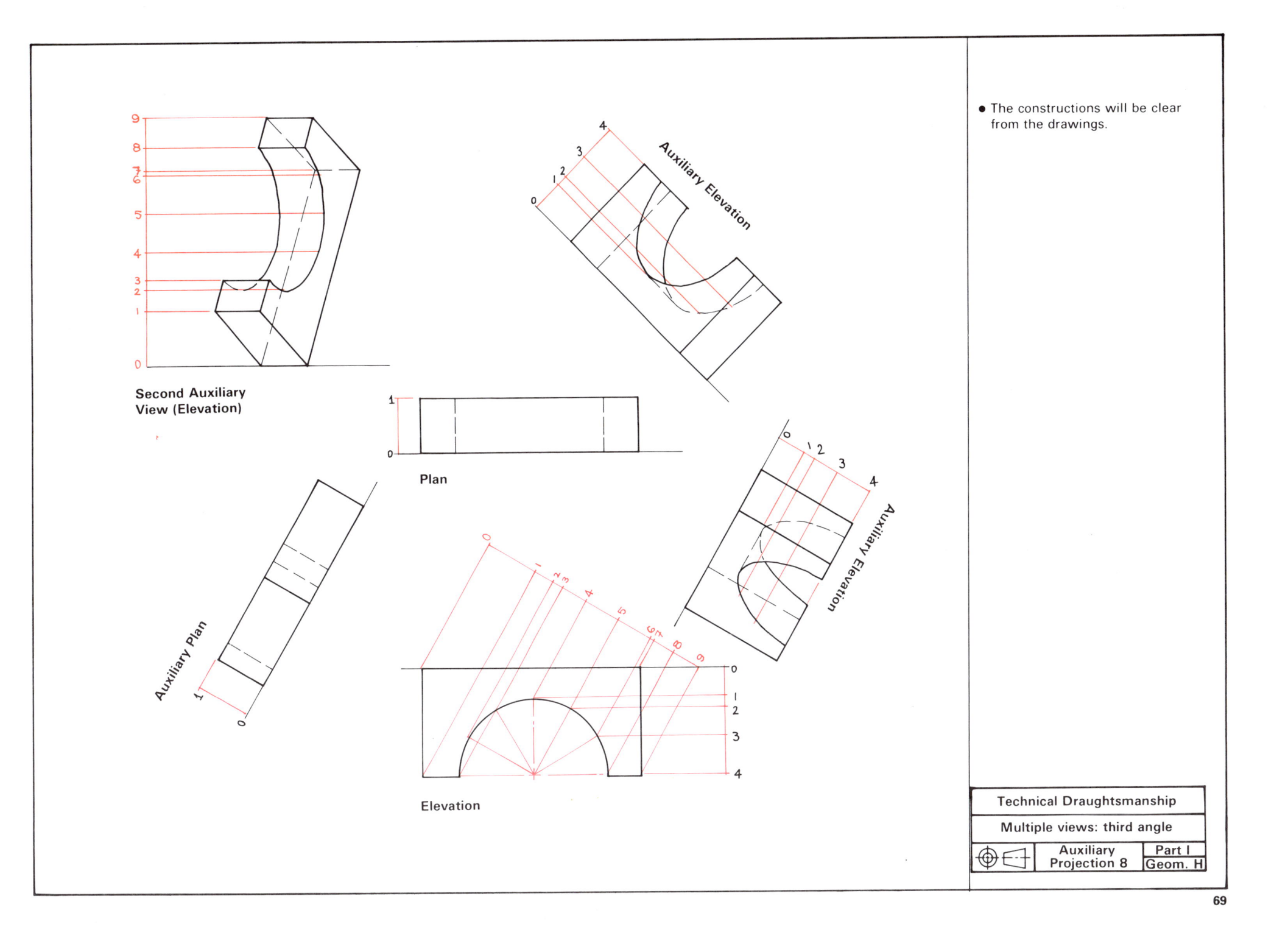

Questions

1 to 11.

In each case project auxiliary elevations across auxiliary plane lines X_1Y_1 and X_2Y_2, then project auxiliary plans across the auxiliary plane lines **AB** or **CD**.

Warning: *Position the given views carefully on the page and check that you have left enough room to fit all of the required auxiliary views.*

Technical Draughtsmanship		
Exercises 1		
NTS	Auxiliary Projection 9	Part I Geom.

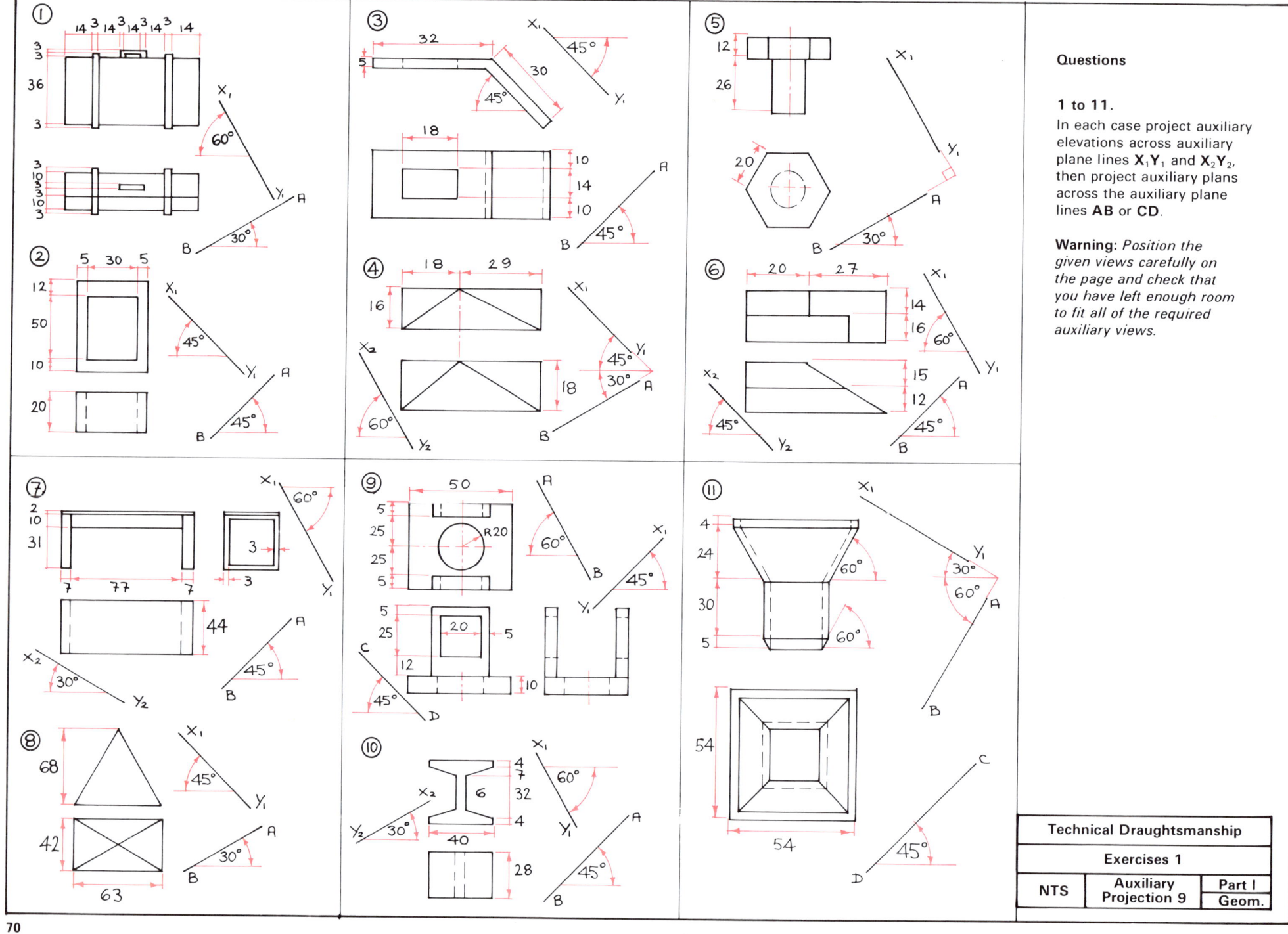

Questions

1 to 6.
Project an auxiliary elevation onto the auxiliary planes X_1Y_1 and X_2Y_2, then project an auxiliary plan across the lines **AB** and **CD**.

Note: Position the given views with great care.

Technical Draughtsmanship		
Exercises 2		
NTS	Auxiliary Projection 10	Part I Geom.

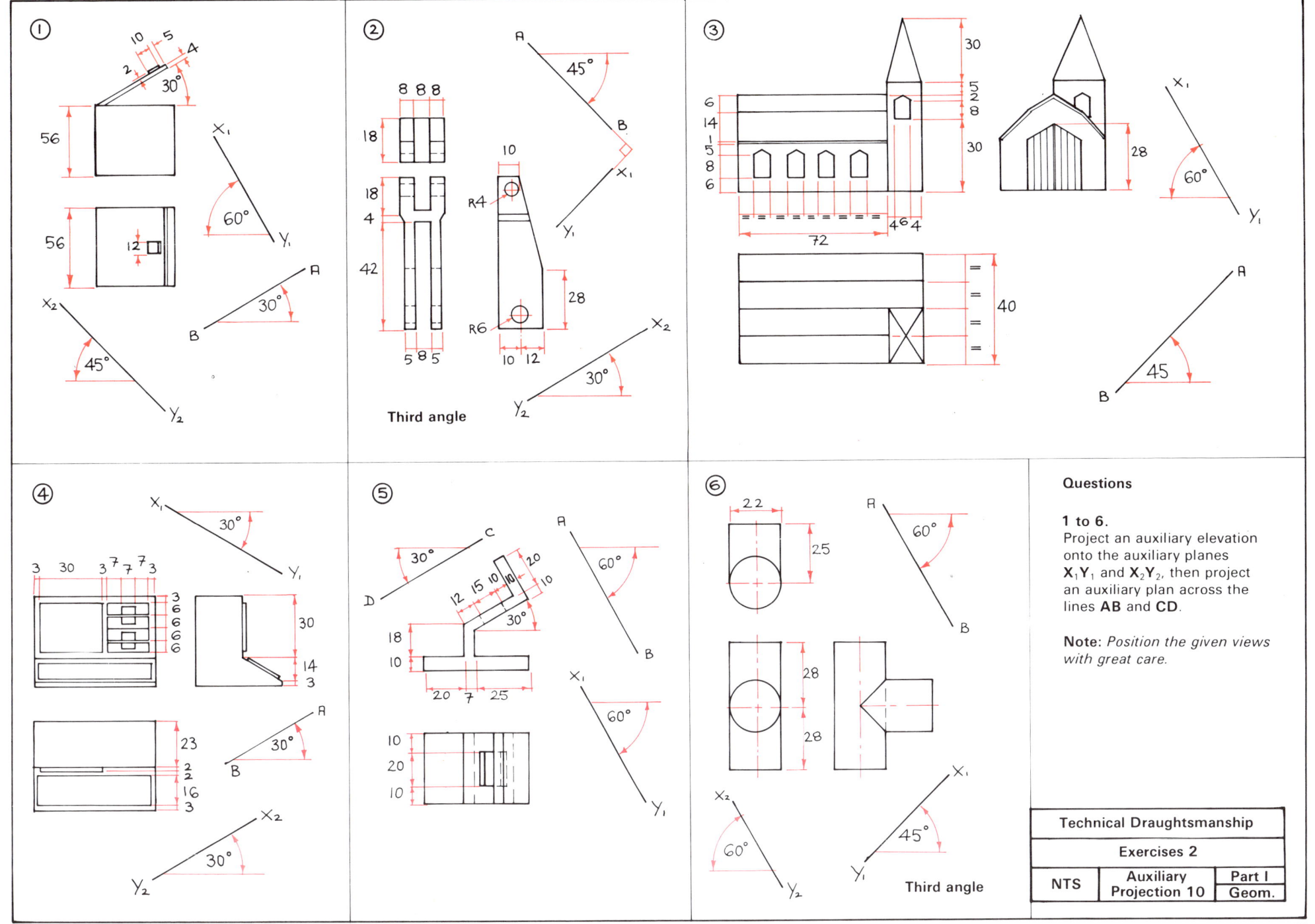

71

Questions

1 to 5. Project an auxiliary elevation of the given figure onto the auxiliary plane X_1Y_1 and then project a second auxiliary view onto X_2Y_2.

6. Project an auxiliary elevation onto X_1Y_1 and then a second auxiliary view onto X_2Y_2. Also draw a first auxiliary plan onto **AB**.

①

②

③ Cam

④ Vee block

⑤ Crank

⑥ Lattice girder

Technical Draughtsmanship		
Exercises 3		
NTS	Auxiliary Projection 11	Part I Geom. H

72

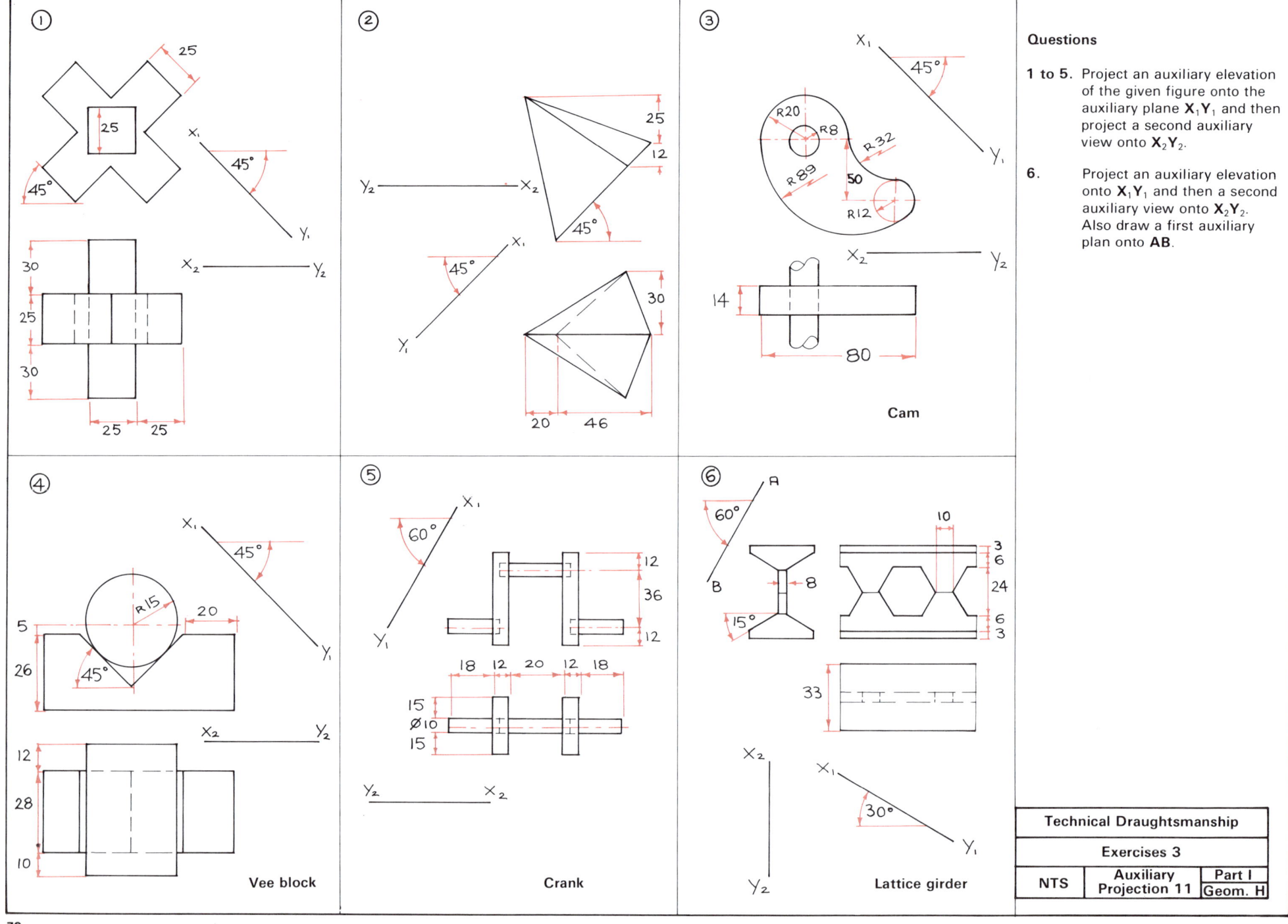

PART I

CHAPTER 7
PICTORIAL PROJECTION

It is easy to misread a complex technical drawing, and such mistakes in design, manufacture, or operation can be costly. A technical illustration will clarify most drawings. There are many ways of projecting an accurate pictorial view and each has its merits and drawbacks. Computer aided manipulation of such an image makes this a most interesting area to work in, see chapter **16**. See also chapter **28** for perspective projection.

CONTENTS

Oblique projection	*Page* **74**
Oblique curves	**75**
Isometric projection	**76**
Crating	**77**
Isometric curves	**78**
Constructing an Isometric Protractor	**79**
The Sphere in Isometric	**80**
Assembly in Isometric	**81**
Planometric and Cutaway	**82**
Isometric: two examples	**83**
Axonometric Axes	**84**
Orthographic to Trimetric 1	**85**
Orthographic to Trimetric 2	**86**
Trimetric to Orthographic	**87**
Exercises	**88**

3RD. ANGLE

Elevation

End view

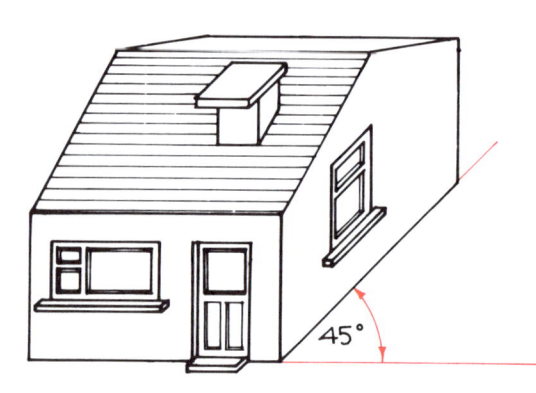

Cavalier projection
All the measurements are transferred directly from the orthographic views. Lines vertical or horizontal on the elevation are unchanged but those on the end view are set out at **45°**. The drawing can still be scaled but there is a visual distortion on the side view as it seems much longer than it really is.

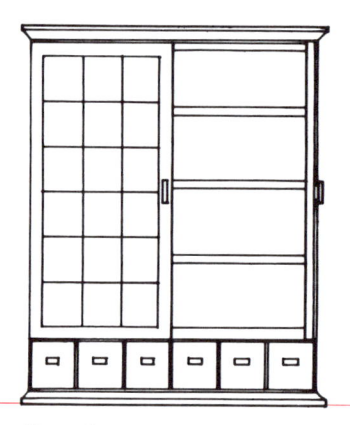

Note: *the oblique axis may be at any angle,* **45°** *being the most popular. Try* **15°**, **30°** *and* **60°** *yourself.*

1ST. ANGLE

Elevation

End view

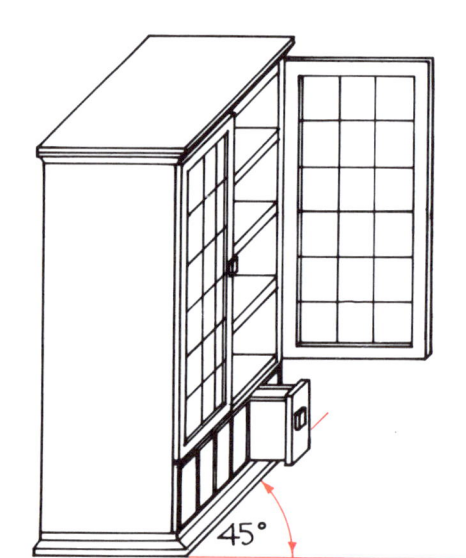

Cabinet projection
To avoid the visual elongation of the side of the object the measurements along the **45°** axis can be reduced. Here they have been halved, but some people prefer to make these measurements *two thirds* of their actual size. Either way, the drawing is much improved in appearance but cannot easily be scaled.

Technical Draughtsmanship		
Oblique Projection		
	Pictorial Projection 1	Part I Geom.

74

①

Elevation

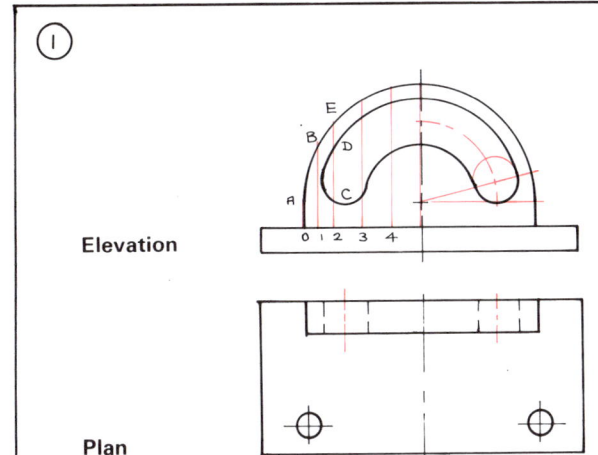

Plan

- Any curve can be transferred to an oblique drawing by drawing a grid onto the orthographic view and marking points on that grid.
- The grid is easily constructed on the oblique projection and once the points are plotted the curve can then be reconstructed.
- Receding circles will appear to be ellipses.
- The tighter the grid the more points can be plotted, and the greater the accuracy of the finished drawing.

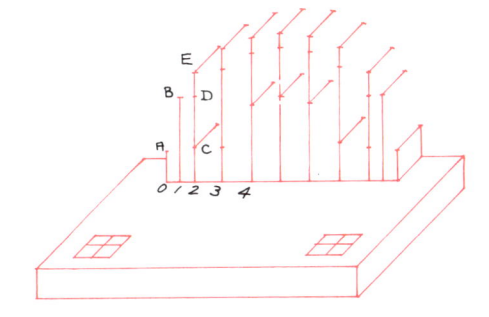

Stage 1: Construction lines.

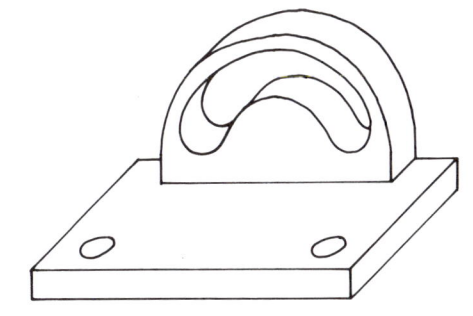

Stage 2: The finished oblique drawing, in cavalier projection.

②

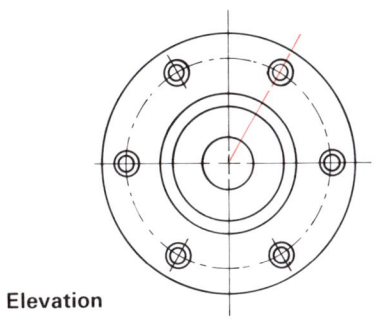

Elevation

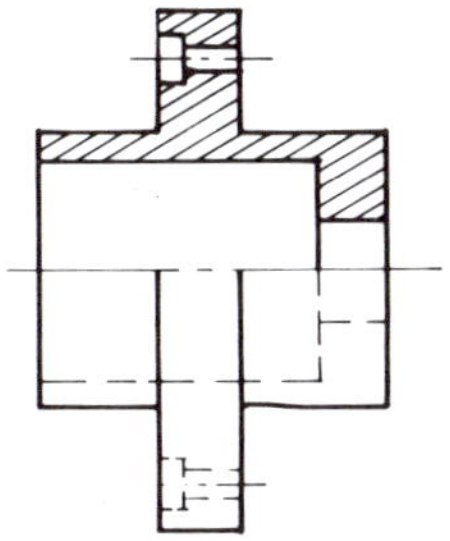

End view and half-section

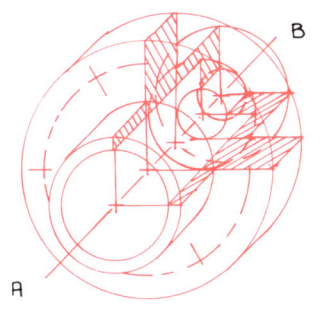

- One of the main advantages of oblique projection is that circles, curves or complicated faces can retain their true shape, making the drawing process simpler.
- Choose an elevation that shows the difficult feature, in this case a series of circles.
- Set up the oblique axis **AB**, and along this, at the appropriate intervals, draw the circles — *undistorted*.
- Complete the figure.
- Half sectioning is also quite straight-forward, as shown.

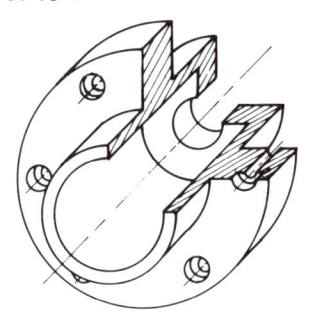

Stage 1: Complete construction outlined with section hatched in. **AB** is at **45°**.

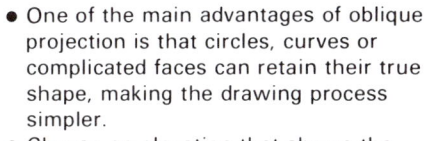

Stage 2: The finished oblique sectioned drawing, in cavalier projection.

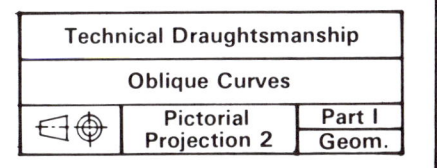

Technical Draughtsmanship		
Oblique Curves		
	Pictorial Projection 2	Part I Geom.

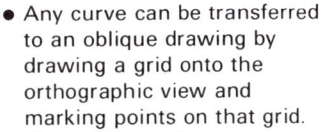

75

3RD. ANGLE

Elevation

End view

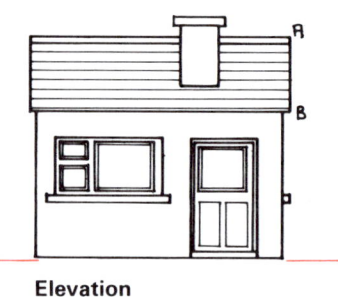

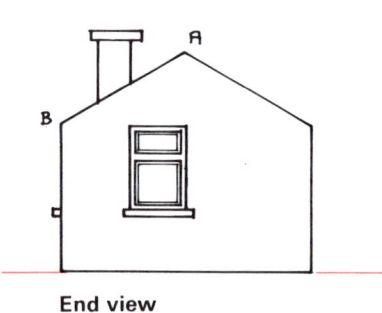

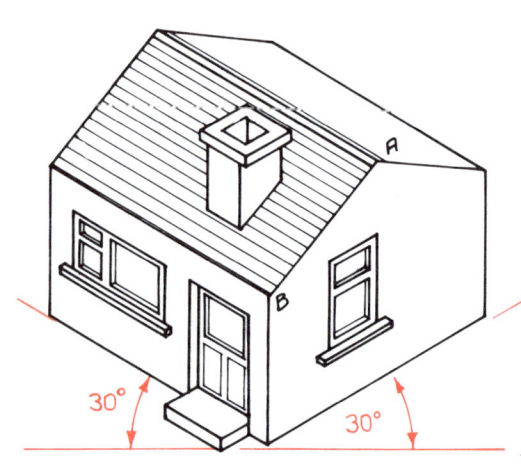

Isometric drawing
- The feeling of seeing a third dimension is greatly enhanced by using *two* oblique axes, set at **30°** each.
- All the measurements are taken from the elevation and end view.
- One exception is the sloping line **AB**. This can *not* be measured directly. Points **A** and **B** are located separately and then joined.
- The horizontal and vertical lines can be scaled, but the overall impression is often too chunky.

The finished isometric drawing

Note: *Both angles and sloping lines are distorted in isometric drawings and cannot be measured directly.*

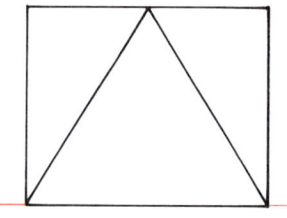

1ST. ANGLE

Elevation

End view

Isometric projection
- To avoid the chunky look often seen in isometric drawing one of the oblique axes can be measured to a reduced scale.
- This scale is found by setting out a true scale at **45°** and dropping these measurements vertically onto a line set at **30°**, as shown.
- Using this isometric scale along one receding axis does improve the visual quality of the drawing.

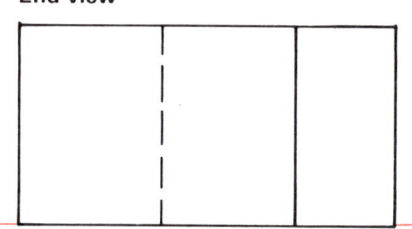

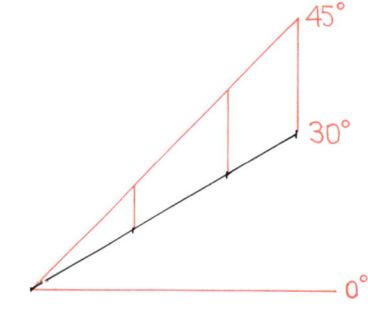

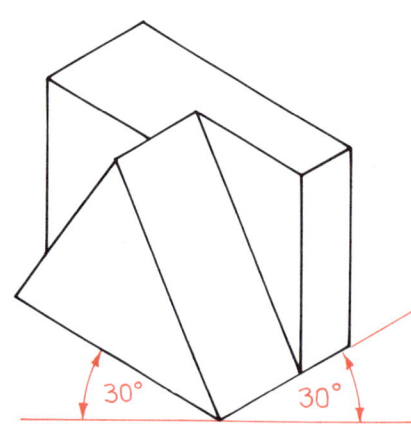

The finished isometric projection

Technical Draughtsmanship
Isometric Projection
Pictorial Projection 3 — Part I Geom.

① Section A — A

Plan

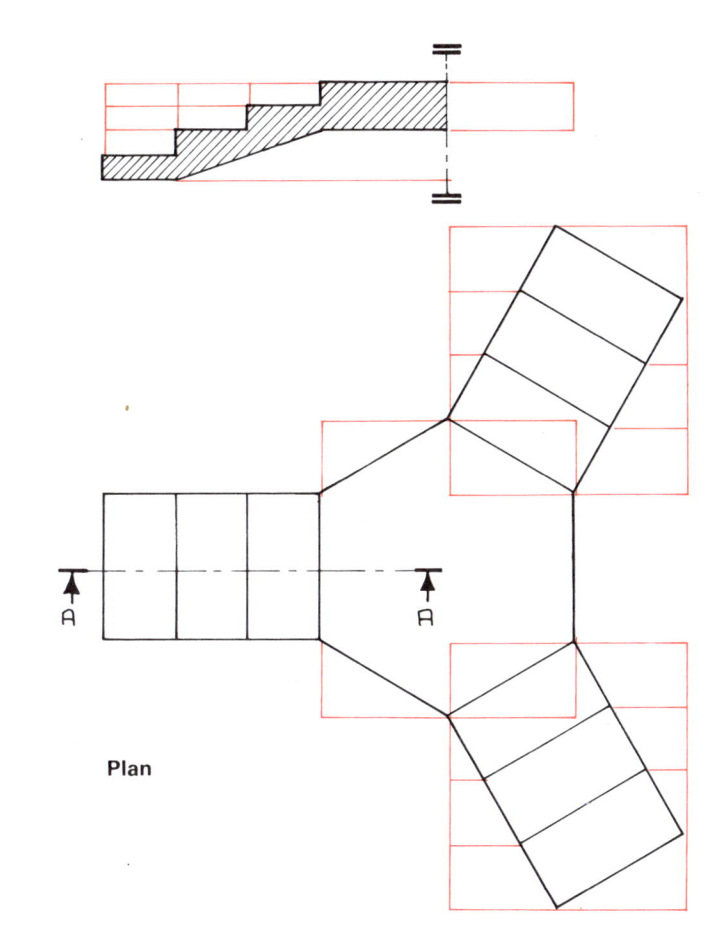

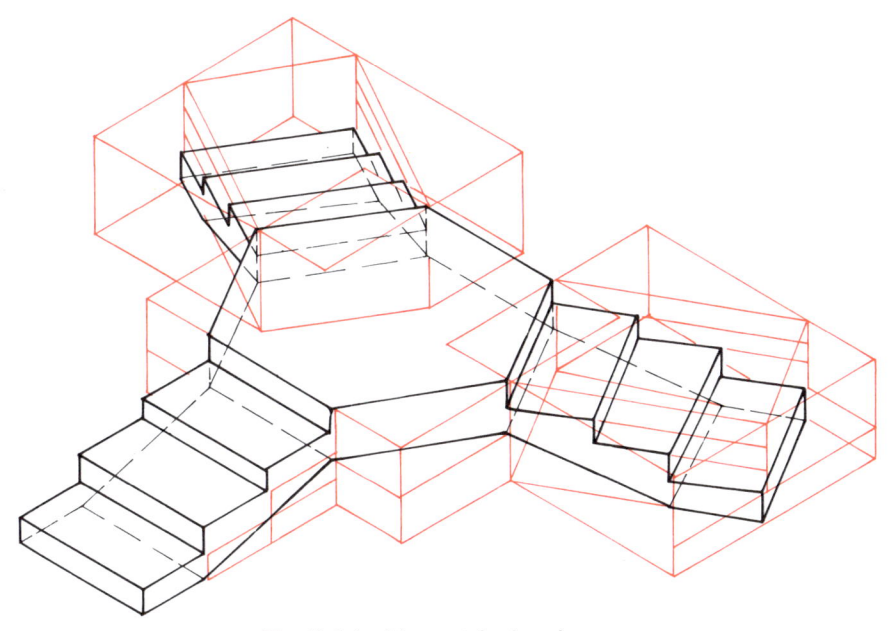

② **The finished isometric drawing**

One of the easiest, and most versatile methods of isometric drawing involves crating. On the standard views, put each part into a box or crate. Then build up the isometric drawing by stacking these crates, as in the above example.

Technical Draughtsmanship		
Crating		
	Pictorial Projection 4	Part I
		Geom.

77

①

Elevation

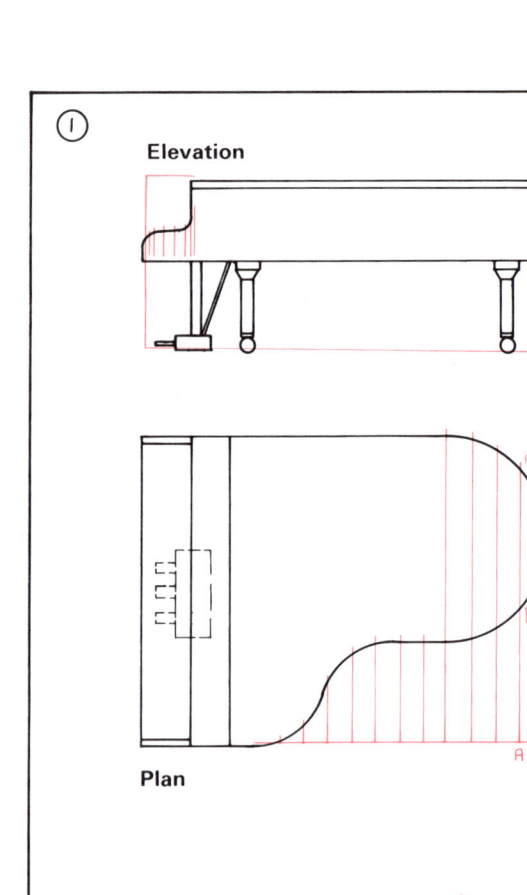

Plan

- Drawing curves in isometric is very similar to drawing them in other projections.
- Draw a grid on the relevant orthographic view and mark the points of the curve on that grid, for example points **A**, **B** and **C**.
- Project the grid in the usual way and plot the points along it.
- Join the points to complete the drawing.
- When needed, intermediate lines can be added to the grid.

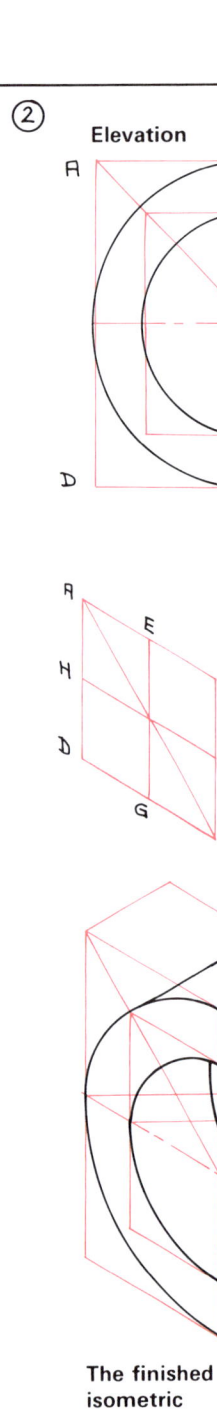

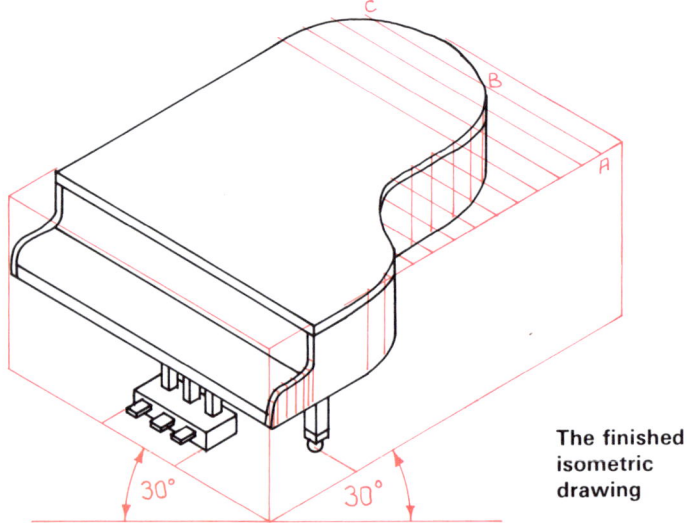

The finished isometric drawing

②

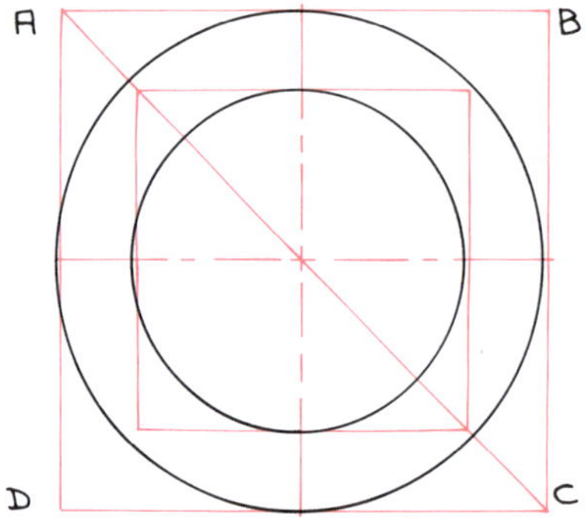

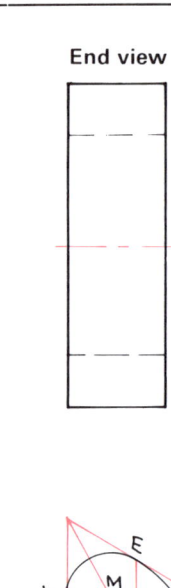

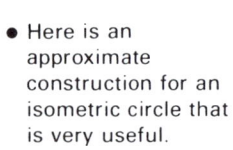

Elevation **End view**

- Here is an approximate construction for an isometric circle that is very useful.
- First box the circle and draw both its diagonal and its mix-axes as shown.

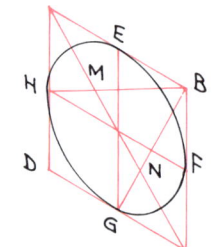

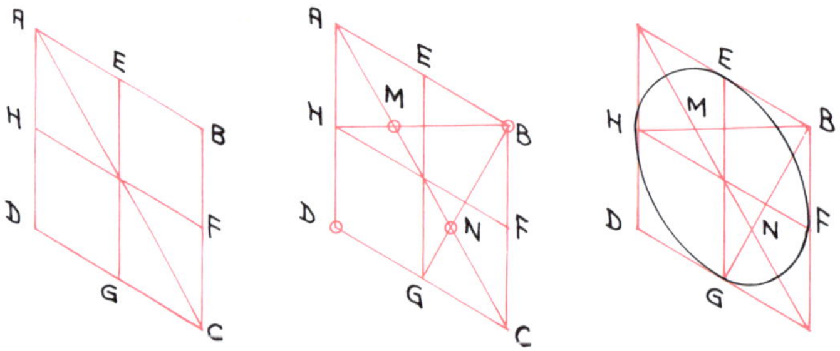

Step by Step

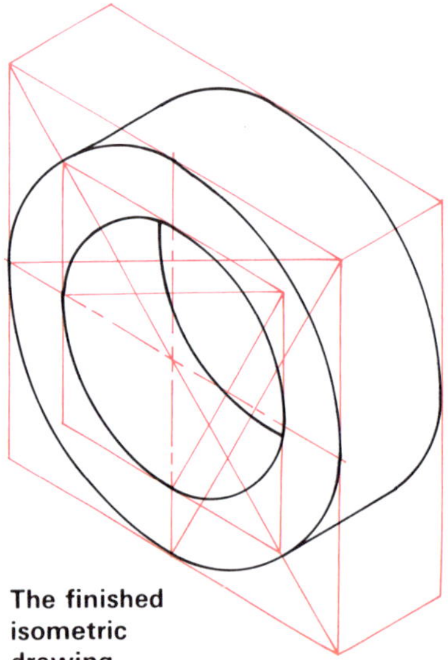

- Project the box and mark its diagonal and mid-axes.
- Join **B** to **H** and to **G**, crossing the diagonal at points **M** and **N**.
- With centre **B** swing an arc from **G** to **H**.
- With centre **D** swing a similar arc from **E** to **F**.
- With centre **M** join **H** to **E**.
- With centre **N** join **F** to **G**.
- Treat the inner circle similarly.

Note: *This construction is not quite exact, but is perfectly adequate for illustrations.*

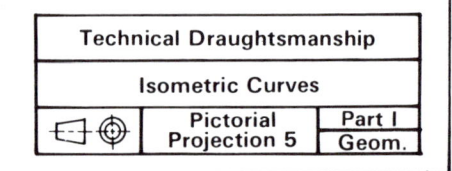

The finished isometric drawing

Technical Draughtsmanship
Isometric Curves
Pictorial Projection 5 — Part I / Geom.

① To construct an isometric protractor

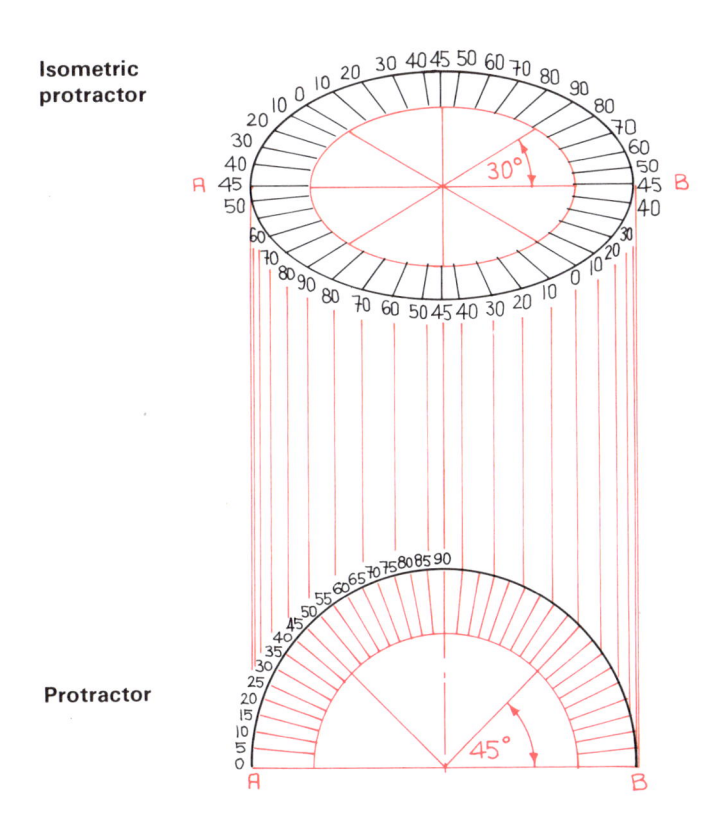

Isometric protractor

Protractor

- Sloping lines and angles are always a nuisance on isometric drawings. The construction, on tracing paper, of an isometric protractor may be of help.
- Trace or construct a drawing of a standard protractor, of base **AB**.
- Project **AB** up to form the major axis of an isometric ellipse.
- The minor axis of the ellipse will be **0.7** times **AB**. Draw the ellipse.
- Project angle points from the circle to the ellipse, here at **10°** intervals.
- Index the ellipse as shown, the isometric axes being **0°** and **90°** respectively.

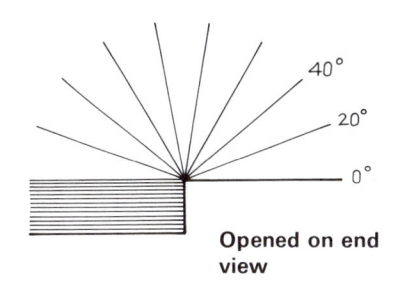

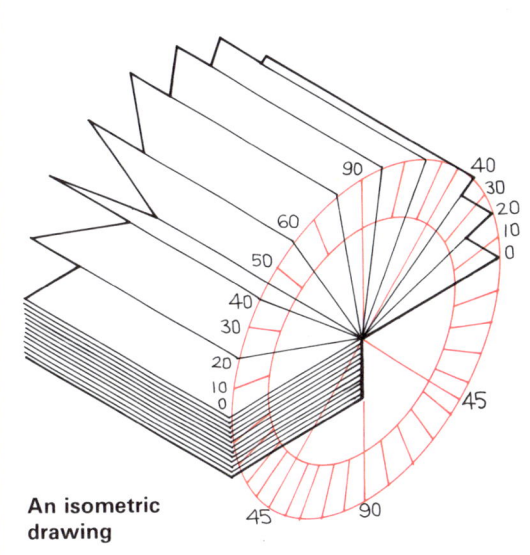

② Example 1

Opened on end view

An isometric drawing

- Here are two examples of an open book showing how the protractor may be used.

③ Example 2

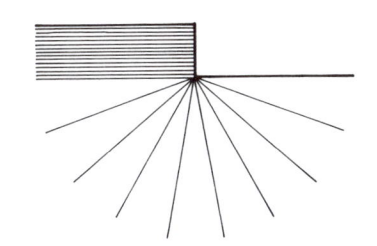

Opened on plan

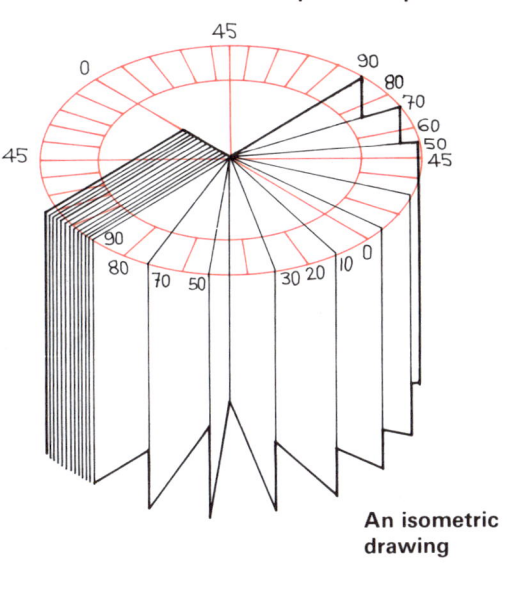

An isometric drawing

Technical Draughtsmanship
Constructing an Isometric Protractor

| Pictorial Projection 6 | Part I Geom. H |

79

①

Elevation

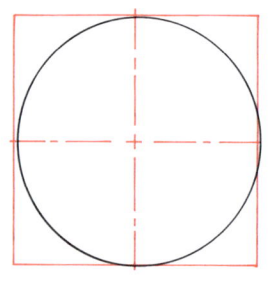

End view

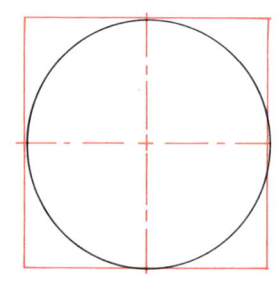

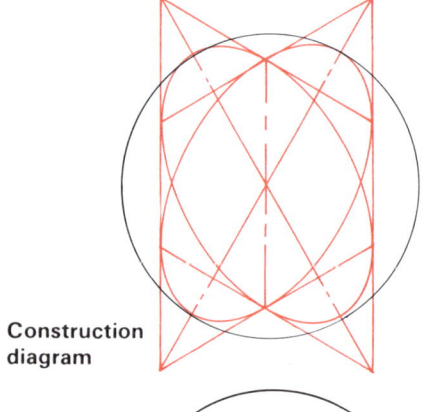

Construction diagram

The completed isometric sphere

- Crate or box both views of the sphere of radius **r**.
- Project these views as isometric ellipses, as shown in the diagram.
- One ellipse is sufficient but the two show clearly the half-sections that are possible.
- With **C** as centre inscribe both ellipses. This circle, of radius **R**, is the isometric drawing of the sphere.
- $R \simeq 1.25\,r$

Note: *Although some texts recommend that a sphere be of the same radius in isometric as in orthographic projection, this will not be in keeping with other elements in the isometric drawing. This can only lead to confusion if the sphere is subdivided, or part of an assembly.*

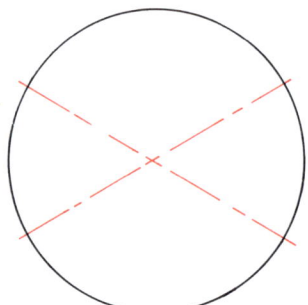

②

Elevation

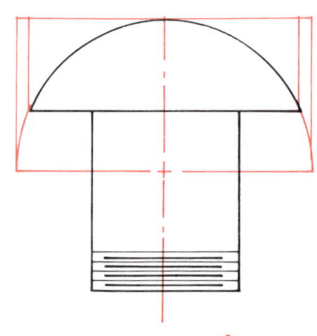

End view

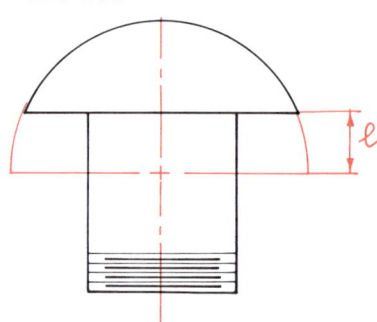

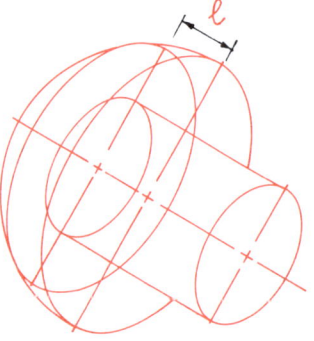

Construction diagram

The completed isometric drawing

- Here only part of a sphere is required.
- Extend this to a hemisphere for construction purposes.
- The rest of the construction will be clear from the diagram.
- The isometric ellipses are based on the information in the orthographic views and can be constructed using the crate, grid or by approximate compass methods.

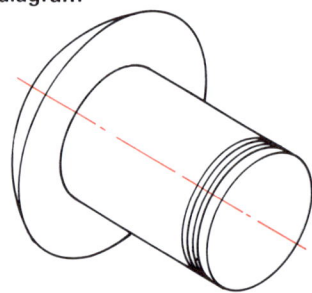

Technical Draughtsmanship		
The Sphere in Isometric		
	Pictorial Projection 7	Part I Geom. H

①

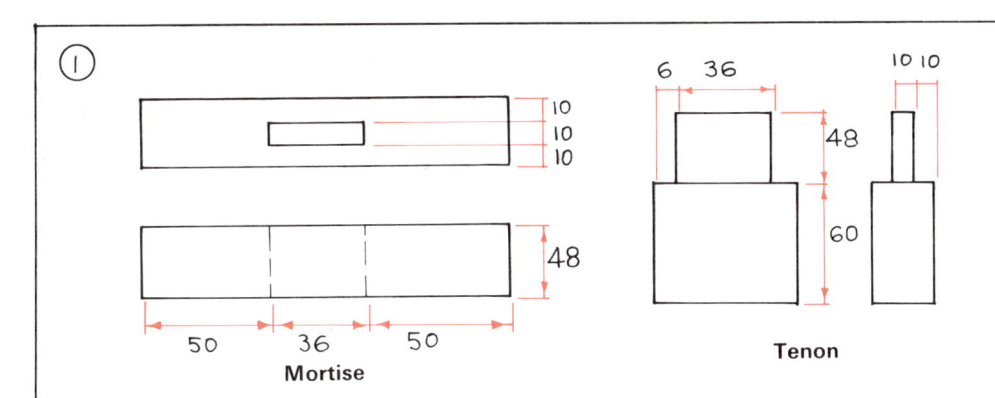

Mortise

Tenon

An exploded assembly drawing in isometric projection

- First draw up one component in isometric, e.g. the mortise. Position this carefully to leave room for the other components.
- Line up the second component fitted into its position, then 'slide' it back along the isometric axis until it is clearly visible.
- Complete the drawing.

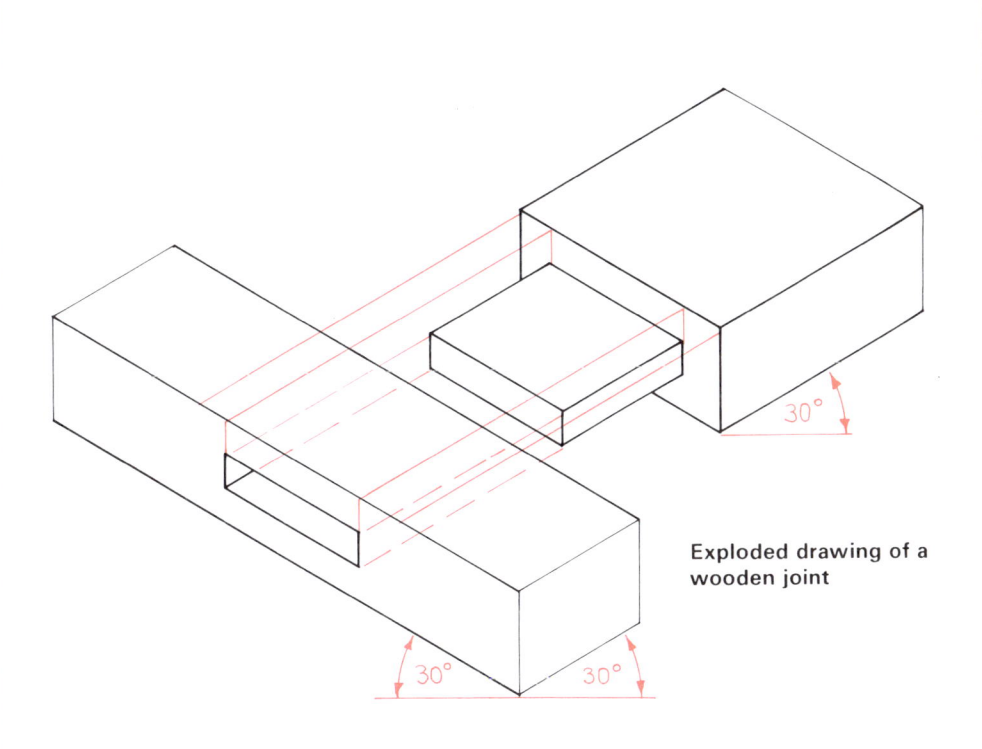

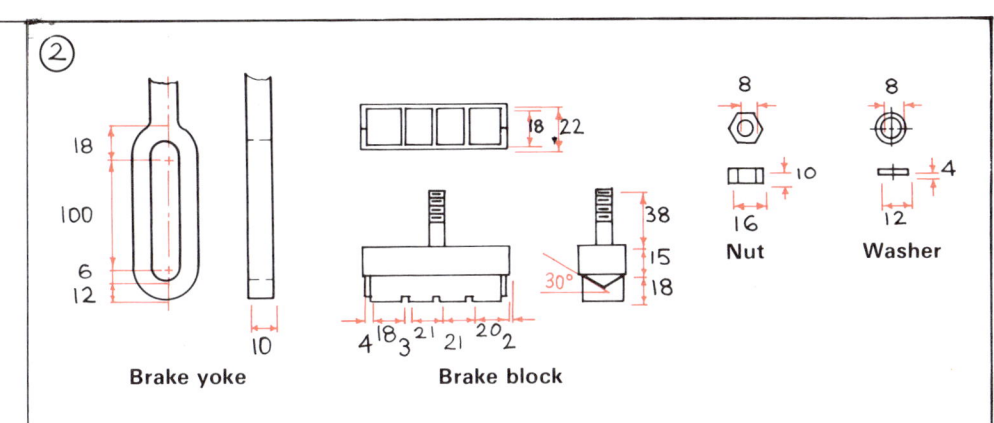

Exploded drawing of a wooden joint

②

Brake yoke **Brake block** **Nut** **Washer**

An exploded assembly drawing of more than two components

- Draw either the nearest, or the most important component in isometric, positioning it carefully on the page.
- Establish the assembly axis or axes, again in isometric.
- Moving back up along this axis draw each component in order of assembly. Each should be clearly separated, as shown.

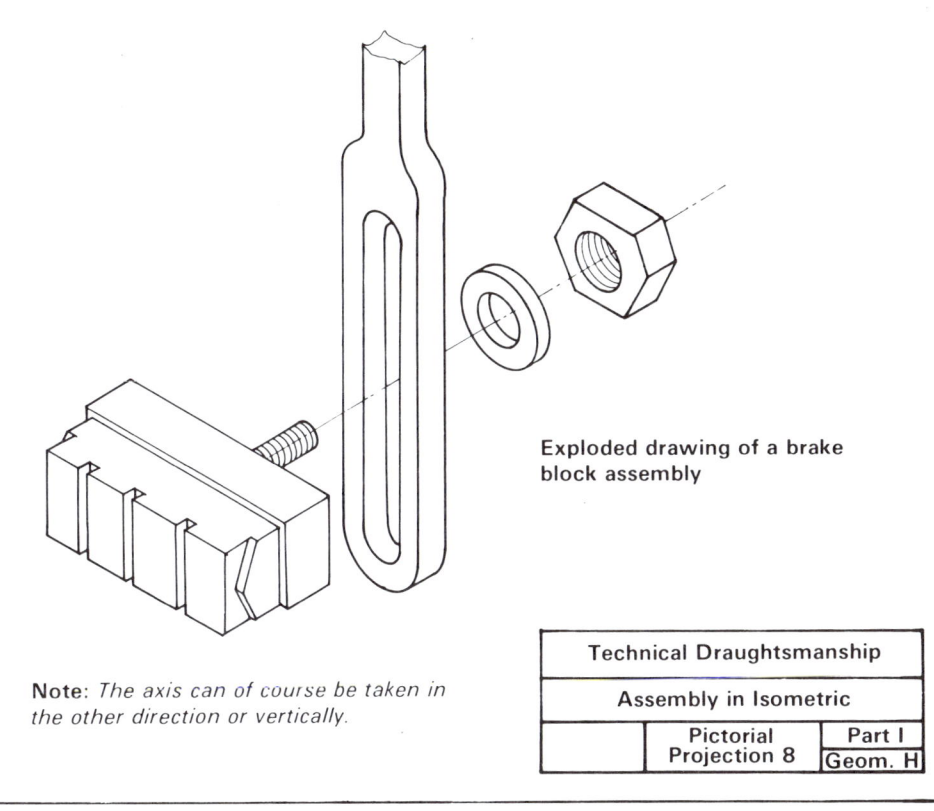

Exploded drawing of a brake block assembly

Note: *The axis can of course be taken in the other direction or vertically.*

Technical Draughtsmanship
Assembly in Isometric
Pictorial Projection 8 — Part I — Geom. H

①

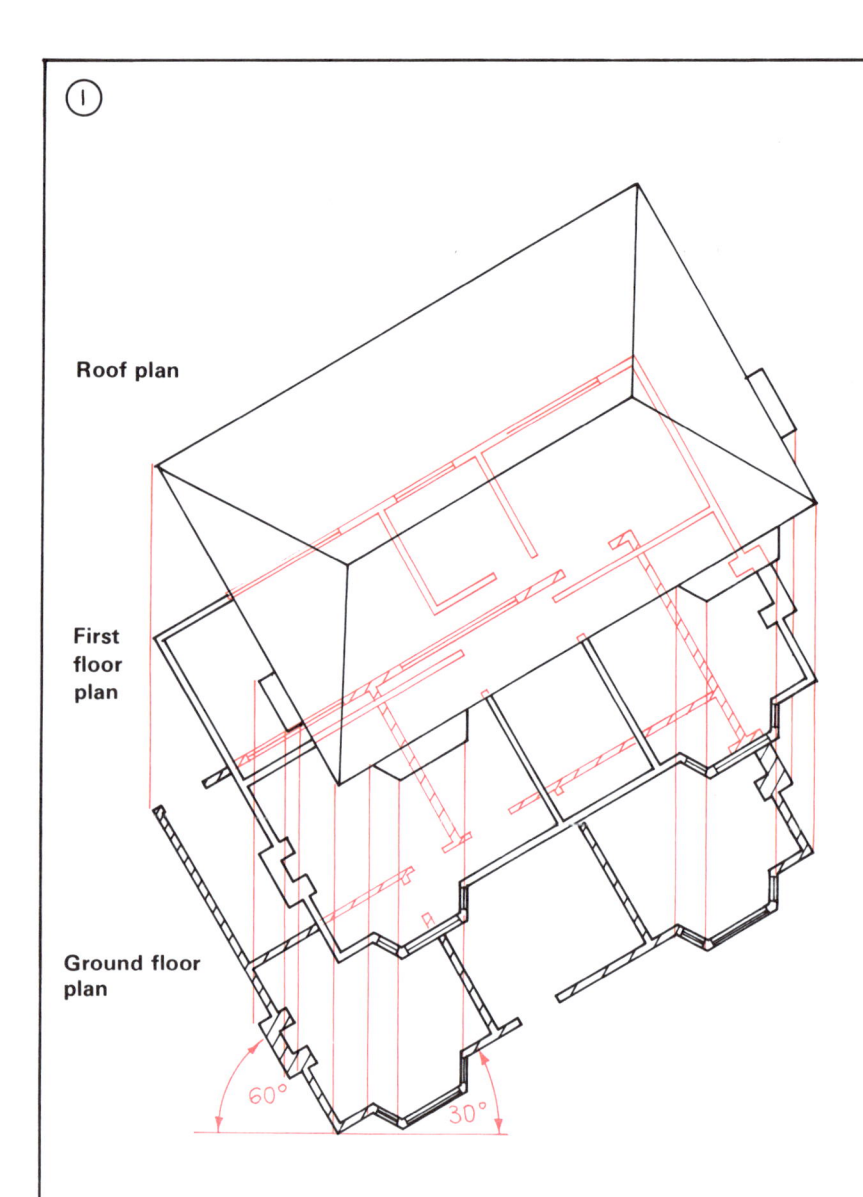

Roof plan

First floor plan

Ground floor plan

60° 30°

Planometric projection: Here the sum of the oblique axes is **90°**. This means that angles are not distorted as they are in isometric. This in turn allows us to trace directly from a plan. By placing further plans over this a solid can be built up, as in the house above.

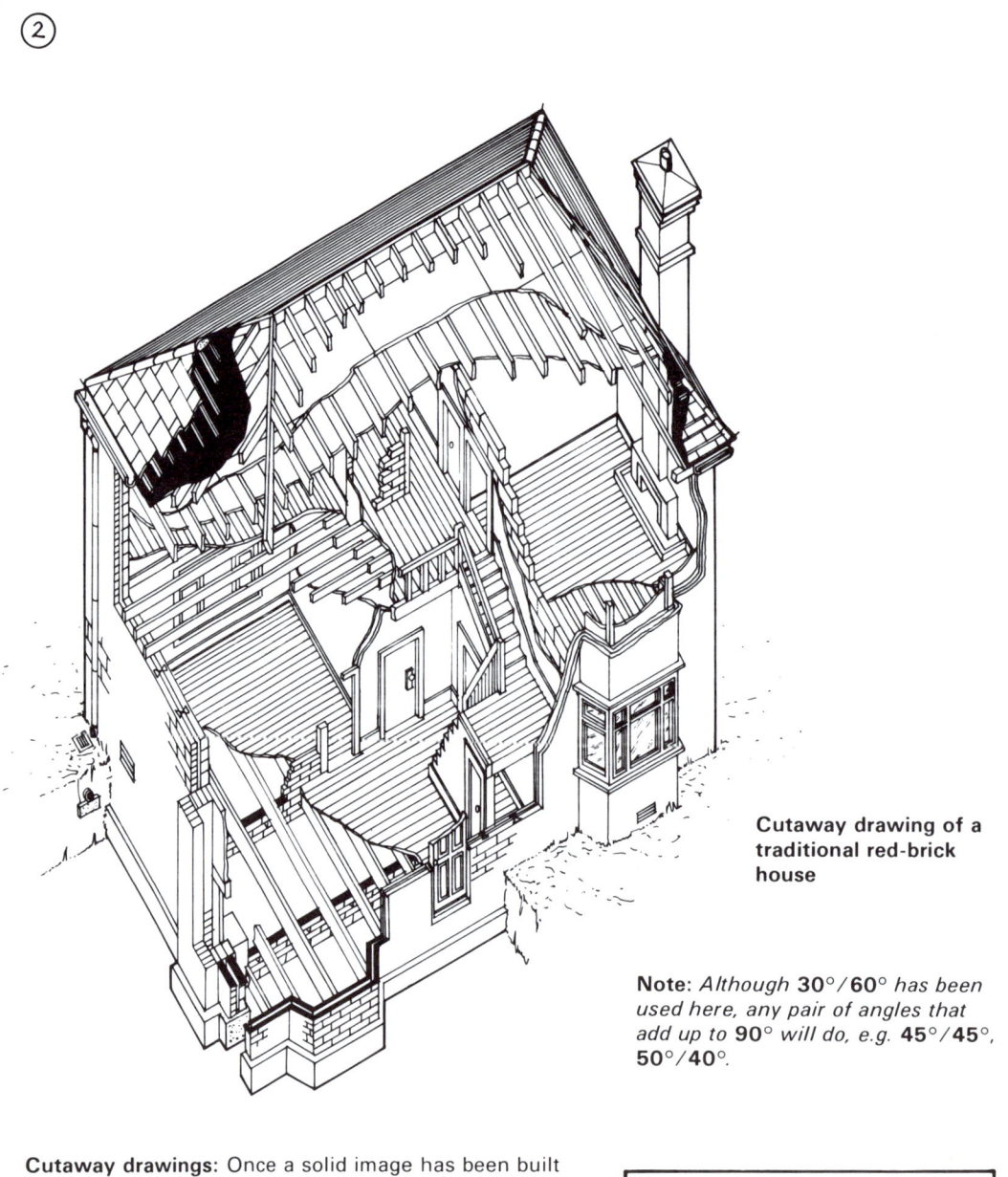

②

Cutaway drawing of a traditional red-brick house

Note: Although **30°/60°** has been used here, any pair of angles that add up to **90°** will do, e.g. **45°/45°**, **50°/40°**.

Cutaway drawings: Once a solid image has been built up, either in planometric as here, or by any other method, it can then be cut away to show its underlying structure. Professionals often use acetate overlays when drawing cutaways.

Technical Draughtsmanship		
Planometric and cutaway		
Pictorial Projection 9	Part I	Geom. H

①

Procedure:
- Draw the given views.
- Set up an outline box in isometric into which the bracket will fit.
- Complete all straight edges, starting at **M**.
- By grid, crate or, as above, by approximate ellipse method draw the curves.
- The corner **N** could also have been chosen as a starting point and the axis set in the other direction.

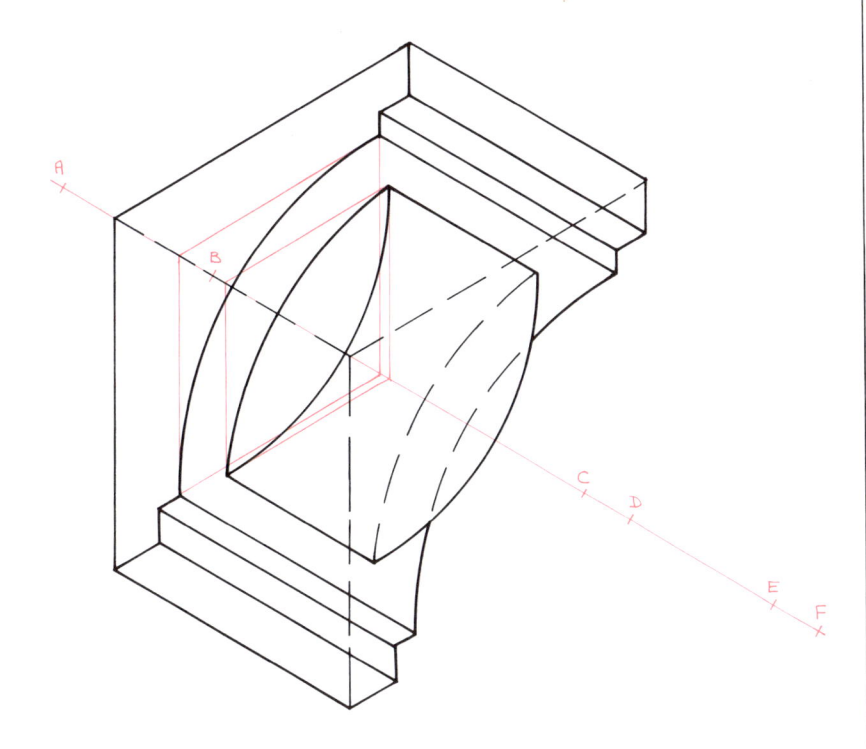

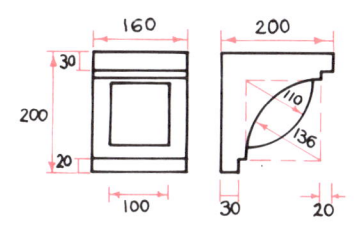

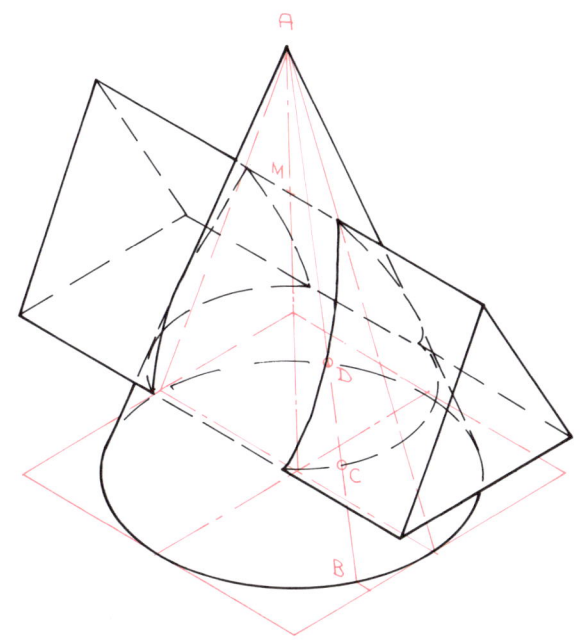

Here are the elevation and end view of a bracket fixed between the wall and ceiling of a room. Draw an isometric view of the bracket when it is viewed from the front looking upwards. Scale **1 : 2**

②

Procedure:
- Draw the given views, plotting the line of interpenetration, see chapter **11**.
- Project an isometric view of the cone.
- Locate point **M** and draw the complete triangular prism.
- To plot the line of interpenetration take a radian **AB** and measure the points **C** and **D**.
- Repeat with other radians to build up the lines.

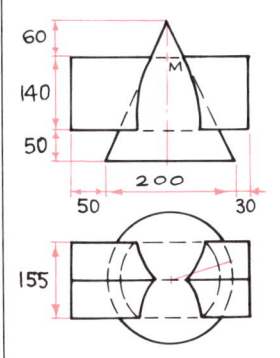

Draw an isometric view of the cone penetrated by a triangular prism shown above. Scale **1 : 2**.

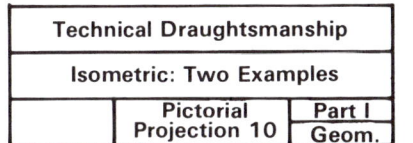

Technical Draughtsmanship		
Isometric: Two Examples		
	Pictorial Projection 10	Part I
		Geom.

① ISOMETRIC (Equal Measures)

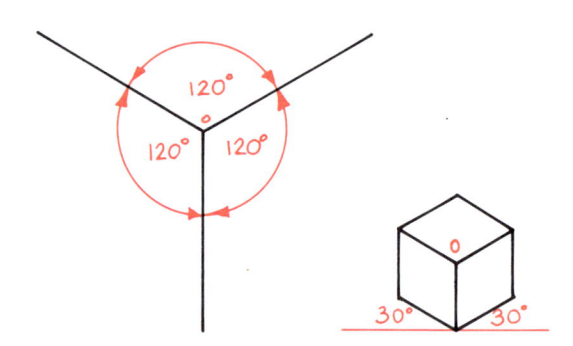

120° / 120° / 120°

Angles at base: 30°/30°

- *All* angles equal.
- *One* angle used throughout.
- *One* scale used.

- **Angles:** 30°/30°

② DIMETRIC (Two Measures)

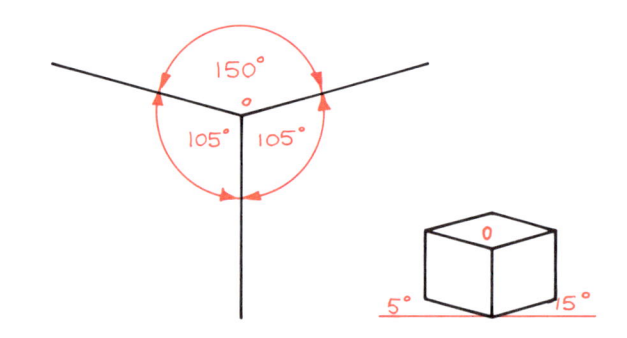

150° / 105° / 105°

Angles at base: 5°/15°

- *Two* angles equal and one other angle.
- *Two* angles used in all.
- *Two* different foreshortened scales used.

- **Common Angles:** 15°/15° for maximum vertical surfaces
  40°/40° for maximum view of the top
  0°/45°

③ TRIMETRIC (Three Measures)

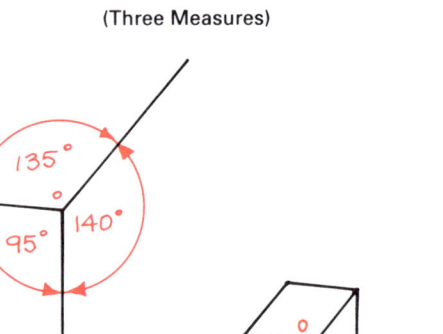

135° / 140° / 95°

Angles at base: 5°/50°

- *Three* different angles.
- *Three* angles used in all.
- *Three* foreshortened scales needed.

- **Common angles:** 5°/50°
  15°/45°

④ TO FIND SCALES FOR TRIMETRIC AXES (e.g. 130°/120°/110°)

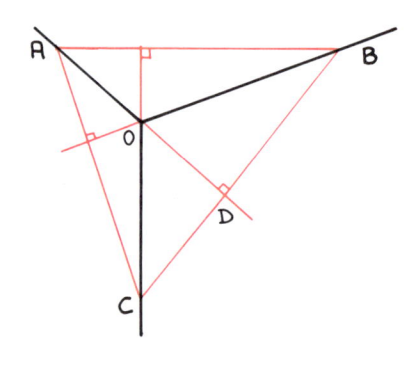

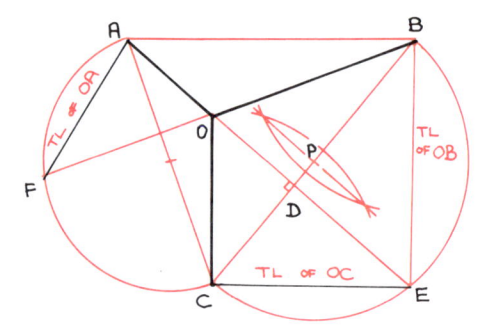

The principle is to rabat the right-angled corner.

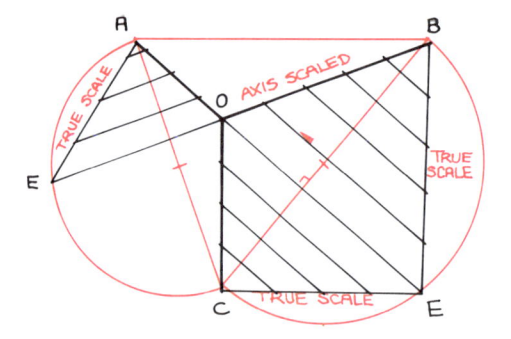

Step One
- Draw the three axes **OA**, **OB**, **OC**.
- Extend **OA** and at any point **D**, draw a line at right angles to fix **B** and **C**.
- Similarly, extend **OB** to find **A** and complete △ **ABC**.

Step Two
- Construct a semicircle on **AB**.
- Extend **AD** to cut the semicircle at **E**.
- **BE** is the true length of **OB** and **CE** the true length of **OC**.
- Similarly, find the true length **AF** of **OA** as shown.

Step Three
- Set true scales on each true length.
- Transfer these across to scale each axis, as shown.

Note:
- **O** is sometimes called the **orthocentre**.

Notes:
- *Using two or three scales can be a nuisance, but grids can be drawn up, or bought, to make it easier in practice.*
- *With a computer, scaling is easily set up. This makes trimetric a versatile method that would include both dimetric and isometric as angle choices.*
- *Can you see how a scaled axis could be worked across to a true scale? How could the ratio of a true to axis scale be measured?*

Technical Draughtsmanship

Axonometric Axes

Pictorial Projection 11 | Part 1 Geom.

① RELATING TRIMETRIC TO ORTHOGRAPHIC VIEWS

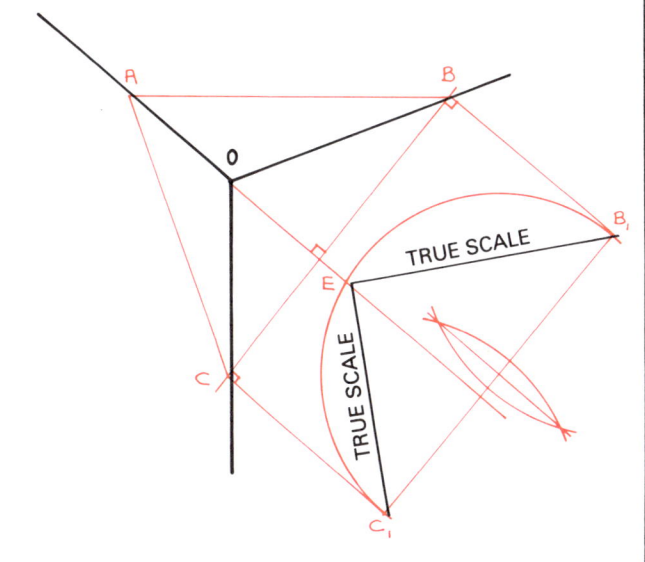

The Principle

- On page **84** we have seen rabatment used to scale three axes.
- We saw that the right angle **CEB** had two true scaled sides, **BE** and **EC** and that these correspond to the two coordinate axes **OB** and **OC**.
- If we slide **CB** out to **C, B**, and draw the triangle **BEC** on the other side, this will allow us to use these two true scales.
- What is a view of one side with two true scales? An elevation.

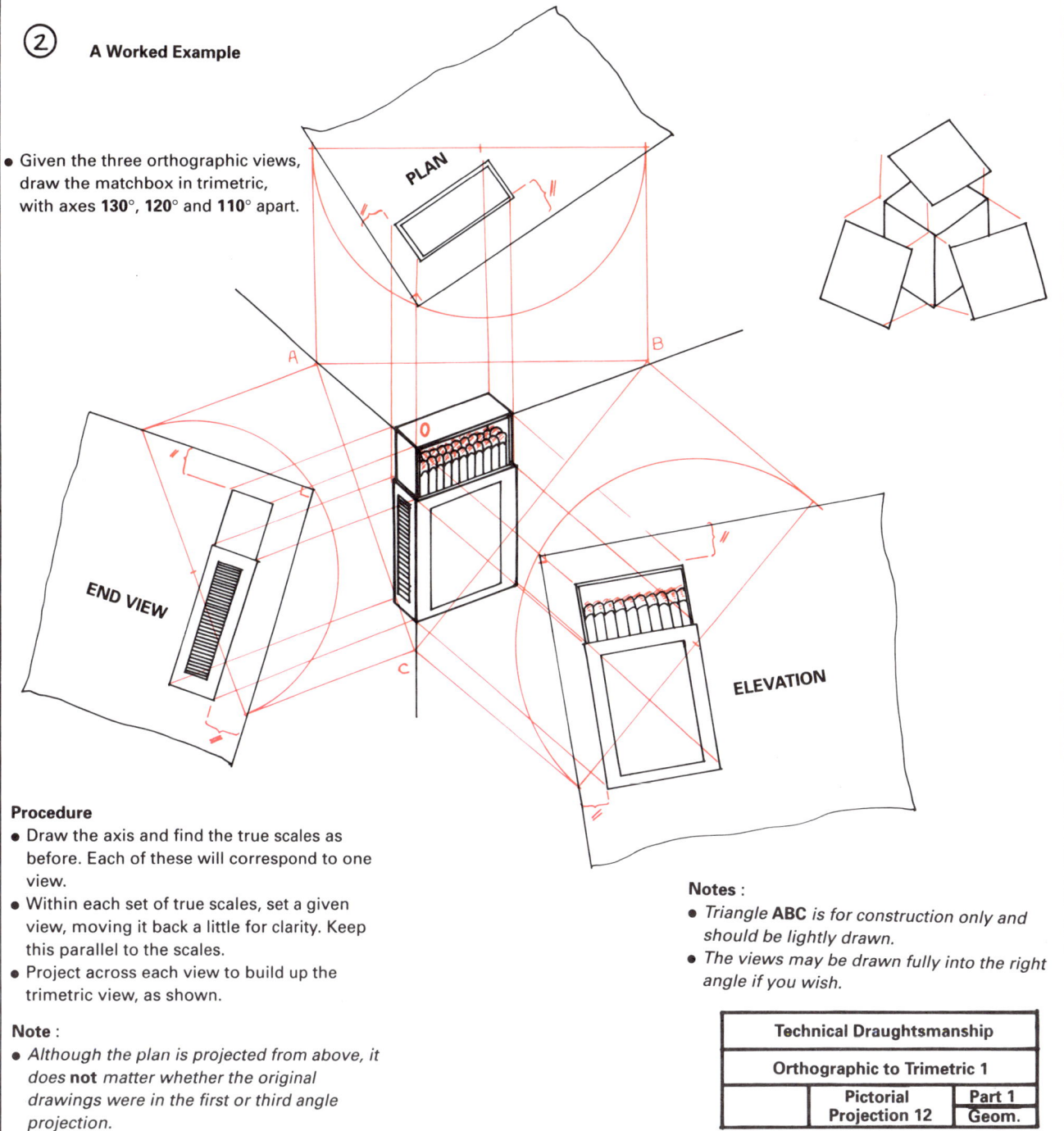

② A Worked Example

- Given the three orthographic views, draw the matchbox in trimetric, with axes **130°**, **120°** and **110°** apart.

Procedure

- Draw the axis and find the true scales as before. Each of these will correspond to one view.
- Within each set of true scales, set a given view, moving it back a little for clarity. Keep this parallel to the scales.
- Project across each view to build up the trimetric view, as shown.

Note:
- Although the plan is projected from above, it does **not** matter whether the original drawings were in the first or third angle projection.

Notes:
- *Triangle **ABC** is for construction only and should be lightly drawn.*
- *The views may be drawn fully into the right angle if you wish.*

Technical Draughtsmanship		
Orthographic to Trimetric 1		
	Pictorial Projection 12	Part 1 Geom.

85

① An Alternative Approach

- If we trace the orthocentre **O**, as the *back* corner, this gives us the above diagram of the axes.
- This method is similar to that used on page **85**.
- This arrangement has distinct advantages, especially when dealing with oblique planes.
- Those trained in first angle projection may find this is a more 'natural' approach, although once the views are separated it is misleading to call it by an angle system.

② A Worked Example

- Given the three orthographic views, make a trimetric drawing with axes **130°**, **120°** and **110°** apart.

- The procedure should be clear from the diagram.
- Trimetric can also be drawn from a transforming grid. The grid is drawn on acetate and tracing paper is used over it, to draw a trimetric more directly.

Technical Draughtsmanship		
Orthographic to Trimetric 2		
	Pictorial Projection 13	Part 1 Geom.

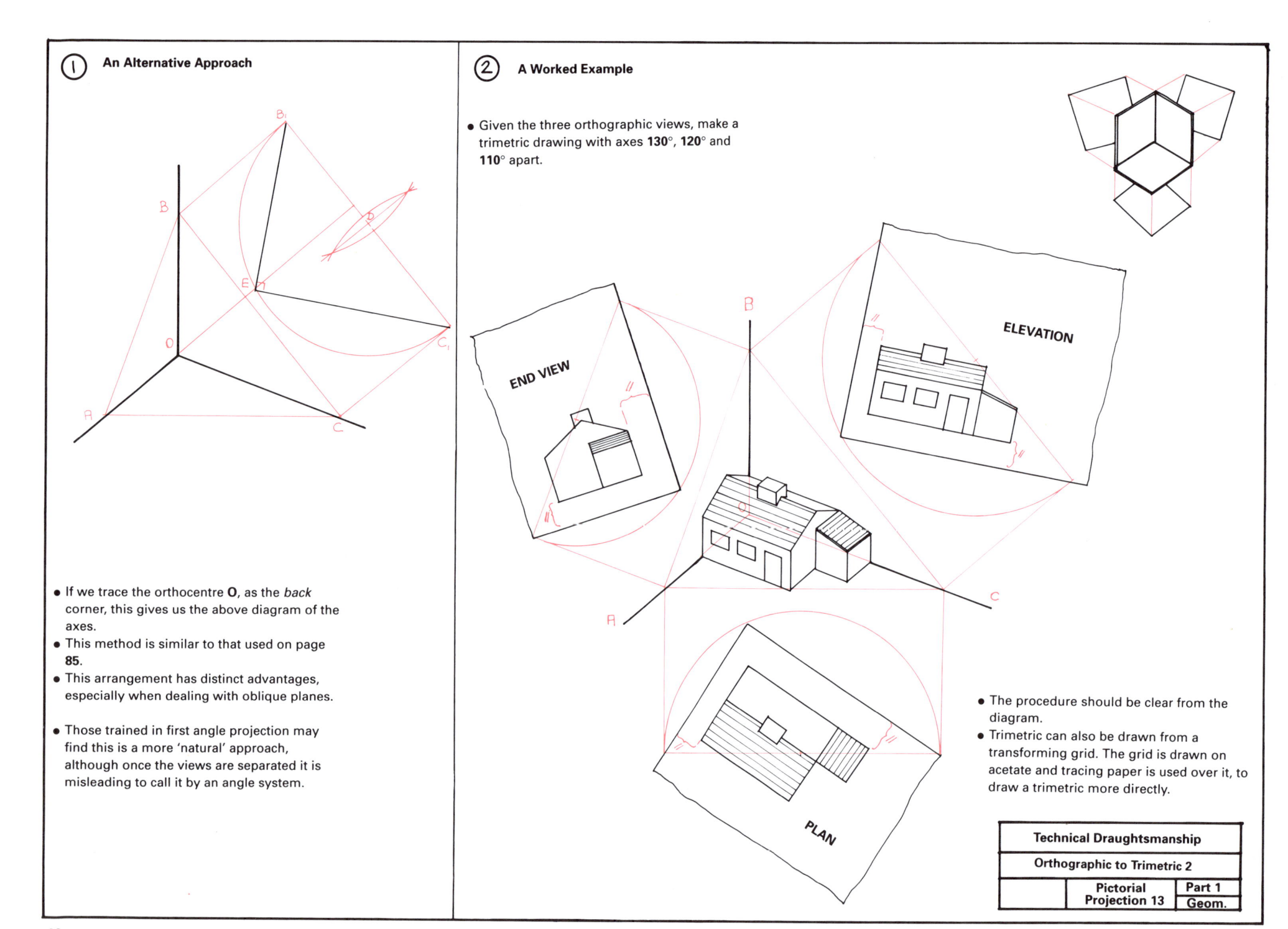

① **Given a trimetric view to plot the three true-scaled orthographic views, the orthocentre being forward.**

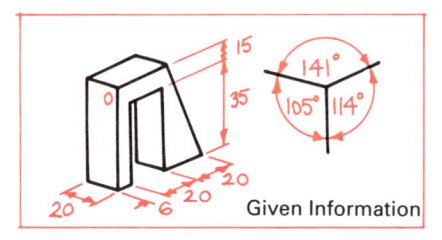

Step 1
- Draw the object as given.
- If the axes are not made clear then extend the lines of the object and measure the angles directly.
- Make sure to leave enough room around your drawing.

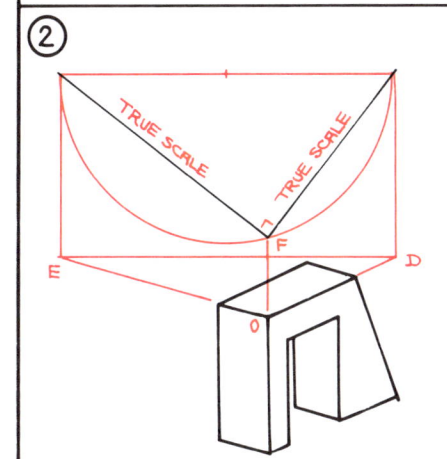

Given Information

② **Step 2**
- Put the object into a crate.
- Take one side e.g. **OD**.
- From **D** draw a line across to **E**, at right angles to **OC**.
- Find the true scales in the usual way.

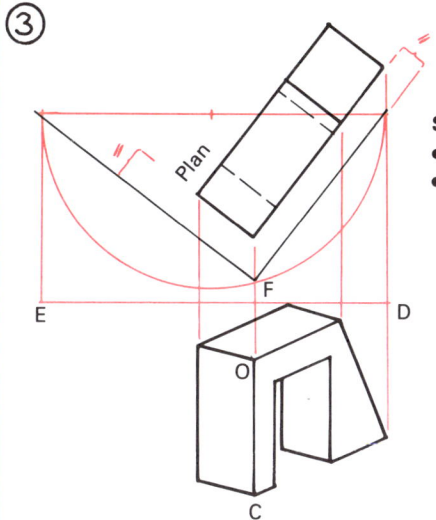

③ **Step 3**
- Build up the view by projection.
- This drawing can be done snug into the corner **F**, but moving it back a bit makes the drawing clearer.

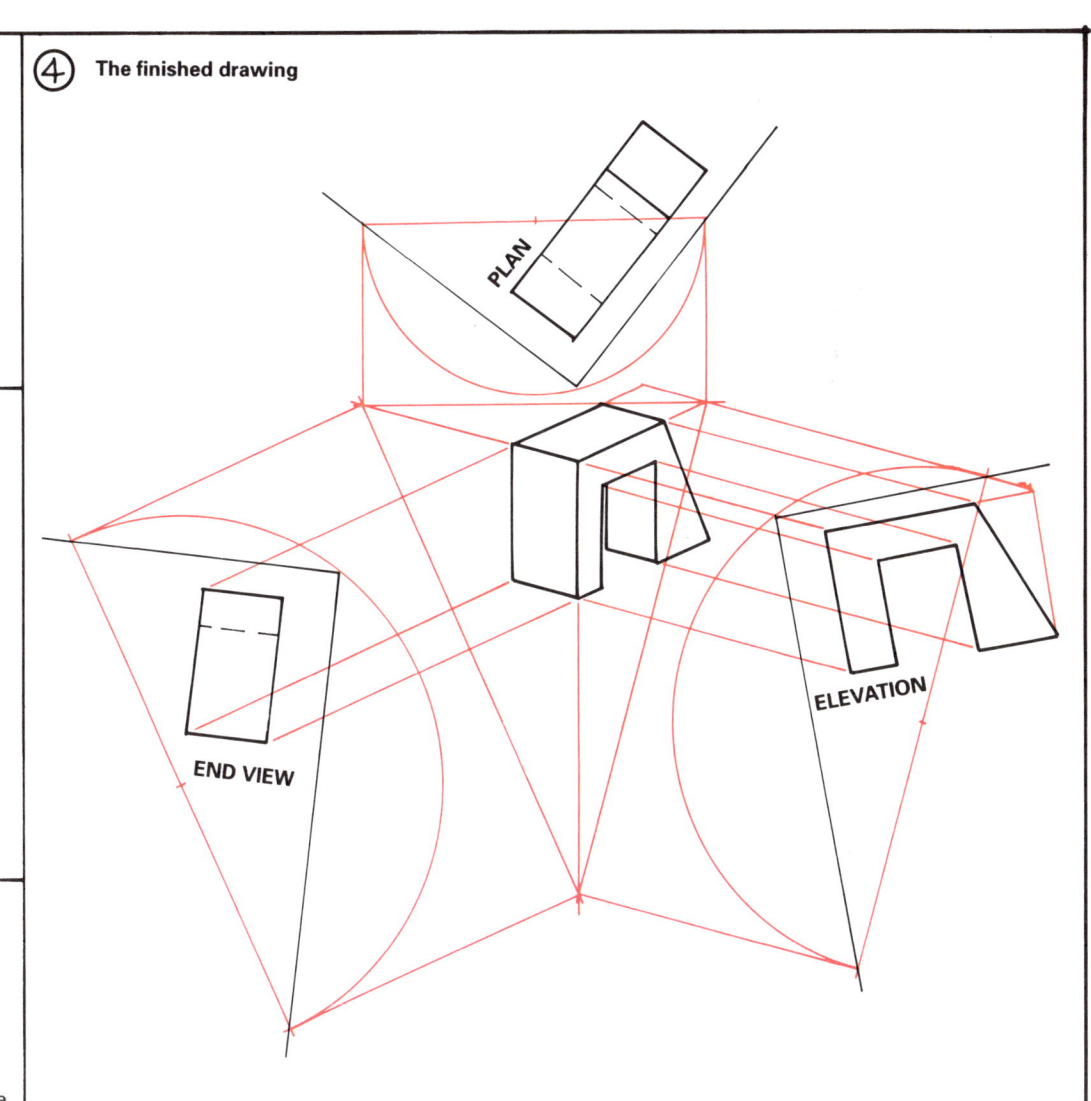

④ **The finished drawing**

Step 4
- Build up the other two views in a similar way.
- How can you work out the ratio of each scaled axis to its true length counterpart?

Note: *Although this is academically interesting it is rarely encountered in practice.*

| Technical Draughtsmanship |
| Trimetric to Orthographic |
| Pictorial Projection 14 | Part 1 Geom. H |

Questions

1 to 4. In each case construct both an isometric drawing and an isometric projection of the given object.

5 to 7. In each case construct both a cavalier and a cabinet projection of the given object.

All measurements are in millimetres.

Technical Draughtsmanship
Exercises 1

| NTS | Pictorial Projection 15 | Part I Geom. |

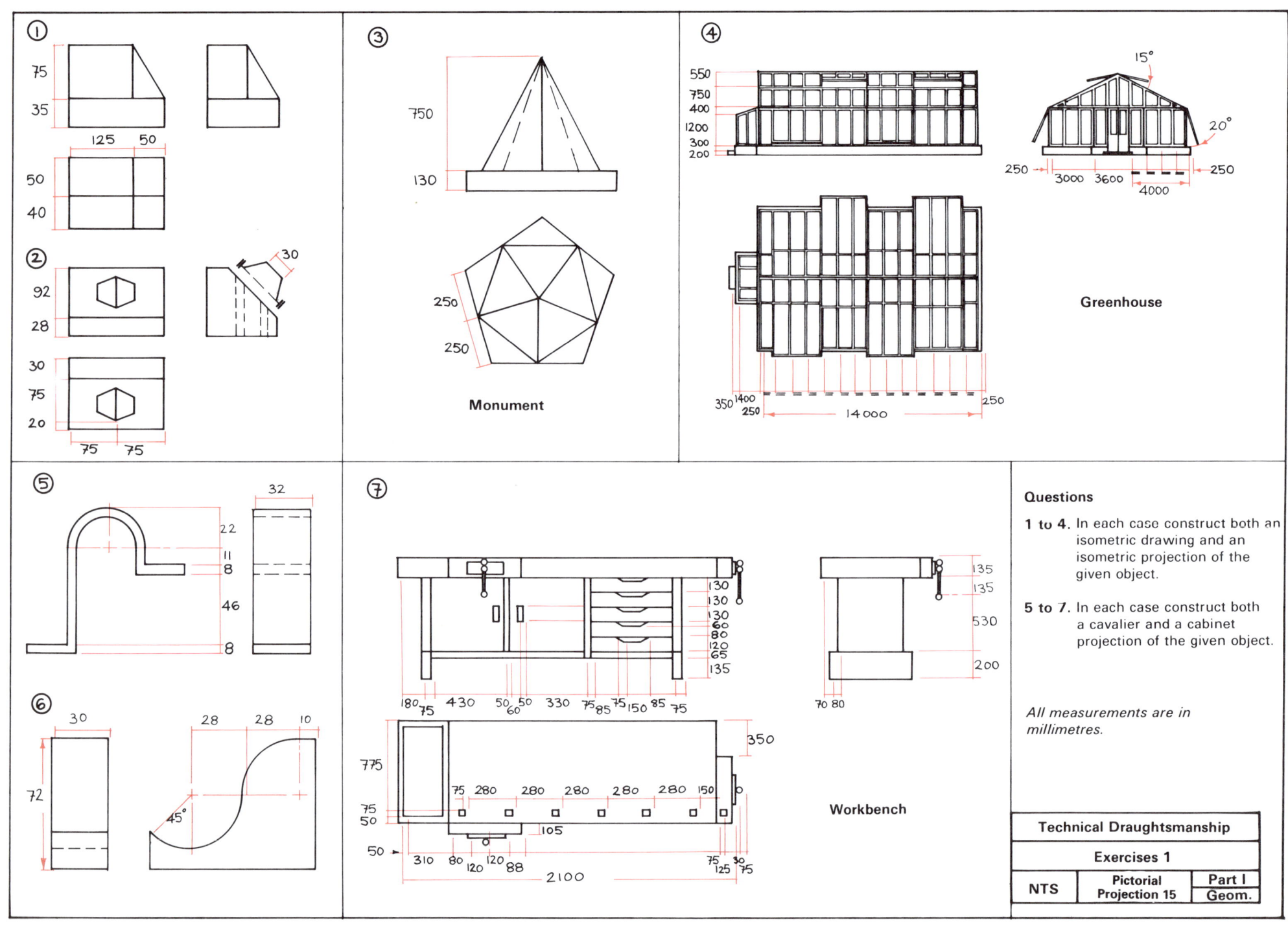

Questions

1 to 3. Make both an oblique and an isometric drawing of the given objects.

4. Draw the assembled clamp in cavalier projection and then as an exploded isometric assembly drawing.

5. Draw the piston in an isometric quarter-sectioned drawing.

6 to 8. Make an isometric drawing of each object.

9. Make an exploded isometric assembly drawing of the saw stool.

All measurements are in millimetres

Technical Draughtsmanship			
Exercises 2			
NTS	Pictorial Projection 16	Part I	Geom.

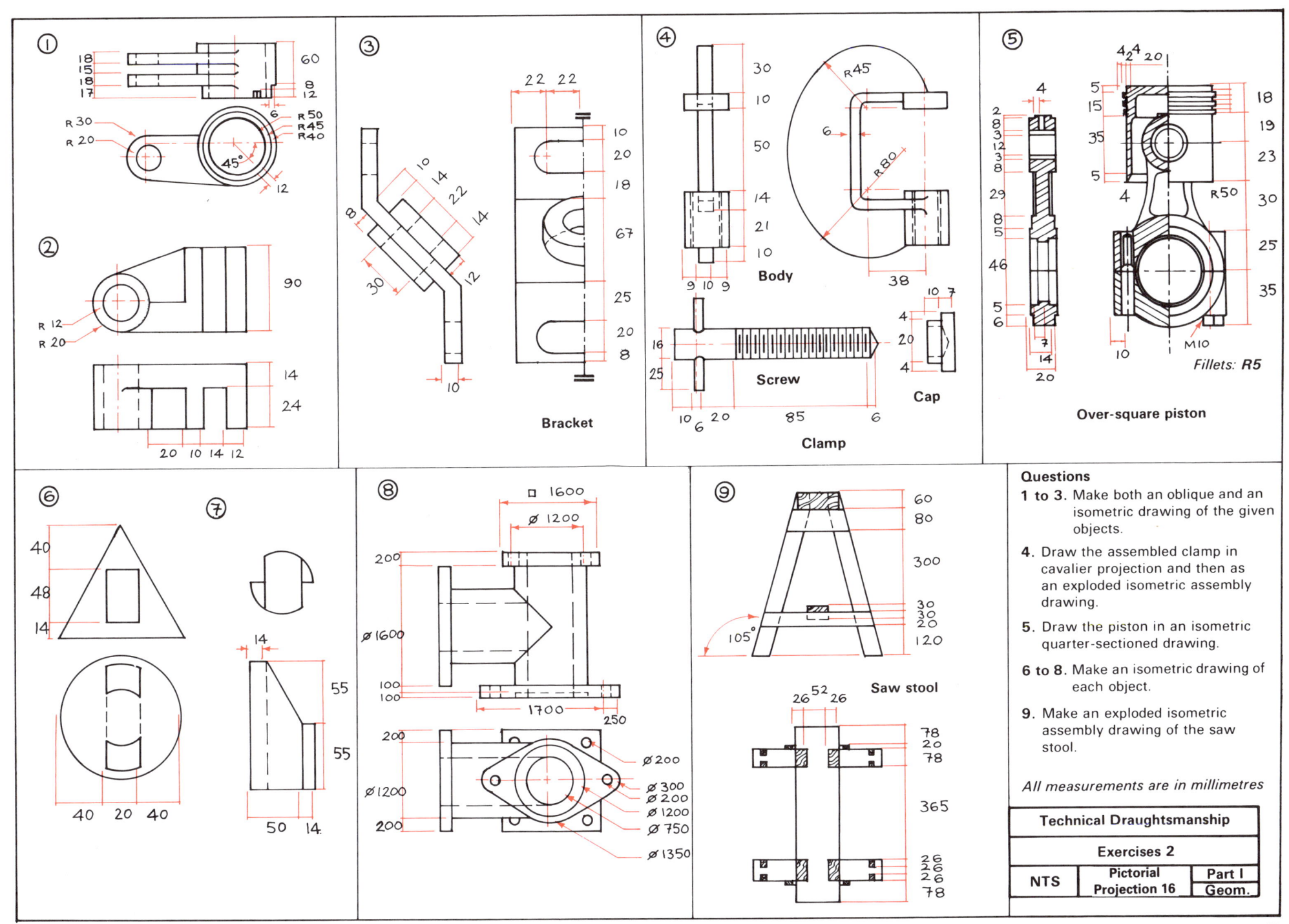

89

Questions

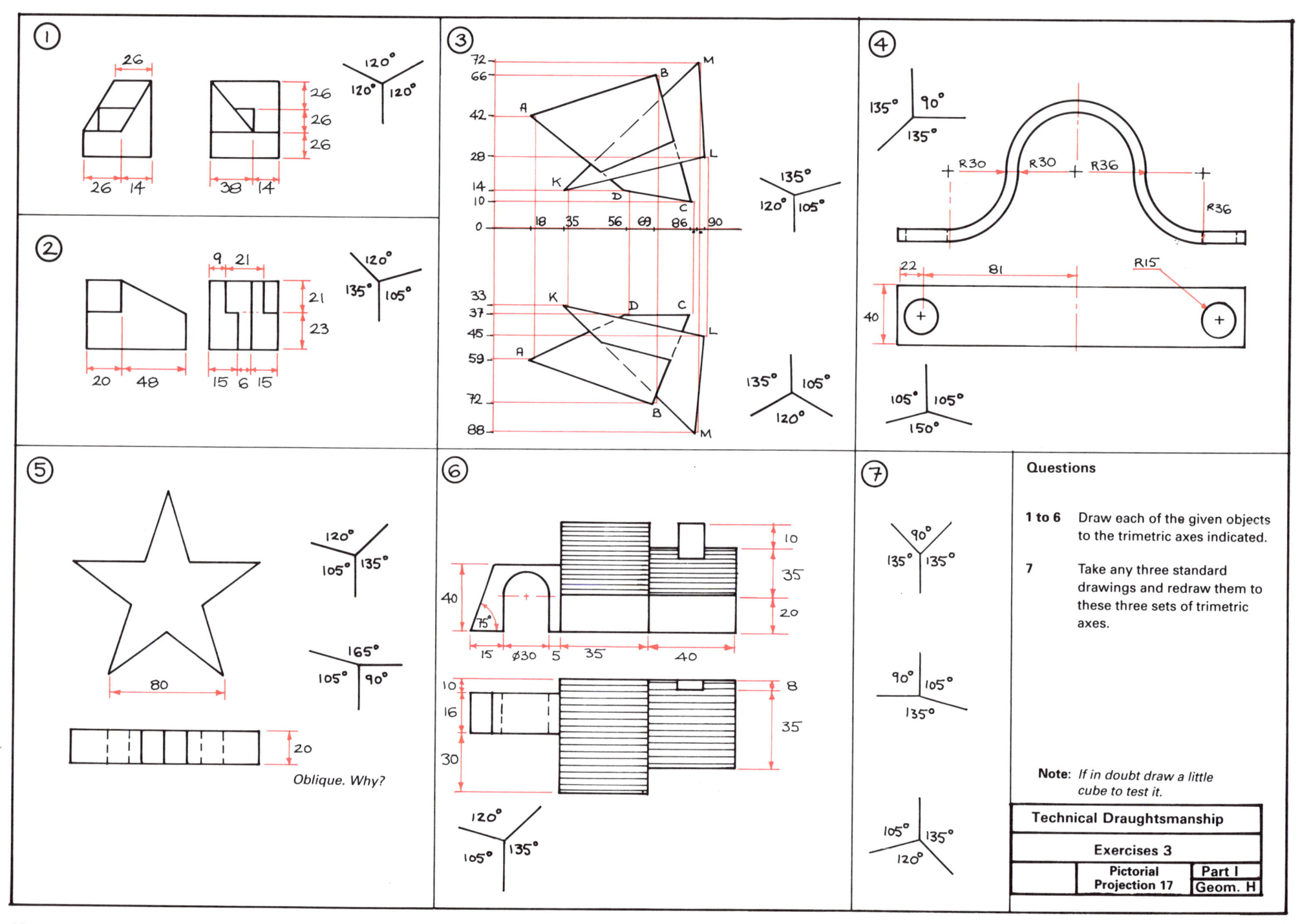

1 to 6 Draw each of the given objects to the trimetric axes indicated.

7 Take any three standard drawings and redraw them to these three sets of trimetric axes.

Note: *If in doubt draw a little cube to test it.*

Technical Draughtsmanship

Exercises 3

| Pictorial Projection 17 | Part I Geom. H |

PART I

CHAPTER 8
POINTS, LINES AND PLANES IN SPACE

Being able to visualize the position of a point, line or plane in space is the most fundamental skill of the draughtsman.
A good grasp of this chapter is essential and will make most other graphic operations easier to follow.

CONTENTS

	Page
Coordinates	92
Laminae by coordinates	93
Lines on V.P. and H.P.	94
Basic line operations	95
Lines and angles	96
Plane shapes and distances	97
Shortest distance between skew lines	98
Interpenetration	99
Dihedral angles	100
Point view example	101
Dihedral by rabatment	102
Exercises	103

Photocopying prohibited by law

①

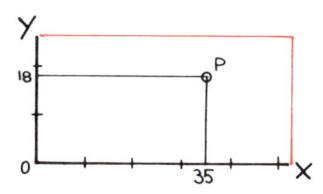

A point on a plane can be located by going over so far and up so far from a given starting point.
- **O** is called the **origin**.
- The horizontal distance is referred to as **X** and is always given first.
- The vertical distance is referred to as **Y** and is always given second.
- The two together are called **coordinates** and are written **(x, y)**, in this case **(35, 18)**.

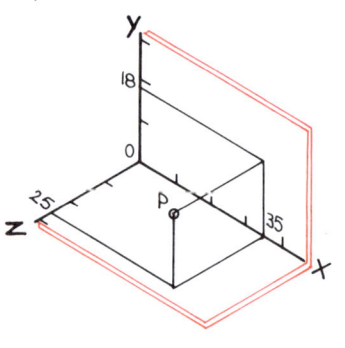

②

A point in space needs a third dimension to fix its position — a third coordinate. A point is so far over **(x)**, so far up **(y)** and so far out from a starting point — the origin.
- This third distance is referred to as **z** and is always given third.
- The three coordinates are written **(x, y, z)**, in this case **(35, 18, 25)**.

Note: *This coding method is of great importance for computer graphics.*

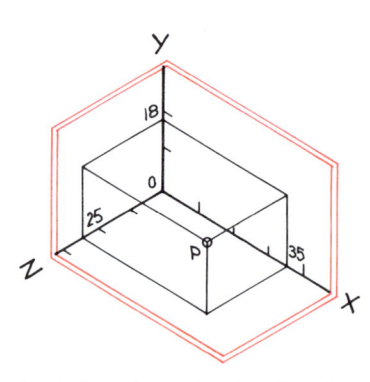

③

In **first angle projection** the planes reflect coordinate planes as shown below:

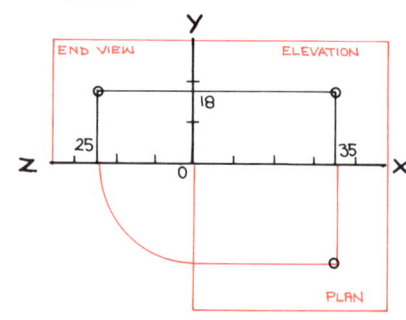

However, this is an uncommon arrangement and in practice the following is the norm:

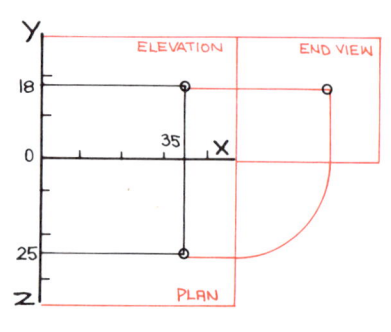

Note: *The third coordinate is measured on the plan and transferred to the end view.*

How would you mark z directly on the end view? Is there a mistake that could easily be made?

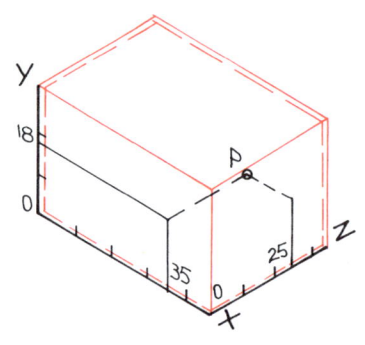

④

In **third angle projection** the planes correspond to the three coordinate planes as shown below:

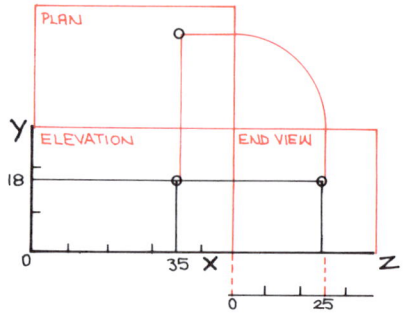

Note: *The origin has to be transferred and the z distance measured separately.*

Another less common arrangement is:

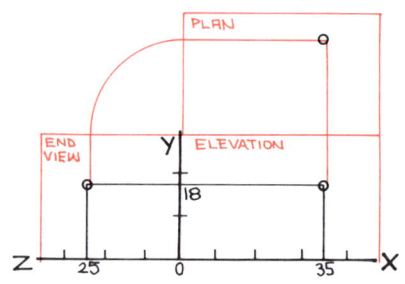

Technical Draughtsmanship
Coordinates
Points in Space 1 — Part I — Geom.

92

A problem

The coordinates of two adjoining triangular laminae **ABC** and **ABD** are given here in tabular form:

	x	y	z
A:	20	45	40
B:	68	10	67
C:	108	50	30
D:	63	70	95

It is required to plot these in first angle orthographic projection.

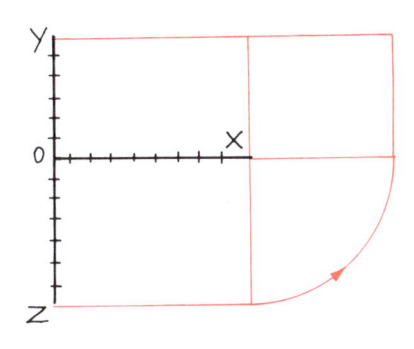

Procedure:

- Mark the distance on the axis as shown in the diagram above.
- In this way plot the points in elevation and in plan.
- Join the points **ABC** and **ABD** to draw the laminae.
- Project the end view.

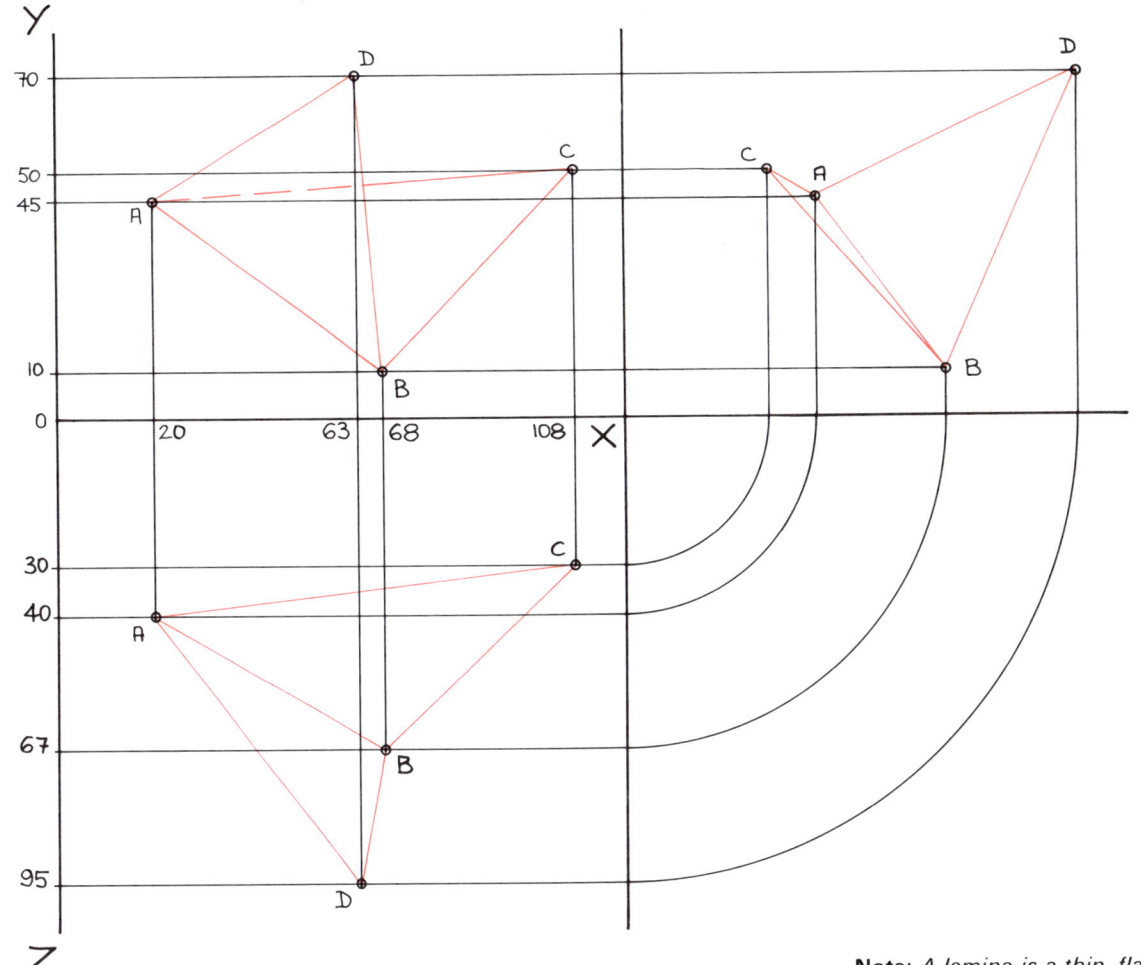

Note: *A lamina is a thin, flat, limited plane of any shape.*

Technical Draughtsmanship

Laminae by Coordinates

Points in Space 2 | Part I
Geom.

① A line parallel to both the vertical plane and to the horizontal plane.

② A line parallel to the horizontal plane and at right angles to the vertical plane.

③ A line parallel to the vertical plane and at right angles to the horizontal plane.

④ A line parallel to the vertical plane and at an angle to the horizontal plane.

⑤ A line parallel to the horizontal plane and at an angle to the vertical plane.

⑥ A line at an angle to both the vertical and to the horizontal plane.

Technical Draughtsmanship
Lines on V.P. and H.P.
Lines in Space 1 — Part I Geom.

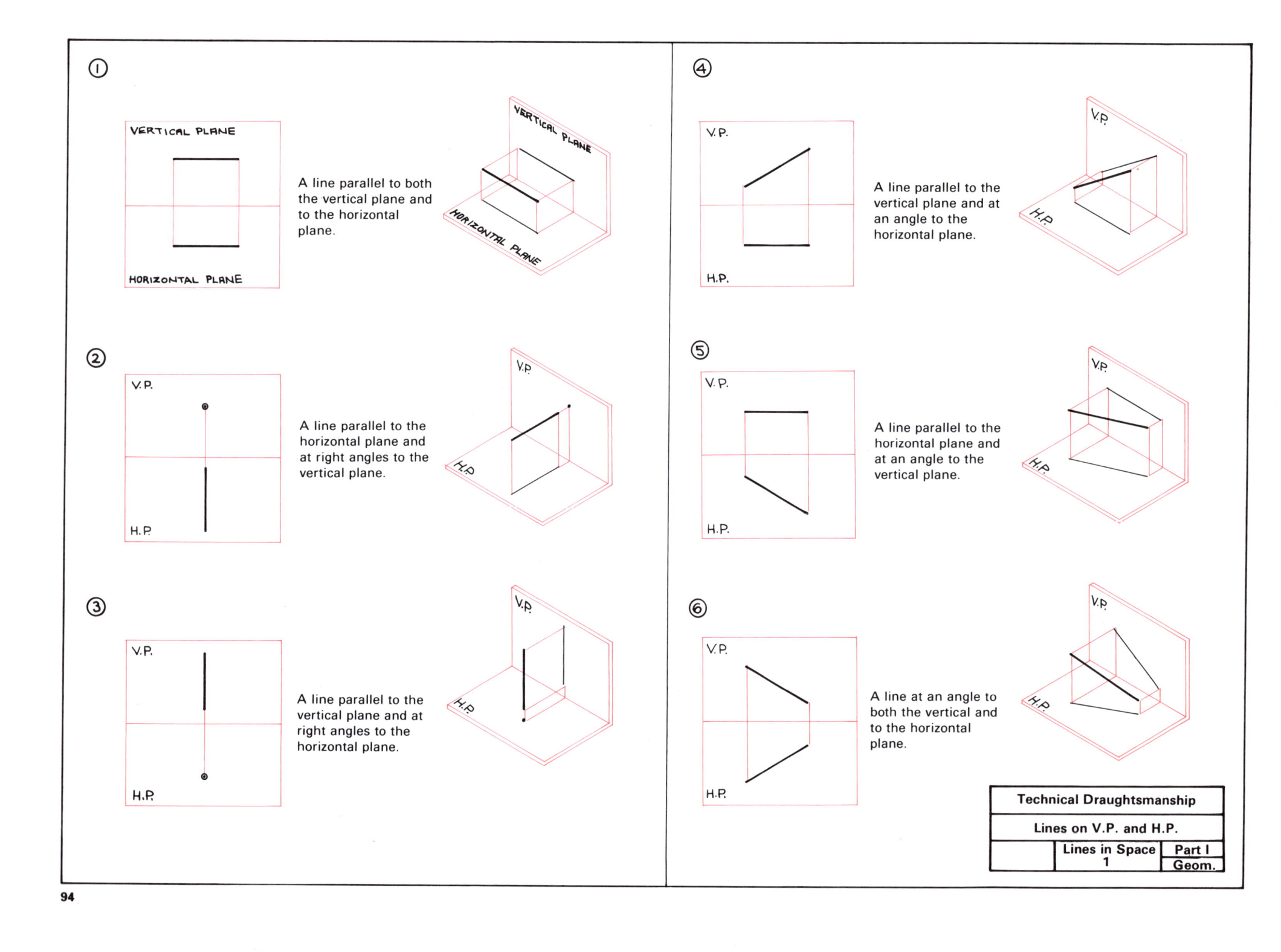

① **True length (a)**
If a line is parallel to the horizontal plane it will appear in its true length on plan.

② **True length (b)**
If a line is parallel to the vertical plane it will appear in its true length in elevation.

③ **True length (c)**
Any line parallel to a projection plane will appear in its true length when it is projected into that plane.

④ **Point view of a line**
A line appears as a point in a view that is perpendicular to a true length view of that line.

⑤ **True angle with the horizontal** (known as the **slope** of a line)

The angle a line makes with the horizontal plane can be measured on any **elevation** in which that line appears in its true length.

⑥ **True angle with the vertical**
The angle a line makes with the vertical plane can be measured on any **plan** in which that line appears in its true length.

Note: *This angle is often quoted in relation to compass points (e.g.* **60° W of N***), in which case it is called the* **bearing** of the line.

Technical Draughtsmanship		
Basic Line Operations		
	Lines in Space 2	Part I Geom.

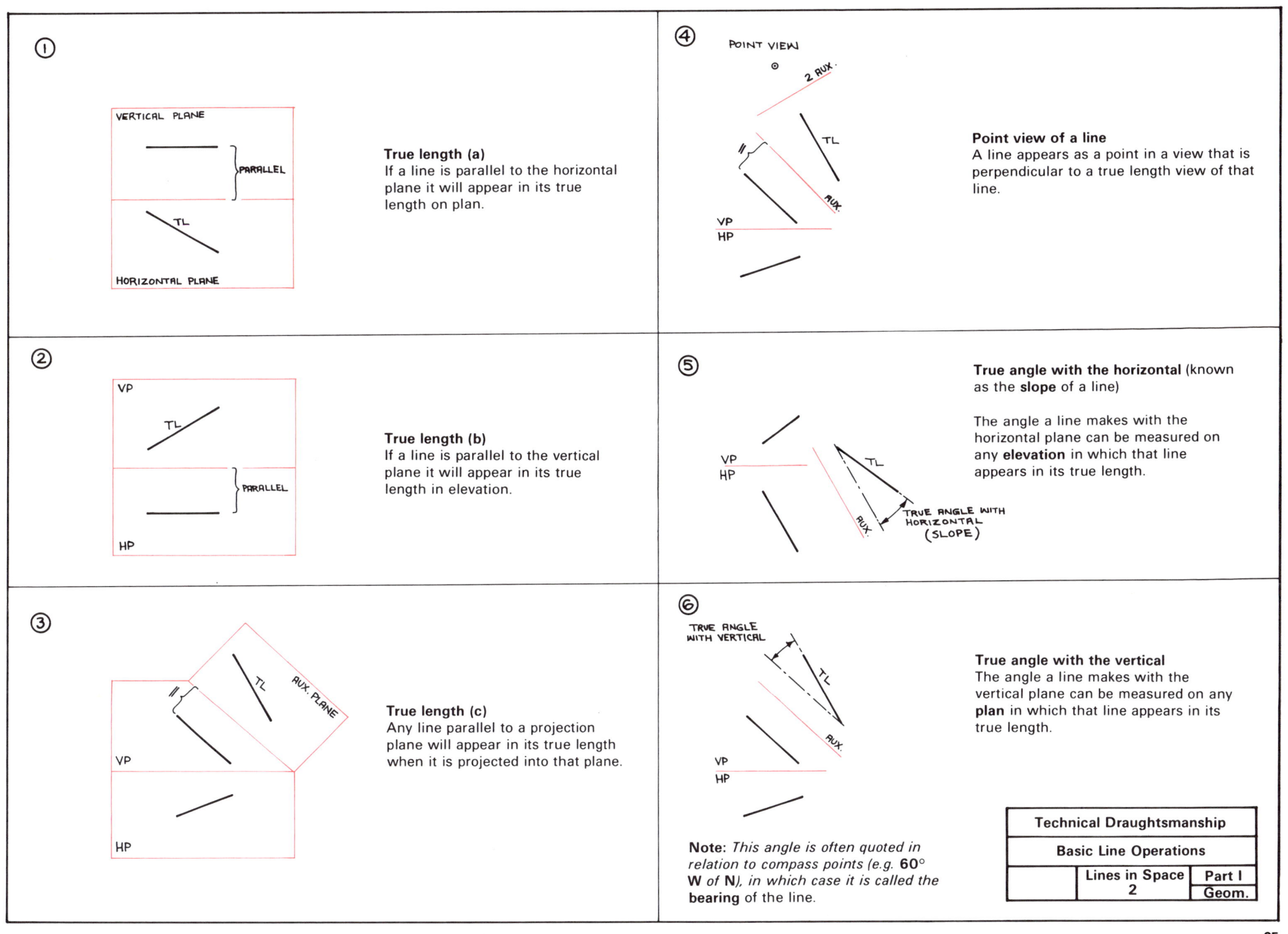

① To draw the projections of a line given its inclination and length.

(a) An example of a line of **60 mm** and of **40°** with the **VP**.

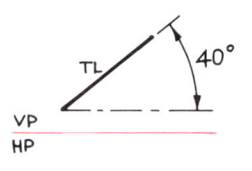

(b) An example of a line of **80 mm** and of **30°** with the **VP**.

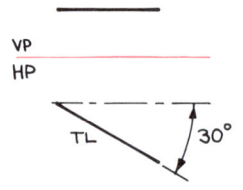

(a)
- Draw the elevation with true length and true angle.
- The plan will be parallel to the projection plane.

or

(b)
- Draw the plan with true length and true angle.
- The elevation will be parallel to the projection plane.

② To project a line given one view and its inclinations

For example an angle of **40°** with the **HP** and **30°** with the **VP**.

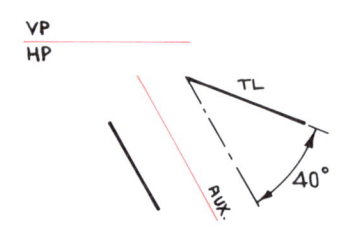

(a) Given the plan
- Parallel to this plan draw an auxiliary projection plane.
- Project the end points of the line across it.
- Set the angle (**40°** here) with the **HP** as shown.
- Draw the line which will appear in true length.

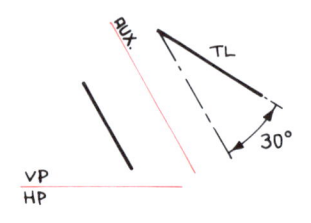

(b) Given the elevation
- Parallel to the elevation draw an auxiliary projection plane.
- Project the end points of the line across it.
- Set the angle (**30°** here) with the **VP** as shown.
- Draw the line, which will appear in true length.

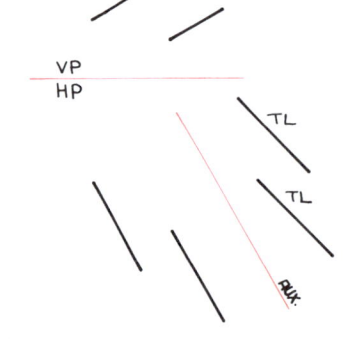

③ Parallel lines

Lines that are parallel in space will appear parallel in all views (except when one lies hidden behind another, or when both are reduced to a point view).

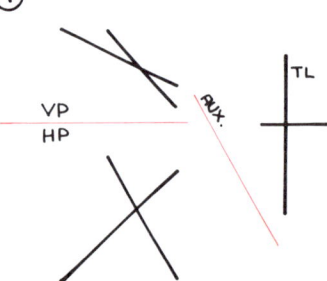

④ Perpendicular lines

Lines that are perpendicular will appear perpendicular in any view that shows either line in its true length (except when one is reduced to a point view).

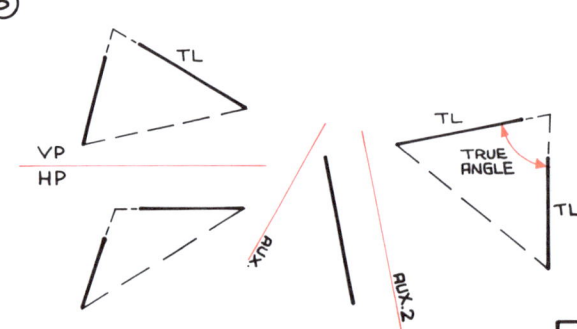

⑤ To find the true angle between two lines

- Join the lines to form a triangle.
- Find one true length.
- Reduce it to a point, thus getting an edge view of the triangle.
- Project onto a plane parallel to this edge view to get both true lengths and the true angle.

Technical Draughtsmanship		
Lines and Angles		
Lines in Space 3		Part I Geom.

① **Plane as a line**

A plane will appear as a line in any view perpendicular to that plane. What does this tell us of line **AB**?

A plane appears as a line in a view where any line which lies on that plane appears as a point

② **The slope of a plane (dip)**
The true angle of a plane to the horizontal is seen on an **elevation** where the plane is seen in an edge view (as a line).

How would the true angle with the vertical be found?

③ **True shape**
The true shape of a lamina (or plane) is seen on a projection plane parallel to that lamina (or plane).

In other words, any plane parallel to an edge view of the lamina will show the true shape of that lamina.

④ **The shortest distance from a point to a line.**

(a) **The line method**
- Reduce the line to a point **P**.
- Measure the distance **d** between what are now two points.

⑤ **The shortest distance from a point to a line**

(b) **The plane method**
- Join the point **P** to both ends of the line, thus forming a lamina.
- Find the true shape of the lamina.
- Drop a perpendicular from the point **P₃** to the line. This will be the shortest distance **d**.

⑥ **The shortest distance from a point to a plane**

- Reduce the plane to an edge view (or line).
- Then drop a perpendicular from the point **P₂** to find the shortest distance **d**.

Technical Draughtsmanship
Plane Shapes and Distances
Planes in Space 1	Part I Geom.

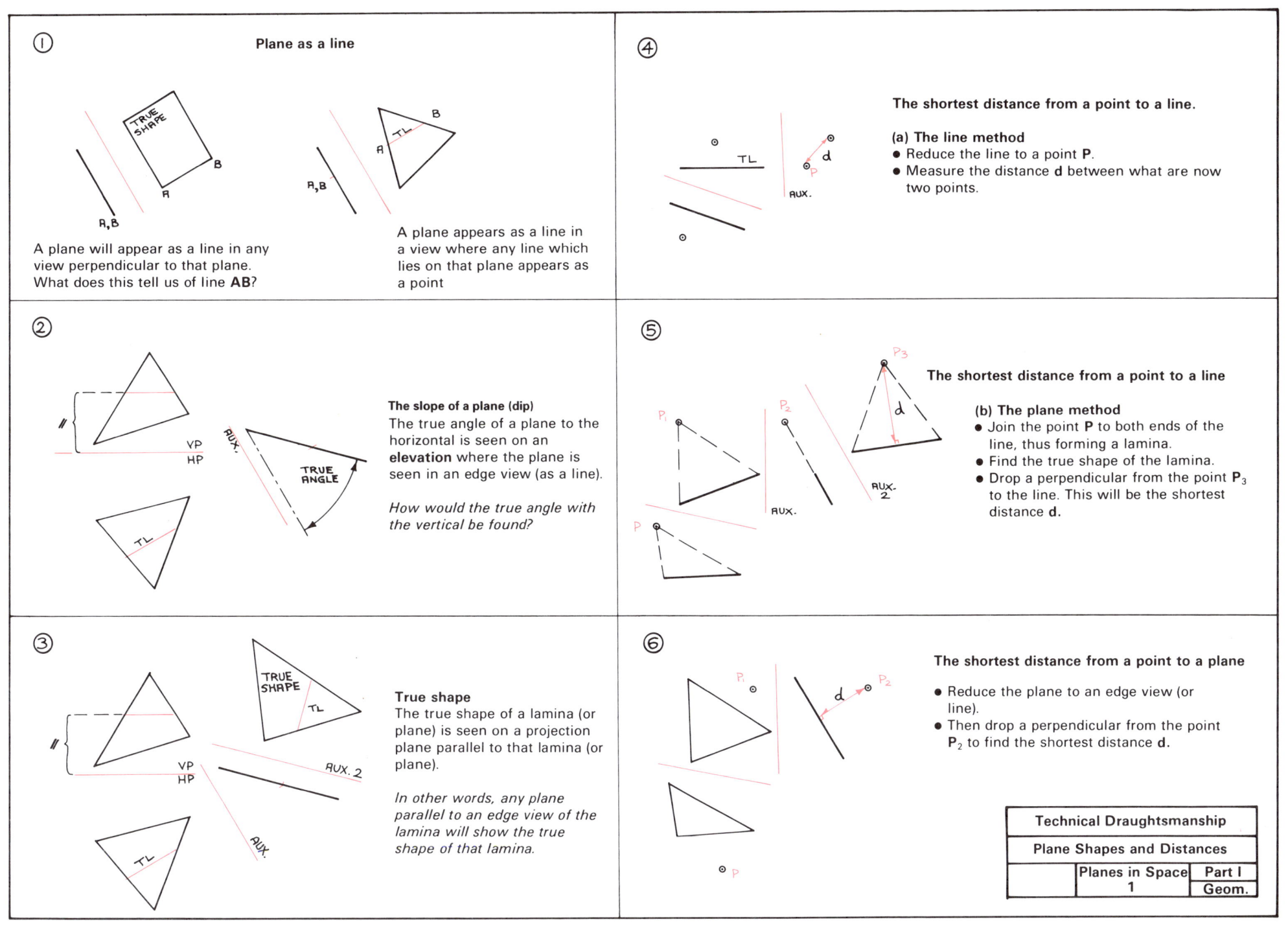

①

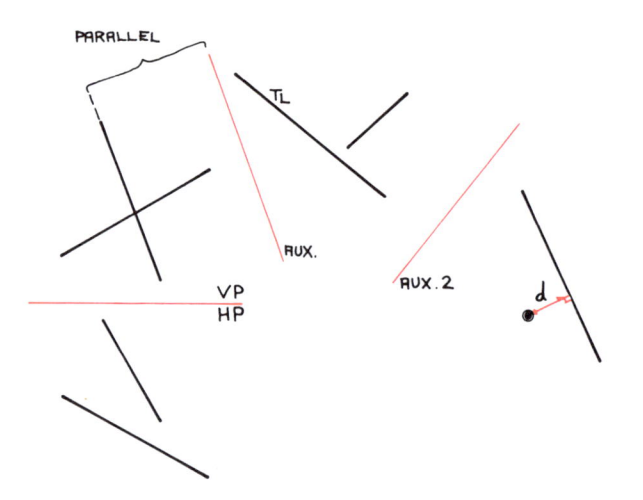

To determine the shortest distance between two skew lines

(A) Line Method

Definition: *Two lines are called skew if they are neither parallel nor intersecting.*

Procedure:
- Reduce one line to a point.
- Drop a perpendicular from this point to the line to find the shortest distance **d**.

②

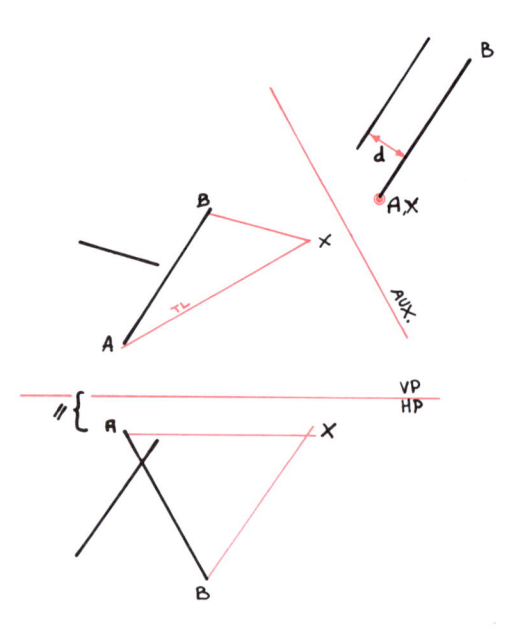

To determine the shortest distance between two skew lines.

(B) Plane Method

- Choose one of the lines and draw a plane containing it, with one edge **BX** parallel to the other line and one edge **AX** parallel to the projection plane.
- Project across the projection plane. **AB** will still be parallel and **AX** will be a true length.
- Reduce the plane to an edge view by projecting at right angles to **AX**. The plane will appear in edge view as a line and both lines will appear parallel.
- The perpendicular distance between these lines is the shortest distance **d**.
- This method will be used again with Mining Strata.

Technical Draughtsmanship		
Shortest distance between Skew Lines		
Planes in Space 2	Part I	Geom. H

98

① **To find the point where a line pierces a plane. Method I.**
- Reduce the plane to a line. The crossing point **P** is the required point and can then be projected back.
- This is called the **edge view method**.

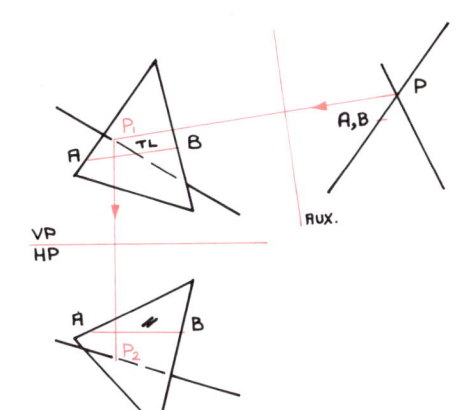

Note: *It can be very helpful to build models of some of these examples. Construct them out of card and hang them from a frame. Graph paper under and behind them makes measuring easier.*

② **To find the point where a line pierces a plane. Method 2**
- In one view imagine the line **LM** to be a cutting plane.
- Project the two extreme points **A** and **B** of the lamina down to the plan.
- Join A_1 to B_1. The point of penetration is where this line A_1B_1 crosses the original line L_1M_1 at **P**.
- Point **P** can then be projected back to the first view.
- This is called the **cutting plane method**.

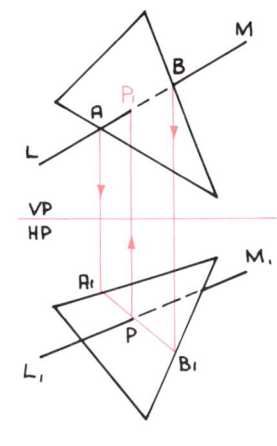

Note: *Although a triangle has been used as an example, the laminae may be of any shape. The approach will be the same.*

③ **The intersection of two planes**
(a). The cutting plane method
- In one view imagine that the overlapping edges **AB** and **CD** are cutting planes.
- Project these down to find two points of intersection **E** and **F**, and therefore the line of intersection **EF**.
- This can then be projected back up.

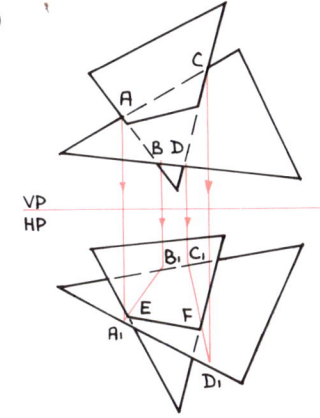

④ **(b). The edge view method**
- Reduce one plane to an edge view and mark the points of intersection **P** and **Q**.
- These can then be projected back to the other views.

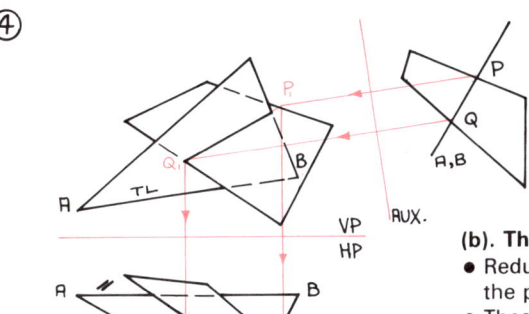

⑤ **(c). The auxiliary plane method**
- On one view draw two lines **AD** and **EH** parallel to the plane of projection.
- Project the lines of intersection onto the plan, and extend these to meet at **Q** and **R**.
- **QR** is the line of intersection of the two planes and it can be projected up to the elevation.

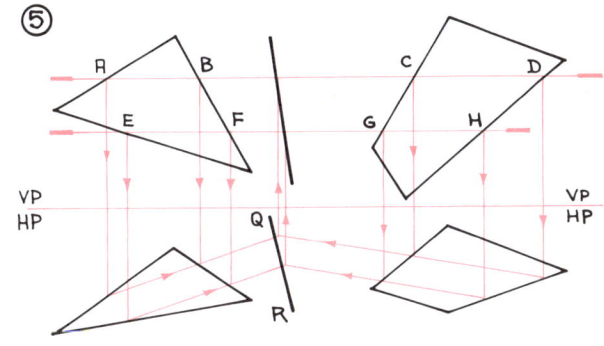

Note: *This is used when the two planes are unlimited and the laminae lie on those planes.*

Technical Draughtsmanship		
Interpenetration		
Planes in Space 3	Part I	Geom.

①

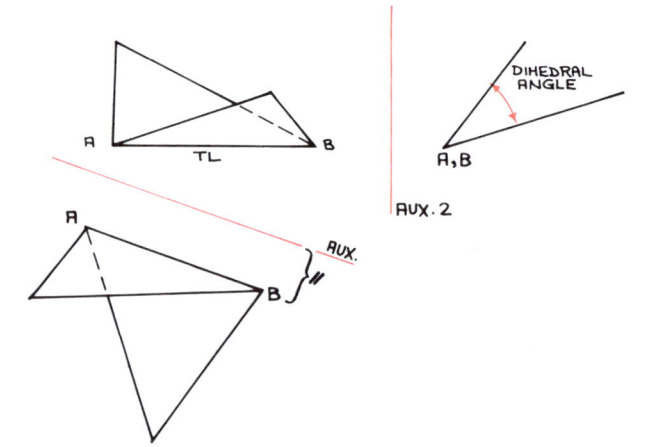

To find the angle between two planes (the dihedral angle)

The point view method
- Reduce the common line to a point view. The two planes will appear as lines and the angle between them may be measured.

②

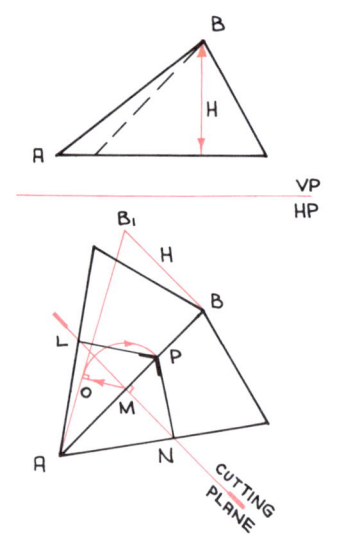

To find the angle between two planes (the dihedral angle)

Rabatment method
- On the plan draw a cutting plane **LN** at right angles to the common line **AB**, cutting it at **M**.
- This plane can be taken anywhere along **AB**.
- On the elevation, measure the height difference between **A** and **B** and transfer this **H** to the plan. Lay out the triangle **ABB**$_1$, where **AB**$_1$ is the true length of **AB**.
- From **M** drop a perpendicular to **AB**$_1$ and, with **M** as centre, swing this around to find **P** as shown.
- Join **L** to **P** to **N**. This is the dihedral angle.

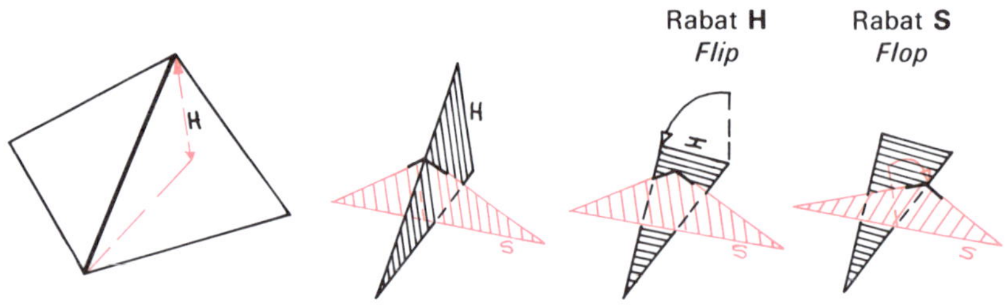

Angle **LPN** is the dihedral angle.

Rabat **H** *Flip*   Rabat **S** *Flop*

Note: *If AC is not parallel to the horizontal plane draw a line from A that is parallel and work from there.*

The principle of the Rabatment method

Technical Draughtsmanship		
Dihedral Angles		
Planes in Space 4	Part I	Geom.

Problem

Find the angle between two adjoining laminae **ABC** and **ABD** whose coordinates are:

	X	Y	Z
A:	20	45	40
B:	68	10	67
C:	108	50	30
D:	63	70	95

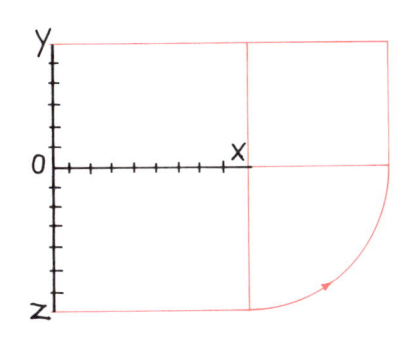

Procedure

- Plot the points on the axis and draw the laminae.
- Reduce the common line to a point by taking an auxiliary plane **Aux.1** parallel to the line **AB**.
- Project onto this plane and **AB** will appear in its true length.
- Take a second auxiliary plane **Aux. 2** perpendicular to **AB** and, by projecting onto it, reduce **AB** to a point view.
- Both planes will be seen as lines and the dihedral angle can then be measured.

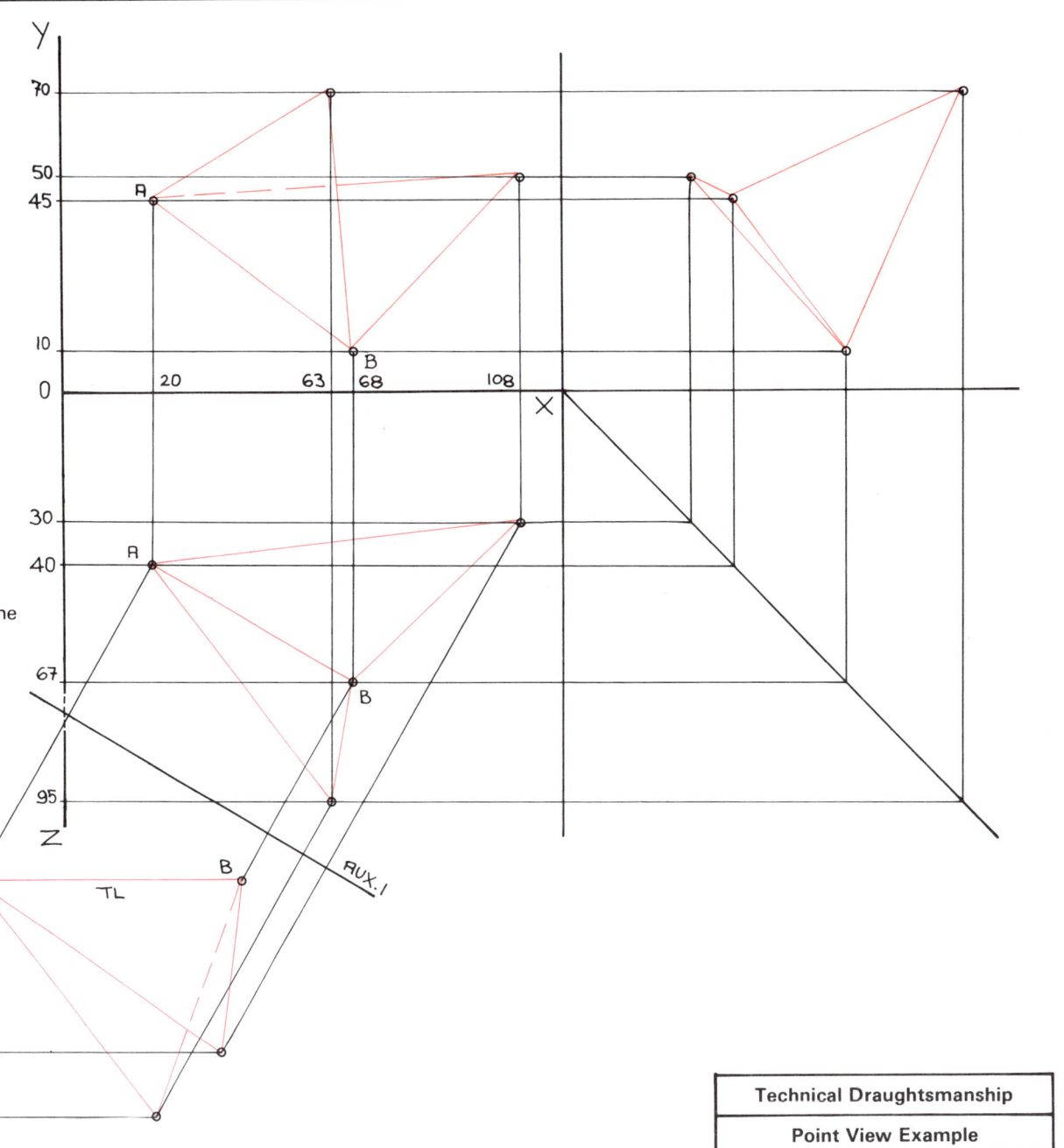

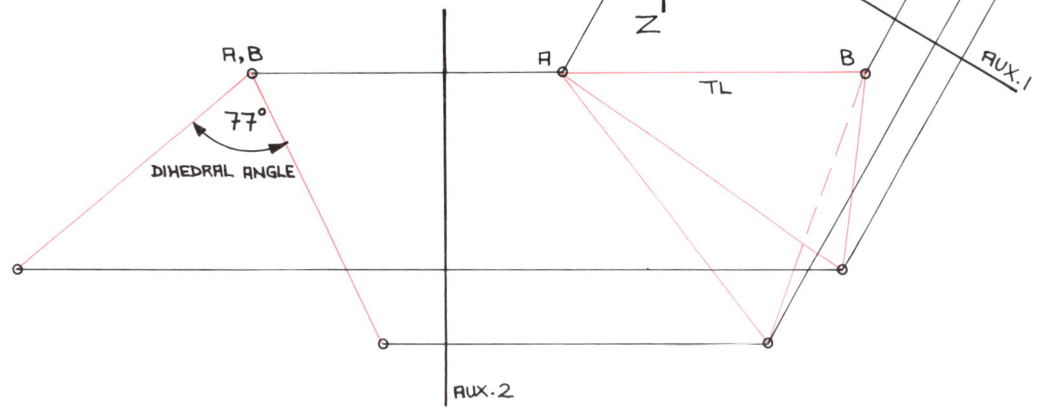

Technical Draughtsmanship
Point View Example
Planes in Space 5 — Part I — Geom. H

101

The Problem
Given the plan and elevation of a roof to find the angle between the roof planes meeting along **AB** (a hip) and along **CD** (a valley).

Note: *The rabatment method will be used.*

Stage 1: To find the dihedral angle along AB.
Procedure
- On the plan, draw a cutting plane **LN** at right angles to **AB**, cutting it at **M**.
- On the elevation, measure the height H_1 between **A** and **B**.
- Transfer this to the plan and lay out the triangle **AA₁B**, where **A₁B** is the true length of **AB**.
- From **M** drop a perpendicular to **A₁B** and, with **M** as centre, swing this back to find **P** as shown.
- Join **L** to **P** to **N**. This is the dihedral angle along **AB**.

Stage 2: To find the dihedral angle along CD.
- This being a valley situation the sectioned triangle will be upside down and the base **GF** will have to be level.
- The section can be taken close up to **C**, but this leaves very little room for drawing. So ...
- On elevation find a point **G** that is on a level with **CE**.
- Project **G** onto the plan and from **G** draw the cutting plane **GF** at right angles to **CD**, extending **CE** to **F**, if necessary.
- Proceed as before to find the dihedral angle.

Note: *For clarity the height H_2 has been set up at **D** rather than at **C**.*

Elevation

Plan

Technical Draughtsmanship
Dihedral by Rabatment
Planes in Space 6 / Part I / Geom.

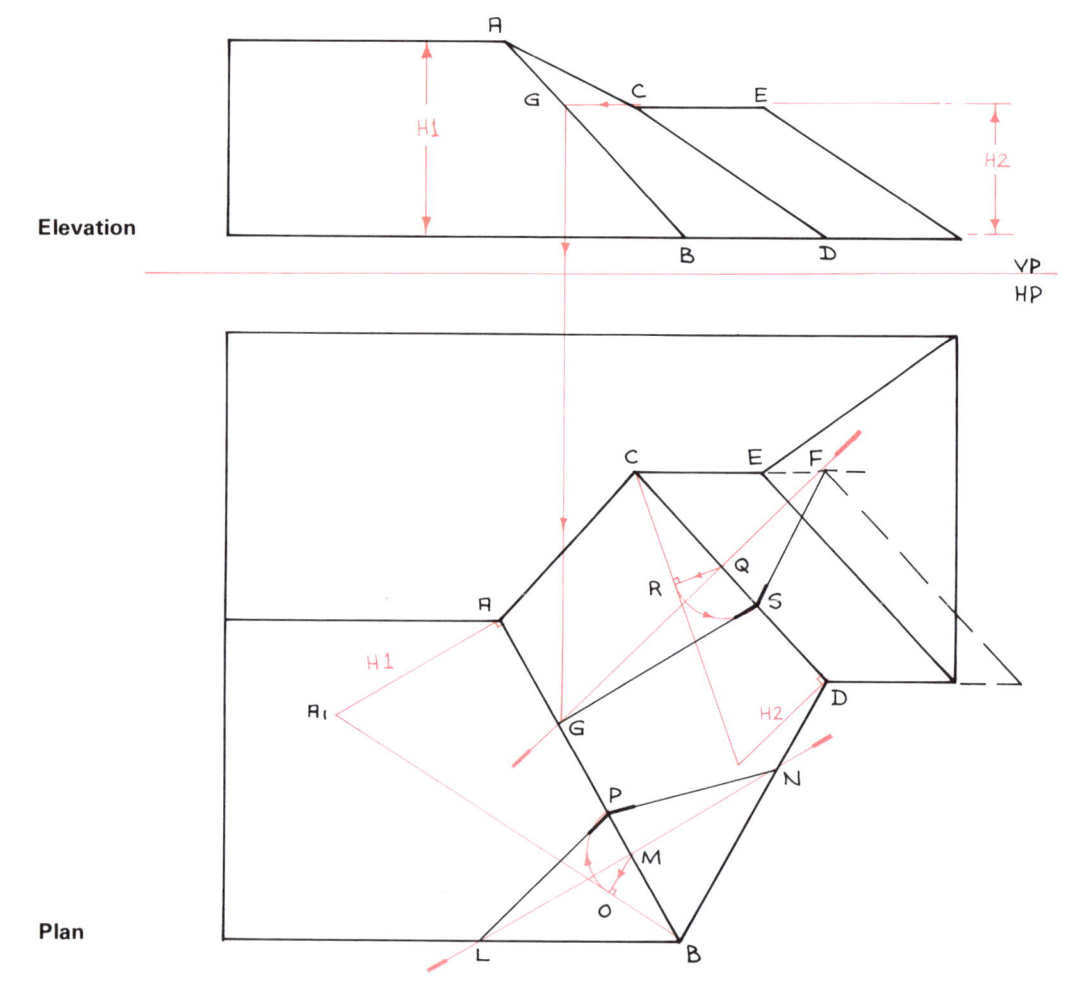

①

	X	Y	Z
A	10	10	22
B	20	35	15
C	45	15	30

	X	Y	Z
A	12	24	36
B	12	24	12
C	48	12	12

	X	Y	Z
A	7.5	72.4	62.3
B	81.6	41.7	9.6
C	49.5	7.2	83.4

	X	Y	Z
A	92	20	44
B	11	20	22
C	31	80	9

② See questions

③

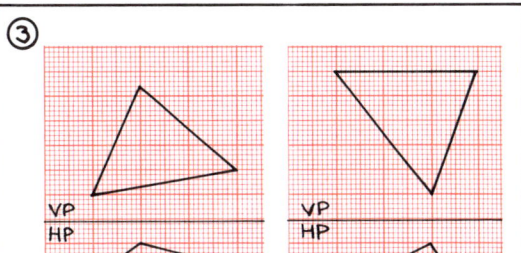

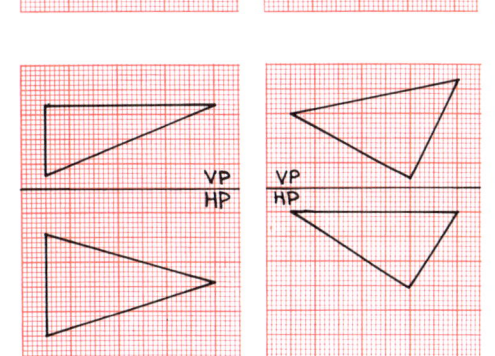

(Orthographic views of four triangular laminae with VP/HP reference lines)

④

	X	Y	Z
A	10	20	5
B	30	30	25
C	36	45	10
D	40	10	10

	X	Y	Z
A	5	30	30
B	25	45	5
C	45	40	30
D	25	10	54

	X	Y	Z
A	0	30	10
B	20	40	15
C	50	5	45
D	25	5	55
E	25	15	40

	X	Y	Z
A	40	25	5
B	40	5	5
C	25	15	20
D	10	5	20
E	10	25	20
F	25	30	5

⑤ See questions

⑥

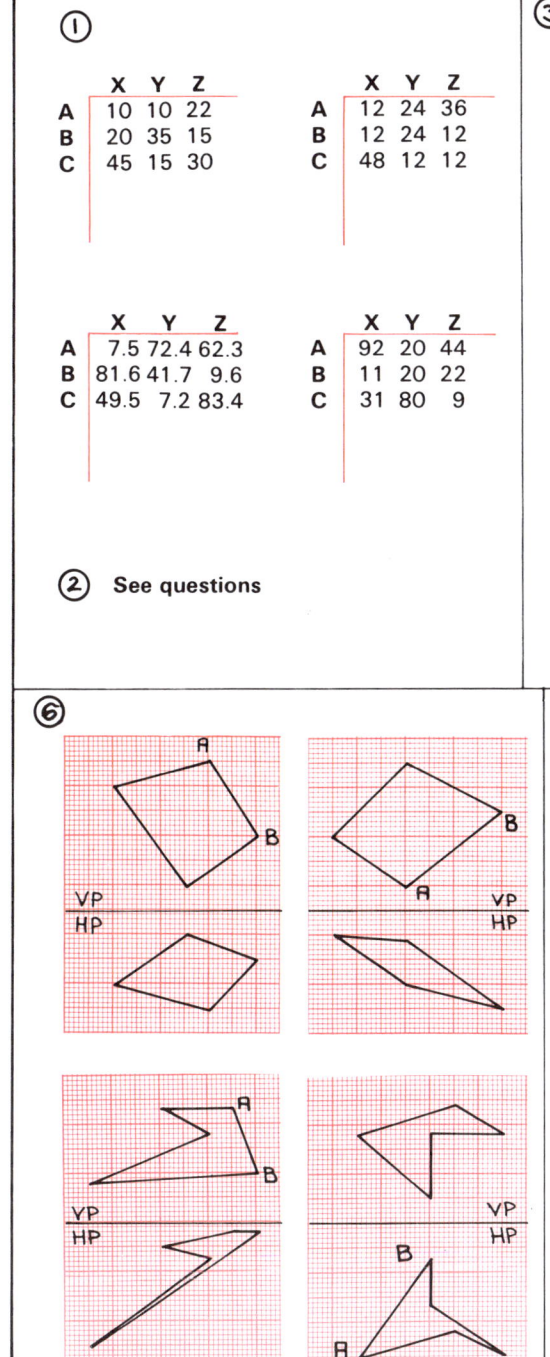

(Orthographic views of quadrilateral and irregular laminae with VP/HP reference lines, points A and B labelled)

⑦

	X	Y	Z
A	15	24	14
B	49	24	27
C	40	3	7
D	5	7	31

	X	Y	Z
A	10	40	42
B	45	27	6
C	49	44	62
D	31	7	6

	X	Y	Z
A	25	40	10
B	25	40	40
C	40	20	10
D	5	20	10

	X	Y	Z
A	5	20	10
B	40	38	10
C	40	38	36
D	16	4	32

⑧ See questions

⑨

	X	Y	Z
A	45	50	45
B	70	5	5
C	20	30	10
D	0	30	5
E	0	30	30

	X	Y	Z
A	30	12	10
B	50	42	10
C	30	0	28
D	50	5	10
E	10	20	10

	X	Y	Z
A	40	10	20
B	40	40	20
C	60	20	5
D	60	35	5
E	5	10	15
F	10	20	10
G	10	40	10

	X	Y	Z
A	60	50	32
B	20	10	50
C	10	20	20
D	50	60	5
E	30	25	20
F	25	45	10
G	45	40	10

All measurements are in millimetres and it is presumed that edges of the lamina follow the alphabetical sequence.

Questions

1. The coordinates of four triangular laminae are given. Draw each in full orthographic projection.

2. Draw each of the laminae in question one, in isometric.

3. Orthographic views of four laminae are given. Project a third view and list the coordinates of each apex.

4. The coordinates of four laminae are given. Draw each lamina in full orthographic projection.

5. Draw each of the laminae in question four, in isometric.

6. Redraw the given views of the laminae. In each case project a third view and calculate the true length of line **AB**.

7. Here are four pairs of triangular laminae. Each pair consists of triangles ABC and ABD, joined along **AB**. Draw each pair in full orthographic projection and determine the true length of line **AB**.

8. Draw each of the laminae in question seven, in isometric.

9. The coordinates of four pairs of laminae are given. Each consists of a triangle ABC joined along **AB** to a second lamina. Draw each pair both in isometric and in orthographic projection, and determine the true length of **AB**.

Technical Draughtsmanship		
Exercises 1		
NTS	Points and Lines	Part 1 Geom.

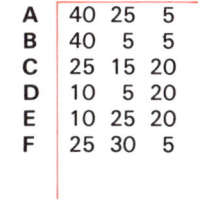

① (diagrams)

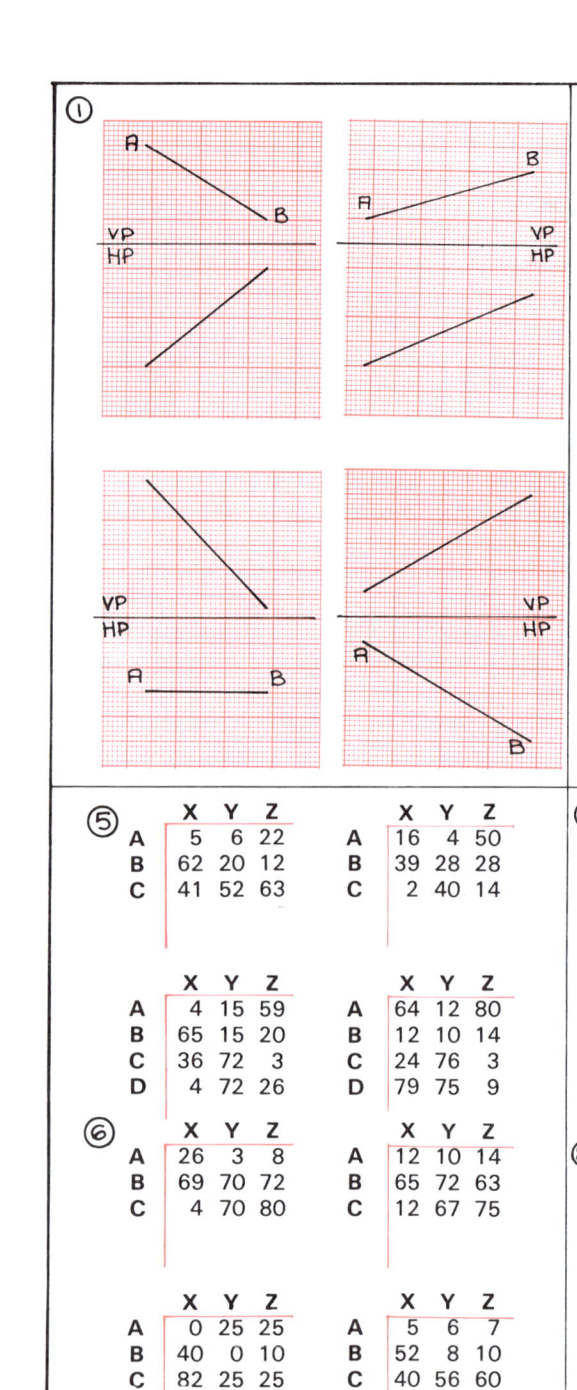

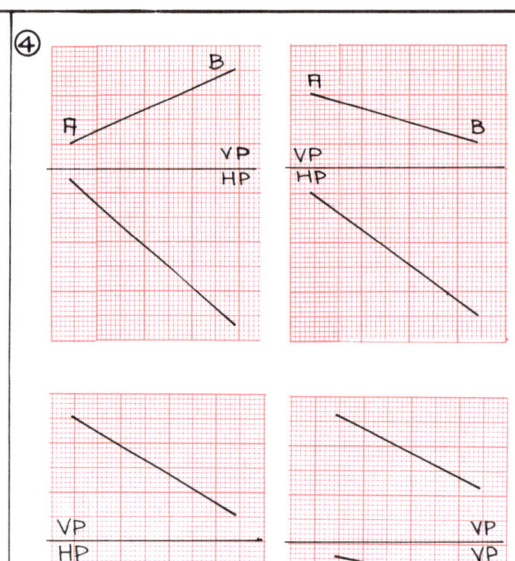

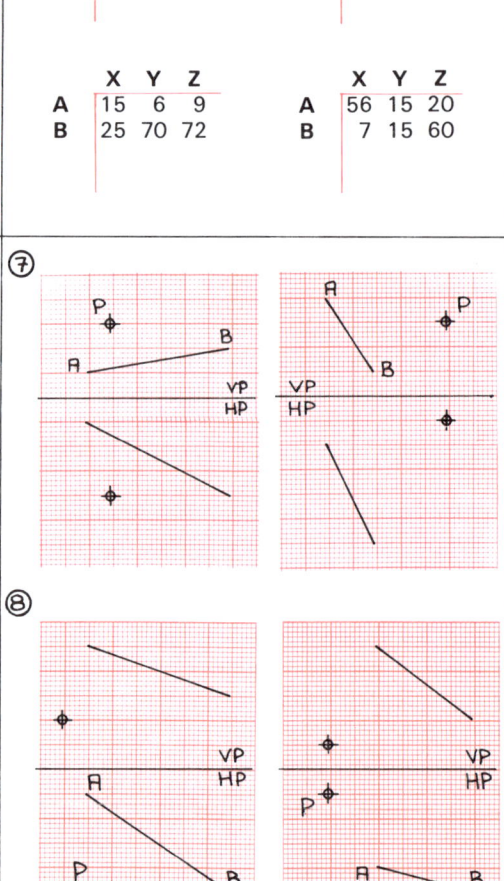

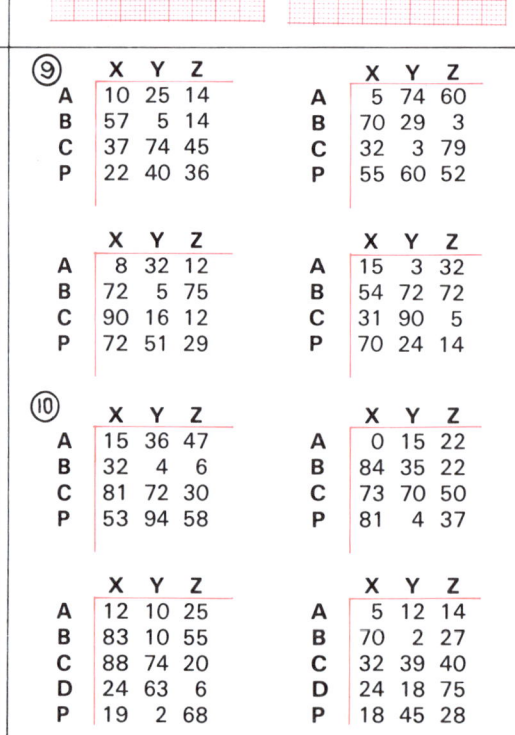

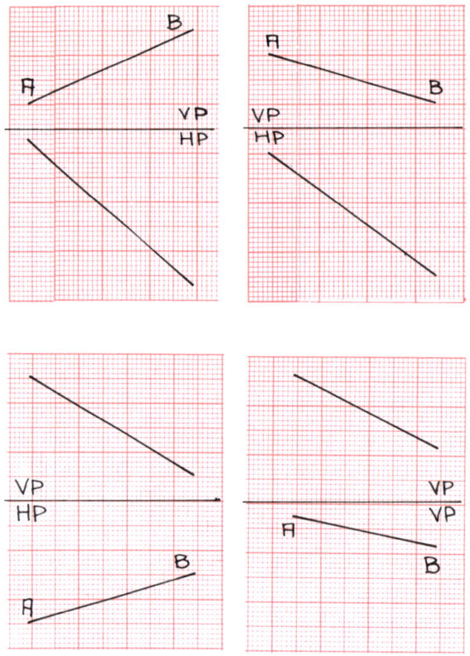

②
	X	Y	Z			X	Y	Z
A	0	24	24		A	12	12	12
B	70	5	5		B	65	40	38

	X	Y	Z			X	Y	Z
A	64	39	8		A	72	6	57
B	8	64	39		B	0	63	2

③
	X	Y	Z			X	Y	Z
A	5	5	5		A	10	60	15
B	42	50	53		B	63	4	75

	X	Y	Z			X	Y	Z
A	15	6	9		A	56	15	20
B	25	70	72		B	7	15	60

④ (diagrams)

All measurements are in millimetres and it is presumed that the edges of the lamina follow the alphabetic sequence.

Questions

1. Find the true length of line **AB** in each of the four examples.

2. Find the true angle with the **HP** of each of the four lines **AB**.

3. Find the true angle with the **VP** of each of the four lines **AB**.

4. Reduce each line **AB** to a point view **A, B**.

5. Find the true angle of each of the four laminae to the **HP**.

6. Project the true shape of each of the four laminae given.

7. Find the shortest distance from point **P** to the given laminae. Use the line method.

8. Measure the shortest distance from point **P** to the line **AB** using the plane method.

9. Show the shortest distance from point **P** to the plane **ABC** for each of the four examples.

10. Draw the true shape of each of the four laminae and also find the shortest distance from point **P** to the given laminae.

⑤
	X	Y	Z			X	Y	Z
A	5	6	22		A	16	4	50
B	62	20	12		B	39	28	28
C	41	52	63		C	2	40	14

	X	Y	Z			X	Y	Z
A	4	15	59		A	64	12	80
B	65	15	20		B	12	10	14
C	36	72	3		C	24	76	3
D	4	72	26		D	79	75	9

⑥
	X	Y	Z			X	Y	Z
A	26	3	8		A	12	10	14
B	69	70	72		B	65	72	63
C	4	70	80		C	12	67	75

	X	Y	Z			X	Y	Z
A	0	25	25		A	5	6	7
B	40	0	10		B	52	8	10
C	82	25	25		C	40	56	60
D	40	40	40		D	0	45	72

⑦ (diagrams)

⑧ (diagrams)

⑨
	X	Y	Z			X	Y	Z
A	10	25	14		A	5	74	60
B	57	5	14		B	70	29	3
C	37	74	45		C	32	3	79
P	22	40	36		P	55	60	52

	X	Y	Z			X	Y	Z
A	8	32	12		A	15	3	32
B	72	5	75		B	54	72	72
C	90	16	12		C	31	90	5
P	72	51	29		P	70	24	14

⑩
	X	Y	Z			X	Y	Z
A	15	36	47		A	0	15	22
B	32	4	6		B	84	35	22
C	81	72	30		C	73	70	50
P	53	94	58		P	81	4	37

	X	Y	Z			X	Y	Z
A	12	10	25		A	5	12	14
B	83	10	55		B	70	2	27
C	88	74	20		C	32	39	40
D	24	63	6		D	24	18	75
P	19	2	68		P	18	45	28

Technical Draughtsmanship		
Exercises 2		
NTS	Lines in Space	Part I Geom.

104

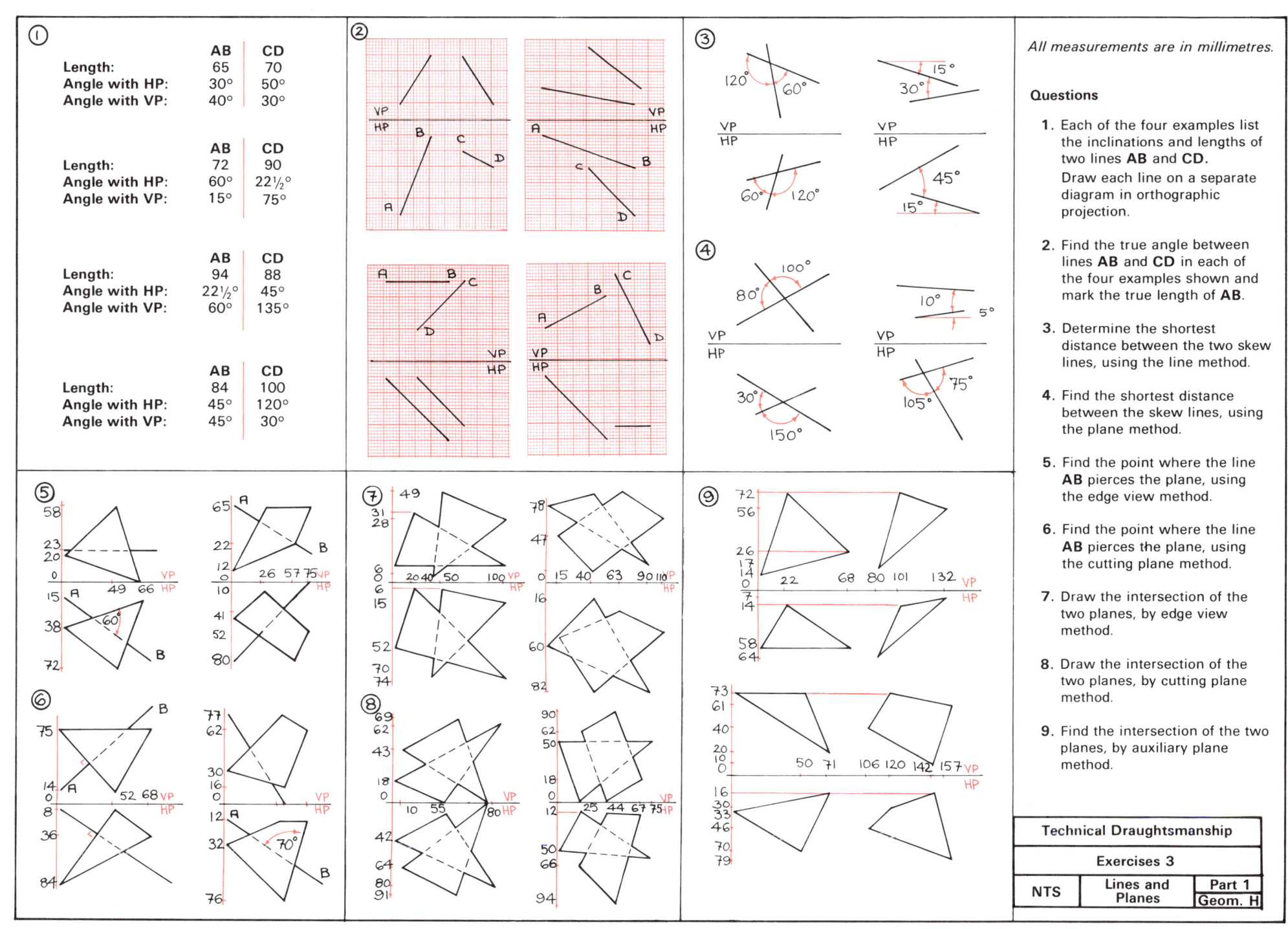

①
	AB	CD
Length:	65	70
Angle with HP:	30°	50°
Angle with VP:	40°	30°

	AB	CD
Length:	72	90
Angle with HP:	60°	22½°
Angle with VP:	15°	75°

	AB	CD
Length:	94	88
Angle with HP:	22½°	45°
Angle with VP:	60°	135°

	AB	CD
Length:	84	100
Angle with HP:	45°	120°
Angle with VP:	45°	30°

All measurements are in millimetres.

Questions

1. Each of the four examples list the inclinations and lengths of two lines **AB** and **CD**. Draw each line on a separate diagram in orthographic projection.

2. Find the true angle between lines **AB** and **CD** in each of the four examples shown and mark the true length of **AB**.

3. Determine the shortest distance between the two skew lines, using the line method.

4. Find the shortest distance between the skew lines, using the plane method.

5. Find the point where the line **AB** pierces the plane, using the edge view method.

6. Find the point where the line **AB** pierces the plane, using the cutting plane method.

7. Draw the intersection of the two planes, by edge view method.

8. Draw the intersection of the two planes, by cutting plane method.

9. Find the intersection of the two planes, by auxiliary plane method.

Technical Draughtsmanship

Exercises 3

NTS | Lines and Planes | Part 1 Geom. H

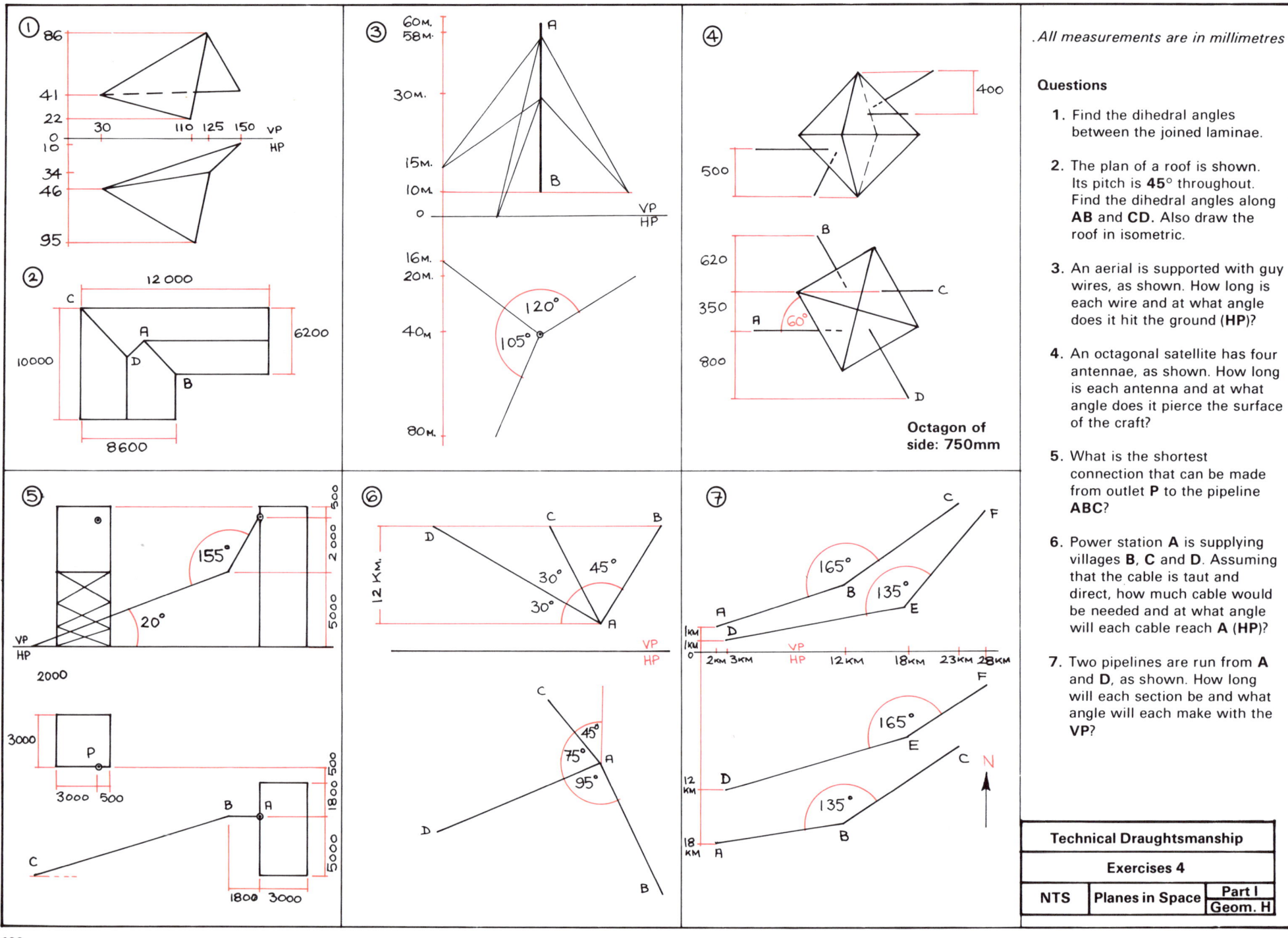

All measurements are in millimetres

Questions

1. Find the dihedral angles between the joined laminae.

2. The plan of a roof is shown. Its pitch is **45°** throughout. Find the dihedral angles along **AB** and **CD**. Also draw the roof in isometric.

3. An aerial is supported with guy wires, as shown. How long is each wire and at what angle does it hit the ground (**HP**)?

4. An octagonal satellite has four antennae, as shown. How long is each antenna and at what angle does it pierce the surface of the craft?

5. What is the shortest connection that can be made from outlet **P** to the pipeline **ABC**?

6. Power station **A** is supplying villages **B**, **C** and **D**. Assuming that the cable is taut and direct, how much cable would be needed and at what angle will each cable reach **A** (**HP**)?

7. Two pipelines are run from **A** and **D**, as shown. How long will each section be and what angle will each make with the **VP**?

Technical Draughtsmanship		
Exercises 4		
NTS	Planes in Space	Part I / Geom. H

106

PART I

CHAPTER 9
THE OBLIQUE PLANE

Not all surfaces are conveniently horizontal or vertical. Some are inclined to one or other plane. Others are at an angle to *both* planes and lie on an oblique plane. It is much simpler to treat these surfaces as oblique planes in space than to try and deal with them on the standard views. Oblique planes are very often used in mining, navigating, and computer graphics.

CONTENTS

Trace of planes	*Page* **108**
Drawing traces, given angles	**109**
Points, lines and laminae	**110**
Traces from a given figure	**111**
Converting the oblique plane	**112**
Sample problem 1	**113**
True shape of laminae	**114**
Sample problem 2	**115**
Dihedral and changing planes	**116**
Sample problem 3	**117**
Exercises	**118**

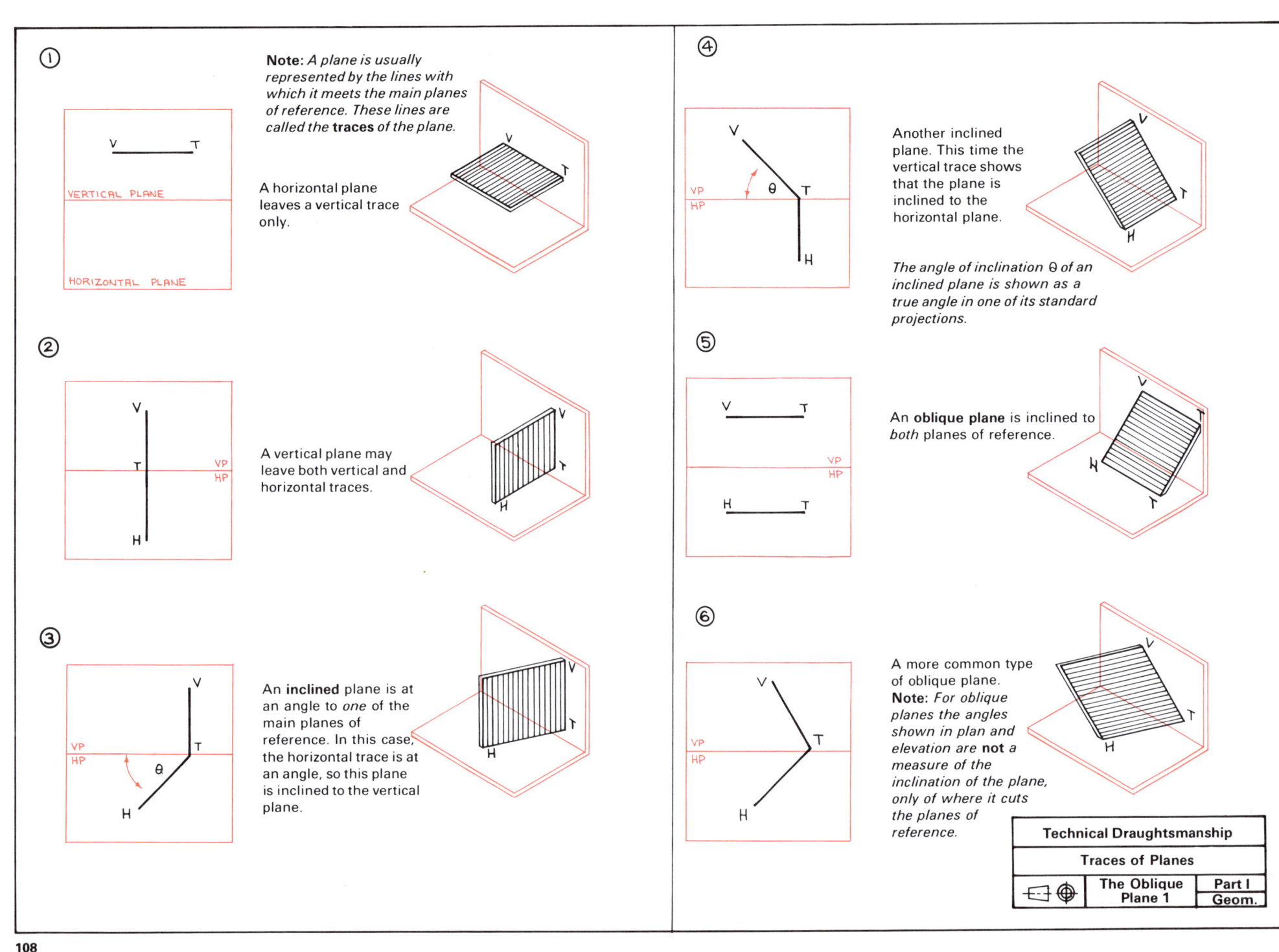

① **Note:** *A plane is usually represented by the lines with which it meets the main planes of reference. These lines are called the* **traces** *of the plane.*

A horizontal plane leaves a vertical trace only.

② A vertical plane may leave both vertical and horizontal traces.

③ An **inclined** plane is at an angle to *one* of the main planes of reference. In this case, the horizontal trace is at an angle, so this plane is inclined to the vertical plane.

④ Another inclined plane. This time the vertical trace shows that the plane is inclined to the horizontal plane.

The angle of inclination θ of an inclined plane is shown as a true angle in one of its standard projections.

⑤ An **oblique plane** is inclined to *both* planes of reference.

⑥ A more common type of oblique plane.
Note: *For oblique planes the angles shown in plan and elevation are* **not** *a measure of the inclination of the plane, only of where it cuts the planes of reference.*

| Technical Draughtsmanship |
| Traces of Planes |
| The Oblique Plane 1 | Part I Geom. |

① **Given the traces to find the true angle with the horizontal plane.**
- Draw a cutting plane **LN** cutting the main axis at **M**.
- From **M** drop a perpendicular to meet **TH** at **P**.
- With centre **M** swing **P** onto the axis at **Q**.
- Join **L** to **Q** to get the required angle α.

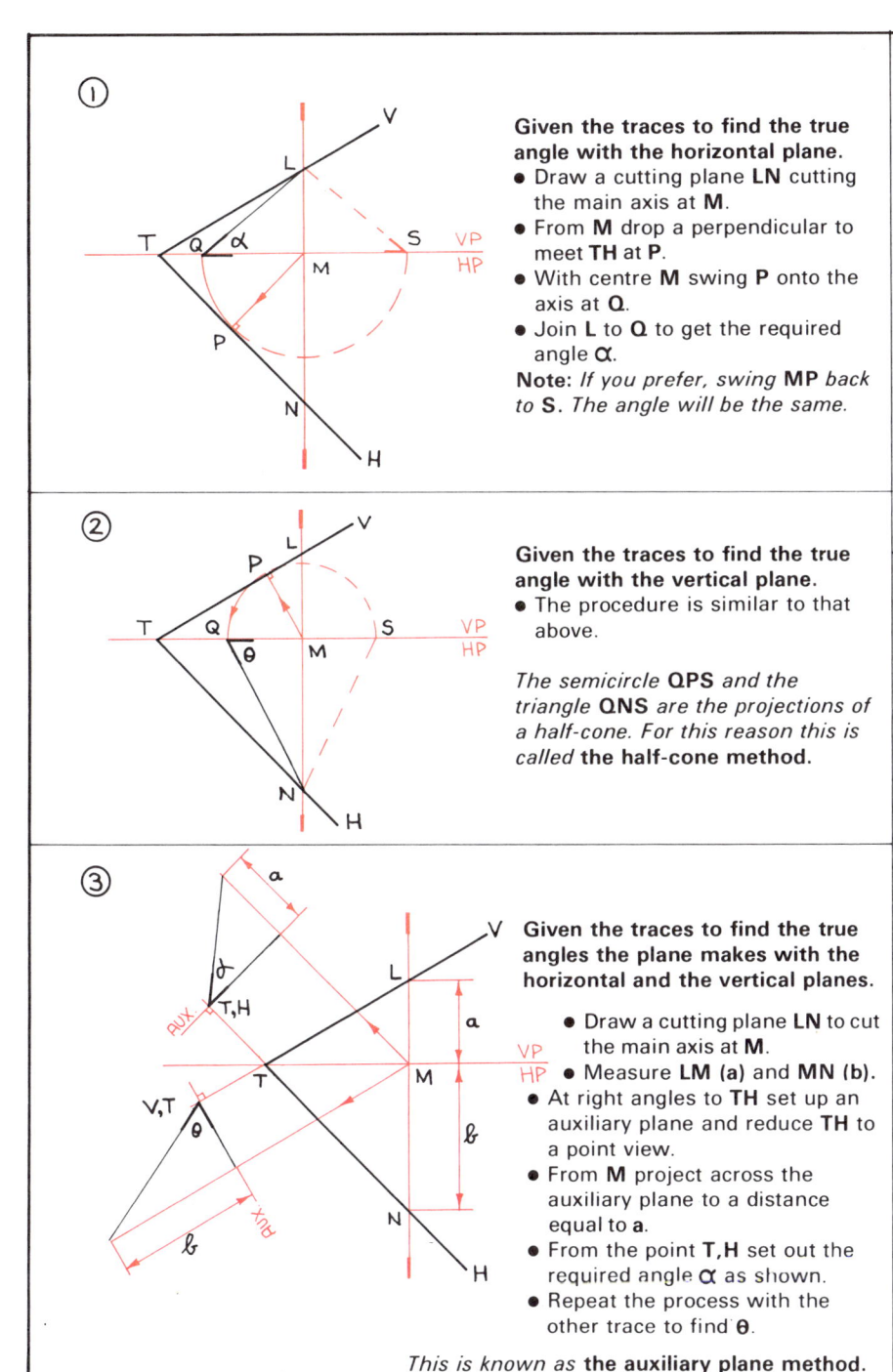

Note: *If you prefer, swing **MP** back to **S**. The angle will be the same.*

② **Given the traces to find the true angle with the vertical plane.**
- The procedure is similar to that above.

*The semicircle **QPS** and the triangle **QNS** are the projections of a half-cone. For this reason this is called **the half-cone method**.*

③ **Given the traces to find the true angles the plane makes with the horizontal and the vertical planes.**
- Draw a cutting plane **LN** to cut the main axis at **M**.
- Measure **LM** (a) and **MN** (b).
- At right angles to **TH** set up an auxiliary plane and reduce **TH** to a point view.
- From **M** project across the auxiliary plane to a distance equal to **a**.
- From the point **T,H** set out the required angle α as shown.
- Repeat the process with the other trace to find θ.

*This is known as **the auxiliary plane method**.*

④ **To draw the traces of a plane that makes an angle of 60° with the HP and of 45° with the VP.**

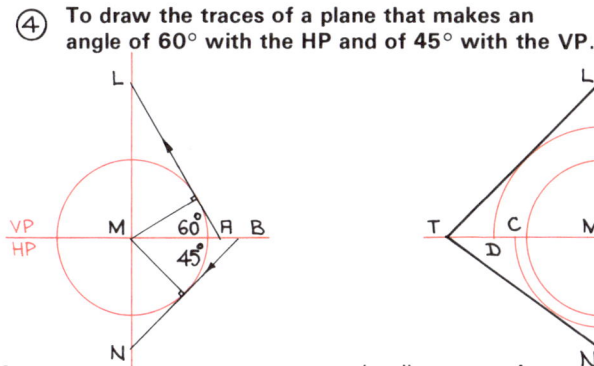

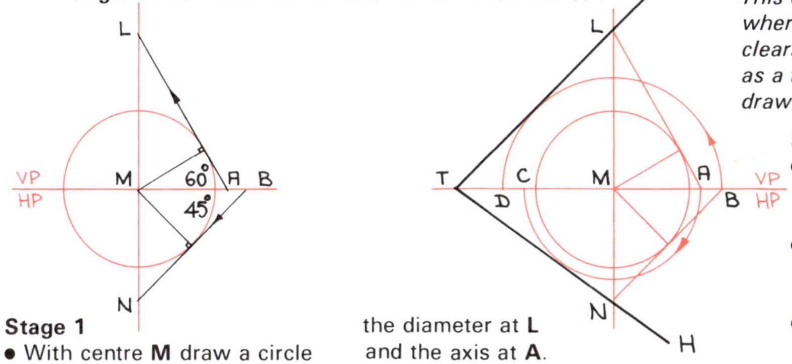

Stage 1
- With centre **M** draw a circle of any radius and extend the vertical diameter.
- Construct a tangent to the circle at 60° to the **HP** to cut the diameter at **L** and the axis at **A**.
- On plan construct a tangent to the circle at 45° to the **VP**, cutting the diameter at **N** and the axis at **B**.

The half-cone method
*This does not work where the semicircle clears the apex (**L** or **N**), as a tangent cannot be drawn.*

Stage 2
- With centre **M** and radius **MA** draw a semicircle **AC**.
- From **N** draw a tangent to this semicircle. This is the trace **HT**.
- With centre **M** and radius **MB** draw the semicircle **BD**.
- From **L** draw the tangent trace **VT**.

⑤ **To draw the trace of a plane that makes an angle of 50° with the HP.**

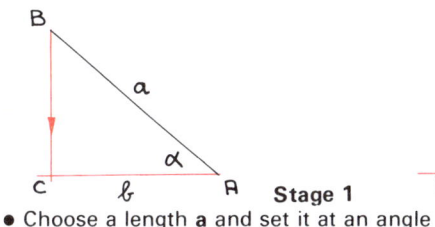

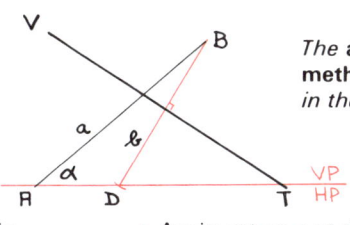

*The **auxiliary plane method** is used in this and in the following example.*

Stage 1
- Choose a length **a** and set it at an angle α equal to 90° – the trace angle, here 90° – 50° = 40°.
- Drop a perpendicular from **B** to mark off a distance **AC**.

Stage 2
- Again set up **a** at the same angle (40°).
- With **B** as centre and radius **AC**, from stage 1, swing an arc to find **D** on the axis.
- Draw the trace **VT** at right angles to **BD** and wherever along it you wish.

⑥ **To draw the trace of a plane that makes an angle of 60° with the VP.**

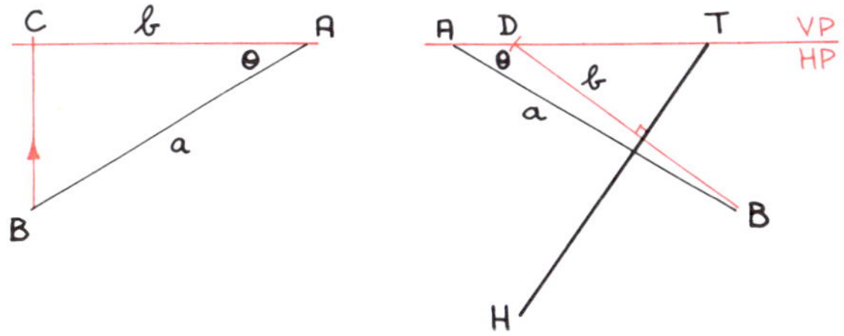

- The procedure is similar to that above, only applied below the axis.

Note: *The point **T** is often given, or else another point **P** through which the trace is required to pass. This should not prove to be a problem.*

Technical Draughtsmanship
Drawing traces, given Angles
The Oblique Plane 2 — Part 1 — Geom.

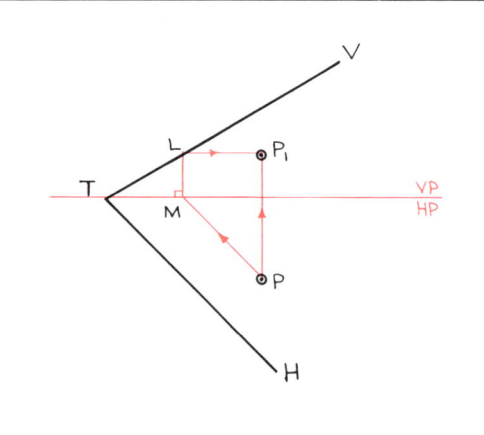

Given the plan of a point P in an oblique plane to find its elevation.

- Parallel to TH draw a line from P to meet the axis at M.
- At M erect a perpendicular to meet the trace VT at L.
- From L project parallel to the main axis towards P_1.
- From P project across the axis to fix P_1 which is the point on elevation.

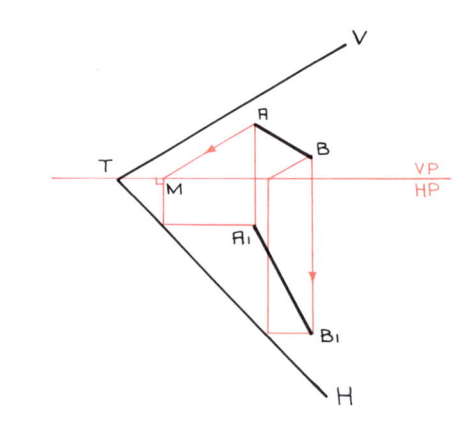

Given the elevation of a line AB in an oblique plane to find its plan.

Note: Here AB is not parallel to the trace VT.

- Each point is taken across and fixed separately, then joined to draw the required plan A_1B_1, as shown.

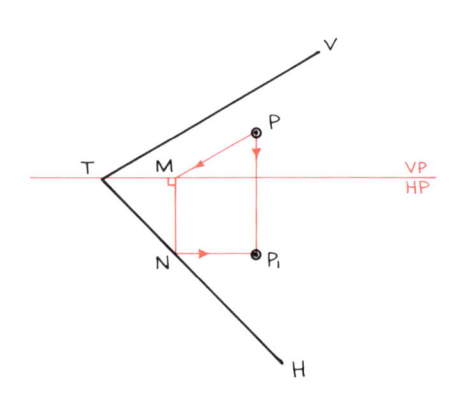

Given the elevation of a point P in an oblique plane to find its plan.
The procedure is similar to that above.

- From P project parallel to the trace VT to meet the main axis at M.
- From M drop a perpendicular to N and then project across towards P_1.
- From P drop a perpendicular to fix P_1, the required point.

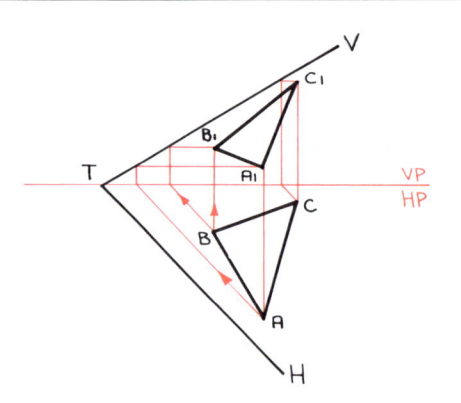

Given the plan of a lamina ABC in an oblique plane to find its elevation.

- Take each point across.
- Then fix and index each separately.
- Join the points to draw the required elevation $A_1B_1C_1$.

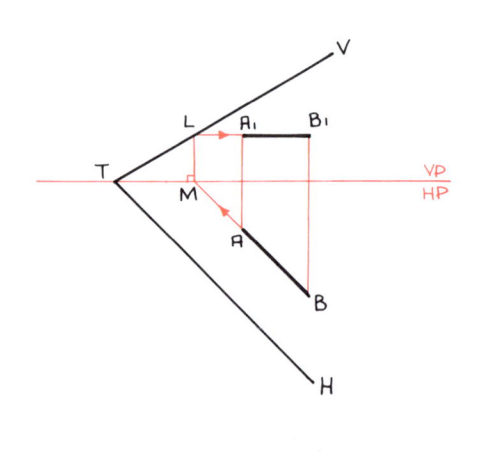

Given the plan of a line AB in an oblique plane to find its elevation.

Note: Here AB is taken as parallel to the trace HT, which makes things easier.

- Extend AB to M.
- Erect a perpendicular at M to meet the trace VT at L.
- From L project across towards A_1B_1.
- Project up from A and B to fix A_1 and B_1.
- A_1B_1 is the required elevation.

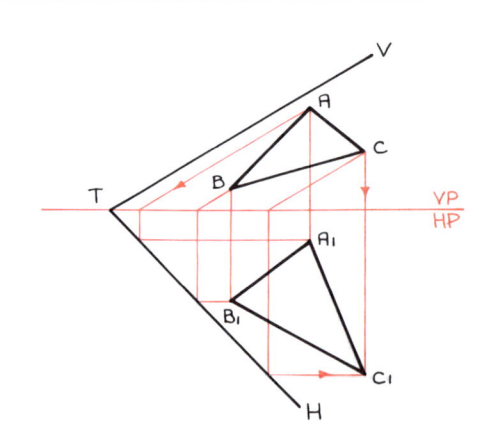

Given the elevation of a lamina ABC in an oblique plane to find its plan.

- The method is similar to that used above.

Technical Draughtsmanship	
Points, Lines and Laminae	
The Oblique Plane 3	Part I
	Geom.

Given the projections of a lamina ABC to find the traces of the plane that contains that lamina.

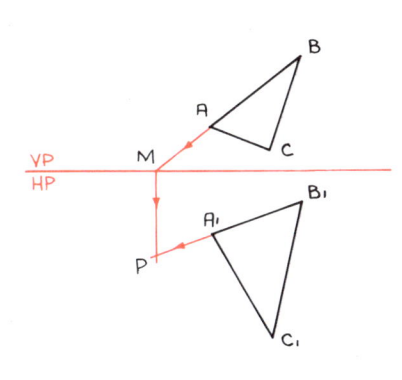

①

Stage 1
- Draw the lamina in position.
- On the elevation take one side **AB** and extend it to meet the main axis at **M**.
- On the plan extend the same side **AB** in a similar direction, towards **P**.
- From **M** drop a perpendicular to fix the position of point **P**.
- This point lies on a trace.

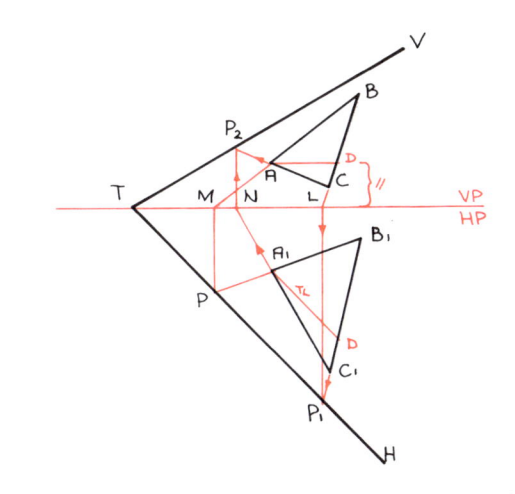

Stage 2
- Take a second side **BC** and by performing the same operation as before find point P_1 on a trace.
- Draw a line through P_1 and **P** to meet the main axis at **T**. This is one trace.
- Take the third side **AC** on plan and extending up find **N** and then the point P_2 on a trace.
- Join **T** through P_2 to complete the traces **VTH**.
- As **AD** is horizontal and is in true length on the plan, it will be parallel to **TH**. This method can be used to find **TH**.

②

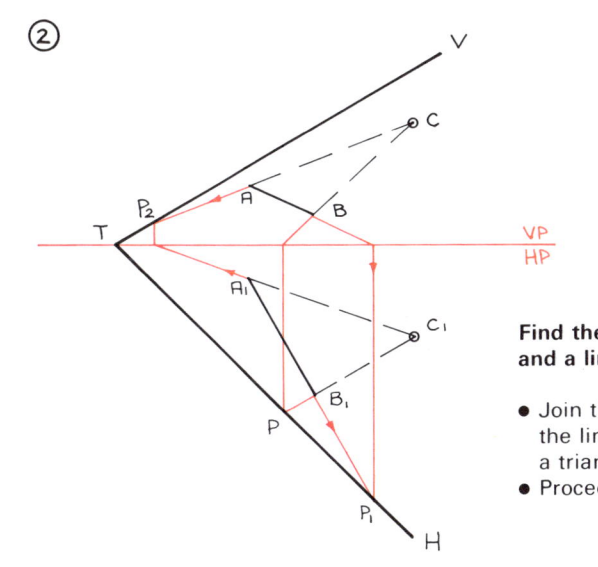

Find the traces given a point **C** and a line **AB** in the plane.

- Join the point **C** to the ends of the line at **A** and **B**, thus making a triangular lamina.
- Proceed as above.

③

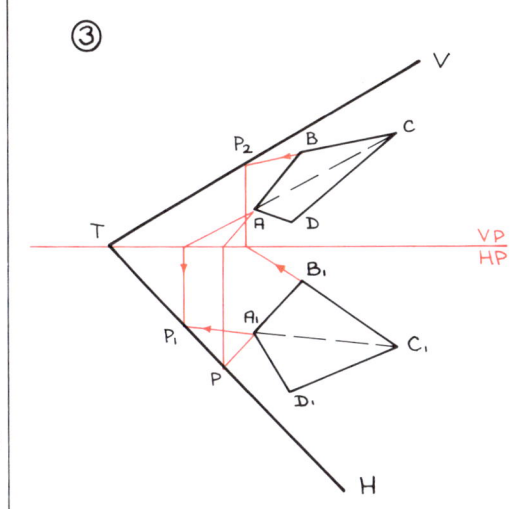

Find the traces given a figure of more than three points ABCD that lies in the oblique plane.

- Take any three points **A**, **B** and **C** on the figure and join them to form a triangular lamina.
- Proceed as before.

Technical Draughtsmanship
Traces from a Given Figure
The Oblique Plane 4	Part I Geom. H

111

①

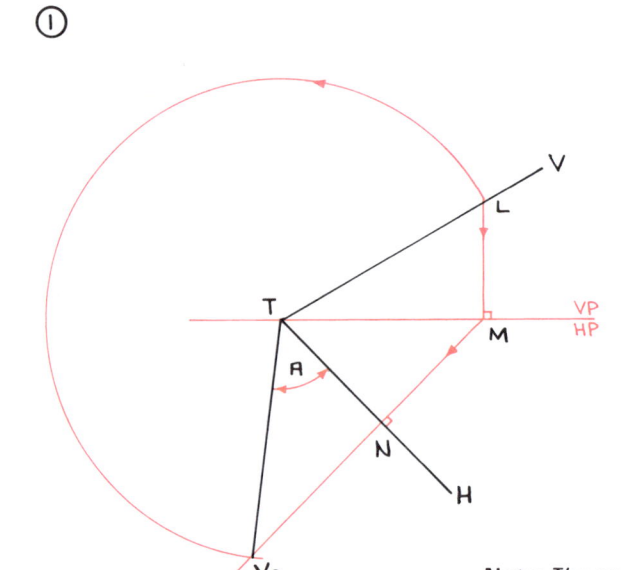

To rabat the oblique plane
i.e. to lay it out horizontally.
- Take any point **L** on **VTH**.
- Drop onto the axis at **M** and then across the other trace **TH** at right angles (**N**) and extend this line towards **V₂**.
- With centre **T** and radius **TL** swing an arc to cut **MN** at **V₂**.
- Join **T** to **V₂**.
- **V₂TH** is the rabatted plane and is now lying on the horizontal plane.

*Note: The angle **A** is the true angle between the traces of the plane.*

②

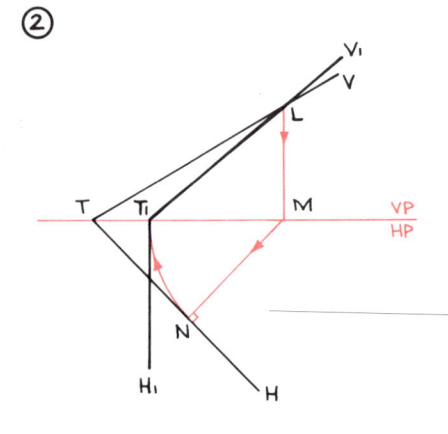

To convert an oblique to an inclined plane
- Choose a point **L** on **VTH**.
- Drop onto the axis **M** and then across to the **TH** trace at right angles (**N**).
- With **M** as centre swing **MN** onto the axis to find **T**.
- Joint **T₁** to **L** and extend. Then set out **T₁H₁** at right angles to the vertical plane.
- **V₁T₁H₁** is an inclined plane derived from the original oblique plane.

Note:
*This is a variation on the rabatment above. It may make things clearer if you imagine yourself pushing **MNH** around until it sticks out at right angles.*

Note: This construction is useful because an inclined plane is much easier to manipulate than an oblique plane.

③

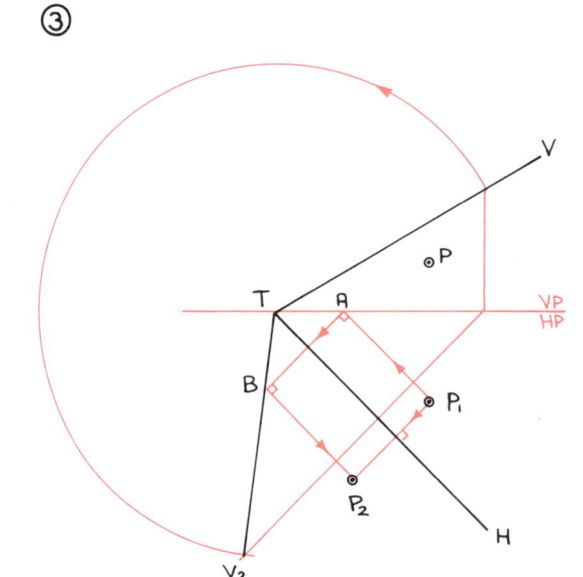

To rabat a point on the oblique plane
Given **VTH** with **P** and **P₁** the projections of a point in the oblique plane.
- Proceed as before and rabat **VTH** to find **V₂TH**.
- Take **P₁** and project it off the axis at **A** and off the **V₂T** trace at **B**, as shown.
- From **P₁** project across the **TH** trace at right angles to meet the previous projection line at **P₂**.
- This is the position of the point on the now horizontal plane.

Note: This construction will later be used to find the true shape of laminae in the plane.

④

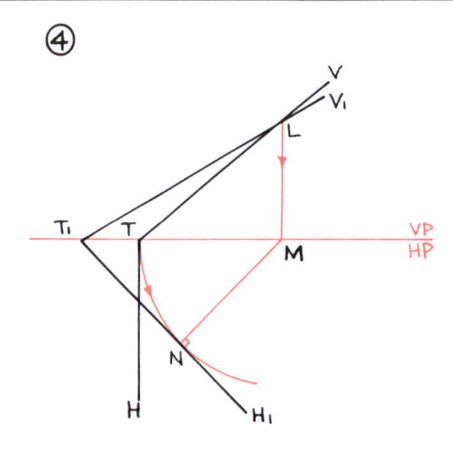

To convert an inclined to an oblique plane
The inclined plane **VTH** is given as is the point **T₁**.
- Choose a point **L** on **VTH** and drop a perpendicular to **M**.
- With **M** as centre and radius **MT** swing an arc.
- Construct a tangent from **T₁** to the arc (**TNH**).
- Join **T₁** to **L** and extend.
- **V₁T₁H₁** is the required oblique plane.

*Note: If **T₁** is not given it may be set anywhere along the axis that will allow a tangent to be drawn to the arc.*

Technical Draughtsmanship
Converting the Oblique Plane
The Oblique Plane 5 — Part I Geom.

112

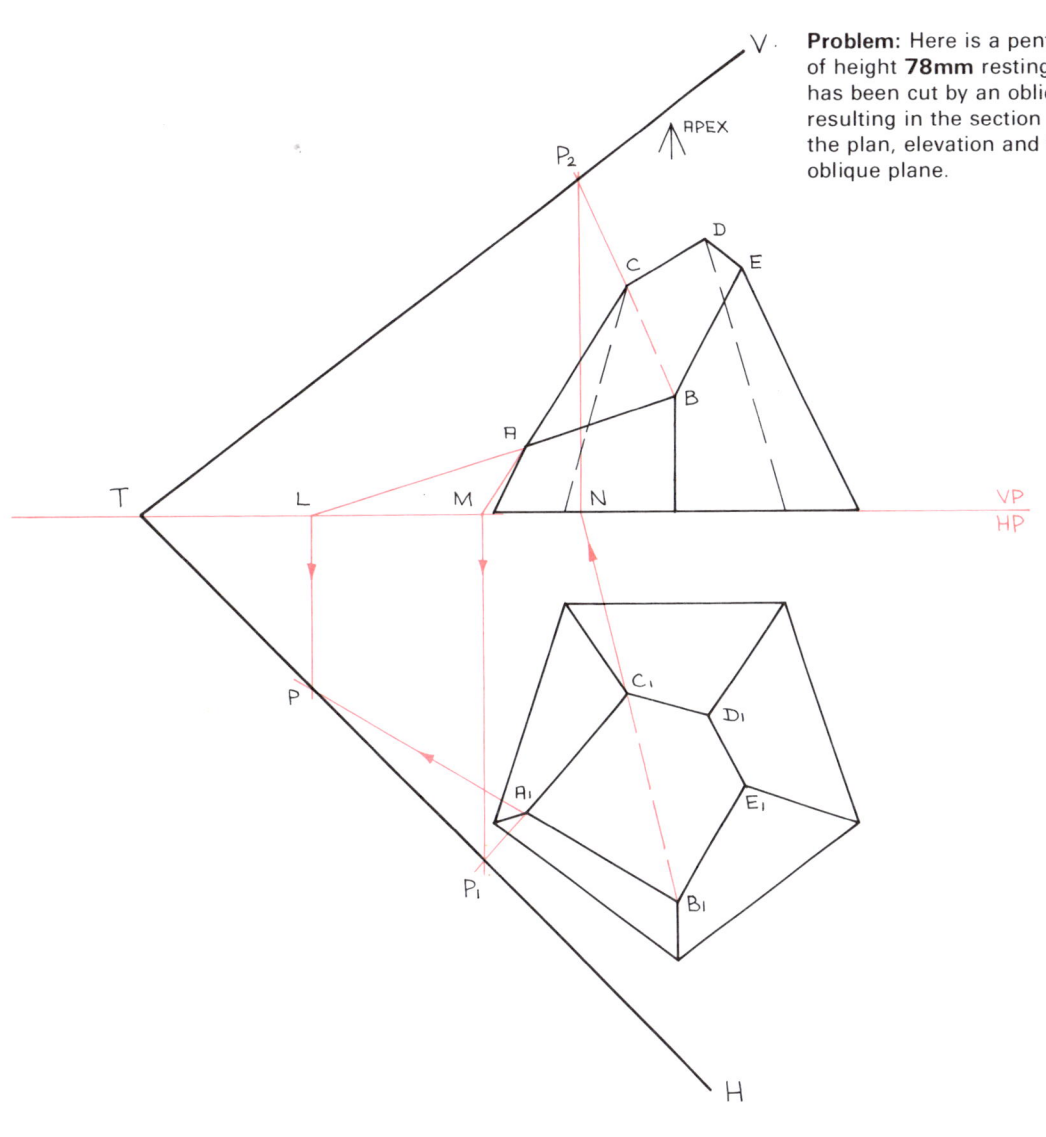

Problem: Here is a pentagonal pyramid of height **78mm** resting on the **HP**. It has been cut by an oblique plane resulting in the section shown. Draw the plan, elevation and the trace of the oblique plane.

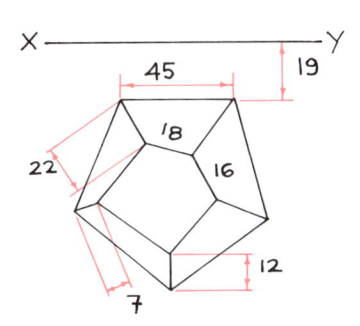

Procedure:
- Draw the plan and project the elevation of the complete pyramid.
- On plan plot the section and project it up onto the elevation.
- Choose three points **A**, **B** and **C** of the section. Join them to form a triangular lamina on the oblique plane.
- Given the lamina now proceed, as on page **110**, to locate the traces of the oblique plane **VTH** as shown.

Note: *A second part of this problem is shown on page 115.*

Technical Draughtsmanship		
Sample Problem 1		
The Oblique Plane 6	Part I	Geom. H

① To find the shape of a lamina in an oblique plane by rabatment.

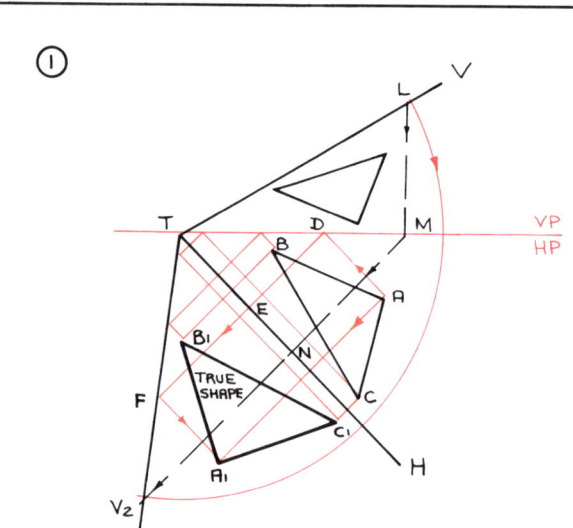

◀ **Method 1** (diagram on left):
- Rabat the oblique plane as on page **112**.
- Take point **A** and project it parallel to **TH** to meet the axis at **D**.
- Project **D** across **TH** at right angles to meet **TV₂** at **F** and finally parallel to **TH** towards **A₁**.
- From **A** project straight across **TH** at right angles to fix **A₁**.
- Locate **B₁** and **C₁** in a similar way.
- Join **A₁** to **B₁** to **C₁** to show the true shape of the lamina.

▶ **Method 2** (diagram on right):
- Rabat the oblique plane as on page **112**.
- Take point **A** and project it parallel to the axis onto trace **VT** at **D**.
- With centre **T** and radius **TD** swing **D** around to meet trace **TV₁** at **E**.
- Finally project **E** parallel to **TH** towards **A₂**.
- From **A₁** project straight across **TH** at right angles to fix **A₂**.
- Similarly locate **B₂** and **C₂** and draw the true shape.

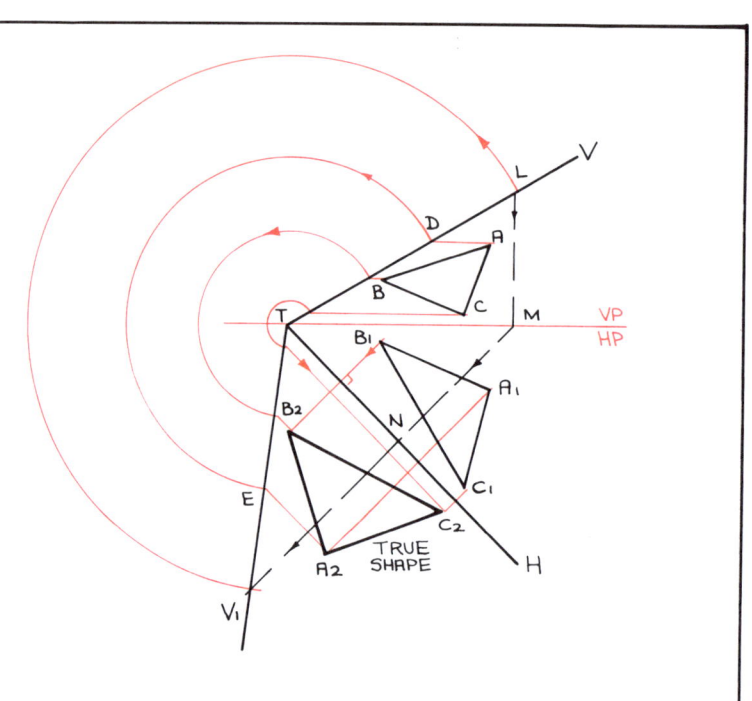

② To find the true shape of a lamina in an oblique plane by auxiliary projection.

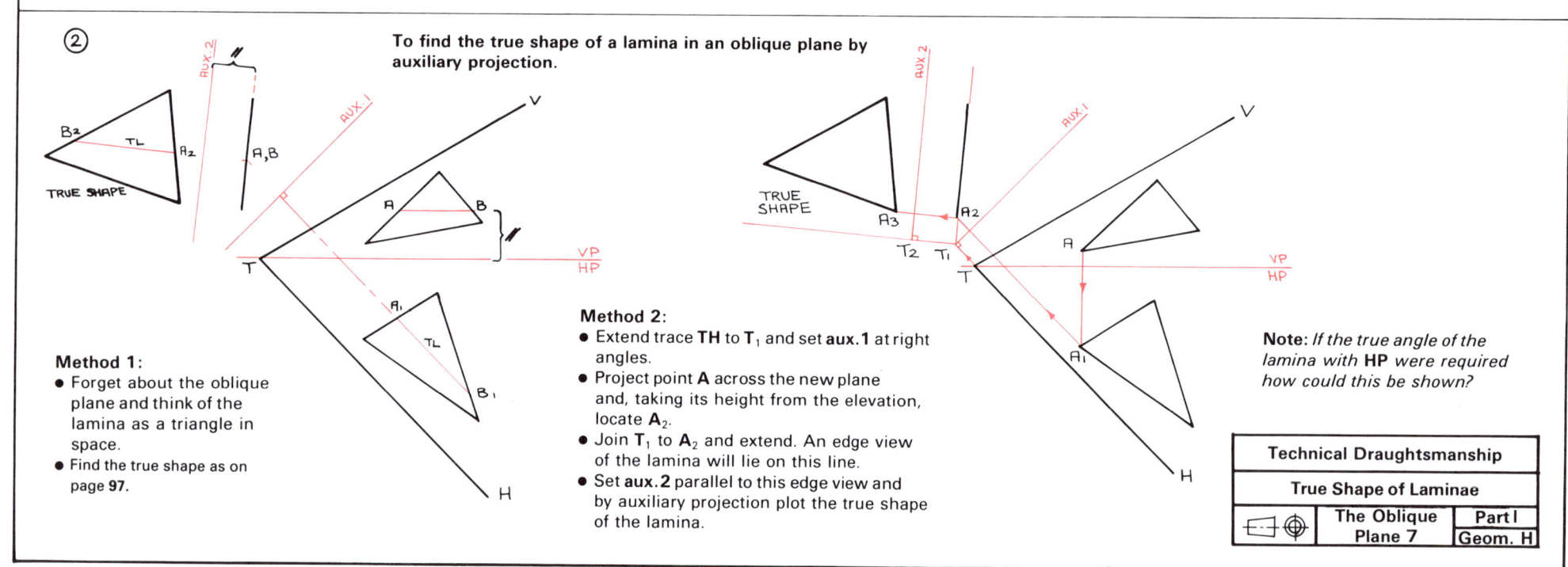

Method 1:
- Forget about the oblique plane and think of the lamina as a triangle in space.
- Find the true shape as on page **97**.

Method 2:
- Extend trace **TH** to **T₁** and set **aux.1** at right angles.
- Project point **A** across the new plane and, taking its height from the elevation, locate **A₂**.
- Join **T₁** to **A₂** and extend. An edge view of the lamina will lie on this line.
- Set **aux.2** parallel to this edge view and by auxiliary projection plot the true shape of the lamina.

*Note: If the true angle of the lamina with **HP** were required how could this be shown?*

Technical Draughtsmanship
True Shape of Laminae
The Oblique Plane 7 — Part I — Geom. H

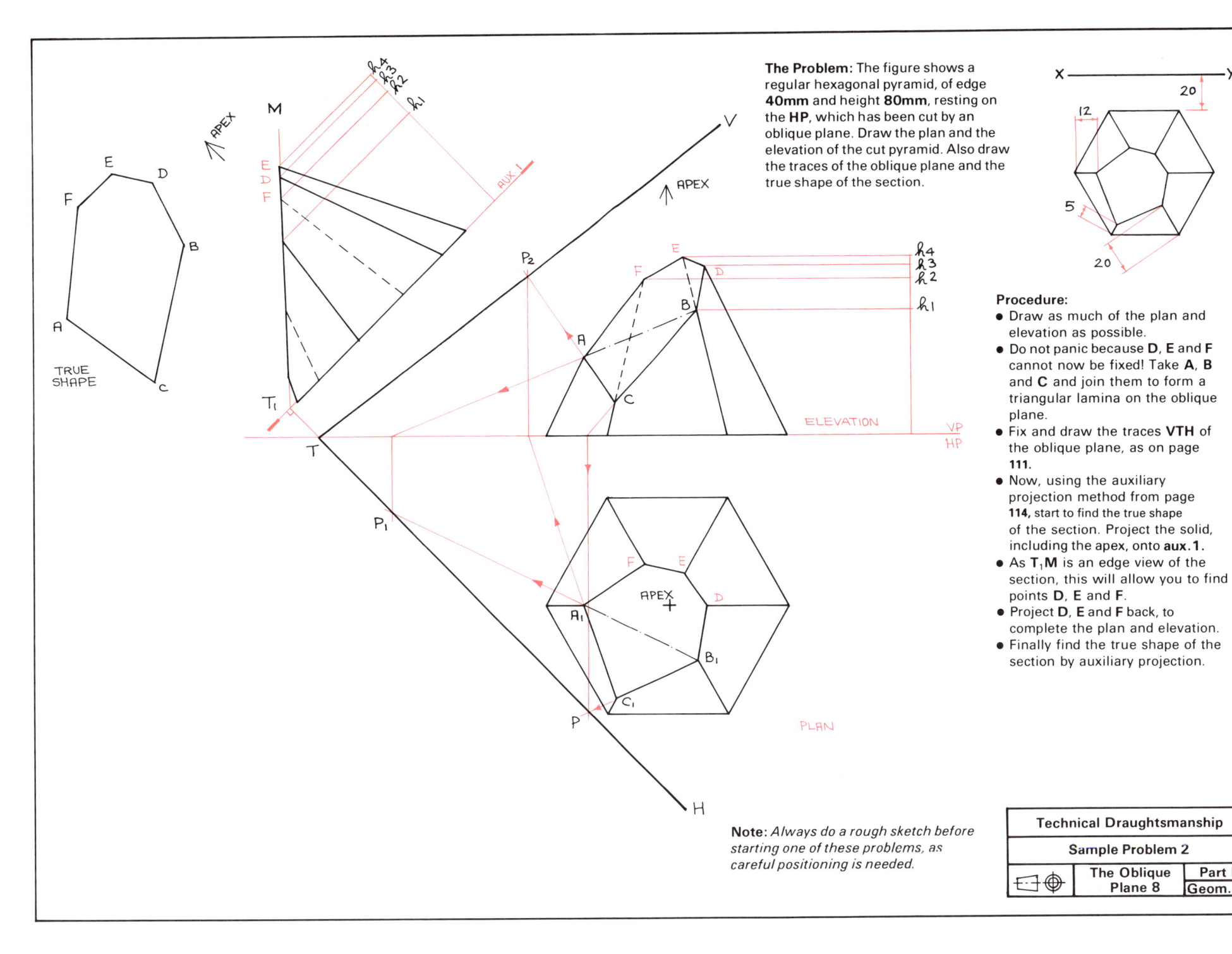

The Problem: The figure shows a regular hexagonal pyramid, of edge **40mm** and height **80mm**, resting on the **HP**, which has been cut by an oblique plane. Draw the plan and the elevation of the cut pyramid. Also draw the traces of the oblique plane and the true shape of the section.

Procedure:
- Draw as much of the plan and elevation as possible.
- Do not panic because **D**, **E** and **F** cannot now be fixed! Take **A**, **B** and **C** and join them to form a triangular lamina on the oblique plane.
- Fix and draw the traces **VTH** of the oblique plane, as on page **111**.
- Now, using the auxiliary projection method from page **114**, start to find the true shape of the section. Project the solid, including the apex, onto **aux.1**.
- As T_1M is an edge view of the section, this will allow you to find points **D**, **E** and **F**.
- Project **D**, **E** and **F** back, to complete the plan and elevation.
- Finally find the true shape of the section by auxiliary projection.

Note: *Always do a rough sketch before starting one of these problems, as careful positioning is needed.*

Technical Draughtsmanship	
Sample Problem 2	
The Oblique Plane 8	Part I Geom. H

① To find the line of intersection of two oblique planes.

Given **VTH** and **V₁T₁H₁** that cross at **A** and **B**.

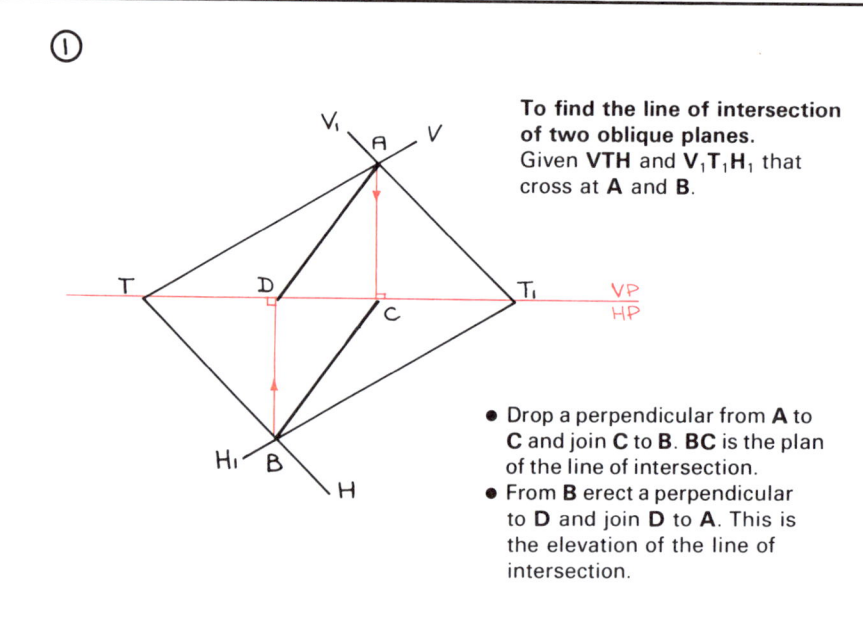

- Drop a perpendicular from **A** to **C** and join **C** to **B**. **BC** is the plan of the line of intersection.
- From **B** erect a perpendicular to **D** and join **D** to **A**. This is the elevation of the line of intersection.

② To find the angle between two oblique planes (the dihedral angle)

Given **VTH** and **V₁T₁H₁** that cross at **A** and **B**.

- Find the line of intersection of the plane in plan and in elevation as in the previous example.
- Now it is a straight dihedral problem (see page **100**).
- Lay the height **H** at right angles to **C**. Join **E** to **B** (the true length of **CB**).
- Now choose a point **M** on **BC** and draw a cutting plane **LMN** at right angles to **BC**.
- From **M** drop a perpendicular **O** onto **BE** and swing it around onto **BC** at **P**.
- Join **L** and **N** to **P**. This is the dihedral angle.

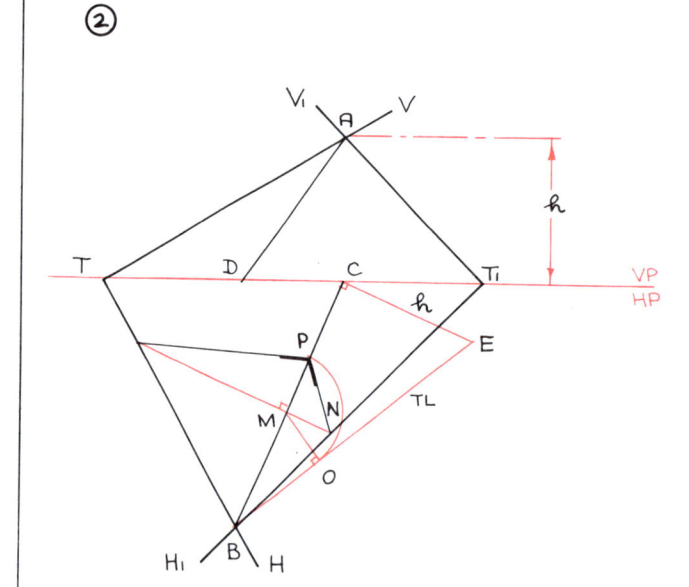

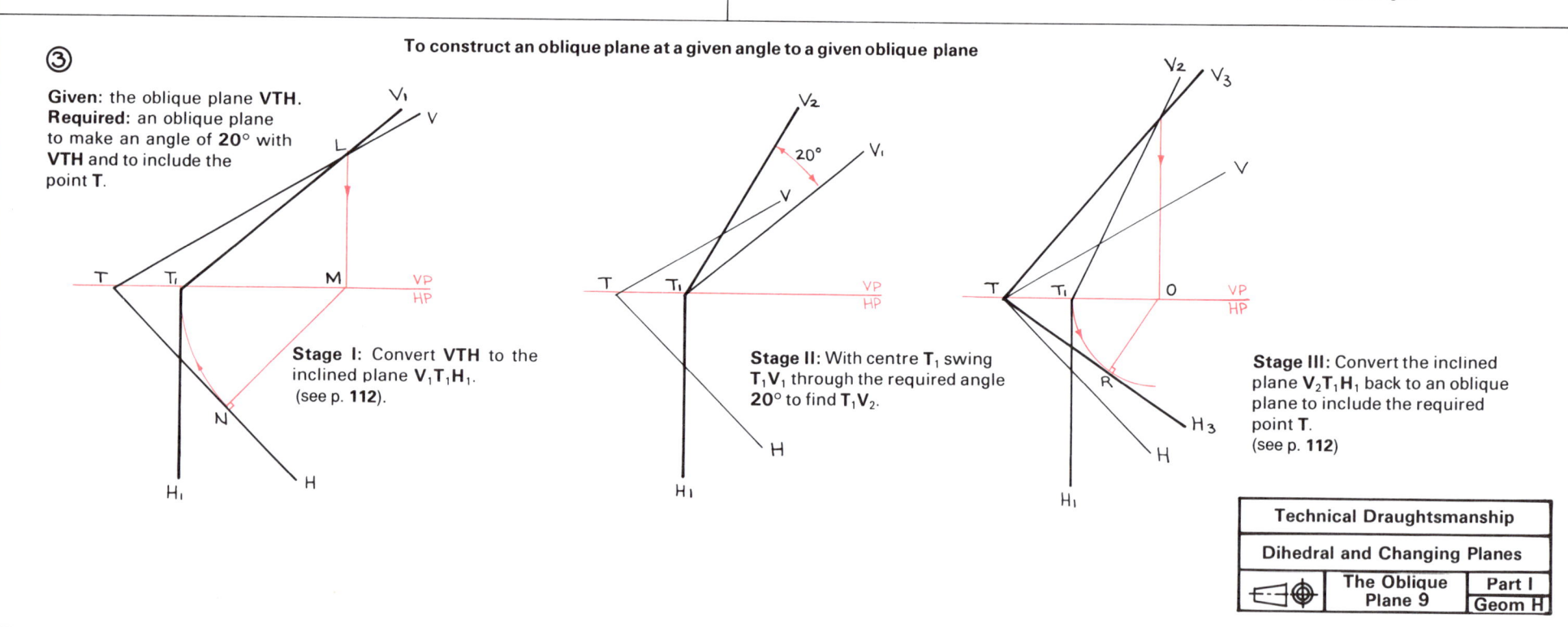

③ To construct an oblique plane at a given angle to a given oblique plane

Given: the oblique plane **VTH**.
Required: an oblique plane to make an angle of **20°** with **VTH** and to include the point **T**.

Stage I: Convert **VTH** to the inclined plane **V₁T₁H₁**. (see p. **112**).

Stage II: With centre **T₁** swing **T₁V₁** through the required angle **20°** to find **T₁V₂**.

Stage III: Convert the inclined plane **V₂T₁H₁** back to an oblique plane to include the required point **T**. (see p. **112**)

Technical Draughtsmanship
Dihedral and Changing Planes
The Oblique Plane 9 — Part I — Geom H

The Problem

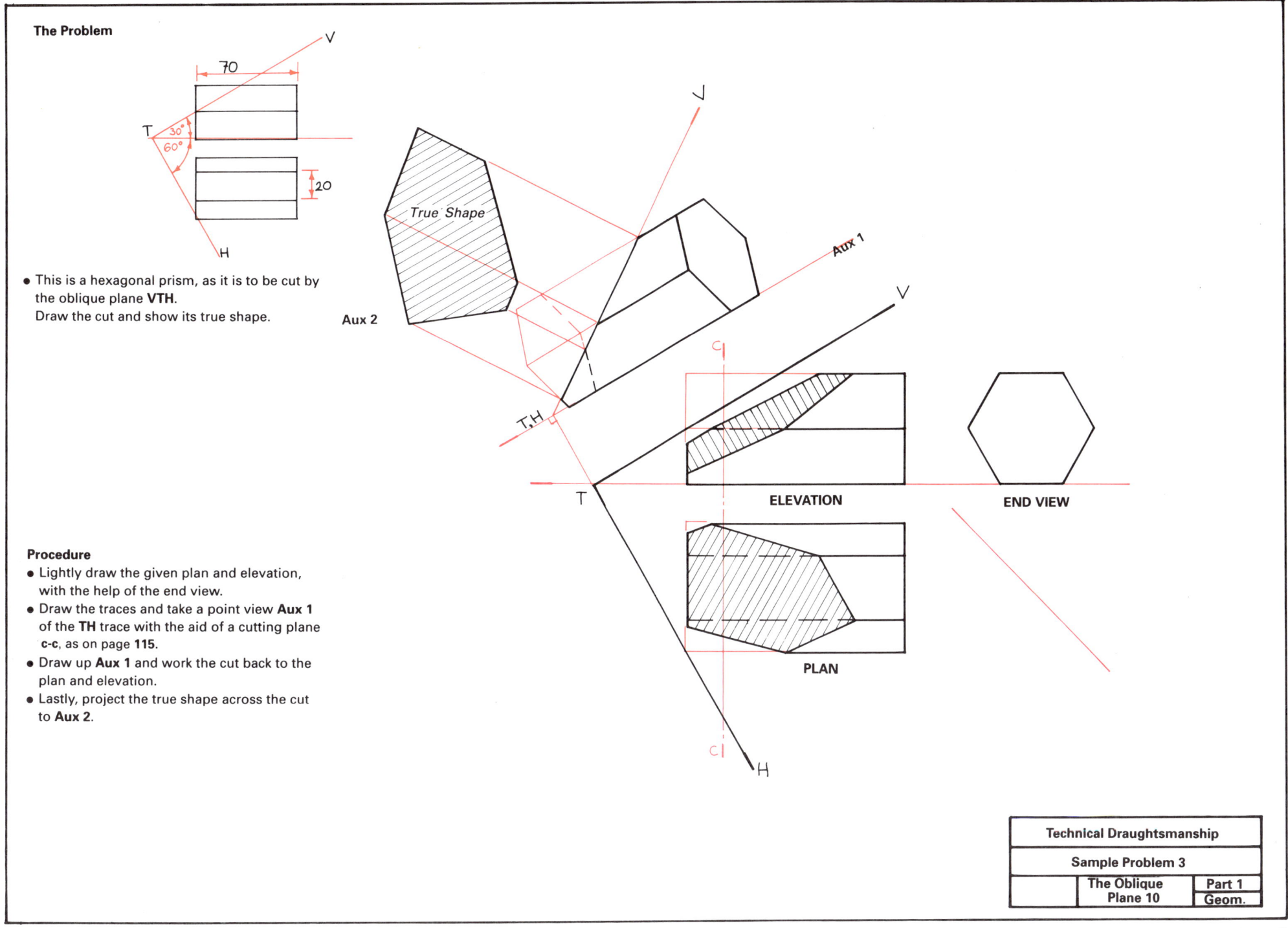

- This is a hexagonal prism, as it is to be cut by the oblique plane **VTH**.
  Draw the cut and show its true shape.

Procedure

- Lightly draw the given plan and elevation, with the help of the end view.
- Draw the traces and take a point view **Aux 1** of the **TH** trace with the aid of a cutting plane **c-c**, as on page **115**.
- Draw up **Aux 1** and work the cut back to the plan and elevation.
- Lastly, project the true shape across the cut to **Aux 2**.

Technical Draughtsmanship

Sample Problem 3

The Oblique Plane 10 — Part 1 — Geom.

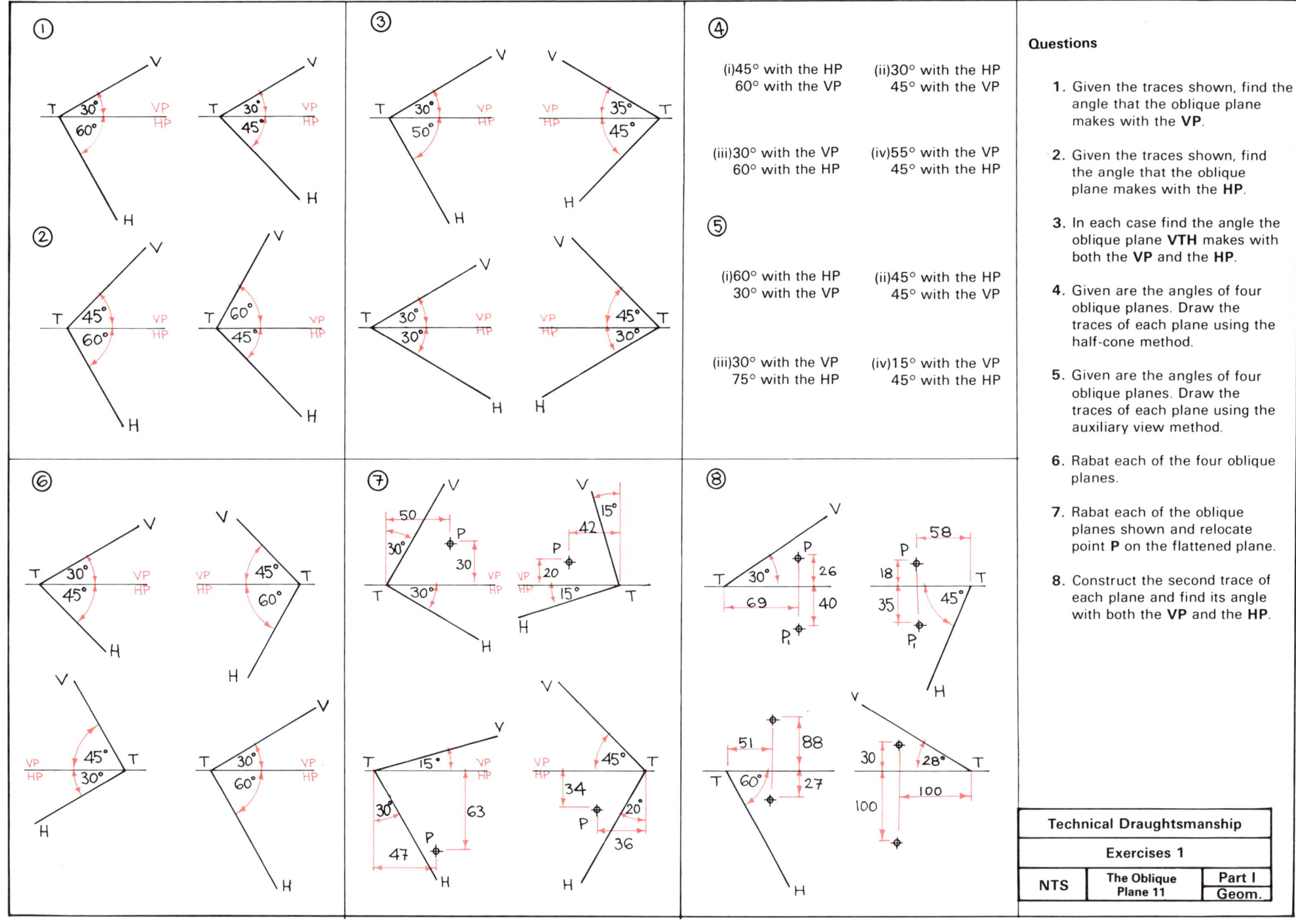

Questions

1. Given the traces shown, find the angle that the oblique plane makes with the **VP**.

2. Given the traces shown, find the angle that the oblique plane makes with the **HP**.

3. In each case find the angle the oblique plane **VTH** makes with both the **VP** and the **HP**.

4. Given are the angles of four oblique planes. Draw the traces of each plane using the half-cone method.

   (i) 45° with the HP / 60° with the VP
   (ii) 30° with the HP / 45° with the VP
   (iii) 30° with the VP / 60° with the HP
   (iv) 55° with the VP / 45° with the HP

5. Given are the angles of four oblique planes. Draw the traces of each plane using the auxiliary view method.

   (i) 60° with the HP / 30° with the VP
   (ii) 45° with the HP / 45° with the VP
   (iii) 30° with the VP / 75° with the HP
   (iv) 15° with the VP / 45° with the HP

6. Rabat each of the four oblique planes.

7. Rabat each of the oblique planes shown and relocate point **P** on the flattened plane.

8. Construct the second trace of each plane and find its angle with both the **VP** and the **HP**.

Technical Draughtsmanship		
Exercises 1		
NTS	The Oblique Plane 11	Part I / Geom.

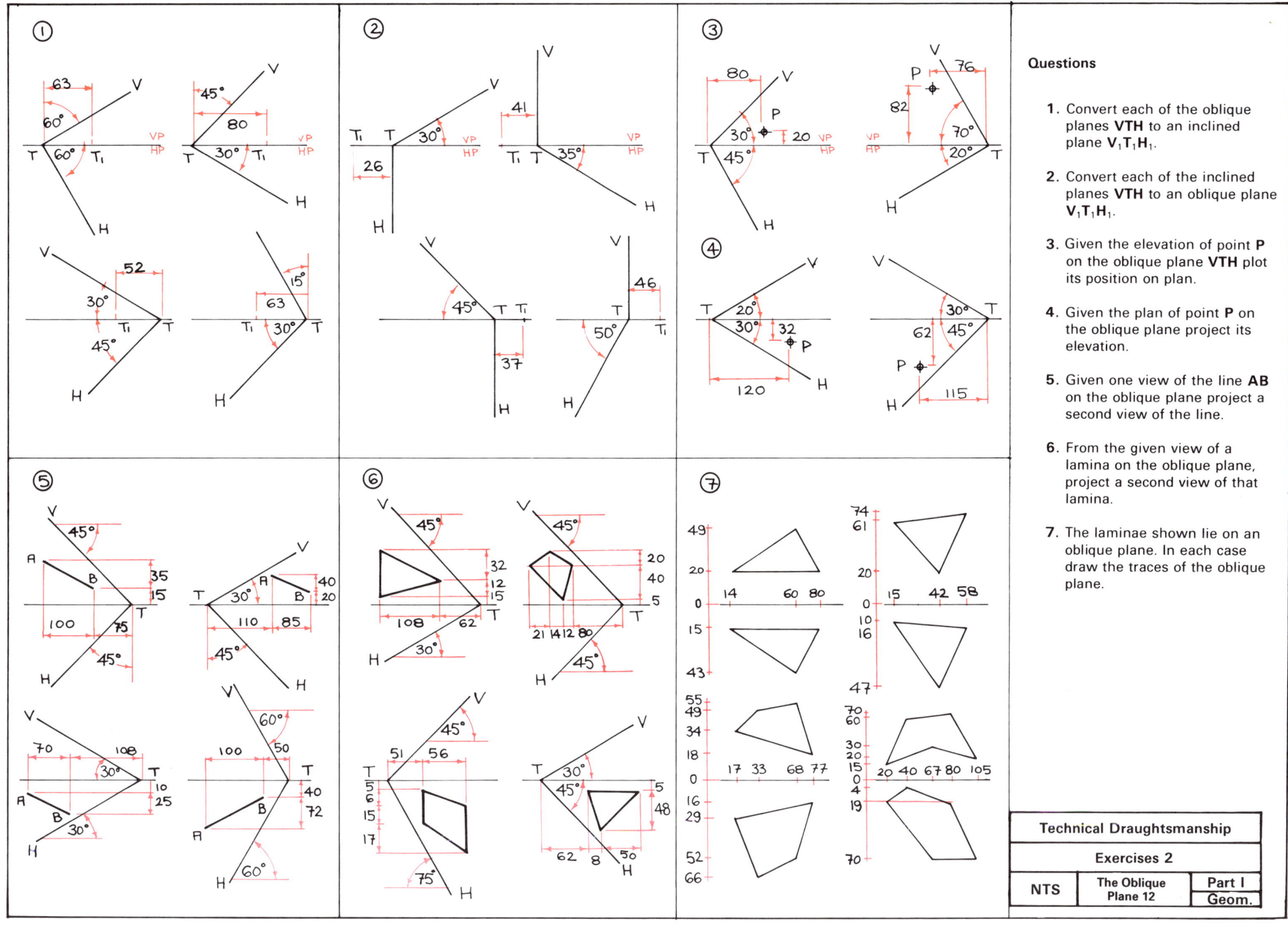

Questions

1. Convert each of the oblique planes **VTH** to an inclined plane $V_1T_1H_1$.

2. Convert each of the inclined planes **VTH** to an oblique plane $V_1T_1H_1$.

3. Given the elevation of point **P** on the oblique plane **VTH** plot its position on plan.

4. Given the plan of point **P** on the oblique plane project its elevation.

5. Given one view of the line **AB** on the oblique plane project a second view of the line.

6. From the given view of a lamina on the oblique plane, project a second view of that lamina.

7. The laminae shown lie on an oblique plane. In each case draw the traces of the oblique plane.

Technical Draughtsmanship		
Exercises 2		
NTS	The Oblique Plane 12	Part I
		Geom.

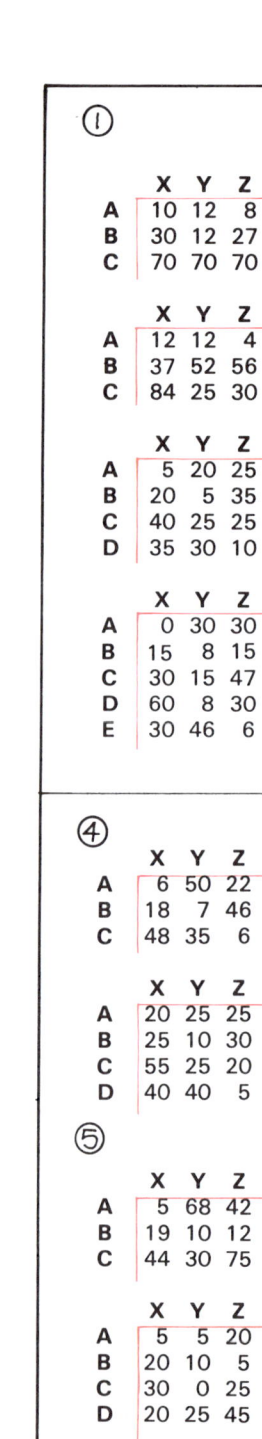

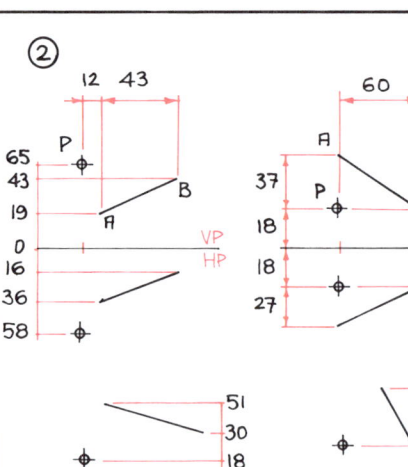

①

	X	Y	Z			X	Y	Z
A	10	12	8		A	10	20	35
B	30	12	27		B	42	5	12
C	70	70	70		C	53	37	36

	X	Y	Z			X	Y	Z
A	12	12	4		A	3	62	27
B	37	52	56		B	28	3	10
C	84	25	30		C	65	53	68

	X	Y	Z			X	Y	Z
A	5	20	25		A	5	25	0
B	20	5	35		B	15	5	10
C	40	25	25		C	30	20	5
D	35	30	10		D	15	45	20

	X	Y	Z			X	Y	Z
A	0	30	30		A	12	44	62
B	15	8	15		B	60	11	51
C	30	15	47		C	70	11	33
D	60	8	30		D	60	52	10
E	30	46	6		E	20	52	22

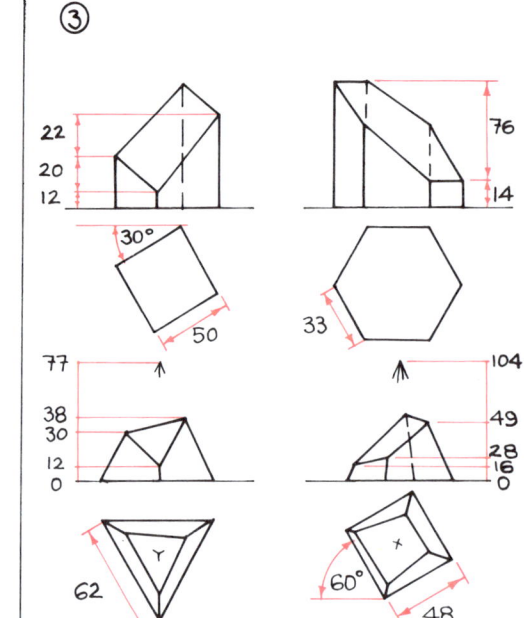

④

	X	Y	Z			X	Y	Z
A	6	50	22		A	0	10	75
B	18	7	46		B	15	42	12
C	48	35	6		C	54	32	39

	X	Y	Z			X	Y	Z
A	20	25	25		A	5	20	15
B	25	10	30		B	25	5	5
C	55	25	20		C	45	5	15
D	40	40	5		D	20	20	30

⑤

	X	Y	Z			X	Y	Z
A	5	68	42		A	0	12	12
B	19	10	12		B	73	0	0
C	44	30	75		C	48	47	56

	X	Y	Z			X	Y	Z
A	5	5	20		A	30	0	20
B	20	10	5		B	50	10	20
C	30	0	25		C	25	15	5
D	20	25	45		D	10	30	5

②

③

⑥

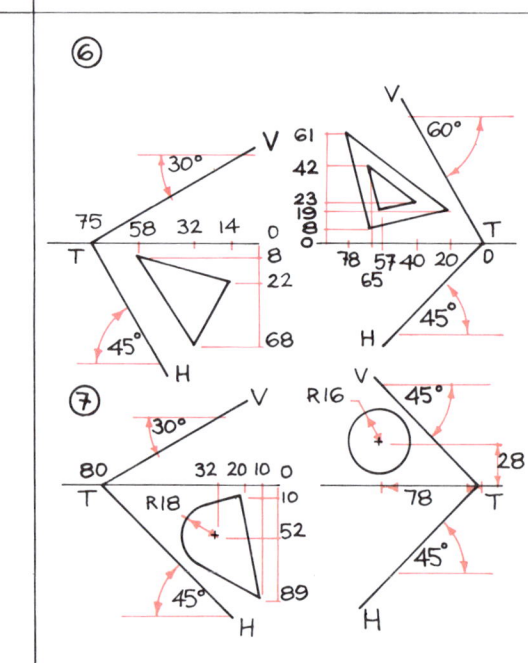

⑦

⑧

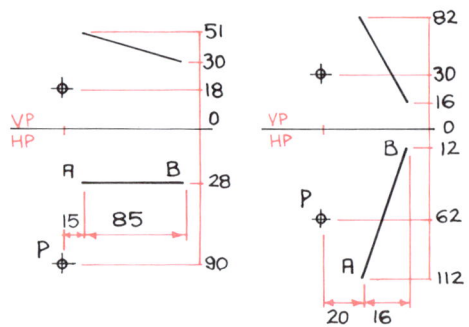

First sighting: 08.03 hrs.

	X	Y	Z
A	15	10	10
B	90	10	55
C	60	40	70
D	60	70	100
E	30	70	85
F	15	100	100

Second Sighting: 14.20 hrs.
Space ship now on an inclined plane making an angle of **45°** with the **HP**.

All measurements are in millimetres

Questions

1. Given are the coordinates of laminae each lying on an oblique plane. Draw each lamina in plan and elevation and indicate the traces of the oblique plane.

2. Each diagram shows a line and a point lying on an oblique plane. Draw the traces of that plane.

3. Shown are four solids cut by an oblique plane. Draw the traces of that plane.

4. Given are the coordinates of four laminae on oblique planes. Find the true shape of each lamina by rabatment, using **method 1** on page **114**.

5. The coordinates of four laminae lying on oblique planes are given. Draw the traces of each plane and find the true shape of the laminae by rabatment, using **method 2**, on page **114**.

6. Find the true shape of each of the given laminae by auxiliary projection, using **method 1**, on page **114**.

7. Find the true shape of each of the given laminae by auxiliary projection, using **method 2**, on page **114**.

8. A flat spacecraft is travelling on an oblique plane. Given are the coordinates of its extremities. At what angle to the **VP** and the **HP** is it travelling? What is its true shape and what change of course does it undergo?

Technical Draughtsmanship		
Exercises 3		
NTS	The Oblique Plane 13	Part I Geom. H

PART 1

CHAPTER 10
SPHERES AND TANGENT PLANES

A further step when dealing with planes is to consider those planes that just touch a solid or a group of solids. The study of the sphere is also a good exercise in tangency.

CONTENTS

	Page
Tangent Spheres	122
Spheres and Planes	123
Sphere with Cone and Cylinder	124
Tangents to Pyramids and Cones	125
Tangents to Sphere, Cone and Cylinder	126
Tangents containing Lines	127
Exercises	128

Photocopying prohibited by law

① Given point P in one view of a sphere to locate its position on a second view.

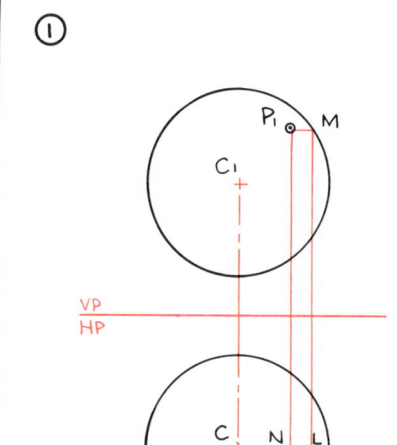

- With centre **C** swing **P** to **L**, so that **CL** is parallel to the **VP**.
- Project **L** up to meet the outline elevation at **M** and then across at right angles towards **P₁**.
- From **P** on the plan project straight up to fix **P₁** on the elevation.

Note: *If P were on the underside of the sphere what difference would this make to the construction?*

② Given point P to find a view in which P is on the outline of the sphere.

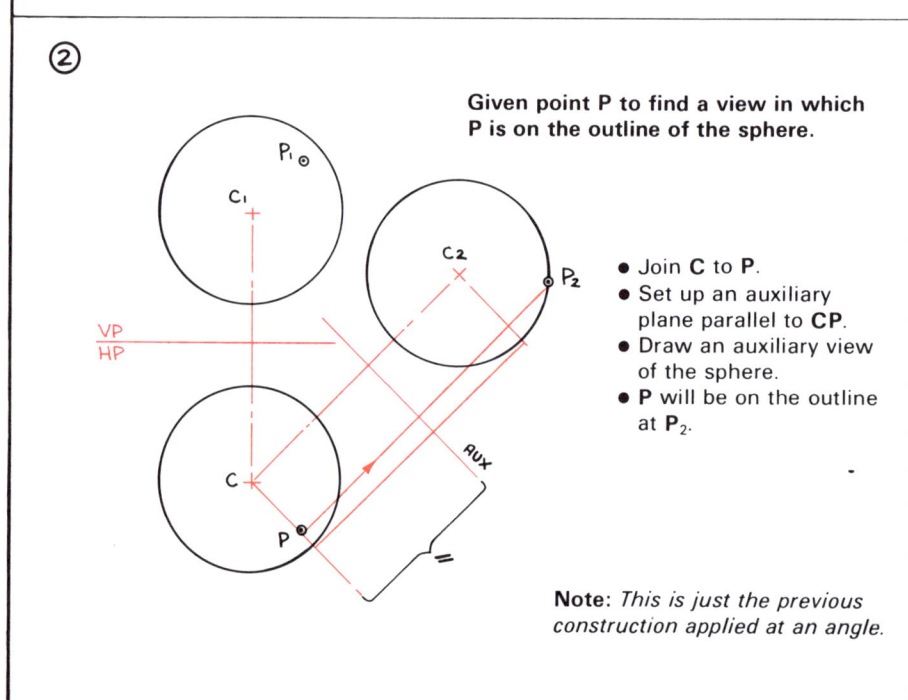

- Join **C** to **P**.
- Set up an auxiliary plane parallel to **CP**.
- Draw an auxiliary view of the sphere.
- **P** will be on the outline at **P₂**.

Note: *This is just the previous construction applied at an angle.*

③ To draw a sphere of radius r to touch point P on a given sphere.

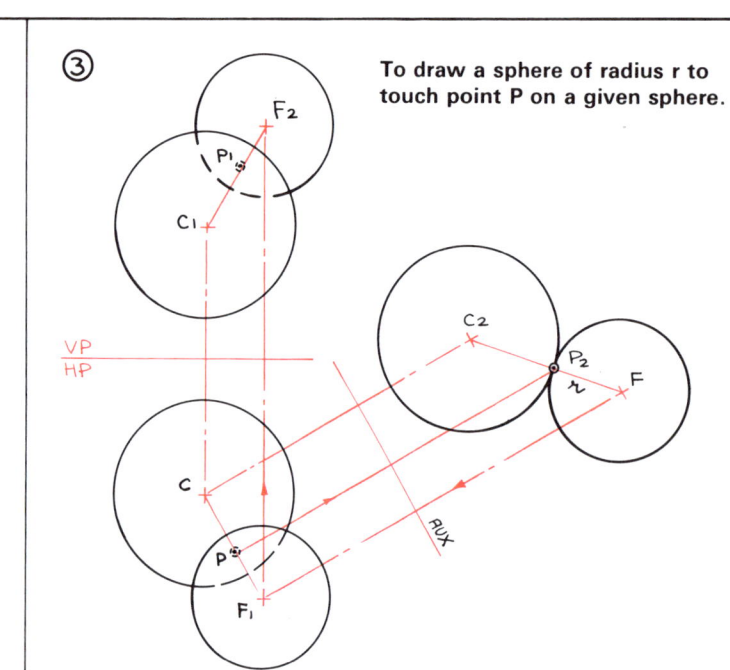

- Project a view in which **P₂** is on the outline of the sphere.
- Join **C₂** to **P₂** and extend by **r** to find **F**.
- With **F** as centre and radius **r** draw the tangent sphere. **C₂F** *is a true length.*
- On plan join **C** to **P** and extend. Then project **F** back to find **F₁**.
- With centre **F₁** and radius **r** draw the sphere on plan. *Why does the outline not pass through P here?*
- On elevation join **C₁** to **P₁** and extend. Then project **F₁** up to find **F₂**.
- With centre **F₂** and radius **r** draw the tangent sphere on elevation.

④ To draw a sphere of radius r tangent to point P on a given sphere.

This is an alternative method to that above in which the auxiliary view is overlaid.

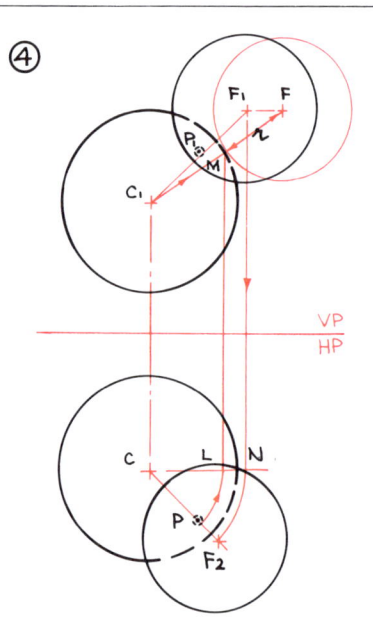

- On plan join **C** to **P** and extend.
- With centre **C** swing **P** to **L** and then project up to meet the outline elevation at **M**.
- Join **C₁** to **M** and extend by **r** to **F**.
- With centre **F** and radius **r** lightly draw a construction circle.
- Join **C₁** to **P₁** and extend towards **F₁**.
- From **F** go straight across to fix **F₁**.
- With centre **F₁** and radius **r** draw the sphere on elevation.
- Project **F₁** down to **N** and with centre **C** swing it onto **CP** at **F₂**.
- With centre **F₂** and radius **r** draw the sphere on plan.

Note: *All of these constructions can be worked starting from the elevation instead of the plan.*

Technical Draughtsmanship
Tangent Spheres
Spheres 1 — Part I Geom.

①　Elevation

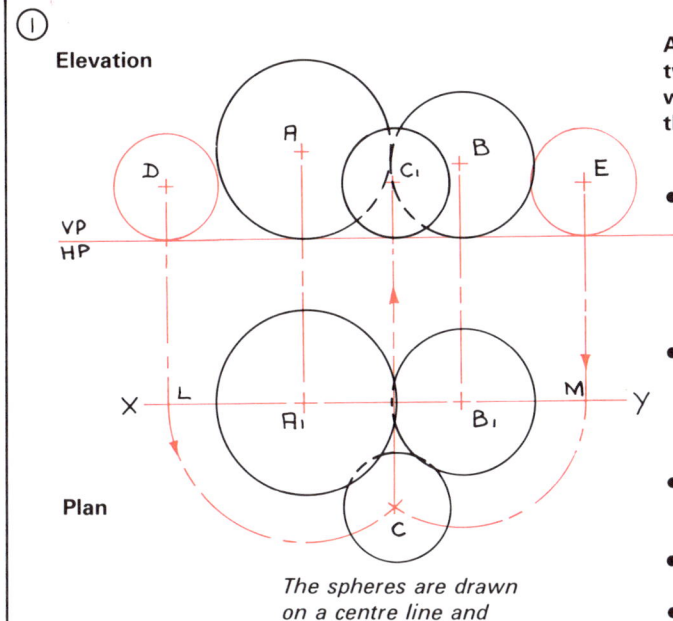

A sphere tangent to two given spheres when all three lie on the HP.

- Draw the given spheres **A** and **B** in elevation and along a chosen centre line **XY** in plan, parallel to the main axis.
- Lightly draw the third sphere twice at **D** and at **E** on elevation, tangent to spheres **A** and **B**.
- Project centres **D** and **E** down onto **XY** at **L** and **M**.
- With centre **A₁** swing **L** around towards **C**.
- With centre **B₁** swing **M** around to fix **C**.
- Draw sphere **C** in plan and elevation.

The spheres are drawn on a centre line and then swung into position.

②　Elevation

A sphere tangent to two given spheres when all three lie against a VP.

- The procedure is similar to that outlined above.

③　Elevation

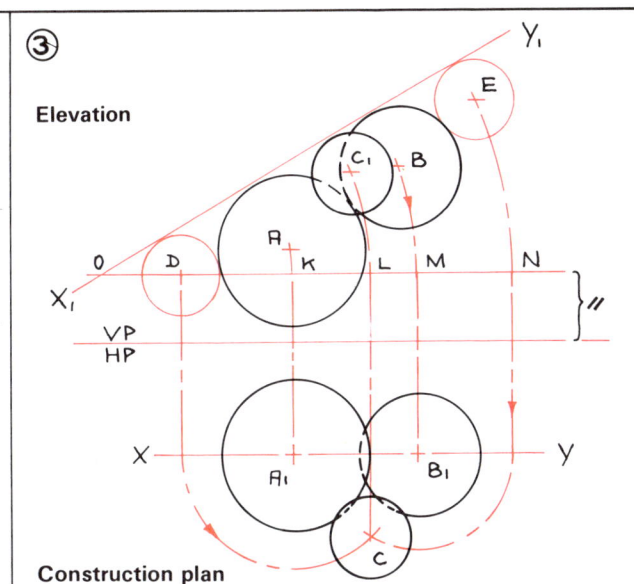

Three tangent spheres lying against a plane XY that is inclined to the HP.

- Draw the inclined plane **XY** and, tangent to it, spheres **A** and **B**.
- Tangent to these draw the two construction spheres **D** and **E**.
- Choose a convenient point **O** along **XY** and draw a line **ON** parallel to the main axis.
- With centre **O** swing the centre of each sphere onto **ON** at **K**, **M** and **N**.
- Proceed as previously to find **C**. Then project **C** to **L** and swing back to find **C₁**, as shown.
- Draw the sphere and project a true plan onto **X₁Y₁**.

*Note: The plan shown is **not** a direct reflection of the elevation. A true plan can be projected down. To keep the diagram clear this last step has not been completed.*

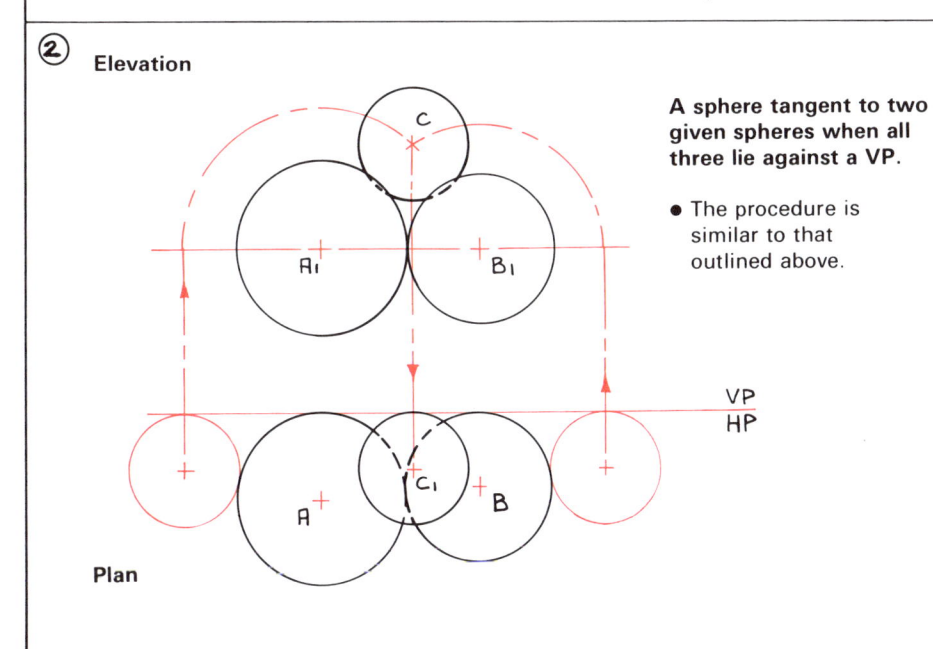

④　Construction elevation

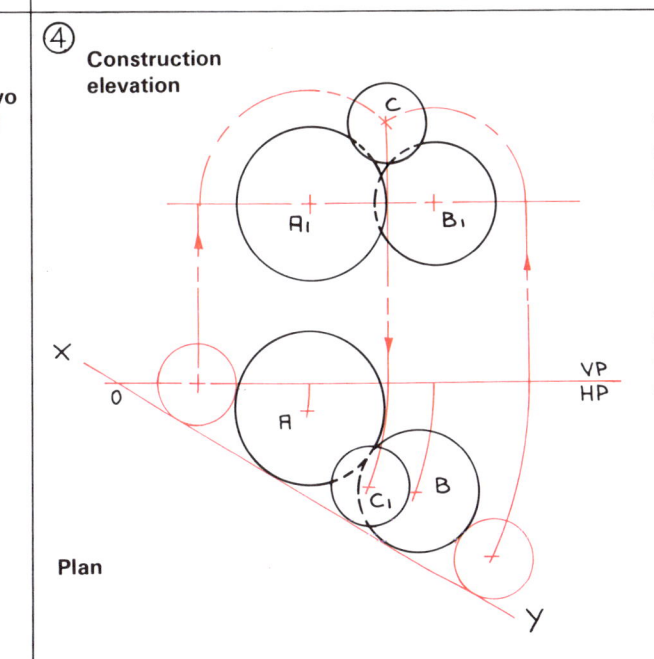

Three tangent spheres lying against a plane XY that is inclined to the VP.

- The procedure is similar to that outlined above.

*Note: For clarity the final elevation has not been shown here. Once the plan is complete a truly aligned elevation can be projected directly onto **X₁Y₁**.*

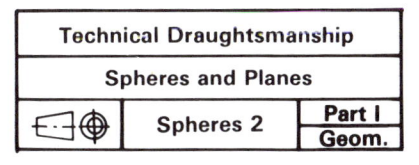

Technical Draughtsmanship
Spheres and Planes
Spheres 2 — Part I Geom.

①

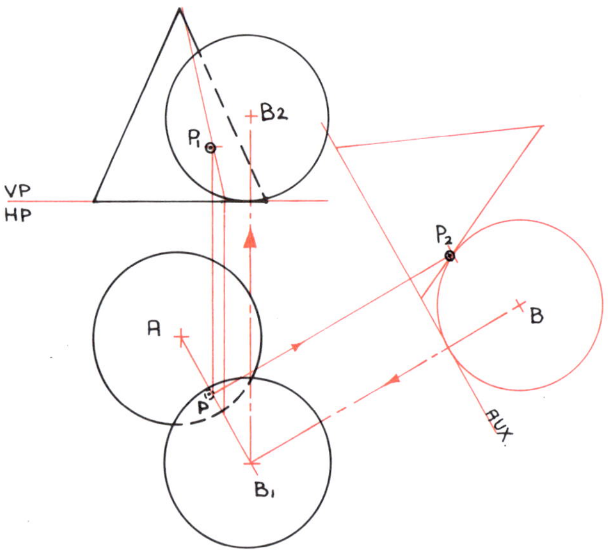

A sphere tangent to a cone at point P.

- Draw the cone and mark point **P** on both views.
- On plan join **A** to **P** and extend.
- Take an auxiliary view parallel to **AP**.
- Locate P_2 on the outline of the cone and draw the tangent sphere on the auxiliary view.
- Project **B** back to B_1 and then draw the sphere on plan and elevation.

②

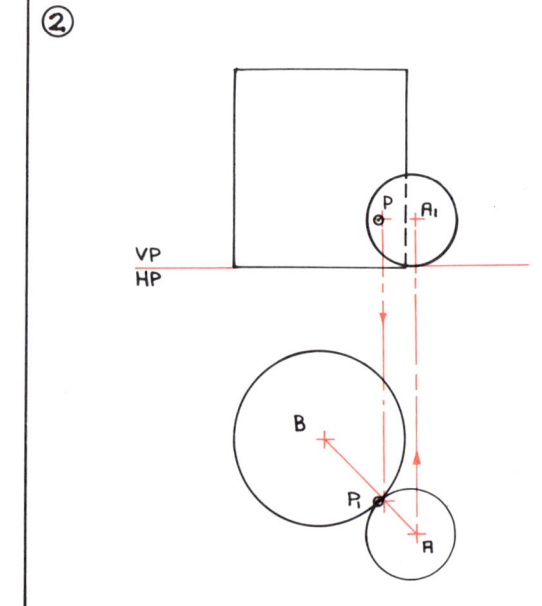

A sphere tangent to a cylinder at point P.

- Draw the cylinder in plan and elevation and mark point **P**. On plan point P_1 will be on the outline.
- Join **B** to P_1 and extend.
- Draw the tangent sphere at **A** through point P_1.
- Project the elevation of the sphere.

③

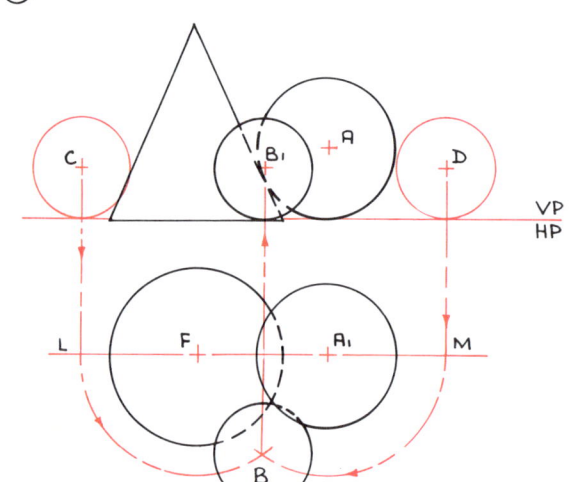

Two spheres tangent to each other and to a given cone.

- Draw the cone in plan and elevation.
- On elevation draw a tangent sphere **A** and project its plan A_1 onto the centre line **LM**.
- On elevation draw the two construction spheres **C** and **D** and project their centres onto the plan at **L** and **M**.
- With centre A_1 swing **M** towards **B**.
- With centre **F** swing **L** around to fix **B**.
- Draw the sphere on plan and project its elevation.

④

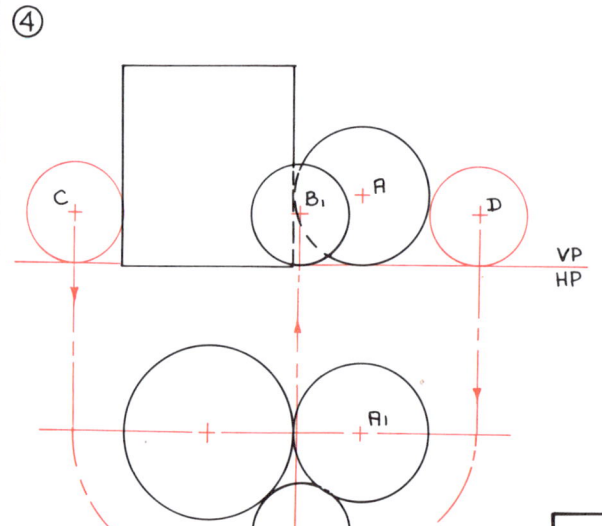

Two spheres tangent to each other and to a cylinder

- Draw one sphere **A** tangent to the cylinder.
- On elevation draw two construction spheres **C** and **D** tangent to the cylinder and to sphere **A** respectively.
- Project **C** and **D** onto the centre line **XY** on plan.
- Locate **B** as outlined above.
- Draw the second sphere **B** and project its elevation.

Technical Draughtsmanship
Sphere with Cone and Cylinder
Spheres 3 — Part I Geom.

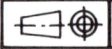

① Two spheres tangent to each other and to a pyramid

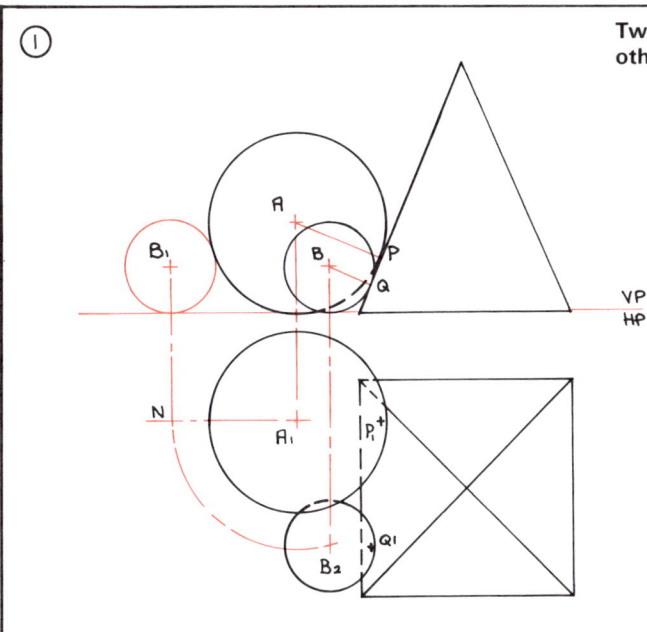

- On elevation draw the two spheres **A** and **B** tangent to the pyramid at points **P** and **Q**.
- Project the plan of one sphere (**A₁**).
- On elevation draw a construction sphere **B₁**.
- On plan draw a line from **A₁** parallel to the main axis to **N**.
- Project **B₁** to **N** and with centre **A₁** swing **N** towards **B₂**.
- Project **B** down to fix **B₂**.
- The points of tangency **P** and **Q** can also be projected, as shown.

② Incomplete elevation

Two spheres tangent to each other and to a given face of a pyramid.

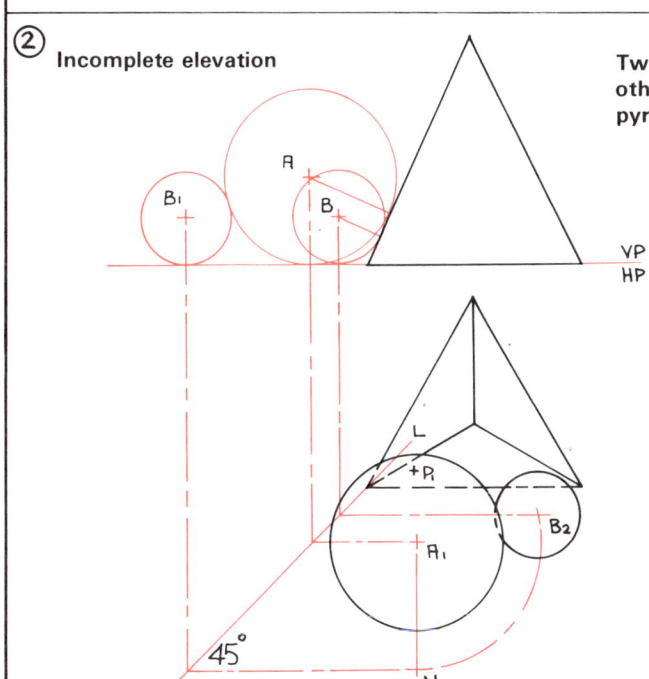

- The procedure is similar to that outlined above, with an additional projection around the corner on plan.
- Once the plan is complete the true elevation can be drawn.

Note: *For clarity this final step has been omitted here.*

③ To draw a cylinder tangent to a given cone.

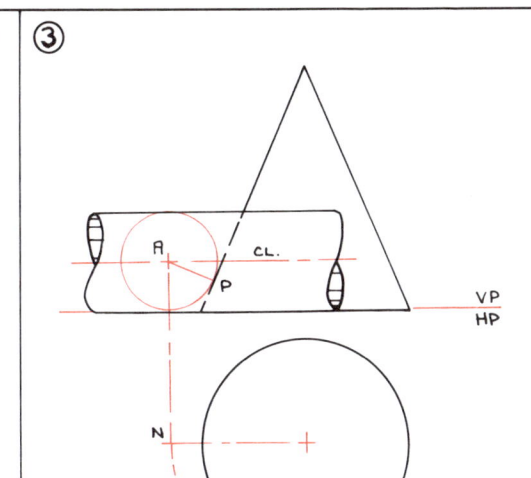

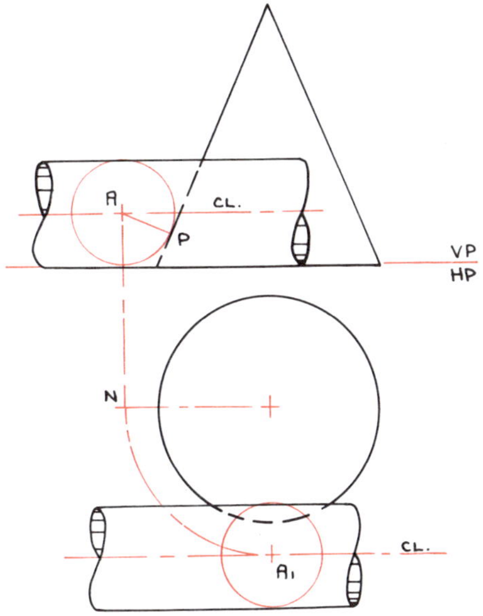

- On the elevation draw a rotated section **A** of the cylinder, tangent to the cone at **P**.
- On plan draw a line from **X**, parallel to the main axis, to **N**.
- Drop **A** to **N** and with centre **X** swing **N** around to **A₁**.
- Draw the centre line of the cylinder **CL** tangent to the curve at **A₁**.
- Construct the plan of the cylinder, as shown.

Note: *A₁ can be anywhere about the circumference of the cone and, therefore, the cylinder can be found at any angle.*

④ A sphere and a cylinder to be tangent to each other and to a given cone.

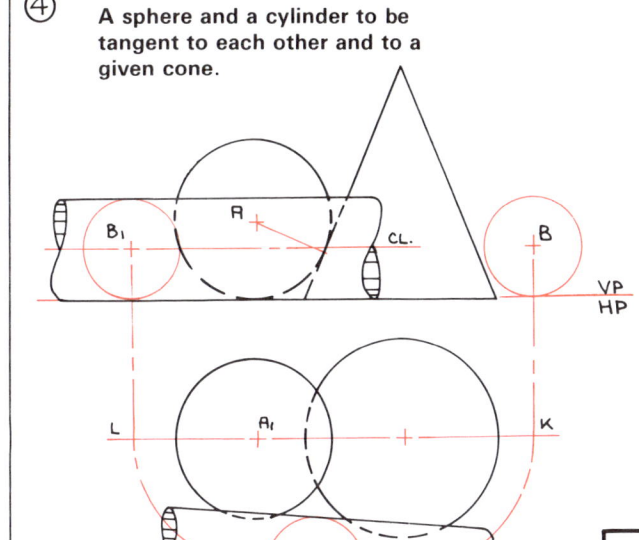

- On the elevation draw the sphere **A** tangent to the cone and project its plan onto centre line **LK** at **A₁**.
- Also on elevation draw two construction spheres **B** and **B₁** tangent to the cone and to the sphere respectively, as shown.
- Project **B** and **B₁** onto the centre line at **L** and **K**.
- With centre **A₁** swing **L** around towards **N**, and with centre **X** swing **K** around towards **M**.
- Draw the centre line of the cylinder tangent to these curves at **M** and **N**.
- Complete the view of the cylinder, as shown.

Technical Draughtsmanship
Tangents to Pyramids and Cones
Spheres 4 — Part I — Geom. H

125

①

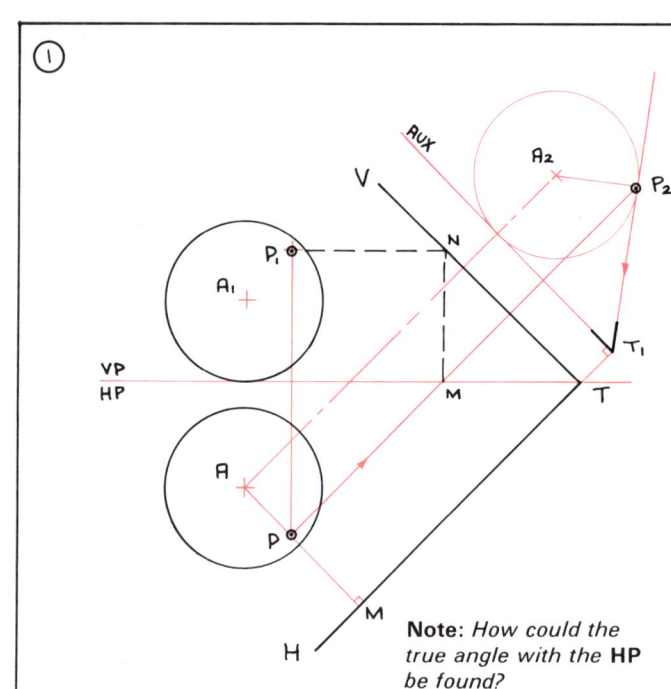

To draw a plane tangent to a sphere at point P.

The plane will usually be oblique.

- Joint **A** to **P** and extend.
- Project an auxiliary view parallel to **AP**.
- Locate **P₂** on the auxiliary view and draw a tangent to **P₂** extending it to **T₁**.
- Project **T₁** back to find trace **TH**.
- The second trace is located in the usual way, as on page **111**.

Note: *How could the true angle with the HP be found?*

②

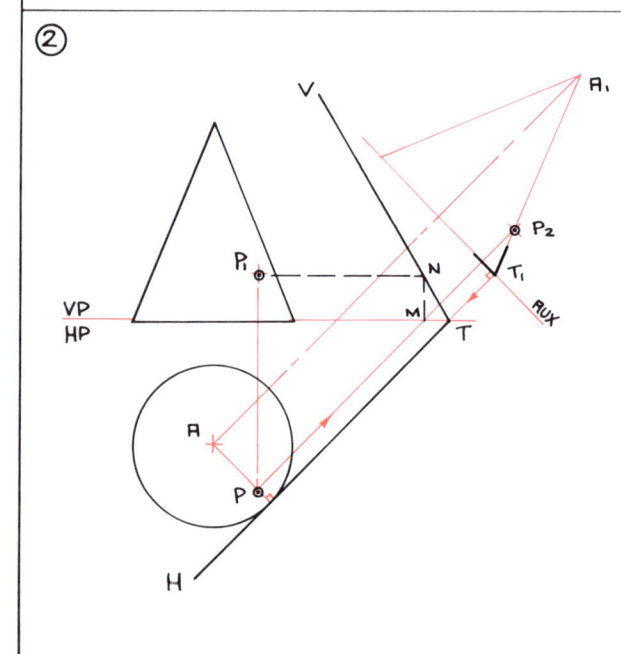

To draw a plane tangent to a cone at point P.

The plane will usually be oblique.

- Join **A** to **P** and extend.
- Construct an auxiliary view parallel to **AP**.
- Locate **P₂** which will be on the outline.
- As **A₁P₂** is already tangent, mark **T₁**.
- Project the trace **TH**.
- The second trace is located in the usual way, as on page **111**.

Note: *A short cut method will be obvious but the above procedure will prove more useful.*

③

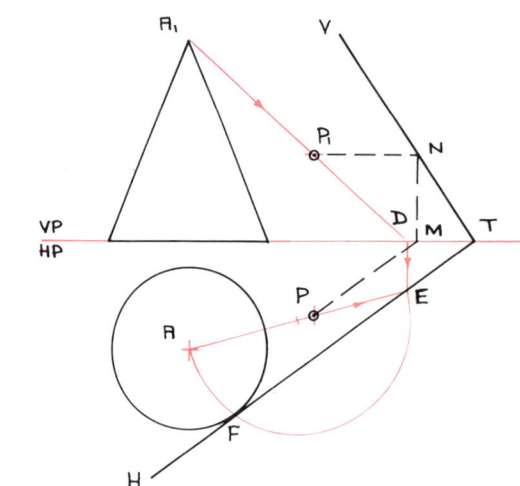

To draw a plane tangent to a cone containing point P.

A tangent plane to a cone must touch the apex.

- Join **A** to **P** and extend towards **E**.
- Join **A₁** to **P₁** and extend to meet the main axis at **D**.
- Drop a perpendicular from **D** to fix point **E**. This is a point on a trace.
- Construct a tangent from **E** to the base circle at **F**, as shown. This is a trace.
- Extend **HE** to **T**.
- Locate the second trace in the usual way, as on page **111**.

Note: *It is possible to draw a second tangent from E to the base A. This is valid, but the drawing gets very cluttered.*

④

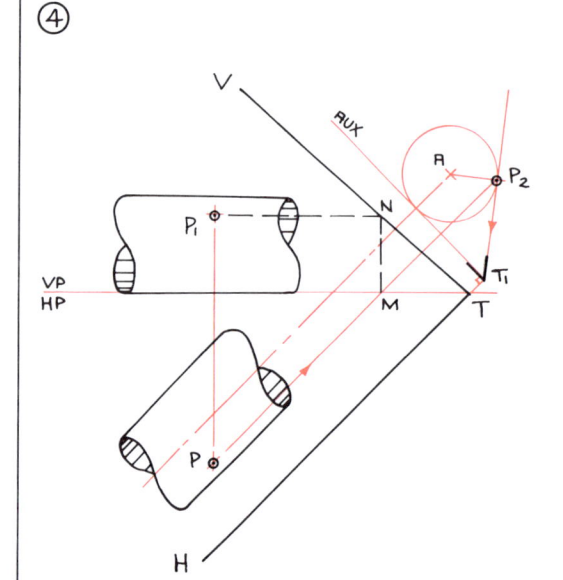

To draw a plane tangent to a cylinder at point P.

- Set up an auxiliary view at right angles to the centre line of the cylinder.
- Locate **P₂** and draw a tangent to find **T₁**.
- Project the trace **TH**.
- Locate the second trace in the usual way, as on page **111**.

Note: *Tangent planes are usually oblique planes. However, if a cylinder is upright the tangent plane would be an inclined plane only.*

Technical Draughtsmanship
Tangents to Sphere, Cone and Cylinder
Tangent Planes 1 — Part I — Geom. H

①

To draw the traces of a plane that contains line AB and that is also tangent to a given cone.

- Join **A** and **B** to **C**. As any plane tangent to the cone touches the apex **C**, then this is a triangle on the oblique plane.
- Use **ABC** to find the traces, as on page **111**.
- Notice that **DB** on plan is parallel to **TH**. Why?

②

To draw the traces of a plane, tangent to a sphere, and that will also contain line AB.

- Reduce **AB** to a point view A_3, B_3, as on page **87**.
- Draw a line through this point A_3, B_3 and tangent to the sphere at point **P**.
- Extend to **T**. This is one trace **VT**.
- Draw the second trace at right angles to the plane and parallel to A_2B_2.

Note: *If the traces are required on the original views, project P back and join the ends of the line AB to the point. This gives a triangular lamina in a plane the traces of which can be found, as on page 111.*

Technical Draughtsmanship
Tangents containing Lines

| Tangent Planes 2 | Part I Geom H |

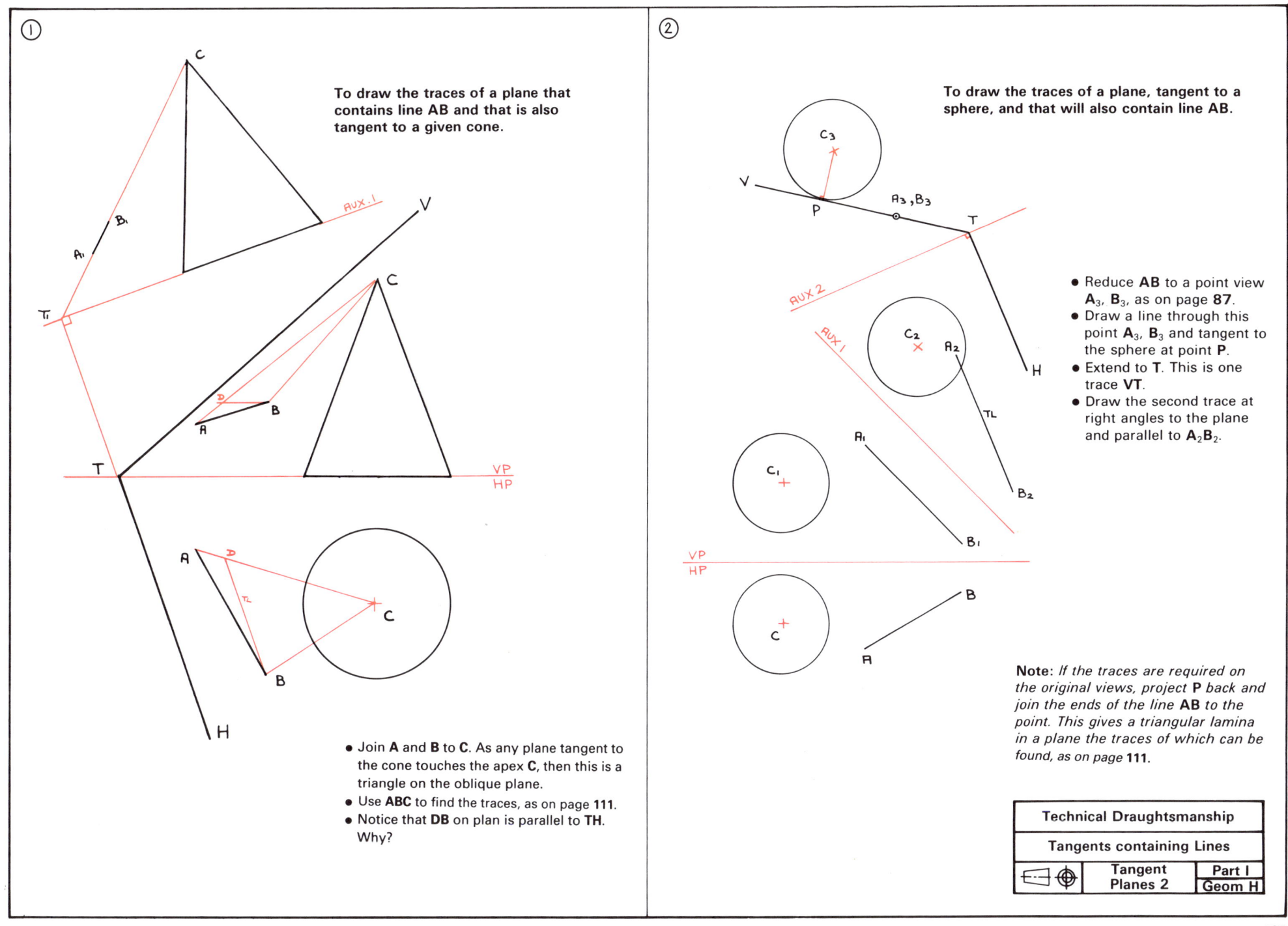

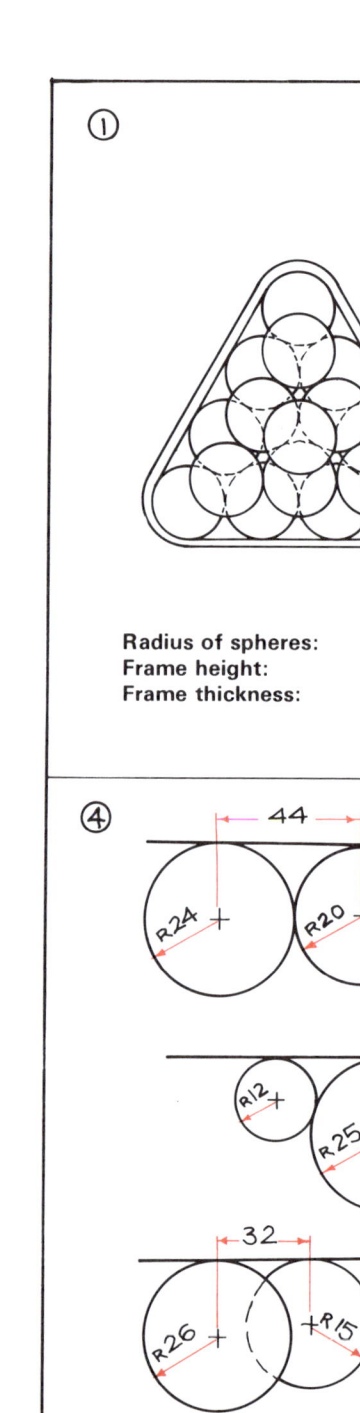

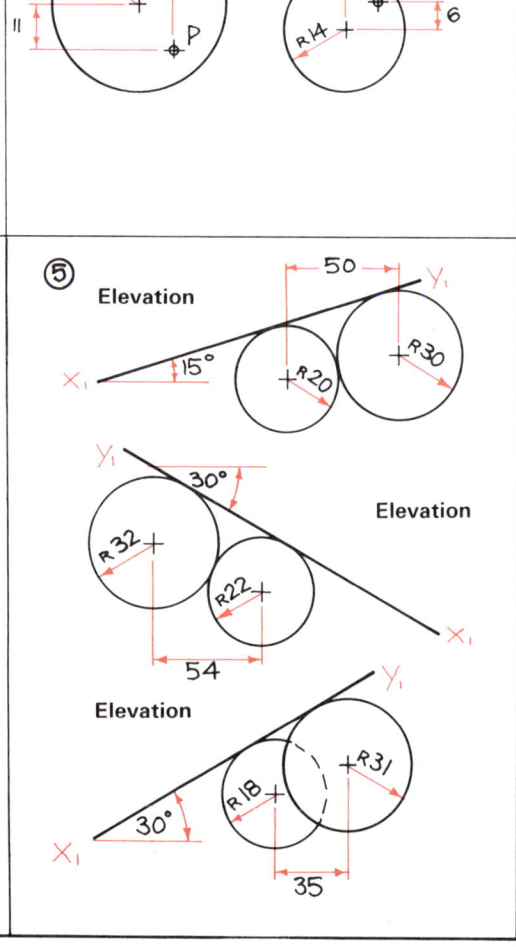

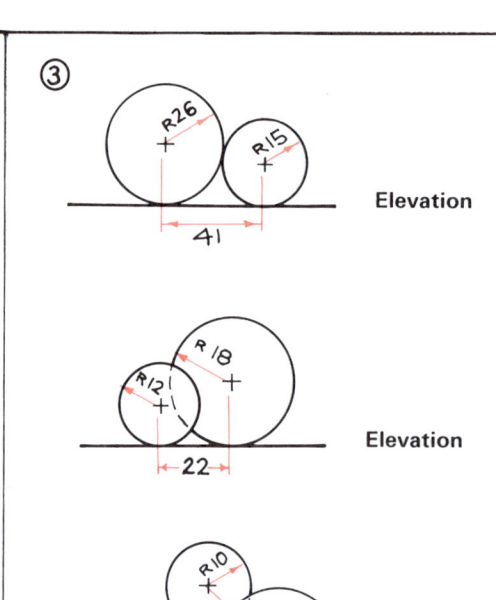

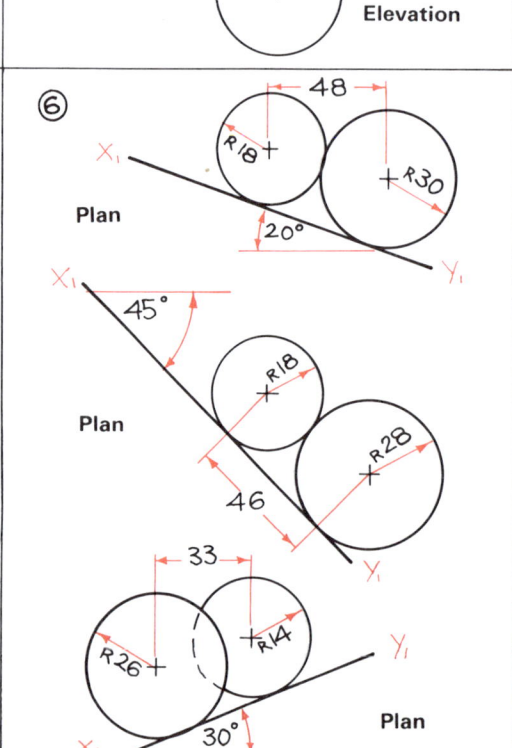

Questions

1. A set of snooker balls has been stacked in its frame as shown. Draw both plan and elevation of this arrangement.

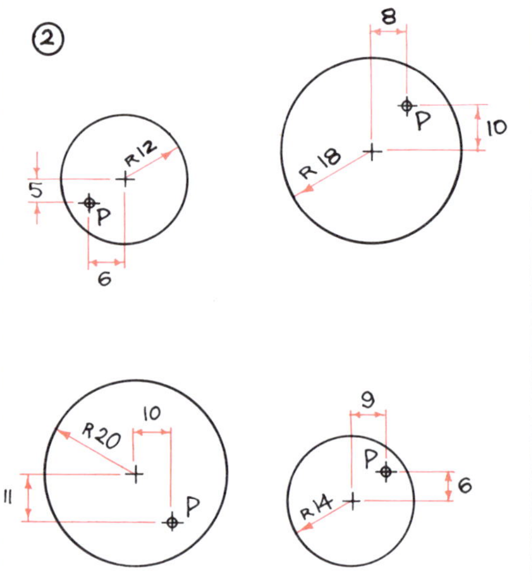

2. Draw a sphere of radius **10 mm** tangent to point **P** on each of the given spheres.

3. In each case draw a sphere of radius **8 mm**, tangent to the two given spheres, when all three lie on the horizontal plane.

4. In all three cases draw a sphere of radius **12 mm**, tangent to the two given spheres, when all three lie on the vertical plane.

5. In each case draw a third sphere of radius **14 mm**, tangent to the two given spheres, when all three lie on the inclined plane X_1Y_1.

6. In each case draw a third sphere of radius **11 mm**, tangent to the two given spheres, when all three lie against the inclined plane X_1Y_1.

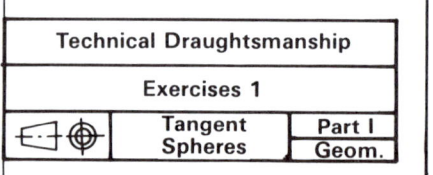

Technical Draughtsmanship

Exercises 1

Tangent Spheres — Part I — Geom.

Questions

1. In each case draw two spheres tangent to each other and to the given cone. One sphere is to be of radius **16 mm** and the second is to touch the cone at point **P**.

2. In both cases draw two spheres tangent to each other and to the given cylinder. One sphere is to be of radius **15 mm** and the second to touch the cylinder at point **P**.

3. Draw two spheres of radii **16 mm** and **11 mm** tangent to each other and to side **A** of each pyramid. Show clearly the points of contact.

4. Draw the plan and elevation of the group of solids in mutual contact, showing the points of contact.

5. A cone of height **82 mm** is leaning on a cylinder as shown. Draw a sphere of radius **25 mm** that is tangent to both solids.

6. A scientist wishes to make two molecular models. The atoms and their radii are shown. In each case combine these as tightly as they will go. Draw each finished model in plan and elevation.

7. In each case draw the group of solids showing the points of contact.

Technical Draughtsmanship		
Exercises 2		
	Tangent Spheres	Part 1
		Geom. H

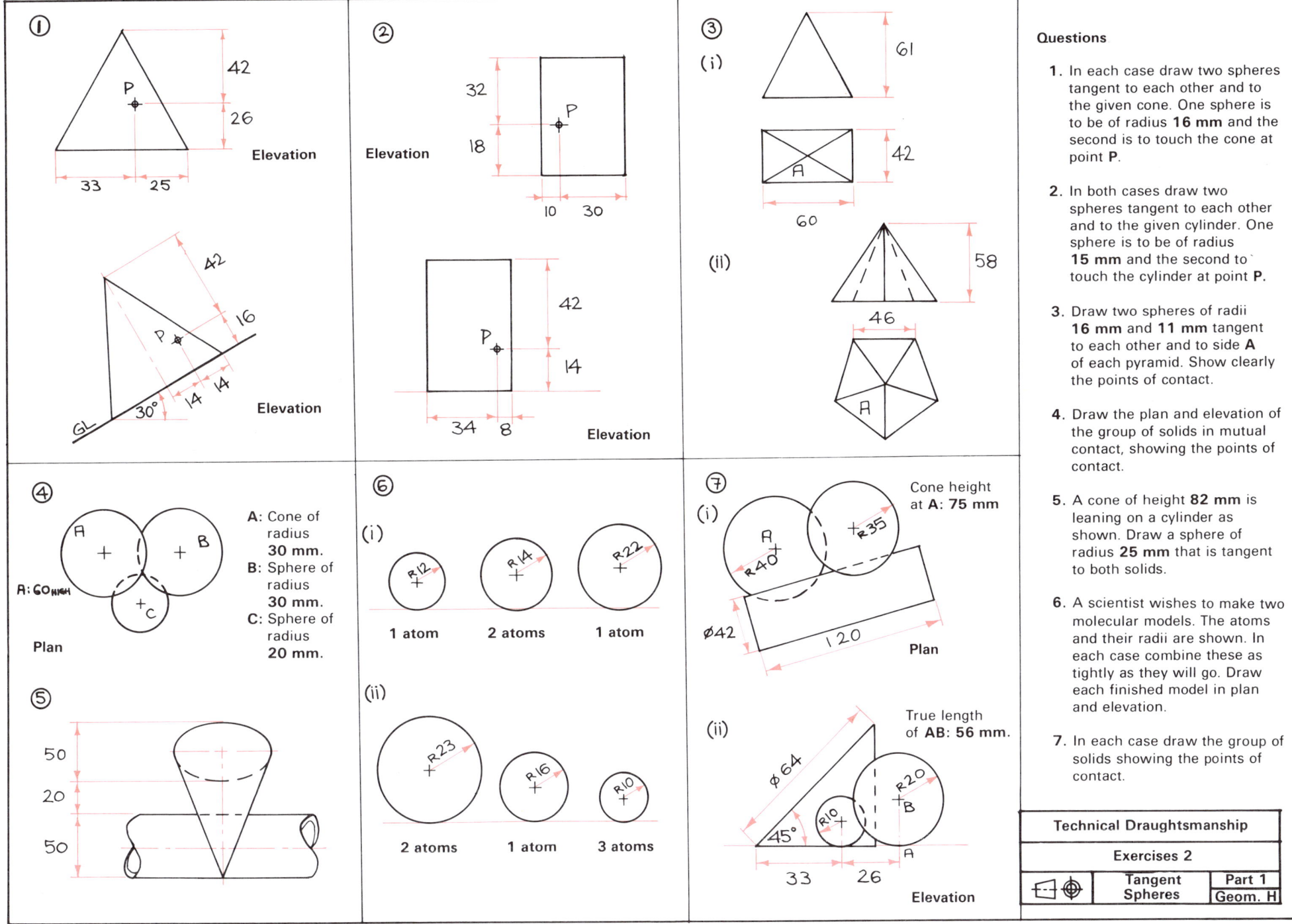

Questions

1. Draw the traces of a plane tangent to each sphere at point **P**.

2. Draw the traces of a plane tangent to each cone at point **P**.

3. Find the traces of a plane tangent to each cone at point **P**.

4. Locate a plane that will be tangent to each cone and will contain point **P**.

5. In each case draw the traces of an oblique plane tangent to the given cylinder at point **P**.

6. In both cases find the traces of a plane tangent to the cone which will also contain the line **AB**.

7. In each case find the traces of a plane tangent to the sphere which will also contain the line **AB**.

8. Draw the true shape of the section cut from the pyramid by a plane that is tangent to the cylinder at point **P**. The cylinder is leaning against the pyramid.

Technical Draughtsmanship

Exercises 3

Tangent Planes — Part I, Geom. H

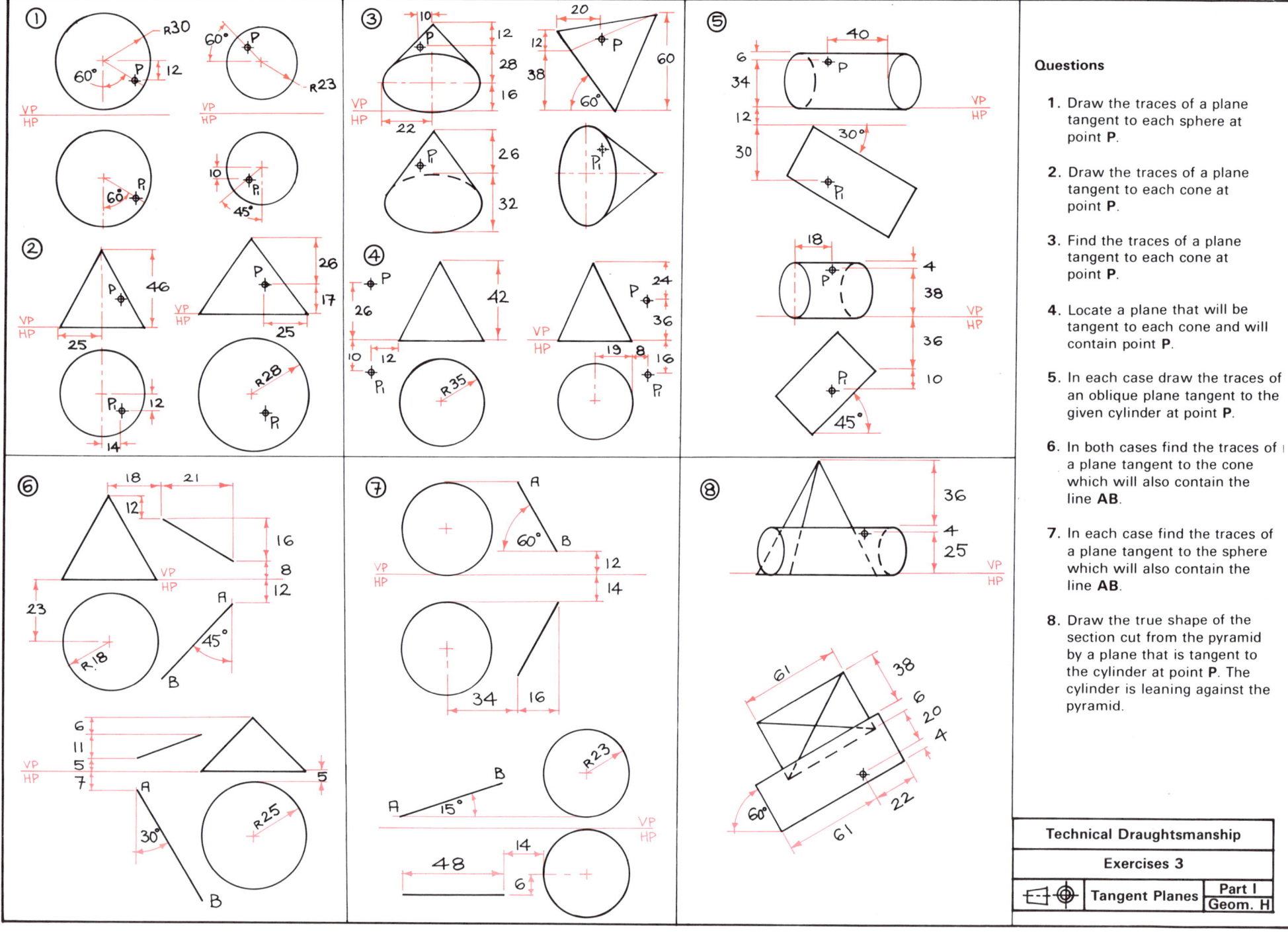

PART 1

CHAPTER 11
SECTIONS AND INTERSECTIONS

A section is a slice through an object made by a cutting plane. Sectional views reveal the inside of an object, or clarify an assembly of objects. Also, when one object penetrates another object the principles of sectioning can be applied when plotting the lines of intersection.

CONTENTS

Sectioning	*Page* 132
Sections of basic solids	133
Sphere and Anchor Ring	134
Irregular sections	135
Oblique cutting planes	136
Points of intersection	137
Prisms interpenetrating	138
Two worked examples	139
A sample problem	140
Machined curves as intersections	141
Exercises	142

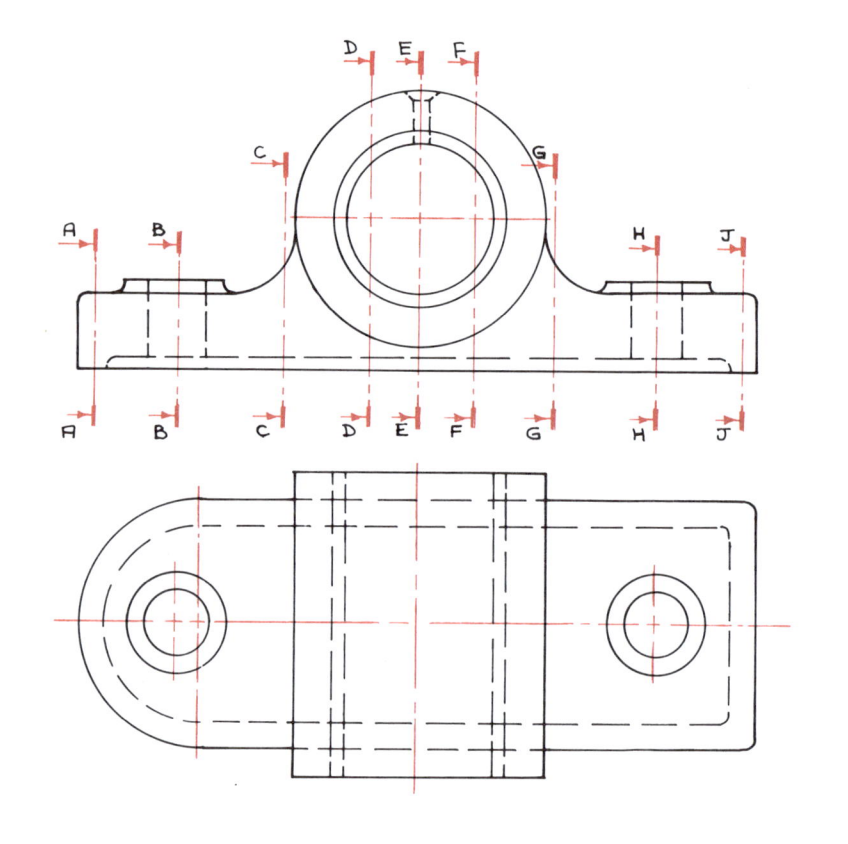

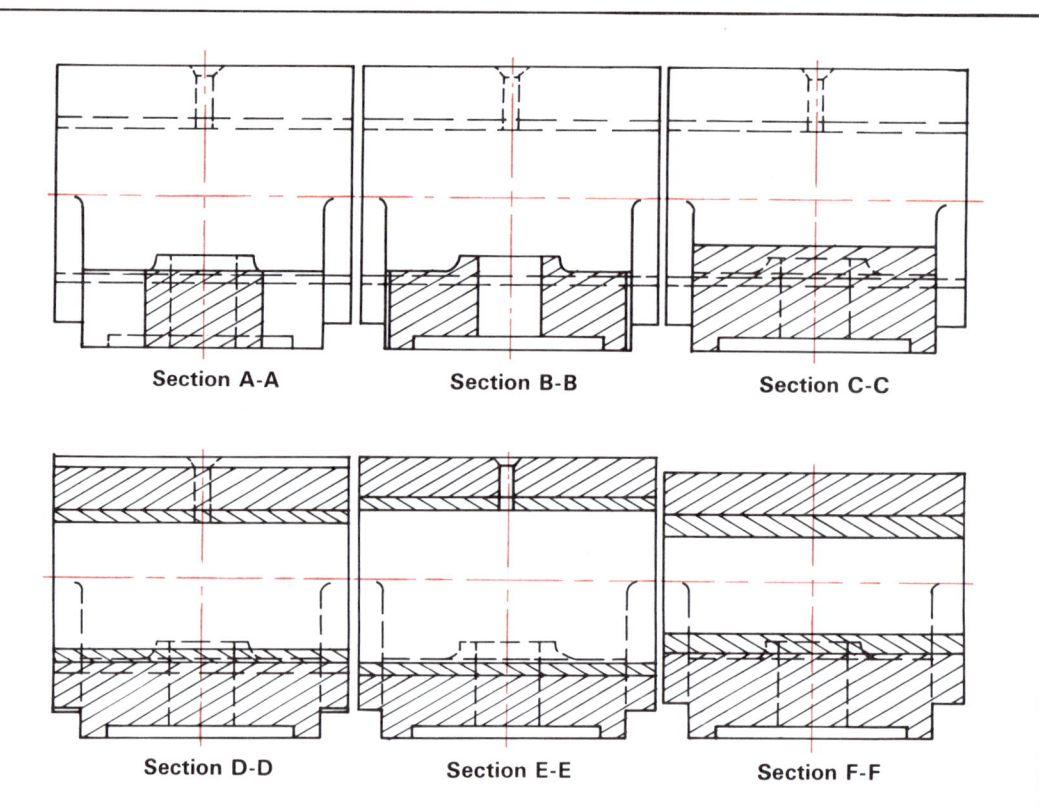

Dead-eye bearing cut by nine vertical cutting planes A-A to J-J
- Cutting planes are shown by a long thin chain line with thickened ends.
- Successive sections are all viewed in the same direction, as shown.
- Hatching lines are usually at **45°** and should not be spaced too closely.
- Separated areas of the same component are hatched in the same direction and with the same spacing.
- Where different adjacent parts meet, the direction of the hatching is usually reversed and staggered. If a change in direction is not practical, then one set of lines should be staggered and more closely spaced.

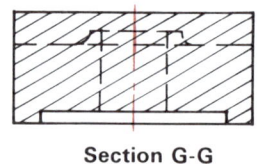

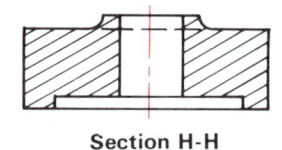

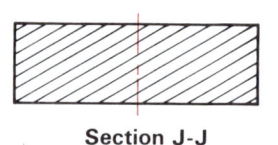

Section A-A

Section B-B

Section C-C

Section D-D

Section E-E

Section F-F

Section G-G

Section H-H

Section J-J

Note:
- *Why is section **C-C** different to section **G-G**?*
- *Also notice that there is an optical illusion when opposed hatching is used. Parallel lines seem to be converging, for example in section **F-F**.*

Technical Draughtsmanship	
Sectioning	
Sections 1	Part 1
	Geom.

① Square prism · Rectangular pyramid · Cone · Cylinder

Horizontal cutting planes

② Hexagonal prism · Triangular pyramid · Cone · Cylinder

Vertical cutting planes

③ Octagonal prism · Pentagonal pyramid · Cone · Cylinder

Cutting planes inclined to the HP

④ Pentagonal prism · Twelve-sided pyramid · Cone · Cylinder

Cutting planes inclined to the VP

Note: Oblique cutting planes and sections of spheres are dealt with on pages **136** and **134** respectively. Conic sections are the subject of chapter **14**, on page **187**.

Technical Draughtsmanship		
Sections of Basic Solids		
	Sections 2	Part I Geom.

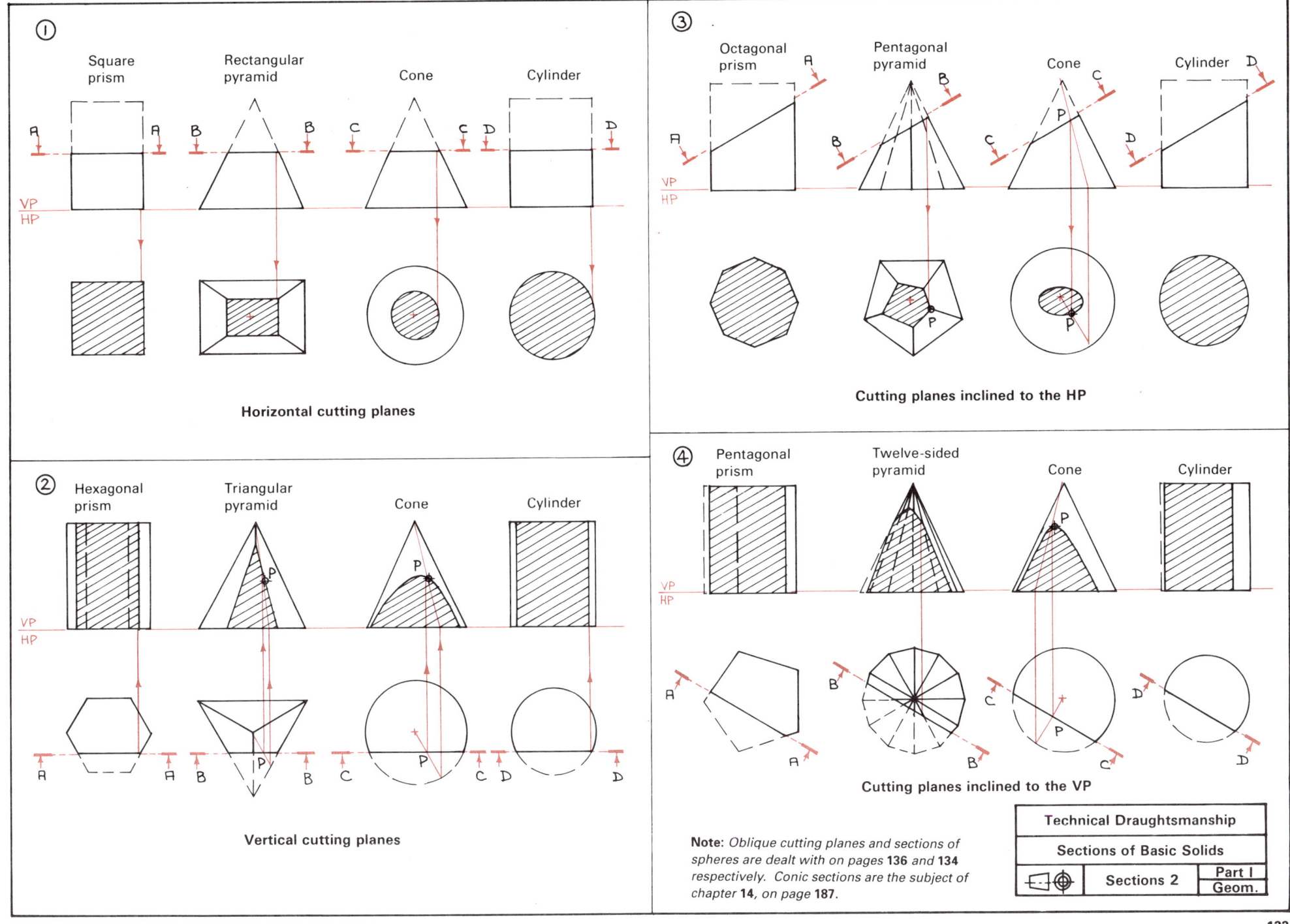

① Sphere cut on elevation by an inclined plane A-A.

- By taking an auxiliary plane parallel to **A-A**, an auxiliary plan showing the true circular section can be projected.
- This can then be used to find the section on the plan, as shown.

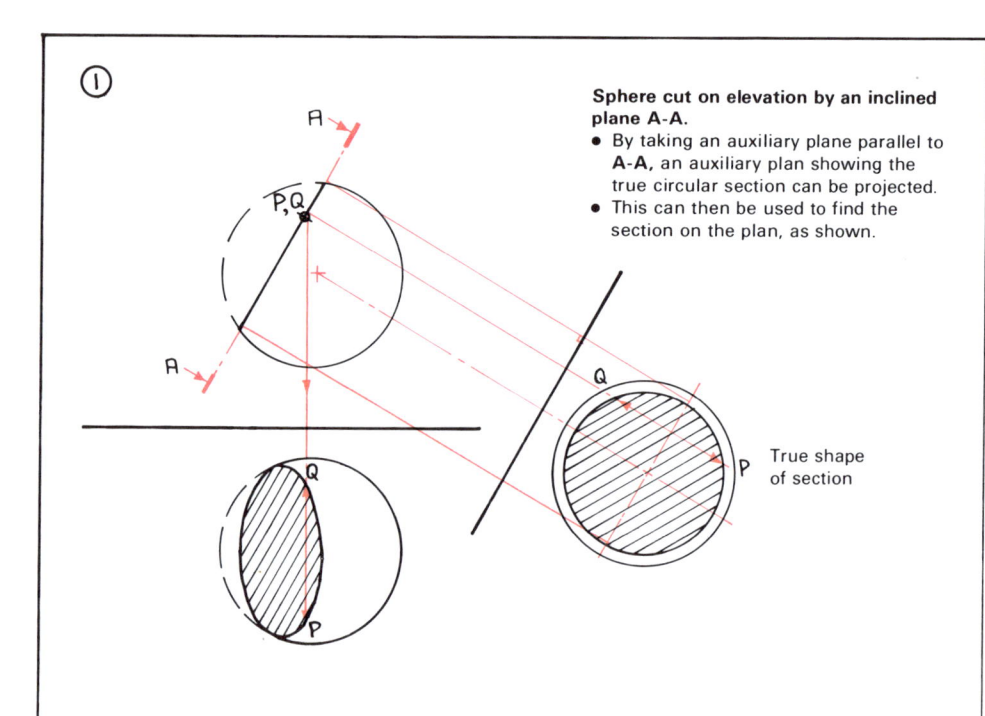

True shape of section

② Sphere cut on plan by an inclined plane A-A

- The procedure is similar to that of the previous construction.

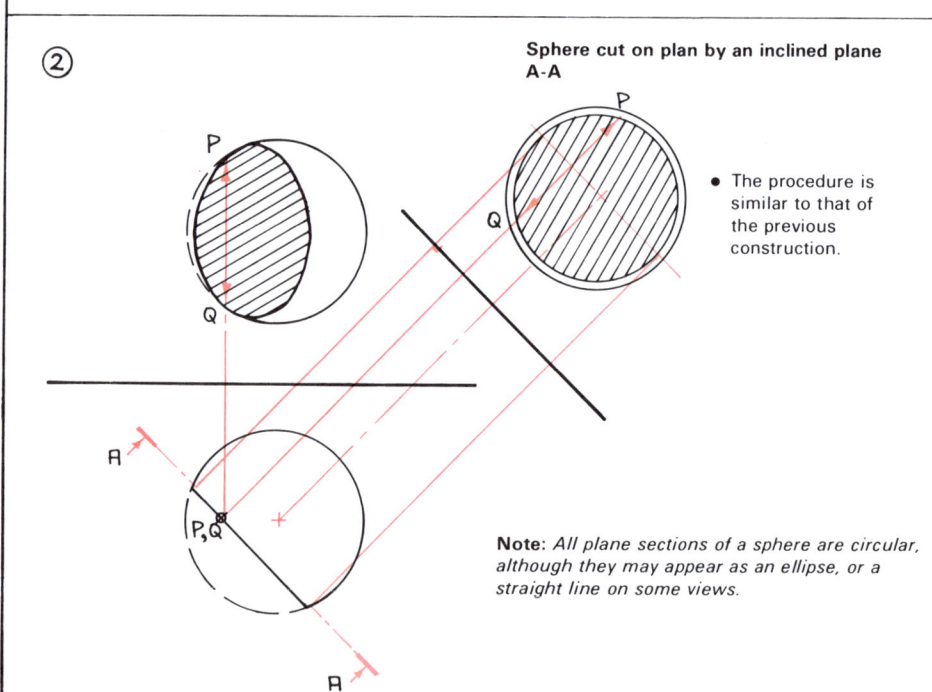

Note: *All plane sections of a sphere are circular, although they may appear as an ellipse, or a straight line on some views.*

③ Vertical sections through a circular torus

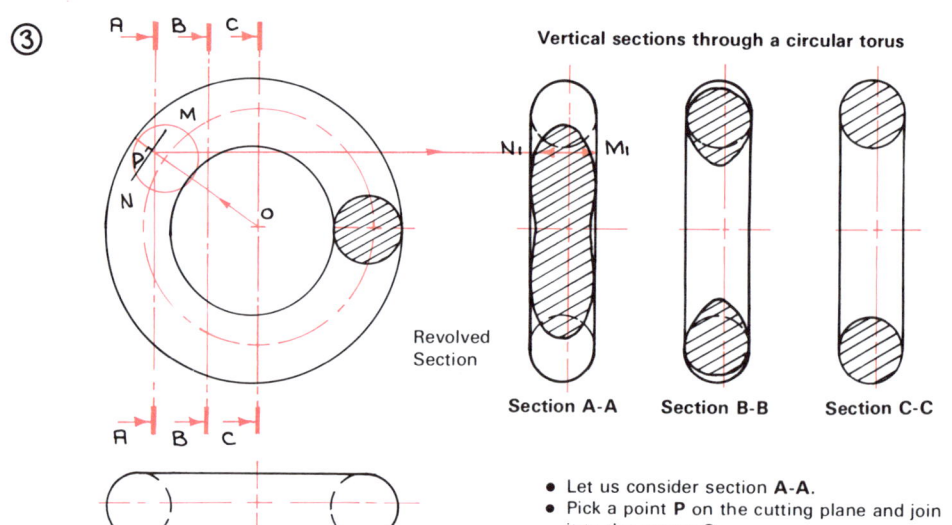

Revolved Section

Section A-A   Section B-B   Section C-C

Note: *A torus is a solid made by a plane figure (e.g. a circle) orbiting a centre. The circular torus is also known as an anchor ring.*

- Let us consider section **A-A**.
- Pick a point **P** on the cutting plane and join it to the centre **C**.
- Draw a revolved section on the radian **CP**.
- At **P** and at right angles to **CP** draw the line **NM**. This is the length of the section at **P**.
- Transfer this to the sectional drawing, as shown.
- Repeat until the section is outlined.

④ An inclined section of a circular torus

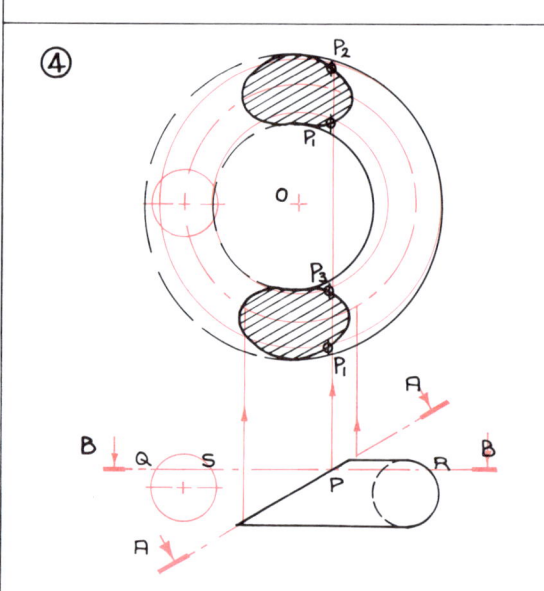

- Let us consider section **A-A**.
- Pick a point **P** on the cutting plane and through **P** draw a horizontal cutting plane **B-B**.
- On elevation, with centre **C** and diameter **QR**, draw a construction circle.
- Project **P** up to meet this circle at P_1 and at P_2.
- With centre **C** and diameter **ST** draw a second construction circle.
- Project **P** up to meet this circle at P_3 and P_4.
- Choose another point on **A-A** and repeat until the section is complete.
- By choosing symmetric points the number of construction circles is reduced.

Technical Draughtsmanship
Sphere and Anchor Ring
Sections 3 | Part I | Geom. H

134

① Half and quarter sections

Half section

Quarter section

Isometric quarter section
Not to scale

- Symmetrical parts can be drawn half in normal view and half in section.
- A quarter-sectioned solid has one quarter of the solid removed to show the internal structure.

② Stepped sections

Plan

Section A-A

- Sections can be taken in two or more parallel planes.
- Such stepped sections are hatched in the normal way.
- Where the cutting plane changes direction, the lines are thickened, as shown.
- The section itself is drawn as continuous and, for this reason, care must be taken to ensure that it is known to be a stepped section. This is done by clearly marking the adjacent view or by drawing an accompanying diagram.

③ Revolved Sections

Bracket with revolved sections

Moulding with revolved section

- The required slice may simply be turned through **90°** to let us see the cross-section.
- There should be no attempt to show depth or background on these sections.
- The drawing is discontinued to allow the revolved sections to be clearly seen.

④ Removed sections

- Here the section is 'removed' and shown to one side of the drawing.
- The background is not shown and it is not a view in the normal sense.
- No arrows are necessary on the cutting planes.

Section A-A

Section B-B

Section C-C

Section D-D

Technical Draughtsmanship
Irregular Sections

| | Sections 4 | Part I Geom. |

135

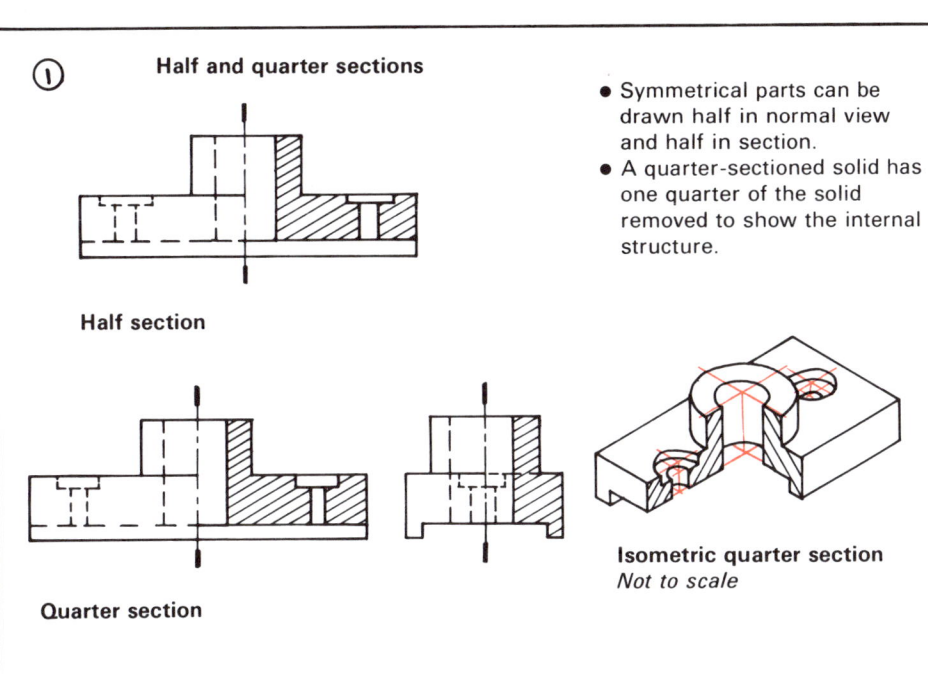

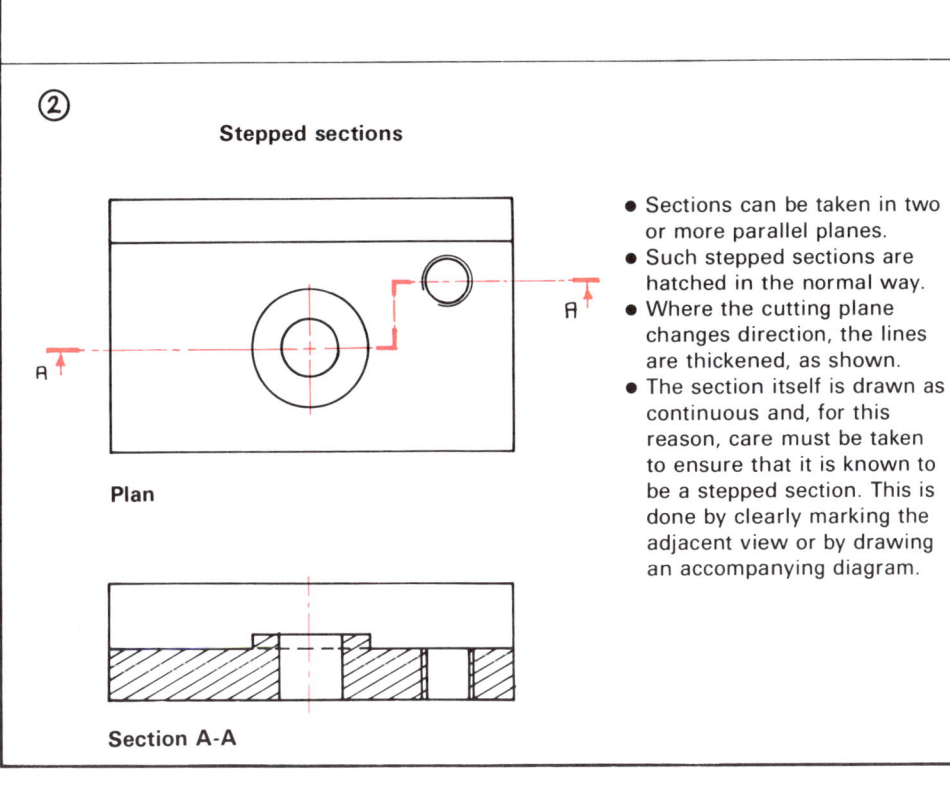

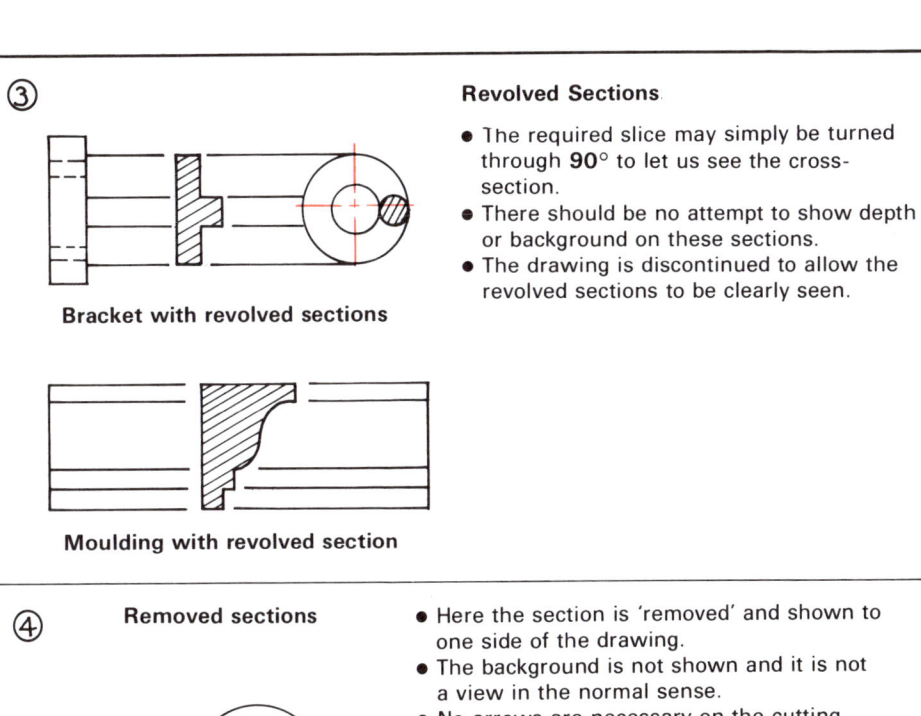

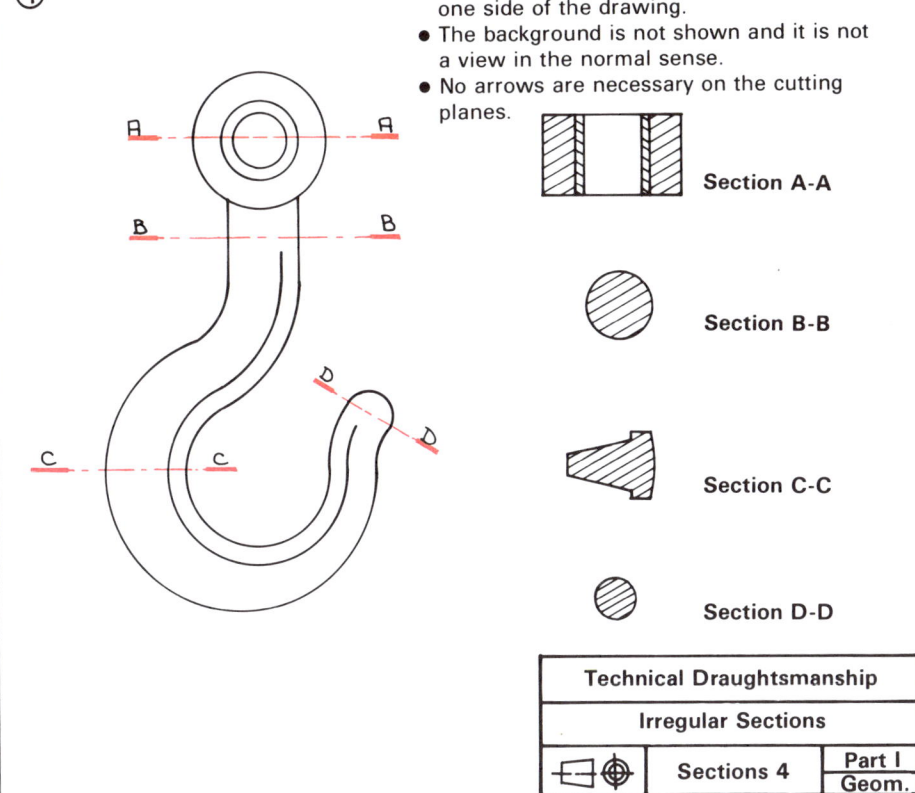

①

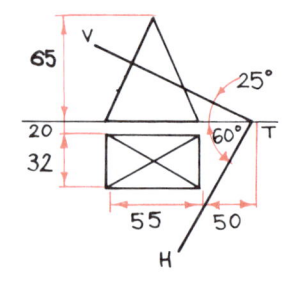

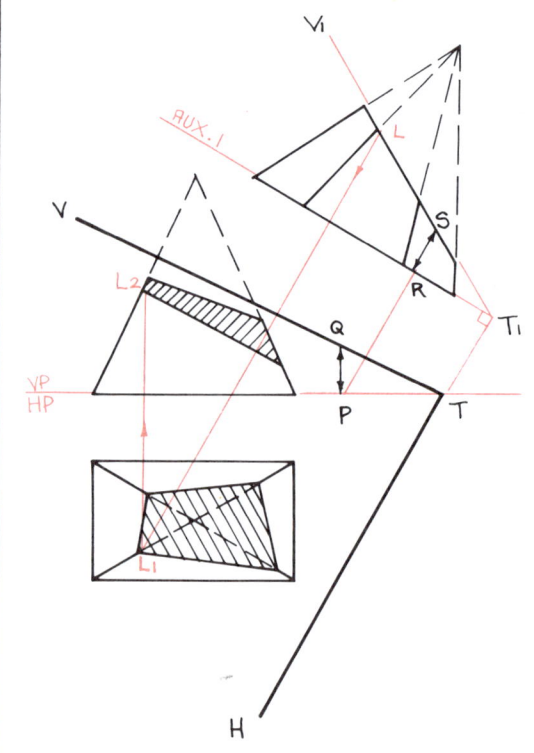

Given:
The solid and the traces of the oblique plane **VTH**.

To Draw:
The section cut by the oblique plane **VTH**.

- Draw the solid and the given traces.
- Choose a point **P** on the main axis and erect a perpendicular to meet the trace **VT** at **Q**.
- Extend trace **HT** clear of the elevation to **T₁**.
- At right angles to trace **HT₁** set an auxiliary plane **Aux 1**.
- Project the solid onto **Aux 1** in the normal way.
- Project point **P** onto **Aux 1** at **R** and extend making **RS** = **PQ**.
- From **T₁** through point **S** draw the line **T₁V₁**. *This is an edge view of the oblique plane.*
- The points of section are now clear and each can be projected back to the main views, as has been done for point **L**.
- Complete the drawing of the section.

Note: *If you prefer, a scale of heights can be taken from the auxiliary elevation and used to find the heights for the section on the elevation. This is also a useful cross check for any doubtful points.*

Note: *Point **T₁** could properly be called **H₁T₁**. Why?*

②

Given:
The solid and the traces of the oblique plane **VTH**.

To Find:
The true shape of the section cut by the oblique plane **VTH**.

True shape

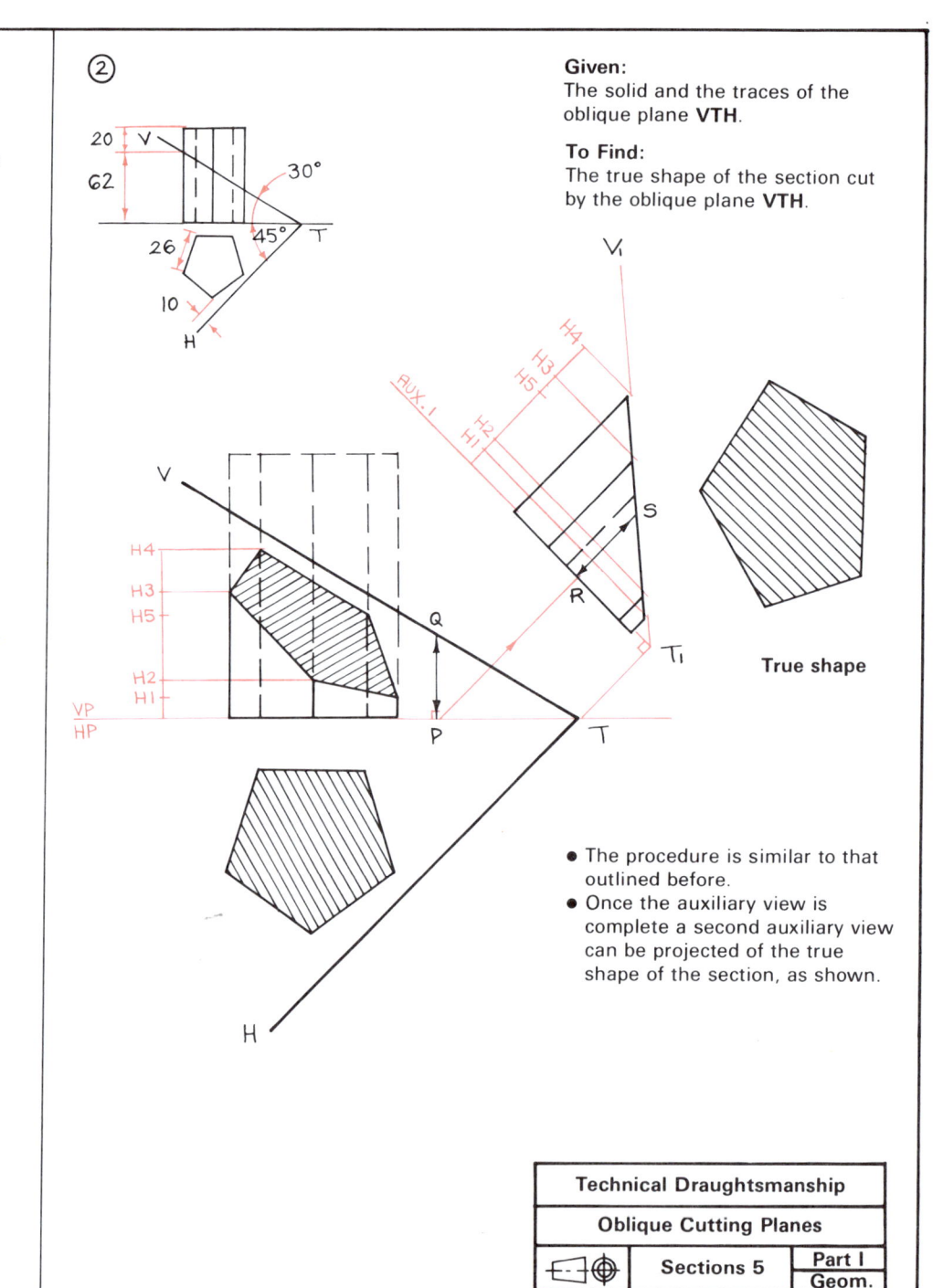

- The procedure is similar to that outlined before.
- Once the auxiliary view is complete a second auxiliary view can be projected of the true shape of the section, as shown.

Technical Draughtsmanship

Oblique Cutting Planes

Sections 5 | Part I | Geom.

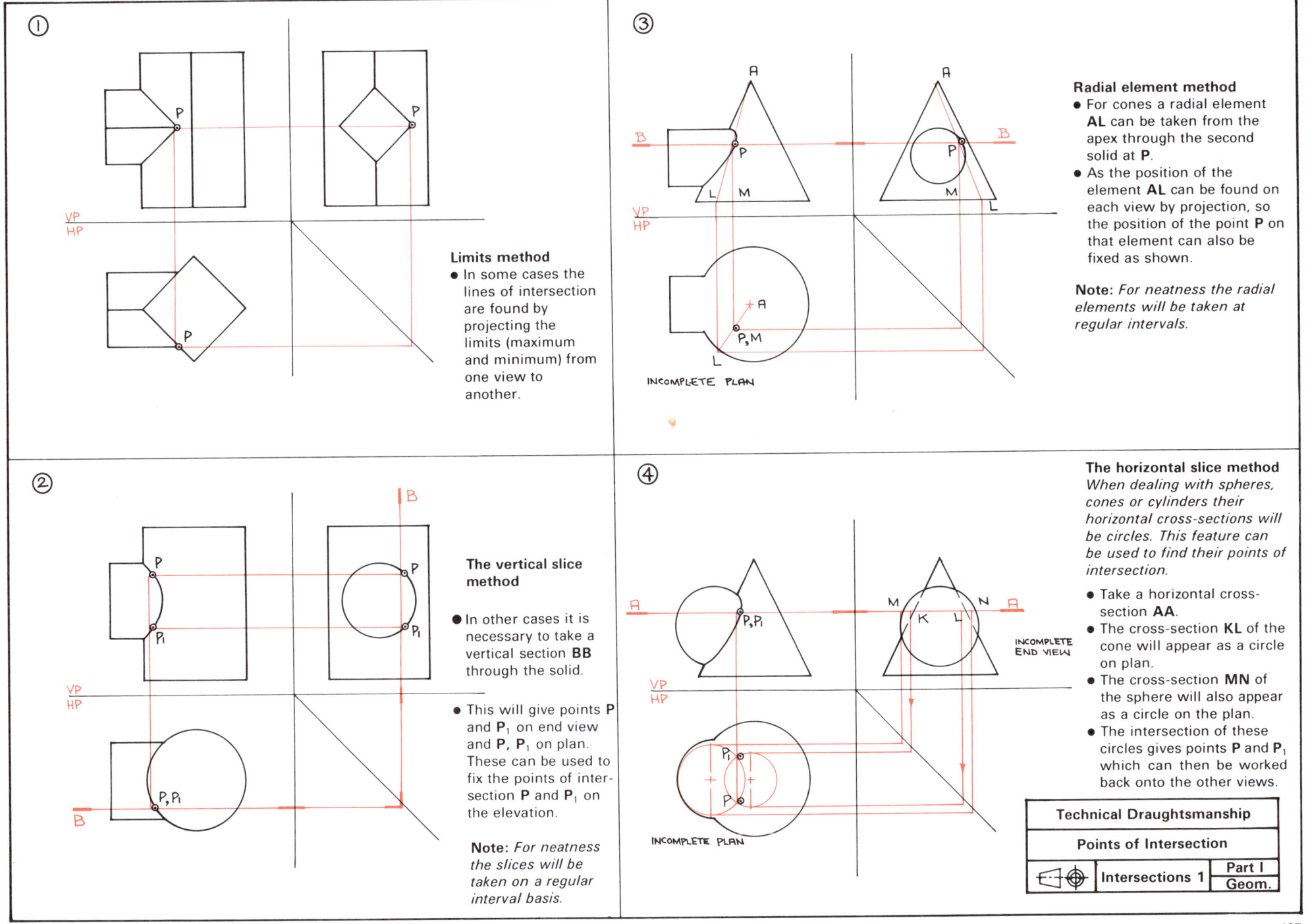

①

Limits method
- In some cases the lines of intersection are found by projecting the limits (maximum and minimum) from one view to another.

②

The vertical slice method
- In other cases it is necessary to take a vertical section **BB** through the solid.
- This will give points **P** and **P₁** on end view and **P**, **P₁** on plan. These can be used to fix the points of intersection **P** and **P₁** on the elevation.

Note: *For neatness the slices will be taken on a regular interval basis.*

③

Radial element method
- For cones a radial element **AL** can be taken from the apex through the second solid at **P**.
- As the position of the element **AL** can be found on each view by projection, so the position of the point **P** on that element can also be fixed as shown.

Note: *For neatness the radial elements will be taken at regular intervals.*

④

The horizontal slice method
When dealing with spheres, cones or cylinders their horizontal cross-sections will be circles. This feature can be used to find their points of intersection.

- Take a horizontal cross-section **AA**.
- The cross-section **KL** of the cone will appear as a circle on plan.
- The cross-section **MN** of the sphere will also appear as a circle on the plan.
- The intersection of these circles gives points **P** and **P₁** which can then be worked back onto the other views.

Technical Draughtsmanship
Points of Intersection
Intersections 1 — Part I / Geom.

137

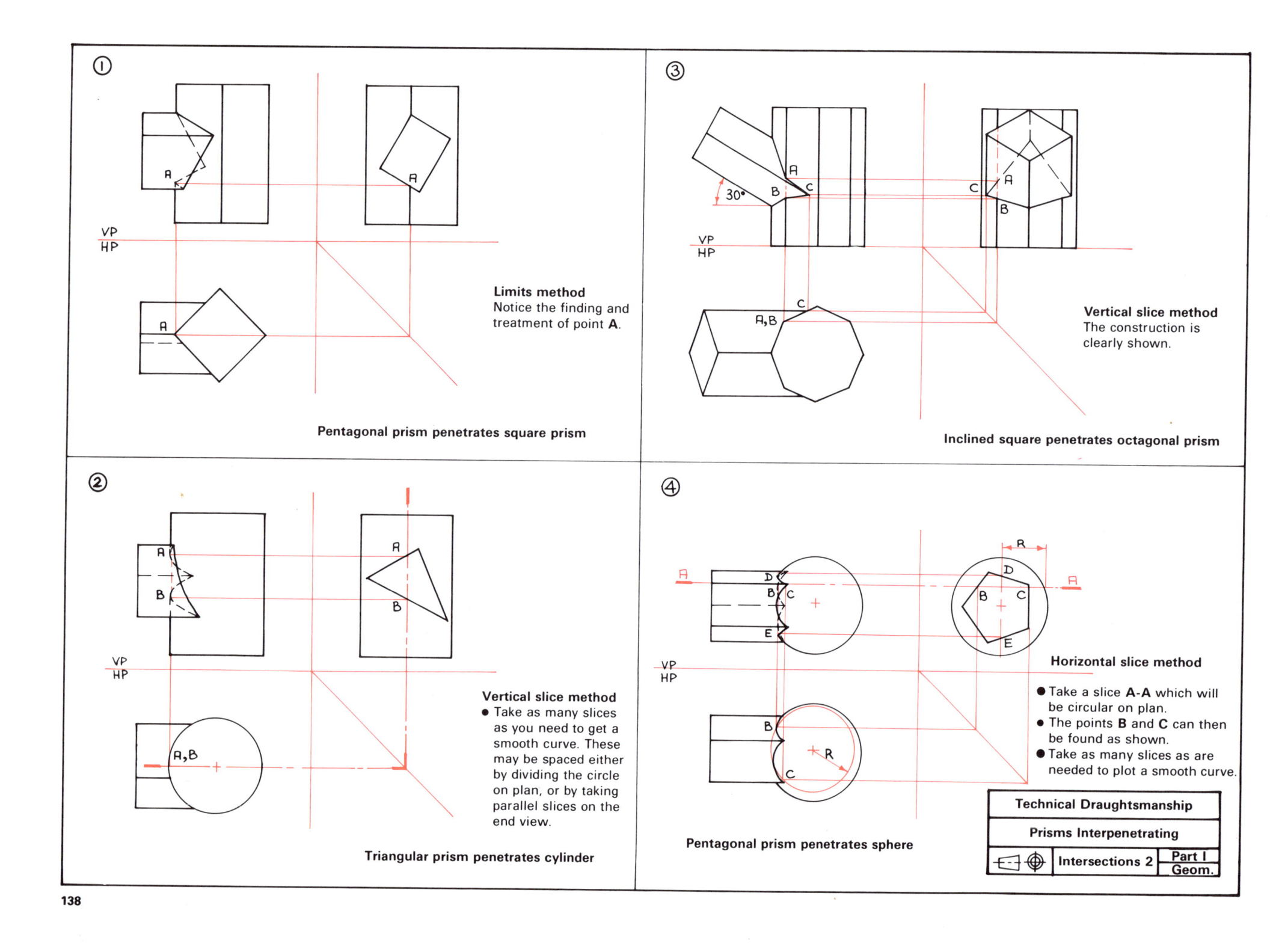

①

Limits method
Notice the finding and treatment of point **A**.

Pentagonal prism penetrates square prism

②

Vertical slice method
- Take as many slices as you need to get a smooth curve. These may be spaced either by dividing the circle on plan, or by taking parallel slices on the end view.

Triangular prism penetrates cylinder

③

Vertical slice method
The construction is clearly shown.

Inclined square penetrates octagonal prism

④

Horizontal slice method
- Take a slice **A-A** which will be circular on plan.
- The points **B** and **C** can then be found as shown.
- Take as many slices as are needed to plot a smooth curve.

Pentagonal prism penetrates sphere

Technical Draughtsmanship
Prisms Interpenetrating
Intersections 2 — Part I Geom.

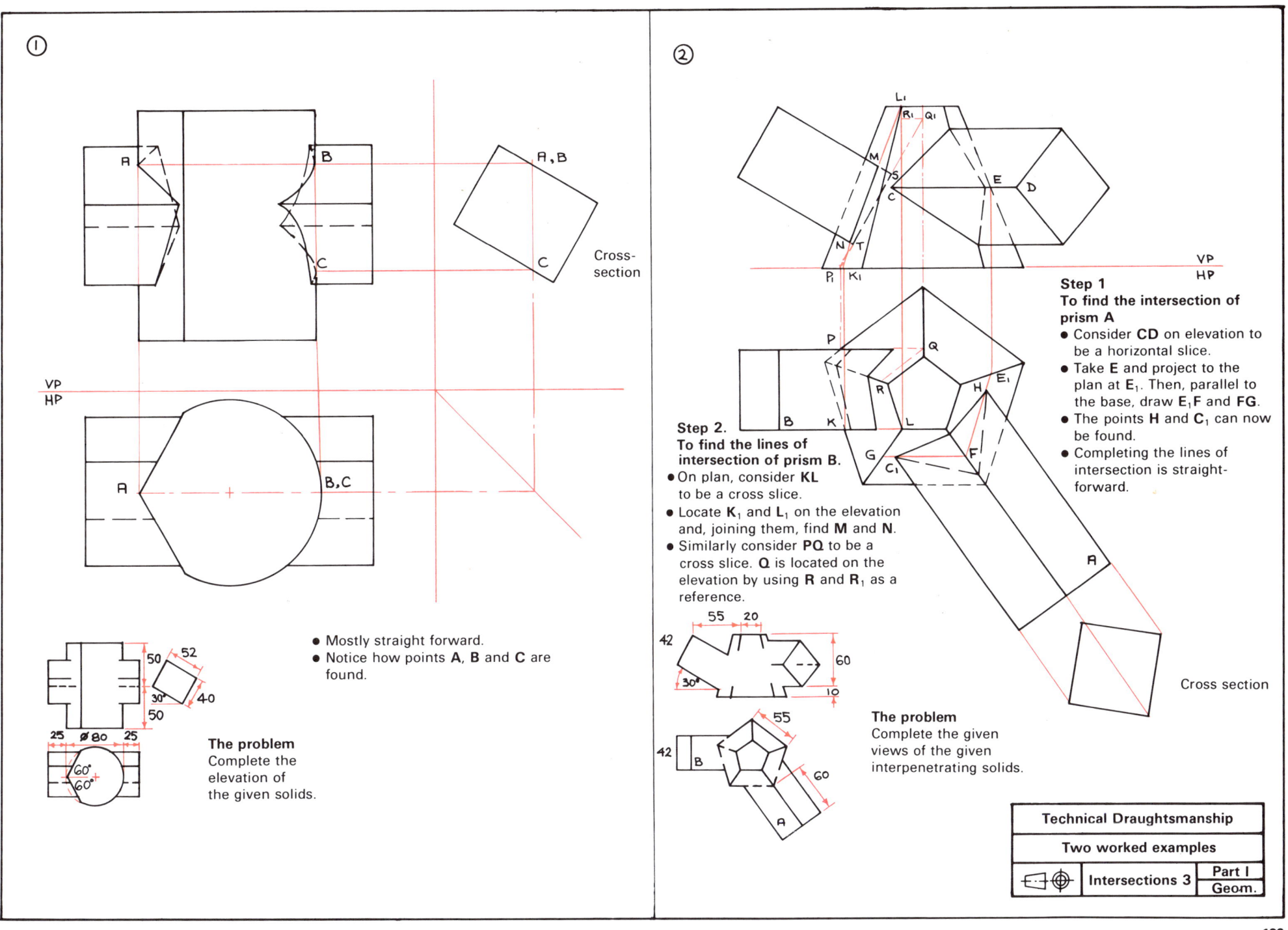

①

Cross-section

VP / HP

- Mostly straight forward.
- Notice how points **A**, **B** and **C** are found.

The problem
Complete the elevation of the given solids.

②

VP / HP

Step 1
To find the intersection of prism A
- Consider **CD** on elevation to be a horizontal slice.
- Take **E** and project to the plan at **E₁**. Then, parallel to the base, draw **E₁F** and **FG**.
- The points **H** and **C₁** can now be found.
- Completing the lines of intersection is straightforward.

Step 2.
To find the lines of intersection of prism B.
- On plan, consider **KL** to be a cross slice.
- Locate **K₁** and **L₁** on the elevation and, joining them, find **M** and **N**.
- Similarly consider **PQ** to be a cross slice. **Q** is located on the elevation by using **R** and **R₁** as a reference.

The problem
Complete the given views of the given interpenetrating solids.

Cross section

| Technical Draughtsmanship |
| Two worked examples |
| Intersections 3 | Part I Geom. |

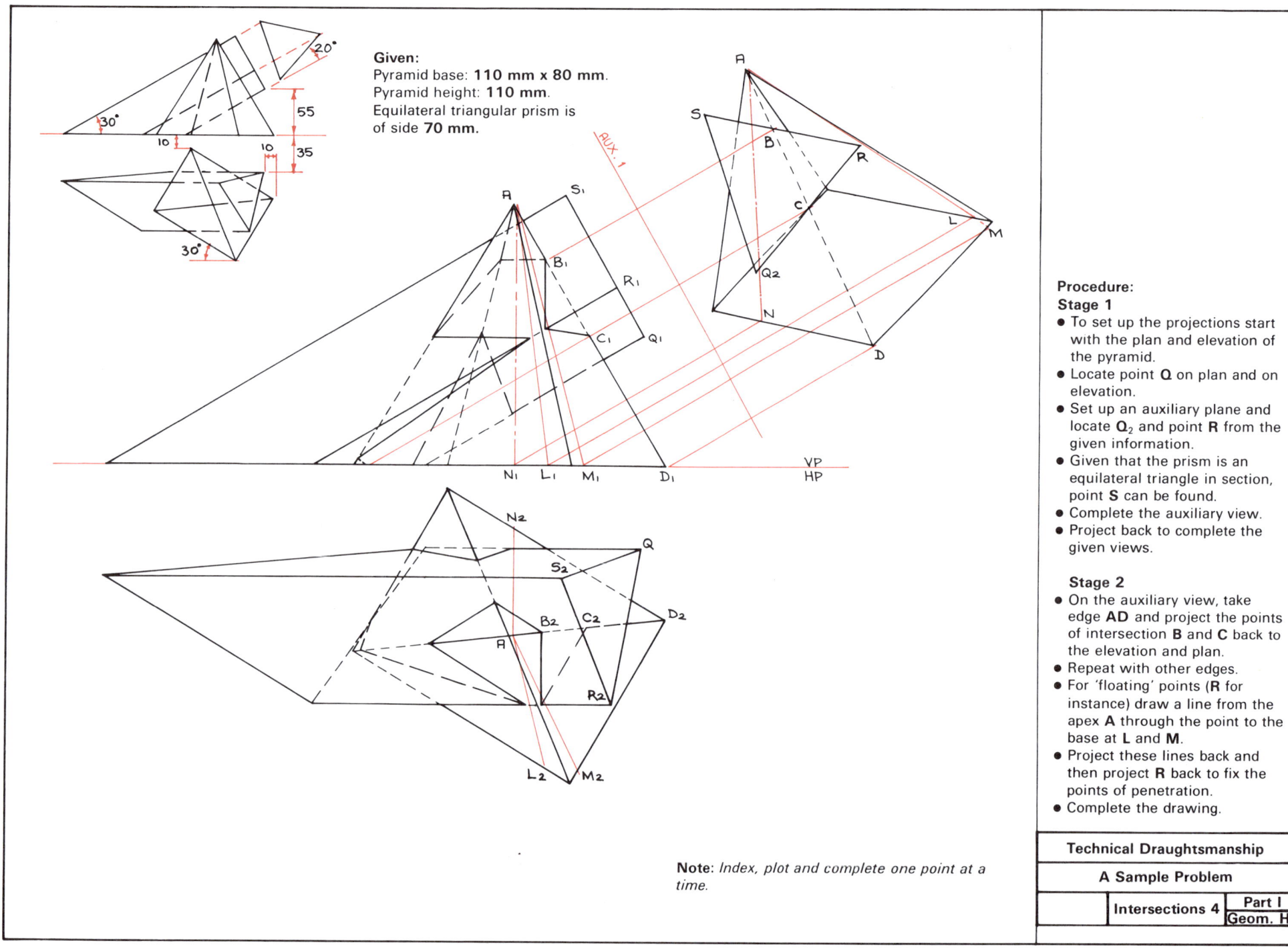

Given:
Pyramid base: **110 mm x 80 mm**.
Pyramid height: **110 mm**.
Equilateral triangular prism is of side **70 mm**.

Procedure:
Stage 1
- To set up the projections start with the plan and elevation of the pyramid.
- Locate point **Q** on plan and on elevation.
- Set up an auxiliary plane and locate **Q₂** and point **R** from the given information.
- Given that the prism is an equilateral triangle in section, point **S** can be found.
- Complete the auxiliary view.
- Project back to complete the given views.

Stage 2
- On the auxiliary view, take edge **AD** and project the points of intersection **B** and **C** back to the elevation and plan.
- Repeat with other edges.
- For 'floating' points (**R** for instance) draw a line from the apex **A** through the point to the base at **L** and **M**.
- Project these lines back and then project **R** back to fix the points of penetration.
- Complete the drawing.

Note: *Index, plot and complete one point at a time.*

| Technical Draughtsmanship |
| A Sample Problem |
| Intersections 4 — Part I / Geom. H |

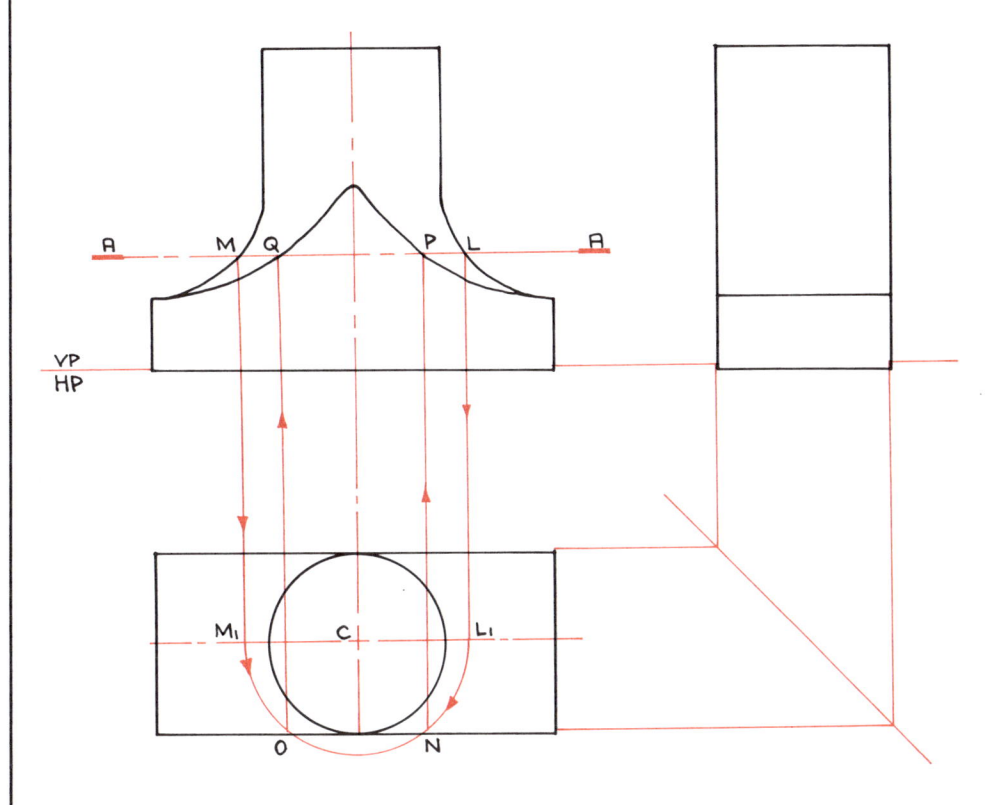

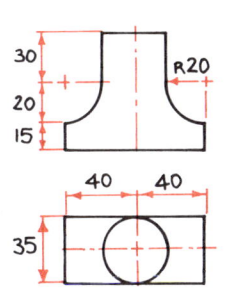

①

- Here a circular bar has been turned and cut. The resulting section is called a **palmate** section.
- The lines of intersection are found by the horizontal slice method, one cut of which is shown.

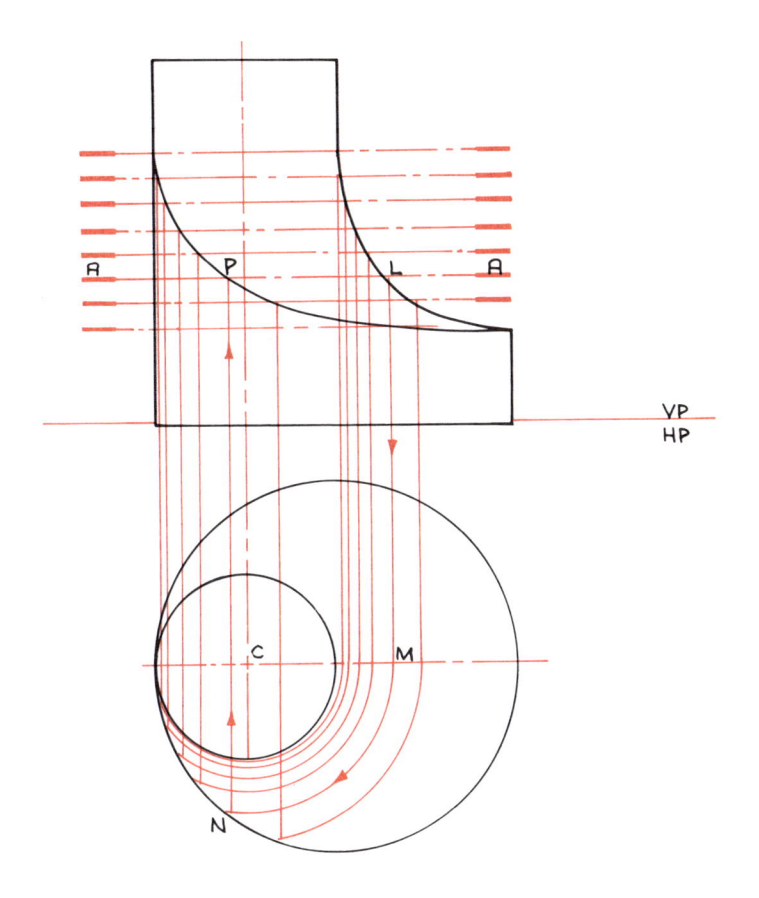

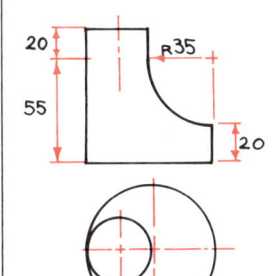

Problem: Complete the given views.

②

- In this case a bar has been turned for a smooth transition to an eccentric cylinder.
- The line of intersection of the surfaces is found by the horizontal slice method, one cut of which is indexed.

Problem: Complete the given views.

Technical Draughtsmanship
Machined Curves as Intersections
Intersections 5 — Part I / Geom. H

141

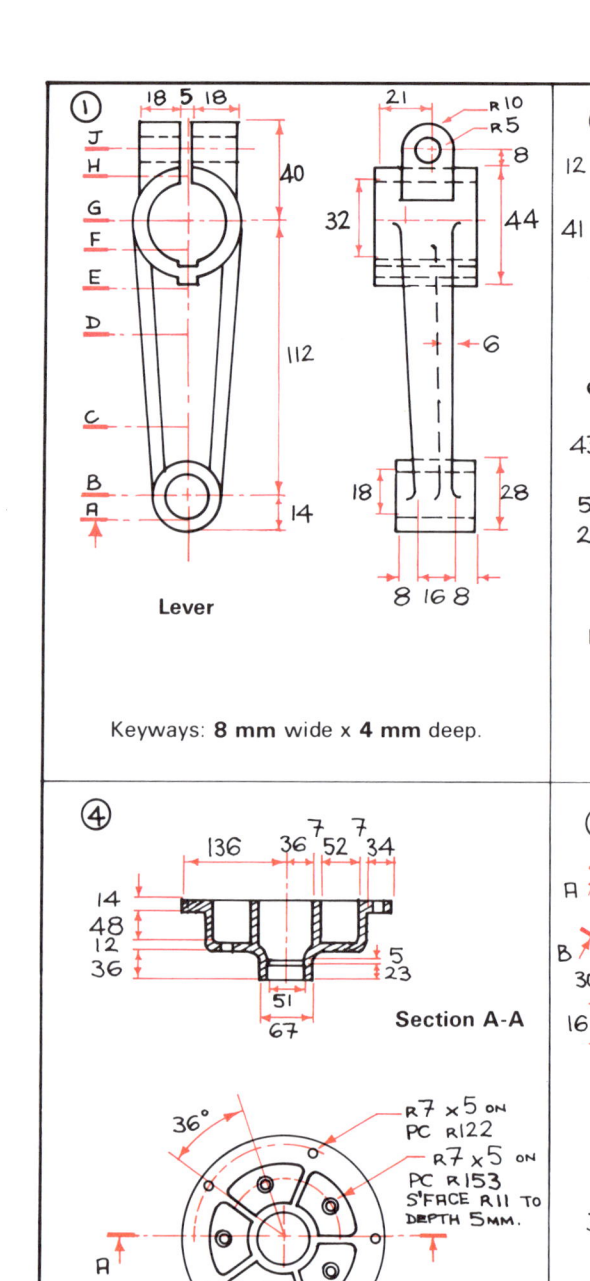

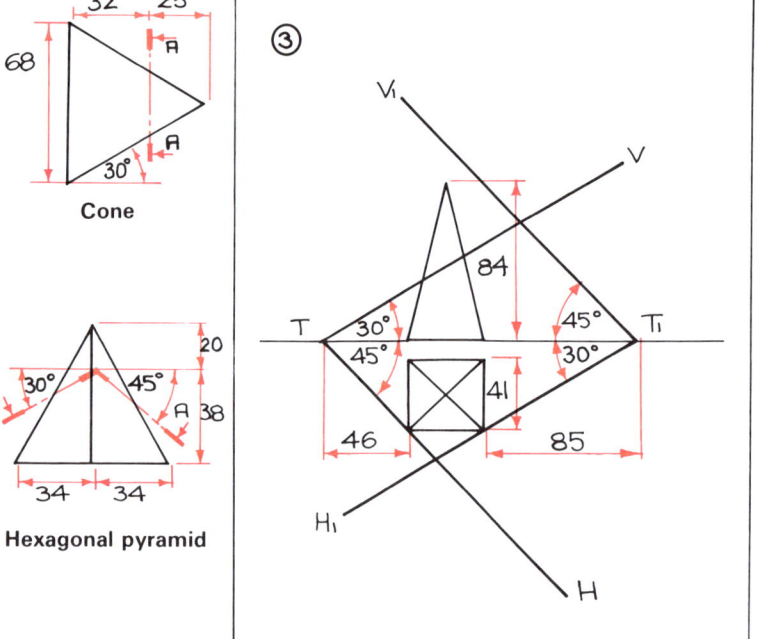

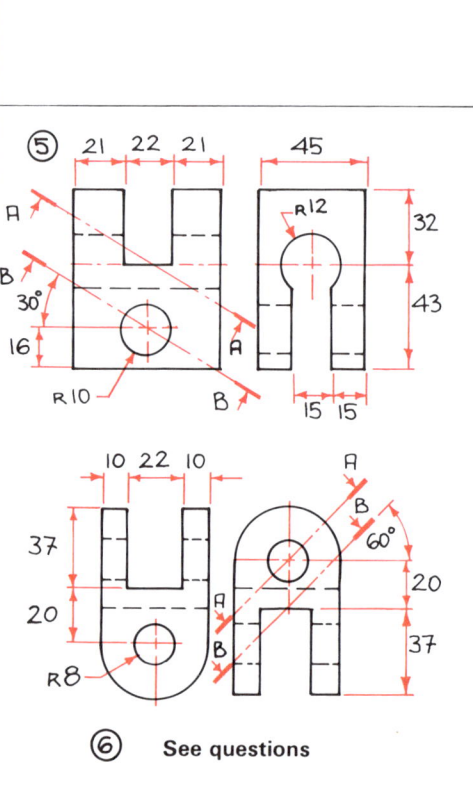

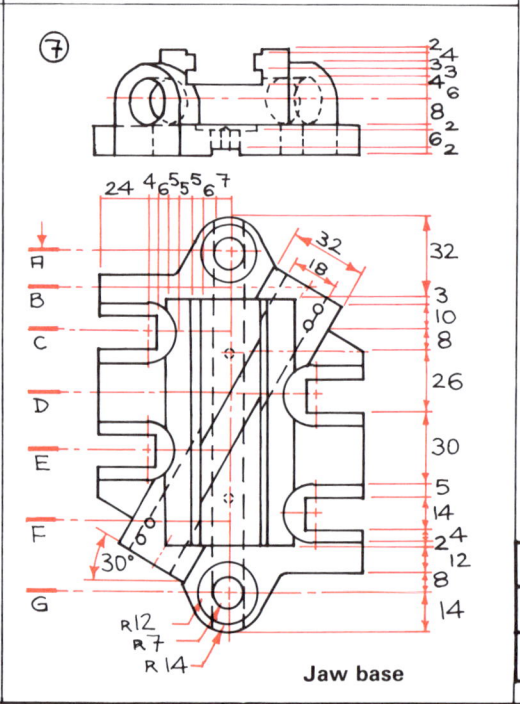

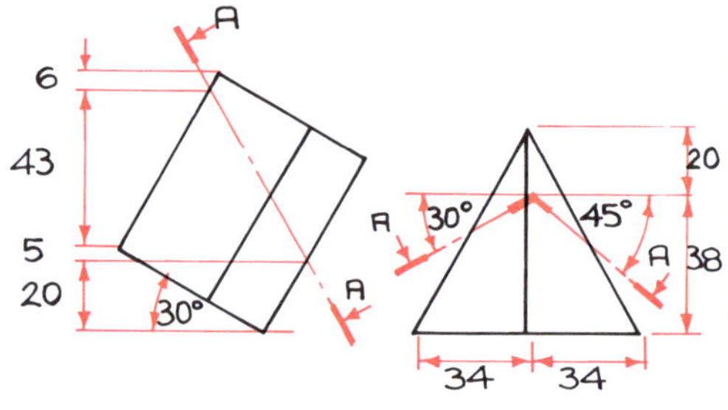

Questions

1. Draw the sections **A-A** to **J-J** of the given lever.

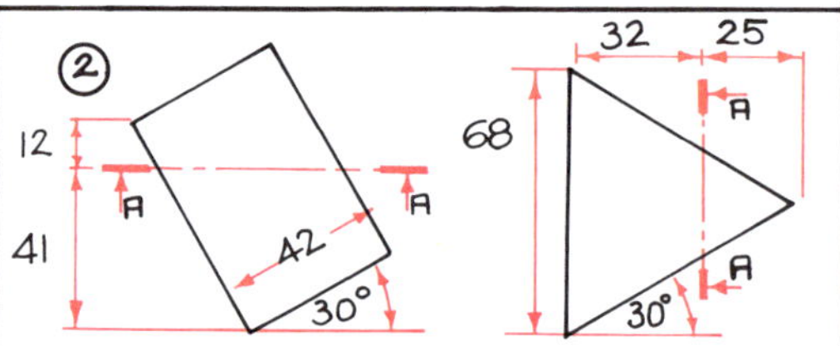

2. In each case draw a full orthographic projection of the solid showing clearly the section cut by **A-A**.

3. A square pyramid has been cut by two oblique planes **VTH** and **V₁T₁H₁**. Draw the solid cut by each plane separately and then by both planes combined.

4. Draw the front wheel hub in half section on all three standard views.

5. Draw the given views and the two parallel sections **A-A** and **B-B** for each solid.

6. (i) Measure and draw a two storey house, then show two vertical sections through that house.

    or

    (ii) Measure and draw a longitudinal half-section through a bicycle. A simplified diagram with enlarged details can be used.

7. Draw the sections **A-A** to **G-G** through the jaw base, the elevation and plan of which are given.

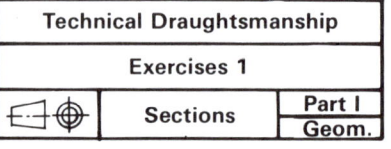

Technical Draughtsmanship

Exercises 1

Sections — Part I Geom.

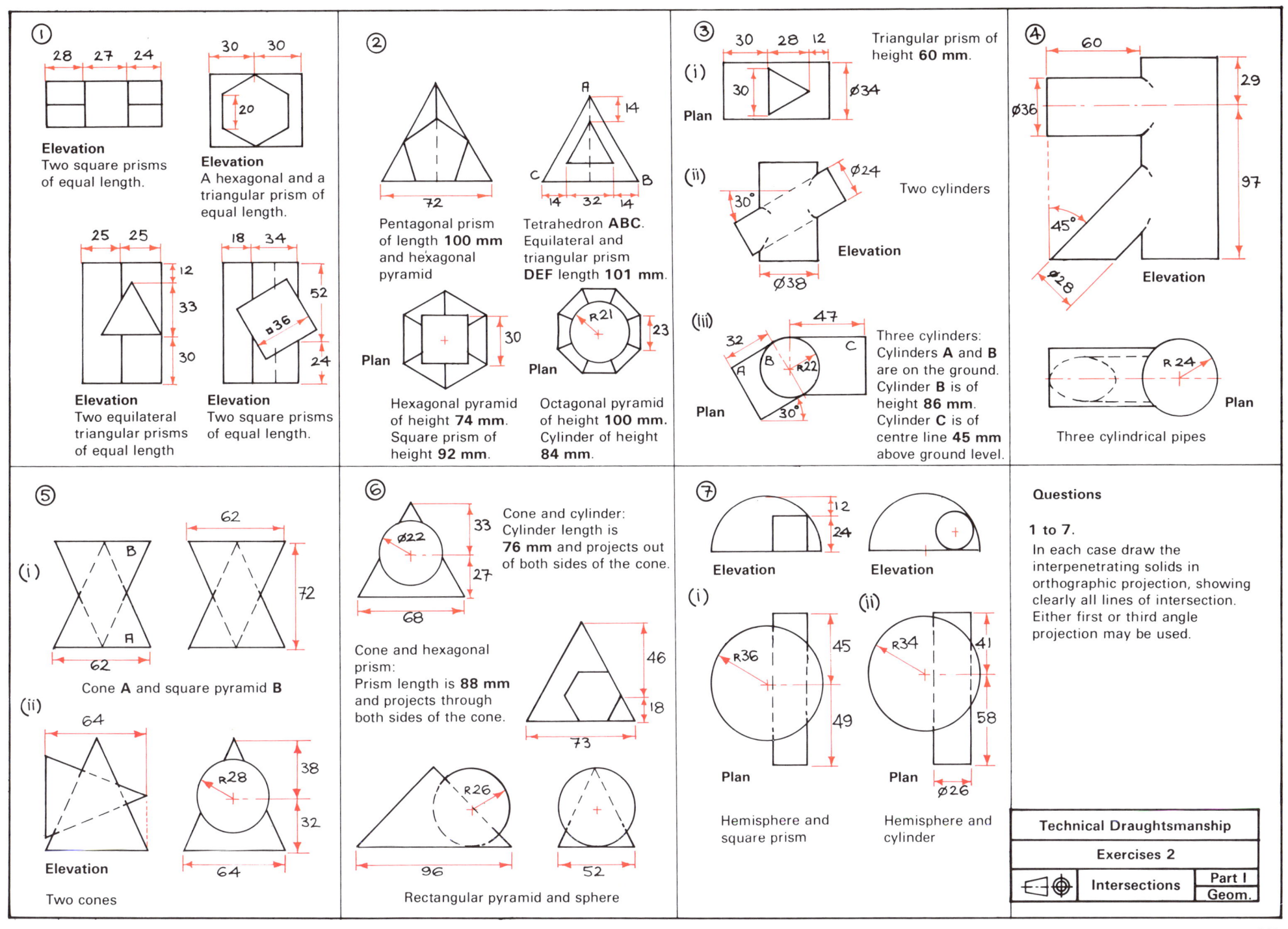

1

Elevation — Two square prisms of equal length. (28, 27, 24)

Elevation — A hexagonal and a triangular prism of equal length. (30, 30, 20)

Elevation — Two equilateral triangular prisms of equal length. (25, 25, 12, 33, 30)

Elevation — Two square prisms of equal length. (18, 34, 52, 24, ⌀36)

2

Pentagonal prism of length **100 mm** and hexagonal pyramid. (72)

Tetrahedron **ABC**. Equilateral and triangular prism **DEF** length **101 mm**. (14, 14, 32, 14)

Plan — Hexagonal pyramid of height **74 mm**. Square prism of height **92 mm**. (30)

Plan — Octagonal pyramid of height **100 mm**. Cylinder of height **84 mm**. (R21, 23)

3

(i) **Plan** — Triangular prism of height **60 mm**. (30, 28, 12, 30, ⌀34)

(ii) **Elevation** — Two cylinders. (⌀24, 30°, ⌀38)

(iii) **Plan** — Three cylinders: Cylinders **A** and **B** are on the ground. Cylinder **B** is of height **86 mm**. Cylinder **C** is of centre line **45 mm** above ground level. (32, 47, R22, 30°)

4

Elevation — (60, 29, ⌀36, 97, 45°, ⌀28)

Plan — Three cylindrical pipes. (R24)

5

(i) Cone **A** and square pyramid **B**. (62, 62, 72)

(ii) **Elevation** — Two cones. (64, 38, 32, R28, 64)

6

Cone and cylinder: Cylinder length is **76 mm** and projects out of both sides of the cone. (⌀22, 33, 27, 68)

Cone and hexagonal prism: Prism length is **88 mm** and projects through both sides of the cone. (46, 18, 73)

Rectangular pyramid and sphere. (R26, 96, 52)

7

(i) **Elevation** / **Plan** — Hemisphere and square prism. (12, 24, R36, 45, 49)

(ii) **Elevation** / **Plan** — Hemisphere and cylinder. (R34, 41, 58, ⌀26)

Questions

1 to 7.

In each case draw the interpenetrating solids in orthographic projection, showing clearly all lines of intersection. Either first or third angle projection may be used.

Technical Draughtsmanship

Exercises 2

Intersections — Part I, Geom.

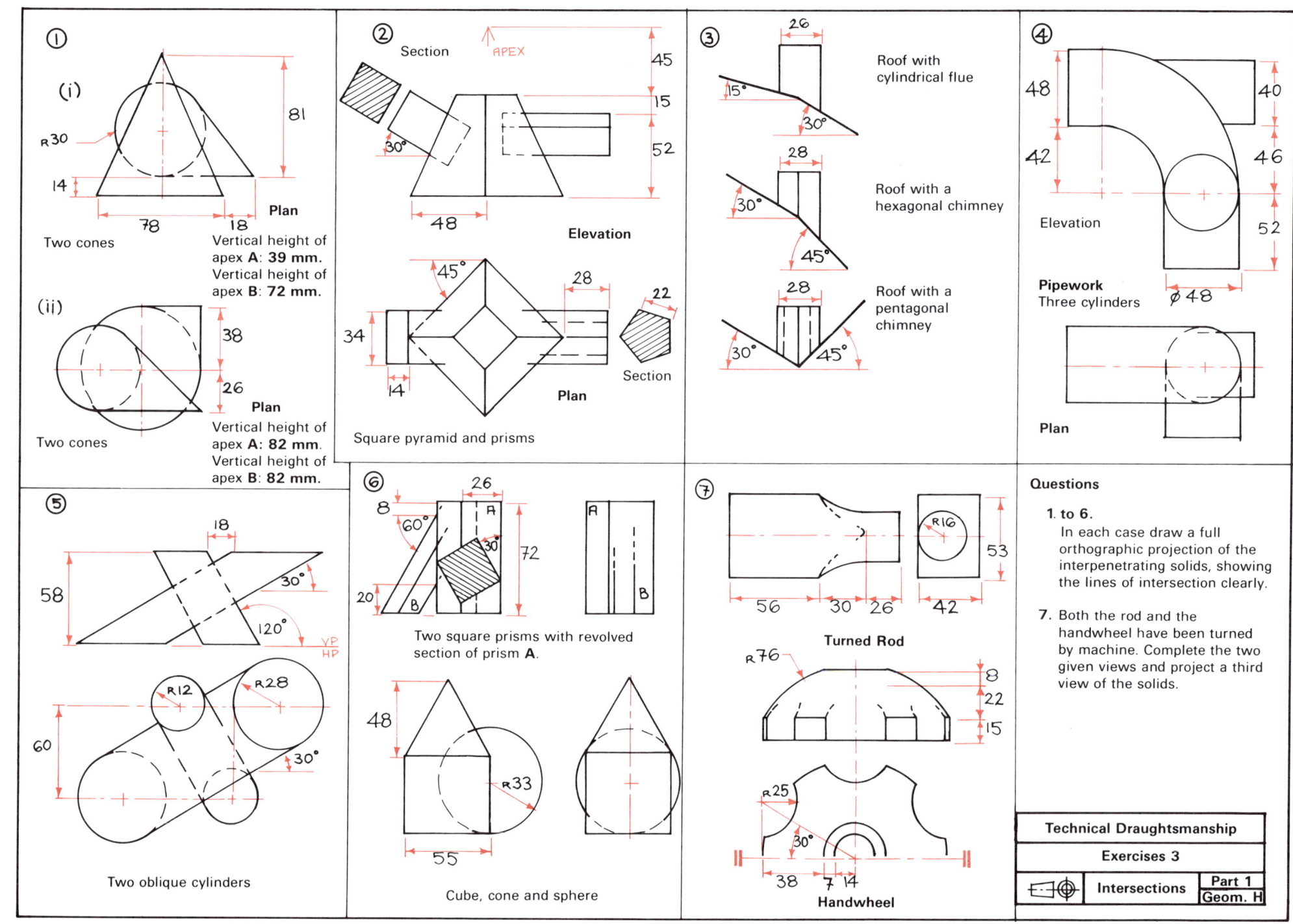

Technical Draughtsmanship

Exercises 3 — Intersections — Part 1 — Geom. H

1. Two cones

(i) Plan — R30, 81, 14, 78, 18
Vertical height of apex **A**: 39 mm.
Vertical height of apex **B**: 72 mm.

(ii) Plan — 38, 26
Two cones
Vertical height of apex **A**: 82 mm.
Vertical height of apex **B**: 82 mm.

2. Square pyramid and prisms

Section, APEX, 45, 15, 52, 30°, 48 — Elevation
45°, 28, 34, 22, 14 — Plan, Section

3.
- Roof with cylindrical flue — 26, 15°, 30°
- Roof with a hexagonal chimney — 28, 30°, 45°
- Roof with a pentagonal chimney — 28, 30°, 45°

4. Pipework — Three cylinders

Elevation — 48, 42, 40, 46, 52, Ø48
Plan

5. Two oblique cylinders

18, 58, 30°, 120°, VP/HP
R12, R28, 60, 30°

6. Two square prisms with revolved section of prism A.

8, 26, 60°, 30, 72, 20, A, B

Cube, cone and sphere — 48, R33, 55

7. Turned Rod

56, 30, 26, 42, 53, R16

Handwheel

R76, 8, 22, 15, R25, 30°, 38, 7, 14

Questions

1. to 6.
In each case draw a full orthographic projection of the interpenetrating solids, showing the lines of intersection clearly.

7. Both the rod and the handwheel have been turned by machine. Complete the two given views and project a third view of the solids.

PART 1

CHAPTER 12
DEVELOPMENT

Development is the laying out flat of the surfaces of a solid. The making of flat two-dimensional patterns enables three-dimensional solids to be fabricated. Tailors, dressmakers, sheetmetal workers and model makers are just a few of the professions that apply the principles of development to their work.

CONTENTS

The three main methods	Page 146
Two truncated prisms	147
Oblique prisms	148
Two worked examples	149
A buttress developed	150
Right cylinders	151
Oblique cylinders	152
Two connecting pipes	153
Elbow joints	154
Right pyramids	155
Oblique pyramids	156
Two pyramid problems	157
Pyramid and cylinder	158
The cone	159
Oblique cones	160
A conic problem	161
An oblique conic problem	162
The regular polyhedra	163
Triangulation	164
Panel and sphere	165
Exercises	166

Photocopying prohibited by law

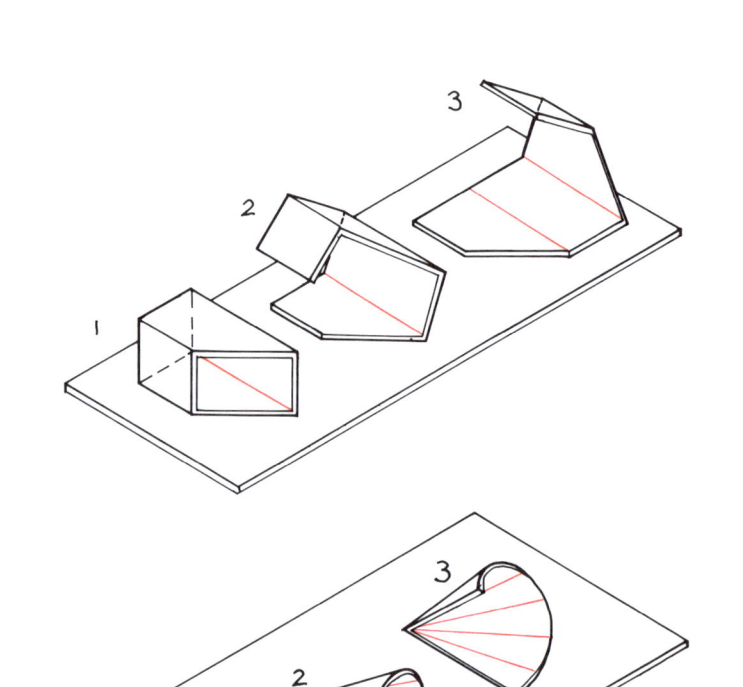

The Parallel line method
- Parallel lines are drawn on the surface in a view that shows them in true length. The distance between the lines and their true lengths being known, the pattern is laid out.
- This is used mainly for prisms and cylinders.

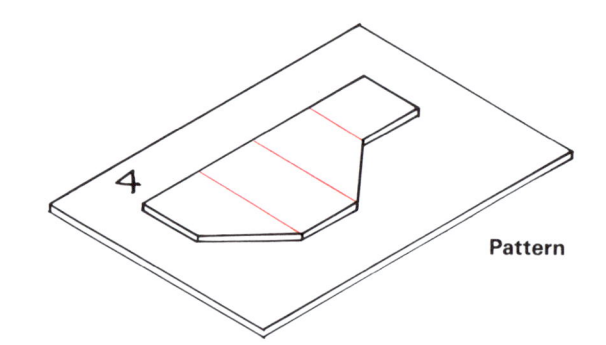

The radial line method
- Used for tapering objects. A spacing is chosen on the base and lines are drawn from the apex to the base. The true lengths of these lines are calculated and the pattern can then be laid out.
- Most useful for cones and for pyramids.

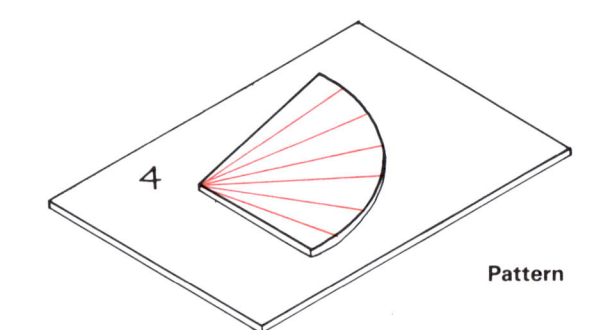

Triangulation
- When the object is not a simple regular solid shape its surface may be developed by reducing it to recognisable shapes. Here triangles are drawn on the surface. Their true shapes are calculated and they are laid out in sequence to form the pattern.
- A further development of this is the square grid used in computers to both draw and develop surfaces.
- Another method is called **Panel Development** and is explained on page **165**.

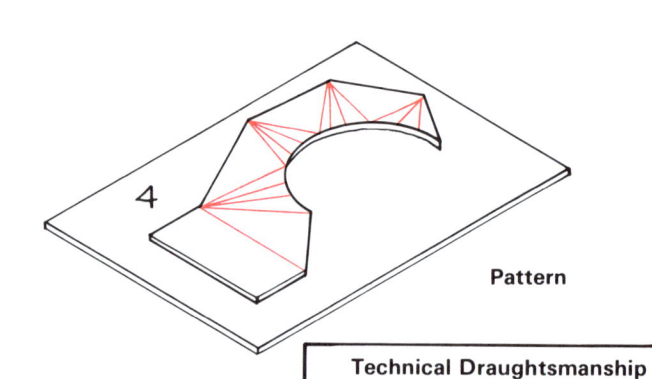

Technical Draughtsmanship		
The Three Main Methods		
Isom.	Development 1	Part I
		Geom.

①

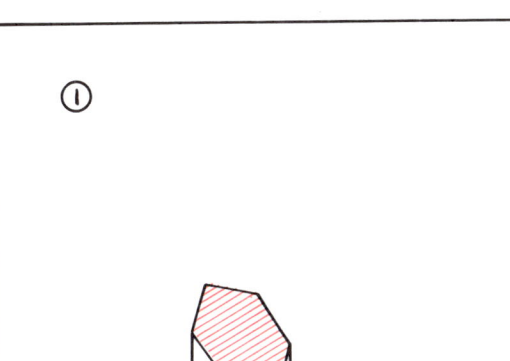

Isometric sketch of a truncated hexagonal prism.

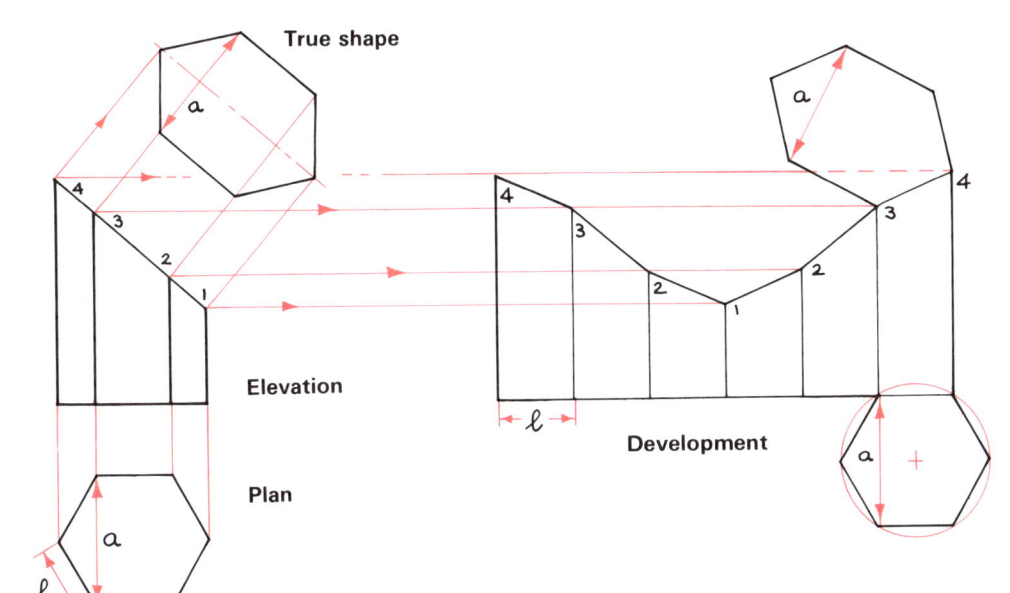

True shape

Elevation

Plan

Development

Procedure:
- Draw the plan and elevation.
- Project and draw the true shape of the cut surface.
- Draw the stretch-out of **6l**.
- As the heights of lines **1, 2, 3** and **4** are true, these may be projected across.
- Join the points, and attach top and base, to complete the developed pattern.

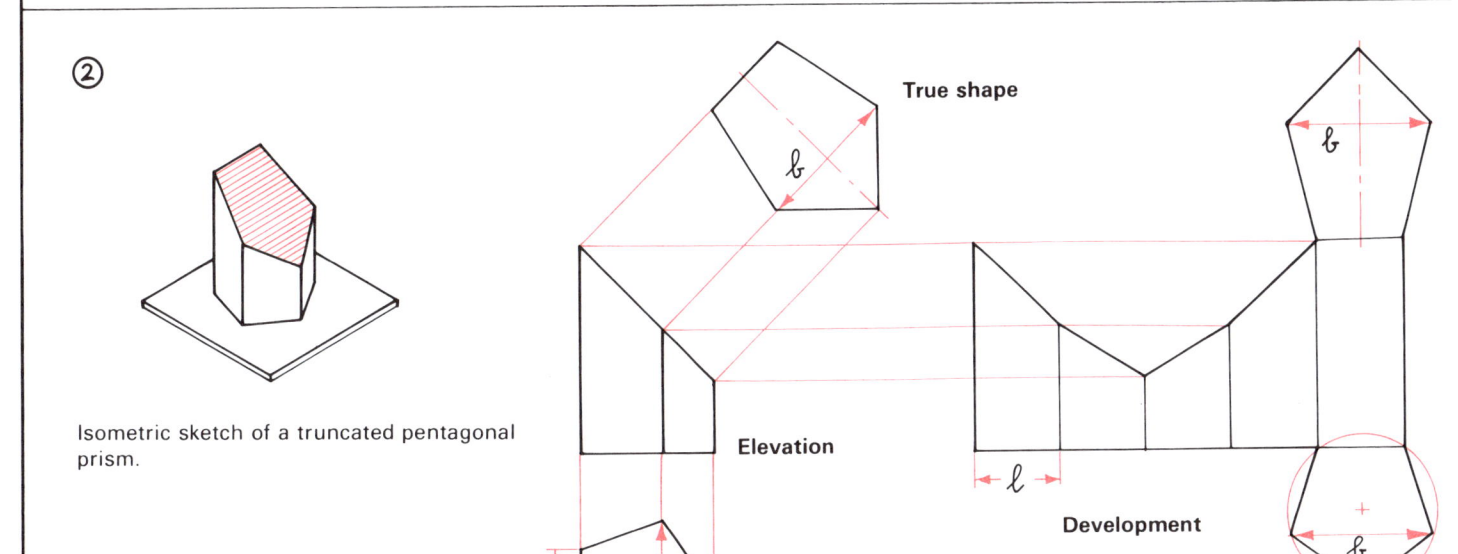

②

Isometric sketch of a truncated pentagonal prism.

True shape

Elevation

Plan

Development

Procedure:
- As above, but with stretch-out of **5l**.

Note: *Draw these larger and transfer the pattern to card. Make up the model using sellotape. How accurate are you?*

Technical Draughtsmanship
Two Truncated Prisms
Development 2 — Part I Geom.

147

①

Elevation

Pattern

An isometric sketch of an oblique heptagonal prism

Plan

Procedure:
- Draw the plan and elevation.
- Although the elevation shows the lines in true length they are oblique (or leaning). To avoid distortion these lengths have to be projected at right angles to their slope.
- Project these true lengths.
- Choose a starting point **A**, and with radius l from the plan, mark off the divisions **B, C, D** etc.
- Complete the pattern by attaching base and top.

②

An isometric sketch of a truncated oblique hexagonal prism.

Elevation

True Shape

Plan

Pattern

Procedure:
- As above, with the addition of finding the true shape of the top.

Note: *Should the base not be horizontal you will need to draw, or project, a flat base for the purposes of construction and to gauge the intervals of l.*

Technical Draughtsmanship
Oblique Prisms
Development 3 — Part I / Geom. H

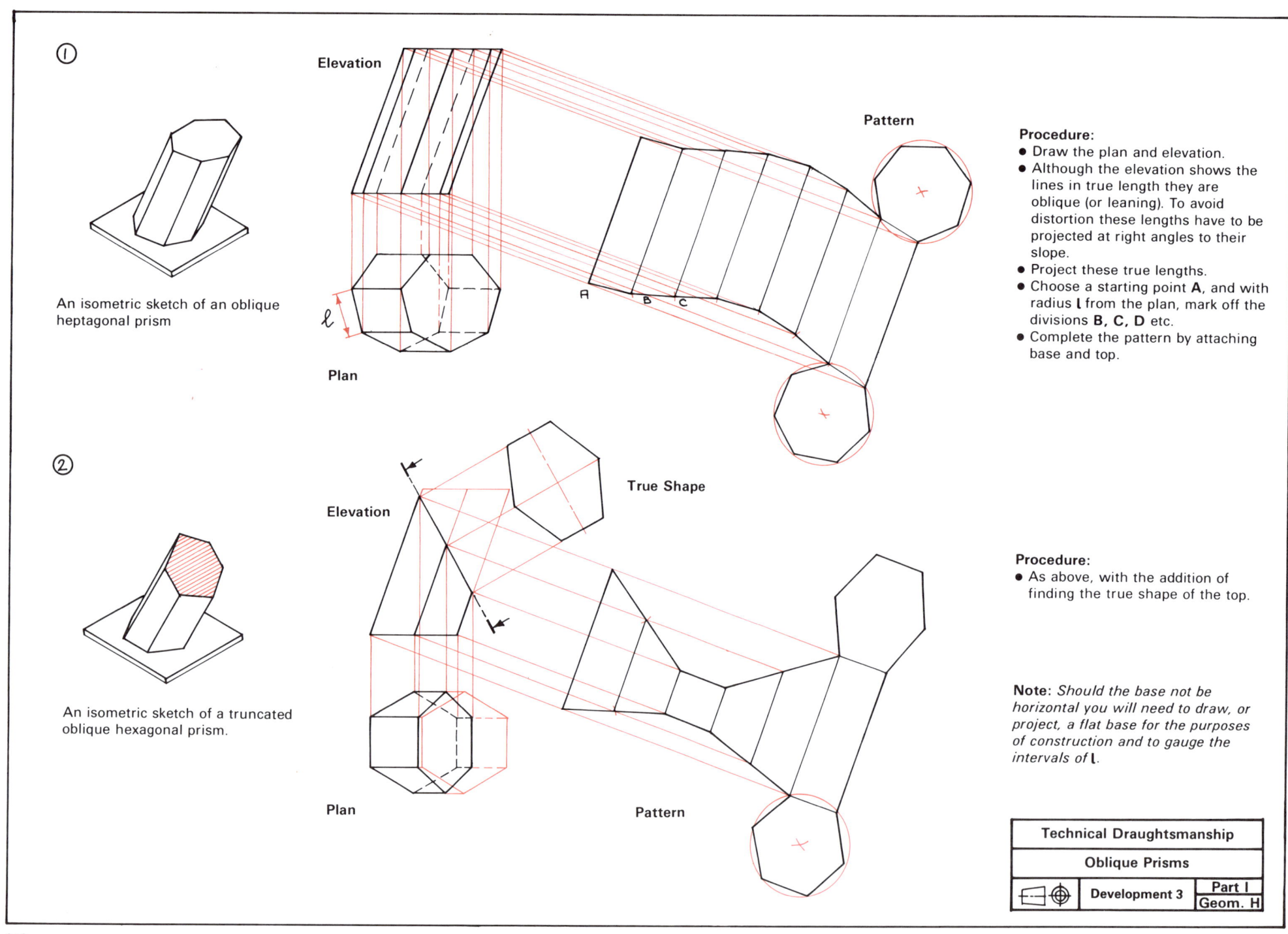

①

Isometric sketch of a metal chimney cowl

Elevation

Plan

Development of Pattern

Procedure:
- Draw the plan and elevation.
- Work out the true length of the leaning edge **TL 1**.
- Set out the pattern, as shown.

Note: *It would probably be more practical to develop the pattern in three pieces: two strips and one piece made by placing the two side pieces together.*

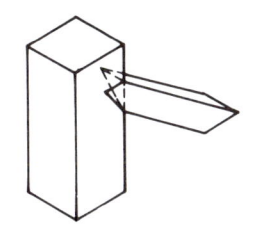

②

Isometric sketch of a newel post and strut

Procedure:
- Draw the plan and elevation.
- Project an auxiliary elevation to establish true lengths. This could also be set up in a separate diagram, if you prefer.
- Draw a rotated section to find the true shape of the section and length of side **l**.
- Set out the pattern by projecting the true lengths against the stretch-out of **4l**.

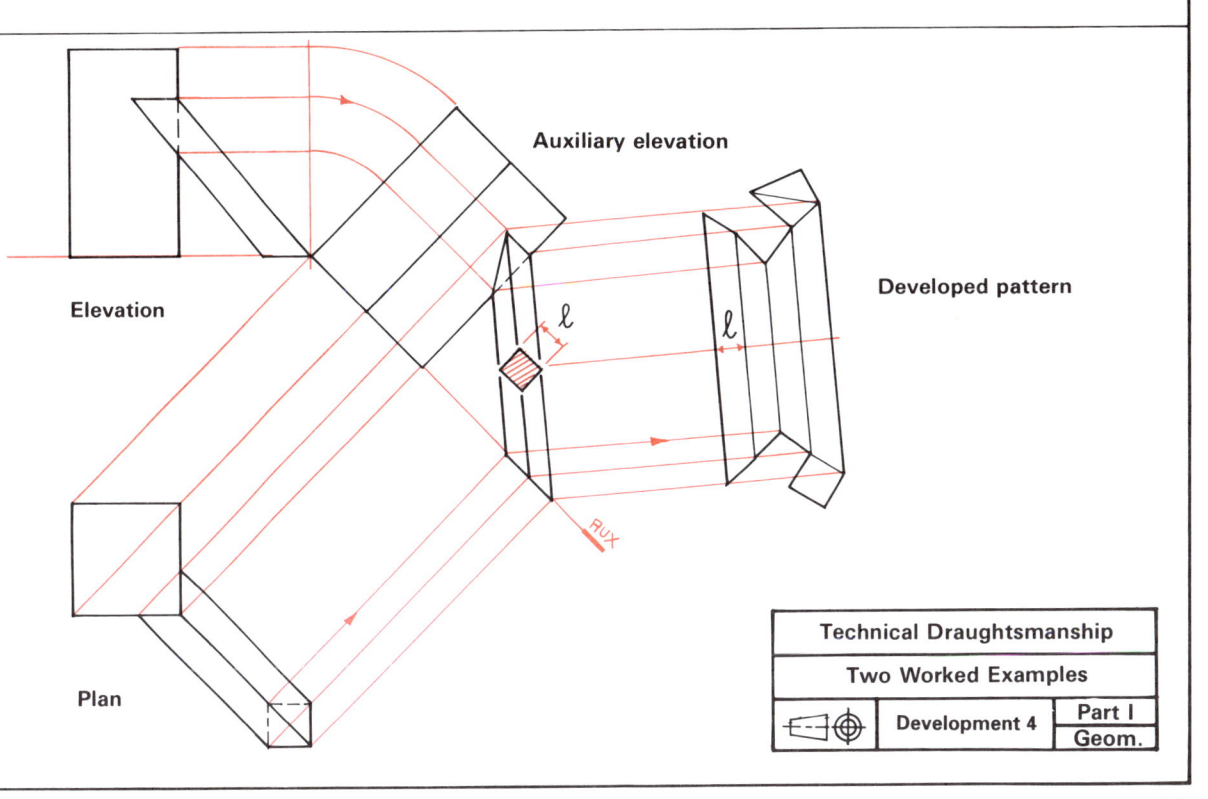

Elevation

Auxiliary elevation

Plan

Developed pattern

Technical Draughtsmanship
Two Worked Examples
Development 4 — Part I / Geom.

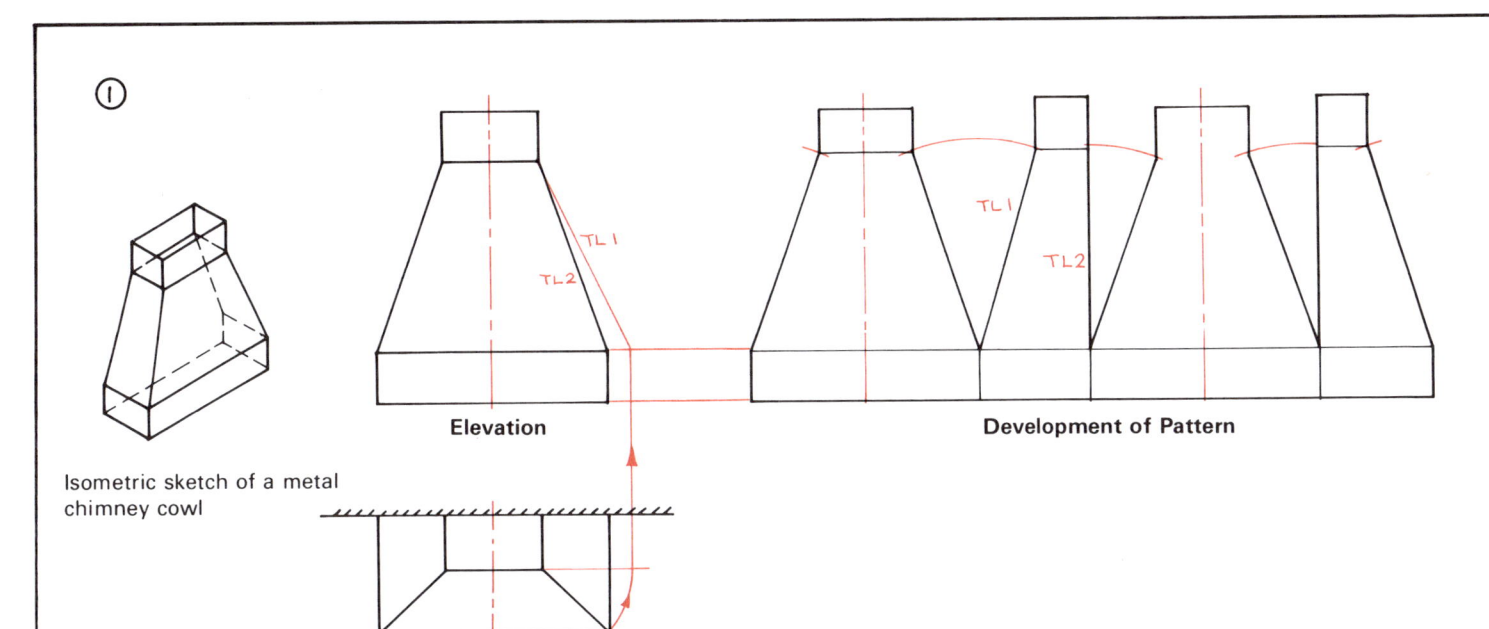

149

The Given Diagram
Required: develop all surfaces.
Scale to suit **A3** sheet.

Development of side

Elevation

Development of front surfaces

Plan

Procedure:
- Draw the plan and elevation.
- Mark the centre line **AE** and extend to any convenient point **P**.
- Rabat lengths **AB, BC, CD** and **DE**.
- Construct true length diagrams by matching heights to lengths rabatted from the plan.
- Use the true lengths to lay out the patterns.

Note: As both sides are identical, there is no need to duplicate the side pattern.

Technical Draughtsmanship
A Buttress Developed
Development 5 — Part I — Geom. H

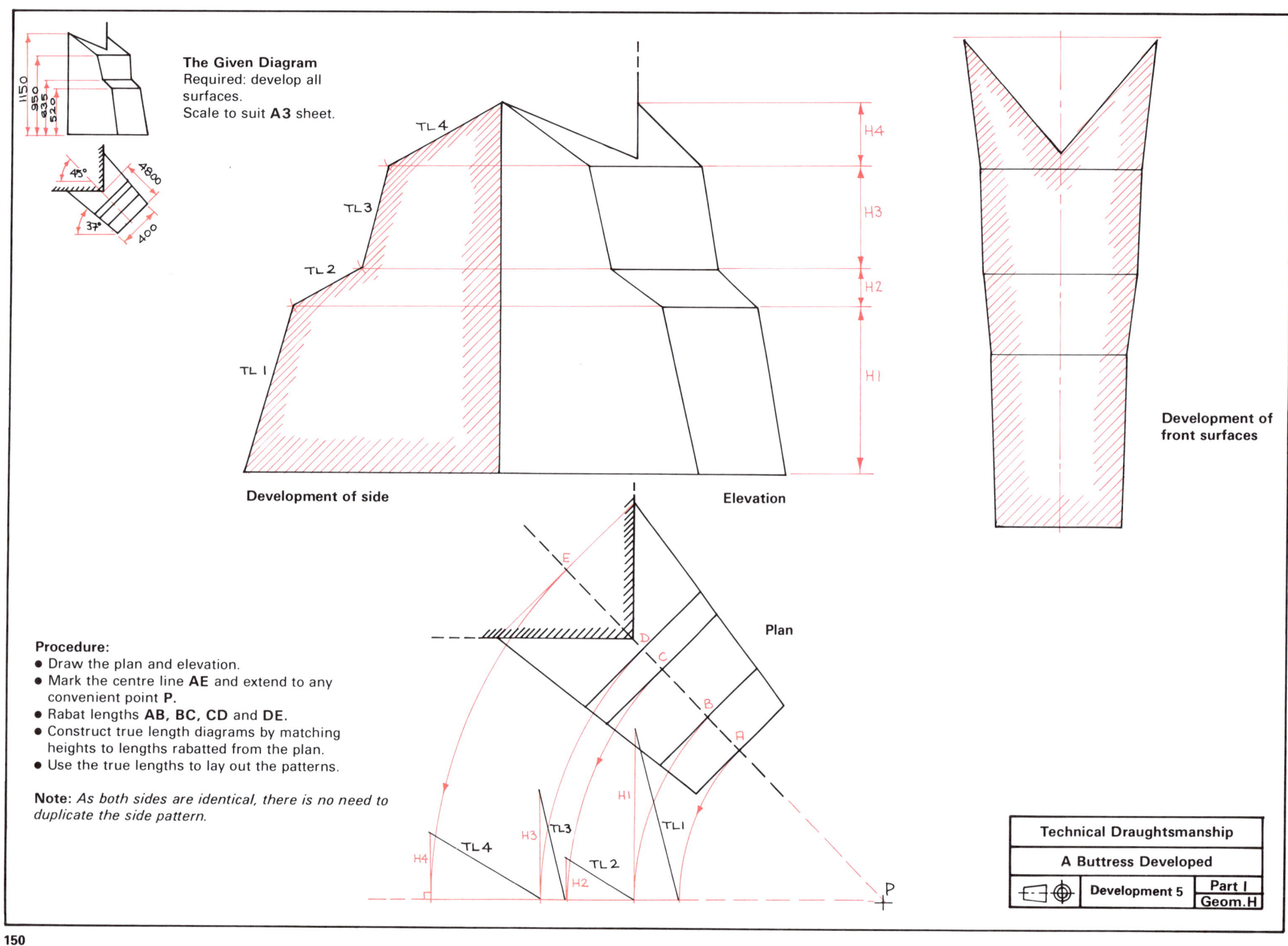

①

Developed pattern

Elevation

Plan

$\ell = \dfrac{\pi R}{6}$

πD

Isometric sketch of a right cylinder

Procedure:
- Draw plan and elevation.
- Divide the plan into a number of pieces, e.g. **12**.
- Project up from the division points on the plan onto the surface of the elevation.
- Lay out the stretch-out = **2πr** and divide this into **12** equal pieces.
- If **l** is measured with a compass and marked out **12** times it gives a fair approximation to **2πr**.
- Draw the panels to the required height and add top and base.

---

②

True shape

Elevation

Plan

Developed pattern

Isometric sketch of a truncated right cylinder

Note: *The true shape of the cut surface of a cylinder is often an ellipse.*

Procedure:
- As above, with two differences.
- Project the true shape of the top surface.
- There are various heights, each of which is projected across, as shown.

| Technical Draughtsmanship |
| Right Cylinders |
| Development 6 — Part 1 / Geom. |

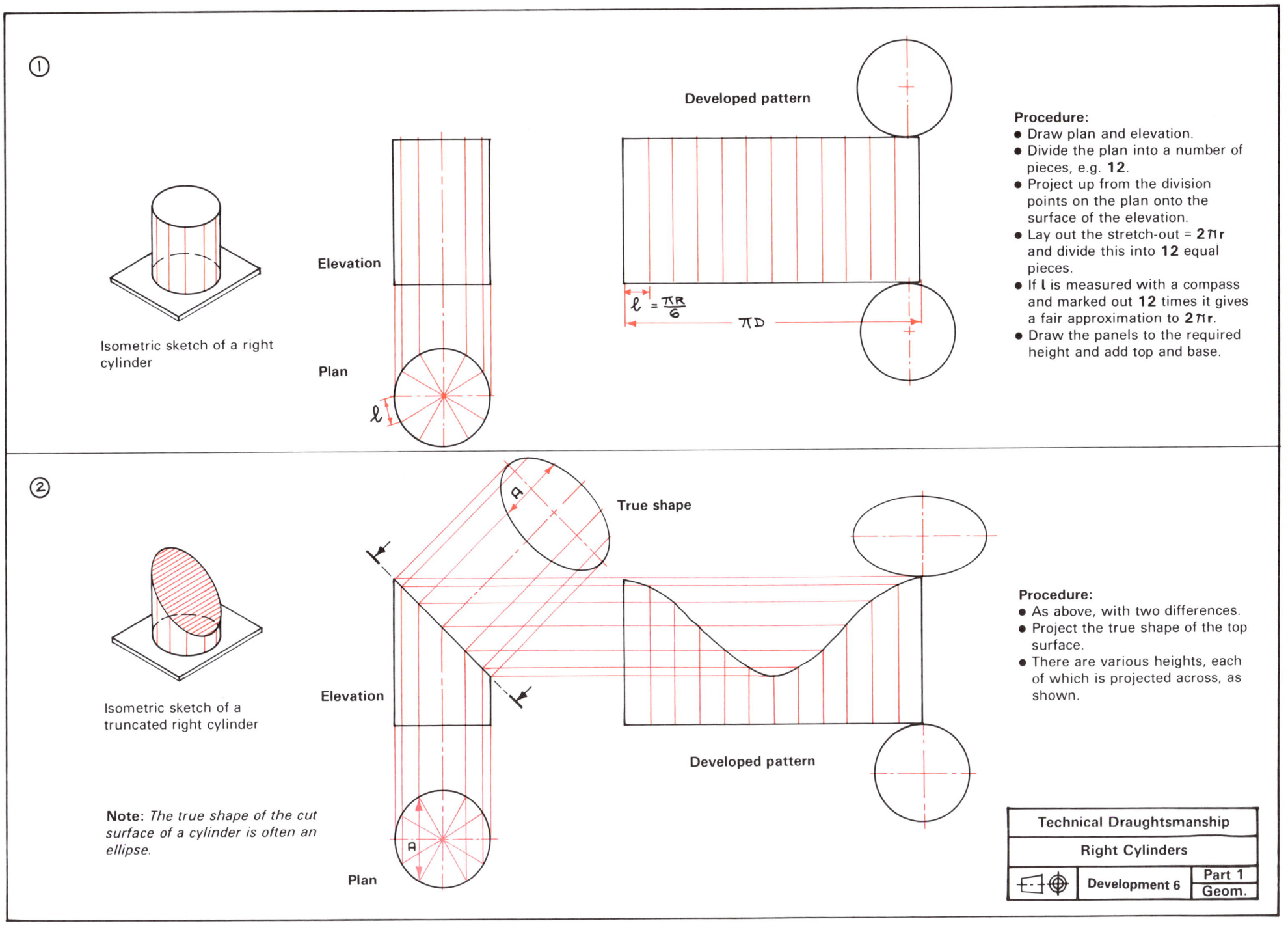

① **Elevation**

Developed pattern

Isometric sketch of an oblique cylinder

Plan

Procedure:
- Draw plan and elevation.
- Divide the base on the plan into a number of parts, e.g. **12**.
- Bring these divisions up to the base in elevation, and then up, parallel to the leaning edge, as shown.
- Project each division line on the elevation at right angles.
- Choose a starting point **A** and, with radius **l** from the plan, swing an arc to find **B**.
- Continue to locate other points.
- Construct the panels and add top and base.

② Isometric sketch of a truncated oblique cylinder

True shape

Elevation

Developed pattern

Plan

Procedure:
- As above, with two differences.
- Project the true shape of the top.
- There are various heights, each of which is projected across, as shown.

Technical Draughtsmanship
Oblique Cylinders
Development 7 — Part 1 / Geom. H

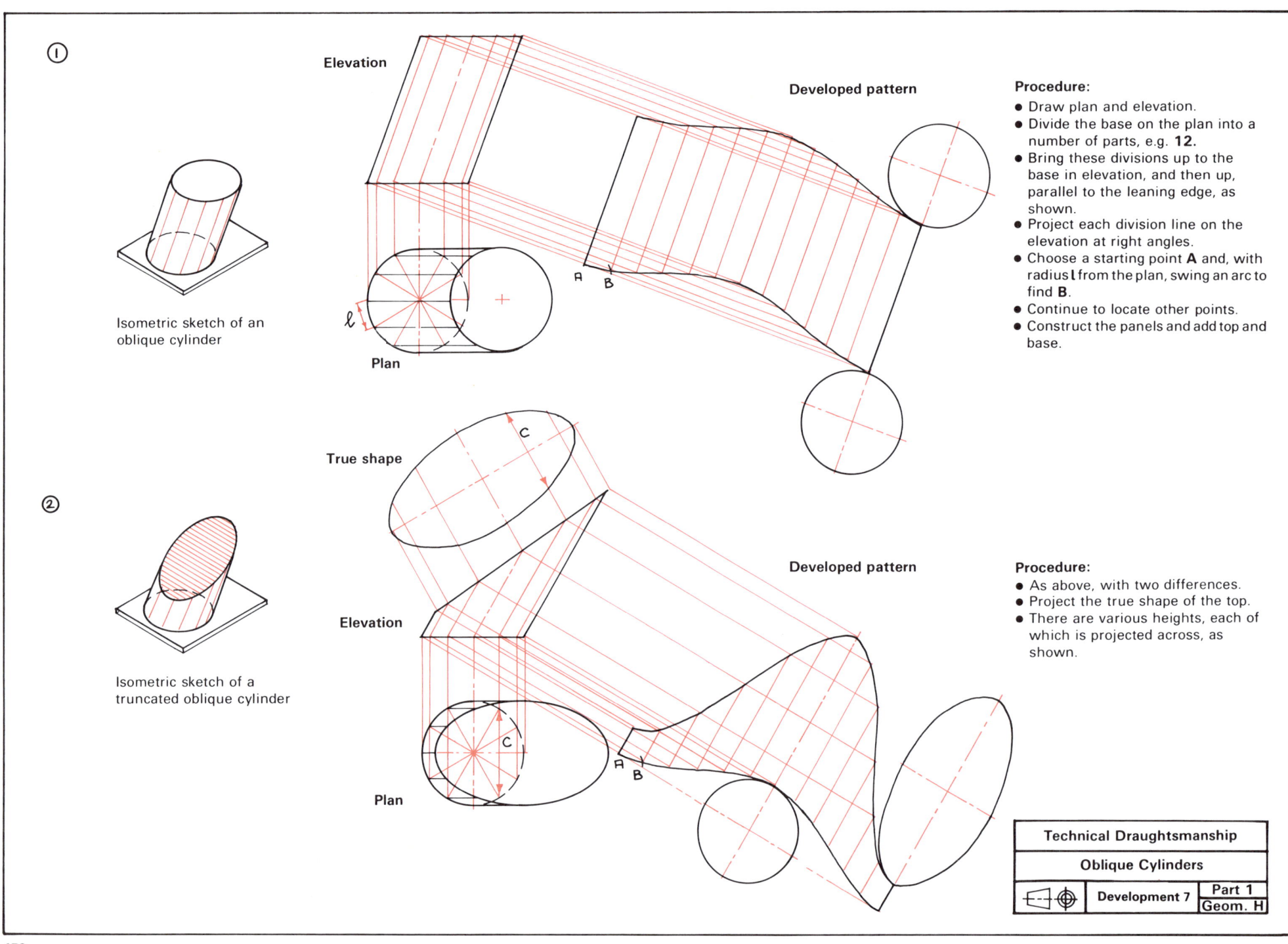

152

Elevation

Development A

Plan

Development B

Isometric sketch

Procedure:
- Draw the plan and project the elevation.
- Divide both cylinders into a number of pieces, e.g. **12**.
- Project and index these divisions.
- Develop the larger cylinder as usual.
- Then project across the points of intersection to define the opening.
- For the smaller cylinder, draw the stretch-out equal to πd.
- Then project across the height for each division line.

Technical Draughtsmanship
Two connecting pipes
Development 8 — Part I — Geom.

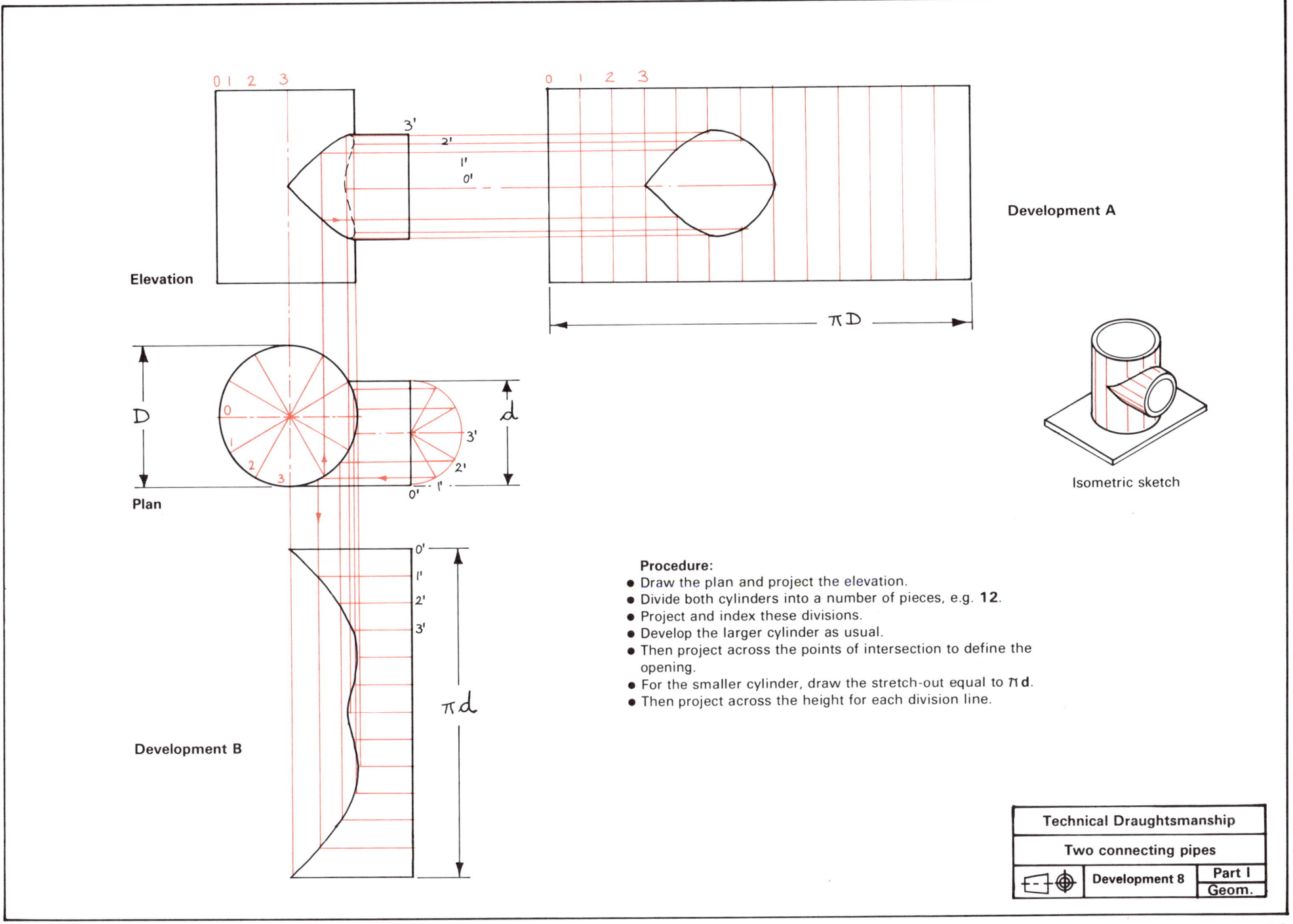

①

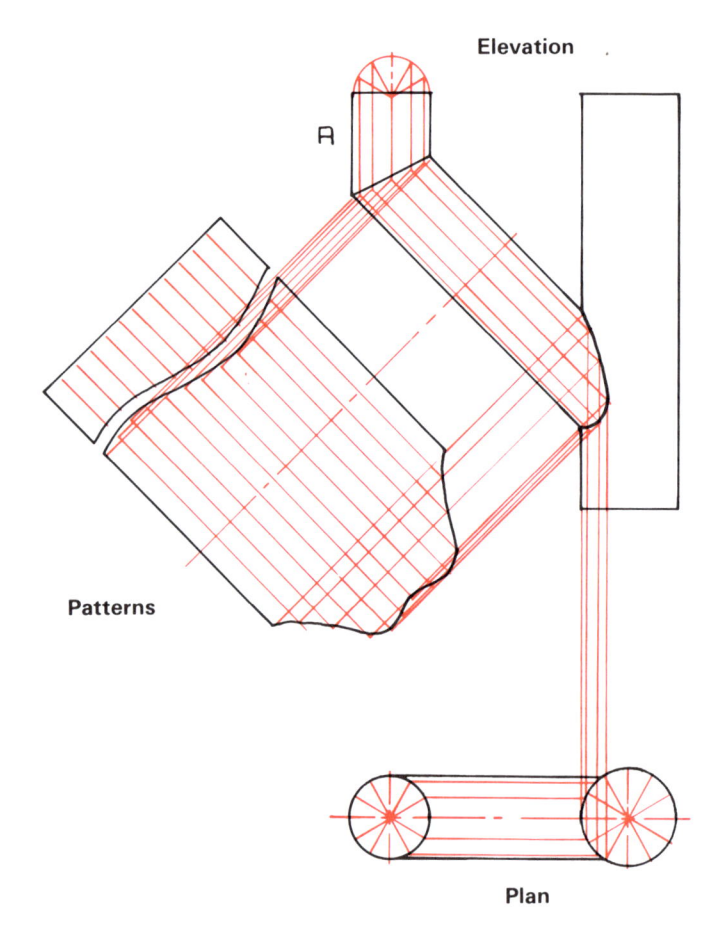

Elevation

Patterns

Plan

Procedure:
- Basically as before.
- The point to note here is that, by rotating the elbow piece **A** through **180°**, a more economical cutting pattern can be made. This is emphasised here by separating the two pattern pieces.

②

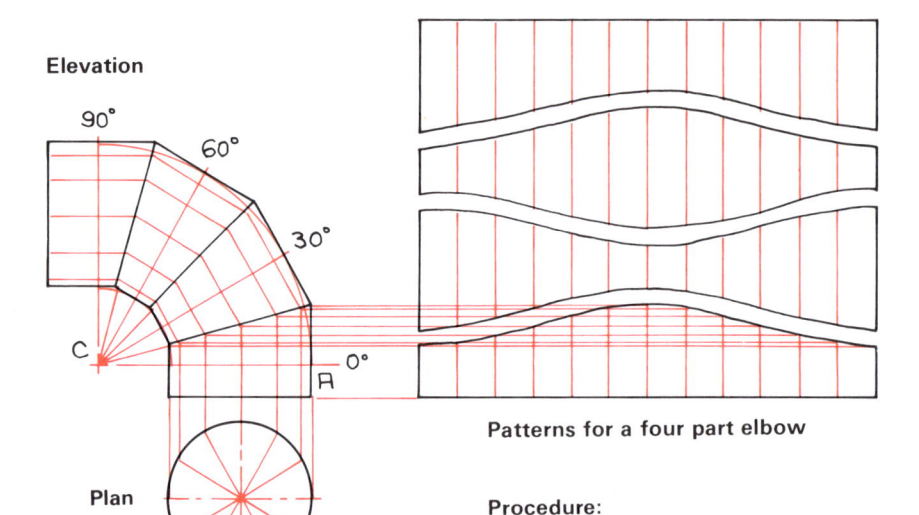

Elevation

Plan

Patterns for a four part elbow

Note: *The economy here is evident. The patterns have been separated for clarity only.*

Procedure:
- Draw the plan.
- To set out the elevation, given **C**, draw two quadrants and the radius for **30°**, and for **60°**.
- Draw tangents at **0°**, **30°**, **60°**, and **90°** on both arcs.
- Bisect each **30°** division, to complete the elevation.
- Open out part **A**, by projection, as usual.
- The other patterns are laid above this, and each measurement is made using pointers to transfer the lengths.

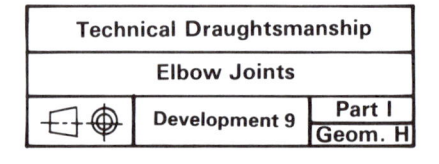

Technical Draughtsmanship		
Elbow Joints		
	Development 9	Part I
		Geom. H

154

① **Elevation** / **Plan** / **Pattern**

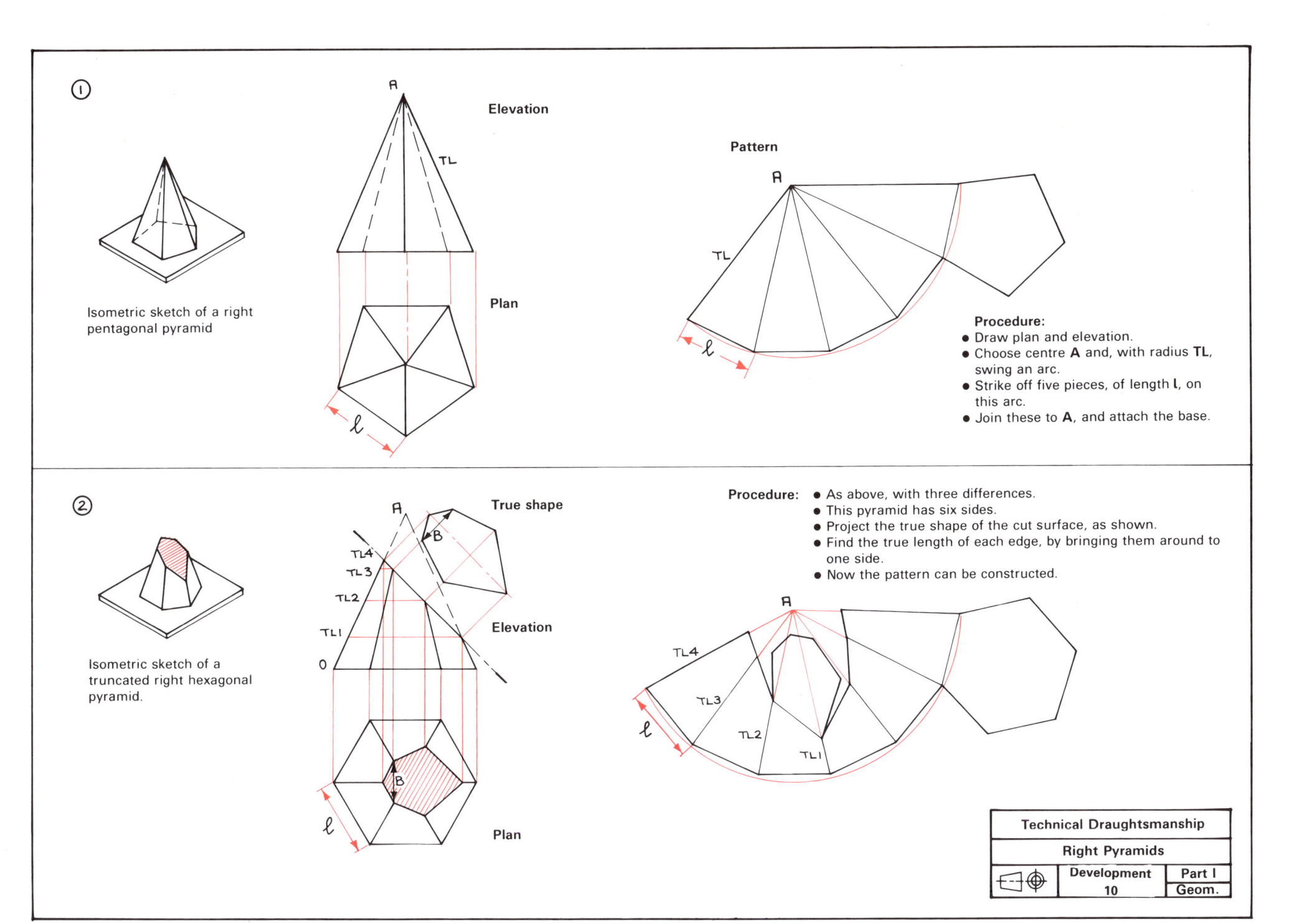

Isometric sketch of a right pentagonal pyramid

Procedure:
- Draw plan and elevation.
- Choose centre **A** and, with radius **TL**, swing an arc.
- Strike off five pieces, of length **l**, on this arc.
- Join these to **A**, and attach the base.

② **True shape** / **Elevation** / **Plan**

Isometric sketch of a truncated right hexagonal pyramid.

Procedure:
- As above, with three differences.
- This pyramid has six sides.
- Project the true shape of the cut surface, as shown.
- Find the true length of each edge, by bringing them around to one side.
- Now the pattern can be constructed.

Technical Draughtsmanship
Right Pyramids

| Development 10 | Part I Geom. |

155

①

Elevation

Plan

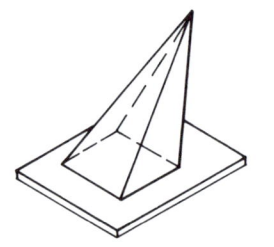

Isometric sketch of an oblique square pyramid.

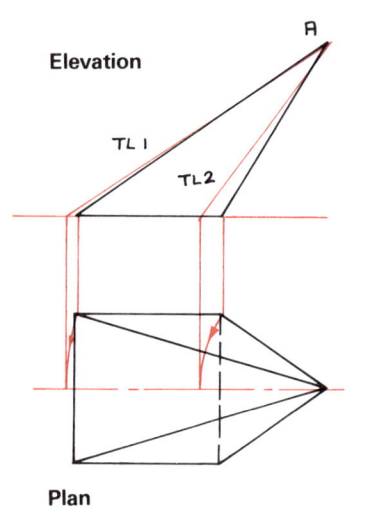

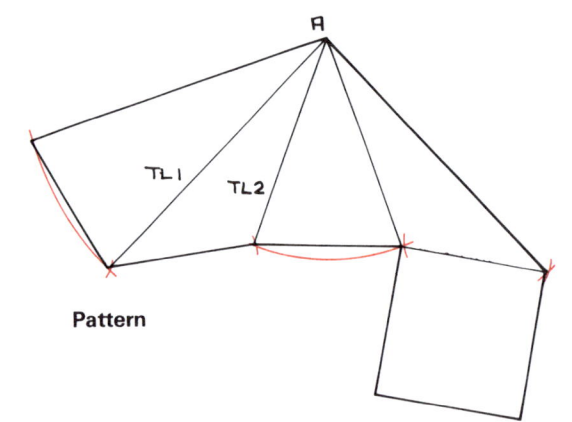

Pattern

Procedure:
- Find the true lengths of the sides, as shown.
- With centre **A**, and all true lengths known, construct each triangle.
- Add the base.

②

Elevation

Plan

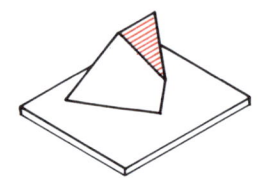

Isometric sketch of a truncated oblique triangular pyramid

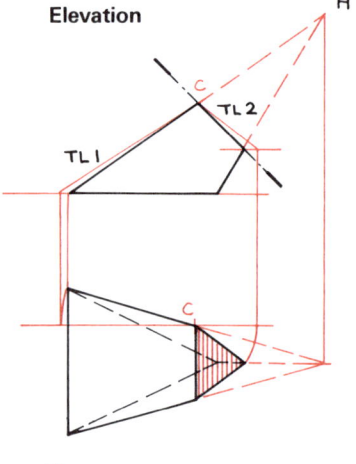

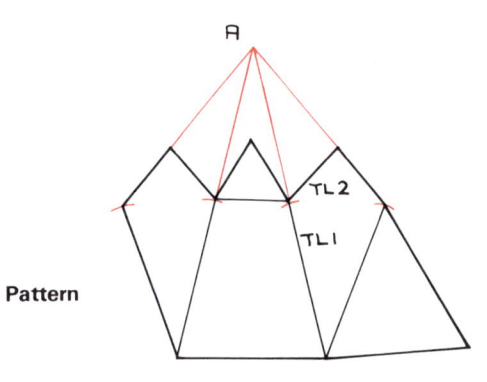

Pattern

Procedure
- Basically as above, with one additional operation.
- Find the true lengths of the cut edges.
- Mark these on the pattern and outline.
- Add the top and base.

Technical Draughtsmanship
Oblique Pyramids
Development 11 — Part 1 / Geom H

① Elevation

Plan

Pattern

Procedure:
- Find true lengths by rabatment, as shown.
- Construct pattern as before.

② Elevation

Plan

Pattern

Procedure:
- Find true lengths, by bringing heights together with apparent lengths on plan.
- You may prefer to set up a separate true length diagram.
- Use these lengths to set out the pattern, around the base.

Note: *Is this the most economic pattern? What would be more economic?*

Technical Draughtsmanship		
Two Pyramid Problems		
	Development 12	Part I Geom. H

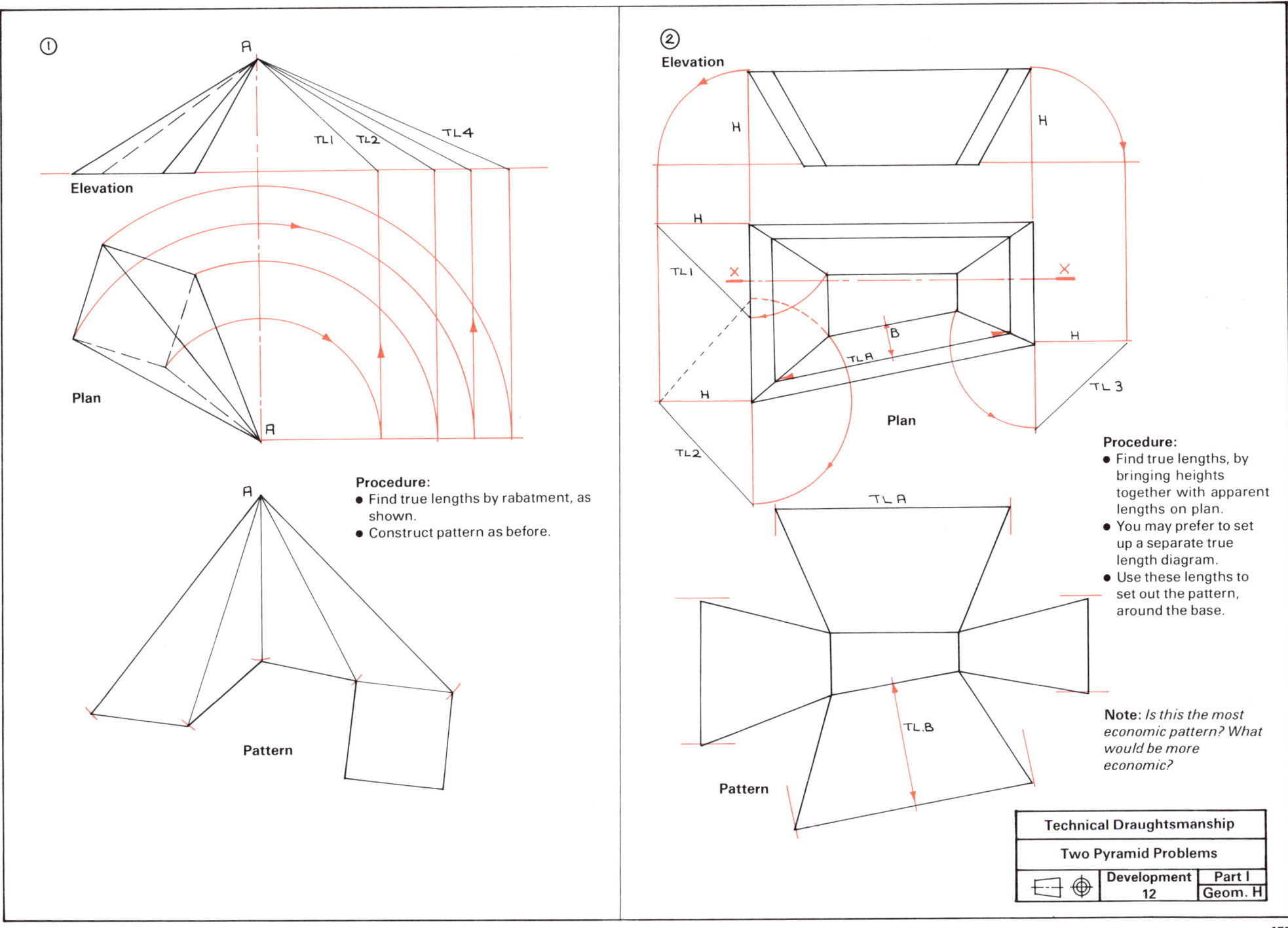

157

Problem
- To develop the surfaces of the given solid.

Procedure
- Draw the elevation, end view and project the plan.
- On elevation divide the arc into sections. Index these **0** to **6**.
- Find **TL 1** and **TL 2** by rabatment.
- Use these to lay out the plane surfaces.
- Bisect **AB** and set a centre line at right angles to **AB**.
- Take chord lengths from the elevation and step these along the centre line of **AB** from **0** to **6**.
- Project the true shape of the cylindrical surface.
- To lay out the sides the lengths **BD, DE, EF,** etc. can be transferred from the cylindrical surface, using a compass, as shown.

Note: *If you prefer, lengths BD, DE, EF, etc. can be calculated mathematically.*

Elevation

End view

Plan and incomplete pattern

First side

Note: *The second side is similar to the first side and has been omitted here in the interests of clarity.*

Technical Draughtsmanship
Pyramid and Cylinder
Development 13 — Part 1 — Geom.

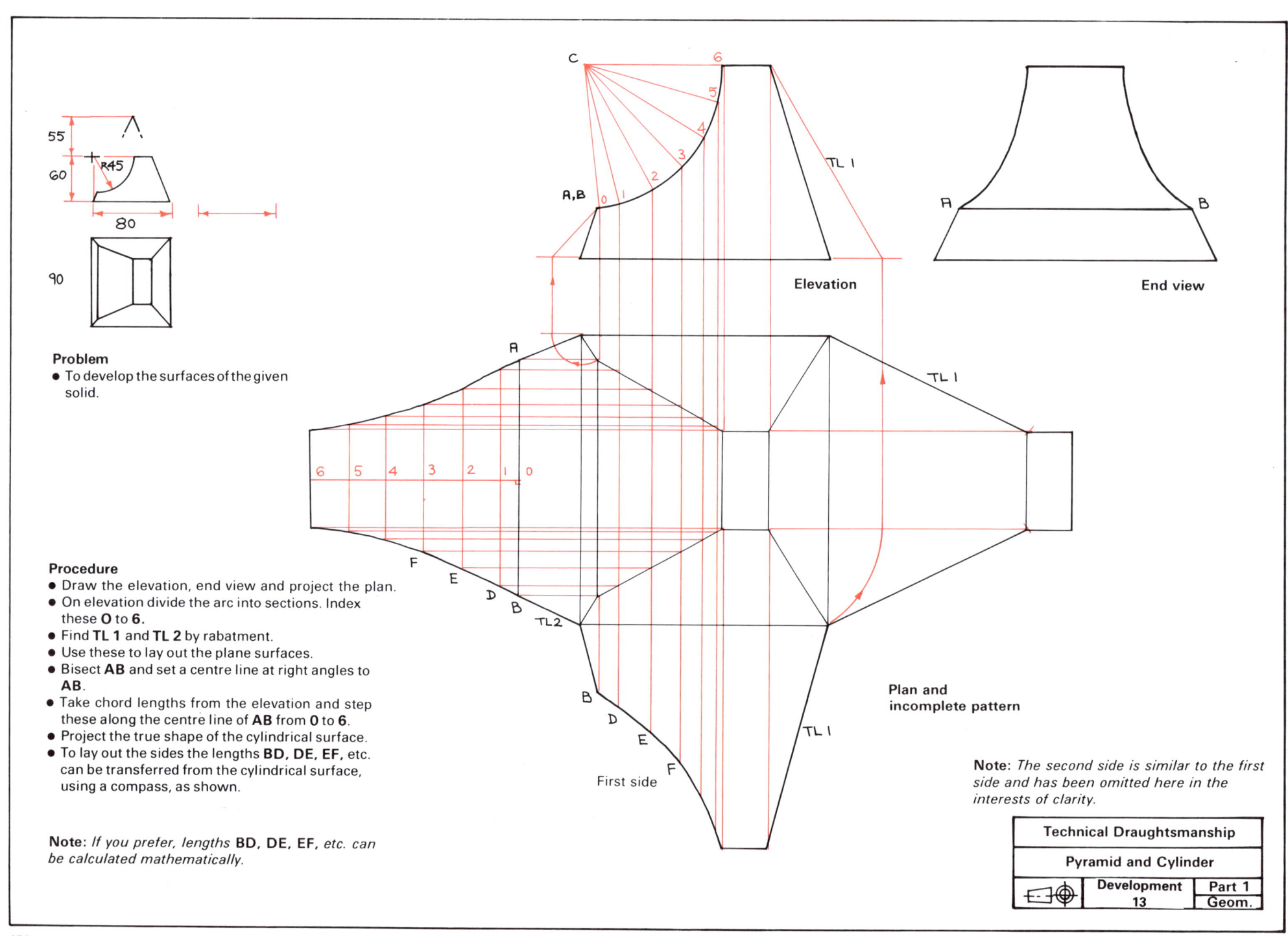

①

Isometric sketch of a cone

Elevation

Plan

Pattern

Procedure:
- Choose centre **A**.
- With radius **L** swing an arc.
- Measure **B°** = **(180 x D) ÷ L** or divide the plan and step chord lengths along the arc.
- Add the circular base.

②

Isometric sketch of a truncated cone

Elevation

Plan

Pattern

Procedure:
- Draw the complete cone, as above.
- Calculate true lengths against the profile of the elevation.
- Use these to measure the radial divisions.
- Project the true shape of the top.
- Outline the pattern and add the top and base.

Technical Draughtsmanship		
The Cone		
	Development 14	Part 1 Geom

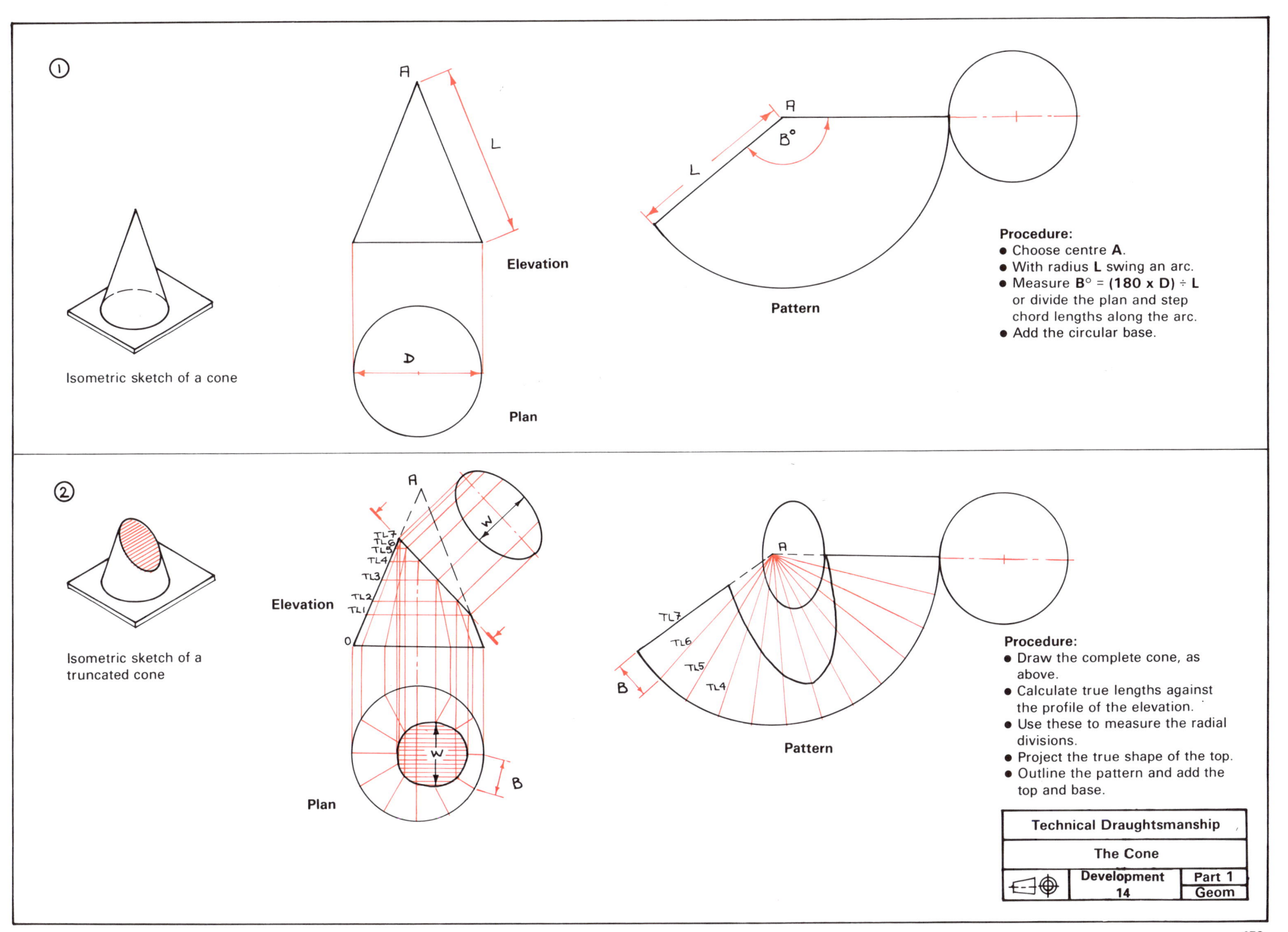

159

① To develop an oblique cone

Sketch

Step 1
- Divide the base of the cone and draw the radians.
- It is necessary to find the true lengths of the radians.
- With A_1 as centre swing the perimeter divisions around onto A_1M.
- Project these up to BN and join them to apex A to find the true lengths.

Step 2
- Choose an apex A_2.
- Set out true length A_2B.
- With true length A_2C and chord length BC fix point C.
- Continue and complete the pattern.

Pattern

② To develop a truncated oblique cone

Sketch

Step 1
- Divide the base and draw the radians
- Set up the full true lengths of the radians as outlined previously.
- Project across the points where the cutting plane cuts the radians to fix true lengths BC, etc.

Step 2
- Choose an apex point A_2.
- Set out true length A_2C and mark off CB.
- With true length A_2D and chord length CD set out A_2D.
- Continue and complete the pattern.

Pattern

Technical Draughtsmanship
Oblique Cones
Development 15 — Part I — Geom. H

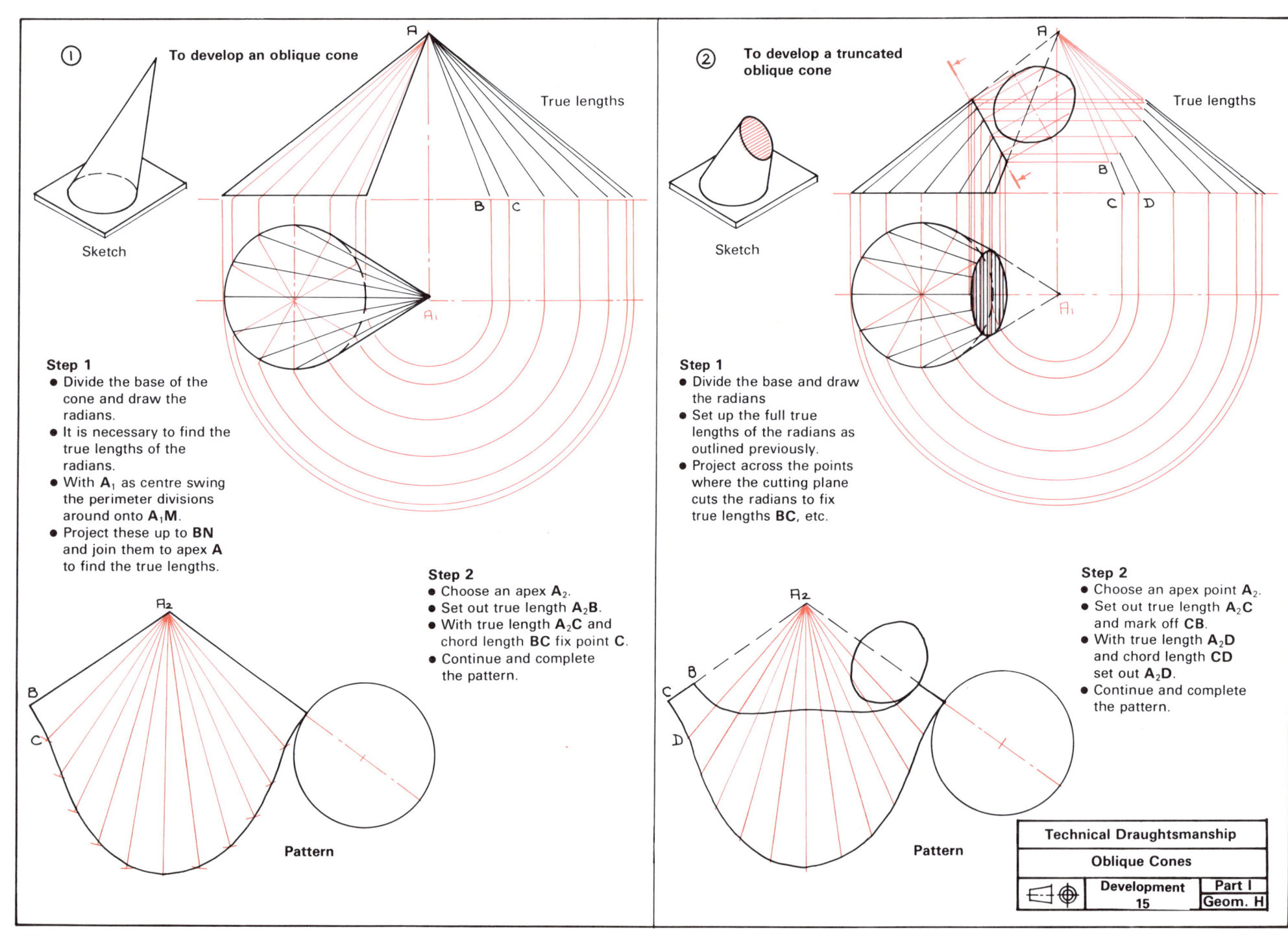

Spout Pattern
- Determine true lengths on the elevation, as shown.
- Choose **A** and with radius **AC** from the elevation draw the pattern, stepping out divisions on the arc.
- Use the true lengths to plot the shape.

Handle Pattern
- Measure the stretch-out along a centre line.
- Take the width from the plan.
- Measure the curves where it meets the body and draw the pattern.

Main body pattern
- Locate **B** and with radius **BD** swing an arc, and step off the divisions.
- Measure the true length **DE** and swing another arc to complete the truncated cone as shown.
- Add the base.

Elevation

Plan

Technical Draughtsmanship
A Conic Problem
Development 16 — Part I — Geom.

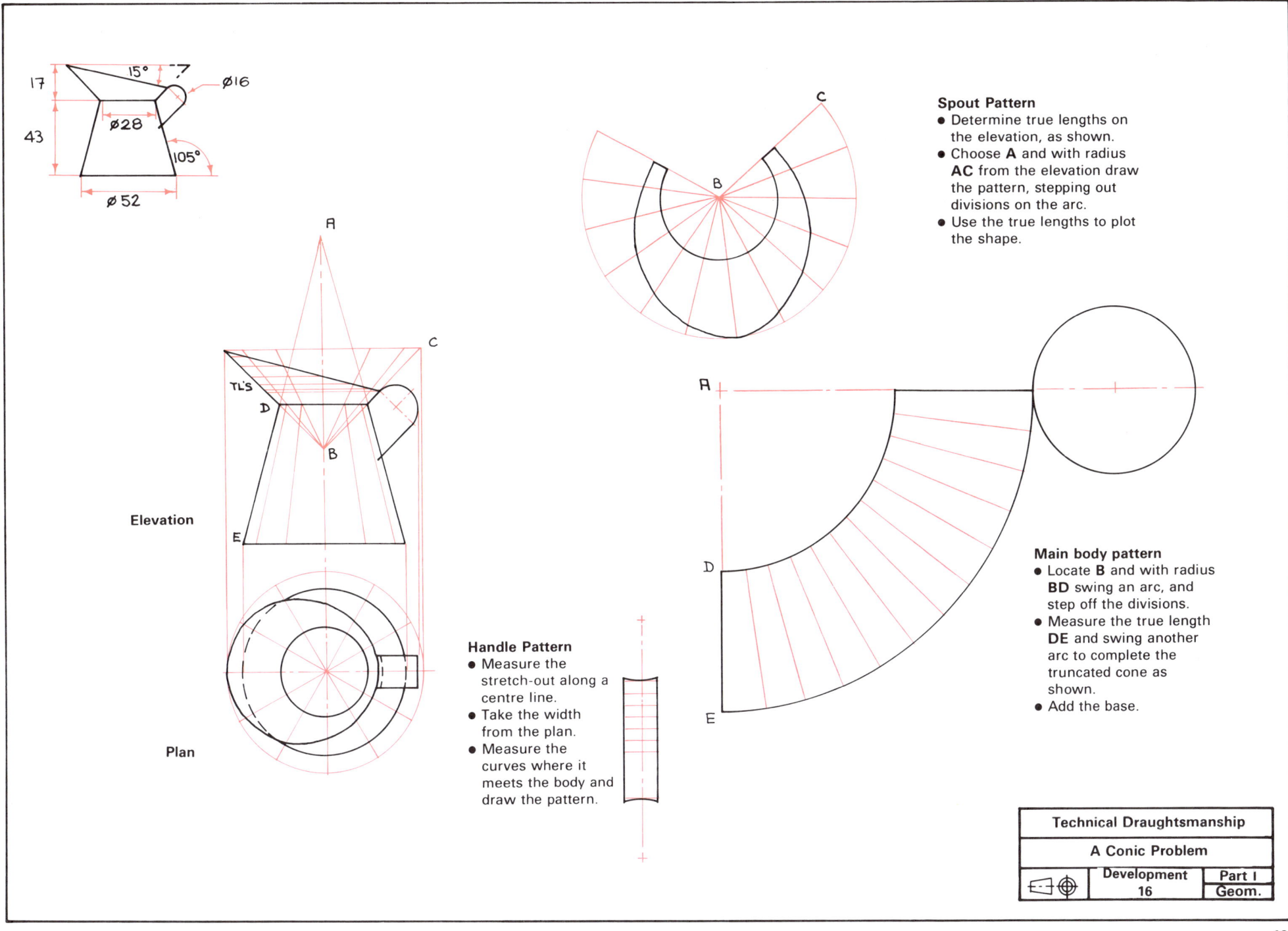

Development of a compound shape
The piece is a hollow funnel.

Elevation

Plan

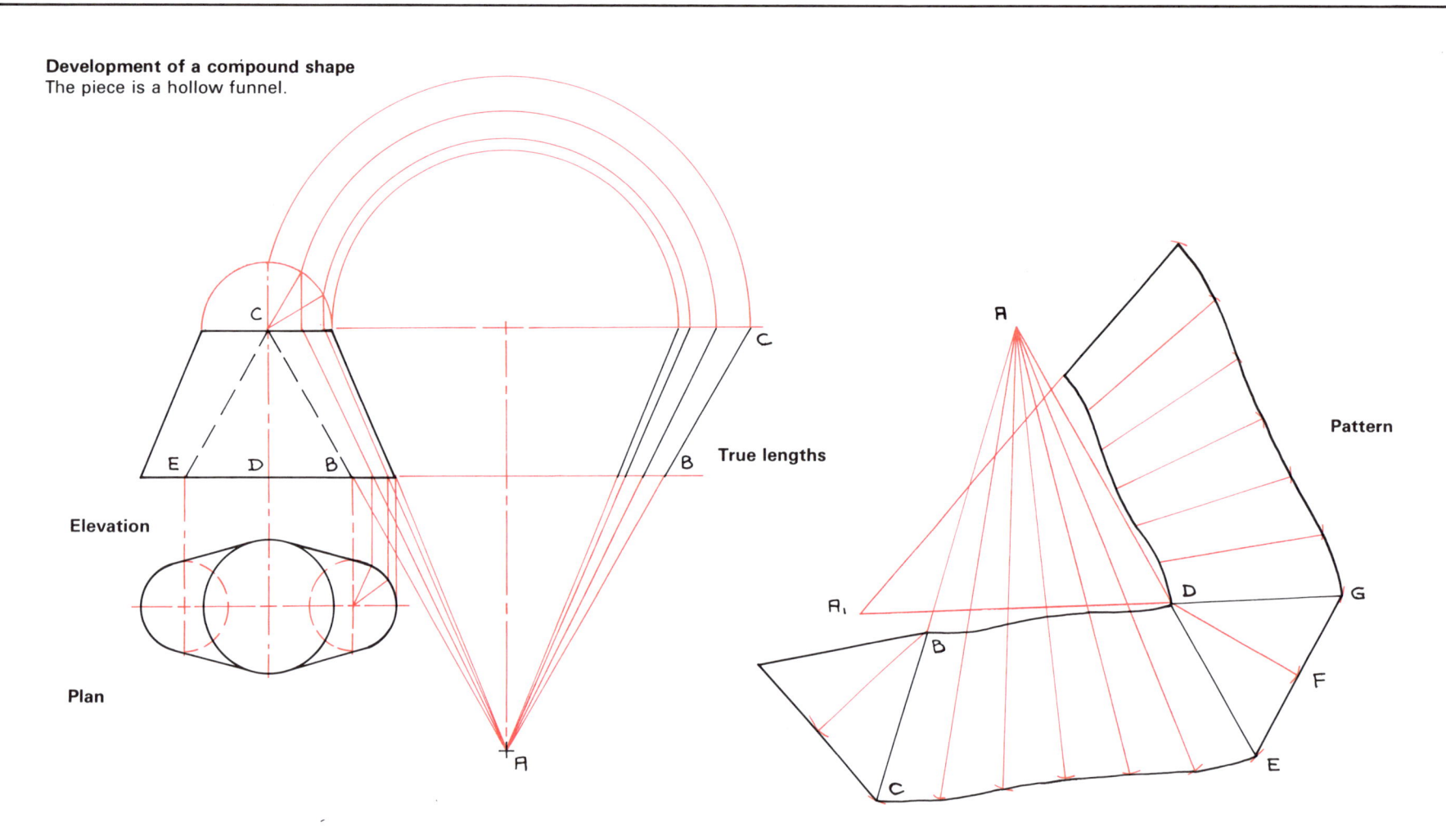

True lengths

Pattern

Step 1
- Divide the surface into areas that can be easily developed. In this case, these will be two conical areas and four triangular areas. The conical areas are seen to be similar.
- For one conical area, extend it to locate the apex **A** and draw a set of radians on its surface.
- Find the true lengths of these radians by rabatment, as shown.

Step 2
- Choose an apex point **A** and, using the true lengths, set out the radians of one conic pattern **BCDE**.
- **EF** and height **DF** can be taken from the plan and elevation. Set out **DEF** and, similarly, **DFG**.
- Continue line **GD** to A_2 and set out the second conic pattern.
- Complete the pattern, shown above.

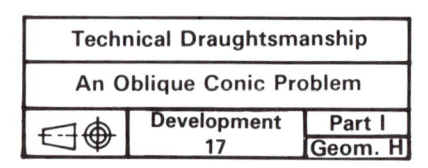

Technical Draughtsmanship		
An Oblique Conic Problem		
	Development 17	Part I Geom. H

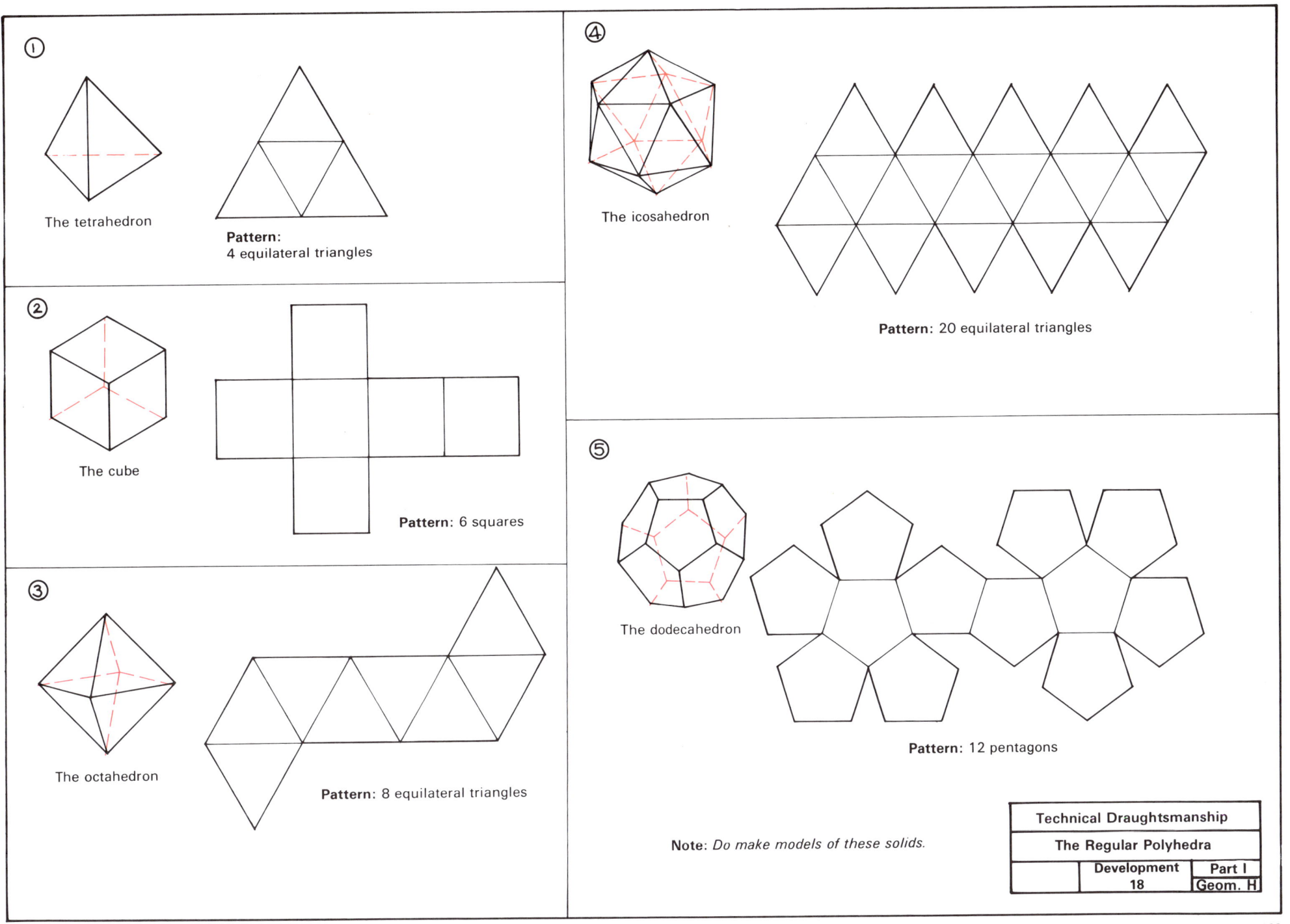

① The tetrahedron
Pattern: 4 equilateral triangles

② The cube
Pattern: 6 squares

③ The octahedron
Pattern: 8 equilateral triangles

④ The icosahedron
Pattern: 20 equilateral triangles

⑤ The dodecahedron
Pattern: 12 pentagons

Note: *Do make models of these solids.*

Technical Draughtsmanship		
The Regular Polyhedra		
Development 18		Part I Geom. H

Development of a transition piece by triangulation
The piece is a hollow duct.

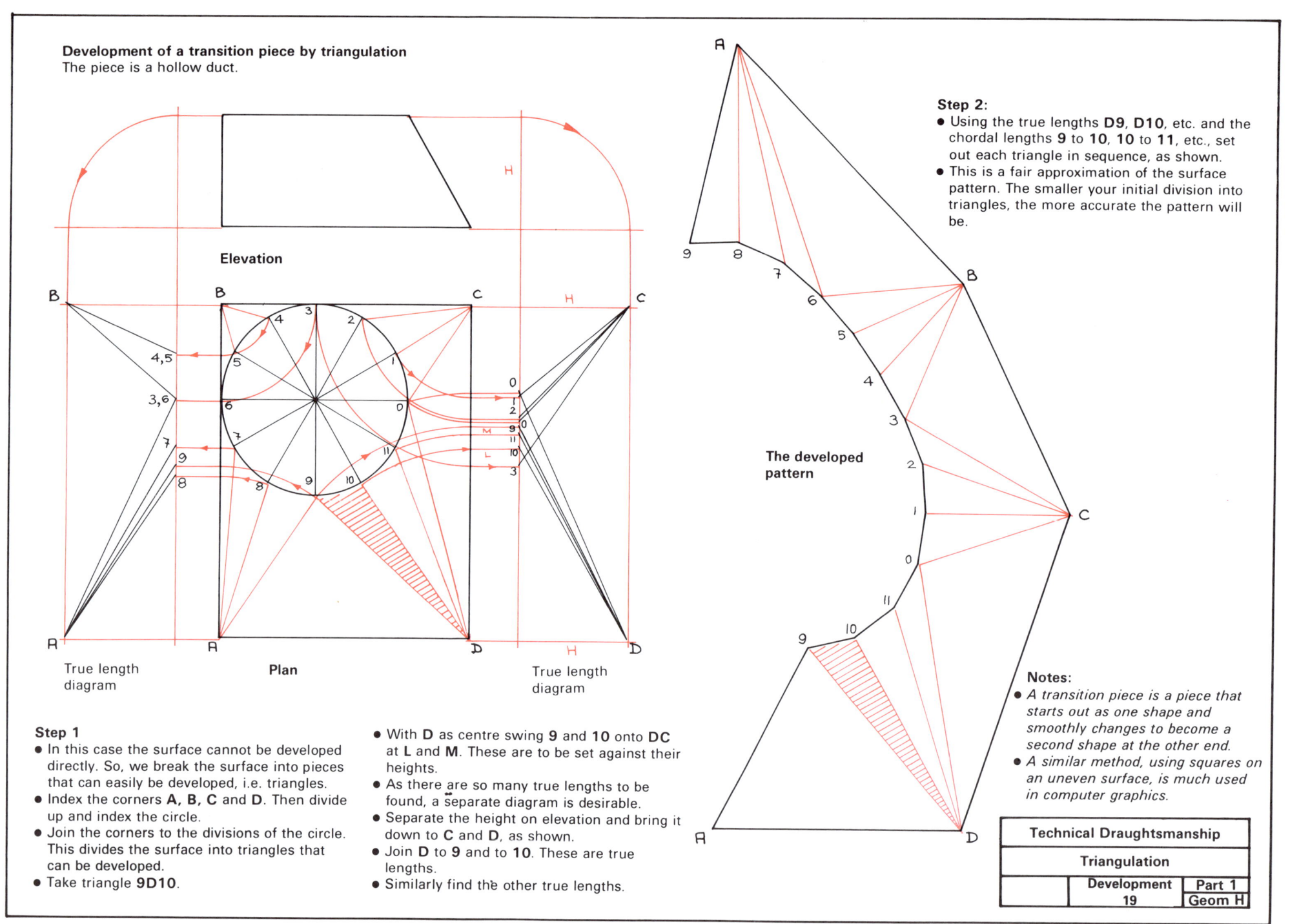

Elevation

Plan

True length diagram

True length diagram

Step 1
- In this case the surface cannot be developed directly. So, we break the surface into pieces that can easily be developed, i.e. triangles.
- Index the corners **A, B, C** and **D**. Then divide up and index the circle.
- Join the corners to the divisions of the circle. This divides the surface into triangles that can be developed.
- Take triangle **9D10**.

- With **D** as centre swing **9** and **10** onto **DC** at **L** and **M**. These are to be set against their heights.
- As there are so many true lengths to be found, a separate diagram is desirable.
- Separate the height on elevation and bring it down to **C** and **D**, as shown.
- Join **D** to **9** and to **10**. These are true lengths.
- Similarly find the other true lengths.

Step 2:
- Using the true lengths **D9**, **D10**, etc. and the chordal lengths **9** to **10**, **10** to **11**, etc., set out each triangle in sequence, as shown.
- This is a fair approximation of the surface pattern. The smaller your initial division into triangles, the more accurate the pattern will be.

The developed pattern

Notes:
- *A transition piece is a piece that starts out as one shape and smoothly changes to become a second shape at the other end.*
- *A similar method, using squares on an uneven surface, is much used in computer graphics.*

Technical Draughtsmanship		
Triangulation		
Development 19		Part 1 Geom H

Hemisphere
From the elevation

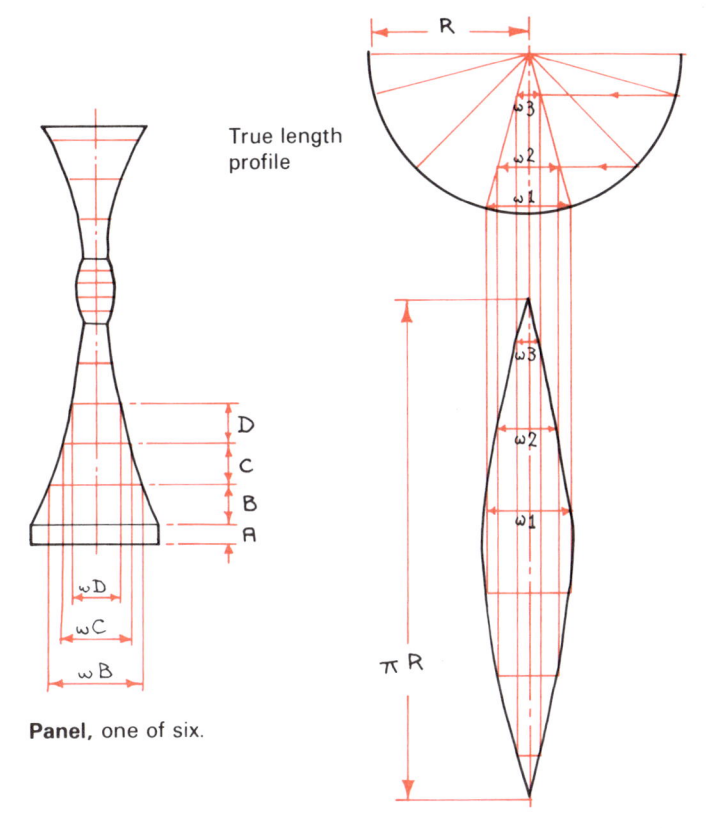

True length profile

Elevation

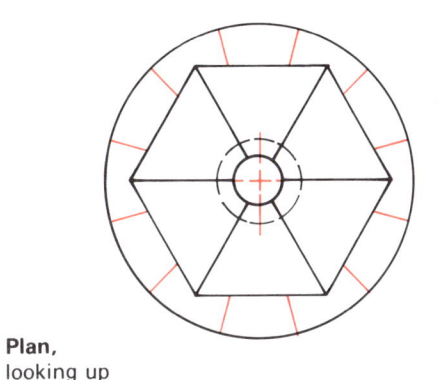

True length profile

Panel, one of six.

Gore, one of five. Two half-gores are also needed.

Plan, looking up

A Goblet

Note: *The panel, or strip of a sphere is called a* **gore**.

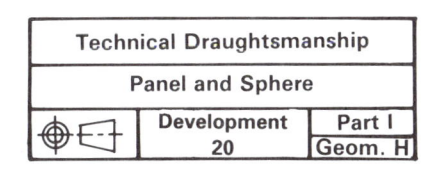

Procedure:
First, develop the stem of the goblet. This is made up of six panels.

To develop a panel.
- Place a panel so that its profile is true length. You may need to find such a profile by rotation.
- Choose a convenient length of arc **B** and cut off equal lengths along the profile **C**, **D** etc. For greater accuracy at the knuckle these divisions have been halved.
- To one side draw a centre line and along it mark the divisions **A, B, C** etc., stretching the profile out straight.
- Match the true widths from the elevation to this centre line, as shown. This a panel.

To develop the hemisphere
- Divide the hemisphere into a number of parts.
- Choose one. Lay out its centre line equal to πr, or step off chord lengths, and divide it into the same number of divisions.
- Project across, as shown, to get the true widths.
- Match these to their place on the centre line.
- Draw the outline to complete the pattern.

Technical Draughtsmanship
Panel and Sphere
Development 20 — Part I — Geom. H

165

Questions

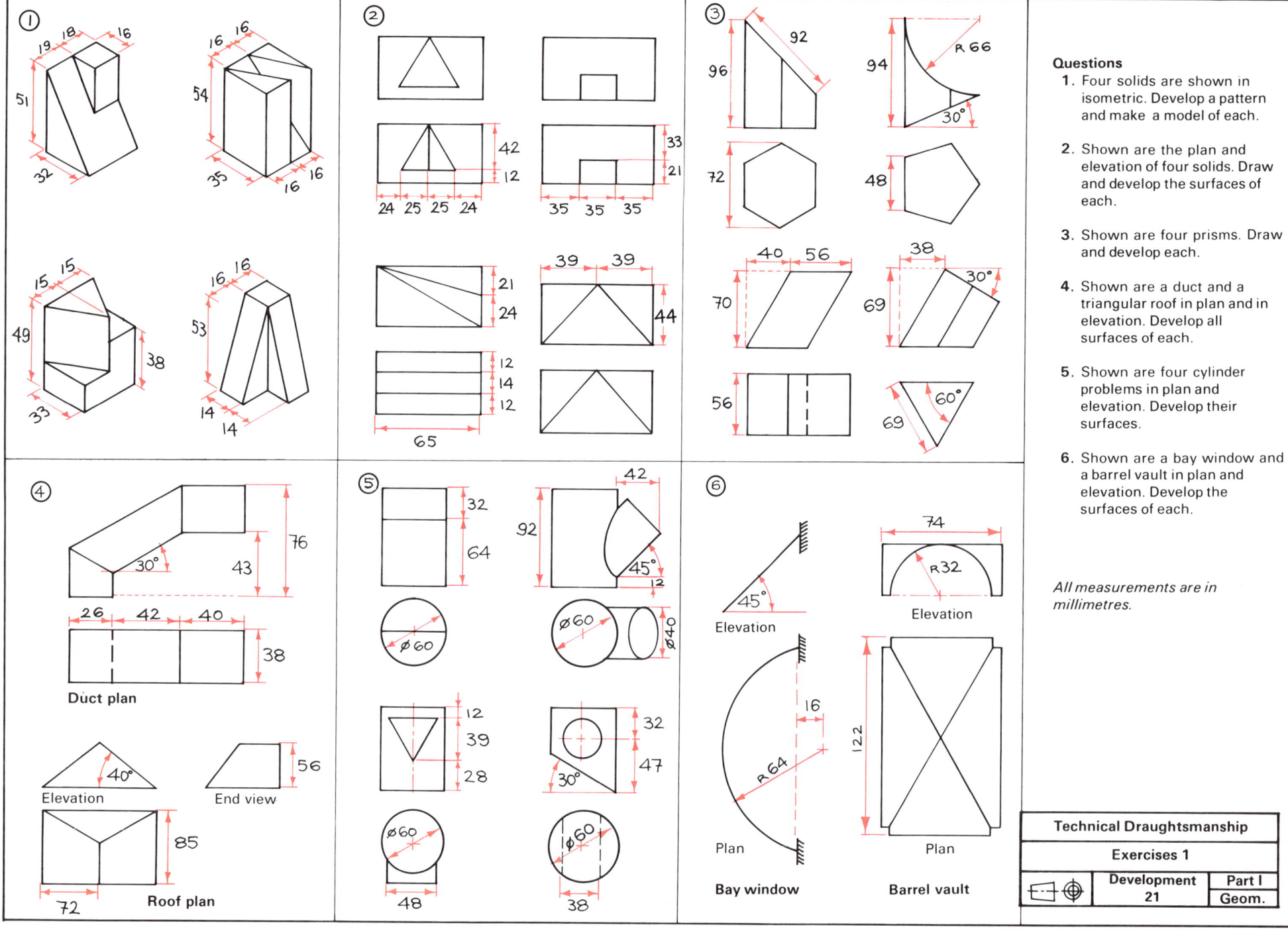

1. Four solids are shown in isometric. Develop a pattern and make a model of each.

2. Shown are the plan and elevation of four solids. Draw and develop the surfaces of each.

3. Shown are four prisms. Draw and develop each.

4. Shown are a duct and a triangular roof in plan and in elevation. Develop all surfaces of each.

5. Shown are four cylinder problems in plan and elevation. Develop their surfaces.

6. Shown are a bay window and a barrel vault in plan and elevation. Develop the surfaces of each.

All measurements are in millimetres.

Technical Draughtsmanship

Exercises 1

Development 21 | **Part I**
Geom.

Questions

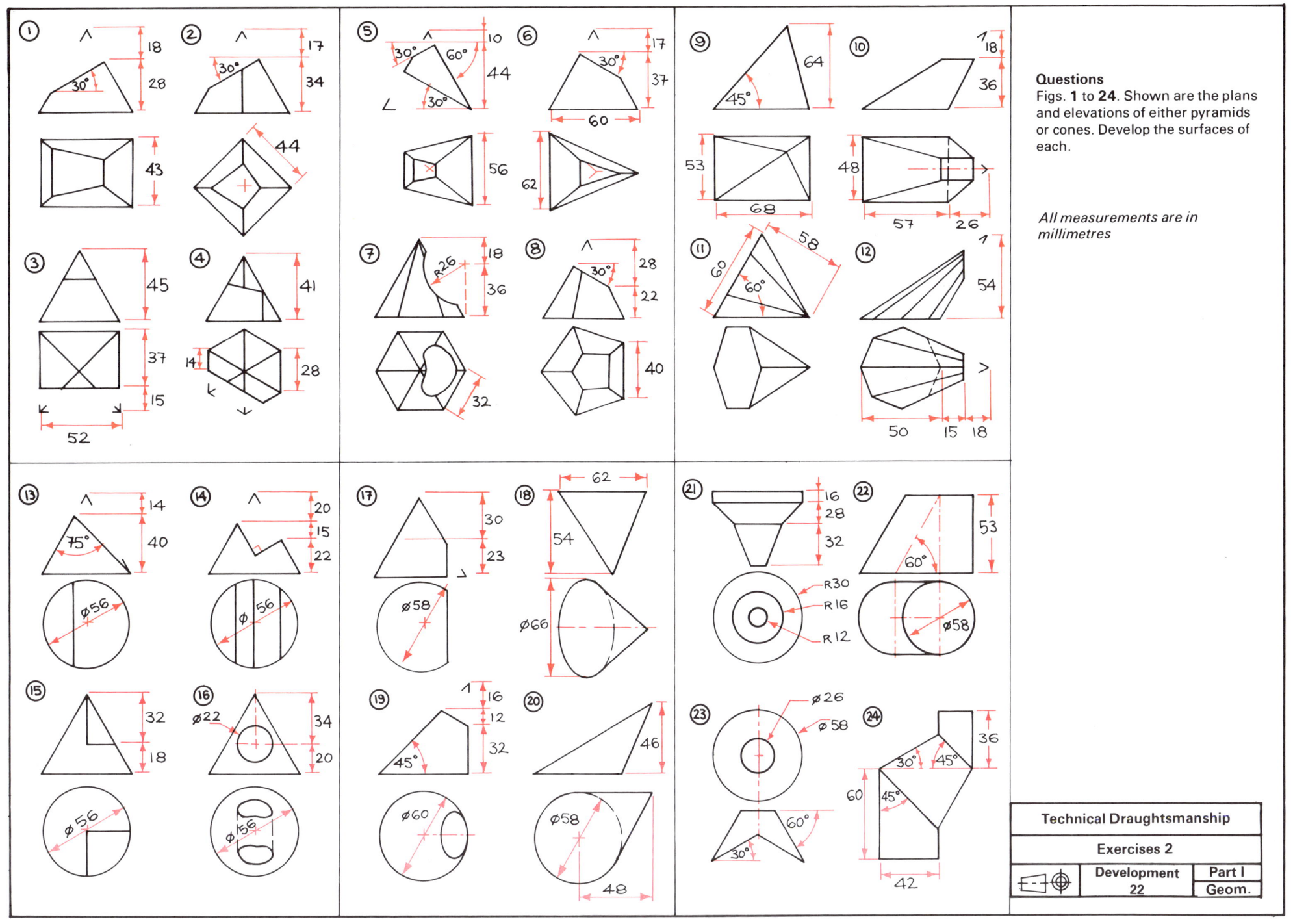

Figs. **1** to **24**. Shown are the plans and elevations of either pyramids or cones. Develop the surfaces of each.

All measurements are in millimetres

Technical Draughtsmanship

Exercises 2

Development 22 — Part I — Geom.

167

All measurements are in millimetres.

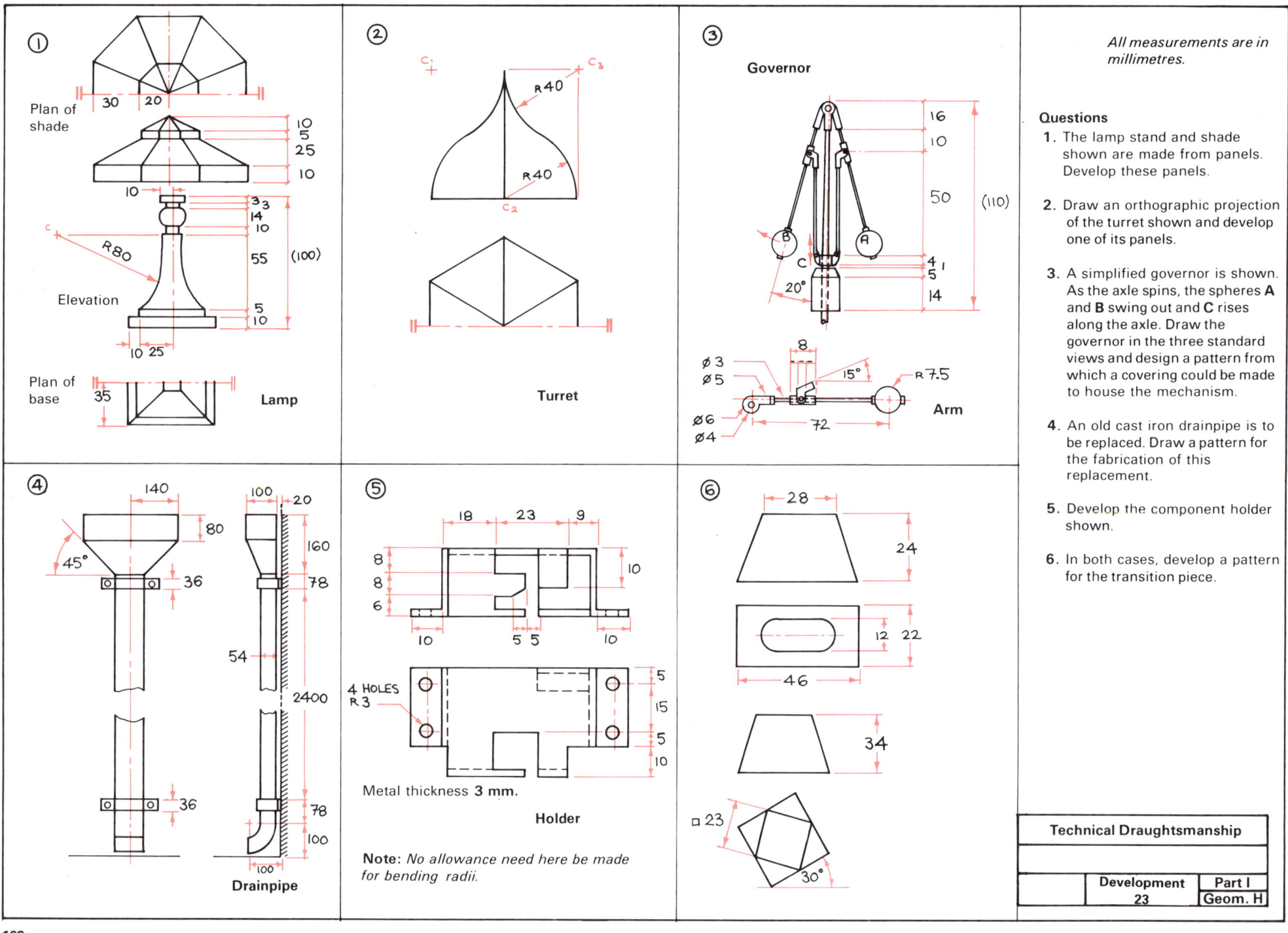

Questions

1. The lamp stand and shade shown are made from panels. Develop these panels.

2. Draw an orthographic projection of the turret shown and develop one of its panels.

3. A simplified governor is shown. As the axle spins, the spheres **A** and **B** swing out and **C** rises along the axle. Draw the governor in the three standard views and design a pattern from which a covering could be made to house the mechanism.

4. An old cast iron drainpipe is to be replaced. Draw a pattern for the fabrication of this replacement.

5. Develop the component holder shown.

6. In both cases, develop a pattern for the transition piece.

Technical Draughtsmanship

Development 23 — Part I — Geom. H

PART 1

**CHAPTER 13
ENVELOPMENTS**

Envelopment is the complete or partial wrapping of an object by packaging, or labelling. The wrapping may be designed in place on the solid and the required pattern then plotted. Alternatively you may wish to plot a given pattern onto various surfaces, or products.

CONTENTS
Labels unwrapped	*Page*	**170**
Labels applied		**171**
Exercises		**172**

Photocopying prohibited by law

Pattern for the neck label.

True length diagram

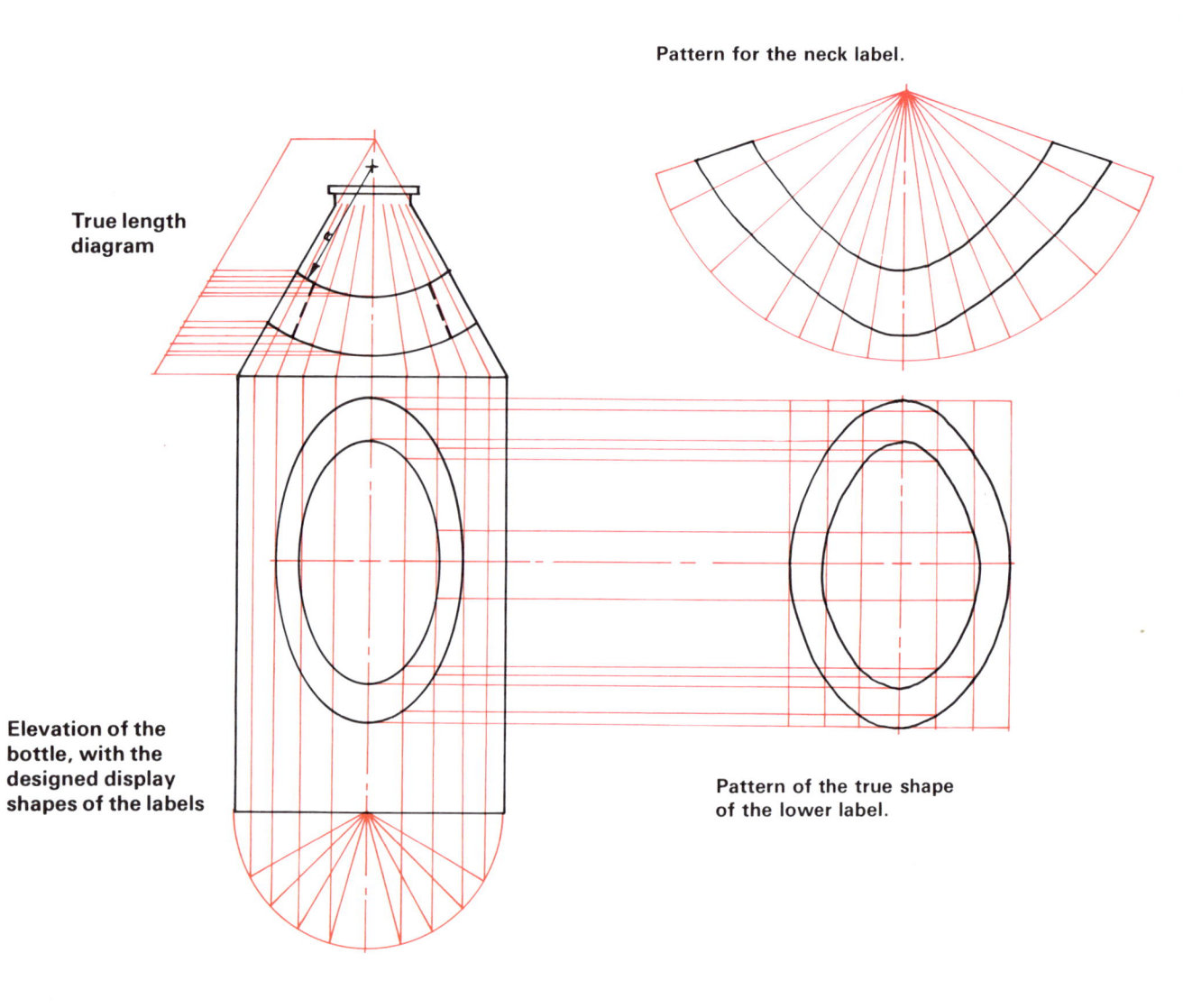

Elevation of the bottle, with the designed display shapes of the labels

Pattern of the true shape of the lower label.

- Labels, or decorations, are designed to look neat and appealing on the surface of a box, or product.
- It is usual first to design the label in place and then to develop a flat pattern, from which the label can be manufactured.
- The pattern can be very different or more complicated in appearance than the design would seem to suggest. This can be seen here in the neck label.
- To develop a label consider it to be part of the surface of the solid. Develop this in the normal way and plot the points of the label as if it were cut from that surface. See chapter **12**.
- It is not usually necessary to develop the complete surface of the solid. Develop only enough to plot the pattern, as shown here.

Technical Draughtsmanship
Labels Unwrapped
Envelopments 1 — Part I / Geom.

①

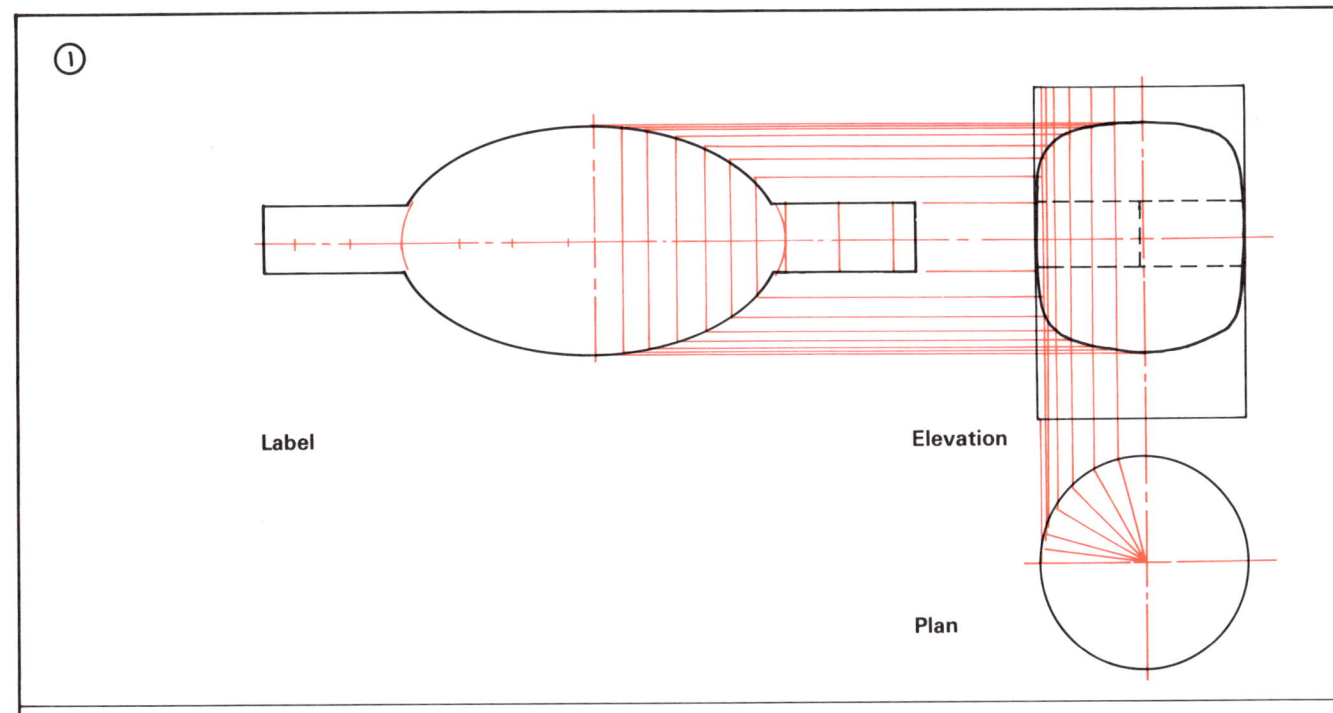

Label   **Elevation**

Plan

To draw the given label in position on the tin
- Lay out the label equal to πD.
- Draw the plan and elevation of the tin. Divide the plan into a number of pieces, set about the vertical centre line.
- Divide the label into the same number of panels, again set about the vertical centre line.
- Subdivide the panels, both on plan and on the label, if required.
- Project each panel of the label onto its corresponding panel on the tin.
- Plot and draw the label in position, as shown.

②

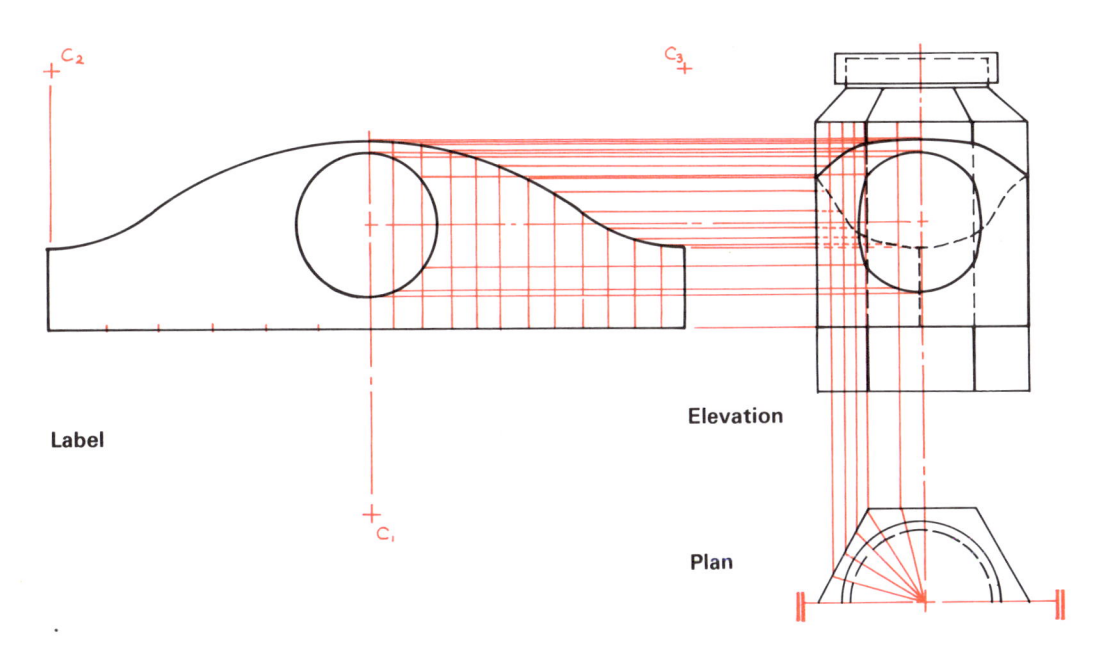

C_2 C_3

C_1

Label   **Elevation**

Plan

Given the label to transfer it to the jar
- Lay out the pattern, equal to the perimeter of the jar on plan.
- Find the centre line and divide the label into panels, each to fit one panel of the jar.
- Subdivide each panel as required, both on plan and on the label. The finer the divisions, the greater the accuracy of the transfer.
- Project over each panel, as shown.
- As both the label and jar are symmetrical, fewer panels need be detailed.

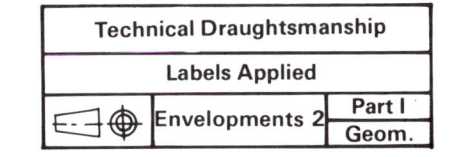

Technical Draughtsmanship		
Labels Applied		
Envelopments 2	Part I
	Geom.

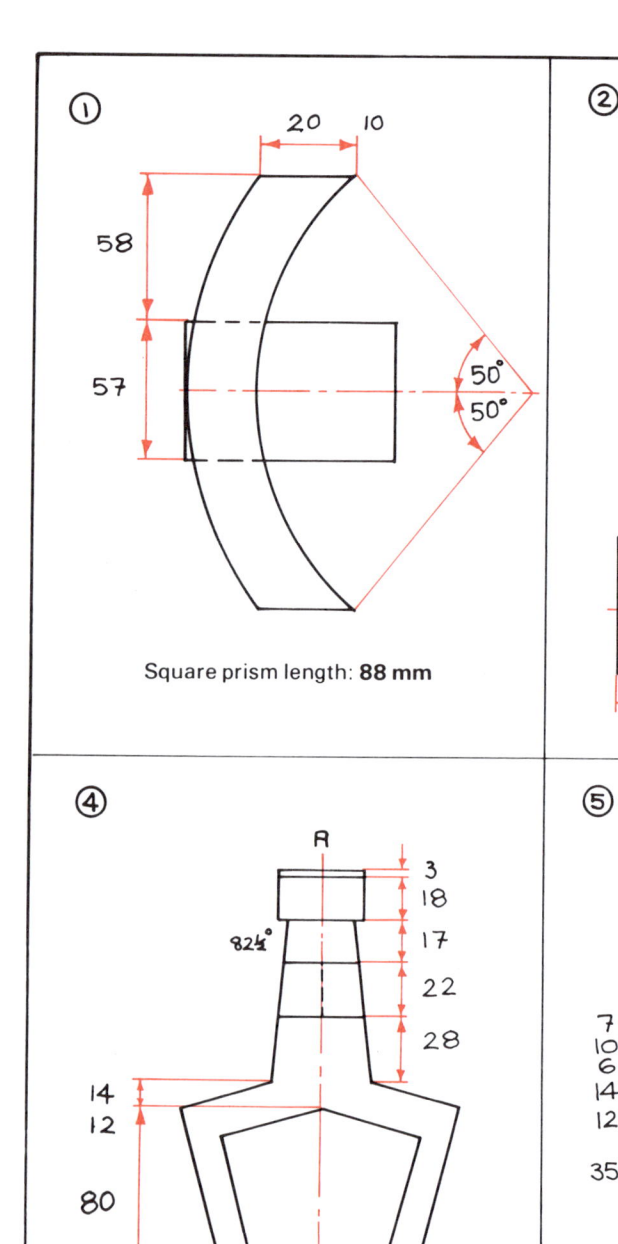

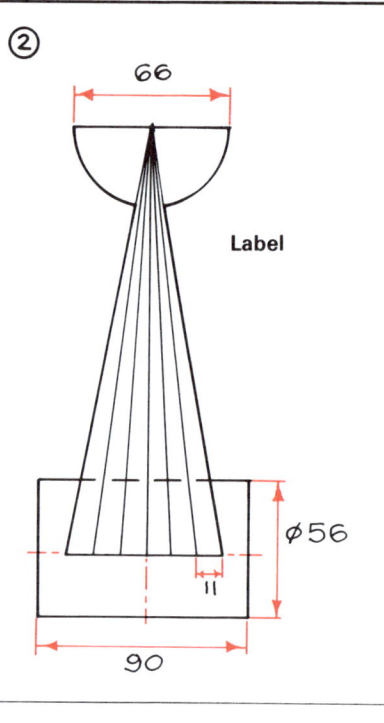

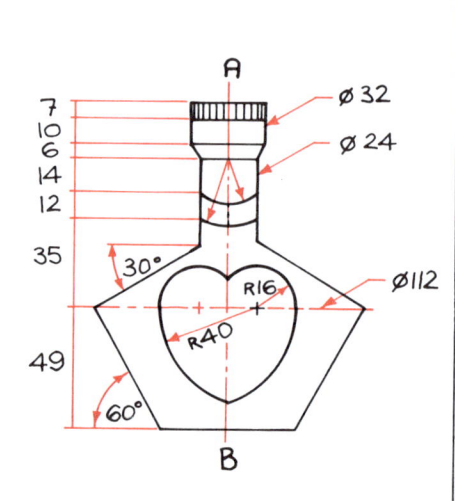

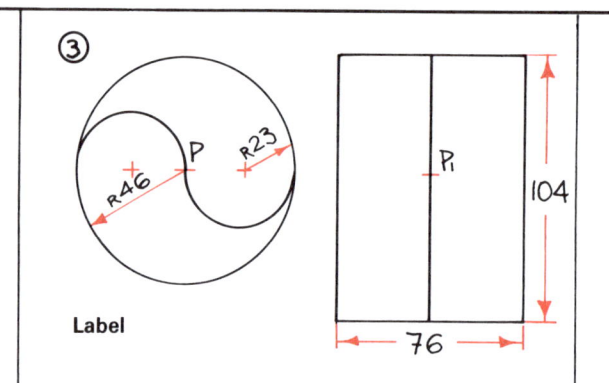

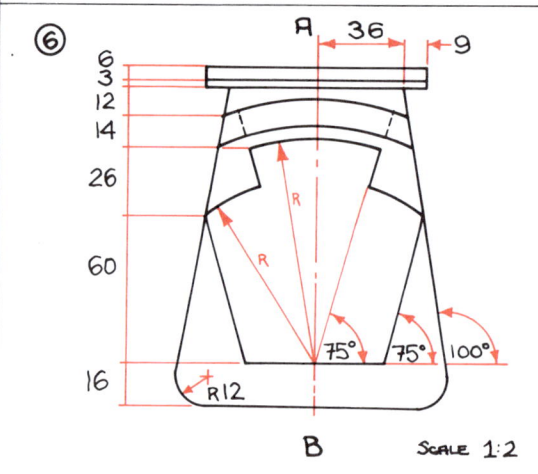

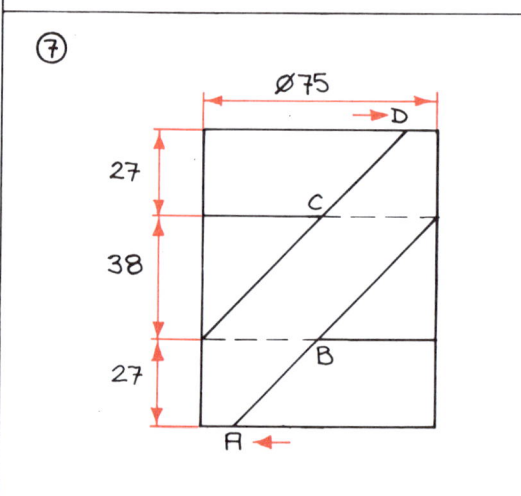

Questions

1. Draw the square prism in full orthographic projection, showing clearly how the label would wrap about it.

2. The label wraps once about the cylinder. Show this in all three orthographic views.

3. If point **P** of the label is placed on point **P₁** of the square prism, how will the label appear when smoothed against the solid? Show this in both elevation and end view.

4 to 6. In each case develop the true shape of both labels. The bottles are symmetrical about the axis **AB**.

7. Develop the pattern of a label that starts at **AB** and, encircling the cylinder as shown, ends at **CD**.

8. Design an imaginative label for the bottle of your choice. Draw the label both as a pattern and in position on the bottle.

Technical Draughtsmanship

Exercises

Envelopments 3 — Part I Geom.

PART 1

CHAPTER 14
LOCI

A locus is the path of a point. The point may itself be moving, or it might be a part of a mechanism which is moving. Sometimes a law, or a machine determines the locus. At other times a required locus determines the law, or the machine. See also chapters **15, 20** and **21**.

CONTENTS
Involutes	*Page*	174
Logarithmic spirals		175
Helices		176
Conical spirals		177
Ionic volutes		178
Cycloids		179
Trochoids		180
Glissette and catenary		181
Sample Problem 1		182
Sample Problem 2		183
Exercises		184

①

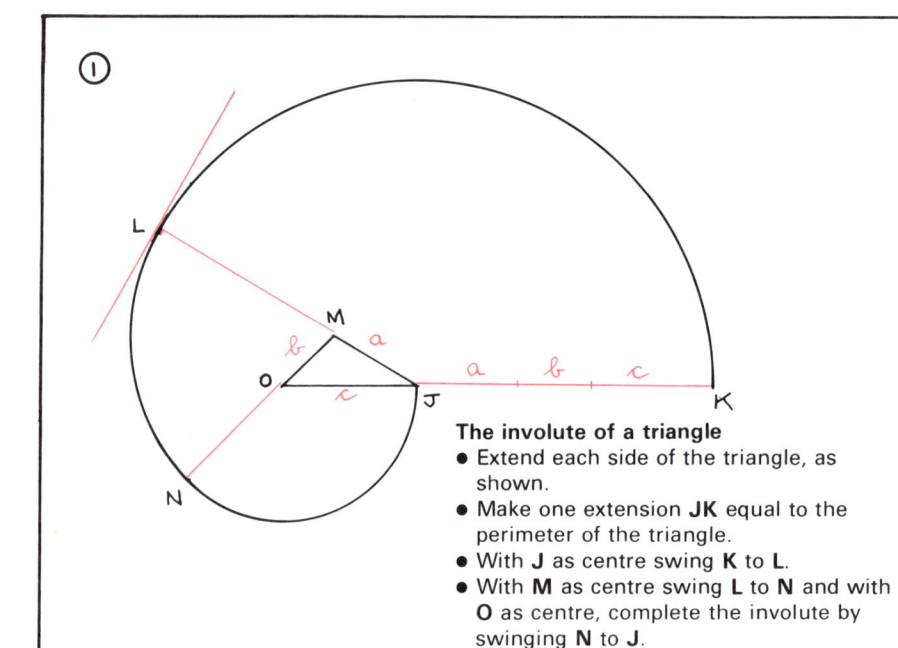

The involute of a triangle
- Extend each side of the triangle, as shown.
- Make one extension **JK** equal to the perimeter of the triangle.
- With **J** as centre swing **K** to **L**.
- With **M** as centre swing **L** to **N** and with **O** as centre, complete the involute by swinging **N** to **J**.
- A tangent may be drawn at **L**, as shown.

②

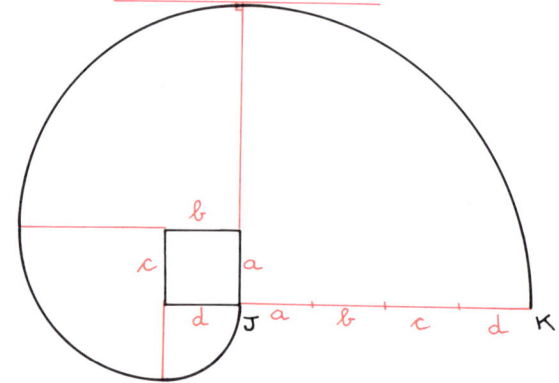

The involute of a square
- Set **JK** equal to the perimeter of the square.
- Proceed, as outlined above, to draw the curve.

③

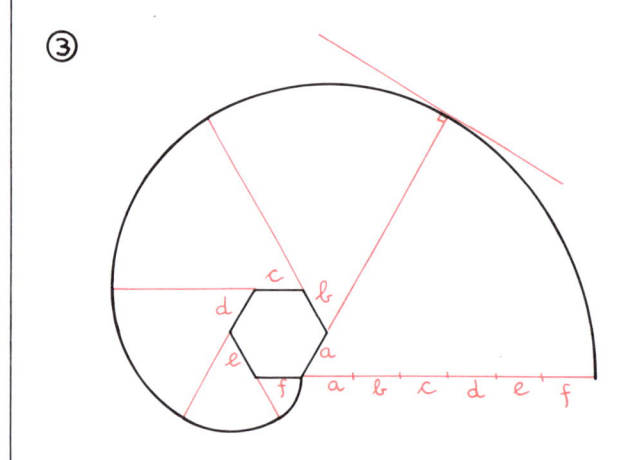

The involute of a polygon
e.g. a hexagon.

- Set out a base line equal to the perimeter of the polygon.
- Proceed, as before, to draw the curve.

Note: *Involutes can be drawn from the inside outwards, if you prefer.*

④

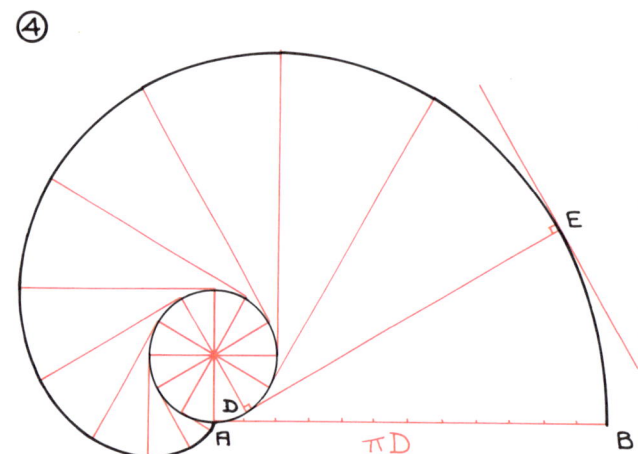

The involute of a circle
- Divide up the circle.
- Set out a base line **AB** equal to πD, where **D** is the diameter of the circle.
- Divide **AB** into the same number of parts as the circle.
- Draw a line **DE** tangent to the first division.
- With centre **A** swing **B** to **E**.
- Continue in this way to complete the involute.

Note: *An involute is the path traced by the end of a taut piece of string when it is unrolled from a basic shape. This basic shape may be called an evolute. The word involute means 'to unfold'.*

Technical Draughtsmanship
Involutes
Loci 1 · Part I · Geom.

174

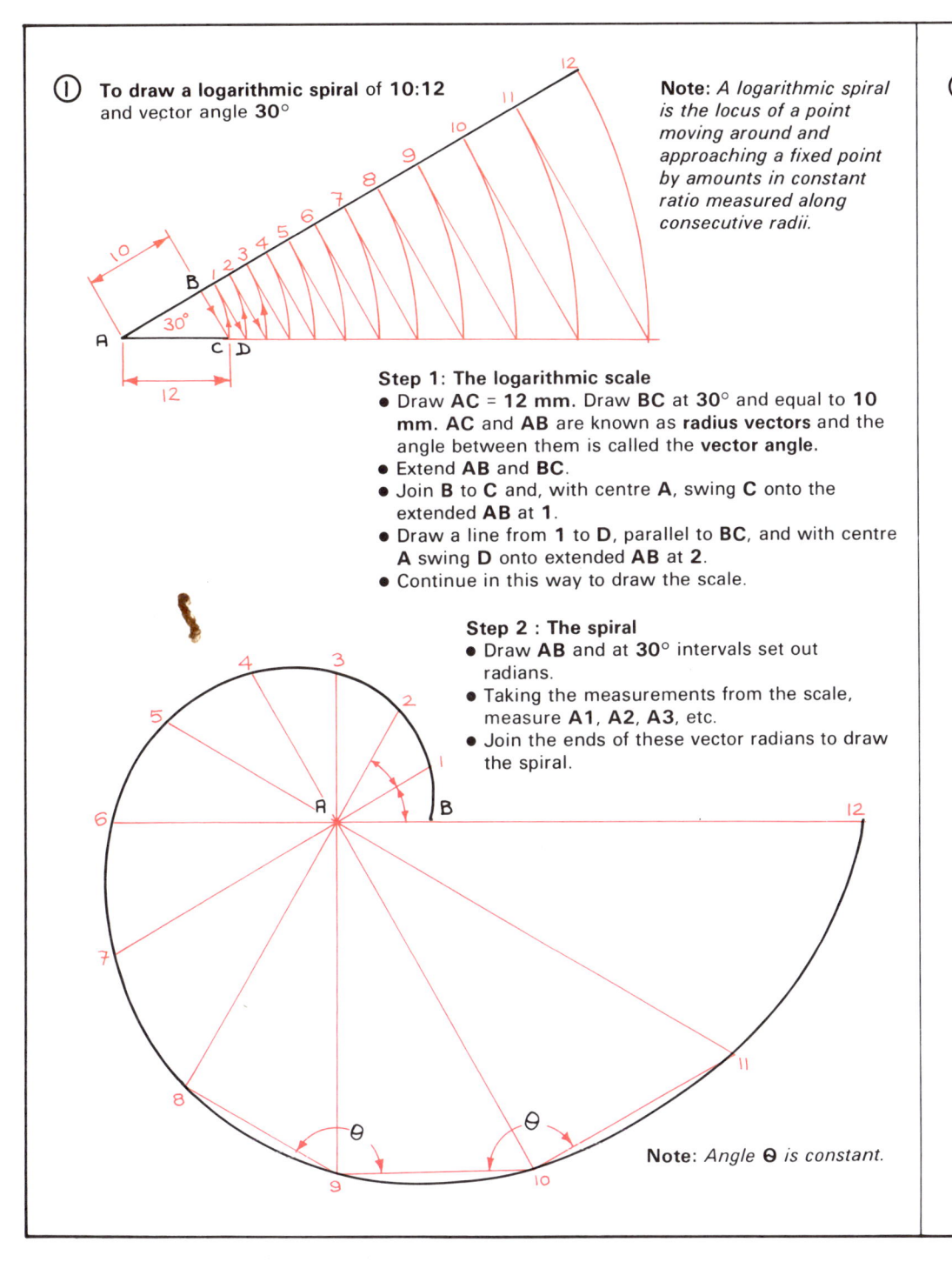

① **To draw a logarithmic spiral** of **10:12** and vector angle **30°**

Note: *A logarithmic spiral is the locus of a point moving around and approaching a fixed point by amounts in constant ratio measured along consecutive radii.*

Step 1: The logarithmic scale
- Draw **AC** = **12 mm**. Draw **BC** at **30°** and equal to **10 mm**. AC and AB are known as **radius vectors** and the angle between them is called the **vector angle**.
- Extend **AB** and **BC**.
- Join **B** to **C** and, with centre **A**, swing **C** onto the extended **AB** at **1**.
- Draw a line from **1** to **D**, parallel to **BC**, and with centre **A** swing **D** onto extended **AB** at **2**.
- Continue in this way to draw the scale.

Step 2 : The spiral
- Draw **AB** and at **30°** intervals set out radians.
- Taking the measurements from the scale, measure **A1, A2, A3**, etc.
- Join the ends of these vector radians to draw the spiral.

Note: *Angle Θ is constant.*

② **To draw a clockwise logarithmic spiral given two vectors and the angle between them**
e.g. **AB** = **15mm.**, **BC** = **18 mm**. and angle **BAC** = **40°**.
- The construction is similar to that outlined before.
- Here, however, the logarithmic scale is used as a basis for the direct construction of the spiral by extension, as shown.

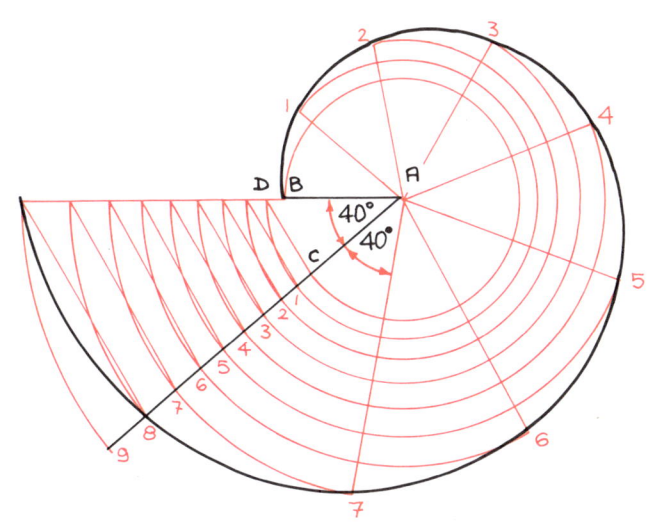

Step 1
- Set out **AB** = **15 mm**. and extend.
- Set **AC** at **40°** to **AB** and equal to **18 mm**. Extend **AC**.
- Join **C** to **B**.
- With centre **A** swing **B** onto the extended **AC** at **1**.
- Draw **1** to **D**, parallel to **CB**.
- With centre **A** swing **D** onto the extended **AC** at **2**.
- Continue to complete the scale.

Step 2
- Set out radius vectors **A7, A6**, etc. at **40°** intervals.
- With centre **A** swing point **7** on the scale onto **A7**, point **6** onto **A6** and so on.
- Join these points to draw the spiral, as shown.

Note: *These steps can be worked together with a little practice.*

Technical Draughtsmanship		
Logarithmic Spirals		
	Loci 2	Part I
		Geom.

175

① Helix

A helix is the curve traced by a point **P** winding around and up a cylinder. If it curls around as does your right hand, it is called a **right handed** helix.

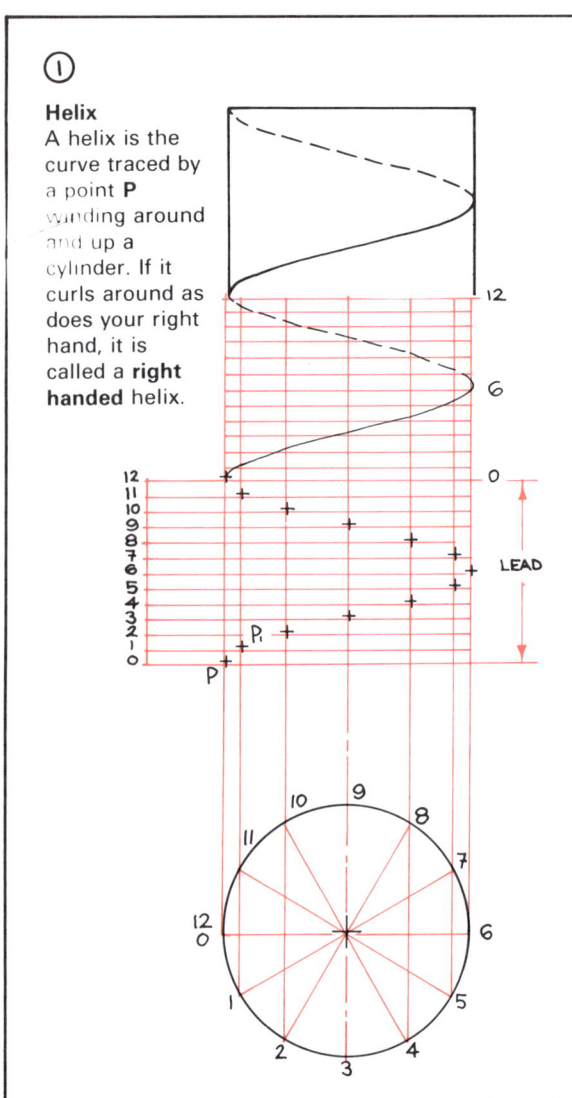

- Draw the plan and elevation of the cylinder and divide it in twelve.
- Mark the height gained in one revolution. This is usually given, and is called the **lead**.
- Divide this lead into twelve.
- Move P over one and up one to find P_1.
- Continue to plot points in this way, and then join the points to draw the helix.

Note: *In some circumstances the lead may be called the pitch. See page* **230**.

② Helical spring of circular section

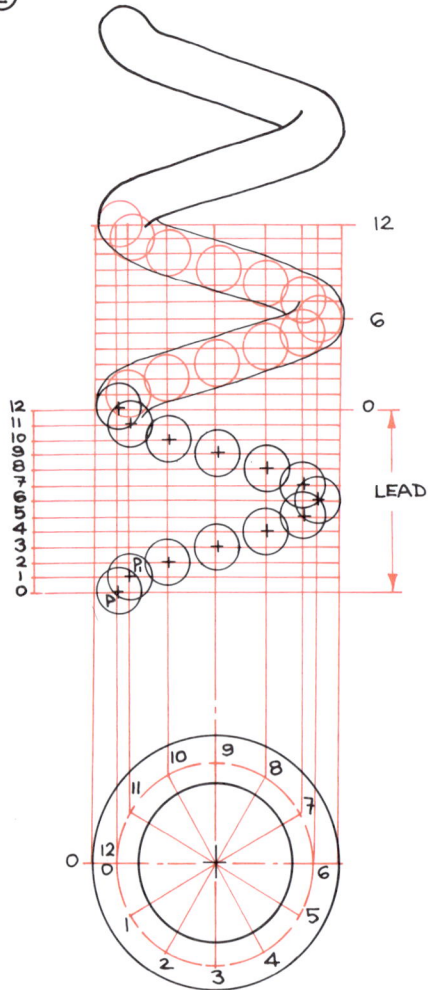

- Draw the plan and divide it in twelve. As the section is circular, draw a circle through the centre points, as shown.
- Index these and project them up to the elevation.
- Plot P, P_1, etc. in the usual way, based on the centre-points circle.
- On each centre P, P_1, etc. lightly draw the circular sections.
- Draw the outline of the spring as shown above.

③ Helical spring of rectangular section

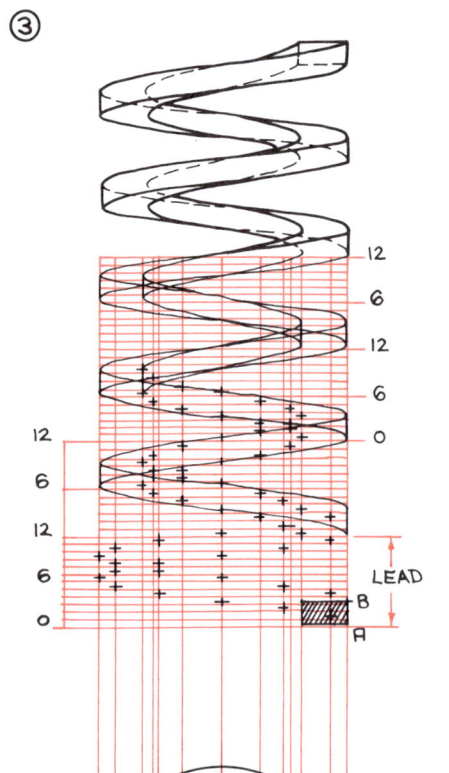

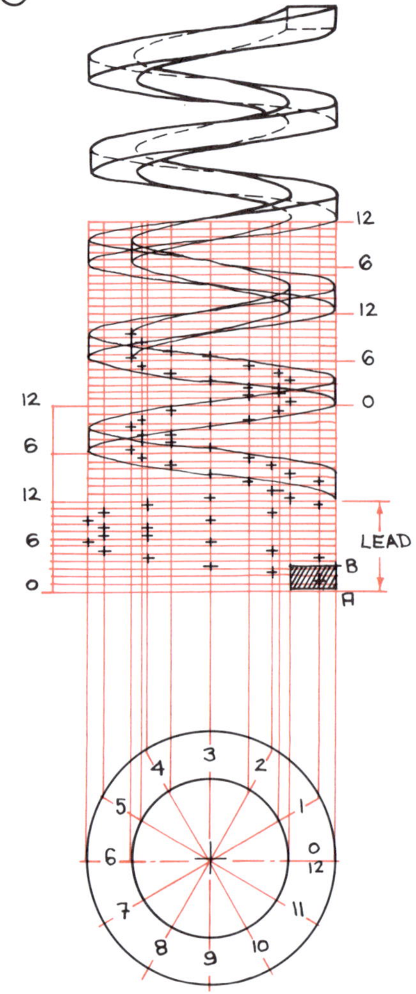

- Take each of the outside corners **A** and **B** and lightly draw their helices.
- Do the same for the inside corners, using the divisions from the inside circle on the plan.
- Strengthen the outline of the spring, as shown above.
- This is a **left handed** helical spring. Why?

Note: *The helix may be the most important curve in the universe. It is the path of the earth through space, and it is also the shape of the DNA molecule.*

Note: *The development of a helix is a straight line.*

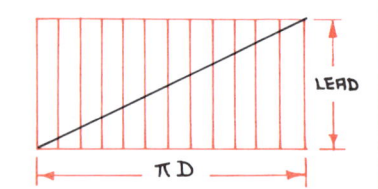

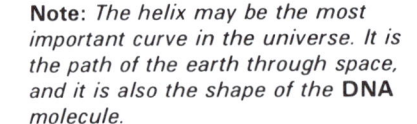

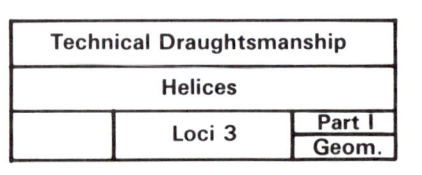

Technical Draughtsmanship		
Helices		
Loci 3		Part I
		Geom.

①

Elevation

Plan

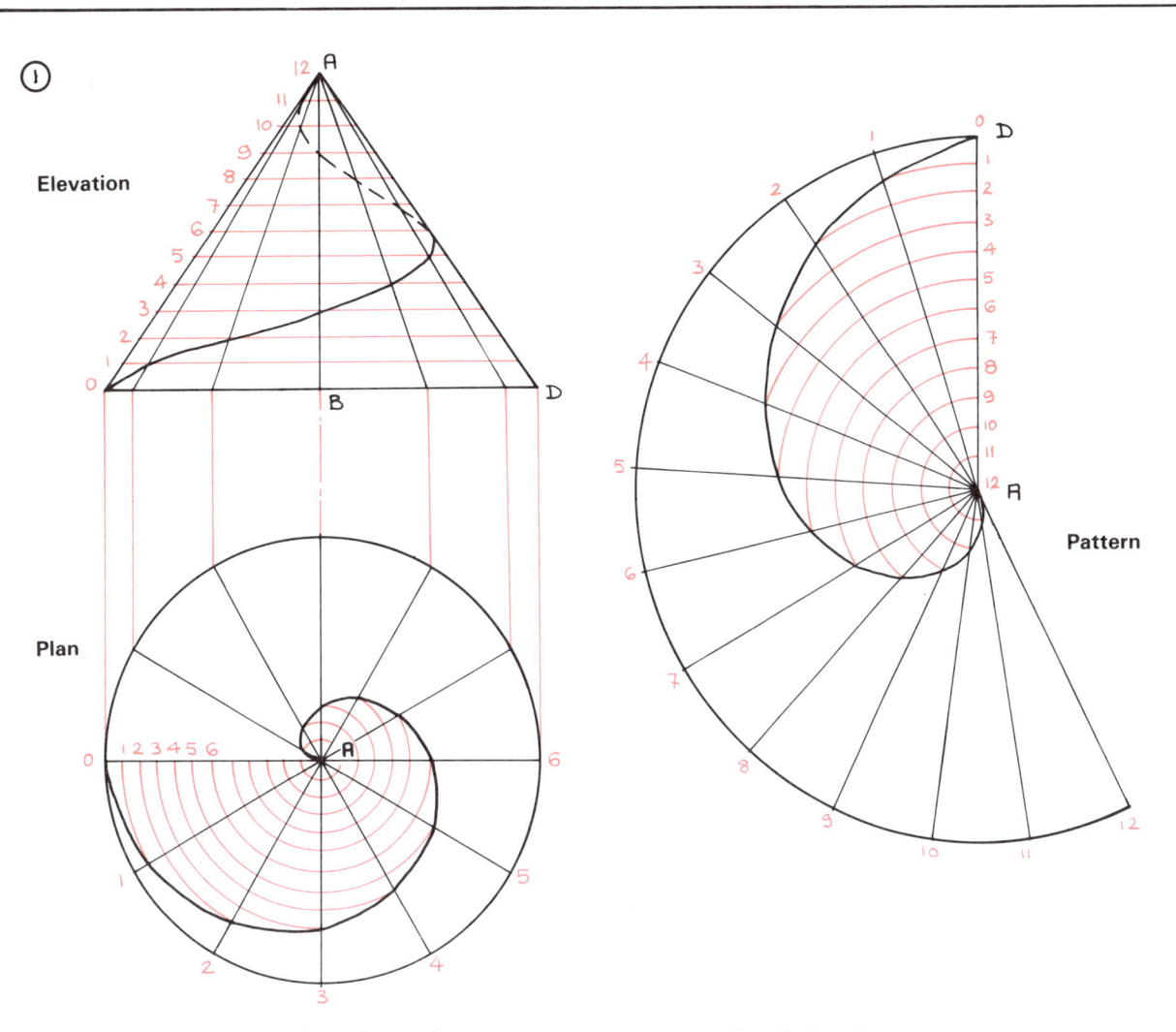

Pattern

Part 1: The plan: An Archimedean spiral.
- Divide the circle into pieces and divide one radius into the same number of pieces. Index, as shown.
- With centre **A** swing point **1** onto radian **1**, point **2** onto radian **2**, and so on.
- Join these points on the radians.

Part 2: The elevation: A conical spiral
- Divide the axis **AB** into the same number of parts as the base circle.
- Plot the points and draw the spiral, as shown above. It is a **right handed** spiral.

Part 3: Development
- Set out the pattern of the cone, in the usual way, see page **159**.
- Using the chord length from the plan, step off the perimeter divisions and join these to **A**, as shown.
- Divide **AD** into twelve and, with centre **A** swing point **1** to radian **1**, point **2** to radian **2**, and so on.
- Join these points on the radians to draw the spiral.

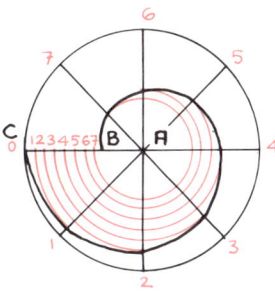

②

Starting off-centre
- Set out the shortest radius **AB** and the longest radius **AC**.
- Divide **BC** into a number of parts, and the circle into the same number of parts.
- With **A** as centre swing point **1** to radian **1**, point **2** to radian **2** and so on.
- Draw the curve, as shown.

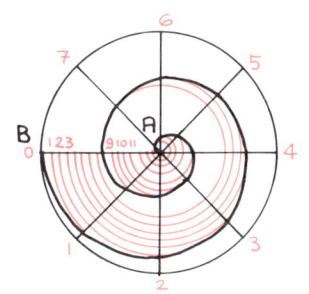

③

A double spiral
- Divide **AB** into *twice* the number of parts as the circle.
- Proceed as usual, going around twice.

Technical Draughtsmanship
Conical Spirals

	Loci 4	Part I
		Geom.

177

① Goldman's method

(a) The centre eye
- Draw a circle of radius $A \div 9$
- Mark points **1** and **4** at the mid-point of the radius.
- Divide the distance **1** to **4** into six equal parts.
- Construct a square of side **1** to **4**.
- Join **C** to **2** and to **3**, and using these as a guide construct two smaller squares on the divisions already marked.
- Index, as shown.

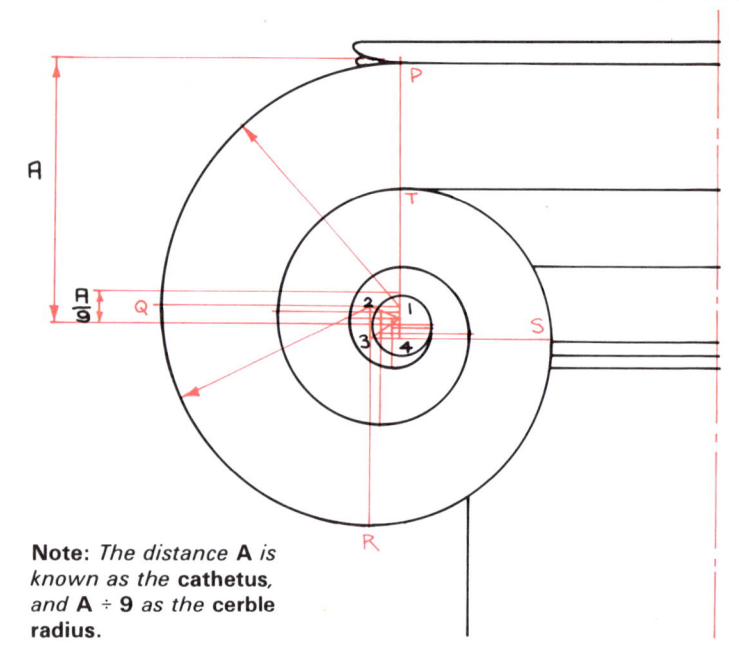

Note: The distance **A** is known as the **cathetus**, and $A \div 9$ as the **cerble radius**.

(B) To draw the volute
- Extend the centre eye to **P, Q, R** and **S**, as indicated in the second diagram above.
- With centre **1**, swing **P** to **Q**.
- With centre **2**, swing **Q** to **R**.
- Continue with centres **3, 4**, etc. to complete the ionic volute.

Note: The Ionians were a race in Greece and volvere is the Latin for 'to roll up'.

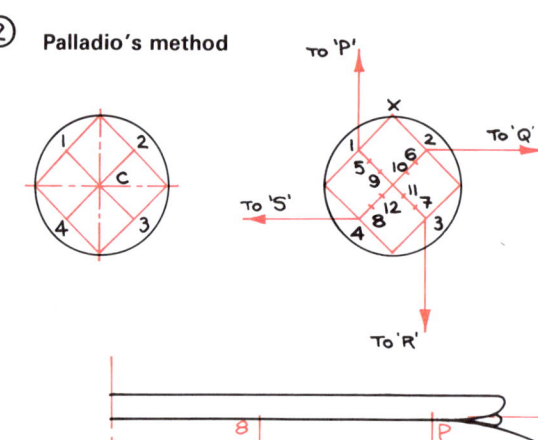

② Palladio's method

(a) The centre eye
- Draw the circle of radius $A \div 9$.
- Inscribe a square on the axis and join the mid-points.
- Subdivide each diagonal, **1** to **3** and **2** to **4**, into six parts. Index, as shown.

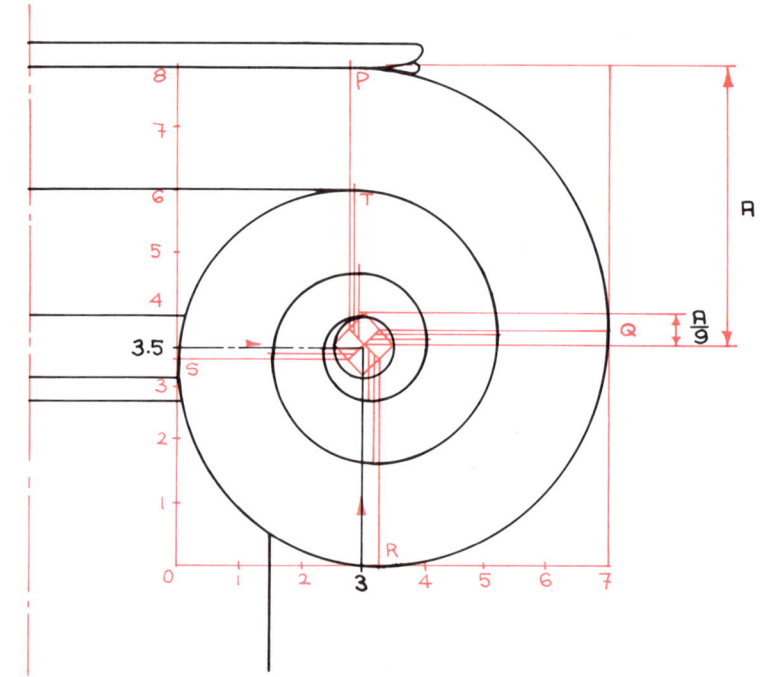

(b) To draw the volute in a rectangle
- Draw a rectangle of side **8** units vertically and **7** units horizontally.
- The centre of the eye will be **3** units across and **3.5** units up.
- Draw the eye and extend it to **P, Q, R** and **S**, as indicated.
- With centre **1**, swing **P** to **Q**.
- With centre **2**, swing **Q** to **R**.
- Continue to draw the volute.

Note: Goldman's volute will **not** fit into Palladio's box.

Technical Draughtsmanship.

Ionic Volutes

Loci 5 | Part I Geom.

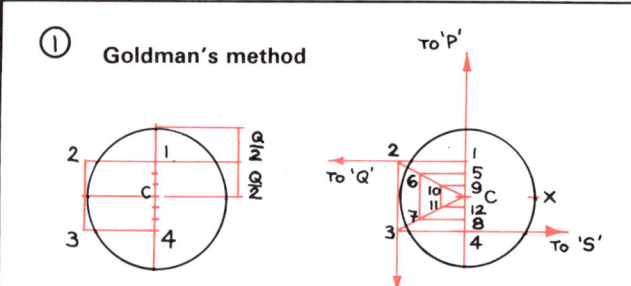

① The cycloid
The path of point **P** as the circle rolls along **AB**.

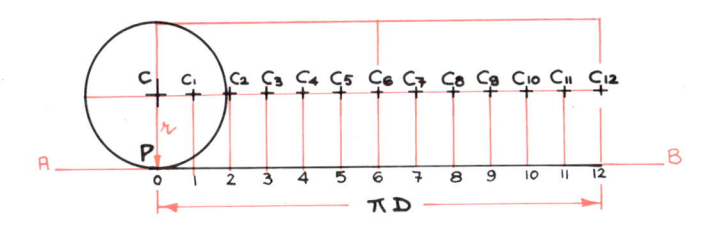

Step 1:
- Mark one revolution πD along **AB** and divide it into twelve.
- Draw CC_{12} parallel to **AB** and mark each of the twelve centres, as shown.

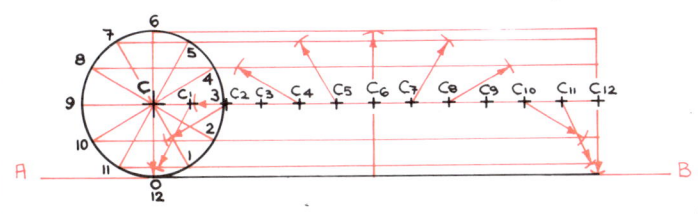

Step 2:
- Divide the circle into twelve and draw lines through the divisions of the perimeter parallel to **AB**.
- With radius **CP** and centre C_1 cut the line from **1**.
- With radius **CP** and centre C_2 cut the line from **2**.
- Continue for centres C_3 to C_{12}, as shown.

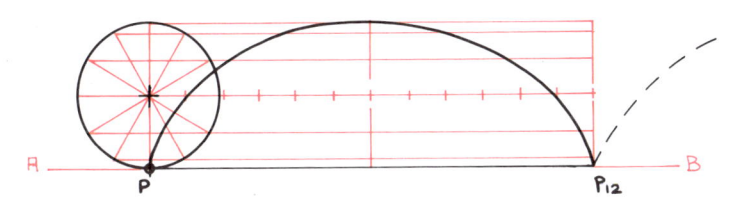

Step 3:
- Join the cut points to draw the cycloid.

Some properties:
- The length of a cycloidal curve = **8r = 4D**.
- The area under a cycloidal arch is equal to 3 × area of the circle = $3\pi r^2$.
- A particle placed anywhere on an upturned cycloid will take the same time to reach the bottom.
- Cycloid in based on the greek word 'kuklos' meaning 'a circle'.

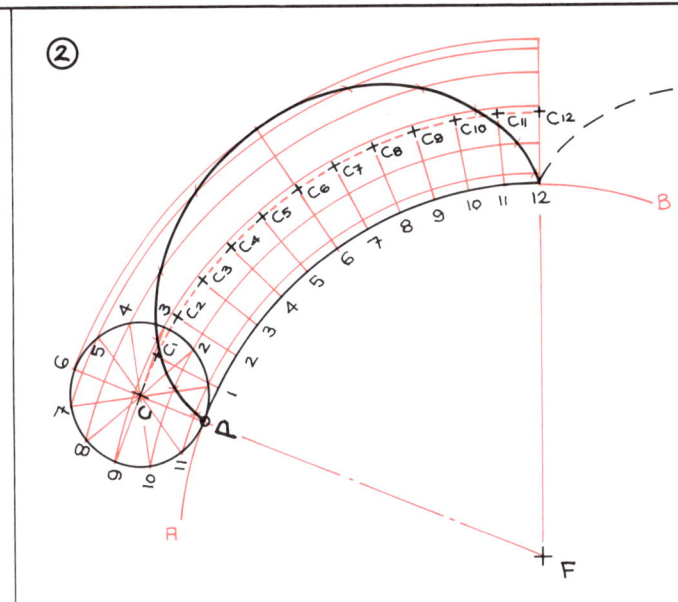

② The epicycloid
The path of point **P** as the circle rolls along the arc **AB**.
- On radian **FP** draw the circle and divide it in twelve.
- Step chordal lengths along the arc to find **1, 2, 3** to **12**.
- Draw a line **F** to **12** and extend.
- With **F** as centre, swing **C** to C_{12}.
- With **F** as centre, draw radians through points **1, 2, 3** etc., to find C_1, C_2, C_3 etc.
- With centre **F** swing the divisions from the *perimeter* of the circle to line **F12**.
- With radius **CP** and centre C_1 cut the arc from **1**.
- With radius **CP** and centre C_2 cut the arc from **2**.
- Continue and draw the curve, as shown.

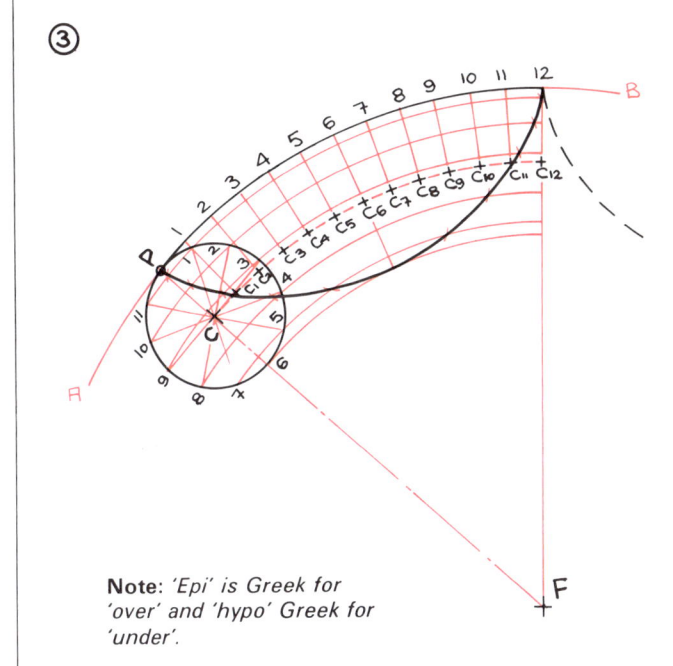

③ The hypocyloid
The path of point **P** as the circle rolls along the underside of arc **AB**.
- On radian **FP** draw the circle and divide it in twelve.
- Step chordal lengths along the arc to find **1, 2, 3** to **12**.
- Join **12** to **F**.
- With **F** as centre, draw the radians from **1, 2, 3** etc. to find C_1, C_2, C_3 etc.
- With centre **F** swing the divisions from the perimeter of the circle to **F12**.
- With radius **CP** and centre C_2 cut the arc from **2**.
- Continue and draw the curve, as shown.

Note: 'Epi' is Greek for 'over' and 'hypo' Greek for 'under'.

Technical Draughtsmanship
Cycloids
Loci 6 — Part I Geom.

179

① Inferior trochoid
The path of P when the outer circle rolls along line **AB**.

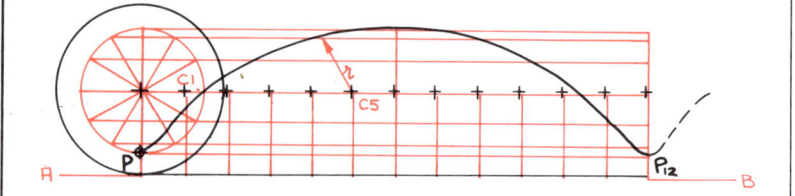

- The distance **P** to **P₁₂** is laid out as the perimeter of the circle rolling along the line, i.e. the *outer* circle.
- However the positions of **P** are plotted from its positions on the *inner* circle.
- So, C_1, C_2 etc. are found and then, with radius **r = CP**, plot the points in the usual way.

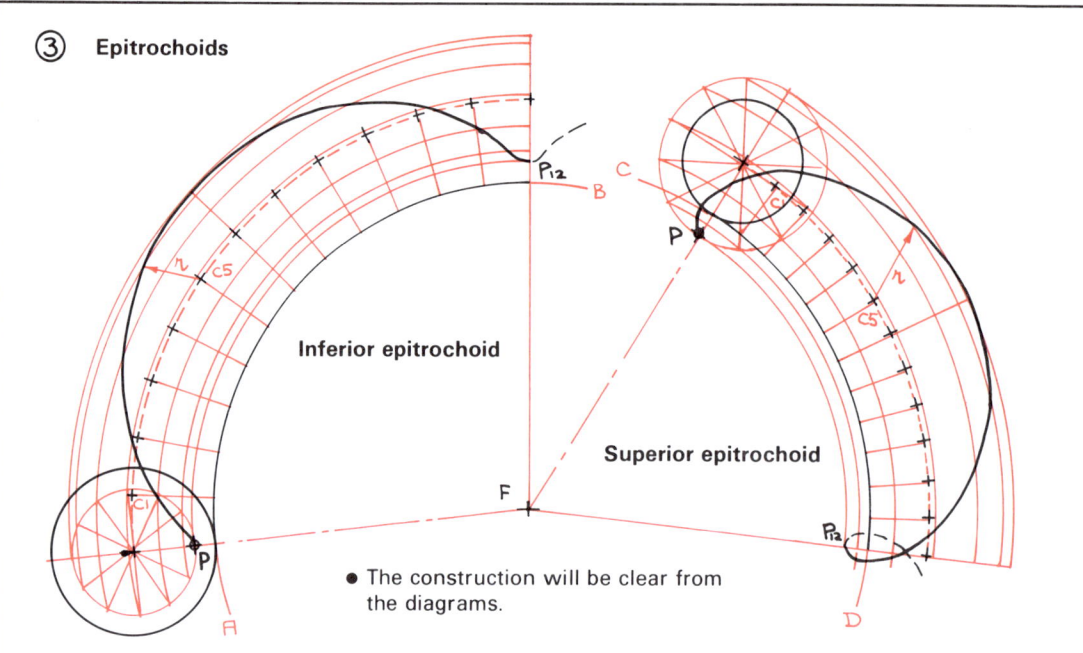

② Superior trochoid
The path of point P when the inner circle rolls along line **AB**.

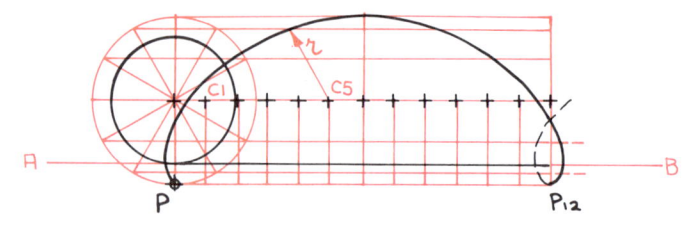

- The distance **P** to **P₁₂** is laid out as the perimeter of the circle rolling along the line, in this case the *inner* circle.
- And the positions of **P** are plotted from its positions on the *outer* circle.
- So, find C_1, C_2 etc. and, with radius **R = CP**, plot the points of the curve in the usual way.

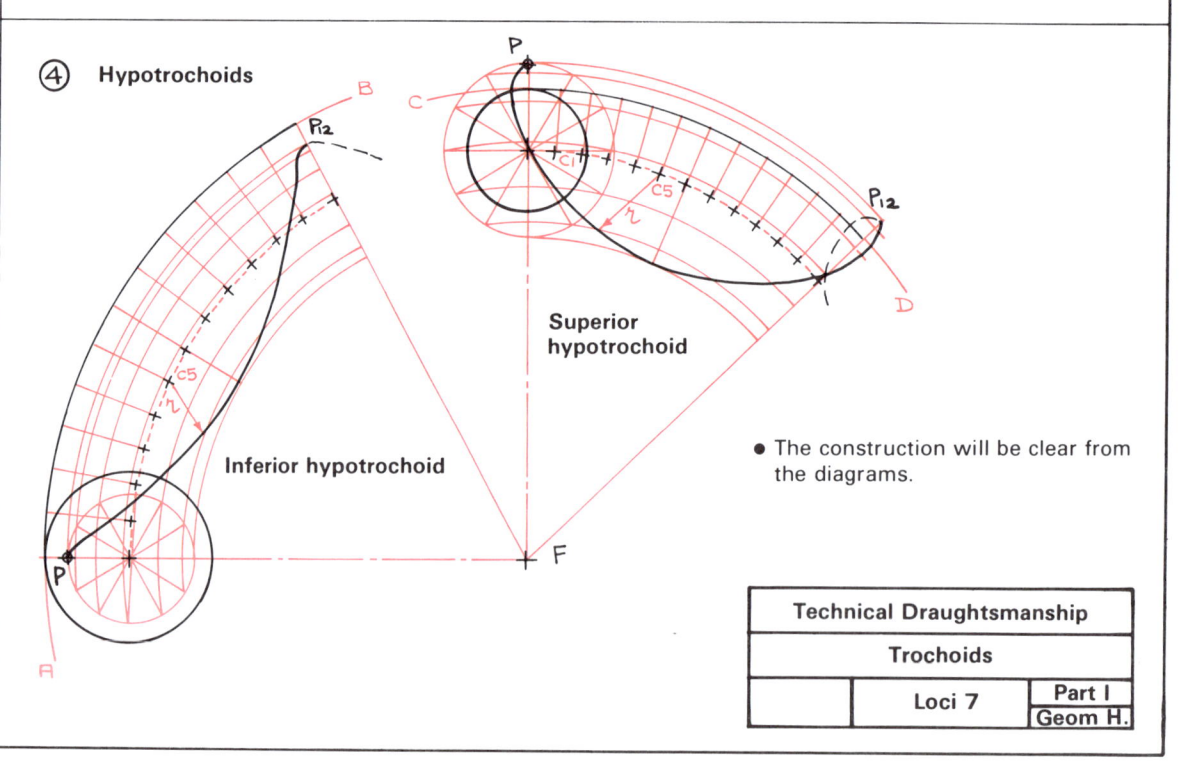

③ Epitrochoids

Inferior epitrochoid

Superior epitrochoid

- The construction will be clear from the diagrams.

④ Hypotrochoids

Superior hypotrochoid

Inferior hypotrochoid

- The construction will be clear from the diagrams.

Technical Draughtsmanship
Trochoids
Loci 7 — Part I — Geom H.

① Glissette on a right angle

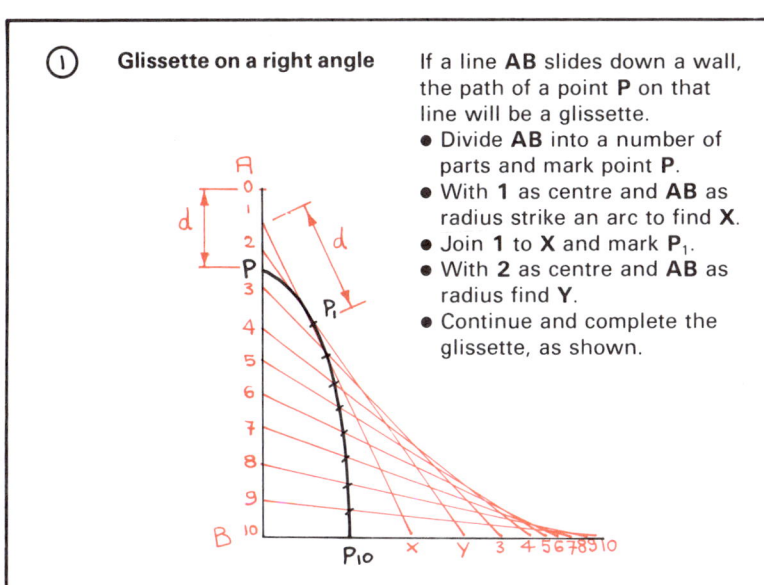

If a line **AB** slides down a wall, the path of a point **P** on that line will be a glissette.
- Divide **AB** into a number of parts and mark point **P**.
- With **1** as centre and **AB** as radius strike an arc to find **X**.
- Join **1** to **X** and mark P_1.
- With **2** as centre and **AB** as radius find **Y**.
- Continue and complete the glissette, as shown.

Note: *Imagine a ladder slipping down a wall.*

② Glissette at an angle

Here the line **OA** slides between two lines that are not at right angles.

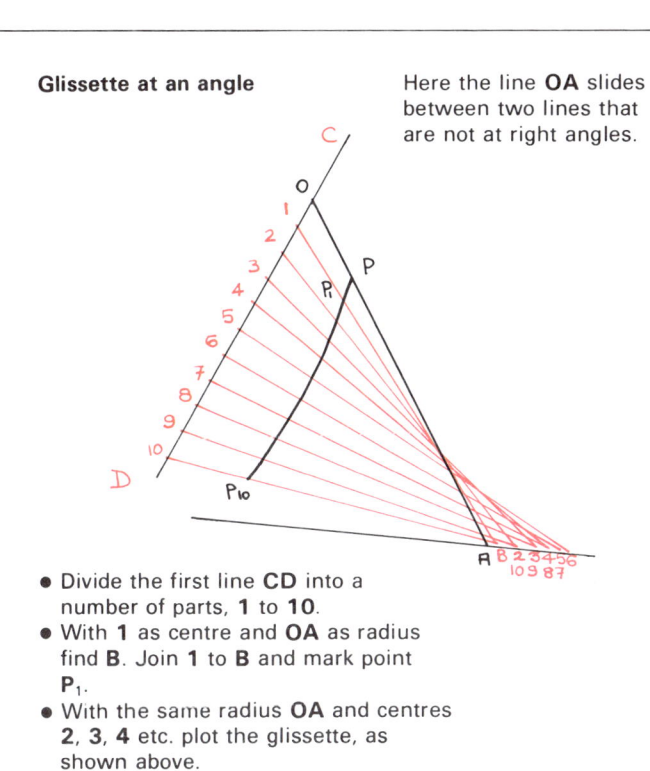

- Divide the first line **CD** into a number of parts, **1** to **10**.
- With **1** as centre and **OA** as radius find **B**. Join **1** to **B** and mark point P_1.
- With the same radius **OA** and centres **2, 3, 4** etc. plot the glissette, as shown above.

③ Roulette

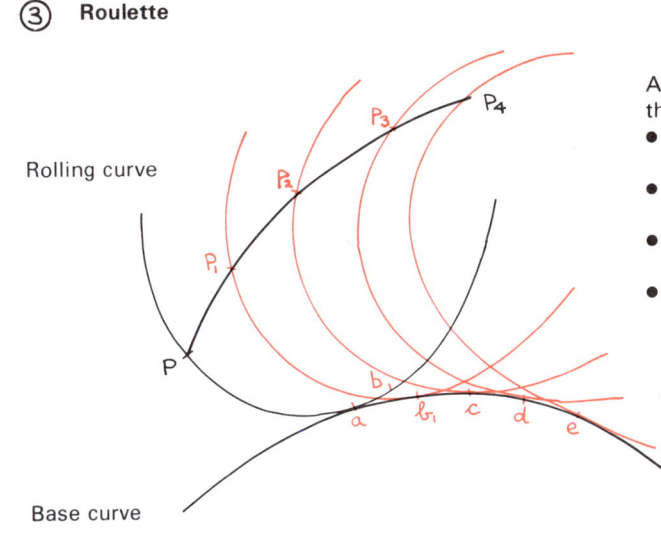

A roulette is the locus of a point **P** on a curve that is rolling on a fixed base curve.
- Draw the base curve and the rolling curve in contact at **a**. Mark point **P**.
- Trace the curve and roll **b** carefully along the base to b_1. Mark point P_1.
- Continue in this way to build up the roulette PP_4.
- This is the usual method, although reconstructing the curve by using **a** as centre and striking an arc from **b** to b_1 and then locating P_1 by triangulation, is possible.

④ Catenary

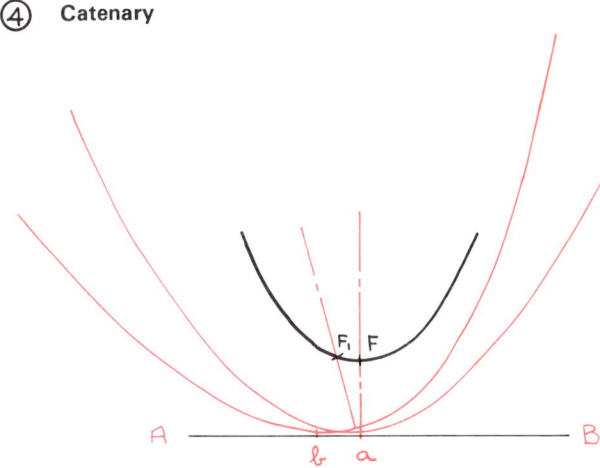

A catenary is the curve made by a chain allowed to hang under its own weight.

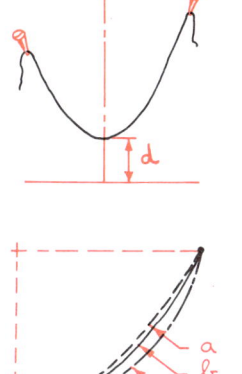

A good catenary can be drawn by hanging a jewellery chain as shown and marking points through it with a pin. Join the points.

A catenary is not quite a parabola.
a. Parabola
b. Catenary
c. Circular arc

- If a parabola is rolled along a line **AB** the path of the focus will be a catenary.
- This is best drawn by tracing a parabola and rolling the tracing along the line while plotting the position of the focus.
- The catenary curve is used in engineering and in aeronautics.

Technical Draughtsmanship
Glissette and Catenary

	Loci 8	Part I
		Geom. H

181

The Problem

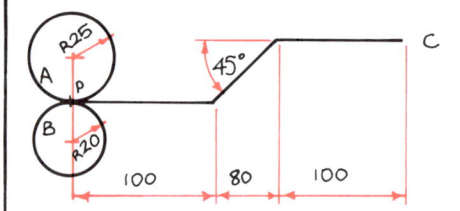

Roll **A** and **B** along the line to **C**. Plot the path of **P** in each case.

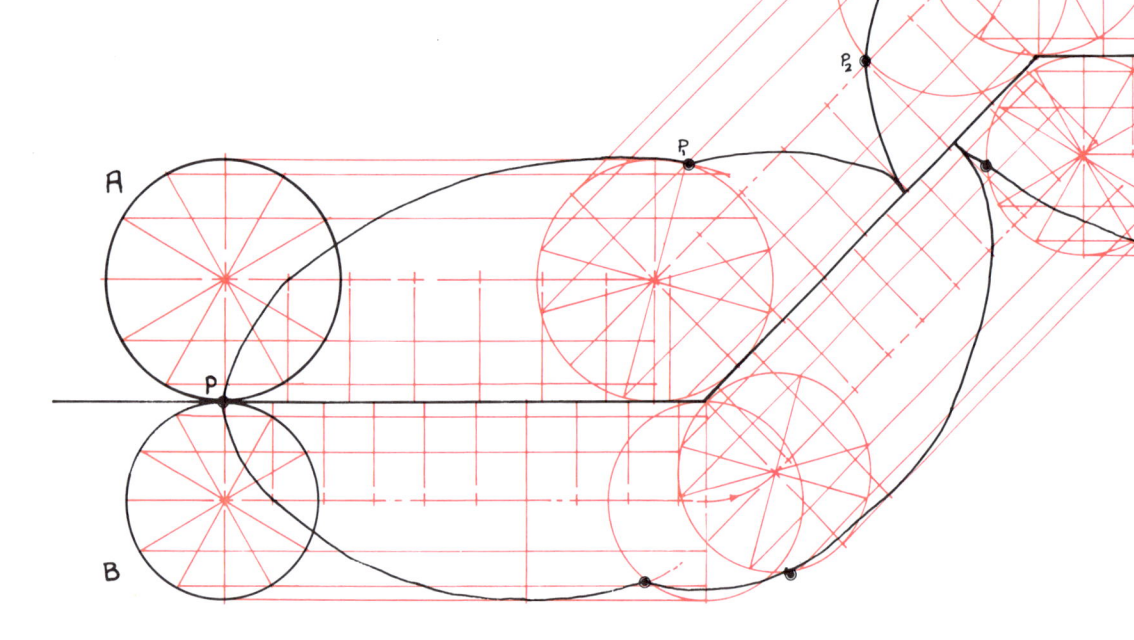

Procedure
- Set up the line and draw **A** in each of its critical positions at **C**, **C₁**, **C₂**, **C₃** and **C₄**.
- Think each step through as a separate run.
- Draw from **C** to **C₁**, then forget about that and imagine a new start from **C₁** to **C₂** with the point at **P**.
- Notice how bridging occurs beneath the circle at **C₁**. Also note how the circle *swings* from **C₂** to **C₃**.
- The cycloid underneath is similar.
- If a point arrives away from a usual division on the circle, then roll it a little to redraw the circle lined up.

Technical Draughtsmanship
Sample Problem 1
Loci 9 — Part 1 / Geom.

The Problem

Plot **P** as the circle rolls from **A** to **B**.

Procedure
- Set up the problem as given.
- Now draw a 'ghost' circle at every point where it changes direction, at **C₁**, **C₂**, **C₃**, and a 'stop' circle at **C₄**.
- *Take only one stage at a time, and try to forget about the others.*
- From **P** to **P₁** is a straightforward cycloid.
- **P₂** starts towards **P₃** as usual. The subtlety occurs when **C₃** turns out to be out of step with the **30°** 'spokes'.
- The extra is **PK**. Use this to take a short 'step' to **K₁**. Find the centre for this and point **P₄**. If it helps, draw a 'ghost' circle here.
- You are now back in step with the **30°** spokes. Continue to **B**.

Technical Draughtsmanship	
Sample Problem 2	
Loci 10	Part 1
	Geom. H

183

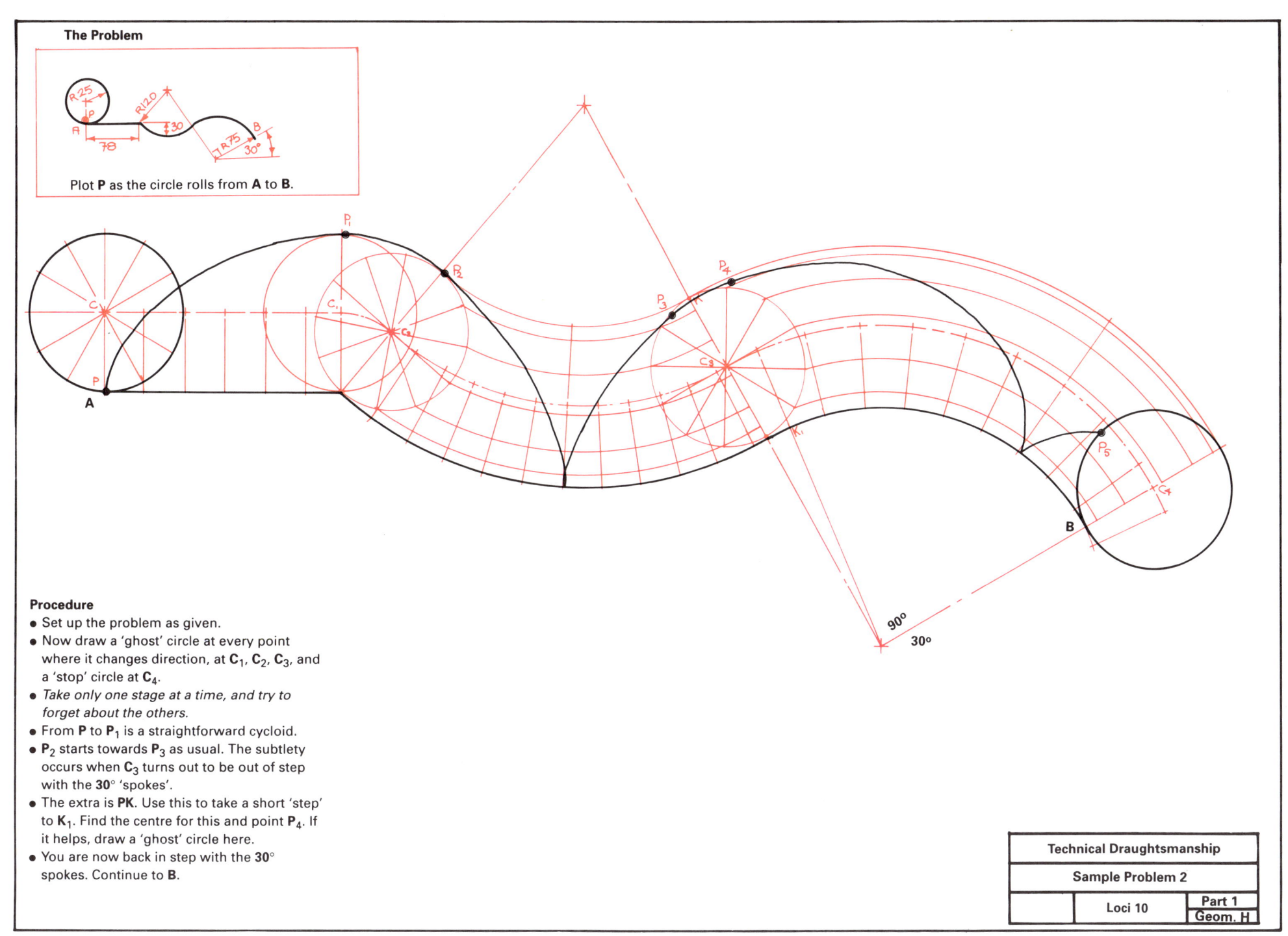

All measurements are in millimetres.

Questions

1. Draw the involute to each of the given solids.

2. For each pair of radian vectors given draw a logarithmic spiral for one revolution.

3. Draw the conical spirals indicated on the diagrams.

4. Draw the helical spirals from the information given.

5. Draw the path of point **P** in each glissette.

6. This snail's shell is an Archimedean spiral of two revolutions. Draw it.

7. The Nautilus' shell is a logarithmic spiral of three revolutions. Draw the shell.

④ (a) **Left hand** helix of diameter **58 mm.**, and lead of **28 mm.**

(b) **Right hand** helix of diameter **62 mm.**, lead of **48 mm.**, and section as shown.

(c) **Left hand** helix of diameter **80 mm.**, lead of **45 mm.**, and section as shown.

(d) **Left hand** helix of diameter **75 mm.**, lead of **80 mm.**, and section as shown.

③ Left hand / Right hand

Two revolutions, right hand / Oblique left hand from **A**

⑥ Snail

⑦ Nautilus

Technical Draughtsmanship

Exercises 1

Loci 11 — Part I — Geom.

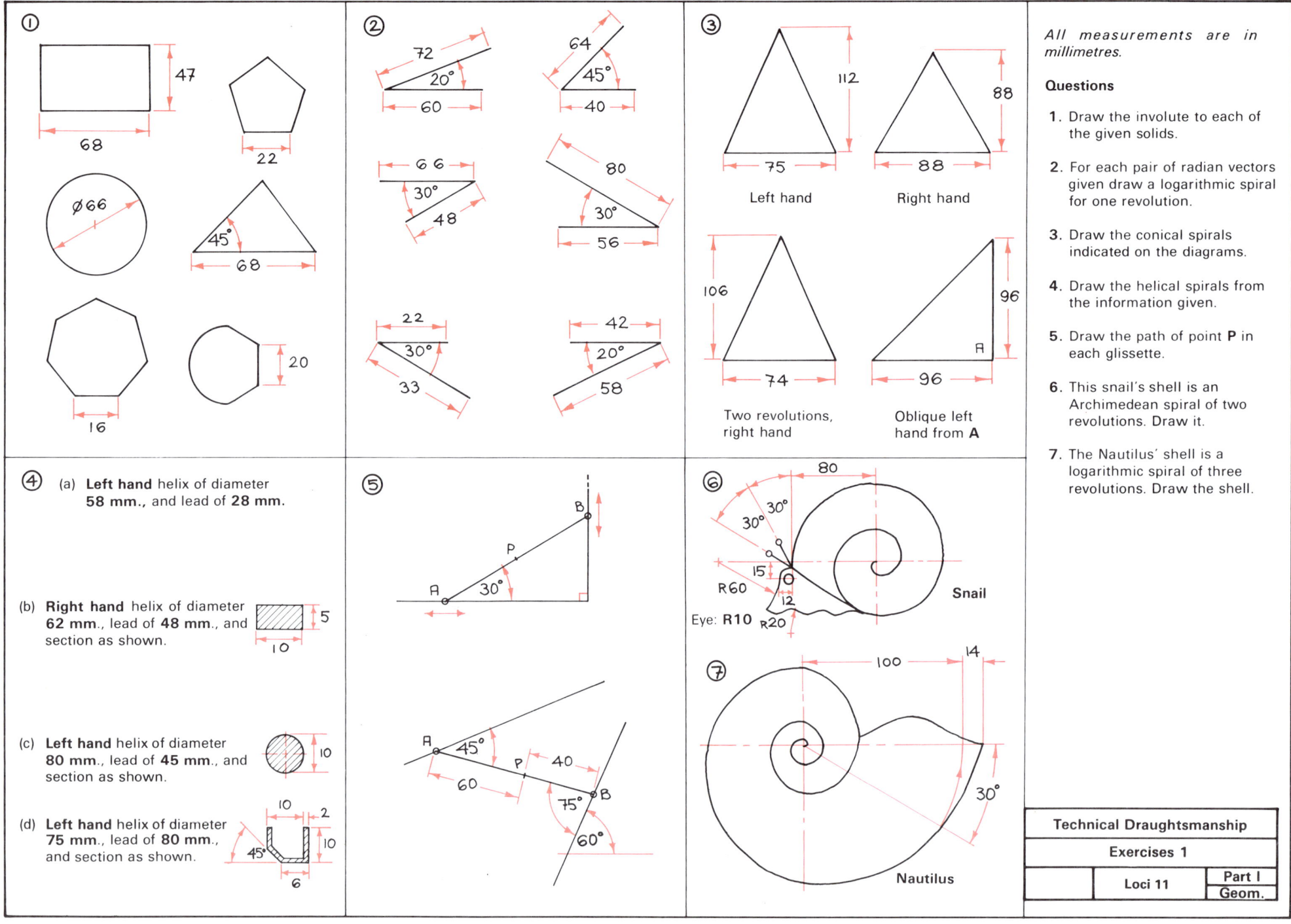

All measurements are in millimetres.

Questions

1. Draw in plan the spiral path of the end of the rope. The thickness of the lamp post need *not* be taken into account.

2. Draw a volute of the height shown.

3. Draw two ionic volutes of cathetus **81mm.**, one using Goldman's, and the other Palladio's method.

4. Draw the path of **P** to **P₂**, as each circle rolls along line **AB**.

5. Draw the path of **P**, on each circle, as they roll along arc **AB**.

6. In each case draw the path of point **P** as the circle rolls along the line **AB**.

7. Circle **M** rolls along **AB** until **P** reaches **P₂**. Circle **N** rolls along **CD** until **Q** also reaches **P₂**. Draw these curves.

8. In each case draw the path of **P** and of **Q** as each circle rolls along an arc **AB**.

Technical Draughtsmanship		
Exercises 2		
Loci 12		Part I Geom.

185

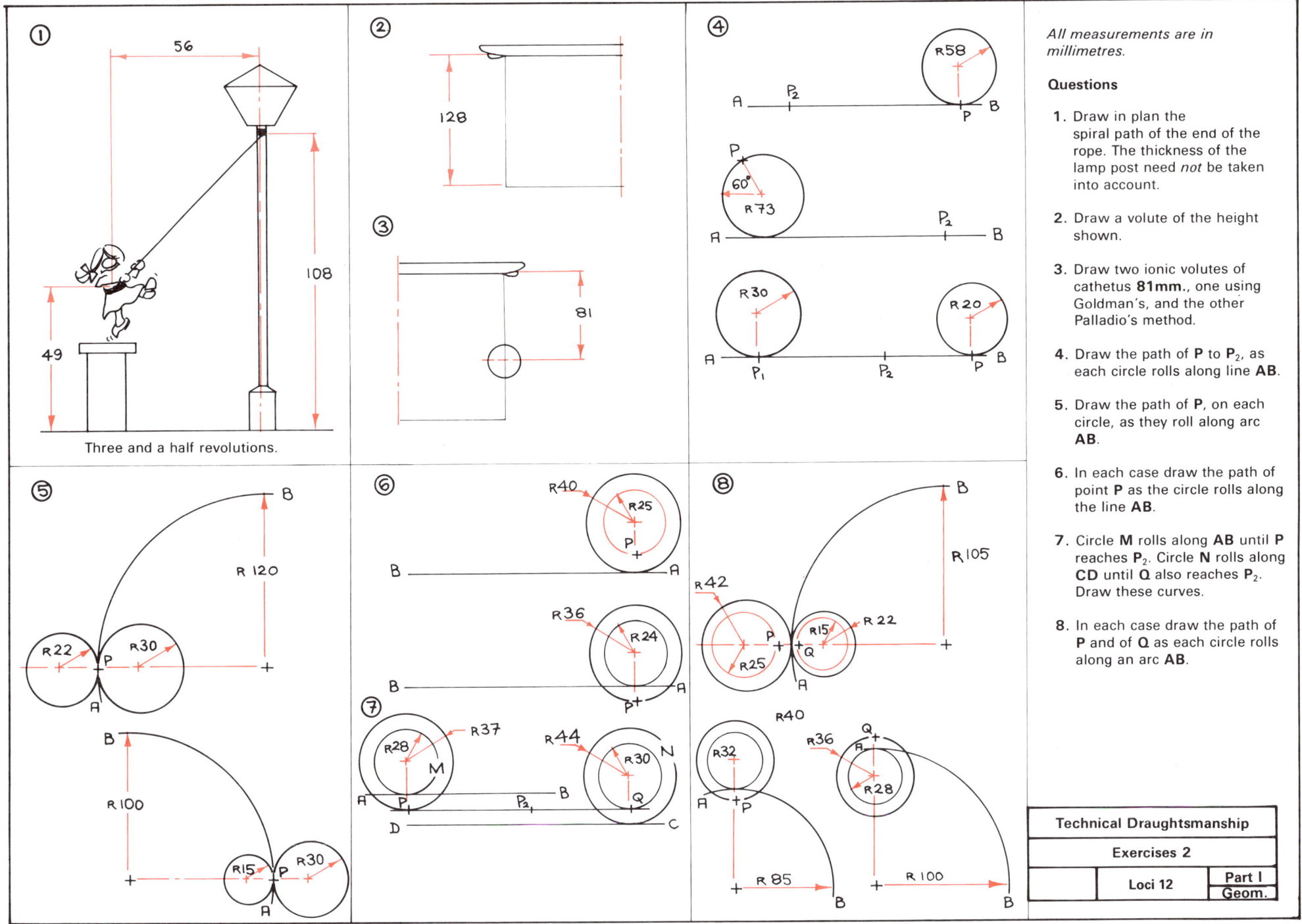

All measurements are in millimetres

Questions

1. When the rocker releases the valve its top rises to position **B**. Draw a half-sectioned elevation of the valve in position **B**.

2. Complete the plan and elevation of the staircase.

3. Draw the completed elevation and plan of the car park exit.

4. Circle **D** rolls along **AB** until **P** is again on the line. Draw the path of **P**.

5. Circle **D** rolls along **AB** until its centre is above **B**. Draw the path of **P** during this movement.

6. Circle **D** rolls along **AB** until **P** is again on the line. Draw the path of **P**.

7. As circle **D** rolls along the line, **AB** rotates about **F** at the same rate. Plot the path of **P** for one revolution of circle **D**.

8. Plot the path of **P** as circle **A** rolls right around circle **B**.

9. Plot the path of **P** as circle **A** makes one circuit of the inside of circle **B**.

Technical Draughtsmanship

Exercises 3

Loci 13 — Part I, Geom. H.

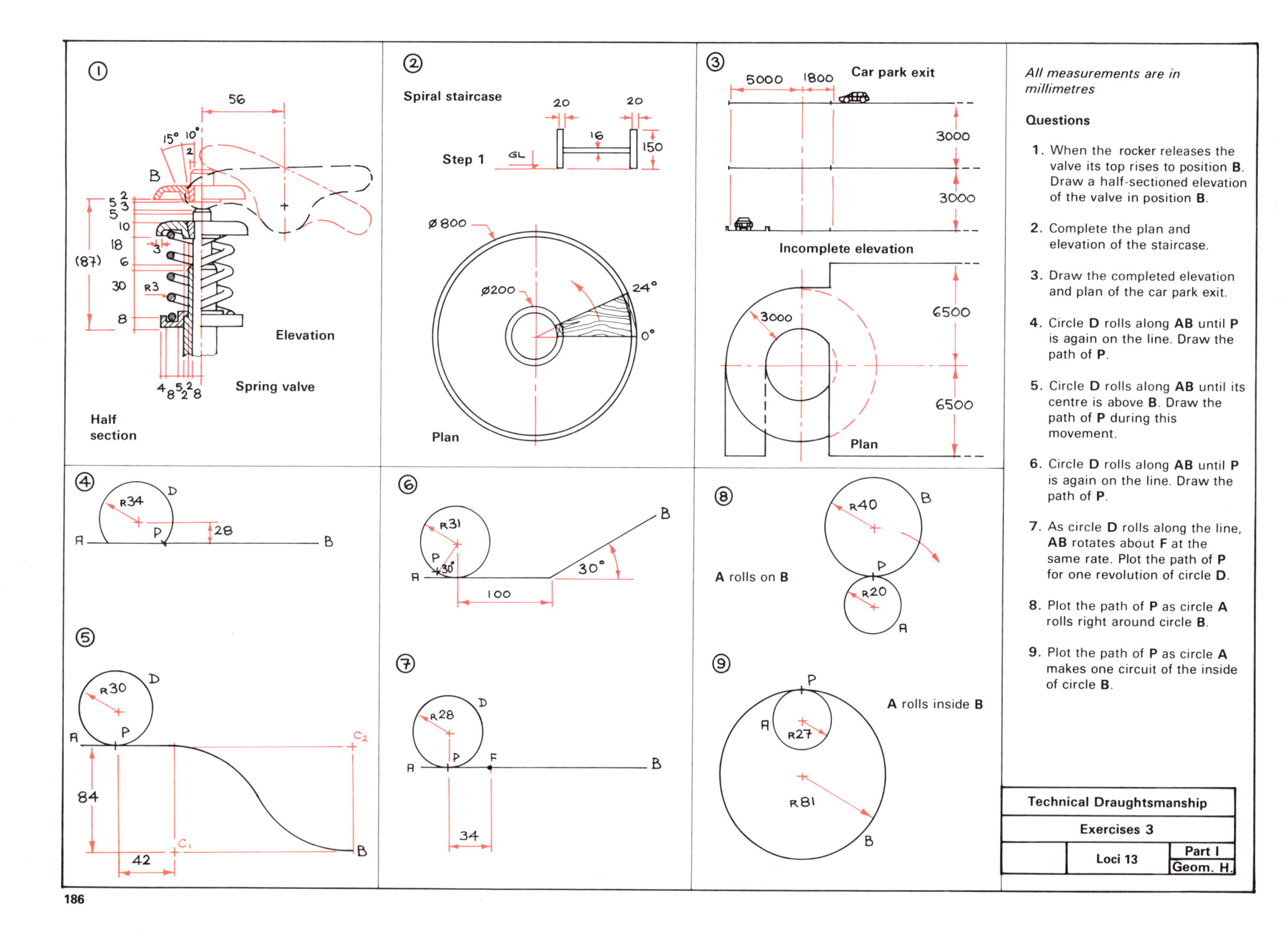

PART 1

CHAPTER 15
CONICS

If a cone is cut the section can be a variety of shapes. These shapes, when studied, have proven not only to be fascinating in themselves but also to have many practical applications.

CONTENTS

Conic sections	*Page*	**188**
True shapes of sections		**189**
Eccentricity		**190**
Sections as Loci		**191**
The Ellipse 1		**192**
The Ellipse 2		**193**
The Parabola 1		**194**
The Parabola 2		**195**
Hyperbolas 1		**196**
Hyperbolas 2		**197**
Exercises		**198**

Photocopying prohibited by law

①
- Conic sections are produced when a plane cuts a right circular cone.

- The surface of a cone can be produced if a sloping line is rotated about a vertical axis. This line would be called a **generator** and each position as it sweeps around is called an **element**. Half of a double cone is called a **nappe**.

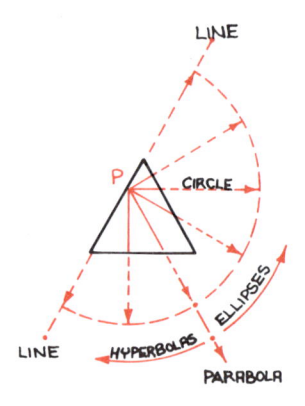

- Depending on where a cone is cut the section may be varied. The section may be either a straight line, a triangle, a circle, an ellipse, a parabola or twin hyperbolas. These are the conic sections and we will study each in turn.

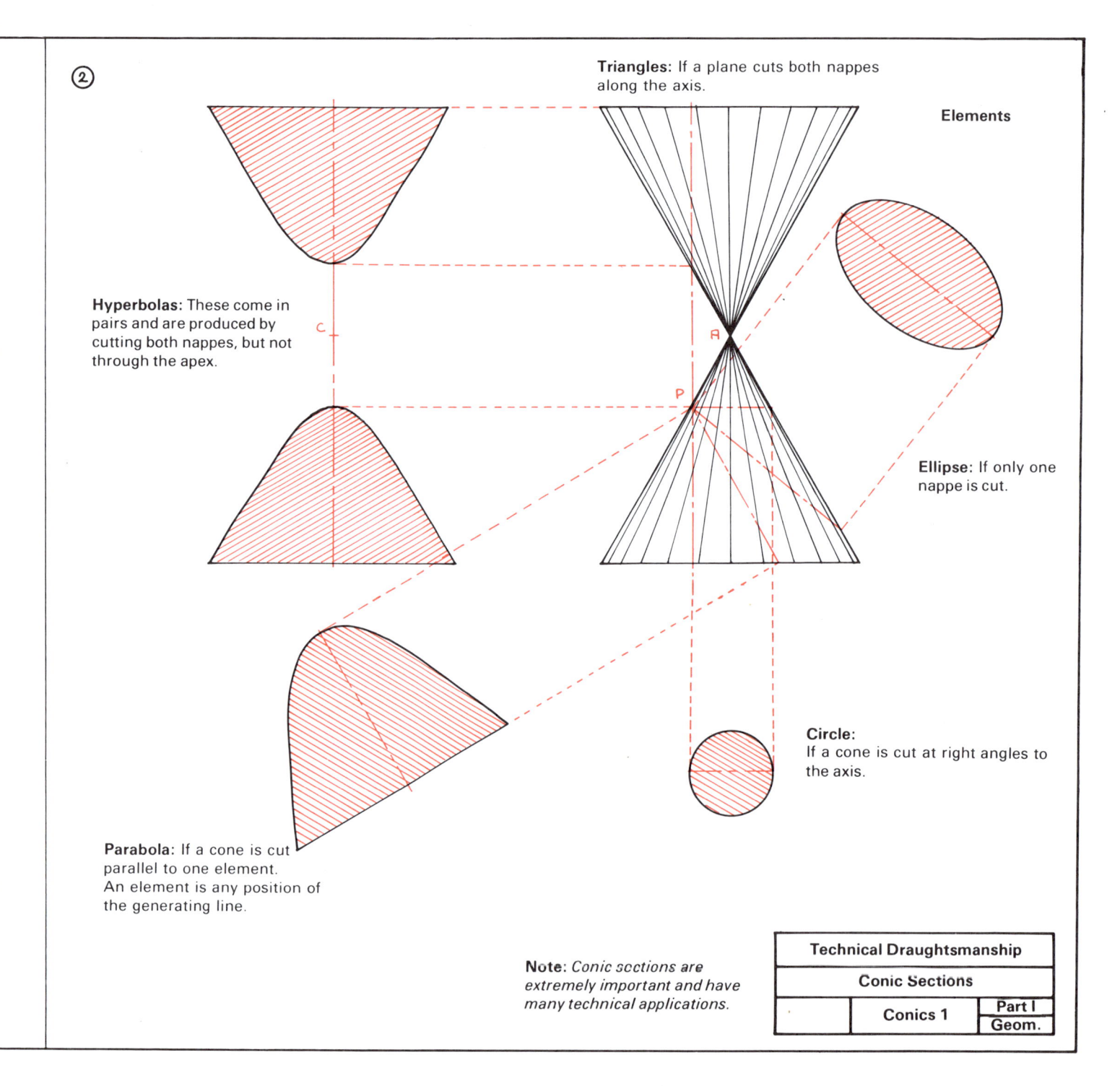

②

Triangles: If a plane cuts both nappes along the axis.

Elements

Hyperbolas: These come in pairs and are produced by cutting both nappes, but not through the apex.

Ellipse: If only one nappe is cut.

Parabola: If a cone is cut parallel to one element. An element is any position of the generating line.

Circle: If a cone is cut at right angles to the axis.

Note: *Conic sections are extremely important and have many technical applications.*

| Technical Draughtsmanship |
| Conic Sections |
| Conics 1 | Part I Geom. |

188

①

Elevation

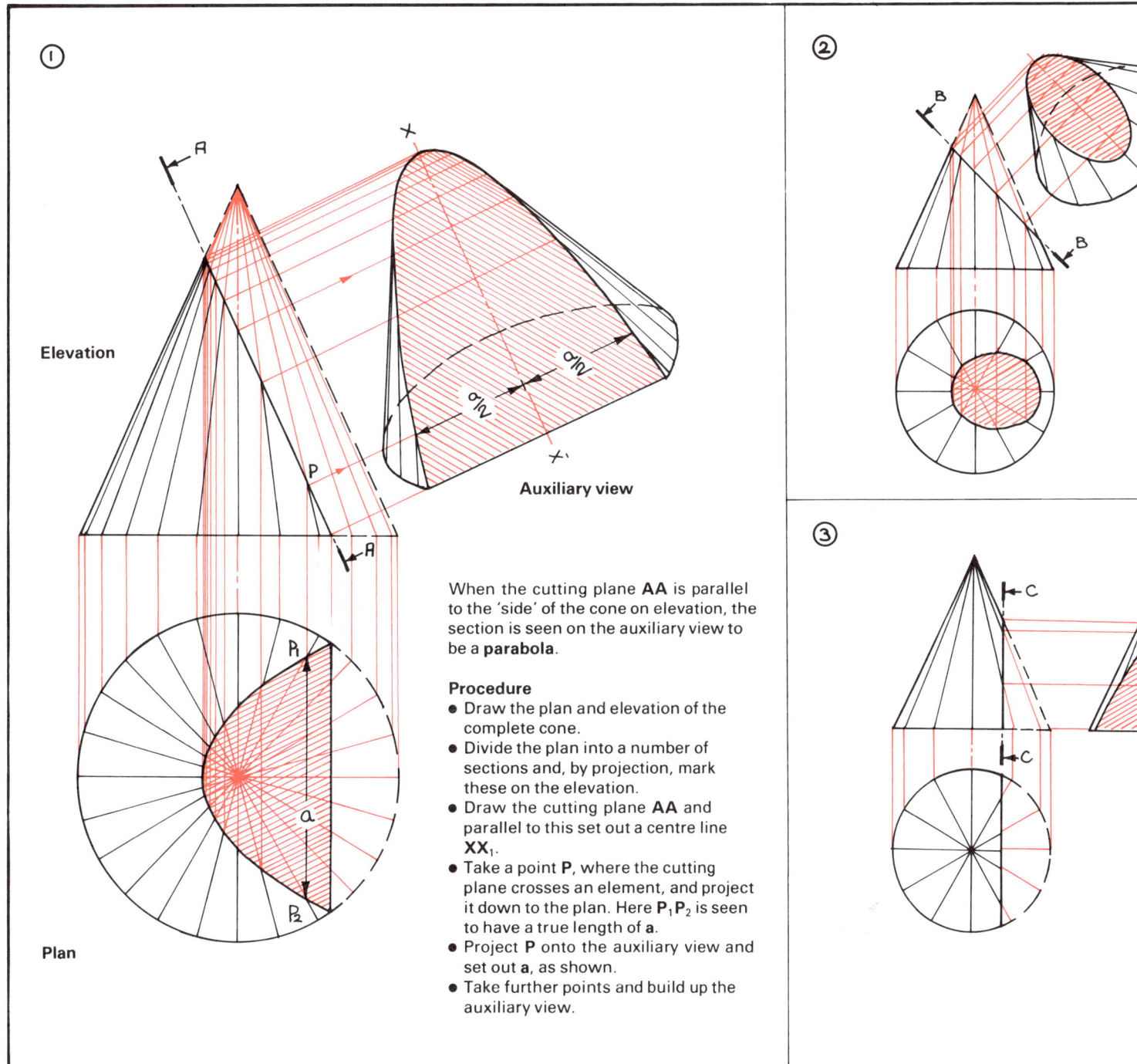

Auxiliary view

Plan

When the cutting plane **AA** is parallel to the 'side' of the cone on elevation, the section is seen on the auxiliary view to be a **parabola**.

Procedure
- Draw the plan and elevation of the complete cone.
- Divide the plan into a number of sections and, by projection, mark these on the elevation.
- Draw the cutting plane **AA** and parallel to this set out a centre line **XX**$_1$.
- Take a point **P**, where the cutting plane crosses an element, and project it down to the plan. Here **P**$_1$**P**$_2$ is seen to have a true length of **a**.
- Project **P** onto the auxiliary view and set out **a**, as shown.
- Take further points and build up the auxiliary view.

②

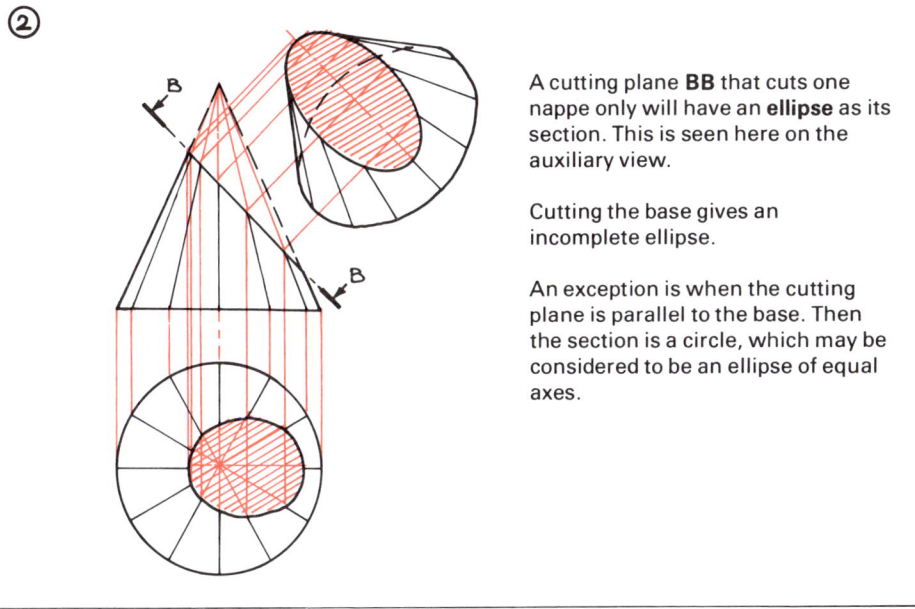

A cutting plane **BB** that cuts one nappe only will have an **ellipse** as its section. This is seen here on the auxiliary view.

Cutting the base gives an incomplete ellipse.

An exception is when the cutting plane is parallel to the base. Then the section is a circle, which may be considered to be an ellipse of equal axes.

③

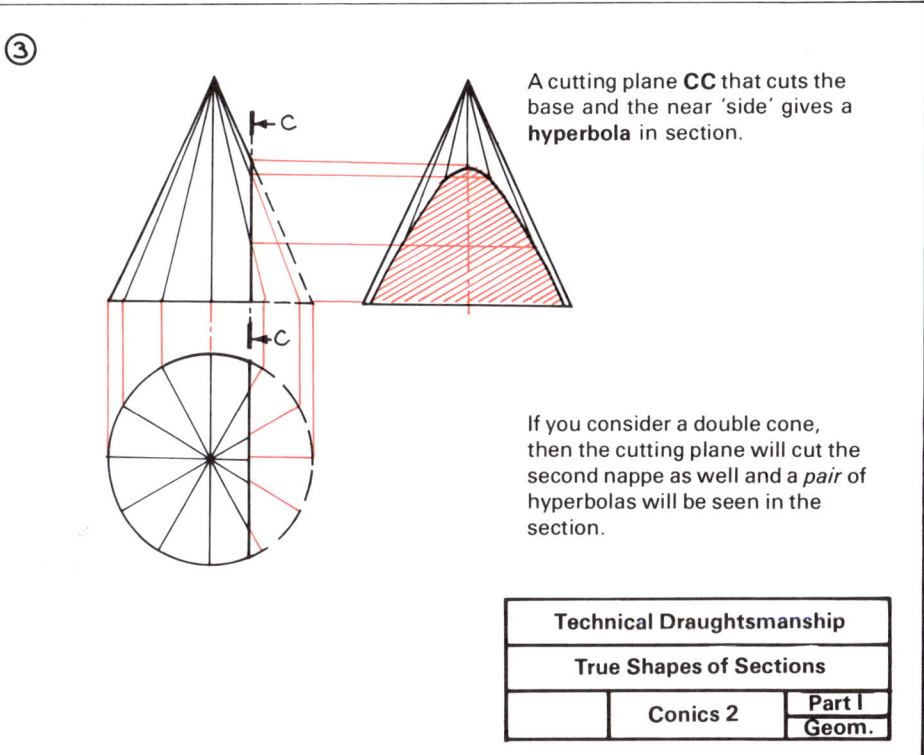

A cutting plane **CC** that cuts the base and the near 'side' gives a **hyperbola** in section.

If you consider a double cone, then the cutting plane will cut the second nappe as well and a *pair* of hyperbolas will be seen in the section.

Technical Draughtsmanship		
True Shapes of Sections		
	Conics 2	Part I
		Geom.

① Eccentricity

The interesting thing about conic curves is that they obey strict laws.

Each may be defined as the path of a point travelling so that its distance from a fixed point (the **focus**) is in an exact and constant ratio to its distance from a fixed line (called the **directrix**).

$$\text{Eccentricity} = \frac{\text{Distance of P from Focus}}{\text{Distance of P from Directrix}}$$

or,

$$\text{Ecc.} = \frac{pF}{pD}$$

- Eccentricity is a ratio.
- If eccentricity is less than one the curve is an ellipse.
- If eccentricity is equal to one it is a parabola.
- If eccentricity is greater than one it is a hyperbola.

or,

Ecc. < 1 ⇒ **Ellipse**
Ecc. = 1 ⇒ **Parabola**
Ecc. > 1 ⇒ **Hyperbola**

Note: *Papphus of Alexandria gave the curves their names about 300 A.D. Ellipse means 'falls short'; Parabola means 'equal by comparison'; and Hyperbola means 'extra by comparison'.*

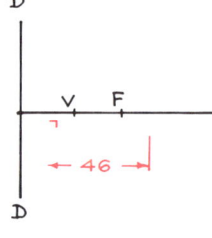

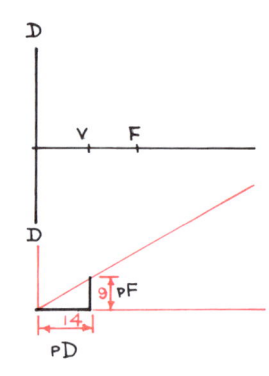

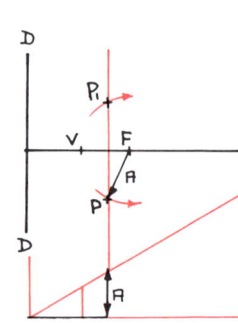

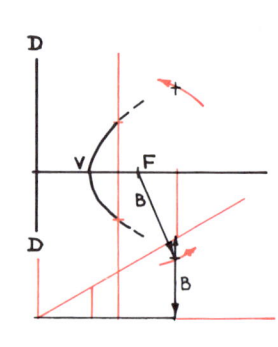

②

To draw any conic curve given its eccentricity
e.g. an eccentricity of $\frac{9}{14}$ and a focus **46 mm.** from its directrix.

Step 1
- Draw an axis and, at right angles, draw the directrix **DD**.
- Mark the focus **F**, as shown.
- The vertex **V** is the limit of the curve and will obey the ratio of eccentricity.

$$\text{Ecc.} = \frac{pF}{pD} = \frac{9}{14}$$

Step 2
- Extend the directrix down well out of the way of the axis.
- Set the distance from the directrix **pD** straight out from the directrix.
- With this as base, construct a triangle using the ratio of eccentricity.

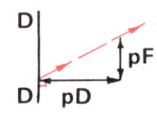

- Extend as far as you wish.

Step 3
- Draw any vertical line, an **ordinate,** and measure its distance **A** within the extended triangle with your compass.
- Transfer **A** as a radius from the focus and strike an arc cutting the vertical line at **P** and **P₁**. These are two points on the curve.

Step 4
- Draw further ordinates and, with the focus as centre, plot more points.

Step 5
- Join the points to draw the curve.

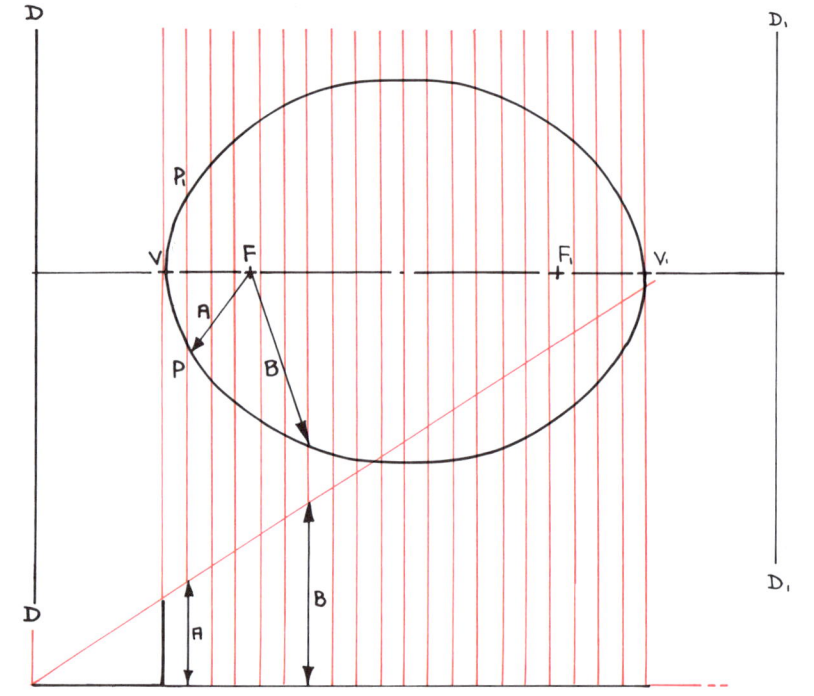

The finished curve: an ellipse

Notes:
- *Spacing the ordinates evenly greatly improves the neatness of the drawing.*
- *The eccentricity may be given in decimal form. If so, convert this to a fraction.*
- *An eccentricity of zero is a straight line and an eccentricity of infinity is a point.*

Technical Draughtsmanship		
Eccentricity		
	Conics 3	Part I
		Geom.

① **Problem:** Given a cutting plane **AA** through a cone to find its axis, vertex, focus, directrix, and eccentricity.

Procedure
- The **axis** is drawn parallel to **AA**, at any convenient distance.
- The **vertex** is found on the axis by projecting across the upper limit of the section.
- To find the **focus** it is necessary to draw a circle tangent to both 'sides' of the cone *and* to the cutting plane. This circle represents the **focal sphere**. Project its centre **C** across to the axis to fix the focus **F**. This line will pass through the point of tangency **T** with the cutting plane.
- To find the **directrix** join the other two points of tangency **T₁** and **T₂** and extend the line to meet the cutting plane at **P**. The projection across of **P** is the directrix **DD**.
- You now have the focus, the directrix and a point **V** on the curve. Calculate the eccentricity as $\frac{vF}{vD}$ and draw the curve, as on page 190.

② In the case of an **ellipse** it will be noticed that *two* focal spheres are possible. In this way both foci **F** and **F₁** can be located.

Note: *a focal sphere is a sphere dropped into a cone that is also tangential to the cutting plane in question.*

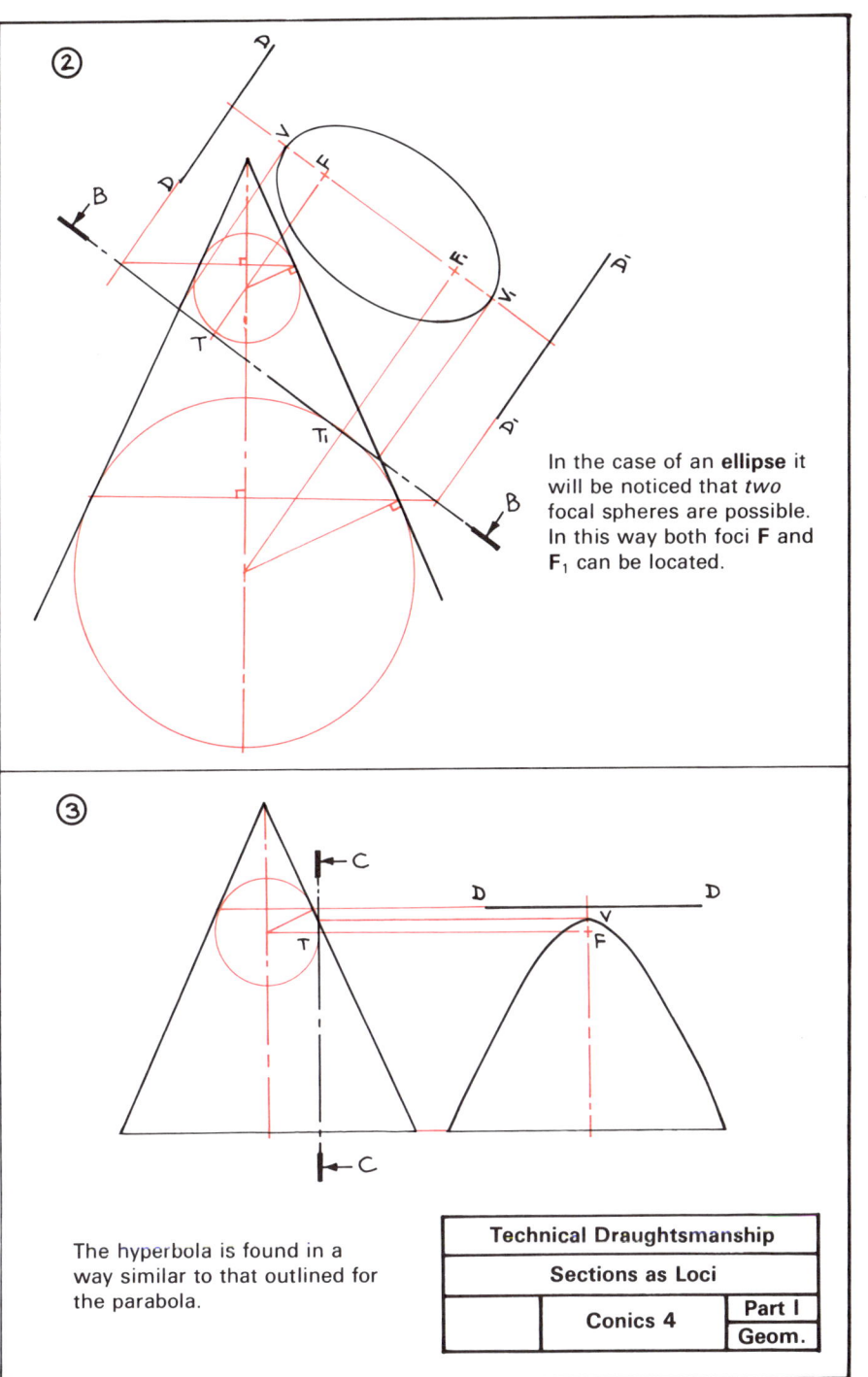

③ The hyperbola is found in a way similar to that outlined for the parabola.

Technical Draughtsmanship		
Sections as Loci		
Conics 4	Part I	
	Geom.	

191

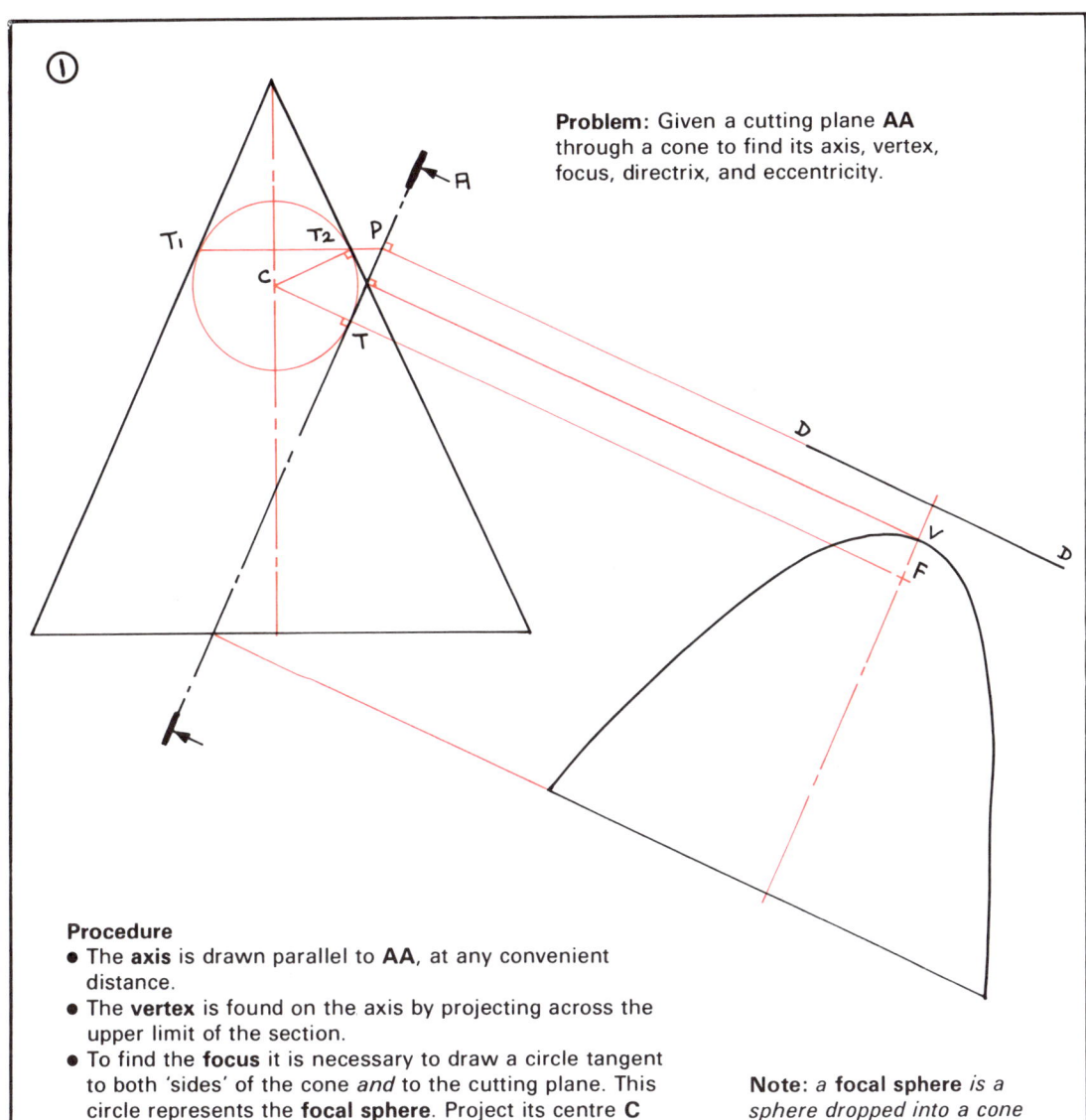

① To draw an ellipse given its eccentricity and focus
e.g. Ecc. = **0.75** and Focus **49 mm** from the Directrix.

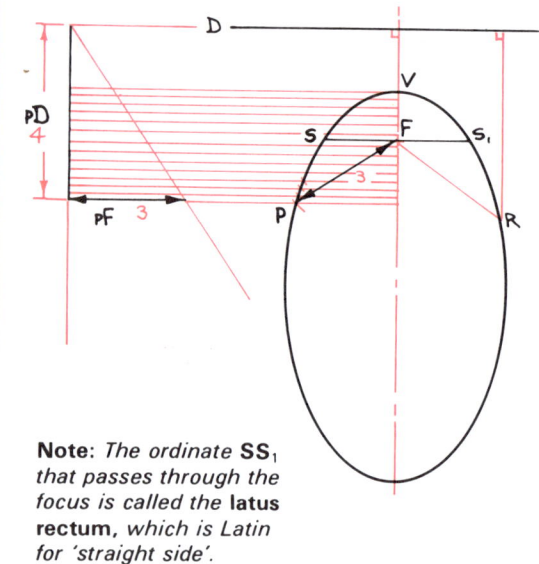

- Draw an axis and a directrix **DD**.
- Go **49 mm**. along the axis from the directrix to locate the focus **F**.
- Convert the eccentricity to a fraction:

$$\text{Ecc.} = \frac{pF}{pD} = 0.75 = \frac{75}{100} = \frac{3}{4}$$

- Use this to locate the vertix **V**.
- Extend the directrix **DD** to one side.
- Set up a proportional triangle and proceed to plot the points of the curve, as on page **190**.

Note: The ordinate **SS₁** that passes through the focus is called the **latus rectum**, which is Latin for 'straight side'.

② To draw an ellipse in a given rectangle

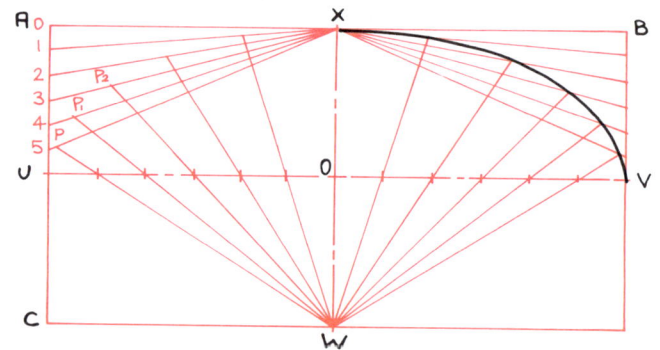

- Draw the rectangle and bisect its sides to get the major axis **UV** and the minor axis **WX**.
- Divide half of one of the short sides **AU** into a number of equal parts and join these to **X**.
- Divide half the major axis **OU** into the same number of parts.
- From **W** draw lines through these divisions.
- Plot the points **P**, **P₁**, etc., as shown.

Note: For an oblique rectangle the procedure is the same.

③ Some properties of an ellipse

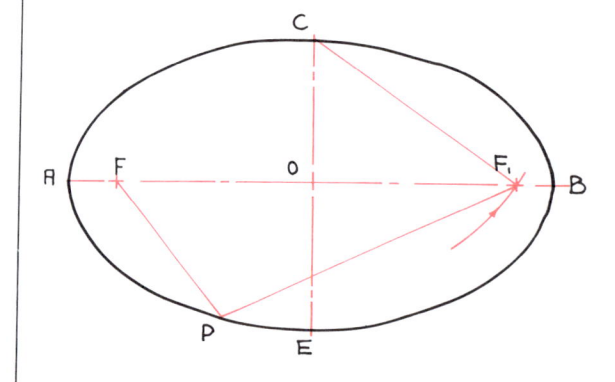

- Ecc. < 1
- $CF_1 = \frac{AB}{2} = AO$
- $AO = OB = \frac{AB}{2}$
- $CO = OE = \frac{CE}{2}$
- $FP + PF_1 = AB$
- Area = $AB \times CE \times \pi$
- The coordinate of any point (**X, Y**) is:
  $$\frac{x^2}{a^2} \times \frac{y^2}{b^2} = 1$$
- A sound, or light, transmitted from one focus when reflected will always pass through the second focus. 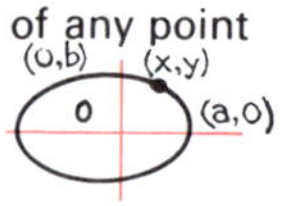
- A circle viewed from an angle appears to be an ellipse.
- An ellipse may be used to measure isometric angles, as on page 79.

④ To draw an ellipse given two conjugate diameters

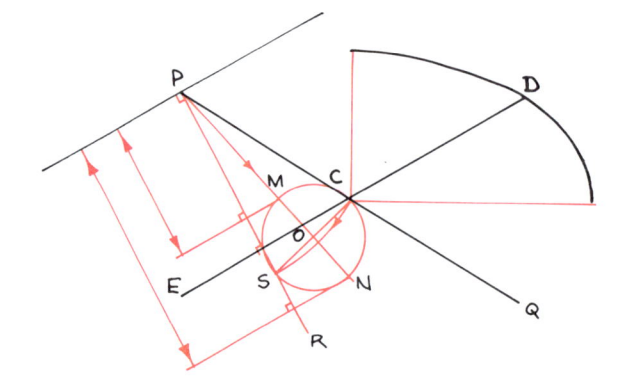

Procedure
- **PQ** and **EF** are the given conjugate diameters. **EF** is parallel to the tangent at **P**.
- From **P** draw **PR** at right angles to **EF**.
- With **P** as centre swing **C** onto **PR** at **S**.
- Join **C** to **S** and on **CS** draw a circle of centre **O**.
- Join **P** to **O** and extend, cutting the circle at **M** and **N**.
- Project **M** and **N** onto **PR** at right angles. This will give the measurement for half the minor axis **CA** and half the major axis **CB**, as shown.
- Complete the ellipse.

Note: Diameters are conjugate when each is parallel to the tangent at the end of the other. An ellipse has many pairs of conjugate diameters.

Technical Draughtsmanship
The Ellipse 1

Conics 5	Part I
	Geom.

192

①

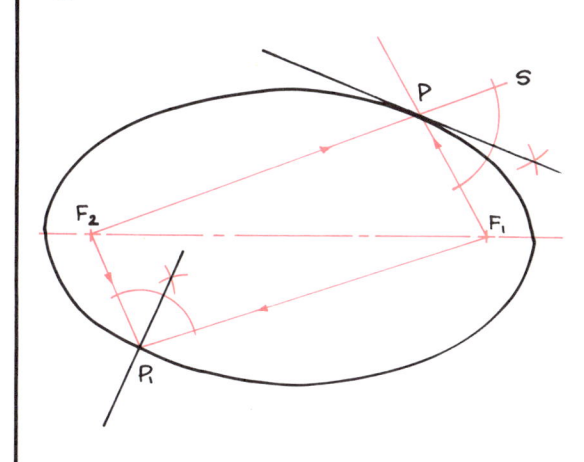

(a) To draw a tangent at point P
- Join **P** to both foci **F₁** and **F₂**.
- Extend **F₂P** to **S** and bisect angle **F₁PS**.
- This bisector is the tangent at point **P**.
- A normal at **P** can be drawn at right angles to the tangent.

(b) To draw a normal at point P₁.
- Join **P₁** to both foci **F₁** and **F₂**.
- Bisect angle **F₁P₁F**.
- This bisector is the normal at point **P₁**.

② To draw tangents from point P to the ellipse.

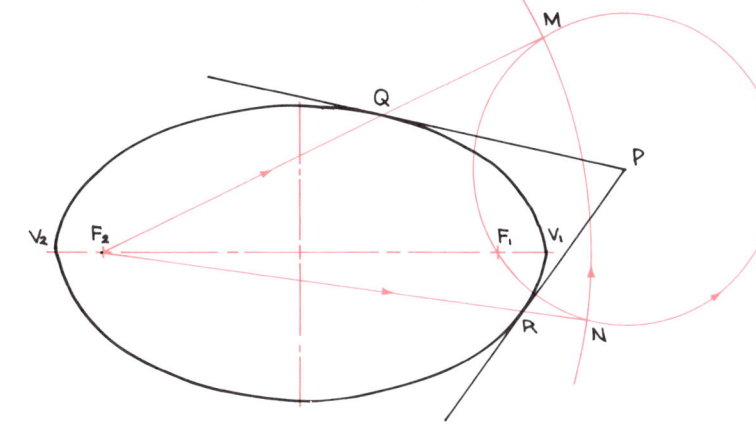

Procedure
- With **P** as centre and **PF₁** as radius draw a circle.
- With **F₂** as centre and **V₁V₂** as radius strike an arc cutting the circle at **M** and **N**.
- Join **F₂** to **M** and to **N** cutting the ellipse at **Q** and **R** respectively.
- Draw the tangents from **P** through **Q** and **R**.

③ To find the centre of curvature for the point P.
- Join **P** to **F₁** and extend.
- Construct a normal **PQ** at **P** by bisecting angle **F₁PF₂**.
- Where the normal crosses the major axis at **A** draw a line, at right angles to **PQ**, towards the focal line at **B**.
- From **B** draw a second line, at right angles to **PB**, back towards the normal, meeting it at **C**.
- Point **C** is the centre of curvature for point **P**.

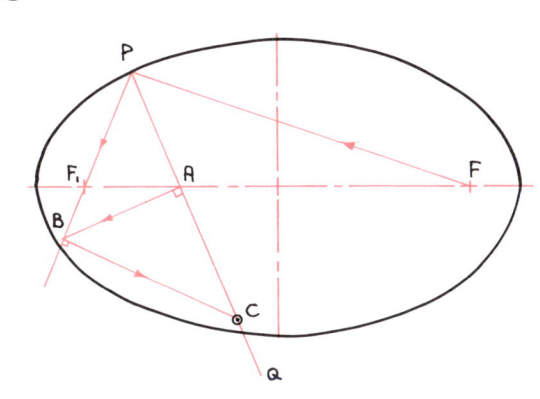

Note: *If you wanted to draw P accurately with a compass, then C would be the centre for the curve. This is useful in drawing evolutes, which are vital to astronomical calculation.*

④

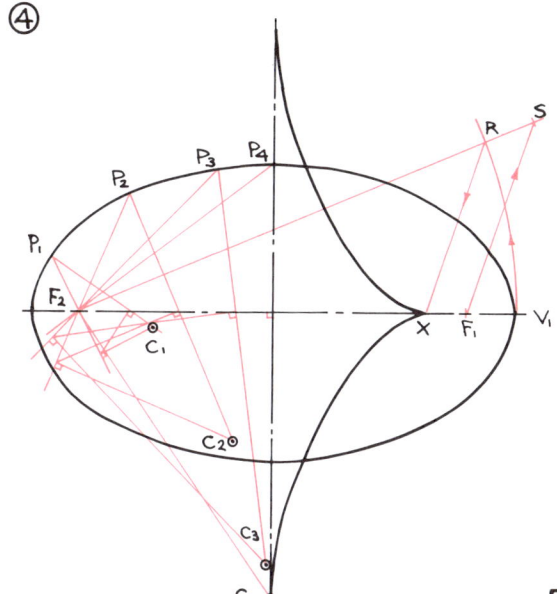

(a) To construct the evolute of an ellipse
- Choose points **P₁**, **P₂**, **P₃** and **P₄** on the ellipse.
- Find the centre of curvature for each point.
- Join the centres of curvature to draw part of the evolute.
- Repeat for the other three quarters to complete the curve.

(b) To find the centre of curvature for the vertex V₁.
- With centre **F₂** swing **V₁** up.
- From **F₂** draw any radian **F₂R** to this arc and extend it so that **RS = F₁V₁**.
- Join **F₁** to **S** and, parallel, draw a line from **R** to **X**, the centre of curvature for the vertex **V₁**.

Notes
- *An evolute is the path of all the centres of curvature.*
- *These drawings need both plenty of room and as big an ellipse as possible.*

Technical Draughtsmanship		
The Ellipse 2		
	Conics 6	Part I
		Geom. H

①

To draw a parabola given its eccentricity and focus.

- Draw an axis and directrix.
- Locate the focus **F**.
- The eccentricity of a parabola is **1**.

$$ECC = \frac{pF}{pD} = 1$$

- Extend the directrix to one side and set up a triangle based on the eccentricity, as shown. In this case it will be a triangle of **45°**.
- Extend the triangle and taking ordinate lines locate points on the curve, as on page **190**.
- Join the points to draw the parabola.

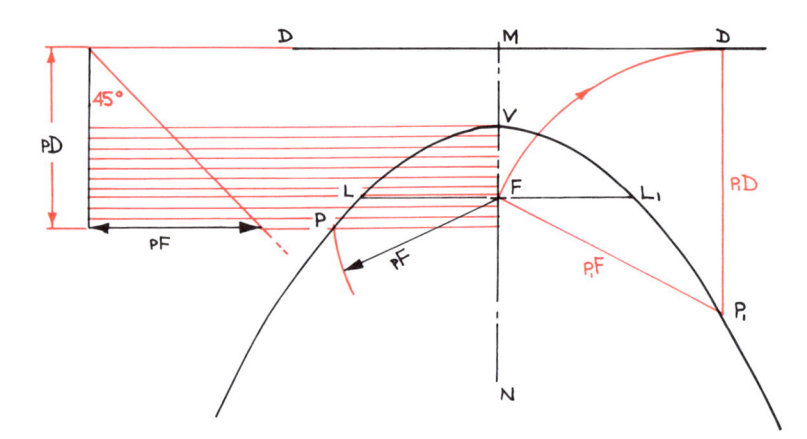

②

Same properties of the parabola

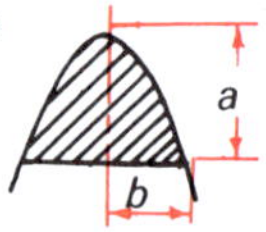

- Ecc. = **1**
- FV = VM
- LL = 4 FV
- Area = $\frac{2}{3}$ ab
- A sound, or light, transmitted from the focus **F** when reflected will always travel out parallel to the axis, e.g. car headlights.
- A sound, or light ray, aimed at any point on a parabola will be reflected through the focus **F**, e.g. radio telescopes.
- The coodinate of any point (**x**, **y**) is:
  $$y = 4\ cx$$

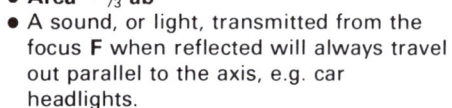

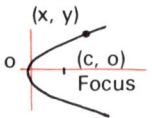

③ To construct a parabola in a rectangle

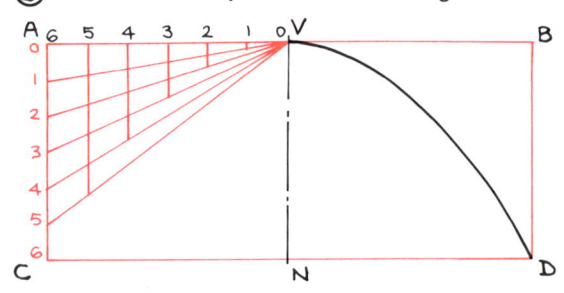

- Draw the centre line **VN**.
- Divide **AC** into a number of units and join these to point **V**.
- Divide **AV** into the same number of parts and drop perpendiculars to the corresponding radians, as shown.
- Join the points of intersection to draw the curve.
- Repeat for the other half.

Note: *An oblique rectangle is treated in a similar way.*

④

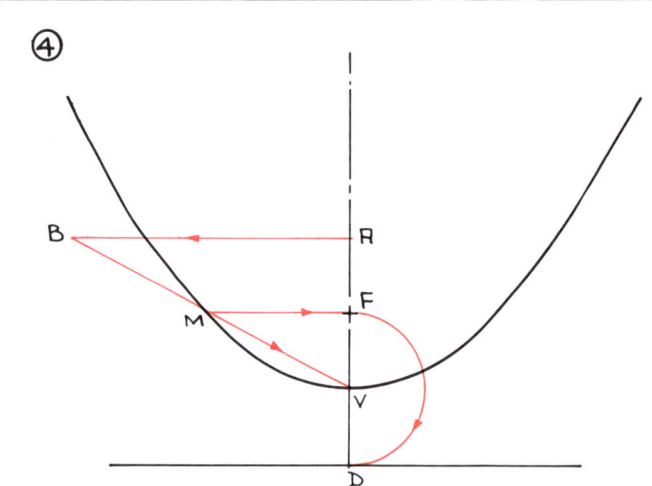

To find the focus and directrix of a given parabola

- Draw any ordinate **AB**, letting **AB = 2AV**.
- Join **B** to **V** cutting the curve at **M**.
- **M** will be a point on the latus rectum, the ordinate that passes through the focus. Draw **MF** to fix **F**.
- With **V** as centre and **VF** as radius swing an arc to find **D**, a point on the directrix. Draw the directrix.

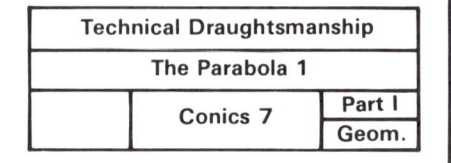

Note: *The parabola turns up in many unexpected applications, such as radar, navigation, ballistic trajectories, bending moments and in graphs of cam movements.*

Technical Draughtsmanship	
The Parabola 1	
Conics 7	Part I
	Geom.

① To construct a tangent at point P

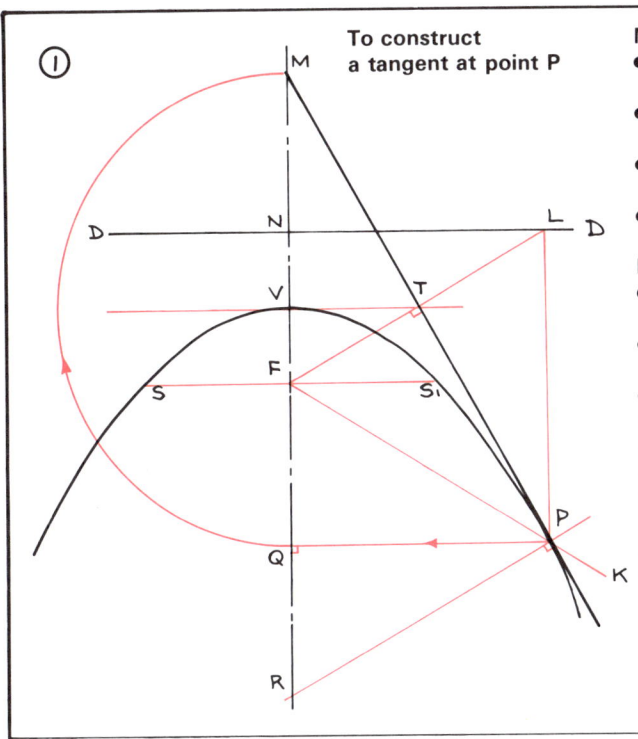

Method 1:
- From **P** draw a line **PL**, parallel to the axis.
- Join **P** to the focus **F** and bisect angle **FPL**.
- This bisector is the tangent at point **P**.
- A normal can be drawn at right angles to this.

Method 2:
- Draw a line **PQ** onto the axis at right angles.
- With centre **V** swing **Q** around to find **M**.
- **MP** is the tangent.
- **PR** is the normal.

Some properties to note:
- ∠ **FPM** = ∠ **LPM**
- **T** is in line with **V**.
- **VM** = **VQ**
- **SS₁** = 4FV
- **QR** = **FS** = 2FV = FN
- **TV** = ½ **QP**
- **PR** is the normal.
- ∠ **QPR** = ∠ **QPF** = ∠ **PFS** = ∠ **SFL**
- **FR** = **LP**.

② To draw tangents from point P to the parabola
- Join **P** to **F** and draw a circle on **PF**.
- Draw a tangent at the vertex **V**, cutting the circle at **R** and **S**. This tangent will be parallel to the directrix.
- From **P**, through **R** and **S**, draw the two tangents **PB** and **PC**.
- Join the point **A**, where the tangent crosses the directrix, to the focus **F**.
- Now, by drawing a line at right angles to **AF**, the point of tangency **B** can be located.

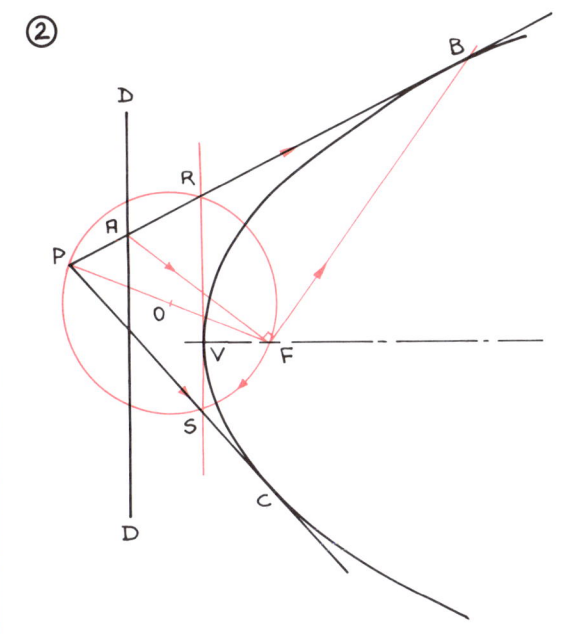

③ To find the centre of curvature for a point P on a parabola
- Draw the tangent at **P**.
- At right angles to the tangent draw the normal **PC**, crossing the axis at **B**.
- Join **P** to the focus **F** and extend.
- From **B** draw a line at right angles to meet the focal line at **E**.
- From **E** draw a second line, at right angles to the focal line, to find point **C**.
- Point **C** is the centre of curvature for point **P**.

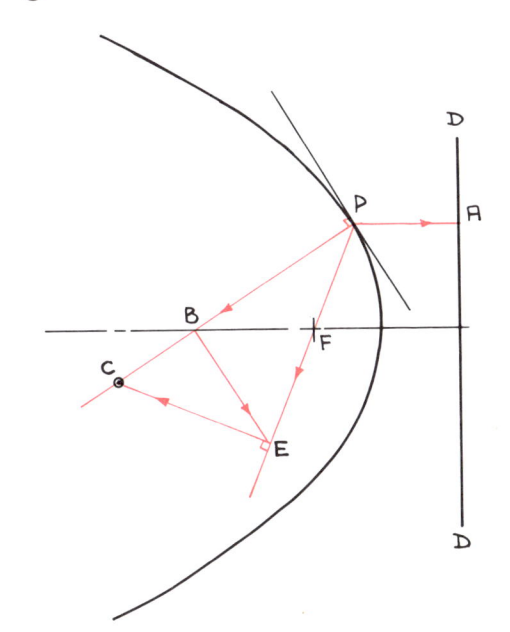

④ To construct the evolute of a parabola
- Choose points **P₁**, **P₂** and **P₃** on the parabola.
- Find the centre of curvature for each of these points.
- Join the centres of curvatures to draw part of the evolute.
- Set **RF** = **FV**. Point **R** is the centre of curvature for the vertex **V**.
- Continue the curve by finding the centres for more points.

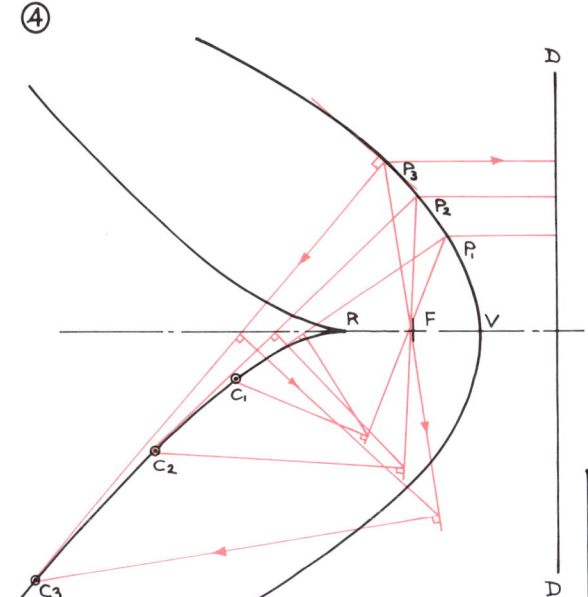

Technical Draughtsmanship		
The Parabola 2		
Conics 8	Part I	Geom. H

① To construct a hyperbola given its eccentricity and focus
e.g. **Ecc: 1.2** and Directrix to focus: **55 mm**.

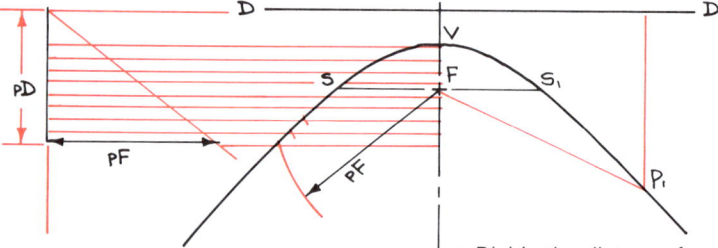

- Draw an axis and directrix.
- Locate the focus.
- Ecc. $= \dfrac{pF}{pD} = 1.2 \Rightarrow \dfrac{12}{10} \Rightarrow \dfrac{6}{5}$
- Divide the distance from focus **F** to directrix **DD** in this proportion and locate the vertex **V**.
- To one side of the directrix set out a triangle based on the eccentricity, as shown.
- Choosing ordinates, proceed to plot the curve, as on page **190**.

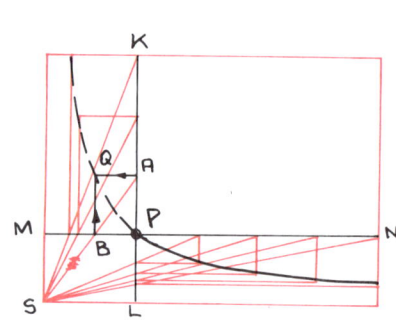

② To draw a hyperbola in a rectangle, given a point P on the curve
- Draw the rectangle and fix point **P**.
- Through **P**, and parallel to the sides, draw **KL** and **MN**.
- From corner **S** draw any radian **SA**, cutting **MN** at **B**.
- From **A** draw a line parallel to **MN** towards **Q**.
- From **B** draw a line parallel to **KL** to fix **Q**, a point on the curve.
- Continue to plot the hyperbola.

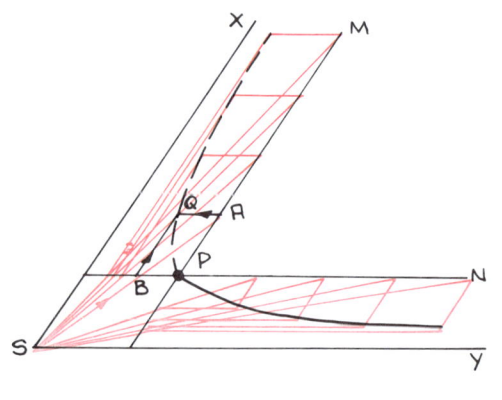

③ To construct a hyperbola given its asymptotes
- The procedure is similar to that outlined above.

Notes:
- *An asymptote is a tangent at infinity, or a line approaching but never quite touching the curve.*
- *In both of these constructions the curve does not fill the rectangle. If that is needed, extend the curve and move the rectangle to fit.*
- *In both constructions point P has been made into the vertex of the curve.*

④ (a) To construct a pair of hyperbolas given their foci and vertices.

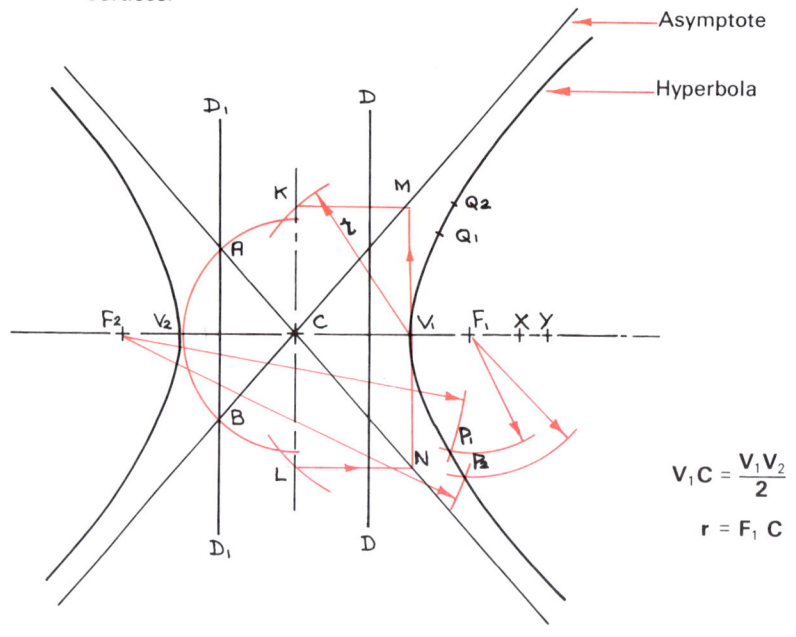

$V_1C = \dfrac{V_1V_2}{2}$

$r = F_1C$

Procedure
- Draw an axis and locate the foci F_1 and F_2, and the vertices V_1 and V_2.
- Beyond F_1 choose a point **X**.
- With centre F_2 and radius V_2X strike an arc.
- With centre F_1 and radius V_1X cut the previous arc at P_1 and Q_1. These are two points on the first hyperbola.
- Choose further points **Y, Z**, etc. and continue the curve.
- Reverse the direction of the process to draw the second hyperbola.

(b) To draw the asymptotes
- With **C** as centre and radius CV_2 draw a circle, cutting the directrix at **A** and **B**. Join **C** to **A** and to **B**, *or*
- With V_1 as centre and radius F_1C cut the centre line at **K** and **L**. Box to find **M** and **N**, as shown.

Note: Sound waves quickly take on hyperbolic shape when transmitted, making hyperbolas vital in techniques of communication and of navigation.

Technical Draughtsmanship		
Hyperbolas 1		
Conics 9	Part I	
	Geom.	

① **To draw a tangent at point P**
- Join **P** to the two foci **F₁** and **F₂**.
- Bisect angle **F₁PF₂**.
- This bisector is the tangent at point **P**.
- A normal at **P** can be drawn at right angles to the tangent.

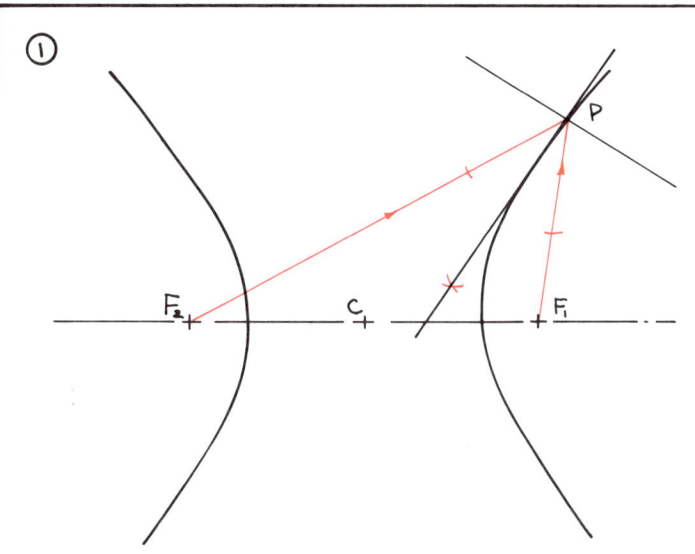

② **To draw tangents from P to a pair of hyperbolas.**
- With centre **P** and radius **PF₂** draw a circle.
- With centre **F₁** and radius **V₁V₂** draw an arc to cut the circle at **A** and **B**.
- Join **A** to **F₁** and extend to find **M**. Draw the tangent **PM**.
- Join **F₁** to **B** and extend to find **N**. Draw the second tangent **PN**.
- Normals can be drawn at right angles to the tangents.

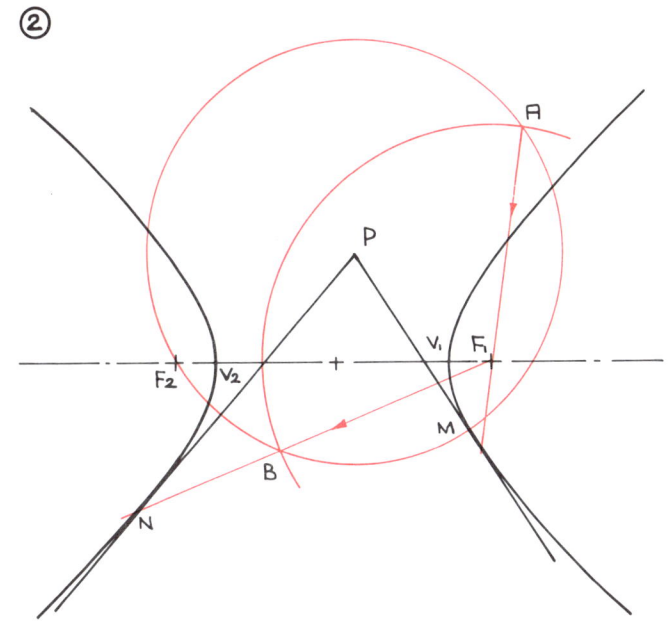

Note: *In this construction point P needs to be chosen carefully, or the drawing will go off the page.*

③ **To find the centre of curvature for point P.**
- Draw a tangent at **P**.
- Draw the normal **PC**, cutting the axis at **A**.
- Join **P** to **F₁** and extend.
- From **A** draw a line at right angles to meet the focal line at **B**.
- From **B** draw a second line, at right angles, back to meet the focal line at **C**.
- Point **C** is the centre of curvature for **P**.

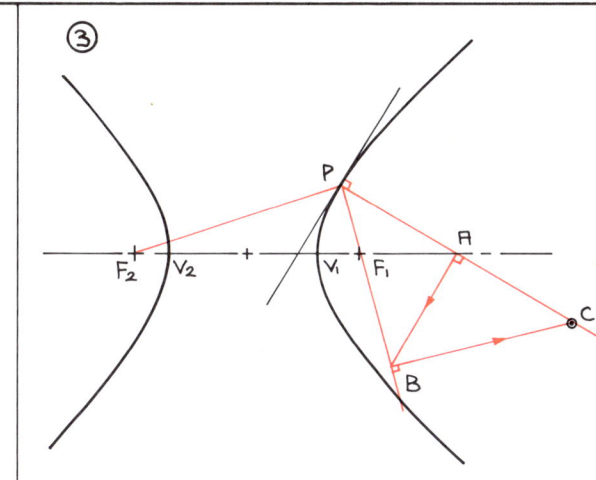

④ (a) **To construct the evolute of a hyperbola**
- Locate the centres of curvature for a series of points on the curve.
- Joining these centres of curvature forms the evolute.

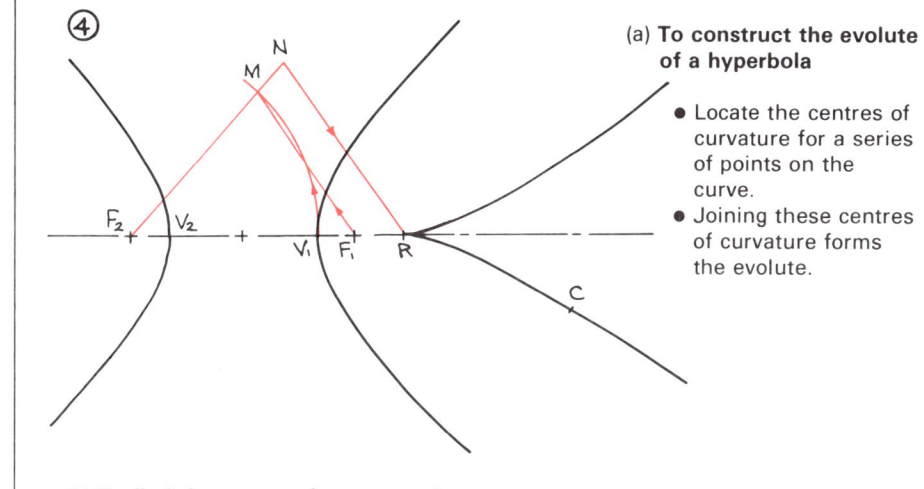

(b) **To find the centre of curvature for the vertex**
- With centre **F₂** swing **V₁** up.
- Draw a radian **F₂M**, at any angle, and extend so that **MN = F₁V₁**.
- Join **F₁** to **M** and, parallel, draw a line from **N** to find **R**.
- Point **R** is the centre of curvature for **V₁**.

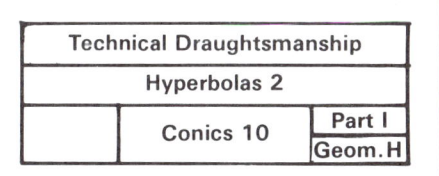

Technical Draughtsmanship		
Hyperbolas 2		
Conics 10	Part I
	Geom. H

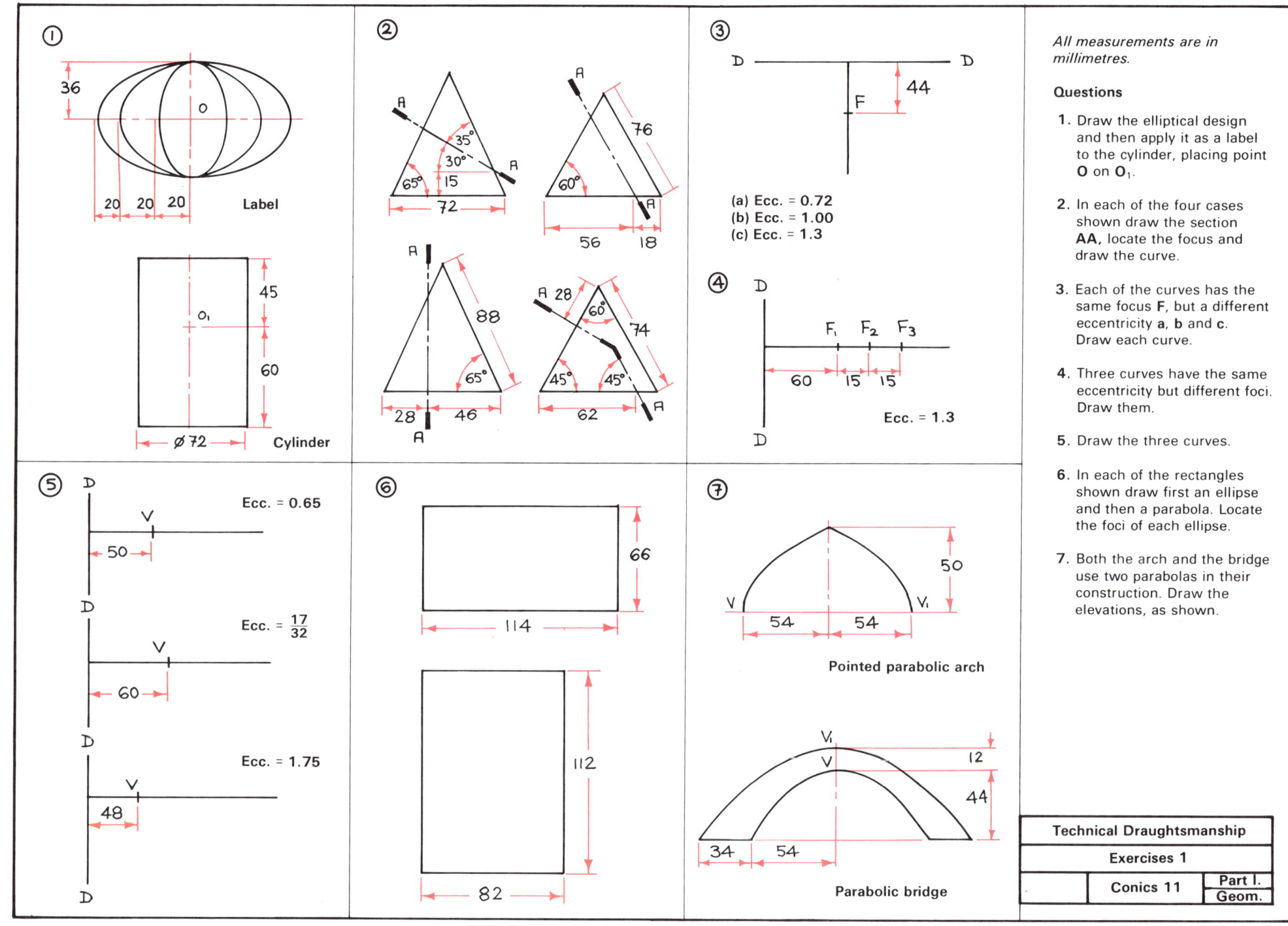

All measurements are in millimetres.

Questions

1. Draw the elliptical design and then apply it as a label to the cylinder, placing point **O** on **O₁**.

2. In each of the four cases shown draw the section **AA**, locate the focus and draw the curve.

3. Each of the curves has the same focus **F**, but a different eccentricity **a**, **b** and **c**. Draw each curve.

   (a) Ecc. = 0.72
   (b) Ecc. = 1.00
   (c) Ecc. = 1.3

4. Three curves have the same eccentricity but different foci. Draw them.

5. Draw the three curves.

6. In each of the rectangles shown draw first an ellipse and then a parabola. Locate the foci of each ellipse.

7. Both the arch and the bridge use two parabolas in their construction. Draw the elevations, as shown.

Technical Draughtsmanship
Exercises 1
Conics 11 — Part I. Geom.

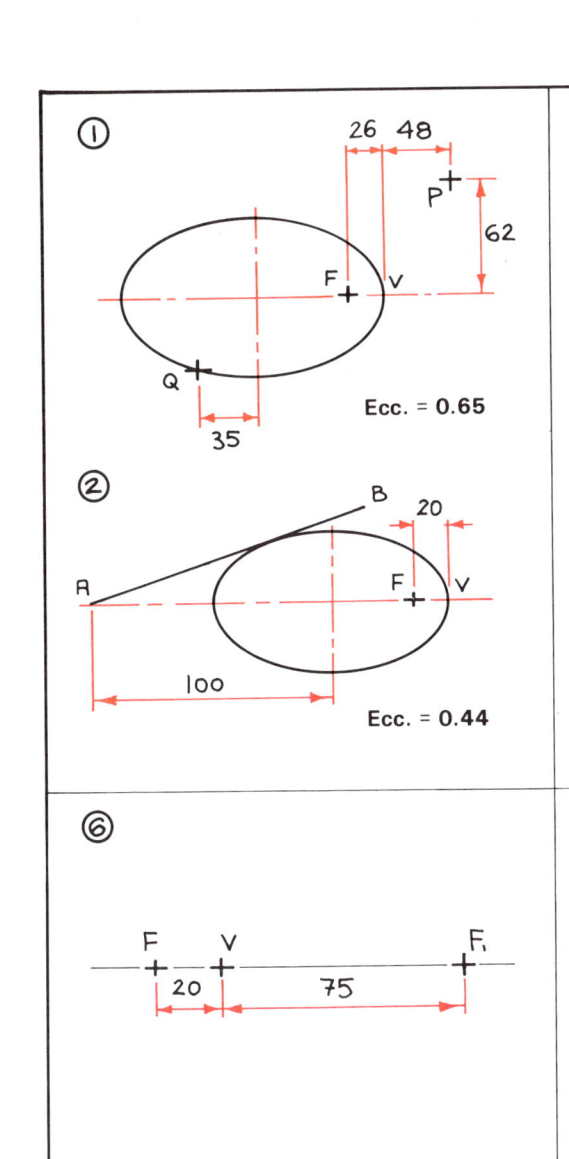

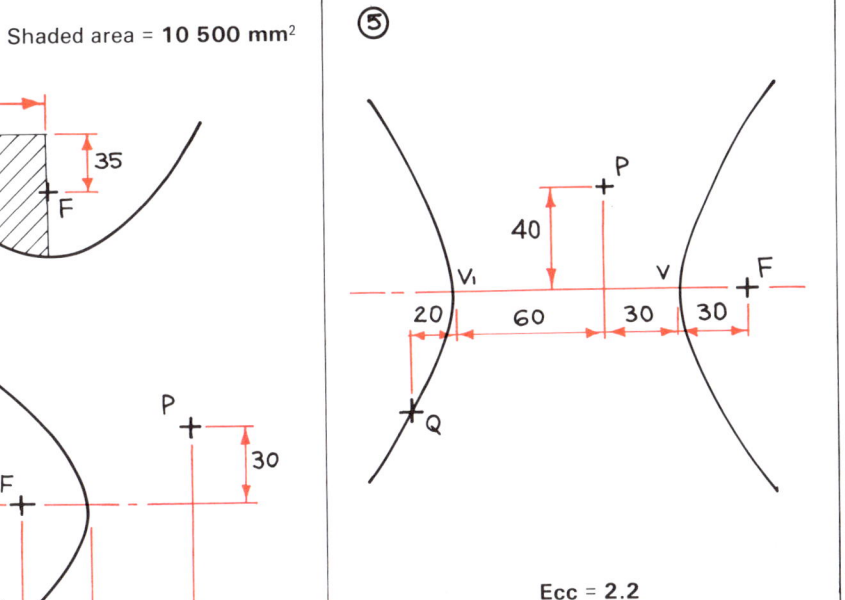

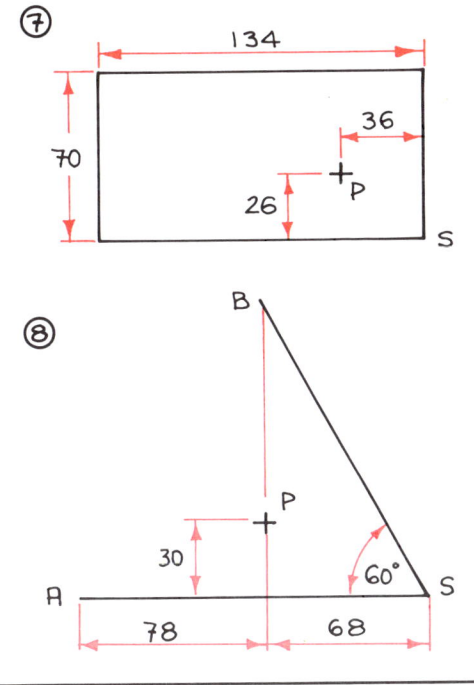

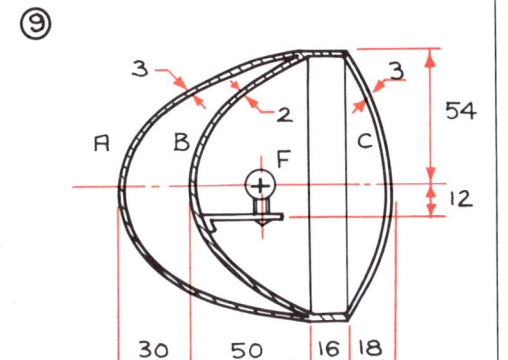

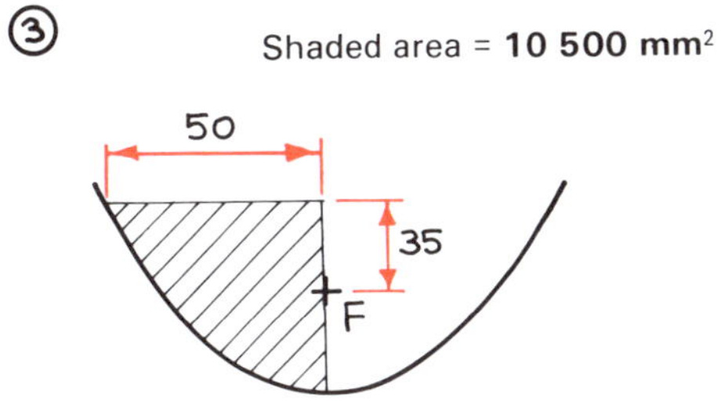

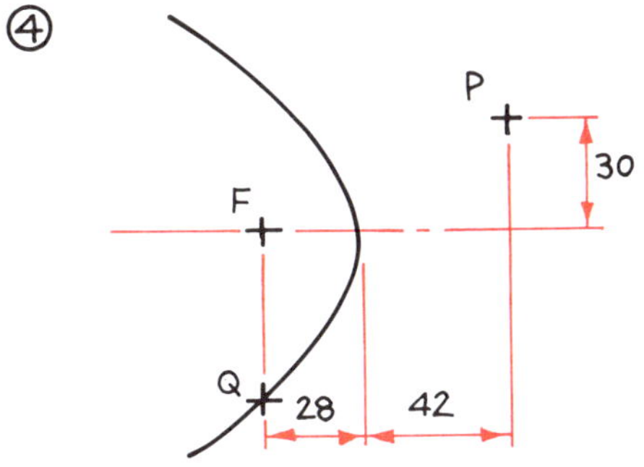

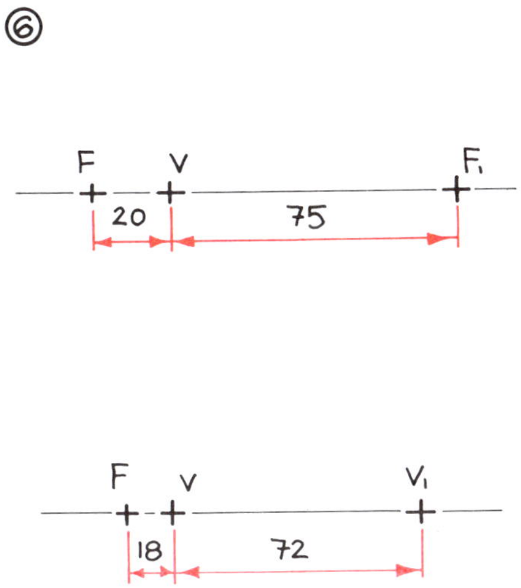

All measurements are in millimetres.

Questions

1. Draw tangents from point **P** and at point **Q** on the ellipse.

2. **AB** is a tangent to the ellipse. Draw the ellipse and the normal to **AB**.

3. Draw the parabola shown.

4. Draw tangents from **P** and at point **Q** on the parabola.

5. Draw tangents from **P** and at **Q** on the hyperbolas.

6. In each case plot the hyperbolas and draw their asymptotes.

7. Draw a hyperbola in the given rectangle. Point **P** is on the curve.

8. **SA** and **SB** are asymptotes, and **P** a point on a hyperbola. Draw the curve.

9. Draw the section through a bicycle front light.

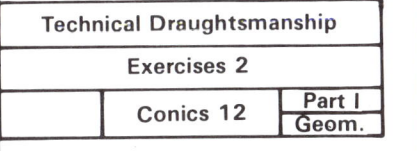

A: Casing: Parabola.
B: Reflector: Parabola of focus **F**.
C: Lens: Parabola.

Headlight

Technical Draughtsmanship
Exercises 2
Conics 12 — Part I — Geom.

199

All measurements are in millimetres.

Questions

1. Draw the two ellipses whose conjugate diameters are shown.

2. Draw the evolutes to each of the three curves.

3. In each of the given parallelograms draw first an ellipse, and then a parabola.

4. A tent design is shown. The ridge is a parabola. Develop the pattern by triangulation.

5. Using the asymptotes given draw both pairs of hyperbolas.

6. Draw the three standard orthographic views of the hyperbolic domed skylight shown. **AB**, **CD**, etc. are similar hyperbolas.

Technical Draughtsmanship

Exercises 3

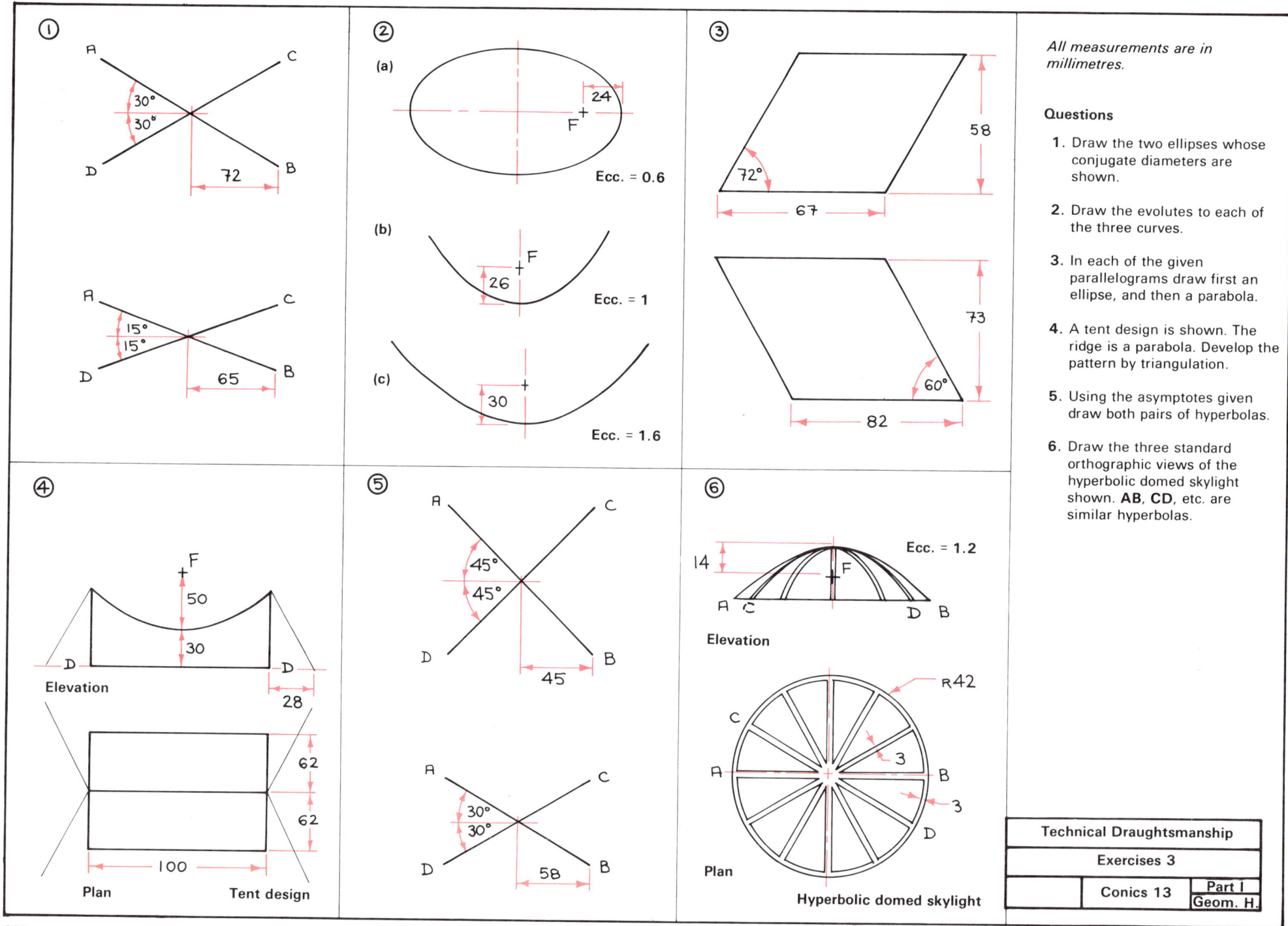

Conics 13 — Part I, Geom. H.

PART 2.
PROFESSIONAL PRACTICE

CHAPTER 16
THE PROFESSION

It is always useful to have an idea of the range of your profession. The processes of designing and dimensioning are also presented here.

CONTENTS
The Range of Professions	*Page* **202**
Designing	**203**
From Client to Contract	**204**
Paperwork	**205**
Computer Aided Design 1	**206**
Computer Aided Design 2	**207**
Some Conventions	**208**
Dimensioning 1	**209**
Dimensioning 2	**210**

Photocopying prohibited by law

There are four main areas where draughtsmanship is of fundamental importance:
- To design anything.
- To draw it.
- To put that drawing into practice.
- To understand the way something works, for servicing or maintenance.

These generate four specific types of drawing:
- Design drawings.
- Detail drawings.
- Working drawings.
- Diagrams.

Each profession has developed its own skills and specialist drawing conventions.

There are many more professions than have been listed here that would require a training in draughtsmanship. Can you think of any?

Some professions that require a training in draughtsmanship.

- Oceanographer
- Aerospace designer
- Circuit designer
- Electrician
- Display artist
- Interior designer
- Commercial artist
- Foundry worker
- Model maker
- Toolmaker
- Jeweller
- Process engineer
- Service engineer
- Mechanical engineer
- Clockmaker
- Plumber
- Carpenter
- Signwriter
- Town planner
- Architect
- Builder
- Surveyor
- Cartographer
- Shipbuilder
- Marine engineer
- Geologist
- Mining engineer
- Meteorologist
- Civil engineer
- Dressmaker
- Tailor
- Tentmaker
- Packaging designer
- Sheetmetal worker
- Stage designer
- Cabinet maker

Technical Draughtsmanship
The Range of Professions
Profession 1 · Part 2 / Gen.

202

①

The design team
In many offices these jobs double up but the functions are much the same. Each job is equally important to the team.

Roles shown: Client → Project Leader → Investigator; Quantity Surveyor ← Designer → Technical Clerks; Computer Operator, Senior Draughtsman, Standards Section; Printer, Draughtsman, Checkers; Specialists, Trainee, Tracers.

②

Evaluation — Performance and how to improve it.

Brief — A short clear description of the problem.

Specification — A detailed list of all requirements.

Investigation — Collect all the information required.

Choices — All possibilities are compared.

Model — Study the chosen design closely.

Construction Drawing — Exact details are drawn up.

Manufacture — Make or build it.

The design loop
Any good design team will go through this process when working to a brief. Especially important is the evaluation stage. This involves not only analysis of the design, but also a hard look at the performance of the design team itself, and of its procedures.

Technical Draughtsmanship		
Designing		
	Profession 2	Part 2 Gen.

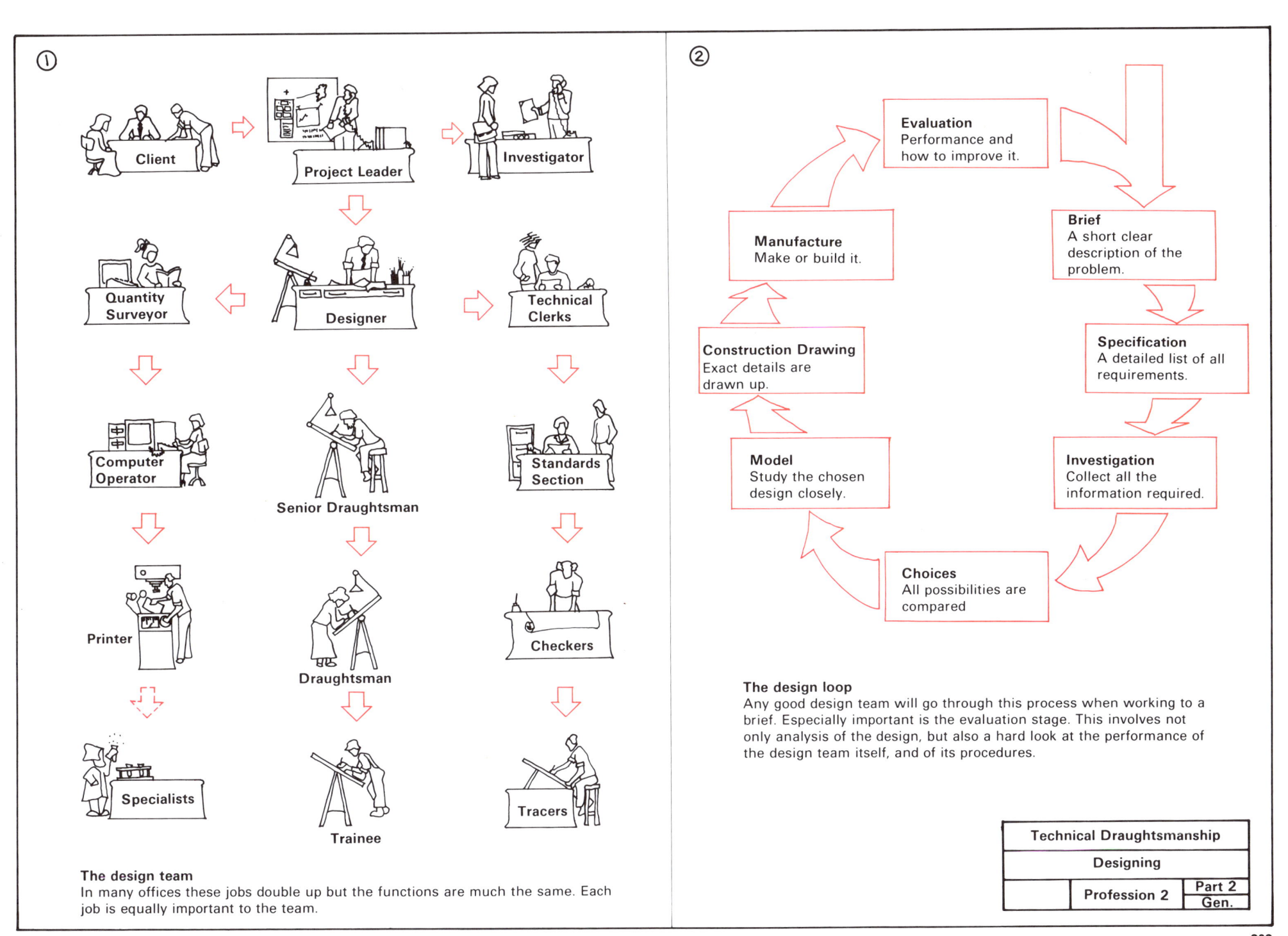

203

① Client

Client comes to the engineer, or architect, with a brief. The project leader will then do the following:

Stage 2
(a) Check ownership, solvency, others involved, etc.
(b) Apply for grants, outline permissions, finance, etc.
(c) List and think about all the potential problems.

Stage 3
(a) Site and amenity survey.
(b) See economist, quantity surveyor and specialists.
(c) Preliminary sketches and estimates to client.

Stage 4
(a) Prepare design drawings and models.
(b) Prepare the general working drawings.
(c) Get all the necessary approvals.

Stage 5
(a) Prepare full working and detail drawings.
(b) Specifications and a bill of quantities are prepared.
(c) A budget is set for the project.

Stage 6
Prepare documents and outline contracts for a tender.

Stage 7
Advertise for contractors to tender their estimates.

② Contractor

Stage 1 The contractor sees the advertisement for tender. He applies for details of the job.

Stage 2
(a) Examines the drawings and documents.
(b) Prepares a list of questions to be answered.
(c) Sends for specialist quotations.

Stage 3
(a) Checks out the designer and any other contractors.
(b) Checks amenity services: site, water, electricity.
(c) Checks his own money situation, insurance etc.

Stage 4
(a) Gets the answers to the list of questions.
(b) Obtains the specialists' replies

Stage 5
(a) Considers labour and plant.
(b) Plans work schedules.
(c) Prices the quantities.

Stage 6
(a) Final check.
(b) Calculates profits.

Stage 7 He bids for the contract.

③

The project leader meets with the client and compares tenders. Then the best contractor is invited to sign a contract. Now the job can get under way.

Note: *Working drawings, tender documents, specifications and bills of quantities have to be precise. Anything unclear, sloppy or incomplete will be a sure source of future troubles and claims.*

Technical Draughtsmanship
From Client to Contract
Profession 3 — Part 2 Gen.

① Paper sizes

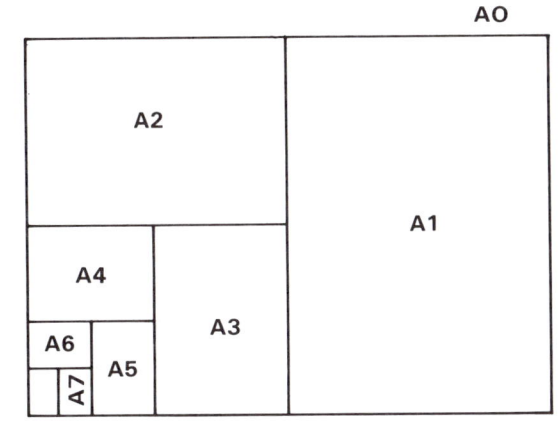

The full **A** series can be produced from a single **A0** sheet.

A0 = 1189 x 841
A1 = 841 x 594
A2 = 594 x 420
A3 = 420 x 297
A4 = 297 x 210
A5 = 210 x 148
A6 = 148 x 105
A7 = 105 x 74

The basis of this series is a rectangle **A0** of an area of one square metre, the sides of which are in the ratio of $1 : \sqrt{2} = 1 : 1.414$. This ratio has the unique property of being unchanged when the longer side is halved, or when the shorter side is doubled. So **A1** is half of **A0**, **A2** is half of **A1**, and so on.

When the longer dimension is horizontal the sheet is described as **landscape** or **oblong**. When the longer dimension is vertical it is described as **portrait** or **upright**.

There are three standard series. The **A** series is for the majority of printed and drawn work. The **B** series is intended for posters, charts and situations that do not quite suit the **A** sizes. The **C** series is for envelopes in which **A** sizes can be enclosed.

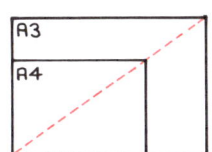

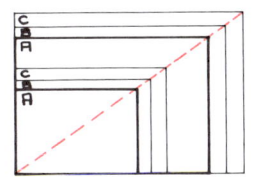

- All metric sizes can be scaled along a diagonal line.

② Filing systems

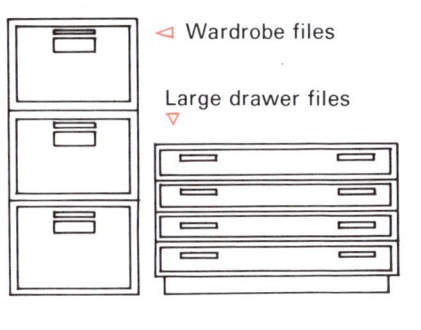

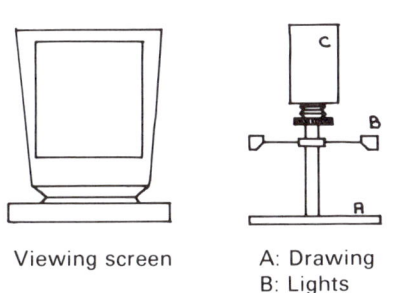

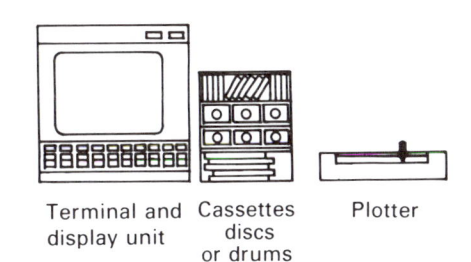

◁ Wardrobe files

▽ Large drawer files

Viewing screen

A: Drawing
B: Lights
C: Camera

Terminal and display unit   Cassettes discs or drums   Plotter

(a) **Paper filing:** This is not very expensive and needs very little hardware or technical skill. But it is bulky, needs a lot of space and does tend to deteriorate with time.

There are many ways of storing large drawings. Drawers and wardrobes are the most common. For legal purposes it may be necessary to keep the original paper drawings for three to five years, but this may change soon.

(b) **Microfilm or microfiche:** This can save up to 95% of the space needed for paper files. Special equipment is needed but this is quick and easy to operate. Large drawings can be a problem. You can put about 1000 A3 pages on a roll of microfilm and about 250 A3 pages onto a microfiche sheet. Microfilm can be transferred to a computer or plotter.

(c) **Computer filing:** Increasingly popular and versatile, these systems are in a state of flux. At present the special digitising, storage and replay equipment is costly and bulkier than microfiche. But the correction, up-dating and manipulation facilities are an enormous advantage.

Note: Most offices use a combination of filing methods. As computer retrieval, search and storage systems become quicker, smaller and easier to operate, these systems will become the norm.

Technical Draughtsmanship		
Paperwork		
	Profession 4	Part 2 Gen.

① CAD: Computer Aided Design

Advantages of CAD
- Given that a design team is always trying to balance a quick and economic design process against a good and thorough one, then **CAD** should, in theory, be an incredible leap forward.
- Checklists, logic and circuit analysis are much improved.
- Design manipulation is greatly increased. A computer can turn out a great range of possible variations in a short time.
- The re-use and combination of proven elements of past design allows systems to be constantly strengthened.
- Stress calculations, quantities, costs and schedules are quick and accurate.
- Up to date reference libraries can be built up.
- Can you think of other advantages?

Disadvantages of CAD
- There is a large initial investment in equipment, training and software.
- The best designers are not necessarily great computer operators. Computers can be frustrating and 'unfriendly' to work with, at times.
- There is a tendency to replace people, whose human subtlety is not replaceable.
- Checklists, programmes and jargon can often become more intricate, demanding, and time consuming than traditional methods of design.
- High costs and quicker results can put enormous pressure on an office to do more work than before. This in turn puts pressure on both the draughtsman and the market.
- At the moment, large digitising tables are very expensive, as are large format display units.

② Work sequence

Drawn work and digitiser

OR

Digitising table and pen

Memory
Terminal
VDU

Hard copier/Printer

OR

Plotter

Note: *The possibilities of relating **CAD** to computer aided manufacture, **CAM**, are clear.*

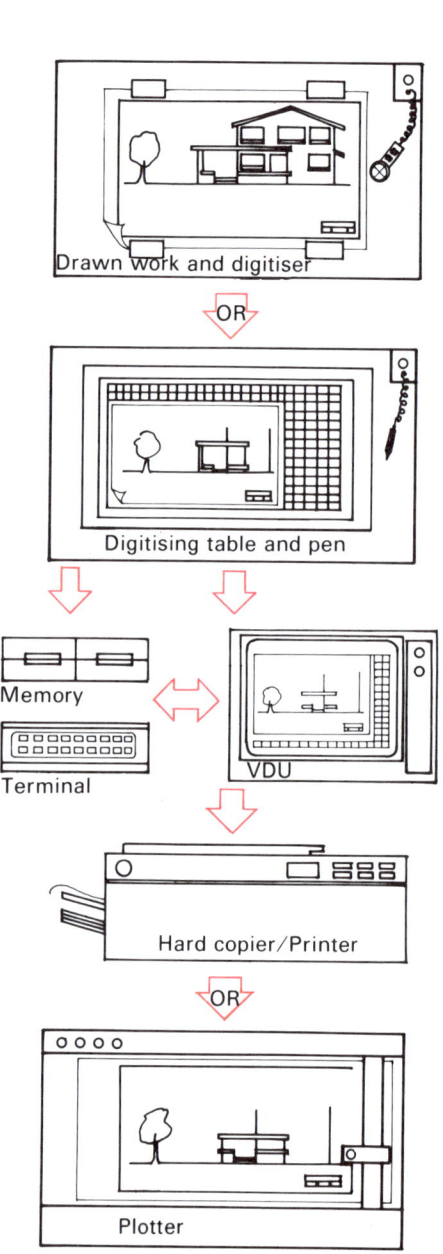

Input
- The method of putting a drawing into a computer is known as **digitising**, as it converts the drawing to a digital form of electronic impulses. This can be done in a variety of ways.
- A crosshair digitiser, known as a **mouse**, has a magnifying lens and a crosshair. The lines can be traced with great accuracy and the buttons on the handle allow editing commands to be made. Automatic scanners are also available.
- A **digitising table** has a pressure pad just beneath the surface and the pressure of drawing sends the coordinates of the lines to the computer. Another variation uses radio waves to pinpoint the position of a pointer on the drawing. Keyboards and a preset list of commands, or **menu**, can be set up to one side of the drawing area.
- **Joysticks**, or **light pens**, can be used to draw directly on a visual display screen. These are very useful for editing but are not the best method for direct technical drawing.

Process
- The manipulation of the drawing by changing, correcting or adding to the drawing. This is usually done on a visual display unit using a special light pen. There are many operations that can be performed at this stage and a menu of these options is shown to one side of the screen. The light pen is used to select a command from this list. See page **207** for further details of menus.

Output
- The various ways in which the drawing is finally presented. This may be as a print out, or plotted full size with technical pens. Alternatively the drawing may be stored on a tape, a disk, simply placed in the computer's memory or added to a graphic 'library'.

Technical Draughtsmanship
Computer Aided Design 1
Profession 5 / Part 2 Gen.

①

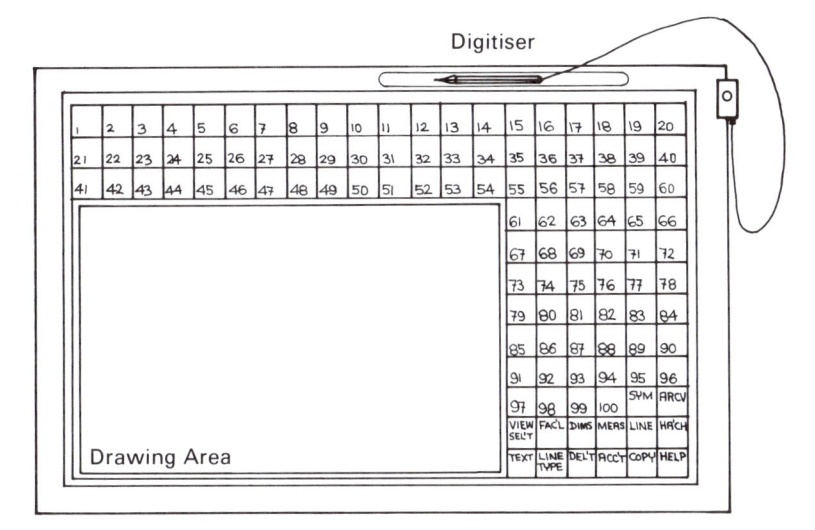

A digitiser drawing board
Digitiser boards can be up to **A0** in size, but **A4** is more usual. The above diagram shows one possible set up. Here the numbered squares are pressure sensitive. Each can be separately set up to correspond to a particular command. More often blocks of numbered squares are related to menus, or prepared blocks of commands or symbols. It is usual to have the most used commands in fixed positions, and then to have a range of menu blocks that can be called up for a particular job. Some of these menus are shown later.

②

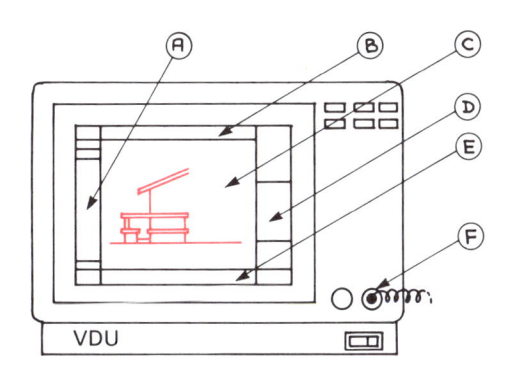

Visual display work
Both original and editing work can be done directly on the screen using a light pen and standard keyboard. A fairly typical display arrangement is shown.

A: Table of user's commands.
B: Grid, line and fount data.
C: Drawing area.
D: Rolling menu display.
E: Guide or menu title.
F: Connection to keyboard and printer or plotter.

③

A selection of menus

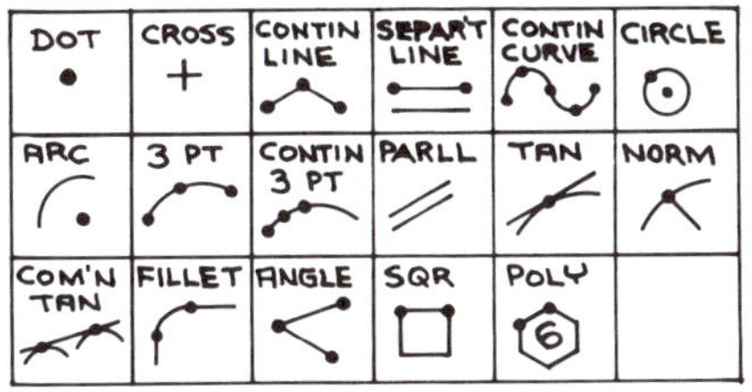

A drawing menu
To draw lines, arcs, curves, etc., it is usually enough to plot a few points and then define the function using a menu like this.

A view manipulation menu
This is quite a short list of the possible manipulations of a drawing. Can you think of others?

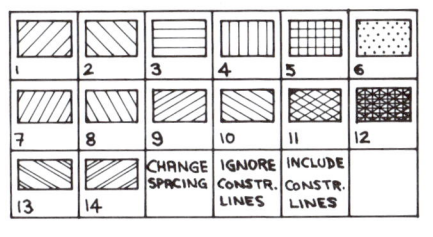

A menu for hatching
The idea is clear. The spacing between the hatching lines can be varied and the range can easily be extended to suit a particular profession.

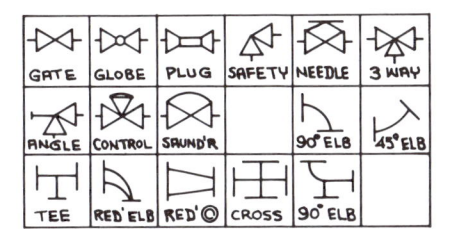

A symbol menu
Blank squares can be used as spaces to visually group and separate related symbols, as shown.

Note: *The above are only a few menus out of the wide and increasingly versatile range available. Menus can be displayed on a screen or printed and laid over an area of the digitising pad.*

Technical Draughtsmanship		
Computer Aided Design 2		
	Profession 6	Part 2 Gen.

207

Abbreviations in common use on orthographic drawings

Term	Abbreviation/Symbol
Across flats	A/F
Approved	APPD
Approximate	APPX
Assembly	ASSY
Auxiliary	AUX
Bench mark	BM
British standard	BS
Cast iron	CI
Centres	CRS
Centre line	CL or ℄
Chamfered	CHAM
Checked	CKD
Cheese head	CH HD
Concrete	CONC
Countersunk	CSK
Counterbore	C'BORE
Cylinder or cylindrical	CYL
Diameter	DIA or ⌀
Dimensions	DIMS
Drawing	DRG
External	EXT
Figure	FIG
Ground level	GL
Hexagonal	HEX
Height	HT
Height line	HL
Horizon	HZ
Hydraulic	HYD
Internal	INT
Left Hand	LH
Long	LG
Material	MATL
Manhole	MH
Maximum	MAX
Mild steel	MS
Minimum	MIN
Not to scale	NTS
Number	NO.
Picture Plane	PP
Pitch circle diameter	PCD
Radius	RAD or R
Reinforced concrete	RC
Right hand	RH
Round head	RD HD
Screwed	SCR
Sheet	SH
Specification	SPEC
Spotface	S'FACE
Square	SQ or □
Standard	STD
Taper	▸
True length	TL
Undercut	U'CUT
Volume	VOL
Weight	WT

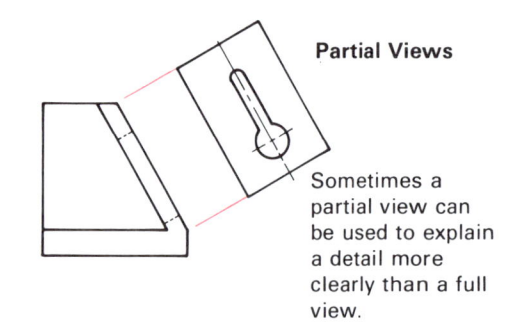

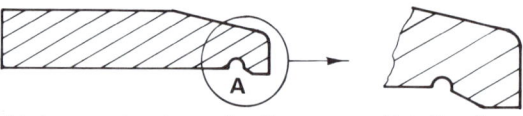

Partial Views

Sometimes a partial view can be used to explain a detail more clearly than a full view.

Enlarged Details

Detail at **A**.

At times enlarging a detail clarifies the drawing. This is very useful where small dimensions are involved.

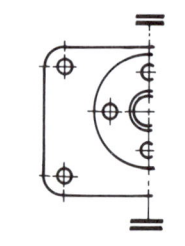

Symmetry: Partial views

When an object is symmetrical it is not always necessary to draw it in full. A partial view with a line of symmetry is sufficient, as shown here.

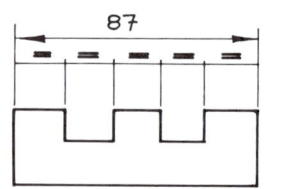

Symmetry: Dimensional

When a series of dimensions is identical this can be indicated as shown.

Note: *Each industry has evolved its own abbreviations and conventions. Many of these are set out in* **BS 308**.

Convention	Representation
Screw Threads	External Internal Assembled
Cylindrical Compression Spring	or
Interrupted Views	General Round shaft Hollow shaft
Knurling — *Knurling is a finish cut into metals to make them easier to grip.*	Straight Diamond

---

Technical Draughtsmanship

Some Conventions

Profession 7 | Part 2 / Gen.

208

①

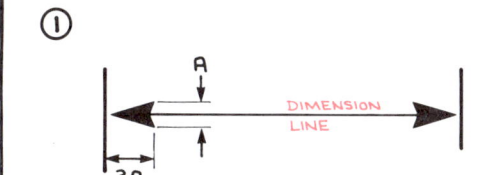

Arrowheads
Dimension lines usually end in an arrowhead. This should be dark and of the proportions shown.

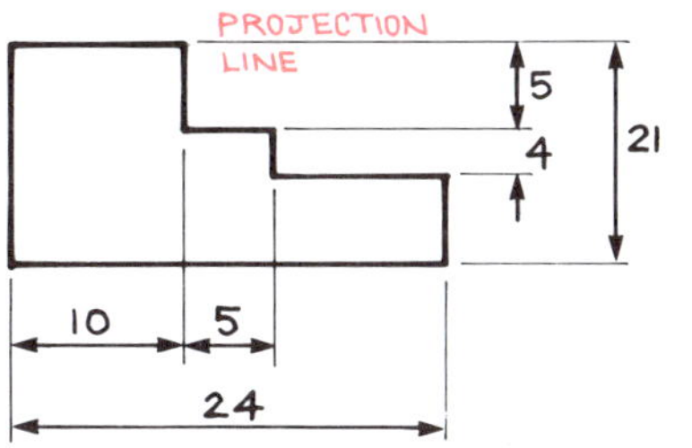

Projection lines
Start with a short gap. The smaller dimensions are shown nearest the drawing and the larger dimensions farther out.

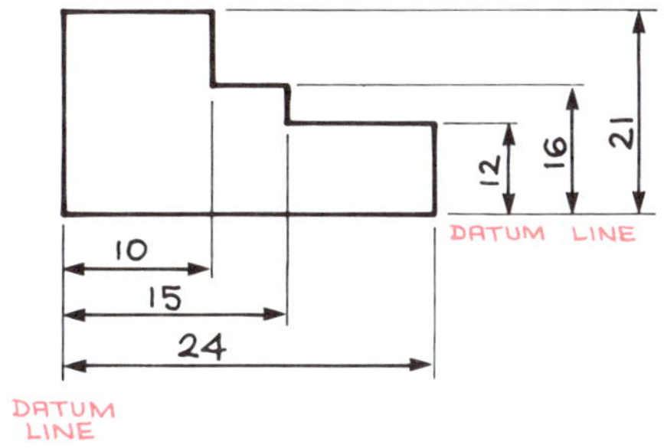

Datum lines
In order to avoid slight inaccuracies accumulating, dimensions are often all taken from a single reference or datum line.

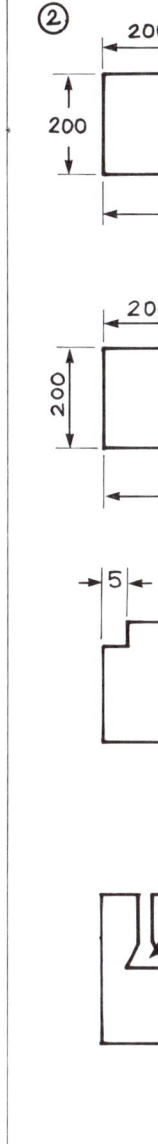

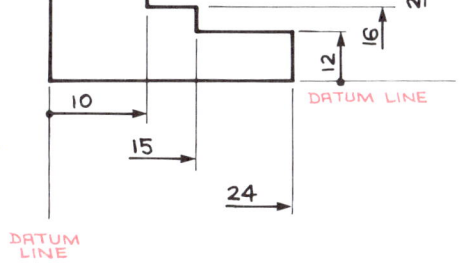

An alternative datum line method for use when space is limited, or when distances are great.

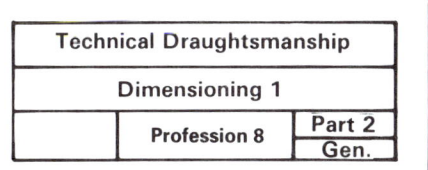

②

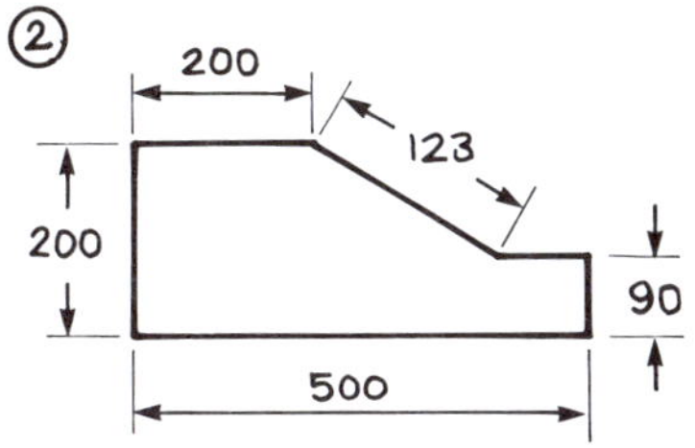

The unidirectional system.
This is the preferred method. All the dimensions are written to be read from one position only, as shown.

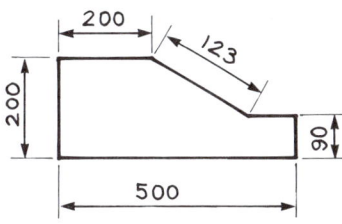

The aligned system.
Here the dimensions are written along and parallel to the dimension lines.

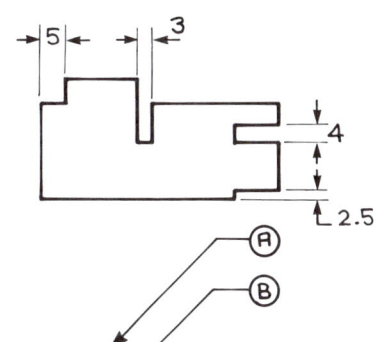

Dimensioning of small linear features.
Avoid situations where the numeral appears to be an extension of a projection or dimension line.

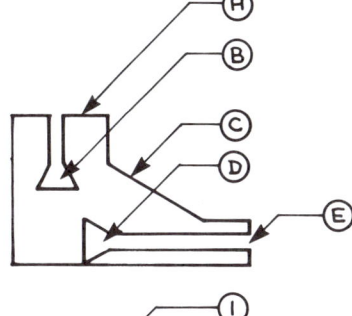

Leader lines and reference bubbles.
(a) With arrowheads: Either letters or numerals can be used and these would refer to an adjacent explanatory list.

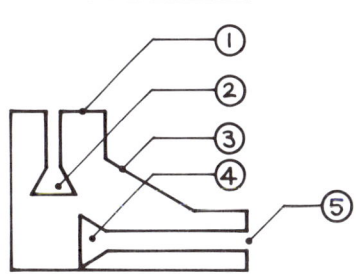

(b) With dot endings: In general, dots are used when most of the references are within the object and arrowheads are used when most of the references are to the surface of the object.

③

Dimensioning principles
1. Dimensions are usually in millimetres. When other units are used these must be clearly shown e.g. **18 cm.**
2. The decimal point should be on the base line e.g. **35.2mm.**
3. When there are more than four numerals to the left of a decimal point they are arranged in groups of three e.g. **16 256.**
4. Dimensions of less than one are preceded by a zero e.g. **0.3 mm.**
5. Do *not* overdimension.
6. Do *not* dimension to a hidden line.
7. Leader lines should not change direction until they have cleared the object.
8. Dimension lines should not cross each other.
9. Dimensions should be placed on the clearest view of the feature concerned.
10. Use *either* the unidirectional *or* the aligned system. Do not mix the two.
11. Dimensions should be drawn so that they can be read from the bottom of the drawing, or from the right-hand side.

Technical Draughtsmanship		
Dimensioning 1		
	Profession 8	Part 2
		Gen.

① Diameters and radii

② Holes

Holes on a pitch circle

2 HOLES X Ø14
4 HOLES Y Ø12

Countersink
Ø6 C'SK AT 90° TO Ø15

Counterbore
Ø6 C'BORE Ø14 × 5 DEEP

Spotface
Ø8 S'FACE Ø16

Axial diameters

Standard notation

Alternative when the complete arrow is not possible.

Angles

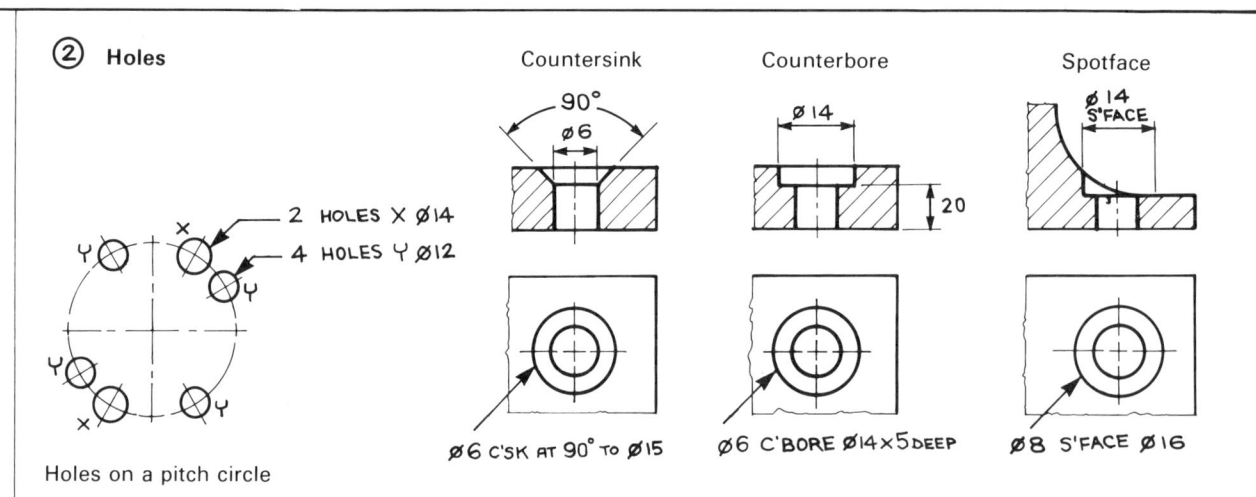

③ Chamfers and tapers

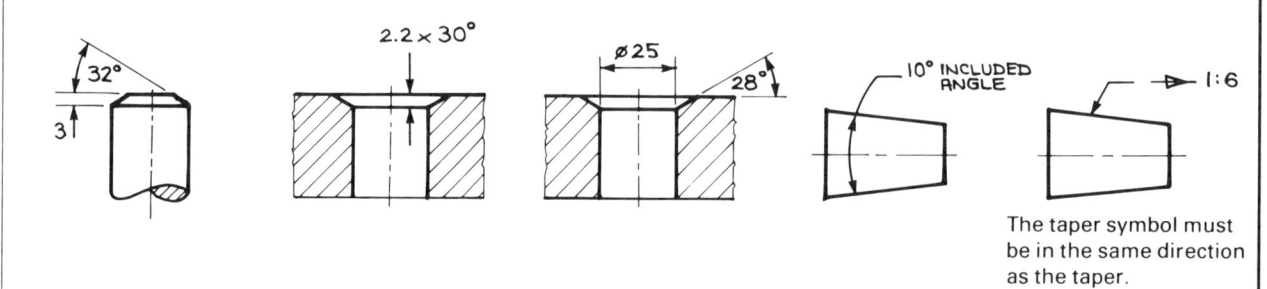

The taper symbol must be in the same direction as the taper.

④ Coordinate and functional dimensions

Datum line

Datum line

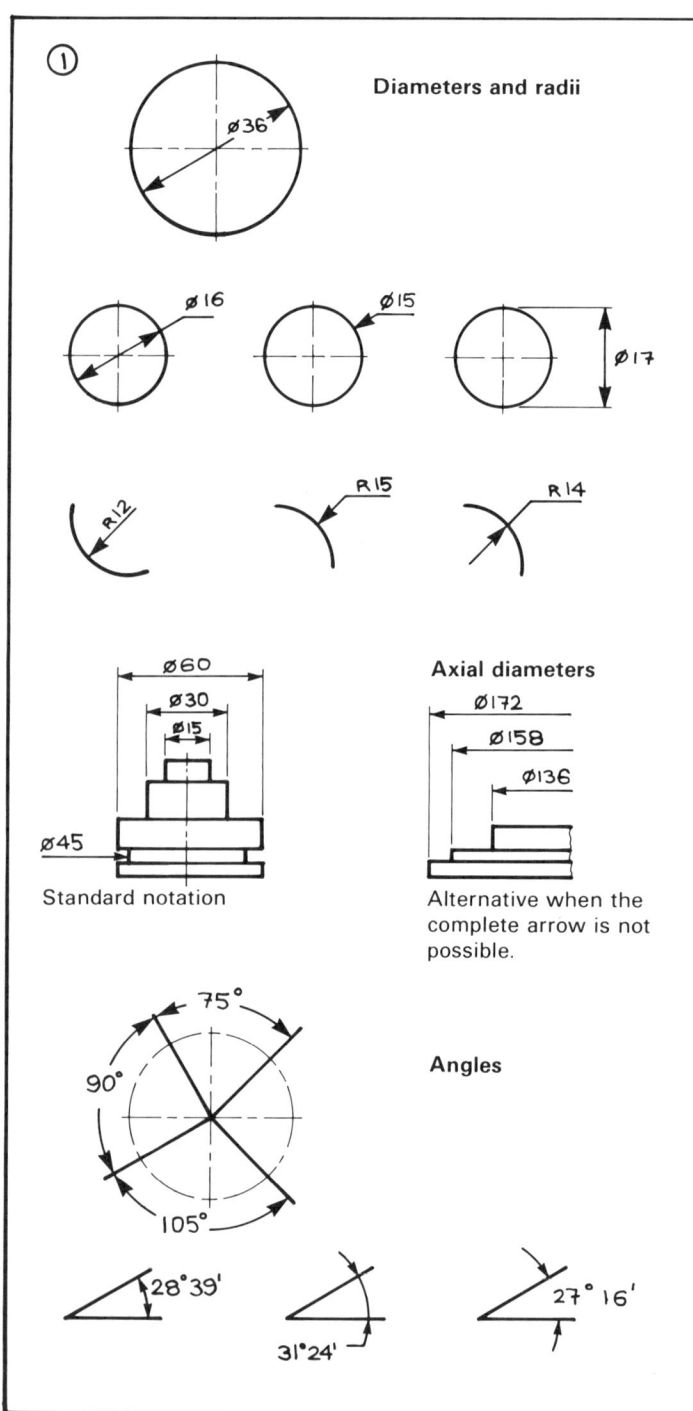

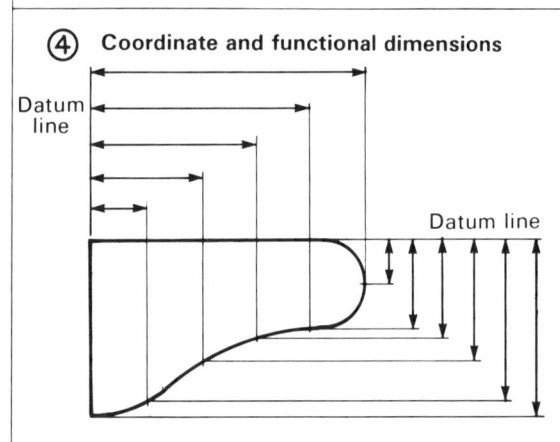

An irregular outline can be measured from two datum lines, as here.

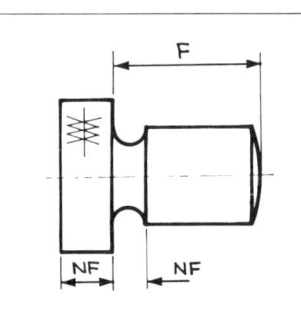

Note: *Tolerances and machining dimensions are outlined in Chapter 23.*

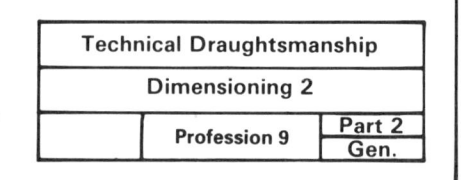

Functional dimensions are those that are vital if the product is to function well and these dimensions should always be clearly shown.
F: Functional dimension
NF: Non-functional dimension.

Technical Draughtsmanship		
Dimensioning 2		
Profession 9	Part 2
	Gen.

**PART 2A
ENGINEERING APPLICATIONS**

CHAPTER 17

AN ENGINEERING PROJECT

As an example of an approach to engineering design this chapter takes a sample brief and follows it through the initial design stages.

CONTENTS
Brainstorming	*Page*	**212**
Design Drawings 1		**213**
Design Drawings 2		**214**
Electrical Circuits		**215**
Detail Drawings		**216**
Final Assembly Drawings		**217**
Exercises		**218**

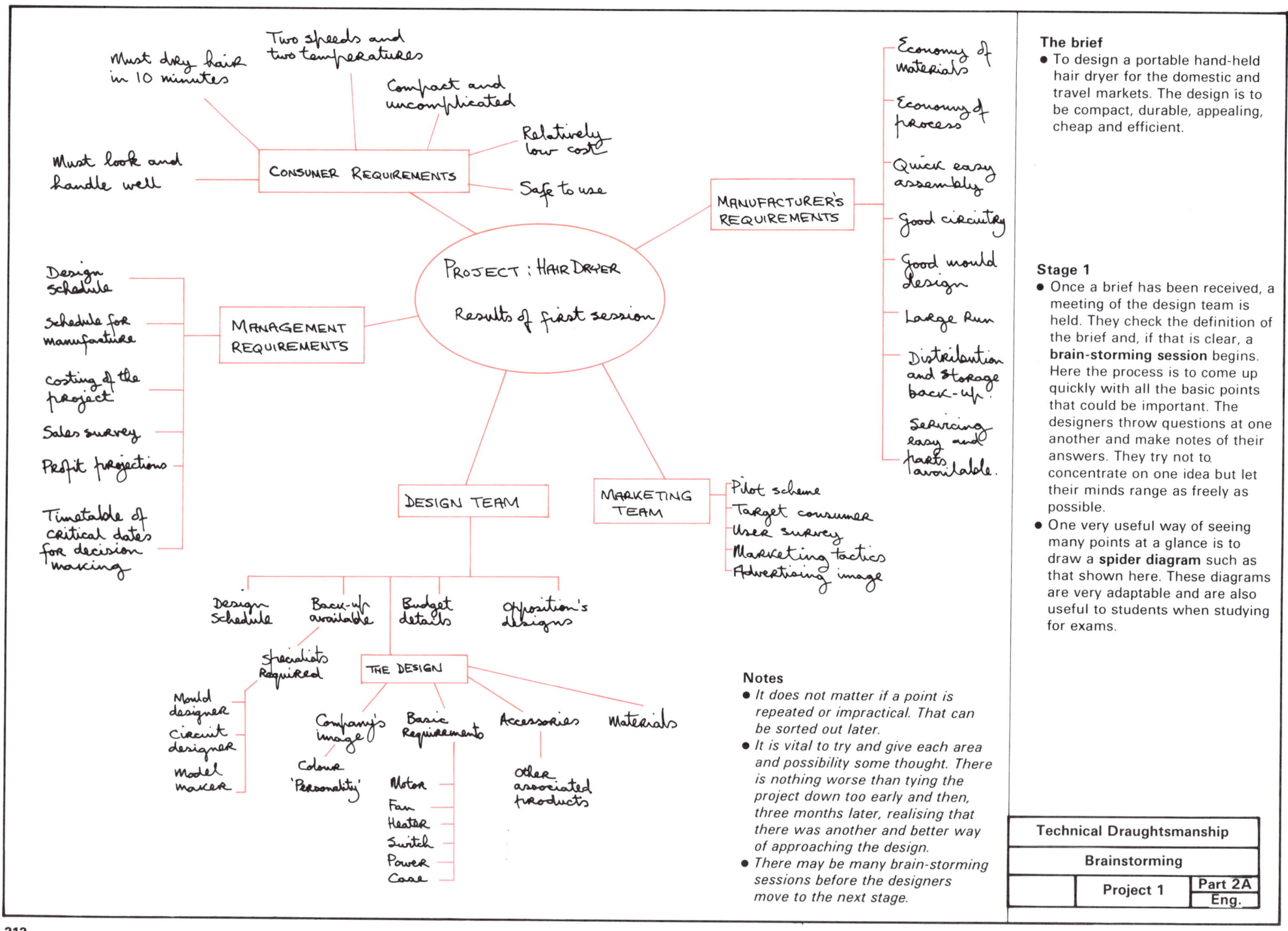

Spider Diagram: Project Hair Dryer — Results of first session

Consumer Requirements
- Must dry hair in 10 minutes
- Two speeds and two temperatures
- Compact and uncomplicated
- Relatively low cost
- Safe to use
- Must look and handle well

Manufacturer's Requirements
- Economy of materials
- Economy of process
- Quick easy assembly
- Good circuitry
- Good mould design
- Large Run
- Distribution and storage back-up
- Servicing easy and parts available

Management Requirements
- Design schedule
- Schedule for manufacture
- Costing of the project
- Sales survey
- Profit projections
- Timetable of critical dates for decision making

Marketing Team
- Pilot scheme
- Target consumer
- User survey
- Marketing tactics
- Advertising image

Design Team
- Design Schedule
- Back-up available
- Budget details
- Opposition's designs
- Specialists Required: Mould designer, Circuit designer, Model maker

The Design
- Company's image / Colour / 'Personality'
- Basic Requirements: Motor, Fan, Heater, Switch, Power, Case
- Accessories
- Other associated products
- Materials

The brief
- To design a portable hand-held hair dryer for the domestic and travel markets. The design is to be compact, durable, appealing, cheap and efficient.

Stage 1
- Once a brief has been received, a meeting of the design team is held. They check the definition of the brief and, if that is clear, a **brain-storming session** begins. Here the process is to come up quickly with all the basic points that could be important. The designers throw questions at one another and make notes of their answers. They try not to concentrate on one idea but let their minds range as freely as possible.
- One very useful way of seeing many points at a glance is to draw a **spider diagram** such as that shown here. These diagrams are very adaptable and are also useful to students when studying for exams.

Notes
- It does not matter if a point is repeated or impractical. That can be sorted out later.
- It is vital to try and give each area and possibility some thought. There is nothing worse than tying the project down too early and then, three months later, realising that there was another and better way of approaching the design.
- There may be many brain-storming sessions before the designers move to the next stage.

Technical Draughtsmanship	
Brainstorming	
Project 1	Part 2A Eng.

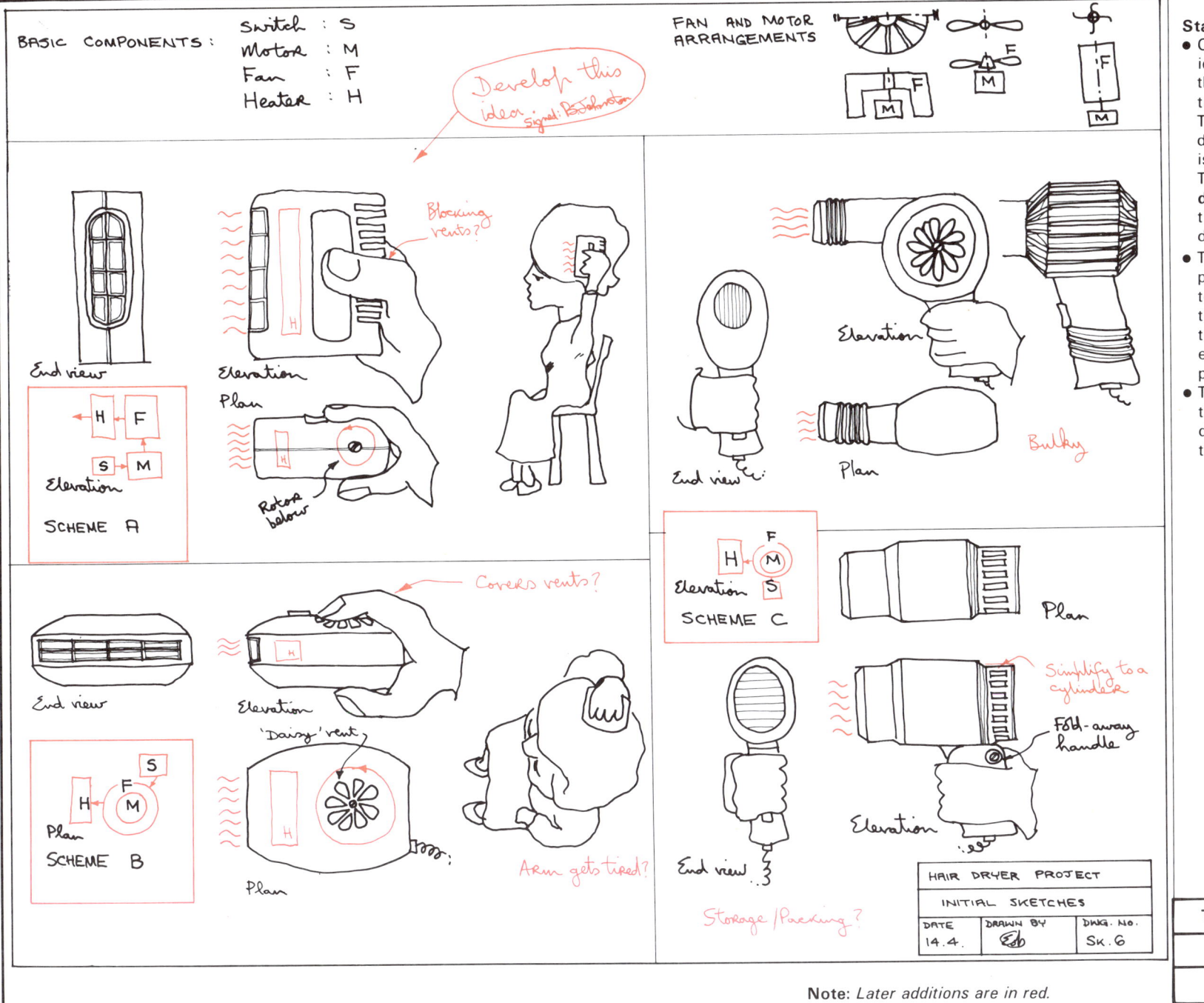

Stage 2

- Once they have got a very good idea of what is required and of the possible lines of enquiry, the designers set to work. They produce sketches and draw them so that each idea is quite clear and no more! These are called **esquisse drawings**. It is foolish to waste time on elaborate or detailed drawings at this stage.
- The esquisse drawings are all pinned to a wall and the design teams criticise and discuss them. They will try to decide on the best ideas and then eliminate those that seem less promising.
- This stage is very important as the decisions made here give direction to the design work that follows.

Note: Later additions are in red.

Technical Draughtsmanship

Design Drawings 1

Project 2 — Part 2A Eng.

213

Stage 3

- A particular design is 'pushed' to see how exactly it might work out in practice.
- Here the designer spends much time and effort in allowing for every detail of a practical design. Later, experts may suggest changes but most of their effort will be in making this design work. If the designer is good there should be little need for drastic changes.
- Once these design drawings have been given the 'go-ahead' the services of specialist designers will be sought, e.g. for designing the machinery and moulds for making the body, or for working out the exact electrical circuits required.

Note: *Later comments are in red.*

Technical Draughtsmanship

Design Drawings 2

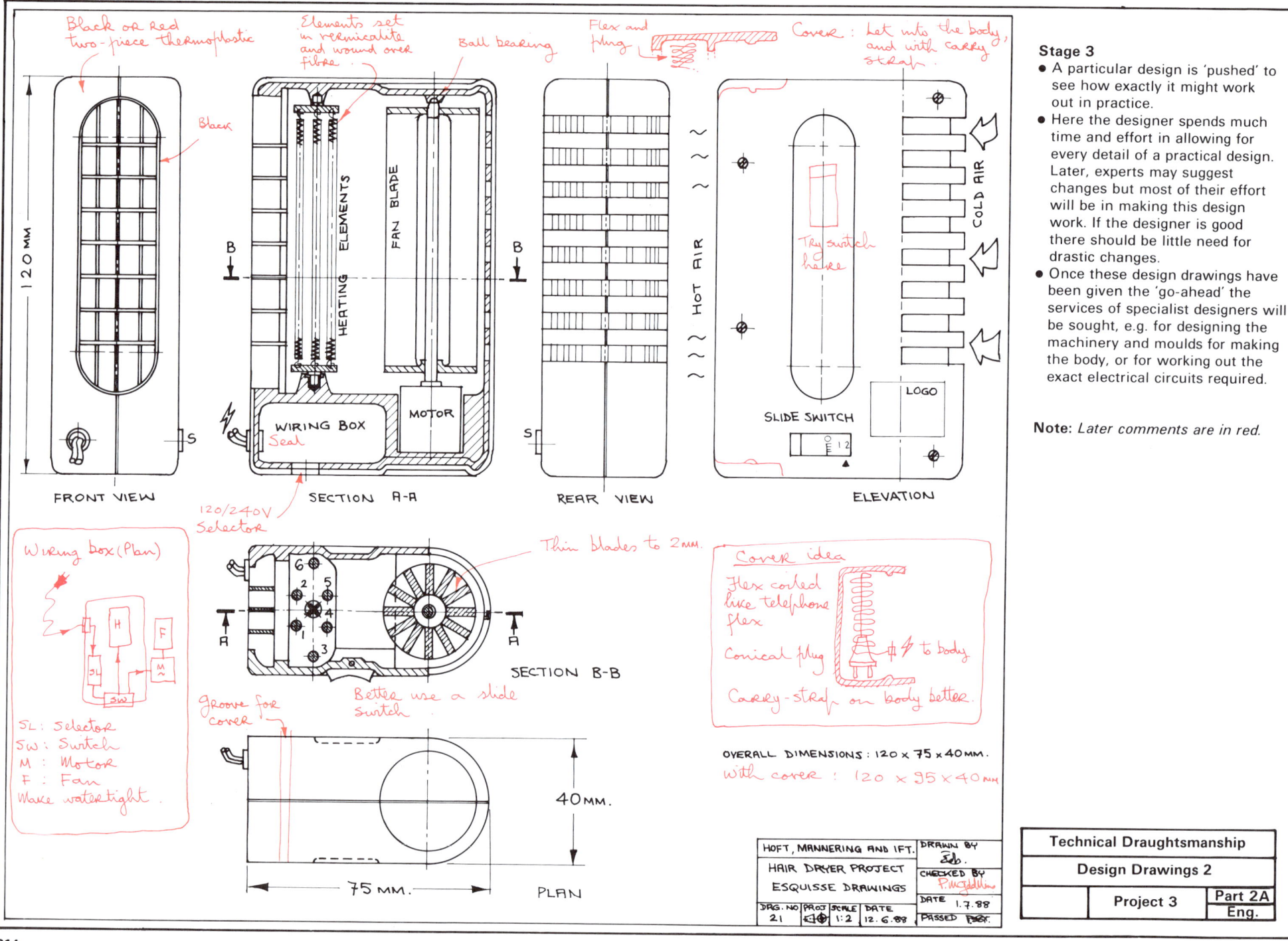

Project 3 — Part 2A — Eng.

① Some electrical symbols

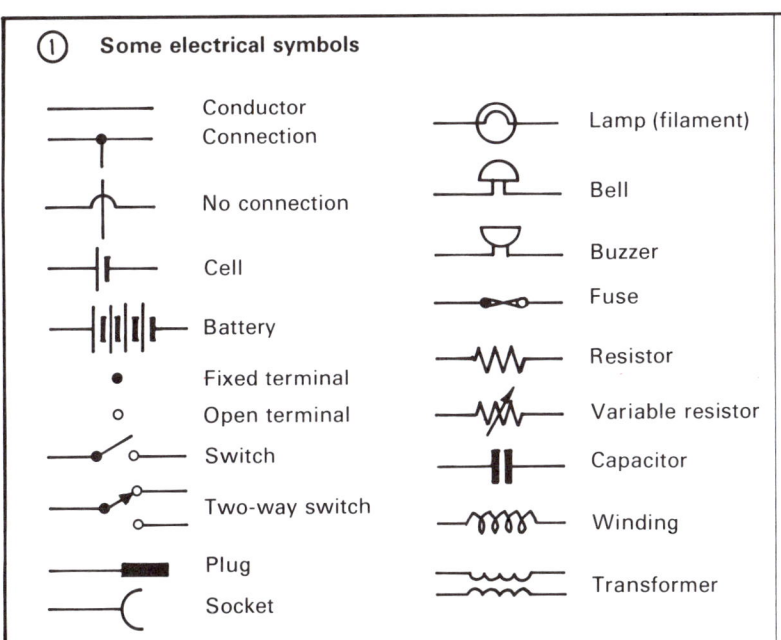

Symbol	Name	Symbol	Name
—	Conductor Connection	Lamp (filament)	Lamp (filament)
	No connection		Bell
	Cell		Buzzer
	Battery		Fuse
•	Fixed terminal		Resistor
○	Open terminal		Variable resistor
	Switch		Capacitor
	Two-way switch		Winding
	Plug		Transformer
	Socket		

② Some basic circuits
Positive lines have been drawn in red and negative lines in black.

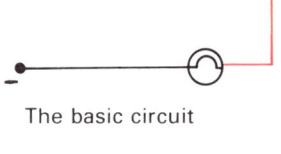

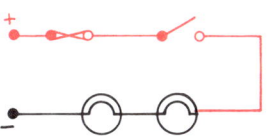

The basic circuit

Two lights (in series). If one light fails the whole system fails.

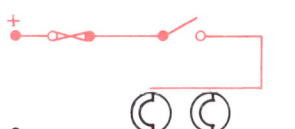

Two lights (in parallel). Each light has its own source and exit (neutral).

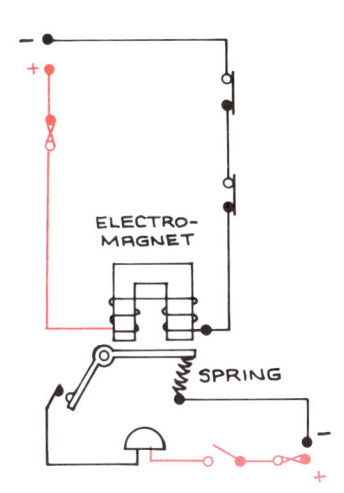

An alarm circuit. If the first circuit is broken the magnet releases the spring and the alarm circuit goes into operation.

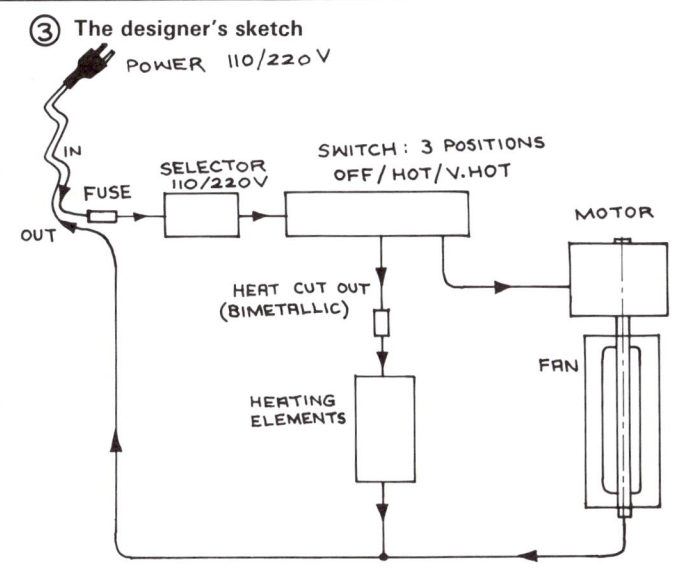

③ The designer's sketch

POWER 110/220V

The designer does his best to set out exactly what he is thinking about and to make the work of the circuit designer easier.

④ The circuit diagram

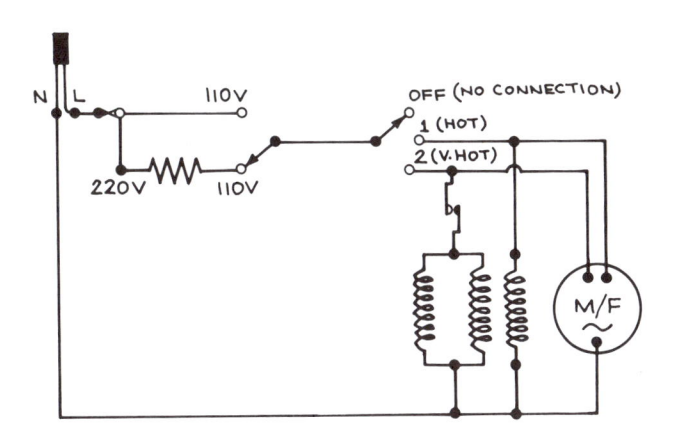

There would also be lists and specifications for each component and, eventually, even the exact lengths of each wire would need to be calculated accurately.

Electrical circuits drawing

A basic circuit has five elements:
- Power in: This is the live wire from either a battery or mains supply.
- Safety: Either a fuse or a circuit breaker.
- Control: Usually a switch.
- Work: A light bulb, machine, or whatever.
- Way out: The negative wire.

The current flows around this circuit and some of it is used as the work is done. By measuring the difference between what goes in and what comes out this loss can be calculated.

To design an electronic circuit using the standard orthographic views would be very confusing and prone to error. So a schematic system has been developed for the design, construction and maintenance of electronic equipment. A few of the graphic symbols used and some simple circuits are shown here.

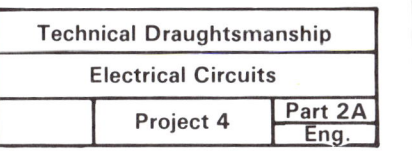

Technical Draughtsmanship

Electrical Circuits

Project 4	Part 2A
	Eng.

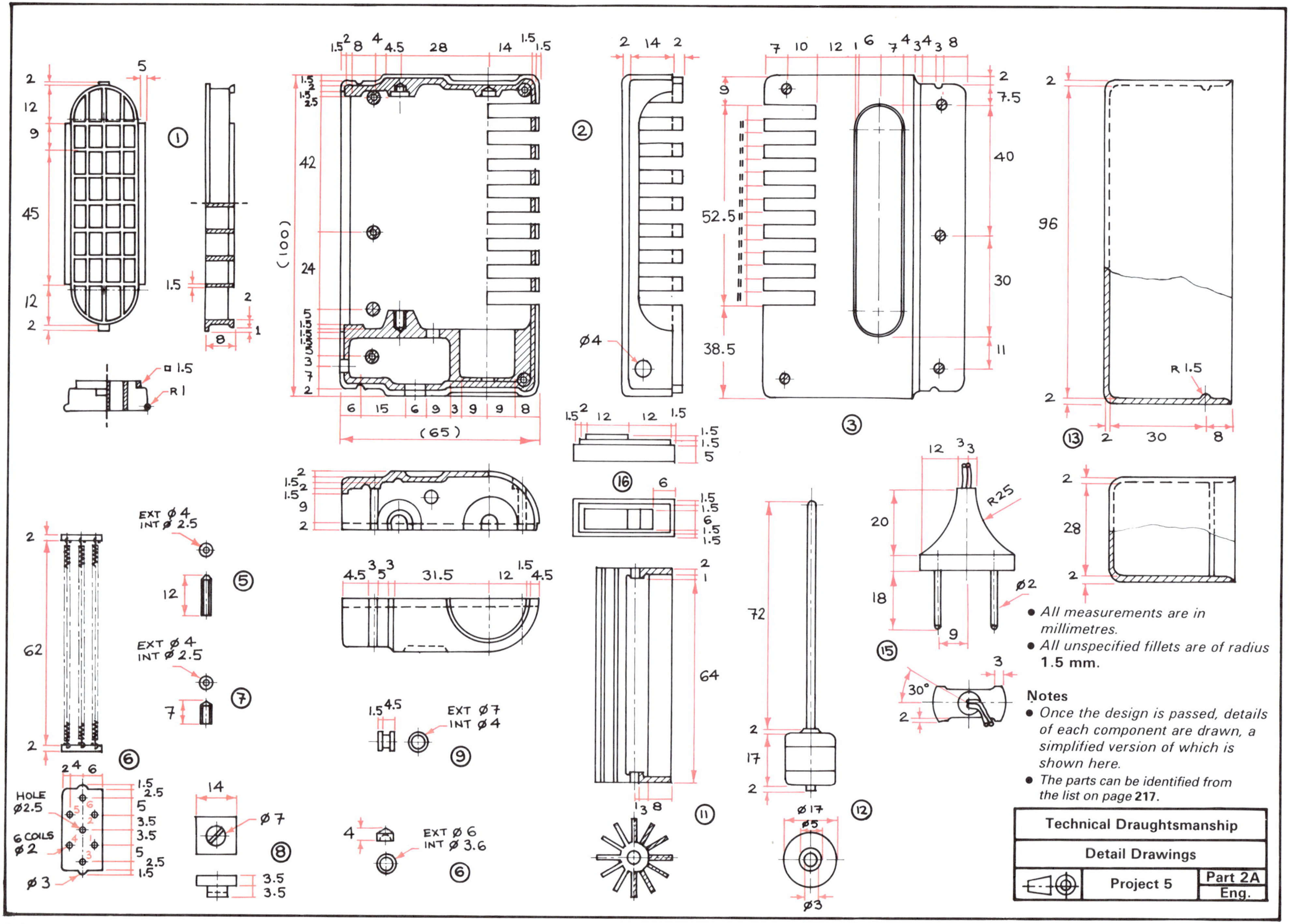

- *All measurements are in millimetres.*
- *All unspecified fillets are of radius* **1.5 mm.**

Notes

- *Once the design is passed, details of each component are drawn, a simplified version of which is shown here.*
- *The parts can be identified from the list on page* **217**.

Technical Draughtsmanship	
Detail Drawings	
Project 5	Part 2A Eng.

Views

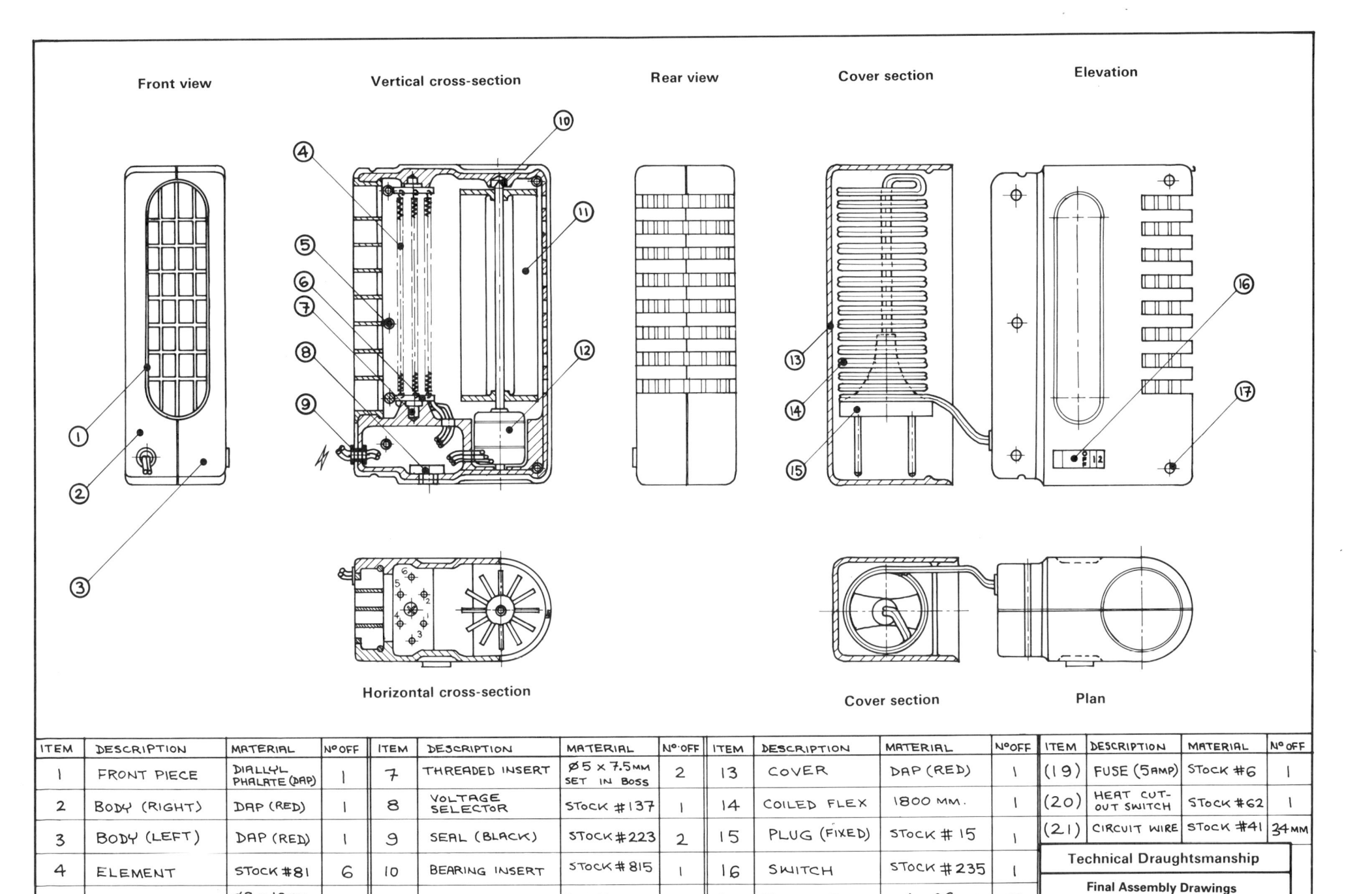

- Front view
- Vertical cross-section
- Rear view
- Cover section
- Elevation
- Horizontal cross-section
- Cover section
- Plan

ITEM	DESCRIPTION	MATERIAL	N° OFF	ITEM	DESCRIPTION	MATERIAL	N° OFF	ITEM	DESCRIPTION	MATERIAL	N° OFF	ITEM	DESCRIPTION	MATERIAL	N° OFF
1	FRONT PIECE	DIALLYL PHALATE (DAP)	1	7	THREADED INSERT	Ø5 x 7.5MM SET IN BOSS	2	13	COVER	DAP (RED)	1	(19)	FUSE (5AMP)	STOCK #6	1
2	BODY (RIGHT)	DAP (RED)	1	8	VOLTAGE SELECTOR	STOCK #137	1	14	COILED FLEX	1800 MM.	1	(20)	HEAT CUT-OUT SWITCH	STOCK #62	1
3	BODY (LEFT)	DAP (RED)	1	9	SEAL (BLACK)	STOCK #223	2	15	PLUG (FIXED)	STOCK #15	1	(21)	CIRCUIT WIRE	STOCK #41	34MM
4	ELEMENT	STOCK #81	6	10	BEARING INSERT	STOCK #815	1	16	SWITCH	STOCK #235	1				
5	THREADED INSERT	Ø3 x 10MM SET IN BOSS	5	11	FAN BLADE	DAP (BLACK)	1	17	FIXING BOLT	M4 x 26MM	5				
6	ELEMENT BASE	VERMICALITE	2	12	MOTOR	STOCK #88	1	(18)	ELEMENT FIXING BOLT	M4 x 6MM	2				

Technical Draughtsmanship

Final Assembly Drawings

Project 6 — Part 2A — Eng.

1 Studio 1

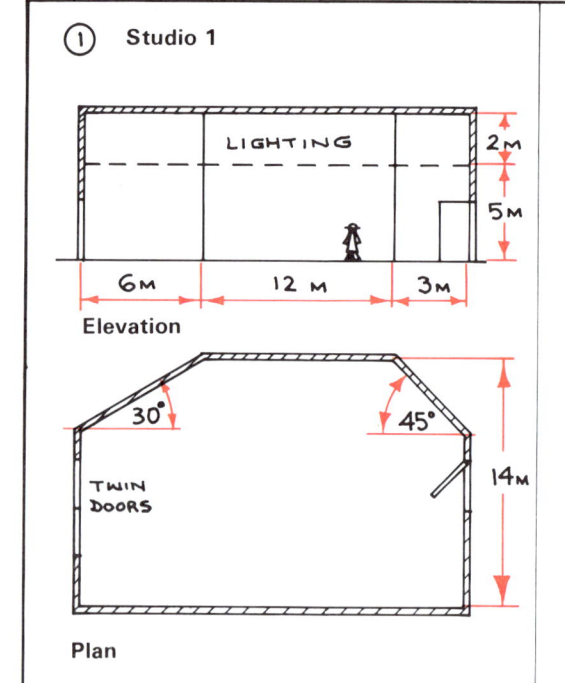

Elevation: 6m, 12m, 3m; 2m, 5m; LIGHTING

Plan: 30°, 45°, 14m; TWIN DOORS

2
Brief: Design an effective scouring brush for domestic use.

3
Brief: A silk-screen printer wants an adjustable 'angle-poise' flourescent tube lamp for use over his **2m x 1m** work table. Design the lamp.

4
Brief: Design a kettle with an automatic cut-out switch.

5
Brief: Design the furniture for your room. This should include both study and leisure facilities and may be in one or more pieces.

6
Brief: Design a gripping device for people with limited reaching ability. This device should be used to extend the reach by **300 mm** and be able to pick up, hold and put down small household objects of up to **2 kg.** in weight. The person's arm is normal in every other way.

Questions

1. Your local television station is about to stage your favourite short story. Design a stage set for Studio 1 for this play. Measured esquisse drawings and a material list are required.

2 to 6. For each brief produce sketch, esquisse, detail and assembly drawings.

7 and 8. Design to the given brief.

9. A simplified sketch of a car's electrical system is shown. Draw a schematic electronic diagram to show the circuit.

10. If the three circuits in the room are wired to the fusebox what would the overall circuit diagram look like? Draw this diagram.

7
Brief: Draw up a table for a 16-team knock-out competition, or ... a club is running an adventure sports week and wants to send application forms to their members. Draw out the form in detail.

8
Brief: Design a bunk bed with storage room and ladder. An isometric sketch, detail and assembly drawings are required.

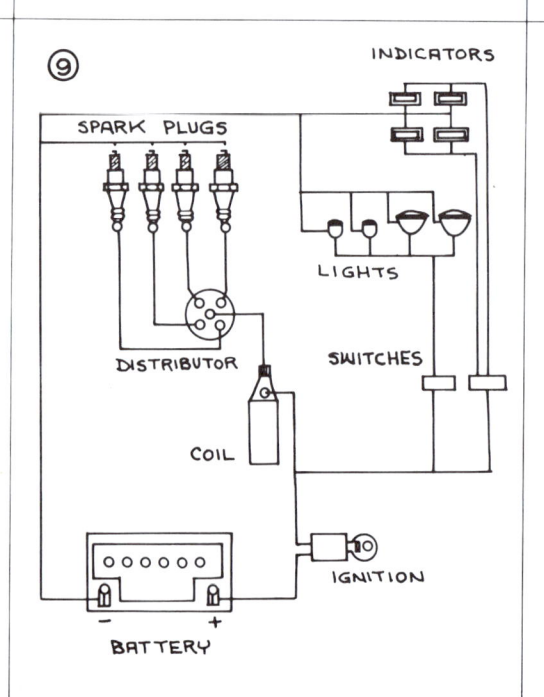

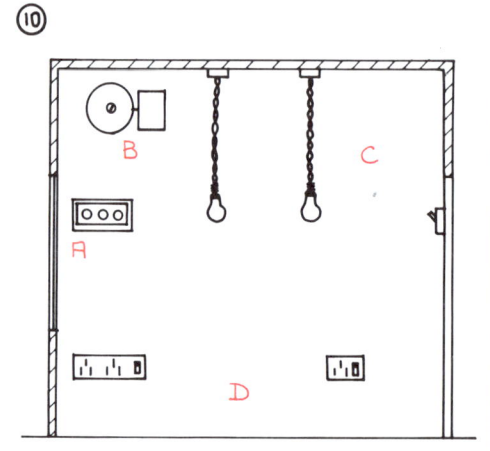

9
SPARK PLUGS, INDICATORS, LIGHTS, SWITCHES, DISTRIBUTOR, COIL, IGNITION, BATTERY

10
A, B, C, D

A: Fusebox with three fuses.
B: Alarm system for the window.
C: Two bulbs and one switch.
D: Double socket with switch and single socket with switch.

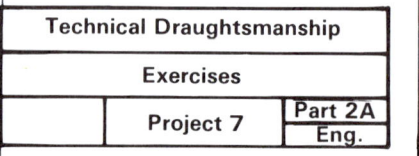

Technical Draughtsmanship
Exercises
Project 7 | Part 2A
| Eng.

218

PART 2A

CHAPTER 18
ENGINEERING STRUCTURES

Here is an introduction to forces and their resolution. There are also some pages on basic structures.

CONTENTS

Forces	*Page*	**220**
Vectors		**221**
Beams		**222**
Frameworks		**223**
Arch and Bridge Types		**224**
Bridge Construction		**225**
Exercises		**226**

Photocopying prohibited by law

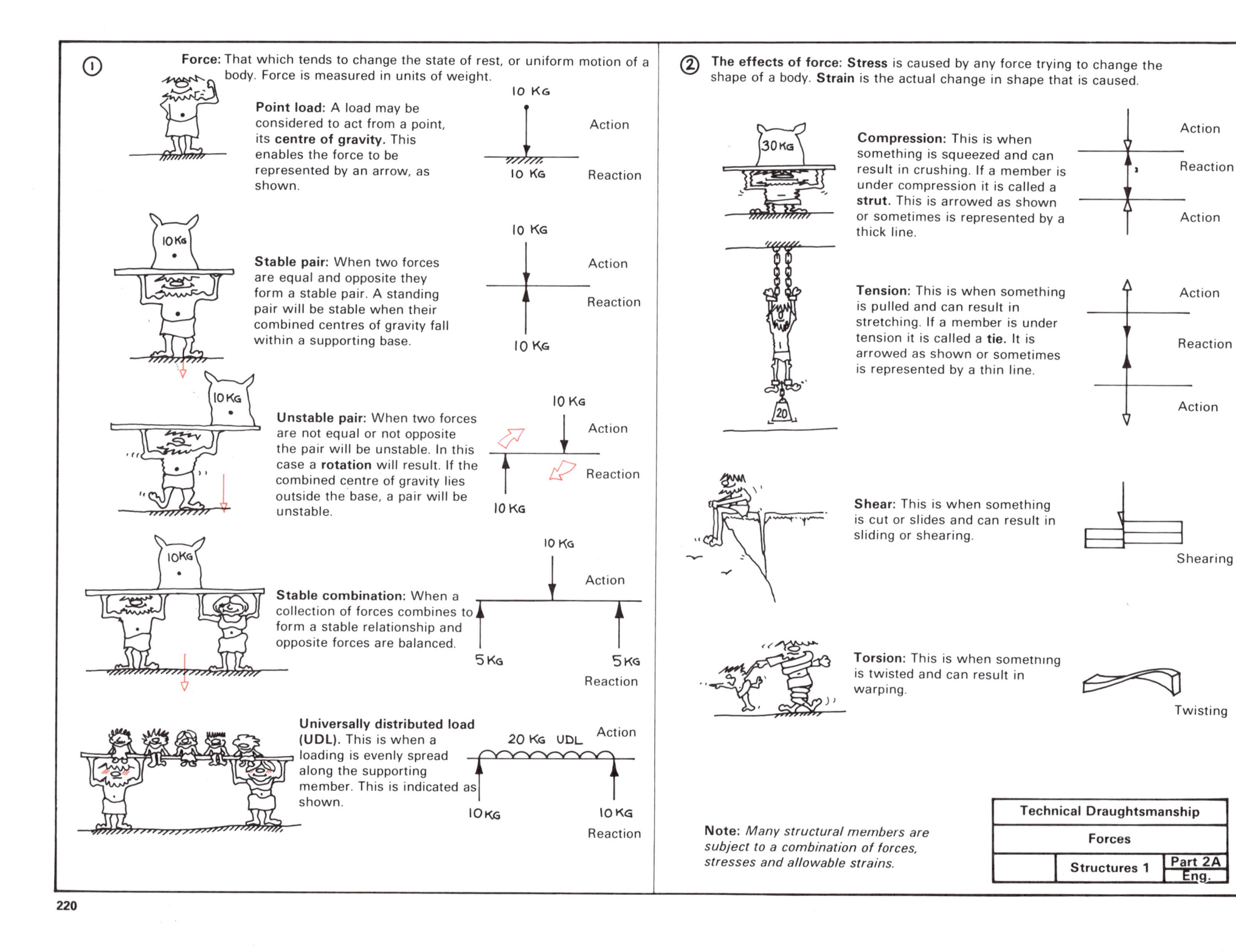

① **Force:** That which tends to change the state of rest, or uniform motion of a body. Force is measured in units of weight.

Point load: A load may be considered to act from a point, its **centre of gravity**. This enables the force to be represented by an arrow, as shown.

Stable pair: When two forces are equal and opposite they form a stable pair. A standing pair will be stable when their combined centres of gravity fall within a supporting base.

Unstable pair: When two forces are not equal or not opposite the pair will be unstable. In this case a **rotation** will result. If the combined centre of gravity lies outside the base, a pair will be unstable.

Stable combination: When a collection of forces combines to form a stable relationship and opposite forces are balanced.

Universally distributed load (UDL). This is when a loading is evenly spread along the supporting member. This is indicated as shown.

② **The effects of force: Stress** is caused by any force trying to change the shape of a body. **Strain** is the actual change in shape that is caused.

Compression: This is when something is squeezed and can result in crushing. If a member is under compression it is called a **strut**. This is arrowed as shown or sometimes is represented by a thick line.

Tension: This is when something is pulled and can result in stretching. If a member is under tension it is called a **tie**. It is arrowed as shown or sometimes is represented by a thin line.

Shear: This is when something is cut or slides and can result in sliding or shearing.

Torsion: This is when something is twisted and can result in warping.

Note: *Many structural members are subject to a combination of forces, stresses and allowable strains.*

Technical Draughtsmanship		
Forces		
	Structures 1	Part 2A Eng.

① Vectors

- Something with magnitude and no direction is called a **scalar** quantity, e.g. **5 Kg**.
- Something which has both magnitude and direction is called a **vector** quantity, e.g. **5 Kg. acting vertically downwards**.
- Vectors can be shown by straight lines. The direction can be indicated by an arrow and the magnitude by figures, or by scaling the length of the line, e.g.:

A move horizontally of **11 m** from **A** towards **B**.

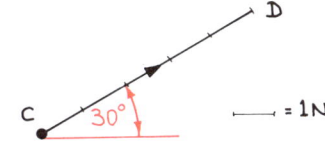

A force of **5 newtons** acting at an angle of **30°** with the horizontal, from **C** towards **D**. A **newton** is a force of **1 kg.m/s²**.

② Resultants

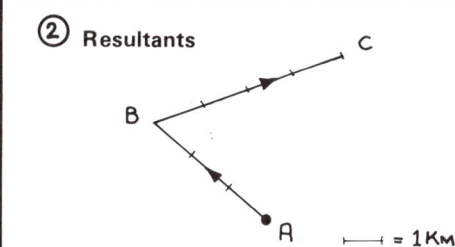

- If a man walks **3 km N.W.** from **A** to **B** and then **4 km E.N.E.** to **C**, his journey can be drawn using the two vectors shown.

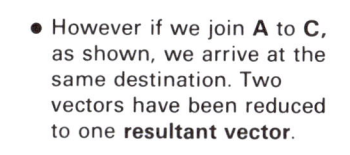

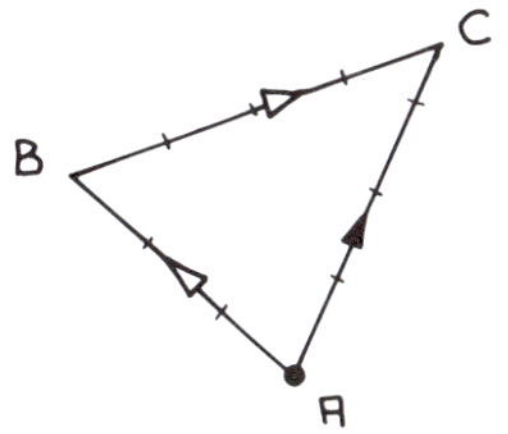

- However if we join **A** to **C**, as shown, we arrive at the same destination. Two vectors have been reduced to one **resultant vector**.

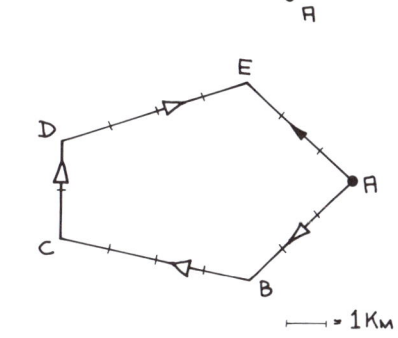

- This method can be used to find the resultant, or overall vector effect, of a number of vectors taken in sequence e.g. the resultant **AE** shown on the left.

Note how the resultant goes against the flow of the arrows.

③ The resolution of forces

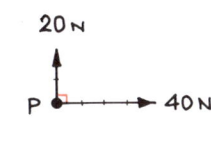

- Two forces act on point **P**. What is the overall effect of these forces? Imagine that the two forces happened one after the other. Find the resultant, as before.

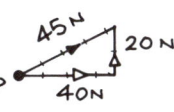

Force diagram 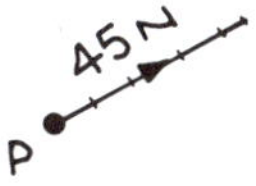 — Resultant force

- Very often the given vector information is not scaled. Scale it and proceed as above. Either force can be taken first.

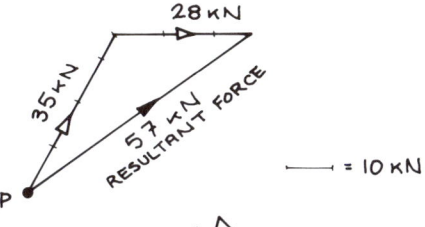

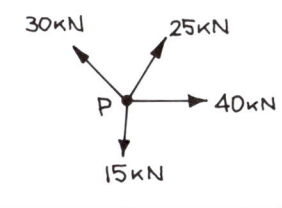

- This method is used to resolve quite complicated forces to a single vector, as shown. The force diagram produced can be called a **polygon of forces**.

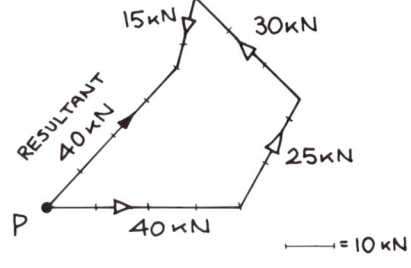

④ Two problems resolved

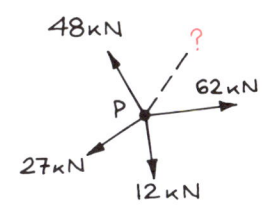

- Point **P** is stable and unmoved. Four forces are known to be acting on **P**. Find the fifth unknown force that keeps **P** stable. Set out each known vector to scale and draw the resultant, as shown.

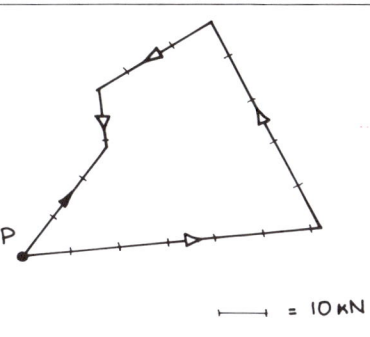

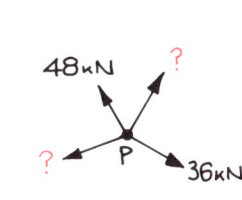

- Point **P** is stable. The lines of action of four forces are given but the magnitudes of two of these are unknown.

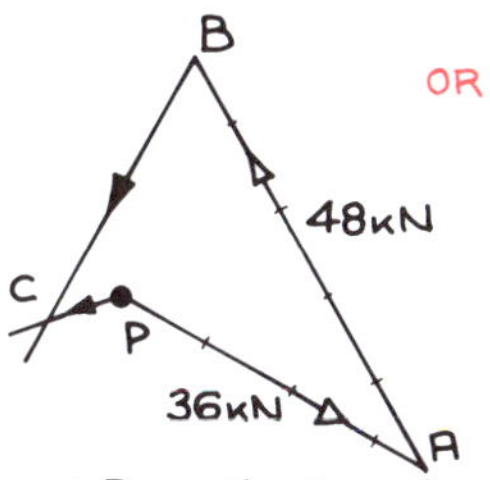

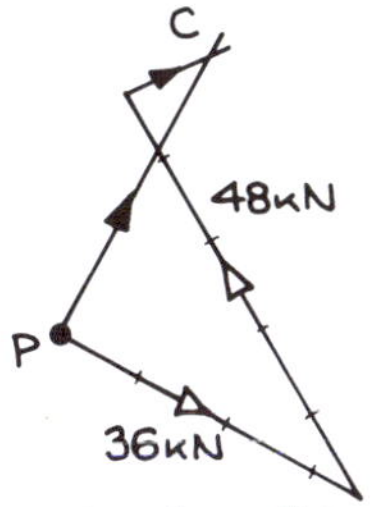

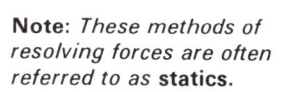

- Draw the two given vectors from **P** to **A** to **B**. Then, following the given directions, draw vectors from **P** and **B** to locate **C**, as shown. Measure the required magnitudes.

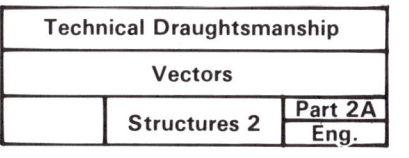

Note: *These methods of resolving forces are often referred to as* **statics**.

Technical Draughtsmanship
Vectors
Structures 2 — Part 2A Eng.

①

Force diagram

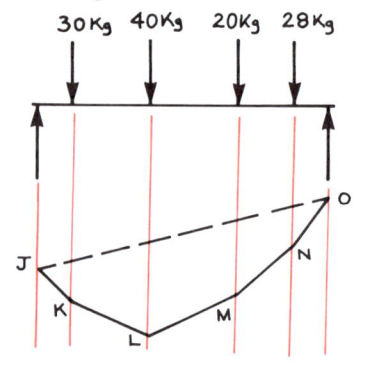

30Kg 40Kg 20Kg 28Kg

Bending moment diagram and funicular polygon.

②

Force diagram

30Kg 40Kg 20Kg 28Kg

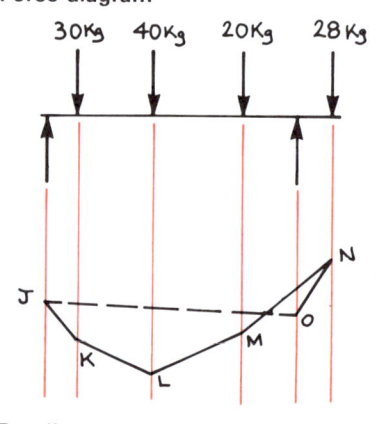

Bending moment diagram and funicular polygon

(a) Bending moment diagrams
- Draw the force diagram and extend each line of action downwards.
- To one side draw a vertical line **AE**, letting each segment be in scale to a downward force. **AB = 30, BC = 40,** etc.
- To one side of **AE** choose a point **Q** and join **Q** to **A, B, C, D** and **E**. This is called a **polar diagram**.
- Beneath the force diagram choose a point **J** and draw **JK** parallel to **AQ**, **KL** parallel to **BQ**, **LM** parallel to **CQ**, etc. This is a **bending moment diagram**.
- Joining **J** to **O** gives the resultant **JO**. By drawing **QF** parallel to **JO** the two supporting forces **AF** and **FE** can be calculated.
- The closed figure **JKLMNO** is called a **funicular polygon**.

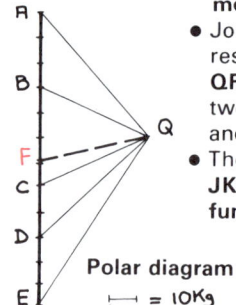

Polar diagram ⊢—⊣ = 10Kg

Note: Funicular means 'rope-like'. If you imagine the weights tied to a rope, you will see why this word is used.

(b) When some loads fall outside the supports
- Draw the force diagram and the polar diagram as outlined above.
- Choose a point **J** and draw **JK** parallel to **AQ**, **KL** parallel to **BQ**, **LM** parallel to **CQ** and **MN** parallel to **DQ**.
- As before **NO** is drawn parallel to **EQ**, but, in this case point **O** is before **N** and not beyond it.
- There is no other change necessary.

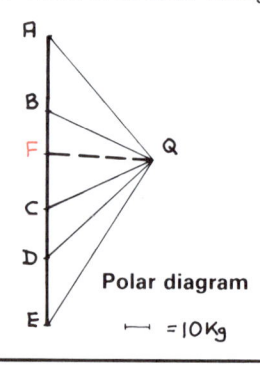

Polar diagram ⊢—⊣ = 10Kg

③

Force diagram

20kN 12kN 18kN 15kN

Bending moment diagram and funicular polygon

Shear force diagram:

Shear force diagrams
- In practice point **Q** is taken to the *left* of line **AE**. This turns the funicular polygon upside down and makes it a 'positive' progression and this simplifies some calculations.
- If you prefer, this can also be done by leaving **Q** to the right of the line and reversing the order of the segments, or by drawing the entire polar diagram on the other side of the force diagrams.

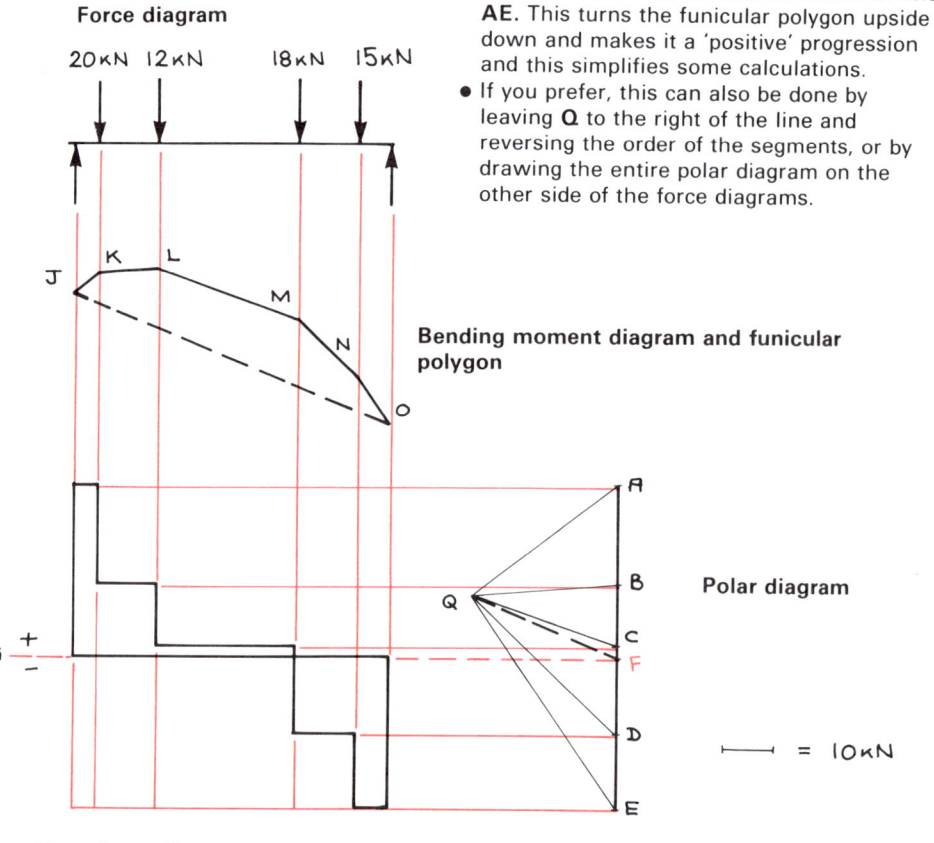

Polar diagram ⊢—⊣ = 10kN

- Extend the lines of force downwards.
- Draw the polar diagram to the right.
- Project across **A, B, C, D,** and **E** as shown.
- Draw **QF** parallel to the resultant **OJ**.
- Project **F** across towards **G**.
- Draw the shear force diagram, as shown above.
- Line **FG** is where one support 'takes over' from the other and is usually indexed as + and −, as indicated.

Notes: *These diagrams allow engineers to calculate the different stresses acting at any point on a beam. This information can then be used to design the beam for optimum performance.*

Technical Draughtsmanship
Beams
Structures 3 — Part 2A / Eng. H.

① Trusses

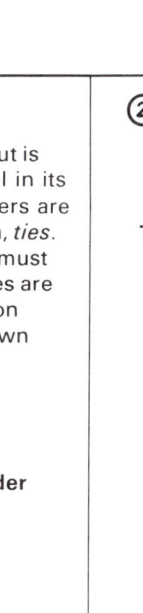

In a trussed girder, material is used only where it contributes strength. It is larger than a solid girder but is only a fraction of the weight and uses less material in its construction. In any trussed structure some members are under compression, *struts*, and others are in tension, *ties*. Struts must take pressure without bending and ties must stretch without snapping. In the diagrams heavy lines are struts and thin lines represent ties. The most common trusses are shown below.

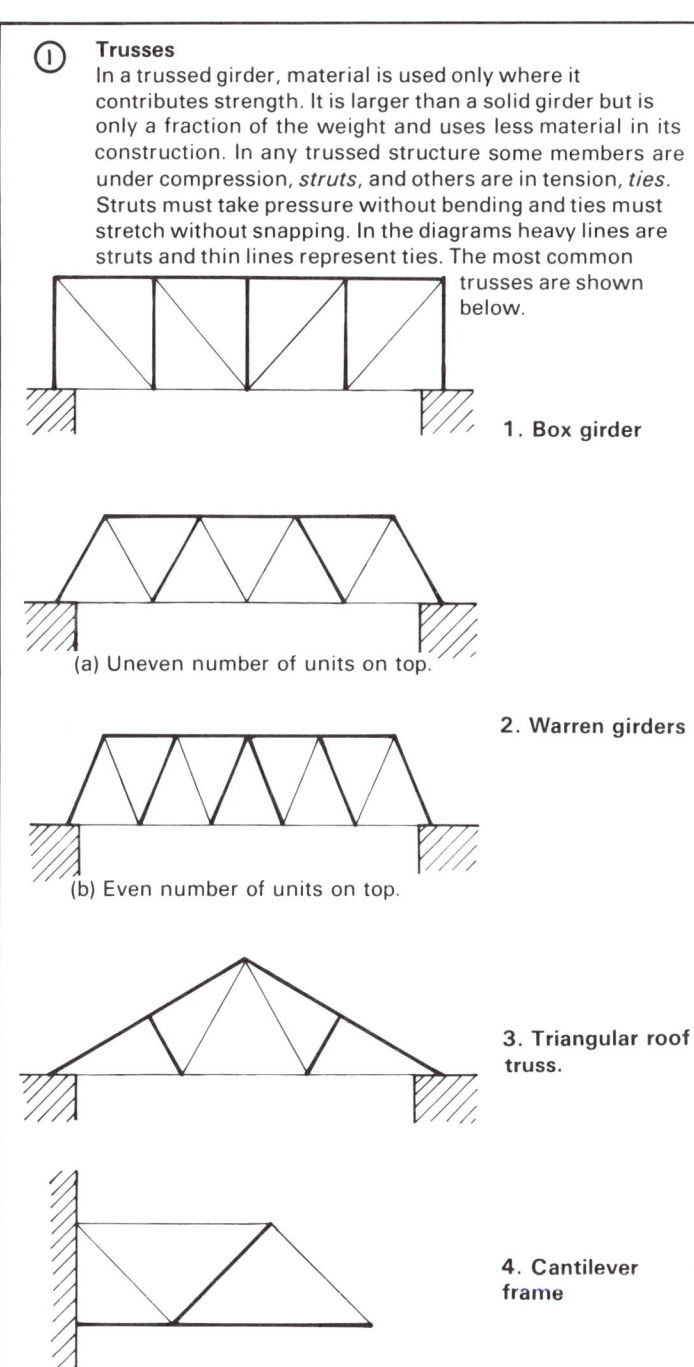

1. Box girder

2. Warren girders
(a) Uneven number of units on top.
(b) Even number of units on top.

3. Triangular roof truss.

4. Cantilever frame

② A framework analysed

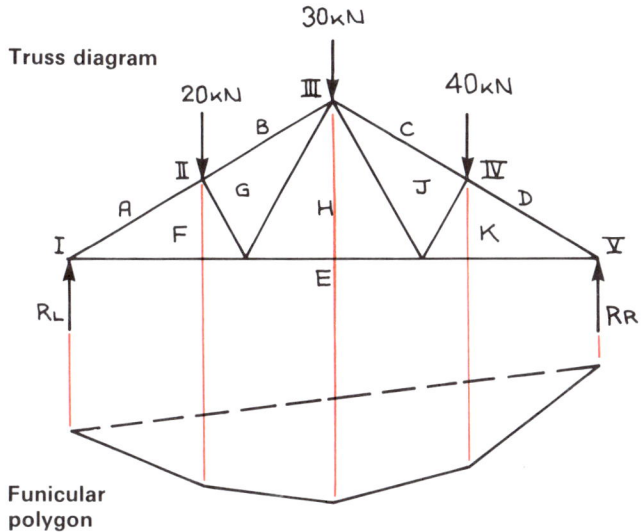

Truss diagram

Funicular polygon

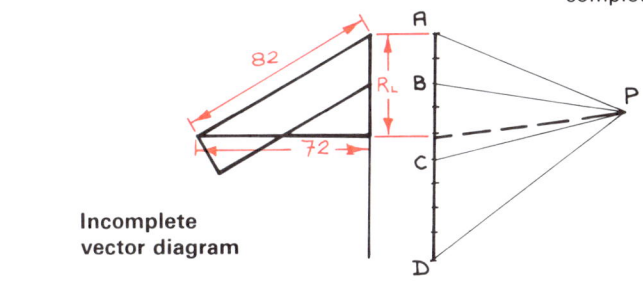

Incomplete vector diagram

$AE \Rightarrow R_L = 42 \text{ kN}$
$ED \Rightarrow R_R = 48 \text{ kN}$
Polar diagram
⊢──⊣ = 10 kN

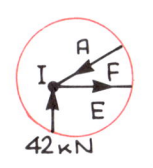

Force diagram of joint I

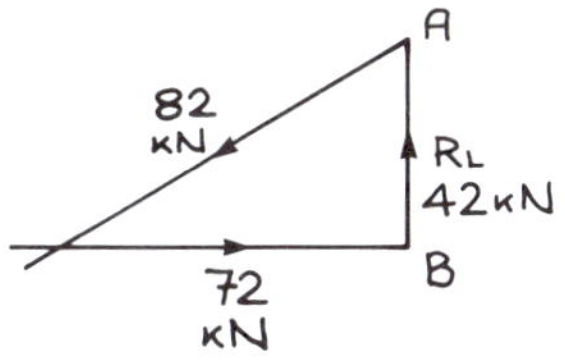

Vector diagram

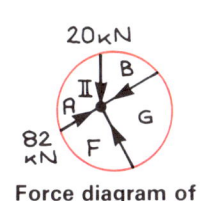

Force diagram of joint II

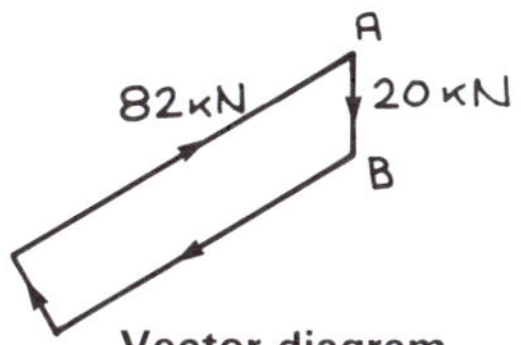

Vector diagram

- Draw the truss diagram.
- Starting from the lower left index the spaces **A, B, C** etc. in a clockwise manner, as shown. This method is known as **Bow's notation** and has definite advantages in complex analyses.
- Construct a polar diagram, as for a beam, see page **222**.
- Plot a funicular polygon and resultant, as on page **222**.
- Another diagram of great use to structural engineers is a **vector diagram**. This is usually drawn across from the polar diagram.
- Take joint **I** The three forces can be drawn in a triangle. As one side of this is **Rl** the triangle can be set out beside the polar diagram as shown.
- Plot the force diagram for joint **II** and, as one side is equal to **AE**, superimpose this on the last diagram.
- Continue for the other joints and complete the vector diagram.

Two individual vector diagrams.
Can you draw the others and complete the overall vector diagram? Make a table of the stress on each member. What would the shear force diagram for this truss look like?

Technical Draughtsmanship
Frameworks
Structures 4 — Part 2A — Eng. H.

223

① Arch types

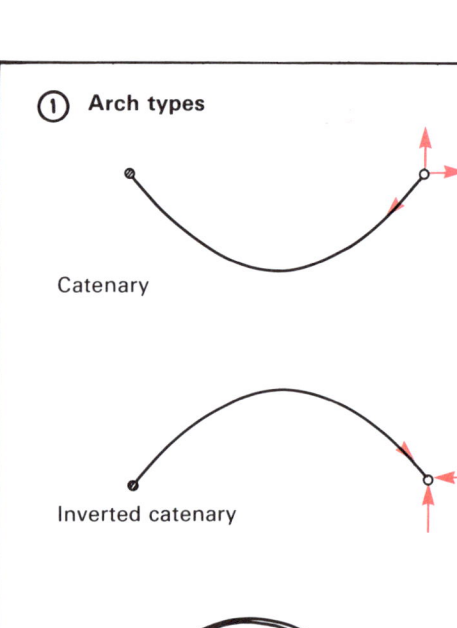

Suspension cable
Has only tensile stresses. This arch tends to pull inwards.

Catenary

Funicular arch
Cable turned upside down. Has only compressive stresses. This arch will tend to thrust outwards.

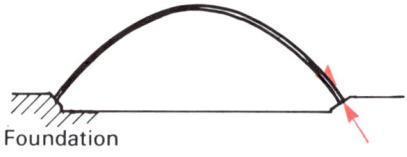

Inverted catenary

Foundation arch
The thrust is resisted by the foundations.

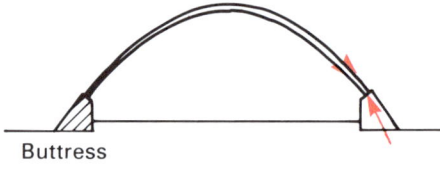

Foundation

Buttressed arch
A buttress takes the thrust.

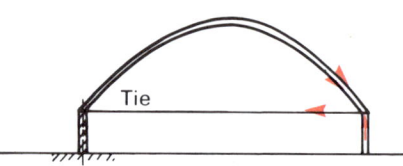

Buttress

Tied arch
A tie takes the thrust and a column takes the weight.

Tie

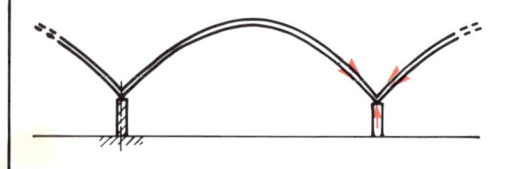

Continuous arch
The other arches take the thrust and a column takes the weight.

② Bridge types

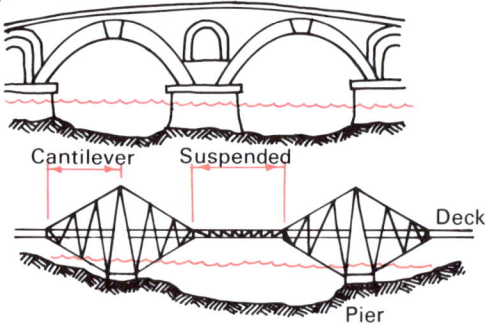

Masonry arch
- Heavy and expensive, this traditional method is little used today. The arches transfer the loads onto the piers.

- **Cantilever**
A frame about a pier supports the deck on either side. A short section can be suspended between two cantilevers, as here. The Forth Railway Bridge is like this and spans 520 m. Such bridges are not economical these days.

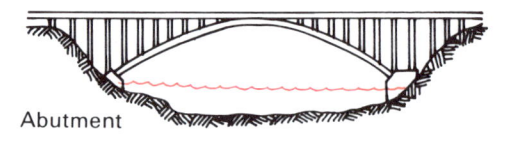

(Cantilever — Suspended — Deck — Pier)

- **Arch (A)**
The deck is supported by an arch. The arch pushes out against the abutments, taking a lot of the stress off the bridge itself. This is a medium span system.

Abutment

- **Arch (B)**
The deck is hung from an arch. These were very popular in the early twentieth century. Sydney Harbour Bridge spans 500 m. in this fashion

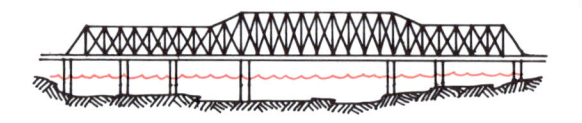

- **Continuous beam (truss)**
The deck is a single trussed girder, box or beam. This is the simplest and most rigid type. It is very economical for short spans.

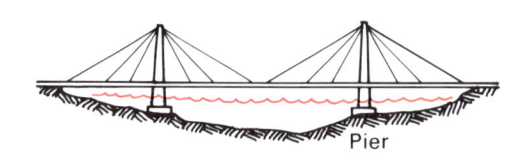

- **Cable-stayed**
The deck is stabilised by cables. These are now very popular. Easy to erect and elegant in design, these can span up to 500 m. They are also economical but must be carefully designed to avoid twisting under load.

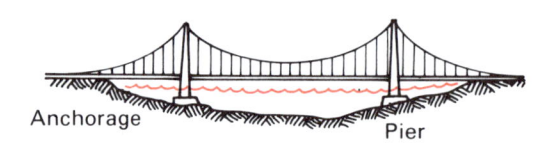

Pier

- **Suspension Bridges**
The deck is suspended from a cable. These can cover amazing spans but tend to be flexible and need to have stabilising features.

Anchorage — Pier

Note: *There are many bridges that are made of combinations or variations of these basic bridge types.*

Technical Draughtsmanship
Arch and Bridge Types
Structures 5 — Part 2A Eng.

① Foundations

Piles
If the material under the site is weak a firm foundation can be built on piles driven deep into the subsoil, or into rock.

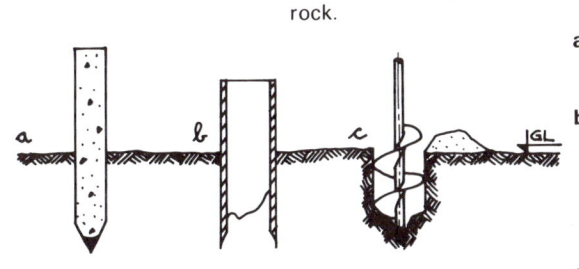

a. A steel or concrete pile is driven straight in, using a mechanical pile driver.
b. A steel cylinder is driven in. Then the soil is taken out of the cylinder and replaced by reinforced concrete. The cylinder is removed for re-use.
c. A drill or auger is used to make a hole, which is then filled with concrete.

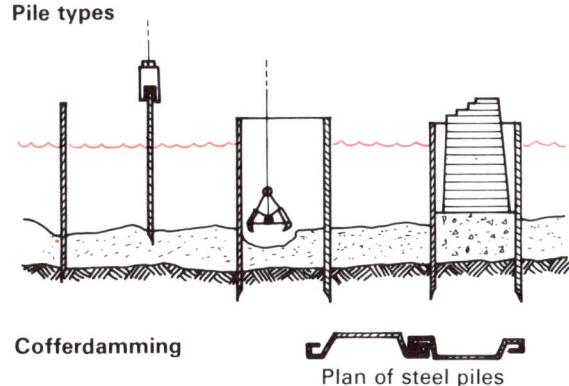

Pile types

Cofferdams
A cofferdam is a temporary watertight box made up of interlocking steel piles. These are pile-driven into the river bed. The mud is then scooped out and men can go in and build up the piers. A pump is needed to keep the inside dry and the piles are pulled out when the pier is finished.

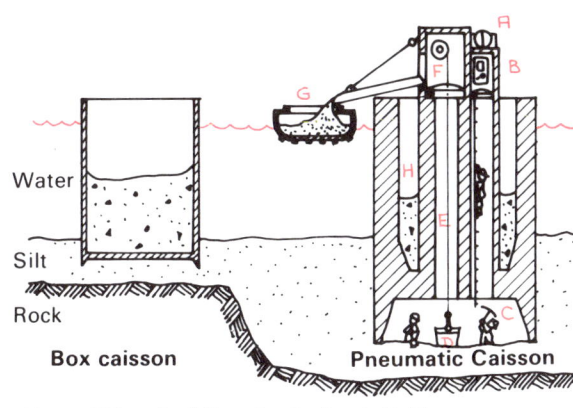

Cofferdamming

Plan of steel piles

Caissons
Caisson is the French word for a chamber. There are two main types. A box caisson is filled with concrete and carefully allowed to sink to the bottom. In a pneumatic caisson men dig out the silt and the caisson is carefully sunk, as shown in the diagram.

A: Compressed-air pump.
B: Workers' airlock.
C: Working chamber.
D: Buckets.
E: Muck shaft.
F: Hoist and airlock.
G: Barge.
H: Concrete to sink the caisson

Box caisson   **Pneumatic Caisson**

Note: *When building the St. Louis Bridge a pneumatic caisson was used to reach the bedrock. This rock was found 30 metres down after going through 4 metres of water and digging out 26 metres of silt!*

② Superstructures

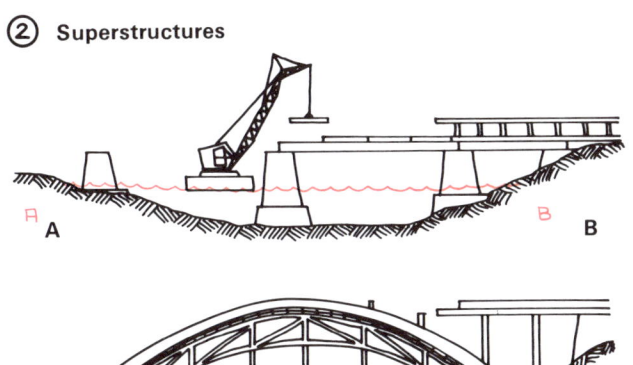

Continuous beam bridge
The piers are completed and then a land-crane, or a floating crane hoists prefabricated units into position. Sometimes the concrete is cast on the site using temporary formwork.

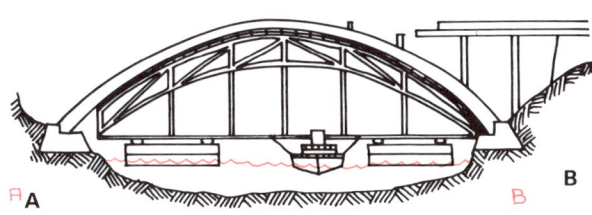

Continuous arch
A temporary wooden, or steel, arch is floated into position. The bridge is built, sets and then the formwork is taken out. The deck is built onto the arch.

Steel arch
The abutments are built and temporary anchors set into the ground. This holds the structure as the arch is built up from each side. Hangers are then dropped from the arch and the deck is fixed to these.

Suspension bridges
The towers are built first. Then a temporary cable is strung between them and secured to each riverbank. On this cable a pulley system operates and hoists cable threads, one at a time, until the full cable is built up. Then this can be used to lift sections of the deck into place.

Cable-stayed bridges (not shown)
These are built in a manner very similar to suspension bridges. In one case, in Düsseldorf, the cable-stayed bridge was built up-river, used while the old bridge was demolished and then floated down to its final position, all 12,500 tonnes of it!

Technical Draughtsmanship		
Bridge Construction		
Structures 6	Part 2A Eng.	

*All linear measurements are in millimetres and all forces are measured in kilonewtons (**kN**).*

Questions

1. Three forces act to keep a point **P** stable. Two of these are given. Find the third force, i.e. the resultant of these two.

2. Plot a fourth force that will balance the three given forces and make the point **P** stable.

3. Plot another force that will balance the given forces.

4. If point **P** is stable what will the two unknown forces be?

5. Draw a series of sketches and diagrams to show how the forces listed on page **220** would act on an elastic band.

6. Draw the bending moment diagram for each of the beams shown.

7. Construct a funicular polygon and a shear force diagram for each of the beams shown.

8. Analyse fully each frame shown.

Technical Draughtsmanship
Exercises
Structures 7 — Part 2A Eng.

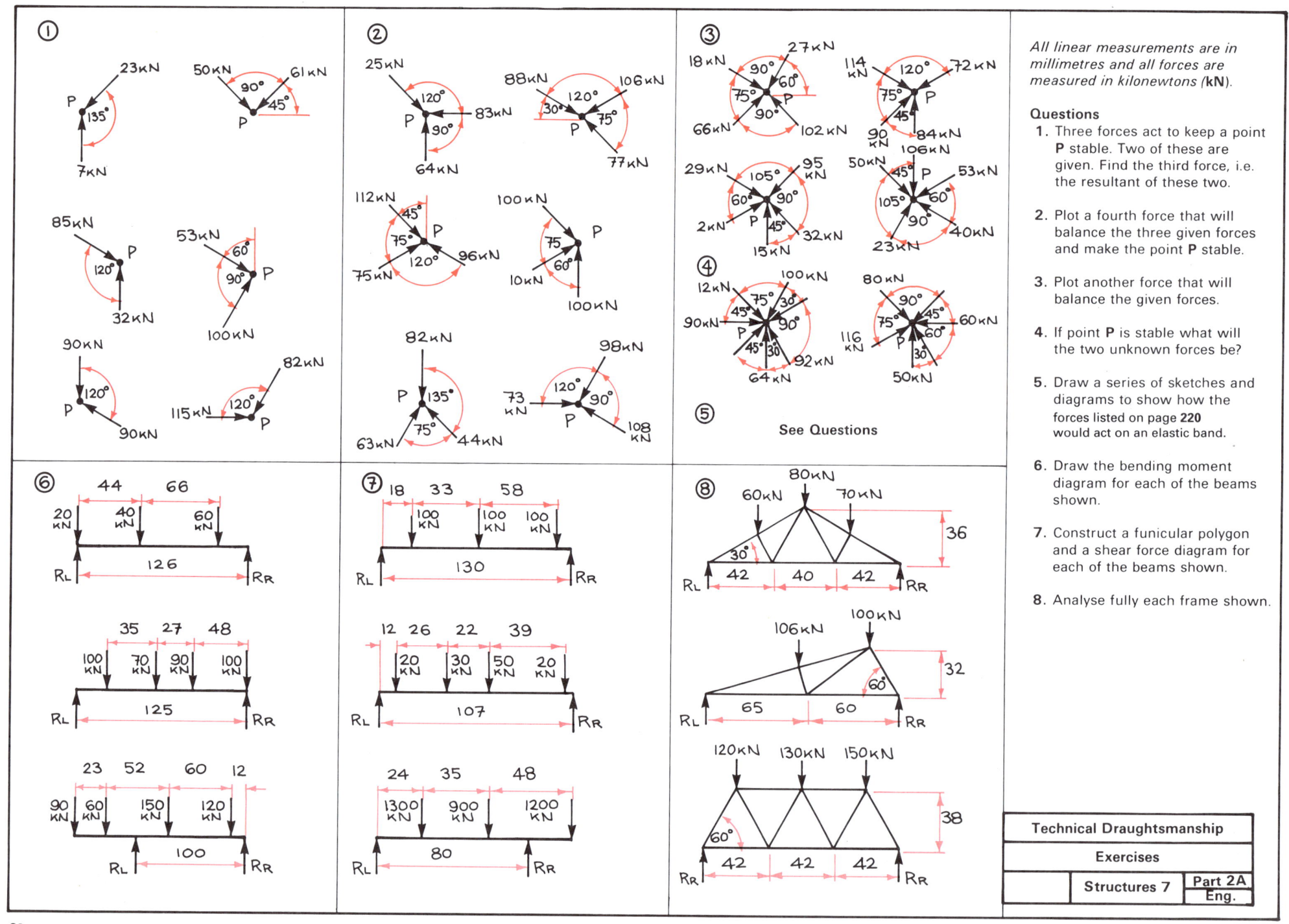

PART 2A

CHAPTER 19
FABRICATION

Fabrication is the method of joining materials. There are many methods of fabrication and some of the main methods are outlined here.

CONTENTS
Screw Threads	*Page* **228**
Nuts and Bolts	**229**
Bends and Seams	**230**
Welding and Riveting	**231**
Steel Sections	**232**
Roof Truss	**233**
Exercises	**234**

① Screw thread terms

A thread is a helical groove cut into a cylinder, or in a cylindrical hole. Threads may be right- or left-handed, and may be single- or multi-start.

Right hand / Left hand

Single start: LEAD = P
Two start: LEAD = 2P

② Head types and their abbreviations

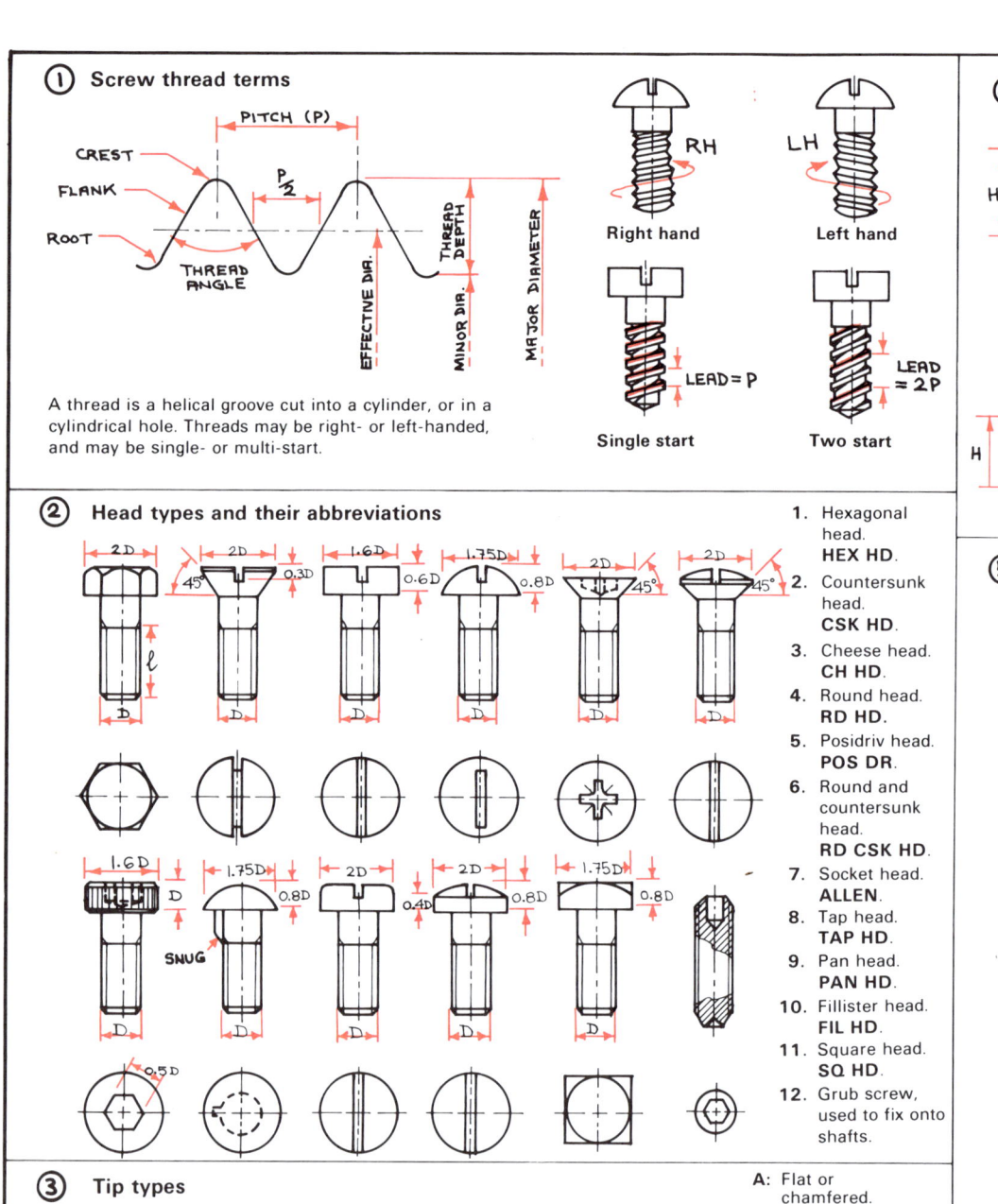

1. Hexagonal head. **HEX HD**.
2. Countersunk head. **CSK HD**.
3. Cheese head. **CH HD**.
4. Round head. **RD HD**.
5. Posidriv head. **POS DR**.
6. Round and countersunk head. **RD CSK HD**.
7. Socket head. **ALLEN**.
8. Tap head. **TAP HD**.
9. Pan head. **PAN HD**.
10. Fillister head. **FIL HD**.
11. Square head. **SQ HD**.
12. Grub screw, used to fix onto shafts.

③ Tip types

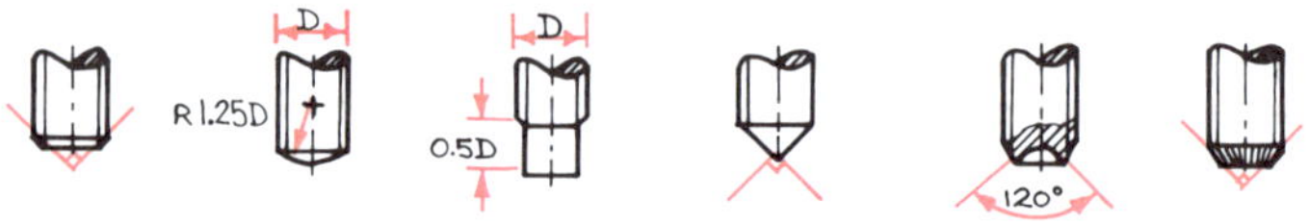

A: Flat or chamfered.
B: Rounded.
C: Dog end, to fit a slot.
D: Cone, to bite into shafts.
E: Cup.
F: Serrated to cut as it goes.

④ ISO threads

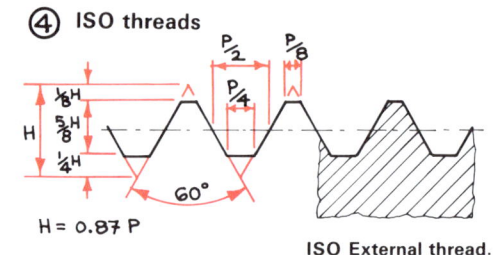

$H = 0.87 P$

ISO External thread.
ISO Internal thread. 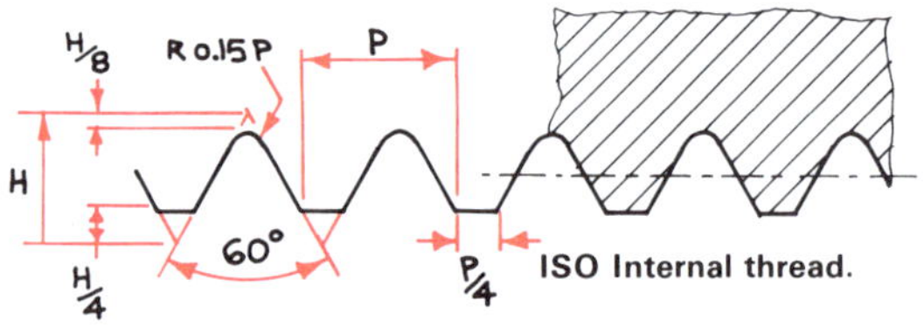

ISO is the International Standards Organisation.
Metric threads are specified as follows:
M 12 x 1.75 - 6g

Where:
M = Metric
12 = Major diameter
1.75 = Pitch
6g = Tolerance class (external)
All dimensions are in millimetres.

Note: See chapter 23 for details of tolerances.

⑤ Some other thread types

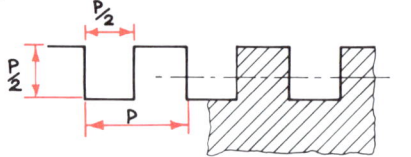

Square thread
Theoretically ideal, these threads are difficult to make and run satisfactorily.

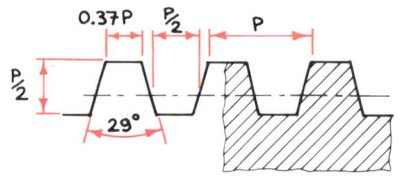

Acme thread
A stronger and more easily manufactured thread.

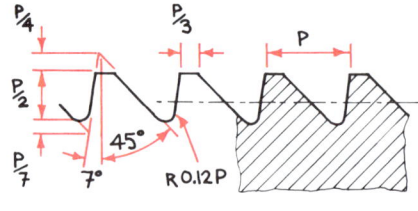

Buttress thread
This thread is used when power is to be transmitted in one direction only, e.g. in a car jack.

Note: These examples have been confined to parallel threads. Taper threads are cut from a conical shape. They are similar in terminology, with the slope being an added specification.

Technical Draughtsmanship
Screw Threads
Fabrication 1 — Part 2A — Eng.

228

① **To draw a hexagonal bolt and nut.** Here the nut is taken at right angles to the view of the bolt.

Stage 1 — 1.75 D, 0.8 D, OVERALL LENGTH, 1 MM, DEPTH OF THREAD, 1 MM, D, 1.5 D, 1 MM, 0.75 D, 1.5 D
- Set out the basic proportions.

Stage 2 — 60°, 60°, C₂, C₃, C₁, 45°, 60°
- Find centres C₁, C₂ and C₃.

Stage 3 — 30°, 60°, LENGTH OF THREAD, 30° TANGENT
- Complete the drawing, as shown above.

② **Basic assemblies**

Set bolt · Nut and bolt · Stud · Nut and stud

Note: *A stud is normally a piece of round bar that is threaded at both ends.*

③ **Locking devices**

Internal Star · Split · Taper · Cotter

0.8 D, 0.5 D

Lock nut · Washer · Spring washer · Pin

Slotted nut · Castle nut · Wiles lock nut · Simmonds lock nut with a plastic ring.

Ring nut · Ring nut at edge · Tab · Tab at edge

Locking plates: There are many types of plates that fit against or over a nut to lock it in position. The plate may be held by a dowel or grubscrew. Some plates are designed to secure more than one nut.

Note: *Shafts and keyways will be dealt with on page 273.*

Technical Draughtsmanship
Nuts and Bolts
Fabrication 2 — Part 2A Eng.

229

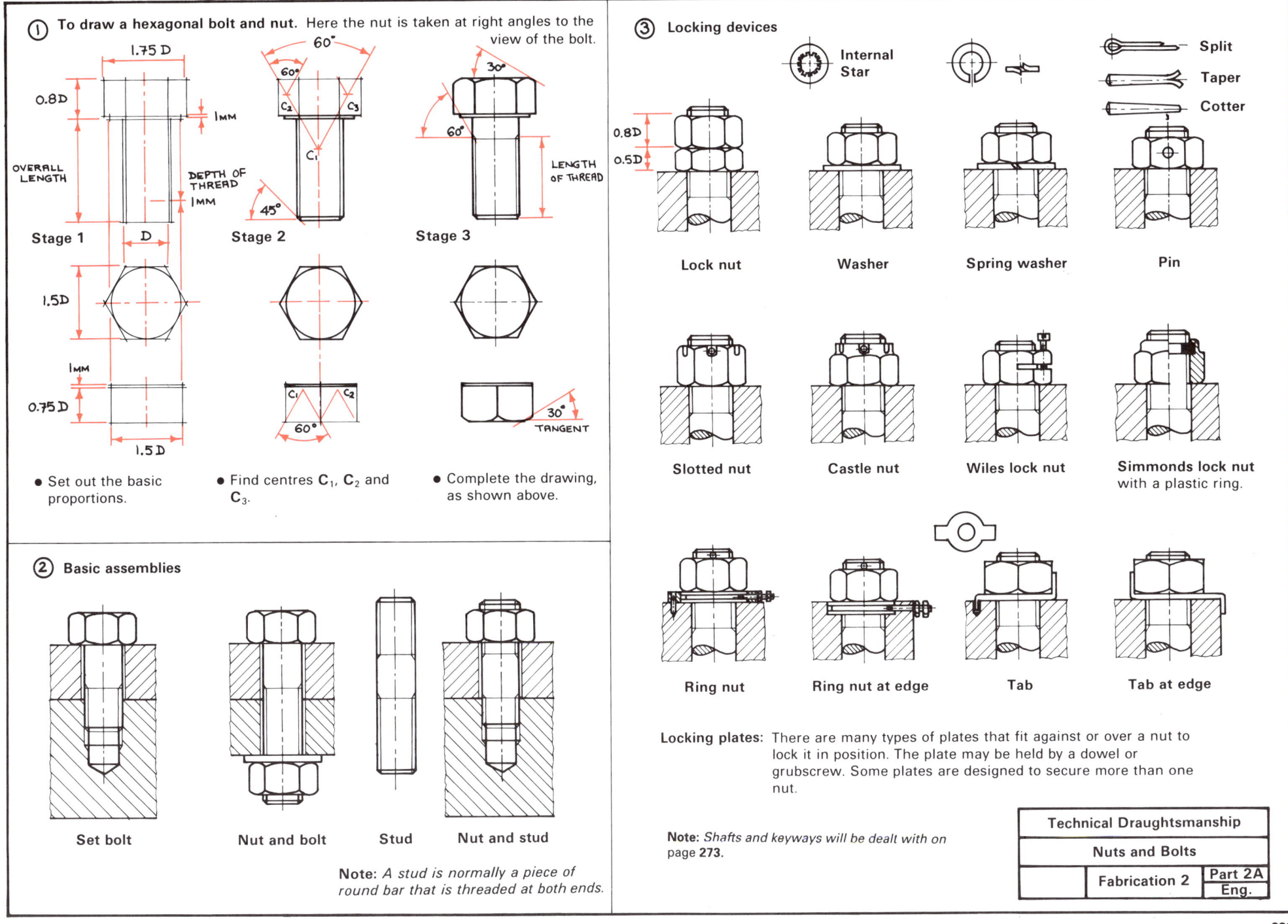

① Bend allowances

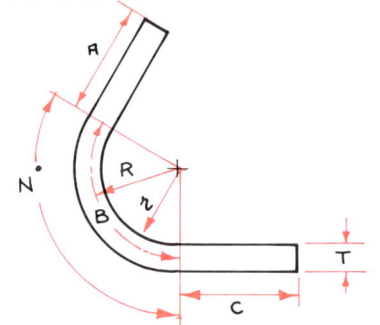

The stretchout = **A** + **B** + **C** where **A** and **C** are straight and **B** is taken **0.45T** from the inside of the bend.

B = (0.0175 R) × N
B = (0.0175r + 0.008T) × N

B: Bending allowance
T: Thickness.
N: The number of degrees in the bend.
r: Inside bend radius.
R: Radius of neutral layer.

- In sheet metalwork allowance must be made for bends. When metal is bent it is compressed on the inside and stretched on the outside. There is, however, a **neutral layer** that is not distorted. This layer **B** is usually taken to be **0.45** of the thickness of the metal measured from the *inside* of the bend.
- The minimum radius of the bend is usually equal to the thickness of the metal.

② Example 1

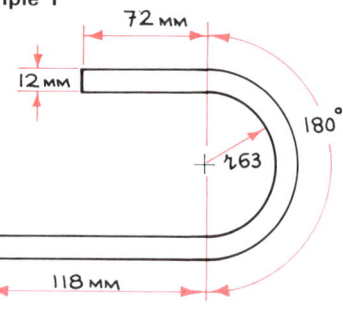

Neutral layer = **0.45 × T**
= 0.45 × 12 ⇨ **5.4**
Therefore R = **r** + **5.4** = 63 + 5.4
= **68.4**

Using the formula
B = **(0.0175 R) × N** we get:
B = (0.0175 × 68.4) × 180
= (1.197) × 180
= **215.46 mm**
Stretchout of the whole piece
is 118 + 215.46 + 72
⇨ **405.46 mm.**

③ Example 2

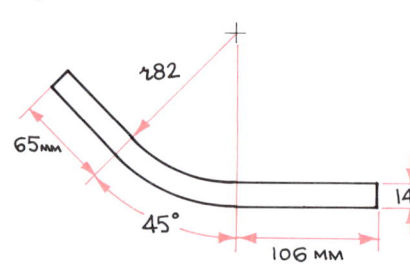

Using the formula
B = (0.0175 r + 0.008T) × N
we get:
B = [(0.0175 × 82) + (0.008 × 14)] × 45
= (1.435 + .112) × 45
= (1.547) × 45
= **69.615 mm**
So, the total stretchout is
65 + 69.615 + 106
⇨ **240.615 mm.**

④ Types of commonly used bends in sheet metalworking

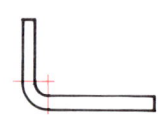

Minimum inside radius = T.

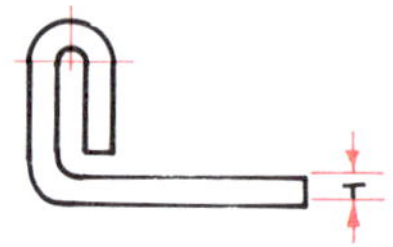

Single flange
Sharp, but economical.

Double flange
Smoother edge.

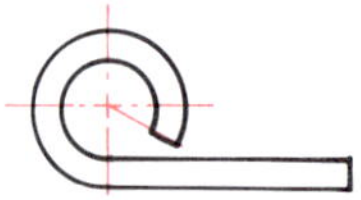

Rolled edge
Very smooth edge.

Single hem
Avoids sharp edge.

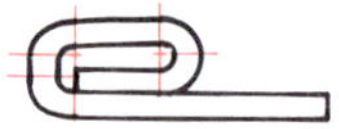

Double hem
Stronger edge.

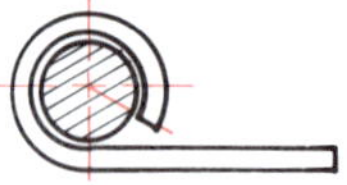

Wired edge
Strengthens an edge.

Plain flat seam
Not very secure, but economical.

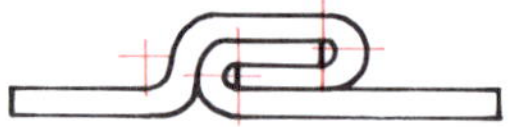

Grooved seam (external)
More secure.

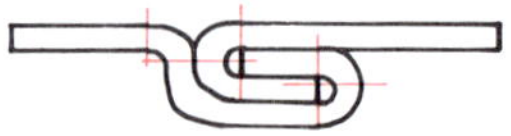

Grooved seam (internal)
Used when a smooth exterior is needed.

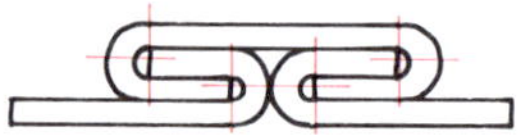

Double grooved joint
Allows for dismantling.

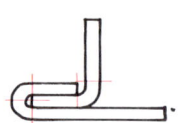

Paned-down joint
Not very secure, but economical.

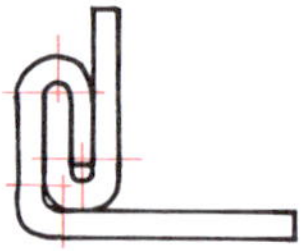

Knocked-up joint
More secure.

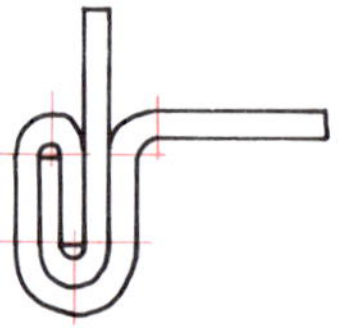

Rebated knocked-up joint
Secure joint used in enclosed forms.

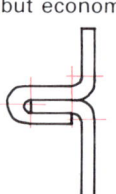

Paned-down seam
Simple, but not very secure.

Pittsburgh lock joint
Secure machine-made joint.

Note: See Chapter 12 for details of development techniques.

Technical Draughtsmanship		
Bends and Seams		
Fabrication 3	Part 2A	Eng.

① Rivet Head Types

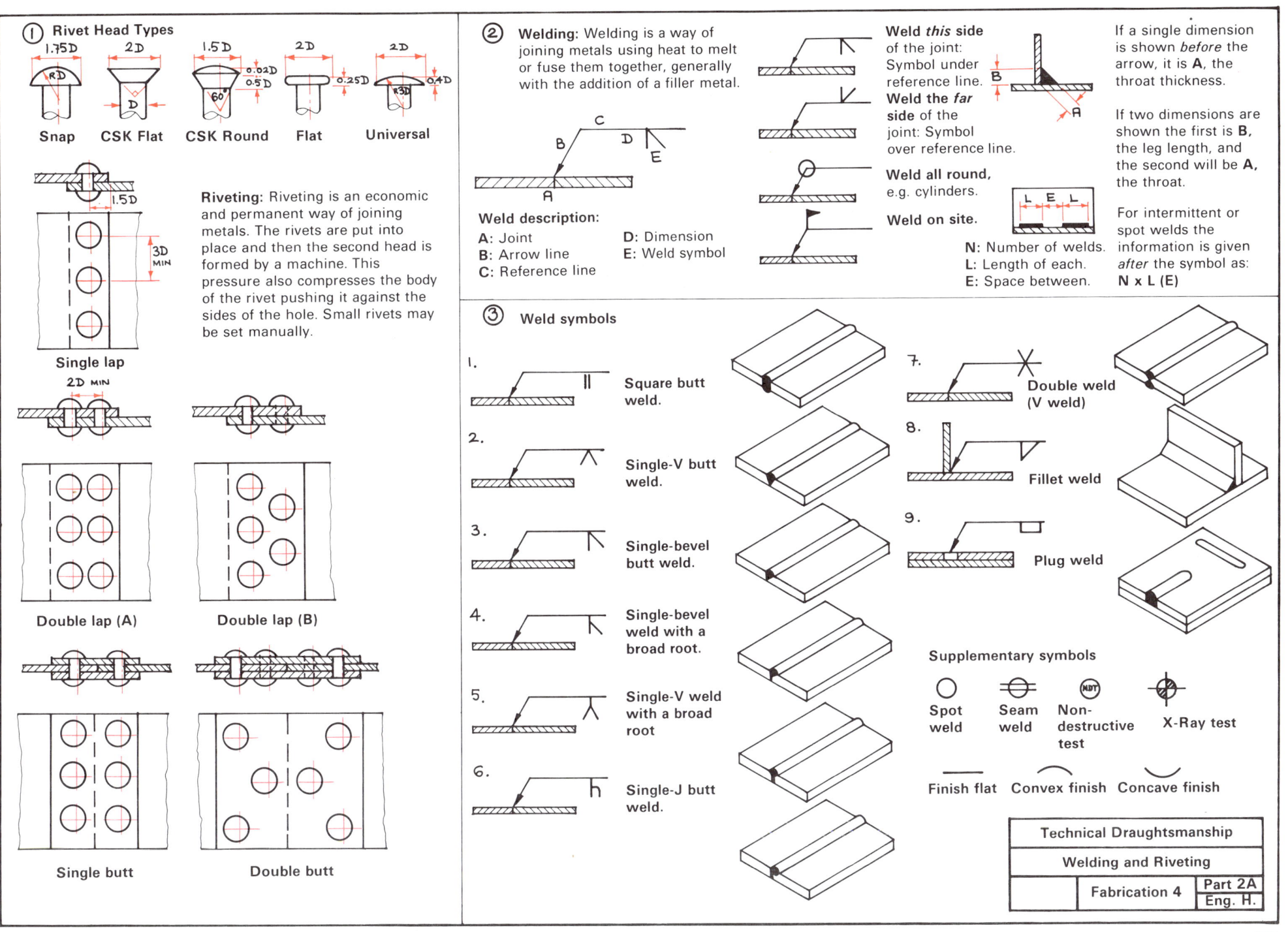

- **Snap** — 1.75D, RD
- **CSK Flat** — 2D, 60°, D
- **CSK Round** — 1.5D, 0.02D / 0.5D, 60°
- **Flat** — 2D, 0.25D
- **Universal** — 2D, R3D, 0.4D

Riveting: Riveting is an economic and permanent way of joining metals. The rivets are put into place and then the second head is formed by a machine. This pressure also compresses the body of the rivet pushing it against the sides of the hole. Small rivets may be set manually.

- **Single lap** (1.5D, 3D MIN)
- **Double lap (A)** (2D MIN)
- **Double lap (B)**
- **Single butt**
- **Double butt**

② Welding

Welding is a way of joining metals using heat to melt or fuse them together, generally with the addition of a filler metal.

Weld description:
- **A:** Joint
- **B:** Arrow line
- **C:** Reference line
- **D:** Dimension
- **E:** Weld symbol

Weld this side of the joint: Symbol under reference line.

Weld the far side of the joint: Symbol over reference line.

Weld all round, e.g. cylinders.

Weld on site.

- **N:** Number of welds.
- **L:** Length of each.
- **E:** Space between.

If a single dimension is shown *before* the arrow, it is **A**, the throat thickness.

If two dimensions are shown the first is **B**, the leg length, and the second will be **A**, the throat.

For intermittent or spot welds the information is given *after* the symbol as: **N x L (E)**

③ Weld symbols

1. Square butt weld.
2. Single-V butt weld.
3. Single-bevel butt weld.
4. Single-bevel weld with a broad root.
5. Single-V weld with a broad root.
6. Single-J butt weld.
7. Double weld (V weld)
8. Fillet weld
9. Plug weld

Supplementary symbols

- Spot weld
- Seam weld
- Non-destructive test (NDT)
- X-Ray test
- Finish flat
- Convex finish
- Concave finish

Technical Draughtsmanship
Welding and Riveting
Fabrication 4 — Part 2A — Eng. H.

① Rolled steel sections

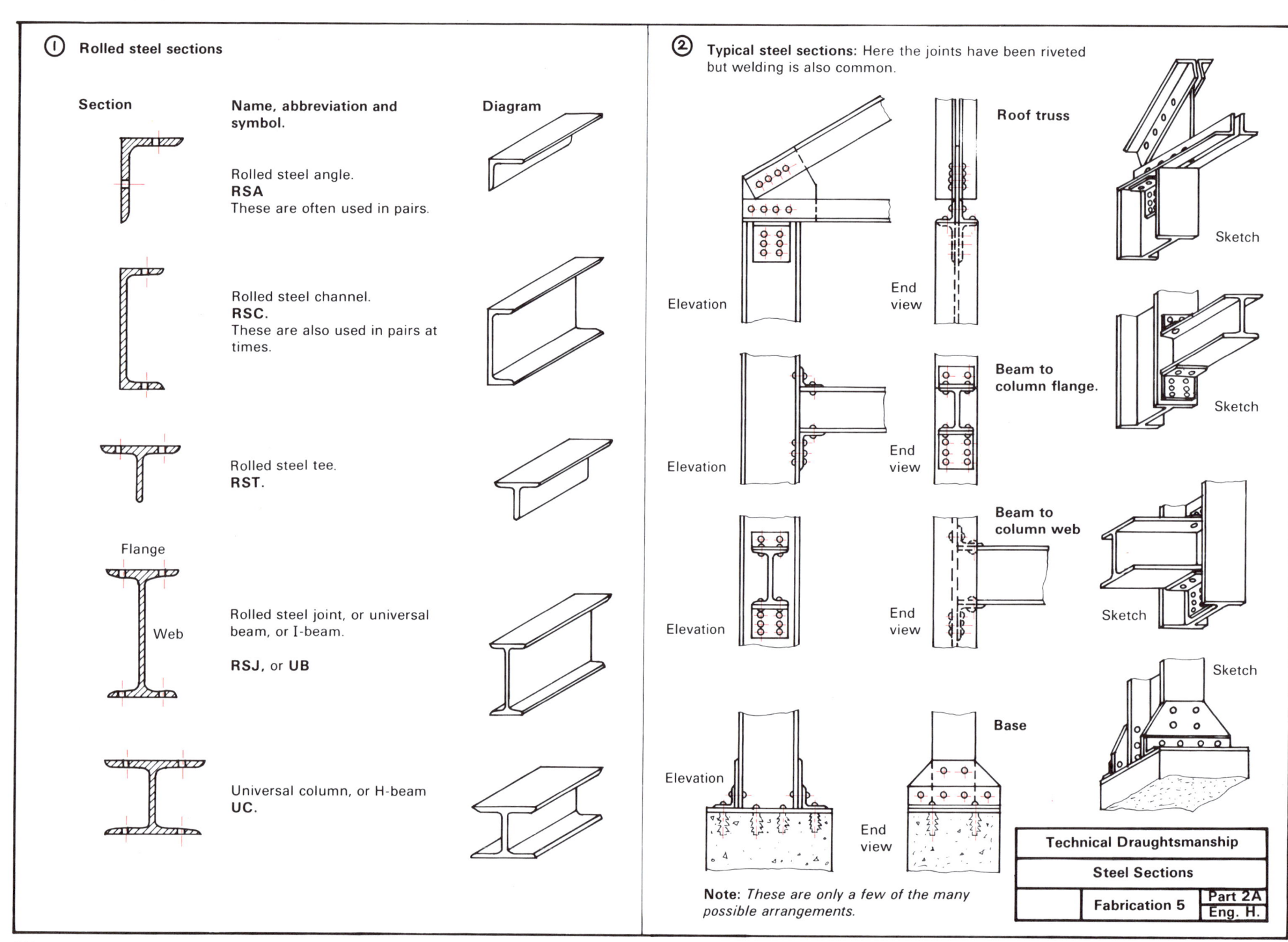

Section	Name, abbreviation and symbol.	Diagram
	Rolled steel angle. **RSA** These are often used in pairs.	
	Rolled steel channel. **RSC.** These are also used in pairs at times.	
	Rolled steel tee. **RST.**	
Flange / Web	**Rolled steel joint, or universal beam, or I-beam.** **RSJ, or UB**	
	Universal column, or H-beam **UC.**	

② Typical steel sections:
Here the joints have been riveted but welding is also common.

Roof truss — Elevation / End view / Sketch

Beam to column flange. — Elevation / End view / Sketch

Beam to column web — Elevation / End view / Sketch

Base — Elevation / End view / Sketch

Note: *These are only a few of the many possible arrangements.*

Technical Draughtsmanship
Steel Sections
Fabrication 5 — Part 2A — Eng. H.

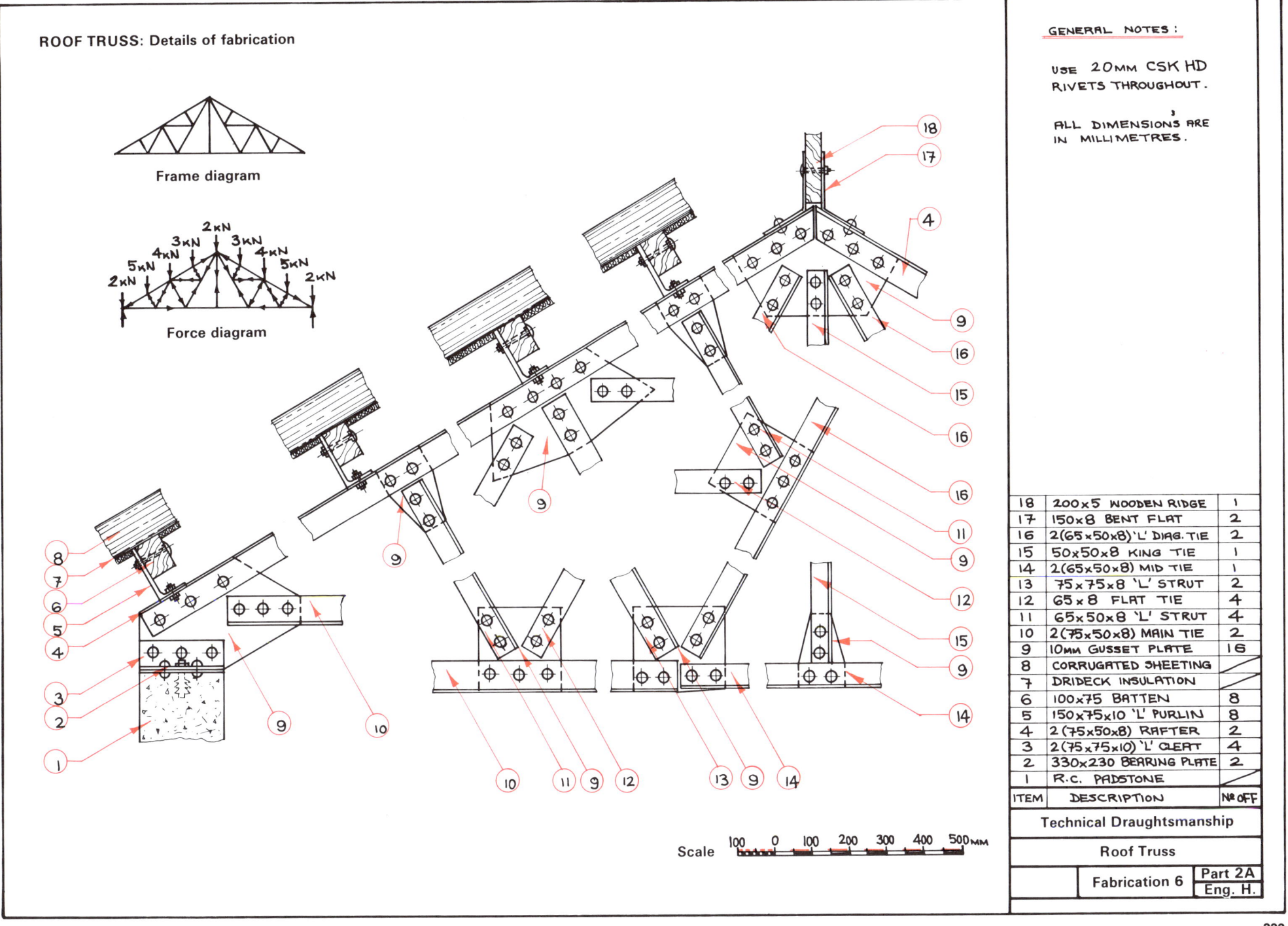

ROOF TRUSS: Details of fabrication

Frame diagram

Force diagram

GENERAL NOTES:

USE 20mm CSK HD RIVETS THROUGHOUT.

ALL DIMENSIONS ARE IN MILLIMETRES.

18	200×5 WOODEN RIDGE	1
17	150×8 BENT FLAT	2
16	2(65×50×8) 'L' DIAG. TIE	2
15	50×50×8 KING TIE	1
14	2(65×50×8) MID TIE	1
13	75×75×8 'L' STRUT	2
12	65×8 FLAT TIE	4
11	65×50×8 'L' STRUT	4
10	2(75×50×8) MAIN TIE	2
9	10mm GUSSET PLATE	16
8	CORRUGATED SHEETING	
7	DRIDECK INSULATION	
6	100×75 BATTEN	8
5	150×75×10 'L' PURLIN	8
4	2(75×50×8) RAFTER	2
3	2(75×75×10) 'L' CLEAT	4
2	330×230 BEARING PLATE	2
1	R.C. PADSTONE	
ITEM	DESCRIPTION	Nº OFF

Technical Draughtsmanship

Roof Truss

Fabrication 6 — Part 2A — Eng. H.

①

(a) M12 × 1.75 RH two-start CSK HD bolt with dog end, length of 50 mm and thread length of 35 mm.

(b) M20 × 2.50 LH single-start CH HD bolt with rounded end, length of 75 mm, thread length of 50 mm and slotted nut with split pin, all set into a steel plate of thickness 50 mm.

②

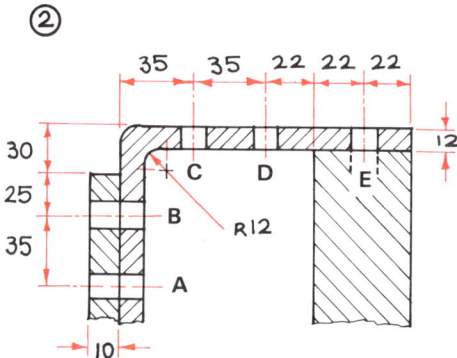

A: M16 × 2.00 SQ HD bolt with locknut on the inside.
B: M20 × 2.50 FIL HD bolt with tab on outside.
C: M20 × 1.50 ALLEN bolt with split pin on inside.
D: M24 × 3.00 HEX HD bolt with nut on inside.
E: M16 × 2.00 stud of length 22 mm and thread length 10 mm with ring nut at edge.

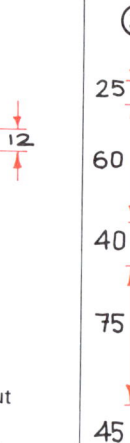

③

Metal thickness: **8 mm**

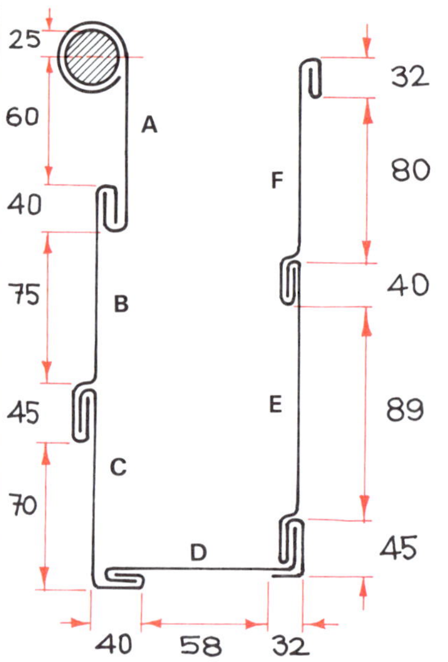

④

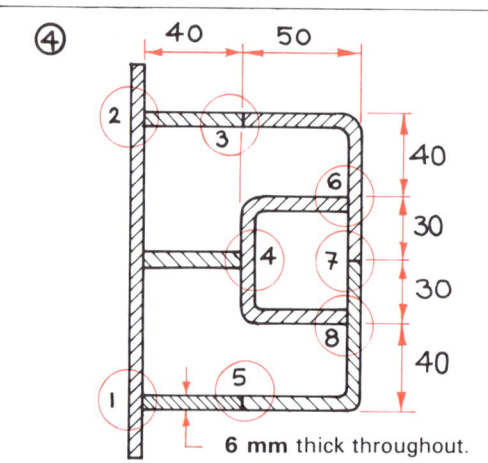

6 mm thick throughout.

Welds
1: Square butt far side.
2: Fillet this side.
3: Single V this side.
4: Broad root single bevel far side.
5: Double fillet.
6: Double J.
7: V this side and bevel far side.
8: J far side and V butt this side.

⑤

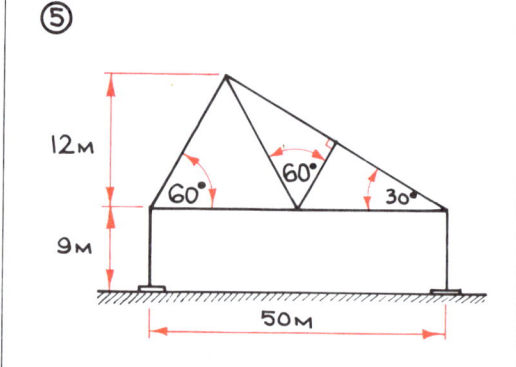

⑥

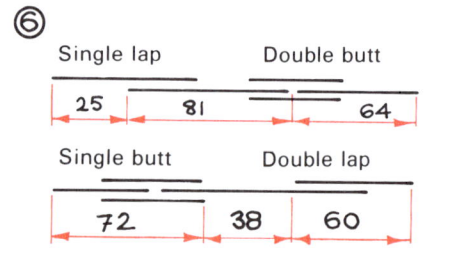

Single lap — Double butt — Single butt — Double lap

⑦

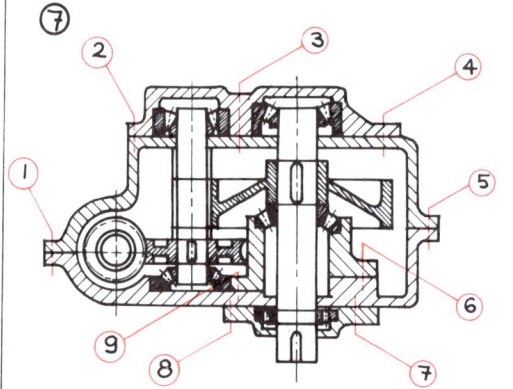

1: HEX nut.
2: ALLEN setscrew.
3: HEX setscrew.
4: CH HD setscrew.
5: Tab washer on HEX nut.
6: RD HD setscrew.
7: Stud with castle nut.
8: Stud with Wiles lock-nut.
9: CSK HD setscrew.

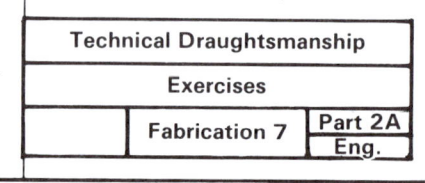

All measurements are in millimetres.

Questions

1. Sketch each of the fastenings as specified.

2. Sketch, in good proportion, the fastenings indicated.

3. Draw each piece of metal and calculate its stretch-out length.

4. Draw this metal frame. Indicate each weld using the correct symbol. Also make an isometric drawing of the frame whose width is **25 mm** throughout.

5. Make a straight and an isometric sketch, in good proportion, of the steel frame shown, showing clearly your joint designs.

6. Draw in section and in plan the riveted sheet metal joints shown. The sheet is **5 mm** thick and **75 mm** wide.

7. Sketch, in good proportion, the gear detail, showing the fixings in place.

Technical Draughtsmanship
Exercises
Fabrication 7 — Part 2A — Eng.

PART 2A

CHAPTER 20
PIPEWORK AND ASSEMBLY

Plumbing, drainage and pipelines of various descriptions are the subject of many engineering drawings. The ability to assemble components is also vital to the draughtsman.

CONTENTS
Pipe Fittings and Couplings	Page	236
Valves		237
Symbols and Pipe Circuits		238
Isometric Pipe Diagrams		239
Detail Drawings		240
Assembly Drawing		241
Exercises		242

Photocopying prohibited by law

① Standard pipe fittings, shown in plain, threaded and flanged forms.

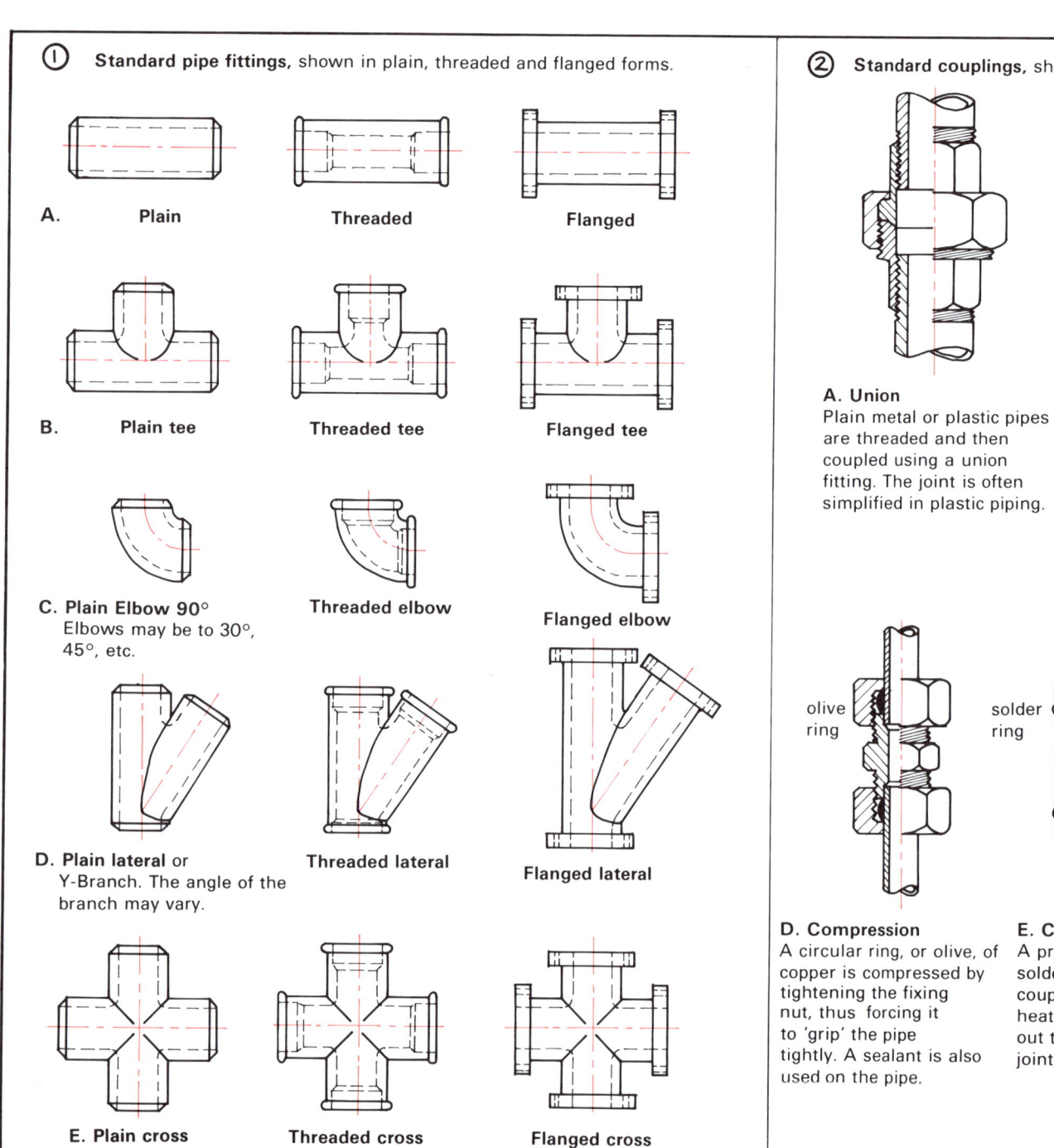

A. Plain — Threaded — Flanged

B. Plain tee — Threaded tee — Flanged tee

C. Plain Elbow 90° — Threaded elbow — Flanged elbow
Elbows may be to 30°, 45°, etc.

D. Plain lateral or Y-Branch. The angle of the branch may vary. — Threaded lateral — Flanged lateral

E. Plain cross — Threaded cross — Flanged cross

② Standard couplings, shown in half section.

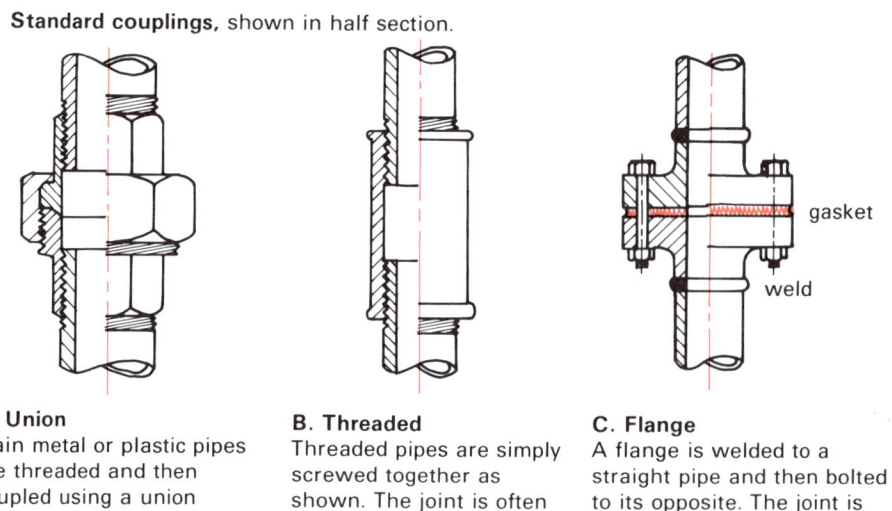

A. Union
Plain metal or plastic pipes are threaded and then coupled using a union fitting. The joint is often simplified in plastic piping.

B. Threaded
Threaded pipes are simply screwed together as shown. The joint is often caulked or sealed. Various spacers and nipple joiners are also available.

C. Flange
A flange is welded to a straight pipe and then bolted to its opposite. The joint is sealed with a ring seal, or gasket.

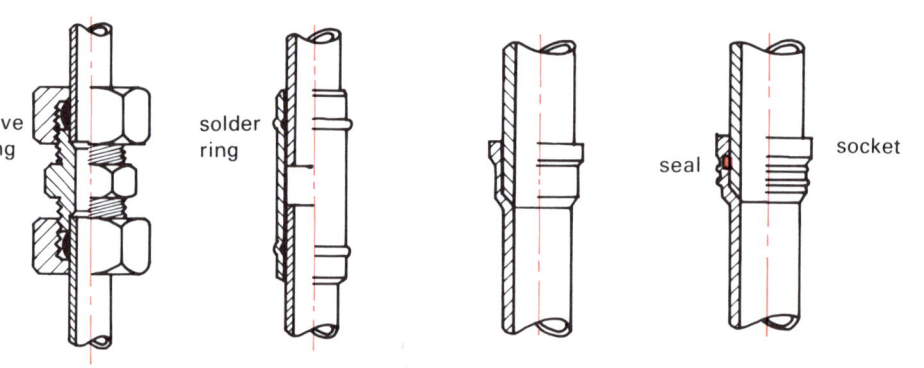

(labels: gasket, weld)

D. Compression
A circular ring, or olive, of copper is compressed by tightening the fixing nut, thus forcing it to 'grip' the pipe tightly. A sealant is also used on the pipe.

E. Capillary
A preset ring of solder is part of the coupling. This is heated and it flows out to seal the joint.

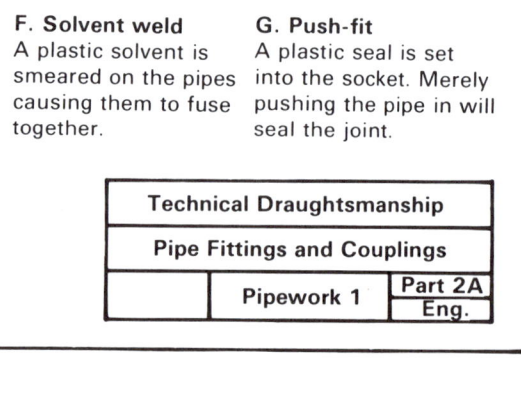

F. Solvent weld
A plastic solvent is smeared on the pipes causing them to fuse together.

G. Push-fit
A plastic seal is set into the socket. Merely pushing the pipe in will seal the joint.

(labels: olive ring, solder ring, seal, socket)

Technical Draughtsmanship		
Pipe Fittings and Couplings		
Pipework 1	Part 2A	Eng.

① Valves

- Valves are used to stop or limit the flow of a liquid, or gas, in a pipeline.

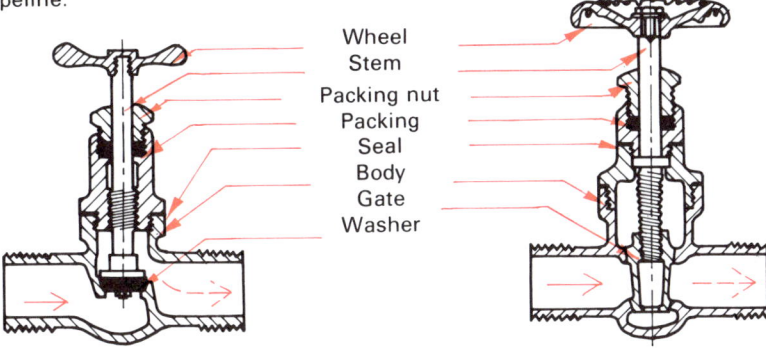

Wheel
Stem
Packing nut
Packing
Seal
Body
Gate
Washer

Globe valve
- Globe valves have an almost spherical body. The stem may be vertical or at an angle.
- These valves are good for the close regulation of flow but also tend to lower the pressure of a system.

Gate valve
- Here a gate is either turned or made to rise and so blocks or opens the pipeline.
- Gate valves are only used in cold low pressure systems.

② Taps
- Taps are used to drain off a liquid from a pipeline.

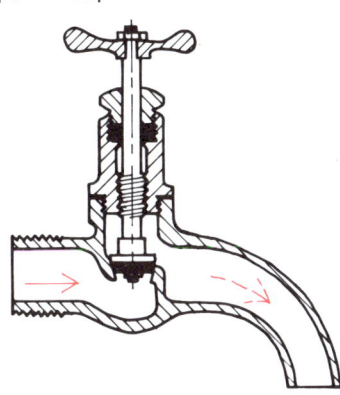

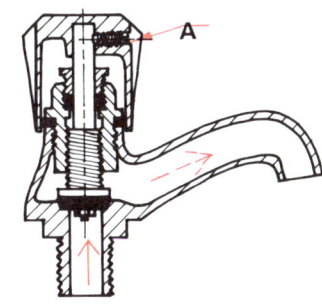

Globe tap
- The principle is similar to that of the globe valve above.
- Regulation is easy and accurate. However, as the water has to swirl around the bends, some pressure is lost.

Pillar tap
- This is similar to a globe tap. However here the water enters vertically, which simplifies the plumbing arrangements.
- Notice also the alternative cap, which is fixed to the stem with the grubscrew **A**.

③ Various valves
- There are dozens of variations on the basic valve design. Two well known variations are shown here.

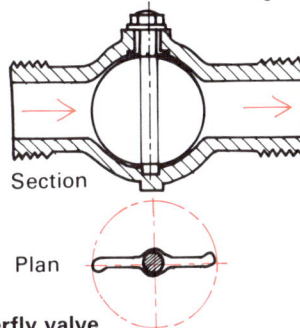

Section
Plan

Butterfly valve
- This is sometimes known as a choke valve from its use in carburettors.

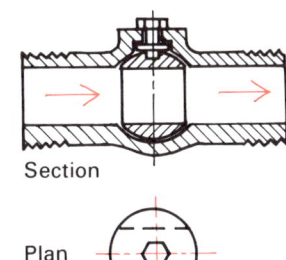

Ball valve
- A bearing is drilled and can be turned to limit or to cut off the supply.

④ Safety valves
- Valves can be designed to work within limits and to react to increases in pressure, or heat, or counterflow.

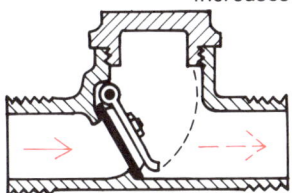

Swing valve
- This is a non-return valve. Pressure is allowed in one direction only. A flow in the other direction closes the valve. Used in gas pipes.

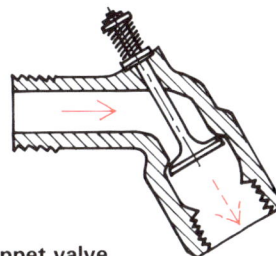

Poppet valve
- This controls the flow and is also a non-return valve. The valve can be opened by the flow or worked by a cam, as in car engines.

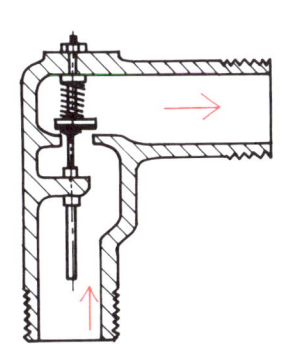

Thermostatic valve
- The rod **A** extends with a rise in temperature and pushes the valve **B** to release the flow.

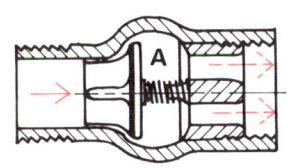

Feed check valve
- A variant of the spring valve. Here the flow is limited or checked by the gap **A**, which is adjustable.

Technical Draughtsmanship
Valves
Pipework 2 — Part 2A Eng.

① Symbols for pipework

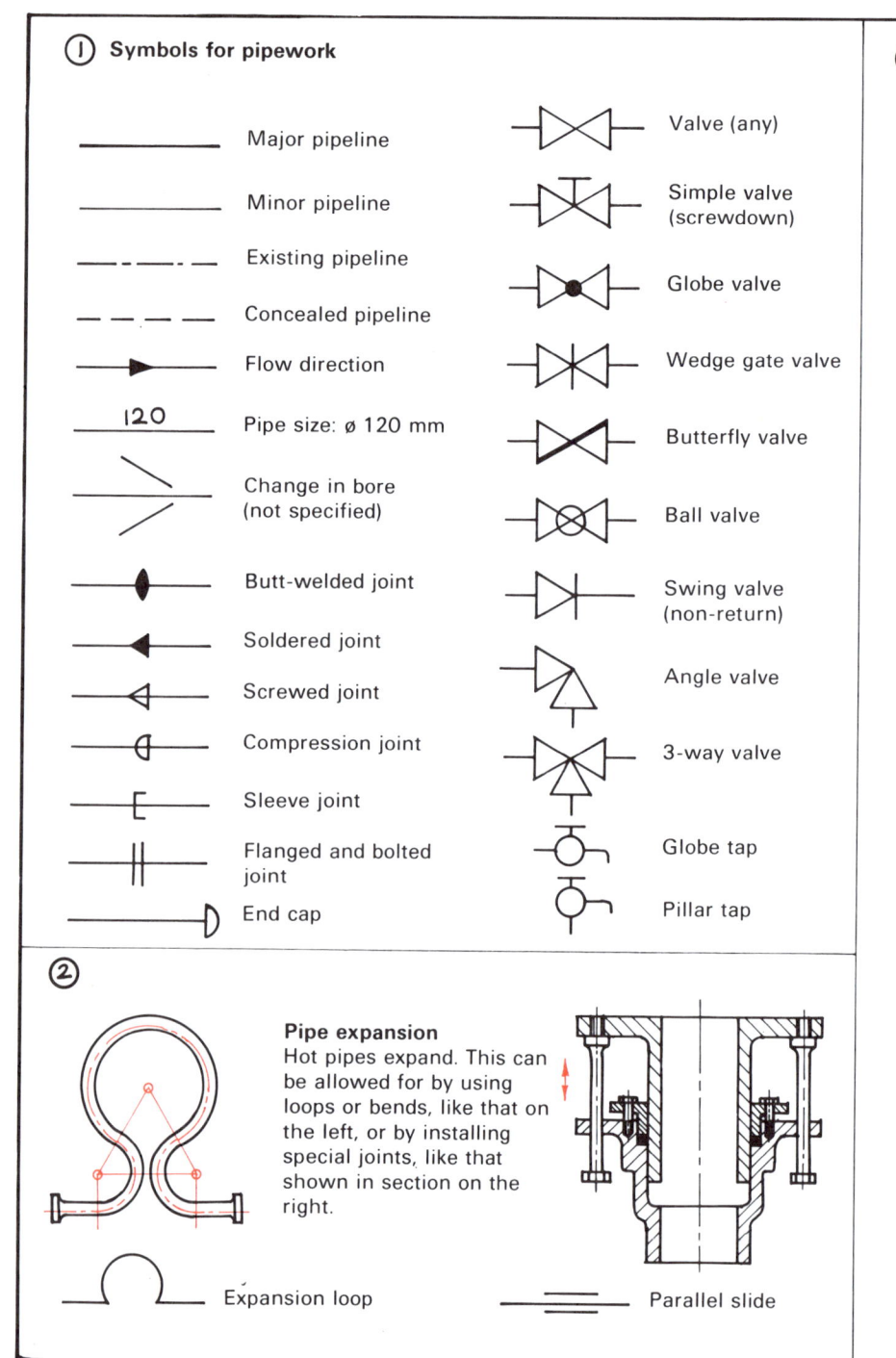

Symbol	Name	Symbol	Name
———	Major pipeline	▷◁	Valve (any)
——	Minor pipeline	▷⋈◁	Simple valve (screwdown)
— — —	Existing pipeline	▶●◁	Globe valve
- - -	Concealed pipeline	▷◁	Wedge gate valve
——▶——	Flow direction	▷╱◁	Butterfly valve
120	Pipe size: ø 120 mm	▷⊗◁	Ball valve
╱╲	Change in bore (not specified)	▷◁	Swing valve (non-return)
◆	Butt-welded joint	▷	Angle valve
◀	Soldered joint	▷⋈◁	3-way valve
◁	Screwed joint	⊖	Globe tap
⊣	Compression joint	⊙	Pillar tap
⊏	Sleeve joint		
⊢⊣	Flanged and bolted joint		
⊃	End cap		

② Pipe expansion

Hot pipes expand. This can be allowed for by using loops or bends, like that on the left, or by installing special joints, like that shown in section on the right.

Expansion loop

Parallel slide

③ Flat representation of a pipe circuit

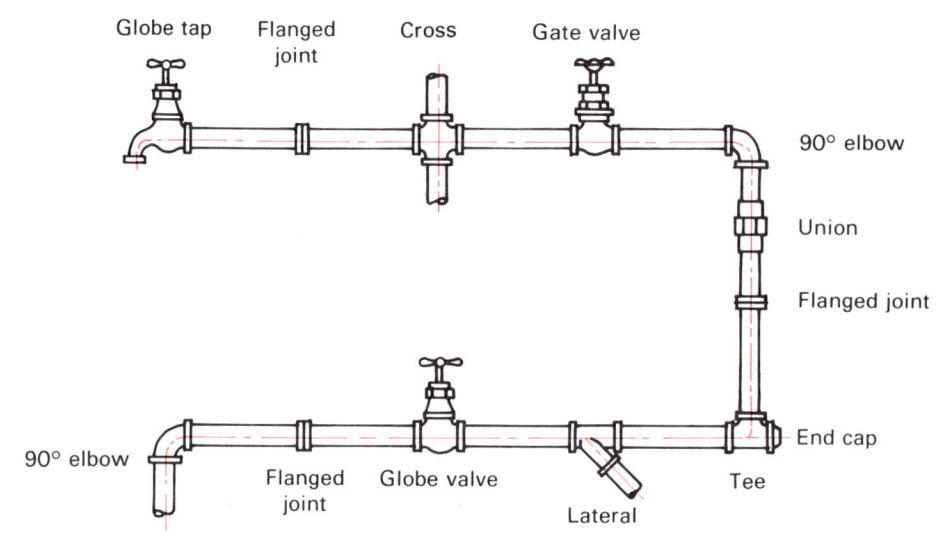

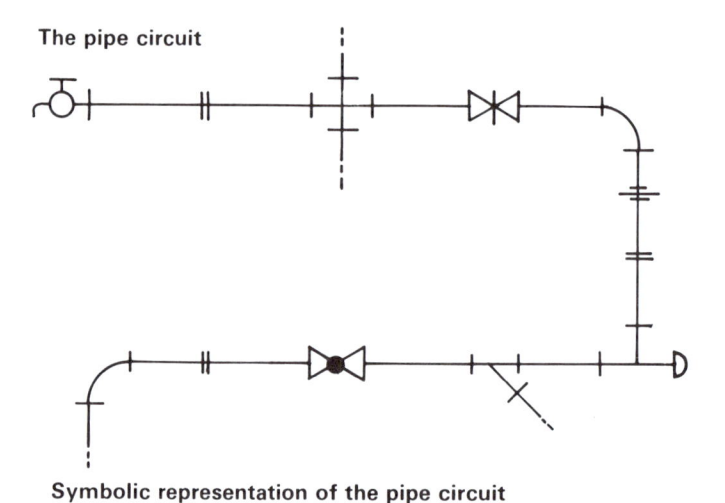

Globe tap — Flanged joint — Cross — Gate valve — 90° elbow — Union — Flanged joint — End cap — Tee — Lateral — Globe valve — Flanged joint — 90° elbow

The pipe circuit

Symbolic representation of the pipe circuit

Note: *Single-line one-view diagrams are very useful for designing a pipe circuit. However for more exact calculations an isometric line diagram is needed.*

Technical Draughtsmanship
Symbols and Pipe Circuits
Pipework 3 — Part 2A Eng.

① The pipework in isometric

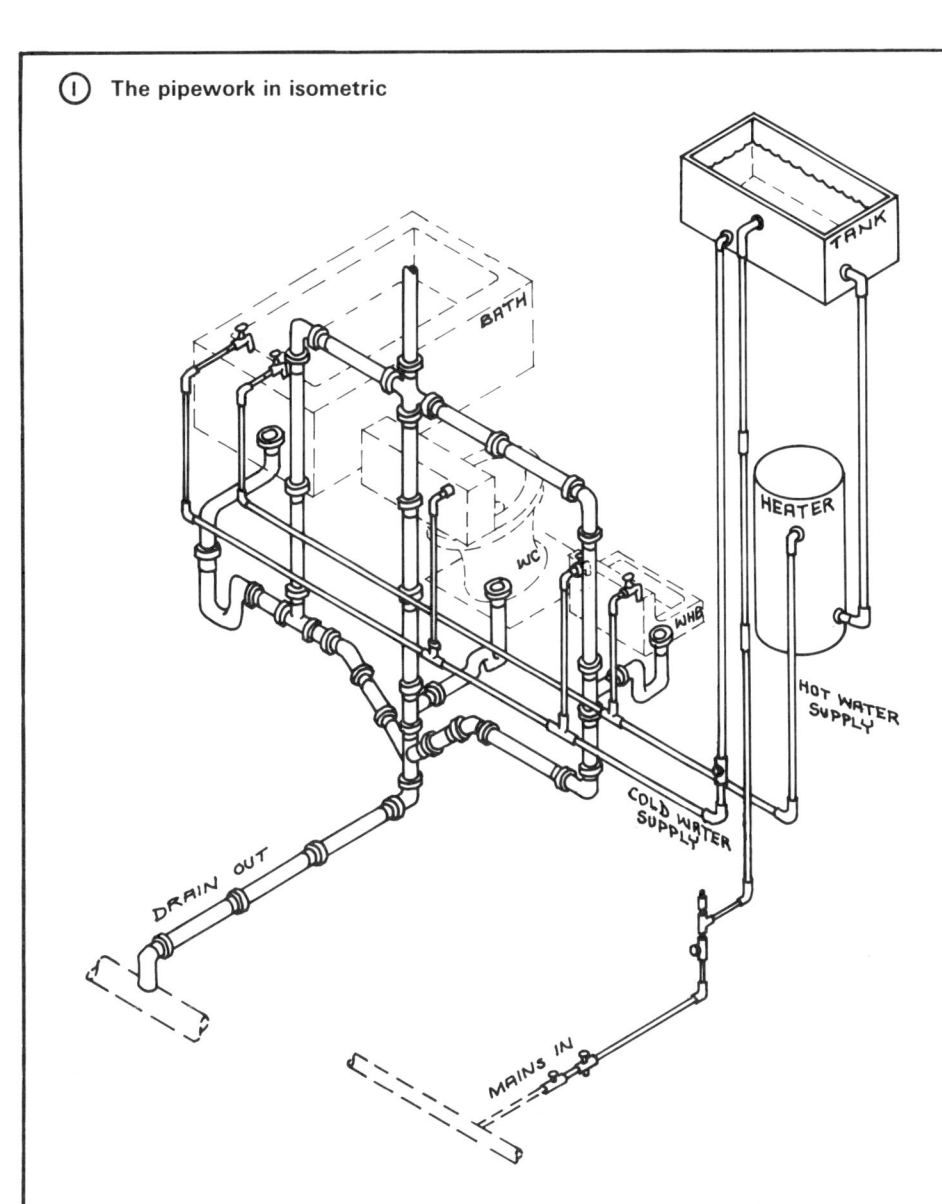

- This is a basic system for a small bungalow and is shown in isometric.
- It can be very confusing to show a pipe system only on orthographic views. An isometric projection is clearer and more useful in costing and planning the installation.
- However the above detailed drawing is both tedious and time-consuming.

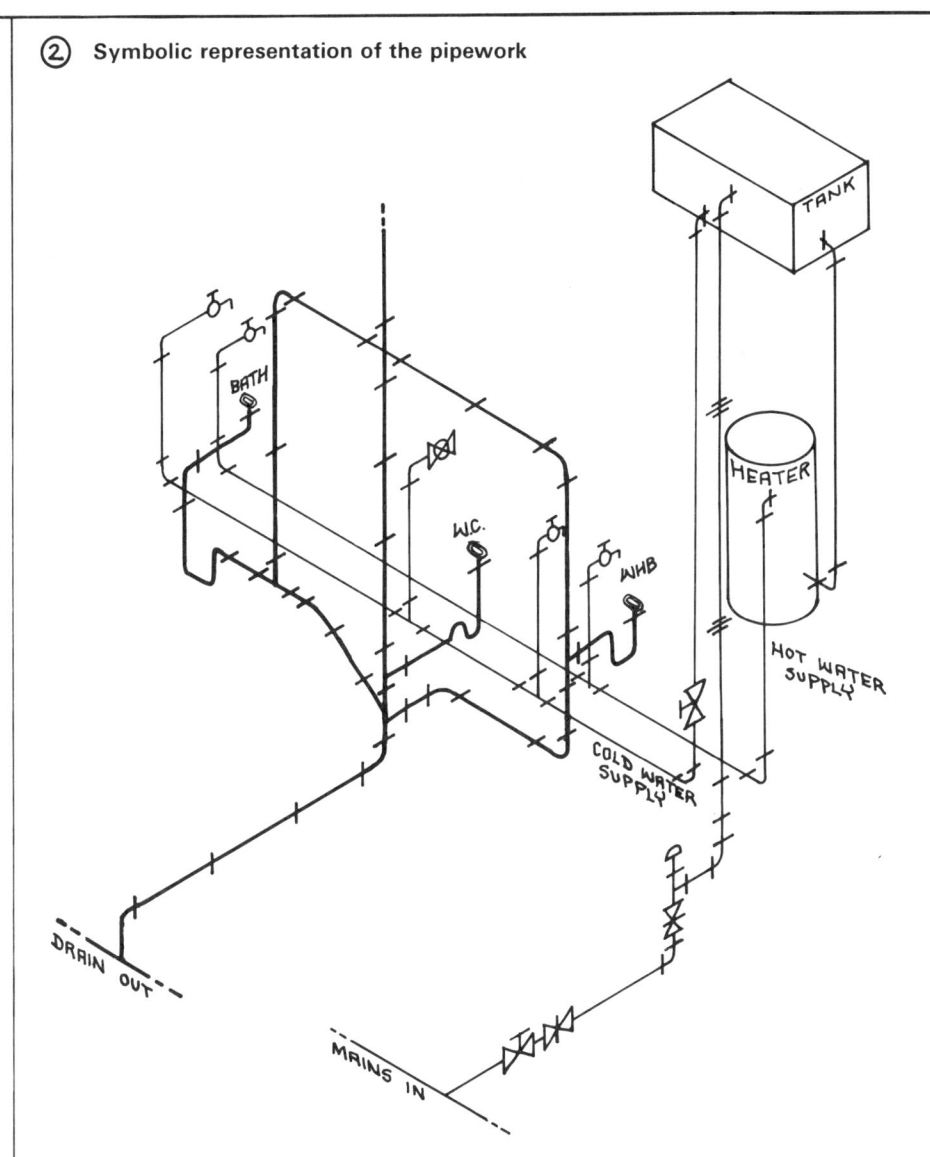

② Symbolic representation of the pipework

- If the pipework is represented in a symbolic way the drawing will be clearer and can be drawn more rapidly.
- The standard symbols are simply drawn in isometric, as shown.
- With computer overlay facilities this type of drawing is becoming more common, and more versatile in its practical applications.

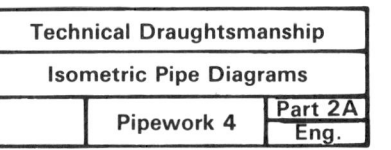

Technical Draughtsmanship
Isometric Pipe Diagrams

| Pipework 4 | Part 2A Eng. |

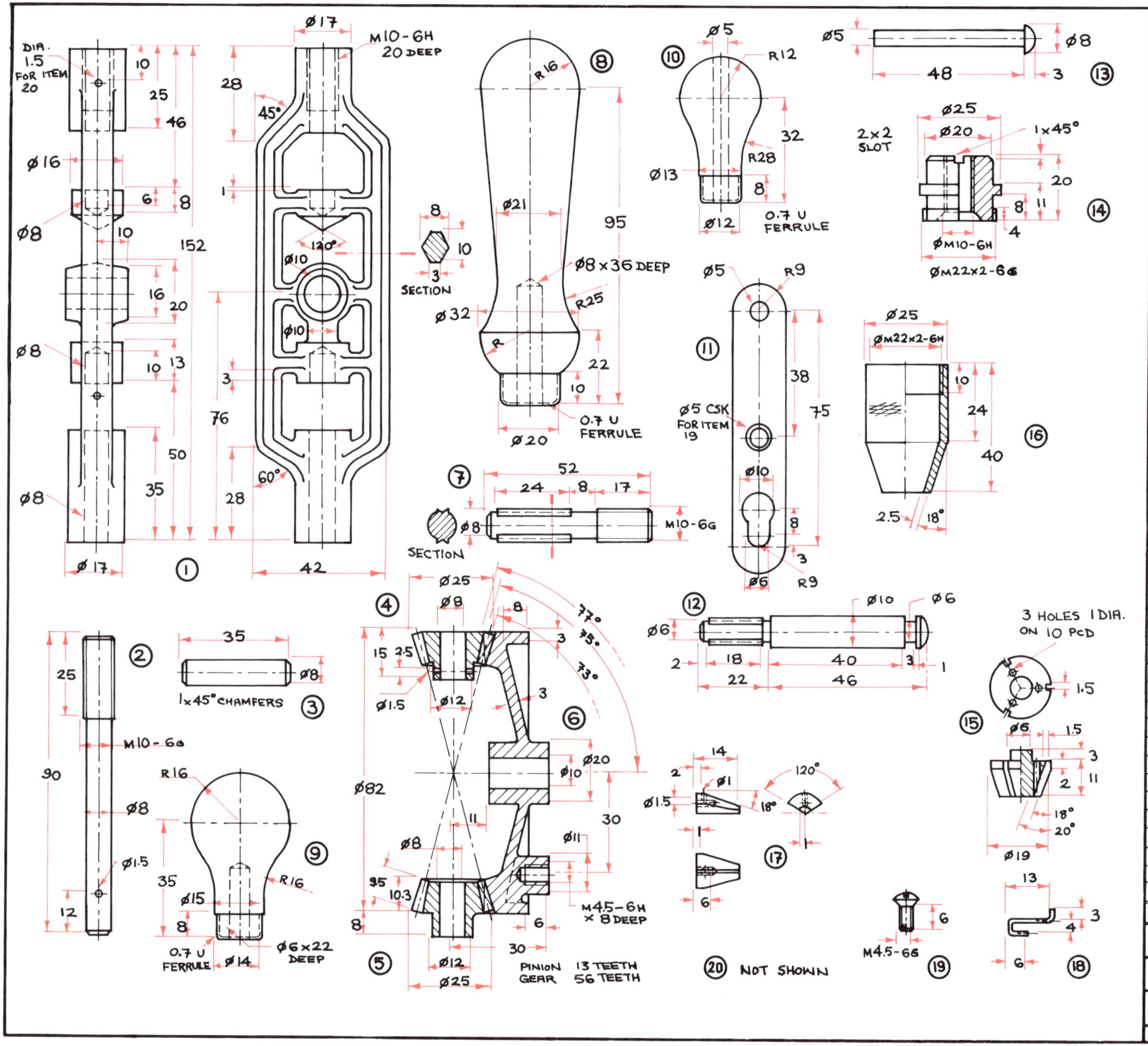

PROJECT DATA	DRG. NO.
HAND DRILL	24

REMARKS

- THIRD ANGLE PROJECTION.
- ASSUME ANY UNSPECIFIED RADII.
- ALL MEASUREMENTS ARE IN MILLIMETRES.

CORRECTIONS

ITEM	DESCRIPTION		MAT'L	NºOFF
20	PINS	TAPER	2	MS
19	SCREW	CSK HD	1	MS
18	SPRING	CHUCK	3	WIRE
17	JAW	CHUCK	3	MS
16	CAP	CHUCK	1	MS
15	COMPRESSOR	CHUCK	1	MS
14	BACK PLATE	CHUCK	1	MS
13	SHAFT	CRANK KNOB	1	MS
12	SHAFT	GEAR	1	MS
11	CRANK		1	MS
10	KNOB	CRANK	1	WOOD
9	KNOB	GEAR	1	WOOD
8	HANDLE		1	WOOD
7	SHAFT	HANDLE	1	MS
6	GEARWHEEL		1	CI
5	PINION	IDLER	1	CI
4	PINION	DRIVING	1	CI
3	SHAFT IDLER PINION		1	MS
2	SHAFT DRIVING PINION		1	MS
1	HOUSING		1	CI

Technical Draughtsmanship

Detail Drawings

Assembly 1 — Part 2A, Eng. H.

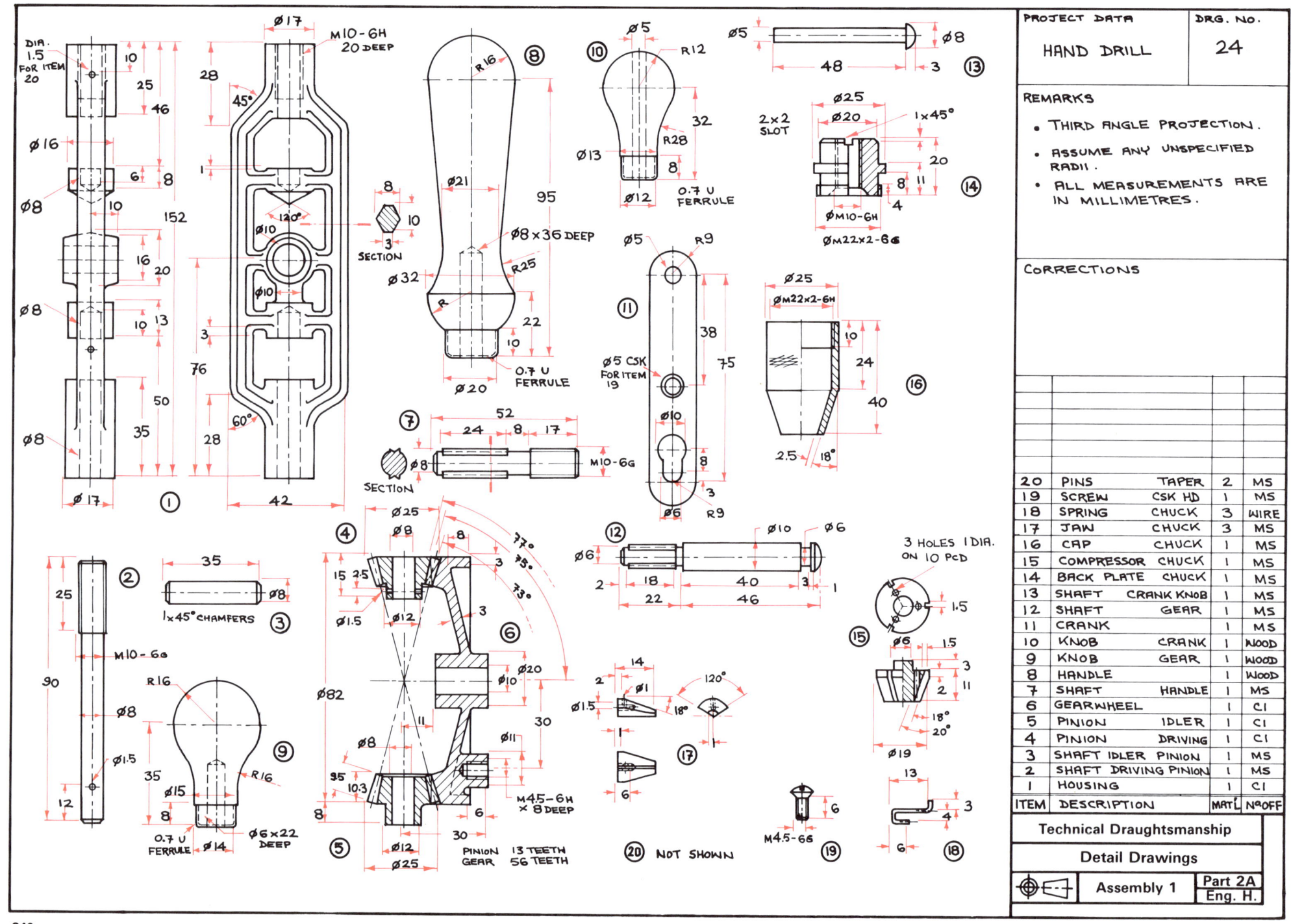

Elevation

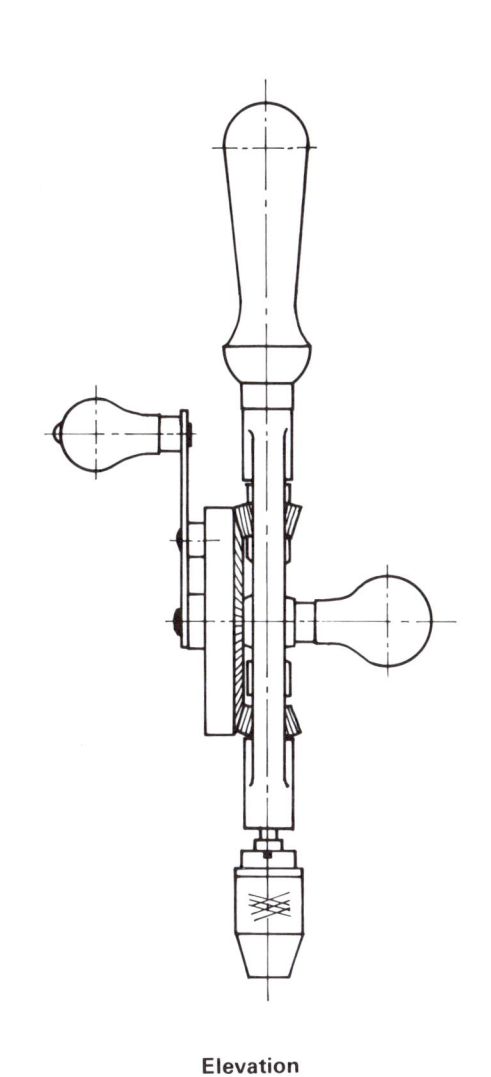

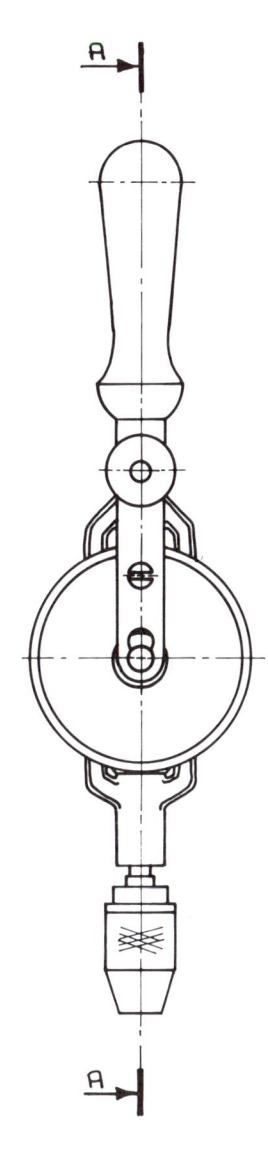

End view

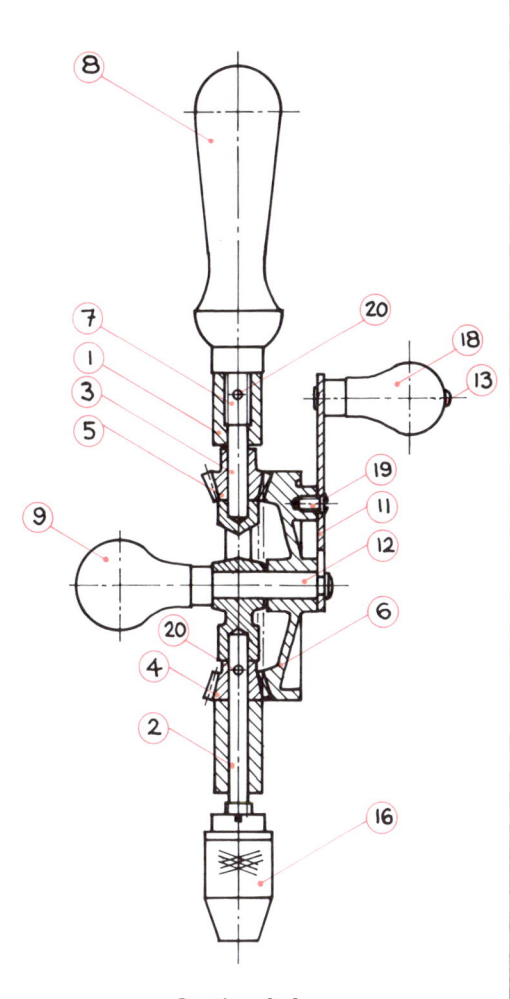

Section A-A

Notes
- *Numbers refer to the parts list on page 240.*
- *The chuck sub-assembly has not been shown here.*

Assembly drawings
- Here the parts on page **240** have been assembled and the assembly has been drawn in elevation, end view and section. An ability to combine details and elements, or to separate an assembly into parts, is invaluable to the draughtsman.
- Always start an assembly by making quick rough sketches of how the parts fit together. Make sure your scheme includes *all* the parts.
- Work out the overall sizes and start to block the layout of your sheet.
- Position the centre lines and check that each view will fit within the page without interfering with any other view.
- To separate an assembly for detail drawings needs even more care.
- Make sure you have enough information to draw the parts. Then 'crate' each part i.e. draw a box around it.
- Lay out each crate on the page and, when you have the best arrangement, draw in the detailed parts.
- A parts-list is best included on the same page, as shown on page **240**.

Technical Draughtsmanship		
Assembly Drawing		
	Assembly 2	Part 2A
		Eng.

241

All measurements are in millimetres

Questions

1. A student plumber has presented this diagram of her work to her teacher. Redraw the diagram and make a list of all the elements used.

2. Draw diagrams of each of the pipework systems listed and sketch in detail a sectioned view of the items marked by a black dot. The length of pipe need not be calculated.

3. This design sketch and part list of a crane hook assembly have been given approval. Make a set of detail and assembly drawings for its manufacture.

4. Copy the given detail drawings and also draw orthographic and half-sectioned views of the completed assembly.

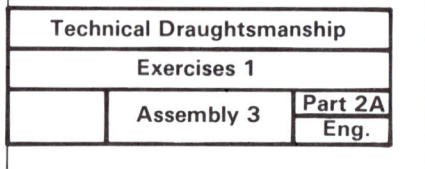

①

(Scale 0–5 M)

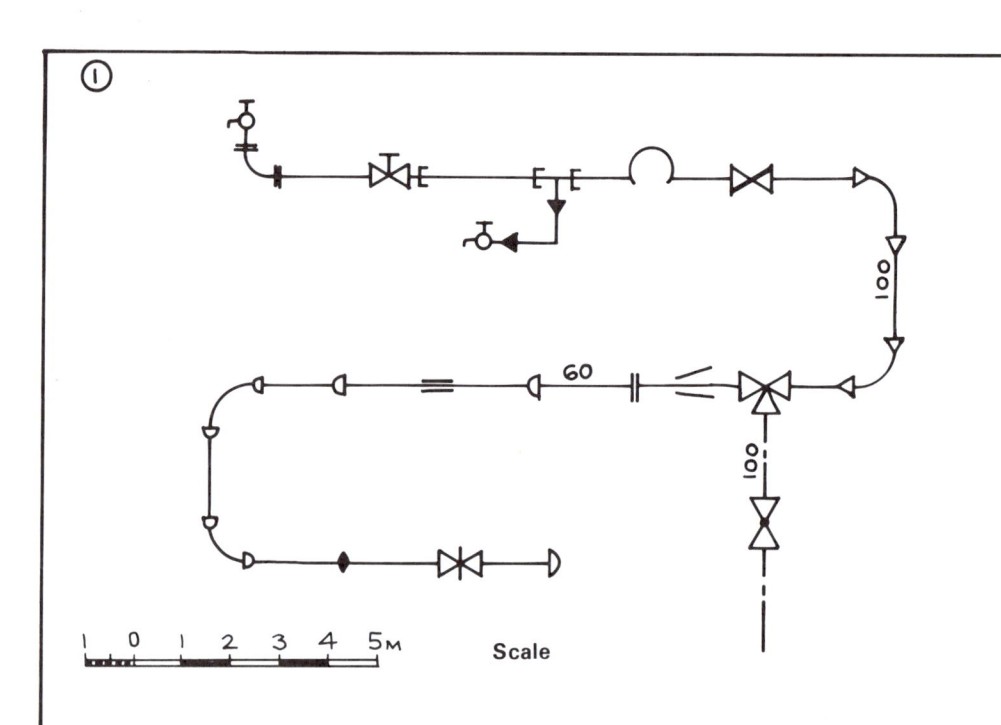

②

(A) Major pipeline in ø **120 mm**, ● Globe valve, ● Threaded T-joint Union, ● Parallel slide expansion joint, and Globe tap.

(B) Major pipeline in ø **120 mm**, ● Check-valve, Bore reduced to ø **80 mm**, Gate valve, ● Butterfly valve and ● Gate tap. Flanged joints throughout.

(C) Minor pipeline ø **25 mm**, solvent welded throughout. Elbow, Simple valve, ● Ball valve, ● Compression joint, Lateral, End cap and ● Pillar tap.

③ Crane hook assembly

SCALE 1:5

8	COTTER PIN	MS	1
7	SPRING PIN	MS	1
6	THREADED HOOK	MS	1
5	SLOTTED HEX NUT	MS	1
4	YOKE	MS	1
3	AXLE	NYLON	1
2	BUSHING	COPPER	1
1	PULLEY	NYLON	1
ITEM	DESCRIPTION	MAT'L	N°. OFF

④ Hand vice assembly

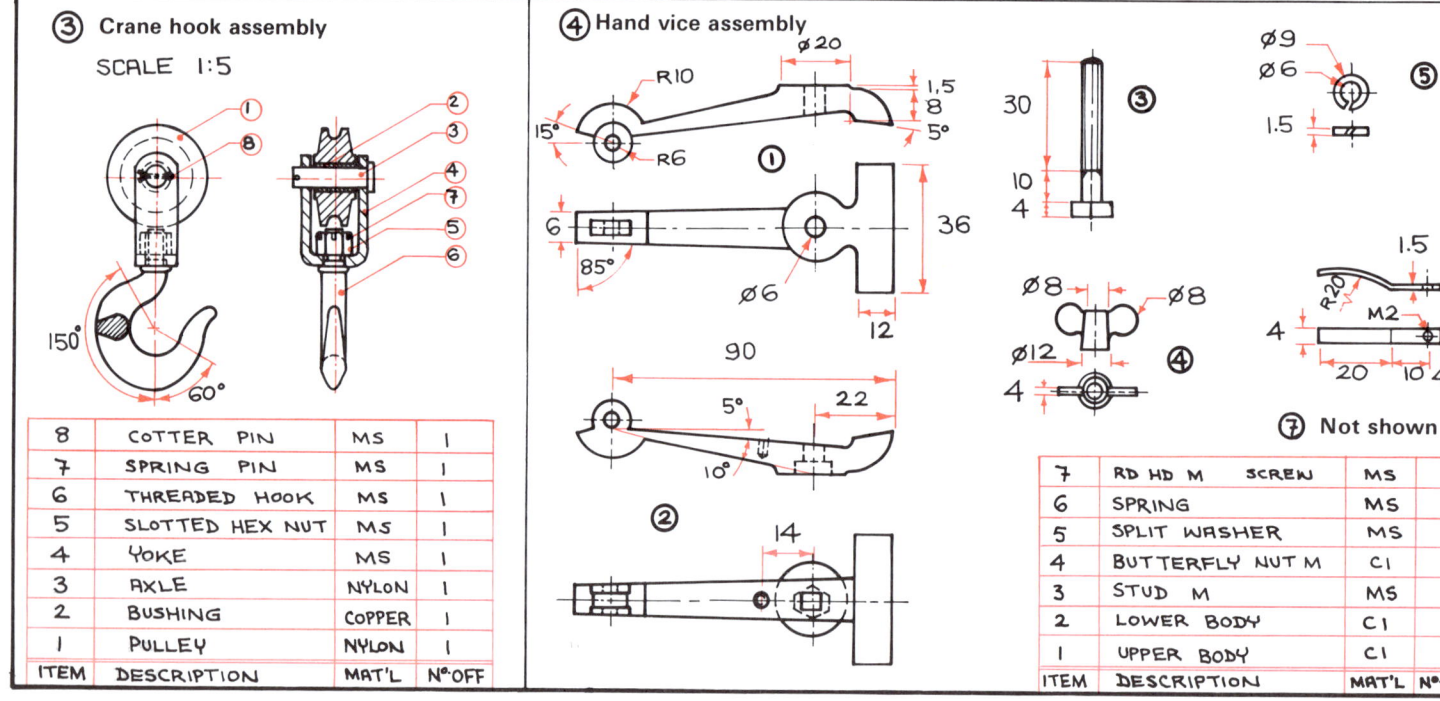

⑦ Not shown

7	RD HD M SCREW	MS	1
6	SPRING	MS	1
5	SPLIT WASHER	MS	1
4	BUTTERFLY NUT M	CI	1
3	STUD M	MS	1
2	LOWER BODY	CI	1
1	UPPER BODY	CI	1
ITEM	DESCRIPTION	MAT'L	N°. OFF

Technical Draughtsmanship

Exercises 1

Assembly 3 — Part 2A Eng.

① Gate valve assembly

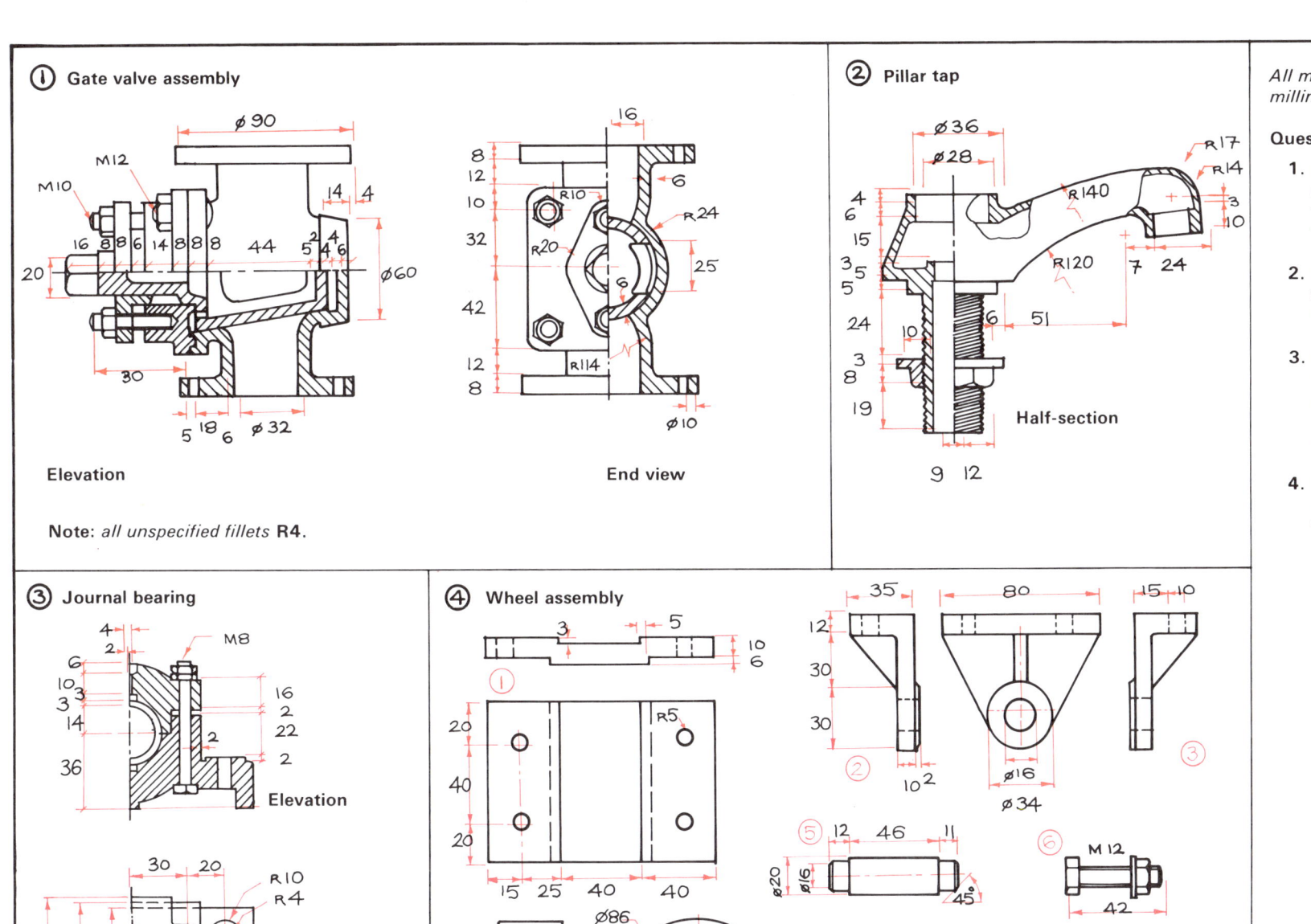

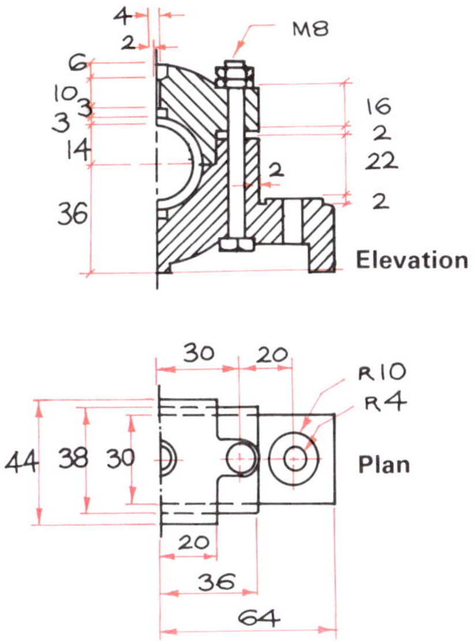

Elevation

End view

Note: *all unspecified fillets* **R4**.

② Pillar tap

Half-section

All measurements are in millimetres

Questions

1. Draw the three standard orthographic views of this gate valve in half-section and with the valve in the open position.

2. In good proportion, complete the pillar tap and make a parts list of the assembly.

3. Draw the journal bearing assembly in full orthographic projection and make detail drawings of each of its component parts.

4. Draw the plan, elevation and end view of the assembled wheel assembly in half-section.

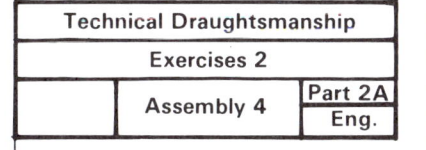

③ Journal bearing

Elevation

Plan

④ Wheel assembly

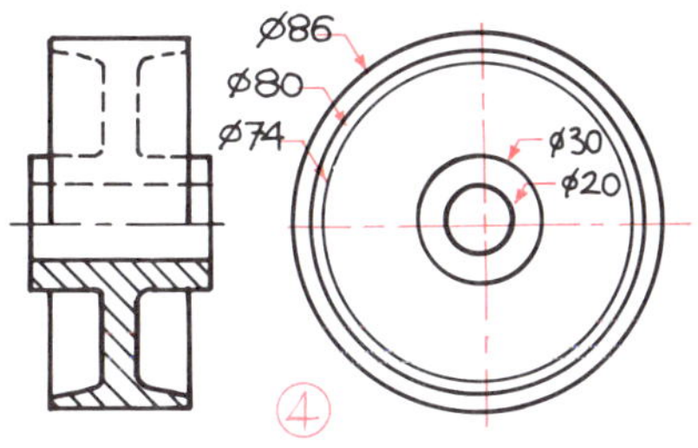

ITEM	DESCRIPTION	MAT'L	NO.OFF
7	SPRING WASHER	MS	1
6	BOLT HEX HD M12 + NUT	MS	1
5	AXLE	MS	1
4	WHEEL	CI	1
3	AXLE SUPPORT (L)	CI	1
2	AXLE SUPPORT (R)	CI	1
1	TOP PLATE	CI	1

Technical Draughtsmanship
Exercises 2
Assembly 4 — Part 2A Eng.

243

① Pipework for a house

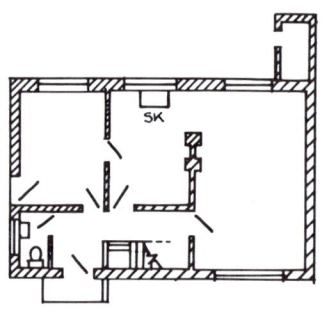

Ground floor plan

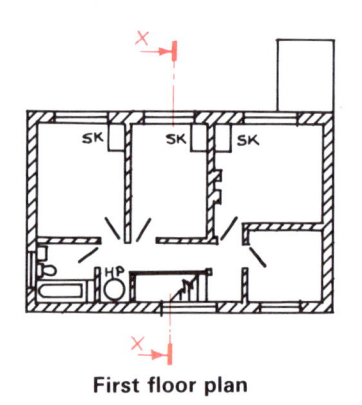

First floor plan

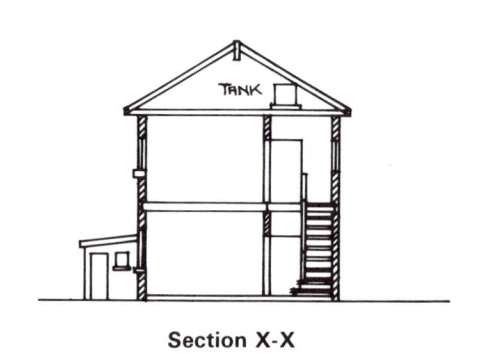

Section X-X

SCALE 1M 0 1 2 3 4 5M

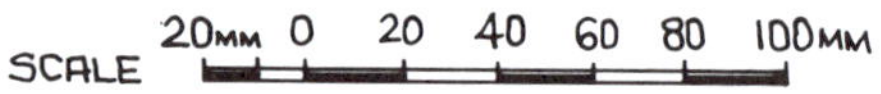

All measurements are to a given scale. In each case set up a Vernier scale on tracing paper and use it to measure the drawings.

Questions

1. Make a flat diagramatic drawing of the pipework for each floor of the given house. Then make an isometric pipeline diagram for the system as a whole. The drawing must be clear but need not be to scale.

2. Make a single-line diagramatic drawing of the pipework shown.

3. Draw the clutch assembly and then make a set of detail drawings of its component parts.

② Pipework system

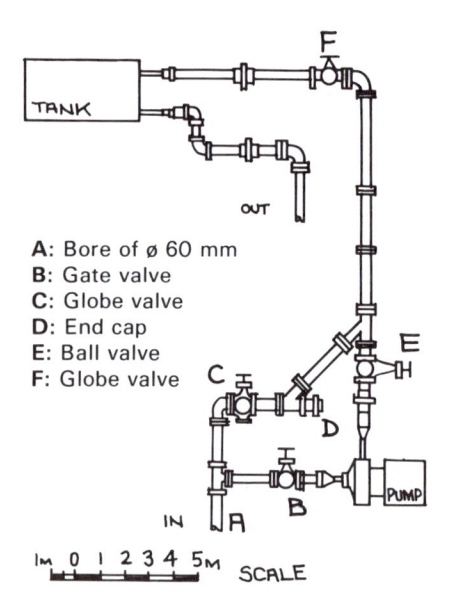

A: Bore of ø 60 mm
B: Gate valve
C: Globe valve
D: End cap
E: Ball valve
F: Globe valve

1M 0 1 2 3 4 5M SCALE

③ Friction clutch assembly

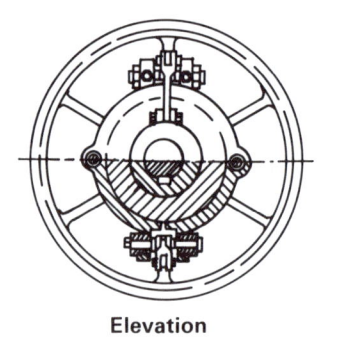

Elevation

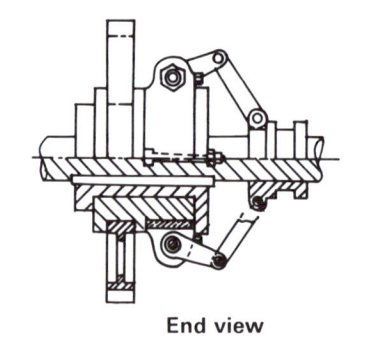

End view

SCALE 20MM 0 20 40 60 80 100MM

Technical Draughtsmanship
Exercises 3
Assembly 5 — Part 2A / Eng. H

244

PART 2A

CHAPTER 21
MECHANISMS

Most of the drawings we have been studying have been of a fixed kind. But what happens when things start to move? Here we will study basic movements, applications and the transmission of movement through gearing.

CONTENTS

	Page	
Loci and Links		246
Linkage Problems 1		247
Linkage Problems 2		248
Linkage Problems 3		249
Cam Types		250
Follower Displacement Diagrams		251
Cam Profile from FDD		252
FDD from Cam Profile		253
Roller Followers		254
Flat Followers		255
Gear Types		256
Gear Terms		257
Spur Gear Profiles		258
Rack and Pinion		259
Bevel Gears		260
Exercises		261

Photocopying prohibited by law

① **Loci:** A locus is the path of a moving point.

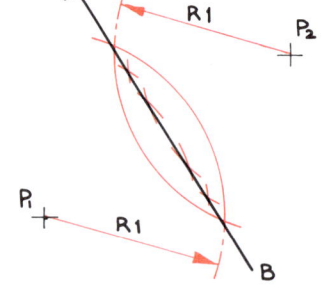

The path of a point that is equidistant from two given points P₁ and P₂
- By swinging equal radii from P₁ and P₂ the locus AB can be plotted.

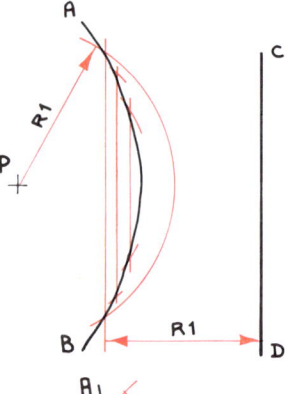

The path of a point that is equidistant from a point P and a line CD.
- Draw a line parallel to CD and at a distance R. With P as centre and R as radius strike an arc. Repeat for new distances and plot AB.

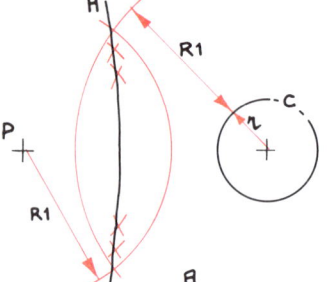

The path of a point equidistant from a point P and a circle C.
- See diagram.

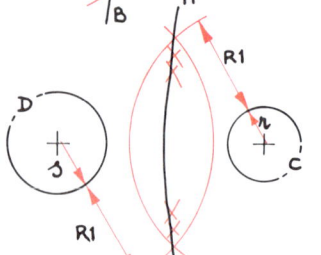

The path of a point equidistant from two circles C and D.
- See diagram.

② **Simple link mechanisms**

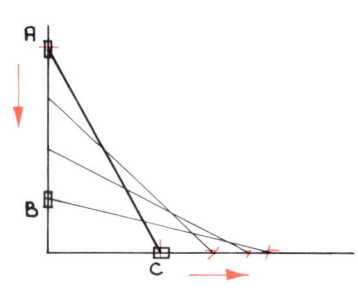

Single sliding link
A slides to B as C slides along the baseline.

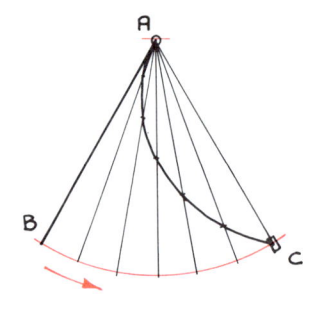

Swinging sliding link
As B swings to C the link A slides down AB to C.

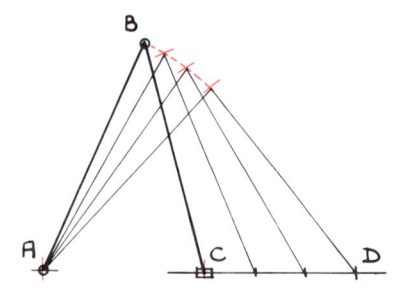

Double link
A is fixed and B is a pivot. C slides to D, or beyond. Note the path of B.

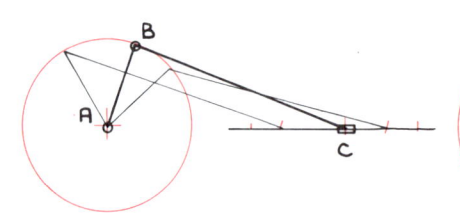

Crank and sliding link
AB is a crank. A is fixed and B rotates. C slides over and back along the line.

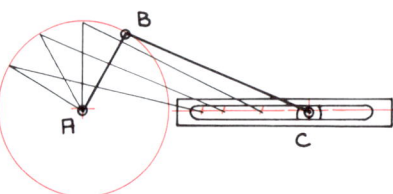

Crank and slotted link
As before, but C moves in a slot. The slot may be curved.

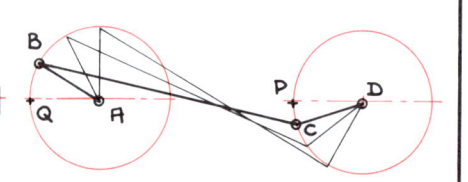

Two cranks
This only works when BC is equal to the distance from P to Q.

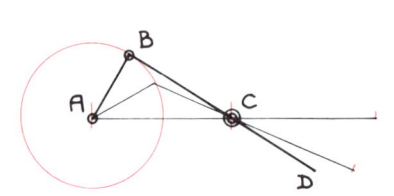

Crank and fixed through-link
As above, but there is a hole drilled through the fixed link C, allowing BD to slide through it.

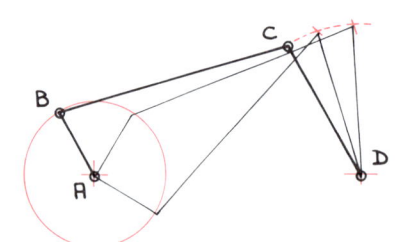

Crank and rocker
As AB rotates CD rocks from side to side. This works if
AB + BC + CD $>$ AD, and
AB + BC − CD $<$ AD.

Note:
Draw each of these figures and complete their movement.

Procedure
All link systems are plotted in one of two ways.
- Plot the mechanism in several different positions, as here, and draw the outline of the movement, *or*
- Make a trammel out of a slip of paper. Mark the functional distances on this and use it to plot the outline of their movements.

Technical Draughtsmanship
Loci and Links
Mechanisms 1 — Part 2A Eng.

① Problem

Plot the locus of point **E** as **AB** rotates about **A**, and **CD** rotates about **D**.

AB: 30 mm
CD: 50 mm
AD: 75 mm
CE: 140 mm

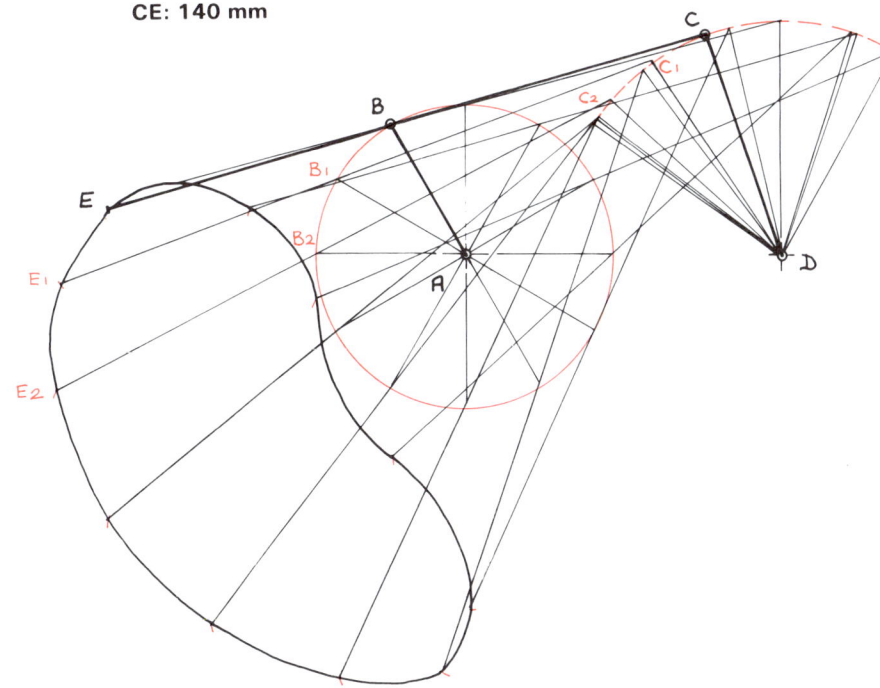

Procedure

- Draw the basic mechanism to the dimensions given.
- With **A** as centre plot the circular path of **B**.
- Divide this circle into a number of pieces e.g. twelve.
- With **D** as centre swing **C** in an arc.
- Take the first position **B₁**. Measure **BC** and with **B₁** as centre and **BC** as radius strike an arc to find **C₁**
- Join **C₁** to **B₁** and extend to locate **E₁**.
- Repeat this process for **B₂**, **B₃** etc.
- Join the positions of **E** to show its locus.

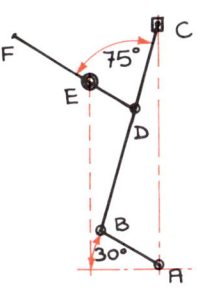

② Problem

AB rotates about **A** as **C** slides up and down the centre line. **E** is a fixed through-pivot. Plot the locus for **D** and then for **F** as **AB** Rotates.

AB: 25 mm
BC: 100 mm
CD: 40 mm
DF: 75 mm

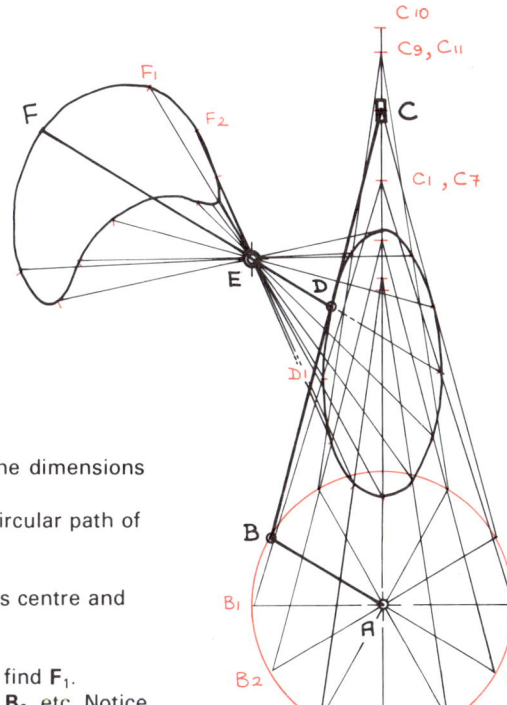

Procedure

- Draw the mechanism to the dimensions given.
- With **A** as centre plot the circular path of **B**.
- Divide this in twelve.
- Take position **B₁**. With **B₁** as centre and **BC** as radius find **C₁**.
- Measure and mark **D₁**.
- Join **D₁** to **E** and extend to find **F₁**.
- Repeat this process for **B₂**, **B₃**, etc. Notice that **C₇** falls on **C₁**, **C₁₁** on **C₉**, etc.
- Join the plotted points to draw the locus of **D** and then of **F**.

Notes:

- *These drawings can seem very confusing. So, plot one move right through before starting the next.*
- *If you use a trammel in an exam, mark it clearly and always hand it in with your answer paper.*

Technical Draughtsmanship	
Linkage Problems 1	
Mechanisms 2	Part 2A Eng.

247

AB: 24 mm
EG: 162 mm

The problem
The circle **A** rolls along the line **CD** until point **B** again meets the line at **D**. **E** is a pivot and **F** is a fixed through-pivot. Plot the locus of **E** and of **G** as **AB** rolls along the line.

Procedure
- Construct the figure as shown.
- Make **BD** equal to the circumference of the circle.
- Divide both the circle and **BD** into a number of pieces e.g. twelve.
- The path of point **E** will be a cycloid. Plot this, as on page **179**.
- Take position **E₁**. Join **E₁** to **F** and extend to find **G₁**.
- Continue from **E₂**, **E₃**, etc. to find **G₂**, **G₃**, etc.
- Join the plotted points to draw the locus.

Note:
Where there is a large distance between points subdivide that step of the movement for greater accuracy.

| Technical Draughtsmanship |
| Linkage Problems 2 |
| Mechanisms 3 | Part 2A Eng. H. |

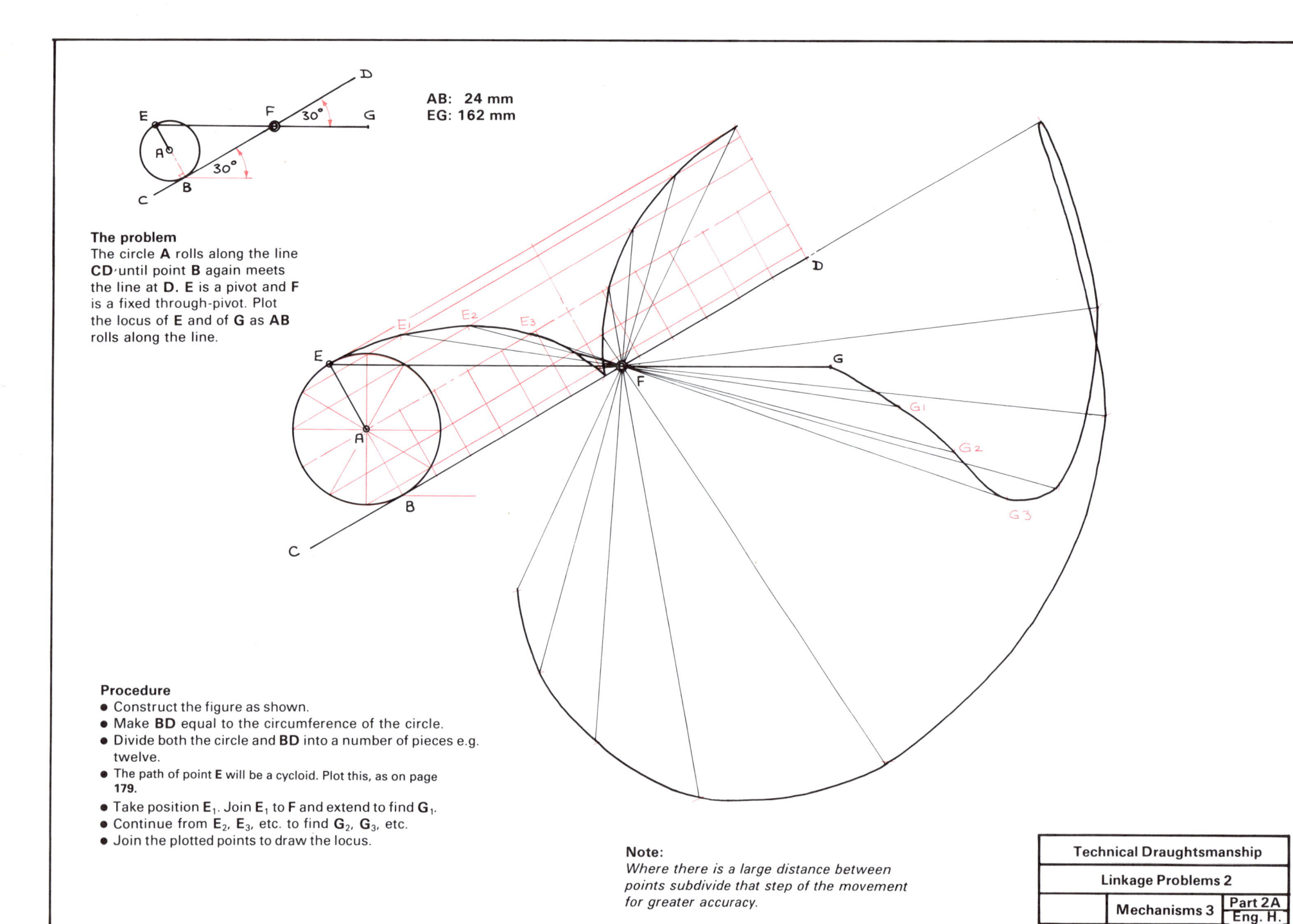

248

The Problem
Cranks **AB** and **CD** are geared so that **CD** turns at twice the speed of **AB** and in the opposite direction.
Draw the locus of **C** and plot a displacement diagram for the sliding link at **F**.

AB: 32 mm
CD: 16 mm
AP: 40 mm
AC: 62 mm
BC = **DE** = **EF** = 102 mm

Procedure
- Draw the mechanism as given.
- With **A** as centre draw the circular path of **B**. Divide this into a number of parts e.g. twelve.
- Similarly draw the path of **D**. As D rotates at twice the speed it need be divided into only half the number of pieces e.g. six. *If you prefer use twelve divisions on the smaller circle and twenty four on the larger circle.*
- Take position **B₁**. **D** will have moved through twice the angle to **D₁**. Plot **E₁** and then **F₁**.
- Continue for the other positions and trace the path of **E**, as shown.

Displacement diagram
This allows the position of **F** to be plotted for any degree of revolution of **AB**, and this can also then be related to time.

Procedure
- Establish the maximum and minimum positions of **F**.
- Set out a graph panel of any convenient length.
- Divide this into pieces, e.g. twelve, and index these from **0°** to **360°**.
- The position of **F** after **30°** of revolution of **AB** is **F₁**. Plot this onto the **30°** line on the graph.
- Repeat for other divisions and trace the curve.

Technical Draughtsmanship		
Linkage Problems 3		
Mechanisms 4	Part 2A
	Eng. H.

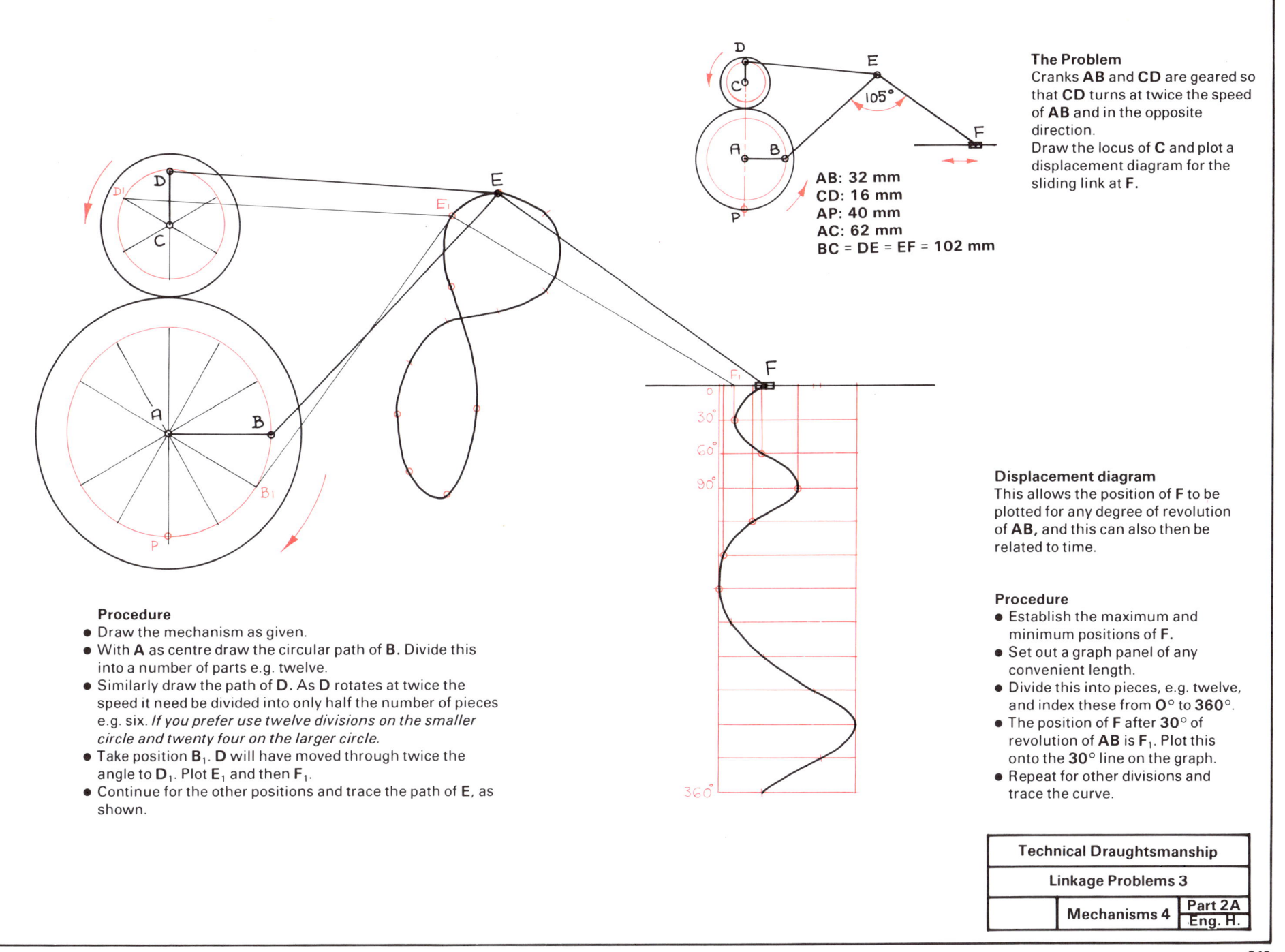

249

① Cam types

- A cam is a specially shaped component designed to transmit a desired motion to another component, a follower, with which it is in contact.
- Cams are used in cars and in automatic equipment e.g. lathes.
- Cams are simple and adaptable. A very simple input motion can be transformed into a wide variety of complex movements, with the great advantage that pauses, or dwell, can be included.
- A wedge demonstrates the principle when it is used to change a sliding movement into a lifting movement, as shown.

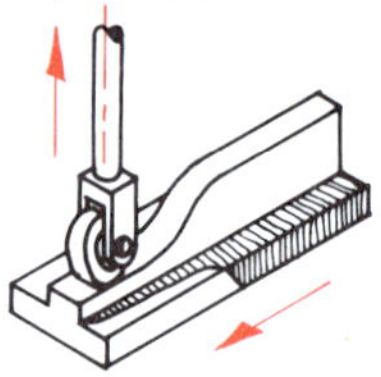

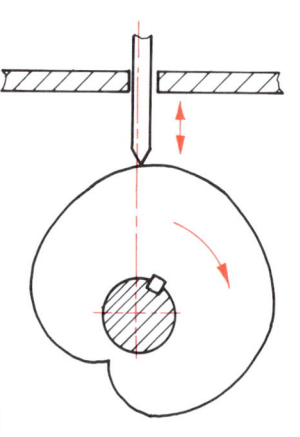

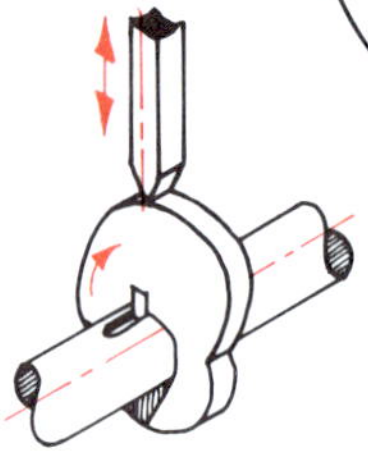

Radial plate cam
- Probably the most widely used type. A spring-loaded follower is kept in contact with the rotating plate.

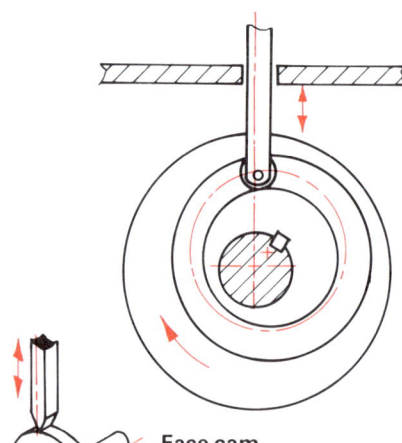

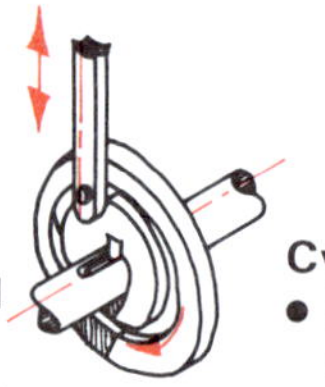

Face cam
- The follower is fitted into a groove machined into the cam.
- This arrangement helps control bounce.

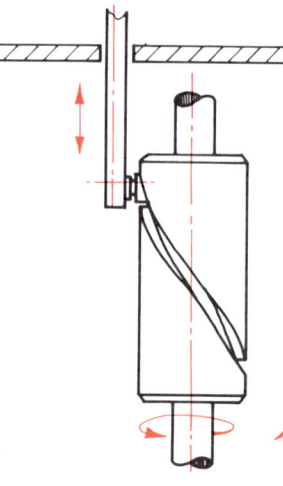

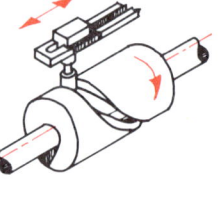

Cylindrical cam
- A cylindrical blank is machined to receive a roller follower.
- The axes of motion are parallel for input and output motions.

② Follower types

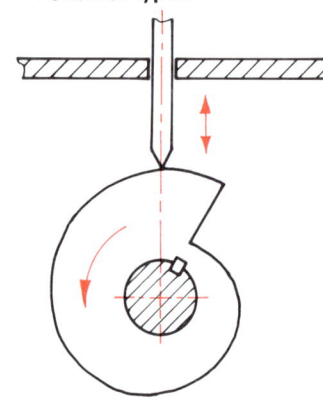

Knife-edge follower
- The point of the follower can follow very complicated cam profiles but wears rapidly and has to be used at slow speeds.
- The above cam is part of a quick-return mechanism. Can you see why?

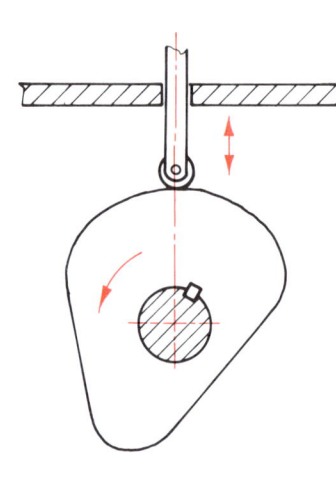

Roller follower
- The roller is more stable at high speeds and, as the surface in contact is greater, it wears better.
- However it is relatively expensive and cannot follow intricate outlines.

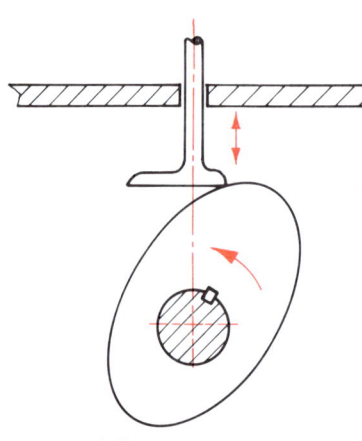

Flat follower
- The foot may be inclined or offset to one side of the centre line.
- It wears better than a knife edge but 'bridging' can occur over hollows.

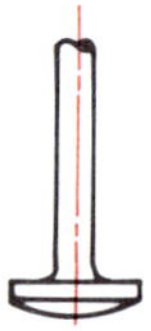

Mushroom follower
- This variation is used in cars.

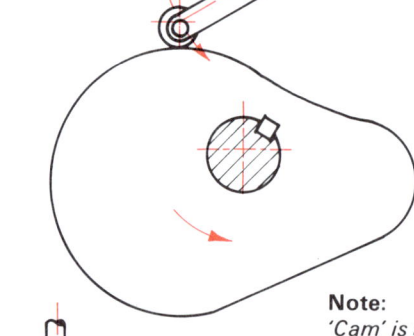

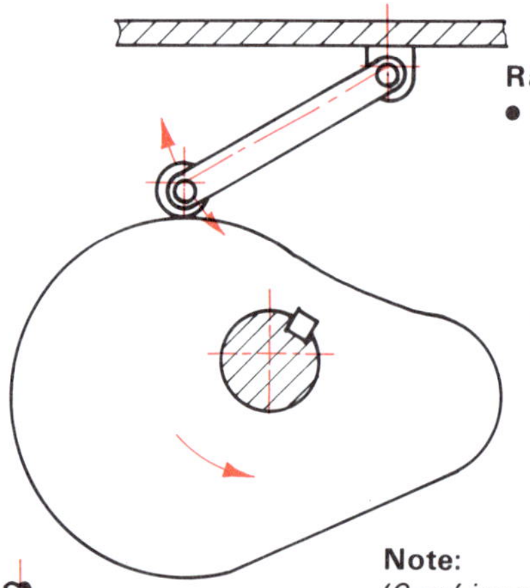

Radial arm follower
- A cam often imparts movement to a complex following mechanism, such as the radial arm follower shown here.

Note:
'Cam' is an old Dutch word for 'wheel'.

Technical Draughtsmanship		
Cam Types		
Mechanisms 5	Part 2A	Eng.

① Uniform velocity (UV)

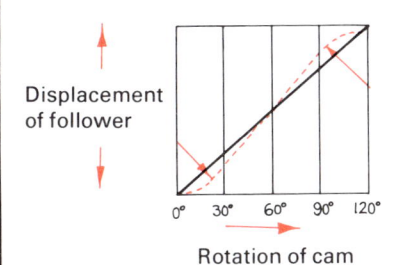

- This follows a straight line on a graph.
- Sometimes the corners may be rounded as shown, to make transitions to other movements smoother.

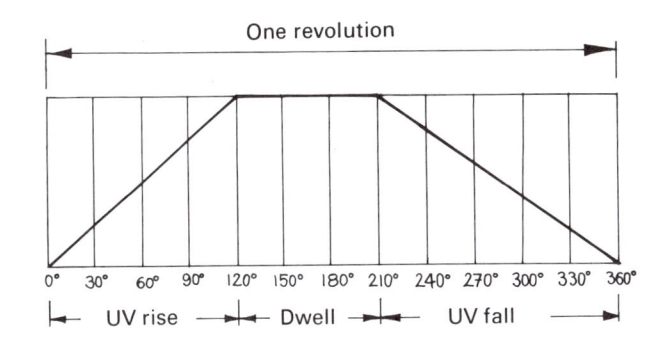

Follower displacement diagram (FDD)

- UV gives a constant speed but the abrupt changes can cause the follower to 'bounce' or to 'chatter' at speed.
- Rounding off corners will ease these defects but will no longer give exactly constant speed.

② Simple harmonic motion (SHM)

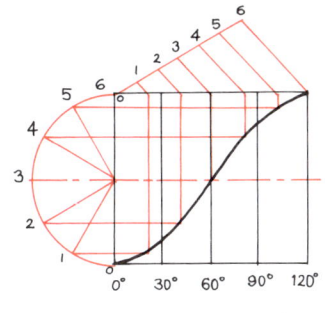

- Draw a semicircle to suit the displacement of the follower.
- Divide this into equal segments.
- Divide the length of rotation into the same number of parts.
- Project the points from the semicircle onto the graph lines, as shown.

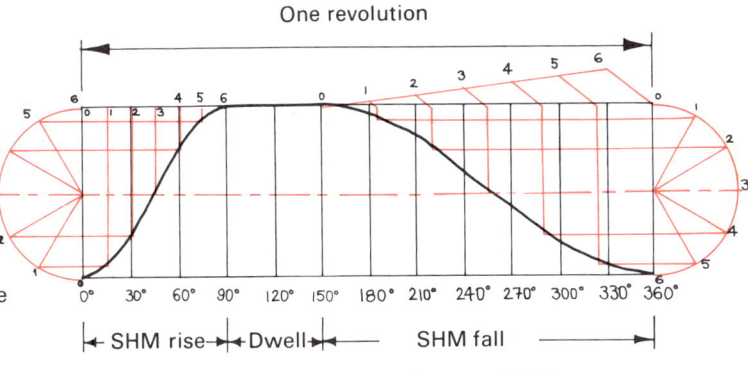

Follower displacement diagram (FDD)

- SHM is based on the circle and the graph is a sine curve.
- Change over of movements is very smooth, but the speed of the follower will be uneven.

③ Uniform acceleration and retardation (UAR)

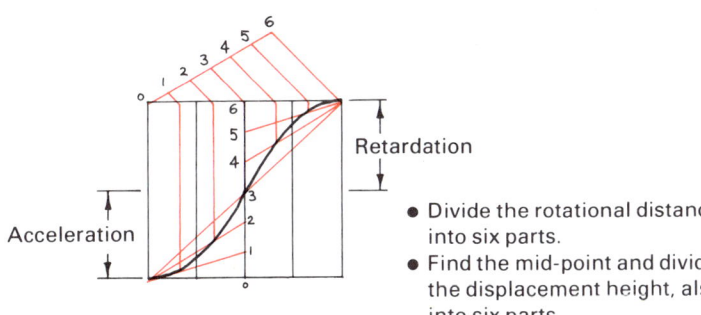

- Divide the rotational distance into six parts.
- Find the mid-point and divide the displacement height, also into six parts.
- Draw six radials from the corners and sketch the curve, as shown.

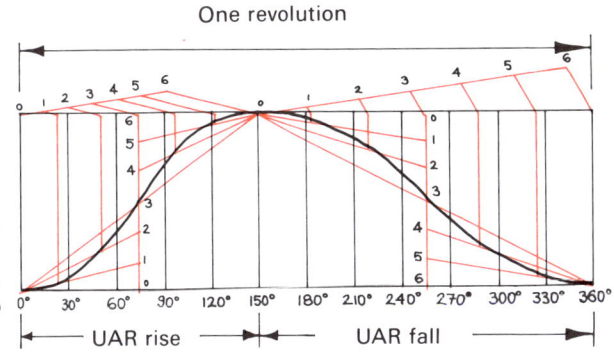

Follower displacement diagram (FDD)

- UAR gives a smooth curve and even speed.
- The graph outline is based on two half-parabolas.

Technical Draughtsmanship		
Follower Displacement Diagrams		
	Mechanisms 6	Part 2A
		Eng.

251

① The problem

- Draw the profile of an anti-clockwise cam to give the following displacements to an in-line knife-edge follower:

   0° to 120° a SHM lift of 52mm
   120° to 180° dwell
   180° to 330° UAR fall of 52mm
   330° to 360° dwell.

   The centre of the cam is **16 mm** below the nearest approach of the follower.

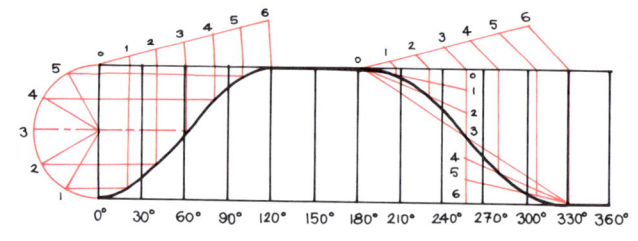

Follower displacement diagram

Procedure: Stage 1
- Lay out a line for **360°** and show the divisions for **0°, 30°, 60°**, etc.
- Proceed as on page **251** to plot the follower displacement diagram for the information given.

②

FDD

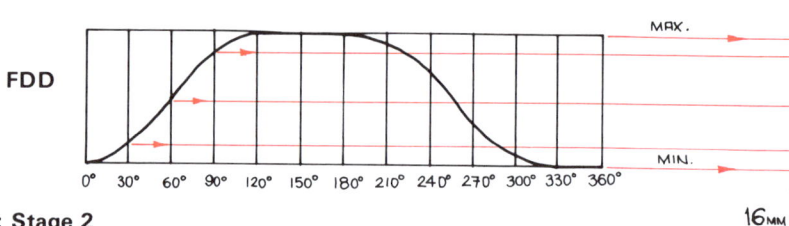

Procedure: Stage 2
- Draw a centre-line **ABCD** to one side and well clear of the **FDD**.
- Project across the minimum, or nearest approach of the follower. Then, **16 mm** below this, mark centre **D**.
- Project across the maximum and with centre **D**, lightly draw the maximum circle. Divide this into twelve and index these divisions, in this case anti-clockwise.
- Project across each point on the **FDD** and, with centre **D**, swing each around to its appropriate division of the circle.

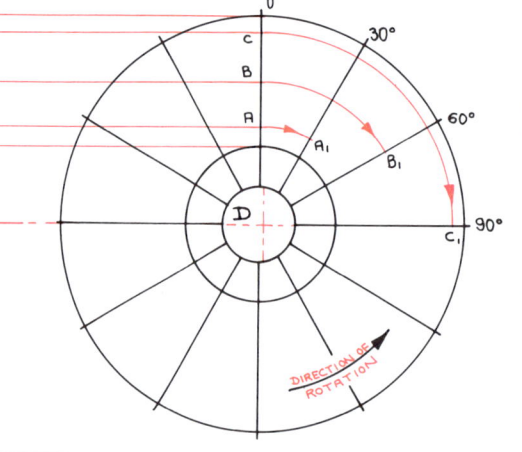

Notes
- *If the direction of rotation were to be clockwise, then the divisions would be indexed from 0° in the other direction. The points **A, B, C**, etc. would then be swung into position in a clockwise direction.*
- *It **is** necessary to indicate the direction of rotation.*

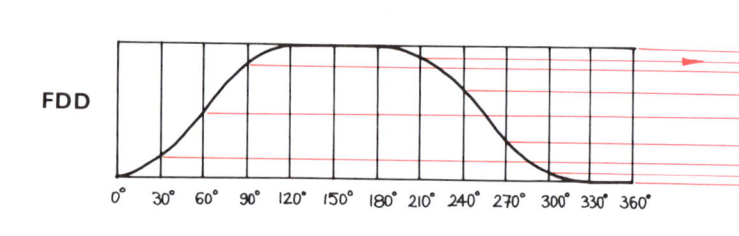

③

FDD

Procedure: Stage 3
- Continue until each major point of the **FDD** has been plotted onto its corresponding position on the circle.
- Join the points in a smooth freehand curve to draw the cam profile.
- Indicate the follower, camshaft and keyway, if required.

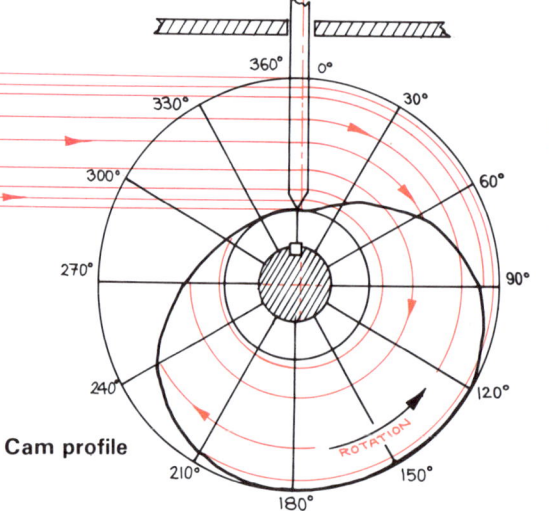

Cam profile

Notes
- *Any division may be sub-divided to increase the accuracy of the cam profile.*
- *In machine design a cam will often be plotted to every degree, or even minute, of its revolution.*

Technical Draughtsmanship
Cam Profile from FDD
Mechanisms 7 — Part 2A / Eng.

①

The problem
- Plot the follower displacement diagram for an in-line knife-edged follower in contact with the cam profile given in the accompanying sketch.
- In other words: Here is a cam. What effect would it have on an in-line knife-edged follower?

Sketch

Cam profile

Procedure: Stage 1
- Draw the cam and with centre **C** draw both the minimum and maximum circles. Divide these into a number of segments e.g. twelve.
- Project the min. and max. points from the centre line **0°** to one side and clear of the cam drawing, as shown.

②

Cam profile

Follower displacement diagram (FDD)

Time scale
*This may be added or may be an alternative method of dividing the FDD into useful units. The cam would then be divided to correspond to the number of time units, in this case into **ten** divisions.*

Procedure: Stage 2
- Along the projected minimum line lay out a suitable length and mark the divisions for one revolution.
- With centre **C** swing the outline at each division of the cam around onto the follower's centre-line. Then project it across to its corresponding position on the **FDD**. Take only one point at a time.
- When each division has been plotted onto the **FDD** draw a fair curve through the points to complete the diagram.

Technical Draughtsmanship		
FDD from Cam Profile		
	Mechanisms 8	Part 2A
		Eng. H.

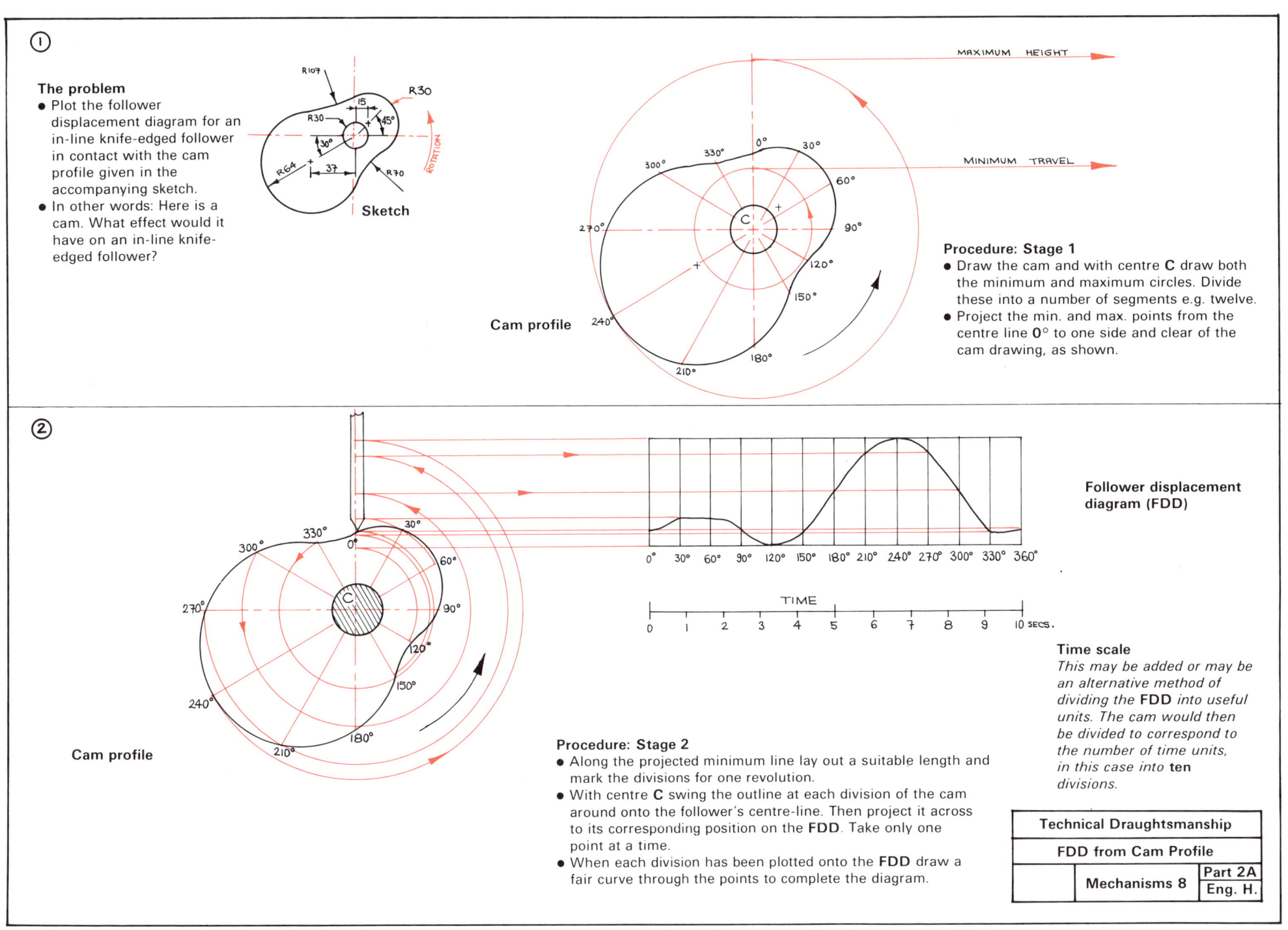

253

① To plot a cam from a FDD when the follower is an in-line roller follower.

Given follower displacement data:
0° to 120° SHM rise of 30 mm,
120° to 180° UV rise of 7 mm,
180° to 240° dwell,
240° to 360° UAR fall of 37 mm.
- The roller is in-line and of DIA 6 mm and its nearest approach to the cam centre is 14 mm centre-to-centre.
- The camshaft is of DIA 15 mm.

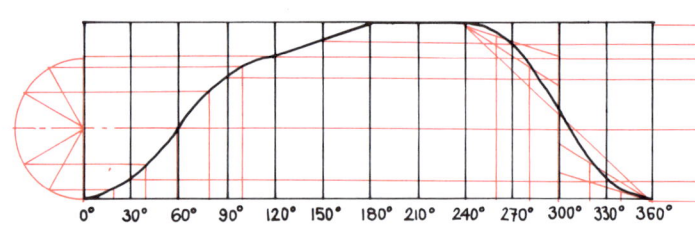

Follower displacement diagram

Cam profile

Procedure
- As on page 252, with one difference.
- The displacement diagram refers to the *centre* of the roller. So plot the diagram onto the divisions of the circle in the usual way and then at each point draw the roller, as shown.
- Finally trace the profile of the cam *tangent* to each position of the roller.

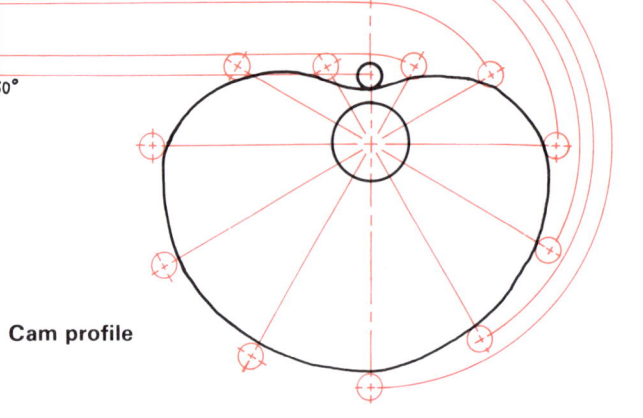

② To plot an FDD for an in-line roller follower acting on a given cam profile

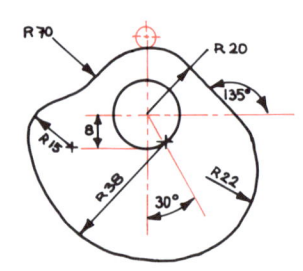

Given profile

- The follower is of a roller type of **DIA 6 mm** and is in line with the centre of the camshaft.

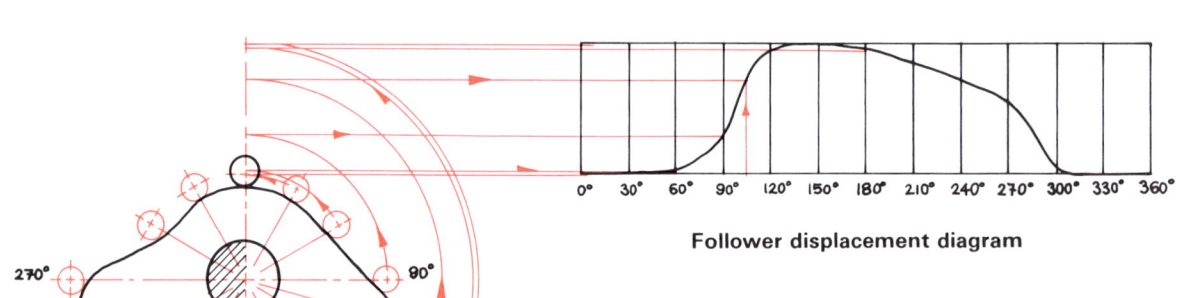

Cam profile

Follower displacement diagram

Procedure
- As on page 253, with one difference.
- Divide up the cam and along each division line draw the roller *tangent* to the cam profile, as shown.
- Now take the *centre* of the roller in each position and use that to find the **FDD** in the normal way.

Technical Draughtsmanship
Roller Followers
Mechanisms 9 — Part 2A / Eng. H

① To draw the profile of a cam with a flat follower given its FDD

Given data:
0° to 110° UAR rise of 18 mm
110° to 180° dwell,
180° to 240° SHM rise of 12 mm,
240° to 330° SHM fall of 27 mm,
330° to 360° UV fall of 3 mm.
- The camshaft is of DIA 14 mm and its centre is 14 mm below the nearest approach of the follower.
- The follower is flat and extends 7 mm to either side of its centre-line.

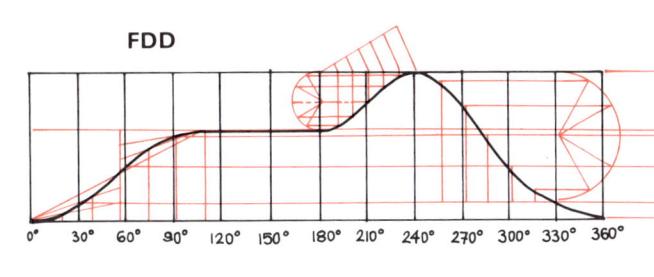

FDD

Procedure
- As on page **252**, with one difference.
- The displacement diagram is for the *centre-line point* **P** on the base of the follower. So, project across the FDD in the usual way and then at each point draw the base of the follower.
- Trace the profile of the cam so that the base touches it in each position, as shown.

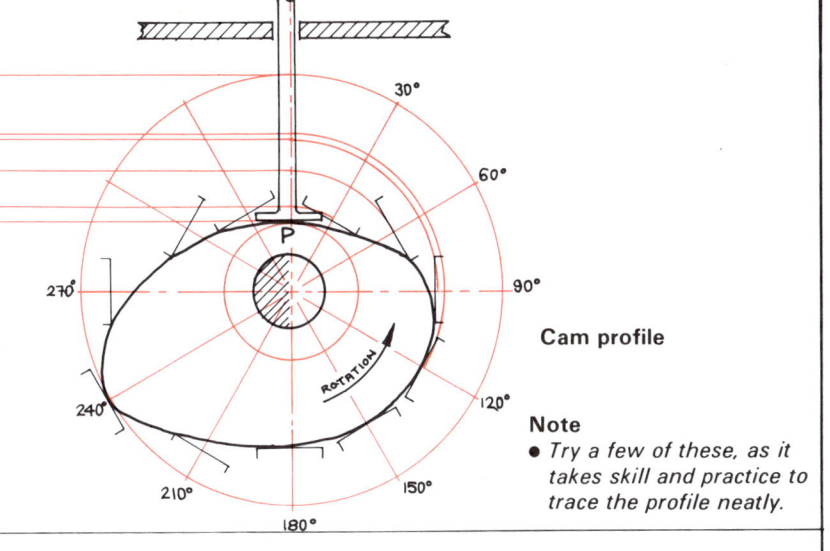

Cam profile

Note
- *Try a few of these, as it takes skill and practice to trace the profile neatly.*

② To plot an FDD for a flat follower given the cam acting upon it

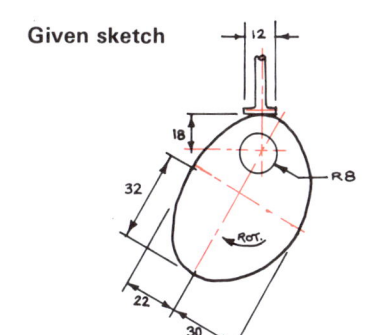

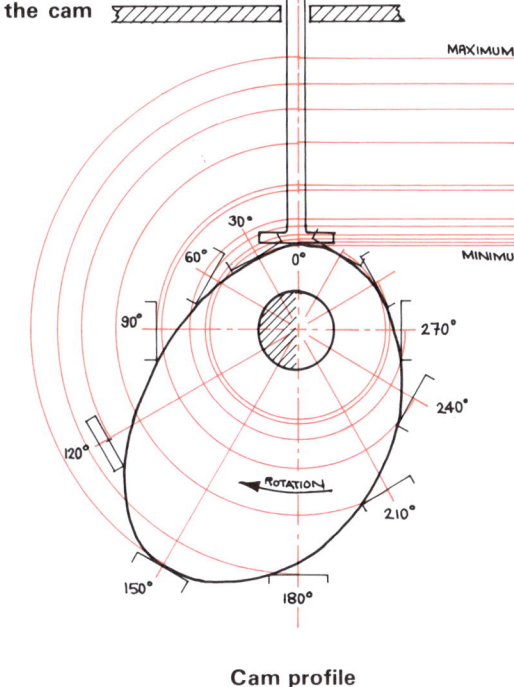

Given sketch

Procedure
- As on page **253**, with one difference.
- Divide the cam and along each division line draw the base of the follower so that it just touches the cam profile, as shown.
- Then take the *centre-line point* of each base of the follower and use that to find the **FDD** in the usual way.

Cam profile

FDD

Note
- *A mushroom follower would be approached in a similar way.*

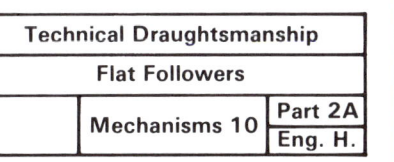

| Technical Draughtsmanship |
| Flat Followers |
| Mechanisms 10 | Part 2A / Eng. H. |

255

① Gear types
- A gear is a wheel with teeth sticking out along its rim. The teeth can fit, or mesh, into the teeth of other gears and so turn them.

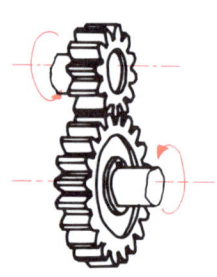

Spur gear pair

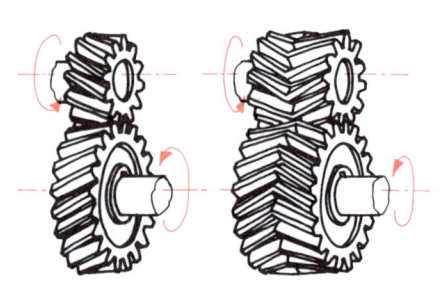

Helical gears **Double helical gears**

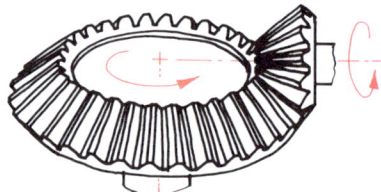

Bevel gear pair

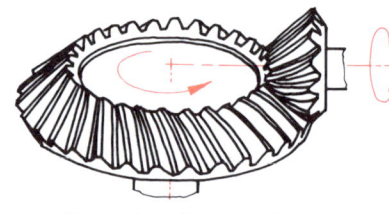

Spiral bevel gear pair

Worm gear and wheel

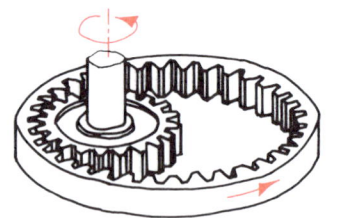

Internal gear system

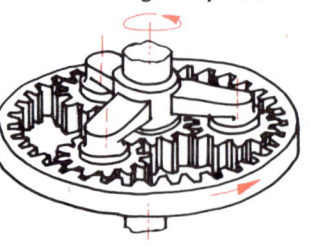

Planetary gear system

- When two gears are meshed directly, and in the same plane, they turn in opposite directions.
- The smaller wheel is called the **pinion** and the larger is called the **spur**.

- When the teeth are curved the next tooth is meshed before the previous tooth disengages.
- The gears run quietly and smoothly and as the contact is over a greater area they are also stronger than spur gears.
- They tend to push sideways and are usually used in pairs.

- The shafts are at right angles and the basic shapes are conical.
- The teeth may be straight, or based on a spiral hyperbola shape.

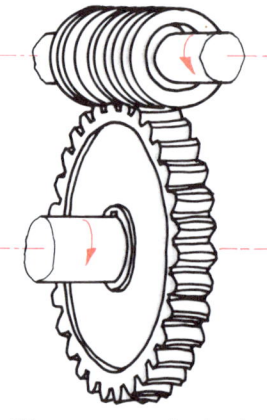

- Shafts are at right angles and in different planes.
- The worm is like a screw and may be multi-start.
- The worm normally drives the wheel.

- The shafts are co-axial and turn in the same direction.
- A variety of these are used in 'automatic' gearboxes.

② Gear drawing conventions

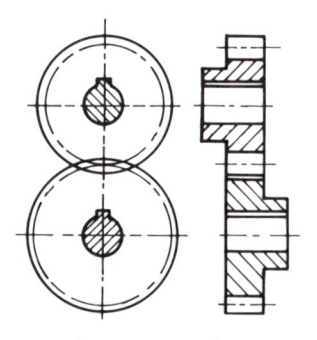

Spur gear pair

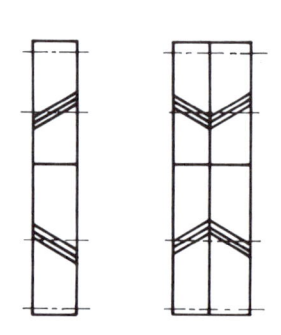

Helical gears

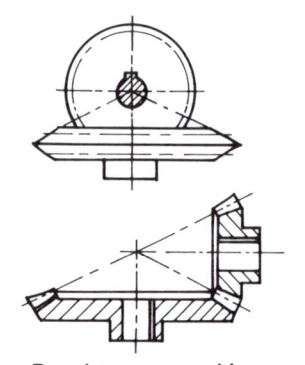

Bevel gear assembly

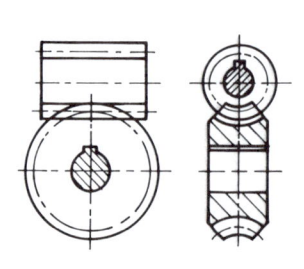

Worm gear and wheel

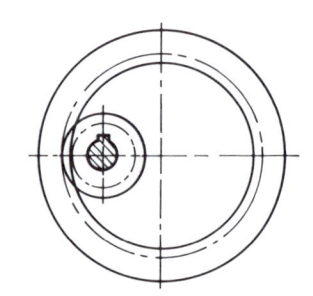

Internal gear and ring

Note
- *The teeth are **not** sectioned, whether cut by a section plane or not.*

Technical Draughtsmanship
Gear Types
Mechanisms 11 — Part 2A Eng.

① Terms used in gearing

Gear pair: Two gears in mesh.
Wheel: The larger of two gears.
Pinion: The smaller of two gears.
Centre distance (c-c): The sum of the pitch radii of the two gears in mesh.
Gear ratio (u): The ratio between the number of teeth on each of the two gears. This also gives the relative speeds of each gear.
Pitch circle (PC): A circle representing the two gears as tangent cylinders. **PCD = mT,** where **T** is the number of teeth and **m** the module.
Pitch point (P): The point of contact of the two pitch circles.
Base circle: An imaginary circle from which the involute profile is generated. **BCD = PCD Cos. 20°**.
Root circle: A circle through the roots of the teeth.
Tip circle: A circle through the tips of the teeth.
Addendum (a): That part of the tooth above the pitch circle, or pitch line. **a = m.**
Dedendum (d): That part of the tooth below the pitch circle, or pitch line **d = a + clearance.**
Clearance (c): The gap left between the tip and root of two meshing teeth. $c = \frac{m}{4} = a - d$
Whole depth: The addendum plus dedendum.
Working depth: The whole depth minus the clearance.
Line of action: A line that with the common tangent contains the pressure angle.
Pressure angle: Normally **20°**, but may be **14½°**.
Module (m): The module is the pitch-circle diameter divided by the number of teeth.

$$m = \frac{PCD}{T} = a$$

Circular pitch (p): The distance from a point on one tooth to a similar point on the next tooth. $p = \pi m$
Tooth thickness: On the pitch circle, the tooth thickness $= \frac{p}{2} = \pi \frac{m}{2}$

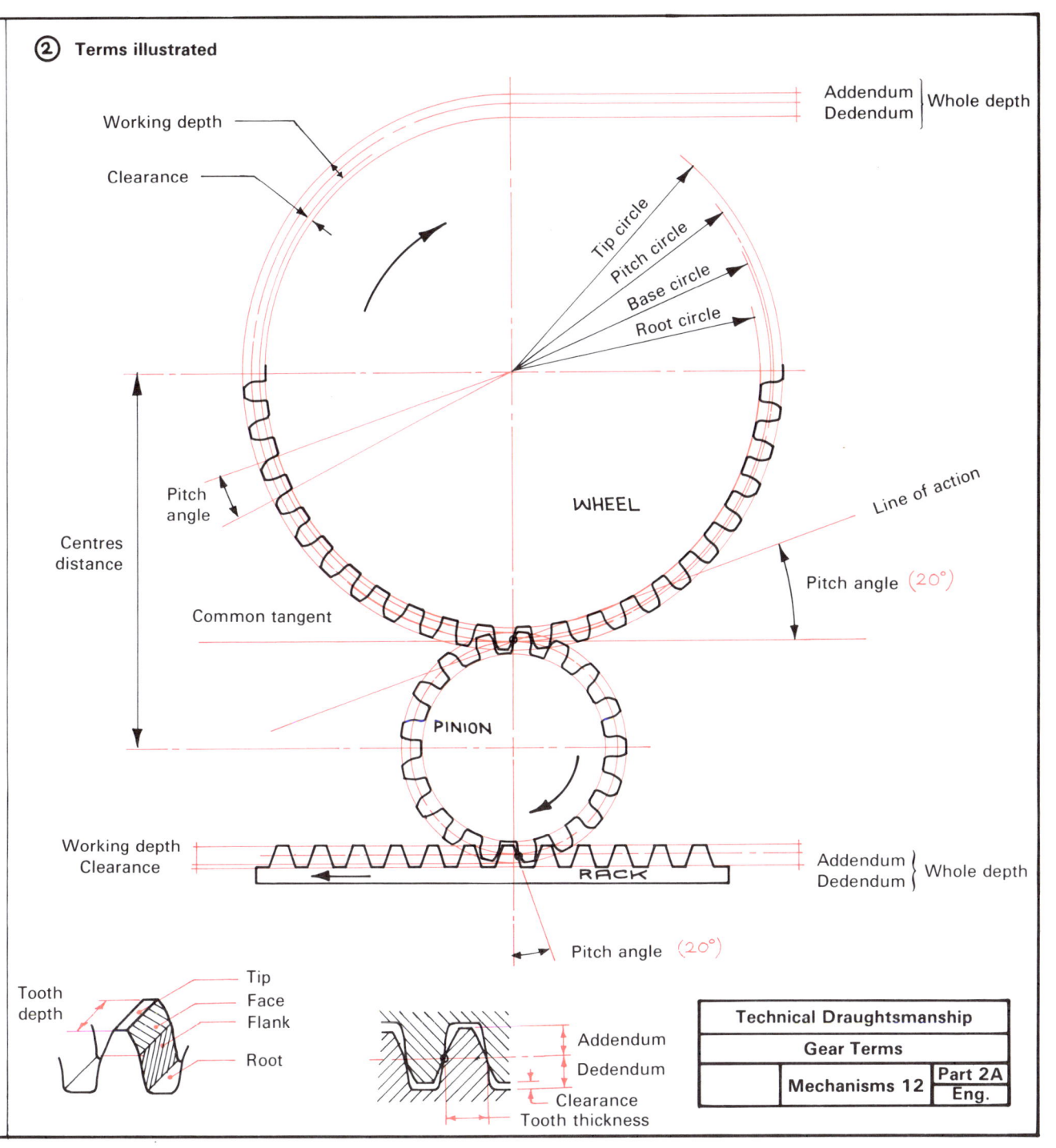

② Terms illustrated

Technical Draughtsmanship
Gear Terms
Mechanisms 12 — Part 2A Eng.

257

① Tooth profile by involute method

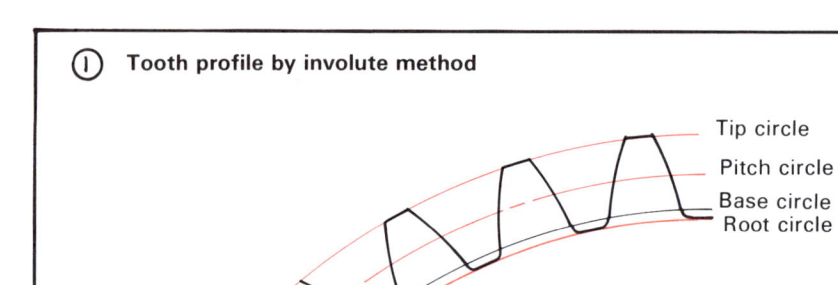

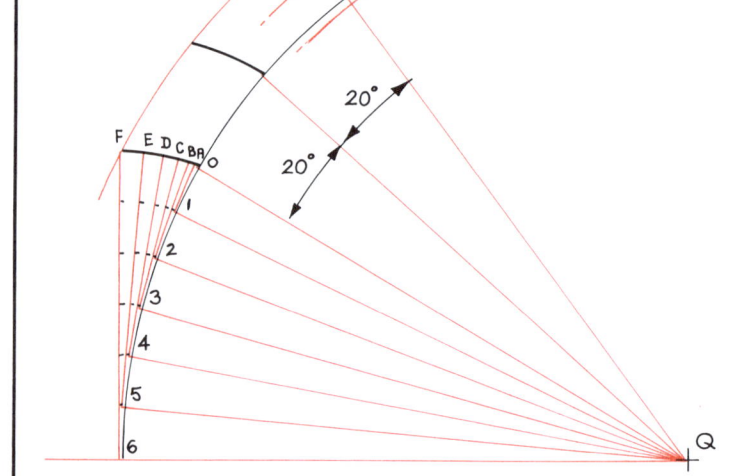

Tip circle
Pitch circle
Base circle
Root circle

Procedure
- Divide an arc of the base circle into a number of parts, e.g. six, and index these **0** to **6**, as above.
- Draw a tangent at **1** and let it be equal to the chord length from **1** to **0**.
- Draw a tangent at **2** and let it be equal to the chord distance from **2** to **0**.
- Continue in this way until the tip circle is reached.
- Further profiles can be traced from the first accurate construction.

② Tooth profile approximated by Unwin's method

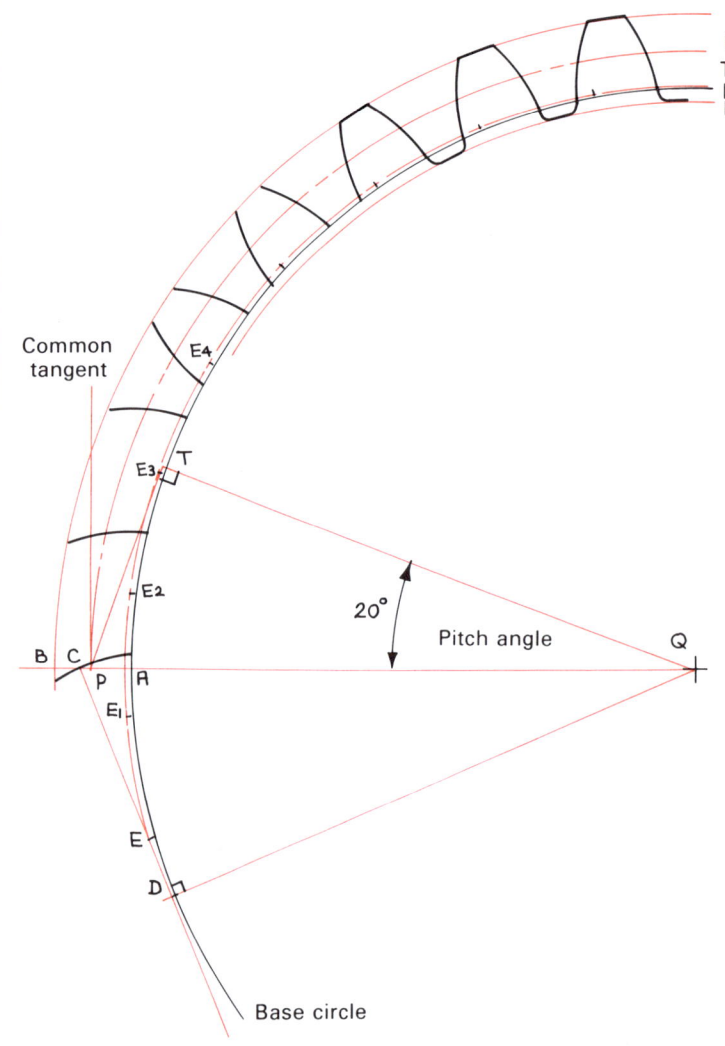

Tip circle
Pitch circle
Tooth centres circle
Base circle
Root circle

Procedure
- Draw the base circle.
- Draw a pitch angle of **20°** and a tangent from **T** to find the pitch point **P**.
- Now draw the pitch circle, the common tangent and the working depth **AB**.
- Divide **AB** into **3** parts and mark **C** one third from **B**, as shown.
- Draw a tangent from **C** to the base circle, finding **D**.
- Divide **CD** into **4** parts and mark **E** one quarter from **D**, as shown.
- With centre **E** and radius **EC** draw the approximate shape of the tooth.
- With radius **OE** draw a tooth centres circle, and, at **20°** intervals, set out **E₁**, **E₂**, etc.
- Continue to draw the tooth profiles.

Note
- If the involute is required at a given pitch point, set up the involute to one side and then transfer it into position.

| Technical Draughtsmanship |
| Spur Gear Profiles |
| Mechanisms 13 | Part 2A Eng. |

Construction by Unwin's method

Construction by involute method

To construct a rack and pinion assembly
- Construct the pinion using either of the methods on page **258**.
- Starting at the pressure point **P** and, using the same addendum, dedendum, and clearance as the pinion, set out the teeth of the rack. The sloping sides will be at an angle of **20°** with the vertical.

PINION

Pitch angle 20°

RACK

Tip line
Pitch line
Base line
Root line

Addendum
Dedendum
Clearance

Worm gears
- These are drawn in a similar way. The rack is drawn and then turned into worm shape by plotting helices, as indicated below. See also page **176**.

Notes
- *The rack may be considered as a spur gear of radius infinity.*
- *Both rack and worm gears are normally reduction gears.*

Technical Draughtsmanship
Rack and Pinion
Mechanisms 14 — Part 2A / Eng. H.

259

① Bevel gears

Two shafts can be fitted with gears and set at right angles. The pitch surfaces of such bevel wheels can be considered as portions of cones with a common apex. The true view of the teeth on the back cone shows them to be similar to those of a spur gear of the same circular pitch.

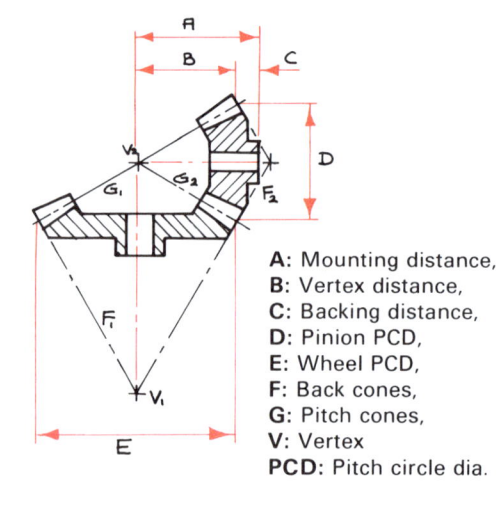

A: Mounting distance,
B: Vertex distance,
C: Backing distance,
D: Pinion PCD,
E: Wheel PCD,
F: Back cones,
G: Pitch cones,
V: Vertex
PCD: Pitch circle dia.

Reduction bevel gears:
The ratio of reduction is **D:E**

Mitre bevel gears: These are two equal bevel gears whose shafts are at right angles.

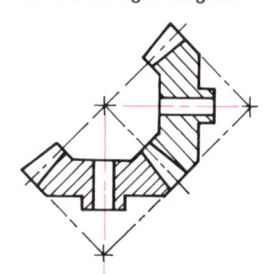

② To construct a bevel gear drawing

Generating tooth profile

Tip circle
Pitch circle
Root circle

A: Root angle
B: Pitch angle
C: Back cone angle

V_1 V_2 V_3

Root diameter
Pitch circle dia.
Tip circle dia.
Root diameter
Pitch circle dia.
Tip circle dia.

Elevation   Tooth face   **End View**

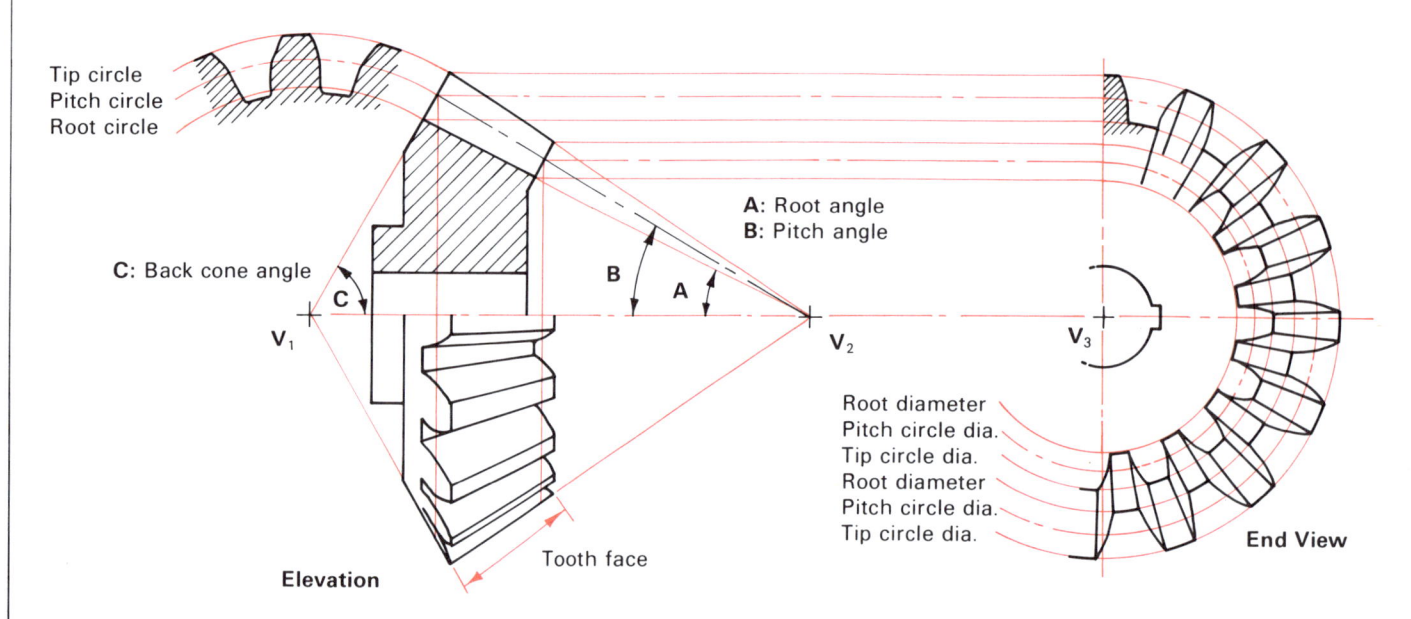

Procedure

- Draw the generating tooth profile in the normal way, as shown on page **258**.
- Using the same centre V_1, set out the back cone of angle **C**.
- Set out the pitch cone, of angle **B**.
- Project the tip, pitch and root circles onto the back cone line and join them to the vertex point V_2.
- To one side choose a centre point V_3 and project across to find both sets of root, pitch and tip circle diameters, as shown.
- Set out the outside tooth profiles and, by using radiating lines from V_3, plot the inside tooth profiles. Complete the end view.
- Project back to plot and draw the elevation.

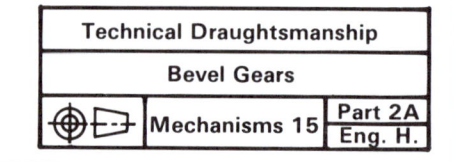

Technical Draughtsmanship
Bevel Gears
Mechanisms 15 — Part 2A / Eng. H.

① See questions

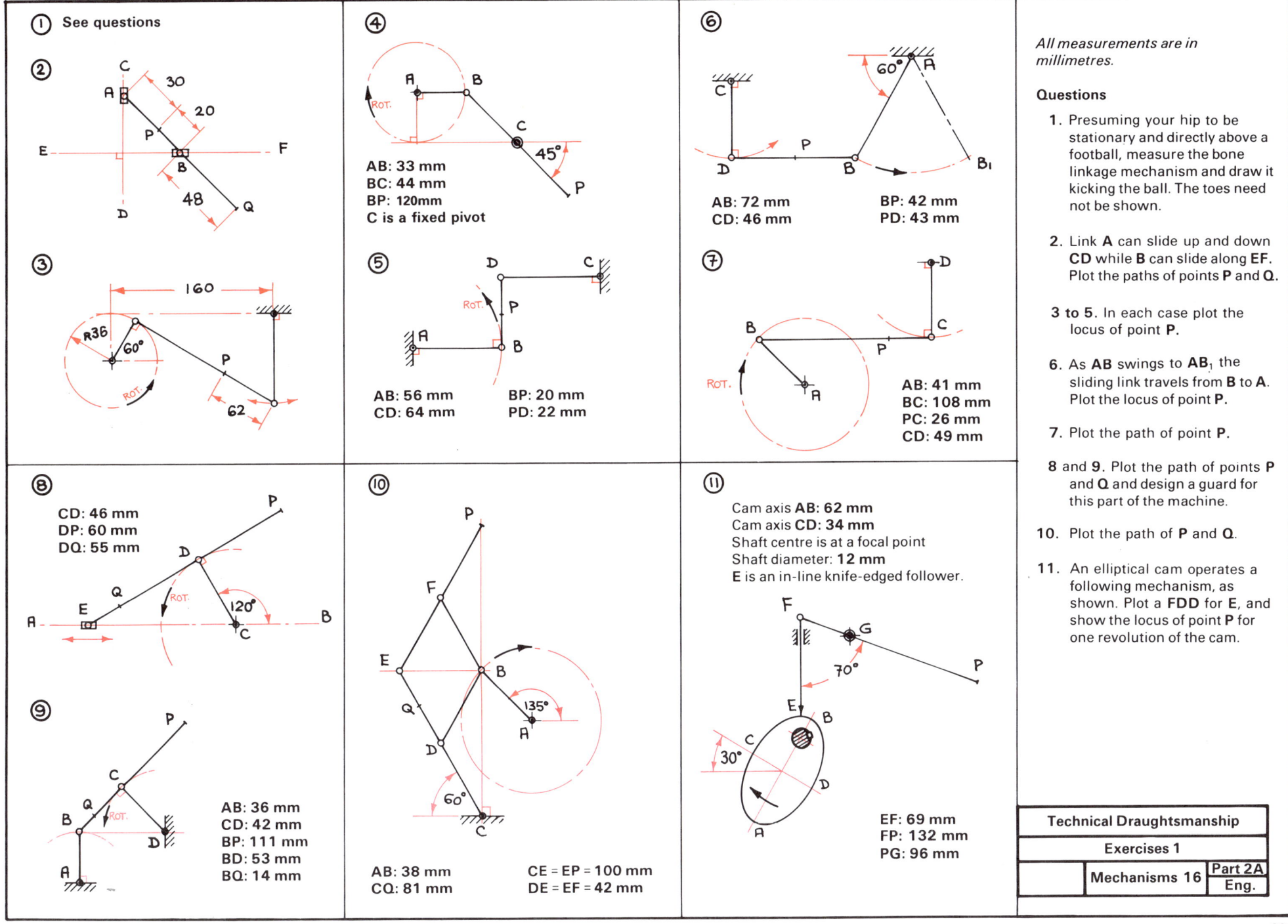

②
AB: (slot with C, 30, 20 measurements)
AC: 30
CP: 20
BQ: 48

③
160
R36
60°
ROT.
62

④
AB: 33 mm
BC: 44 mm
BP: 120 mm
C is a fixed pivot
45°

⑤
AB: 56 mm   BP: 20 mm
CD: 64 mm   PD: 22 mm

⑥
60°
AB: 72 mm   BP: 42 mm
CD: 46 mm   PD: 43 mm

⑦
AB: 41 mm
BC: 108 mm
PC: 26 mm
CD: 49 mm

⑧
CD: 46 mm
DP: 60 mm
DQ: 55 mm
120°

⑨
AB: 36 mm
CD: 42 mm
BP: 111 mm
BD: 53 mm
BQ: 14 mm

⑩
135°
60°
AB: 38 mm   CE = EP = 100 mm
CQ: 81 mm   DE = EF = 42 mm

⑪
Cam axis AB: 62 mm
Cam axis CD: 34 mm
Shaft centre is at a focal point
Shaft diameter: 12 mm
E is an in-line knife-edged follower.
70°
30°
EF: 69 mm
FP: 132 mm
PG: 96 mm

All measurements are in millimetres.

Questions

1. Presuming your hip to be stationary and directly above a football, measure the bone linkage mechanism and draw it kicking the ball. The toes need not be shown.

2. Link **A** can slide up and down **CD** while **B** can slide along **EF**. Plot the paths of points **P** and **Q**.

3 to 5. In each case plot the locus of point **P**.

6. As **AB** swings to **AB₁** the sliding link travels from **B** to **A**. Plot the locus of point **P**.

7. Plot the path of point **P**.

8 and 9. Plot the path of points **P** and **Q** and design a guard for this part of the machine.

10. Plot the path of **P** and **Q**.

11. An elliptical cam operates a following mechanism, as shown. Plot a FDD for **E**, and show the locus of point **P** for one revolution of the cam.

Technical Draughtsmanship
Exercises 1
Mechanisms 16 — Part 2A Eng.

261

1
Cam profile

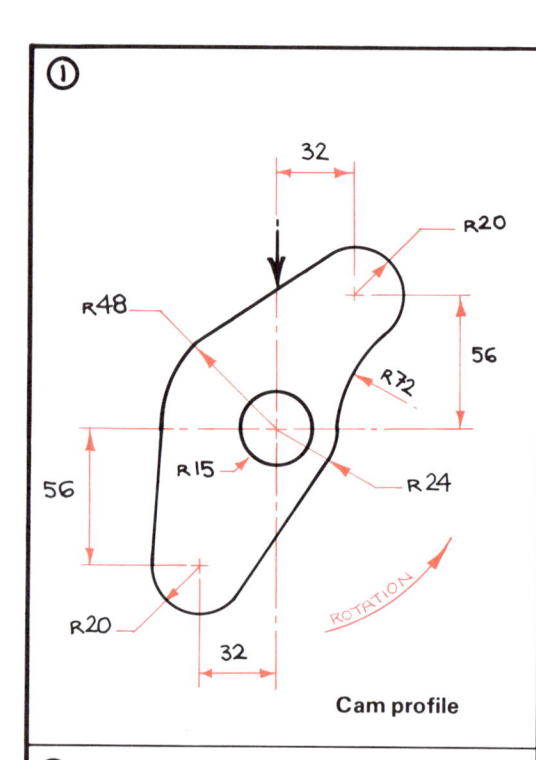

(dimensions: 32, R20, R48, R72, R20, R15, R24, 56, 56, 32, rotation indicated)

2
(a) 0° to 90° SHM lift of 40 mm
   90° to 120° SHM fall of 16 mm
   120° to 180° Dwell,
   180° to 360° UAR fall of 24 mm
   Shaft Dia. 10 mm
   Nearest approach 15 mm from centre.

(b) 0° to 120° UAR rise of 30 mm
   120° to 165° UV fall of 12 mm
   165° to 270° SHM fall of 18 mm
   270° to 360° Dwell
   Shaft Dia. 12 mm
   Nearest approach 14 mm from centre

(c) 0° to 60° Dwell
   60° to 150° SHM fall of 25 mm,
   150° to 270° UAR rise of 48 mm,
   270° to 360° SHM fall of 23 mm,
   Shaft Dia. 14 mm,
   Nearest approach to shaft 5 mm.

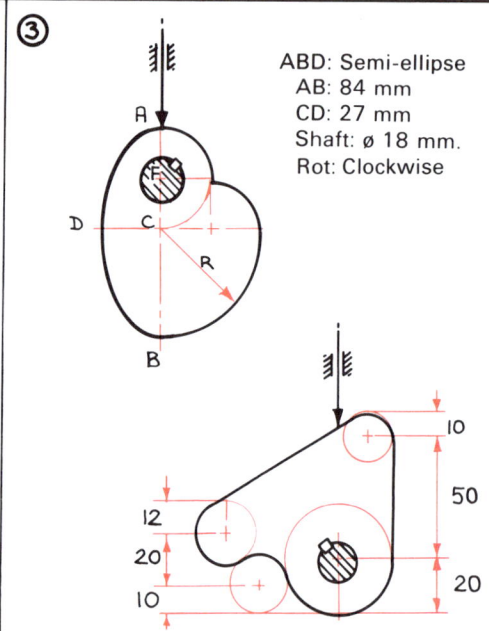

3
ABD: Semi-ellipse
AB: 84 mm
CD: 27 mm
Shaft: ø 18 mm.
Rot: Clockwise

Rot: Anticlockwise
Shaft: ø 16 mm

All measurements are in millimetres

Questions

1. Plot the **FDD** for an in-line knife-edged follower in contact with the given cam profile.

2. In each case draw the **FDD** to the given specifications and plot the profile of a cam that will give that performance to an in-line knife-edged follower. The rotation is anti-clockwise.

3. Plot the **FDD** for a in-line knife-edged follower for each of the given cam profiles.

4. In each case draw the **FDD** and plot the cam profile to the given specifications. The rotation is clockwise.

5. A shop-window display is shown. Draw only the cam and the **FDD** for the follower. How would a child interpret the clown's movements?

6. Draw the **FDD** for point **P**, when **A** is a roller follower set as shown.

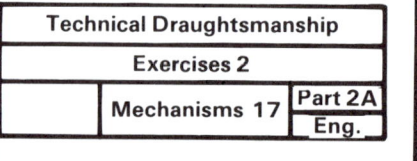

4
(a) 0° to 30° UAR fall of 30 mm,
   30° to 120° UAR fall of 24 mm,
   120° to 150° Dwell
   150° to 360° SHM rise of 54 mm,
   Knife-edge in-line follower,
   Shaft Dia. 12 mm,
   Nearest approach to centre 15 mm

(b) 0 to 15 secs UAR fall of 28 mm,
   15 to 28 secs SHM fall of 14 mm,
   28 to 65 secs UAR rise of 50 mm,
   65 to 100 secs SHM back to start
   Knife-edged follower in-line
   Shaft Dia. 110 mm
   Nearest approach to centre: 14 mm.

(c) 0° to 45° Dwell
   45° to 150° UAR rise of 56 mm,
   150° to 195° Dwell
   195° to 240° SHM fall of 24 mm,
   240° 360° SHM fall of 32 mm,
   Roller in-line follower Dia. 12 mm,
   Shaft Dia. 8 mm,
   Nearest approach to shaft: 12 mm.

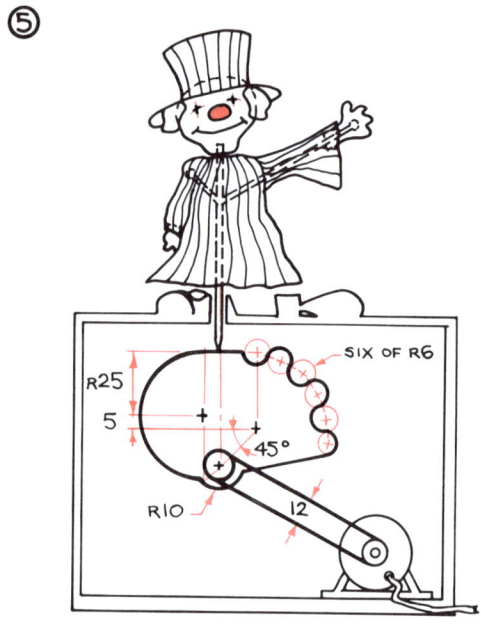

5
One revolution: **60 secs**

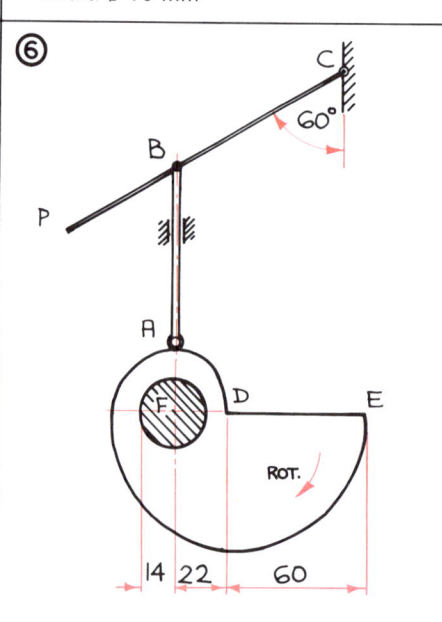

6
EAD is an Archimidean spiral about F.
A: ø 10 mm.   BC: 80 mm.
AB: 70 mm.   BP: 72 mm.

Technical Draughtsmanship
Exercises 2
Mechanisms 17 | **Part 2A** | **Eng.**

①
A: 24 teeth
B: 14 teeth
Pressure angle: **20°**
Module: **8 mm.**

105

②
A: 27 teeth
Pressure angle: **20°**
Module: **6 mm**

16

③
A: Use Unwin's method.
B: Use the involute method.
Number of teeth: **20**
Pressure angle: **20°**
Module: **12 mm.**

④
22
A: A two-start worm.
B: 20 teeth
Pressure angle: **20°**
Module: **8.5 mm**

⑤
210
A: 20 teeth
B: 10 teeth
C: 15 teeth
Pressure angle: **20°**
Module: **9 mm**

⑥
AP: 23 mm
CP: 27 mm
60°

⑦
CD: 25 mm
DP: 120 mm

⑧
AC: 13 mm   CF: 37 mm
BD: 29 mm   EP: 48 mm
AF: 20 mm   Module: 4 mm
45°

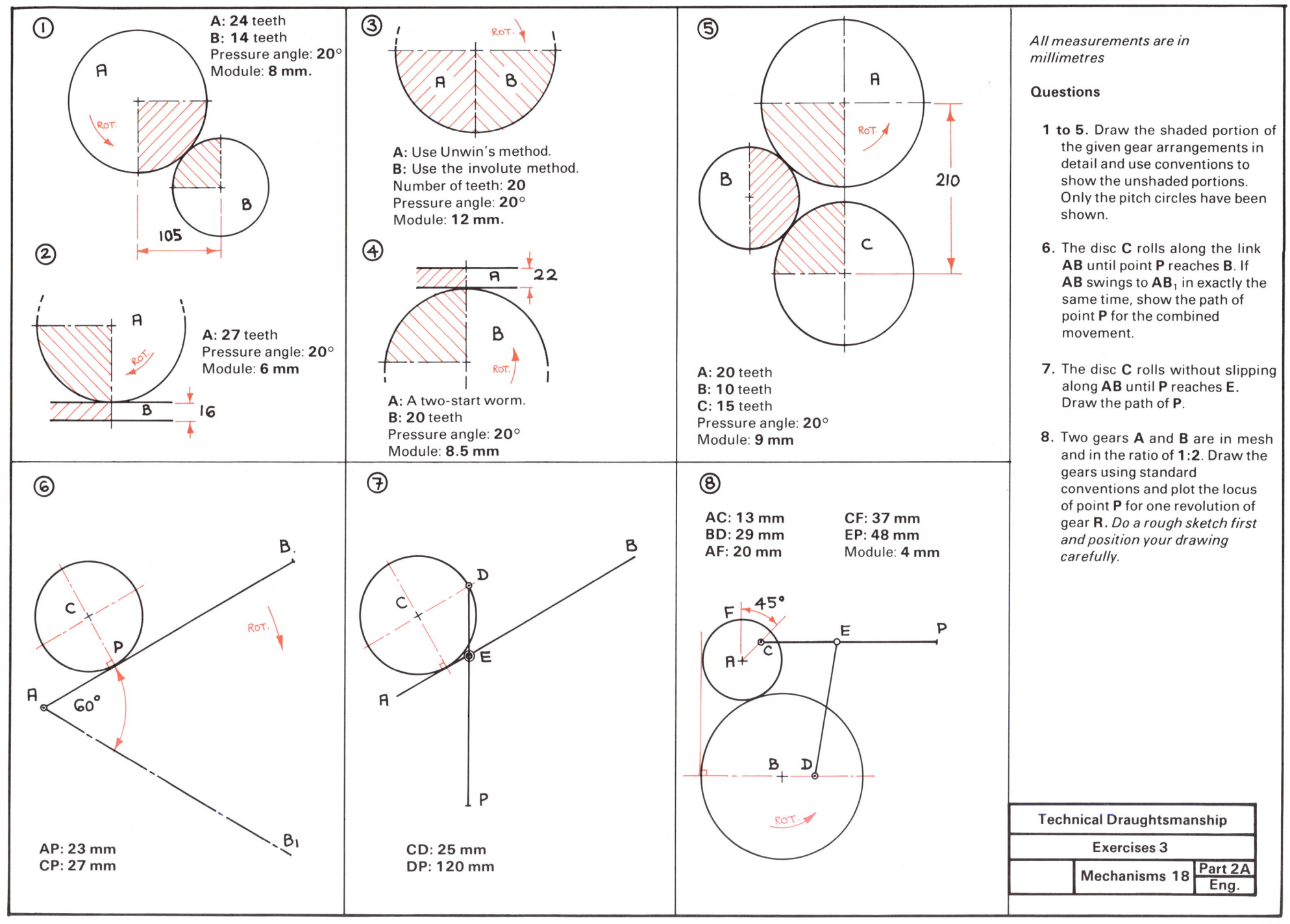

All measurements are in millimetres

Questions

1 to 5. Draw the shaded portion of the given gear arrangements in detail and use conventions to show the unshaded portions. Only the pitch circles have been shown.

6. The disc **C** rolls along the link **AB** until point **P** reaches **B**. If **AB** swings to **AB₁** in exactly the same time, show the path of point **P** for the combined movement.

7. The disc **C** rolls without slipping along **AB** until **P** reaches **E**. Draw the path of **P**.

8. Two gears **A** and **B** are in mesh and in the ratio of **1:2**. Draw the gears using standard conventions and plot the locus of point **P** for one revolution of gear **R**. *Do a rough sketch first and position your drawing carefully.*

Technical Draughtsmanship		
Exercises 3		
Mechanisms 18	Part 2A	
	Eng.	

263

① Chain driven link system

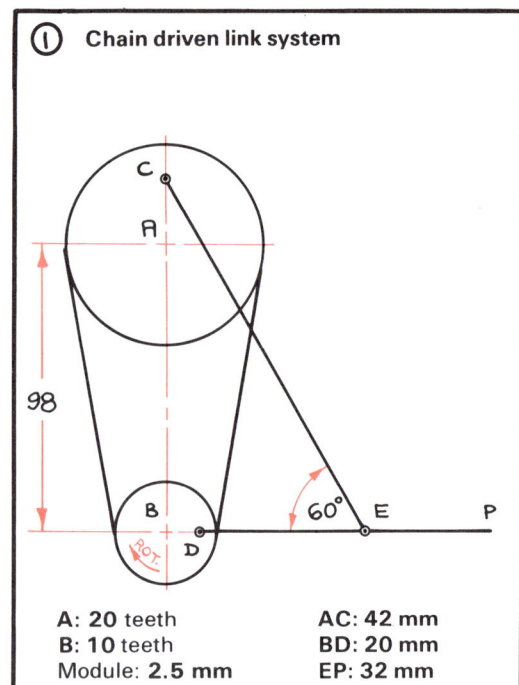

A: 20 teeth
B: 10 teeth
Module: 2.5 mm
AC: 42 mm
BD: 20 mm
EP: 32 mm

② Rack, pinion and linkage

CE: 25 mm
CF: 20 mm
FG: 36 mm
Circle CD: 9 teeth
Module: 5 mm
Pressure angle: 20°

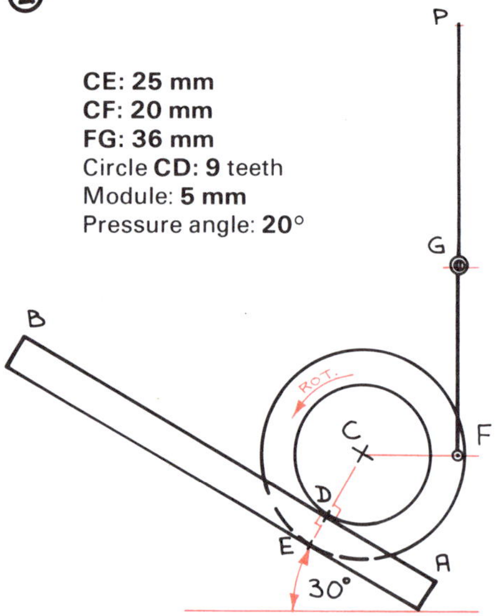

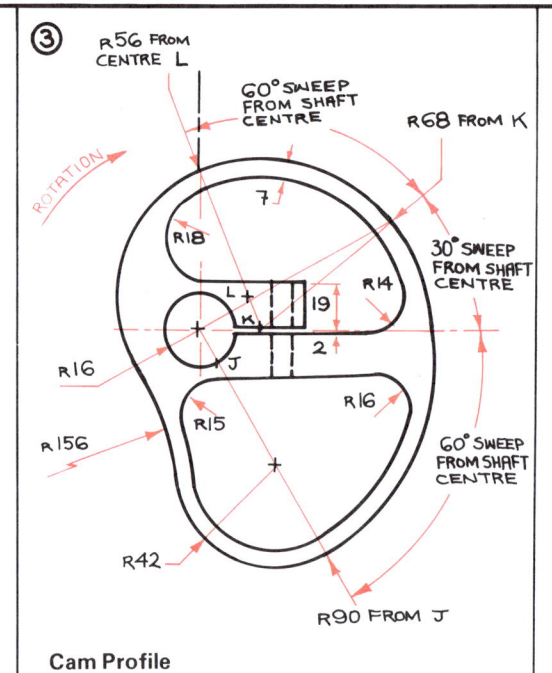

③ Cam Profile

④

(a) 0° to 75° SHM rise of 52 mm
75° fall of 52 mm,
75° to 300° UAR rise of 60 mm,
300° to 360° Dwell,
Rotation anticlockwise,
Roller in-line follower Dia. 12 mm,
Shaft Dia. 16 mm,
Nearest centre to centre 18 mm.

(b) 60° datum 0, rotation clockwise,
60° to 180° UAR fall of 20 mm,
180° to 255° SHM rise of 48 mm,
255° to 300° Dwell,
300° to 60° UAR fall of 28 mm,
Flat in-line follower of base length 15 mm,
Shaft Dia. 12 mm,
Nearest approach to centre is 10 mm.

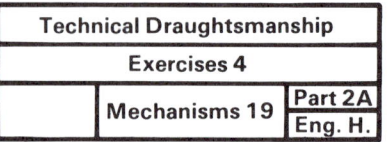

⑤

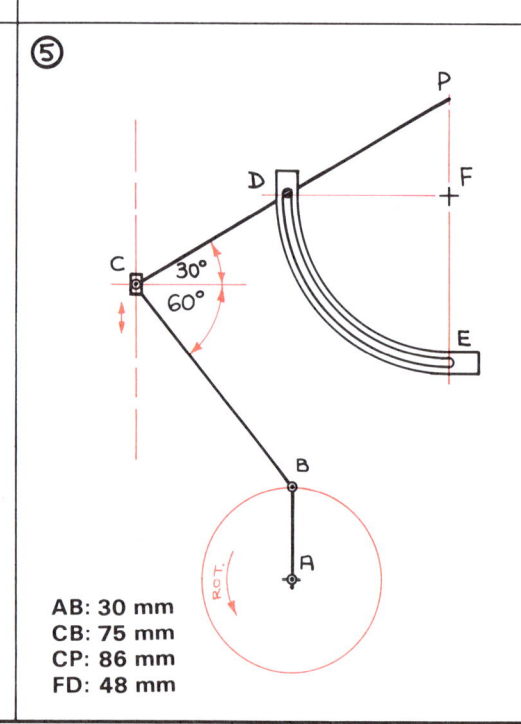

AB: 30 mm
CB: 75 mm
CP: 86 mm
FD: 48 mm

⑥

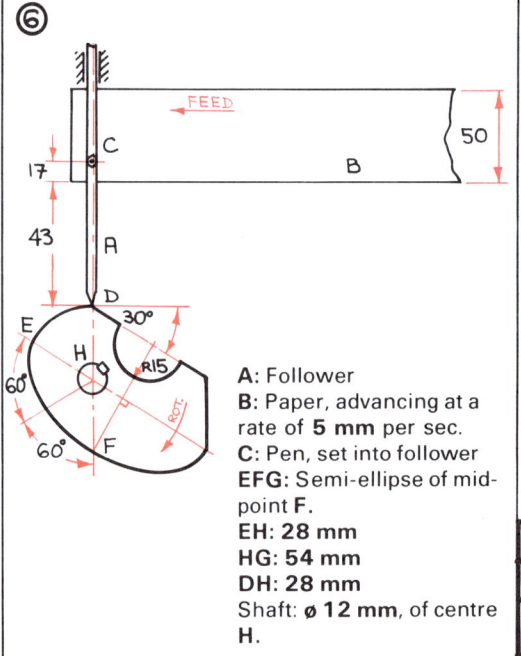

A: Follower
B: Paper, advancing at a rate of 5 mm per sec.
C: Pen, set into follower
EFG: Semi-ellipse of mid-point F.
EH: 28 mm
HG: 54 mm
DH: 28 mm
Shaft: ø 12 mm, of centre H.

All measurements are in millimetres

Questions

1. Plot the locus of point **P** as **D** rotates twice.

2. The pinion **PD** rolls along **AB** until point **D** is again a pressure point. What is the shortest length of **FP** so that it approaches but does not slip through the fixed pivot **G**?

3. This cam operates an in-line roller follower of ø **8 mm**. Plot the **FDD**.

4. Draw the cam profiles necessary to produce each of these performances.

5. As **AB** rotates once, the slotted link slides from **D** to **E** and back. Plot the locus of **P** during this movement.

6. A cam works an in-line knife-edged follower that has an inset pen, as shown. This pen writes on a moving sheet of paper. Plot the written graph for one revolution of the cam, which takes **18 secs**.

Technical Draughtsmanship	
Exercises 4	
Mechanisms 19	Part 2A
	Eng. H.

PART 2A

CHAPTER 22
ENGINES

The most obvious extension of mechanisms is to study prime movers, and their application in the car. A look at bearings and pumps is also included in this chapter.

CONTENTS
Steam Engines	*Page*	**266**
The Four-stroke Engine		**267**
The Two-stroke Engine		**268**
Rotary and Diesel Engines		**269**
Transmission 1		**270**
Transmission 2		**271**
Steering and Braking		**272**
Keyways and Bearings		**273**
Pumps 1		**274**
Pumps 2		**275**
Exercises		**276**

Photocopying prohibited by law

① **The steam engine**
One of the earliest engines to use steam was the pump shown below, built by Thomas Newcomen in 1712. It was called an atmospheric steam engine and was used to pump water from flooding mineshafts.

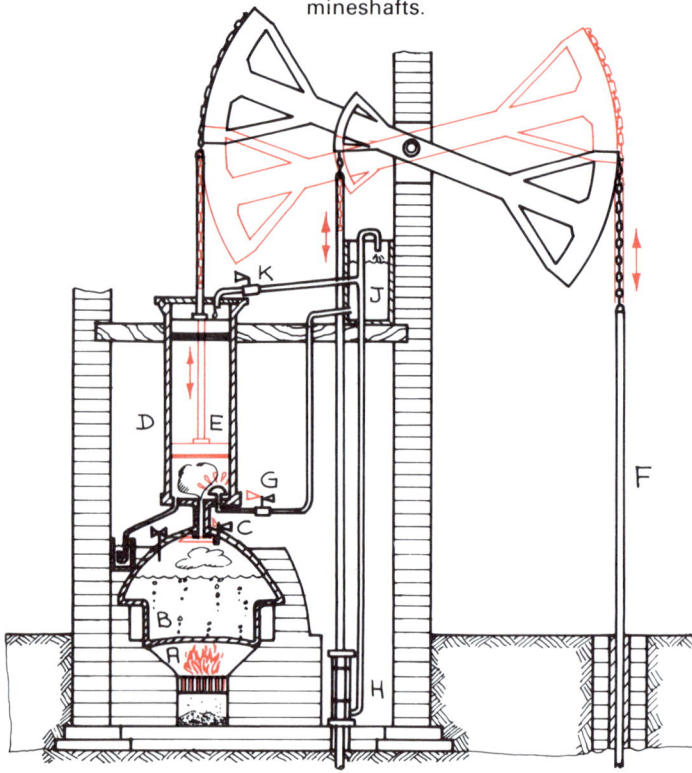

How it works
- The fire **A** heats the water **B** and produces steam.
- The tap **C** is opened and lets the steam into the cylinder **D**. This forces the piston **E** up, helped by the falling pump rod **F**.
- Now tap **C** is shut and tap **G** is opened, spraying cold water into the cylinder.
  This condenses the steam causing a near vacuum in the cylinder.
- Pushed by the outside air and sucked by the vacuum inside, the piston is forced down.
- A smaller pump **H** feeds the tank **J** and piston cooling tap **K**.

② **Watt's improvements**
Newcomen's engine required an enormous amount of steam and, therefore, of fuel. Watt's first improvement was to keep the main cylinder hot and to cool the steam in a separate condenser. He later thought up the centrifugal governor to regulate the speed and also introduced a double-acting piston. This last may be explained with Corliss's slide valve, as below.

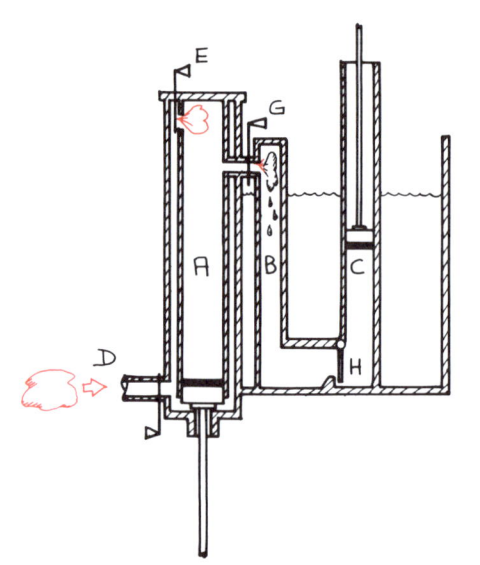

Watt's separate condenser
- Steam enters at **D** and surrounds cylinder **A**, keeping it warm.
- Then valve **E** is opened to let the steam into cylinder **A**, pushing down piston **F**.
- Now **E** is closed and valve **G** is opened. At the same time piston **C** is pulled up. The steam is sucked into the cold cylinder **B**, where it condenses, causing the vacuum that sucks the working piston **F** up along cylinder **A**.
- Note the non-return valve **H**.

Watt's centrifugal governor
- This is shown on page **168**.
- The faster it spins the wider the spheres fly. This is then changed to a sliding movement that works a throttle valve.

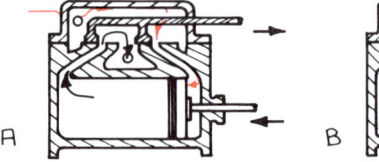

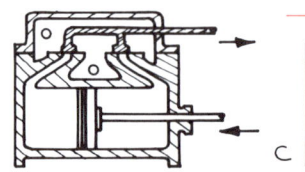

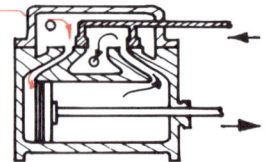

③ **Corliss's slide valve:** This proved a most economical idea.

- In position **A** the steam enters behind the piston and there is suction ahead of the piston.
- Position **B** allows for compression.
- In position **C** steam enters ahead of the piston and there is suction behind.
- The slide is connected to a governor.

Technical Draughtsmanship
Steam Engines
Engines 1 — Part 2A / Eng. H.

① The four-stroke sequence

Down stroke

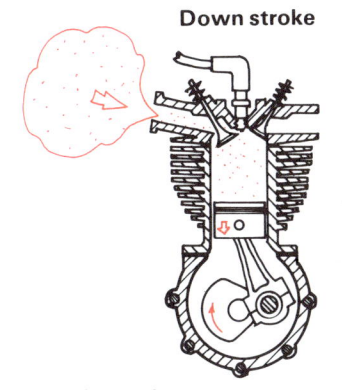

Induction
- The inlet valve opens and the dropping piston sucks the petrol-and-air mixture into the cylinder.

Up stroke

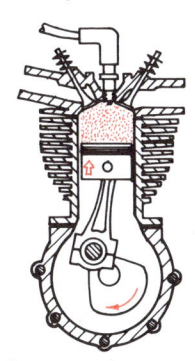

Compression
- Both valves close. The piston rises, compressing and heating the mixture.
- The compression ratio is about 8:1.

Down stroke

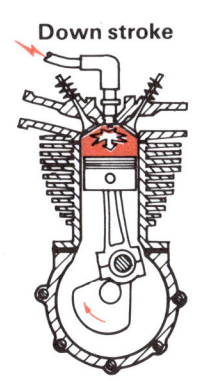

Power
- As the piston reaches its top dead-centre (TDC) a spark ignites the mixture.
- The explosion generates power and forces the piston down, turning the crankshaft.

Up stroke

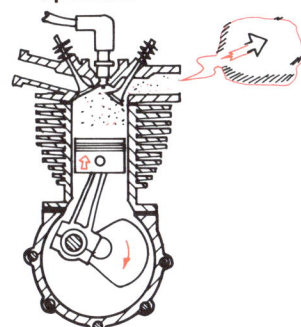

Exhaust
- When the piston is just past its bottom dead-centre (BDC) the exhaust valve opens.
- As the piston rises it pushes the fumes out of the cylinder.

② Parts of the engine

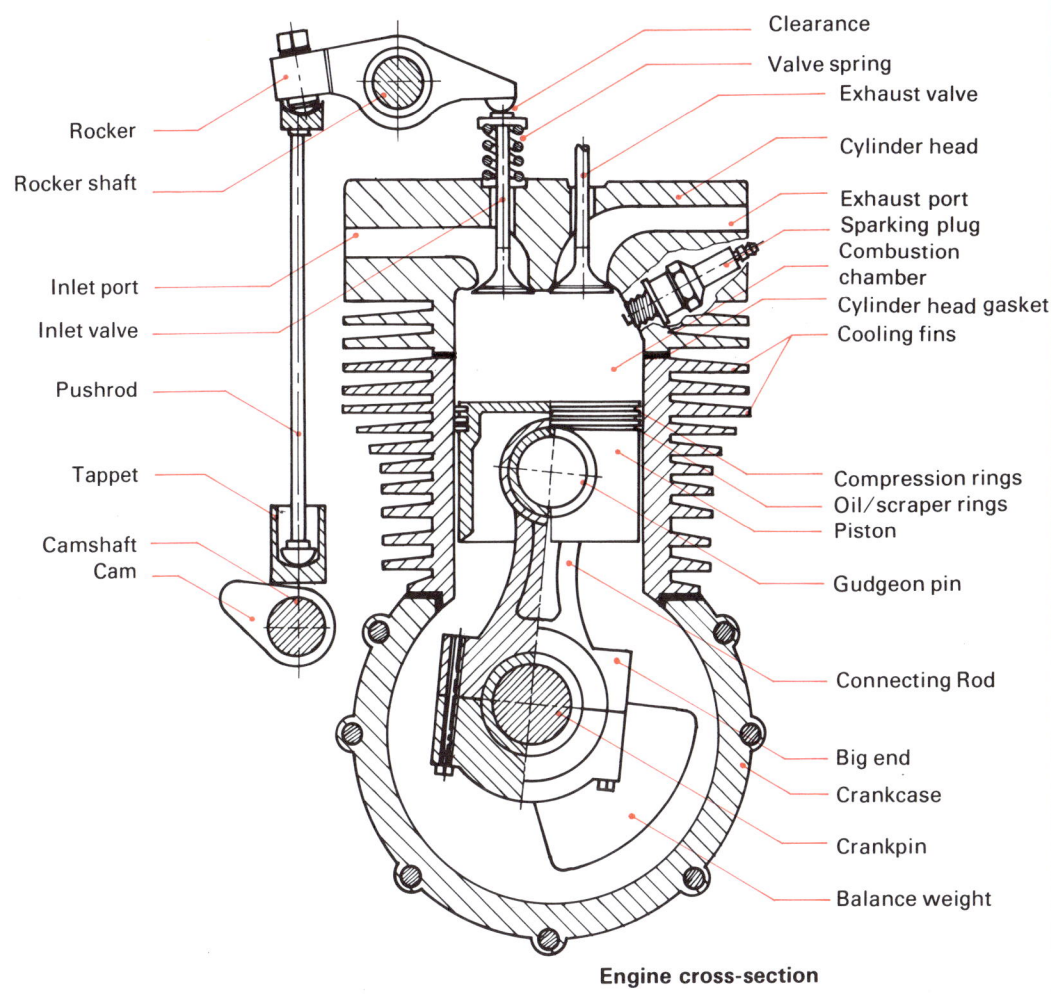

Labels: Rocker, Rocker shaft, Inlet port, Inlet valve, Pushrod, Tappet, Camshaft, Cam, Clearance, Valve spring, Exhaust valve, Cylinder head, Exhaust port, Sparking plug, Combustion chamber, Cylinder head gasket, Cooling fins, Compression rings, Oil/scraper rings, Piston, Gudgeon pin, Connecting Rod, Big end, Crankcase, Crankpin, Balance weight

Engine cross-section

Notes
- *There are often six, eight or more of these cylinders working together. Some aero-engines have up to forty cylinders.*
- *Most combustion engines use the four-stroke sequence.*
- *The engine shown here is called a spark ignition engine.*

Technical Draughtsmanship
The Four-stroke Engine

| Engines 2 | Part 2A Eng. |

267

1 Operational sequence

Down stroke

Above piston:
- Ignition and power develop as the piston drops.
- When exhaust port **B** is open the burnt gas escapes.

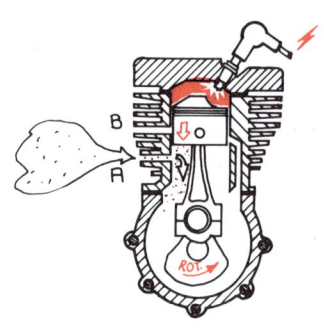

Below piston:
- Inlet port **A** is open and fresh petrol-and-air mixture enters the crankcase.
- The mixture in the crankcase is compressed.

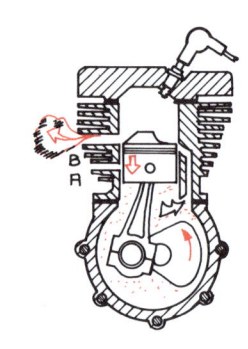

Up stroke

Above piston:
- (See below)
- The piston rises closing the ports and compressing the mixture.

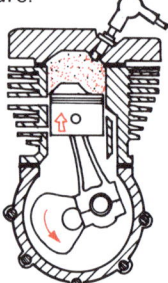

Below piston:
- When the transfer port **C** is open the mixture flows from the crankcase into the cylinder.
- After the ports are closed further rising of the piston produces suction in the crankcase.

2 Parts of the engine

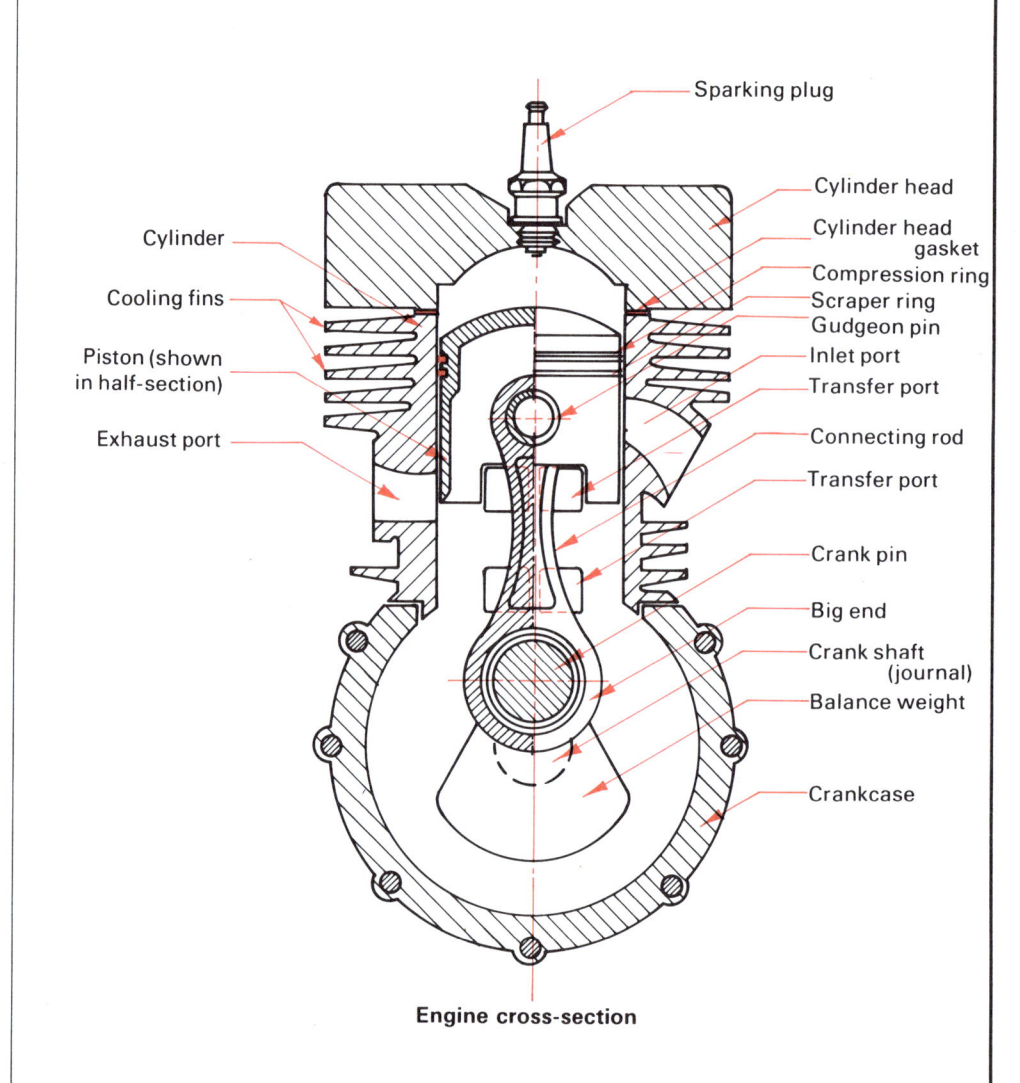

Labels on engine cross-section:
- Sparking plug
- Cylinder head
- Cylinder head gasket
- Compression ring
- Scraper ring
- Gudgeon pin
- Inlet port
- Transfer port
- Connecting rod
- Transfer port
- Crank pin
- Big end
- Crank shaft (journal)
- Balance weight
- Crankcase
- Cylinder
- Cooling fins
- Piston (shown in half-section)
- Exhaust port

Engine cross-section

Notes
- The two stroke engine is generally used in motor-cycles, lawn mowers, small boats, etc.
- It is not as economic as the four-stroke, but is smaller, lighter and cheaper to produce.
- This is also a spark ignition engine.

Technical Draughtsmanship		
The Two-stroke Engine		
Engines 3	Part 2A	Eng.

1. The Rotary Engine

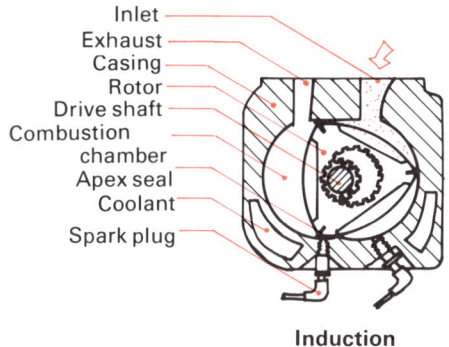

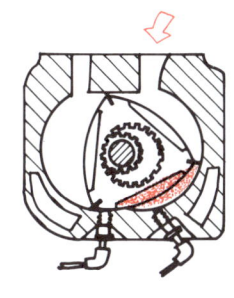

Labels on diagrams:
- Inlet
- Exhaust
- Casing
- Rotor
- Drive shaft
- Combustion chamber
- Apex seal
- Coolant
- Spark plug

Induction | **Compression**

Power | **Exhaust**

Note
- As the inlet and exhaust are always open no timing diagram is given.

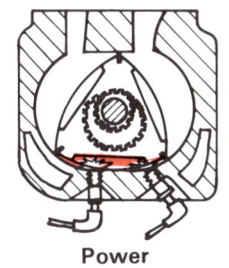

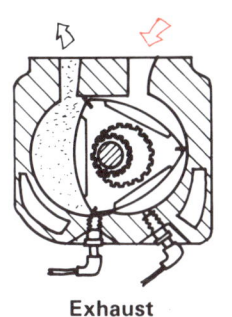

Operation
- The rotary engine operates on the same principles as the reciprocating piston engine on page **267**.
- The rotor has an internally toothed gear meshing with a gear on the drive shaft. The ratio is **2:3**, causing the drive shaft to rotate three times for one turn of the rotor.
- As there is a simultaneous sequence of operations in each chamber there will be three power impulses for each turn of the rotor.
- This engine is compact and has few moving parts. It is capable of high speeds, with little vibration and low noise.
- Unfortunately production, running and service costs are, as yet, uncompetitive.

2. The Diesel engine

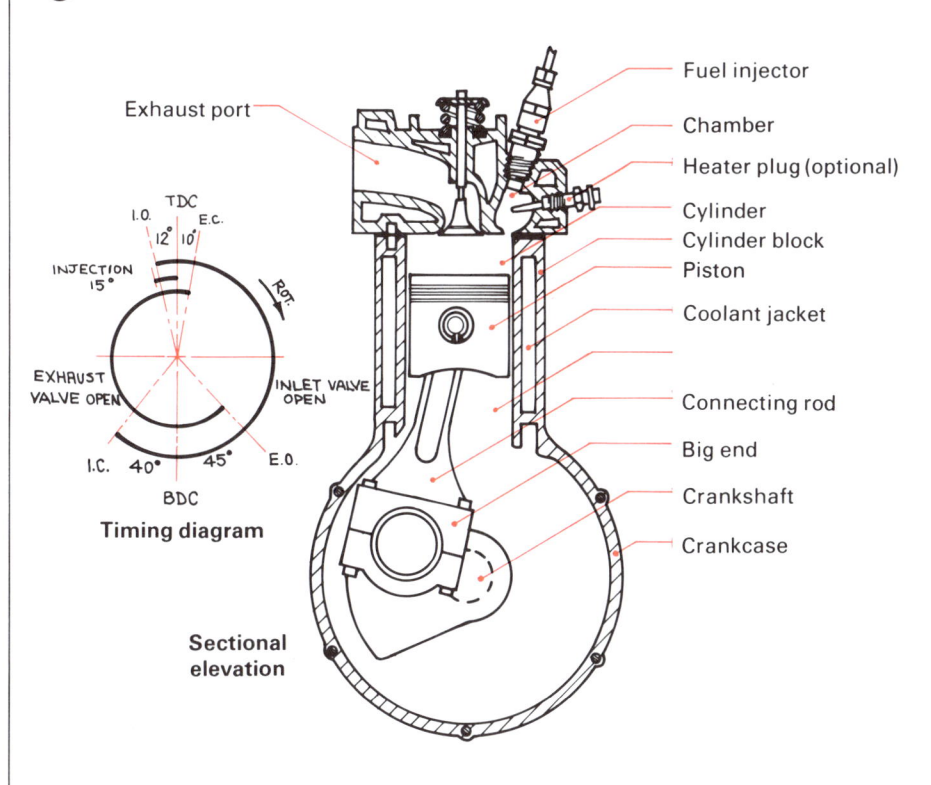

Labels on sectional elevation:
- Exhaust port
- Fuel injector
- Chamber
- Heater plug (optional)
- Cylinder
- Cylinder block
- Piston
- Coolant jacket
- Connecting rod
- Big end
- Crankshaft
- Crankcase

Timing diagram labels:
- TDC
- I.O. 12°
- E.C. 10°
- INJECTION 15°
- ROT.
- EXHAUST VALVE OPEN
- INLET VALVE OPEN
- I.C. 40°
- E.O. 45°
- BDC

Timing diagram

Sectional elevation

Operation
- A diesel engine both looks and works much like a four-stroke petrol engine.
- The important difference is that the air is so compressed, **20:1,** and is so hot, **500°C,** that the fuel will explode without the need of a spark.
- To aid this process the fuel used, derv, is thinner and more easily ignited.
- As the piston reaches its top dead centre, **TDC,** the diesel fuel is injected into the chamber and explodes.
- The resulting temperature is over **1500°C** and the pressure is about **5000 kN/m²**.
- The rest of the cycle is similar to that of a spark ignition engine.
- The diesel engine is a compression ignition engine.
- Some diesel engines work on a two-stroke system, but this is fairly rare.

Technical Draughtsmanship		
Rotary and Diesel Engines		
	Engines 4	Part 2A Eng. H

① The transmission of power (A)

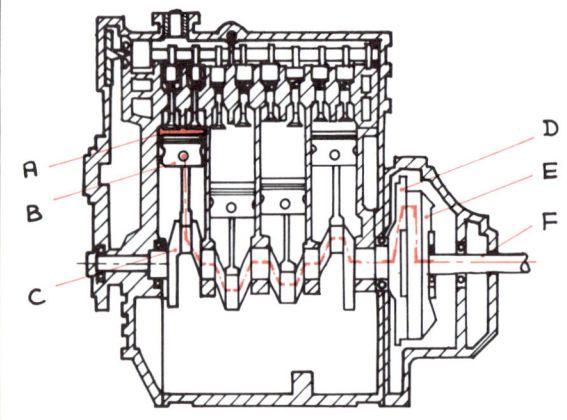

Engine cross-section (simplified)

- An explosion at **A** drives the piston **B** downwards.
- This turns the crankshaft **C**.
- The camshaft is fitted to a flywheel **D**.
- The clutch **E** is tight against the flywheel, but slides out of contact when gears are to be changed.
- The clutch is fitted to the driveshaft **F**.

② The transmission of power (B)

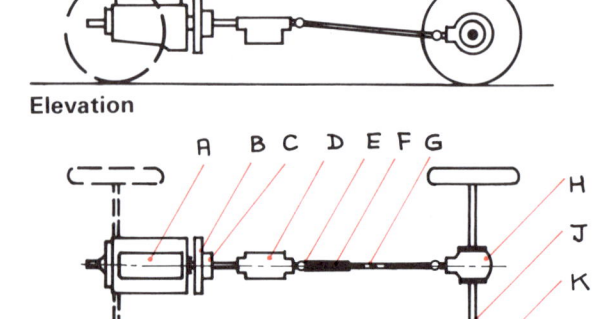

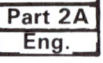

Elevation

Plan

- The engine **A** passes the turning power, or torque, to the flywheel **B**.
- The clutch **C** takes this and passes it on to the gearbox **D**.
- From the gearbox power is transmitted through a universal joint **E** and a sliding joint **F** to the propeller shaft **G**.
- Having passed a second universal joint the power is transmitted through a differential **H** to the live axles **J**.
- This turns the wheels **K**.

③ Single plate clutch

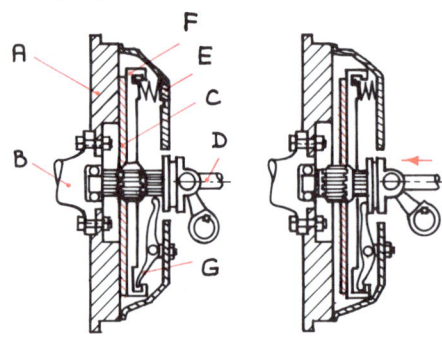

- The flywheel **A** is fixed to the engine shaft **B** and rotates with it.
- The driven plate **C** is attached to the gearbox shaft with a sliding joint.
- Normally the springs **E** push the pressure plate **F** and the whole system is clamped together.
- When the clutch pedal is depressed it pushes the release lever **G** which lifts the pressure plate and the driven plate clear of the flywheel.

④ Diaphragm clutch

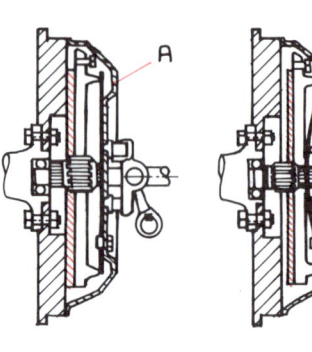

- Here a diaphragm **A**, a saucer shaped metal disk, flips back when the clutch pedal is depressed, bringing the driven plate clear of the flywheel.
- A clutch is a smooth and sophisticated clamp.
- Sometimes a small brake is added to stop residual rotation of the driven plate.

⑤ Universal joint and sliding joint

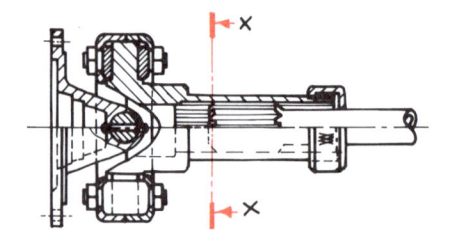

Sectional plan 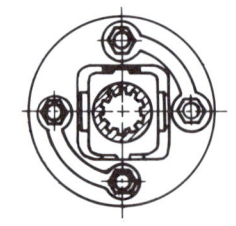   **Section X-X**

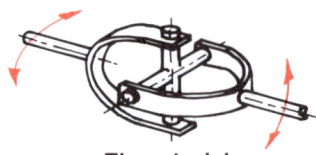

The principle

- Allowance must be made for the movement of a car's suspension system.
- A universal joint allows for a change in angle as the wheel base moves up, down, over or back.
- A sliding joint allows for slight shortening and lengthening of the propeller shaft due to road slope, braking etc.

Technical Draughtsmanship
Transmission 1
Engines 5 — Part 2A Eng.

270

1. The gearbox

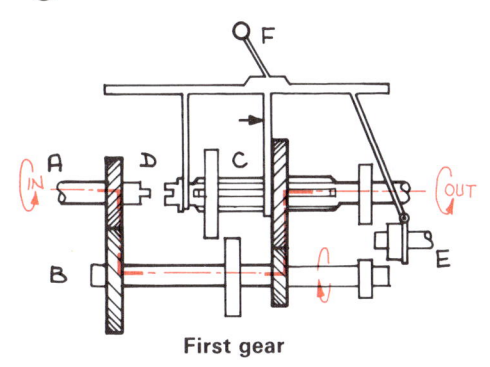

First gear

Second gear

Top gear

Reverse

Neutral

Operation
- An engine has to turn very quickly. Wheels turn at a variety of speeds. A gearbox allows a choice of output speeds and torques, or turning powers.
- The gearbox has three shafts, the primary shaft **A**, the layshaft **B** and the mainshaft **C**, which is splined to allow a sliding movement of two gear wheels.
- In first and second gears one of these gearwheels is slid along the splined mainshaft to mesh with a gear wheel on the layshaft.
- In top gear the primary shaft is connected directly to the mainshaft by the dog clutch **D**.
- Reverse is made possible by bringing a reverse roller **E** to mesh with wheels on both the primary shaft and the mainshaft.

Note:
The system shown here is a simplification. Modern gearboxes are a bit more complicated than this.

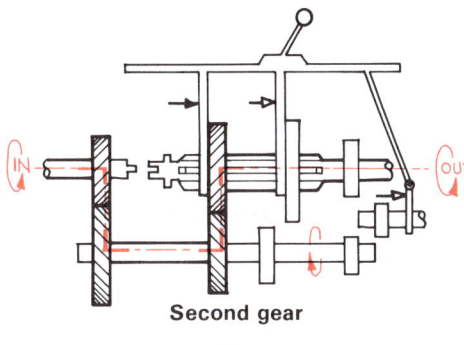

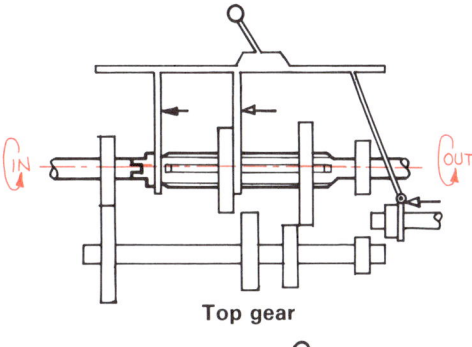

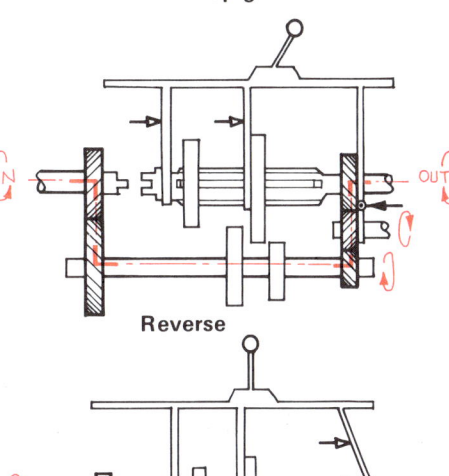

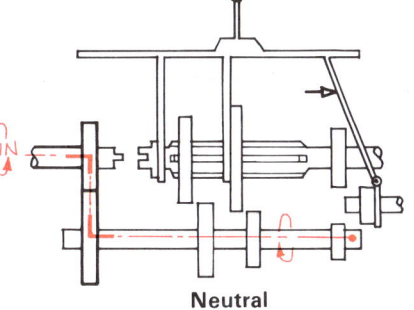

2. The final drive

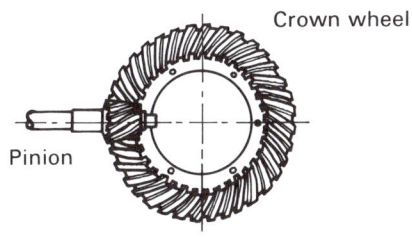

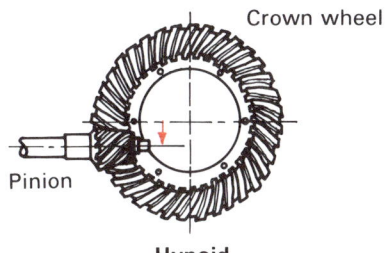

Spiral bevel

Hypoid

- The final increase in torque and decrease in engine speed takes place at the rear axle. Two matched bevel gears reduce and transmit the power from the propeller shaft to the half-axles. The pinion is often dropped to allow the transmission tunnel, that passes through the car, to be lowered.

3. The differential

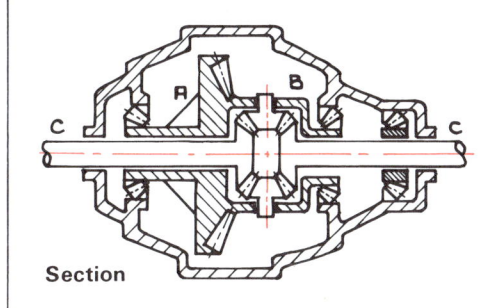

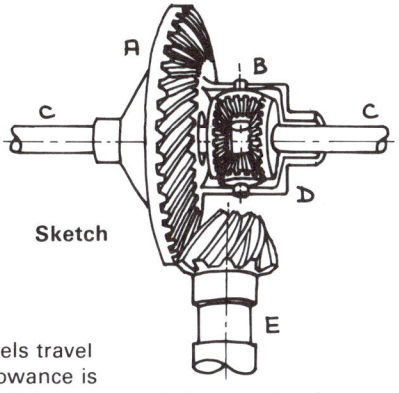

Section

Sketch

- When a car turns a corner its outside wheels travel farther than the inside wheels. If some allowance is not made for this, the tyres will wear and skid.
- The differential is set in a frame **B** and, when the car is travelling in a straight line, the whole frame rotates while the gear wheels inside are locked and do not move.
- However the unequal pressure when cornering *will* set the gears in motion, driving the far half shaft faster than the near one.

A: Crown wheel
B: Frame
C: Half shafts
D: Differential
E: Pinion

Note:
This can be confusing until you actually see it in action.

Technical Draughtsmanship
Transmission 2
Engines 6 — Part 2A Eng.

① Steering

- The steering wheel **A** is fixed to the steering column **B** and this ends in the steering box **C**.
- Within the box a rack-and-pinion system converts the turning of the wheel into a to-and-fro movement.

Detail at C

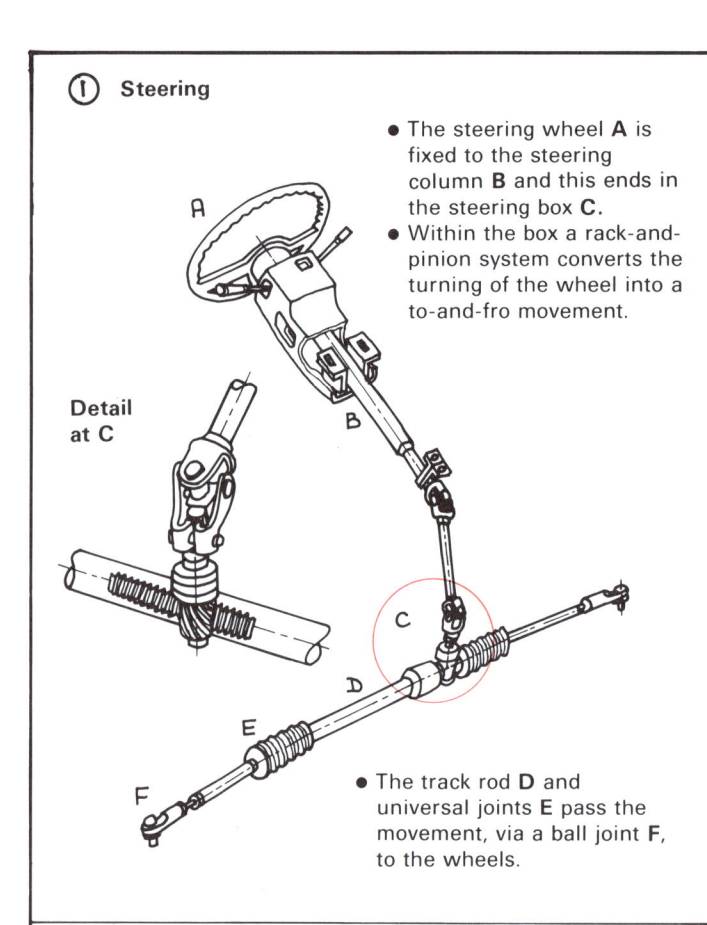

- The track rod **D** and universal joints **E** pass the movement, via a ball joint **F**, to the wheels.

② Suspension and wheel

- The ball joint **A** steers the wheel via the link system **B**.
- The half shaft **C** is joined by a universal joint **D** to the wheel hub **E**, nave **F**, rim **G** and tyre **H**.
- The suspension system has a helical spring **J** and a shock absorber, or damper, **K**.

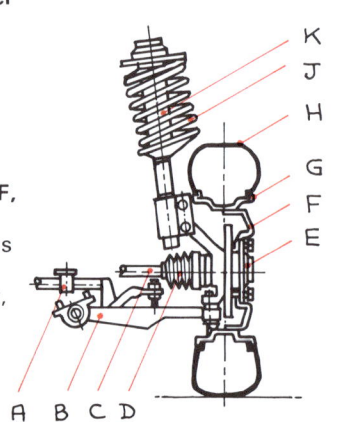

③ Brake control: hydraulics

- Most vehicles have dual-circuit braking systems and self-adjusting devices to avoid brake failure. 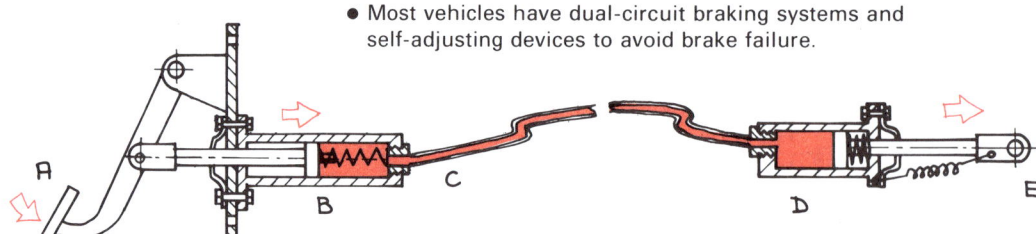
- When the driver pushes the pedal **A** it works a piston in the master cylinder **B** forcing fluid out through nozzle **C**.
- This passes to a series of slave cylinders **D** where a second piston reacts and works an appliance **E**.
- By varying the design, a little pressure at **A** can cause a great pressure at **D** and **E**.

④ Drum brakes

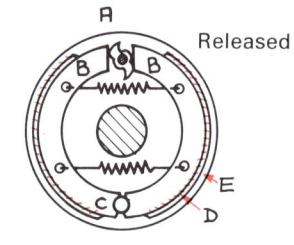

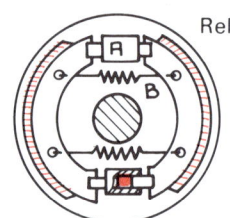

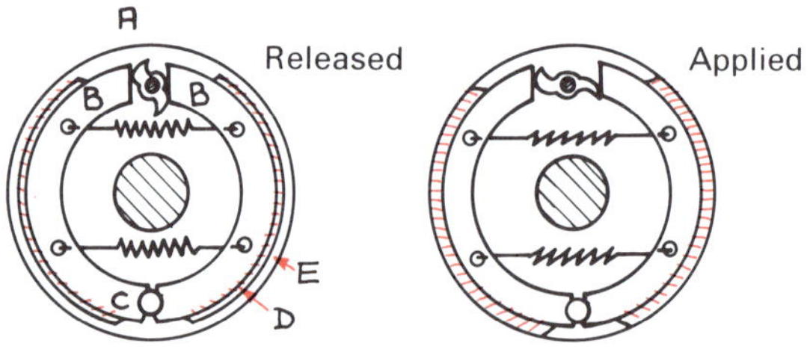

Released   Applied   Released   Applied

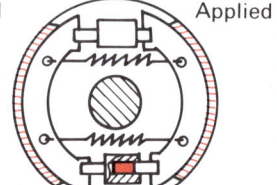

Cam operated system
- An 'S' cam **A** is turned and forces the brake shoes **B** outwards about the pivot **C**.
- This forces the friction pads **D** against the lining of the brake drum **E**, which is fixed to the wheel.

Expanding cylinder system
- The two cylinders **A** each have two pistons that are hydraulically pushed outwards.
- In both systems pull-off springs **B** help release the brakes.

⑤ Disc brakes

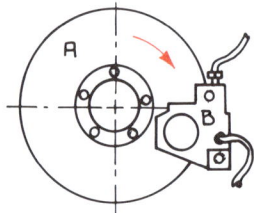

- A steel disc **A** is fixed to the wheel and rotates with it.
- The brake unit **B** is set up to straddle the disc.
- Brake fluid **C** enters a chamber **D** into which is set a piston **E** with friction pads **F**. 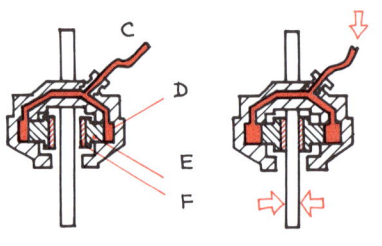
- When braking, the fluid pushes the pistons and pads against the disc.

Note
- *Disc brakes do not need pull-off springs and they are easier to cool. But the area of braking surface is less than in drum brakes.*
- *Generally a car will have disc brakes on the front and drum brakes on the rear wheels.*

Technical Draughtsmanship
Steering and Braking

Engines 7	Part 2A Eng.

272

1 Keys and keyways

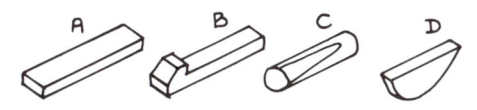

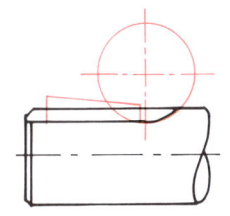

Keys (A, B, C, D)

Edge-milled keyway
With tapered key.

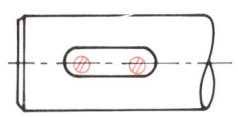

Edge-milled keyway
With feathered key.

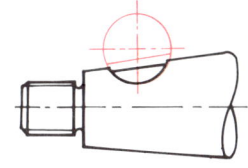

Woodruff keyway
In a tapered shaft.

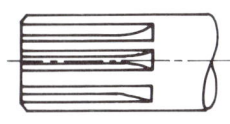

Splined shaft
To allow for a sliding component

- One way to prevent a part slipping on its shaft is to machine a slot, a *keyway,* in both and to insert a tight fitting steel piece or *key,* so that no relative movement is possible.
- Keys may be rectangular **A**, or square, or round. A gib-head key **B** is easier to knock into place and to remove. These may be straight edged or tapered for a forced fit.
- A cotter pin **C** is a piece of round bar with a tapered flat milled into it. These are used to good effect on bicycle pedal shafts.
- A Woodruff key **D** is a segment of a disc and has the advantage that it can be fitted into a tapered shaft.
- Keyways are cut on machines, or may be milled or slotted. Their proportions vary to suit the strength required.
- A form of multi-key is a spline. This is a very strong joint that allows a component to slide but not slip.

2 Rolling bearings:
These are hardened steel balls or cylinders held between two rings called races. A cage is usually included to correctly position the rollers.

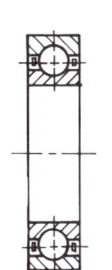

Ball-bearing

Roller-bearing

Ball-bearing
The standard design. These can also be shown on a drawing by a crossed square, as at **B** above.

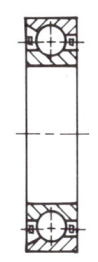

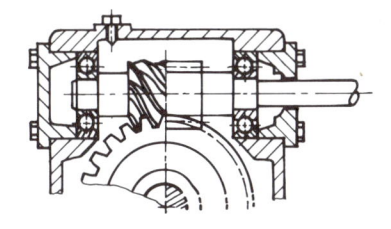

Angular contact ball-bearing
These are designed to take thrust forces as well as journal forces, but in one direction only. They are used in opposing pairs.

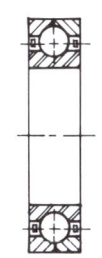

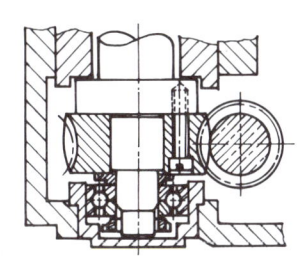

Duplex bearing
These are deep-set stiff bearings. One of the rings is split to allow for assembly.

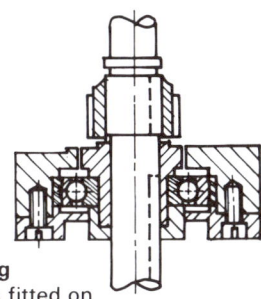

Self-aligning bearing
Here an extra ring is fitted on the outside to allow for slight wobbles.

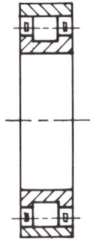

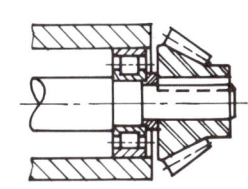

Roller bearing
A ball-bearing makes a point contact. For larger forces roller-bearings are used as they can spread the forces along the length of the roller.

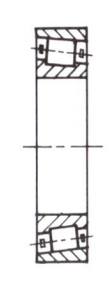

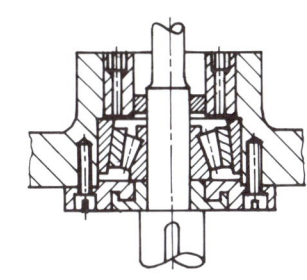

Taper roller-bearing
These act like angular-contact bearings and are often used in opposing pairs to take thrust forces.

Note
Bearings are often used in pairs and sequences, or made with double or multiple races.

Technical Draughtsmanship		
Keyways and Bearings		
Engines 8	Part 2A Eng.	

273

① Lift pump, or atmospheric pressure pump, or cylinder pump, or reciprocating positive displacement pump, alias the village pump.

Operation
- As the piston **A** is pulled up, valve **B** closes and water is sucked into chamber **C**.
- Now the piston is pushed down. Valve **D** is shut and, as valve **B** opens, the piston can move through the trapped water.
- Another upward stroke of the piston lifts this water until it overflows at **F**, while at the same time sucking more water into chamber **C**.
- Water can be 'lifted' up to **10 m** by this method.

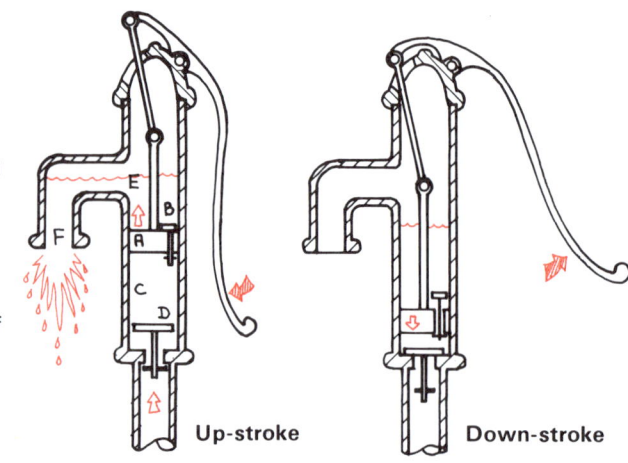

Up-stroke **Down-stroke**

Note: *The valves are non-return valves.*

② Compressor.
Most often used to compress air, this can also be used to give greater pressure to water, and to pump it. A bicycle pump is a simple compressor. The compressor below is a two-stage piston compressor with a cooling chamber.

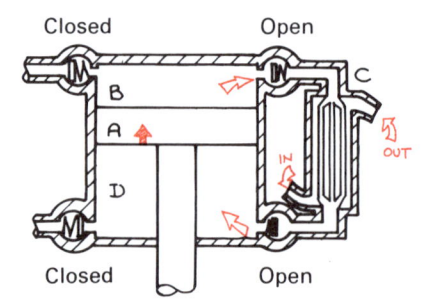

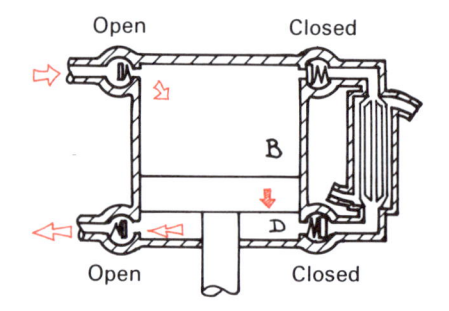

Closed | Open — Open | Closed
Closed | Open — Open | Closed

Stage 1: Up-stroke
- The piston **A** rises compressing the water in chamber **B** and driving it into the cooling chamber **C**.
- At the same time similar compressed and cooled water is sucked into chamber **D** behind the piston.

Stage 2: Down-stroke
- The piston descends reversing the non-return valves.
- The water in chamber **D** is further compressed and expelled.
- At the same time fresh water is sucked into chamber **B**.
- Sometimes an aftercooler is also necessary.

③ Ram and cam pump
- As the piston **A** is pushed forward by the cam **B** the ball valve at **C** is sealed and the water is pushed out past **D**.
- On the back-stroke the valve at **D** is sealed and water is sucked in at **C**.

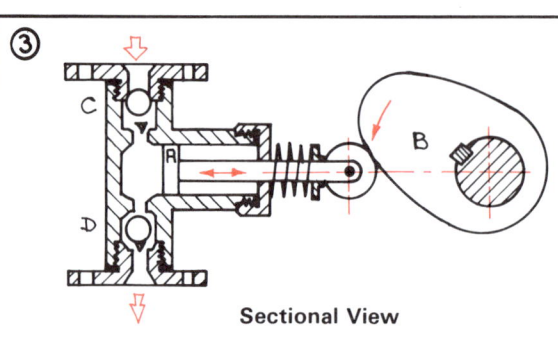

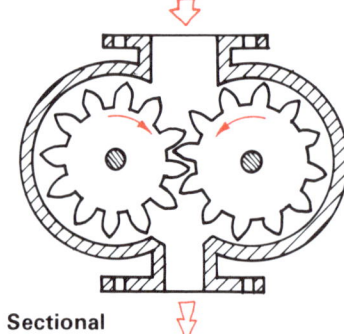

Sectional View

④ Gear pump
- Two equal gears suck, compress and expel water, or oil, between their meshing teeth.
- This system is used in many automobile lubrication systems.

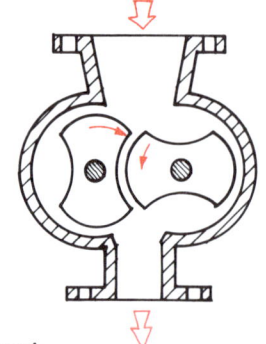

Sectional diagram

⑤ Root's vacuum pump
- The closely meshing wheels suck, trap, compress and expel liquids or gases.
- This is used as a de-gassing device in foundrywork.

Sectional diagram

Technical Draughtsmanship
Pumps 1
Engines 9 — Part 2A Eng.

① Centrifugal vane pump

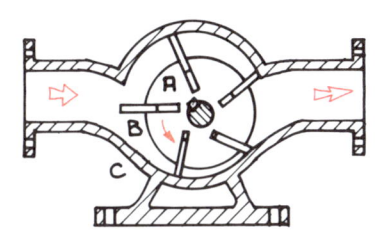

Sectional diagram

- The rotor **A** is offset and carries a number of sliding vanes **B**.
- As the rotor turns the vanes slide in and out, keeping in contact with the outer casing **C**.
- These trap, compress and expel the water, as shown.
- This is a rotary pump and has the advantage of requiring no valves.

② Rotary pump with rubber lobe

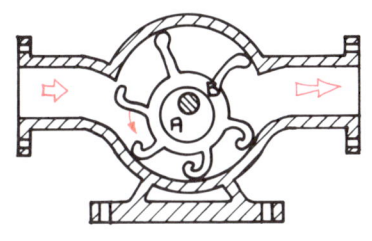

Sectional diagram

- A cam rotor **A** has a rubber lobe **B** fixed about it.
- As the rotor turns the lobe arms, being flexible, trap, compress and expel the water as shown.
- The rubber wears easily but is easily replaced.

③ Peristaltic pump

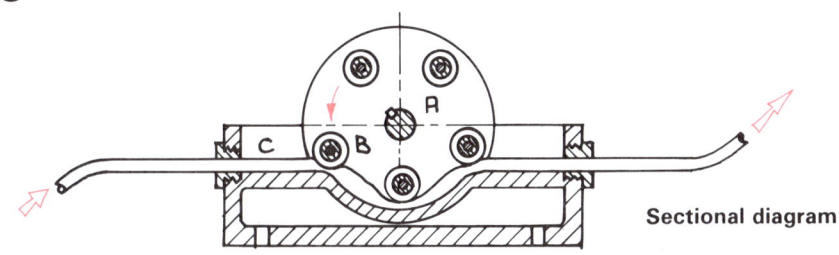

Sectional diagram

- This is also a valve-less rotary pump.
- The rotor **A** has rollers **B** and these squeeze a flexible tube **C**.
- The water is trapped, pushed along and expelled.
- These pumps work well with thick liquids and are used in medicine to pump blood.

④ Centrifugal pump

These are often arranged in series with the outlet of one unit leading to the inlet of the next unit.

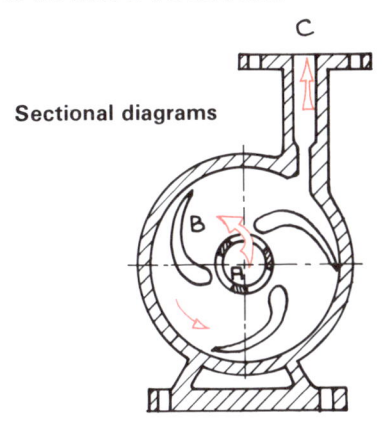

Sectional diagrams

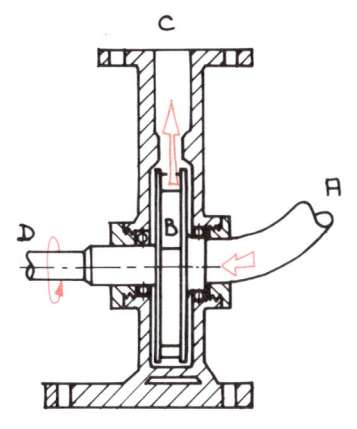

- Water is sucked into the 'eye' of the pump at **A**.
- The impeller **B** has fixed vanes and, as it turns, it whisks the water to the outside.
- The water at the edge of the impeller is thrown outwards at speed and escapes through outlet **C**.
- The pump is coupled to an engine along axle **D**.

⑤ Diaphragm pump

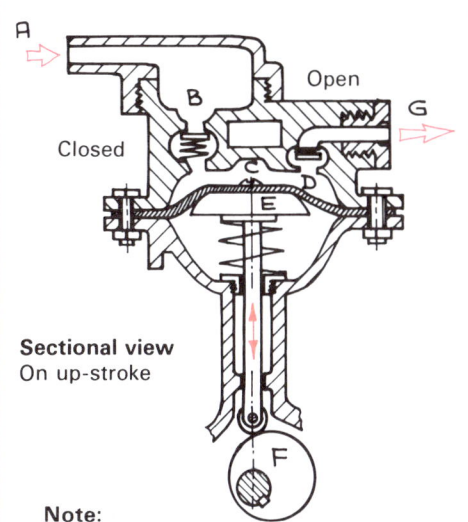

Sectional view
On up-stroke

- The pumps shown before are all wet pumps. They all allowed the liquid to enter and surround the works. The diaphragm pump does not do this and is a 'dry' pump.
- The liquid is sucked in at **A**, then through the inlet non-return valve **B** to the chamber **C**.
- A plastic diaphragm **D** is fixed to the piston **E**, which is worked by a cam **F**. The exclusion of liquid from the works keeps the liquid uncontaminated and also stops it clogging the works.
- The up-stroke reverses the valves and expels the liquid at **G**.
- These pumps are used in cars.

Note:
There are many other types of pump, notably electric pumps, that are not shown here.

Technical Draughtsmanship
Pumps 2
Engines 10 · Part 2A Eng.

All measurements are in millimetres.

Questions

1. Sketch the two engines shown, identify the engine type and write a short note on the function of each item indicated.

2. Proceed as in question 1.

3. Given are an elevation and a half-sectioned elevation of Hooke's universal coupling. Make a quarter-sectioned orthographic projection of the assembly, and a set of detail drawings of the components.

4. Measure your own leg and calculate distances A and B. Design a comfortable pedal and calculate 'l', the length of pedal movement. Then draw panel C with pedal and brake chamber in position.

5. Draw the shaft and bearings, as shown, and sketch an alternative arrangement.

6. A friction brake is shown. Draw half-sectioned orthographic views of the assembly.

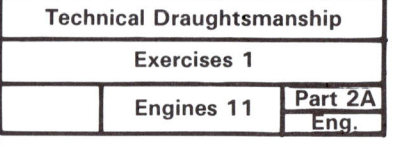

Panel 4 — Brake chamber
- Pistons D and E are set to work in tandem.
- Fluid inlets have been omitted.

Panel 5:
- A: Circlip
- B: Ball bearing
- C: Roller bearing
- D: Oil seal

Technical Draughtsmanship

Exercises 1

Engines 11 — Part 2A Eng.

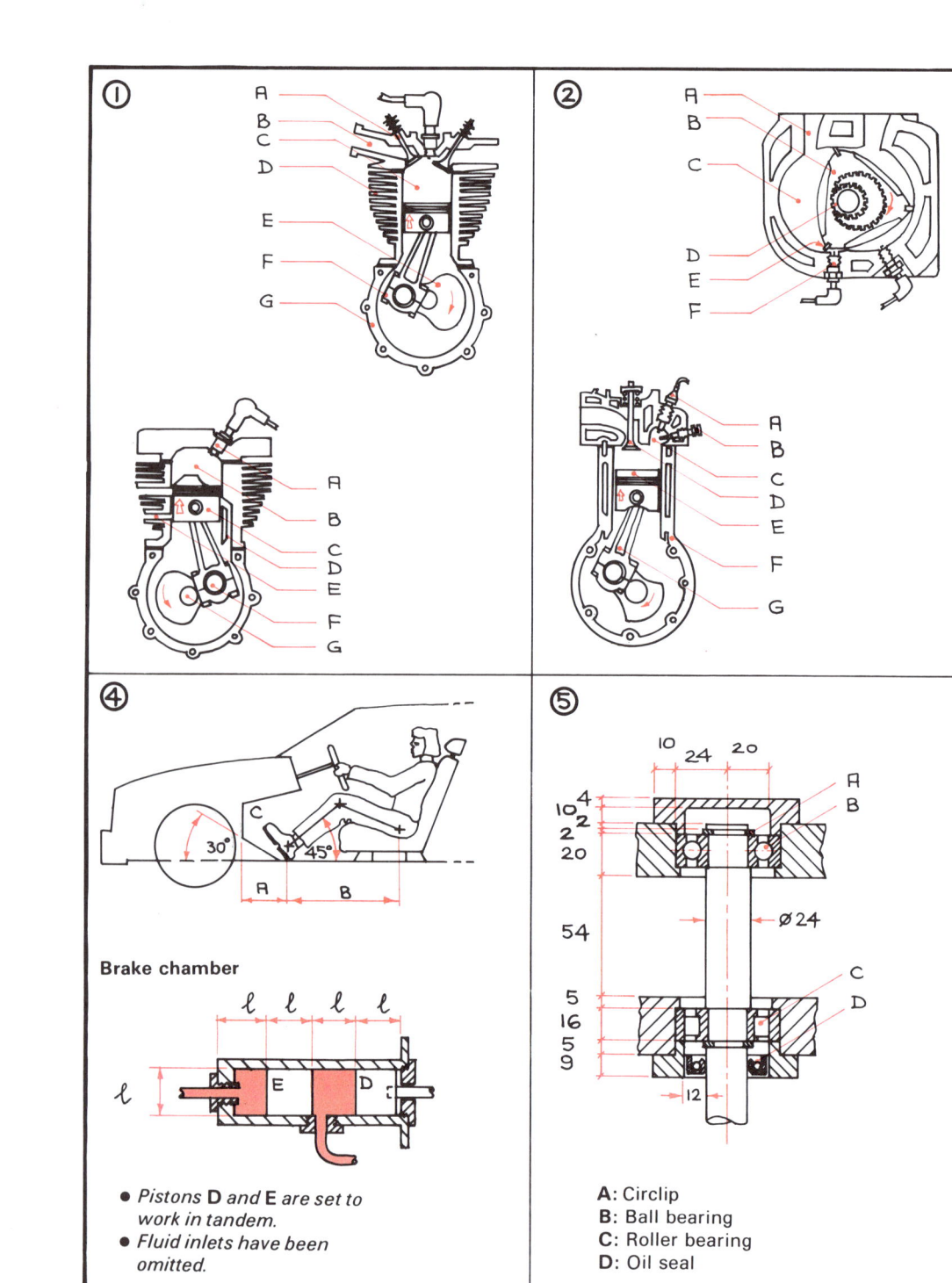

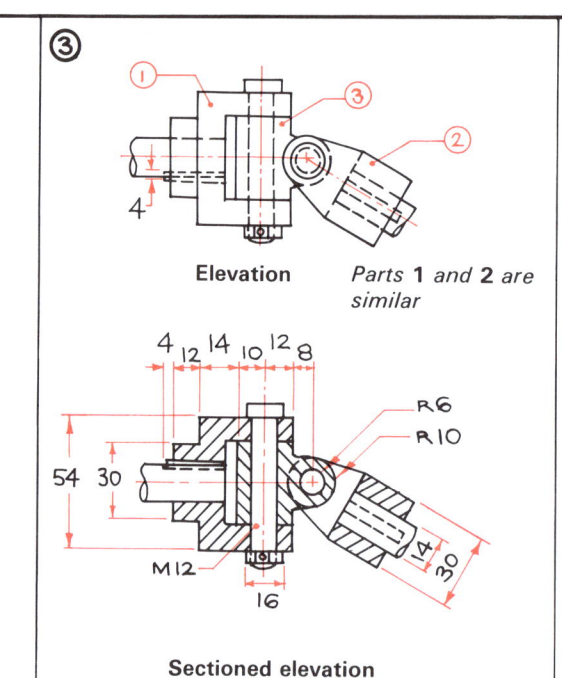

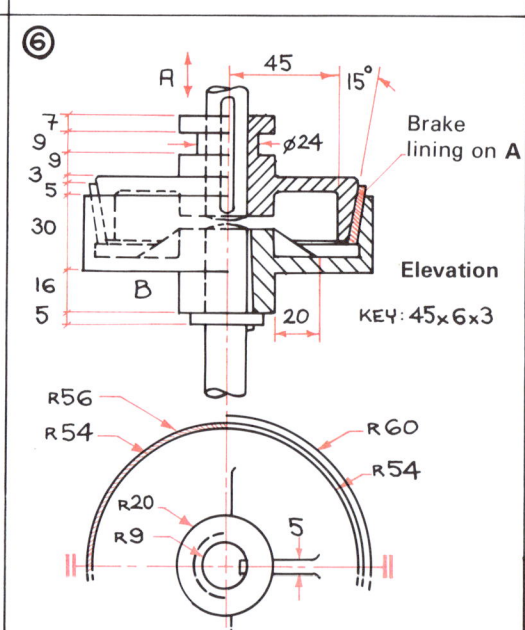

276

① Plummer block (journal bearing)

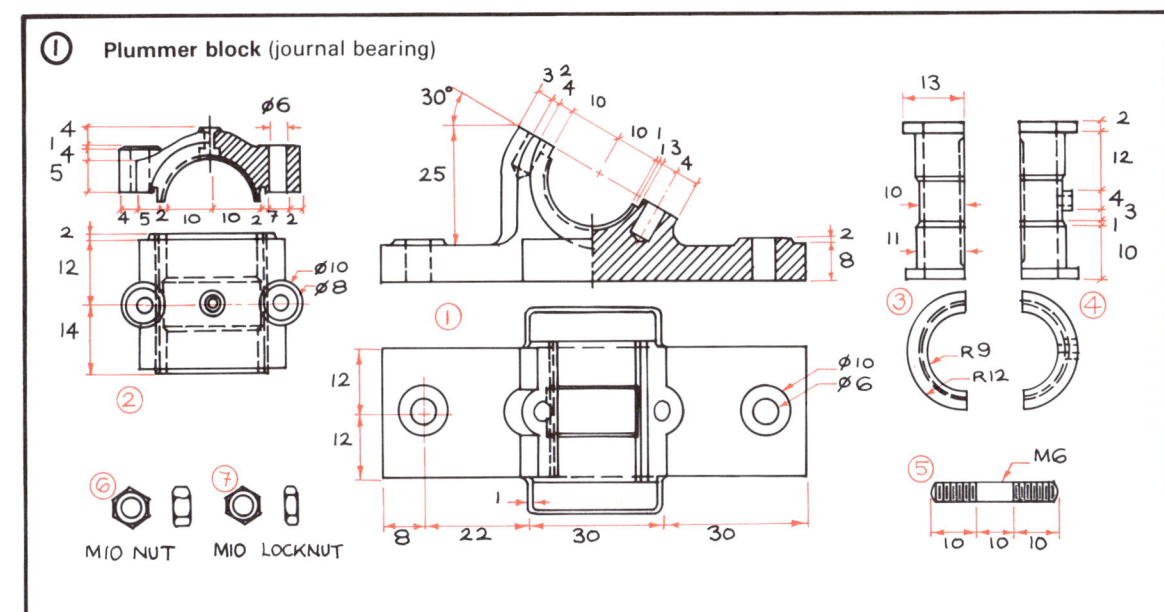

ITEM	DESCRIPTION	NO. OFF
1	BODY C.I.	1
2	CAP C.I.	1
3	UNDER BUSH BRASS	1
4	OVER BUSH BRASS	1
5	STUD	2
6	NUT	2
7	LOCKNUT	2

Note: *All unspecified fillets R5.*

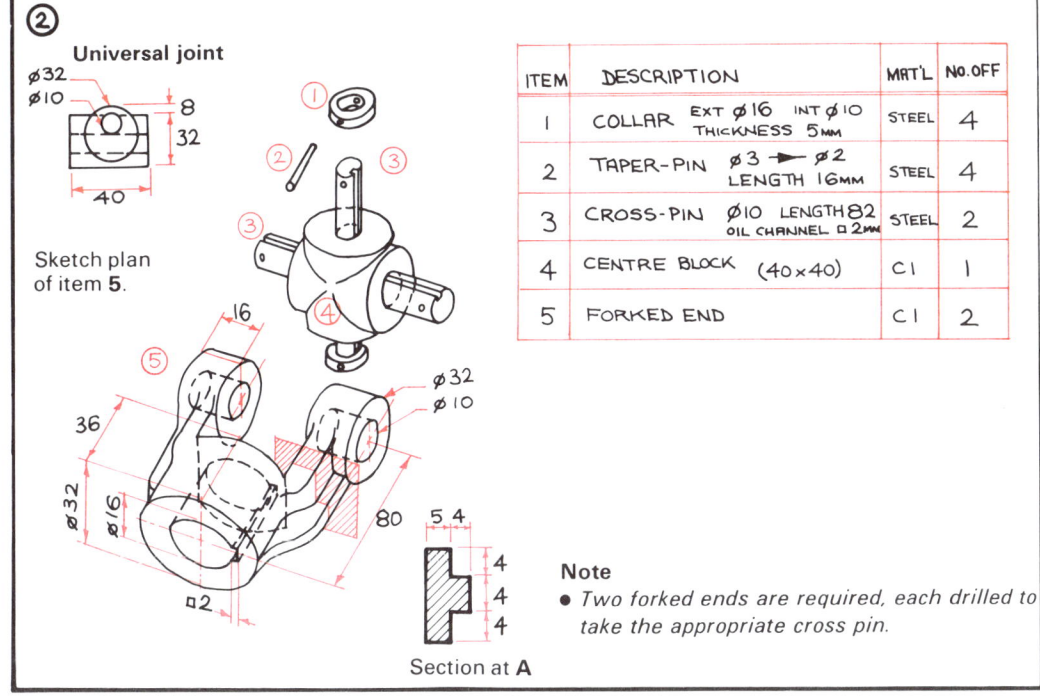

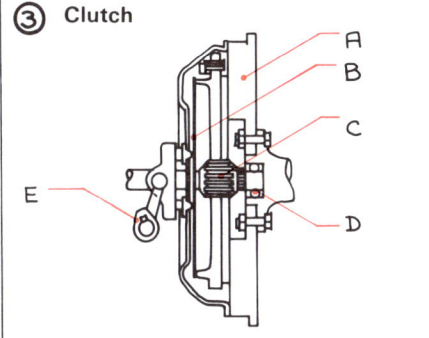

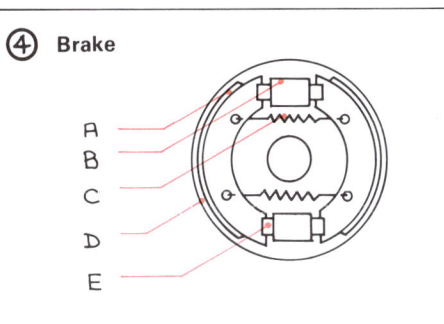

② Universal joint

ITEM	DESCRIPTION	MAT'L	NO.OFF
1	COLLAR EXT ⌀16 INT ⌀10 THICKNESS 5mm	STEEL	4
2	TAPER-PIN ⌀3 → ⌀2 LENGTH 16mm	STEEL	4
3	CROSS-PIN ⌀10 LENGTH 82 OIL CHANNEL □2mm	STEEL	2
4	CENTRE BLOCK (40×40)	CI	1
5	FORKED END	CI	2

Sketch plan of item **5**.

Note
- *Two forked ends are required, each drilled to take the appropriate cross pin.*

Section at **A**

③ Clutch

④ Brake

All measurements are in millimetres

Questions

1. Draw the assembled Plummer block in half-sectioned orthographic projection and index each item clearly.

2. Draw the assembled universal joint in half-sectioned orthographic projection. Also make an isometric projection of the assembled joint, indicating its range of movement.

3. Sketch the given assembly when the clutch is applied and write a note on the function of each item indicated.

4. Sketch the assembly shown when the brake is applied and write a note on the function of each item indicated.

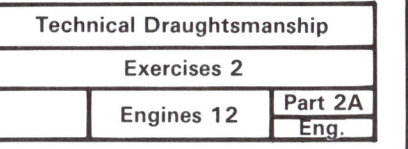

Technical Draughtsmanship

Exercises 2

Engines 12 — Part 2A Eng.

All measurements are in millimetres

Questions

1. Make a half-sectioned set of orthographic drawings of the assembled motorbike piston and connecting rod.

2. (i) Make a half-sectioned set of orthographic views of the assembled crankshaft. There are two connecting rods **A** and **B**, whose line of action is vertical.
   (ii) Plot the two follower displacement diagrams for **C** for one revolution of the crankshaft.
   (iii) If the crankshaft is rotating at **600 RPM**, plot the timing scale against the follower displacement diagrams.
   (iv) What timing gap should there be between the sparkplug in the cylinder above **A** and that above **B**?

Technical Draughtsmanship

Exercises 3

Engines 13 — Part 2A, Eng. H.

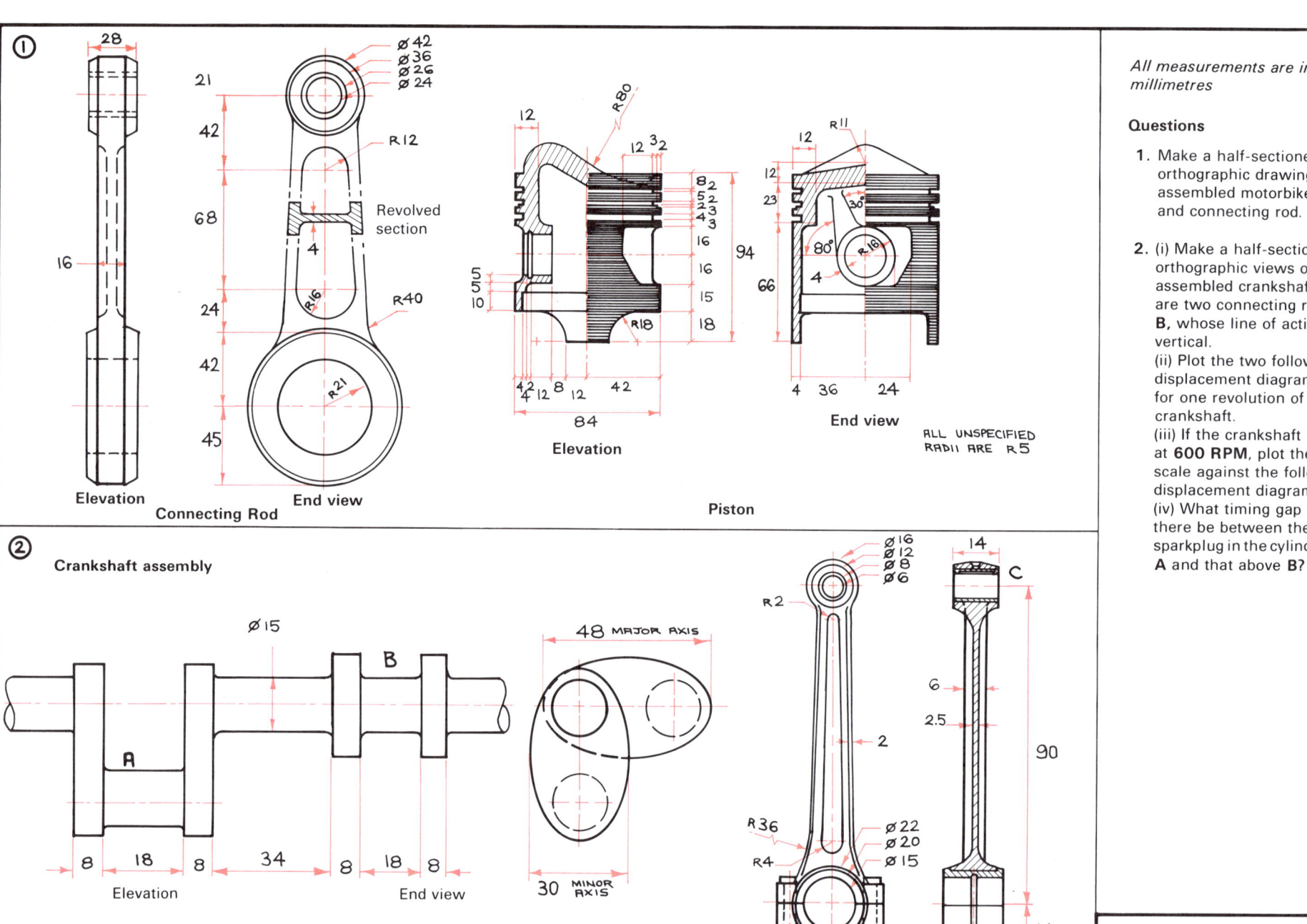

PART 2A

CHAPTER 23
LIMITS AND FITS

Accuracy is essential to good design, and an international system exists to define the accuracy required, both in the manufacturing and the fitting of a component.

CONTENTS
Tolerances	*Page*	**280**
Fits		**281**
Machining		**282**
Exercises		**283**

① ISO tolerance symbols

- A tolerance is an allowable zone of accuracy. In some cases, if a machine part is a millimetre above or below the required dimension it is still acceptable. In other precision jobs it is not acceptable to be even a micron (**0.0001 mm**) out! The tolerance must be shown clearly and this is done by using standard symbols in a tolerance frame, or a control box, as it is sometimes called.

Symbol	Type of Tolerance	Abbreviation
—	Straightness	**STR TOL**
▱	Flatness	**FLAT TOL**
○	Roundness	**RD TOL**
⌭	Cylindricity	**CYL TOL**
⌒	Profile (line)	—
⌓	Profile (surface)	—
//	Parallel to	**PAR TOL**
⊥	Perpendicular to	**SQ TOL**
∠	Angle with	**ANG TOL**
⊕	Position	**POSN TOL**
◎	Concentricity	**CONC TOL**
≡	Symmetry	**SYM TOL**

- Tolerances are usually quoted in millimetres.
- The greater the accuracy the more time and expense will be needed in manufacture. So always use the maximum acceptable tolerance.
- When indicating a tolerance zone always make clear where it is to be measured from, or what it is to relate to.

② Tolerance frames, also called control frames.

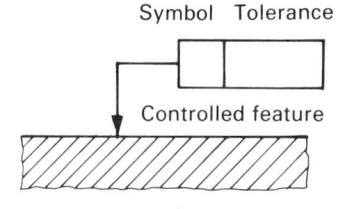

- The frame is a box in two parts. The symbol is placed in the first box and the total amount of tolerance is placed in the second box. An arrowhead points to the feature that is controlled.

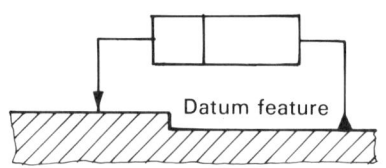

- Here the tolerance is related to a second or datum feature. The arrow that leaves the datum feature goes to the frame and the other leader points to the controlled feature.

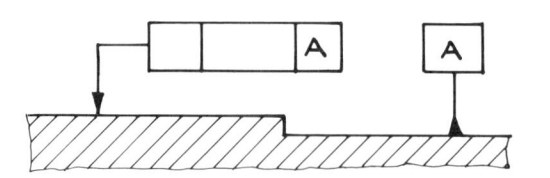

- Here the datum feature is separate and is cross-referenced to an extension of the frame. Note the arrow directions.

- Ⓜ This symbol is sometimes also added and it denotes that the minimum amount of metal should be removed. This is called the maximum material condition or **MMC**.

③ Examples of the frame in use

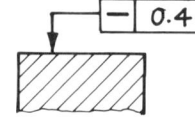

- The surface must lie between two parallel lines **0.4 mm** apart.

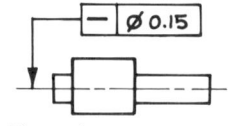

- The axis must not vary outside a circular zone of **0.15 mm** diameter.

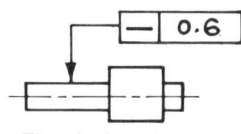

- The surface indicated must be straight within a tolerance zone of **0.6 mm** along its whole length.

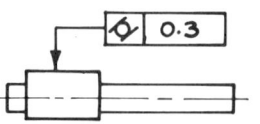

- The curved surface indicated must lie between two coaxial cylinders **0.3 mm** apart.

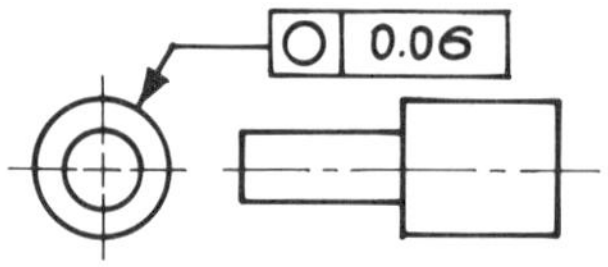

- The outline of the cylinder indicated is to lie between two concentric circles **0.06 mm** apart.

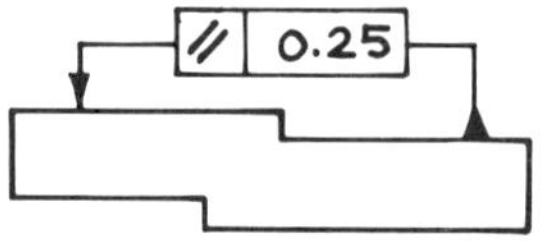

- The surface must lie between two planes **0.25 mm** apart and be parallel to the datum surface.

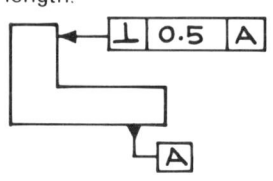

- The indicated surface is to lie between two planes **0.5 mm** apart and be perpendicular to the datum surface.

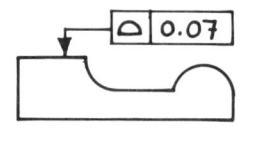

- The profile indicated should not deviate more than **0.035 mm** above or below the 'perfect' outline.

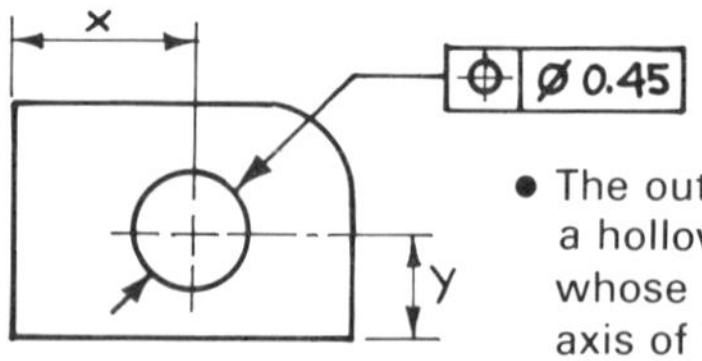

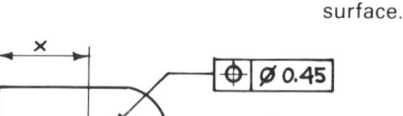

- The outline of the hole must lie within a hollow cylinder, **0.45 mm** thick, whose axis is the true position of the axis of the hole.

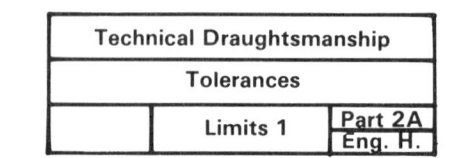

Technical Draughtsmanship
Tolerances
Limits 1 — Part 2A — Eng. H.

① Fits
- Tolerances are brackets within which a part is manufactured.
- However a problem arises when two parts are to be fitted together. A system of allowances has been designed for these circumstances.

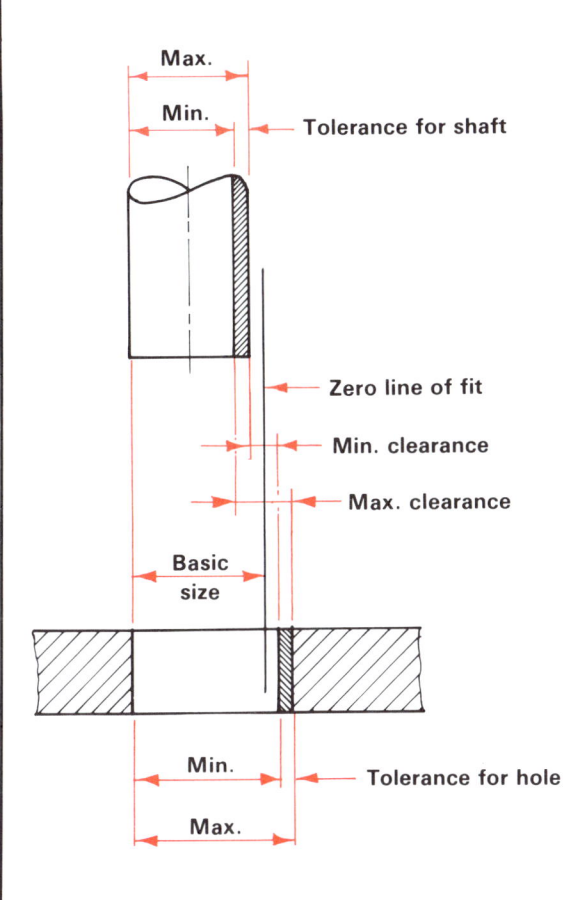

(Diagram labels: Max., Min., Tolerance for shaft, Zero line of fit, Min. clearance, Max. clearance, Basic size, Min., Max., Tolerance for hole)

- There are three sets of allowances: The tolerance allowance for the shaft, the tolerance allowance for the hole, and the clearance allowance for the fit which is set out either side of a *basic size line* or a *zero line* as it is called.
- However there are different types of fit.

② Types of fit. Engineering fits are of three basic types.

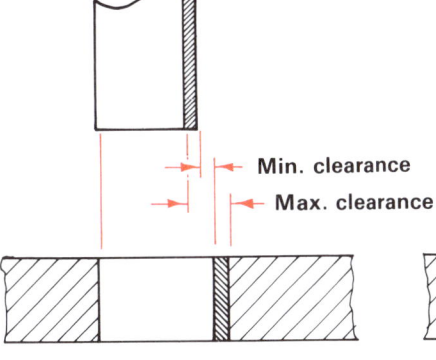

(Diagram labels: Min. clearance, Max. clearance, Min. clearance, Max. interference, Min. interference, Max. interference)

Clearance fit
- The shaft is always smaller than the hole.
- Used for running parts, or parts subject to temperature changes.

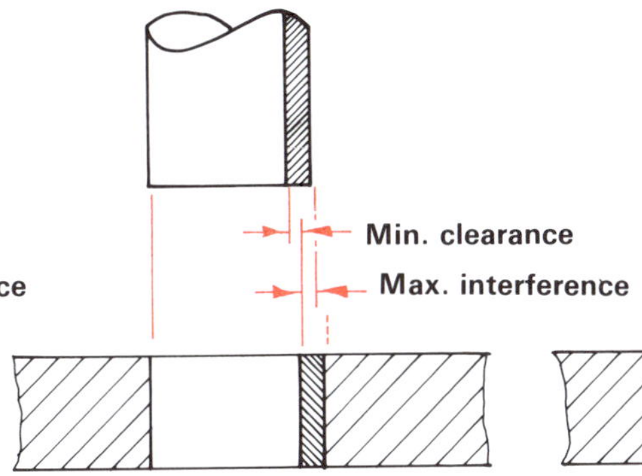

Transition fit
- The shaft may be a little smaller or bigger than the hole.
- Used for precisely located parts.

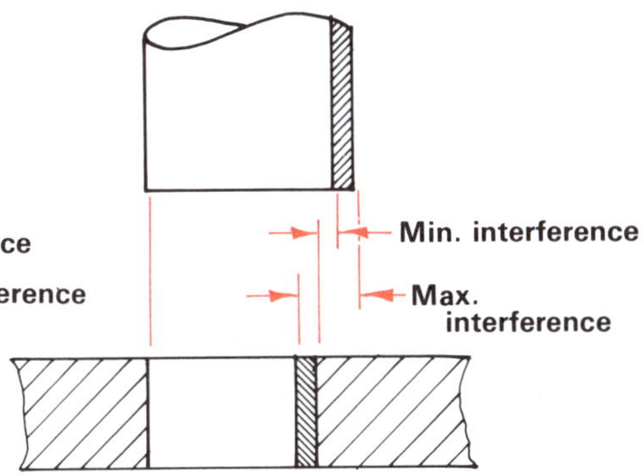

Interference fit
- The shaft is always bigger than the hole.
- Used for tight permanent assemblies. The parts are forced into position.

③ I.S.O. Fits
There are two international standard fit systems. One is the *hole basis* system in which, as above, the hole diameter is constant while the shaft fit varies. This is the usual, and more economical system. However, some situations require different fits along one shaft and a *shaft basis* system is used where the hole size varies to fit with a constant diameter shaft. The tolerance unit must be stated and is, usually, **0.001 mm**.

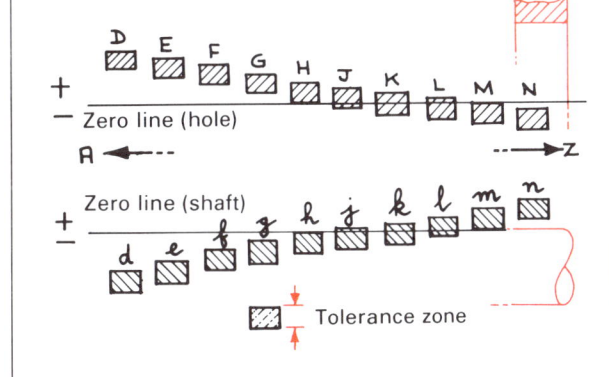

(Diagram: Zero line (hole) with tolerance zones D E F G H J K L M N, A ← → Z; Zero line (shaft) with d e f g h j k l m n; Tolerance zone)

Tolerance zones by letters
Tolerances are shown by a system of letters. **A** to **Z** for holes, **a** to **z** for shafts. Some of these are shown above. Notice **H** and **M** in particular.

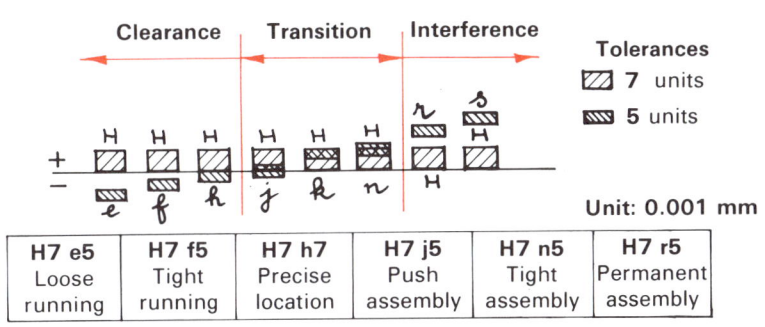

(Diagram: Clearance | Transition | Interference; Tolerances: 7 units, 5 units; Unit: 0.001 mm)

Sample fits

H7 e5	H7 f5	H7 h7	H7 j5	H7 n5	H7 r5
Loose running	Tight running	Precise location	Push assembly	Tight assembly	Permanent assembly

Notes
- There are various subdivisions possible e.g. H7 ef 5, H7 ef4.3 etc.
- See Table, page 349 for standard fits.

Technical Draughtsmanship		
Fits		
	Limits 2	Part 2A Eng. H

① Machine control symbols

- These symbols are often encountered on machines to indicate how a control functions. They are not widely used on finished drawings but are a great help on sketches.

Movement

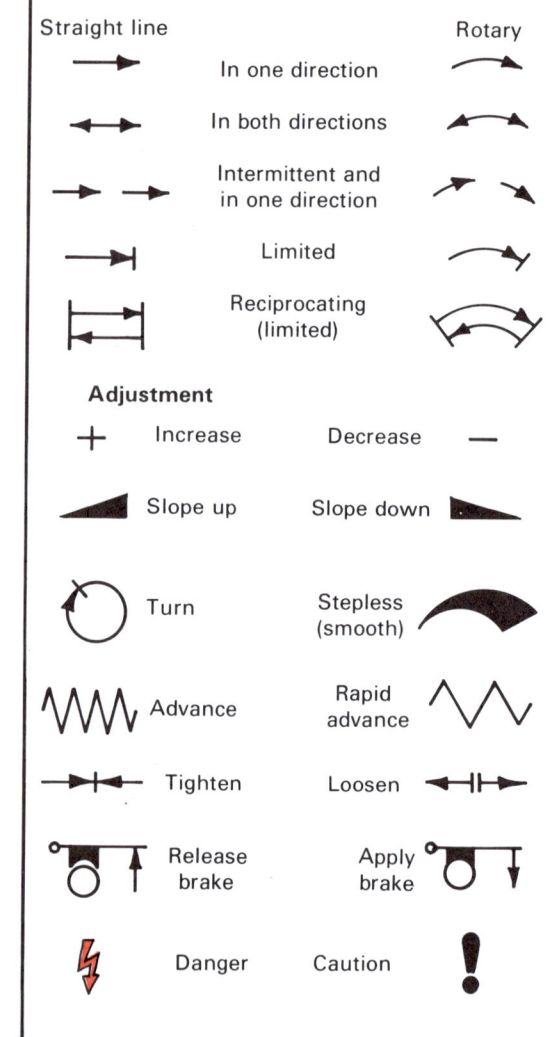

Straight line
- → In one direction
- ←→ In both directions
- →→ Intermittent and in one direction
- →| Limited
- |←→| Reciprocating (limited)

Rotary
- ⌢→ In one direction
- ←⌢→ In both directions
- ⌢→→ (intermittent)
- ⌢ Limited
- reciprocating arc

Adjustment

- + Increase
- − Decrease
- ◤ Slope up
- ◣ Slope down
- ⊙ Turn
- ▰ Stepless (smooth)
- ∿ Advance
- ∧∧ Rapid advance
- →|← Tighten
- →|← Loosen
- Release brake
- Apply brake
- ⚡ Danger
- ! Caution

- There are many other symbols in use on machines. Can you think of any?

② Machining and finishing

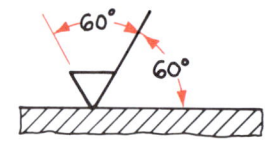

The standard symbol (60°/60° V symbol)

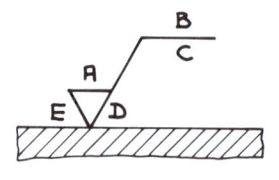

Information layout
- A: Roughness value.
- B: Method of treatment.
- C: Sampling length.
- D: Direction of lay.
- E: Machining allowance

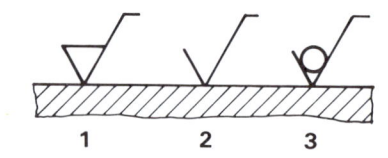

Options
1: Machine.
2: Machining may be done, but another method of finishing may be used.
3: Machining is *not* to be done and another method of finishing *must* be used.

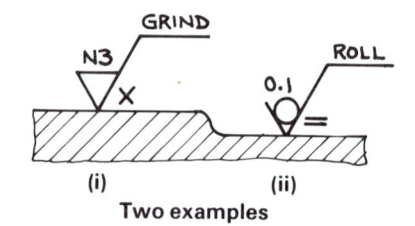

Two examples (i) N3 GRIND × ; (ii) 0.1 ROLL =

When a surface is to be machined or finished to fine limits, a standard symbol is used. As with tolerances, the introduction of fine machining raises costs and such a demand should not be made without good reason.

A: Roughness value: This is a measure of how un-smooth the surface is to be and is measured in microns (**μm**), or by roughness number (**N**). These are related, as shown below.

Microns	0.025	0.05	0.1	0.2	0.4	0.8	1.6	etc.
Roughness No.	N1	N2	N3	N4	N5	N6	N7	→

1 Micron = 1 μm = 0.0001 mm.

B: Method of treatment: This could refer to machining or finishing, or both, and would include such orders as:

GRIND: Grinding **PLAT:** Electroplating
LAP: Lapping **CHEM:** Chemical treatment
HONE: Honing. **ROLL:** Roller burnishing

C: Sampling length: The length over which the treatment is to be applied. This order is not often necessary.

D: Direction of lay: The direction, or directions, in which the finish is to be laid down. These are indicated as shown below.

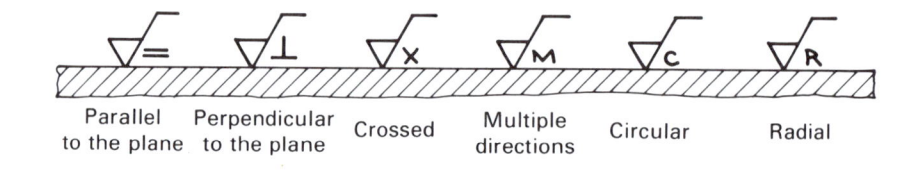

= Parallel to the plane ⊥ Perpendicular to the plane × Crossed M Multiple directions C Circular R Radial

E: Machining allowance: This is the amount that is to be removed from a stock or standard size.

Example (i): A finish of roughness N3 is to be cross-ground.
Example (ii): A burnished finish of roughness 0.1 μm is to be laid parallel to the place indicated.

Technical Draughtsmanship
Machining
Limits 3 — Part 2A — Eng. H

①

(a) ▱   (b) ◯ ⌀ 1.23

⌖

≡   ─ 0.05

▭▭   ⌒

▭▭   Ⓜ

CONC TOL   B⌐

▭▭   PAR TOL

⌓   // 0.44 A

②

(a) Controlled feature
Tolerance
SQ TOL
Transition fit

(b) **SYM TOL**
Datum feature
Cylindricity
SQ TOL

(c) Clearance fit
Zero line
ISO fits
Interference fit

③

(a)
(i) A parallelism tolerance of **0.05 mm** relative to datum **A**.
(ii) A flatness tolerance of **0.3 mm**
(iii) A squareness tolerance of **0.06 mm** relative to datum **F**.
(iv) A position tolerance of **0.02 mm**.
(v) A straightness tolerance of **0.36 mm**.

(b)
(i) A parallelism tolerance of **0.1 mm** relative to datums **C** and **D**.
(ii) A profile tolerance of **0.14 mm**.
(iii) A concentricity tolerance of **0.03 mm** relative to datum **G**.
(iv) A squareness tolerance of **0.2 mm** relative to datum **32**.
(v) A cylindricity tolerance of **0.07 mm**.

All measurements are in millimetres.

Questions

1. Write an explanatory note on each of the symbols shown. Show one example of where each could be used.

2. Write a note and draw a sketch to explain each term shown.

3. Draw a simple component to include and illustrate each of the given tolerances.

4. Draw the crank, dimension it and draw control boxes to indicate the required tolerances.

5. Explain with the aid of a sketch each of the given terms.

6. Draw the universal coupling and draw control boxes to indicate the required tolerances.

④

Elevation

Plan

(i): PAR TOL 0.04 mm A to E.
(ii): SQ TOL 0.025 mm A to B and C.
(iii): CYL TOL 0.015 mm for D.
(iv): PAR TOL 0.3 mm B to C.

⑤

Tolerance unit! **0.0001 mm**

(a) A6   (d) H7
f8   z12
C4   M6
m5   l6

(b) G5/g5   (e) H8/h8
G5/r5   H7/f5
A6/a7   H5/r7
M9/h4   H6/j4

(c) Hole basis   (f) Shaft basis
PLAT   **CHEM**
ROLL   Sampling length
Roughness value   **GRIND**

⑥

Elevation

Section X-X

(i) SQ TOL 0.015 mm EF to GH
(ii) PAR TOL 0.02 mm A to B.
(iii) CYL TOL 0.025 mm for C and D.
(iv) RD TOL 0.018 mm for J.

Technical Draughtsmanship

Exercises 1

Limits 4 | Part 1A Eng. H.

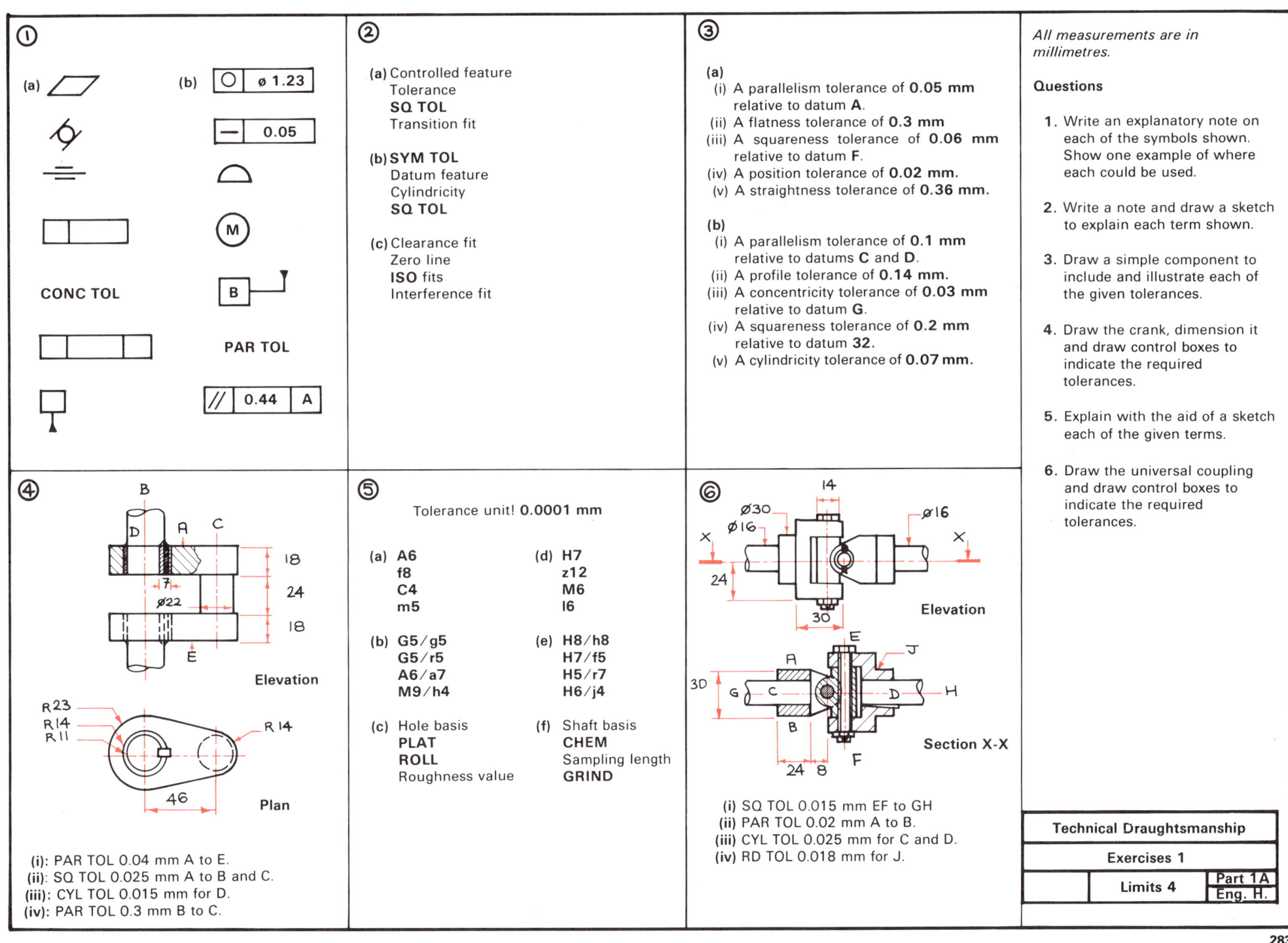

All dimensions are in millimetres

Questions

1. Explain accurately the meaning of each of the symbolic representations shown.

2. Draw the cross-head and indicate on your drawing the machining instructions required.

3. Draw the solid in both orthographic and isometric projections and indicate on the orthographic views the machinery instructions required.

4. Complete the detail drawings of the given assembly. Draw the assembly in half sectioned orthographic projection.

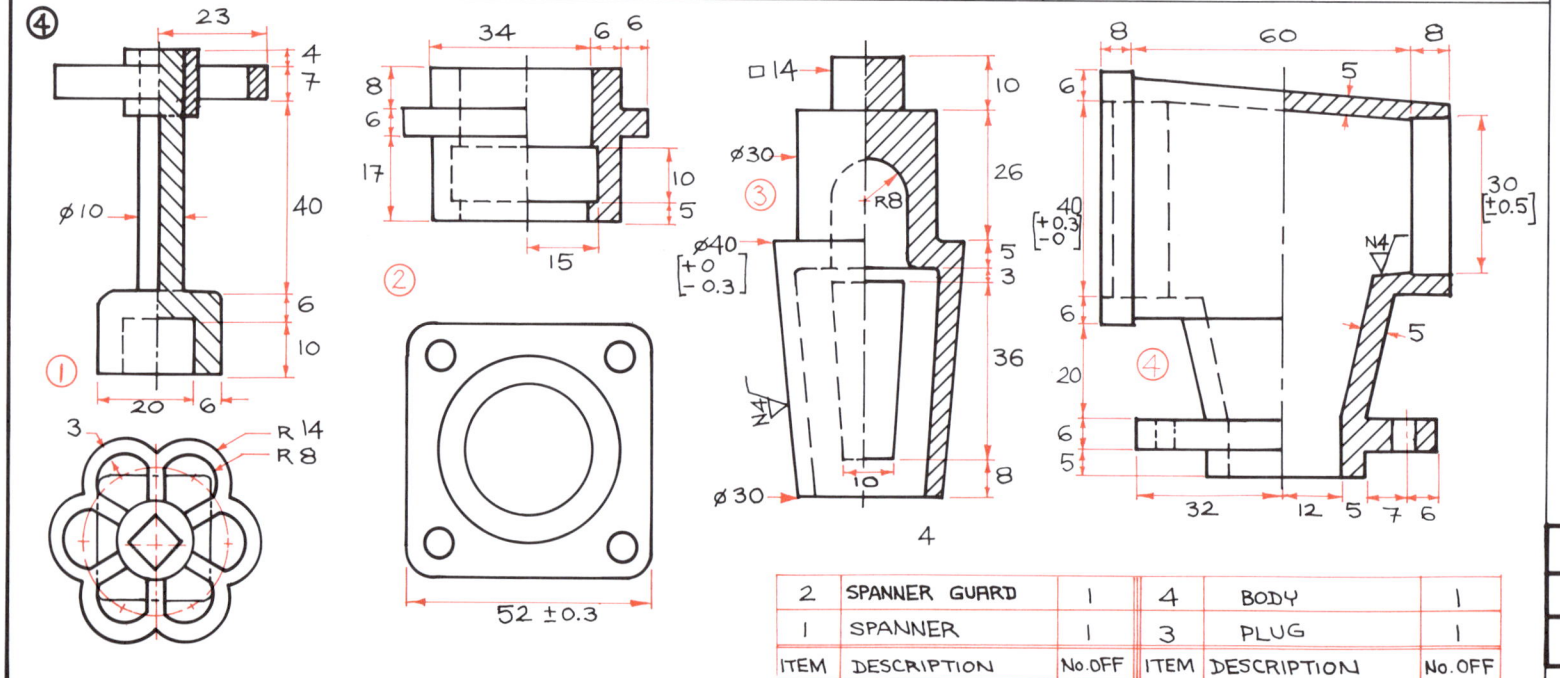

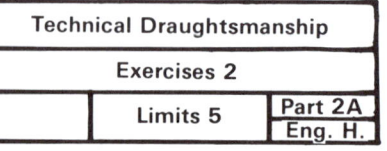

Panel 2:
- A: Finish to roughness **N3** by cross-grinding.
- B: Hone to **N2**.
- C: Burnish perpendicular to **N4**.
- D: Grind parallel **0.05 um**.

Panel 3:
- A: Cylindricity of ± **0.1 mm**.
- B: Parallelism of ± **0.05 mm** to E.
- D: Perpendicularity of ± **0.03** to C.

ITEM	DESCRIPTION	No.OFF	ITEM	DESCRIPTION	No.OFF
2	SPANNER GUARD	1	4	BODY	1
1	SPANNER	1	3	PLUG	1

Technical Draughtsmanship
Exercises 2
Limits 5 — Part 2A — Eng. H.

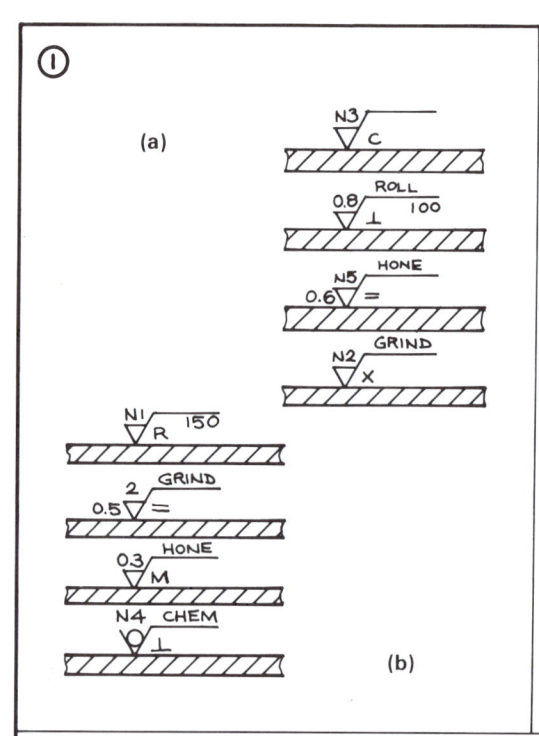

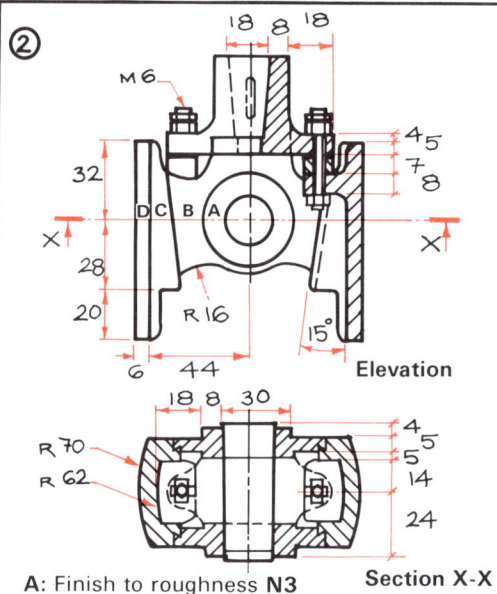

284

PART 2B
BUILDING APPLICATIONS

CHAPTER 24
A BUILDING PROJECT

Here we will look at the drawings required in the design of a standard semi-detached house. Other projects might be more complicated but the approach would be similar.

CONTENTS
Site Surveys	*Page* **286**
Preliminary Sketches	**287**
Working Drawings	**288**
Detail Drawings	**289**
Site Plans	**290**
Building Drawings	**291**
Exercises	**292**

① The brief

- The builders, Chett and Co. have got the contract and planning permission to build six semi-detached houses on a new estate. They want these to be three-bedroomed, of sound construction and design, and economically profitable. The area is likely to attract purchasers of moderate income and medium range mortgage potential. Design the houses in question.

② A visit to the site

- The first thing to do is to locate the site and take a good look at it.
- Make a list of points to check out on your visit to the site. These should include those listed below.
- Is there access, or temporary access to the site for trucks, etc.?
- Is there room on the site for storage and plant?
- What is the soil like? Will drainage or water disposal be a problem?
- Once building has started will movement be hindered?
- Are there existing services? Exactly where are their nearest points of contact?
- Imagine the most logical positions for services, buildings, huts, fences, etc.

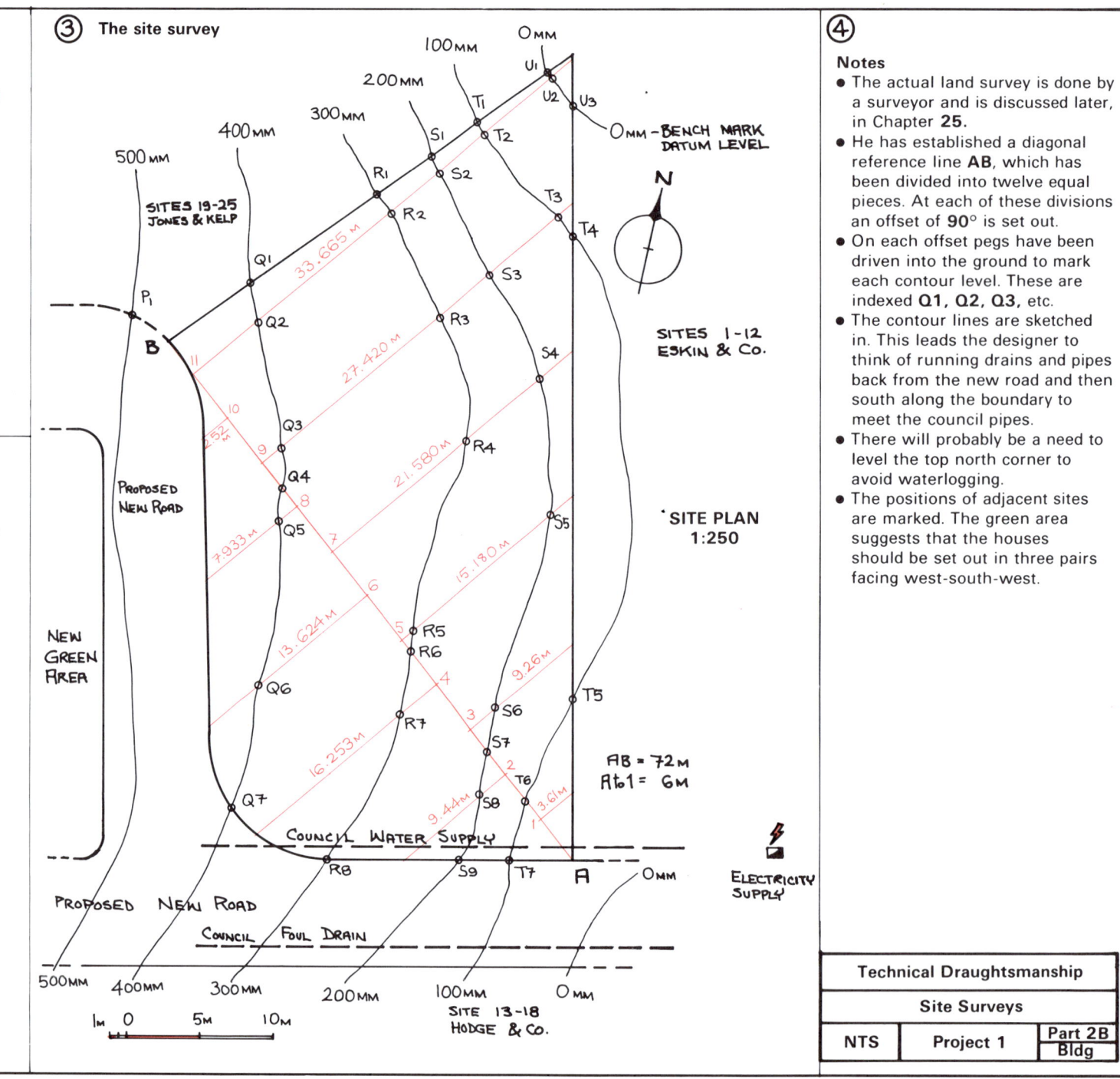

③ The site survey

SITE PLAN 1:250

④ Notes

- The actual land survey is done by a surveyor and is discussed later, in Chapter **25**.
- He has established a diagonal reference line **AB**, which has been divided into twelve equal pieces. At each of these divisions an offset of **90°** is set out.
- On each offset pegs have been driven into the ground to mark each contour level. These are indexed **Q1, Q2, Q3,** etc.
- The contour lines are sketched in. This leads the designer to think of running drains and pipes back from the new road and then south along the boundary to meet the council pipes.
- There will probably be a need to level the top north corner to avoid waterlogging.
- The positions of adjacent sites are marked. The green area suggests that the houses should be set out in three pairs facing west-south-west.

Technical Draughtsmanship		
Site Surveys		
NTS	Project 1	Part 2B Bldg

286

① General orientation of houses

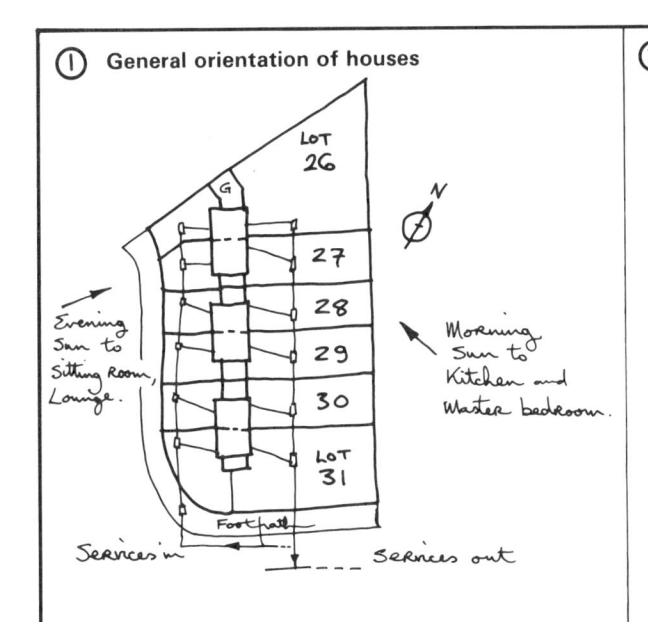

LOT 26, 27, 28, 29, 30, LOT 31
Evening Sun to Sitting Room, Lounge.
Morning Sun to Kitchen and Master bedroom.
Services in — Footpath — Services out

② General layouts

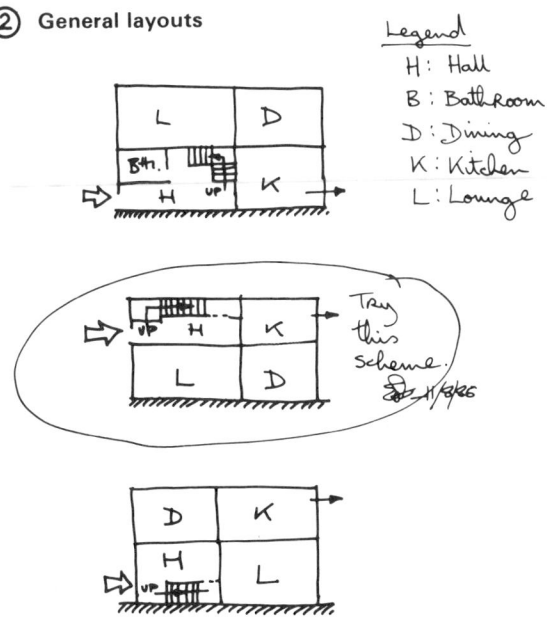

Legend
H: Hall
B: Bathroom
D: Dining
K: Kitchen
L: Lounge

Try this scheme. 11/9/85

- It is usual to draw many quick sketches before a few promising schemes are found.
- Similar sketches would be drawn for the first-floor plans.

③ Esquisse sketches

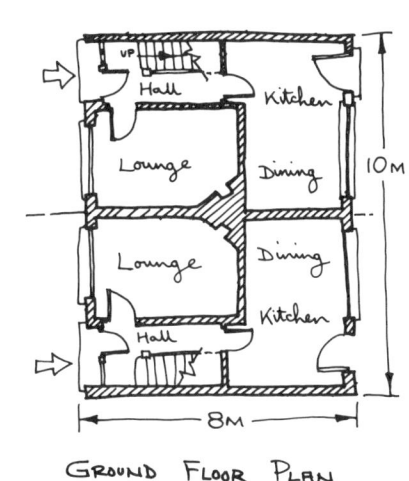

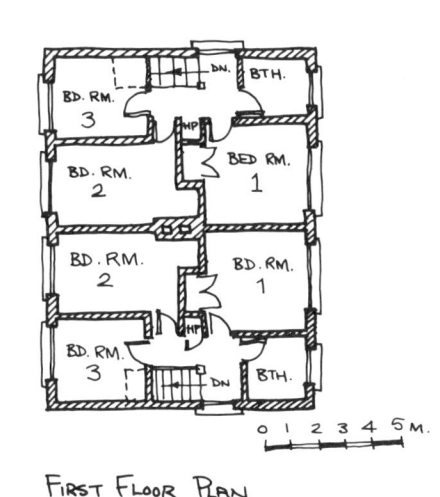

Ground Floor Plan (8M × 10M): Hall, Kitchen, Lounge, Dining (×2 units)

First Floor Plan: BD. RM. 3, BD. RM. 2, BED RM. 1, BTH. (×2 units)

0 1 2 3 4 5 M

④ Interior sketches

Hallway — Kitchen — Lounge

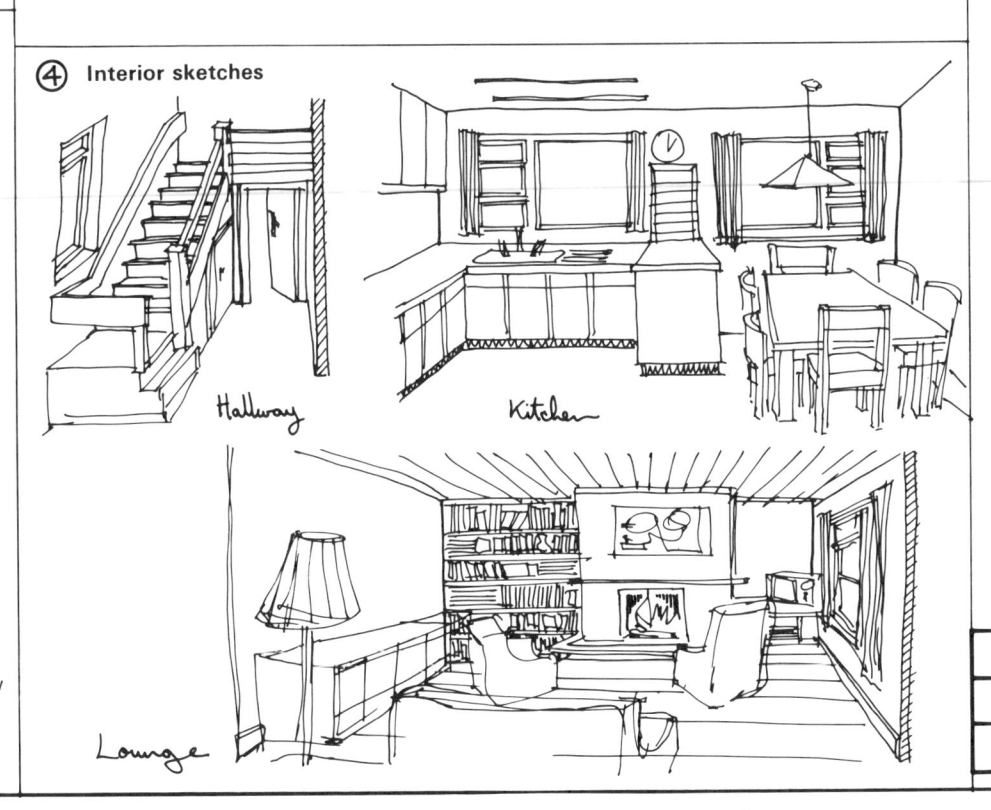

Notes

- First of all the general orientation of the building is to be decided. This will depend on access, views, sunlight, other boundary walls, etc. A quick sketch can settle the matter. Always check that the north-sign is marked correctly.
- Then down to the general layout. In large buildings this can be extremely complex, e.g. a hospital. Keep sketching until you get the best arrangement. Do not waste time on details at this stage.
- Esquisse drawings show exactly how a layout works, no more and no less. They are drawn to a scale, often over graph paper. The first floor plan is usually traced above the ground floor drawing to keep walls in line. Changes are still easy to make.
- Once a scheme is chosen some three-dimensional sketches are made to see if it would really fit together as a place to live in.
- These sketches may later be worked into finished publicity drawings, or form the basis for a show-house. See page **333** for perspective drawing.

Technical Draughtsmanship		
Preliminary Sketches		
NTS	Project 2	Part 2B Bldg.

Working plan of the ground floor of site No. 28

Working drawings

- These are drawings that show the builder exactly what is to be done and where everything is to go.
- If the drawing gets very confusing a symbol system and note references can be added.
- If there is a larger set of detailed working drawings for plumbing, electrical, joinery work, etc., reference would be made to these above the title block.
- Nevertheless, it is always a good idea to have at least one drawing with all the main details on it.
- Although such a drawing looks very detailed, to each individual workman it is simplicity itself.

LEGEND

- SWITCH
- SWITCH (2-WAY)
- CEILING ROSE
- C.R. (VARIABLE HT.)
- POWER PT. (DOUBLE)
- DIMMER SWITCH
- FUSEBOX

Technical Draughtsmanship
Working Drawings

| NTS | Project 3 | Part 2B Bldg |

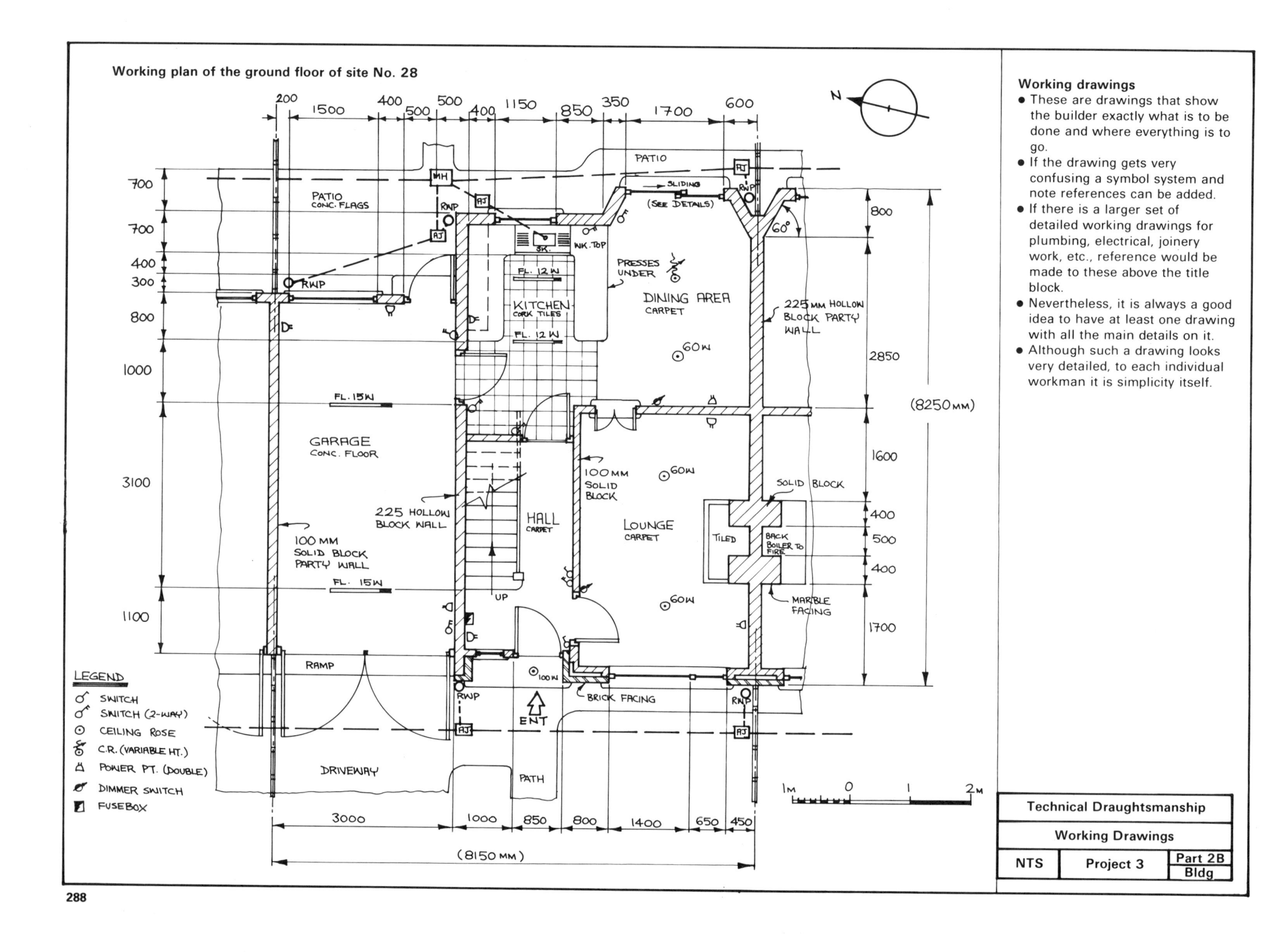

① Representation of materials

▨	Brickwork
▦	Concrete
⊠	Unwrot wood (sawn)
〰	Wrot wood (planed)
▧	Insulation
⋈	Hardcore
▨	Earth
▨	Stone
▨	Blockwork
H I	Steel sections
Large Small	

② Structural details

CEMENT MORTAR BED
RIDGE TILE
200 × 30 RIDGE PIECE
INTERLOCKING TILE
125 × 50 RAFTER
20 × 40 BATTENS @ 300 c-c.
SARKING FELT
100 × 75 WALL PLATE
50 × 25 BRACKET
R.C. LINTOL
50 × 25 BRACKET
PVC GUTTER ON FASCIA
20 SOFFIT BOARD
70 × 50 HEAD
DPC
TOP RAIL
6MM GLASS
70 × 50 TRANSOM
70 × 50 SILL
R.C. SILL
DPC
HALF-BRICK FACING
METAL FLASHING
BUILT-UP FELT
FIRRING PIECES
125 × 50 JOIST
VENTS
CONC. LEVELLING
150 CONC. SLAB
DPM
150 HARDCORE, CONSOLIDATED
250 GRAVEL, CONSOLIDATED
R.C. FOOTING
CONC. BLINDING

ATTIC
20 INSULATION BOARD
125 × 50 JOIST
PLASTERBOARD
FIRST FLOOR
200 × 25 BOARDS
DPC
100 CAVITY
400 × 200 × 100 HOLLOW CONC. BLOCK
20 SKIRTING
22 T&G BOARDS
100 × 50 JOISTS
PLASTERBOARD
HALLWAY
GARAGE
100 × 50 JOISTS
100 × 75 WALL PLATE
150 TASSEL WALL
100 SITE CONC.
150 HARDCORE, CONSOLIDATED
BEARING SOIL

SECTIONAL DRAWING OF HOUSE STRUCTURE

100mm 0 100 200 300mm

Detail Drawings

- Usually specialist in character, these drawings define the exact details of a construction, installation or assembly.
- If there is any deviation from standard procedure, a detailed drawing should be made to avoid confusion, or mistakes.
- Detailed drawings are usually accompanied by specifications. These are written descriptions of the work to be done, e.g.: 90 × 22 T&G Boarding on 100 × 50 Joists at 400 c-c on 100 × 75 wall plates ... etc.
- Both detail drawings and specifications are vital pieces of evidence should any dispute arise.

Technical Draughtmanship		
Detail Drawings		
NTS	Project 4	Part 2B
		Bldg

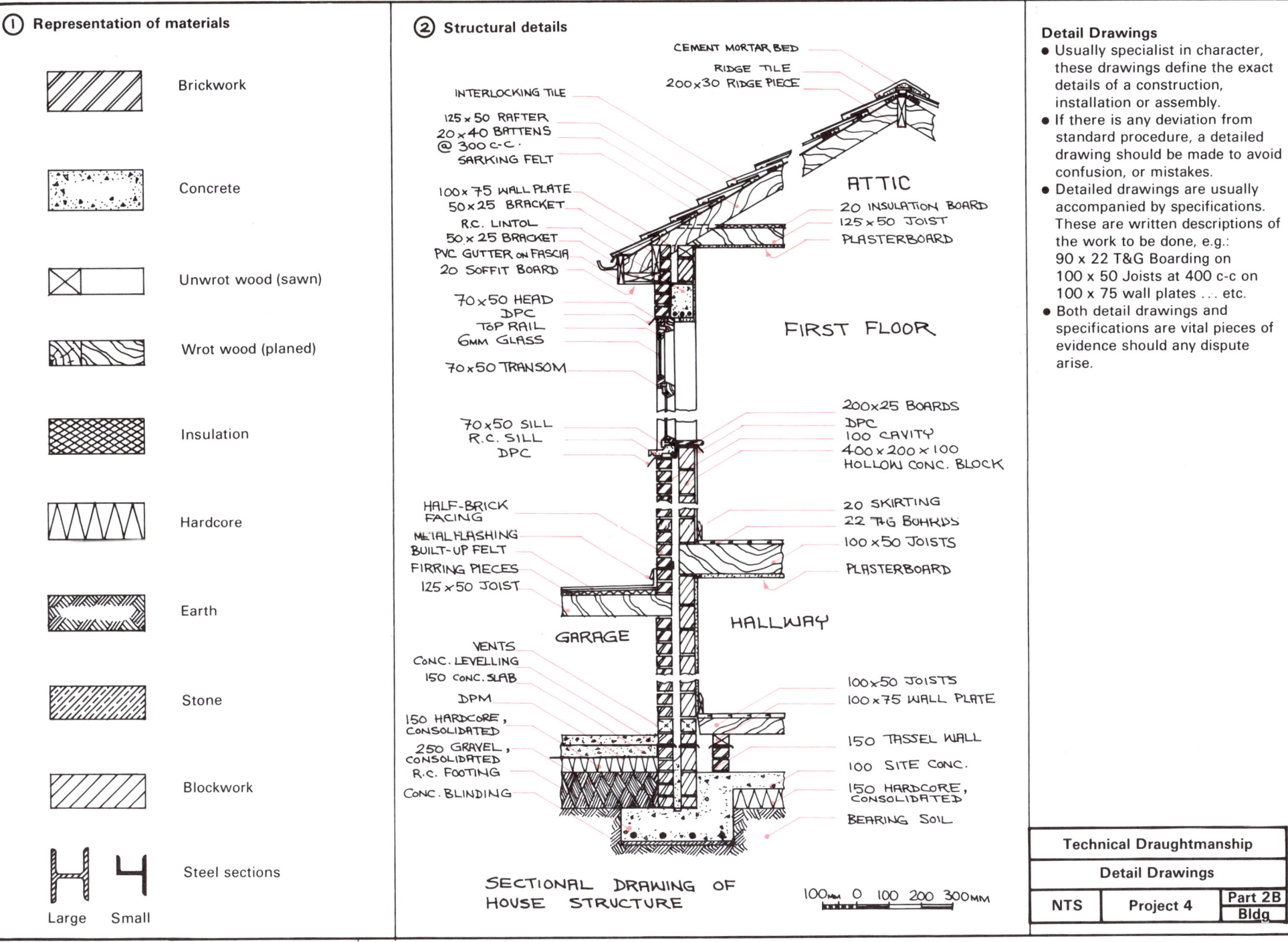

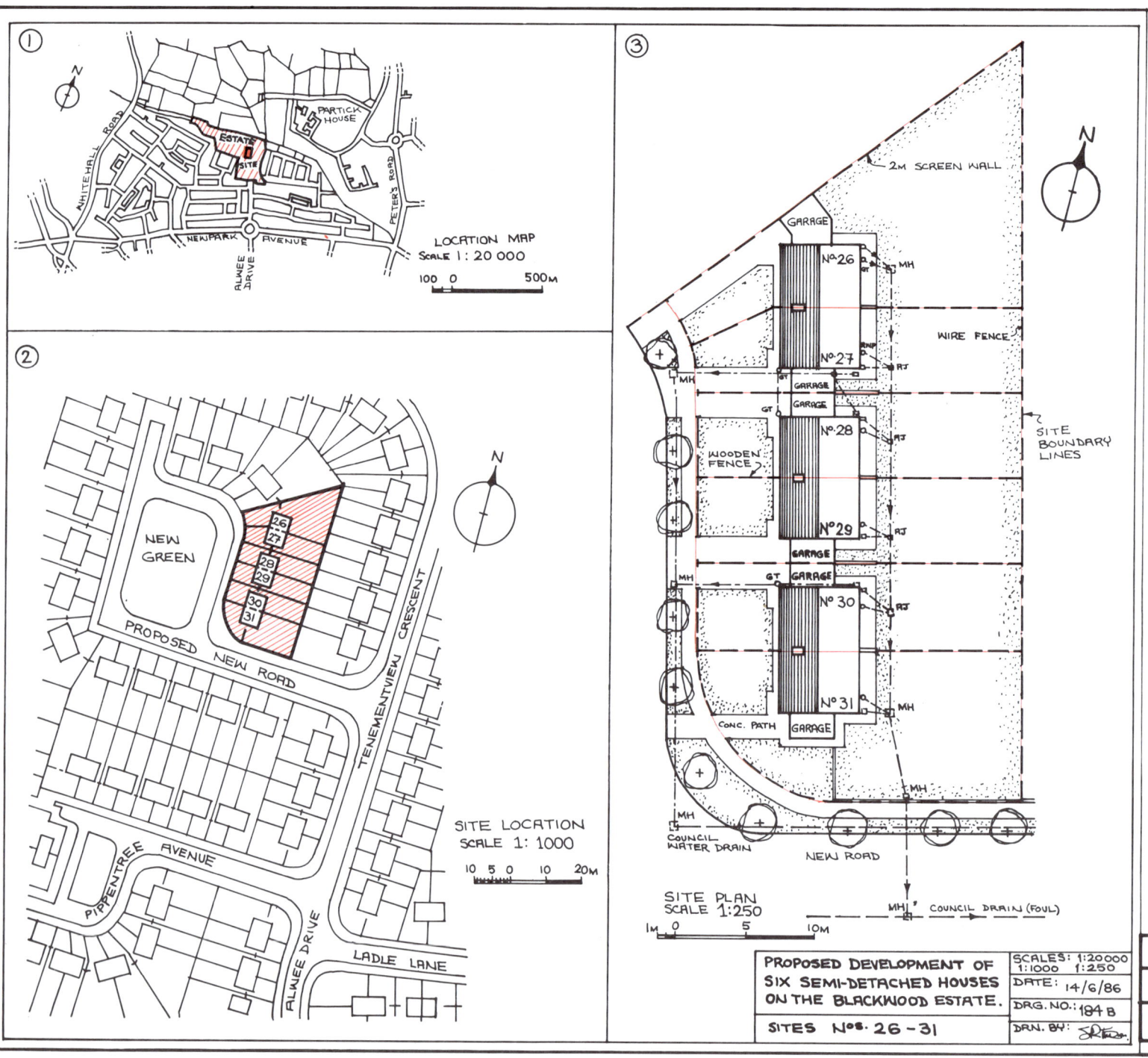

Site Plans

- These are used to give the precise location of the site. They are important to the client, the planning office, the builder and for legal purposes.
- They define the location and extent of the property.
- A sheet similar to this one must be lodged with the local government offices before planning permission can be given.

Building drawings

- These are usually for the client, the planning office and the builder.
- They show on one sheet the building, its basic structure, and its leading dimensions.
- Sometimes a set of building drawings will have many sheets and will include working and detail drawings.
- For the client some presentation drawings may be added, e.g. coloured perspectives, sketches, etc.

Technical Draughtsmanship

Building Drawings

NTS | Project 6 | Part 2B Bldg

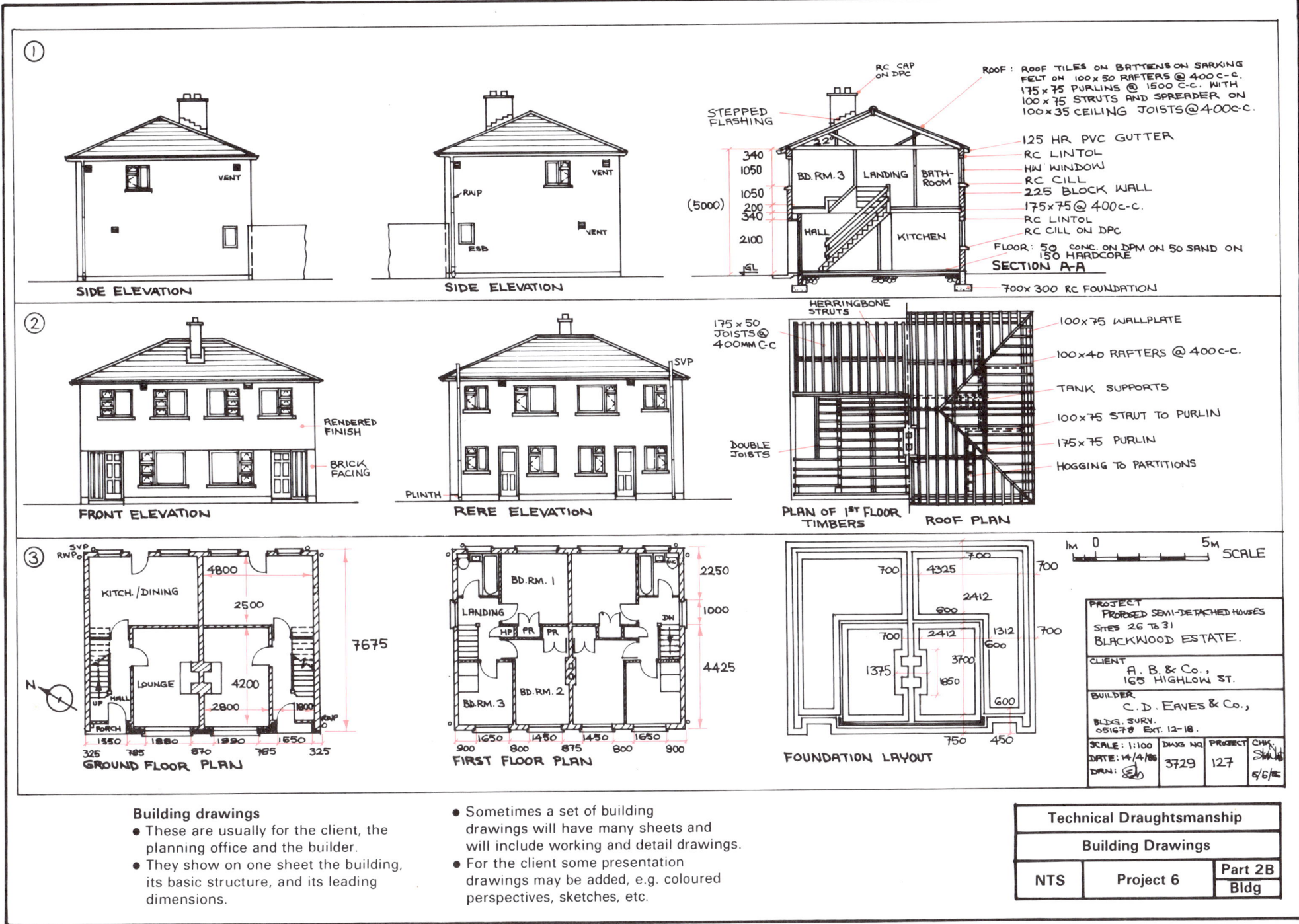

All measurements are in millimetres.

Questions

1. Given is the site plan of your new house. Make a list of your initial observations. Draw sketches of a three-roomed chalet for the site and show how you would position the house on the site.

2. Choose a site near you. Survey it, listing its advantages and drawbacks. Draw it and show how you would place a building on it.

3. Make a set of design sketches for the conversion of this room to an apartment.

4. A client has set out a space for her garage workshop. She is very interested in do-it-yourself work of all kinds and wants a good versatile workshop. Draw a plan and sketches of such a workshop.

5. This householder wants to build a new kitchen and dining room onto his house. Design this for him. Show sketches and working drawings.

Technical Draughtsmanship

Exercises

Project 7 — Part 2B Bldg

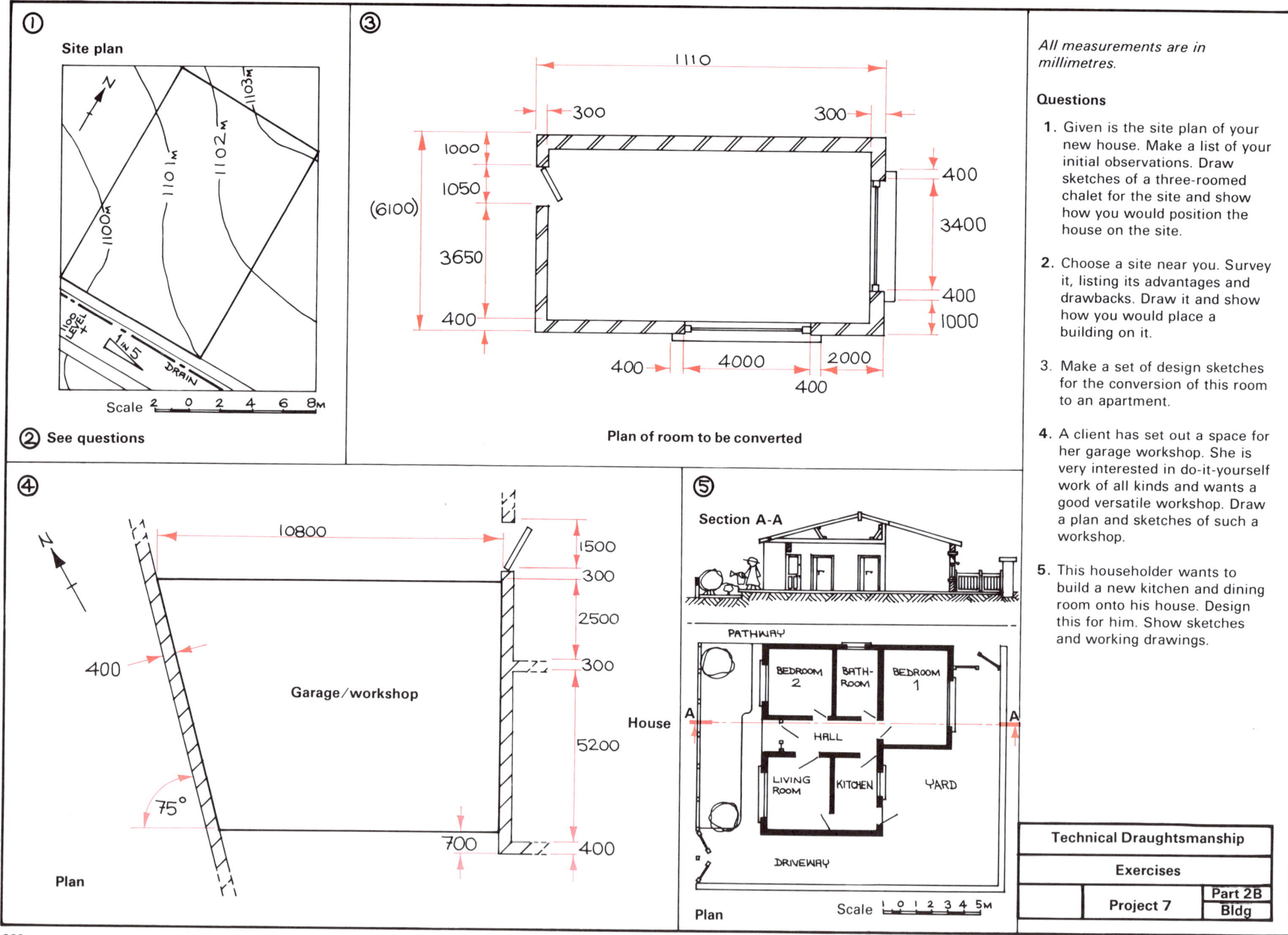

PART 2B

CHAPTER 25
SURVEYING AND MINING

Before any building can start a good survey of the terrain must be made and its contours taken into account.

CONTENTS
Measuring Distances	*Page* **294**
Measuring Heights	**295**
Contouring	**296**
Grids	**297**
Road Building	**298**
A Worked Example	**299**
Curved Roads and Platforms	**300**
Sloping Roads	**301**
Mining Strata	**302**
Dip and Strike 1	**303**
Dip and Strike 2	**304**
Two Skew Boreholes	**305**
Exercises	**306**

Photocopying prohibited by law

① **Surveying** is the three-dimensional measurement of a piece of the earth's surface. This involves two problem areas: measuring flat distances and measuring heights.

② **Distances** (For the moment, ignore heights).
There are four basic approaches. In each approach two control points **A** and **B** are chosen and a control line **AB** is fixed. The problem is to use this to pin-point all the other features of the area e.g. a tree **C**.

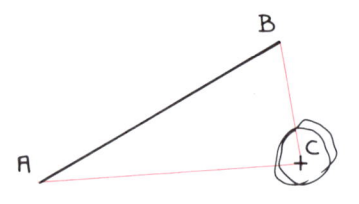

(i) Measure the distances AC and BC
- This is called chain surveying and was often done using chains with fixed-length links. It is effective, but time consuming. It has been made easier through laser beam and radio wave equipment, but still requires a lot of walking.

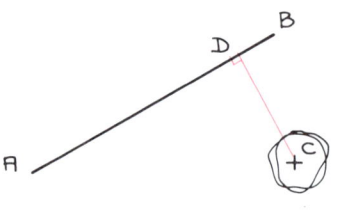

(ii) The point D is found and the right-angled offset DC is measured.
- This allows the surveyor to walk from **A** to **B** and measure all the features to either side of him. This also makes drawing easier, and is a form of chain surveying.

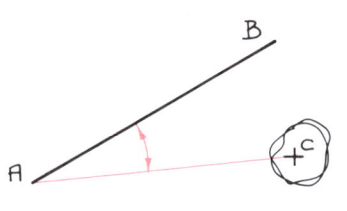

(iii) The angle BAC is measured, as is the distance AC.
- Using a telescope, or theodolite, the surveyor at **A** can measure the angle as he swings from viewing **B** to viewing point **C**.

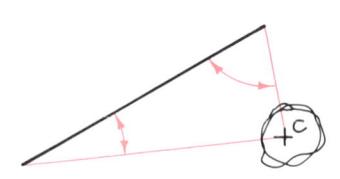

(iv) Both the angles BAC and ABC are measured.
- This eliminates much of the walking as the readings are all taken from **A** or **B**. The angular data is easily translated to distances with a calculator.

Note: *Very often, two methods will be used to ensure accuracy.*

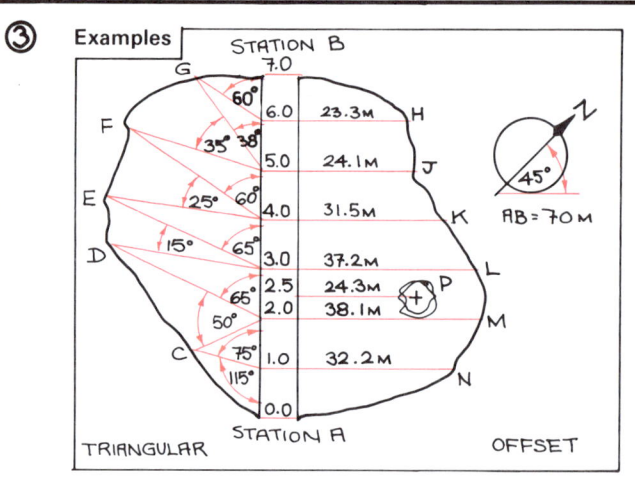

③ **Examples**

Page from a log book.
- Two methods are shown: triangulation on the left and perpendicular offsets to the right.
- The centre line **AB** has been 'opened out' into a strip to allow for the divisions to be indexed.
- For clarity in the drawing the triangles are taken as shown and not just from **A** and **B**. In practice, these are taken from the station points and tracings or overlays used to avoid confusion.

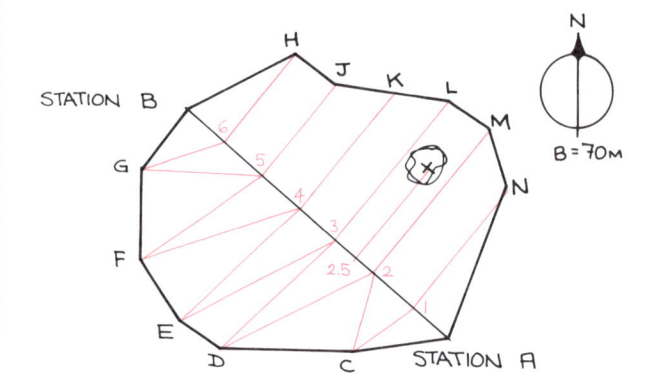

A drawing based on the log book above
- Here the site plan is turned and read in the more usual north-orientation.
- The control line **AB** is drawn and the various points on the boundary are plotted.
- Features, such as the tree, are similarly plotted.

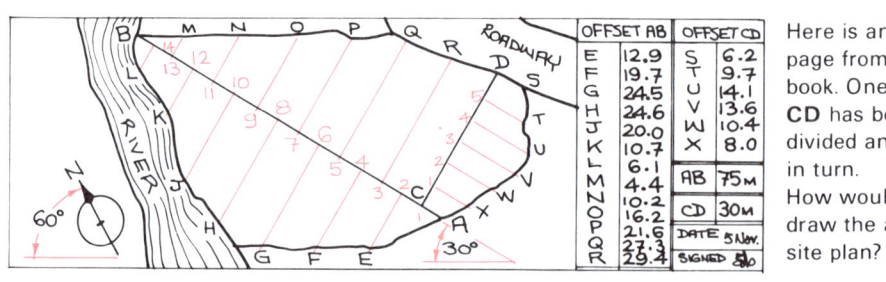

Here is another page from a log book. One offset **CD** has been sub-divided and offset in turn.
How would you draw the adjusted site plan?

Note: *Most important surveys these days are plotted by laser, or radio waves, onto an electronic log, which is later connected to a computer and plotter. Quality fieldwork is as vital as ever.*

Technical Draughtsmanship
Measuring Distances
Surveying 1 — Part 2B Bldg

① Levelling, or the measurement of heights

Levelling instruments may be visual, electronic, or laser. In each case they record accurately both horizontal and vertical angles. In the case of electronic or laser instruments the distance from the station point is calculated directly. With visual instruments distances can also be read, there being a system of allowance for the 'fore-shortening' effect of viewing an object from a vertical angle.

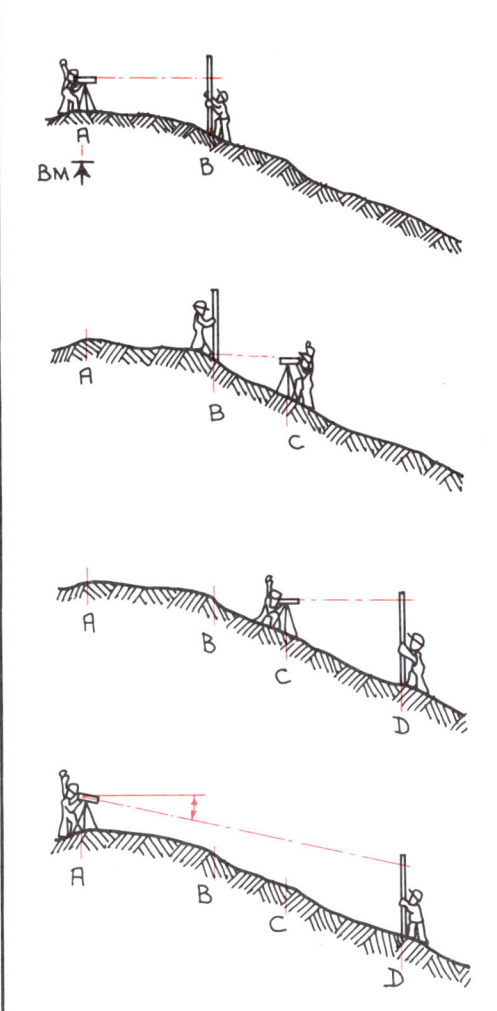

How to get levels

- A point **A** is chosen as a starting point or *datum level*. This is often a local *bench mark*. These marks were made by the Ordnance Survey and show the height above sea level.
- At **B** a man stands with a staff, a rigid stick marked in centimetres.
- The surveyor reads the height of the staff at **B**.
- He then moves to **C** and takes a *back sighting* to **B**.
- The man moves the staff to **D** and a *fore sighting* is made.
- The leap-frog continues and by simple calculation the levels of **B, C,** and **D** are found. These are usually written on pegs driven into the ground.
- The whole system is simplified if the views can all be taken from **A** and an allowance made for the angles of inclination.

② A sample levelling survey, for laying a drain

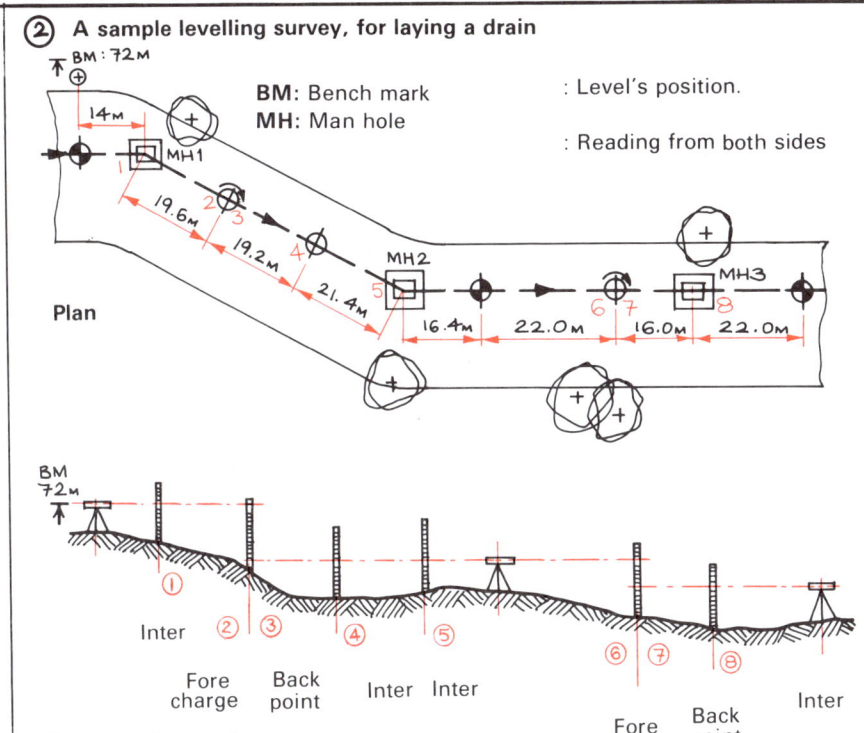

BM: Bench mark
MH: Man hole

: Level's position.

: Reading from both sides

Plan

Diagram of procedure

Reading	1	2	3	4	5	6	7	8
FORE		2.41				2.63		
INTER	1.33			1.75	1.34			1.80
BACK			0.26				0.92	
LEVEL	70.67	69.57	69.57	68.08	68.49	67.2	67.2	66.32

Log

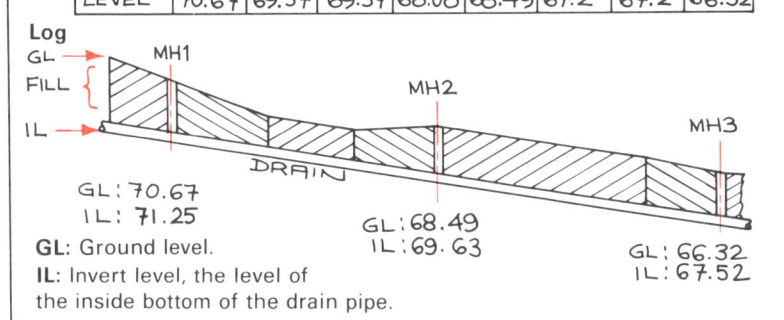

GL: 70.67
IL: 71.25

GL: 68.49
IL: 69.63

GL: 66.32
IL: 67.52

GL: Ground level.
IL: Invert level, the level of the inside bottom of the drain pipe.

Elevation of readings

Note:
These days surveyors use an electronic log that records the positions and heights in a computer memory system.

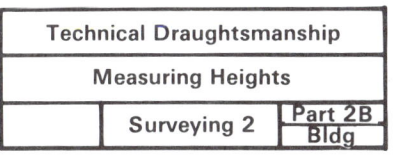

Procedure

- Locate a bench mark, or set up a starting datum level of your own.
- On plan mark your various station points. Then mark the proposed line of the drain and its manholes.
- Show clearly the sighting positions and index them.
- Sightings are taken and logged, as shown. Notice how fore, back and intermediate sightings are taken and entered in the surveyor's log book.
- The information can then be used to draw a diagram of the levels. This is then used to plot the drain levels and manhole depths, as shown.
- Notice how the drain has been set out in one plane.

Technical Draughtsmanship
Measuring Heights
Surveying 2 — Part 2B Bldg

① Contours

- A contour is a line that joins all points of the same height above or below a chosen datum level.

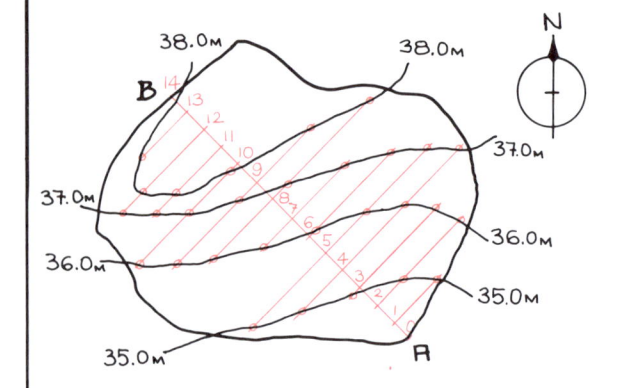

- A contour may be plotted using a control line **AB** and perpendicular offsets, as shown above.
- Choose the interval you require between contour lines, here **1.0 m**. This is called the *vertical interval*.
- Now sight a theodolite along an offset and set down pegs to mark the points on the offset that are at the required levels.
- Plot points on each offset and then draw a contour line through the points of equal height.

② Profiles

- Take the line **AB**. You now know the points where the contours cross that line. Set the heights of these contours to draw the profile of a section along **AB**.

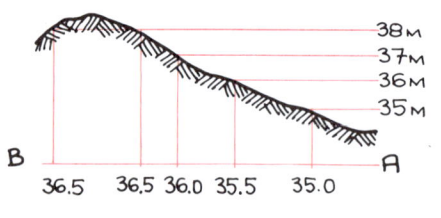

Profile of the line AB

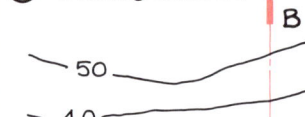

③ Reading contours

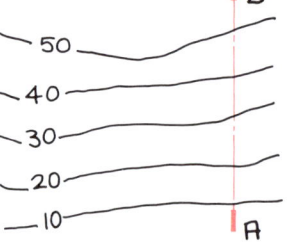

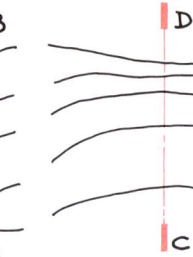

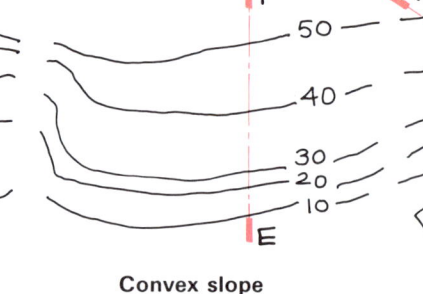

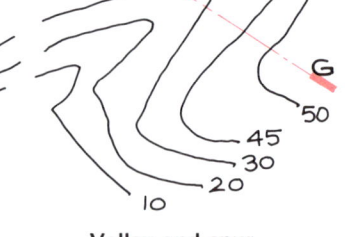

Regular slope
- The contours are evenly spaced up the slope

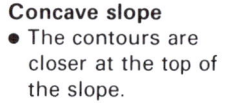

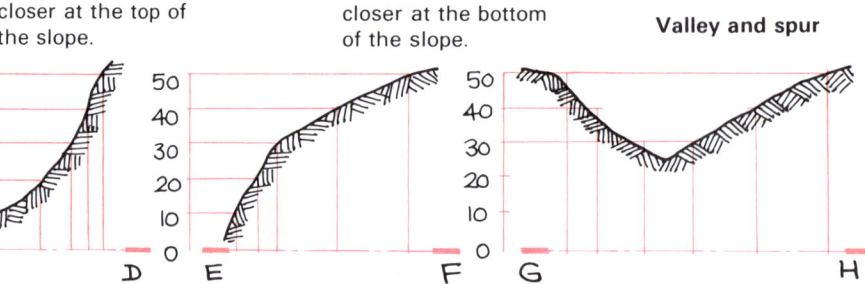

Concave slope
- The contours are closer at the top of the slope.

Convex slope
- The contours are closer at the bottom of the slope.

Valley and spur

Profile of AB   Profile of CD   Profile of EF   Profile of GH

- The horizontal distance between two contours is known as the *horizontal equivalent,* for reasons outlined below.

④ Gradients:

This is the slope of the ground and is shown either as a ratio or as a proportional triangle.

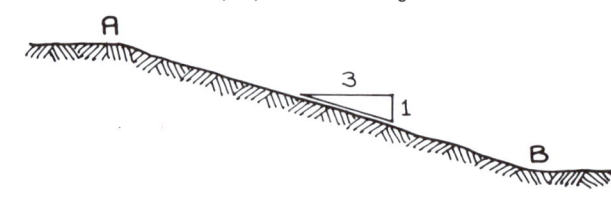

- Gradient along **AB = 1 in 3**, i.e. one step vertically for every three steps horizontally.
- Contours can also be used to find the gradient.
- When the contours are close together the gradient is steep and when the contours are widely spaced the gradient is shallow, or even flat.

- The gradient can also be found by dividing the vertical interval **EF** by the horizontal equivalent **DF**.

Gradient of DE $= \dfrac{EF}{DF} = \dfrac{10}{25} = \dfrac{1}{2.5} = $ **1 in 2.5**

Note: *Contours can also be fairly accurately plotted mathematically from a grid of spot levels, as seen on page* **297**.

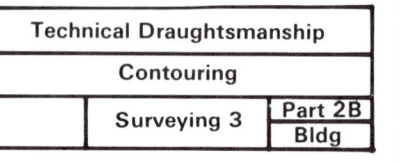

Technical Draughtsmanship		
Contouring		
	Surveying 3	Part 2B Bldg

① Setting out a grid

- Pegging contours by offsets is a time-consuming job and operating on a site with widely scattered pegs can be confusing.
- To simplify things a grid system is often set up, as below.
- It is also possible to deduce fairly accurate contours from grid system readings.

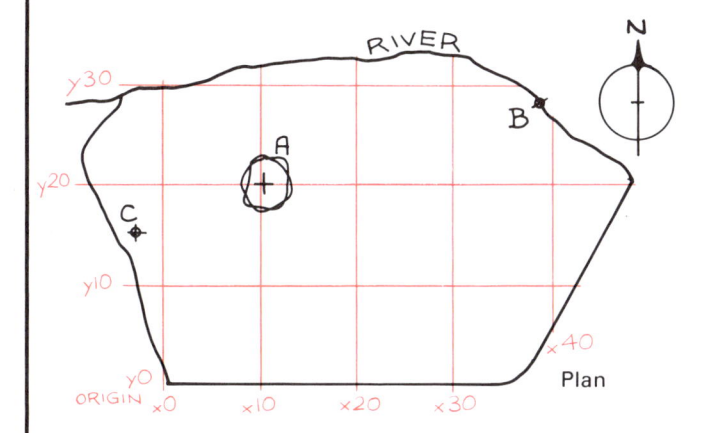

Plan

Procedure
- Choose a suitable origin and an appropriate interval, here **10 m**, and set out the grid.
- The grid reference of **A** is **x10y20**, of **B** is **x38y27** and of **C** is **x-4 y16**.
- Levels are taken and marked at intersections.

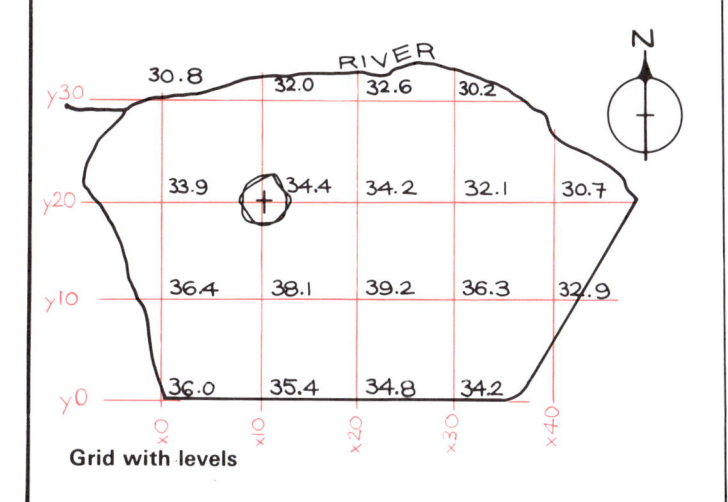

Grid with levels

② Interpolation of contours: This is an approximate method of deducing contour points from grid levels.

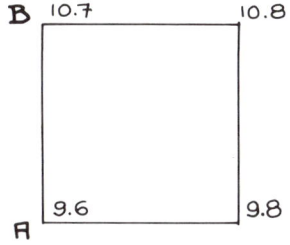

- Take one grid square at a time.
- It will be noticed that the difference from **A** to **B** is **1.1 units**

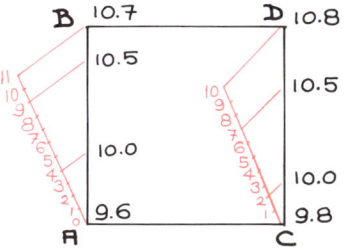

- By proportional division of **AB** a reasonable position for **10.0** and **10.5** can be deduced.
- Similarly **CD** can be divided to find contour points.

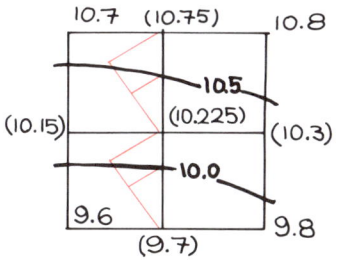

- This technique can be extended to sub-divide the grid square, as above.
- This allows further points to be found.
- Draw contours through the points.

③ Interpolation template
- On tracing paper draw a line **AB** of any chosen length.
- At right angles and to one end of **AB** draw a line **CD**.
- Divide **CD** into twenty equal divisions, as shown.
- Join each division to point **A**.
- This template can be used to rapidly find contour points.

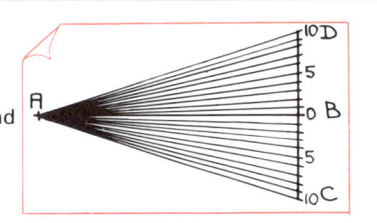

Template

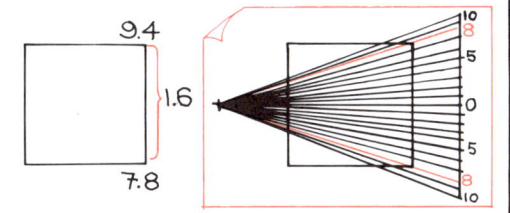

- Slide the template over the grid line until this is divided into the required number of units, here **16**.
- Mark the contour points with a pin.

④ An example of interpolation

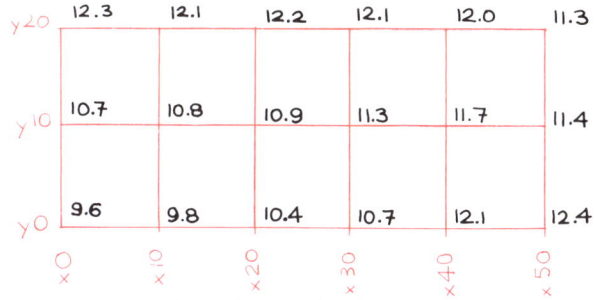

The grid with levels

Notes:
- Interpolation is tedious and ideally suited to computers.
- The smaller the grid interval, the more accurate the contours.
- The word comes from Latin: Inter meaning 'between' and polire 'to make smooth'.

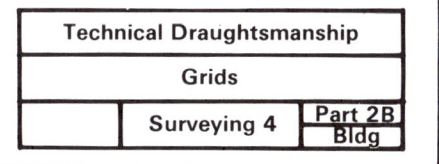

The interpolated contours

Technical Draughtsmanship
Grids
Surveying 4 — Part 2B Bldg

297

① Road profiles

To plot a road from **A** to **B** that will have a gradient of **1 in 6** over its entire length. The width of the road is not to be taken into account.

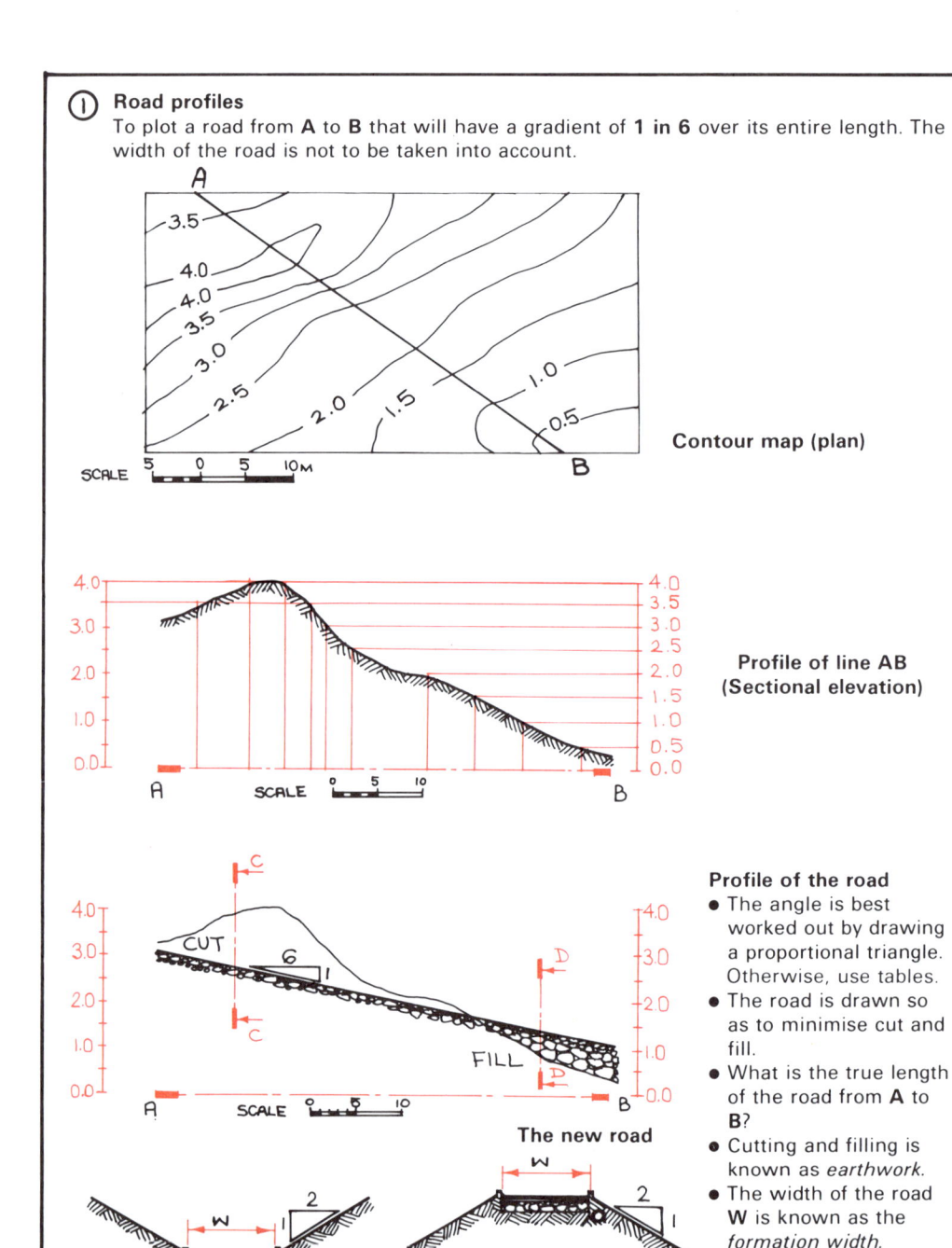

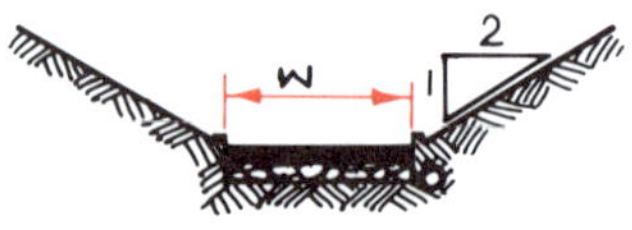

Contour map (plan)

Profile of line AB (Sectional elevation)

Profile of the road
- The angle is best worked out by drawing a proportional triangle. Otherwise, use tables.
- The road is drawn so as to minimise cut and fill.
- What is the true length of the road from **A** to **B**?
- Cutting and filling is known as *earthwork*.
- The width of the road **W** is known as the *formation width*.
- The gradient of a sloping side can be referred to as an *angle of repose*.

The new road

Section C-C — A cutting

Section D-D — An embankment

② Road plans when the road is level (no gradient).

- The profile **AB** will be retained here.
- The road is to be horizontal, to have a formation width of **5 m** and to have a gradient of **1 in 2** on all cutting and embankment side slopes.

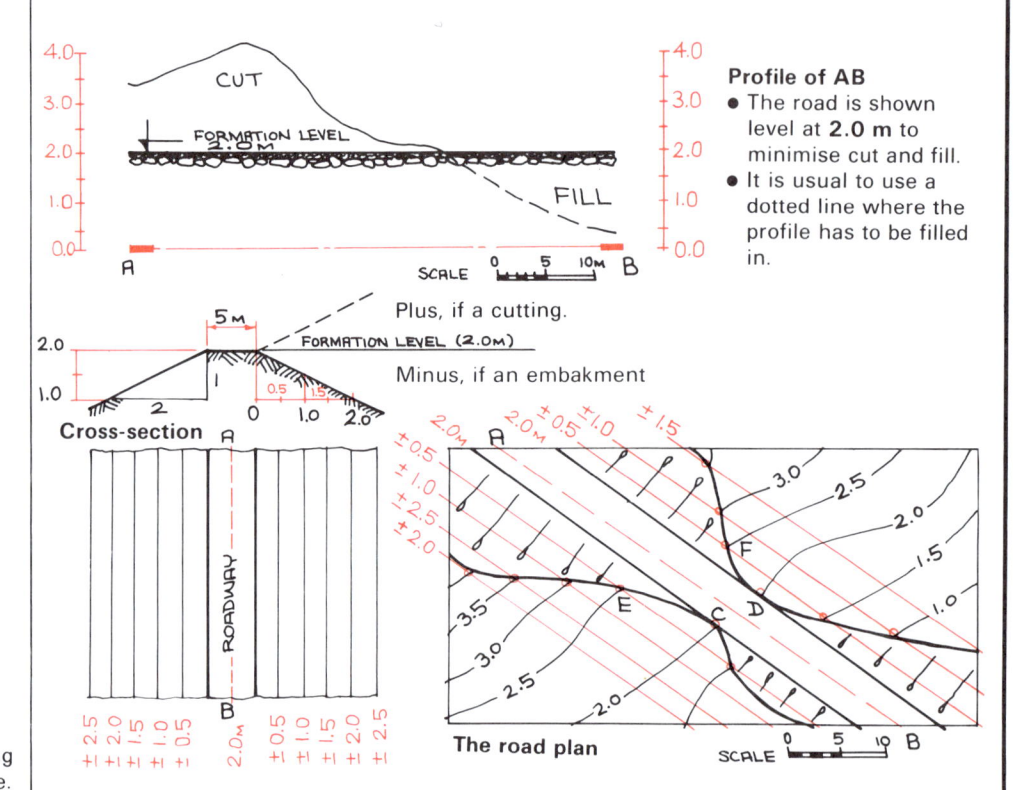

Profile of AB
- The road is shown level at **2.0 m** to minimise cut and fill.
- It is usual to use a dotted line where the profile has to be filled in.

Cross-section — Plus, if a cutting. Minus, if an embankment.

Plan (template)
- First, let us look at the road, regardless of the terrain.
- Draw any cross-section and, working out the gradient, draw two side slopes.
- Sub-divide the horizontal, as shown, to coincide with the intervals on the contour map.
- From this project a plan, as shown, onto tracing paper.
- Notice how the lines will mean height added for a cutting, and subtracted for an embankment.
- Now place the tracing about the centre line **AB** and over the contour map.
- Draw the road **5.0m** wide.

The road plan
- The road has a formation level of **2.0 m**, so, mark **C** and **D** on the **2.0 m** contour.
- Now take lines **2.0 m + 0.5** on the template and mark **E** and **F** on the **2.5 m** contour. Continue to plot the outline of the cut and fill, as shown.
- 'Tadpole' symbols are used to show the direction of the slope, using the rule: *Tadpoles always swim uphill*.

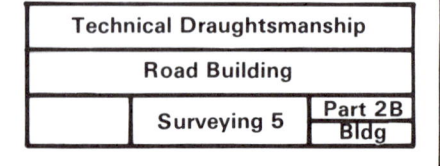

Technical Draughtsmanship
Road Building
Surveying 5 — Part 2B Bldg

The Problem

Given the map with points **A** and **B**, plot the earthworks for a road from **A** to **B** of:
- Formation Level : **100m** throughout
- Formation width : **10m**
- Angle of cut : **45°**
- Angle of fill : **30°**

Procedure

Stage 1
- Draw the road itself.
- At right angles to this, project the profile of **AB** and draw the road on the profile. This will give a good idea of where the cut and fill will be needed.

Stage 2
- Extend the road and set up the fill diagram at one end. It will help to draw the workman on the road. Plot the fill by bringing the levels back to match up with the contours.
- Notice the interpolation of **85m** to find **P** and **Q**.

Stage 3
- Extend the road at the other end, draw the cut diagram and plot the cut.
- Add the tadpoles.

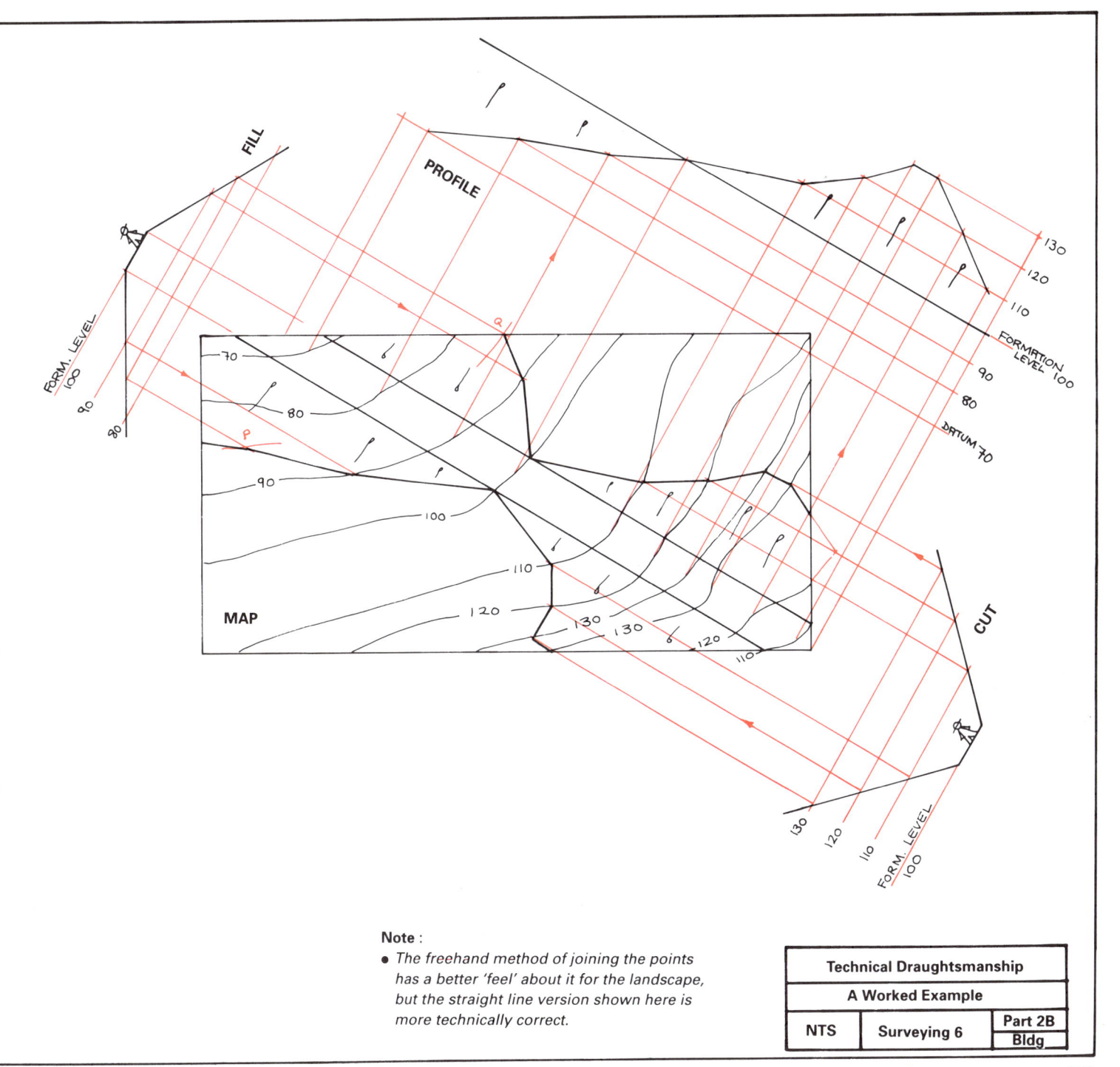

Note:
- *The freehand method of joining the points has a better 'feel' about it for the landscape, but the straight line version shown here is more technically correct.*

Technical Draughtsmanship		
A Worked Example		
NTS	Surveying 6	Part 2B
		Bldg

1. CURVING ROADWAYS

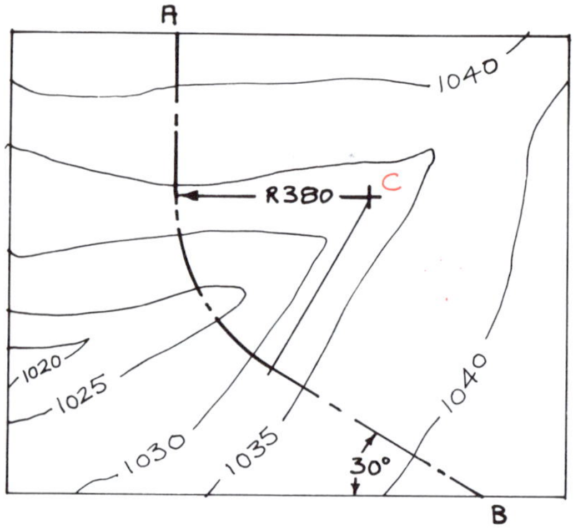

The Problem
Given is the centre line of a level roadway, **10m** wide at formation level **1030m**, with a fill angle of repose of **1 in 2** and a cut angle of repose of **1 in 1**.
Show the limits of cut and fill needed.
Scale **1:100**.

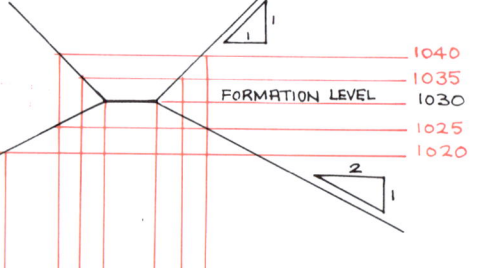

Stage 1
- Make a cross-sectional diagram for cut and fill.

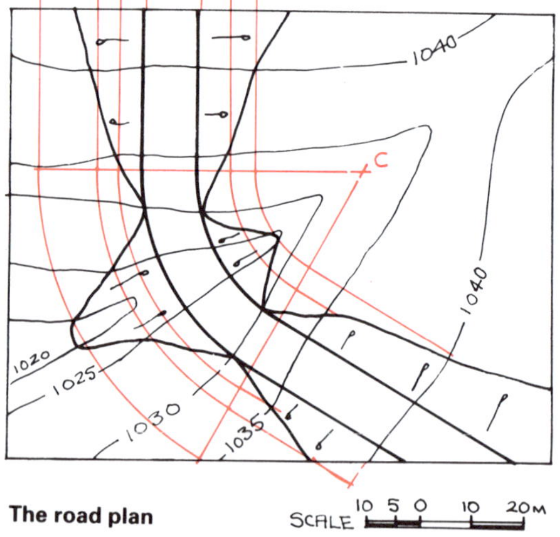

Stage 2
- Plot these onto the map as shown.
- The curve of the road is from **CE** to **CF**, with centre **C**. Using **C** as centre, swing the lines from the cross-section around, from **CE** to **CF**.
- The road meets both **CE** and **CF** at right angles.
- The cut and fill can now be plotted in the usual way.
- Add the tadpoles and the scales.

The road plan

2. PLATFORMS

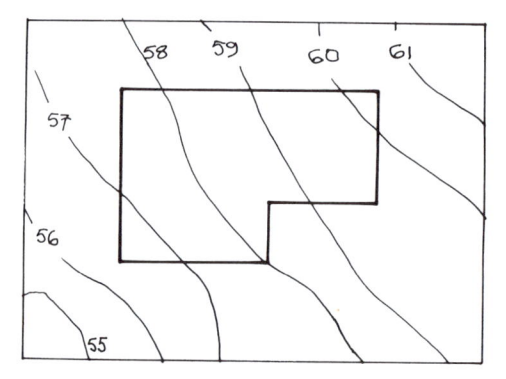

The Problem
A house is to be built on the given platform.
The platform is at a formation level of **59m** and the angle of both cut and fill is **50°**.
Show the limits of cut and fill needed.
Scale **1:50**.

Given information
Cross-section

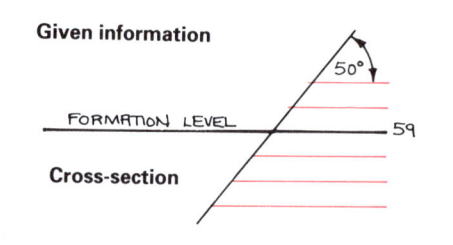

Stage 1
- Make a diagram of the cross-section to calculate spacing for cut and fill.

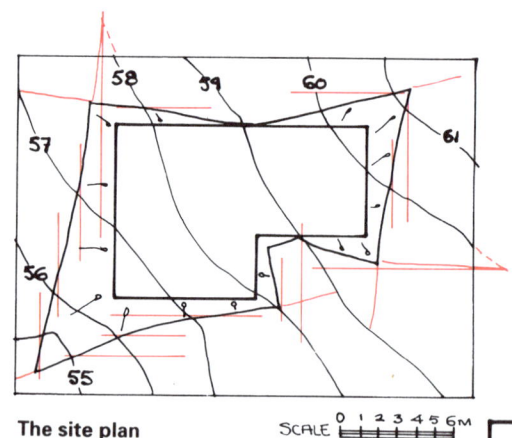

Stage 2
- Using the measurements from the cross-section, parallel to each side plot cut and fill as for the side of a road, extending slightly beyond the side. Where these plot lines intersect will complete the overall map of cut and fill.

The site plan

Technical Draughtsmanship		
Curved Roads and Platforms		
NTS	Surveying 7	Part 2B
		Bldg H

The Problem
Given the map and position of **A** and **B**, construct a road from **A** to **B** to be of:

Formation Width: **12m**
Formation Level at **A**: **125m**
Gradient: **1: 6.6** falling from **A**
Angle of Cut: **60°**
Angle of Fill: **30°**

Plot all the necessary earthworks.
What will be the level of the road at **B**?

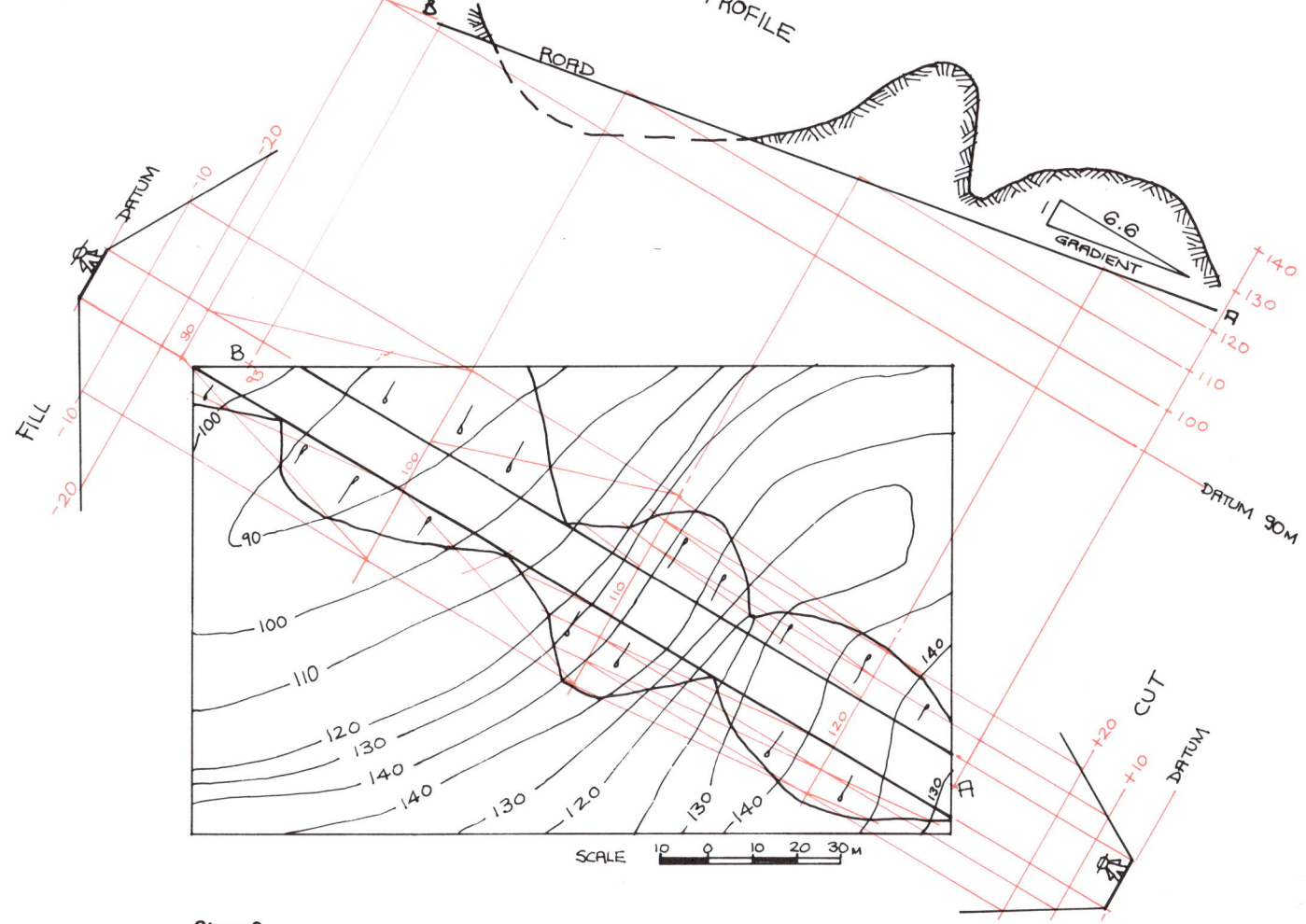

Procedure

Stage 1
- Project the profile and draw in the road, using the gradient triangle as a guide.
- Now forget about the profile for a minute; concentrate on the sloping road. Find the various levels (**120, 110** etc.) on the road. Project these back onto the road on the map.

Stage 2
- To one end, draw the fill diagram. As the road itself is changing level, this gives us **-10**, **-20** etc., from whatever level it is at. For instance, draw **-10** back until it is alongside **110**. This will be level **100**. As we know another point at level **100**, join these, and project to cut the contour **100**.
- Continue in this way to plot the fill.

Stage 3
- In a similar way, plot the cut. Be careful, as this will give **+10, +20** etc., and the lines will splay out in the opposite direction to the lines for fill.
- Sometimes it is necessary to overshoot the road to find where the earthworks strike it. After a while, you will find the rhythm of it and see some shortcuts.

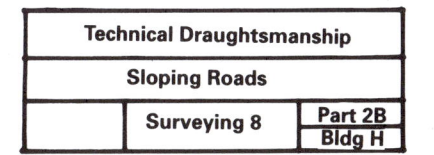

Technical Draughtsmanship		
Sloping Roads		
	Surveying 8	Part 2B
		Bldg H

301

1. MINING EXPLORATIONS

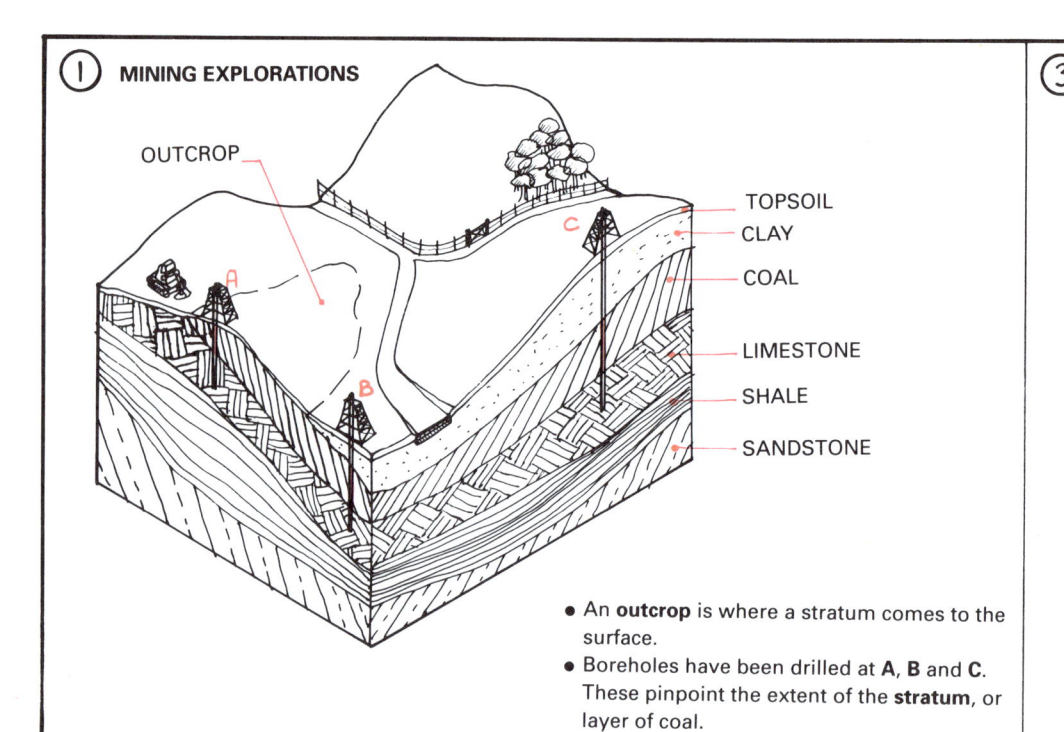

Labels: OUTCROP, TOPSOIL, CLAY, COAL, LIMESTONE, SHALE, SANDSTONE

- An **outcrop** is where a stratum comes to the surface.
- Boreholes have been drilled at **A**, **B** and **C**. These pinpoint the extent of the **stratum**, or layer of coal.

2. A STRATUM WEDGE

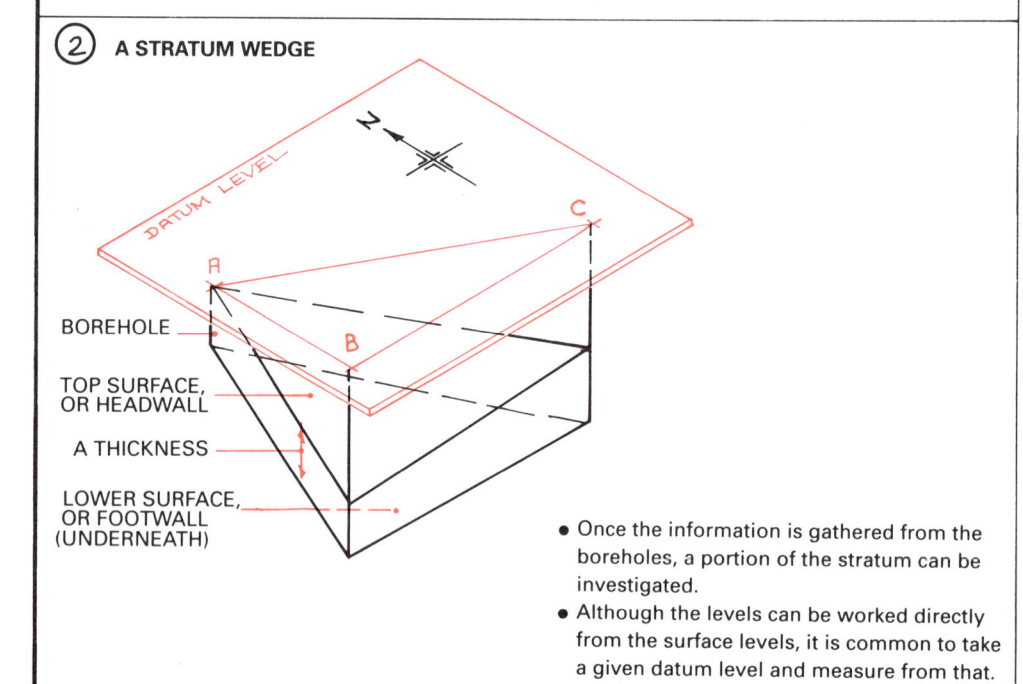

Labels: DATUM LEVEL, BOREHOLE, TOP SURFACE, OR HEADWALL, A THICKNESS, LOWER SURFACE, OR FOOTWALL (UNDERNEATH)

- Once the information is gathered from the boreholes, a portion of the stratum can be investigated.
- Although the levels can be worked directly from the surface levels, it is common to take a given datum level and measure from that.

3. PLOTTING A STRATUM WEDGE FROM SURFACE LEVELS

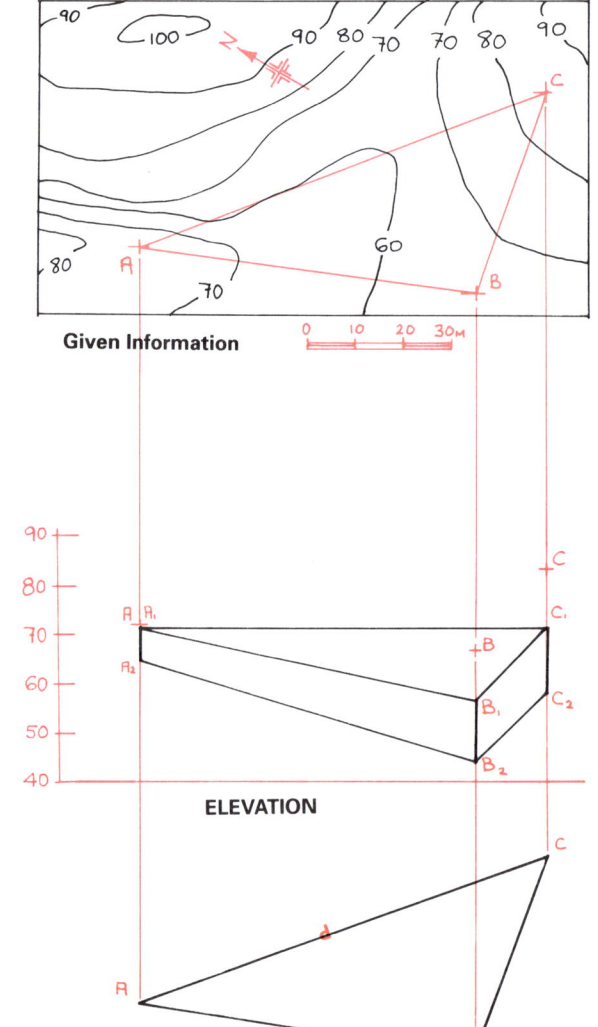

Given Information

- **Borehole Data**

  A: Surface elevation is of **72.0m** and coal was found from **0.0m** down to **6.5m**.
  B: Surface elevation is of **66.4m** and coal was found from **14.2m** down to **21.4m**.
  C: Surface elevation is of **83.0m** and coal was found from **11.7m** down to **24.6m**.

Procedure

Step 1
- Join **A** to **B** to **C**.
- Set up a scale of heights.
- Project each borehole down and set the limits of the stratum.
- Draw the Headwall A_1, B_1, C_1.
- Draw the Footwall A_2, B_2, C_2 and the thickness.
- This is an elevation of the wedge.

ELEVATION

Step 2
- To draw the plan, simply transfer **ABC** from the given map as shown.

PLAN

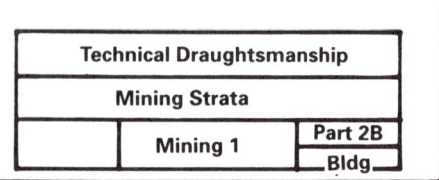

Note:
- *Due to drilling considerations on site, boreholes are not always straight down, but may be skew. See page 98.*

Technical Draughtsmanship		
Mining Strata		
Mining 1	Part 2B	Bldg

① DIP

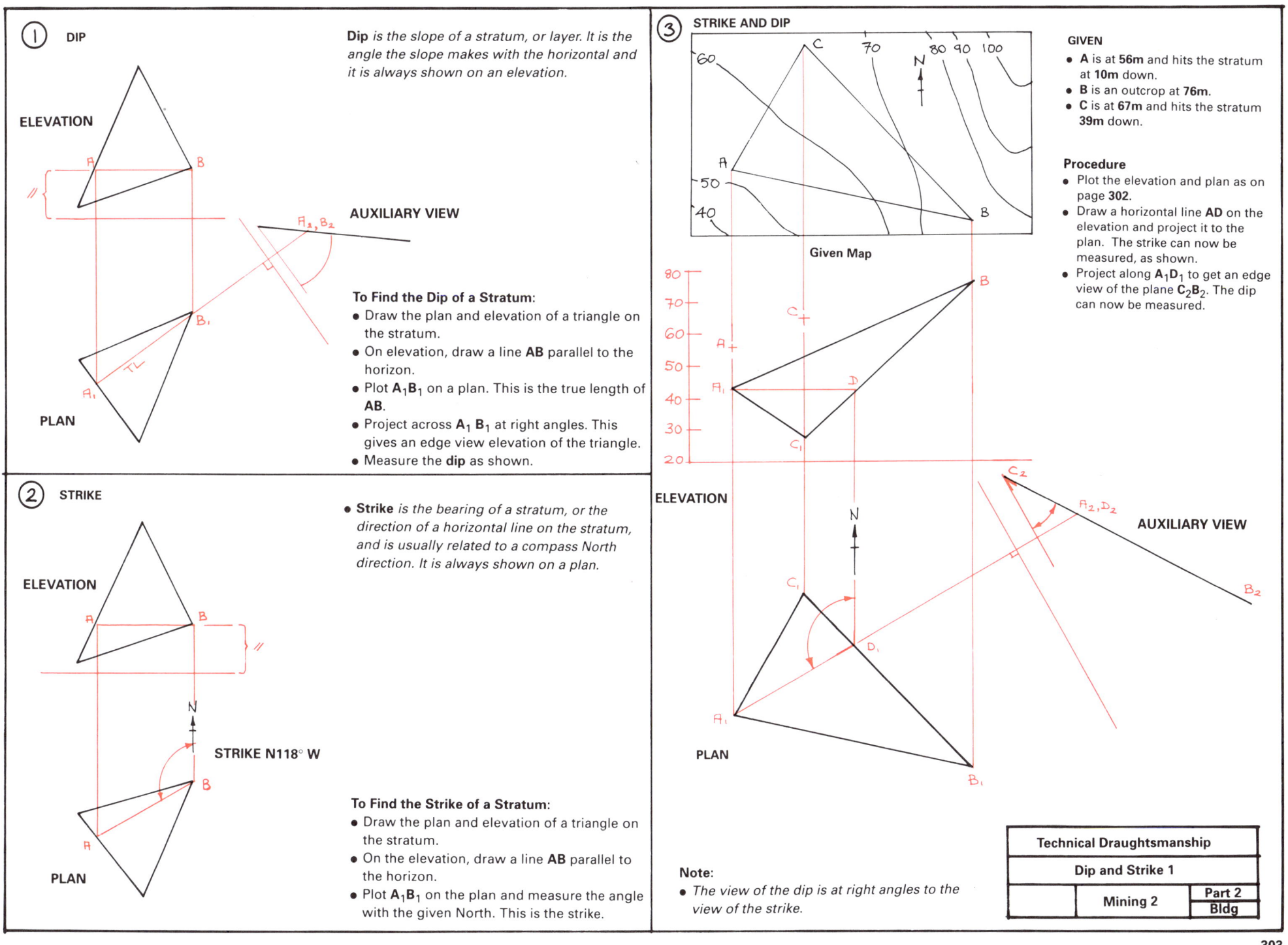

Dip *is the slope of a stratum, or layer. It is the angle the slope makes with the horizontal and it is always shown on an elevation.*

ELEVATION

PLAN

AUXILIARY VIEW

To Find the Dip of a Stratum:
- Draw the plan and elevation of a triangle on the stratum.
- On elevation, draw a line **AB** parallel to the horizon.
- Plot A_1B_1 on a plan. This is the true length of **AB**.
- Project across $A_1 B_1$ at right angles. This gives an edge view elevation of the triangle.
- Measure the **dip** as shown.

② STRIKE

ELEVATION

STRIKE N118° W

PLAN

- **Strike** *is the bearing of a stratum, or the direction of a horizontal line on the stratum, and is usually related to a compass North direction. It is always shown on a plan.*

To Find the Strike of a Stratum:
- Draw the plan and elevation of a triangle on the stratum.
- On the elevation, draw a line **AB** parallel to the horizon.
- Plot A_1B_1 on the plan and measure the angle with the given North. This is the strike.

③ STRIKE AND DIP

Given Map

ELEVATION

PLAN

AUXILIARY VIEW

GIVEN
- **A** is at **56m** and hits the stratum at **10m** down.
- **B** is an outcrop at **76m**.
- **C** is at **67m** and hits the stratum **39m** down.

Procedure
- Plot the elevation and plan as on page **302**.
- Draw a horizontal line **AD** on the elevation and project it to the plan. The strike can now be measured, as shown.
- Project along A_1D_1 to get an edge view of the plane C_2B_2. The dip can now be measured.

Note:
- *The view of the dip is at right angles to the view of the strike.*

Technical Draughtsmanship		
Dip and Strike 1		
	Mining 2	Part 2
		Bldg

303

Dip and Strike - an alternative method

PLAN

- P, Q and R are on a stratum of ore and have elevation heights of **53**, **34** and **20m** respectively. Plot the dip and strike of the stratum.

PLAN (STRIKE: N88°W)

Procedure
Step 1
- R is the lowest and may be taken as a datum level.
- From P, set a right angle and measure the distance of P above R along this line to find S.
- Likewise, at Q, set a right angle and measure QT.
- Join U to R. This is the strike and can be measured relative to North.

PLAN (DIP 42°)

Step 2
- From P, drop a perpendicular to UR at V.
- With P as centre, swing V up to find W on PQU.
- Join W to S to find the dip of the given stratum.
- See also pages **93**, **110**, **114** for laminae in space.

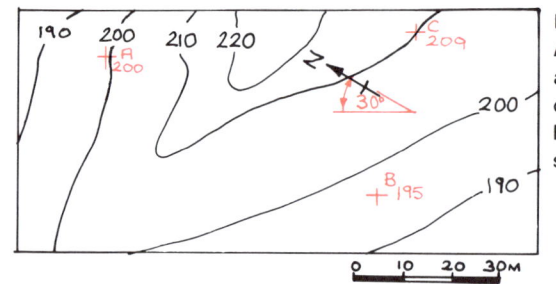

Notes:
- The principle is one of rabatment.
- **UVR** is a horizontal trace of the oblique plane containing **PQR**. How could the vertical trace be found?

A Sample Problem Using this Method

PLAN

Borehole Information:
A struck gold at a depth of **17m**, **B** at a depth of **4m** and **C** at a depth of **9m** below the surface.
Find the dip and strike of the stratum that contains **A**, **B** and **C**.

PLAN (STRIKE: N17½°E, DIP 19°)

Procedure

Step 1: Strike
- If the points on the stratum are **A**, **B** and **C**, these would be at levels of **183**, **191** and **200m** respectively.
- A is the lowest and may be taken as the datum. Join C to B.
- C is **18m** higher, so set **18m** at right angles to CB to find D.
- B is **8m** higher than A, so set **8m** at right angles to find E.
- Join D to E and extend to meet CB at F.
- Join F to A. This is the strike and is measured as shown.

Step 2: Dip
- From C drop a perpendicular to AF at G.
- With C as centre, swing G to H.
- Join H to D to find the angle of dip.

Notes:
- CD can be taken either side of CB, but the side away from the third point A, gives the clearest drawing.
- Notice that the North sign can be at any angle and how the strike is written.

Technical Draughtsmanship
Dip and Strike 2
Mining 3 — Part 2B — Bldg H

304

① The Principle

Create a plane that contains one skew line and also contains a line parallel to the second skew line. Then get an edge view of this plane. This will give a view where the skew lines *appear* parallel. *See page 98.*

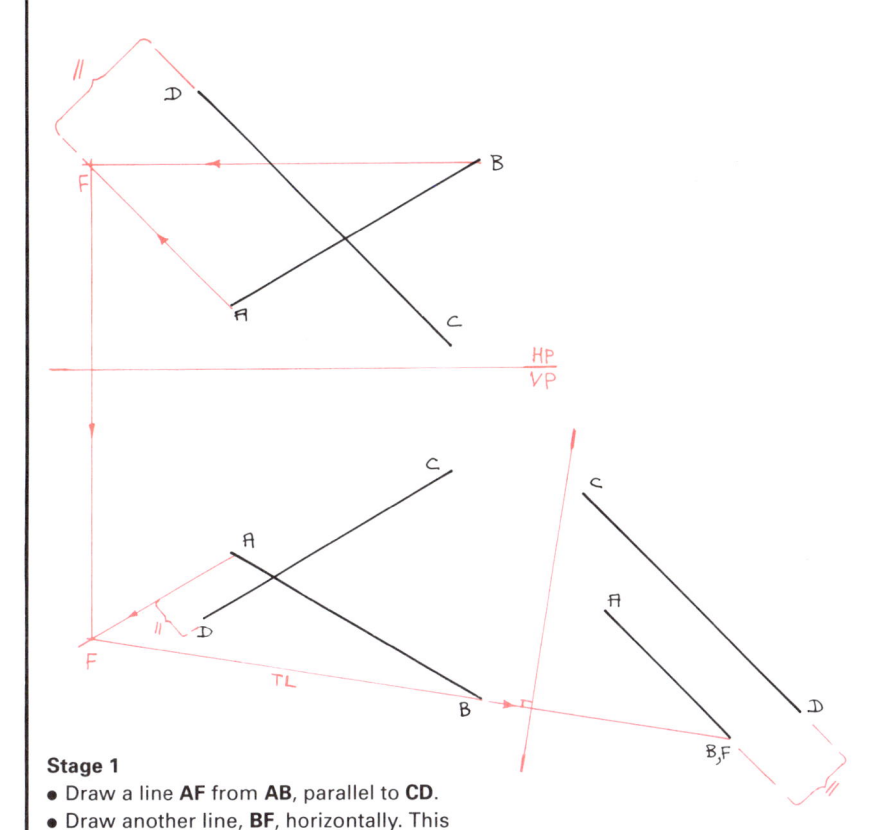

Stage 1
- Draw a line **AF** from **AB**, parallel to **CD**.
- Draw another line, **BF**, horizontally. This makes finding an edge view easier.
- Find **ABF** on the plan, **AF** being parallel to **CD**.

Stage 2
- Project a view along **FB** to get an edge view **ABF** - the construction triangle 'disappears'.
- As **FA** was set up parallel to **CD**, the two skew lines will now appear parallel.

② The Principle Applied to Mining

The Problem
Two skew boreholes are drilled as follows:

Borehole A: Level **45m**.
Drilled **S45°E** and at **30°** to **HP**.
Hit gold from levels **40** to **17m**.

Borehole B: Located **74m N60°E** of **A**
Level **76m**.
Drilled **S15°W** and at **45°** to **HP**.
Hit gold from levels **64** to **34m**.

Stage 1
- Using the auxiliary views, set up the boreholes and find the ore.
- Join **P** to **Q** to find a line on the headwall.
- Join **R** to **S** to find a line on the footwall.

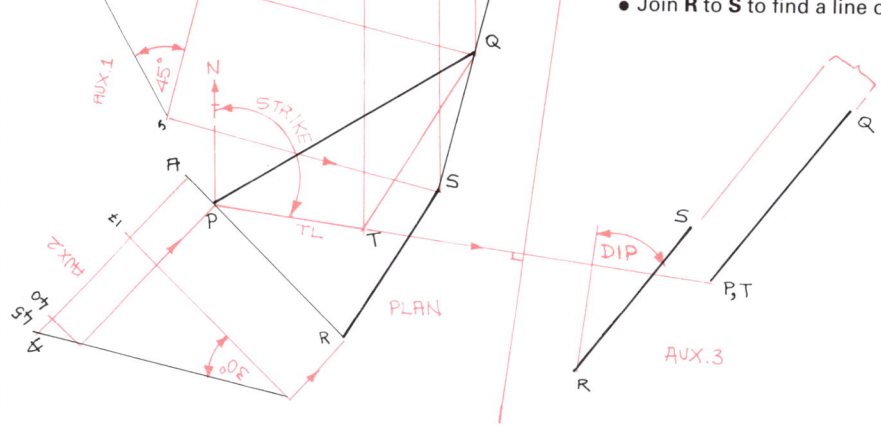

Stage 2
- Set up a triangle **PQT**, where **QT** is parallel to **RS** and **PT** is horizontal.
- Find **PQT** on the plan. **QT** is parallel to **RS**. As **PT** is a true length it will give us the strike.
- Trace an auxiliary view along **PT** to get the dip and a thickness for the ore-bearing stratum.

Technical Draughtsmanship		
Two Skew Boreholes		
	Mining 4	Part 2B
		Bldg H

305

Note: *Tracing paper will be required for these exercises.*

Questions

1. Trace this site. Set out a control line and survey it, using the perpendicular offset method. Use this information to redraw the site to a more appropriate scale.

2. Trace and then survey this site by the triangulation method. Use the survey to redraw the site to a larger scale.

3. Trace, survey and redraw both sites using the offset method.

4. Trace and survey this site using control line **AB** in general and the offset **CD** as a control line for the quarry boundary. Redraw the survey on an A3 sheet.

5. Take one of the above sites and sketch a house design for it.

6. Plot the cut and fill for a road of width **10m** from **A** to **B** at formation level **30m** throughout.

Technical Draughtsmanship

Exercises 1

Surveying — Part 2B / Bldg.

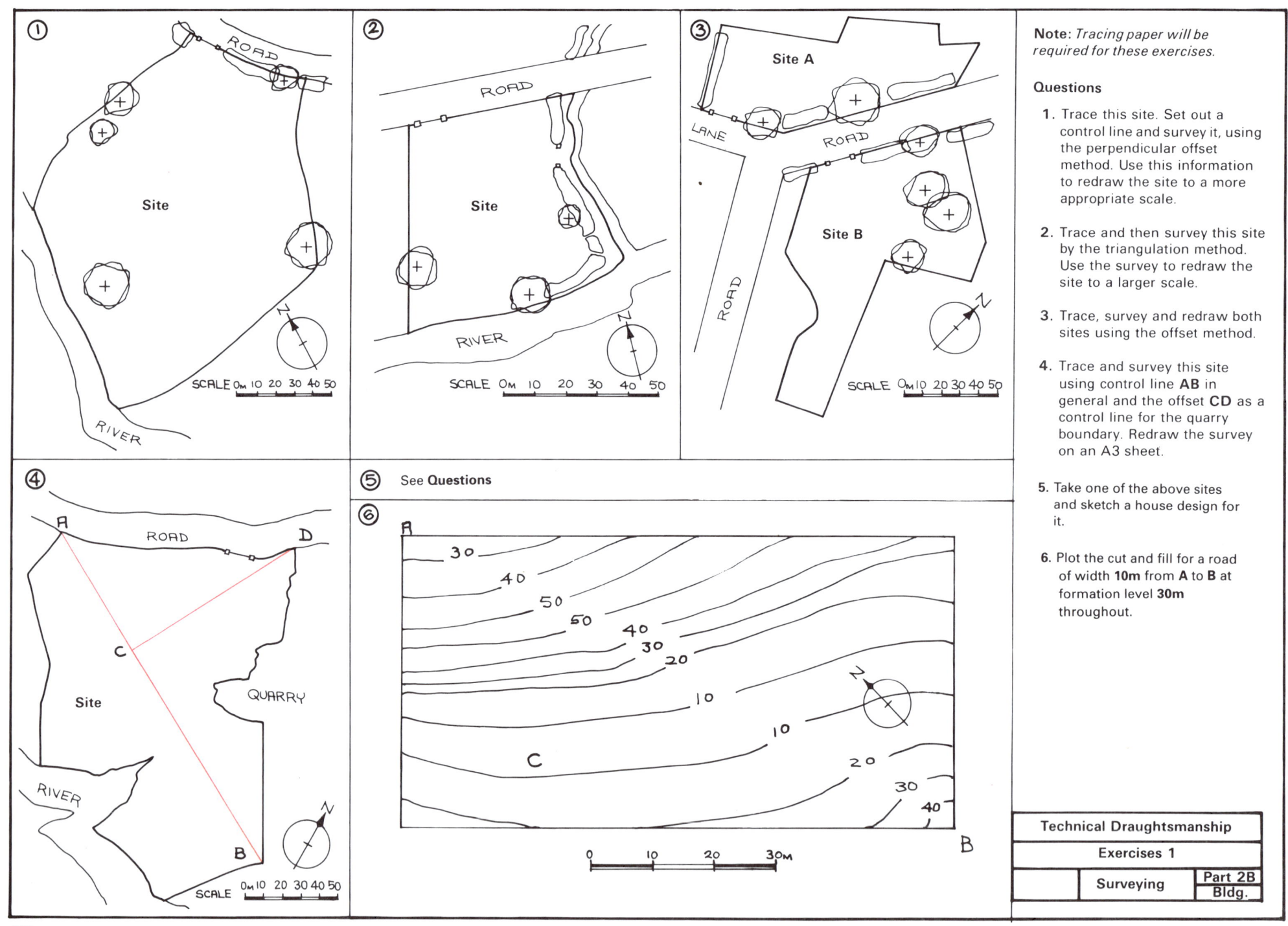

①

Site with contours 1057–1065, Roadway, Cottage, point A
Scale 0 10 20 30 m

②

Contours 2745–2751, points L, M, N, line A–B
Gradient from **A** to **B** is **1 in 6**.
Formation width **8m**.
Angles of repose: **30°** on fill, **45°** on cut.
Scale 0 1 2 3 4 5 M

③

Contours 878–883, points L, M, N, line A–B
Gradient from **A** to **B** is **1 in 7**.
Formation width **4m**.
Angles of repost: **1 in 2** on fill, **1 in 3** on cut.
Scale 0 2 4 6 8 10 M

④

Contours 455–480, points L, M, N, O, lines A–B and C–D
Gradient from **A** to **B** is **1 in 6**.
Gradient from **C** to **D** is **1 in 8**.
Angle of repose **45°** for both cut and fill.
Scale 0 10 20 25 M

Note: *All contours are given in metres above sea level.*

Questions

1. Trace and redraw this site to a suitable scale. An access road is required from **A** to **B** of formation width **4m**. Draw this road in plan and profile. The road is of even gradient throughout with a **1 in 2** angle of repose to both cut and fill.

2 & 3. Plot the earthworks and also find the dip and strike of the stratum whose outcrops are indicated.

4. Plot the earthworks. Make two triangular strata of the outcrops shown and find their dip and strike.

5. Draw any one of these questions in isometric or trimetric.

Technical Draughtsmanship		
Exercises 2		
Surveying	Part 2B	Bldg. H

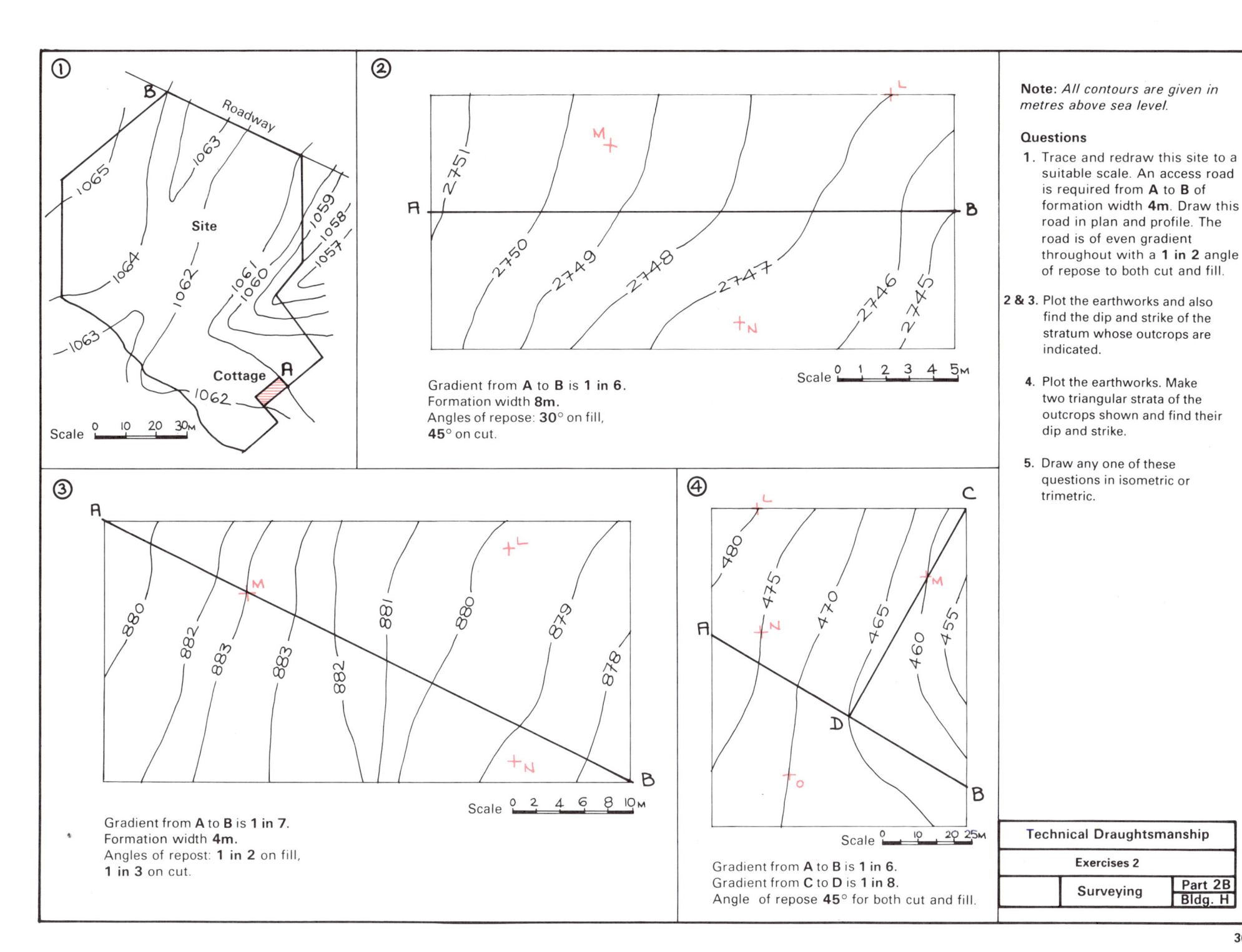

307

①
Borehole A: Altitude: **95m**
Drilled: **Vertical**
Hit gold from altitude **65** down to **28m**.

Borehole B: Situated **80m S30°E** of **A**
Altitude: **75m**
Drilled: **Vertical**
Hit gold from altitude **60** down to **54m**.

Borehole C: Situated **66m N45°E** of **B**
Altitude: **60m**
Drilled: **Vertical**
Hit gold from altitude **60** down to **14m**.

②
Borehole A: Altitude: **186m**
Drilled: **Vertical**
Hit coal from **184** to **156m**.

Borehole B: Situated **45m S60°W** of **A**
Altitude: **148m**
Drilled: **Vertical**
Hit coal from **140** to **130m**.

Borehole C: Situated **70m N30°W** of **B**
Altitude: **155m**
Drilled: **Vertical**
Hit coal from **120** to **100m**.

③
Borehole A: Altitude: **80m**
Drilled: **Vertical**
Hit rubbish tip from level **60m** to **20m**.

Borehole B: Situated **60m S** of **A**
Altitude: **52m**
Drilled: **Vertical**
Hit rubbish tip from **30** to **10m**.

Borehole C: Situated **80m E** of **A**
Altitude: **72m**
Drilled: **Vertical**
Hit rubbish tip from **50** to **30m**.

Verdict: Re-site the office block.

④
Borehole # 665: Altitude: **1086m**
Drilled: **Vertical**
Hit Uranium from **1060** to **1050m**.

Borehole # 666: Situated **90m W** of **#665**
Altitude: **1044m**
Drilled: **Vertical**
Hit Uranium from **1022** to **1010m**.

Borehole # 667: Situated **80m S75°E** of **#666**
Altitude: **1110m**
Drilled: **S45°E** at **45°** to **HP**
Hit Uranium from **1108** to **1080m**.

⑤
Borehole A: Situated **50m N45°W** of **C**
Altitude: **100m**
Drilled: **Vertical**
Hit diamonds from **15** to **27m** down.

Borehole B: Situated **70m S60°W** of **A**
Altitude: **90m**
Drilled: **W** at **45°** to **HP**
Hit diamonds from **0** to **18m** down.

Borehole C: Altitude: **88m**
Situated: **SE** at **75°** to **HP**
Hit diamonds from **48** to **70m** down.

⑥
Drill 1: Altitude: **90m**
Drilled: **S30°E** at **60°** to **HP**
Hit gas from altitudes **50** to **10m**.

Drill 2: Situated **75m W** of **Drill 1**
Altitude: **37m**
Drilled: **S30°W** at **45°** to **HP**
Hit gas from **29** to **3m**.

Drill 3: Situated **60m S60°E** of **Drill 2**
Altitude: **82m**
Drilled: **N45°E** at **60°** to **HP**
Hit gas from **70** to **61m**.

⑦
Borehole A: Altitude: **180m**
Drilled: **Vertical**
Hit slate from **160** to **140m**.

Borehole B: Situated **60m N30°E** of **A**
Altitude: **172m**
Drilled: **S45°E** at **45°** to **HP**
Hit slate from **139** to **129m**.

Borehole C: Situated **75m S15°E** of **B**
Altitude: **198m**
Drilled: **SW** at **15°** to **HP**
Hit slate from levels **196** to **188m**.

⑧
Borehole A: Situated **75m E** of **B**
Altitude: **40m**
Drilled: **SW** at **45°** to **HP**
Hit copper from **35** to **23m**.

Borehole B: Altitude: **88m**
Drilled: **S45°E** at **60°** to **HP**
Hit copper from **67** to **40m**.

⑨
Borehole #736: Altitude: **2400m**
Drilled: Due **E** at **75°** to **HP**
Found silver from **2350** to **2000** and from **1950** to **1550m**.

Borehole #737: Situated **7km W30°N** of **#736**
Altitude: **2200m**
Drilled: **S30°W** at **45°** to **HP**
Found silver from **2150** to **1950** and from **1800** to **1650m**.

Questions
1 to 7
Plot the strike and dip of the headwall of each stratum

8. Find a dip, strike and thickness for the stratum.
9. Find a dip, strike and thickness for the stratum.
10. Draw two of these problems in isometric or trimetric.
11. Take two of these problems and set out the coordinates of the stratum. Choose your origin with care and relate it to the boreholes.

Technical Draughtsmanship		
	Exercises 3	
	Mining	Part 2B
		Bldg H

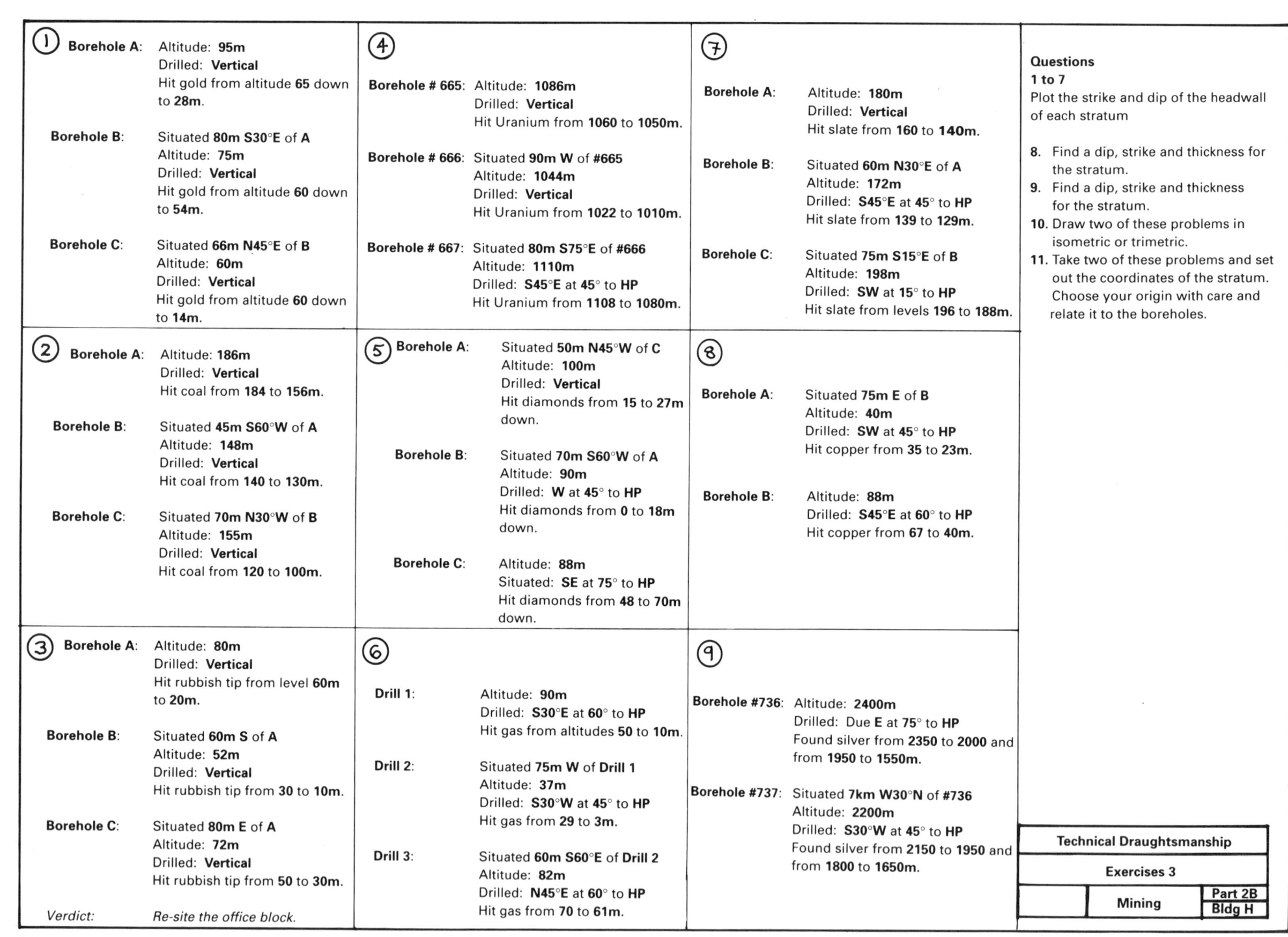

PART 2B

CHAPTER 26
BUILDING STRUCTURES

This chapter considers the basic forms of building structures and their immediate applications.

CONTENTS
Posts and Beams	*Page* **310**
Arches, Vaults and Domes	**311**
Skeletal Structures	**312**
Surface Structures	**313**
Defining a Ruled Parabaloid 1	**314**
Defining a Ruled Parabaloid 2	**315**
Finding the Three Axes	**316**
Some Roof Shells	**317**
The Hypar as a Translation	**318**
A Worked Example	**319**
Exercises	**320**

① Solid structures

- The most intuitive structure is that made out of solid rock, or blocks of solid material such as concrete, brick, stone or even ice, piled on top of each other. Stresses are transmitted through heavy walls to a foundation. Solid structures are of limited height and of a high material cost for the space enclosed. On the positive side they are good for fire resistance, thermal insulation and protection.
- Many structural methods were first devised to transfer stresses through solid buildings.

② Post and beam construction

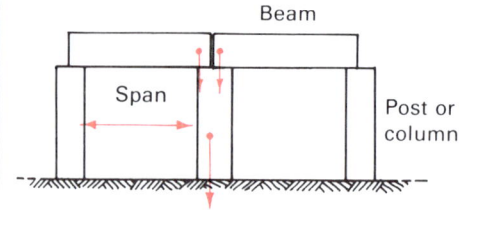

Stable
- The loads on the beam are passed down the columns to the ground.

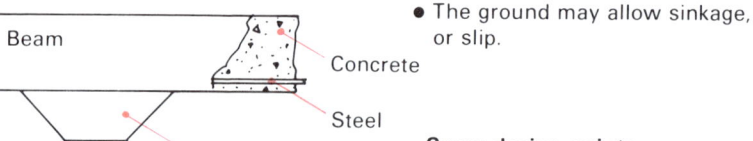

Failure
- The beam crushes on top and tears underneath.
- Columns buckle, as shown.
- The ground may allow sinkage, or slip.

Some design points
- Concrete is good in compression e.g. at the top of the beam.
- Steel is good in tension and is set within the concrete e.g. underneath the beam.
- A head 'funnels' the weight more evenly.
- Again concrete and steel counteract compression and tension in the column.
- By using steel ties the column is not allowed to 'belly' out.
- A base spreads the weight.

③ Setting out an entasis

- The Greeks were very clever architects. In designing columns they used an entasis, which means a 'bellying', along its height. This was not only structurally correct but it was also visually correct. The columns actually looked very straight and sturdy. There are two standard methods of setting out an entasis.

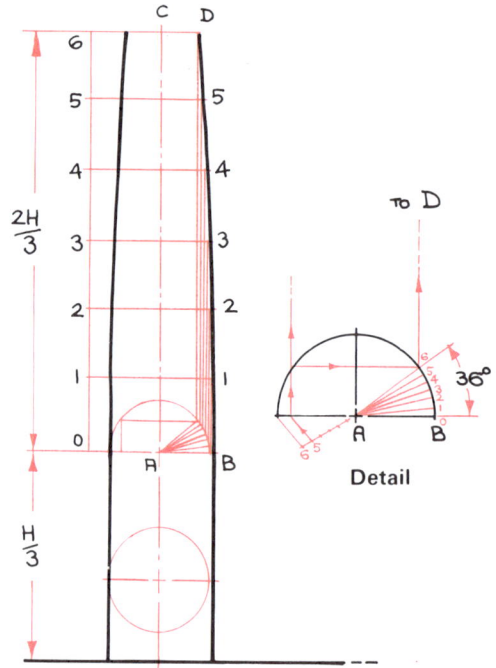

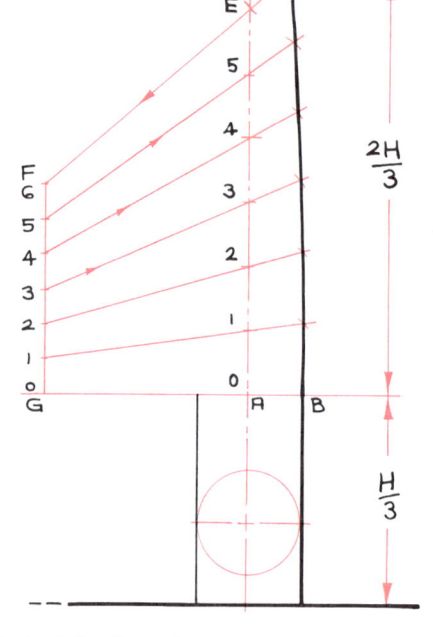

Method 1: Normand's Method
- Divide the height of the column into three parts. The bottom third is cylindrical and is not affected by entasis.
- Draw a semi-circle on **AB**.
- **CD** will be given, or will be presumed to be **5/6** of **AB**. This can be found either by proportional division, or by drawing an angle of **36°** from **A**, as shown in the detail.
- Now divide the height to be treated by entasis into a number of parts e.g. **6**.
- Divide the **36°** angle into the same number of parts and index these, as shown.
- Angle **6** will go to **D**, angle **5** to vertical division **5**, **4** to **4**, etc.
- Draw the profile of the column through these points.

Method 2: The polar method
- The bottom third is unaffected.
- Draw **FG** parallel to **AC** and to one side.
- Set out **CD** as given, or find it, as before.
- With centre **D** and radius **AB** cut the axis at **E**.
- Join **D** to **E** and extend to **F**.
- Divide **AE** and **GF** into pieces e.g. **6**.
- Join **5** on **GF** to **5** on **AE** and extend.
- With centre **5** on **AE** and radius **AB** cut the extension to find a point on the profile.
- Plot further points and draw the profile.

Technical Draughtsmanship		
Posts and Beams		
Structures 1	Part 2B	Bldg.

① The arch

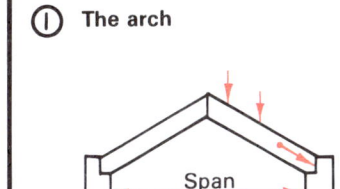

A triangular arch (stable)
- The downward forces are transmitted to each side and down the columns to the ground.

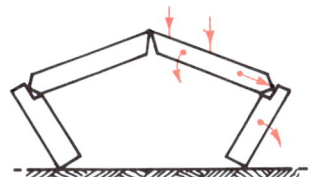

Failure
- The arch collapses and opens at its centre.
- This pushes the supports outwards and causes stress on the foundations.

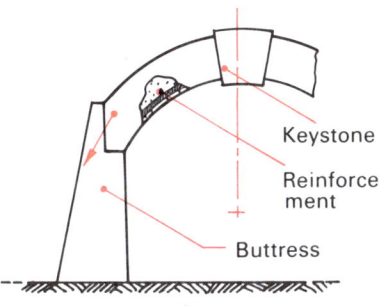

Some design points
- The arch is rounded to transmit the forces more evenly.
- The centre has a keystone to strengthen it.
- Reinforcement is usually given to the underside.
- The supporting column has its base widened to prevent rotation. This is called a **buttress.** Walls often act as buttresses to an arch.

② The vault

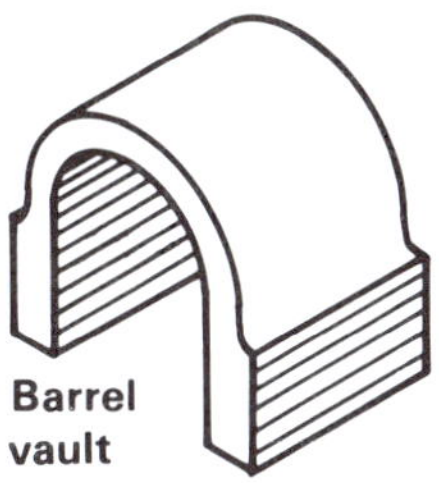

- A vault is an arch that is extended to form a cylinder, or barrel.
- When two barrel vaults intersect they form a groin vault.
- Medieval cathedrals show amazing virtuosity in the use of the vault.

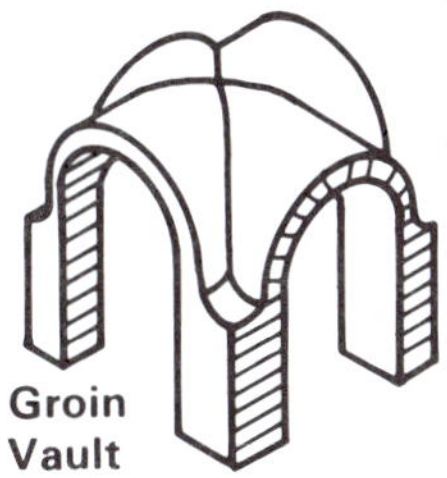

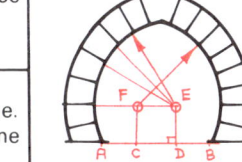

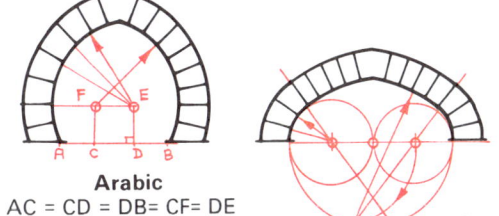

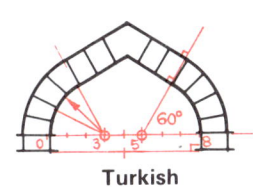

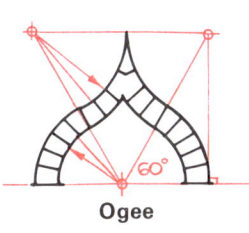

Barrel vault | **Groin Vault**

③ The dome

- A dome is an arch that is rotated about its centre line.
- The forces acting on a dome are evenly spread out.
- The dome can be mounted on a ring beam and columns, or it can be extended as pendentives with arched 'cut-outs'.

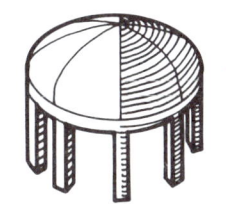

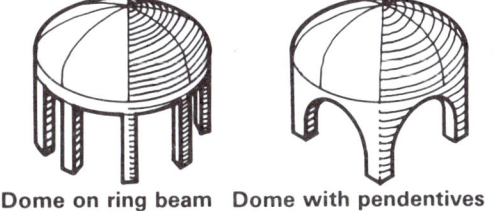

Dome on ring beam | **Dome with pendentives**

④ Terms for a semi-circular arch

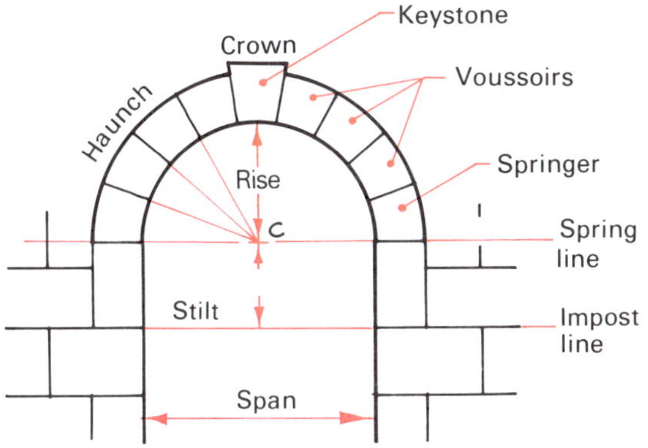

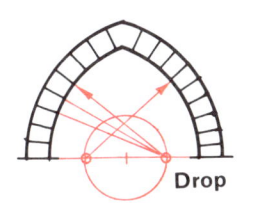

Crown, Keystone, Haunch, Voussoirs, Rise, Springer, Spring line, Stilt, Impost line, Span

- The outer or upper side of a voussoir is called the *extrado*.
- The inner or lower side of a voussoir is called the *intrado*.
- Point **C** is called the *centre* of the arch. Arches may have more than one centre, as seen below.
- When the swing of the arch is cut short it is called a *segmented arch*.
- An arch that starts from one side and finishes before it comes down on the other is called a *rampant arch*.

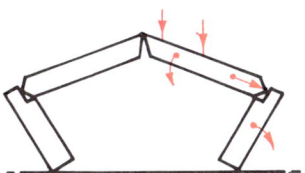

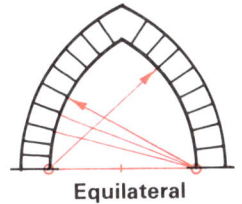

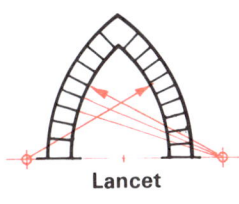

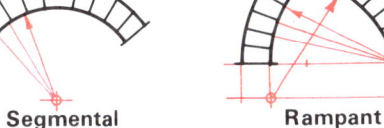

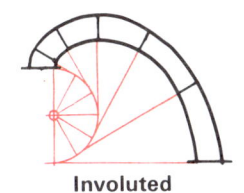

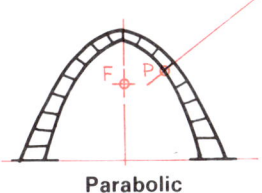

⑤ Some arch types

Corbelled | **Equilateral** | **Drop** | **Lancet**

Segmental | **Rampant** | **Involuted** | **Parabolic**

Arabic
AC = CD = DB = CF = DE

Tudor | **Turkish** | **Ogee**

Notes:
- *The division lines of the arch are usually normal to the inside of the arch.*
- *These are only a few of the very many variations of the arch that have been developed.*

Technical Draughtsmanship
Arches, Vaults and Domes
Structures 2 | **Part 2B** | **Bldg.**

311

① Skeletal structures:
The idea of a 'skeletal' or thin frame construction is as old as the tent. Long thin units are connected to form a load-carrying arrangement. A sufficient number of component parts form a *simply stiff structure*. Any additional members are *redundant,* but may be included for special reasons. If there are too few members the arrangement is a *mechanism,* structurally unacceptable but it may be mechanically useful. Sometimes a stiff structure will have pin joints to allow for a little rotation.

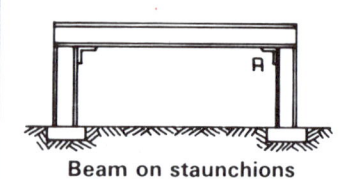

Standard Frames

Beam on staunchions

- The simplest is the post and beam construction, as on page **310**. A beam on staunchions is subject to bending moments and severe loads may cause the connecting angle **A** to yield.

Lattice girder on staunchions

- By using a lattice girder the span is increased and the weight of the girder is reduced. Laminated wood box girders can also be used in this way

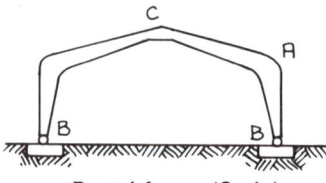

Truss on staunchions

- A triangular truss is a most economic system. Not only is the strength high in relation to the material used, but the shape of the roof is also suited to weather proofing. Triangular trusses may be of steel or wood and they are examined in more detail in Chapter **18**.

Portal frame (2 pin)

- The portal frame is really an arch. By thickening the knee **A** the material is strongest where its strength is most needed. Portal frames may be of reinforced concrete, steel or of laminated wood. Pin joints may be used at **B** and at **C** to allow a certain amount of bending to take place.

Cantilever truss on column

- Another variation is to build a cantilever truss, as in many garage forecourts, where the 'span' **A** is limited.

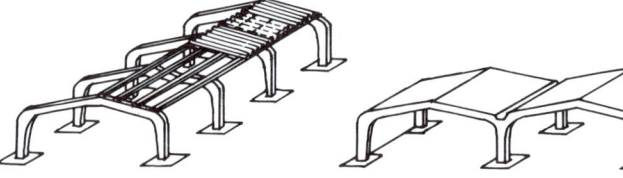

② Extending the basic unit

Multiple units
- The units are set up parallel to each other and joined by *purlins,* which are in turn covered by sheeting, and lighting or window units.

Extended units
- The units are set side by side and roofed as before. The units are often joined or adapted along their common edge.

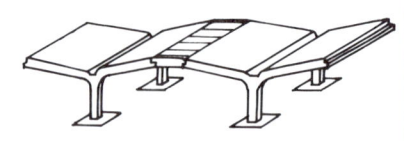

Cantilevers extended
- The units are extended, unsupported, to each side. These 'wings' are cantilevers. These are much used in garage forecourts.

③ A timber framed house

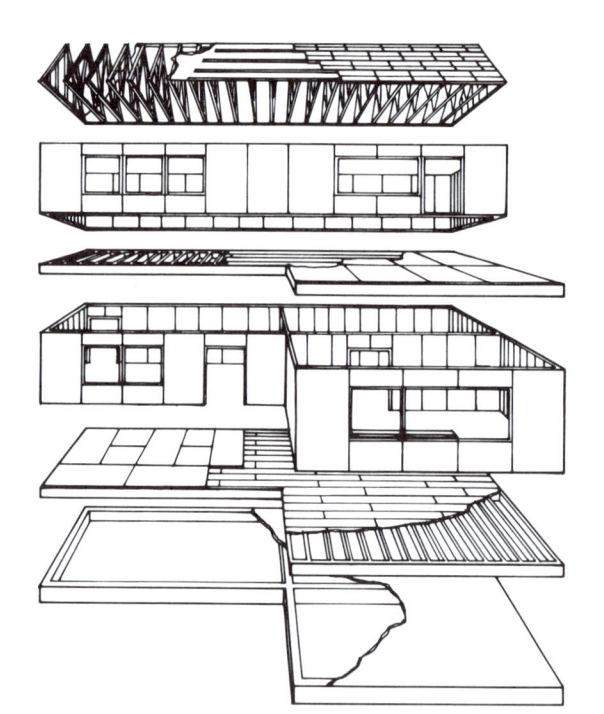

Specification (in millimetres)

The roof:
25 cladding on 50 x 25 battens on 38 x 100 trussed rafters at 450 centres on 50 x 100 wall plates.

The upper storey:
100 x 75 post and lintel frame with 100 x 50 studs clad on both sides and insulated in between.

The upper floor:
25 flooring slabs on a 100 x 50 wooden frame.

The lower storey:
100 x 75 post and lintel frame with 100 x 50 studs clad on both sides and insulated in between.

The ground floor:
25 flooring slabs on 100 x 50 wooden frame made to suit the house plan.

The foundation:
A 100 x 150 R.C. ring beam. This varies with soil conditions and is placed on 125 hardcore.

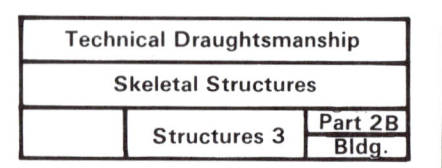

Notes:
- *All the components can be prefabricated or delivered ready to be assembled.*
- *Cable frames can also be designed.*
- *There is an incredible number of ways in which simple frames can be modified or extended. Can you sketch some of these possibilities?*

Technical Draughtsmanship	
Skeletal Structures	
Structures 3	Part 2B Bldg.

① Surface structures

- These are structures whose surfaces both enclose the space and provide support.
- These surfaces are usually made of reinforced concrete. They may take the form of plates or of shells and may be prefabricated or cast on site.
- We will look at plates first and then examine shells.

② Plates

Horizontal plate: Slab

Vertical plate: Panel

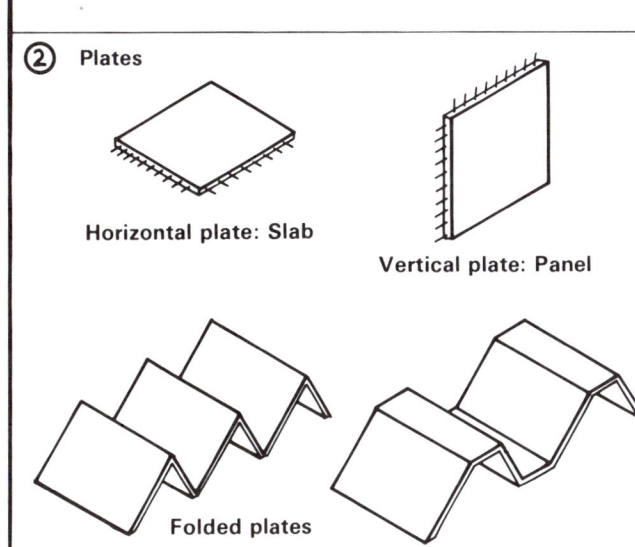

Folded plates

- By 'folding', the stiffness of thin slabs is increased and stresses are more easily transferred to their supports.
- There are many variations of the folded plate and some of these incorporate glazing panels.

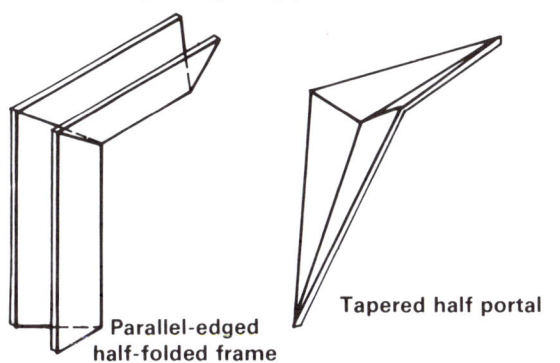

Parallel-edged half-folded frame

Tapered half portal

- These frames can be joined in series or spaced with lighting frames or panels
- They can also be set to curved or circular building plans.

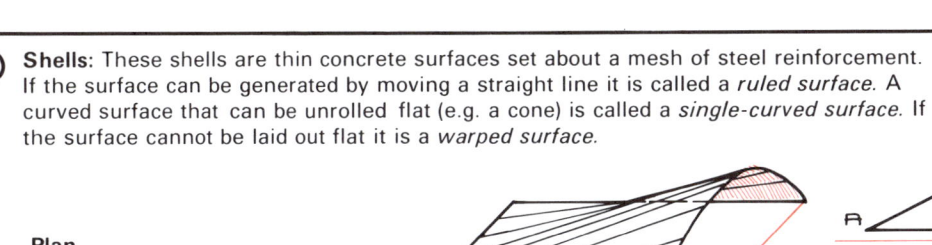

③ Shells

These shells are thin concrete surfaces set about a mesh of steel reinforcement. If the surface can be generated by moving a straight line it is called a *ruled surface*. A curved surface that can be unrolled flat (e.g. a cone) is called a *single-curved surface*. If the surface cannot be laid out flat it is a *warped surface*.

Plan

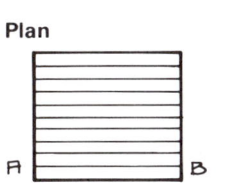

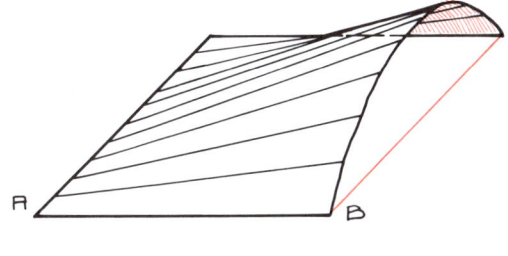

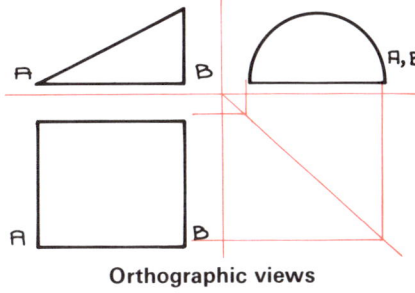

The conoid

Orthographic views

- If one end of a generating line runs along a straight line and the other end runs along a semicircle, or other curve, the surface is called a *conoid*.
- These surfaces can be grouped in series and the raised end glazed, as in conoidal roofs.

The hyperbolic paraboloid
High saddle type.

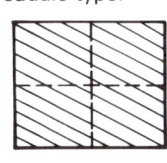

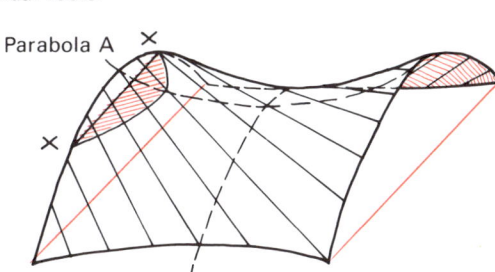

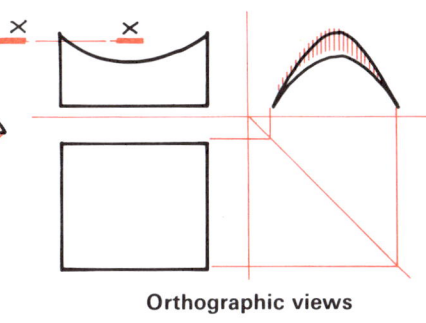

Plan

Orthographic views

- If a parabola **A** runs along a second parabola **B**, the surface is a hyperbolic parabaloid.
- Vertical sections will be parabolas and horizontal sections will be hyperbolas.

The hyperbolic paraboloid, shallow saddle type.

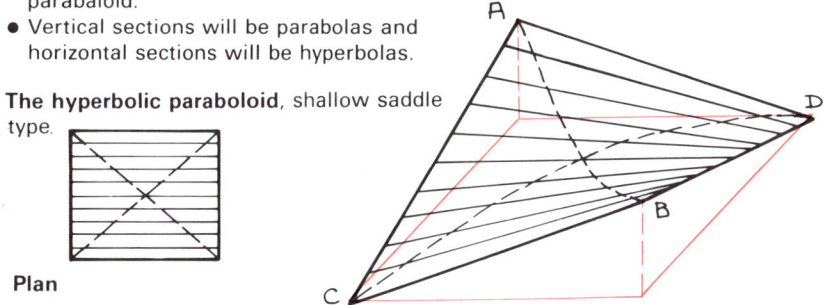

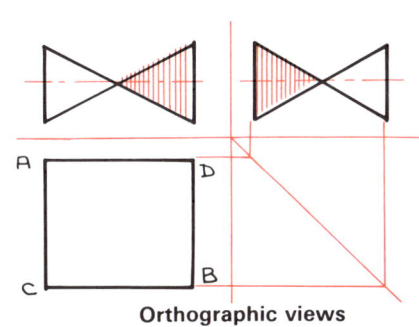

Plan

Orthographic views

- The alternative position where the parabola **AB** travels along a second parabola **CD**. The sections are as before.
- This can also be seen as a square whose corners are displaced, a warped square, or rectangle.

Note: *In the orthographic views the underside of the elevations have been shaded for clarity.*

Relation to high saddle type above.

Technical Draughtsmanship
Surface Structures 1
Structures 4 — Part 2B Bldg.

Defining a Hyperbolic Paraboloid as a Ruled Surface

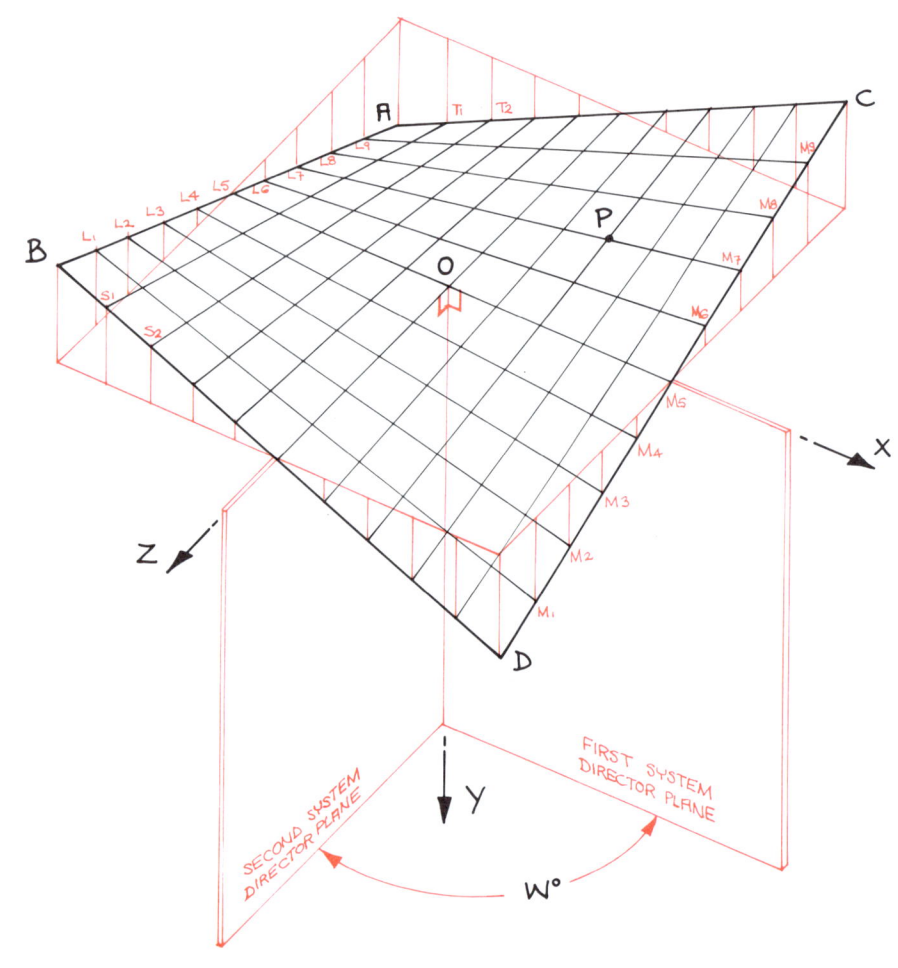

Properties
- The hyperbolic paraboloid may be treated as a ruled surface and may be defined using either of two systems of generating lines.
- The first system uses two straight, non-parallel, non-intersecting lines, **AB** and **CD**. These skew lines are called its directrices. 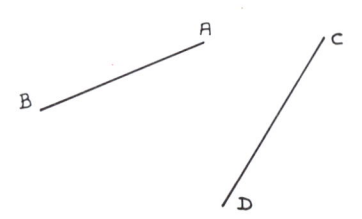
- Straight lines L_1M_1, L_2M_2, etc. generate the surface if they touch both directrices and are all parallel to one plane **XOY**. This is called a director plane. 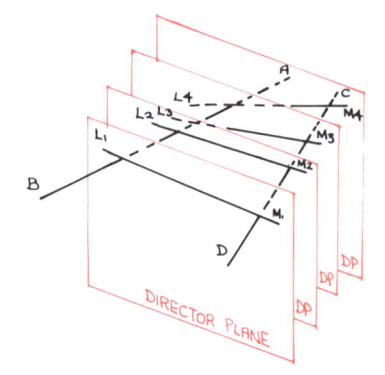
- The second system would use directrices **AC** and **BD**, generating lines S_1T_1, S_2T_2, that are parallel to director plane **ZOY**.
- The angles **XOY** and **ZOY** are right angles but **W°** is variable. If **W°** is 90° then the hypar will be rectangular. If **W°** is not 90° the hypar will be oblique.

Notes:
- The angle between the two director planes **W°** is fixed for a given surface, but will vary from one paraboloid to another.
- Point **O** has been taken as central, but this need not be the case. Any point **O** may be chosen.
- Any point **P** on the surface will be at the intersection of two straight lines contained within the surface.
- As the surface is warped, it cannot be developed.

Technical Draughtsmanship		
Defining a Ruled Paraboloid 1		
	Structures 5	Part 2B
		Bldg

314

① The Angle W° Between the Two Director Planes

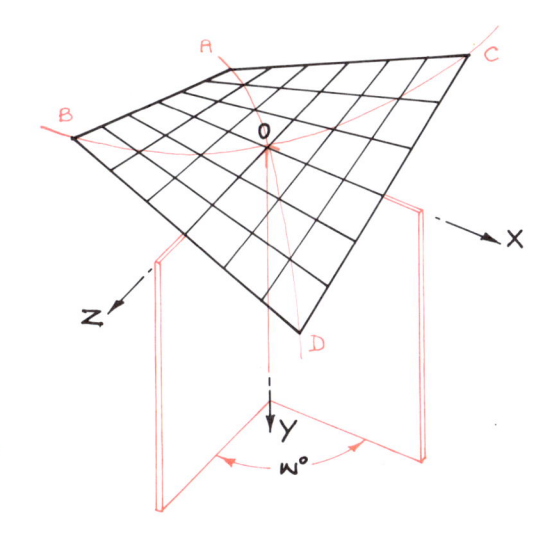

- The angle **W°** between the two director planes is fixed for a given surface, but may vary from one paraboloid to another.
- If **W°** is 90°, the hypar will be rectangular or square.
- If **W°** is *any* other angle then the hypar will be oblique.
- If **W°** is bisected, the bisecting plane will contain the principle parabola **AOD**. All sections parallel to this plane will also be parabolas.
- The bisecting plane for **BOC** can be found in a similar way.

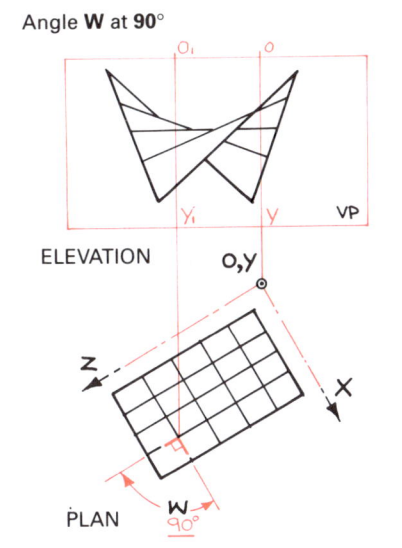

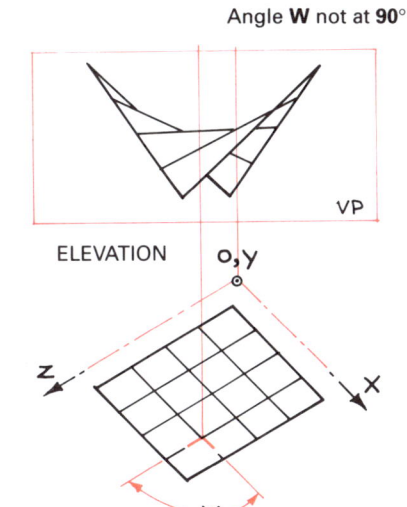

Angle W at 90°

ELEVATION

PLAN — W 90°

Angle W not at 90°

ELEVATION

PLAN — W NOT 90°

Note:
- *If* **OY** *is vertical, then the VP can be seen as a director plane, governed by plane director* **OY**.

② The Third Plane Director OY

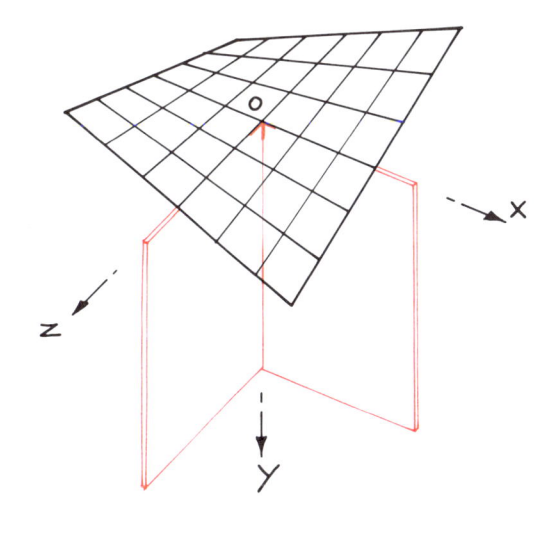

- The angles **XOY** and **ZOY** are right angles.
- A point view of one line element will also be an edge view of a director plane.
- But **OY** is *not* always vertical. If **OY** is not vertical, then **OX** and **OZ** will not be horizontal. If this is so, then the generating lines on the plan will not appear parallel.

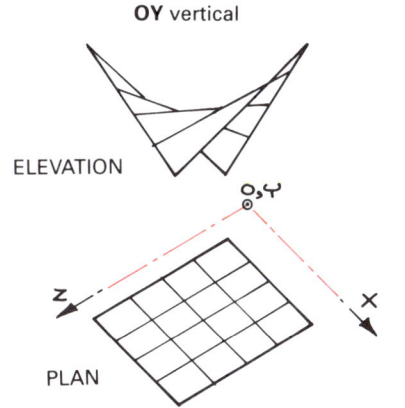

OY vertical

ELEVATION

PLAN

- Here **OY** is vertical and the elements *are* parallel on the plan and all the axes are clearly identifiable.

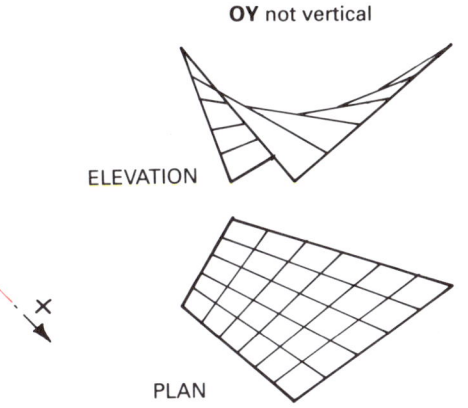

OY not vertical

ELEVATION

PLAN

- Here **OY** is not vertical and the elements are *not* parallel on the plan. An extra view will be needed to find the axes.

Technical Draughtsmanship		
Defining a Ruled Paraboloid 2		
	Structures 6	Part 2B
		Bldg

To Find the Axes when OY is not Vertical

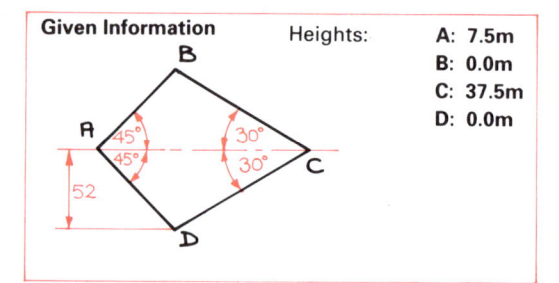

Given Information

Heights:
- A: 7.5m
- B: 0.0m
- C: 37.5m
- D: 0.0m

Method 2: If one plane director is required.
- Trace any generating line **BC** and make auxiliary views **Aux 2** and **Aux 3**, reducing it to a point **B,C**.
- It will be found that the second set of generating lines will appear parallel to each other, giving us the direction of their generator plane **X**.

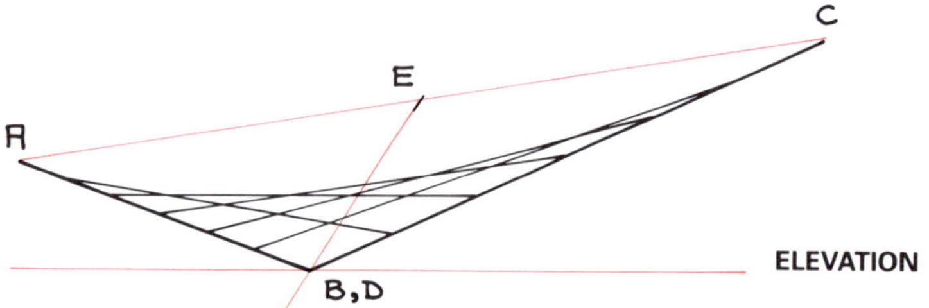

Method 1: If all three axes are required.
- Draw an elevation where the two low corners **B** and **D** are in line.
- Now join the high points **A** and **C** and bisect this to find point **E**.
- Join **E** through **BD**. This is the direction of one plane director **OY**.
- Draw an auxiliary view **Aux 1** in the direction of **Y** to find the other two plane directors **OX** and **OZ**.

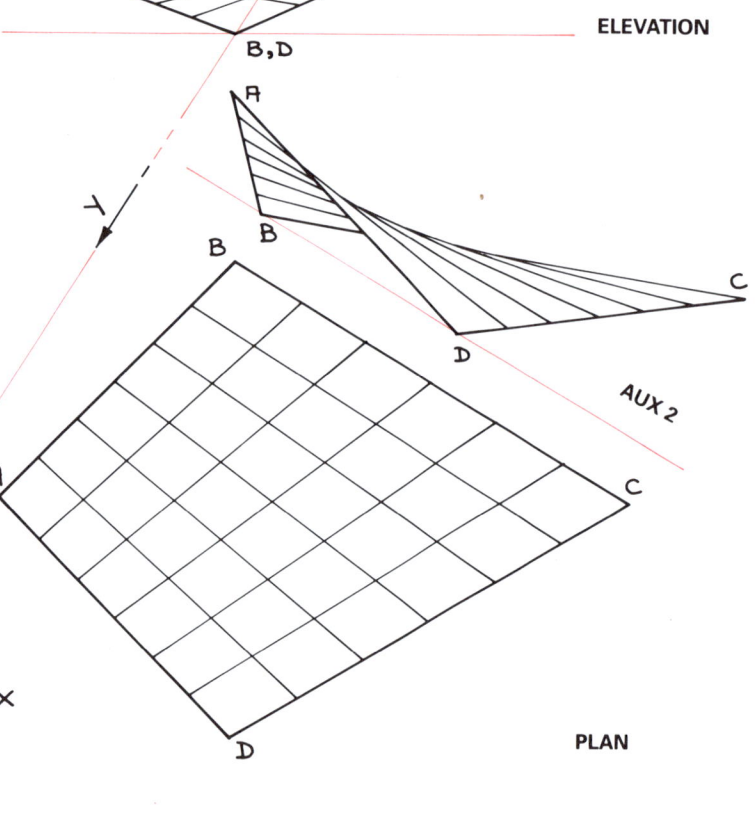

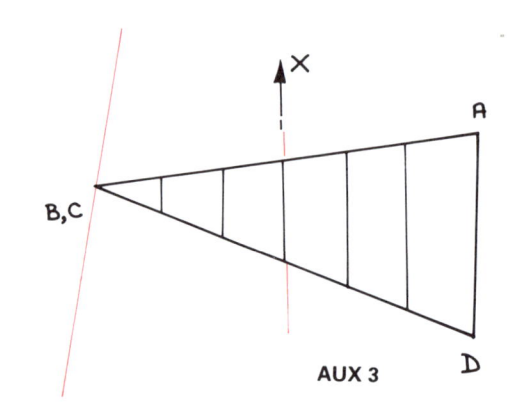

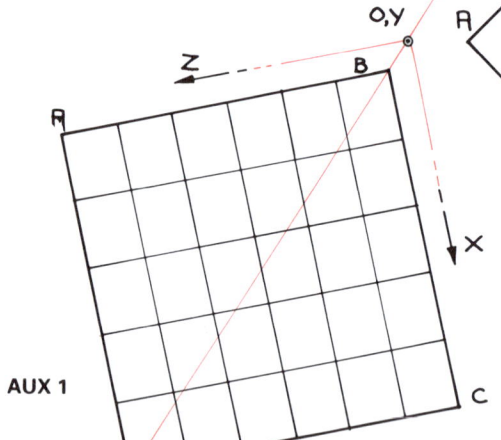

ELEVATION

AUX 2

PLAN

AUX 1

AUX 3

Note:
- *How could further axes be found using **Method 2**?*

| Technical Draughtsmanship |
| Finding the Three Axes |
| Structures 7 | Part 2B |
| | Bldg H |

① Surfaces of revolution

Sphere (Circle)
Oblate ellipsoid (Half-ellipse)
Prolate ellipsoid (Half-ellipse)
Paraboloid (Parabola)

- These are the surfaces generated when a shape is rotated about its axis. They have positive curvature.

Hyperboloid of Revolution (Hyperbolas)
- If a pair of hyperbolas are rotated about their conjugate axis **AB**, they generate a hyperboloid of revolution.
- As this shape is not within the hyperbolas themselves it is said to have a negative curvature.

② Some Roof Shell Combinations

- The architect Felix Candela has designed many beautiful shell buildings.

③ Conoidal sections

Procedure
- Mark ruled lines on the plan.
- Project these via the end view onto the elevation.
- A point **P** can now be found on section **A-A**, as shown.
- Plot further points and draw the section. Complete the end view.

④ The hyperbolic paraboloid:
These are used in cooling towers and in gear profiles.

Section **A-A** will be a circle.

Section **B-B** will be an ellipse

Section **C-C** will be a hyperbola.

Sketch of a generating line.

Procedure
- Given an asymptote, a vertex or a focus and the height **H**.
- Find the throat and thus the generating circle on plan.
- Project the asymptote down to find generating line **AB**.
- Plot further positions of **AB** on plan and project their elevations to draw the hyperboloid.
- As the throat narrows the hyperboloid becomes more like a cone, and a wider throat makes it more cylindrical.

Technical Draughtsmanship
Some Roof Shells
Structures 8 — Part 2B / Bldg. H

317

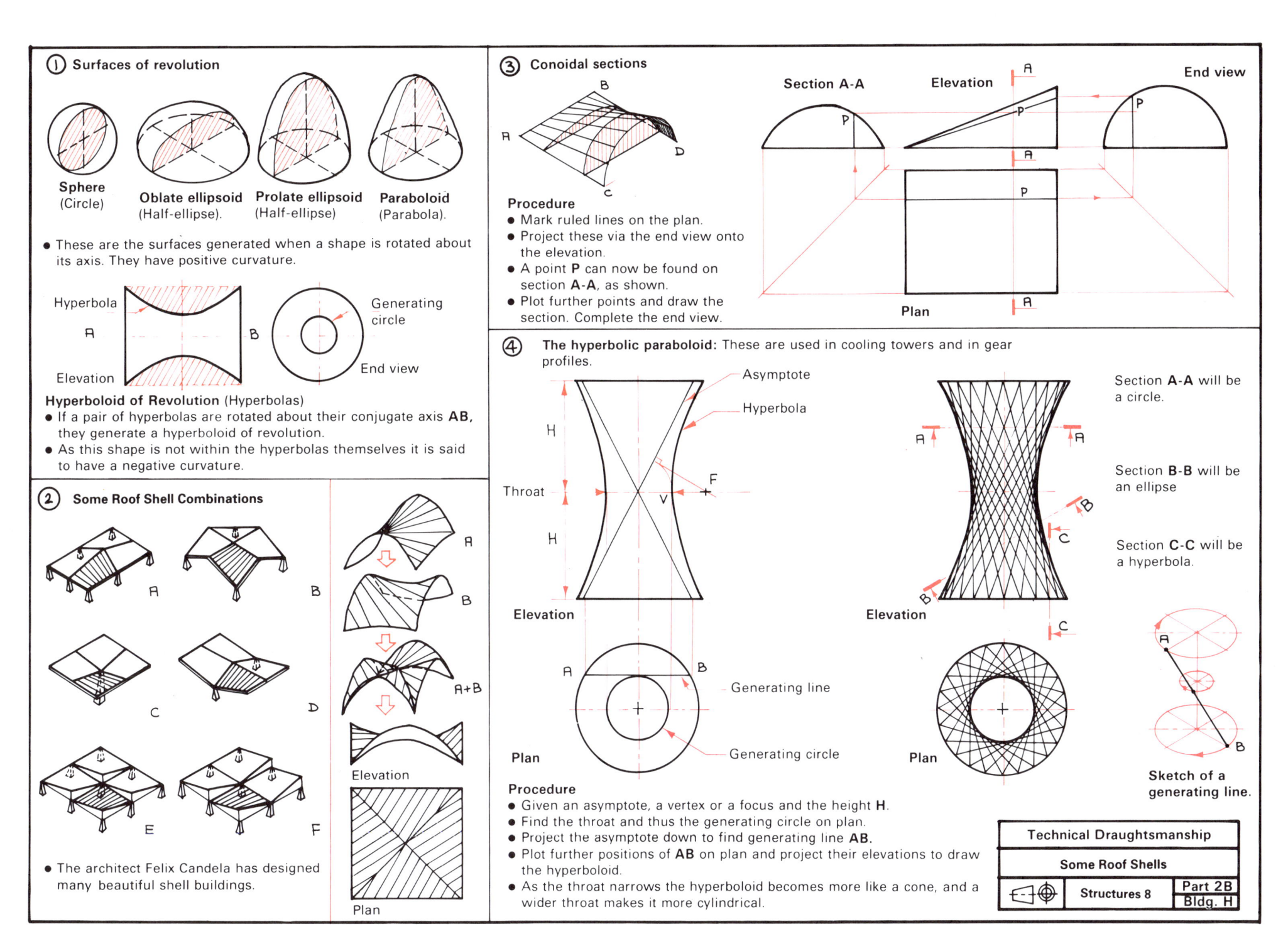

Step 1
- Take a parabola **AOB**.

Sketch ELEVATION END VIEW

Step 2
- Hang another parabola **COD** onto the first one.

Sketch ELEVATION END VIEW

Step 3
- Move parabola **COD** along the first parabola. This will generate a hypar, as shown.

Note
- *Some problems arise when it is required to have the hypar sit on the ground (the HP).*

Sketch ELEVATION PLAN END VIEW

Technical Draughtsmanship
The Hypar as a Translation
Structures 9 — Part 2B — Bldg H

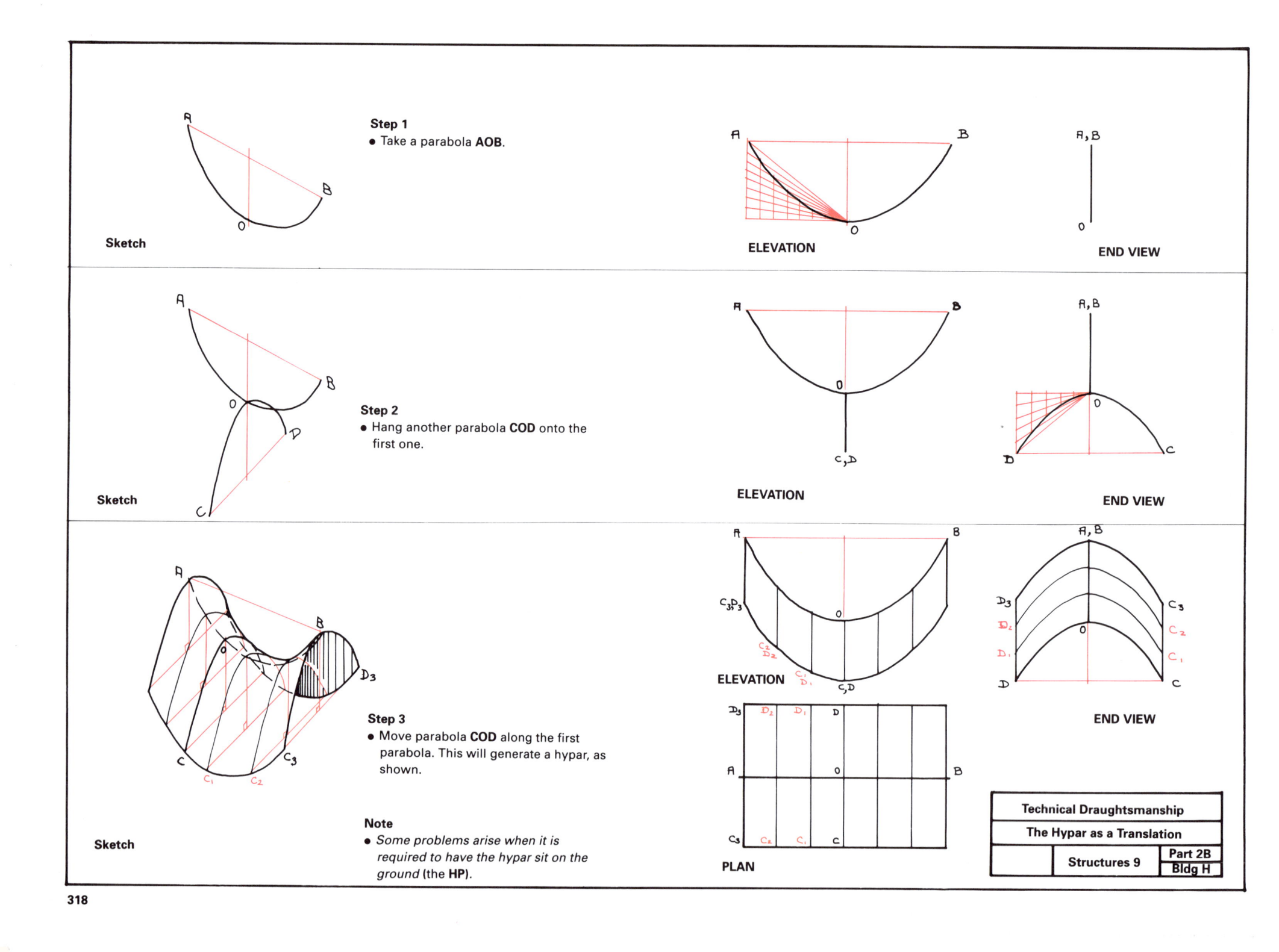

① The Principle

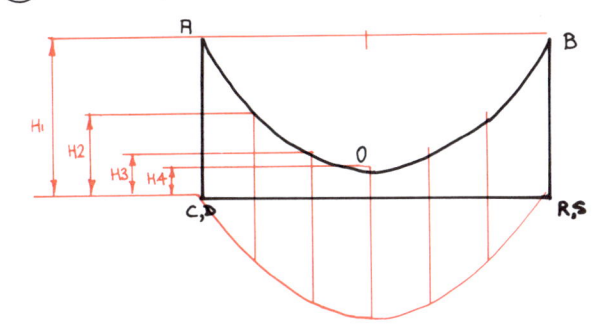

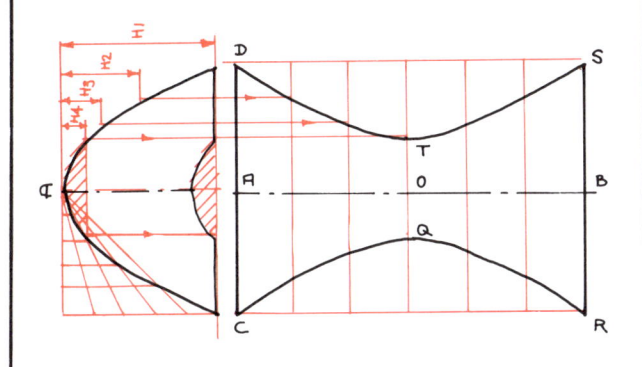

- Imagine the parabolas sinking into the ground, with their heads **H2**, **H3**, **H4** sticking out of it.
- Draw the end view of the main parabola **C3AD3**; set the heads **H2**, **H3**, **H4** against this and plot the plan as shown.
- It will be found that **C3QR** and **D3TS** are hyperbolas.
- To complete the end view, slide or copy the shaded piece, **H4**, into position.

② The Problem

Given the dimensions indicated, complete the three views. Height of **A**: 75, Height at **O**: 33, Width of **CD**: 80, Angle of cut **AQ**: 75°.

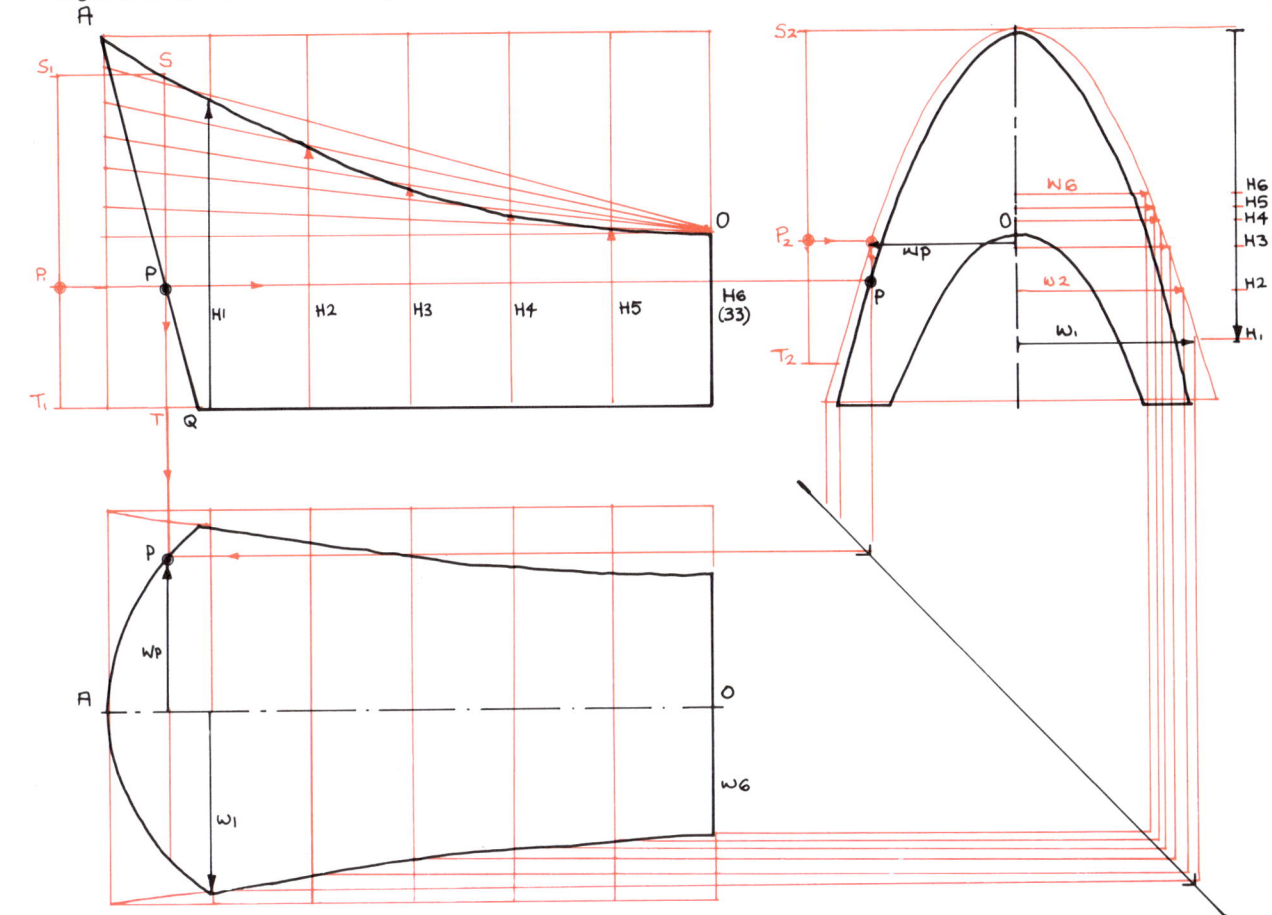

Procedure
- Set out the given dimensions and plot the parabolas **AO** and **CAD**, as on page **318**.
- Divide the elevation into pieces and note the head-heights **H1**, **H2**, etc. This is the amount of the parabola **CAD**, that will stick out of the ground.
- Use these heights to locate their shape and their widths, **W1**, **W2**, etc. on the end view. Project these to complete the basic plan.
- To plot the cut **AQ**, subdivide it. Take one division **ST** and set its head-height and that of **P**, out to one side.
- Set these against the end view to find the width at **P**.
- Plot this on plan and end view. Continue like this to complete the three views.

Note:
- *If you use tracing paper the first time you do this, it will help clarify the procedure.*

Technical Draughtsmanship
A Worked Example
Structures 10 — Part 2B, Bldg H

319

All measurements are in millimetres

Questions

1. Draw the two classical columns. Use Normand's Method for **A** and the polar method for **B**. The spiral may be approximated.

2. Design a petrol station forecourt with a cantilevered trussed concrete roof. Draw this is isometric and in orthographic projections.

3. Plot the elevation and the end view of this roof.

4. Draw a traditional groin vault in orthographic projection.

5. Draw the given arch in orthographic projection.

6. Plot the elevation and end view of this roof.

7. Complete the orthographic views and draw the sections **A-A**, **B-B** and **C-C**. In each case plot generating lines lightly on the surface of the shell.

8. As for question **7** above.

9. As for question **7** above.

Technical Draughtsmanship

Exercises 1

Structures 11 — **Part 2B Bldg**

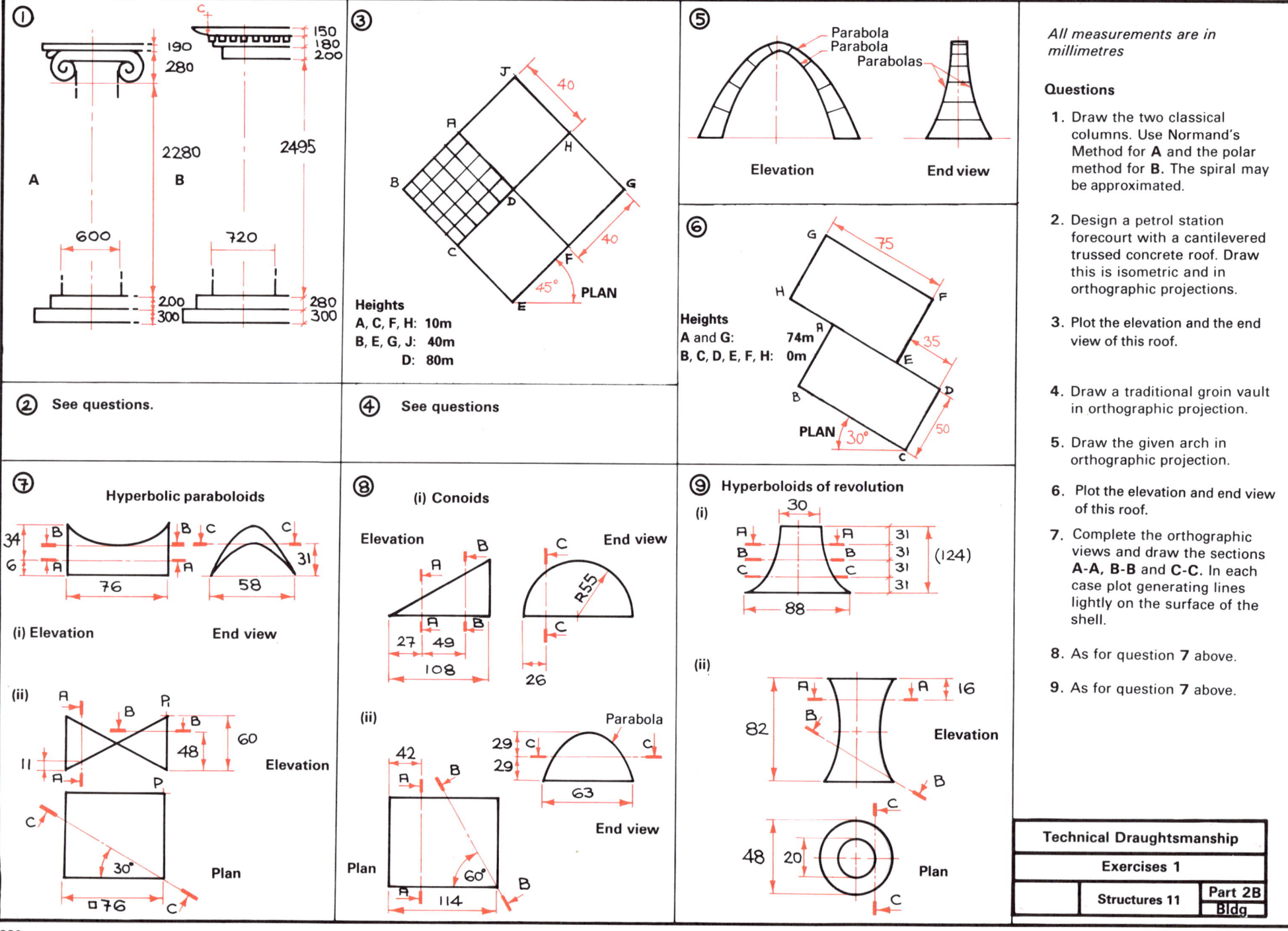

Questions

1. Draw each of the generated surfaces shown in orthographic projection and locate point **P** on each view.

2. Two asymptotes **AB** and **CD** of a hyperboloid of revolution are given. Draw the hyperboloid.

3. Design a warehouse to be built with folded plates and frames, and then make a model of your design.

4. and 5. Given are the elevation and end view of two conoidal roofs. Draw each in orthographic projection and plot sections **A-A**, **B-B** and **C-C**.

6. Draw the high saddle roof, shown in plan, in orthographic projection and plot the section **M-M**.

7. Draw each shallow saddle combination in orthographic projection, to a suitable scale.

8. Draw orthographic views of the given church to a suitable scale.

Technical Draughtsmanship

Exercises 2

Structures 12 — **Part 2B** — **Bldg. H**

321

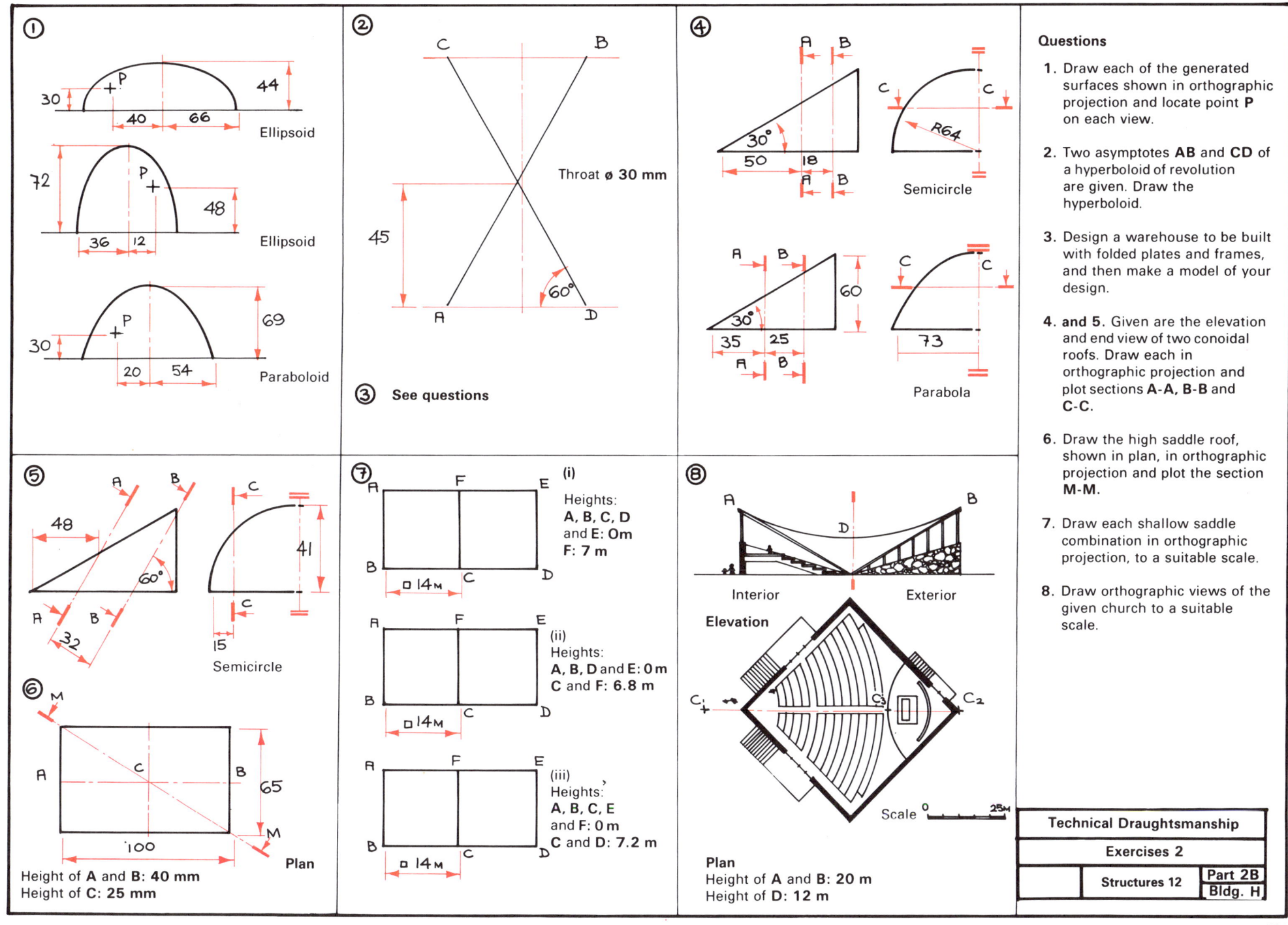

Questions

1. Draw the plan and elevation of this factory roof and find the plane directors of **ABCD**.

2. Draw the elevation, find the plane directors of **ABCD** and adapt the corner, **PQ**, as shown.

3. Plot the end view and find a plane director for **ABCD**.

4 and 5
Draw the plan of these shells.

6. Draw the plan and plot the path of the focus of parabola **ABC** on the elevation.

7. Plot the plan and find the plane directors.

8. Draw the elevation and end view of this roof and find the plane generators of **ABCD**.

9. Draw the three standard views and find the plane directors of **ABCD**.

Technical Draughtsmanship

Exercises 3

Structures 13 — Part 2B — Bldg H

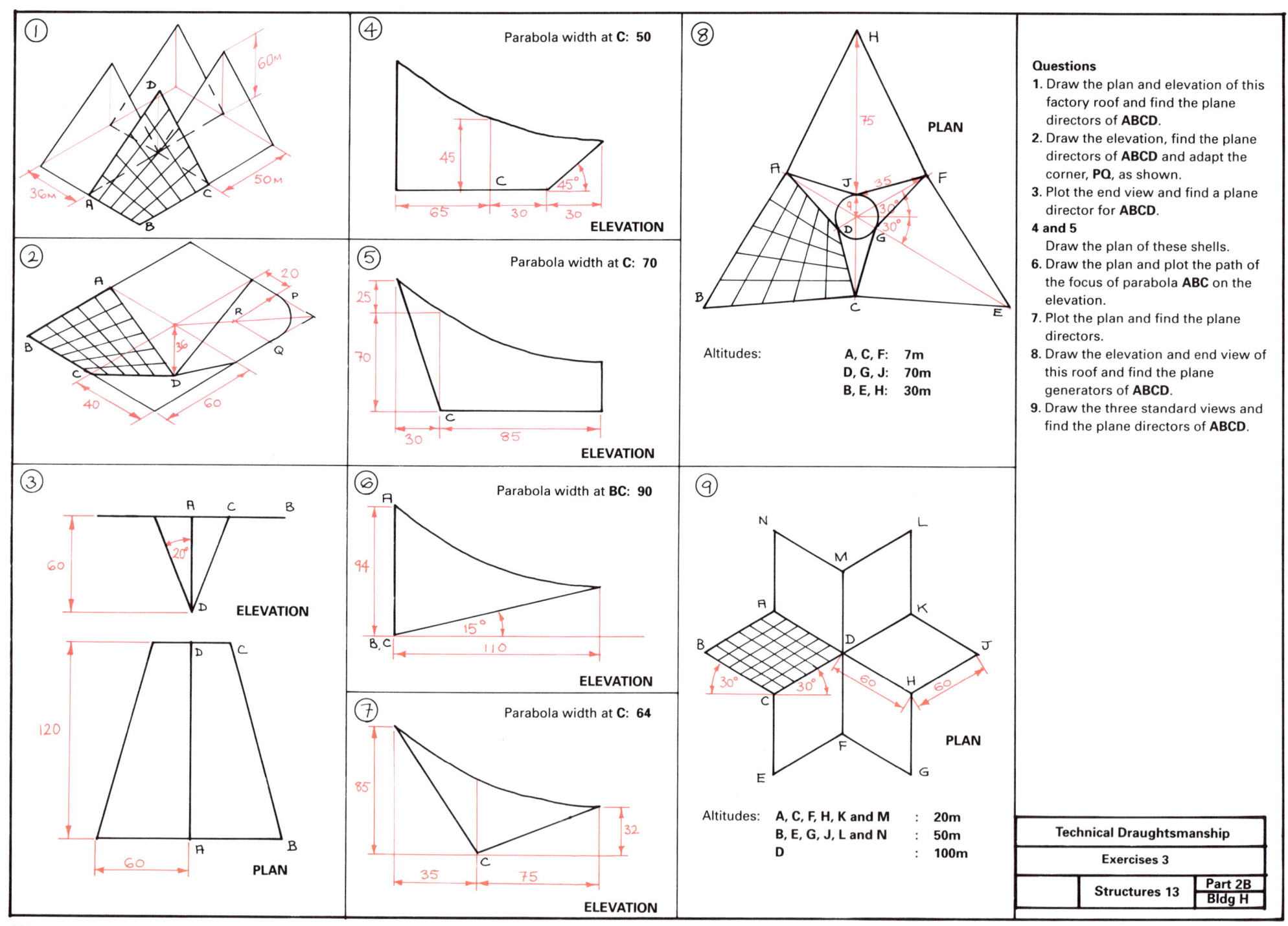

PART 2B

CHAPTER 27
BUILDING GEOMETRY

There are various building specialities that require a good knowledge of basic geometry. Some of these are considered here.

CONTENTS
Tracery	*Page* **324**
Mouldings	**325**
Roof Development	**326**
Sample Problem	**327**
Exercises	**328**

Photocopying prohibited by law

① Tracery panels

Trefoil

Pointed trefoil

Quatrefoil

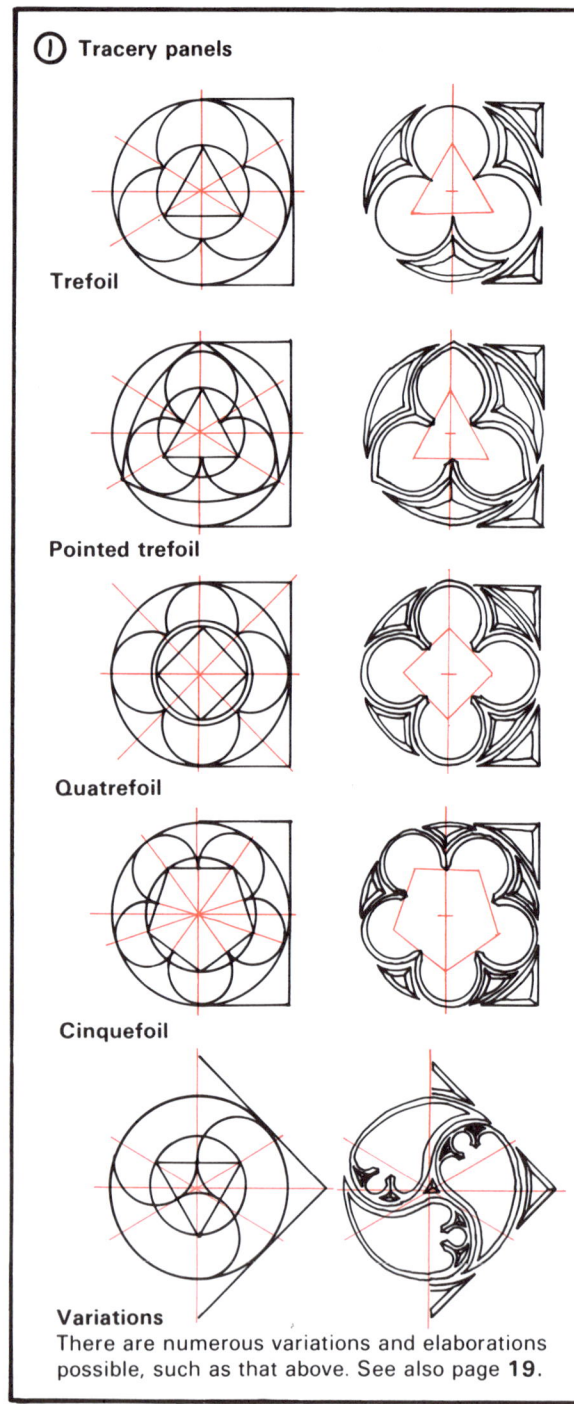

Cinquefoil

Variations
There are numerous variations and elaborations possible, such as that above. See also page **19**.

② Setting out

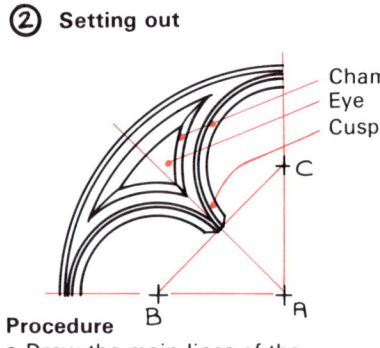

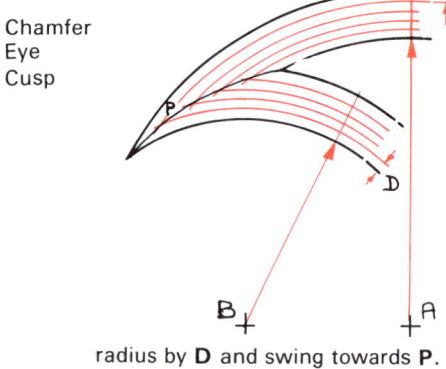

Chamfer
Eye
Cusp

Procedure
- Draw the main lines of the construction e.g. quatrefoil.
- Set out the outlines to the required sections.
- Plot the intersections of chamfers.

The intersection of chamfers
- With centre **A** increase the radius by **D** and swing towards **P**.
- Increase the radius from **B** by the same amount **D** and fix point **P**.
- Continue to find further points.
- The sectional profile is vital to setting out. This is usually given, as there are many profiles that can be used.

Sections (enlarged)

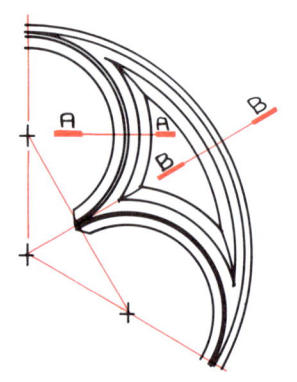

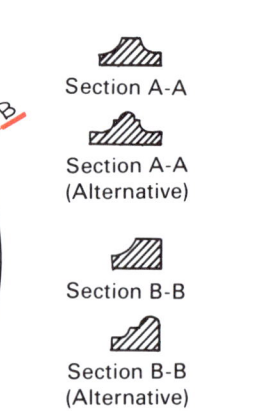

Section A-A

Section A-A (Alternative)

Section B-B

Section B-B (Alternative)

③ Two sample tracery panels

A window panel
The construction should be clear from the drawing.

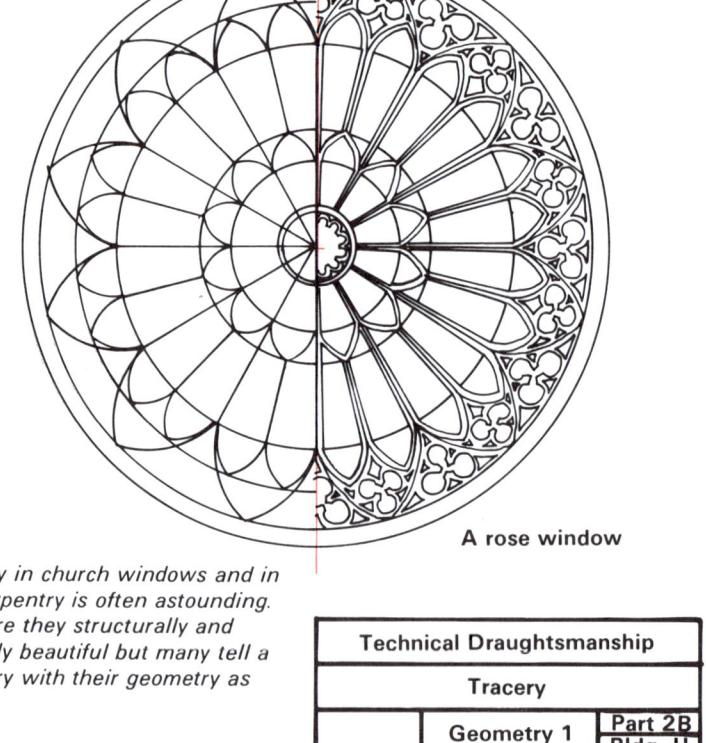

Note
- *The tracery in church windows and in church carpentry is often astounding. Not only are they structurally and decoratively beautiful but many tell a tantric story with their geometry as well.*

A rose window

Technical Draughtsmanship
Tracery
Geometry 1	Part 2B
	Bldg. H

① Typical mouldings

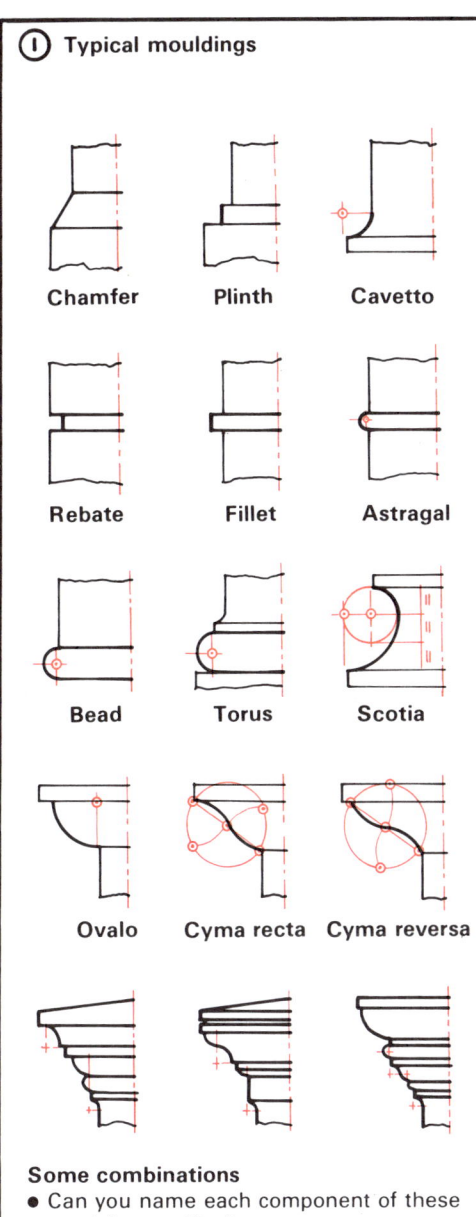

Chamfer, **Plinth**, **Cavetto**

Rebate, **Fillet**, **Astragal**

Bead, **Torus**, **Scotia**

Ovalo, **Cyma recta**, **Cyma reversa**

Some combinations
- Can you name each component of these moulding profiles?
- The above curves are based on radii and are known as Roman mouldings.
- The Greeks based their equivalent curves on ellipses, parabolas and hyperbolas.
- Mouldings may be made from many materials e.g. stone, wood, plaster.

② Sections and intersections of mouldings

The given plan and section

- When mouldings meet they should join together cleanly and completely. This means that mouldings meeting at an angle, or curve, must each be made to a slightly different profile.

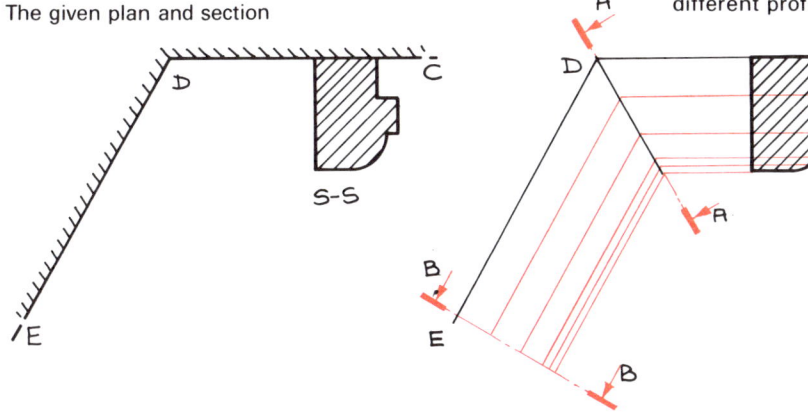

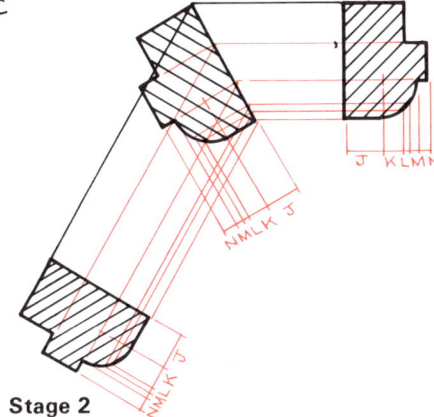

The problem
- A moulding of section **S-S** is to be set against wall **CDE**. Draw the section along the mitre and the section along the wall **DE**.

Stage 1
- Bisect angle **CDE** to find the mitre **A-A** and set a section line **B-B** at right angles to **DE**.
- Project across the main points, as shown.

Stage 2
- Mark the dimensions **J**, **K**, **L**, **M** and **N** and use these to plot each section, as shown.
- These are revolved sections and may be shown to left or right of the section line.

③ Mouldings on curved walls

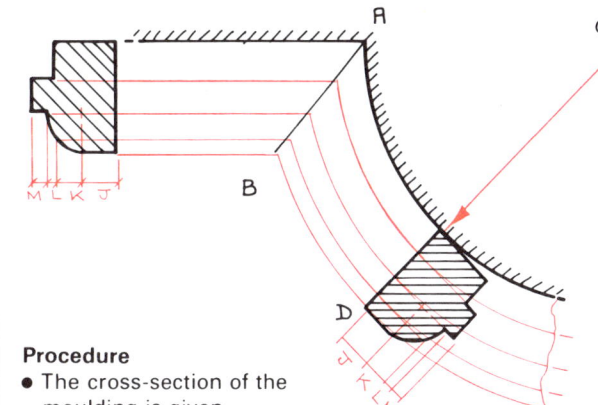

Procedure
- The cross-section of the moulding is given.
- The mitre **AB** is straight. If a curved mitre is to be used the curve of intersection is found as on page **306**. The rest of the procedure will be the same.
- Take a radian **CD** and set out a section, as before.

④ Changes in levels (Raking mouldings)

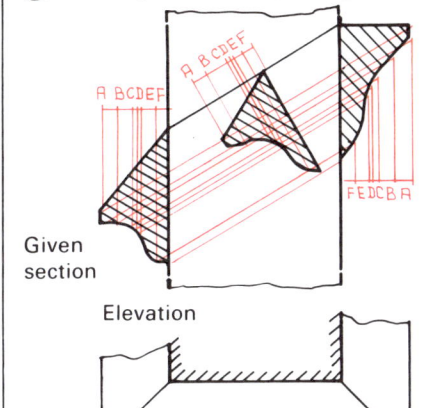

Given section

Elevation

Plan

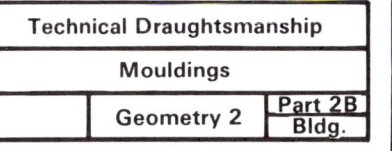

Procedure
- The construction will be clear from the drawing.
- Do have a look around and notice the subtlety of the mouldings that you may never have thought about before.

Note
An irregular shape is grid-lined and points are relocated one at a time.

Technical Draughtsmanship
Mouldings
Geometry 2 — Part 2B Bldg.

325

① A roof problem step by step.

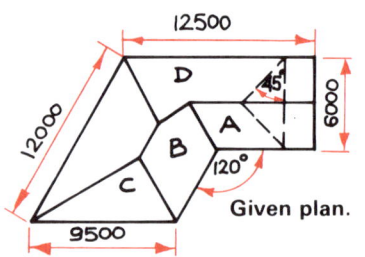

- All the roof surfaces have the same pitch of **45°**.
- Draw the plan, develop surfaces **B**, **C** and **D**, and determine the angle between surfaces **A** and **B**.

Given plan.

Procedure

Step 1
- Set out the roof plan. It may be necessary to draw an end view and an auxiliary view to locate the points where the lines meet, as shown.
- As the pitch is known each height can also be calculated.

Step 2
- Lines parallel to the ground will already be their true lengths, but the true lengths of the sloping lines will have to be found.
- Set the height at right angles and at one end of such a line. Join the extremities of both lines. This is the required true length.
- All the lengths being known, lay out the patterns.

Step 3
- To find the dihedral angle between surfaces **A** and **B**: Draw a line **DF** from **DG** and parallel to the bottom edge of surface **B**.
- Draw **GF** across **DC** at right angles and rabat the true length of **DC**, as shown.
- Drop perpendicular **JK** onto **EC** and swing **K** to **M** to define the dihedral angle **FMG**.

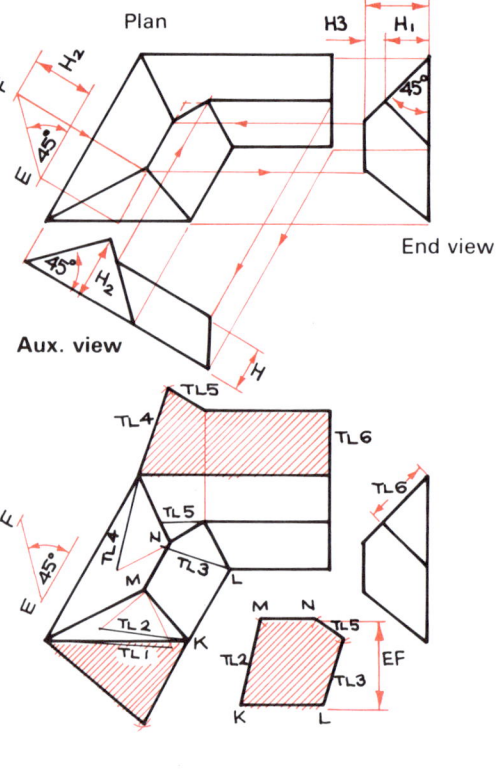

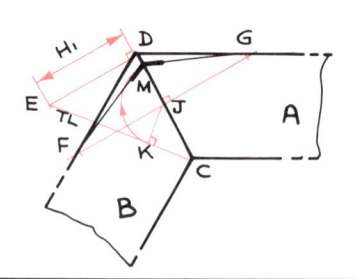

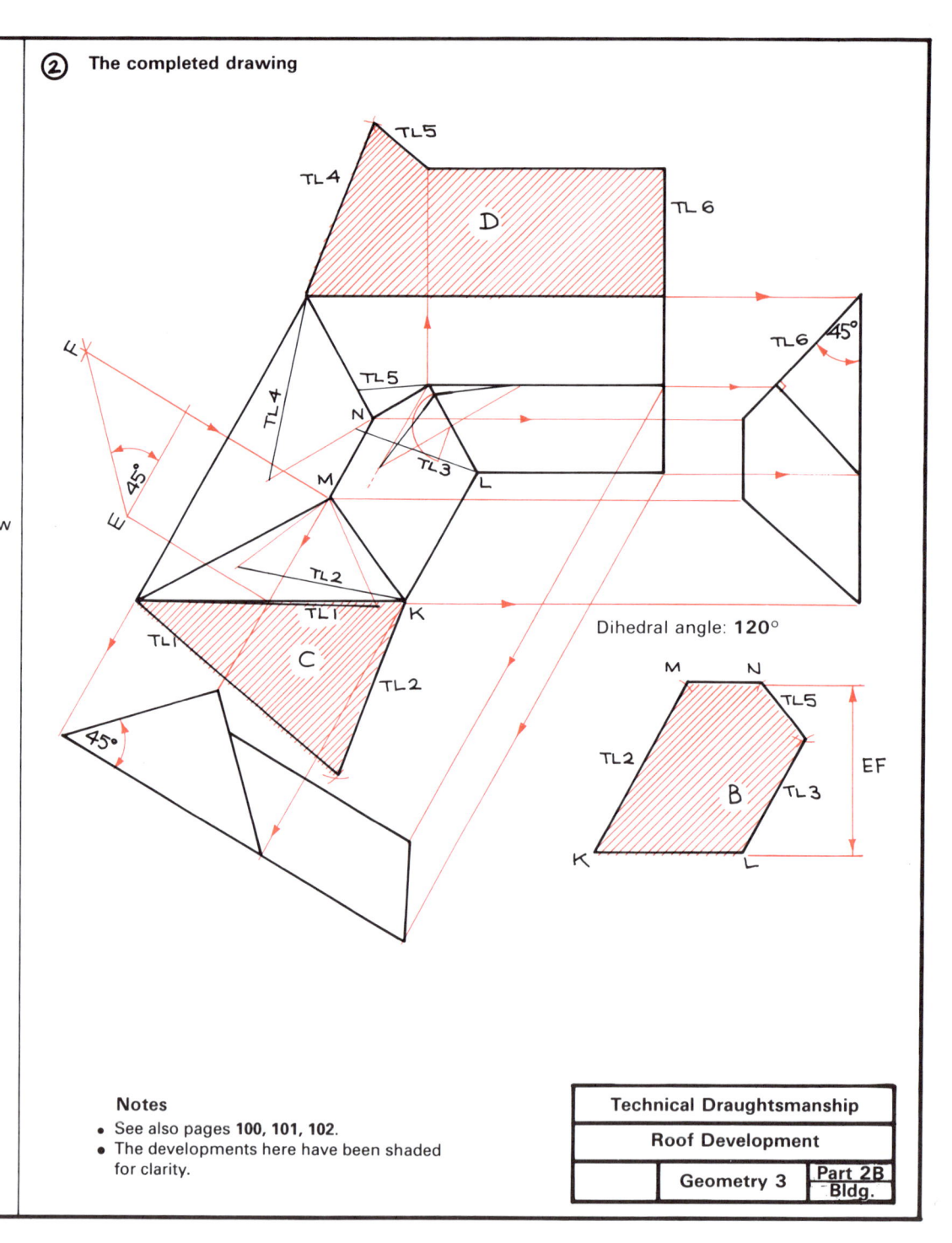

② The completed drawing

Dihedral angle: **120°**

Notes
- See also pages **100, 101, 102**.
- The developments here have been shaded for clarity.

Technical Draughtsmanship
Roof Development
Geometry 3 — Part 2B Bldg.

326

The Problem

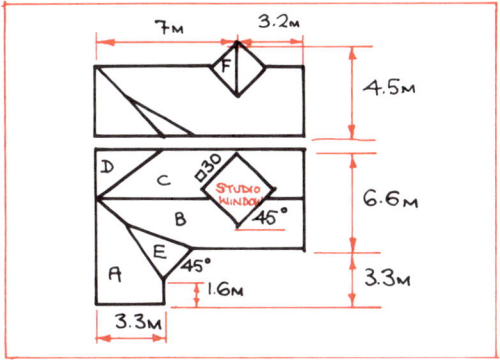

Roof surfaces **ABC** and **D** are of pitch **45°** and surface **E** is of **25°**.

(a) Find the dihedral angle between surface **A** and **E**.
(b) Find also the dihedral angle between surface **B** and dormer **F**.

Scale 1:100

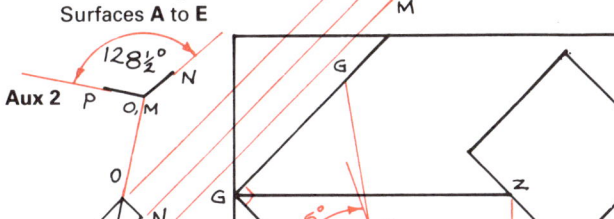

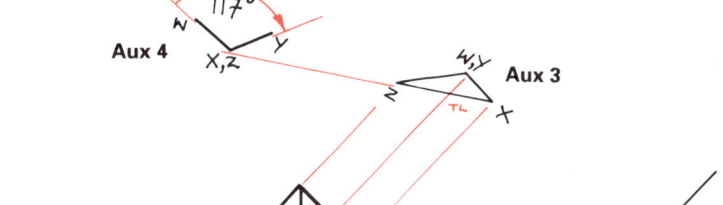

Procedure

- Draw up the roof in elevation and plan with the help of a partial end view. To find the top of surface **E**, take a line along **NG** and rabat it as if **E** did not exist, giving **NGG**$_1$. Draw the **25°** pitch from **J** to find **H**. Work **H** back.

- To get the dihedral angle for **A** and **E** mark off a sample rectangle **MNOP**. Project this to get the true length of **MO** as in **Aux 1**, then project along **MO** to reduce it to a point view in **Aux 2**. The angle will now be clear.

- Equally, take a sample **WXYZ** and project it to find the dihedral angle between surfaces **B** and **E**.

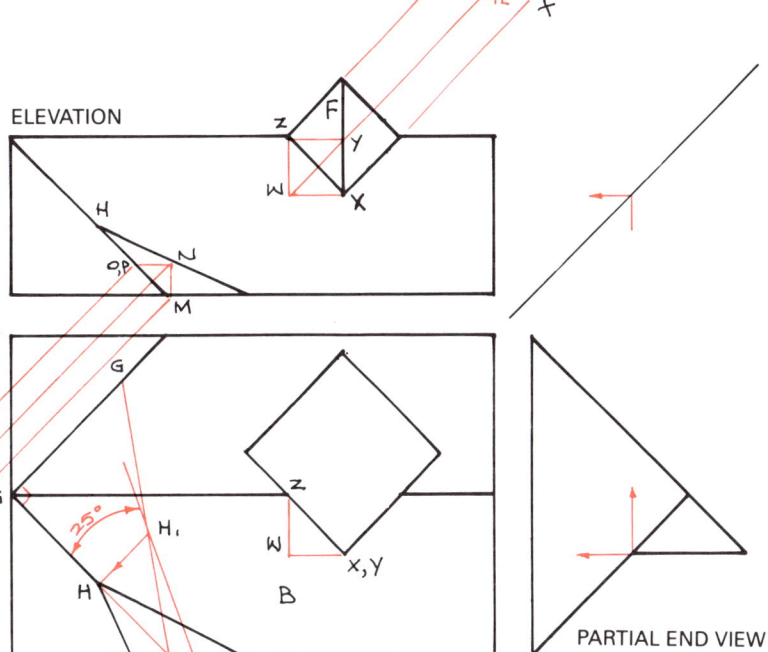

Technical Draughtsmanship
Sample Problem
Geometry 4 — **Part 2B / Bldg H**

327

①

Trefoil — □84

Cinquefoil — R43

Quatrefoil — □72, 45°

Pointed trefoil — □86

②

East window: 60°, R60, 108, 60

West window (Rose window): R75, A, B, C

Note: A, B and C are to be equal in area.

③

Section A-A: 8, 12, 12

Section B-B: 8, 4, 8, 12

Carving — Pentagon side: 75 mm

④

(i) **30** block on **R30** ovals on **20** block on overall **R50** cyma reversa on **R80** column.

(ii) **15°** chamfer to **14** block on scotia of base circle **R7** on **14** block on Ionic volute of cathetus **63** with column underneath.

(iii) Column of height **180** and base radius **20**, with entasis, on **R6** cavetto on **4** block on **R12** torus on **20** block plinth.

⑤

30, 24, 14, 120°, 90, B

12, 12, 45, 210°, B

90, B, 24, 12, 12, 12

All measurements are in millimetres.

Questions

1. Set out the tracery panels as required.

2. Design tracery panels for the windows shown. Do *not* simply copy those on page **324**.

3. The main lines and removed sections of a hardwood tracery carving are shown. Draw the finished carving to scale.

4. Draw the profile of each of the specified pieces.

5. Three hardwood handrails are shown in revolved section against the walls along which they are to be installed. Draw the completed plan of each installation and a second section along the wall marked **B**.

Technical Draughtsmanship

Exercises 1

Geometry 5 | **Part 2B** | **Bldg**

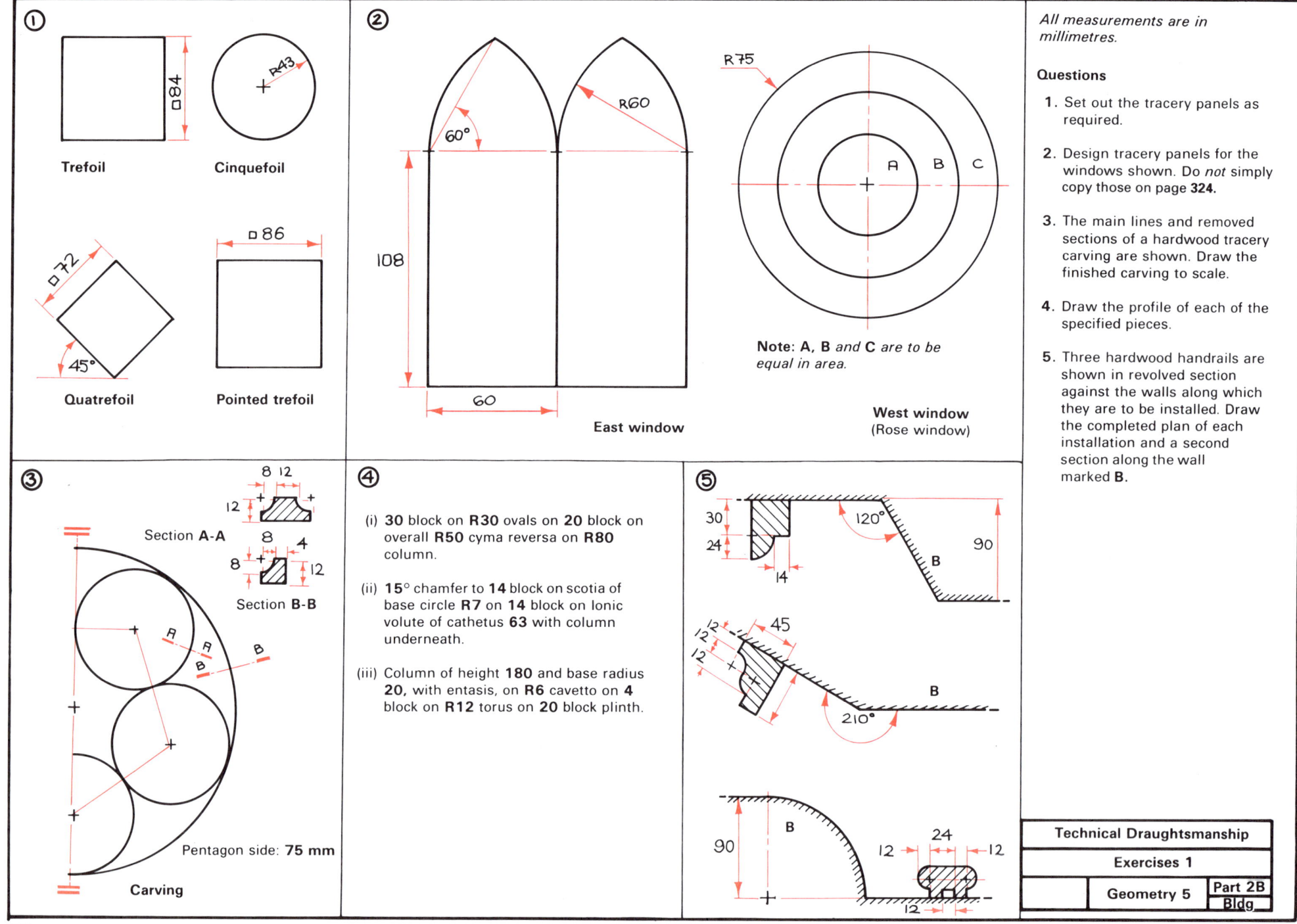

Questions

1. Develop the roof surfaces and find the dihedral angles between surfaces **A** and **B**.

2. Develop surfaces **A**, **B** and **D**, then find the dihedral angles between **A** and **B**, and between **C** and **D**.

3. Complete the views of both newel posts and develop a pattern for the struts.

4. Develop the lining of each semicircular arch.

5. Develop the linings of the arch shown.

6. Develop the linings of the given arch.

Technical Draughtsmanship

Exercises 2

Geometry 6 — Part 2B — Bldg

329

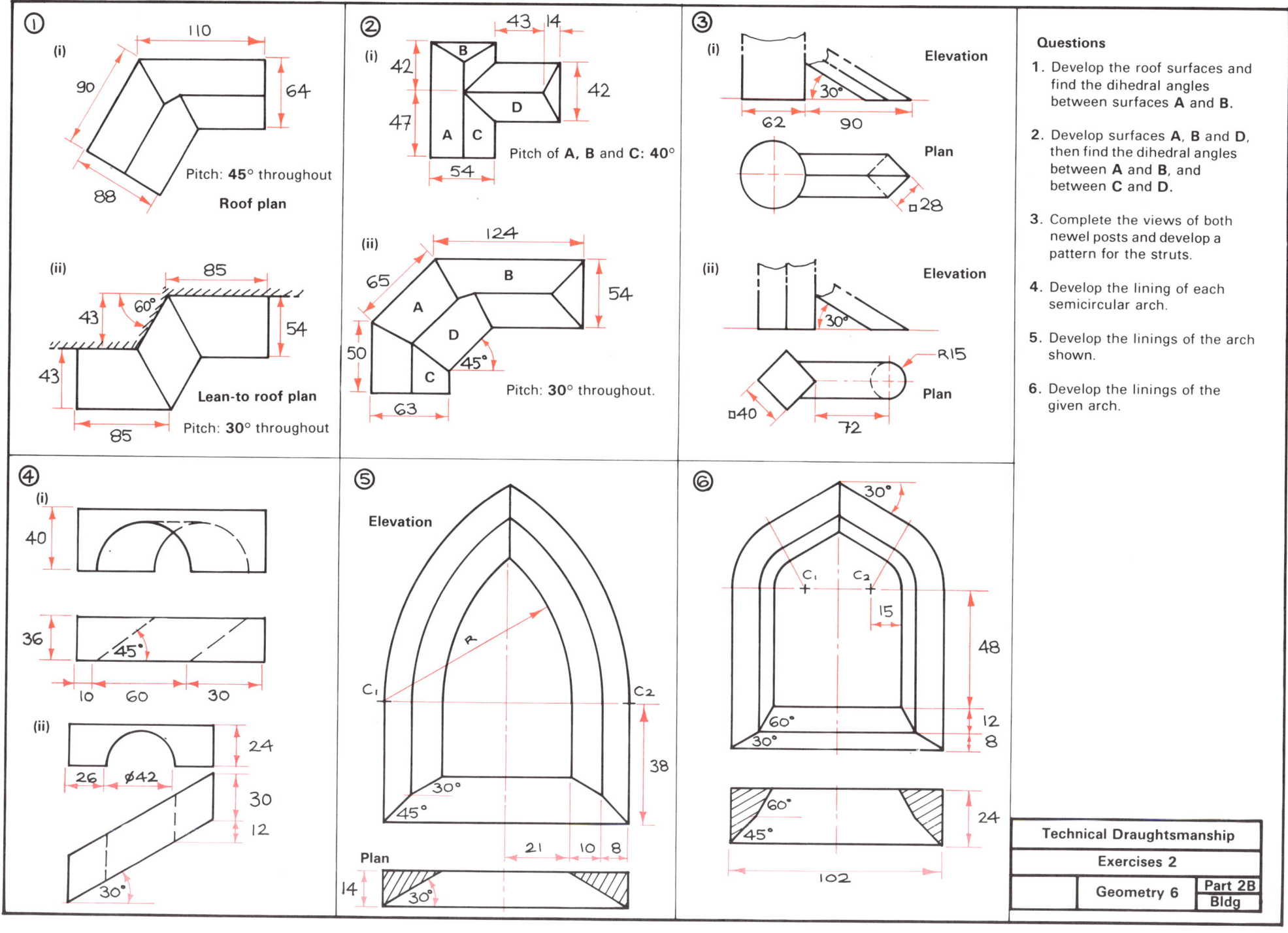

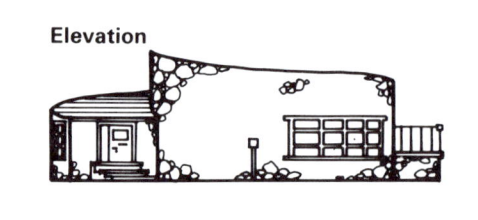

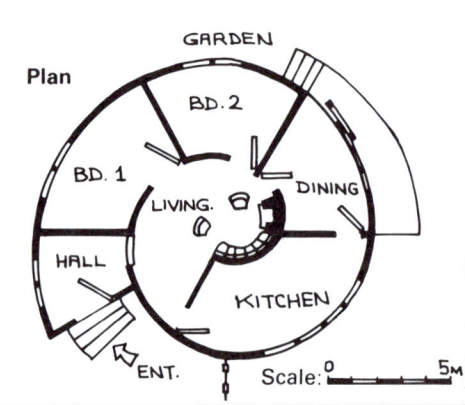

Questions

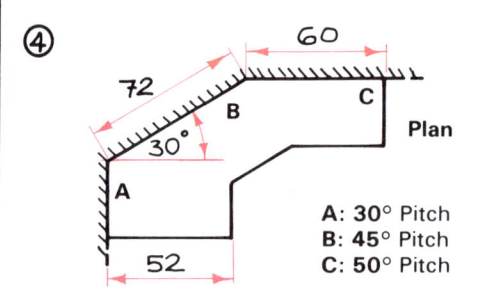

1. In each case a moulding of the given cross-section is to be continued from **A** to **B**. Draw the cross-sections needed along **AB** and at **B**.

2. Complete the orthographic views of the newel posts and develop the surfaces of the struts.

3. Complete the roof plan, develop surfaces **A**, **B** and **C**, and then find the dihedral angles between **A** and **B**, and between **C** and **D**.

4. Each of the lean-to roof surfaces is of equal height but of different pitch. Complete the plan and develop each surface.

5. Develop the lining of the arch of the bridge.

6. Complete the roof views and develop surfaces **A**, **B** and **C**.

7. This architect's plan is based on an Archimedean spiral and the roof is a helix. Draw the plan, elevation and end view. There is a skylight over the living room.

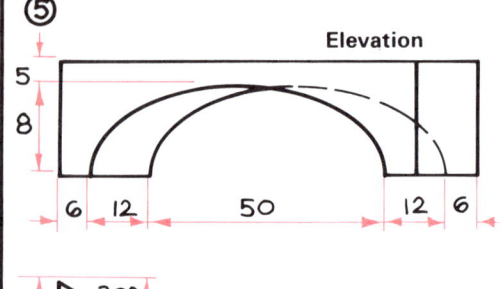

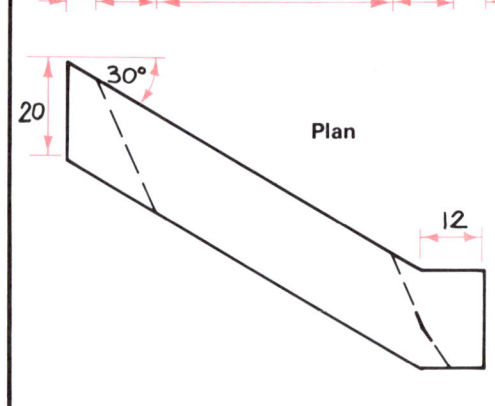

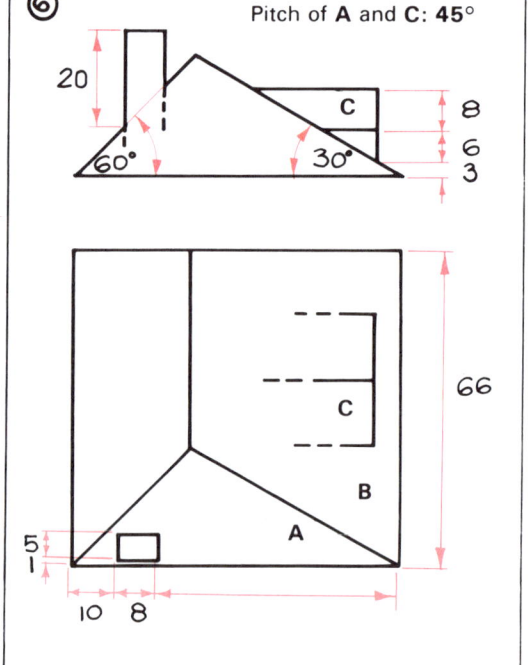

Technical Draughtsmanship

Exercises 3

Geometry 7 — Part 2B, Bldg H

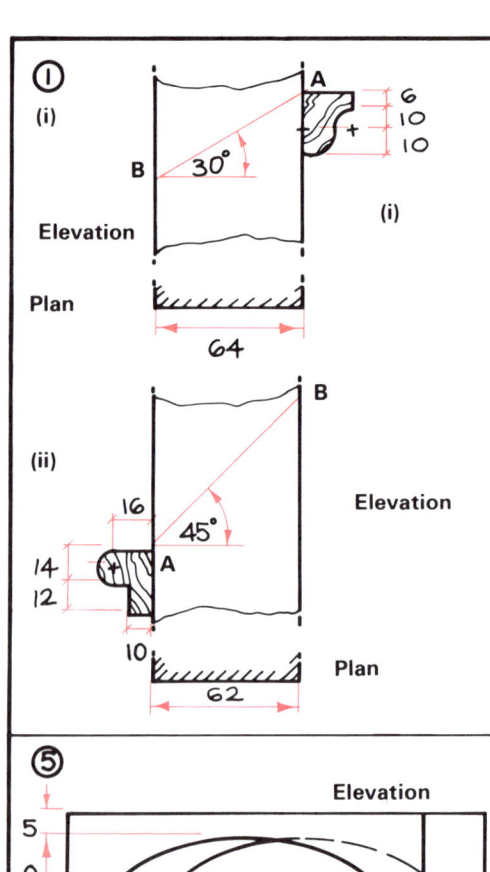

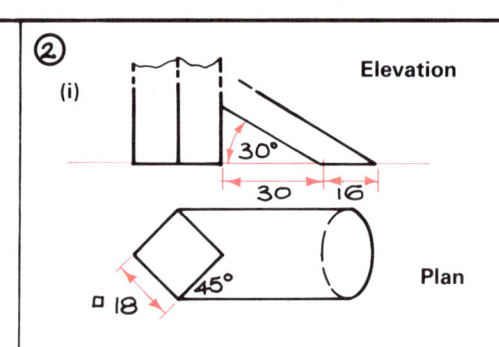

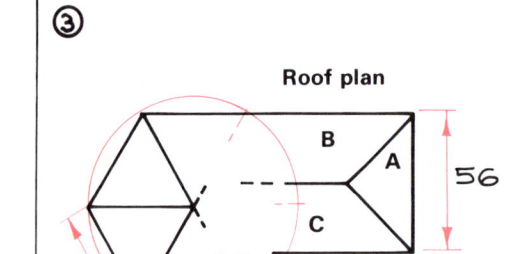

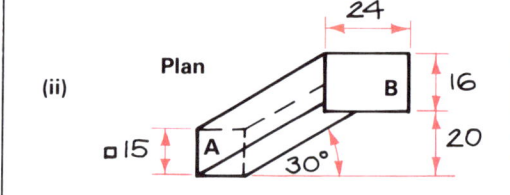

PART 2B

CHAPTER 28
PRESENTATION DRAWINGS

It is often an advantage to be able to see an object in a convincingly 'real' way, especially when presenting designs to a client who is not used to technical drawings. The addition of shadows will enhance the realism of the drawings.

CONTENTS
Terms in Perspective	Page **332**
One-point Interiors	**333**
Two point Perspective	**334**
Variables	**335**
Scales and an Example	**336**
Three and Multi-point	**337**
Sample Problem 1	**338**
Basic Shadow Projection	**339**
Shadows on Houses	**340**
Standard Shadow Shapes	**341**
Sample Problem 2	**342**
Shadows in Perspective	**343**
Exercises	**344**

Photocopying prohibited by law

① Terms used in perspective drawing

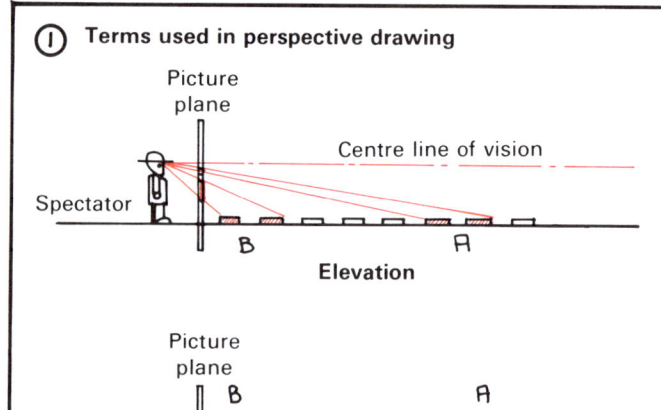

- If a sheet of glass is placed in front of a spectator a far away object **A** will take up less space and will be higher up than a nearer object **B**.
- Likewise, on plan, **A** will take up noticeably less space on the sheet of glass than **B**.
- The sheet of glass is called the *picture plane*. It controls the size of the image. The farther the picture plane is from the spectator the larger the image will be.
- A line drawn from the spectator in the direction and at the height that he is viewing is called the *centre line of vision*.

② The cone of vision

- If you look straight ahead you will see things in focus but objects over to one side will not be clear unless you turn your head.
- Similarly in perspective there is a limited area within which objects are clear and undistorted.
- This area is set **30°** to either side of the centre line of vision, both in plan and elevation, and is called the *cone of vision*.
- All objects that fall outside the cone of vision will appear distorted when drawn in perspective. This gives us a useful method of avoiding such distortions.

③ Basic types of perspective drawing

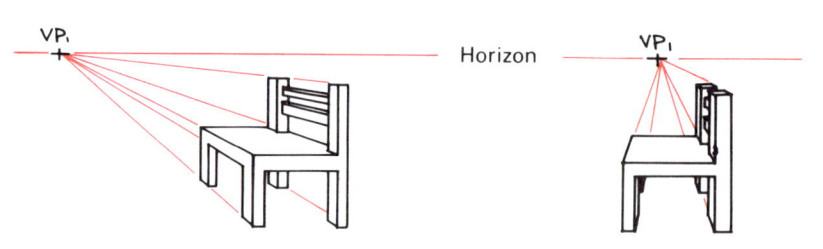

One-point perspective
- This is a variation of oblique projection. There is one vanishing point **VP1** and the lines of one axis are directed towards it. A one-point interior perspective is particularly useful. See page **333**.

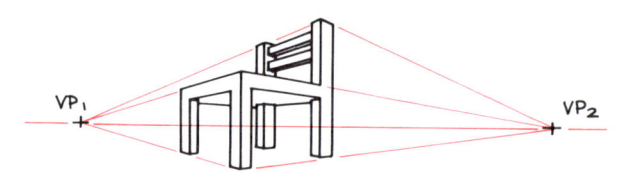

Two-point perspective
- This is the most useful and realistic form. The vertical lines stay vertical but lines recede to right and left towards two vanishing points **VP1** and **VP2**.

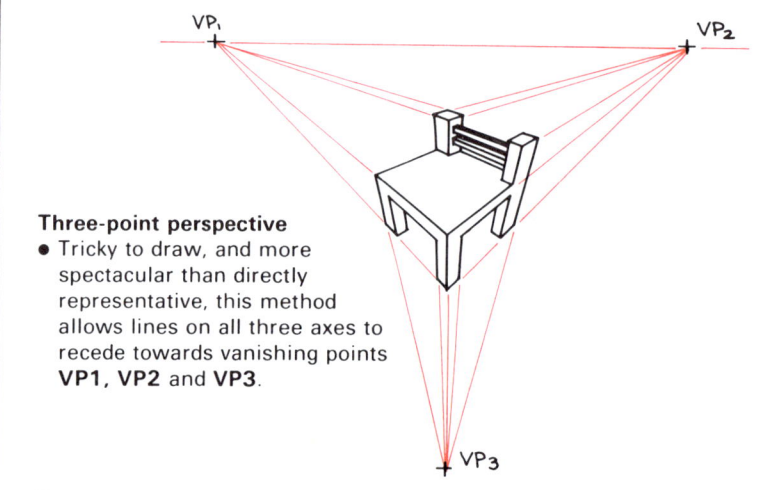

Three-point perspective
- Tricky to draw, and more spectacular than directly representative, this method allows lines on all three axes to recede towards vanishing points **VP1**, **VP2** and **VP3**.

Notes
- *Perspective drawings are spectacular and, even if time consuming, are very satisfying.*
- *However, there is little advantage over a good isometric projection in practical terms.*

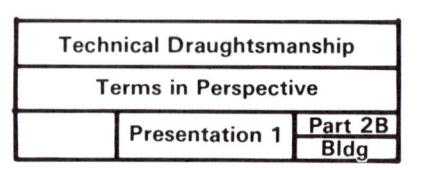

Technical Draughtsmanship		
Terms in Perspective		
Presentation 1	Part 2B	Bldg

1. Procedure step by step

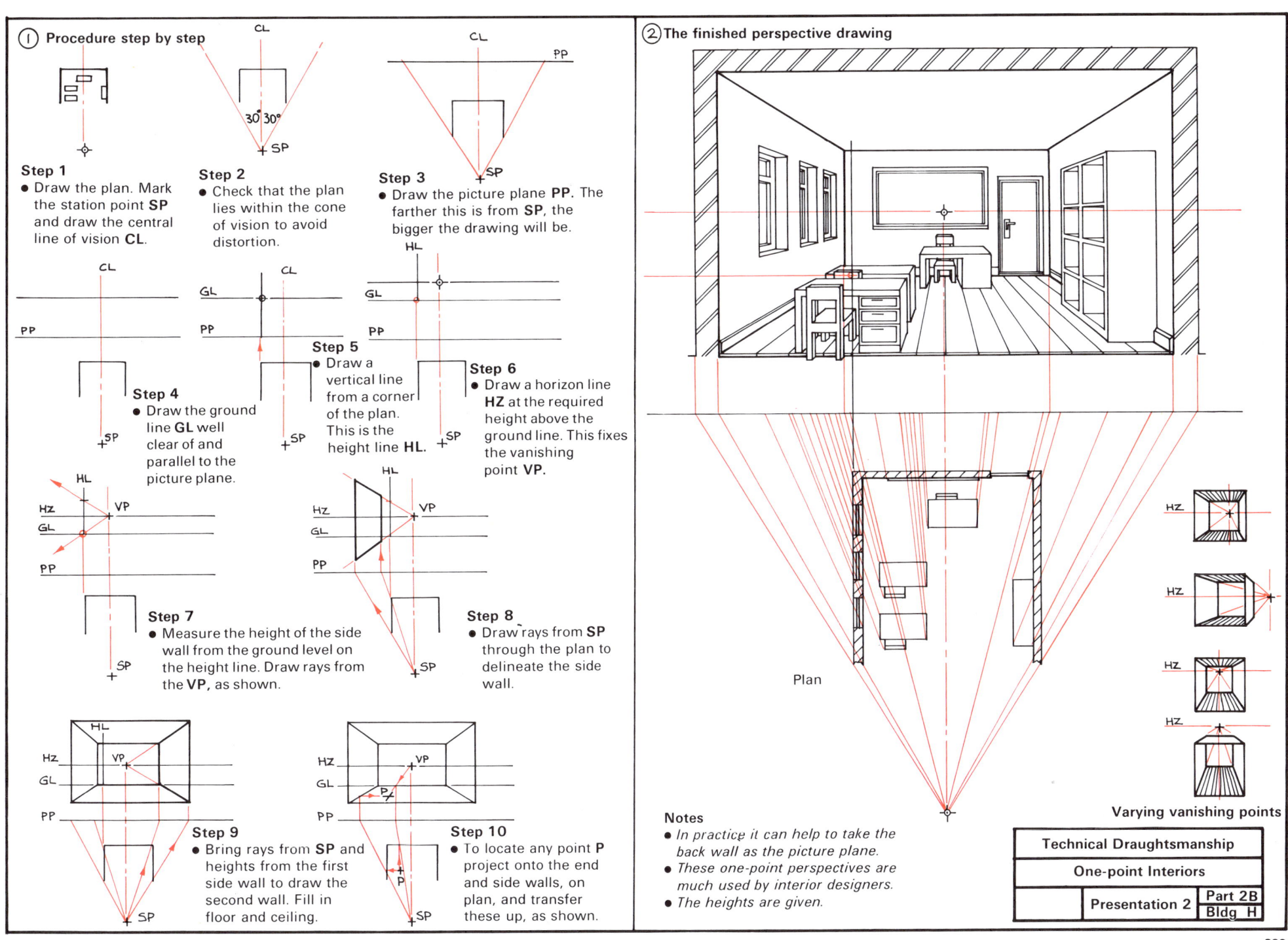

Step 1
- Draw the plan. Mark the station point **SP** and draw the central line of vision **CL**.

Step 2
- Check that the plan lies within the cone of vision to avoid distortion.

Step 3
- Draw the picture plane **PP**. The farther this is from **SP**, the bigger the drawing will be.

Step 4
- Draw the ground line **GL** well clear of and parallel to the picture plane.

Step 5
- Draw a vertical line from a corner of the plan. This is the height line **HL**.

Step 6
- Draw a horizon line **HZ** at the required height above the ground line. This fixes the vanishing point **VP**.

Step 7
- Measure the height of the side wall from the ground level on the height line. Draw rays from the **VP**, as shown.

Step 8
- Draw rays from **SP** through the plan to delineate the side wall.

Step 9
- Bring rays from **SP** and heights from the first side wall to draw the second wall. Fill in floor and ceiling.

Step 10
- To locate any point **P** project onto the end and side walls, on plan, and transfer these up, as shown.

2. The finished perspective drawing

Plan

Varying vanishing points

Notes
- *In practice it can help to take the back wall as the picture plane.*
- *These one-point perspectives are much used by interior designers.*
- *The heights are given.*

Technical Draughtsmanship
One-point Interiors
Presentation 2 — Part 2B — Bldg. H

333

① Procedure step by step

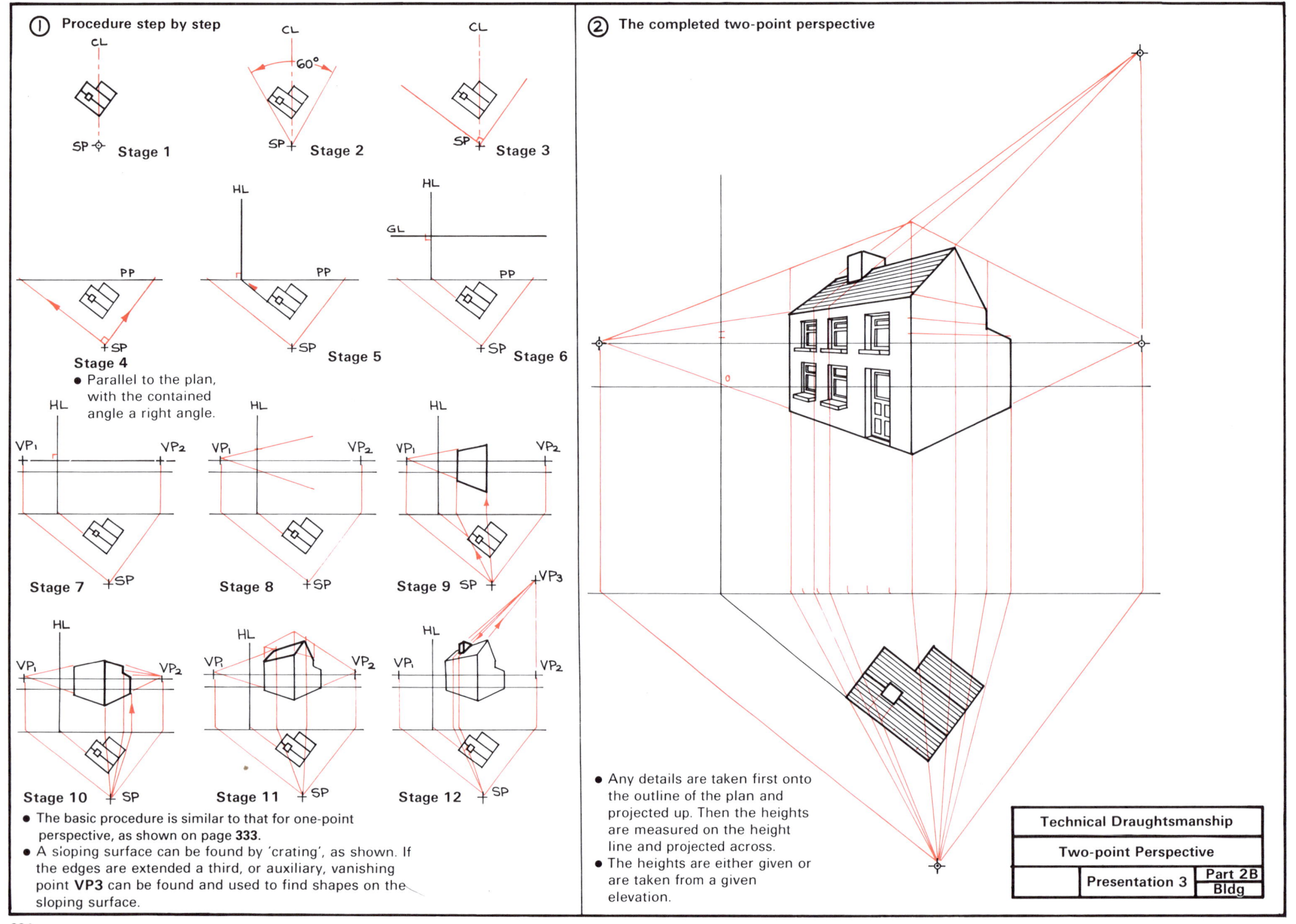

Stage 1
Stage 2 — 60°
Stage 3
Stage 4
Stage 5
Stage 6
- Parallel to the plan, with the contained angle a right angle.
Stage 7
Stage 8
Stage 9
Stage 10
Stage 11
Stage 12

- The basic procedure is similar to that for one-point perspective, as shown on page **333**.
- A sloping surface can be found by 'crating', as shown. If the edges are extended a third, or auxiliary, vanishing point **VP3** can be found and used to find shapes on the sloping surface.

② The completed two-point perspective

- Any details are taken first onto the outline of the plan and projected up. Then the heights are measured on the height line and projected across.
- The heights are either given or are taken from a given elevation.

Technical Draughtsmanship		
Two-point Perspective		
	Presentation 3	Part 2B
		Bldg

① Varying the picture plane

Situation 1
- The picture plane is on the opposite side of the plan to the spectator and the perspective drawing is projected up above the **PP**.
- This is the least confusing arrangement.

Situation 2
- The plan is large and the picture plane is between the plan and the spectator.
- The drawing may be projected up above the plan or down, as in this example.
- Notice how it is also possible to use one line for both **PP** and horizon.

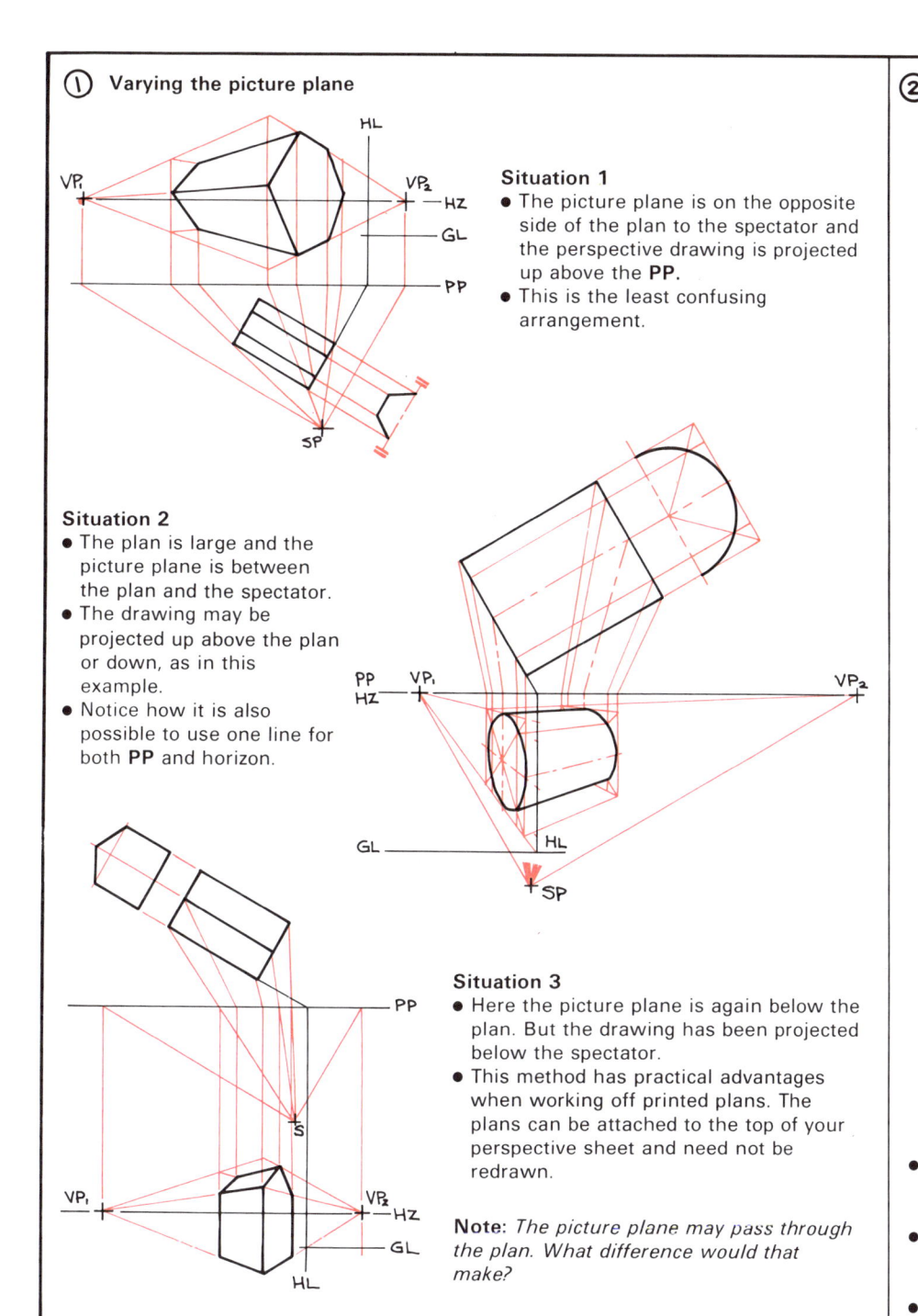

Situation 3
- Here the picture plane is again below the plan. But the drawing has been projected below the spectator.
- This method has practical advantages when working off printed plans. The plans can be attached to the top of your perspective sheet and need not be redrawn.

Note: *The picture plane may pass through the plan. What difference would that make?*

② Varying the distance between eye level (horizon) and the ground.

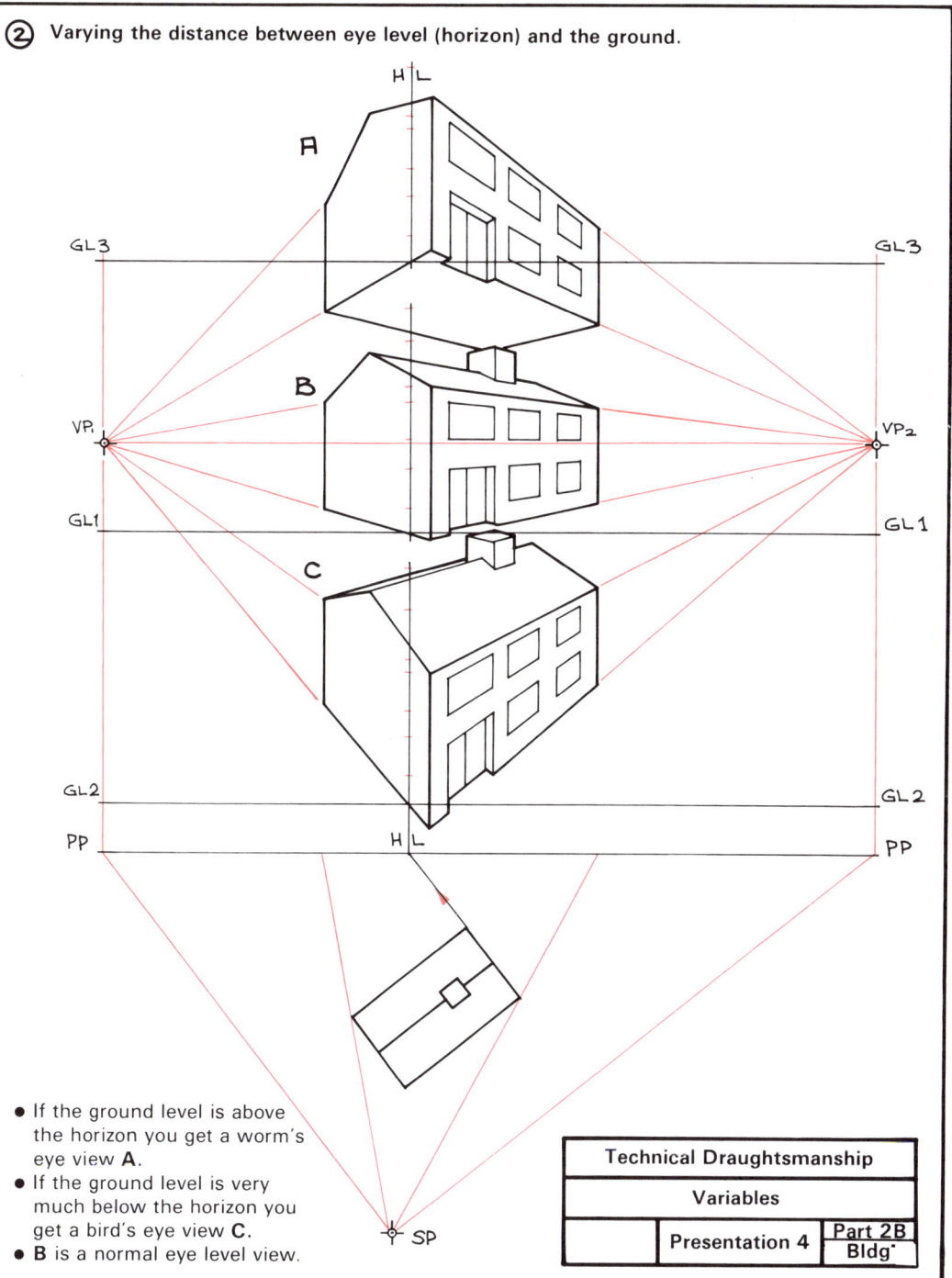

- If the ground level is above the horizon you get a worm's eye view **A**.
- If the ground level is very much below the horizon you get a bird's eye view **C**.
- **B** is a normal eye level view.

Technical Draughtsmanship		
Variables		
Presentation 4	Part 2B	Bldg

335

① Scales and grids

- Can perspective drawings be measured? How can a complicated or detailed surface be transfered to a perspective view? The answer is a grid system.

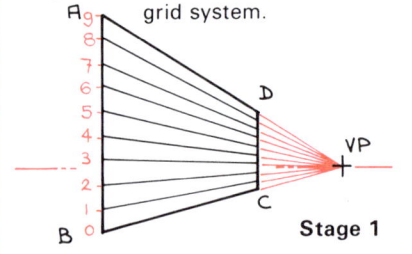

Stage 1

- Take a surface **ABCD** where the height of **AB** is **9m**.
- Divide **AB** into its nine metres. Join each to the **VP**, as shown.

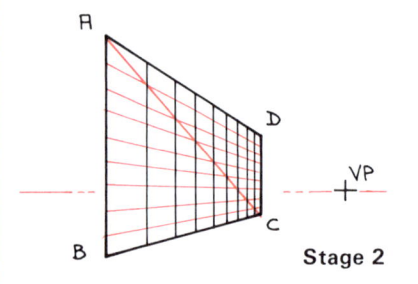

Stage 2

- Now draw the diagonal **AC** and draw a vertical line through each point where **AC** crosses a receding line.
- This is a grid in perspective and can be related to a grid on the orthographic view.
- An entire coordinate grid can easily be built up in this way.
- Alternatively points or shapes can be pin-pointed without difficulty.
- Patterns can also be drawn in perspective using grids.
- Grids can be set out in any direction.

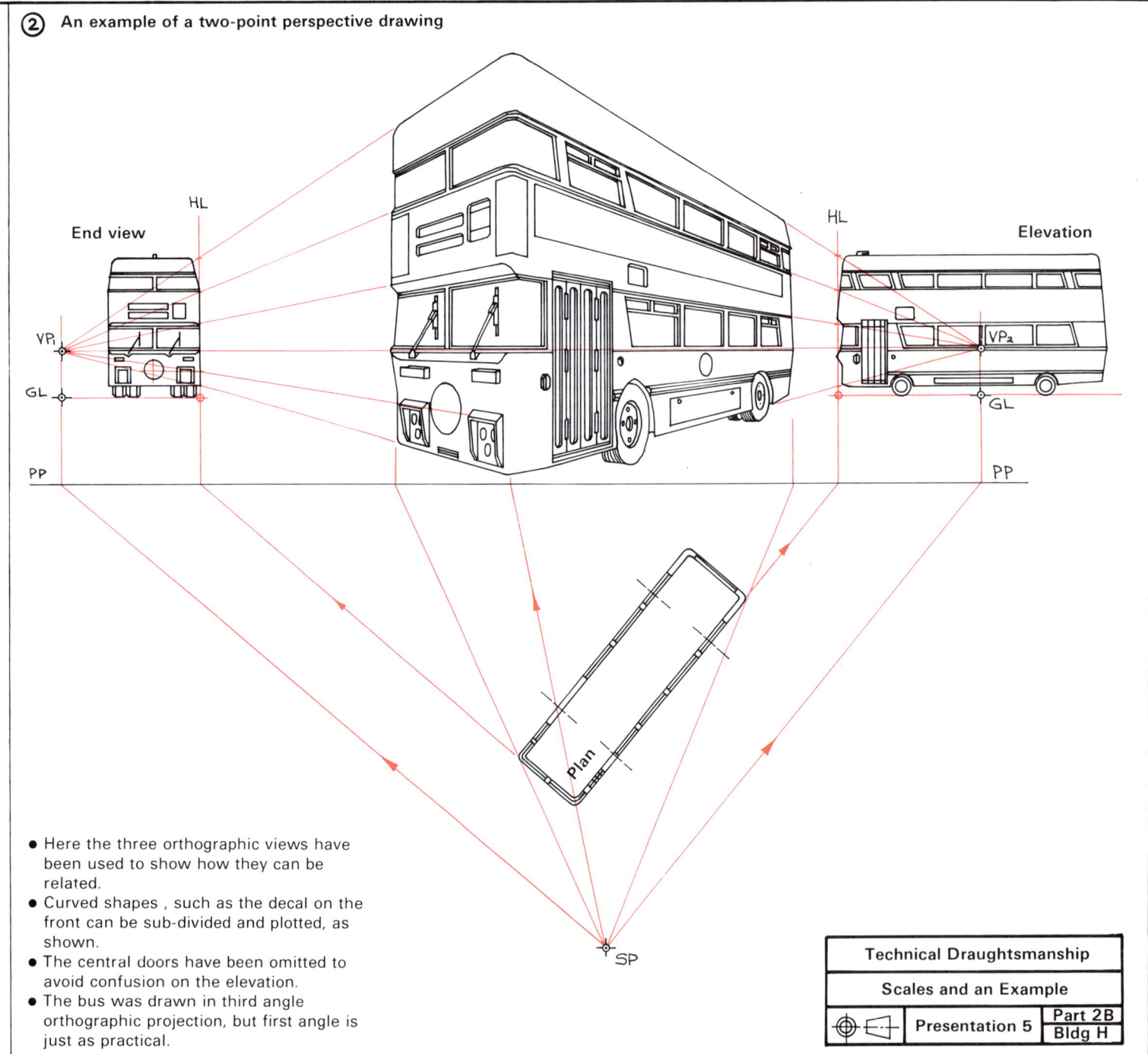

② An example of a two-point perspective drawing

- Here the three orthographic views have been used to show how they can be related.
- Curved shapes, such as the decal on the front can be sub-divided and plotted, as shown.
- The central doors have been omitted to avoid confusion on the elevation.
- The bus was drawn in third angle orthographic projection, but first angle is just as practical.

Technical Draughtsmanship

Scales and an Example

Presentation 5 | Part 2B | Bldg H

① Auxiliary vanishing points

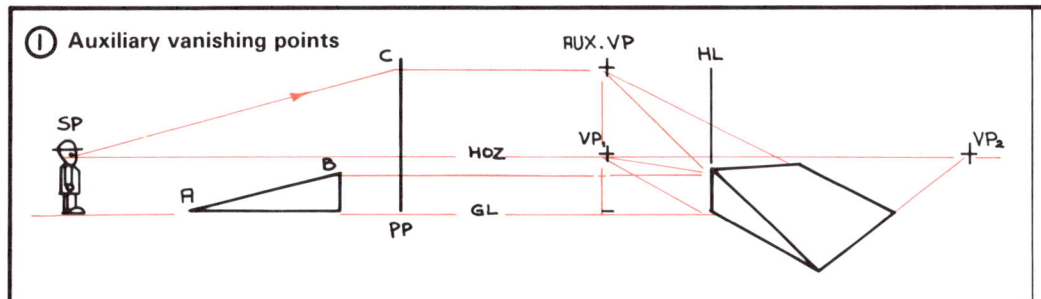

- To find a vanishing point for an inclined surface **AB** take an orthographic view showing the true slope of the line, and the respective positions of both the station point and the picture plane.
- From the station point draw a line parallel to **AB** to find **C** on the picture plane. This will be the height of the vanishing point for the sloping surface **AB**.
- On the perspective drawing use the height of **C** to mark **Aux. VP**, as shown.
- This can be used with any view or perspective method.
- For a simple slope 'crating' is equally effective.

② Multi-point perspective

- This is where a variety of vanishing points is required.

End view

Perspective drawing

Note: See also page 79.

③ Three-point perspective

Procedure

- Draw the horizon and mark points **VP1** and **VP2**.
- With a centre **A** draw a semicircle from **VP1** to **VP2**.
- With the same radius and centre **VP2** swing **A** onto the semicircle at **B**.
- With centre **B** swing **A** through **C** towards **VP3**.
- With centre **C** swing **A** through **B** to fix **VP3**.
- A cube can be projected from the three vanishing points, as shown.
- To project a given shape crate it and relate it to a cube. Then project the cube and use a grid to subdivide it. See page **336**.

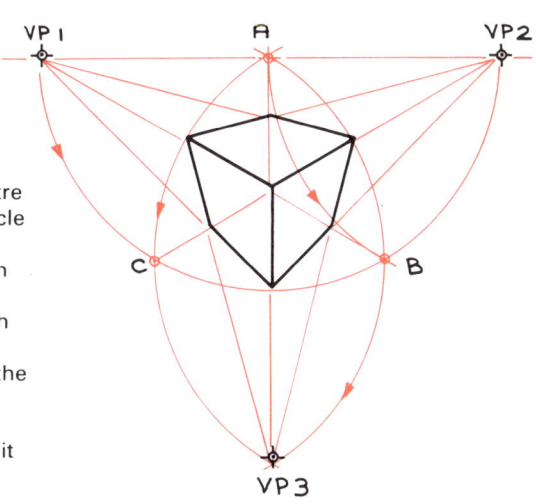

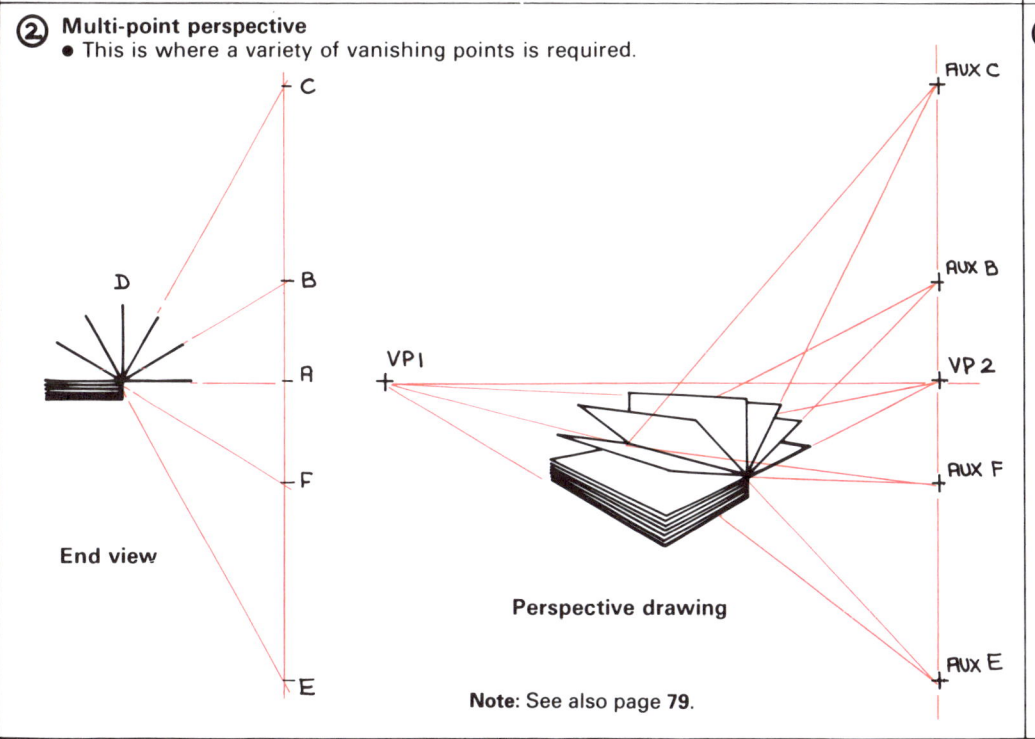

④ To extend a three-point cube

Procedure

- To extend side **ABCD**, drop a perpendicular from **VP2**.
- Join **A** to **D** and extend this diagonal to find **Aux. 1**.
- Join **Aux. 1** to point **C**, crossing the **BDVP2** line at **E**.
- Join **VP3** through **E** to **F**. This defines a perspective doubling of **ABCD** to **ABEF**.
- This process can be continued and the cube can be extended in any direction in a similar way.
- The extended cube can still be sub-divided by the standard grid method.

Note
The three-point cube method has been chosen for its simplicity and its application to computer graphics.

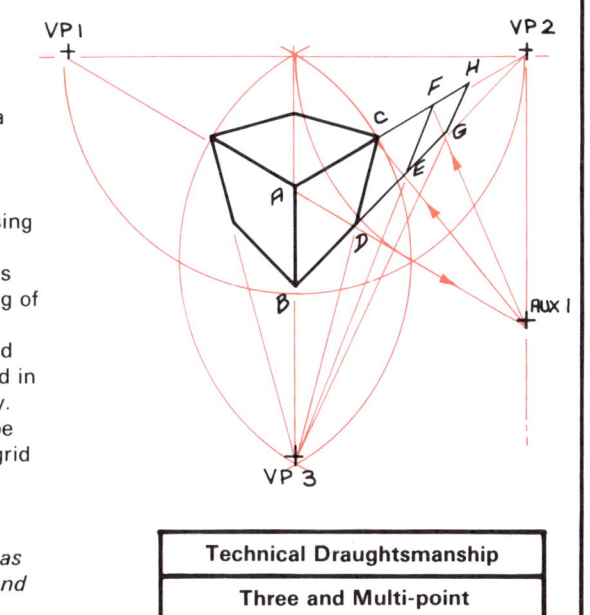

Technical Draughtsmanship		
Three and Multi-point		
	Presentation 6	Part 2B
		Bldg H

337

The Problem

This is the plan of a building, all of whose roofs are pitched at **30°**. Construct a perspective view of the building when the **Sp** is **6.5m** from the corner **A**, the picture plane passes through **B**, and the horizon is **4m** above the ground line. **Scale 1:100**

Procedure

- Draw the basic set up and with the help of the end view **Aux 1** complete the plan.
- Plot the basic shape through ground level **0**. It is usually handier to trace the biggest outline you will need on the ground and then work in and up from this. Here it is the outline of the roof edge.
- By taking lines **Q, R, S, T**, etc. on to the outline on plan, it allows you to fix heights easily and to work them back as shown.
- Build up the perspective view block by block.

Note:
Imagine a child dragging a crayon along a wall and around the corner. That is how to transfer a height from the HL to wherever you want it.

Technical Draughtsmanship		
Sample Problem 1		
	Presentation 7	Part 2B Bldg H

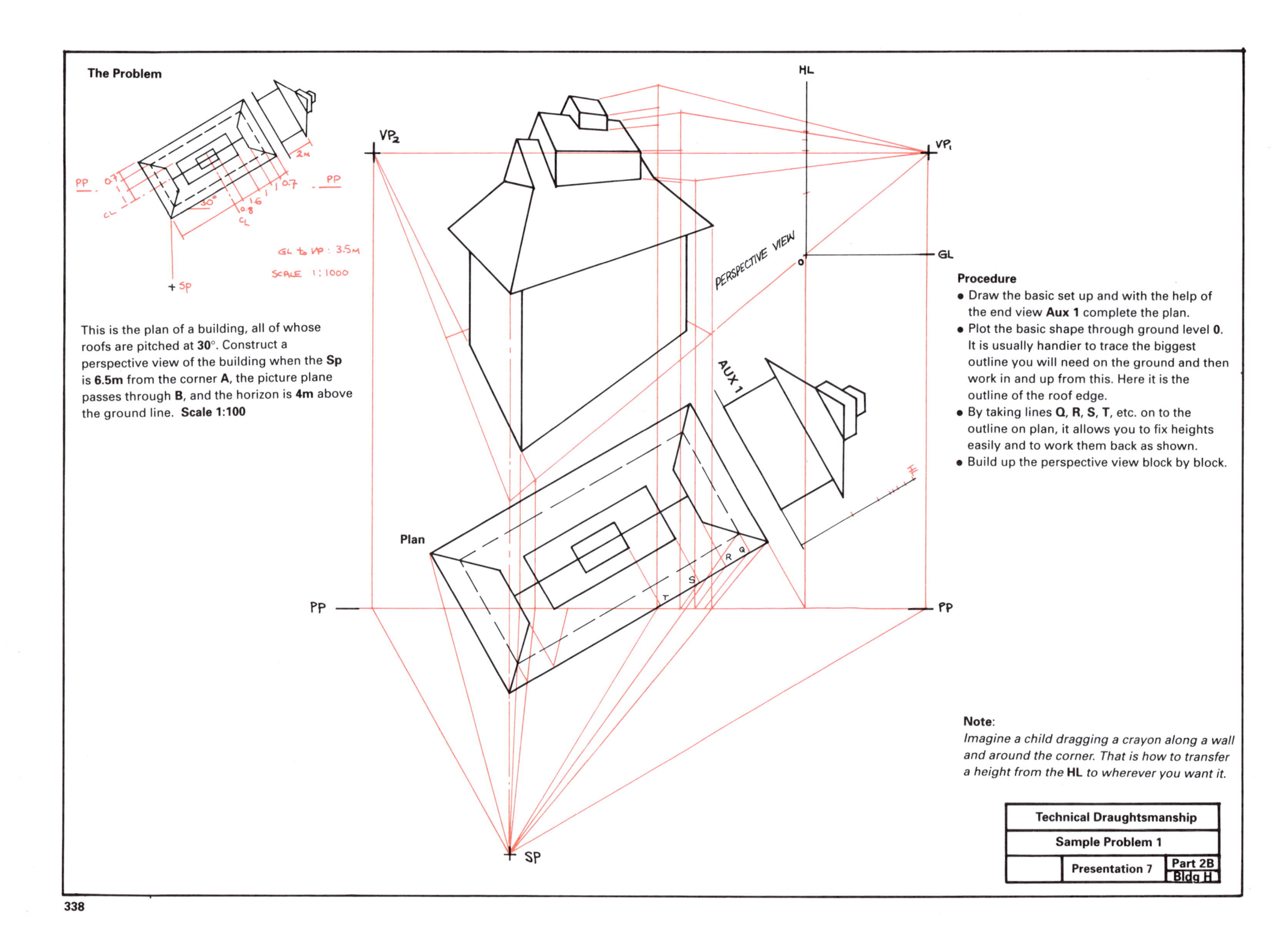

① To find the shadow of a point P

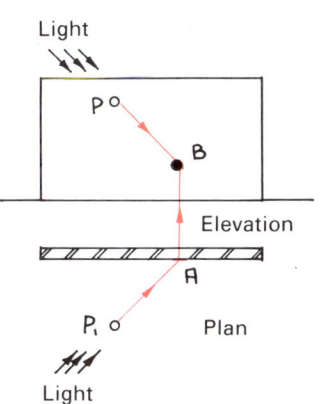

- The direction of the light is given as an angle to the horizontal, i.e. on elevation, and as an angle to the vertical, i.e. on plan.
- Use these angles to project the point onto the wall and locate its shadow, as shown.

② To find the shadow of a line AB (i)

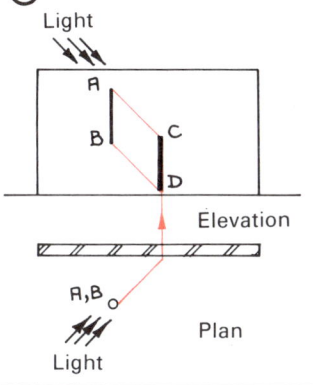

- Proceed as before and project the extremities of the line to plot the shadow **CD**.

③ To find the shadow of a line AB (ii)

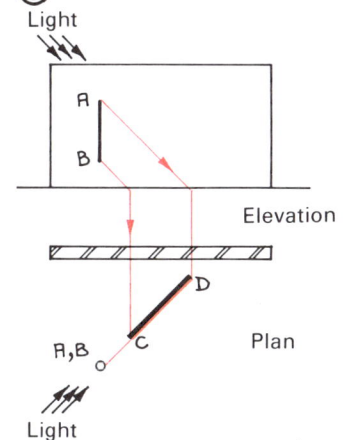

- In this case the shadow is not on the wall but on the ground.
- Project **A** and **B** onto the ground on the elevation and project across to the plan to fix the shadow **CD**.

④ To find the shadows of a rectangle

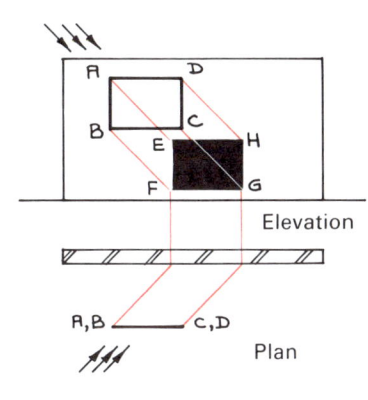

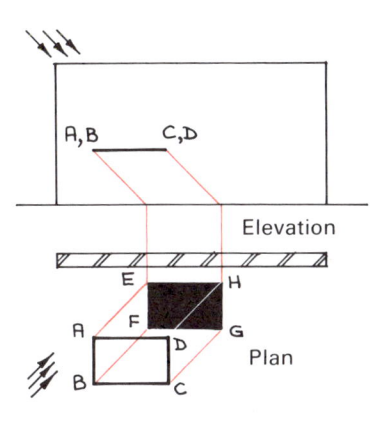

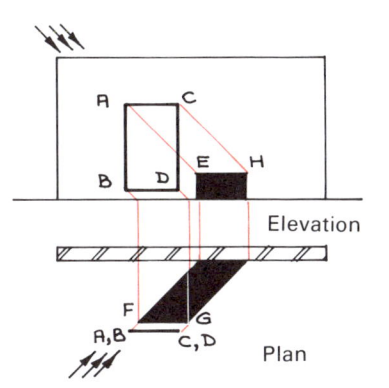

- The shadow is on the wall and is located by projecting each corner of the rectangle, as shown.
- Here the shadow is on the ground and is found as before.
- In this case the shadow lies on both the wall and the ground. The projections will be clear from the diagram.

⑤ To find the shadows of a rectangular solid

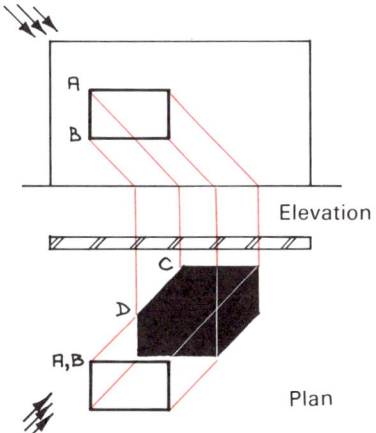

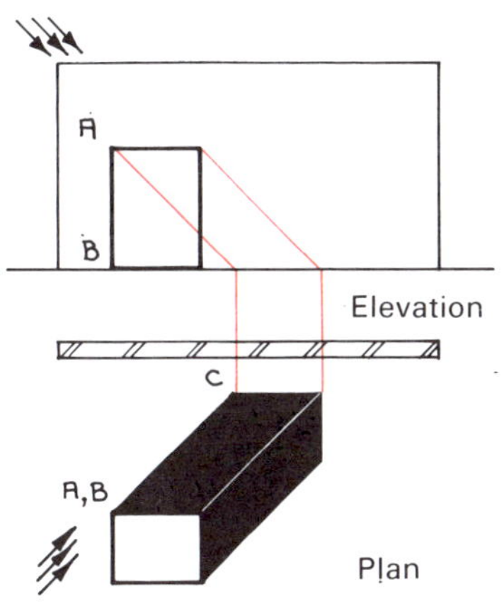

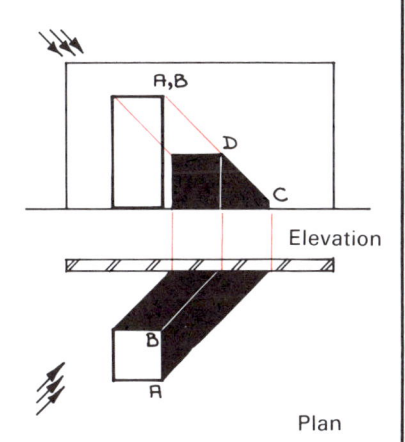

- In each case the constructions will be clear from the diagrams.

Note:
*The angles used here have been of **45°** with the horizontal and **45°** with the vertical. A different set of given angles would be treated in a similar way.*

| Technical Draughtsmanship |
| Basic Shadow Projection |
| Presentation 8 | Part 2B Bldg |

1. Doorway

- The construction will be clear from the diagram.

Elevation — Section — Plan

2. Doorway with lintel

- The construction will be clear from the diagram.

Elevation — Section — Plan

3. Porch

- The construction will be clear from the diagram.

Elevation — Section — Plan

4. Shadows on a sloping ground

Light — Shade — Shadow

- To plot the shadow on a sloping ground it is necessary to show the slope in profile. This allows the shadow to be located, as shown.
- In a complicated drawing a diagram of the sloping plane may be sufficient.

Section

Note
- *Notice the different treatment of a plane in light, shade and shadow.*

5. Shadows of a two-storey house

- Each recognisable basic shape is projected separately, to build up the compound shadows and shades as shown.

Technical Draughtsmanship
Shadows on Houses
Presentation 9 — Part 2B Bldg

340

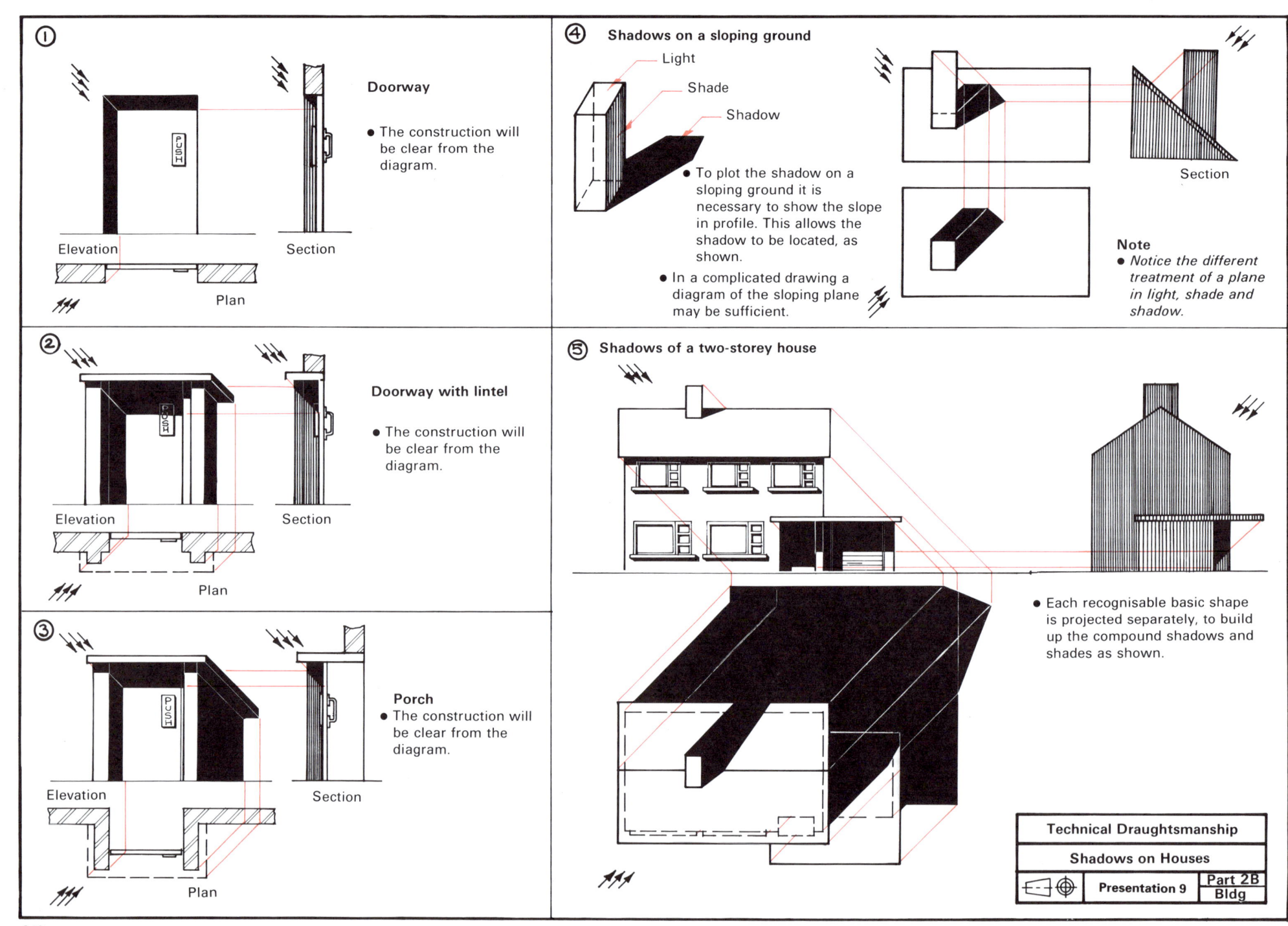

① Shadow of a vertical disc

- In this case the shadow is a circle.
- If the angle of the light is varied crate the circle and proceed as below.

② Shadow of a suspended horizontal disc

- Crate the circle and project the outline of the crate. Then relocate the profile of the circle to find the shadow.

③ Shadow of disc on a wall and on the ground

- The construction will be clear from the diagram.

④ The shadows of standard solids

- In each case the constructions should be clear from the diagrams

⑤ The effects of varied standard shapes on standard uprights.

- In each case take a number of points on the top shape and find each point's shadow to build up the compound shadow.

⑥ Shadow of a sphere

- The shadow is an ellipse the axes of which are found as shown.

⑦ An alternative method for finding the shadow of a sphere

- By auxiliary projection set a circle **A** parallel to the direction of light.
- Locate **B**, as shown, on the auxiliary plane. This enables **B**, **C** and **D** to be found.
- Bring these back on the centre line **EF** to find the axis of the ellipse.

Technical Draughtsmanship		
Standard Shadow Shapes		
	Presentation 10	Part 2B
		Bldg H.

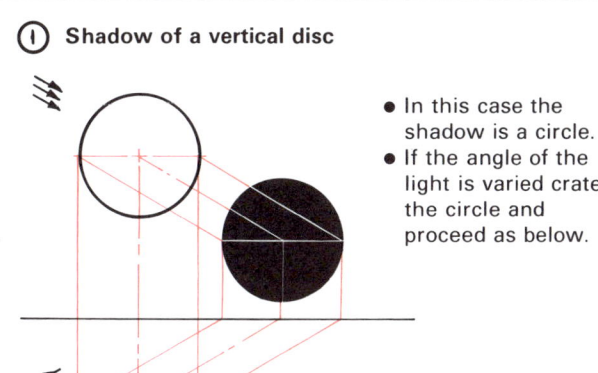

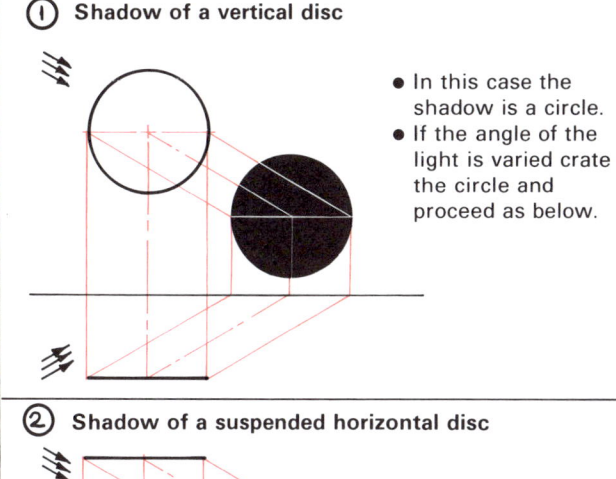

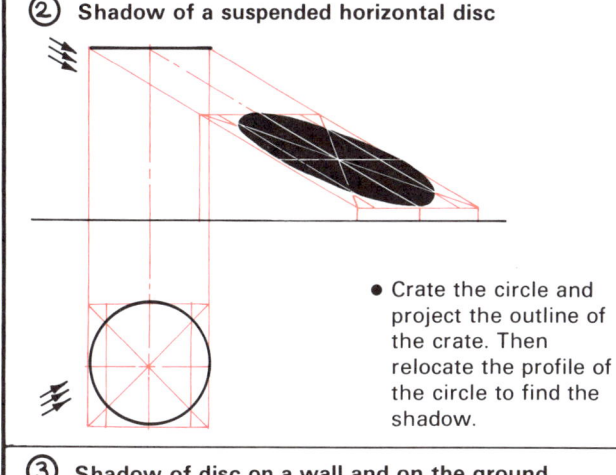

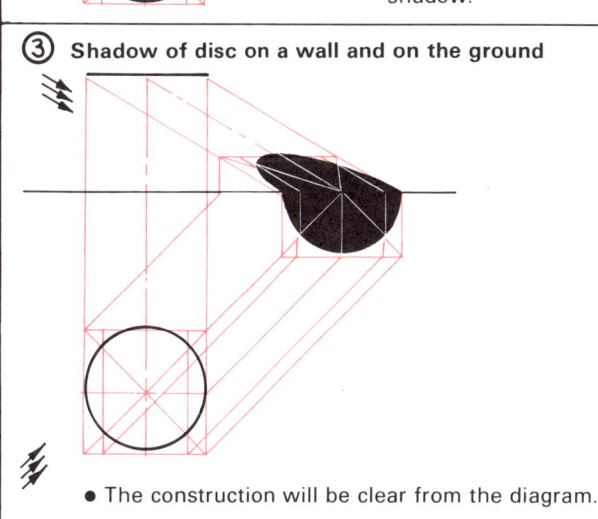

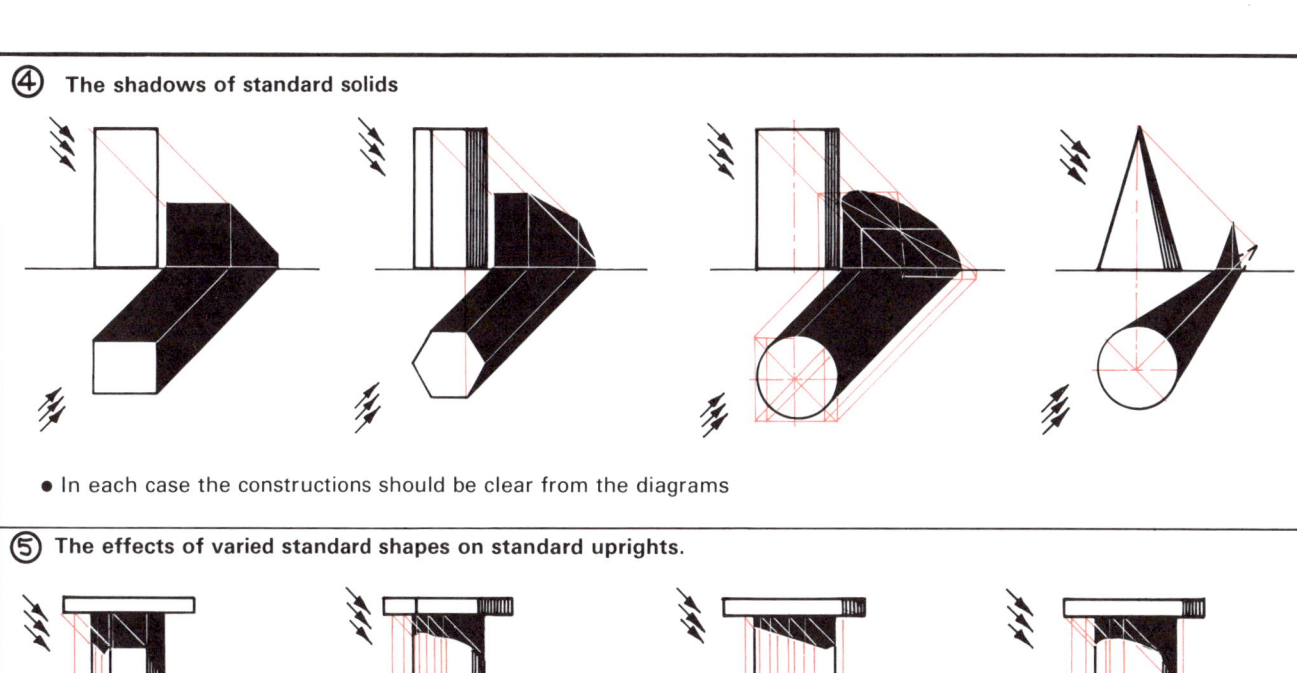

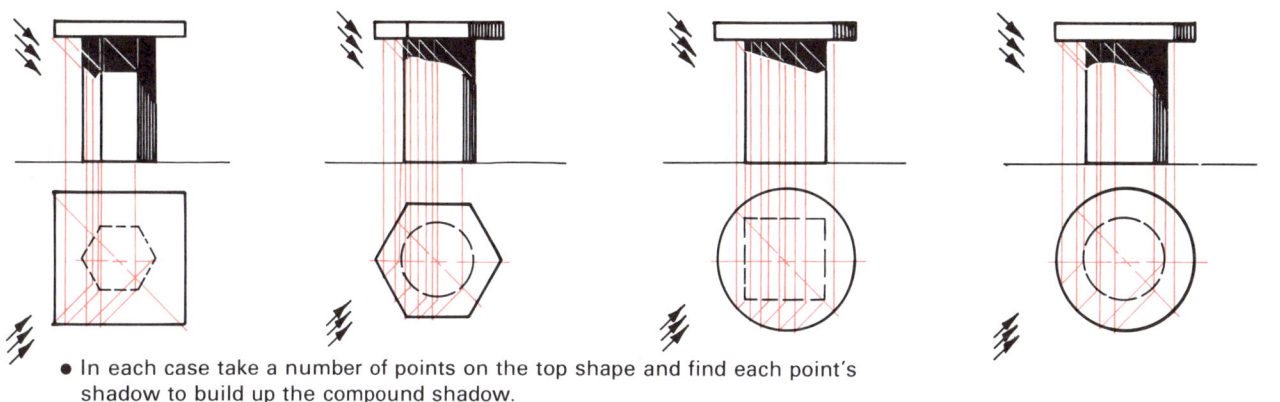

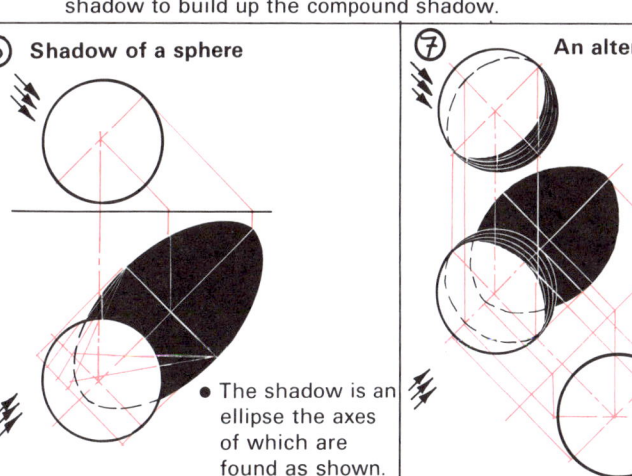

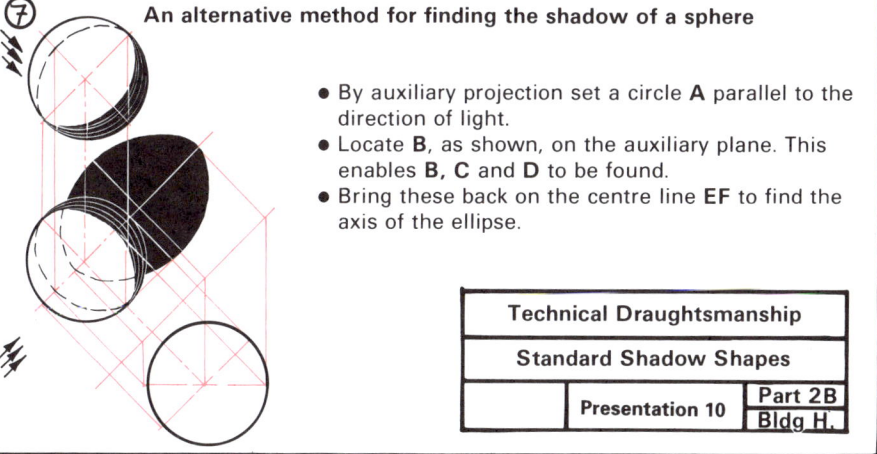

The Problem

Plot the shadows when the sun is as indicated.
Scale 1:100.

Procedure
- Draw the three views.
- Locate the sun on plan and elevation.
- To find the direction of the sun on the plan, box off a piece of the arrow and project it as shown.
- Now, take the easiest shape and project it to the shadow, step by step.
- For the shadow of the chimney, the base is clear, but the point at the top of the wall will need the use of **R** on the end view. Why?
- The end view will also be needed for the shadow on the roof.

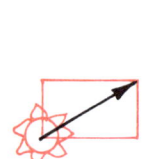

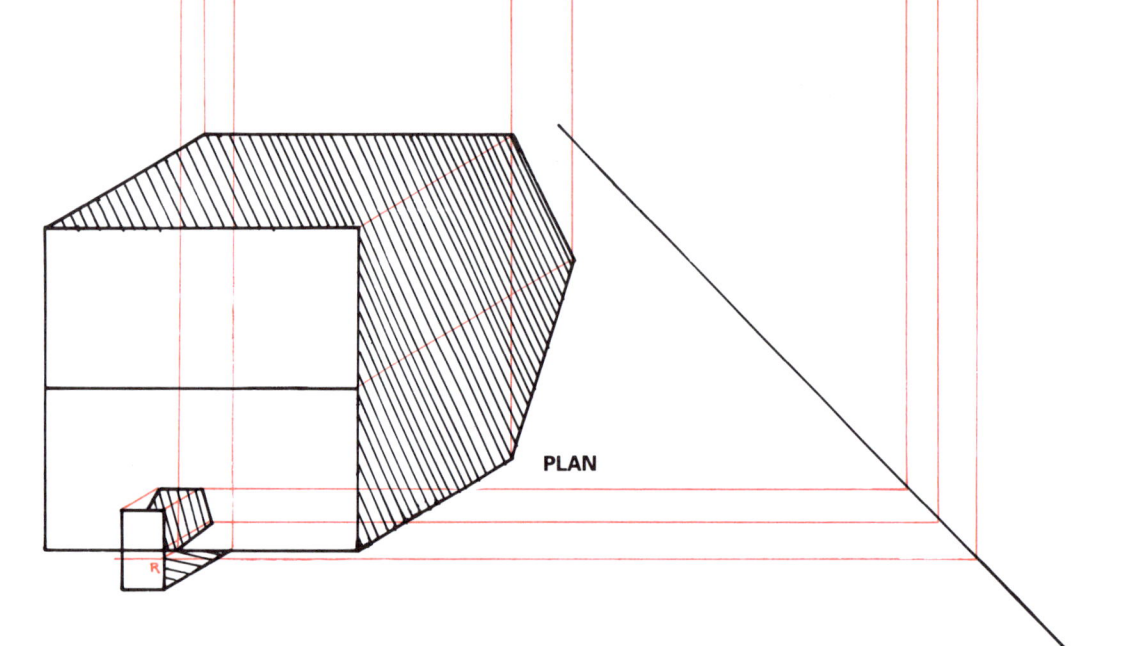

ELEVATION

END VIEW

PLAN

Technical Draughtsmanship
Sample Problem 2

| Presentation 11 | Part 2B Bldg |

342

① Projecting shadows on a perspective drawing

- The position of the sun may be given, as in this case, at **LS**, i.e. *light source*.
- Drop a perpendicular to the horizon to locate the *light base*, **LB**.
- Take line **AB**. From **LS** draw a line through **A** towards **C**.
- From **LB** then draw a line through **B** to fix **C**.
- Repeat with other lines to build up the shadow, as shown.

Note:
An interior can be treated in a similar way, the LB being a spot on the floor directly below the LS.

② To locate the light source and light base when the light source is in front of the spectator

- Given is the angle with the horizontal **Y** and with the vertical **X**. The sun is, we are told, in front of the spectator.
- From **SP** draw a line at angle **X** to find **C**.
- Erect a perpendicular to find **LB** and continue towards **LS**.
- With centre **C** swing **SP** to **A** and project up to **B**.
- Draw an angle of **Y** at **B** to find **LS**.

③ To locate the light source and light base when the light source is behind the spectator

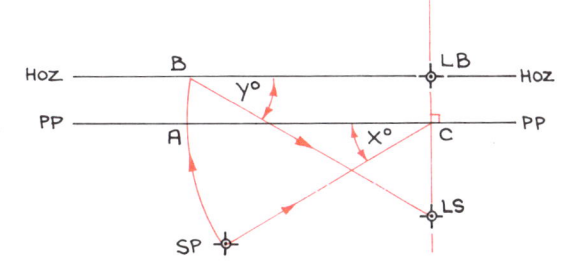

- **LB** is found as before.
- Again swing **SP** around to find **A** and then project up to **B**.
- The difference is that the angle **Y** is set out from **B** *below* the horizon.

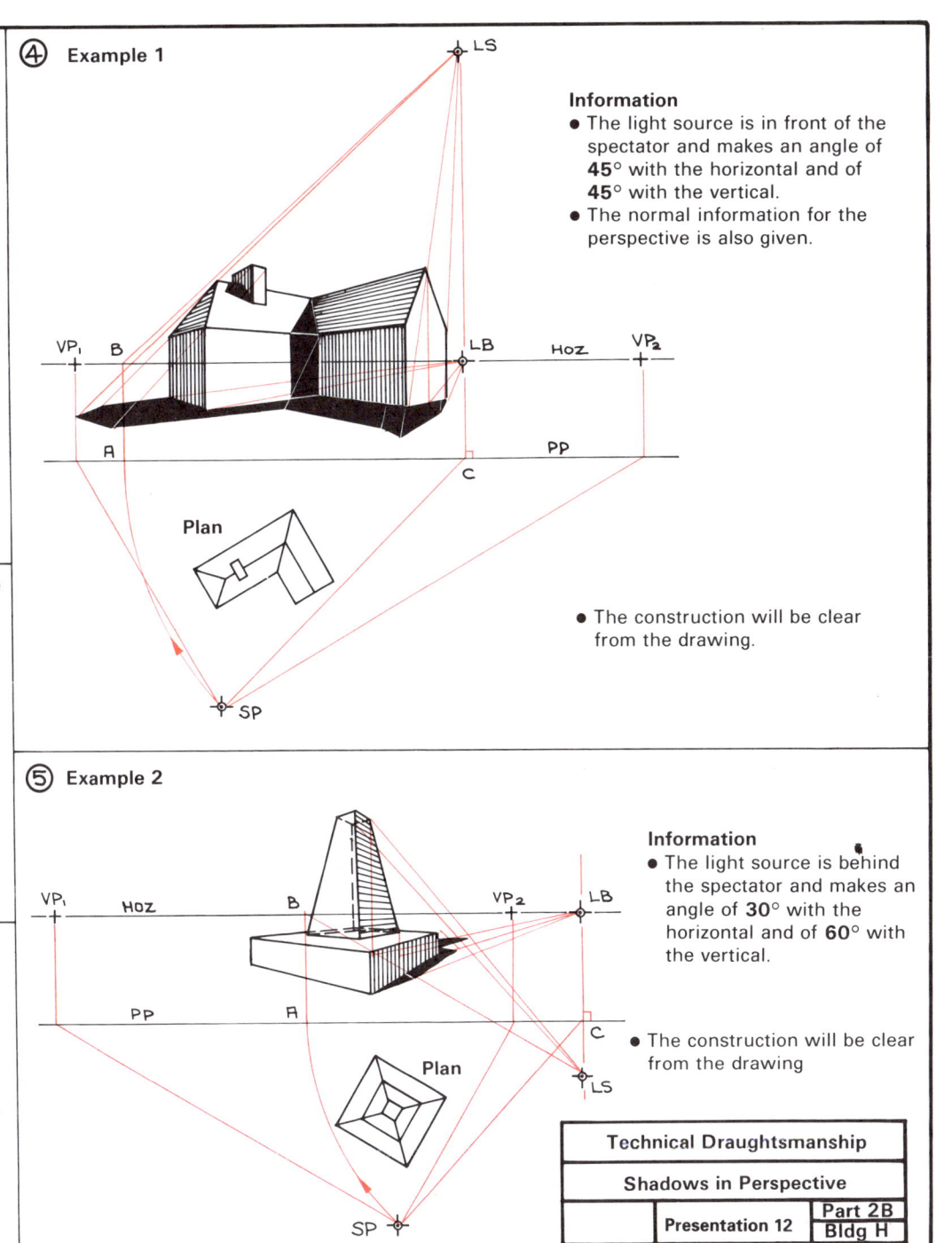

④ Example 1

Information
- The light source is in front of the spectator and makes an angle of **45°** with the horizontal and of **45°** with the vertical.
- The normal information for the perspective is also given.

Plan

- The construction will be clear from the drawing.

⑤ Example 2

Information
- The light source is behind the spectator and makes an angle of **30°** with the horizontal and of **60°** with the vertical.

Plan

- The construction will be clear from the drawing

Technical Draughtsmanship
Shadows in Perspective

Presentation 12	Part 2B
	Bldg H

343

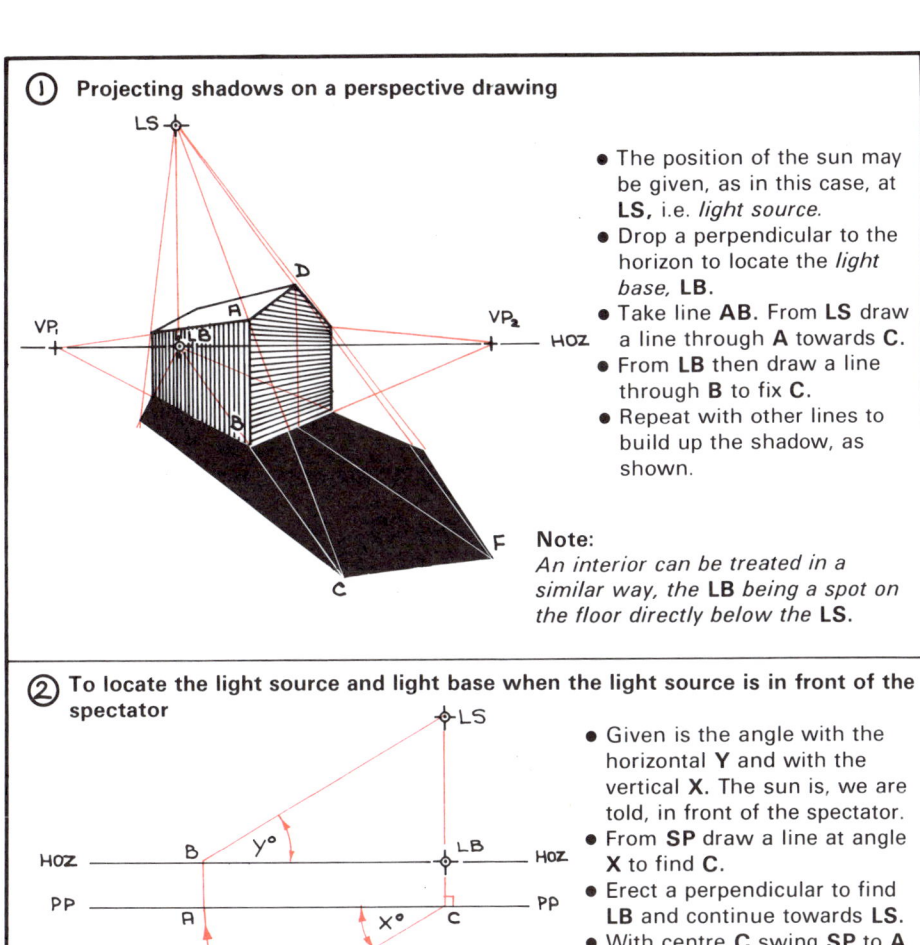

All measurements are in millimetres.

Questions

1. Make a two-point perspective drawing of the cottage using the information given.

2. From the given information construct a two-point perspective drawing of the house.

3. Plot a two-point perspective view of the steps shown.

4. Make a two-point perspective drawing of the given solid.

5. Construct a one-point interior perspective of the office shown.

6. Make a one-point interior perspective of the kitchenette. Add the necessary details and furniture to your finished drawing.

Note
SP: *Spectator.*
PP: *Picture plane.*
VP: *Vanishing point.*
GL: *Ground level.*

Technical Draughtsmanship

Exercises 1

Presentation 13 — **Part 2B Bldg**

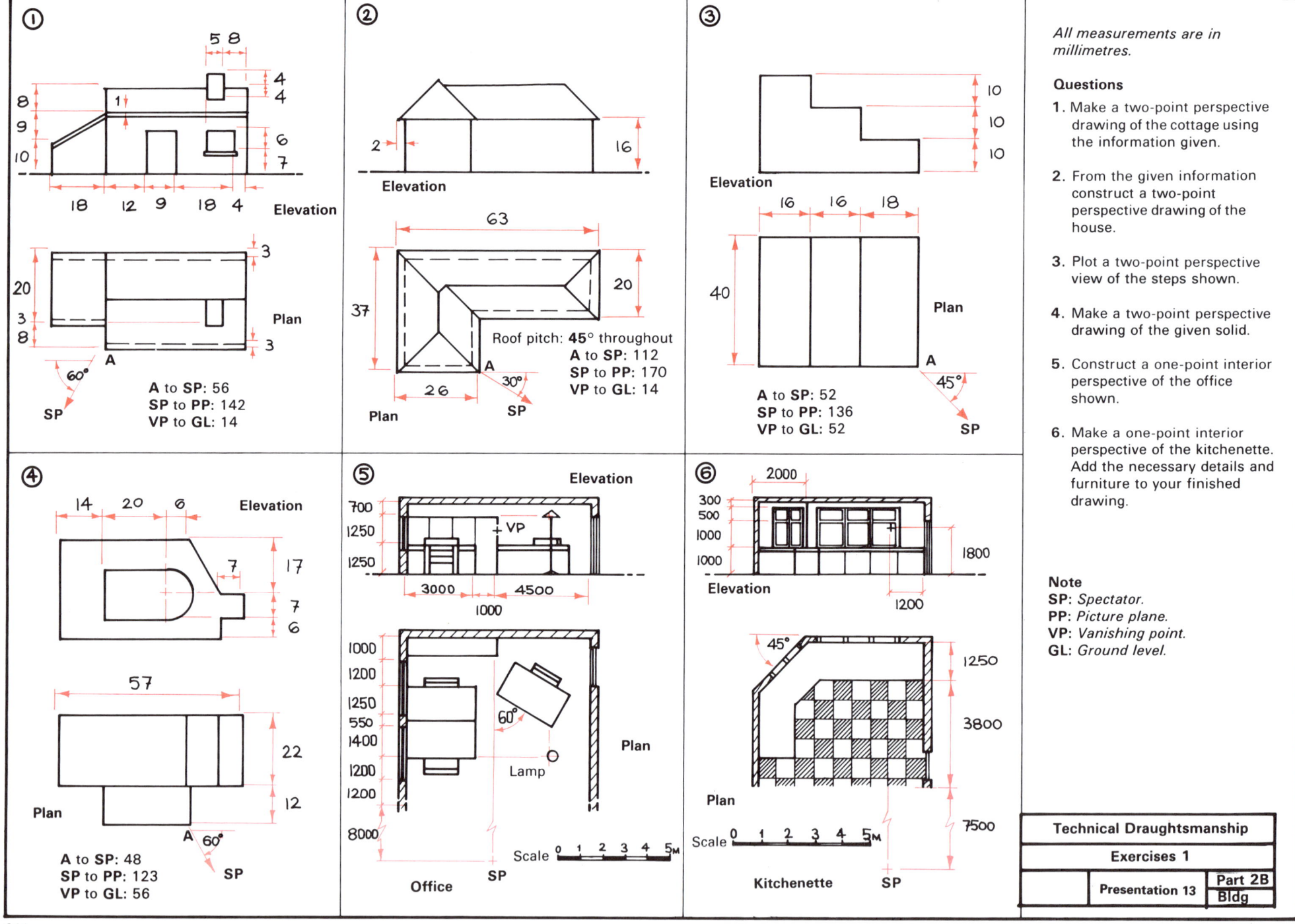

All measurements are in millimetres.

Questions

1. Draw the bus-shelter and plot the shade and shadows cast. Leave plenty of room between each view.

2. Draw the orthographic views of the postbox and indicate the shade and shadows cast.

3. Complete the given views and project the shadows of each object when the light makes an angle of **30°** with the **HP** and **45°** with the **VP**.

4. Project the shade and shadows of the given house.

5. Project the shade and shadows of the given solids.

6. Project the shade and shadows cast when the light is turned on in the given cell. Two end views are required, **A-A** and **B-B**.

Technical Draughtsmanship	
Exercises 2	
Presentation 14	Part 2B Bldg

345

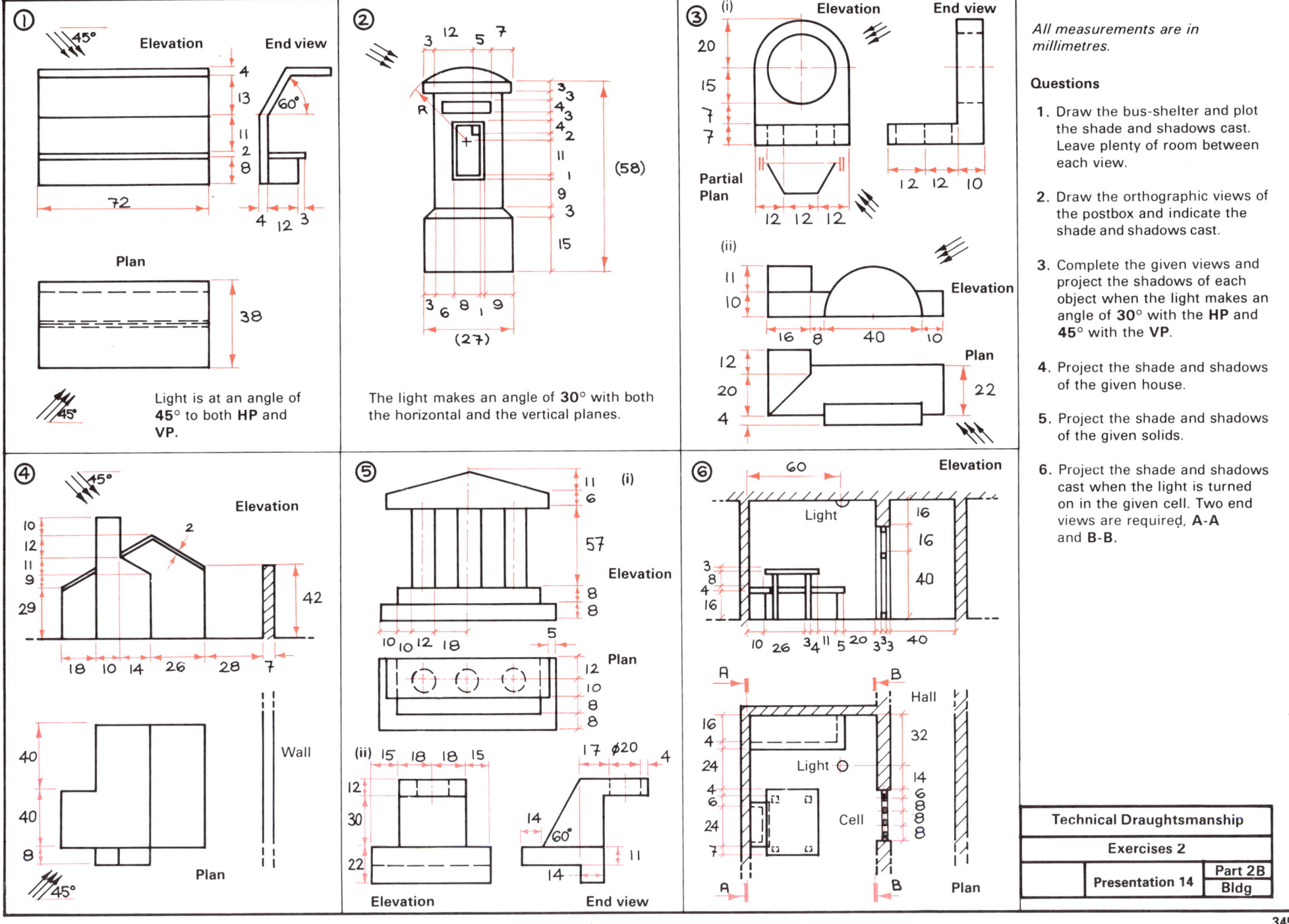

All measurements are millimetres

Questions

1. Project the shadows of both structures onto the ground. The sun makes an angle of **45°** with the horizontal and of **30°** with the vertical.

2. Draw the church in orthographic projection and use this information to construct a perspective view. Take the **VP** height as that of point **P**.

3. Make a three-point perspective drawing of the house shown.

4. Using the interior perspective from question 5 on page **344**, project the shadows when the lamp is turned on at night.

5. Make a perspective drawing of the open cigar box.

6. Draw the desk in perspective projection and plot the shade and shadows cast.

7. Draw a perspective with shade and shadows cast of the open stall shown.

The light source is behind the spectator and makes an angle of **30°** with the horizontal and of **45°** with the vertical plane.

The light source is in front of the spectator and is at an angle of **30°** with both **HP** and **VP**.

Box thickness is **6 mm** throughout.

Technical Draughtsmanship
Exercises 3
Presentation 15 — Part 2B / Bldg H

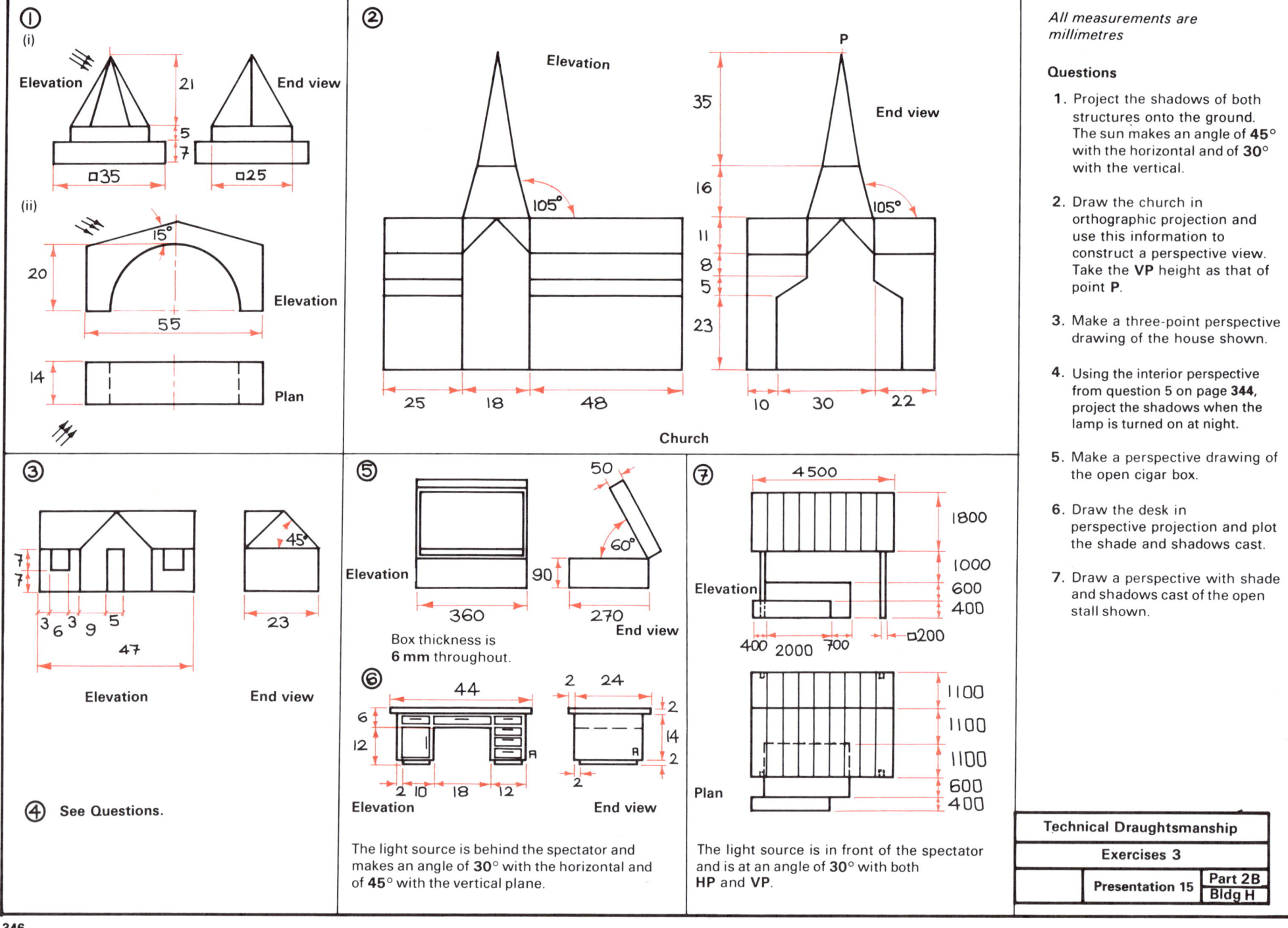

General advice

- Practice *is* needed to prepare for an examination. You are deceiving yourself and will be disappointed if you enter an examination without proper preparation.

- Setting a weekly pattern of study and practice *will* pay dividends. Sporadic 'hit-and-miss' study is not effective.

- You will need to know and understand the constructions well enough to handle the problems that will be presented to you. That needs practice and *more* practice.

- Looking at a drawing is *not* a true revision. Redraw it if you want to learn it well.

- Drawing takes time. Leaving things to be crammed into a few hours before an examination is folly and will *not* work at this level.

- Know your weak points and practise in those areas. This is difficult but is the best way to get on top of the subject.

- Time yourself regularly. It is very helpful to be able to pace yourself under pressure. Try to build up a quick decisive unrushed style. You will be surprised how much 'free-wheeling' you can eliminate.

- Make yourself familiar with the format of the examination. Try to answer past papers and be clear as to the choices you will have to make.

Tackling the examination

- Check and clean your instruments a few days before your examination, and in good time to replace any item you may need.

- In an examination read each question *three* times. Read *all* the questions before you make a choice. Satisfy yourself that you know *exactly* what the examiners require of each answer.

- Pace yourself and allocate your time per question.

- There is a maximum mark for each question. Do *not* waste time chasing stray marks when whole questions are being left unanswered. Be prepared to leave an unfinished question, if necessary.

- Plot your layout and make *sure* the drawing will fit on the page. *Always* draw a quick sketch before you commit yourself to working in detail.

- Some questions look easy but need a lot of time to plot the constructions. Take this into account.

- Leave your construction lines on the drawing. This helps the examiner to give you every credit possible.

- In orthographic or other projections marks will be given for each view. You will do better with two good views than with one highly finished one.

- Remember that marks will be given for draughtsmanship, layout and knowledge of the construction in question, as well as for solving a particular problem.

- Present your work neatly and label it clearly.

- Good luck in all your examinations.

Technical Draughtsmanship
Examination Hints
Appendix 1

① Some SI Units

Quantity	Name of Unit	Symbol
Length	metre	m
Mass	kilogram	kg
Time	second	s
Force	newton	N
Work	joule	J
Power	watt	W
Area	square metre	m²
Volume	cubic metre	m³
Velocity	metre per second	ms
Moment of force	newton metre	Nm

Notes:
- 1 kg mass = 9.81 N
- Force x distance = work done
  1 newton x 1 metre = 1 joule
- 1 radian = 57.3 degrees
- 1 degree = π/180 radians.

② SI prefixes

Prefix	Symbol	Factor	Example
Giga	G	10^5	Gm
Mega	M	10^4	Mm
Kilo	k	10^3	km
Hecto	h	10^2	hm
Deca	da	10	da m
Basic unit	—	1	m
Deci	d	10^{-1}	dm
Centi	c	10^{-2}	cm
Milli	m	10^{-3}	mm
Micro	μ	10^{-4}	μm
Nano	n	10^{-5}	nm

Note
- Although all of these units are valid, for convenience particular multiples are preferred e.g.: mm, m, km.

③ TRIGONOMETRIC FUNCTIONS (See page 9)

Angle	Sine	Cosine	Tan	Cotan	Angle
0°	.0000	1.0000	.0000	∞	90°
1°	.0175	.9998	.0175	57.290	89°
2°	.0349	.9994	.0349	28.636	88°
3°	.0523	.9986	.0524	19.081	87°
4°	.0698	.9976	.0699	14.301	86°
5°	.0872	.9962	.0875	11.430	85°
6°	.1045	.9945	.1051	9.5144	84°
7°	.1219	.9925	.1228	8.1443	83°
8°	.1392	.9903	.1405	7.1154	82°
9°	.1564	.9877	.1584	6.3138	81°
10°	.1736	.9848	.1763	5.6713	80°
11°	.1908	.9816	.1944	5.1446	79°
12°	.2079	.9781	.2126	4.7046	78°
13°	.2250	.9744	.2309	4.3315	77°
14°	.2419	.9703	.2493	4.0108	76°
15°	.2588	.9659	.2679	3.7321	75°
16°	.2756	.9613	.2867	3.4874	74°
17°	.2924	.9563	.3057	3.2709	73°
18°	.3090	.9511	.3249	3.0777	72°
19°	.3256	.9455	.3443	2.9042	71°
20°	.3420	.9397	.3640	2.7475	70°
21°	.3584	.9336	.3839	2.6051	69°
22°	.3746	.9272	.4040	2.4751	68°
23°	.3907	.9205	.4245	2.3559	67°
24°	.4067	.9135	.4452	2.2460	66°
25°	.4226	.9063	.4663	2.1445	65°
26°	.4384	.8988	.4877	2.0503	64°
27°	.4540	.8910	.5095	1.9626	63°
28°	.4695	.8829	.5317	1.8807	62°
29°	.4848	.8746	.5543	1.8040	61°
30°	.5000	.8660	.5774	1.7321	60°
31°	.5150	.8572	.6009	1.6643	59°
32°	.5299	.8480	.6249	1.6003	58°
33°	.5446	.8387	.6494	1.5399	57°
34°	.5592	.8290	.6745	1.4826	56°
35°	.5736	.8192	.7002	1.4281	55°
36°	.5878	.8090	.7265	1.3764	54°
37°	.6018	.7986	.7536	1.3270	53°
38°	.6157	.7880	.7813	1.2799	52°
39°	.6293	.7771	.8098	1.2349	51°
40°	.6428	.7660	.8391	1.1918	50°
41°	.6561	.7547	.8693	1.1504	49°
42°	.6691	.7431	.9004	1.1106	48°
43°	.6820	.7314	.9325	1.0724	47°
44°	.6947	.7193	.9657	1.0355	46°
45°	.7071	.7071	.0000	1.0000	45°
Angle	Cosine	Sine	Cotan	Tan	Angle

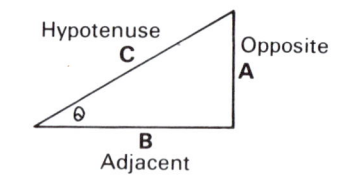

The hypotenuse is the longest side

$\text{Sin } ø = \dfrac{A}{C} = \dfrac{\text{Opposite}}{\text{Hypotenuse}}$

$\text{Cosine } ø = \dfrac{B}{C} = \dfrac{\text{Adjacent}}{\text{Hypotenuse}}$

$\text{Tan } ø = \dfrac{A}{B} = \dfrac{\text{Opposite}}{\text{Adjacent}} = \dfrac{\text{Sin } ø}{\text{Cos } ø}$

$\text{Cosec } ø = \dfrac{C}{A} = \dfrac{\text{Opposite}}{\text{Adjacent}} = \dfrac{1}{\text{Sin } ø}$

$\text{Sec } ø = \dfrac{C}{B} = \dfrac{\text{Hypotenuse}}{\text{Adjacent}} = \dfrac{1}{\text{Cos } ø}$

$\text{Cot } ø = \dfrac{B}{A} = \dfrac{\text{Adjacent}}{\text{Opposite}} = \dfrac{1}{\tan ø}$

Some functions to note:
- Sin 30° = 0.5
- Cos 60° = 0.5
- Cosec 30° = 2.0
- Sec 60° = 2.0
- Tan 45° = 1.0
- Sin 90° = 1.0

Note:
*To use this table read from the top titles for angles up to **45°**, and from the bottom titles for angles between **45°** and **90°**.*

Technical Draughtsmanship

Tables 1

Appendix 2

① Metric Paper sizes

A0	1189 x 841
A1	841 x 594
A2	594 x 420
A3	420 x 297
A4	297 x 210
A5	210 x 148
A6	148 x 105

Notes
- **A0** = One square metre.
- **A1** is half of **A0**, **A2** half of **A1**, etc.
- The sides of all sheets are in the ratio $1:\sqrt{2}$.
- There is a **B** series, for use when the **A** series is not acceptable.
- The **C** series is used for envelopes into which the **A** series will fit.

② Regular Polygons

Name	Number of sides	Angle at centre
Equilateral triangle	3	120°
Square	4	90°
Pentagon	5	72°
Hexagon	6	60°
Heptagon	7	51.43°
Octagon	8	45°
Nonagon	9	40°
Decagon	10	36°

Notes

Dodecagon	12	30°
Icosagon	20	18°

③ Designation of Metric Screwthreads

Order of indication:
1. Material
2. Head shape
3. Bolt or nut
4. Metric M
5. Diameter
6. Pitch
7. Length
8. Type of Fit

Example:
Steel Hex. Hd. Bolt M10 x 1.5 x 30 8g.

⑥ Some Hole and Shaft Fits

(i) **Clearance Fit**

	Hole	Shaft
Average	H8	f7
Fine	H7	g6

Example: Clearance Fit H8-f7

(ii) **Transition Fit**

	Hole	Shaft
Average	H7	n6
Fine	H7	k6

Example: Transition Fit H7-n6

(iii) **Interference Fit**

	Hole	Shaft
Average	H7	s6
Fine	H7	n6

Example: Interference Fit H7-s6

BS 4500: 1A, B for details.

④ ISO Metric Screwthreads

Measurements are in millimetres

Diameter	Pitch
1.6	0.35
2	0.4
2.5	0.45
3	0.5
4	0.7
5	0.8
6	1.0
8	1.25
10	1.5
12	1.75
16	2.0
20	2.5

BS 3643: 1963 Part I for details

⑦ Metric Spur Gears Formulae

Name	Symbol	Formula
Module	m	$m = \dfrac{PCD}{T}$
Pitch Circle Dia.	PCD	PCD = T x m
Teeth	T	$T = \dfrac{PCD}{m}$
Addendum	A	A = m
Clearance	C	C = 0.157 m
Dedendum	D	D = 1.157 m
Outside Dia.	OD	OD = (T + 2) m
Centre Distance	CD	CD = ½(T + t) m
Root Dia.	RD	RD = (T − 2.314) m

BS 436 and 4582 for details

⑧ Bolts and Nuts

Class of Fits for general use

	Bolt	Nut
Close	4h	5H
Medium	6g	6H
Free	8g	7H

⑤ Rivets

Measurements are in millimetres

Rivet Diameter	Plate Thickness
2	0.11
2.5	0.2
3	0.3
4	0.5
5	0.7
6	1.0
8	2.0
10	3.0
12	4.0
16	8.0
20	12.0

Note
Rivet Diameter $= 6\sqrt{plate\ thickness}$
BS 4620: 1970 for details.

Note
- More detailed tables will be readily available at most local libraries.

Technical Draughtsmanship
Tables 2
Appendix 3

349

GLOSSARY

Acute angle: An angle between 0° and 90°.
Addendum: The radial distance from the pitch circle to the tip of a gear tooth.
Arc: Part of the profile of a circle.
Assembly: Two or more parts attached to perform a particular function.
Asymptote: A straight line that approaches but never quite touches a hyperbola.
Auxiliary: A helpful extra view, projection or plane.
Axonometric: Any pictorial drawing with receding, but not converging, axes.

Bench mark: A level set and marked by the Ordnance Survey.
Bending moments: Forces trying to bend a body.
Bow's notation: A method of indexing that simplifies structural analysis.
Bushing: A replaceable lining or sleeve for a bearing.

Cabinet drawing: An oblique pictorial drawing with a receding axis measured to half scale.
Cam: A rotating piece shaped to impart a specific movement to a follower.
Cantilever: A structural element that projects beyond its support.
Casting: A piece made by pouring molten metal into a mould.
Catenary: The line of a slack chain whose ends are fixed.
Cavalier drawing: An oblique pictorial drawing with a 45° receding axis.
Centre of curvature: The point where a compass would be located to properly draw the curve.
Chamfer: A bevel, usually along an edge.
Chord: A straight line across a circle.
Clearance: The gap between the tip and root of two meshing gear teeth.
Coordinates: References from an origin that locate a point in space.
Contour: A line through points of equal height.
Counterbore: To enlarge a hole cylindrically.
Countersink: To enlarge a hole conically.

Datum: A line, or level, from which measurements are to be taken.
Dedendum: The part of a gear tooth inside the pitch circle.
Development: Unfolding the surface of an object onto a plane.

Diagonal scale: A very accurate method of subdividing a ruler.
Dimetric: A pictorial drawing with two receding axes, e.g. isometric.
Directrix: A reference line for plotting conic curves.

Eccentricity: A ratio that enables conic curves to be plotted.
Envelopment: The wrapping of an object by a sheet of any shape.
Exploded drawing: When each part of an assembly is drawn separately in a position that clearly suggests how the parts fit together.

Fillet: A rounded intersection between two surfaces.
Focal sphere: A sphere touching both sides of a cone and a cutting plane.

Gasket: A thin layer sealing two joined surfaces.
Gear pair: Two mating spur gears.
Gradient: The inclination of a plane expressed as a ratio of vertical to horizontal.

Inclined plane: A plane at an angle to either the horizontal or the vertical reference planes.
Index: To label points for easy reference.
Isometric drawing: A pictorial drawing, whose two receding axes are at 30°.
Isometric scale: A reduced scale used on one receding isometric axis to enhance the pictorial effect.

Key: A small piece of metal sunk partly into a shaft and a hub to prevent slipping.
Keyway: The slot into which a key fits.

Legend: An explanation of the symbols used in a diagram.
Locus: The path of a moving point.

Normal: A line at right angles to a tangent at its point of tangency.

Oblique: Any straight line that is neither vertical nor horizontal.
Oblique plane: A plane inclined to both vertical and horizontal planes of reference.
Orthographic projection: A multi-view drawing in two-dimensions.

Pattern: A flat development of a surface.
Perspective: A pictorial drawing with converging lines.
Pinion: The smaller of two mating gears.
Pitch circle: A circle representing a gear as a tangent cylinder.
Planometric: A pictorial drawing whose receding axes are set at complementary angles, i.e. add up to 90°.
Platonic solids: The five regular polyhedra.
Polyhedra: Many-faceted solids.
Polygon: A many-sided flat figure.
Proportion: A comparison of two ratios.
Pyramid: A solid with a polygonal base whose sloping sides meet at an apex.

Rabat: To beat down flat.
Rack: A flat bar with gear teeth cut into it.
Radian: The angle made by an arc equal to the radius.
Ratio: A comparison of two sizes, quantities or areas.
Rendering: A shaded or coloured presentation drawing.

Scale: The relation of dimension as shown to their actual sizes.
Section: A cut through a solid.
Skew lines: Two lines that are neither perpendicular nor parallel to each other.
Strain: Any change caused by stress.
Stress: When forces are trying to change the shape of an object.
Stretch-out: The overall length of a pattern.

Tangent: A line just touching a curve without crossing it.
Tolerance: The amount of variation permitted.
Traces of a plane: The lines of interpenetration of an oblique plane on the vertical and horizontal reference planes.
Transition piece: A piece of metal that joins two differently shaped ducts.
Trimetric: A pictorial drawing with three measured axes.
Truncated: A solid with a piece cut off it.
True: Actual as opposed to apparent length or shape.

Universal joint: A joint that allows movement in any direction.

Vanishing point: The meeting point of converging lines in perspective drawing.

Weld: A joint made with melting metals.
Wheel: The larger of two mating gears.

INDEX

Addendum, 257.
Angles, 9.
Arches, 224, 311, 324.
Archimedean spiral, 177.
Arcs, tangent, 16.
Areas, 23-32.
Assemblies, 81, 225, 235-44.
Asymptotes, 196.
Auxiliary projection, 46, 61-72, 109, 114.
Axonometric, 84-87.

Basic geometry, 8-22.
Beams, 222, 310.
Bearings, 273.
Bending moments, 222.
Bends and seams, 230.
Bevel gears, 256, 260.
Bolts, 229.
Bow's notation, 223.
Brainstorming, 212.
Brakes, 272.
Bridges, 224, 225.
Building geometry, 323-30.
Building project, 285-92.
Building structures, 309-22.

Cabinet projection, 74.
Cams, 250-55, 272.
Car systems, 265-72.
Catenary, 181, 224, 314.
Cathetus, 178.
Cavalier projection, 74.
Centre eye, 178.
Centre of curvature, 193, 195, 197.
Centrifugal pump, 275.
Cerble radius, 178.
Circle, 15, 17, 18.
Circumscribing, 15.
Clutches, 270.
Compass bearing, 9.
Compressor, 274.
Computers, 206, 207.
Cone, 187-200.
Conic sections, 187-200.
Conical spiral, 177.
Conjugate diameters, 192.
Conoids, 313, 314.
Contours, 293, 307.
Contracts, 204.

Conventions, 208.
Coordinates, 92, 93, 101.
Crating, 77.
Curves of intersection, 141.
Cut and fill, 298, 299.
Cutaway drawing, 82.
Cutting lists, 4.
Cycloids, 179.

Datum lines, 209.
Dedendum, 257.
Designing, 203.
Development, 145-68, 326, 328.
Diagonal scales, 38.
Diaphragm pump, 275.
Diesel engine, 269.
Differential, 271.
Digitising, 206, 207.
Dihedral angle, 100-102, 116.
Dimensioning, 209, 210.
Dip, 302-5.
Directrix, 190.
Division of figures, 29.
Dodecahedron, 55.
Domes, 55.

Eccentricity, 190-92.
Elbow joint, 154.
Electrical circuits, 215.
Ellipse, 189-91, 193, 194.
Engineering project, 211-18.
Engineering structures, 219-26.
Engines, 265-78.
Enlargement, 30-33.
Envelopment, 169-72.
Epicycloid, 179.
Epitrochoid, 180.
Equipment, 2.
Escribing, 18.
Evolute, 193, 195, 197.
Examination hints, 347.
Exploded assemblies, 81.
Extreme ratio, 12, 28.

Fabrication, 227-34.
First angle projection, 46-8.
Fits, 250.

Focal sphere, 191.
Follower displacement diagrams, 251-5.
Followers, 250.
Forces, 220, 222, 223.
Four-stroke engine, 267.
Frameworks, 223.
Funicular polygon, 222, 223.

Gears, 256-60, 271.
Generator, 189.
Glissette, 181.
Glossary, 350.
Golden mean, 12, 28.
Goldman's method, 178.
Graphic calculation, 12, 23-32.

Half-cone method, 109.
Helical gears, 256.
Helices, 176, 256.
Hyperbolas, 189-91, 196, 197.
Hyperbolic paraboloids, 313-19.
Hyperboloids, 313, 314.
Hypocycloid, 179.
Hypotrochoid, 180.

Icosahedron, 54.
Ionic volute, 178.
Inclined planes, 108.
Inferior epitrochoid, 180.
Inferior hypotrochoid, 180.
Inferior trochoid, 180.
Inking, 6.
Inscribing, 18, 19.
Internal gear, 256.
Interpenetration, 99, 131-44.
Interpolation, 297.
Intersections, 131-44, 153.
Involutes, 174, 258, 259.
Isometric drawing, 76-82, 83-90, 135, 239.
Isometric scale, 76.
Isometric protractor, 79.

Joints, 154.

Keyways, 273.
Knife-edged followers, 250-55.

Labels, 169-72.
Laminae, 93, 110, 114.
Left-hand helix, 184.
Levelling, 295.
Limits and fits, 279-84.
Lines, hidden, 4.
Lines in space, 93-7.
Linings, 328.
Linkages, 246-9.
Loci, 173-86, 245-64.
Logarithmic scale, 175.
Logarithmic spiral, 175.

Machining and fits, 279-84.
Mean ratio, 12, 28.
Mechanisms, 245-64.
Menus, 207.
Mining, 302-5.
Module, 257.
Mouldings, 325.

Nappes, 189.
Normal, 15.
Nuts, 219, 231.

Oblique cutting planes, 136.
Oblique planes, 107-20.
Oblique projection, 74, 75.
Orthographic projection, 43-60.

Palladio, 178.
Palmate sections, 141.
Panel development, 166.
Paper, 205.
Parabola, 181, 189-91, 194, 195.
Paraboloid, 313-19.
Pentagons, 13.
Perspective, 331-7, 343.
Pictoral projections, 73-90.
Pinions, 256, 260.
Pipework, 235-44.
Planometric projection, 82.
Platonic solids, 11.
Points, lines and planes, 91-106.
Polar diagrams, 222.
Polygons, 10, 13.
Polyhedra, regular, 11, 53-6, 163.

Presentation drawings, 331-46.
Projections, 44-6.
Proportionals, 12, 28.
Pumps, 274, 275.
Pyramids, 157, 158.

Quadrilaterals, 10.

Rabatment, 100, 102, 112, 114.
Rack, 259.
Radians, 9.
Ratios, 12, 28.
Reduction and enlargement, 30-33.
Resultant, 220, 222, 223.
Revolved sections, 135.
Right-hand helix, 184.
Roads, 296-301.
Roof surfaces, 102, 326.
Roof truss, 232, 233.
Rotary engine, 269.
Roulette, 181.

Scale of chords, 12.

Scales, 35-42.
Screw threads, 228.
Seams, 230.
Sections and intersections, 131-44.
Sector, 15.
Segment, 15.
Set squares, 3.
Shadows, 339-43.
Shear force diagram, 222.
Shortest distances, 97, 98.
Simple harmonic motion, 251-5.
Site plans, 290.
Skew lines, 98.
Sliding joint, 270.
Solids, 11.
Spheres, 80, 121-30.
Spirals, 175-7, 256.
Spur gears, 256.
Square roots, 28.
Statics, 220, 222, 223.
Steam engine, 266.
Steel sections, 234.
Steering mechanisms, 272.

Strike, 302-5.
Structures, building, 309-21.
Structures, engineering, 219-26.
Struts, 328.
Studs, 231.
Subdivision of figures, 29.
Superior epitrochoid, 180.
Superior hypotrochoid, 180.
Superior trochoid, 180.
Surface structures, 313, 317.
Surveying, 293-308.

Tables, 348.
Tangent planes and spheres, 121-30.
Tangents, 16-17.
Taps, 237.
Third angle projection, 46, 48, 50, 65, 69.
Title blocks, 5.
Tolerances, 280.
Torus, 134.
Traces, 108-11.
Tracery, 324.
Triangles, 11, 14.

Triangulation, 164.
Trigonometry, 9, 348.
Trimetric, 84-7.
Trochoids, 180.
True angle, 95-7, 109.
True lengths, 51, 95, 96.
True shape, 52, 97, 114, 115, 136.
Trusses, 223.
Two-stroke engine, 268.

Uniform acceleration and retardation, 251-5.
Uniform velocity, 251-5.
Universal joint, 270, 277.

Valves, 237.
Vane pump, 275.
Vectors, 221.
Vernier scales, 39.

Warren girders, 223.
Welding, 231.
Worm gear, 256.
Wrapped labels, 169-72.